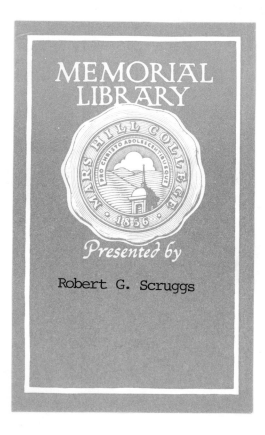

The Encyclopedia of

WITCHCRAFT AND

DEMONOLOGY

The Encyclopedia of

WITCHCRAFT AND

DEMONOLOGY

by ROSSELL HOPE ROBBINS

Fellow of the Royal Society of Literature

CROWN PUBLISHERS, INC. • NEW YORK

for

H. A. M. R.

© 1959 by Crown Publishers, Inc., New York, N. Y.
Library of Congress Catalog Card Number: 59-9155

Printed in the United States of America.

Although widely discussed, witchcraft is, in fact, an almost unknown subject. Most people think of a witch as an old crone out of Walt Disney, with a peaked hat and a broomstick, accompanied by a cat, poking her long bony fingers at her cowering victim—a misconception reinforced every year by the traditions of Halloween. The distinction between this kind of comic-book witchcraft, which is never more than simple sorcery, and witchcraft as a Christian heresy is generally obscured. The Introduction and various entries in this *Encyclopedia* will, it is hoped, explain and illustrate this distinction, and show what witchcraft meant to the men and women accused as witches and to the judges who condemned them.

This *Encyclopedia* attempts a rational, balanced history of the three centuries of this horror, from its beginnings in the fifteenth century, through its peak about 1600, to its ending in the eighteenth century. Since witchcraft is a Christian heresy, the subject is clearly delimited to western Europe, and, by extension, to the brief flicker at Salem. Witchcraft is not a department of anthropology, folklore, mythology, or legend; its relations to magic are very limited; to modern Satanism, nil; its links to demonology subordinated to witchology: in a word, witchcraft lies in the province of theology. Sorcery, as practiced in Africa, Central and South America, or elsewhere, is not treated in this volume.

With all the difficulties inherent in a book of this scope, omissions and errors inevitably creep in. To be inclusive, the history of witchcraft would be the history of European civilization, or rather un-civilization, and one hundred volumes of similar size to this *Encyclopedia* would be inadequate—and unreadable. I have selected what I conclude to be most significant for the total picture of witchcraft presented here: a colossal fraud and delusion, impossible because the "crime" of witchcraft was an impossible crime. The present entries could have been doubled and trebled, but the reader would not necessarily be that much the richer or wiser. Errors of omission are, indeed, best known to the author. For the errors of commission, I tender my apologies, and, as my teacher, the late George G. Coulton of Cambridge University, always promised with his great historical monuments, offer to correct in future editions any inaccuracies of fact.

Even a cursory glance through this *Encyclopedia* will show that the sources of information will be found only in America's greatest libraries which contain at least two million volumes. The biggest and best collection in the world for a study of witchcraft is at Cornell University, lovingly and painstakingly assembled over a period of some forty years by its first president, Andrew Dickson White, especially during his service as minister plenipotentiary to Berlin. In his searches and purchases he was advised by his librarian, a professor of history, George Lincoln Burr. It is regrettable that Burr, who possessed the most detailed and extensive knowledge of witchcraft of any student of the subject, published so very little and left no literary remains. That other great scholar, Henry Charles Lea, left his personal collection to the University of Pennsylvania; but his library, though outstanding, remains inferior in witchcraft materials to the White collection at Cornell University. Lea's three-volumed *Materials Toward a History of Witchcraft*, published posthumously in 1939 with an introduction by Burr, and recently reissued, is a treasure trove. Lea's work, however, is best appreciated by the reader who knows Latin, French, and German, and already is acquainted with the subject. Although invited many times, Lea never made use of the Cornell books; thus, many of the unique volumes gathered by White and Burr are introduced to the public for the first time in this *Encyclopedia.* To the librarians at Cornell University goes my gratitude for their many kindnesses.

Even the White collection is not exhaustive, and, apart from the six million volumes at Harvard, the reader who wants to read from original sources will best go to the Reserve Room of the New York Public Library, especially rich in American materials. In New York will be found three other collections of importance for witchcraft: Columbia University Library, rich in rare French works (in its Jeanne d'Arc collection); Union Theological Seminary Library, with a huge holding (the McAlpin collection) of some 5000 choice sixteenth- and seventeenth-century English theological books; and the new and tiny Bollingen Library, which, among its books on magic, has a few treasures pertaining to witches. The books left to the Library of Congress by Houdini are of greater interest to the historian of magic than of witchcraft. Other libraries used in the preparation of this book for material not available in the United States, primarily contemporary printed pamphlets or chapbooks on English trials, include, of course, the British Museum, the Bodleian Library at Oxford, and Lambeth Palace Library, many of whose books survived the Nazi incendiary bombing which destroyed the edifice in World War II. Specialized French materials have been drawn from the Bibliothèque nationale in Paris.

These references to the great libraries indicate some of the value of this *Encyclopedia:* a distillation of more than a thousand primary works on witchcraft. By culling and arranging even a tiny fragment of the total body of materials available, perhaps the impact these books make on the scholar will be conveyed to the non-specialist reader. Witchcraft is an ugly subject; it is difficult not to be revolted at the turn of every page—handling the copy of the first edition of the first book ever printed on witchcraft (in 1467), for example, and realizing this very book was owned by the Monastery of St. Maximin at Treves and helped form the intellectual background of the monks who sentenced 300 persons to

death as witches. This was just one of the treasures Burr brought back to Cornell; how human was his comment that we "can hardly turn these pages without a shudder." After reading so many similar accounts, all faithfully described in this present volume, it is difficult to preserve the equanimity scholarship expects; nor do I apologize if very occasionally a word of my own personal shock has slipped into these pages. Yet a reader will see that the subject matter of witchcraft is even more terrible when presented without editorial comment; the words of the official scribes, not writing for posterity, cry out more effectively than any others against this inhumanity.

If witchcraft reveals the lapse of the human being into the foulest animal, it can also show the occasional spark of the godlike in men such as Löher, Meyfarth, Spee, Stapirius, or Scot, Bordelon, or Calef, who wrote whatever they could against the delusion; and in the accused, named as well as nameless, who fought back against the mania and who by their courage in dying laid a seed of doubt in the validity and honesty of witch believers and witch trials. The end of witchcraft persecutions was hastened by a few such courageous men and women who opposed the dominant ideologies to the best of their abilities, and gave leadership to millions terrified by the extent and control of a crushing superstition.

If the cries and shrieks of these martyrs for humanity—for such the "witches" and their defenders were—and the protests of writers can be taken from the steel-doored vaults of libraries to show the present-day reader the dangers of bigotry and rigidity of thought, and the prerequisite of the inquiring mind in all phases of man's activities, this work will hold more than either antiquarian or sensational values. It will have fulfilled the main purpose of scholarly research—namely, understanding the past the better to understand the present and anticipate the future.

To the following, who have helped in various ways with the preparation of this *Encyclopedia,* I wish to acknowledge my thanks: Mr. Lee Ash, New York; Mr. E. G. W. Bill, Lambeth Palace Library,

London; Dr. Curt Bühler, Pierpont Morgan Library, New York; Mrs. Maud Cole, Reserve Room, New York Public Library; Mlle. Thérèse d'Alverny, Bibliothèque nationale, Paris; Mrs. Alexander Dobkin, New York; Mrs. Richard Fried, New York; Dr. Albert Friedman, Harvard University; Miss Vaughan Gilmore, Bollingen Foundation Library, New York; Mr. Johann S. Hannesson, Fiske Icelandic Collection, Cornell University Library; Dr. George Harris Healey, Cornell University Library; Miss Edith Henderson, Harvard Law Library; Dr. Rudolf Hirsch, Lea Library; Mrs. Philomena Houlihan, Reserve Room, New York Public Library; Dr. Richard W. Hunt, Bodleian Library, Oxford; Miss Frja Järvii, Helsinki University, Finland; Professor William R. Keast, Cornell University; Professor John E. Keller, University of North Carolina; Mrs. Henry Kroul, New York; Mr. Gerritt Lancing, New York; Mr. Gene Liberty, New York; Dr. Henry F. Mins, Clinton, New Jersey; Mr. Leonard E. Mins, Woodstock, New York; Dr. Tauno Mustanoja, Helsinki University, Finland; Mr. Edward Neil, Harvard University; Mrs. Lisbeth E. Rawski, Cornell University Library; Mr. Derek Roper, Lincoln College, Oxford; Professor James L. Rosier, Cornell University; Miss Marie Salvatore, New York; Dr. Kenneth M. Setton, University of Pennsylvania Library; Mr. Lewis M. Stark, Reserve Room, New York Public Library; Professor Francis Lee Utley, Ohio State University; and Professor Beatrice E. White, Westfield College, University of London. For their personal interest and concern in this work special thanks are due the publishers.

As throughout the past twenty years, I am under the deepest debt of affection to my wife, Helen Ann Mins Robbins, for her constant wisdom and loyal encouragement; during the years of the writing of this *Encyclopedia* she has given of herself above and beyond the call of spousehood.

Katsbaan Onderheugel,
Saugerties, New York
Candlemas, 1959   R.H.R.

The words *witch* and *witchcraft*, in everyday usage for over a thousand years, have undergone several changes of meaning; and today witchcraft, having reverted to its original connotation of magic and sorcery, does not convey the precise and limited definition it once had during the sixteenth and seventeenth centuries. If witchcraft had never meant anything more than the craft of "an old, weather-beaten crone, leaning on a staff, hollow-eyed, untoothed, going mumbling in the streets," Europe would not have suffered, for three centuries from 1450 to 1750, the shocking nightmare, the foulest crime and deepest shame of western civilization, the blackout of everything that *homo sapiens*, the reasoning man, has ever upheld. This book is about that crime and shame.

The record of witchcraft is horrible and brutal: degradation stifled decency, the filthiest passions masqueraded under the cover of religion, and man's intellect was subverted to condone bestialities that even Swift's Yahoos would blush to commit.

Never were so many so wrong, so long. Witchcraft destroyed the principles of honor and justice; it opened wide the rosters for the Hall of Shame. Here are some examples of what witchcraft did to the persecutors:

A lord chief justice of England closes his eyes to proven fraud by a prosecution witness, even when it is drawn to his attention by his associate judges.

A trial judge in Germany, repulsed by a woman to whom he made improper advances, in revenge seizes her sister, accuses her of witchcraft, cruelly tortures her, and burns her alive the same day.

A distinguished professor of law at the University of Toulouse advocates the suspension of rules in witch trials, because "not one out of a million witches would be accused or punished, if regular legal procedure were followed."

A bishop in Germany burns a minimum of 900 men and women, including many respected and wealthy citizens, as witches, and confiscates their estates and properties for his own enjoyment.

A Protestant minister in Scotland refuses Christian burial to a woman crushed to death by a mob because she had been accused as a witch by a sixteen-year-old lad.

A famous French magistrate regrets that, instead of burning young children accused of witchcraft, he had merely sentenced them to be flogged while they watched their parents burn as witches.

"One can but exclaim," a Catholic priest and confessor cried in despair in 1592, "O Christian religion, how long shalt thou be vexed with this direst of superstitions? and cry aloud, O Christian commonwealth, how long in thee shall the life of the innocent be imperilled?"

Consider some of the varied tortures and injustices witchcraft inflicted on the persecuted:

At Salem two young men are trussed at their neck and heels until the blood drips from their noses, to force a statement used to convict those accused.

A woman in Scotland is burned as a witch for stroking a cat at an open window at the same time the householder finds his brew of beer turning sour.

A mother and daughter in England are executed as witches on accusations by a ten-year-old girl of bewitching her with fits.

A witness in a witch trial in France makes a dying confession that his evidence had been dictated by the prosecutor; nothing is done to reopen the case, and the accused, a nun, dies in solitary confinement.

A woman in Scotland is convicted as a witch for curing unhealthy children by washing them.

A poor immigrant in Boston, speaking only Irish and saying her simple prayers in Latin, is hanged as a witch because she could not repeat the Lord's prayer in English.

Admittedly, these represent the more infamous incidents in the history of witchcraft; but they are neither exceptional nor unusual. If a professor of law advocated suspension of customary legal procedures in witch trials, he was merely justifying the common practice: trials for witchcraft were not designed to establish guilt or innocence, but to condemn the accused as soon as possible. If a child sent two women to their death by her hysterics, she was but one of many young people (including the Salem "witch bitches") who faked epileptic fits; the accounts of "possessed" children are so frequent and uniform that their recital becomes almost monotonous.

Happening day after day for centuries, resulting in torture and horrible death for tens of thousands, the following examples of witchcraft in action are perhaps even more terrifying than the preceding, just because they are so routine:

Any person having a mole, wen, scar, or bunion is considered to possess a devil's mark, and is therefore to be executed as a witch. A celebrated professor of law at Cologne said no one with such a mark could have lived a blameless life.

Every witch had her familiars or imps, disguised as household animals or insects, sent to her by the devil. While imprisoned, her cell is to be carefully watched for spiders and flies; any insect not caught is presumed to have escaped because of its diabolical powers, thus proving the accused guilty.

Common report or rumor or gossip was sufficient ground to bring an accusation of witchcraft; once arrested, the accused was tortured until he confessed his guilt. Ignoring common report was considered an indication of guilt.

What a gulf separates the Hansel and Gretel witch from the witch against whom the most highly trained minds of western Europe for three centuries mobilized the entire resources of church and state. "Germany is almost entirely occupied with building fires for the witches," wrote an experienced witch judge about 1600.

"Switzerland has been compelled to wipe out many of her villages on their account. Travelers in Lorraine may see thousands and thousands of the stakes to which witches are bound."

The old hag was no doubt objectionable, undesirable, malicious, but of herself presented no clear and present danger to the stability of society; no more than the Gypsy with a bad reputation for a vagabond existence, pilfering, and fortunetelling is any menace to modern society. Yet the authorities devoted so much effort to counteract witchcraft that they clearly believed an attack from some direction was imminent. The person hunted by the inquisitors, ecclesiastical and secular alike, from 1450 to 1750, was no hag; he was a member of an international movement, a powerful subversive force working day and night to destroy true religion and to prevent the establishment of God's kingdom. The powers of evil were very strong, and it was touch and go whether the Christian God or the Christian Devil would be victorious. To side with Satan was a crime far worse than treason to earthly rulers, for man's life was an infinitesimal speck on the limitless canvas of eternity. Witchcraft was treason against God, and therefore justified whatever measures of suppression were successful.

"Whatever punishment we can order against witches by roasting and cooking them over a slow fire is not really very much," said Jean Bodin, eminent French lawyer, economist, and political theorist, whose book on witches was a standard text, "and not as bad as . . . the eternal agonies which are prepared for them in hell, for the fire here cannot last much more than an hour or so until the witches have died."

The following instances, both superficially similar, may help clarify the historical concept of witchcraft as it is presented in this *Encyclopedia,* and distinguish it from the modern loose interpretation of witchcraft as sorcery or magic—between the heretic and the hag.

The first example comes from St. Osyth,

Essex (England), in 1582. Here, fourteen women were tried at the county sessions at Chelmsford, largely on two sets of allegations: acts of malice, and murder by bewitching. Most of the women had at one time or another feuded with their neighbors; consequently, suspicion pointed to them whenever a man had trouble with his cows or geese, or when the butter would not churn. Moreover, several of the women were charged with causing death by witchcraft. Mrs. Harrison, the wife of a minister, believed that a number of mishaps, including her own ill health, was due to hexing by Agnes Heard. Her husband promised to question the suspect: "You vile strumpet! I do think you have bewitched my wife, and, as truly as God doth live, if I can perceive that she be troubled any more as she hath been, I will not leave a whole bone about thee. And besides, I will seek to have thee hanged." A few months later, Mrs. Harrison again took ill, and her suspicions against Agnes Heard intensified. "Husband, God bless you and your children, for I am now utterly consumed with yonder wicked creature." After two days, Mrs. Harrison died, her last words being, "Oh, Agnes Heard, Agnes Heard, she hath consumed me." Agnes Heard was tried and, surprisingly, found Not Guilty.

The second example is from Tring, Leicestershire (England), in 1757. Ruth Osborne and her husband were old and poor, supporters of the unpopular Stuart rebellion of 1745, and regarded as witches. Whenever trouble happened, the Osbornes were blamed. Especially were they blamed by a farmer named Butterfield. Mother Osborne had begged some buttermilk from him

> but Butterfield told her with great brutality that he had not enough for his hogs. This provoked the old woman, who went away, telling him that the [Stuart] pretender [to the English throne] would have him and his hogs too. Soon afterwards several of Butterfield's calves became distempered; upon which, some ignorant people, who had been told the story of the buttermilk,

gave out that the [calves] were bewitched by old Mother Osborne.

Butterfield then sold his farm and, in the hope of diverting the spell he assumed Ruth Osborne had cast on him, opened a tavern. But things got worse, and Butterfield was himself taken with fits. Then word was spread that suspected "witches" were to be given the water ordeal: if they floated, they were witches; if they sank, they were innocent. A mob rounded up the Osbornes, manhandled them, and thrust them in the river. Mother Osborne was tied in a sheet and did not sink; so the ringleader of the crowd poked and prodded her. Eventually, she was taken out of the water, "thrown quite naked on the bank, almost choked with mud, and expired in a few minutes." Her husband died shortly after. The ringleader thought himself a popular hero and took up a collection.

In these two accounts, the incidents are similar. Commonplace accidents happen about a farm, and a person becomes sick (and in one story dies); an unpopular neighbor is accused as the cause of these ills. What makes the trial of Agnes Heard a case of witchcraft and the lynching of Ruth Osborne, though she was labeled a "witch," a case of sorcery?

Throughout the report of the evil acts or *maleficia* of Mrs. Osborne and of assuming she had certain occult or magical powers, the devil is never mentioned or implied. The action against her was for something she was supposed to have done; it was not sanctioned by any religious or secular authority and its perpetrators were punished. Mrs. Osborne was, in common parlance, a "witch." By the historical and legal definition of the word used exclusively to the mid-eighteenth century, she was not a witch.

On the other hand, Agnes Heard was tried by statute law for practicing "invocations and conjurations of evil and wicked spirits," whereby property was destroyed and a woman killed. Agnes Heard's occult powers were derived specifically from the Devil, a fact evident, as her seven-year-old daughter was permitted to testify, from her keeping six pet blackbirds. These birds were actually demons or familiars, proved by Agnes' possession of witch's marks.

The theory of witchcraft underlying familiars and witch's marks was assumed. In reward for her allegiance, the Devil presented the witch with demons disguised as small household animals, birds, or insects, to carry out her orders to work evil. These familiars the witch fed on delicacies (as one would feed a pet), but the choicest delicacy was her own blood. Any little wen or similar protuberance on the body was regarded as a teat to suckle the familiars. Consequently, every suspected witch was completely shaved and probed for any such mark—one was always found somewhere, even under the eyelids, under the tongue, or in the genitals. In 1604 the theory was formally embodied in the statute of King James which made it a felony "to consult, covenant with, entertain, employ, feed, or reward any evil and wicked spirit."

In an atmosphere of arbitrarily ascribing motives to people on the basis of skin blemishes, the reason of men atrophied. In 1681, a master of arts of Cambridge University, Henry Hallywell, attempted a scientific explanation of "an unquestionable matter of fact." The demons, said Hallywell

being so mightily debauched . . . wear away by a continual deflux of particles, and therefore require some nutriment to supply the place of the fugacious atoms, which is done by sucking the blood and spirits of these forlorn wretches [witches]. . . . And no doubt but these impure devils may take as much pleasure in sucking the warm blood of men or beasts, as a cheerful and healthy constitution in drawing in the refreshing gales of pure and sincere air.

Cats, white mice, and blackbirds, along with little irregularities on the body, were but the outward indications of the pact with the Devil—the essence of witchcraft. On this essential, English Protestants were in complete agreement with Continental Catholics. The decision to aid Satan, which caused the witch to enter the pact, could be inferred from what a wicked witch did; but the subtle witch tried to deceive men by living an outwardly virtuous life. One who never went to church and one who regularly attended services might be equally guilty of witchcraft. What linked them was the denial of God in their minds and, by an act of decision, joining the spiritual forces of what the church called evil. Consequently, the assumed pact with the Devil, or the agreement to work against the Christian God and the Christian church, became a "crime of conscience," or a crime in the mind or imagination. Witchcraft was not primarily concerned with acts; it was concerned with opinions and ideas; no one had ever seen a witch flying on a broomstick, but thousands of people described how and why she flew. Agnes Heard was tried, not for her acts of witchcraft, but for what she was presumed to have believed, that is, for witchcraft-ism.

In practice, in England (unlike France or Germany) a witch was generally accused of some evil *act*. Practice implied theory. But the English theorists were unanimous that allegiance to the Devil determined a witch. This intangible pact, not the tangible *maleficia*, constituted the offense. A noted Protestant preacher, George Gifford, summed up:

> A witch by the word of God ought to die the death not because she killeth men —for that she cannot, unless it be those witches which kill by poison, which either they receive from the devil or he teacheth them to make—but because she dealeth with devils.

By this reasoning, the "white witch," ostensibly doing good to her neighbors, was just as damnable as the really bad witch. One of the most celebrated Protestant theologians, William Perkins, in his own day reckoned second only to Calvin, wrote:

> In like manner, though the witch were in many respects profitable, and did not hurt but procured much good, yet, because he hath renounced God his king and governor and hath bound himself by other laws to the service of the enemies of God and his church, death is his portion

justly assigned him by God: he may not live.

Witchcraft, then, differed from sorcery in that it was a form of religion, a Christian heresy. Witchcraft was restricted to a few countries of western Europe, especially France, Germany, Scotland, England, and to some extent, Italy; Holland, the Scandinavian countries, Ireland, and (for other reasons) Spain were virtually free of the delusion. Witchcraft was limited in time to, say, the period from 1484, the date of Pope Innocent's bull which opened the floodgates of witch persecution, to 1692, the trials at Salem, plus an introductory and concluding period of about fifty years on either side. Witchcraft was remorselessly attacked by both civil and church authorities; it resulted in tens of thousands of people being legally murdered. Contrariwise, sorcery is universal: the witch of Endor summoning Samuel at the request of Saul, Medea bewitching the dragons to let Jason fetch the Golden Fleece, are examples of sorcery. Sorcery extends from Europe to Africa to the West Indies to China, is not limited to any special period of time, has nothing to do with Christianity (and in fact existed before it), is seldom persecuted by the authorities, and never results in mass slaughter. Sorcery has persisted as an effort to control natural forces, for good or evil, and has developed whenever a certain stage of culture was reached. Witchcraft was a part of religion; sorcery part of folklore.

This definition of witchcraft, considered from the religious view as a crime of the mind, the imagination, or motives, is not arbitrary; the word had no other meaning at the time when witchcraft dominated men's thinking, living, and dying. To every theologian, judge, lawyer, professor, administrator, Catholic and Protestant, witchcraft meant just this. The jurist, Jean Bodin, in 1580, gave the legal definition of a witch as "one who knowing God's law tries to bring about some act *through an agreement with the devil.*" The Catholic demonologist Del Rio, in 1599, defined witchcraft as "an art by which, *by the power of a contract entered into with the devil,* some wonders are wrought which pass the common understanding of men." In 1653, the Anglican judge Sir Robert Filmer echoed Del Rio in almost identical terms: "Witchcraft is an art serving for the working of wonders, *by the assistance of the devil,* so far as God shall permit." Edward Phillips, the nephew of John Milton, wrote in 1671 that witchcraft is "a certain evil art, *whereby with the assistance of the devil, or evil spirits,* some wonders may be wrought which exceed the common comprehension of men." Cotton Mather placed the American colonies on record: "Witchcraft is the doing of strange and for the most part ill things *by the help of evil spirits.*" Even when belief in devils was waning, a professor of law at Glasgow University was still repeating in 1730 the old formulation as it had been known and acted on for three centuries: "Witchcraft is the black art whereby strange and wonderful things are wrought *by a power derived from the devil.*"

By 1736, when witchcraft was removed from the list of felonies in England, traffic with the devil had become a superstition (for which any fortuneteller could be prosecuted) ; but the word continued current to describe what had formerly been the trappings of witchcraft—the petty irritations and mishaps of life, the *maleficia,* for which a rational explanation was hard to come by. The thing disappeared; the word continued.

The ascription of guilt and the severest punishment to people for what they thought, or imagined, or were forced to admit having thought or imagined, was the achievement of the Inquisition. The function of the Inquisition was to change the opinion of anyone who thought differently from what the Church told him; if he refused to alter his beliefs, it was the additional function of the Inquisition to see that he was destroyed. "Faith must be persuaded to men, and not imposed upon them," said St. Bernard. But he added in his next sentence, "Yet it would be better that they were coerced by the sword of that magistrate who beareth not the sword in vain, than that they should be suffered to bring many others into their own error."

Intolerance began in the twelfth century,

and was promoted by both church and state—the state in the persons of the Count of Toulouse (before 1194), the King of Aragon (1197), and the Emperor Frederick II (1224). The Church kept pace. Pope Lucius III in 1184 (exactly 300 years before Pope Innocent VIII) had created an episcopal inquisition for a tri-annual inquiry, an *inquisitio,* into heresy. In 1199, Pope Innocent III expanded the prohibitions against heresy, and encouraged their enforcement by permitting confiscation of a heretic's possessions; his instructions later became part of the Canon Law of the Church. By a decree, *Excommunicamus,* in 1215, Innocent III forced the secular authorities, on pain of heresy, to swear "that they will strive faithfully, to the utmost of their ability, to exterminate from their territories subject to their rule all heretics who have been proscribed by the Church."

For a century, the Inquisition attacked the Waldenses and Cathari and other heretical sects in southern France; it worked so successfully that it killed most of the heretics and so dried up the sources of its funds. In 1375, the Inquisitor Eymeric lamented: "In our days, there are no more rich heretics, so that princes, not seeing much money in prospect, will not put themselves to any expense; it is a pity that so salutary an institution as ours should be so uncertain of its future."

Ways and means to forestall the diminution of potential victims had been broached as early as 1258, when the Inquisition asked the Pope "whether it ought not to take cognizance of divination and sorcery." Permission was denied, unless the sorcery involved manifest heresy—the detection and removal of which were the Inquisition's primary purposes. After 1320, when Pope John XXII empowered the Inquisition at Carcassonne to prosecute those who worshiped demons, entered a pact with them, made images, or used sacred objects to work magic, the Inquisition slowly and unevenly developed its concept of witchcraft—heresy superimposed on magic. Trials for heretical sorcery occurred at Carcassonne in 1330 and 1335 (when seventy-four persons were accused), and regularly thereafter. By 1350, in Carcassonne and Toulouse, the Inquisition had burned 600 persons as heretics for practicing the new sorcery. Trials for witchcraft spread from inquisitor to inquisitor, throughout southern France, to south and western Switzerland, and into French Savoy and northern Italy and up into the Rhineland.

Pope John's permission was reformulated in later bulls, and continued operative until 1451, when Pope Nicholas V extended the inquisitors' authority to deal with all kinds of sorcery, even not "manifestly savoring of heresy." Inquisitors were the first to write on witchcraft, including the first vernacular works in French and Spanish; among others were the Dominican inquisitors Nicholas Eymeric, Nicholas Jacquier, Jean Vineti, and Girolamo Visconti. The *Malleus Maleficarum*, printed about 1486 and the most celebrated of all books on witchcraft, was the work of Jakob Sprenger and Heinrich Kramer, two such inquisitors; it became the first manual to codify the heresy of witchcraft as including pact, sabbat, and night flight: "A belief that there are such things as witches is so essential a part of the Catholic faith that obstinately to maintain the opposite opinion savors of heresy."

The concept of the heresy of witchcraft was frankly regarded as a new invention, both by the theologians and by the public. Having to hurdle an early church law, the Canon Episcopi, which said in effect that belief in witchcraft was superstitious and heretical, the inquisitors cavilled by arguing that the witchcraft of the Canon Episcopi and the witchcraft of the Inquisition were different. The new witchcraft was certainly a heresy and the prohibitions of the Canon Episcopi did not apply to it. At this stage, numerous theologians could refuse to accept all the contentions of the Inquisition, as did the famous Franciscans Alphonsus de Spina in the fifteenth and Samuel de Cassini in the early sixteenth century. Indeed, the inquisitors met with considerable opposition to their witch hunts and even more considerable apathy. Those two infamous men, Sprenger and Kramer, bitterly complained of the hostility of rulers and people throughout Germany, and had Pope Innocent VIII in his bull of 1484 command that their investigations should not be obstructed.

The early witch hunters all tell of encountering skeptics. Jacquier said "many" opposed the Inquisition; Visconti and Pico that "many" thought the confessions were extorted only by torture. Murner was shocked that some theologians explained disasters by natural causes rather than by witchcraft. And about 1514 Alciatus said the peasants in the subalpine valleys broke into rebellion at the wholesale burnings by the local inquisitor. Only years later, after decades of pounding in the new doctrine and the squelching of opposition, did public support for the delusion grow.

In this, witchcraft differed from sorcery: it was never "of the people." Witchcraft was an intellectual aberration, devised by inquisitors with the exceptional powers of torture and confiscation, and soon taken over and shared by civil authorities (who vaguely recognized that witchcraft was a method of government). An indifferent public was ruthlessly lashed into believing it. Where the methods of the Inquisition were adopted, that is, in Germany and France, tens of thousands of witches were discovered. In England, where torture was not permitted and the property of the witch was not (generally) confiscated, but the hundredth part of the executions of Germany or France were committed. In those occasional autonomous areas in Europe which prohibited torture, such as the Duchy of Juliers-Berg, although surrounded by virtual pogroms of witches, no person was burned for witchcraft after 1609. The town of Cologne prohibited confiscation of property, with the result that, apart from two bad outbreaks, it had far fewer executions for witchcraft than the other components of the Empire. When in 1630-31 the Holy Roman Emperor forbade the appropriation of property by the courts, persecutions for witchcraft decreased immediately, as at Bamberg, where an average of 100 a year had been burned from 1626 to 1629; in 1630 only twenty-four were executed, and in 1631 none.

With the bull of Pope Innocent VIII in

1484, witchcraft came of age—long after the dark Middle Ages. Armed with their manuals of procedure, such as the *Malleus Maleficarum,* and with power to torture those brought before them, the inquisitors roamed Europe hunting witches. Secular judges got into the act. Obeying the instructions given in the rapidly multiplying manuals, they forced the accused under torture to admit the crimes enumerated and reveal their wicked accomplices. The confessions of witches authenticated the experts, and the denunciations ensured a continuing supply of victims. Throughout France and Germany this procedure became standardized; repeated year after year, in time it built up a huge mass of "evidence," all duly authorized, from the mouths of the accused. On these confessions, later demonologists based their compendiums and so formulated the classic conceptions of witchcraft, which never existed save in their own minds.

One typical set of standardized questions was used at Colmar, in Lorraine, over the three centuries of the witch mania:

1. How long have you been a witch?
2. Why did you become a witch?
3. How did you become a witch and what happened on that occasion?
4. Who is the one you chose to be your incubus? What was his name?
5. What was the name of your master among the evil demons?
6. What was the oath you were forced to render him?

The questions continued:

21. What animals have you bewitched to sickness or death, and why did you commit such acts?
22. Who are your accomplices in evil . . . ?
24. What is the ointment with which you rub your broomstick made of . . . ?
26. What tempests have you raised, and who helped you to produce them?

When it is remembered that the accused had to answer, that refusal was deemed taciturnity necessitating harsher torture, that judges or torturers would prompt the accused's memory, the uniformity of confessions is no mystery.

The nature of witchcraft is best understood by reading court reports of witch trials to see how admissions of guilt were secured. The most detailed were those of the early seventeenth century, but the procedures were about the same as those of the sixteenth century. Three such court records will be briefly noted here; they are described in full in the appropriate individual entries in this *Encyclopedia.*

Exhibit One is typical of tens of thousands of trials in the Rhineland. It took place at Eichstätt in 1637. The accused was a poor peasant woman. None of the crimes of which she was accused—night rides, sabbat banquets, storm-raising, exhumation of corpses, passing through locked doors—was real or possible of proof; nor was any proof offered. The judges were interested solely in extracting a confession of guilt and securing names of alleged accomplices, who sooner or later would be subjected to a similar fate.

We pick up the thread of the court report on November 15, 1637, after the prisoner has denied being a witch. She is examined for the devil's marks. The report (written in a German dialect, in the third person) continues:

Where had she received these devil's marks?

She does not know. She had nothing to do with the devil.

Inasmuch as the accused does not respond to merciful treatment, she is brought into the torture chamber.

Evidence taken down in the torture chamber: After being put on the ladder, and the ropes tightened a little, she says, Yes, she could be a witch. When released, she announces she is not a witch. Therefore she is put back on the ladder and drawn once, twice, and thrice; finally, she is released on the admission that she is a witch. But immediately she becomes stubborn and denies that she is a witch. Then again she is drawn even more tightly on the ladder.

She confesses it is true that fourteen years ago, when she was unmarried, she had become a witch.

But since she had testified that she had been married for twenty-three years, how could it be only fourteen years ago that she became a witch?

At this, she asked to be taken off the ladder, when she would tell the truth. No, she must first make a start at confessing; she deserves to remain on the ladder. When she finds out she is not going to be released, she says that about eighteen years ago, once her husband had come home drunk and wished the devil would take her (at that time she had just given birth to another child) and her children, young and old alike. . . .

[The next day, after further lengthy questioning, the report goes on:]

Since the prisoner feigns sickness and seems to want to deny her evidence, and since the signs of her piety of yesterday seem to fade, she is ordered to be flogged in the torture chamber to induce fear and a true testimony. After three floggings, she says that the devil, dressed in black, came to her prison cell last night and this morning. Last night he arrived precisely between eleven and twelve o'clock and had intercourse with her, but he caused her so much pain that she could hardly hold him, and she thinks her back and thighs are falling apart. Furthermore, she promised to surrender her body and soul to him again, to reveal nothing of this pact, and to remain true to him only, and to oppose the judges as long as she can. In return, her incubus promised to help her and ordered her to think how she could commit suicide. To this end, she continued scratching open with her fingernails the middle veins on her right arm, a half *bazen* wide, where she had had a blood-letting two weeks ago, because the scars were very recent and the veins could be opened very easily. In this way she could kill herself without attracting attention and go to the devil in both body and soul.

[On November 27, the prisoner again becomes reluctant.] She says her testimony so far is true, but then she sighs heavily.

This seems to be another revocation. So she is again confronted with the hangman and questioned.

How did she influence the weather?

She does not know what to say and can only whisper, "Oh, Heavenly Queen, protect me!" . . .

The torture of the Spanish boots was applied to one foot, but the screws were not tightened. . . .

Inasmuch as her answers are unsatisfactory, and she still seems to be under the domination of the devil, she is tied with ropes in order to receive a flogging. Several lashes are administered. Thereupon she confesses that she and N.N., fifteen years ago, buried in her garden the powder she had received from the devil, in the hope that it would cause bad weather and prevent the fruit from ripening that year. And thus it happened.

She does not want to continue.

She says the devil commanded her not to say anything else. Whatever they asked her, she balked at, and recited the creed. And after long and repeated orders to confess, she was lashed three times with the whip while the bells tolled the Ave Maria.

The trial continues and the end looms near. On December 11 she is led back into the torture chamber and confirms the names of forty-five accomplices. For three following days, December 13, 14, and 15, she confirms her testimony of the preceding month. On December 17, she is burned as a witch.

Exhibit Two is the ecclesiastical trial of a parish priest, Father Dominic Gordel, in 1631, before the Bishop of Sitie, acting as Vicar-General of Lorraine. The original charges which implicated Father Gordel had been made by persons under torture and themselves accused of witchcraft.

In the tower called La Joliette in the episcopal palace of Toul, April 26, 1631, at one o'clock in the afternoon, in the presence of the Reverend Master Jean Midot, Grand Archdeacon and Canon of the said Church of Toul, Master Antoine l'Antan, priest almoner of the Squire of Sitie, and in addition, Charles Mathiot, doctor of medicine, and Jean Marson, surgeon of Toul, whom we asked to assist in conducting the trial and to see that no unreasonable violence be inflicted on the said Gordel. Declared to the said Gordel, after being seriously admonished about the gravity of the charges laid against him, that he should freely confess his crime without forcing us to resort to the tortures which were being prepared for him, and, after we had made him swear on the Holy Gospels of our Lord, laying his hands on the book, to speak the truth. He replied that he was no sorcerer and that he never had any pact, implied or overt, with the devil.

Upon which, we ordered Master Poirson, hangman of the town of Toul, to apply the thumbscrews on the left hand (except the fingers used for benediction). The accused called on "Jesus, Maria," and said that he had never been a sorcerer. Then we had the thumbscrews applied on the same fingers of the right hand, whereupon he said, "St. Nicholas!"

Questioned if he had any kind of pact with the devil, he said No, and that he wished only to die in the arms of God.

Then we caused the aforesaid screws to be applied to his big toes, at which he said he had never seen nor been at a sabbat, and cried out, "Jesus, Maria! St. Nicholas!" and "St. Mary, Mother of God! Sweet Jesus!"

Questioned if he had not conducted Claude Cathelinotte to a sabbat, he replied he had not and that he had never been to one.

After this, we had him put on the ladder and stretched out, and we ordered him hoisted to the first rung. Questioned if he had ever been to a sabbat and made a pact with the devil, he said only, "Jesus, Maria!" adding, "I am dying!" Admonished to tell if he had ever committed any act of sorcery or pretended to act as a priest joining persons in matrimony at a sabbat, he said No. We observed, however, that all this time he had said nothing but Jesus, Maria, and that he had never made any compact, secret or open, with the devil, and that he had not been to a sabbat.

[Torture was increased, and Father Gordel was put to the strappado, and, while he was hanging by his arms bound behind his back, the vise was applied.]

After this, we ordered the vise applied to the left arm, thigh, and left leg; to all this he said that he had never been at a sabbat and, "I am dying! I am broken! Jesus, Maria! I renounce the devil!" With this, we ordered him to be crushed

more severely, whereupon he cried that he told the truth and that he had never been at a sabbat, always saying, "Jesus, Maria! Mother of God have pity on me! Never have I had any compact with the devil, secret or otherwise. I have never consented to his temptings." Pressed more tightly, he said, "Jesus, Maria! Father everlasting, help me! I am broken! I never saw a sabbat. I was never at a sabbat. I renounce the devil and confess the Holy Trinity. I deliver myself into the hands of the good angels. Mercy, I beg God for mercy!"

Exhibit Three, for an incidental reason, is perhaps the most moving of all the court records, although again the procedures are commonplace. In 1628, a burgomaster of Bamberg, the 55-year-old Johannes Junius, was accused of witchcraft by his friends under torture. Like all the other accused, on his first interrogation he said he knew nothing of the crime of witchcraft. Two days later, "the aforesaid Junius was again without torture exhorted to confess, but again confessed nothing. Whereupon, since he would confess nothing, he was put to the torture."

Unique in this case is the letter Junius managed to smuggle out of jail to his daughter Veronica, wherein he told what happened to him.

And then came also—God in highest Heaven have mercy—the executioner and put the thumbscrews on me, both hands bound together, so that the blood spurted from the nails and everywhere, so that for four weeks I could not use my hands, as you can see from my writing.

Thereafter they stripped me, bound my hands behind me, and drew me up on the ladder. Then I thought heaven and earth were at an end. Eight times did they draw me up and let me fall again, so that I suffered terrible agony. I said to Dr. Braun, "God forgive you for thus misusing an innocent and honorable man." He replied, "You are a knave."

And this happened on Friday, June 30, and with God's help I had to bear the torture. When at last the excutioner led me back to the cell, he said to me, "Sir, I beg you, for God's sake, confess something, whether it be true or not. Invent something, for you cannot endure the torture which you will be put to; and, even if you bear it all, yet you will not escape, not even if you were an earl, but one torture will follow another until you say you are a witch. Not before that," he said, "will they let you go, as you may see by all their trials, for one is just like another. . . ."

Then I had to tell what people I had seen [at the sabbat]. I said that I had not recognized them. "You old knave, I must put the torturer at your throat. Say—was not the chancellor there?" So I said Yes. "Who besides?" I had not recognized anybody. So he said: "Take one street after another. Begin at the market, go out on one street and back on the next." I had to name several persons there. Then came the long street. I knew nobody. Had to name eight persons there. Then the Zinkenwort—one person more. Then over the upper bridge to the Georgthor, on both sides. Knew nobody again. Did I know anybody in the castle—whoever it might be, I should speak without fear. And thus continuously they asked me on all the streets, though I could not and would not say more. So they gave me to the torturer, told him to strip me, shave me all over, and put me to the torture. "The rascal knows one on the market place, is with him daily, and yet won't name him." By this they meant Burgomaster Dietmeyer; so I had to name him too.

Then I had to tell what crimes I had committed. I said nothing. "Hoist the knave up!" So I said that I was to kill my children, but I had killed a horse instead. It did not help. I had also taken a sacred wafer, and had buried it. When I said this, they left me in peace.

Now, my dearest child, here you have all my acts and confession, for which I must die. And it is all sheer lies and inventions, so help me God. For all this I was forced to say through dread of torture beyond what I had already endured. For they never cease the torture till one confesses something; be he ever so pious, he must be a witch. Nobody escapes, though he were an earl. If God send no means of bringing the truth to light, our whole kindred will be burned. God in heaven knows that I know not the slight-

est thing. I die innocent and as a martyr.

Dear child, keep this letter secret, so that people do not find it, else I shall be tortured most piteously and the jailers will be beheaded. So strictly is it forbidden . . . Dear child, pay this man a thaler . . . I have taken several days to write this—my hands are crippled. I am in a sad plight. . . .

Good night, for your father Johannes Junius will never see you more.

Such was the pattern of witch trials throughout Europe.

To those reared in the pagan, common-law tradition of the Anglo-Saxons, where the prosecution has to prove the accused guilty, the inquisitorial law of the Roman Catholic Church and the Continental countries, both deriving from the classical codes of ancient Rome, must seem repugnant—the accused had to prove himself innocent, otherwise his guilt was assumed. In crimes of conscience—that is, of ideas, thoughts, or motives—this task is, of course, impossible. Other aspects of inquisitorial laws are just as intolerable:

1. The procedure was secret.

2. Common report was accepted as an indication of guilt. In theory this consisted of the testimony of several trustworthy persons; in practice, hearsay gossip or denunciations given under torture. The accused had to disprove the rumors.

3. Frequently, the precise charges were concealed from the accused. Very occasionally, he was allowed a lawyer appointed by the court, but the lawyer had to take care lest he defend the accused too well and so himself be accused of befriending a heretic. Finally, even this pretense was abolished.

4. Witnesses or informers were kept secret, but if they desired, they might confront the accused.

5. Persons normally debarred from giving evidence in all other trials were permitted and encouraged to testify in witch trials—children of ten years and younger, perjurers, felons, and excommunicates.

6. No favorable evidence was permitted about the accused's previous life and character. In crimes of conscience, a man's actions counted for nought.

7. A witness for the accused would be presumed to be a friend, and therefore guilty by association of the same crime.

8. Torture was always employed, nor was there any limit to its severity or duration. If the accused died under torture, it was said the devil broke his neck. Even if the accused confessed without torture, nevertheless he had to make his confession under torture; it was assumed he might have confessed falsely just to avoid being tortured. After torture, the accused had to repeat his confession "freely," and the court record would so state.

9. The most severe torture was reserved to make the accused an informer; often the names of "accomplices" were suggested to him by the judges or hangmen.

10. No one accused was ever found innocent. At best, his case would be declared Not Proven, and the trial could be reopened at any time. However, this was theoretical, for in practice the accused was tortured until he confessed, or died under the torture.

The procedure of a witch trial, a *crimen exceptum*, an "exceptional crime," was therefore accurately summarized in 1580 by Jean Bodin, as observed at the beginning of this Introduction:

> Wherefore it is that one accused of being a witch ought never to be fully acquitted and set free unless the calumny of the accuser is clearer than the sun, inasmuch as the proof of such crimes is so obscure and so difficult that *not one witch in a million would be accused or punished if the procedure were governed by the ordinary rules.*

Victims kept silent about the methods used to force them to become informers, for any attempt to make a public recantation of the falsity of their denunciations brought on an even more grievous torment: such relapsed or obdurate victims would forego the customary clemency of being strangled before being burned.

Occasionally, a witch confided his perjury to his father confessor, who left some brief record. One such, now lost and known only by a description in a book which itself has survived in a single copy, was made about 1630 by an obscure clergyman of Hirschberg, near Paderborn, Michael Stapirius. He recounted a typical answer from one witch whom he urged to retract the false witnessing.

> I was tortured, and I was asked, "What do you know about so-and-so and so-and-so who live by the cemetery?" I was asked so often that I could not help seeing what people he [the inquisitor] wanted me to denounce. So I mentioned the names of the persons about whom people had been whispering. But I really don't know anything bad about them . . . I begged the commissioner to strike out their names, but he answered that if I should declare them innocent I should be tortured again.

When the chaplain pleaded with another convicted witch to rehabilitate the innocent persons she had been forced to name, the woman replied:

> But look, Father, look at my legs! They are like fire—ready to burn up— so excruciating is the pain. I could not stand so much as a fly touching them, to say nothing of submitting again to torture. I would a hundred times rather die than endure such frightful agony again. I cannot describe to any human being how terrific the pain actually is.

Another woman told the priest she feared her informing on others would bring her eternal damnation:

> I never dreamed that by means of the torture a person could be brought to the point of telling such lies as I have told. I am not a witch, and I have never seen the devil, and still I had to plead guilty myself and denounce others. I beseech you, for God's sake, help me to be saved.

With such unimpeachable exposés as these, it is no wonder that the authorities saw to it that all copies of Michael Stapirius' little book were destroyed.

In England it was somewhat easier for condemned persons to proclaim their innocence—not that it affected their execution. One woman, about 1662, told the Lord Advocate:

. . . under secrecy, that she had not confessed because she was guilty, but, being a poor creature who wrought for her meat, and being defamed for a witch, she knew she would starve, for no person thereafter would either give her meat or lodgings, and that all men would beat her, and hound dogs at her, and that therefore she desired to be out of the world. Whereupon she wept most bitterly, and, upon her knees, called God to witness to what she said.

A highly damning indictment of witchcraft was made by a famous Jesuit, a theologian and poet, Friedrich von Spee, in his *Cautio Criminalis* [*Precautions for Prosecutors*] (1631). Not only was Spee a trained scholar, but a working parish priest whose office it was to accompany condemned witches to the stake. From his experience with the trials, Father Spee concluded: "Previously I never thought of doubting that there were many witches in the world; now, however, when I examine the public record, I find myself believing that there are hardly any."

The whole of Spee's summary of the nightmare of the witch trials deserves the most careful attention. He wrote:

When, under stress of pain, the witch has confessed, her plight is indescribable. Not only cannot she escape herself, but she is also compelled to accuse others whom she does not know, whose names are frequently put into her mouth by the investigators or suggested by the executioner, or of whom she has heard as suspected or accused. Those in turn are forced to accuse others, and these still others, and so it goes on. Who can help seeing that it must go on and on? . . . It is the same with those who are calumniated maliciously; if they do not seek redress, their silence is proof of guilt; if they do seek it, the calumny is spread, suspicions are aroused, and it becomes common fame. Thus those forced under torture to denounce are likely to name names. From all which follows this corollary, worthy to be noted in red ink: that, if only the trials be steadily continued, nobody is safe, no matter of what sex, fortune, condition, or dignity, if any

enemy or detractor wishes to bring a person under suspicion of witchcraft.

To insure greater acceptance of the executions and to convince the multitude of the enormity and reality of witchcraft, the confessions were publicly read at the executions. In Germany, the court scribe used his notes of the questions and answers to write a formal "relation," which had to be signed by the accused as a voluntary statement of guilt. In England, in addition to the public reading of the confessions, little pamphlets or chapbooks giving the witches' confessions were immediately printed and widely distributed. By such means, from their earliest and most impressionable years, children were brainwashed into accepting witchcraft as something which existed in fact, and adults were terrorized into fearful silence and nervous conformity. Yet why should they not believe what their pastors and priests, judges and jurists, professors and theologians, all told them was true? Would such leaders mislead?

How quickly public opinion could be manipulated and changed is seen in Hermann Löher's observation that in the Bonn region, in 1601, a late killing frost was ascribed to an act of God; by 1631, after the witch judges had been active, similar disasters were universally ascribed to the malice of witches. By thus associating physical damage experienced by ordinary people with their sophisticated theory of heresy, the civil and ecclesiastical inquisitors could pose as friends to mankind.

One important aspect of witchcraft is often ignored: by the beginning of the seventeenth century, witchcraft had developed into a vested interest and an industry. The courts, secular and religious, were self-sustaining. The witch or his relatives paid for the salaries and perquisites of the judges, court officials, torturers, physicians, clergymen, scribes, guards, attendants. Every act of torture, every banquet which the judges held whenever a suspect appeared before them, the very food the prisoner was given, had to be paid for. The workmen who erected the stakes and scaffolds and the men who brought the wood and tar for the executions profited by the death of each witch. Less directly, inn-keepers profited by the crowds who came to watch the executions. The need to keep the organization functioning and thereby pro-viding a livelihood for so many people was a major factor in the insistence that witches be tortured into confession and denuncia-tion of accomplices, for a supply of poten-tial victims was essential. "Wretched crea-tures are compelled by the severity of the torture to confess things they have never done," said Father Cornelius Loos in 1592, "and so by cruel butchery innocent lives are taken; *and, by a new alchemy, gold and silver are coined from human blood.*"

The big-business aspect of witchcraft was explicitly censured by a canon of Treves Cathedral in the early seventeenth century. Canon Linden noted how, as at Bonn, a season of severe damage to the crops now incited animosity to any suspected of work-ing harm.

> *This movement was promoted by many in office, who looked for wealth in the ashes of the victims.* And so, from court to court, throughout all the towns and villages of the diocese, scurried special accusers, inquisitors, notaries, jurors, judges, constables, dragging to trial and torture human beings of both sexes and burning them in great numbers. Scarcely any of those who were accused escaped punishment. Nor were even the leading men spared in the city of Treves. For the judge, two burgomasters, several coun-cilors and associate judges were burned. Canons of sundry collegiate churches, parish priests, rural deans, were swept away in this ruin. So far, at length, did the madness of the furious populace and of the courts go in this thirst for blood *and booty* that there was scarcely any-body who was not smirched by some suspicion of this crime. *Meanwhile, nota-ries, copyists, and innkeepers grew rich.* The executioner rode a blooded horse, like a noble of the court, and went clad in gold and silver; his wife vied with noble dames in the richness of her array.

How far removed is the penniless hag from the typical witch burned in the trials (although, of course, many old women were

slaughtered), is seen in a letter to a Count Werner from the parish priest of a village near Bonn, in the early seventeenth cen-tury:

> The victims of the funeral pyres are for the most part male witches. Half the city must be implicated; for already professors, law students, pastors, canons, vicars, and monks have been arrested and burned. His Princely Grace has seventy seminarians training to become priests, one of whom, eminent as a musician, was arrested yesterday; two others were sought, but have escaped. The Chancellor and his wife and the Private Secretary's wife have already been apprehended and executed. On the Eve of Our Lady's Day there was executed here a girl of nineteen who had the reputation of being the love-liest and most virtuous in all the city, and who from her childhood had been brought up by the Prince-Bishop himself. A canon of the cathedral, named Roten-sahe, I saw beheaded and burned. Chil-dren of three or four years have devils for their paramours. Students and boys of noble birth, of nine, ten, eleven, twelve, thirteen, and fourteen years of age, have here been burned. To sum up, things are in such a pitiful state, that one does not know with what people one may talk and associate.

While providing a living for those con-nected with the trials, the property of the condemned witches also yielded extensive booty for whatever local authority had jurisdiction. After paying the expenses, the property of the witch was confiscated either by the autonomous town, the local noble-man, the king, the bishop, or the Inquisi-tion; sometimes several courts, secular and ecclesiastical, shared the loot. With such an easy source of funds, it is not strange that the leaders of Germany and France were for a long time content to let witch persecu-tions continue.

To a century which has seen—and is forgetting—Belsen and Lidice, and the an-nihilation of an estimated 15,000,000 human beings in five years by the Nazis, the cruelty and injustice of the witch judges may seem inconsequential. It took 200 years to burn, at a conservative estimate,

200,000 witches. Obviously, in respect to genocide, witchcraft cannot be compared to fascism. But in another respect, the theory of witchcraft was worse than fascism. In Nazi Germany, torture and extermination were justified as practical politics or done with no justification. Nazi apologists did not appeal to Christianity; at the most, they synthesized an emotional mysticism and spurious reasoning. Furthermore, in the rest of the world, the majority of the spiritual and intellectual leaders were firmly opposed to fascism, long before the outbreak of war. What makes witchcraft so repellent, and morally lower than fascism, is that throughout civilized Europe, in every country (with the possible later exception of Holland), the clergy led the persecutions and condoned them in the name of Christianity, while the lawyers and judges and professors abetted them in the name of reason.

One courageous judge, Hermann Löher, at length became so horrified at the witch persecution (in which he had taken part) that he expressed dissent. He barely escaped with his family from Germany to Holland in 1636; but for fear of reprisals he delayed forty years, until he was eighty-one, before publishing his account of the trials. Löher asked:

> Who would assume such a dangerous task? Should anyone undertake it, out of Christian charity, then people would somehow manage to prevent him from being heard; and if he were heard, then those who began the unjust burnings would cry out they mistrust that he is a witch patron.

Nor was repression the idea of just a handful of sinful individuals; it was the official policy of the churches, Roman Catholic and Protestant. Some of the last to keep the delusion alive, long after it had been rejected by the other leaders of society, were to be found among the clergy. Richard Baxter makes a good example; a renowned Presbyterian teacher, in 1691 he wrote his *Certainty of the World of Spirits*, a work in support of belief in witchcraft. At a time when his contemporaries were opposing the delusion, Baxter came down on the side of superstition and obscurantism.

The men on the side of humanity were those priests and ministers who revolted against their religion, often in the process suffering as "witch lovers," along with those skeptics labeled by their opponents as "sadducees and atheists." Shaming the cowards and addleheads, the sycophants and opportunists, these people showed the alternative way. They shine like bright stars, redeeming one's faith in human nature. On a key issue of the sixteenth and seventeenth centuries, "Do you or do you not approve the trials, the methods used to produce confessions, and the whole apparatus of witch hunting?" only a few replied Nay. These men, the "witch defenders," had become the real enemy, witches a mere pretext to attack them for discussing a condition of society and reaching their own conclusions. These courageous few shook off the burden of credulity and opened the way for the age of reason and new mental horizons free from thought control.

Throughout these centuries, those who should, by their birth, training, and position, have been the conscience of the world, accepted the delusion and promoted it. Such men not only appealed to the emotions of religion, but perverted the entire structure of logic and reason. Everything was sacrificed to a preconceived prejudice. The logic of the demonologists, all highly educated men, leaders in their own disciplines, is the most terrifying feature of witchcraft. Because of their turning rational thinking on its head—far more than the most foul act of a torturer or witch judge—the centuries of the witchcraft mania may be called the centuries of un-civilization.

Johann Meyfarth, a Protestant professor and contemporary of Father Spee, graphically described the logic of witch hunters. The judges of a witch pose certain alternative questions in reaching their verdict: Is Anna in good or bad repute? If in bad, she is a witch; if in good, she is undoubtedly a witch, for witches always seek to be well thought of. Anna is arrested. The judges ask if she is frightened or not. If yes, she is a witch; if not, she is just as certainly a witch, for witches always represent themselves as innocent.

These dilemmas, selected from the procedures Dr. Meyfarth witnessed at the trials, were paralleled by the explanations of the demonologists, who applied Ockham's law in reverse: the most roundabout, tortuous, illogical explanation of any simple action was the best. The Italian friar Guazzo in 1608 commented on a ninety-year-old priest, waiting to be burned as a witch, who cut his throat. The explanation that an old man, after torture and in desperation at his impending fate, committed suicide was not acceptable. Guazzo told what really happened:

> A demon appeared to him and tempted him so that . . . he cut his own throat with his knife, and although the wound was not serious enough to cause instant death, yet the demon, in that very act of desperation, seized violently on this soul and carried it to hell, to the great astonishment of all. I saw the man dead, and still warm, lying on the straw; and as he had led the life of a beast, so he lay on the provender of beasts. For so did Divine Justice dispose, which rewards every man according to his works; and God willed that he, who had for ninety years lived a follower of Satan, should also entl his life at the hands of Satan.

Paulus Grillandus, a papal judge, gave an explanation of why a witch, kept in fetters in a strong prison and watched by guards, did not escape. The devil, said Grillandus, could very easily help the woman change her shape and crawl through the keyhole. But "the reason why no witch can escape from prison is that, when the devil has once got control over them, he is eager that they should be put to death, in order that they should not escape him by recanting and penitence." The Inquisitor Bartolommeo Spina explained why oxen, left unattended and killed by witches, are later found in their original condition, apparently unmolested. Witches, said Spina, slay the ox and feast on it, and then, with the help of

the devil, put back the skin over its bones and revive it.

The most common sleight of the demonologists was explaining how a woman could be watched in her bed by her husband during the whole night and still be miles away at a devil's sabbat. This marital deception might be achieved in several ways: the witch could leave a pillow and bewitch her husband into imagining it his wife; or the devil might impersonate the body of the woman while she was away. In 1515, a Milanese lawyer could ask the obvious question: "Why not rather presume the demon to be with his demons and the woman with her husband? Why invent a real body in a fictitious sabbat and a fantastic one in a real bed?" A few years later, no one could pose such a question and expect to escape punishment.

When the majority of educated men think in such a frame of reference, and the majority of poorly educated men follow them, humanity's chances for survival become dim. Other facets of witchcraft discussed in this book may be far more striking and sensational than these intellectual perversities: the detailed analyses of the techniques of copulation between devils and humans, the odd survival into the twentieth century of a belief in noisy demons or poltergeists, the accounts of werewolves and vampires, the description of epileptic children considered suffering from demoniacal possession, the flare-up of a sophisticated Satanism in the black masses said for the courtiers of Louis XIV. Just because they are sensational, not disturbing, and escapist, these aspects of witchcraft generally dominate the average book about witches. As absorbing and valid as they indeed are, these subjects do not give the essence of witchcraft or reveal its real horror. Nothing about witchcraft is more ominous than the suppression and destruction of man's power to think and his right to ask questions. Those who set up the witchcraft delusion and spread it damaged Europe's culture for as long as that delusion was not rejected. Our civilization today is that much retarded.

Aberdeen Witches. Inspired by the publication in 1597 of King James's *Demonology*, a witch craze swept over Aberdeen which resulted in the burning of twenty-four men and women. The accusations ran the gamut of witchcraft: dancing with the devil round the town cross, using ligature to cause married men to be untrue to their wives, making milk sour, bewitching animals, or giving love charms of bent pennies tied in a cloth with a piece of red wax.

Old Janet Wishart, representative of the cases, was indicted for casting a *cantrip* or spell on Alexander Thomson, so that he suffered from alternate shivering and sweating. She similarly bewitched Andrew Webster so that he died. Others, too, died because of her evil eye. She raised storms by throwing out live coals; she sent nightmare cats to cause horrible dreams; and she dismembered a corpse hanging on the gallows. She was burned with another witch at the cost of eleven pounds and ten shillings, for the "peat, tar barrels, and coals," and the executioner's fees.

Some of the others accused as witches were identified by a convicted witch who made herself useful to the judges by finding them new victims and thus prolonged her life. She swore she had been at a great gathering in Atholl, and had seen over two thousand witches. "She knew them all well enough, and what mark the devil had given severally to every one of them. There was many of them tried by swimming in the water, by binding of their two thumbs and their great toes together; for being thus cast in the water, they floated always above."

See also Costs of Witch Trials.

Ady, Thomas. Many English polemics on witchcraft sought to convince potential jurors on the fiction or actuality of witchcraft. Thus Thomas Ady's book, quoted vainly by Rev. George Burroughs at his trial in Salem, has for its full title: *A Candle in the Dark, or a Treatise concerning the nature of witches and witchcraft: being advice to the judges, sheriffs, justices of the peace and grandjurymen what to do before they pass sentence on such as are arraigned for their lives as witches* (London, 1656). Ady wrote against the delusion, and attacked the belief head on, using the weapon of the "witchmongers" themselves, the Bible. George L. Burr called it "one of the bravest and most rational of the early protests."

A Candle in the Dark is in three parts.

The first, by the multiple meanings of "witch," disproves the contemporary application of the biblical injunction, "Thou shalt not suffer a witch to live." Deuteronomy xviii. 10-11, for example, makes nine classifications, including astrologer, enchanter, pythonist (e.g., the Endor Witch), soothsayer, necromancer, and juggler (as in Exodus xii. 15). According to these definitions, the real witches were "the popish rout, the contrivers of charms to *delude the people*."

The second book shows that the contemporary proofs of witchcraft are nowhere found in the Bible.

> Where is it written in all the Old and New Testaments that a witch is a murderer, or hath power to kill by witchcraft, or to afflict with any disease or infirmity? Where is it written that witches have imps sucking of their bodies? Where is it written that witches have biggs [nipples] for imps to suck on . . . that the devil setteth privy marks upon witches . . . that witches can hurt corn or cattle . . . or can fly in the air. . . . Where do we read of a he-devil or a she-devil, called incubus or succubus, that useth generation or copulation?

The third book attacks "the vanity of some English writers concerning witches," especially King James, whose *Demonology*

"There is a sabbat every day. . . . The witches are gathered together by the sound of the cornet which is winded by a devil."—Sister Madeleine de Demandolx (1611). From Ricchierus, *Lectionum Antiquarum* (1517).

Ady suggests was ghostwritten by "James, Bishop of Winton [Winchester]." He opposes Thomas Cooper, "a bloody persecutor of the poor," and Matthew Perkins' *Discovery*, "a collection of mingled notions" from Bodin, Spina, and "other popish blood suckers," who composed "great volumes of horrible lies and impossibilities." Less adamantly, he corrects Gaule and Gifford. Throughout, remembering the function of

his book to sway judges and juries, Ady (following Reginald Scot) exposes swimming, witch's marks, malediction by witches, reliance on charms and amulets, ventriloqual speaking from the belly, and jugglers (who often use an imitation mouse on a springy wire as a familiar).

The tenets of evangelical Protestantism were rooted in the Bible, and the Protestant belief in witchcraft, although originally carried over from Roman Catholicism, was therefore easily vulnerable. Once the biblical sanction for witchcraft had been disproved, the Protestants had less resort: they could not claim (as did the Roman Catholic demonologists) the tradition of the Church. Ady was thus very perspicacious in basing his entire argument, not on discrediting individual stories or trials of witches, but on the absence of scriptural authority.

Aix-en-Provence Nuns. "It is true, Madeleine, thou art a witch, and hast performed whatsoever belongeth thereunto in great solemnity; thou hast renounced God at three several masses, one at midnight, another at the dawning of the day, and the third was at high mass."

This accusation of Sister Madeleine de Demandolx de la Palud by her possessing devil, Beelzebub, was a high spot in Grand Inquisitor Sebastian Michaëlis' exorcism of the young penitent. The story of the nuns bewitched by Father Louis Gaufridi, a handsome parish priest of Marseilles, lacks the lurid details of such later accusations as were made against Father Urbain Grandier in 1634, Father Thomas Boullé in 1647, or Father Jean-Baptiste Girard a hundred years later (in 1731). Yet the trial of Father Gaufridi in 1611 (coming soon after the Labourd scares, investigated by De Lancre) attracted much attention, not only locally in Aix-en-Provence and Marseilles, but throughout western Europe. It was immediately reported and quickly translated into foreign languages. Thanks to the smug pride of Inquisitor Michaëlis, it provided one of the most detailed accounts of prolonged daily exorcisms of two tormented girls ever written. His *Admirable History of a Penitent Woman who was seduced by a magician in the country of Provence in France, and of the end of the said magician* displayed his skill in exposing the wizard who had sent devils into the nuns, but the English translation (London, 1613) by "W. B." thought it showed the "poor estate of popery." Fortunately, Michaëlis' account can be corrected by the thousand pages of trial reports now in the Bibliothèque nationale in Paris.

Madeleine de Demandolx came of a very aristocratic and rich Provençal family. A nervous child, somewhat vain and affected, she was deeply religious. In 1605, at the age of twelve, she went to reside in the newly formed Ursuline convent at Aix-en-Provence, a tiny group of only six nuns, all of noble birth. Their spiritual director was the founder of the convent, Father Jean-Baptiste Romillon, S.J., who also superintended the sister house at Marseilles. After being in the convent school for over two years, Madeleine became very depressed and was sent back to her parents at Marseilles. Her spirits improved by contact with a friend of the family, Louis Gaufridi, parish priest of Accoules in Marseilles. Though of humble birth and scant education, he was welcomed by several wealthy families. He was gay, even boisterous, occasionally playfully tossing soft cheese [*brousse*] across the dinner table to the guests. Some two dozen women, single and married, had selected him for their confessor, and apparently enjoyed his society; maybe six were in love with him.

Now approaching fourteen, Madeleine fell in love with Father Gaufridi, aged thirty-four, who frequently visited her at home. When gossip of a prolonged stay of an hour and a half with Madeleine, while everybody was out of the house, got rumored abroad, the aristocratic head of the Ursuline convent at Marseilles, Mother Catherine de Gaumer, warned Madame Demandolx about her daughter. Madeleine told her mother the priest had stolen her most beautiful rose. Mother Catherine also cautioned Father Gaufridi about the dangers of this liaison.

Immorality among the clergy appeared less shocking in the seventeenth than in the twentieth century. The biography [*Vie*] of Father Romillon by Bourguignon (Marseilles, 1669), for example, described a traditional party given a monk after his first mass. A local family paid for the feast, and the daughter acted as "Maraine" or partner for the new priest during the festivities, which included dancing, kissing, and "other liberties." All the monks appeared in secular garb, bedecked with ribbons. When Father Romillon tried to prevent such a festival in his own town, the monks waylaid and beat him with clubs they had concealed under their robes. Apparently, few thought the custom blameworthy. In such a climate, license by an attractive parish priest would excite little attention, unless complicated by witchcraft.

The next year (1607), Madeleine entered the convent as a novice. To Mother Catherine she confessed Father Gaufridi's intimacies with her. Nothing ensued, except that Madeleine was transferred to the more distant convent at Aix, where Father Gaufridi could not visit her. Here, after a year or two, Madeleine, by now sixteen or seventeen, manifested severe shaking fits and convulsive cramps, and had visions of devils. Just before Christmas, 1609, during confession, she smashed a crucifix.

Old Father Romillon decided to exorcize, but without success; and Madeleine's symptoms spread to three other nuns who went into convulsions, lost their speech, and could not swallow. At Easter, 1610, Father Romillon and another priest warned Father Gaufridi about Madeleine's symptoms, and in June they questioned him about his conduct with her. Gaufridi denied sexual relations. Under exorcism, however, Madeleine continued accusing Father Gaufridi: he had denied God, had given her a "green devil" for familiar, and had copulated with her since she was thirteen (later, she said since nine). He told her, "Since I would enjoy your favors, I will give you a drink made of a special powder to make sure that any babies you may get by me won't look at all like me: in this way no one will suspect me of immorality."

Father Romillon persevered with his

Heads of Evil Demons

Sister Louise Capeau taunted Sister Madeleine with demoniacal possession by Astaroth and 6,665 other devils. An illustration from the rare and curious work by Francis Barrett, *The Magus* (1801).

secret exorcisms of this sex-starved girl throughout the year. Her hysteria spread to five other nuns. One of these, Sister Louise Capeau (or Capelle), evidently jealous of the richer and more notorious Madeleine, tried to rival her signs of demoniacal possession. Finally, in desperation, Father Romillon took both girls to the aged Sebastian Michaëlis, the famous Grand Inquisitor in Avignon. Father Michaëlis had much experience with sorcery, for in 1582 he had burned eighteen witches at Avignon. He tried public exorcism in the celebrated shrine of St. Mary Magdalene in

the grotto at Ste-Baume, but fared no better than Father Romillon.

The two girls next were taken to the Royal Convent of St. Maximin, to be treated by another celebrated exorcist, the Flemish Dominican, François Domptius. Here Louise became his star attraction, revealing in a deep bass voice, before numerous spectators, the three devils which possessed her—Vérin, Grésil, and Sonnillon. She taunted Sister Madeleine with possession by Beelzebub, Leviathan, Baalberith, Asmodeus, and Astoroth, and 6,661 other devils [see Demonology]. Madeleine, in reply, blasphemed, "howling and crying with a loud mouth." On December 15, Louise, as the devil Vérin, publicly identified Father Gaufridi as the source of Madeleine's possession: "Thou [Madeleine] wast deceived by a priest who was thy confessor. . . . He is of Marseilles, and is called Louis." The exorcists were "confident that the two girls were indeed possessed."

The Inquisitor decided to summon the alleged cause of this bewitchment, Father Louis Gaufridi, to try his hand at exorcism to get the girls well. On December 30, 1610, accompanied by three priests, Father Gaufridi arrived at Ste-Baume in a raging snowstorm. He knew nothing of exorcism; the two girls mocked his inability. Louise accused him as a magician, forcing him to retort: "If I were a witch, I would certainly give my soul to a thousand devils!" On this proof(!) Gaufridi was put behind bars in a corner of the grotto with its "vile and offensive savors."

Sister Madeleine expanded the accusations, charging Gaufridi with practically every obscenity known to the demonologists. Even at the altar she mocked him: *"Tu non lou dises pas de bon cor."* ["You do not pray with a clean heart."] Meanwhile, Father Gaufridi's rooms in Marseilles were searched for "any schedules or characters of magic," but nothing was found. Apparently, he had sufficient friends, especially among the Capuchin friars, to forestall a "plant."·In fact, all the evidence the Inquisitor could gather was favorable to Gaufridi, and he reluctantly let the priest return to his parish.

The calumnies not being proved, Father Gaufridi determined on a clear-cut vindication. Many clergy agreed the allegations were "merely practice and fooling." Gaufridi appealed to the Bishop of Marseilles and to the Pope; he sought further the suppression of the Ursuline convents and the jailing of the nuns of Ste-Baume.

Madeleine was confined to Ste-Baume by the Inquisitor and developed manic-depressive traits: she had visions, danced and laughed, sang love songs, neighed like a horse, disrupted the services (snatching birettas and tearing a chasuble), told fan-

tastic tales of sabbats (with sodomy and eating of little children). She spit up globs of frothy matter, looking like "a mingle of honey and pitch." Beelzebub caused "her bones to crack and grate one against the other." In her paroxysms, her bowels were displaced "and turned topsy-turvy . . . so that the sounds of these unnatural motions were easily heard. When these tortures were ended, then did [the devils] cast her into a dead sleep or lethargy, so that she seemed stark dead."

The second half of the story of the possessed nuns of Aix-en-Provence moved to the civil courts, inevitable with the spreading notoriety of demoniacal possession,

Relations between confessors and their penitents were frequently satirized in eighteenth-century France. Typical of many tracts and novels is *Les amours de Sainfroid, Jesuite, et d'Eulalie, fille dévote* (La Haye, 1729).

Father Gaufridi's attempts to clear himself of suspected witchcraft, and Inquisitor Michaëlis' political pressure for punishment of the accused sorcerer. In February, 1611, the Parlement of Aix, under its superstitious President, Guillaume de Vair, with nothing except "spiritual evidence" to go on, opened the procès verbal.

The testimony largely recapitulated what happened at the exorcisms; during the trial Madeleine and Louise often went into fits. The girls spoke Provençal, which had to be translated into French for the record. Sister Madeleine acted alternately lucid and demented. She anticipated the Salem girls in her impudence to the priests in court, telling one of them to prove his ordination by showing his tonsure! Then she quietened and confessed her allegations were "all imaginings, illusions, and [had] not a word of truth in them"—*Procès verbal*, February 21, 1611. She swooned for love of Gaufridi: *"O! que si aqueste lengo li poudié pourta uno bonero paraulo à l'aureillo, que contentamen!"* ["Oh! If his tongue could bear to her ears a friendly word, what happiness!"] After this, she was seized with lascivious tremblings, "representing the sexual act, with violent movements of the lower parts of her belly." She displayed devil's marks on her feet and under her left breast, into which physicians stuck pins without causing loss of blood or pain. These stigmata disappeared without warning. Every day she contradicted herself, accusing and then retracting. As the trial continued, Madeleine appeared very much depressed and twice tried to commit suicide.

In March, Father Gaufridi was interrogated. He had been harassed by the Inquisition for a year and was worn out in health, having been kept in an underground dungeon, fettered with heavy chains, among rats and vermin. After his whole body had been meticulously shaved, three devil's marks were found. At the end of the month, Gaufridi confessed to being the "Prince of the Synagogue." He had signed a pact with his own blood, and the devil had promised that all women would "affect and follow" him. (Michaëlis) He invented an elaborate account of a sabbat, more like a formal

ecclesiastical reception, however, than a libidinous revel. Inquisitor Michaëlis was jubilant, and printed a bogus confession ascribed to Gaufridi, comprising fifty-two items. Regaining some strength, Gaufridi denied all these confessions, saying they were forced from him by torture: "All are false, by him composed and invented to give more color and belief to what he says."

Ignoring his retraction, on April 18, 1611, the court found the accused guilty on his own confession of all the indictments: magic, sorcery, idolatry, and fornication (physicians said Sister Madeleine was no virgin). Father Gaufridi was sentenced to be burned alive *"sur un feu de busches"*— on a pyre of bushes, because these burned more slowly than faggots. Even after sentencing, the interrogations went on, with Gaufridi often demented. On his last appearance before the judges, on April 28, he denied intercourse with Madeleine, although admitting he had been a good friend of the family. Then he complained that no one believed what he said, and that he would confess anything the judges wanted. Yes, he ate roasted babies at the sabbat— the truth no longer mattered.

The death warrant was signed on April 29, and on April 30, 1611, the execution took place. Father Louis Gaufridi was first defrocked and degraded by the church authorities, and then handed back to the Parlement of Aix. In order to make his death more horrible, Gaufridi was put to torture, technically to force from him the names of his accomplices. Thrice he was put to the strappado: his arms bound behind his back, he was hoisted on a rope and dropped to the floor. *"Mon Dieu,"* he cried, *"je ne scay point de complices. Ay, laisso, siou mouert."* ["Oh, God, I know of no accomplices. Ah, leave me, I am dying."] At the third drop, he said, in Provençal: *"Yo àiriou, Messiés, non siou pas christian; si noun lou disiot, ay conegut Magdalens a la sinagogo, parce que la conession de deca."* ["I tell you, messieurs, no, I am not a Christian. If I said I did not know Madeleine at the sabbat, it was because I had known her before."]

After the strappado came the *question*

extraordinaire, the brutal torture of squassation. Monsieur Ollivier, the excutioner, attached heavy weights to his feet, and four times hoisted and dropped the victim to within a few inches of the floor, until his body was dislocated by the awful jerking. Still Father Gaufridi could give no names.

Flanked by ten archers, Gaufridi went through the motions of making the *amende honorable*, of asking pardon of God and the court. Then, bound to a hurdle or wooden sled, he was dragged through the crowded streets of Aix. The cortège took five hours to reach the Place des Prêcheurs. By special dispensation (probably by the Bishop of Marseilles), Gaufridi was strangled before being burned. The next day, according to the *Chronique de l'Ordre des Ursulines* (1673), Madeleine de Demandolx de la Palud was cured of her diabolical possession.

Louise Capeau was not cured. She continued to see witches. She was directly responsible for the burning of a blind girl, Honorée, so accused, on July 19, 1611. And other nuns in other convents (e.g., St. Claire's at Aix, and St. Bridget's, in faraway Lille) also caught the original infection. Fathers Michaëlis and Domptius set off to Flanders to exorcize Sister Marie de Sains, who, having recently been in Aix, had spread the contagion to St. Bridget's, Lille. Fortunately, the Archbishop of Malines intervened, and mad Sister Marie was quietly put away in the prison of Tournai.

The closing years of Madeleine's life were as troubled as those of her youth. In 1642, when forty-nine, she was accused of witchcraft. Rejected by her relatives, she had to defend herself alone; some inherited money helped her. Again, in 1652, she was accused and, although she contributed to the Trinitarian order of friars, she was imprisoned the following year. Many witnesses came forward against her; devil's marks were found, and on December 12, 1652, Madeleine de Demandolx was condemned to pay a heavy fine and spend the rest of her life in perpetual imprisonment. After ten years, she was released in custody of a relative to Chateauvieux (Fréjus), and

there, on December 20, 1670, aged seventy-seven, she died.

Alexander VI, Pope. At the end of the fifteenth century, the Inquisition was spreading the witch delusion throughout Europe. Extending the authority Pope Innocent VIII gave to the inquisitors in Germany, Pope Alexander VI in his bull *"Cum acceperimus"* (1501) confirmed the authority of the Inquisitor Angelo of Verona over the whole of Lombardy.

> Inasmuch as we have learned that in the province of Lombardy men and women have abandoned themselves to divers incantations and devilish superstitions, committing infamous crimes by means of poisons [*veneficia*] and divers other practices to destroy men, beasts, and crops, spreading scandalous errors, [therefore] for the accomplishment of our pastoral duty, as charged by God, we are resolved to suppress such crimes and to prevent, as far as lies in our power, God helping us, the promotion of these scandals and errors.
>
> For these reasons we thus command you, as well as your successors in Lombardy, in whom by these presents we place our complete confidence, and we order you to seek out diligently, either alone or in the company of such honest colleagues as you will select, men and women [as described above], and punish and chastise them according to law.
>
> And so that you can the better fulfill this mission, by these presents we give you full power against them, notwithstanding any constitutions or apostolic regulations, dispensations, or ordinary privileges which have been accorded at other times, and notwithstanding any provisions to the contrary, no matter what they may be.

A similar bull was addressed by Julius II (1503) to the Inquisitor of Cremona, Giorgio de Casale, urging him to extirpate "by fire and sword" the sorcerers of Lombardy, especially odious and dangerous because of their ability to transform themselves into cats. He was to disregard the opposition of clerics and laymen. Later, on July 20, 1523, Pope Adrian VI referred to

cõdigna caſtigacõe p̃pl'i xp̃iaɩ̃ deſtruereɛ̃
imperiũ ſarracenoꝛ̃ et ſic ceſſabit eoꝛ̃ ſup
ſticioſa ſecta ſiue lex.

Q Vare⁹ paſſ⁹ et vlti⁹ eſt de ppe=
tua captiuitate ſeu buitute ſar=
raceõꝛ̃ ſub ɩugo xp̃ianoꝛ̃. Hãc
aũt buitutẽ predixit meetbodi⁹ martir lo
quẽs de fine ſeculi Vñ poſtꝗ̃ p̃munciauit
caſtigacõez xp̃ianoꝛ̃ p ſarracenos. Subſe
quenē dixit et p⁹ tribulacõz dieꝛ̃ que fca
erit a filɩɩs yſmael' deſolata erit oĩs terra
ab eis et erũt oĩes amicti oꝛnamentis ex
auro et purpura et ſplendidis vos veſti=
mẽtis tanꝗ̃ ſponſi dicẽtes. Ecce vicim⁹
terrã in foꝛtitudie nr̃a et oĩs ꝗ̃ biⱦãt ĩ
ea. Tũc recoꝛdabit dñs de⁹ ſcm̃ ſuã mi=
ſericoꝛdiã quã p̃miſit diligẽtibꝫ ſe et eis
qui ĩ xp̃o ſue creditur et liberabit eos de
manu ſarracenoꝛ̃. Surget aũt xp̃ianoꝛ̃
gens et pliabit cũ eis et occidet eos gladio
et captiuas ducet m'ieres eoꝛ̃ et inficiet
infantes eoꝛ̃ et deſcendẽt filɩɩ yſmaelis in
gladiũ et tribulacõz et afflictionẽ & re=
det illis dñs mala que ipſi alɩɩs fecerãt et
irruet ſup eos malicia ſepcies tm̃ quantũ
in alɩɩs geſſerũt et occidet illos dñs ĩ mã⁹
xp̃ianoꝛ̃ et erit regnũ xp̃ianoꝛ̃ exaltatũ
ſup oĩa regna et imponet xp̃iani ɩugum
ſup eos graue et erũt ſerui ꝗ̃ remanebunt
et tũc pacificabit terra que ab eis fuerat
deſtructa et qui captiui fuerãt ab eis reti=
rent in terrã ſuã et m'tiplicabunt boïes
ſup terrã et erit indignacio magna regi
romanoꝛ̃ ſup eos qui xp̃m negauerũt &
erit pax et trãquillitas magna ſup terrã
qualis nõ fuit antea nec erit ſil'is p⁹ illã
ꝓ eo ꝗ̃ in fine ſeculoꝛ̃ et erit leticia et pax
ſup omẽz terrã et requieſcet a laboꝛibus.
Hec erit pax de qua dicit apl'⁹. Cũ fuerit
tranquillitas magna et ſecuritas tũc ve=
niet repentin⁹ interoi⁹ a quo liberari me=
reanſ felicė p ib̃m xp̃m dñm nr̃m qui eſt
turris foꝛtitudis a facie inimici cui ſit bo
noꝛ et gloꝛia ſine fine amen.

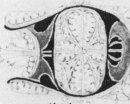

Iſſolutis hereticoꝛ̃ iu=
deoꝛ̃ et ſarraceoꝛ̃ bel
lis. Reſtat expiri ĩ hoc
libro quinto et vltimo
bui⁹ volumis de demo
nũ viribꝫ quid ſez poſ
ſint cont nr̃m fidei foꝛ
talicɩũ. et ut mei⁹ poſſem explicari conce
peũ duodecim cõſideracões circa bellũ de=
monũ occurrunt intellectũ ꝑtractande⸴
Prima erit an ſint temones & de quiddi
tate demonũ et eoꝛ̃ nobilitate ac natura⸴
Scda de eoꝛ̃ ſciencia ❡ Tercia de bello de=
monũ in celo ❡ Quarta de eoꝛ̃ habitacõe
Quita de eoꝛ̃ p̃tate et feminécia ❡ Sexta
de bello demonũ cont humanũ gen⁹ poſt
ꝗ̃ ceciderũt de celo vſqꝫ ad xp̃i aduentũ⸴
Septima de pditione dominɩɩ eoꝛ̃ p iuſti
ciã in xp̃i aduentu⸴ Octaua de ꝓpetatibꝫ
et malicia demonũ ❡ Nona de bello demo
nũ poſt aduentũ xp̃i ❡ Decima de diuerſi
tate demonũ et ſi poſſunt bri ſpiritꝫ fa=
miliares ❡ Vndecĩa de qualitate et figu=
ris coꝛpũ ĩ quibꝫ apparet & ſi poſſunt hu
mana coꝛpa vel aĩas ſubintrare ❡ Duode
cima ꝗ̃ fine debet termiari bella demonũ.

P Ria cõſideracõ é an ſint demões
et de quidditate demonũ et de
eoꝛ̃ nobilitate ac natura. qua
tuor ergo puncta in hac cõſideracõe ſunt
videnda. Primo an ſint demones. Secun
do quid eſt diaboi⁹. Tercio qualis eſt ei⁹
nobilitas. Quarto qualis eſt ei⁹ natura
An ſint demones in mũdo et ſi ſue ꝗ̃ ſunt
eoꝛ̃ noĩa ❡ Prim⁹ punct⁹ eſt an ſint de=
mones et que noĩa eoꝛ̃. Quo ad p̃mũ nõ
diſcrepãt iudei et ſarraceni a xp̃ianis ꝗ̃a
apud iudeos ſcriptũ eſt et diabolos et de
p̃cipibꝫ eoꝛ̃ huſa et azael eſſe appellatos
dicebat etiã iudei in euangelio inſultãtes
contra xp̃m demonũ habet et inſanit. Et
iteꝝ in belzebub p̃ncipe demonioꝛ̃ eicit de
monia qui nõ affirmaret ñ diabolos cre
derent eſſe. Nõ eni poſſunt negare qñ ſcri
ptũ ſit in p̃mo regũ ꝗ̃ ſp̃ũs mal⁹ agita=
bat ſaul. Sarraceni etiã cõcedũt demones
eſſe et illos p̃ncipes demonũ quos vocant

A page from the first book ever printed on witchcraft, Alphonsus de Spina's *Fortalicium Fidei*, printed in exquisite Roman type by Mentelin in Strasbourg (1467). This copy, now in Cornell University Library, originally belonged to the Benedictine Monastery of St. Maximin at Treves [Trier]. Its lessons were not wasted on the monks, observed George Lincoln Burr: "Nowhere in all Europe did the persecution of these unfortunates rage with greater this bull and, because the crime of witch-craft still continued, re-emphasized its provisions in a bull to Modestus Vincen-tinus, Inquisitor of Como.

Allier, Elisabeth. During the seven-teenth century, French witchcraft was characterized by a phenomenal number of young women, especially novices and nuns, possessed by devils. In some of the more famous examples of possession, bewitching by a specific person was alleged (e.g., Ur-bain Grandier and the Loudun Nuns). In many others, however, the possessing devils entered apparently because of their own evil designs or some unidentified malefice. When priests felt they had accomplished exorcism, they made known their success.

One such *True Relation* concerns Elisa-beth Allier, possessed for twenty years by two devils calling themselves Orgeuil and Boniface, and liberated after six exorcisms by a Dominican of Grenoble, François Farconnet. He started on a Saturday, Au-gust 18, 1639. Although Sister Elisabeth did not move her lips, the devils revealed in gruff voices they had entered her body on a crust of bread when she was seven; they would leave only three days before her death. (St. Gregory tells how a devil entered a nun as she was eating lettuce; she had forgotten to make the sign of the cross.) After five fruitless exorcisms, the services continued into the Sunday. Father François finally exposed the Sacrament, saying, "Go, then, miserable creature." The more pressure he put on the devils, the more was Sister Elisabeth seized with strange convulsions—her tongue twisted out of her mouth to the extent "of more than four fingers." At last the remaining devil left, saying with humble voice, "*Jésus, sortit*—Jesus, I go!"

Alphonsus de Spina. Alphonsus de Spina's *Fortalicium Fidei* [*Fortress of the Faith*], written about 1459, was published in 1467—the first book ever printed to dis-cuss witchcraft. Its five parts discuss the "armor" of all the faithful, and the wars against heretics, Jews, Saracens (i.e., Mo-hammedans), and demons. This last section describes ten kinds of demons, the last of which deceives old women [*bruxae*] into imagining they can work evil [see Demon-ology]. Such deluded people are especially numerous in Dauphiné and Gascony, where they all assemble at a rock, *el Boch de Biterne,* and adore a boar by kissing its posteriors. Many of these wretches have been burned, and in the house of the In-quisitor at Toulouse one can see paintings of their assemblies and punishments. Com-pared to other writers of his period, Al-phonsus was, in witchcraft, a moderate (e.g., transvection is only a delusion).

Alphonsus de Spina (not to be confused with Bartolommeo Spina) was converted from Judaism and joined the Franciscans. He became Confessor to King John of Cas-tile, professor at Salamanca, and, before his death in 1491, Bishop of Thermopolis. His work is full of anti-Semitic fables, such as the Jew who threw the sacred host into boiling water. Alphonsus included also the legend of Hugh of Lincoln, who, after he was said to have been murdered by the Jews and cast into a cesspool (*in loco profundissimo et immundo fetoribusque plano*), kept on praising the Virgin Mary. Modern readers will see here an analogue of Chaucer's *Prioress's Tale.*

Amber Witch. Maria Schweidler, the "Amber witch," was a celebrated hoax in-vented by Rev. Dr. Wilhelm Meinhold. His brilliant re-creation of the witch terror in

---

violence than within the jurisdiction of this old abbey during the last decades of the 16th century. From its twenty villages or so, hundreds went to the stake. A still extant list drawn up by its court (I have myself studied the autograph document) names over 300 of these who perished between 1587 and 1594, and even for this brief period the list is professedly incomplete. An old court record which I found (in 1885) in the possession of a peasant woman at Fell, the old seat of the court of St. Maximin, shows that this persecution was already under headway in 1572. Remembering this and the part which this volume may have taken in suggesting it, one can hardly turn these pages without a shudder."

a small hamlet in Pomerania during the Thirty Years' War (1630), his use of authentic dialect, and his reconstruction of typical procedures of witch trials passed as the fascinating biography of an enlightened seventeenth-century parson. Only in the final chapters did romance break the illusion, with Maria Schweidler, the poor parson's daughter who found the vein of precious amber that saved her village from destitution, rescued from the witch stake by her noble lover with a troop of armed men. The work, which was praised by King Frederick William IV of Prussia, stimulated the research on German witchcraft which produced so many monographs in the later nineteenth century. A few years after the book's publication, Dr. Meinhold freely admitted his authorship.

Amulets: see Charms.

Aquinas, Thomas. Among the five great theologians of the Church is the Dominican Thomas Aquinas (about 1227-74); as late as 1879, Pope Leo XIII ordered all Roman Catholic clergy "to take the teachings of Aquinas as the basis of their theological position."

Professor George L. Burr, the learned historian of witchcraft, placed a major responsibility on Aquinas: "These human allies and servants of Satan [were] postulated into existence by the brain of a monkish logician." Early writers on witchcraft constantly quoted him; Nider, Vineti, and Sprenger and Kramer (the authors of the *Malleus Maleficarum*) cited Aquinas, with the Bible and Augustine, as their principal authority. In turn, later witch experts used the *Malleus*. Aquinas denied the *formal* pact between man and the Devil, but his concept of association with the Devil, implied or expressed, laid the foundation for the ensuing witchcraft mania.

Aquinas notably influenced thinking in the five core areas of practical witchcraft:

1. *Sexual Relations with Devils.* The sexual perversions of the witches' sabbat evolved from and were justified by Aquinas' theory (taken from a Byzantine theorist) that humans could copulate with devils, and that as a result, by a lightning transfer of semen from a male unsuspectingly masturbating or fornicating with a succubus, women could bear babies. In his *Quaestiones Quodlibetales,* for example, Aquinas wrote:

> Because the incubus demon is able to steal the semen of an innocent youth in nocturnal emissions and pour it into the womb of a woman, she is able by this semen to conceive an offspring, whose father is not the demon incubus, but the man whose semen impregnated her, because it took effect by the virtue of him from whom it was dissipated. Therefore it seems that a man is able without a miracle to be at one and the same time both a virgin and a father.

Even in witch trials where sabbat-going was minimized, sexual relations with the devil were a standard charge.

2. *Transvection.* Aquinas borrowed the speculations of Albertus Magnus that Satan, in tempting Christ on the mountaintop, had assumed a body and carried Christ (who rendered himself invisible) on his shoulders—walking, however, rather than flying. From this came the corollary that devils, within certain divine limits, could transport witches through the air. Aquinas added Augustine's doctrine of *raptus*, an early form of astral projection in which the soul could have experiences outside the body. (Other contemporary scholars, such as John of Salisbury, criticized belief in transvection as illusory.)

3. *Metamorphosis.* Aquinas accepted without dissent the popular theories, sanctioned by Augustine, of the Devil's ability to transform men into animals (as Circe had changed the followers of Odysseus into beasts). His reasoning was extremely involved: The Devil creates an illusion in the mind of a man, and then from a body of air makes a second outward illusion to correspond to the mental illusion. Thus the metamorphosis is not actual but imaginary, although the effect on men is the same, just as alchemists produce imitation gold which looks genuine. Both Augustine and Aquinas rejected literal lycanthropy, but applied the "imaginary appearance" [*phantasticam ap-*

paritionem] theory. Later demonologists, however, cited Aquinas in support of transformation.

4. *Storm-Raising.* Aquinas believed in the power of devils, with God's permission, to work *maleficia,* including storm-raising (as he explained in his commentary on Job). In addition, Aquinas set down rules for the use of charms.

5. *Ligature.* In his *Quaestiones Quodlibetales,* Aquinas wrote: "The Catholic faith maintains that demons are something and that they can do harm by their operations and impede carnal copulation." They might effect this very simply, for example, by causing a man to have an aversion for some particular woman. Aquinas also believed that old women, by an accord [*foedus*] with the Devil, could harm children by the evil eye or fascination.

Having granted an agreement with the Devil, implying heresy, in addition Aquinas promoted the thesis that heretics should be burned, since in the New Testament they were called thieves and wolves, and it was customary to hang thieves and kill wolves. When the Dominican-controlled Inquisition turned heretics over to the civil authorities for execution, it went back to the words of Aquinas: "If false coiners or other felons are justly committed to death without delay by worldly princes, much more may heretics, from the moment that they are convicted, be not only excommunicated, but slain justly out of hand." (*Summa Theologica,* II. xi)

> "It is clear that Thomas Aquinas, directly or indirectly, afforded both explanation and support for the witchcraft delusion in most of its important features, and that his theories were extended to give credence to others."—*Charles E. Hopkins* (1940)

Arras Witches. In 1459-60 the Inquisition organized a witch hunt at Arras, among the earliest in northern France. At this date, just what constituted witchcraft had still not been precisely defined, and the

Inquisition's loose conduct was denounced by several bishops. Thirty years later, the Parlement of Paris ordered rehabilitation of the victims. After 1500, few would have dared—or desired—to criticize.

The accusations against these new heretics, the witches, were founded on those leveled against the earlier heretics, the Waldensians or Vaudois, who likewise were said to have adored devils and eaten human flesh. The parallels were so

A witch condemned by the Inquisition to wear the opprobrious heretic's miter. From Philip van Limborch, *Historia Inquisitionis* (1692).

The earliest known picture of witches flying on broomsticks, from a manuscript (about 1440) of *Le Champion des dames*, by Martin le Franc. The text states that not one, two, or three, but three thousand witches go to see their familiar devils.

close that *"aller en vaudois"* became the term for going to the sabbat. Burning was the fate for both Vaudois and witches.

On the denunciations of one Robinet de Vaulx (a condemned prisoner), the Inquisitor Pierre le Broussart seized as a Vaudois heretic a weak-minded woman, called Deniselle Grenières. Deniselle was tortured several times until she identified four women and an old painter, Jehan la Vitte, nicknamed derisively the *Abbé-de-peu-de-sens*, as accomplices. Jehan la Vitte tried to cut out his tongue to avoid answering under torture, but only lacerated his mouth; since he could write, he too had to name names. The contemporary chronicler, Jacques du Clercq, told what evil these early witches were supposed to have done. Men and women were suddenly transported to a meeting place, where they found the devil

in human shape, whose face was never revealed, and who read or delivered his commandments and ordinances, telling how they should serve him. Then he made them all kiss his backside and gave them a few coins. Finally, he presided at a sumptuous banquet, of which everybody partook. Then, all at once, the lights went out, and each one took a partner and knew each other carnally. Which done, everyone suddenly returned to the place where he or she had been originally.

A contemporary Latin tract, written in May, 1460, perhaps by the Inquisitor to justify the mass arrests, included a detailed description of the alleged orgies [see Sexual Relations with Devils].

According to custom, the reports of the trial were·submitted for review to theological experts, Dr. Gilles Cartier and Canon Grégoire Nicolai, both of Cambrai, who recommended that since neither murder nor desecration of the host had been charged, the judges should show leniency. The Inquisitor ignored this advice and arranged an auto-da-fé. On May 9, 1460, Deniselle Grenière and four she had named (the fifth committed suicide in jail) were marshaled on a platform in front of the episcopal palace. They were garbed in the uniforms of heretics, with opprobrious miters decorated with devils on their heads. The Inquisitor himself preached a sermon, declaring them Vaudois and detailing their crimes, but omitting mention of copulation with demons "lest innocent ears should be pricked by such heinous offenses, so horrendous and remorseless." The five victims were accused of flying on sticks [*baguettes*], adoring the devil, and trampling the cross. Thereupon they were handed over to the "secular arm." Shrieking their innocence, they were burned alive.

The next month, June, 1460, the Inquisitor resumed his activities, on the basis of the names he had forced from those already burned. Du Clercq wrote:

Many notable persons were imprisoned, as well as lesser folk, crazy women, and others, who were so horribly tortured [*géhenés*] and so terribly tormented, that some admitted they had done exactly what was charged, and moreover confessed they had seen and recognized at their nocturnal assemblies many gentlefolk, prelates, lords, and other administrators of counties and towns. These accused were tortured "so long and so frequently" that they confessed what suited the judges.

Some of the richer and more influential of the accused bought their way out of ignominy and torture. [The poor were burned.] Some of the most important of those accused were encouraged and seduced by the inquisitors who gave them to understand (and, in fact, promised) that, if they admitted the allegations, they would forfeit neither life nor property

—a promise which was, of course, not kept. Their estates were confiscated by their feudal overlord and their movable property by the bishopric. Some few, said Du Clercq, denied the charges and refused to bribe the judges.

While the Inquisitor was seizing and torturing the townspeople, some clergymen suggested an amnesty, but they were overruled. By the end of the year, merchants could not be sure of honoring business contracts, and the trading prosperity of Arras began to suffer. In some embarrassment, the Inquisitor appealed for support to Philip the Good, Duke of Burgundy; but he was still more embarrassed when the Archbishop of Rheims and the Bishops of Amiens and Paris declared the sabbat illu-

In the fifteenth century, witches were often identified with the heretical sect of the Waldensians or Vaudois and were similarly accused of worshiping the goat. This illustration comes from a French translation of a Latin tract by Johann Tinctor, *Of the Sect Which Is Called Vaudois:* "Truly, then there will be no acceptance of customs, obedience to the law, respect for justice, concern for life, protection and defense of the state, or fear and reverence for God. All will be turned into upset and confusion, each wicked sinner will live by his own will, the wicked will subvert local and national government, and the lowly but God-fearing people will groan and beg in desolation."

sory and dismissed charges of witchcraft brought before their tribunals. In 1461, the Parlement of Paris insisted some of those imprisoned be released, and the Bishop of Arras, Jean Jouffroy, who had been away in Rome during the witch hunts, came home and freed the rest. Finally, on July 10, 1491, the Parlement of Paris declared the Inquisition had acted "in error and against the order and dignity of justice— a false trial and one conducted without due process." Furthermore, it condemned the "inhuman and cruel interrogation and tortures of the Inquisition, like squeezing the limbs, putting the soles of the feet in the fire, and making the accused swallow oil and vinegar." It asked for prayers for those who had been put to death.

Auldearne Witches: see Gowdie, Isobel.

Austria, Witchcraft in. Here, the worst period of the witchcraft delusion occurred under the Emperor Rudolph II (1576-1612), and was spread by the Jesuits seeking to roll back Protestantism. A secondary period came at the end of the seventeenth century in the Austrian provinces of Styria and the Tyrol, finding expression in the *Halsgerichtsordnung,* a severe anti-witchcraft code adopted in 1707.

Before 1570 prosecution was infrequent and, with the exception of the Carolina Code of 1532, the laws dismissed witchcraft lightly. The criminal ordinance for the Tyrol in 1499 did not refer to either sorcery or witchcraft; in 1544 sorcery and divination were treated as delusions; and even in 1573 another *Policey-Ordnung* (again for the Tyrol) ranked witchcraft with blasphemy, punishable by a fine (of which the informer got a quarter, the judge a quarter, and charity half). Credit for such moderation went to the Emperor Maximilian II (1564-76), educated in Spain (where he had the model of the Spanish Inquisition, which discouraged loose accusations), and opposed to violence. To him, witches and those who resorted to fortunetellers were idiots. The exception to this tradition in Austria was the Carolina Code, with its new theory of burning those

convicted of heresy or malicious sorcery. Although this code, designed for all electoral states of the Empire, was quoted by all later witch hunters, it was often ignored, not only in the Protestant states, but even in Roman Catholic Bavaria.

With the coronation of Maximilian's successor in 1576, witch trials increased. Rudolph II was himself superstitious and a believer in witchcraft—he thought he was bewitched. He was dominated by the Jesuits, who equated sorcery and heresy, and in their zeal interpreted many harmless acts in this light. The changed attitude showed up in the trial of sixteen-year-old Anna Schlutterbauer, a demoniac exorcized at Mariazell [see Christoph Haizmann] and in 1583 at St. Barbara's in Vienna by the Bishop of Breisgau (Baden). An old woman relative, accused of causing her possession, was seized as a witch. After being tortured several times, she confessed she had copulated with the devil, raised storms for fifteen years, and gone to the sabbat. The elderly municipal judge, appointed during the reign of the skeptical Maximilian II, found the old woman insane and committed her to an asylum; but he was overruled by the newly appointed judges, who condemned the accused to be dragged on a hurdle to the stake and there burned [see Possession].

Such was the attitude for the next 150 years. For example, a *Landgerichtsordnung* of 1656 included among the signs justifying arrest for witchcraft the discovery of oil, ointment, pots of vermin, or human bones in the witch's possession. In 1679, however, the Emperor Leopold I forbade the introduction of new tortures, particularly the gruesome *Nagelbett,* or bed of nails. On the other hand, a revival of persecution occurred in Salzburg from 1677 to 1681, necessitating the building of a special prison. About a hundred persons were tortured into confession, beheaded, strangled or burned; the youngest was ten, the oldest eighty—Riezler, *Hexenprozesse in Bayern.* Just when the delusion seemed to be tapering off, it was stimulated by the *Halsgerichtsordnung* of 1707 (under the Emperor Joseph I), which revived the principles and practices of the *Malleus Maleficarum*. In Austria proper, however, there were no further executions, and trials occurred only in outlying regions. The Empress Maria-Theresa issued her famous *Constitutio Criminalis Theresiana . . . peinliche Gerichtsordnung* in 1769, which limited persecutions: no sentence for witchcraft, for example, was permitted without government approval (Article 58). In spite of such reforms, the volume describing the code is mainly filled with descriptions and thirty plates of legal torture, not abolished until 1776. Eleven years later, on January 13, 1787, all witchcraft laws were repealed.

In the German-speaking areas of the Tyrol there were few trials before 1600. In 1637 the Attorney General of Innsbruck, Dr. Volpert Mozel, drew up a set of instructions to help local magistrates discover and punish witches. The compilation somewhat resembled the guides issued by officers of the Inquisition, such as Bordonus (1648), and showed a similar credulity. Mozel added to Bordonus' list one more indication of sorcery: a man's finding a woman's girdle or other article of female apparel in his room indicated a witch was abroad! The accused witch was never to be told the facts or circumstances of the accusation; if she revoked a confession given under torture, she was to be tortured again; names of accomplices had to be revealed under "moderate torture" to ensure their accuracy. Mozel limited torture to three one-hour periods. At the end of the century, in 1696, a similar handbook was published at Innsbruck by a professor of law and rector of the university, Dr. Johann Christoph Frölich. Since the crime was so serious, Frölich contended, normal legal safeguards must be bypassed. Evil repute, being the child of a witch, inability to look a person in the face, sufficed to bring on a trial. Interrogation should immediately follow arrest, so the devil would not have time to coach the prisoner. The torture chamber should be sprinkled with holy water and fumigated with blessed herbs. Accusations (from other witches under torture) of presence at a sabbat proved guilt. Lesser crimes, such as divining for

water, might be punished by flogging, exile, or fines. Children under seven were exempt from punishment; over fourteen they were considered adults. Anyone convicted forfeited his wealth and property. This horrible book was reprinted in 1714.

With such directions, the records of provincial trials in Austria should cause no shock. In 1673 at Gutenhag (Styria), a judge kept a 57-year-old woman eleven days and nights kneeling on a torture stool (with sharp prongs), burning her feet with sulphur, because she would not confess to a pact with the devil. She died insane under torture (Holzinger, *Zur Naturgeschichte der Hexen*, 1883). In 1679, Emerenziane Pichler was tried at Linz (Tyrol), and after a year condemned with her two eldest children. She was burned September 25, 1680; her two children, aged twelve and fourteen, on September 27, 1680. In 1679 at Meran (Tyrol), a fourteen-year-old beggar boy was suspected by the police of causing tempests. He was so ignorant he did not know his own name, but under torture he confessed the charge and implicated three others, aged eighteen to twenty-five. All four were burned on December 13, 1679 (Rapp). So extensive were the executions in this area that a priest, Laurenz Paumgartner, wrote in his diary that in his small parish alone, within fifteen months (about 1680), thirteen witches had been executed. In 1688 in Styria a whole family, including the children and a servant, were burned as witches. In 1695 at Steiermark (southern Styria), Märina Schepp, under the jurisdiction of the Dominicans at Pettau, confessed after six and a half hours on the torture stool, beginning at four o'clock in the morning, to sexual relations with the devil; she was burned. After the two major outbreaks around 1670 and 1690, the trials gradually ceased with the general demise of witch hunts throughout Europe.

See also Carolina Code, Witchcraft in Germany.

Auxonne Nuns. The nuns of the Ursuline convent of Auxonne, allegedly possessed by devils from 1658 to 1663, are less known than their sisters at Aix-en-Provence (1611), Loudun (1634), or Louviers (1647); but their story is similar and almost as lurid. Its chief difference is that the sex-starved girls made accusations of improper conduct, not against their father-confessors, but against their 47-year-old Mother Superior, Sister St. Colombe (Barbara Buvée). Accusations of Lesbianism in convents were not often publicized. Coming later than the other demonstrations of possession, however, the attacks at Auxonne were subject to closer scrutiny; consequently, the accused Mother Superior was found innocent, and physicians testified that the possession was fraudulent.

The story built up over five years but did not break into the open until 1660, when charges of witchcraft were made against Barbara Buvée. Eight nuns were sexually stimulated by one of the convent's two confessors, the ugly but young Father Nouvelet. One nun, Marie Borthon, "on his account suffered great temptations of the flesh." Others, especially during menstruation, had erotic fantasies. Only witchcraft could be the cause. Because he was linked with the nuns' temptations, Father Nouvelet suggested he too had been bewitched. Two peasants were therefore seized and accused of witchcraft, but since no evidence was produced, the court sentenced them merely to banishment. As they left the court, however, a mob lynched them. The next step was exorcism. Father Nouvelet conducted some services in the chapel, where amazing spectacles occurred. Sister Denise with only two fingers lifted a heavy vase which two strong men could scarce move; other nuns adored the sacrament by lying on their bellies, head and arms raised off the ground and their legs bent backward to form an arc. Father Nouvelet conducted other exorcisms lying in bed with the girls, so close that "only the sister's veil separated her face from that of the priest." The confessor also spent considerable time traveling with Sister Claudine Bourgeot; they slept in the same bedroom but, they said, in separate beds.

Barbara Buvée, Mother Superior since 1651, had quarreled with Father Nouvelet's predecessor, Father Borthon, whose three sisters were members of the convent. For her insubordination she had been punished with fastings and floggings. Since she had also opposed the exorcisms by Father Nouvelet, she seemed the cause of the nuns' possession. On October 28, 1660, Sister St. Colombe was formally accused of witchcraft; on November 13, she was put in heavy shackles in solitary confinement; and on January 5, 1661, was brought to trial for witchcraft before the Parlement at Dijon.

The nuns were unanimous in their attacks on Sister St. Colombe, Barbara Buvée. Sister Henriette Cousin testified that Barbara Buvée put her hand on her bosom [*gorge*] and passionately kissed her; when Sister Henriette protested, the Mother Superior (she said) replied she thought she was kissing a holy statue. Sister Humberte Borthon had visions of hell, in which the Mother Superior had put "*un serpent dans les parties*," and, having embraced her, "lay down on her like a man on a woman." Sister Charlotte Joly had seen the Mother Superior kiss with the tongue Sister Gabrielle de Malo and place her hand under her petticoat, while both made "reciprocal touchings." Sister Françoise Borthon, often violated by the devil Asmodeus, swore Barbara Buvée "had once made her sit across her knees and had put her finger into her private parts just like a man would have done." Furthermore, Barbara Buvée had said the nun was pregnant, and had "put her hand in her and pried open her secret place, causing a lot of blood, both clear and clotted, to issue out." Another sister had a vision of Barbara Buvée, who appeared to her holding in one hand a stolen sacred host on which reposed "*la partie honteuse*" of a man, and in the other an artificial phallus made of linen with which "she committed on herself impure acts." So the testimony went on. But the Parlement of Dijon, on March 18, 1661, ordered a further investigation. Finally, in August, 1662, it dismissed the charges. Sister St. Colombe then changed her convent, and the nuns' hysteria gradually disappeared.

The special prison for witches, or *Hexenhaus*, erected in 1627 by the Prince-Bishop of Bamberg, Gottfried Johann Georg II Fuchs von Dornheim, who burned a minimum of six hundred witches.

During these years, several physicians had examined the nuns. On a certain occasion, one doctor declared them all frauds, with possibly a few sick; another believed them genuinely possessed by devils; and a third thought that nothing demoniacal was proved. On June 15, 1662, Dr. Bachet wrote an official report to the Chancellor, in which he stated:

> I can assure your honor that in all their acts, whether bodily or mental, the nuns have never displayed any legitimate or convincing sign of true demoniacal possession, neither in understanding foreign tongues, knowledge of hidden secrets, revelations, levitation of their bodies in the air, movement from one spot to another, nor in their extraordinary contortions which exceed those normally found.

Bamberg Witch Trials. The slaughter of witches in Germany was greatest in the territories ruled by the prince-bishops— Treves, Strasbourg, Breslau, and Fulda, for example, and in Würzburg and Bamberg. These last two principalities were ruled by exceptionally brutal cousins, Prince-Bishop Philipp Adolf von Ehrenberg (1623-31), who burned 900 witches, and the *Hexenbischof*, Gottfried Johann Georg II Fuchs

von Dornheim (1623-33), who burned a minimum of 600 persons. There is a similar pattern of persecution in these areas.

Witch hunting reached Bamberg later than other German states. It began under Bishop Johann Gottfried von Aschhausen (1609-22), who burned about 300 persons accused as witches—1617 was a bad year; 102 were burned. But Witch Bishop Johann Georg II got better results with the aid of his Vicar-General, Suffragan Bishop Friedrich Förner, and a secular council of doctors of law. These bigots resumed persecutions in 1624 and in 1627, and erected a special *Drudenhaus* with room for thirty or forty prisoners, and probably similar witch prisons in the smaller towns of the bishopric, Zeil, Hallstadt, and Kronach. From 1626 to 1630 witch trials were especially irregular and vicious; one commissioner, Dr. Ernst Vasolt, executed 400 denounced as witches.

The Vice-Chancellor of Bamberg, Dr. George Haan, had some limited success in checking the trials, but his relative moderation made him (like Dietrich Flade) suspect as a witch lover, and with his wife and daughter he himself was burned in 1628— this despite an Imperial order for their release, because "their arrest was a violation of the law of the Empire not to be tolerated." In fact, all the burgomasters were accused and condemned; the most heart-rending trial of all is that of Johannes Junius, whose dying letter to his daughter survived to reveal the sickening degradation of the witch persecutions.

The victims included many other leading citizens. In April, 1631, when the terror was diminishing, the witch prison contained twenty-two inmates, including the Bishop's treasurer. Their combined property, which had already been confiscated, amounted to 220,000 florins. All this money lined the pockets of the Bishop. In addition, prisoners (their estate or their families) had to pay high fees to everyone connected with their execution [see Costs].

The spate of accusations, tortures, burnings increased, and some prominent people managed to flee to Rome, Bohemia, or to the Emperor's court at Regensburg. But the Prince-Bishop cared little for the Emperor, who in any case was otherwise occupied. Even Ferdinand's intervention for Dorothea Block, the wife of a rich citizen of Bamberg, was disregarded. The accusations against her were not made known, nor was a lawyer permitted; she was burned like the rest, in May, 1630. Her father fled.

The speed of these "trials" was amazing, even at the period. For example, the calendar of Frau Anna Hansen in 1629 reads:

June 17 Imprisoned on suspicion of witchcraft.

June 18 Refused to confess; scourged.

June 20 Tortured with the thumb screws; confessed.

June 28 Her confession read to her.

June 30 Voluntarily confirmed her confession; sentenced.

July 4 Informed of the date of her execution.

July 7 Beheaded and burned.

Bamberg had become synonymous with torture. Among the devices routinely employed in extracting confessions from anyone accused as a witch were:

1. The thumbscrews (*Daumenstock*), used in conjunction with

2. The leg vises (*Beinschraube*).

Instruments of torture used at Bamberg for the witch trials. From *Bambergische Halsgerichtsordnung* (1508).

3. Scourging either off or while hanging on

4. The ladder, a form of strappado.

In addition, special tortures were employed, such as

5. The stocks (*Bock*), furnished with iron spikes, a torment which might be continued for as long as six hours.

6. Strappado (*Zug*), a modification of squassation.

7. Severe friction with a rope around the neck, to cut to the bone (*Schnur*).

8. Cold water baths.

9. Burning feathers (*Schwefelfedern*) held under the arms and groin, frequently dipped in burning sulphur.

10. Prayer stool (*Betstuhl*), a kneeling board with sharp wooden pegs.

11. Forcible feeding on herring cooked in salt, and denial of water.

12. Scalding water baths to which lime had been added (in 1630, six persons had been killed at Zeil by this method).

After sentencing and on the way to being burned, additional punishment could be imposed, including cutting off the right hand and tearing the breasts of women with red-hot pincers.

Such ruthlessness, however, began to attract unfavorable attention to Bamberg, and the Emperor was under pressure to do something. Lamormaini, Ferdinand's Jesuit confessor, told him: "It was horrifying what prominent men everywhere were thinking and saying about the procedure in the courts." Another Jesuit (Heinrich Türck of Paderborn) protested:

Some people began to feel great sympathy for the unfortunate victims; and grave doubts were raised as to whether the numerous persons who perished in the flames were really guilty and deserving so horrible a death. In fact, many people thought that this treatment of human beings, who had been bought with the precious blood of Christ, was cruel and more than barbaric.

The refugees from Bamberg also added their complaints: Councillor Dümler, whose pregnant wife had been horribly tortured and burned, told the Emperor: "People are protesting that it is impossible that justice has been done to all the people in Bamberg." He suggested that the confiscation of the prisoners' property be halted. One man who had escaped from the *Drudenhaus* presented a written petition from Barbara Schwarz, tortured eight times without confessing and confined three years in a dungeon.

The Prince-Bishop of Bamberg sent special emissaries to Regensburg to plead his case, but they were coldly received. By September, 1630, Father Lamormaini told the Emperor that hostility at his inaction was preventing the election of his son as Emperor, and that, if he continued to ignore the lawlessness of the Bamberg courts, Lamormaini could hardly give him absolution. Some time later, Ferdinand II subpoenaed the court records for examination, and ordered that in future trials the basis for accusation be made public (simple defamation or ill fame were the commonest grounds), legal counsel be allowed the defendant (usually kept incommunicado), and confiscation of property cease. Torture, however, was not abolished.

The terror receded in the early summer of 1631, owing partly to the death of Suffragan Bishop Förner in December, 1630, partly to the threats of the Swedish King Gustavus (who entered Leipzig in September), diverting attention to the war, and partly to the opposition (in mandates of 1630 and 1631) of the Emperor. In 1630, twenty-four were executed, but none in 1631. The Bishop of Bamberg died in 1632. With his death, that of his cousin, the Bishop of Würzburg, in 1631, and the death of the Cardinal Bishop of Vienna in 1630, three of the fiercest promoters of persecution were gone.

Barclay, Margaret

It is scarce possible that, after reading such a story, a man of sense can listen for an instant to the evidence founded on confession thus obtained, which has been almost the sole reason by which a few individuals, even in modern times, have endeavored to justify a belief in the existence of witchcraft.

So wrote Sir Walter Scott, who first reported from the town records of Irvine in Ayrshire the execution of Margaret Barclay in 1618. Yet her trial is typical, no better and no worse than thousands of other witch trials in Scotland.

Margaret Barclay, the wife of Archibald Dean, a burgess of Irvine, was not on the best of terms with her brother-in-law and his wife. At length, after some particular acrimony, Margaret took action against her in-laws before the church court. The Kirk recommended a reconciliation. Margaret still retained rancor, however, and when her brother-in-law set sail for France with Andrew Tran, the provost of the town, it was alleged she wished the ship would sink and that "partans [crabs] might eat the crew at the bottom of the sea."

Some time later, a vagabond, John Stewart, passing through Irvine, told of the sinking of a ship near Padstow, England, a loss later confirmed by the two surviving sailors. John Stewart was arrested for precognition, and Margaret Barclay for witchcraft. Stewart, in prison and doubtless under torture, told how Margaret had sought his aid against "such persons as had done her wrong," and how he had visited her in a deserted house where she was making waxen images of Tran and the ship. Stewart gave her an accomplice, Isobel Insh (or Taylor). Isobel's eight-year-old daughter was seized and "confessed" that she too was present in the deserted house. The child added that when it became dark, a devilish dog emitted light from its jaws and nostrils so the women could work on their figurines. Margaret Barclay swore the child to secrecy with a promise of a new pair of shoes. Although he had previously made no mention of the child, John Stewart later agreed that the "little snatchet" was there.

Such was the evidence, and everything was ready for the trial.

First, Isobel Insh was tortured into confession. She was confined in the belfry, but managed to escape onto the roof of the church. She slipped and fell. Five days later she died.

Second, the beggar, John Stewart, although under heavy guard and with his arms in fetters, contrived on the morning of his trial to strangle himself with the ribbons of his bonnet.

Third, Margaret Barclay was now the only surviving accused. She was put to what a local nobleman, the Earl of Eglinton, called a "most safe and gentle torture," namely, setting her "two bare legs in a pair of stocks, and thereafter by on-laying of certain iron gauds [bars]." Finally, she could endure no more and cried, "Take off, take off! And before God I shall show you the whole form." The iron bars were removed and kept before her, so that her confession could be accepted by the jury as technically made "without any kind of demand, freely." During the trial, her husband appeared with a lawyer, and this gave Margaret sufficient hope to recant. "All I have confessed was in agony of torture, and before God, all I have spoken is false and untrue." She was convicted, strangled, and burned to ashes.

There was a fourth victim. Under torture, Margaret implicated one Isobel Crawford. She too was tortured and confessed, but not without a remarkable display of courage. Isobel did "admirably, without any kind of din or exclamation, suffer above thirty stone [420 pounds] of iron to be laid on her legs, never shrinking thereat in any sort, but remaining, as it were, steady." But the weights got heavier and heavier, until she said what was required of her, including relations with the devil. Released from torture, she denied all, and died impenitent and absolutely refusing to pardon the executioner.

Bargarran Impostor. Many men and women have been murdered by children, and the murderers praised rather than punished. Almost a hundred years after the Warboys trial in England came its Scottish equivalent, the trial in 1697 of the Renfrewshire witches. At a time when the witch mania was expiring in England, one eleven-year-old girl, Christine [Christian] Shaw, third child of John Shaw, Laird of Bargarran, near Paisley, in Renfrewshire, could cause twenty-one persons to be indicted, and seven of them burned at the stake in Paisley. The symptoms of hysteria and malice of this "Impostor of Bargarran," as Hugo Arnot termed her in 1785, resemble closely those of her equally perverted but less destructive American counterparts— the Goodwin Children or Margaret Rule, who brought worry and ill repute to Cotton Mather in 1693. Like these, Christine Shaw knew of other possessed children; the memory of Janet Douglas' bewitching of Sir George Maxwell in the same county was only twenty years old.

On Monday, August 17, 1696, little Christine saw "a young well-formed lass" stealing a drink of milk and threatened to expose her. The lass, Katherine Campbell, "of a proud and revengeful humor," wished the devil might hurl Christine's soul through hell! On August 21, an old woman of bad reputation, Agnes Naismith, asked Christine how she fared, but the child sassed her. On August 22, Christine was taken with fits, jackknifing her body, swallowing her tongue, and crying out that Katherine and Agnes were tormenting her. In these fits, or demoniacal possessions, the child apparently vomited scraps which she claimed her spirit tormentors forced her to swallow—crooked pins, small bones, cinders, hay, gravel, balls of hair, candle grease, feathers, and egg shells. She argued with these specters, quoting the Bible at them. The doctor, Dr. Matthew Brisbane, reported that Christine, when out of her hysterical convulsions, was "in every way healthful," but admitted his inability to diagnose her trouble. A second physician, Dr. Marshall, concurred.

Five months later, on January 19, 1697, the Privy Council of Scotland appointed an investigating commission to report on suspected witchcraft at Bargarran. Christine meantime had extended her accusations: Elizabeth Anderson, aged seventeen; her father, Alexander, a beggar; Jean Fulton, her grandmother; and her two young cousins, "squint-eyed" James, aged fourteen,

and Thomas Lindsay, aged eleven. Two upper-class women were also accused: Margaret Lang, "a person of extraordinary gravity and wisdom" (*Relation*, 1697), and her seventeen-year-old daughter, Martha Semple. These two boldly faced their accuser, when they could easily have fled, Margaret saying scornfully: "Let them quake that dread and fear that need; but I will not gang [flee]." Her disdain for the whole proceedings recalls the bravery of Agnes Samuel at the Warboys trial.

Some of the accused, especially Elizabeth Anderson, themselves accused others, until twenty-one men and women were indicted. Christine alleged these witches as specters molested her, and she threw a fit whenever one of them was forced to touch her. Just like the Salem Church in 1692, the Kirk held a public fast day on February 11 for Christine's release. In fact, the ministers constantly attended Christine and seemed to have encouraged her delusions (Arnot).

The investigating committee had not been idle, and within two months submitted its report, including the confessions of Jean Fulton's three grandchildren—Elizabeth Anderson, and James and Thomas Lindsay. These children complemented Christine's charges. They described being taken to sabbats by their grandmother, and being given each a piece of liver of an unbaptized child —they refused to eat this and so were free to make confessions, unlike the other accused witches who partook of the flesh and therefore would not confess. They said they had killed a minister (he had been dead some time) by sticking pins into his waxen image; had strangled two children (also dead), and overturned a ferryboat, causing two drownings. Elizabeth told how she had seen the devil talking to her father and Agnes Naismith and others in Bargarran's yard, plotting to kill Christine Shaw "by the stopping of her breath." She dipped into her memory and told of devilish meetings seven years before, and of flying with her father.

These children's fantasies were more than sufficient evidence to authorize a new commission on April 5, 1697, with power to sentence to death. The new judges got two other confessions, and on April 13, 1697, presented their indictments to the jury. The prosecution, led by the Lord Advocate himself, warned the jurors that, if they acquitted the prisoners (already proved witches by the presence of devil's marks), "they would be accessory to all the blasphemies, apostasies, murders, tortures, and seductions, whereof these enemies of heaven and earth should be guilty." So warned, the jury took seven hours and returned seven Guilty verdicts: three men (including fourteen-year-old James Lindsay) and four women—the two gentlewomen, Margaret Lang and her daughter, the maid-servant Katherine Campbell, and Agnes Naismith. These seven were burned on June 10, 1697, at Paisley. A horseshoe in George Street still commemorates the place of execution. One account says the condemned were too quickly taken from the gallows and thrown into the fire; so apparently some may have been still living when burned. A man whose stick had been used to poke back the legs of the witches as they thrust them out of the flames refused to take it back, declaring angrily: "I'll take no stick home with me to my house that has touched a witch."

After the burnings, Christine Shaw stopped her fits, vomited trash no longer, and no longer saw apparitions. In 1839, two writers visited the Shaw house and discovered a tiny hole in the wall of Christine's room, normally hidden by the bed (the room had been kept as it was). "Supposing, then," wrote Mitchell and Dirkie, "Christine Shaw to have had an accomplice, of which there seems no reason to doubt, how easily could pins, straw, bones of fowls, etc., have been transmitted through the perforation to the bed on which she lay"—*Philosophy of Witchcraft*, 1839. The prosecution noted, incidentally, these articles came from her mouth "so dry, that they appeared not to have come out of her stomach." (*Sadducismus Debellatus*, 1698)

In 1718, Christine married a minister and, after his death seven years later, became celebrated for introducing machinery from Holland to manufacture fine sewing thread (called after her family name,

"Bargarran"), which ultimately led to the growth of Paisley as a wool center.

It might be observed that the acceptance of these indictments in 1697 contrasts unfavorably with the punishment of six residents of Paisley in 1692 for defaming twelve prominent local gentlefolk as witches. The slanderers had to pay damages and appear in public bearing a placard: "We stand here for scandalizing the good names of . . ." and listing those so libeled.

Basque Witches. When Pierre de Lancre wrote his *Tableau* (1612) to convert "the very many who deny the principles of witchcraft, believing it is nothing but a delusion, a dream, and self-deception," and to demand stronger measures against witches, he utilized his experiences as an investigator in 1609 in the Basque-speaking Pays de Labourd, Béarn, in the southwest of Guienne, adjoining the Spanish frontier. Consequently, the *Tableau* provides a detailed account of a typical mass witch hunt in France during the early seventeenth century, similar to those conducted by Remy in Lorraine or Boguet in Franche-Comté.

In all the major witch persecutions throughout France and Germany, an irresponsible tribunal was created, with power to override local and regional courts. Thus De Lancre received his appointment from the King, and when he admitted "questioning about what a suspect has done is merely a trick to trap him into confessing," no one could protest his unethical procedures.

Labourd became the haven of devils thrown out of Japan and the East Indies by Christian missionaries, De Lancre maintained. English wine-buyers had seen their hordes flying the skies. As early as 1576, witches had been hunted there, and forty burned. The devils rapidly converted the majority of the 30,000 population, including the priests, so that the area became "a hive of witches." Sabbats were held in the public square at Bordeaux; sometimes 12,000 witches assembled at Hendaye, and sometimes all flew to Newfoundland! Some sabbats saw 100,000 witches in attendance, and 2,000 children were common! The sab-

Young nude woman, with kitten and toads, anointing herself with oil in typical Basque kitchen. Modern illustration, inspired by De Lancre, for Witchcraft Museum at Bayonne, France.

bats were well-organized, and a fine of one-eighth of a crown or ten sous was assessed for non-attendance.

Under torture, many confessions, very likely suggested by De Lancre, were recorded (and translated into French). Seventeen-year-old Marie Dindarte described how, on the night of September 27, 1609, she anointed herself and flew through the air. She could not produce the ointment in court because the devil was angry at her revealing his secrets and had hidden it. Saubadine de Subiette and her sixteen-year-old daughter, Marie de Naguille, told how the devil always wakened

them when it was time for the sabbat and opened the windows for them to fly out. Marie de Marigrane, fifteen, and three friends rode the devil in the form of an ass to Biarritz. Father Pierre Bocal of Siboro confessed to singing a devil's mass at a sabbat, for which he had been paid twice his usual stipend. Judge de Lancre's skill in questioning extracted from the girls minute details of their sexual relations with the devil. Henry C. Lea described the value of such forced confessions for evidence of witchcraft thus: "To a mind not wholly prejudiced in advance, the extracts which he gives from the depositions would have led to the conclusion that the culprits were seeking merely to invent stories that would satisfy their judges." But De Lancre dismissed any doubt that the confessions were valid by arguing that the Catholic Church would criminally err if it punished witches for illusions and not for real attendance at a real sabbat. Therefore anyone who questioned the executions also questioned the Church and gravely sinned.

De Lancre's wholesale burnings produced a state of complete chaos in Labourd. The violent hostility of the populace he ascribed to the Devil: the leading families preferred the discomfort of sorcerers to the execution of their relatives; the 5,000 fishermen returning from Newfoundland became howling mobs who held up justice when they learned their loved ones had been burned. Finally, after De Lancre had burned three priests, the Bishop of Bayonne, Bertrand d'Echaux, rescued five other priests from jail and joined the opposition to the witch hunt. De Lancre was fully aware of the hatred he inspired, and he complained that while he was asleep on the night of September 24, 1609, a black mass was celebrated in his bedroom. The witch judge also strove to convince the Labourdins and other Frenchmen of the reality of the Devil on the theoretical level. Having praised Del Rio as the first to establish the reality of the sabbat as "what every good Christian should believe about a matter which has always until now seemed uncertain and doubtful," he found that the most clear-minded and "the majority of the judges and almost everybody still have some doubt" about the crime of witchcraft.

Bateman, Mary. The case of Mary Bateman, the Yorkshire witch, "almost unrivaled in the annals of British atrocities," shows how generally the term witchcraft was loosely applied to sorcery. Born in 1768 at Topcliffe, Yorkshire, Mary Bateman, after a life of petty crime, was convicted of the murder of Rebecca Perigo in 1808 and hanged the following year. Her crimes, including murder, were all involved with fortunetelling, charmed emetics to produce abortion, tricks to procure husbands—the typical acts of white magic. By such means, Mary Bateman made her living; in one instance she mulcted £70 from a literally starving family. "Credulity and vice were Mary's best friends," says the prosy and moralizing tract published at her execution. Had she lived two centuries earlier, she would have been charged with witchcraft. In the nineteenth century, however, the courts acted on legal evidence, not on unprovable allegations.

Bavaria, Witchcraft in. Maximilian I of Bavaria (1597-1651), by his sweeping anti-witchcraft laws of 1611, 1612, and 1622, intensified the work of his superstitious father, William V, who had started the repression in 1590. During the forty years from 1590 to 1630, the two dukes had as counselors Jesuit fanatics, who pressed for ferocious action against alleged witches. By 1631, however, the influence of moderate Jesuits like Adam Tanner, the friend of the humanitarian Father Friedrich von Spee, began to be felt. In that year, Maximilian proclaimed a sort of Edict of Grace; while it encouraged informers, in practice it marked a slow and uneven decline in persecutions.

The Jesuits had come into the Duchy in 1541, but because of public hostility worked unostentatiously at training the future ruler, William V. In 1590 he asked his *Hofrat* [palace council] and the Jesuit University of Ingolstadt for advice on exterminating witches. On April 28 the University replied that, since the crime of witchcraft was new in Bavaria, judges needed help. They should be guided by the *Malleus Maleficarum*, by the work of the Jesuit-trained Binsfeld (just published in German at Munich), and by the available records of previous trials. Furthermore, "the Duke should make it a penal offense not to denounce every one suspected of witchcraft; the torture could be applied more promptly than in other trials." Another Jesuit adviser, the influential Gregory de Valentia (1595), averred the best evidence in trials was the witch's own confession under torture.

The kind of trials the University recommended (though did not specify) may be illustrated from Schongau, Freising, or Werdenfels. In Schongau, in 1587-89, Duke Ferdinand, William's brother, suspended all other trials for a general inquisition into witchcraft. Sixty-three women were beheaded or burned. The Hofrat at Munich supervised the procedure, in one instance ordering a woman to be tortured *continuously* until she confessed. At Freising, after a hailstorm, a woman remarked that worse weather was to be expected. She was denounced as a witch, tortured into confessing and accusing many other women, who were arrested and executed. In the small Alpine town of Werdenfels, forty-nine women of a total population of 4,700 were burned in twenty months in 1590-91. The villagers had to pay the huge amount of 4,000 florins for this holocaust. The special judge finally petitioned the bishopric at Freising to stop the trials, for, said he, if the witchcraft continued as it had begun, very few women would be left alive.

Just as at Treves, the public executioner of Schongau, Jörg Abriel, grew powerful and wealthy, discovering witches all through the German states. The charge for looking for the devil's mark was two florins, irrespective of results, and for an execution eight florins. When Abriel, a Bavarian counterpart of the English Matthew Hopkins, could not find a mark on one woman, he said she looked like a witch to him. She was therefore arrested and tortured into confession.

In 1597, William abdicated in favor of his son Maximilian and entered a monastery. Maximilian also had been trained by Jesuits; his tutor, Johann Baptist Fickler, had in 1582 advocated extreme penalties against witches, and had imbued the future duke with his ideas. When Maximilian was only seventeen, he had watched witches being tortured at Ingolstadt, and had written to his father that soon five of them would be ready for burning. Maximilian felt a personal hatred for witches, since he thought their ligature responsible for his wife's barrenness. The witchcraft hysteria was kept raging at the court by the official preacher, the Jesuit Jeremiah Drexel, who proclaimed that those who opposed the persecution of witches were unworthy of the name of Christian.

During Maximilian's long reign, numerous laws were issued against witchcraft. He made no fine distinction between the superstition of sorcery and the heresy of witchcraft; all black arts were covered by his edict of 1611: "All those who made a pact with the devil should be punished with torture, death by fire, and confiscation of property." The next year he urged the Bavarian judges to hunt down witches with greater vigor. In 1616 came further laws, ordering that a victim who retracted her confession was to be tortured a second time, and if necessary a third time. In 1619, Maximilian personally intervened (just like James I) in a trial at Ingolstadt, where a judge had dropped charges of witchcraft against a woman and three children for insufficient evidence. His Instructions on Witchcraft (1622) ranks with the most vicious legislation in the history of witchcraft. Here Maximilian reversed his rule of 1616 and allowed no revocation after torture—otherwise the trials would never end. Priests were to be admitted to victims only to hear confessions and not to encourage retractions. Denunciation under torture was grounds for arrest, and fear after arrest was proof of guilt!

How the mania spread is shown in detail in this *Encyclopedia* in the 1637 trial at Eichstätt, a few miles northwest of Ingolstadt. The trial was conducted in the epis-copal court, but the procedure was that of the Duke. In this small town alone, Riezler, the nineteenth-century Bavarian historian, estimated that between 1,000 and 2,000 persons were burned as witches, and a similar number in each of the other two episcopal enclaves at Freising and Augsburg.

As in so many other parts of Germany, the witch mania was abated in Bavaria by the entry of the Swedish army in 1632. Thus, in 1634, damage to the crops was no longer attributed to witchcraft, but to natural causes. But some persecutions persisted, and the statute of 1611 was repeated in 1665 and 1746. In Munich, on January 9, 1666, a seventy-year-old man was convicted of raising storms. Duke Ferdinand Maria commuted more severe penalties, and the victim was merely torn three times with red-hot pincers before being burned alive.

The brief recrudescence of persecution in the early eighteenth century from about 1715 to 1722 is marked by the perjury of young boys, similar to that which a century earlier had convicted many English witches [see Burton Boy]. In 1715, at Wasserburg, about thirty-five miles southeast of Munich, nine schoolboys accused their teacher, Caspar Schwaiger, of going to the sabbat. He was savagely tortured, but refused to confess; when brought for a second torment he admitted his guilt and incriminated others. Later he withdrew his statements, but not being able to bear further torture, he let them stand. A similar trial occurred in 1722, at Moosburg, near Freising, when boys accused Georg Pröls of witchcraft. The torture chamber was censed, and the whips blessed before the flogging. Under torture, he confessed, then later revoked. Pröls was beheaded and burned. The authorities, however, feared widespread hysteria and freed thirteen others accused with Pröls, some of whom had already confessed. A year earlier, at Freising, some adolescents had themselves been indicted; of eleven persons executed there, one was a boy of thirteen, three others were fourteen, and one each aged sixteen, seventeen, and eighteen.

A late trial, at Eichstätt in 1723, shows clearly the position of the Church in keeping alive the delusion. Maria Walburga Rung, aged twenty-two, had been tried in a secular court at Mannheim as a witch, but the judge had decided she was merely a prostitute. She was eventually picked up by the episcopal court at Eichstätt, tortured until she confessed she was a witch, and burned.

Among the last sentences for witchcraft in this region were those given at the mass trial of some twenty persons in 1728-34 at Augsburg, when several women were executed. The Criminal Code of 1751 reaffirmed death by burning for the pact, and beheading for *maleficia*. The last execution for witchcraft in Germany took place in 1775 in the episcopal town of Kempten in Swabia, later a province of Bavaria [see Anna Maria Schwägel]. Two other late executions in Bavaria, thirteen-year-old Veronica Zerritsch in 1754 and Marie Klossner in 1756, have not been completely documented.

> "Who could dare accuse of error and injustice the judges, who, with fire and sword, proceed against this pest of witchcraft? Yet there are Christians unworthy of the name, who oppose with might and main the extirpation of this vice, lest perhaps, they say, the innocent suffer. O, ye enemies of the divine honor! Does not the law of God command, 'You shall not suffer a witch to live'? And I cry out as loud as I can, at the divine bidding, to bishops, princes and kings: You shall not suffer witches to live. Exterminate this pest with fire and sword."
> —Father Jeremiah Drexel, S.J. (1637)

Bavent, Madeleine: see Louviers Nuns.

Baxter, Richard. In all the standard biographical works about Richard Baxter (1615-91), a renowned Presbyterian teacher and author, no mention is made of witchcraft. Only one of the 150 entries in the New York Public Library catalogue refers to the *Certainty of the World of Spirits* (1691), a key book on witchcraft, published at the end of Baxter's life. At a time when his contemporaries were op-

posing the witchcraft delusion, Baxter supported superstition, obscurantism, and degradation. Does a celebrity's folly and stupidity on a critical contemporary issue sully his judgments on other subjects—else why this silence?

Baxter's *Certainty of the World of Spirits* is one of the last English works to defend witch beliefs, more reprehensible in that it tried to bolster the ebbing acceptance in England by calling in the witch terrors of New England. Richard Baxter had a curious life. The son of a profligate turned evangelical, Baxter was courtier, student of theology, schoolteacher, preacher, army chaplain, and author. In 1685 he was imprisoned for a year by the notorious Judge Jeffreys for "libeling the church."

At various periods of his life he was the friend of well-known witch believers, such as Judge Matthew Hale and Increase Mather, to whom Baxter dedicated his *Glorious Kingdom of God* (1691). Another believer in witches, John Wesley, edited Baxter's writings. Baxter's most significant work was the *Saints Everlasting Rest* (1650), but modern readers might prefer his comments on plunging necklines, in his *A Just and Seasonable Reprehension of Naked Breasts and Shoulders*, an English translation of Jacques Boileau (1675).

The *Certainty of the World of Spirits* is similar to Joseph Glanvill's *Saducismus Triumphatus* (1681), Richard Bovet's *Pandaemonium* (1684), or George Sinclair's *Satan's Invisible World Discovered* (1685): numerous "relations" of allegedly supranormal events to convince those "drowned in sadducism and bestiality" (the skeptics) of "invisible powers or spirits." Baxter praises all the classic demonologists, Bodin, Remy, Grillandus, Lavater, and the *Malleus Maleficarum*, and some lesser-known authorities such as Zanchy and Danaes, and the two Mathers who "hath most convincing evidence." In spite of his caveats against papist-inspired boy demoniacs and "lustful rank girls and young widows," the credulity of Baxter is amazing:

Storm-Raising: The raising of storms by witches is attested by so many, that I think it needless to recite them.

Bier Right: What shall we say to the many certain histories of the fresh bleeding of murdered bodies, when the murderer is brought to it, or at least, when he toucheth it, whether it be by the soul of the dead, or by a good spirit that hateth murder, or by the devil appointed for revenge, it seems plainly to be an invisible spirit's operation.

Possession: She vomited a thousand and two hundred worms, some as long as one finger, and some longer.

Incubi: And that many devils which the French call *ducii,* do daily attempt this uncleanness, and effect it, is reported by so many, that 'tis impudence to deny it.

Such a man did the celebrated witch judge Matthew Hale commend as "a person of great devotion and piety, and of a very subtile and quick apprehension."

Bekker, Balthasar. The Dutchman, Rev. Dr. Balthasar Bekker (1634-98), in his *De Betoverde Weereld* or *The World Bewitched* (1691), "openly assaulted the doctrines of witchcraft and of the devil. . . . As a reward for his exertions to enlighten his fellow-creatures, he was turned out of the ministry, and assaulted by nearly all the writers of his age"—Charles W. Upham. Bekker followed Descartes and another Dutch rationalist, Simon Stevin, who rejected belief in miracles. He was the last of the Dutch thinkers from Johan Weyer to Grevius who had kept Holland free from the abuses of the witch hunters. The liberal climate thus engendered had made Holland the only country where Reginald Scot had been translated. In 1683, Bekker had attracted attention by publishing his *Inquiry into Comets,* showing that they were not portents of evil. In 1691, first in Dutch, then in 1693 in German, he published his attack on belief in witchcraft, on the only logical basis possible: that spirits, either good or bad (the existence of which Bekker did not deny), could exercise no influence over human affairs; nor should

Balthasar Bekker's *The World Bewitched* (1691) was one of the last works attacking the witchcraft delusion. From *Fürstellung vier neuer Welt-Weisen* (1702).

seemingly paranormal effects be attributed to witchcraft. Since the belief in the influence of spirits had crept into Christianity from paganism, said Bekker, there was no reason to credit the pact between the witch and the Devil, the core of the theory. In fact, Bekker added, the theory of witchcraft was invented by the papacy "to warm the fires of purgatory and to fill the pockets of the clergy," who burned witches to confiscate their property and to pay the salaries of the inquisitors.

The English translation (1695) put it:

It has come to that pass that men think it piety and godliness to ascribe a great many wonders to the devil, and impiety and heresy, if a man will not believe that the devil can do what a thousand persons says he does. It is now reckoned godliness, if a man who fears God fear also the devil. If he be not afraid of the devil, he passes for an atheist, who does not believe in God, because he cannot think there are two gods, the one good, the other bad. But these, I think, with much more reason, may be called ditheists. For my part, if, on account of my opinion, they will give me a new name, let them call me a monotheist, a believer of but one God.

As Bekker had foreseen, he was himself called an atheist for questioning the whole system of the witch delusion, and was attacked by the Calvinist divines. "They protected the survival of superstitions of the pagan past in order to save the future from losing faith in the revealed word of God"—Adrian J. Barnouw. Refusing to recant, on August 21, 1692, Bekker was expelled by the Reformed Dutch church, but the Amsterdam magistrates prevented a public burning of his book and continued to pay his ministerial stipend. He was still outside the church at his death, June 11, 1698.

Many writers engaged in a war of words, attacking and defending Bekker's views, especially his denial of demoniacal possession. Bekker himself refused to participate in the debate, but in 1692 defended himself in *Die Friesche Godgelehrheid*. After his death, rumors circulated that he had changed his views, but this suggestion was repudiated by his son, Jan Hendrik Bekker. Balthasar's stand was continued by Christian Thomasius.

Bible Witchcraft. One of history's ironies is the justification of witchcraft on biblical texts, written originally for a religion which had no devil. Catholics and Protestants quoted Exodus xxii. 18, "Thou shalt not suffer a witch to live." But the Hebrew word *kaskagh* (occurring twelve times in the Old Testament with various meanings) here means, as Reginald Scot pointed out in 1584, "poisoner," and certainly had nothing to do with the highly sophisticated Christian conception of a witch. Yet the domination of Holy Scriptures was such that these mistranslations fostered the delusion. After the execution of Goody Knapp at Fairfield (Kent) in 1653, a neighbor said "it was long before she could believe this poor woman was a witch, or that there were any witches, till the word of God convinced her, which saith, Thou shalt not suffer a witch to live."

Another text which changed the Hebrew meaning—"a woman with a familiar spirit" for "pythoness"—occurred in I Samuel xxviii, the miscalled Witch of Endor.

Writers who tried to expose the witchcraft superstition, such as Reginald Scot or Thomas Ady, had to clear up two fallacies: (1) The numerous Hebrew words, uniformly translated by *veneficus* or *maleficus* or *witch*, covered many different practitioners of the occult, from jugglers to astrologers. To refer to all these different classes by one word (witch) was inadequate and erroneous. (2) The definition of witch based on the pact with Satan, transvection, metamorphosis, sabbat and *maleficia* was neither implied nor defined anywhere in the Bible. That the Old Testament did not deal with witchcraft is hardly surprising, for witchcraft depended on a Christian demonology. Thus Sir Walter Scott observed:

> It cannot be said that, in any part of that sacred volume [Old Testament], a text occurs indicating the existence of a system of witchcraft, under the Jewish dispensation, in any respect similar to that against which the law-books of so many European nations have, till very lately, denounced punishment. . . . In the four Gospels, the word, under any sense, does not occur. (*Letters on Demonology and Witchcraft*)

Lea suggested the biblical denunciations against sorcery were directed almost exclusively against divination.

In fact, therefore, while it may discuss magic and occult customs, the Bible has nothing to do with heretical witchcraft. The following quotations (Authorized Version), those most often cited in debates on the subject, are included here to show how erroneous translation and tendentious interpretation fostered the growth of obscurantism.

Exodus xxii. 18: "Thou shalt not suffer a witch to live."
Leviticus xix. 26: "Neither shall ye use enchantment, nor observe times [dreams]."
Leviticus xix. 31: "Regard not them that have familiar spirits, neither seek after wizards, to be defiled by them: I am the Lord your God."

Leviticus xx. 6: "And the soul that turneth after such as have familiar spirits, and after wizards, to go a whoring after them, I will even set my face against that soul, and will cut him off from among his people."

Leviticus xx. 27: "A man also or woman that hath a familiar spirit, or that is a wizard, shall surely be put to death: they shall stone them with stones; their blood shall be upon them."

Deuteronomy xviii. 10-12: "There shall not be found among you any one that maketh his son or his daughter to pass through the fire, or that useth divination, or an observer of times, or an enchanter, or a witch, or a charmer, or a consulter with familiar spirits, or a wizard, or a necromancer. For all that do these things are an abomination unto the Lord: and because of these abominations the Lord thy God doth drive them out from before thee."

Deuteronomy xviii. 20: "But the prophet . . . that shall speak in the name of other gods, even that prophet shall die."

I Samuel xv. 23: "For rebellion is as the sin of witchcraft [*gloss*: divination], and stubbornness is as iniquity and idolatry."

II Kings ix. 22: "What peace, so long as the whoredoms of thy mother Jezebel and her witchcrafts are so many?"

II Kings xxi. 6: "And he made his son pass through the fire, and observed times, and used enchantments, and dealt with familiar spirits and wizards: he wrought much wickedness in the sight of the Lord, to provoke him to anger."

II Kings xxiii. 24: "Moreover the workers with familiar spirits, and the wizards, and the images, and the idols, and all the abominations . . . did Josiah put away."

Isaiah viii. 19: "When they say unto you, Seek unto them that have familiar spirits, and unto wizards, that peep and that mutter, should not a people seek unto their God?"

Bier Right. Occasionally in witchcraft trials, evidence was introduced which depended on some primitive folklore belief. The various kinds of ordeals used to detect offenders long before witchcraft was invented often survived in the public memory, and were tolerated, especially by the clergy, in historical times. Bier right was reintroduced at the end of the twelfth century. The ordeal of bier right—the capacity of a corpse to bleed on the approach of the murderer—was considered especially valuable when all other legal methods of proving guilt had failed; it was allowed, for example, in a murder trial in 1628 at the Hartford Assizes. The blood of the murdered would gush out, wrote King James in his *Demonology* (1597), "as if the blood were crying to heaven for revenge." In Shakespeare's *Richard III*, Lady Anne expressed the same sentiments, when she declaimed against the Duke of Gloucester's interruption of the funeral procession of her husband, whom he had slain:

O gentlemen, see, see! dead Henry's wounds
Open their congealed mouths and bleed afresh.

Later, the ordeal was sometimes used in witchcraft trials whenever any person was accused of bewitching to death.

Bier right was approved by such celebrated demonologists as Del Rio, De Lancre, Binsfeld, and Lavater. Del Rio explained the phenomenon as caused by the hatred of the murdered for the murderer, which aggravated certain latent or hidden qualities in the corpse. This somewhat vague opinion was endorsed by Dr. Walter Charleton, physician to King Charles I, in his *Physiologia* (London, 1654) as "the noblest of antipathies."

An account of the Dalkeith witch trial in Scotland, in 1661, from a manuscript belonging to the (Scottish) National Museum of Antiquities, related how a woman, Christine Wilson, protesting her innocence

refused to come nigh the corpse or to touch it, saying that she never touched a dead corpse in her life. But being earnestly desired by the minister and bailiffs . . . that she would but touch the corpse softly, she granted to do it . . . she touching the wound of the dead man very softly, it being white and clean without any spot of blood or the like, yet immediately, while her finger was upon it, the blood rushed out of it to the great admiration [astonishment] of all the beholders, who took it as a discovery of the murder.

Bilson Boy. One of a long line of juvenile impostors in the history of English witchcraft, coming four years after the exposure of John Smith, the Leicester Boy. In 1620, William Perry, known as the Boy of Bilson, accused an old woman, Jane Clark, of bewitching him and provoking fits. King James's skepticism about the Leicester affair no doubt caused the judges at Stafford to examine William more closely, for they dismissed his accusations. The boy finally confessed he had faked the fits because he enjoyed the attention they brought.

Soon afterward, the same boy was caught repeating the fraud, and presumably imperiling other lives. Thomas Mor-

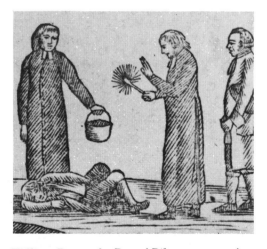

William Perry, the Boy of Bilson, a young impostor who faked fits, and whose accusations of witchcraft against an old woman were dismissed by the judges at Stafford in 1620. This engraving represents a late eighteenth-century German conception of William Perry receiving exorcism.

ton, then Bishop of Lichfield, became interested in the charges, and ultimately found that Perry had been trained by a Roman Catholic priest to feign possession by vomiting "out of his mouth rags, thread, straw, crooked pins."

Perry almost outwitted Bishop Morton by apparently passing black urine, for even "the physicians were of the opinion that nature had left her usual operations." Bishop Morton had resolved to "make no further trial," but as a last gamble "he set a trusty servant to watch him through a hole that looked into the chamber upon the bed." The whole household going to church, the boy thought himself alone. "Finding all quiet, [Perry] lifts up himself, and stares, and listens, and at length gets out of his bed, and in the straw or mat under it, takes out an inkpot and makes water in the chamber-pot." The lad then added the ink, and "for a reserve, if he should be forced to make water before company," saturated a piece of cotton with the ink, and put it "into his prepuce, covering it with the [fore-]skin." The Bishop's reputation was saved.

The devil who was supposed to afflict the boy sent him into fits at the reading of the first verse of the first chapter of St. John's Gospel. However, the devil did not always respond as he should, if the verse were read in foreign languages. Thomas Morton then admonished William:

"Boy, it is either thou or the devil that abhorrest these words of the Gospel; and if it be the devil, he (being so ancient a scholar, as of almost six thousand years' standing) knows and understands all languages, so that he cannot but know when I recite the same sentence out of the Greek text. But if it be thyself, then thou art an execrable wretch, who plays the devil's part. . . . Wherefore, look to thyself, for now thou art to be put to trial, and mark diligently, whether it be that same Scripture shall be read." . . . The Bishop then read out another verse in Greek, and the boy, thinking it was the first verse, had at once a furious seizure. Later, when the Bishop read out the first verse in Greek, the boy, believing that this

TRACTAT

Von Bekanntnuß der Zau=
berer vnd Heren. Ob vnd wie viel
denselben zu glauben.

Anfängklich durch den Hochwürdigen Herrn
Petrum Binsfeldium, Trierischen Suffraganten/ vnd
der H.Schrifft Doctorn/ kurtz vnd summarischer
Weiß in Latein beschrieben.

Jetzt aber der Warheit zu stewr in vnser Teutsche Sprach
vertiert/ durch den Wolgelerten M.Bernhart Vogel/ deß löblichen
Stattgerichts in München/ Assessorn.

Exod. XXII. Cap.
Die Zauberer solt du nicht leben lassen.

Gedruckt zu München bey Adam Berg.
Anno Domini M. D. XCI.
Mit Röm: Bay: May: Freyheit/ nit nachzudrucken.

Title page of the first edition in German (1591) of Bishop Peter Binsfeld's *De Confessionibus Maleficorum et Sagarum* [*Treatise on Confessions of Witches*] (1589), a bigoted and savage work which exercised tremendous influence in promoting the witchcraft delusion.

verse had already been read, remained unmoved.

Binsfeld, Peter. A major German authority on procedure, trained by the Jesuits in Rome, as Suffragan Bishop [*Weihbischof*] who stimulated the Treves witch trials, Peter Binsfeld (about 1540-1603) was quoted throughout Germany for the next century by Protestants as well as Catholics. His *Tractatus de Confessionibus Maleficorum et Sagarum* [*Treatise on Confessions by Evildoers and Witches*] was written with the trial of Dietrich Flade in mind: "I have wished the principal scope of my treatise to be the question whether faith is to be put in the confessions of witches against their accomplices." The second edition was extended to include a similar refutation of Loos, who had been forced to abjure his errors publicly before Binsfeld.

Binsfeld's *Tractatus* shows how the works of the demonologists were built up, using stories from earlier authorities (such as the maiden's successful excuse when caught fornicating, from Spina), citations of other experts (e.g., the *Malleus*, Grillandus, Bodin), and experiences drawn from the cases he had judged. While Binsfeld tries to appear "fair" according to the irrational code he followed—for example, he doubts metamorphosis and devil's marks—yet his learned bigotry oozes through. He discredits deathbed recantation because it is made without judicial solemnities; he admits that to exclude denunciations by witches would preclude any further trials; he terms light torture no torture at all; he agrees the law forbids repetition of torture but sanctions it in practice; by a subtle wordplay on presumption of guilt, he allows judges (in his later *Commentarius*) to question the accused on the names of suspects; he maintains the devil cannot appear in the shape of an innocent person; and he justifies secret informers. In all other crimes, it is better to absolve the guilty than condemn the innocent, yet in witchcraft every one is presumed to be a heretic.

Black Mass. In certain popular accounts of witchcraft, the black mass, a blasphemous parody of the Catholic mass involving sexual obscenities, figures prominently. A few scholars have elaborated on this idea. Thus Jules Michelet, an otherwise reputable French historian of the nineteenth century, saw the black mass as the symbol of the peasant's rebellion against the Church. "Fraternity of man with man, defiance of the Christians' heaven, worship of Nature's God, under unnatural and perverted forms—such was the inner significance of the black mass." From the position of Catholic orthodoxy, Montague Summers saw the black mass as the rallying point of the adherents of a real physical devil.

Every witches' sabbat was supposed to include a diabolical service, but the "black mass" as such is not found in any contemporary account of witchcraft, and the term became current only at the end of the nineteenth century in connection with Satanism (first used in English in 1896). No matter how titillating, all accounts of black masses (with one exception) must be dismissed as unfounded speculation. Both Michelet and Summers accepted as true the confessions of witches; but absolutely no credence can be placed in statements previously prepared by the interrogators and confirmed by the accused only under severe torture. Some accused, thinking to lighten their torture, elaborated on the questions asked them. But the black mass, as something that historically occurred, is one of the biggest intellectual frauds ever imposed on the lay public.

It was only natural that the inquisitors and the lay witch hunters who aped them would think of witchcraft in inverse terms to the religion they knew; witchcraft was made a conscious parody of Christianity.

To emphasize the crimes of witchcraft and to justify its extirpation, the demonologists emphasized the caricature of the most holy service of the church, the mass. Thus Father Gaufridi at his trial at Aix-en-Provence in 1611 made a brief reference (under torture) to a mass wherein he made the sign of the cross backward, and replaced the benediction with "Go, in the name of the Devil." Once the fantasies of the demonologists had been clad with the robe of authority, who would dare question them?

Among the stories of the desecration of the host (standard in all accusations against heretics and witches from early times), Nicholas Jacquier (1458), an inquisitor in France and Bohemia, told how a priest copulated in a church, and collected his semen and mixed it with the holy chrism oil. This act did not foreshadow any black mass, but was simply an instance of idolatry or sacrilege. Another early witch judge, Paulus Grillandus (about 1525), described solemn services to the Devil, with candles and prayers. The Inquisitor at Carcassonne in 1335 found a shepherd parodying the mass in a state of nudity, as Adam had been. On such hints, later writers built their stories, so that in a century or two, the most obscene practices would be believed, such as the rites of Father Picard and Father Boullé for the nuns at Louviers.

The credulous monk, Francesco-Maria Guazzo (1608), a prominent witch hunter, quoted Florin de Raemond's account of a trial in 1594 in Aquitaine [Haute-Garonne]. A young girl described the typical sabbat, with signing the pact, dancing, and intercourse with the goat, the god of the witches.

They also performed a travesty of the mass, celebrated by one clothed in a black cope with no cross woven into it. At the time of the holy sacrifice and the elevation of the host, he lifted a segment or round of turnip stained black, upon which they all with one voice cried out, "Master, help us!" The chalice contained water instead of wine; and they made their holy water as follows: the goat pissed into a hole dug in the ground, and with this undiluted water the celebrant sprinkled them all with a black aspergillum.

Another notorious demonologist, Pierre de Lancre (1612), made a unique allusion to a goat, wearing a chasuble, reading from a missal bound in wolf's skin, with red, white, and black pages.

In historical witchcraft (to 1750), satanic masses were actually celebrated only very late in the seventeenth century, in the Chambre Ardente Affair. Sophisticatedly accepting the thrill of sorcery as an influence on future events, the nobles of the court of Louis XIV hired a corps of some fifty or sixty priests of the Roman Catholic Church, all identified and known by name, to conduct special masses. The idea of a priest's celebrating mass on the belly of a nude girl stretched across the altar, and adding to the regular liturgy a few charms to secure her lover's fidelity, had its origin in the earlier orthodox amatory masses. If the mass was performed to provoke love, opined Grillandus, "it seems not to savor of heresy, because the divine precepts urge love and charity." When a Spanish priest, visiting Rome, fell in love with four nuns and had some monks celebrate mass with special prayers for success in venery, he was merely temporarily banished from the city. Dr. Johan Weyer (1563) described how a priest tried to exorcize a young nun from a very strict convent by performing mass on her belly. In the same way, mortuary masses, said to secure the death of a living person, were not considered heretical; however, the one who paid for the mass, as well as the priest who performed it, was liable to banishment (Grillandus). It should be remembered that the orgies of the "Guibourg" masses of the Chambre Ardente trials were developed only toward the end of the investigation and in confessions made under threats or under torture. Thus La Voisin's daughter, Marguerite, amplified the originally simple and guileless amatory mass as follows:

Every time during the course of the mass when the priest had to kiss the altar, instead he kissed the body of the girl. He consecrated the host over her private parts, into which he inserted a small portion of the host. At last the mass was finished, and the priest went into the woman, and, with his hands dipped in the chalice, washed all her genital areas.

The satanic mass was virtually a literary creation. One famous description was given by the Marquis de Sade in *Justine*. Some wicked monks dressed a young girl, Florette, to represent the Virgin Mary; by making some seemingly miraculous gestures she could win fame and fortune for their chapel. Justine related how, after this blasphemy—

our libertine monks, to compound their impieties, wished Florette to appear at their nightly orgies in the same vestments which had brought her so much veneration as the Blessed Virgin. Each one of them whipped up his filthy desires to commit the vagaries of his lusts with her in this costume. Excited by this first blasphemy, they counted other sacrileges for naught. The monks made this virgin strip and lie down flat on her belly on a big table. They lit the holy candles and placed a statue of our Lord between her legs, and had the audacity to celebrate the most holy of our sacraments on the buttocks of this young girl. At this horrible spectacle I fainted, for I could not endure it. Father Severino saw me in this condition, and told me that in order to be humbled I had to serve, in my turn, as the altar. They grasped me and laid me where Florette had been. The sacrifice of the mass was consummated. Severino seized the host, that sacred symbol of our venerable religion, and pushed it in the obscene entrance he used for his perverted pleasures, abusively pressing it in; then he ignominiously crushed it under the repeated lunges of his monstrous tool [*dard*], and, shouting blasphemies, emitted the foul surges of the torrent of his lubricity over the very body of his Saviour.

Not until the nineteenth century, when witchcraft had ceased to exist, did a few wayward minds create the black mass as it is thought of today, a service dedicated to anti-Christ, or a supposed relic of anti-Christian folklore. Only by distorting an occasional reference to an isolated perverse Christian practice and by ignoring the whole historical development and meaning of witchcraft can writers claim any relation between the hoaxes of a Léo Taxil, the recreations of the "Work of Mercy" of Pierre Ventras and Abbé Boullan (portrayed by Joris-Karl Huysmans in *Là Bas*), the occultism of a Guaita or a Jules Bois, and, on the other hand, the accounts of the witches' sabbats given by the demonologists. The so-called mortuary mass of St. Sécaire in Basque-speaking territories and the mass of the Holy Ghost in Normandy belong to folklore or anthropology, but not to witchcraft.

Blanckenstein Tragedy. "I have gone through much deplorable reading in my researches," wrote Henry C. Lea, "but I have never met anything that was so depressing as the blind and stupid cruelty of this superstition [of witchcraft]." What provoked this outburst from the great historian was a verbatim report of a trial near Naumburg (possibly at Altendorf), in Saxony, in the year 1676 (the documents identify persons and places by initials). More than other witch trials, that of Chatrina Blanckenstein, resulting in her acquittal, followed by the trial and conviction of her 44-year-old daughter, shows how once an *idée fixe* has obsessed a person, a group, or a nation, then every word and deed, no matter how disparate or irrelevant, serve to confirm the mania.

Chatrina Blanckenstein was a widow, sixty-six, well respected and comfortably situated, with four grown sons and two daughters. The tragedy started on March 10, 1676, when her daughter went to a neighbor's to get some fuel. Having no money with her, she offered to give in exchange some of her mother's jam, a local delicacy. The neighbor accepted the jam and gave some to her baby. The child became ill, passed four curious worms, and died within four days. Clearly, it had suffered from the *maleficia* of a witch. The

next day, March 15, the town council started to investigate Frau Blanckenstein. Evidence rapidly accumulated. A hare pursued by a crowd of boys and dogs miraculously escaped near the Blanckenstein house. The town watchman had seen in the public square three cats with red eyes. A court official who went to take inventory of Frau Blanckenstein's possessions (for confiscation on her anticipated conviction) walked heavily over a weak floor and saw his inkstand topple off three sacks of corn. A tax collector recalled that Chatrina's payments were unaccountably short when he made his returns. By March 25, the council received permission from a university law faculty (probably Jena or Leipzig) to charge Chatrina Blanckenstein with murder by witchcraft.

Her sons became active in her defense, but the court held all the trumps. The sons protested her imprisonment when she could easily furnish bail; they demanded opportunity for a defense lawyer (possible only at this late stage in the witchcraft delusion), and the release of their sister, jailed for opposing her mother's arrest. During April, the defense submitted its brief to the university, stressing the flimsiness of the charges but carefully answering every one of them in detail. On April 28, the council reconvened and heard further witnesses. A prison guard said Chatrina's unconcern at the prospect of torture indicated her a witch; another guard said her grief at the disgrace she had caused her family was equally a sign. A driver complained his cart upset outside Chatrina's garden (the road was very uneven at this point and the cart was badly loaded). More reports were sent for review by the university during May, and within the month the council court was told to question the physician attending the baby and to proceed to the torture of Frau Blanckenstein by ladder and boots. The physician believed the worms came from witchcraft— they had many legs and big red heads. The sons managed to delay the torture a few days, while they appealed to the Elector, but without effect. On June 9, beginning at 11:00 P.M., Chatrina Blanckenstein was tortured for two hours. She was cruelly tormented, not only with thumbscrews, boots, and ladder, but with hair ropes which scraped off the flesh from her legs, and with the *Schnur*, the ropes biting her neck and so twisting her head that the torturer feared she might die. She confessed nothing; her silence, naturally, was another indication of guilt. When the sixty-year-old woman collapsed on the ladder, it was said she was sleeping.

Later in June, the prisoner was searched for the devil's mark, her body being shaved all over by two women, but the hangman could find no insensitive spot. "You may look at me where you will, there is nothing anywhere. I trust in God my Creator and Christ Jesus my Saviour," she told the torturer. Further reports went to the university. On June 23, it ordered the case dismissed, but Chatrina had to take the *Urfehde* (the oath not to seek revenge) and pay court costs of seventy thalers, a considerable sum—even though found innocent, she still had to pay for the agony of her torture! Not until July 16 did her sons secure her freedom.

Yet, as the defense lawyer observed, "To be imprisoned for this offense was an irreparable injury, because she suffered harm to the reputation of her name." Common gossip against her continued and increased so that Frau Blanckenstein had to leave town. Her disappearance was another proof of guilt, and the magistrates quickly sought authorization to seek out and arrest her. This time, however, the university insisted on stronger indications of witchcraft. Apparently Chatrina later returned home, for she was buried in the local churchyard.

The tragedy of the Blanckensteins does not end here.

Suspicion of witchcraft had always fallen on the daughter of a witch. Thirteen years after the trial of the mother (who had meanwhile died), her daughter L—— was accused of bewitching to death a nine-month-old child on May 1, 1689. The only connection between the daughter and the child's father was the latter's indebtedness of thirty thalers, which L—— had lent him.

The town council took evidence about the baby's death, as well as the death of various animals attributed to L——, and an alleged injury to a tax collector. Without waiting for permission from the university, the council held five hearings during May, at which similar allegations were presented. On May 28, her estranged husband, living some miles away at Güsten in the neighboring state of Anhalt, appeared and forbade her to use her money for a lawyer—her brothers or the court could see to that, if they wanted. However, when an advocate was found, he examined the records and then refused to defend her.

During early June, five more hearings were held and the reports forwarded for evaluation to the university, which by this time had sanctioned the trial. Then on June 17, 1689, L—— was prepared for torture in the vault of the constable's house. The sight of the instruments broke her spirit. "What shall I confess?" she asked. "If she is guilty of the death of the child." After some reflection, she replied, "Yes." Then she admitted the conventional charges against all witches: she had given herself to a man with a dark plume (a devil named Heinrich), and had continued relations with him; she had killed cows and horses; she had renounced the Trinity; and she named accomplices. Two days later, she attempted to commit suicide with her belt, but was resuscitated after her face had already turned black. She then withdrew her accusations against accomplices. The university reviewed the whole trial and ordered her to be burned alive; those she had accused were to be secretly but thoroughly investigated.

Blocula: see Mora Witches.

Bodenham, Anne: see Dr. Lamb's Darling.

Bodin, Jean. Bodin's *De la Démonomanie des sorciers* [*Demonomania of witches*] (Paris, 1580), is a landmark in the history of witchcraft, but views on its merit differ. Archbishop Samuel Harsnett, for example, in 1605 mocked Bodin for believing in

"For it is recommended in crimes so conspiratorial that presumption and conjecture are sufficient proofs."—Jean Bodin, famous French lawyer, philosopher, and demonologist (1580).

transvection, ligature, and lycanthropy, and "above all," stung to the quick by a slur on his country, because Bodin told "that unsavory, melancholy and ridiculous tale of an egg which a witch sold to an Englishman and by the same transformed him into an ass." Bishop Francis Hutchinson in 1718 dismissed Bodin as "a pure sot." Henry More, the Cambridge philosopher, in 1653 thought Bodin's opinions "not at all unworthy of a rational and sagacious man."

Jean Bodin was highly educated in classics, law, philosophy, and economy, and therefore his opinions encouraging the witch delusion are the more blameworthy. Born in 1529 at Angers, he attended the local university, became a Carmelite monk, but left for the University of Toulouse (for twelve years), later becoming professor of Roman law there. In 1561 he went to Paris to serve the king, and began publishing his many learned dissertations. Fifteen years later, Bodin published his *Republic*, which, with some public speeches, lost him royal favor, for he argued that the royal domain was vested in the people and the king simply a commoner—the *Republic* was full

of such ideas, far in advance of the age. The same year, 1576, he married the daughter of a King's Prosecutor at Laon, and settled down as a provincial lawyer, later becoming a public prosecutor. In 1581 he visited England in the retinue of the Duke of Alençon, a suitor to Queen Elizabeth. Jean Bodin died of the plague at his birthplace in 1596, a proud Angevin.

Of his dozen works, the most notorious is the *Démonomanie,* published first in French in 1580, and in Latin [*De Magorum Daemonomania*] the following year; it had ten editions before 1604. The 1698 (Hamburg) German translation was conflated into a refutation of Balthasar Bekker. The *Démonomanie* was acceptable to Protestants, for Bodin advocated religious toleration of the French Calvinists. Indeed, because of suspected Calvinist leaning, he was marked for murder at the St. Bartholomew's Day Massacre, but luckily escaped. And all his works were condemned by the Inquisition. About witchcraft, however, Roman Catholics and Calvinists were of one mind.

The *Démonomanie,* written to help judges counter witchcraft, was based on Bodin's personal experience as judge in many witch trials, as well as on his erudition. Witchcraft had been removed from the ecclesiastical courts to the secular by a decree of 1390, and Bodin was one of the first to attempt a *legal* definition of a witch: "One who knowing God's law tries to bring about some act through an agreement with the Devil [*par moyens diaboliques*]."

The third part tells how to torture, interrogate, condemn, and execute witches. While from time to time the trained legal mind shines through—"I confess it is far better to absolve the guilty than condemn the innocent"—for the most part Bodin writes as an unmitigated bigot, infuriated by the acceptance of the more moderate views of Johan Weyer (whose *De Praestigiis* had been reprinted at Basel in 1578).

Bodin discredits in advance those who doubt witchcraft, by giving examples of skeptics later proved leading witches themselves. For witchcraft must be extirpated: "One must not adhere to the ordinary rules of prosecution," he says, for "proof of such evil is so obscure and difficult that not one out of a million witches would be accused or punished, if regular legal procedure were followed." So Bodin adds his arguments and examples to bolster the worst features of the witch persecutions initiated in the *Malleus Maleficarum* and in so doing becomes more priest than the priests.

In witch trials, but in no other trials, Bodin thus interprets the law:

A prisoner may be promised immunity or reduced punishment if he accuses his accomplices.

The names of informers are to be kept secret.

Children are to be forced to testify against their parents.

Crafty and experienced *agents-pro-vocateurs* are to cajole the accused into confessing.

Suspicion is sufficient ground for torture, for popular rumor is almost never misinformed.

A person once accused should never be acquitted, unless the falsity of the accuser or informer is clearer than the sun.

In addition, Bodin urged brutal treatment of suspects; he himself, as a trial judge, tortured children and invalids [*"une jeune fille, un jeune enfant, ou une femme délicate, ou quelque mignard"*]. No punishment [*peine*] was too cruel for witches. To put the fear of God into them, Bodin advocated using cautery and hot irons so that the putrefied flesh would have to be cut out: *"Il faut appliquer les cautères et*

DEMONOMANIE
DES SORCIERS
A MONSEIGNEVR M. CHRE-
stofle de Thou Cheualier Seigneur de Cœli, premier President en la Cour de Parlement, & Conseiller
du Roy en son priué Conseil.

PAR I. BODIN ANGEVIN.

A PARIS,
Chez Iacques du Puys Libraire Iuré, à la Samaritaine,
M. D. LXXX.
AVEC PRIVILEGE DV ROY.

Title page of the first edition of Jean Bodin's *Démonomanie* (Paris, 1580), a horrible landmark in the history of the witch delusion.

A Visit from the Devil.

The 1698 German translation of Bodin's *Démonomanie* (1580) added some 500 pages on seventeenth-century witchcraft (including Salem). Some of the examples are illustrated. The above engraving depicts a drunken youth who awakens to find little creatures crawling everywhere. A tall stranger (the Devil) presses him to conviviality, on pain of a broken neck, but a figure of light urges prayer. The stranger orders his creatures to torture the youth, who is saved by the crowing of the cock.

fers chauds et couper les parties putréfiées." Burning by a slow fire was too good for witches, for burning lasted only half an hour or so [see Executions]. It was impossible to be lenient to witches; in fact, the judge who did not execute a convicted witch should himself be put to death.

Note should be made of the gentlemanly silence which shields witch hunters. In Vermandois, near St.-Quentin, in 1566 a woman was mistakenly burned alive; the executioner forgot to strangle her first. Bodin did not cry out at this miscarriage of justice; instead he rationalized: "Not a mistake—it is better to say the just judgment of God, who thus reminds us . . . there is no crime more worthy of burning."

Such were the procedures which Bodin's precept and prestige fostered. And such was the man whom Montaigne described as "having far more judgment than the mob of scribblers of that century."

Boguet, Henri. *Grand Juge de St.-Claude, au Comté de Bourgogne,* Henri Boguet (about 1550-1619) was an eminent lawyer, and author of a legal textbook that was a standard for over a century. His *Discours des sorciers,* with twelve editions in twenty years, rapidly became an authoritative work on demonology. Its wealth of carefully verified human interest stories sheds much light on the psychology of witchcraft in the early seventeenth century. "I have founded the following treatise upon certain trials which I myself conducted, during the last two years, of several members of this sect, whom I have seen and heard and probed as carefully as I possibly could in order to draw the truth from them."

While he was chief judge at St.-Claude, an eight-year-old child, Loyse Maillat, was exorcized against possession. She said the devils had been sent by Françoise Secretain, a woman of hitherto unblemished reputation. Boguet systematically tortured her until she named many accomplices and created the basis for a mass witch hunt. In the *Discours,* Boguet described forty witches he had examined, all presumably burned. He included in his holocaust children below puberty, because their crime was so horrible and because once in the clutches of Satan they seldom reformed. Many of his victims were not strangled before being burned. Claude Janguillaume, for example, tore herself from the stake three times, and was three times thrust back into the flames by the executioner.

In repute, the *Discours* rivaled the *Malleus Maleficarum,* and surpassed similar works by noted contemporaries like Bodin, Remy, or De Lancre by virtue of its appendix, "The Manner of Procedure of a Judge in a Case of Witchcraft," seventy articles codifying existing statutes and court methods. The success of *Discours des sorciers* was helped by the lavish praise of many professors and church dignitaries, who seconded Boguet's wish that all witches might "be united in one single body, so that they might all be burned at once in a single fire." Some of the chapter headings suggest the contents of the book:

Of the power used by witches.
How witches afflict the herds.
Witches are unable to shed tears in the presence of the judge.
The marks on the bodies of witches.
Whether one accused of witchcraft who dies in prison may be buried in consecrated soil.
Of the might and virtue of holy water against devils.

Boguet's family tried to suppress the book; possibly his relatives were secretly sympathetic to the victims of witchcraft.

Boots. The boots, sometimes called the "Spanish boots," was an instrument of torture reserved for such crimes as treason and witchcraft. It consisted of a vise enclosing the legs from ankles to the knees, operated by screws or wedges. When this vise was forced together tightly, the bones and flesh of the legs would be severely lacerated and crushed. A graphic account of the use of the boots or "bootikins" in Scotland occurs in the trial of Dr. John Fian, the alleged leader of the North Berwick witches; at each stroke of a large hammer which forced the wedges to tighten the vise, the question was repeated. Official records are still extant describing the French fortune-tellers tortured with the boots [*brodequins*] in the Chambre Ardente Affair.

Bordelon, Laurent. Laurent Bordelon (1653-1730) was born at Bourges and died in Paris; he was chaplain of St.-Eustache and moved in the ruling and intellectual circles of the capital. A minor writer, he is typical of the nascent movement that included Cyrano de Bergerac (died 1655) at the end of the seventeenth century

The History of the Ridiculous Extravagances of Monsieur Oufle (1711).
"It also frequently happens that even those of riper years are yet full as weak as children in swallowing whatever they read, if it does but seem uncommon, wonderful, and prodigious."

which ultimately led to the acceptance of rationalism.

In over thirty works (including drama and pedagogy) combating superstition, Bordelon occasionally employed the weapons of ridicule: he parodied Apuleius' *Golden Ass,* he satirized credulity in *Mital,* and in his somewhat pedantic *L'Histoire des imaginations extravagantes de Monsieur Oufle* (Paris, 1710) successfully poked fun at all the traditional aspects of witchcraft and demonology. "It is better to utilize ridicule rather than reason with such blockheads," he said. *Oufle,* is, of course, an anagram for *le fou* [the madman], and this Don Quixote of demonography has amazing adventures into the magical arts, meeting lycanthropes, apparitions, astrologers, devils, and sorcerers. Bordelon added pertinence and sting to his fantasy by giving accurate footnotes from the recognized demonologists to emphasize the folly of their labors. If his endeavors do not seem remarkable to us, we must remember that in his time the official religious view was that belief in witches was "an article of faith which it was impossible to deny without falling into heresy"—Daugis, *Traité sur la magie,* 1732. And even a half-century after *L'Histoire,* the Abbey of Poissy annually celebrated a mass to protect its nuns against goblins (*fées*).

Boullé, Thomas: see Louviers Nuns.

Bouvet, Le Sieur. Le Sieur Bouvet's *Manières admirables* [*Excellent Ways and Means to Investigate All Kinds of Crimes and Witchcraft*] is a technical manual on how to conduct a *procès-verbal.* While his comments pertain also to other crimes, nevertheless it is the treason of witchcraft on which Bouvet concentrates his attention; like heresy, it merits burning *sans rémission.* The book is crammed with vivid accounts of what goes on in the courtroom and torture chamber, drawn from Bouvet's own experience as Provost General of the French armies in Italy. He anticipates unusual situations and tells how to overcome them (e.g., how to torture a prisoner sick with syphilis); he notes where the prisoner

should shriek out in pain and when the judge must harden his heart. In this grotesque but homely fashion, the *Manières admirables* (1659) is perhaps the most inhumanly· human of all the manuals for secular judges.

Two chapters deserve special mention.

"How a good judge should superintend the torture, and how he should interrogate the accused, and what he should watch out for during the process"—Chapter 18. The judge should have the accused shaved and bound, and then, unemotionally and composedly, have him tortured until the prisoner can stand no more. The judge must proceed neither too lightly nor too severely, always show mercy and moderation, and take into account either the extreme age or youth of the accused, and his good or bad reputation. The judge must not desist on account of the cries and shrieks that will be made, lest feeling too much pity he lose the chance to find out the truth. His rules are not those of his own heart, but those of the civil and ecclesiastical law; yet he must not be tyrannical but dispense what justice demands.

"What should be done if the prisoner is suspected of using charms to endure torture"—Chapter 20. The prisoner must be stripped nude (*dépouillé nue*). Every single part of his body must be scrutinized, especially the nostrils, ears, privy parts, and even wounds and sores, for any little bits of paper or parchment or old skin, in which could be hidden a tiny piece of wax with some words inscribed on it. If no charm is found, then the hair, beard, and pubic hair must be burned off, for sometimes a prisoner, almost imperceptibly, can just rub his hair, and, by the aid of the devil hiding there, not feel the pain. But if all this avails naught, and a charm is not found, it follows the prisoner must have swallowed it. He must be given an emetic to cause evacuation; invariably the charm is passed out. When the accused sees what is happening, he is so panicked that he doesn't know what to say. Very often he confesses immediately without waiting for further tortures.

A note of dissent cited in this chapter highlights the strangling irrationality of the witch delusion [see also Heinrich von Schultheis]. It is ridiculous, says Bouvet, to believe that a prisoner endures torture without pain because he is firm and resolute (as *beaucoup d'esprits* think). All the facts prove the contrary; he is a witch sustained by a charm—and Bouvet could more than fill a book with examples he has seen in Italy.

Bovet, Richard. A minor English demonologist, born 1641, died early eighteenth century, educated at Oxford, author of *Pandaemonium* (1684). Bovet was introduced to modern readers by Montague Summers in a limited edition. The work is in two parts. The first consists of unoriginal comment on witchcraft, violently antipapist, some borrowed from Glanvill and the rest from the mystical theology of the unreliable Daniel Brevint, Dean of Lincoln Cathedral; it has little interest to the general reader, save for the admission that confessions of witches may be due to "a deep melancholy, or some terror that they may have been under." The second part, however, contains fifteen quite amusing ghost stories (including Poltergeists), one of which, "The Demon of Spreyton," was retold by Andrew Lang, *Cock Lane and Common Sense* (1894), and by others. Bovet's point of view is clearly stated: "The more unaccountable these things seem to be in themselves (the real matter of fact being proved) it ought the more to prevail toward a belief of these extraordinary agencies." In collecting such stories from his friends, Bovet shows the contemporary interest in experimental philosophy, in common with Dr. Henry More (to whom his book is dedicated) and Glanvill, which "in its search for proofs of the reality of spirit is apt to pursue spirits." (Douglas Bush, *Oxford History of Literature*, Vol. IV, 1945)

Broomstick: see Transvection.

Buirmann, Franz. The exploits of Franz Buirmann, judge and mass murderer, surely the most degenerate of all the hundreds of degenerate witch judges in

A A Witch.   B A Spirit raised by the Witch.
C A Friar raising his Imps.   D A Fairy Ring.
E A Witch riding on the Devill through the Aire.
F An Inchanted Castle.

An Enchanted Castle, the frontispiece of Richard Bovet's *Pandaemonium* (1684), in the Bodleian Library, Oxford.

Germany, were recorded from personal knowledge by the seventeenth-century humanitarian, Hermann Löher: "I would rather be judged by wild animals, would rather fall into a den of lions, wolves and bears, than into the hands of a witch judge." In Buirmann's two visits in 1631 and 1636 to the little villages of Rheinbach, Meckenheim, and Flerzheim (near Bonn), out of 300 households he burned alive 150 persons.

Franz Buirmann was an itinerant judge appointed by the Prince-Archbishop of Cologne, and he could override the local authorities. He was active not only in the Cologne archdiocese, but in Juliers, Cleves-Berg, and the abbey town of Siegburg. He was, says Lois Gibbons, "a shrewd man of low birth, a rough tool in the hands of persons higher than himself." Since the property of his victims was forfeit, he took free rein in his activities.

The following are some typical examples

Torture of Christine Böffgen in 1631 by Judge Franz
Buirmann at Rheinbach;
she died on the fourth day
of torture. From Hermann
Löher, *Hochnötige Klage.*

of the men and women he murdered at Rheinbach in 1631:

1. Christine Böffgen, a prosperous elderly widow, childless, generous, and highly respected. Either on "presumption" or denunciation by two prisoners, Buirmann arrested her on suspicion of witchcraft. In a kangaroo court (five of the seven assessors refused to take part in the trial), Frau Böffgen was blindfolded, exorcized, shaved, and pricked [see Pricking]; she was placed on the torture stool, and the vise was tightened around her legs until she confessed. When released from the torture, she recanted. Back under torture, she refused to name "accomplices." Christine Böffgen died on the fourth day of torture, and Judge Buirmann confiscated her property. As late as 1926, masses for the repose of her soul were said in St. George's Church in Rheinbach.

2. Frau Peller, wife of a court assessor, guilty by association with her sister, who had repulsed Buirmann's advances. Unknown to the local justices, Frau Peller was arrested in the morning and by two o'clock in the afternoon was under torture. Judge Buirmann had her protesting husband thrown out of the courtroom. Like Frau Böffgen, she was exorcized, shaved, searched—the torturer's assistant raped her during this process—and tortured. To stifle her cries, Judge Buirmann stuffed a dirty handkerchief into her mouth. Asked to name her accomplices, she gave so many names that the question was hurriedly dropped. She was immediately convicted and burned alive in a hut of dry straw, the usual method in this part of the Rhineland. Her terrified husband died a few months later.

3. Herr Lirtzen, burgomaster of Rheinbach and brother-in-law to an assessor. Even after application of the leg vises and of the "crocodile jaws," he would not confess. Herr Lirtzen was then bound to a St. Andrew's cross, loosely fixed in the floor, with a jagged iron collar around his neck, with four iron rings, from each of which ropes stretched to the corners of the room. The torturer shook the cross so that the iron collar lacerated the neck. Herr Lirtzen still refused to confess. He was fastened in a metal witch's chair under which a fire was burning. After continuous torture for twenty-four hours, he still refused to bear false witness. Two days later, he was burnt alive with Frau Peller.

One other typical trial of Judge Buirmann's came in 1636:

4. The mayor of Rheinbach, the educated and wealthy Dr. Schultheis Schweigel, had been Buirmann's most formidable opponent. In 1631 he had opposed the trial of Christine Böffgen, and so Buirmann, on his return in 1636, arrested Schweigel as a "witch patron." After seven hours of continuous torture, Schweigel died. His corpse was dragged from prison and burned. He had willed considerable wealth to the poor; Judge Buirmann took it.

Buirmann was faced with widespread but unavailing opposition by the townspeople and clergy of Rheinbach. Prominent among the dissenting priests in 1636 were the Dominican Johann Freylinck; the parish priest of Rheinbach, Father Weynhart Hartmann, who publicly remonstrated with Buirmann's henchmen; and Father Hubertus of Meckenheim, who preached against the persecution (and found himself called a witch). Finally, in his persecutions at Siegburg in 1636, Buirmann discovered that his own executioner was a witch. Buirmann promptly had him burned, too.

Burning Court: see Chambre Ardente Affair.

Burning of Witches: see Executions.

Burroughs, George. "The most important personage executed during this period [1692, at Salem], and one of the most noted of witchcraft victims in the history of the world." So wrote Winfield S. Nevins, a standard authority on the Salem witch trials.

Whereas in Europe many priests suffered death on charges of sorcery, in England and America ministers were the exception. In America (though not in England) the accused were often of middle or upper class, but Rev. George Burroughs was the only clergyman indicted as a servant of the devil. He had been minister at Salem Village for only a couple of years, from 1680 to 1682. The parish had been recently created, having been split off from Salem Town in 1672. It had a record of disputes over stipends between congregation and minister. From his predecessor, James Bayley, Burroughs inherited feuds and a di-

The torture of Herr Lirtzen, Burgomaster of Rheinbach, in 1631. His legs were broken, and his neck lacerated with an iron collar. This torture was described by a contemporary witness, Hermann Löher, who later published a denunciation of Buirmann, with illustrations of the agonies of the victims. The only known copy of this book was in 1939 at Münster; these engravings come from the duplicate set in Cornell University Library.

vided parish. When he revisited Salem Village in 1683, from Maine, in the middle of a formal settlement with the village elders, he was arrested on complaint of John Putnam for nonpayment of debts. Since the parish owed him several times the amount of the debts, however, the suit was dismissed. It took the church two years to overcome its bad reputation and get Deodat Lawson, who resigned in 1688; then the congregation was left without a minister until Rev. Samuel Parris came in November, 1689.

The Putnam family was Burroughs' *bête noir*. The parsonage being in disrepair, Burroughs had for a time lodged with John Putnam and his wife, both of whom pried into his personal life. When Burroughs' second wife died in 1681, the Putnams hinted the minister had not been as kind to her as he might. Burroughs returned to his home in Maine in 1682, and left with Thomas Putnam a young girl, Mercy Lewis, a waif he had taken into his home in Portland. This girl whom he had befriended and Thomas Putnam's daughter Ann (John's niece) were the two chief accusers of Burroughs and were responsible for his hanging.

Accusations had been thrown by the "afflicted" young women of Salem for two months before the "little black minister that lived at Casco Bay" was identified with Burroughs. Before this, there had been talk by the girls of assemblies in a pasture of Rev. Samuel Parris; and confessions of accused witches told of broomstick nightrides, of feasts "of roast and boiled meat," of unholy communions with "red bread and red wine like blood" (most Puritans considered transubstantiation to be of the Devil), and of proselytizing sermons. Most of the interrogations were thereafter devoted to finding out who was this "tall black man with a high crowned hat."

On April 20, 1692, twelve-year-old Ann Putnam deposed she was "grievously affrighted" by the apparition of a minister, who choked her and urged her to write in his book. "[I] told him that it was a dreadful thing that he which was a minister that should teach children to fear God should come to persuade poor creatures to give their souls to the Devil." She continued: "Oh, dreadful creature, tell me your name that I may know who you are. Then again he tortured me and urged me to write in his book, which I refused. And then presently he told me that his name was George Burroughs." On May 3, Ann amplified her first deposition to include charges of murder against Burroughs for killing both his first and second wife [see Ann Putnam].

Mercy Lewis, nineteen, testified on May 7, and identified the devil's book of names as one "that was in [Burroughs'] study when I lived with them; but I told him I did not believe him, for I had been often in his study but I never saw that book there. But he told me that he had several books in his study which I never saw in his study, and he could raise the devil." She also confirmed Ann's vision of the dead wives, but added: "The next night he told me I should not see his two wives if he could help it, because I should not witness against him."

Then Mercy recalled a Bible story and continued:

This ninth [of] May, Mr. Burroughs carried me up to an exceeding high mountain and showed me all the kingdoms of the earth, and told me that he would give them all to me if I would write in his book, and if I would not he would throw me down and break my neck. But I told him they were none of his to give, and I would not write if he throwed me down on a hundred pitchforks.

The most extreme statement by any of the possessed accusers came from Abigail Hobbs, who confessed that on May 12 the devil in the shape of Burroughs brought her poppets to stick pins into.

Q. Who brought the images to you?
A. It was Mr. Burroughs.
Q. How did he bring it you?
A. In his own person, bodily.

The shape of Mr. Burroughs was not simply an apparition or specter; it could be touched by the hand. At this time, Abigail was in jail and Burroughs eighty miles away in Maine. That her testimony was not a slip is seen by a further question:

Q. Was [Burroughs] there himself with you in bodily person?
A. Yes, and so he was when he appeared to tempt me to set my hand to the book. He then appeared in person, and I felt his hand at the same time.

Other spectral evidence was introduced at the trial on August 5 by Benjamin Hutchinson, who recalled that on April 21, Abigail Williams had seen Burroughs' specter in front of Ingersoll's inn.

I asked her where about the little man stood. Said she, "Just where the cart wheel went along." I had a three grained iron fork in my hand, and I threw it where she said he stood. And she presently [immediately] fell in a little fit, and when it was over said she, "You have torn his coat, for I heard it tear." "Whereabouts?" said I. "On one side," said she.

Hutchinson went into the "great room" of the inn, and Abigail cried out:

"There he stands!" I said, "Where, where?" and presently drew my rapier. But he immediately was gone, as she said. "Then," said she, "there is a gray cat." Then I said, "Whereabouts doth she stand?" "There," said she, "there." Then I struck with my rapier. Then she fell in a fit, and when it was over, she said, "You have killed her; and immediately Sarah Good come and carried her away."

This story Abigail had got from Mary Walcott, who told it on April 19 against Bridget Bishop, with her brother Jonathan striking the specter so that "he tore her coat in striking, and she heard it tear."

On this evidence of six "witch bitches" and eight confessing witches, plus nine depositions (only two eyewitness) of Burroughs' phenomenal strength—although short, he had been known as an athlete at Harvard—Burroughs was condemned. The clinching evidence came at his trial, when the girls accused Burroughs, who was kept in jail, of biting them. They displayed the toothmarks, and the judges pried open Burroughs' mouth to compare the impressions, "which could be distinguished from those of some other men's." Cotton Mather, who recorded this proof, concluded the thirty testimonies against Burroughs "were enough to fix the character of a witch upon him." (*Wonders of the Invisible World.*)

The verdict was, of course, assured before the trial began. Quoting the skeptic Thomas Ady, Burroughs unreservedly denounced the whole delusion: "There neither are nor ever were witches that having made a compact with the Devil can send a devil to torment other people at a distance." A statement like this was just as damning evidence as the fullest confession.

On the scaffold, Burroughs maintained his innocence and flawlessly recited the Lord's Prayer (which no "firebrand of hell"—Pastor Noyes's term—could ever speak without stumbling), a demonstration so inflammatory that Cotton Mather, who was watching the hanging, had to pacify the onlookers by suggesting that the devil was most dangerous when appearing as an angel of light (Calef, *More Wonders of the Invisible World*).

See also Salem Witch Trials, Ann Putnam.

Burton Boy. The Boy of Burton, Thomas Darling, is one of the many English adolescents who, by going into convulsions, condemned numerous old women as witches. In this respect, he echoes the Throckmorton girls [see Warboys Witches] and foreshadows the "witch bitches" of Salem. Thomas was, to be sure, eventually exposed through a lengthy pamphlet war between Archbishop Samuel Harsnett and John Darrell, who connived with young Darling in his "exorcism." The contemporary accounts include striking examples of the boy's murderous fantasies.

Tommy's accusations against Alice Gooderidge, aged sixty, and her mother, Elizabeth Wright, at any other period in history would have earned him perhaps a sound thrashing or a psychiatrist's couch. But in 1596 judges accepted the wildest inventions of delinquent or disturbed children as weighty matter; they sought, not to determine the truth, but to confirm their own prejudices. Without going into the legal

SEMPER EADEM

Province of the
Massachusetts=Bay.

AN ACT.

Made and Passed by the Great and General Court or
Assembly of Her Majesty's Province of the Massachusetts
Bay in New=England, Held at Boston the 17th
Day of October, 1711.

An Act to Reverse the Attainders of George Burroughs and others for Witchcraft.

FORASMUCH as in the Year of our Lord One Thousand
Six Hundred Ninety Two, Several Towns within this Province were Infested with a horrible Witchcraft or Possession
of Devils ; And at a Special Court of Oyer and Terminer
holden at Salem, in the County of Essex in the same Year
One Thousand Six Hundred Ninety Two, George Burroughs of Wells,
John Procter, George Jacob, John Willard, Giles Core, and
his Wife, Rebecca Nurse, and Sarah Good, all of Salem aforesaid :
Elizabeth How of Ipswich, Mary Eastey, Sarah Wild and Abigail Hobbs all of Topsfield : Samuel Wardell, Mary Parker,
Martha Carrier, Abigail Falkner, Anne Foster, Rebecca Eames,
Mary Post, and Mary Lacey, all of Andover : Mary Bradbury
of Salisbury : and Dorcas Hoar of Beverly ; Were severally Indicted, Convicted and Attained of Witchcraft, and some of them put
to Death, Others lying still under the like Sentence of the said Court,
and liable to have the same Executed upon them.

acrobatics of the German jurists, the English judges in their own pragmatic way achieved a similar result: the accused was executed as a witch.

Fourteen-year-old Thomas Darling, on February 27, 1596, becoming separated from his uncle while hunting in the woods, returned home feeling sick. Next day he had fits, seeing a green cat and green angels, and some time later "a man come out of a chamber pot, flames of hell, and the heavens open." A physician's diagnosis that the boy had worms was rejected, and an alternative explanation of bewitchment advocated in detail in the youth's hearing. His fits continued, and in a few weeks Thomas could describe the manner of his enchantment. While lost, he had inadvertently broken wind as a "little old woman with . . . three warts on her face" passed by. She took umbrage at his action, and presumably to bewitch him and cause his fits, said (according to Thomas):

Gyp with a mischief and fart with a bell,
I will go to heaven and thou shalt go to hell.

The boy's relatives then started looking for a likely suspect, and by April 8 had come up with Alice Gooderidge. Within two days Alice admitted being in the woods that day, but she had merely scolded another boy who once had broken her basket of eggs. Later, she admitted meeting Tommy, who had derided her as "the witch of Stapenhill." She retorted:

Every boy doth call me witch,
But did I ever make thy arse to itch?

The case against Alice was built up along traditional lines. Tommy accused her of bewitching him; when she was removed from his presence, his convulsions stopped. One day he had twenty-seven fits within six hours, "shrieking pitifully, blearing out the tongue, his neck so wrythen [twisted] that his face seemed to stand backward." Alice was, of course, searched for the witch's mark, and she failed to recite the

Lord's Prayer. A neighbor added the charge of bewitching his cow. To get her to confess, a type of torture was employed which is rarely mentioned in English records. A "cunning man" put on her a new pair of shoes, and "set her close to the fire till the shoes became extreme hot . . . She being thoroughly heated, desired a release and she would disclose all. Which granted, she confessed nothing." Later, however, she admitted help from the devil "in likeness of a little parti-colored dog, red and white, and I called him Minny." A neighbor's dog, supposed to look like Minny, was exonerated when Alice said she got her Minny from her mother, Elizabeth Wright.

By this association, Elizabeth Wright and Alice's husband and daughter were implicated. Only Elizabeth was accused; she, too, could provoke Tommy's fits, which now included visions of hell. "Yonder comes Mother Red Cap. Look how they beat her brains out! See what it is to be a witch! See how the toads gnaw the flesh from her bones!"

The climax came on May 27, 1596, with the arrival of the notorious exorcist, John Darrell. Somewhat of a ventriloquist, he staged the following conversation, supposedly "delivered by a wicked spirit or by an holy angel":

> *Small voice*: Brother Glassap, we cannot prevail, his strength is so strong, and they fast and pray, and a preacher prayeth as fast as they.
> *Big and hollow voice*: Brother Radulphus, I will go unto my master Beelzebub, and he shall double their tongues.
> *Another voice*: We cannot prevail. Let us go out of him, and enter into some of those here.
> *Finally a voice*: My son, arise up and walk; the evil spirit is gone from thee. Arise and walk.

This exorcism allegedly cured Thomas, for he got up and walked (though partly paralyzed for the first three months); at

---

The Act of 1711 cleared some of those executed for witchcraft at Salem in 1692; others had to wait for justice until 1957.

Fourteen-year-old Thomas Darling's visions of hell, with three devils torturing witches. From the very rare tract (1597) in Lambeth Palace Library.

it was widely known throughout New England and influenced the conduct of the Salem trials. Rev. John Hale, whose wife was accused at Salem, in his *Modest Inquiry into the Nature of Witchcraft* (1702), noted how the judges consulted precedents for witch trial procedures, among whom were Glanvill, Cotton Mather, and *A Trial of Witches . . . at Bury St. Edmunds*. The importance of this trial, therefore, extended across the ocean from Suffolk to Massachusetts, and surpassed that of the earlier mass executions of sixty or seventy witches at Bury St. Edmunds in 1645 [see Matthew Hopkins].

> "In conclusion, the judge and all the court were fully satisfied with the verdict."—*A Trial of Witches* (1682).

least no more fits were reported. Soon afterward, Darling was examined by Samuel Harsnett, to whom he admitted he had counterfeited. Darrell, however, rejoindered that the confession had been extorted from his patient only after seven weeks imprisonment and threats to "throttle him and . . . whip him," and that Darling had signed a blank page which was afterward filled in by Harsnett. Darrell's belief that Alice Gooderidge caused Darling's fits, however, no matter how the retraction was obtained, makes all his evidence tainted.

Alice Gooderidge died in prison at Derby, while serving her sentence of twelve months. The disposition of her mother, Elizabeth Wright, is not known. Thomas Darling achieved a second bout of notoriety when, in 1603 at Oxford University, he was sentenced to be whipped and lose his ears for libeling the Vice-Chancellor.

Bury St. Edmunds Witches. "A most lamentable exhibition of credulity and inhumanity." Such was the opinion of Lord Campbell, in his *Lives of the Chief Justices* (1849), of the famous witch trial heard in 1662 before Sir Matthew Hale, later Chief Justice. Not only was it one of the most thoroughly documented trials (the descriptive pamphlet consists of sixty pages), but

The initial situation, the accusers and the defendants, the type of evidence, the attitude of the judges, and the verdict are all very similar to the events at Salem thirty years later; they recall, too, the whole case of the Warboys Witches seventy years earlier. The indictment charged that Rose Cullender and Amy Duny, two old widows of Lowestoft, Suffolk, had bewitched seven children ranging in age from a few months to eighteen years, one of the children dying supposedly as a result, and in addition had, over a period of several years, practiced various acts of sorcery or *maleficia*. After Judge Hale's direction to the jurymen, the two defendants were found guilty within half an hour on thirteen indictments. They maintained their innocence, but four days later were hanged. "The judge and all the court were fully satisfied with the verdict."

The following illustrations (taken from the original pamphlet of 1682) show the kinds of evidence admitted by the court.

1. Unsupported assumptions of cause and effect, especially in regard to *maleficia*.

Mrs. Dorothy Durent hired Amy Duny as a baby sitter. Amy, against instructions, tried to nurse the infant. When reprimanded, Amy muttered "that [Mrs. Durent] had as good to have done otherwise than to have found fault with her." When the baby had fits soon after this incident,

Mrs. Durent took it to a "white witch," a Dr. Jacob, who prescribed wrapping the child in a blanket previously hung in a chimney, and burning anything that should happen to fall out of the blanket. A toad was found and burned with "a flashing in the fire like gunpowder." Amy reputedly was seen with her face, legs, and thighs scorched. Although Amy again threatened the Durents, the child recovered. [Francis Hutchinson in 1720 noted that by burning the toad and scorching Amy, Mrs. Durent was herself a witch.]

> "It was a trial much considered by the judges of New England."—Cotton Mather (1693).

While nine-year-old Deborah Pacy, suffering lameness, was sitting in the sun, Amy Duny came to the house to buy herrings. Having the reputation of being a witch, she was sent packing. After the third refusal, "she went away grumbling, but what she said was not perfectly understood. But at the very instant of time, the said child was taken with most violent fits, feeling most extreme pain in her stomach." The child accused Amy of causing her trouble.

Besides the charges of bewitching the children, a number of neighbors testified to certain supposed acts of *maleficia*, dating back several years. Three such statements may be noted here. The first (a) relates typical annoyances with a rickety farm cart on a hot summer day. The second (b) is a side light on seventeenth-century personal cleanliness. The third (c) is an anecdote to delight any tenant who ever complained to the landlord that the refrigerator needed fixing, only to be told that it worked perfectly and was a new machine!

a) One John Soam of Lowestoft, aforesaid, yeoman, a sufficient person, deposeth that not long since, in harvest time, he had three carts, which brought home his harvest. And as they were going into the field to load, one of the carts wrenched the window of Rose Cullender's house, whereupon she came out in great rage and threatened this deponent for doing that wrong. And so they passed along into the fields and loaded all the three carts. The other two carts returned safe home and back again, twice loaded that day afterwards. But as to this cart which touched Rose Cullender's house, after it was loaded, it was overturned twice or thrice that day. And after that they had loaded it again the second or third time, as they brought it through the gate which leadeth out of the field into the town, the cart stuck so fast in the gate's head, that they could not possibly get it through, but were enforced to cut down the post of the gate to make the cart pass through, although they could not perceive that the cart did of either side touch the gateposts. [Hutchinson comments: "But if it did not touch the posts, what made them cut the posts down?"] And this deponent further saith, that after they had got it through the gateway, they did with much difficulty get it home into the yard. But for all that they could do, they could not get the cart near unto the place where they should unload the corn, but were fain to unload it at a great distance from the place. And when they began to unload they found much difficulty therein, it being so hard a labor that they were tired that first came; and when others came to assist them, their noses burst forth a-bleeding, so they were fain to desist, and leave it until the next morning. [Hutchinson: "And if a man's nose bleed in the harvest, might not heat and labor cause that without a devil?"] And they unloaded it without any difficulty at all.

b) Robert Sherringham also deposeth against Rose Cullender, that about two years since . . . he was very much vexed with great number of lice of an extraordinary bigness. And although he many times shifted himself [changed clothing], yet he was not anything the better, but would swarm again with them. So that in the conclusion he was forced to burn all his clothes, being two suits of apparel, and then was clear from them.

c) The said Amy [Duny] became tenant to this deponent's husband for a house, who told [the deponent] that if she looked not well to such a chimney in her house that the same would fall.

Whereupon this deponent replied that it was a new one; but not minding much [Amy's] words, at that time they parted. But in a short time the chimney fell down, according as the said Amy had said.

2. Hysterical accusations by children, including throwing of fits.

Eleven-year-old Elizabeth Pacy during the trial "for the most part . . . remained as one wholly senseless as one in a deep sleep, and could move no part of her body—her stomach and belly by the drawing of her breath would arise to a great height." When Amy Duny was forced to touch the child, Elizabeth leaped up, scratching Amy's face "till blood came."

Both the Pacy girls suffered hysteria. The pamphlet gives a full account:

> Their fits were various. Sometimes they would be lame on one side of their bodies, sometimes on the other. Sometimes a soreness over their whole bodies, so as they could endure none to touch them. At other times they would be restored to the perfect use of their limbs and deprived of their hearing. At other times of their sight; at other times of their speech, sometimes by the space of one day, sometimes for two, and once they were wholly deprived of their speech for eight days together and then restored to their speech again. At other times they would fall into swoonings, and upon the recovery to their speech they would cough extremely and bring up much phlegm, and with the same crooked pins, and one time a two-penny nail with a very broad head. Which pins, amounting to forty or more, together with the two-penny nail, were produced in court, with the affirmation of the said deponent that he was present when the said nail was vomited up, and also most of the pins. Commonly at the end of every fit they would cast up a pin, and sometimes they would have four or five fits in one day.

Another young demoniac, Mercy Short, had similar experiences, swallowing pins and distending her abdomen. Like Margaret Rule, Jane Bocking, another of the Bury St. Edmunds children, would eat no food

for several weeks. Both Mercy and Margaret were assisted by Cotton Mather, who was fully conversant with this trial, and abstracted its main features a little later in his *Wonders of the Invisible World* (1693). The Salem children stumbled or balked at holy names, another lesson apparently learned from these Bury depositions:

> In this manner the said children continued with this deponent for the space of two months, during which time in their intervals this deponent would cause them to read some chapters in the New Testament. Whereupon this deponent several times observed that they would read till they came to the name of Lord, or Jesus, or Christ, and then before they could pronounce either of the said words they would suddenly fall into their fits. But when they came to the name of Satan, or Devil, they would clap their fingers upon the Book, crying out, "This bites, but makes me speak right well."

3. Employment of interested parties as court-appointed professional witnesses.

Mrs. Mary Chandler was the mother of eighteen-year-old Susan, who was one of the complainants. Yet Mrs. Chandler was appointed to search Amy Duny for witch's marks, and to give evidence of what she found:

> They began at her head, and so stripped her naked, and in the lower part of her belly they found a thing like a teat of an inch long. They questioned her about it, and she said that she had got a strain by carrying of water which caused that excrescence. But upon narrower search, they found in her privy parts three more excrescences or teats, but smaller than the former. This deponent further saith that in the long teat at the end thereof there was a little hole, and it appeared unto them as if it had been lately sucked, and upon the straining of it there issued out some white milky matter.

4. Spectral evidence by single witnesses.

Elizabeth and Deborah both maintained they saw apparitions of Amy Duny and Rose Cullender which frightened them.

In their fits they would cry out, "There stands Amy Duny or Rose Cullender"; and sometimes in one place and sometimes in another, running with great violence to the place where they fancied them to stand, striking at them as if they were present. They would appear to them sometimes spinning and sometimes resting or in other postures, deriding or threatening them.

After Rose Cullender had also been refused herrings at the Durents', fisherfolk like the Pacys, the daughter Ann said "she had seen the apparition of the said Rose who threatened to torment her."

Two other features of this trial are worthy of comment.

Sir Thomas Browne, a physician and the well-known author of the *Religio Medici* (1642), gave expert evidence. While he cautiously refused to state clearly that he believed the children were bewitched, nevertheless any jury would certainly get that impression.

> And his opinion was that the devil in such cases did work upon the bodies of men and women upon a natural foundation, that is, to stir up and excite such humors super-abounding in their bodies to a great excess; whereby he did in an extraordinary manner afflict them with such distempers as their bodies were not subject to, as particularly appeared in these children. For he conceived that these swooning fits were natural, and nothing else but that they call the "mother," but only heightened to a great excess by the subtlety of the devil, co-operating with the malice of these which we term witches, at whose instance he doth these villainies.

The most revolting aspect of this trial to the twentieth-century reader is the court's ignoring proof of fraud by a witness, and its continued acceptance of bogus spectral evidence. Some of the judges suspected the children might be counterfeiting when they screamed at the touch of the supposed witch. Consequently they made a test:

> Wherefore to avoid this scruple it was privately desired by the Judge that the Lord Cornwallis, Sir Edmund Bacon,

and Mr. Sergeant Keeling, and some other gentlemen there in court, would attend one of the distempered persons in the further part of the hall, whilst she was in her fits, and then to send for one of the witches to try what would then happen. Which they did accordingly. And Amy Duny was conveyed from the bar and brought to the maid. They put an apron before her eyes, and then one other person touched her hand, which produced the same effect as the touch of the witch did in the court. Whereupon the gentlemen returned, openly protesting, that they did believe the whole transaction of this business was a mere imposture.

The presiding judge, Sir Matthew Hale, however, was a convinced believer in witchcraft, and he gladly accepted the "explanation" of the girl's father "that possibly the maid might be deceived by a suspicion that the witch touched her when she did not." Another Chief Justice, Sir John Holt, at a later witch trial in 1694 at Bury St. Edmunds, took a different position and made history by forcing the acquittal of Mother Munnings on charges of prognostications causing death. Had Sir Matthew behaved like his successor, the verdict might have been different and Salem averted.

Buvée, Barbara: See Auxonne Nuns.

Cadière, Catherine. The legal battle between Father Jean-Baptiste Girard, S.J., and young Catherine Cadière before the Parlement of Aix-en-Provence in 1731 intrigued the whole of western Europe, and book after book poured forth supporting one side or the other. The notoriety came from such unsavory scandals as a priest's practicing sexual aberrations with a young girl, who herself employed crude deceptions (such as smearing herself with menstrual blood) to pass herself off as a saint. At the time, the importance of this trial in the history of witchcraft seemed subordinate to a titillating charge of seduction; Father Girard's lawyer, indeed, answered the charge of witchcraft only because it had allegedly resulted in fornication. "Otherwise, we frankly own that we should have thought our time lost in refuting such a charge as that of sorcery." In effect, however, the case of Girard and La Cadière marked the end of formal trials for witchcraft in France.

The two protagonists recall figures in earlier famous French trials, where epileptic nuns accused their confessors of satanic immorality: Sister Madeleine Demandolx de la Palud against Father Louis Gaufridi in 1611 (also at Aix-en-Provence), Sister Jeanne des Anges against Father Urbain Grandier in 1634 at Loudun, and Sister Madeleine Bavent against Father Thomas Boullé in 1647 at Louviers. No fantastic allegations of black masses were made in this present case, however, possibly because of the famous Edict of Louis XIV in 1682. Father Girard's alleged crime was fundamentally bewitching (or hypnotizing) a girl for immoral purposes, although the indictment charged sorcery, quietism [a dangerous heresy], spiritual incest, procurement of abortion, and subornation by perjury. Either Father Girard was guilty of immorality or Catherine Cadière was guilty of perjury. This basic issue was obscured by Catherine's obsessive religiosity and her brother's scheming publicity about her saintliness, as well as by the hostility whipped up by the monks and friars against the Jesuits. Whether or not Father Girard ever molested Catherine, at any rate he had plenty of opportunities; he sent her love letters, and admitted to certain actions which (if he were not completely without guile) were open to the ugliest interpretation.

Marie-Catherine Cadière, born at Toulon in 1709, was brought up by her widowed mother in a deeply religious household: of her three brothers, the second, Etienne Thomas Cadière, became a Jacobin (Dominican) friar, and the youngest a parish priest. While still a teen-ager, Catherine showed "extraordinary gifts of prayer" and was wont to swoon in church. At eighteen, a ravishingly beautiful young lady, she joined a loosely organized group of women who, though living in their own homes, were dedicated to prayer and medi-

tation. The spiritual director of these devotees of the Third Order of St. Theresa was a well-known and highly respected Jesuit, Father Girard, formerly a schoolteacher and, since 1728, rector of the Royal Seminary of Chaplains of the Navy at Toulon.

Catherine was ambitious to become a saint, and sought a privileged position as Father Girard's special *protégée;* she told him God had recommended him in a vision. She clearly had a young girl's infatuation for an older man of fifty. (This very attraction was proof enough of sorcery!) His presence, whether actual or imagined, gave her great emotional satisfaction; she testified "feeling something like a finger moving about my entrails and making me feel quite wet; and this happened every time Father Girard came to the house."

After a year or more of encouraging her spiritual quest, Father Girard decided that her signs of holiness were of dubious validity. When she became despondent at her confessor's rejection of her aspirations, on his advice, in the spring of 1730, she made a retreat to the convent of Ste-Claire-d'Ollioules. Here she acted as if possessed, manifesting nervous prostration, convulsions, epileptic hysteria, hallucinations, and traces of insanity. The Bishop of Toulon sent her home to her mother, and in September assigned her a new confessor, 38-year-old Father Nicholas of St. Joseph, Prior of the Barefooted Carmelites at Toulon. Father Nicholas attempted exorcism, and Catherine saw her campaign to become a saint failing. Instigated by her brother, she revealed her bewitchment by Father Girard and her consequent seduction: her "miracles" were no longer holy but the work of the Devil. Father Etienne Cadière also persuaded two of Father Girard's devotees, a 65-year-old woman and 23-year-old La Baratille (with a weak head and a strong imagination) to join Catherine in charging seduction by the Jesuit. The Cadière lawyers eventually produced four other devotees and four nuns who swore Father Girard had been intimate with them.

Father Girard appealed these calumnies to his Bishop, while the friends of La Cadière went to the police lieutenant at Toulon. The Bishop said he lacked jurisdiction, and the matter came to the civil courts. By now, the scandal was wide open, and therefore, by order of the King, the Parlement of Aix on January 10, 1731, undertook to hear the dispute. The excitement generated by the trial can only be compared to the *affaire Dreyfus* two centuries later.

Just before the trial, to gain public support for the accusations of bewitchment, Catherine and her brother attracted huge crowds by midnight exorcisms. Catherine appeared "senseless and motionless, with her neck swollen and the swelling rising toward her mouth." Etienne exorcized his sister, "standing naked to his shirt, with a violet stole about his neck, in one hand holy water, and in the other a *rituale* [service book], which Father Nicholas had taken care to bring with him." Other priests, who arrived soon after, denied any possession, and Catherine took care to recover before a physician might examine her. The following night, until four in the morning, La Cadière "rolled about the room, and screamed out, so as to be heard in the middle of the street." Catherine alleged the Jesuits tried to prevent her getting a lawyer, and that while waiting trial in a convent (like Madeleine Bavent) she was mistreated.

Father Girard had faced a difficult situation with Catherine Cadière. In her determination to become a saint, she studied the lives of such famous mystics as St. Theresa and St. Catherine of Siena, and modeled her actions on them. In June, 1729, she claimed "intimate communion with God." In November, God told her she should suffer in place of a soul in mortal sin; she went into convulsions and contortions, with loss of speech, until in February, 1730, realizing Father Girard was still unimpressed, she miraculously found deliverance through the prayers of a recently deceased nun! Meanwhile, her brother Etienne was keeping an exact journal of his sister's trances, stigmata, and visions (which included a bleeding heart and naked men and women), presumably with a view to her hoped-for beatification.

During her abnormal manifestations, Father Girard naturally spent much time with her. He received special dispensation from the Abbess to write to Catherine without censorship and to visit her privately. From this point it is difficult to separate fact from fantasy, as nearly all the evidence on both sides is streaked with perjury, the allegations becoming wilder and wilder to score a needed point. At times, the charges seem copied from the heresies revealed at Louviers in 1647. It is quite possible, of course, that, although both protagonists were clearly neurotic, under all the accusations there was some element of truth.

Justification de demoiselle Catherine Cadière (1731), from which some of the following passages are translated, was written "to teach persons of my sex that they must be on guard against the appearance of piety." Realizing that she would be compromised by her apparent acquiescence in Father Girard's lubricities, Catherine stressed how he had bewitched her. The English *Case of Mistress Mary Catherine Cadiere* (1732) explained how:

> Then stooping down and putting his mouth close to hers, he breathed upon her, which had such a powerful effect upon the young lady's mind that she was immediately transported with love and consented to give herself up to him. Thus did he bewitch the mind and inclinations of his unhappy penitent.

This infatuation laid the basis for the charge of sorcery, as well as saving "the young woman's honor." Catherine was thus in a position to make a sobbing appeal to the court: "You see here before you a young girl of twenty years, plunged into an abyss of evils, but whose heart is still unsullied."

Catherine described step by step how Father Girard had seduced her, claiming everything he did was by God's will. A witness testified she had seen the priest embracing and kissing Catherine, and placing her hands under his cassock. "My dear child," he was reported saying, "I want to lead you to perfection; don't be disturbed by what happens to your body; banish your scruples, your fears and doubtings. By this

"He breathed on me in a way that had something very peculiar about it." From *Recueil de pièces* (1731).

means, your soul will become stronger, purer, more illuminated. It will acquire a holy freedom."

"One day, I remember among others," wrote Catherine, "as I was coming out of a severe fainting spell, I found myself stretched out on the floor with Father Girard behind me, running his hands over my breasts, which he had uncovered." When Catherine asked him what he was doing, Father Girard told her it was the will of God she experience humiliation in order to proceed to perfection. "He told me that one day God would wish him to put his belly to hers."

On another occasion, Catherine Cadière claimed:

Father Girard found me in bed, and having locked the door he lay down beside me. Drawing me to the edge of the bed, he put one hand under my buttocks, and the other in front; then he undressed me and without any warning kissed me. Often he made me expose myself, while his hands explored every nook of my body. As I was subject to fainting spells, I could not answer for what he did when

I was in that state. I can only recall that when I came to, I found myself in such a condition that I knew only too well that Father Girard had not been content just to look at me.

Almost every day he visited her, sometimes making love to her for two or three hours.

With a surprising understanding of the psychology of a man of fifty, Catherine graphically described how Father Girard was stimulated by erotic sadistic flagellation:

"Sometimes he would give me strokes with a cane, and then immediately afterwards kiss the places where he had beaten me. One day, coming to see me to punish me for refusing God's grace, having locked the door, he ordered me to kneel before him. He held in his hand a cane and told me I deserved the whole world should see what he was going to do to me, but nevertheless he made me swear faithfully and promise him never to speak about it. I promised him, not knowing what he was going to do. Evidently reassured by my promise, he told me that it was the will of God, that divine justice, seeing I had

"My daughter, I want to lead you to the highest stage of perfection. Do not be distressed about what may happen to your body."

refused to accept God's grace, demanded I should take off my clothes and stand naked before him. At these words I was revolted, my mind went blank, and I fell senseless [*en défaillance*] to the floor. He lifted me up. To my surprise I found myself so dazed that thereafter I obeyed him without question and allowed him to do whatever he wished. He ordered me first of all to remove my veil, then my coif, my belt, and finally my dress; to put it bluntly, he left me nude except for a chemise. In this undressed condition, I felt him kiss my buttocks. I am not sure what he did next, but I felt a kind of sadness which I had not known before. After this, he helped me to get dressed. More than once, he made me lie on the bed, and in this position he whipped me and then kissed me without the least inhibition or decorum, always telling me that this was the new way to reach the highest stages of perfection."

Another day, the said Father Girard made her take off even the chemise and place it on the bed, telling her she must be punished for the sin she had committed of not freeing herself [of scruples], at which she felt moist [*mouillé*] and ticklish [*chatouillé*] in her private parts. Again, he gave her a whipping on both her buttocks [*fesses*] and then kissed them; and it was then that he gently scratched her until she was all moist.

"Sometimes he gave me blows with a whip, and then he kissed the spot where he had beaten me."

Elsewhere, Catherine described the position she took for this ritual: Father Girard "ordered her to climb on the bed and put a hassock under her elbows in order to raise her up." The English *Case of Mistress Mary Catherine Cadiere* coyly added: "It is not proper to express what followed, but 'tis easily imagined." When the Abbess forbade his prolonged visits, Father Girard discovered a window from which he could pry off the grille; through this aperture he was able to kiss Catherine and from time to time practice flagellation.

Father Girard did not take these charges lightly. Some of them he answered directly. He agreed he had locked the door for as long as three hours on his visits to Catherine, because he wished to conceal her angelic possession. When Father Etienne

Cadière started to publicize her "miracles," Father Girard persuaded Catherine to go to a convent lest her sanctity be prematurely divulged. Since he was deaf, he had to bend his head to listen to her—he was not kissing her. When she was thirsty, he brought her a bowl of water, which she had charged was a potion to secure an abortion. His letters were to be construed only in terms of heavenly love: "Do not have any will of your own, and do not feel the least repugnance. Do everything I tell you, like a good [little] girl who finds nothing difficult where her father asks for it."

Only later did Father Girard suspect Catherine was an impostor. To this end he unearthed some devastating counterevidence. She had suborned three maids, promising one of them a pension for giving favorable evidence. [This evidence was curious: the girl found Father Girard and Catherine *in flagrante delicto*, but had merely inquired what color vestments Father Girard needed for the next service.] On May 7, 1730, Catherine fabricated a "transfiguration" or death trance in honor of Christ's passion, her face all bloody. This "miracle" occurred again on June 6 and July 7, whereupon Father Girard concluded that Catherine had smeared her visage with her own menstrual flow. Her lawyer argued she had another "transfiguration" on July 20, and no woman had two "incommodities" a month. Her regularity also disproved Catherine's charge that Father Girard had aborted her. For further proof he produced her diary, which marked regular periods on March 8, April 4, May 8, June 11, July 4, August 8, and September 9. "Consequently there were no suppressions, no suspicions of pregnancy within the time [midsummer] limited by La Cadière to make her charge of procuring abortion so much as probable."

Catherine claimed to fast for several days on end, but at night she stole into the convent garden to gorge on peaches. One night she found herself trapped there by angry nuns; she wriggled out of this net by saying God had caused her gluttony to humble her, and, by pruning selected fruit, make the tree bear better peaches! Father Girard sprang another surprise by producing the original "Holy Cross" sent her from heaven, which Catherine had surprisingly duplicated. His lawyer found Catherine "a cunning, artful, girl." In addition, Girard's lawyer attempted to discredit the opposition, and produced a prostitute to accuse Prior Nicholas of immorality.

The trial concluded in a welter of accusations. Catherine apparently had some running sores on her body which she claimed as stigmata. As a special mark of devotion, Father Girard was accustomed to remove her veil and suck the sore or ulcer on her throat. This he did every day for three months. He also admitted kissing the ulcer or stigma near her left breast (incidentally, Madeleine de Demandolx and Madeleine Bavent both had stigmata or ulcers there). Catherine in her account added that "this one he kissed with much sensuality." The Cadière lawyer seized on this admission to ridicule Father Girard. "Here is an angel of purity, indeed," he told the court, "who teaches us the art of gazing on the naked body of a girl or woman whom he loves passionately, and

even flagellating her, without any trace of erotic emotion and without peril to his soul. What a prodigy of chastity!" Father Girard's lawyer retorted: "Can anyone really believe that such objects [as ulcers] should be meet fuel for a lewd flame?"

The Parlement at Aix had taken evidence for nearly a year. It returned its verdict on October 11, 1731. The judges were divided, twelve holding Father Girard should be burned, and twelve condemning La Cadière to hanging. The deciding vote was cast by President Lebret, who returned Father Girard to the ecclesiastical authorities for his irregular conduct as a priest, and sent Catherine back to her mother. By this dismissal he indicated the charges of sorcery were not proved. President Lebret's decision was unpopular with the mob, which manhandled Father Girard, but raised Catherine's lawyer on their shoulders in triumph. Catherine lived quietly at her home; and Father Girard, cleared by the Church, retired to his native Dôle, where he died in 1733.

Canon Episcopi. Until the thirteenth century, the official and accepted position of the Church theoreticians was that the acts of witches were all illusions or fantasies originating in dreams, and that consequently belief in the actuality of witchcraft was pagan and therefore heretical. This position is the precise opposite of the later views of the inquisitors when sorcery had been equated with heresy—that witchcraft, night flights, intercourse with demons, transformation into animals, really occurred and that therefore *disbelief* in witchcraft was heretical [see Innocent VIII].

One of the earliest and most continuously quoted documents presenting the earlier view is the Canon or Capitulum Episcopi, erroneously attributed to the Council of Ancyra (A.D. 314) by Regino of Prüm, Abbot of Treves, who was the first (about 906) to present the text. Whatever the origin of this canon, it was nevertheless for many centuries accepted as the highest authority. It was incorporated in the *Corpus Juris Canonici* by Gratian of Bologna in the twelfth century, and thus became part of the Canon Law.

After the sixteenth century, transvection was an accepted belief of the witch mania; in the tenth century, the Canon Episcopi had classified belief in night flight as heresy. By Bonaventura von Genelli, *Das Leben einer Hexe* (1847).

Since it flatly contradicted the whole theory of witchcraft as established by both clerical and secular demonologists, it had to be continually undermined and whittled away and even expressly denied (e.g., by Thomas Aquinas).

One method was to say that even if the witch had only dreamed about her magical activities, nevertheless her recollection of the dream made her as guilty as if what had transpired in the dream had been a reality (e.g., Pedro Cirvelo). Surprisingly enough, this casuistry passed into Protestant thinking, and the materialist philosopher Thomas Hobbes, in his *Leviathan* (1651), found himself keeping company with the *Malleus Maleficarum:* "As for witches, I think not that their witchcraft is a real power; but yet that they are justly punished for the false belief they have that they can do such mischief, joined with their purpose to do it if they can."

Another means of altering the dogma was to argue that the statements of the Canon Episcopi applied only to the times when it was written, and that since then a *new* sect of witches had arisen which could do all the impossibilities the demonologists imputed to them. The inquisitor who was among the first to get rid of the Canon was Nicholas Jacquier in 1458, who maintained that the man who believed in corporeal transvection had the true and catholic faith. Yet as late as 1613, however, De Lancre had to pay lip service to the Canon, which had been retained by Pope Gregory XIII (1572-85) in the *Decretum.* He used the

escape hatch constructed by Del Rio, which admitted that some witches have only the illusion of going to the sabbat. These, he said, may be reconciled to the Church, but —and here he nullified his proviso—they may also be tortured to produce a confession.

The broad influence of the Canon Episcopi and how it filtered down to the typical layman is illustrated by its presence in Chaucer's *Canterbury Tales*, where the parson distinguishes between *maleficium* (black magic or witchcraft) and white magic (the semi-Christianized pagan charms; for example, the Night Spell).

What say we of them that believe in divinations, as by flight or by noise of birds, or of beasts, or by sort [lot], by geomancy [divination by figures and lines], by dreams, by chirking [creaking] of doors, or cracking of houses, by gnawing of rats, and such manner wretchedness? Certes, all this is defended [forbidden] by God and by all Holy Church. For which they be accursed, till they come to amendment, that on such filth set their belief. Charms for wounds or malady of men, or of beasts, if they have any effect, it may be peradventure that God suffereth it, for folk should give the more faith and reverence to his name. (*Parson's Tale*)

The Canon Episcopi

Bishops and their officials must labor with all their strength to uproot thoroughly from their parishes the pernicious art of sorcery and malefice invented by

The Canon Episcopi insisted that transvection was a superstitious delusion. Goya's satirical drawing of two witches on a broomstick has this caption: "The broom is perhaps the most essential tool for a witch. For besides being useful for sweeping, it can, according to many a story, be changed into a mule that runs so fast that even the Devil can't catch up with it."— Goya (1799).

the devil, and if they find a man or woman follower of this wickedness to eject them foully disgraced from their parishes. For the Apostle says, "A man that is a heretic after the first and second admonition avoid." Those are held captive by the devil who, leaving their creator, seek the aid of the devil. And so Holy Church must be cleansed of this pest.

It is also not to be omitted that certain abandoned women perverted by Satan, seduced by illusions and phantasms of demons, believe and openly profess that, in the dead of night, they ride upon certain beasts with the pagan goddess Diana, with a countless horde of women, and in the silence of the dead of night fly over vast tracts of country, and obey her

commands as their mistress, while they are summoned to her service on other nights.

But it were well if they alone perished in their infidelity and did not draw so many others along with them into the pit of their faithlessness. For an innumerable multitude, deceived by this false opinion, believe this to be true and, so believing, wander from the right faith and relapse into pagan errors when they think that there is any divinity or power except the one God.

Wherefore the priests throughout their churches should preach with all insistence to the people that they may know this to be in every way false, and that such phantasms are sent by the devil who deludes them in dreams. Thus Satan himself, who transfigures himself into an angel of light, when he has captured the mind of a miserable woman and has subjected her to himself by infidelity and incredulity, immediately changes himself into the likeness of different personages and deluding the mind which he holds captive and exhibiting things (joyful or sorrowful) and persons (known and unknown), leads her faithless mind through devious ways. And while the spirit alone endures this, she thinks these things happen not in the spirit but in the body.

Who is there that is not led out of himself in dreams and nocturnal visions, and sees much when sleeping which he had never seen waking?

Who is so stupid and foolish as to think that all these things which are done only in spirit happen in the body, when the prophet Ezekiel saw visions of God in spirit and not in body, and the apostle John saw and heard the mysteries of the Apocalypse in the spirit and not in the body, as he himself says, "I was rapt in spirit." And Paul does not dare to say that he was rapt in his body.

It is therefore to be publicly proclaimed to all, that whoever believes such things or similar things loses the faith, and he who has not the right faith in God is not of God, but of him in whom he believes, that is, the devil. For of our Lord it is written, "All things were made by him." Whoever therefore believes that anything can be made, or that any creature can be changed to better or worse or be transformed into another species or likeness, except by God himself who made everything and through whom all things were made, is beyond doubt an infidel.

Carolina Code. The criminal code for the states comprising the Holy Roman Empire was introduced in the Regensburg Reichstag in 1532 during the reign of Charles V. Under these laws, derived from the famous *Bambergische Halsgerichtsordnung* (1508), most of the prosecutions for witchcraft were conducted. At the end of the sixteenth century, however, witch judges often ignored the Code's provisions and tried the accused according to their own whim; thus, at Bamberg, for example, accused witches or their relatives appealed to the Emperor to enforce the Carolina Code, as it was called, as protection against such extra-legal procedures.

The following paragraphs governed the trials against witches.

21. Concerning proof of those who presume to tell fortunes by sorcery. Likewise, on mere indictment, no one of those who presume to tell fortunes by sorcery or other magic arts is to be imprisoned or put to torture. However, those who themselves claim to be fortunetellers, being so accused, are to be punished for this. Should the accused fortuneteller be found guilty under oath of causing financial loss, afflictions, injuries or harm to his victim, the judge may proceed further in the case against him, as is set forth in a following separate paragraph.

44. Concerning sufficient proof of witchcraft. If anyone teaches others witchcraft; or if he misleads people into bewitching and in addition brings those he has deceived to effect bewitchment; also if he has associated with witches, either male or female; or with such suspected things, actions, words and ways as imply witchcraft; and, moreover, if he is defamed by these same witches; these indications give just proof of witchcraft and sufficient grounds for torture.

52. How the person is to be questioned into admitting witchcraft. If someone admits to witchcraft, she should be questioned under oath about its origin and the details; furthermore, with whom, how and when she practiced witchcraft, and with what words or actions. Then, if it appears that the interrogated person has buried or withheld something, which might be connected with such witchcraft, the same should be sought out, if it can be found. But if these acts of witchcraft were done through words or deeds, she must be examined, to see if it means a charge of witchcraft. She must also be questioned from whom she learned witchcraft, and how she came into it, whether she also used this witchcraft against other persons, specifically whom, and what injuries occurred as a result.

109. Penalty for witchcraft. If someone did injury or damage to people through witchcraft, she must be punished from

life to death, and this punishment must be done by burning. But where someone uses witchcraft without causing injury, she should be punished in another way, according to the magnitude of the crime; here the advice of the council should be followed, according to the permission provided hereafter.

116. Penalty for the lewd, who work contrary to nature. If a man has lascivious relations with a beast, or a man with a man, or a woman with a woman, they shall lose their life, and following general custom they should be sentenced to death by burning.

Carpzov, Benedict. Benedict Carpzov (1595-1666) was reputed to have signed the death warrants of 20,000 persons. Philipp Andreas Oldenburger, who started this legend in 1675, may have exaggerated, but his estimate, made when the memory of the man was still fresh, could not have been improbable; furthermore, Oldenburger quoted the figure in admiration. Whether it is accurate or not, Carpzov exercised more influence over German witchcraft than any other person. Called "the lawgiver of Saxony," he was the son of a celebrated law professor at Wittenberg, and was himself professor at Leipzig; he sat on the Collegium Scabinorum Lipsienium, the Leipzig Supreme Court, deciding thousands of difficult cases sent there for review. Local judges were generally so uneducated that in many parts of Germany they had to submit trial records to the law faculty of some neighboring university; but often this obligation was either not in force or disregarded. Carpzov, however, upheld the custom, and thus influenced verdicts throughout all Saxony, and, by publishing his opinions, indirectly in Protestant courts in other German states.

His *Practica Rerum Criminalum* [*Concerning Criminal Law*], first published in 1635, and reprinted nine times by 1723, was the *Malleus Maleficarum* of Protestantism. But little about it was Protestant, for Carpzov's sources were the famous Catholic demonologists, the *Malleus* itself, Grillandus, Remy, Binsfeld, Del Rio, and especially Bodin. What gave Carpzov greater

scope than these earlier authorities was his own reputation within Saxony. Binsfeld's activity was confined largely to Treves; Bodin was a witch judge for only a brief time. Carpzov controlled the laws of his state for many years.

Carpzov introduced nothing original into the theory either of witchcraft or of law; he was not a great intellect. He merely interpreted the merciless laws introduced into Saxony by the Elector Augustus in 1579 (as a substitute for the imperial Carolina Code), dressing them up in legal finery, quoting references, and, in the name of Lutheranism, expounding his views from the eminence of his professorship. A devout man, going to church every Sunday and to holy communion every month, and claiming to have read the Bible fifty-three times, he was nevertheless a ruthless bigot. Malblanc, the eighteenth-century historian, thought "his blind and at times stupid religious zeal befogged his intelligence." During the cruel period of the Thirty Years' War, his dogmatic rulings against the witches who supposedly caused the disasters swept away any voices of reason. He was especially opposed to Johan Weyer, holding that for such crimes the inquisitorial was the only proper procedure, and that since witchcraft was so secret and heinous, local judges should not be restricted by legal technicalities in obtaining evidence. Time and time again, he returned to the dictum that the local judge had wide discretionary powers in "exceptional" crimes.

No doubt Carpzov considered himself a reformer. He opposed keeping prisoners in an underground dungeon, where they might be killed by snakes. A prisoner should have three days' notification of his execution, during which time he should have good food and wine. Ignorant novices should not sit as judges in local courts.

However, when it came down to basic principles, Carpzov was no whit different from the demonologists. There was no "statute of limitations" for witchcraft. In witchcraft, intention was sufficient proof. Witches flew to the Blocksberg. The sabbat was real and not an illusion. Witches had sexual relations with devils two or three times a week, and sometimes gave birth to elves. Sorcery and witchcraft were the same, because both depended on the Devil. Carpzov recommended torture, justifying it from the Bible, and specified seventeen different methods, including slowly burning the body with candles, and driving wooden wedges under the nails and then setting fire to them. If the prisoner retracted his confession, he should be tortured again. Burial should not be permitted, for the decaying corpse of a witch was a deterrent to others.

Sometimes Carpzov argued with subtlety: Denunciation by an accomplice was by itself no basis for arrest; however, the accused should be examined, and if his statement disagreed with the denunciation, he then gave grounds for suspicion, therefore arrest, and therefore torture. Again, wrote Carpzov, the accused should not be allowed to question witnesses, because he might confuse them and thus escape the punishment he deserved.

At the end of the *Practica*, Carpzov printed thirty-six decisions of the Leipzig Supreme Court, from 1558 to 1622, which were constantly quoted in later trials, and Carpzov became an oracle.

The continuing influence of Carpzov is seen almost a century after the appearance of the *Practica*, when one of his opinions was quoted to send a poor woman, Anna Maria Rosenthal, to her death in Winterberg (Westphalia) in 1728. The Attorney General referred to the "celebrated criminalist" Carpzov for proofs of witchcraft— Carpzov had let the judge decide in each individual case—and the review board at Arnsberg gave Carpzov and Del Rio precedence over the contradictory Carolina Code which made specific indications. At the end of the seventeenth century, Carpzov was answered by another lawyer, also a Protestant, Christian Thomasius.

Cassini, Samuel de. Cassini, a Franciscan friar, born in Turin, educated in Paris, and resident of Milan, was one of the handful of early theologians to oppose witchcraft. The idea of witchcraft developed slowly during the fifteenth century; when the demonology developed by the desert saints

A page from the *Question de le Strie* (1505), by Franciscan Friar Samuel de Cassini, one of the very few works before 1550 to refute the idea of witchcraft. Only two copies are extant, one in Milan and the other in Cornell University Library.

of Egypt was added to the age-old tradition of magic (both black and white), a new heresy was born. After the publication of the *Malleus Maleficarum*, in 1486, only three major writers opposed it: Symphorien Champier (about 1500), Samuel de Cassini (about 1505), and Gianfrancesco Ponzinibio (about 1520).

Basically, Cassini hewed to the Canon Episcopi, which condemned *belief* in the night flight of witches as heresy. For centuries, inquisitors had to continue to deny or explain away this established belief. Not for very many years to come were such outspoken attacks on the witch delusion made. Cassini accused the inquisitors themselves of heresy, for they were flouting church tradition; instead of countenancing false accusations, they should restore the property and good name of those accused.

Cat: see Familiars.

Chambre Ardente Affair. Fantastic is the only word to describe the black masses, with Catholic priests gashing newborn babies over the breasts of naked girls stretched out over the altars, described by the witnesses before the *Chambre ardente*, the star chamber set up by Louis XIV to investigate widespread poisoning among the French nobility. This investigation, extending from January, 1679 to July, 1682, is probably the only witch trial based on some element of factual truth, rather than on the wild imaginings of young neurotics or the morbid logic of perverse witch judges and inquisitors. An eager police commissioner, personally responsible to the King himself, said of the evidence: "I have gone over and over everything that might persuade me the accusations were false, but such a conclusion is just not possible." Yet the charges, involving the greatest lords and ladies of France, depended largely on evidence secured under torture, from women with their legs eight times smashed in the boots.

The investigation grew out of poisonings. As early as 1673 two prominent priests at Notre-Dame-de-Paris told the police, without revealing any names, that most of their penitents confessed either attempted or actual murder to straighten out matrimonial triangles. In 1677, the Police Commissioner of Paris, Nicholas de la Reynie, uncovered a well-established international poison ring, with connections in Portugal, Italy, and England. Headed by several noblemen, a lawyer, and a banker, it distributed poisons throughout France. Huge stores of poison were discovered. The aristocratic ringleader, François Galaup de Chasteuil, escaped. (He led one of the most colorful lives of a colorful century—son of the Attorney General of Aix, a doctor of law, a knight of Malta, a freebooter in Algeria, and a Carmelite prior who kept a mistress in his cell.) The rest of the gang were questioned for over a year, but the police got no definite leads, although one suspect, Vanens, later proved the contact man for the small distributors, the fortunetellers, who doubled as bawds and abortionists.

A break in the case came from a chance conversation of Marie Bosse, a *devineresse*: "What a lovely occupation is mine! What classy clients! Nothing lower than duchesses, marquises, princes, and lords. Three more poisonings and I retire, my fortune made!" A woman police agent followed up the clue, posed as desirous of getting rid of her husband, and came away with a bottle of poison. The police moved in and found a cache of poisons in Madame Bosse's establishment.

On January 4, 1679, Police Commissioner Reynie started questioning Widow Bosse, her daughter, and her two sons, along with another fortuneteller, La Dame Vigoreux, who had been the accepted mistress of both previous husbands of La Bosse. It was an odd crew: all five slept together in one bed. To stop the use of poisons, Monsieur Reynie had to get the names of customers. Madame de Poulaillon was the first *femme de qualité* accused; during the following months, some several hundred of the highest courtiers were implicated. The pattern in each instance was the same. Madame de Poulaillon, for example, had a lover; her old husband clutched his money bags. Madame therefore bought *poudres de succession* (or poisons), but her husband grew suspicious and took refuge in a monastery. The typical method of administering the poison was to soak a shirt in arsenic acid, which caused body inflammation resembling syphilis. The woman then brought allegedly healing salves, actually poisonous, which, rubbed into the skin of her sick husband, would bring on his death within a couple of months.

On this kind of evidence, on March 8, 1679, King Louis XIV agreed to create a special *commission de l'Arsenal*, a star chamber court, sitting in secret and permitting no appeal, popularly called *la Chambre ardente* (because the room was draped in black and lit with candles). It seized another fortuneteller, the celebrated Catherine Deshayes, Widow Montvoisin, commonly known as La Voisin. She pleaded her trade was chiromancy and physiognomy, and countered with allegations against La Bosse. In the cross fire, two widows of Paris magistrates were named as buyers of poison from La Voisin; they were also arrested. A third *sage femme*, La Lepère, was imprisoned as an accomplice of La Voisin; her specialty was abortions. She explained that she helped only women whose menstrual periods were delayed, never any women who were pregnant. She would never take money from virgins who thought themselves in trouble, but La Voisin consoled her that if these girls thought themselves tramps [*putains*], she should believe them! Many babies and fetuses, however, were allegedly buried in a garden at Villeneuve-sur-Gravois, a Paris suburb. One witness charged La Voisin with getting rid of 2,500 unwanted babies.

Thinking to get the whole investigation over quickly, on May 6, 1678, the *Chambre ardente* condemned La Vigoreux and La Bosse to be burned alive, and the son, François Bosse, hanged. Madame de Poulaillon was let off with banishment. The court reserved judgment on La Voisin and La Lepère, and the go-between, Vanens.

To this point, witchcraft was not involved. Sorcery, yes—the fortunetellers sold love philtres [*poudres pour l'amour*] and mixed their arsenic, sulphur, and vitriol with dried bats and toads, semen, and menstrual blood. Nor did witchcraft figure in the evidence collected later from other fortunetellers during the summer and fall sessions, and testimony largely concerned the placing of ladies-in-waiting to the King's several mistresses as potential poison "pushers." Among the notables involved was the great dramatist, Jean Racine; a warrant charging him with poisoning his mistress was signed, but it was never served.

After a year's investigation, with more and more of the royal circle implicated in using poisons, on January 23, 1680, the *Chambre* ordered the arrest of the Countess of Soissons, the Marquise d'Alluye, Madame de Polignac (a favorite of the King), Madame de Tingry, the Duchess of Bouillon, the Marquise du Roure, the Duke of Luxembourg (Captain of the King's Guard), and the Marquis de Feuquières. They were imprisoned in the palace at Vincennes or in the Bastille. All French high society was in an uproar, and several of the accused fled the country. Corneille's *La Devineresse*, playing in Paris, took on added significance.

The Duchess of Bouillon appeared in court, escorted by her husband (whom she was accused of trying to poison) and her lover. Her appearance was brief:

Q. Do you know La Vigoreux?
A. No.
Q. Do you know La Voisin?
A. Yes.
Q. Why do you wish to do away with your husband?
A. Me—do away with him! You had better ask my husband what he thinks about that. He escorted me to the door of this courtroom.
Q. But why do you go so often to see La Voisin?
A. I wish to find out what the sybils have in store for me; you have got to know how to tread these days.
Q. Did you dangle a bag of gold before this woman?
A. No—no more than was reasonable. Is that all, gentlemen, you wish to question me about?

Whereupon the Duchess left the court, Madame de Sévigné reported, saying, "Truly, I would never have believed that intelligent men could ask such silly questions." This and other tart replies were, of course, deleted from the official records. The Marquis de Pas summarized the sentiments of the nobility: "Some professional poisoners, male and female, have figured out a way to prolong their own condemned lives by denouncing every so often various aristocrats, whose arrest and interrogation give these wretches a bit more time."

Sensible of the growing antagonism to him, Police Commissioner Reynie applied pressure to his little stable of accused fortunetellers, especially one Lesage, a former galley convict now turned professional witness. Monsieur Reynie used torture, starting with the *sellette*, the torture chair, and then the *brodequins*, where wedges hammered into the boots with mallets crushed the legs. Under three days of horrible pain, La Voisin still denied all charges of poisoning. The verbatim account of the scribe records her shrieks at each successive crushing of her legs. At the second blow, she cried, "Oh, my God! Holy Virgin! I have nothing to say." At the third, she cried out loud and said she had told the truth. At the fourth, the scribe recorded she cried out "extraordinarily," but said nothing. The torture continued. The Police Commissioner ascribed her taciturnity to too gentle treatment. The Attorney General demanded her tongue be cut out and her hands chopped off, but the court was satisfied with burning alive. She had a hard death (February 22, 1680). She was forced to the stake, "tied and bound with iron. Cursing all the time, she was covered with straw, which five or six times she threw off her, but at last the flames grew fiercer, and she was lost to sight." (Madame de Sévigné, *Letters*)

Witchcraft had already been introduced when Lesage accused two priests, Fathers Davot and Mariette, of saying black masses over the naked bellies of young girls. Father Gérard, priest of St.-Sauveur, was charged with saying a similar mass, at which he had debauched the girl serving as an altar. But only after torture was regularly applied did the accusations of black magic amount to anything. To get the evidence he needed, Reynie used the more horrible tortures of the rack and *question de l'eau* (pouring down the throat eight pitchers of water!). He even had the idea of subpoenaing Madeleine Bavent [see Louviers Nuns], who allegedly had contact with several fortunetellers. Commissioner Reynie was overruled, and Madeleine stayed uneventfully in her Normandy convent. On February 24, 1680, the scope of the *Chambre ardente* was extended to "sacrilege, impiety, and profanation."

The Abbé Mariette was arrested at Toulouse and brought to Paris. La Voisin's 21-year-old daughter and Lesage (the professional witness) told how the priest had sacrificed white pigeons and made wax figures. Another fortuneteller, La Filastre, confessed to sacrificing a child to the devil in the middle of a circle of black candles,

and renouncing the sacraments. At one black mass, celebrated by Abbé Deshayes and Abbé Cotton, she sacrificed her own newborn baby, and the priest said mass over the placenta. The priests baptized little figurines, giving them godparents, with the intention to provoke love or death.

Numerous other priests had performed blasphemous rites. Father Davot, for example, said an amatory mass over a naked girl, throughout ceremonially kissing her *parties honteuses*. Madame de Lusignan and her priest, naked in the woods of Fontainbleau, practiced abominations with a big Easter candle. Father Tournet said three amatory masses, during one of which he publicly lay with the girl on the altar.

The 66-year-old hunchback Abbé Guibourg, the illegitimate son of Henri de Montmorency, the sacristan of St.-Marcel in Saint-Denis, was involved as an accomplice of La Voisin. He, too, had said a placenta mass for Mademoiselle La Coudraye (for whom he forged a marriage certificate), and other masses over naked women. Sometimes, at the elevation of the host, he inserted conjurations for hidden treasure or for sexual attraction. One such

Asmodeus, the destroyer demon, who seduced Eve. From Collin de Plancy, *Dictionnaire infernal* (1863).

was addressed to the two traditional devils of lust:

> Astaroth and Asmodeus, princes of fellowship, I invoke you to accept the oblation of this child for that which I ask [on her behalf for whom this mass is celebrated]: that the King and the Dauphin will continue their friendship toward her, that she will be honored by the princes and princesses of the royal family, that the King will deny nothing she asks of him for her relations or household.

La Voisin's daughter described a midnight mass in greater detail: "She had seen the woman stretch out on a mattress, her head extending over the edge and supported by a pillow on a chair turned upside down, her legs hanging down, a napkin with a cross on it covering her breasts, and the chalice resting on her belly." Lesage, the escaped convict, added that the woman held candles in her hands throughout the service.

Father Guibourg described another mass at which he said he had murdered a child. His testimony was confirmed by La Voisin's daughter (only sixteen at the time) and by one of his three mistresses, Jeanne Chaufrain (by whom he had seven children).

> He had bought a child to sacrifice at the mass, said on behalf of a great lady. He had cut the child's throat with a knife, and drawing its blood, had poured it into the chalice; after which he had the body taken away into another place, so that later he could use the heart and entrails for another mass. . . . He said this second mass in a hovel on the ramparts of Saint-Denis, over the same woman, and with the same ceremonies. . . . The body of the child would, he was told, be used to make magic powders.

Another variant of the amatory mass was celebrated for the King's mistress.

> Robed in his aube, stole, and manciple, [Guibourg] had read a conjuration in the presence of Mademoiselle des Oeillets, who was making a charm for the [king]. She was accompanied by a man who gave him the words of the conjuration. For

Astaroth, who obtains the friendship of great lords. From Collin de Plancy, *Dictionnaire infernal* (1863).

this rite it was necessary to have the sperm of both sexes, but Mademoiselle des Oeillets, since she had her *mois*, was incapacitated, so instead she put into the chalice some menstrual blood. The gentleman who was with her went into the space between the bed and the wall, and Guibourg directed his semen into the chalice. Into this mixture, each put a powder made from the blood of bats, and added some flour to give it a firm consistency. Then [Father Guibourg] recited the conjuration, and poured what was in the chalice into a little bottle which Mademoiselle Oeillets and the gentleman took away with them.

Such ceremonies were but an extension of two centuries' acceptance of witchcraft, growing out of still earlier theories of the great powers of the Devil. While theologians might explain Satan did nothing not permitted by God, the mass of the people could not resolve the contradictions of an all good and all powerful God who sanctioned evil. It was easier to accept the continuing heresy of Manicheism, with a good God and a bad Devil; and if God could not help, perhaps the Devil could. In this dualism, blasphemous rites mingle with orthodoxy. La Voisin was arrested coming from Sunday morning mass; La Lepère was most scrupulous in baptizing the premature babies she procured for the black masses. On a sophisticated plane, the French nobles were acting like French peasants, seeking help from friends of the Devil. In addition, since masses were said with special intentions—for rain, health, victory—their extension to love seemed logical.

The accusations, in spite of the Police Commissioner's conviction that they were true, remain tainted. All the witnesses were of bad reputation, and in any other trial their word would have been suspect. The most sensational revelations were given only under excruciating torture. Yet La Voisin constantly denied all witchcraft. Her daughter flatly contradicted her own lurid testimony on two occasions. La Filastre, before being burned alive, retracted her confessions made under torture, telling the Police Commissioner that "everything that she had said in this respect had been only to free herself from the pain and agony of the torture and in fear lest it be continued." On the other hand, more compelling is the apparatus of witchcraft found at the fortunetellers'—not simply poisons, but wax figures, charms for abortion, books on magic, and black candles. Such candles were not intended for shining shoes, despite the avowals of La Trianon, another fortuneteller. Receipts for large sums of money paid to the Abbé Guibourg are likewise damning evidence. It may well be that when love philters failed, French ladies turned to black masses. The description of a service in 1668 (for assisting at which the prize informer, Lesage, had been sent to the galleys) was simply a regular service said with amatory intent, a written request for success in *amour* being kept on the altar. By 1680, however, the mass came replete with slashed babies and nude bellies.

Nevertheless, French society accepted these accusations, and the King's problem was how to stifle the biggest scandal of the century. He suspended the *Chambre ardente* in August, 1680, but since the evidence pointed to the attempt of his former mistress, Madame de Montespan, to poison Louis himself and his new young mistress (Mademoiselle de Fontanges), Louis or-

dered Reynie to continue super-secret investigations. Evidence piled up to show that Madame de Montespan was the key to all this Satanism. The need became even more urgent to conceal the disgrace. Commissioner Reynie continued his work until July, 1682, indiscriminately torturing and burning many lower-class men and women accused of selling poisons and assisting in witchcraft. In all the four years, however, no noble person was tortured or executed. Justice was blindfolded indeed.

During the investigations, 319 persons had been arrested, and 104 sentenced: 36 to death, 4 to slavery in the galleys, 34 to banishment, and 30 acquitted. Ensuing legislation banned fortunetellers, controlled the sale of poisons, and declared witchcraft a superstition [see Edict of Louis XIV]. In 1709, at the age of seventy, Louis XIV decided to destroy the records, and on July 13 they were burned. But somehow copies of the official transcripts and the Police Commissioner's notes escaped destruction, and the King's attempt to erase a page of history failed.

Channel Islands, Witchcraft in the. The Channel Islands suffered possibly more than any other part of Great Britain from witch persecutions. In the first place, the Islands were politically English (with the English monarchs confiscating the goods and property of the convicted), but culturally French; consequently, the apprehension and trial of witches followed the rougher customs of France; for example, witches were burned rather than hanged. In the second place, the percentage of convictions was surprisingly high. In Guernsey, a small island with only a few thousand inhabitants, during the reigns of Elizabeth, James I, and Charles I, 58 women and 20 men, mostly natives of Guernsey, were tried for sorcery, and all except 8 convicted; for example:

3 women and 1 man were burned alive
24 women and 4 men were hanged first and then burned
1 woman was banished, but hanged when she returned

3 women and 1 man were whipped and
   had an ear cut off
22 women and 5 men were banished

These figures are the complete opposite
of those given by the most reliable authorities in England, where only one out of five
is said to have been convicted after trial
[see Witchcraft in England]. Jersey was
somewhat less fanatical than Guernsey, but
between 1562 and 1736, sixty-six trials were
held, at least half the accused being hanged
or burned.

No special legislation was passed against
witchcraft, but Jersey passed a curious ordinance in 1591 forbidding those who have
sought "assistance from witches and diviners in their ills and afflictions . . . to
receive any such assistance on pain of imprisonment" for one month on bread and
water. Throughout the records, the stress
is on *maleficia*, such as maggots infesting
a bed, or lice a shirt, or the drying up of a
cow (perhaps by some black powder). The
witch was apparently either one who might
help (a *quéraude*, a white witch) or, more
probably, one who would work harm.

The witch's subjugation to the devil was,
of course, not forgotten. A typical confession, such as that of Collette du Mont in
1617, mentions a sabbat. She undressed,
rubbed a black ointment into her back,
belly, and stomach, dressed again, and flew
to the sabbat, where a group of fifteen or
sixteen had assembled (no coven of thirteen here!). At first she said she was "unable to recognize [anyone] because they
were all blackened and disfigured" [*tous
noircis et deffigurés*]. Collette had copulation with the devil (as a black dog who
stood on his hind legs and whose paw felt
very much like a human hand), and attended a feast, lacking salt, with wine of
poor quality. In the same year, Isabel Dec-
quet went to the sabbat on the nights her
husband was out fishing, and she kissed the
devil's posteriors. She was marked on the
upper part of her thigh, "which mark having been examined by the midwives, they
reported that they stuck a small pin [*une
petite espinge*] into it, and that she had not
felt it, and that no blood had issued."

An unusual feature of Channel Islands
trials is the employment of torture to extract a confession *after* sentence of death
had been passed. The strappado was the
most common method, but here the rope
was tied to the two *thumbs* (the hands
bound behind the back) so that when the
prisoner was dropped, his thumbs might
be torn off. The torture, naturally, was not
to get admission of guilt, but to obtain
names of accomplices. Since a person so
named would fall under suspicion on the
basis of common rumor and report [*cou-
tume renomée et bruit des gens*], and since
common rumor was grounds for accusation
(and therefore conviction), the courts did
not lack business.

> "How many innocent people have per-
> ished in the flames on the asserted testi-
> mony of supernatural circumstances? I
> will not say there are no witches; but
> ever since the difficulty of convicting
> them has been recognized in the island,
> they all seem to have disappeared, as
> though the evidence of times gone by had
> been but an illusion."—Philippe le Geyt
> (1635-1715), Lieutenant Bailiff of Jersey.

Charms. The distinction between a charm
and a prayer was subtle, especially since, in
the Christian period, charms incorporated
holy names, used Latin phrases similar to
those of the liturgy, and based their efficacy on the power of the Christian God.
The famous White Paternoster—

Matthew, Mark, Luke and John,
Bless the bed that I lie on

could serve as a bedtime prayer or a night
spell. One charm to staunch blood, widespread in English, French, and German,
illustrates this dualism and establishes the
typical literary form of the charm: (1) a
reference to a precedent of the sickness or
injury, successfully cured, and (2) a petition that the sufferer will similarly recover.
A fifteenth-century English version reads:

When our Lord Jesus Christ was done
on the cross, then Longius came with his
spear and pierced him in the side. Blood

and water came out at the wound. Longius wiped his eyes and saw a man through the holy virtue that God showed there. I conjure thee, blood, that thou come not out of this Christian man.

The plea is sealed by the repetition of *"In nomine patris et filii et spiritus sancti. Amen."*

Witches who reputedly possessed occult knowledge used traditional charms to reinforce the properties of their herbs or amulets, and consequently charms sometimes appeared as evidence in witch trials. A charm to cure a bewitched person, recited in court by James Device, became famous at the trial of the Lancashire witches in 1612:

Upon Good Friday, I will fast while I
   may,
Until I hear them knell
Our Lord's own bell;
Lord in his mass
With his twelve apostles good,
What hath he in his hand?
Liking, lithe wand [pleasing, flexible
   rod of office].
What hath he in his other hand?
Heaven's door key.
Open, open, Heaven, door keys.
Steck, steck [shut], hell door.
Let chrisom child
Go to its mother mild.
What is yonder that casts a light so
   farrandly [splendidly]?
My own dear son that's nailed to the
   tree.
He is nailed sore by the heart and hand,
And holy harn-pan [skull].
Well is that man
That Friday spell can,
His child to learn;
A cross of blue, and another of red,
As good Lord was to the rood [cross].
Gabriel laid him down to sleep
Upon the ground of holy weep [i.e.,
   Gethsemane].
Good Lord came walking by:
Sleepest thou, wakest thou, Gabriel?
No, Lord, I am sted [beset] with stick
   and stake,
That I can neither sleep nor wake.
Rise up, Gabriel, and go with me,
The stick nor the stake shall never deer
   [harm] thee.
Sweet Jesus, our Lord, Amen.

On such evidence, James Device was condemned for "as dangerous and malicious a witch as ever lived in these parts of Lancashire."

The use of written charms placed in amulets was indeed sanctioned by the Church, and won the approval of Thomas Aquinas: "To attach holy words about the neck, provided they contain nothing false or suspect, is certainly not unlawful, although it would be better to refrain [from such use]." Protestants regarded charms as superstitions; Thomas Ady, for example, referred to "Pope Leo's amulet" against harm in battle, which relied on the repetition of names of God and three paternosters. "Many of the poor idolatrous Irish rebels," he wrote, "[were] found slain with charms in their pockets, composed by the popish clergy, the witches of these latter times." William Perkins likewise condemned charms using the names of Jesus to drive away the devil or prevent witchcraft, because "the ignorant people think that Christ is a conjurer, and that there is virtue in naming of his name to do some strange thing."

In the early *Malleus Maleficarum* (1486), seven rules were given to distinguish good and wicked charms. A charm was licit if it contained:

1. No suggestion in words of any pact with the Devil (and if the user had no such intention).
2. No unknown names.
3. Nothing untrue.
4. The only ritual the signing of the cross.
5. No credence in the *manner* of writing or reciting the charm, or of wearing or using it.
6. Only biblical phrases in their original context.
7. Assurances that the efficacy depended wholly on the will of God.

As a safety precaution, the *Malleus* recommended as charms only the standard Catholic prayers, such as the paternoster, the Ave Maria, or Christ's seven words on the cross. Most of the prayers used in exorcism, such as the blessing of salt for animals, and the litany against ligature, however, are very close to pagan charms.

No witch was given the benefit of the doubt that her charm might be a prayer. William Perkins in his *Discourse of Witchcraft* (1608) defined the "nature and proper end of a charm" as a spell or verse "used for a sign and watchword to the devil to cause him to work wonders." Vairo (1583) said charms were invented by devils to gratify their "furious rage" against mankind. In Scotland, the use of charms merited death by burning, and in 1678 the famous lawyer Sir George Mackenzie justified such punishment for witches:

> Though charms be not able to produce the effects that are punishable in witches, yet since these effects cannot be produced without the devil, and [since] he will not employ himself at the desire of any who have not resigned themselves wholly to him, it is very just that the users of these should be punished, being guilty at least of apostasy and heresy.

From amulets ostensibly religious, the transition to diabolical amulets and magical tokens was easy. James I believed the devil taught witches how to contrive murders by waxen images. At the witch trial at St. Osyth in 1582, Ursula Kempe confessed how a wise woman had given her a cure for arthritis—a factor in her conviction and execution. She had to—

> take hog's dung and charnell and put them together and hold them in her left hand, and to take in the other hand a knife, and to prick the medicine three times, and then to cast the same into the fire, and to take the said knife, and to make three pricks under a table, and to let the knife stick there. And after that to take three leaves of sage, and as much of herb John (alias herb grace) and put them into ale, and drink it last at night and first in the morning; and that she taking the same had ease of her lameness. (*A True and Just Record*)

The harrowing trial of Dr. John Fian in 1590 produced one almost comical charge. Dr. Fian supposedly sought the love of the sister of one of his students. Promising "to teach him without stripes [whippings]" if the boy brought "three hairs of his sister's privities," Dr. Fian gave the lad "a piece of conjured paper . . . to lap them in when he had gotten them." The boy, who slept with his sister, was not very adept. "Being one night in a sleep, and her brother in bed with her, [she] suddenly cried out to her mother, declaring that her brother would not suffer her to sleep." The cry wakened the mother, who, being a witch herself, knew what tricks her son was up to. She "beat him sundry stripes, whereby he discovered the truth unto her." So the mother "went to a young heifer which never had born calf nor gone to the bull, and with a pair of shears, clipped off three hairs from the udder of the cow, and wrapped them in the same paper which she again delivered to the boy, then willing him to give the same to his said master, which he immediately did." Dr. Fian took the hairs, thinking them from the young lady, and "wrought his art upon them." At once the heifer came to the door of the church "and made toward the schoolmaster, leaping and dancing upon him," and followed Dr. Fian all over the church and through the town. People thought he did this by the help of the devil, and his fame grew as a "notable conjurer."

Protection against the malicious charms and harmful amulets of witches could be secured by counter charms. Guazzo, for example, suggested recitation of prayers and the use of religious tokens, "for such devotions are the safest protection and bulwark against the wiles of the Prince of Darkness." Mary Hortado, who suffered from poltergeist troubles at Salmon Falls, Massachusetts, in 1638, got relief by placing bay branches in her house. "And as long as the bays continued green, she had quiet." Herbs were regularly used in exorcism. Sinistrari listed many ingredients to drive away demons, ranging from the castor oil plant through coral, jet, and jasper, to menstrual blood. He included a curious incense against the incubus, made of medicinal herbs (most of them stimulants and aphrodisiacs!): "Sweet flag, cubeb seed, roots of aristolochia, great and small cardamon, ginger, long pepper, clove-

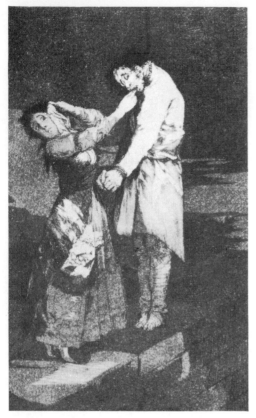

"People believe that the teeth of hanged men are very important to sorcery; that without them it cannot succeed. What a pity that the people should believe such nonsense!"—Goya (1799)

pink, cinnamon, cloves, mace, nutmegs, resin, benzoin, aloe wood and root, and fragrant sandal. These ingredients were to be brewed in three and a half quarts of brandy and water." In 1597 a Scottish woman, Janet Leisk, listed red thread and rowan wood (tied inside a person's clothes) as a preventive against bewitchment. In 1665 a woman was indicted at York for a charm she considered religious; she had freed a man from a possessing devil, she said, by laying a silver crucifix on him. A Cambridge clergyman, Henry Hallywell (1681), however, had a simpler method for resisting witches and devils: "It is possible for the soul to arise to such a height, and become so divine, that no witchcraft or evil demons can have any power upon the body." The same thought had been ex-

pressed in simpler language by Perkins, that the only sure and lawful remedies were "the covenant of grace, made and confirmed in the Gospel by the blood of Christ." Bodin, the Catholic demonologist, agreed in principle: charity was the best safeguard, for witches could not injure a charitable man, even if he were otherwise vicious.

Chelmsford Witches. At Chelmsford, Essex, in the summer term of 1566, occurred the first really notable trial for witchcraft in England resulting from the bill of 1563 passed under Queen Elizabeth. The proceedings have the added distinction of being the first to be presented in a topical and sensational chapbook, heralding hundreds of successors in the next two centuries: *The Examination and Confession of Certain Witches at Chelmsford in the County of Essex before the Queen's Majesty's Judges, the 26th Day of July, Anno 1566. At the Assize held there as then, and one of them put to death for the same offense, as their examination declareth more at large.*

The trial is as typical an illustration of English witchcraft practices as could be found, for it incorporates all the traditional factors of later witch trials. The prestige of the judges made the court's decisions a precedent to be followed by later justices; the first day the trial was conducted by Rev. Thomas Cole, rector of a church near Chelmsford, and Sir John Fortescue, later Chancellor of the Exchequer; the second day by Sir Gilbert Gerard, the Attorney General, and John Southcote, a Justice of the Queen's Bench. That the Attorney General intervened indicates how a minor affair was blown up into a key trial.

Witchcraft took different forms in various countries, depending on many factors of historical and economic development. English witchcraft, according to this first Chelmsford trial, was signalized by the absence of any involved pact with the Devil (as claimed throughout the Salem trials) or of any organized gathering at infamous sabbats (the staple of European records); by the importance of familiars; and by the extent of simple acts of *maleficia*, all seemingly typical domestic accidents attributed to the spite of a neighbor, who by this attribution became a witch.

More important for the future history of witchcraft in England was the court's accepting as valid evidence the highly imaginative stories of children (when the legal minimum age of witnesses in other trials was fourteen), spectral evidence, the finding of witch's marks, and the unsupported confessions of the accused.

The charges against the three defendants, Elizabeth Francis, Agnes Waterhouse, and her daughter Joan, were not related; the only connection was that all three came from Hatfield Peverell, a little village in Essex, and that Mrs. Francis had given Mrs. Waterhouse her old pet cat, Sathan.

Elizabeth Francis, wife of Christopher Francis, a yeoman, was charged with bewitching the infant child of William Auger, "who became decrepit." She confessed to various other villainies, was found Guilty and sentenced to one year's imprisonment. Under the witchcraft act of James I she would have been hanged. Later, Elizabeth was indicted for bewitching Mary Cocke, "who languished for ten days following"; she pleaded innocent, but was found Guilty and (instead of being hanged as a second offender) got off with a year in jail and four appearances in the pillory. In 1579 Elizabeth was charged again, for bewitching Alice Poole, "who languished until November 1 [1578] when she died." Although pleading innocent, Elizabeth was convicted and hanged.

Her confession in 1566 is supposedly verbatim, but the pamphlet omits any mention of the actual indictment. Since court records about Elizabeth Francis are extant, the pamphlet cannot be fictitious. But where was William Auger, the father of the bewitched child, and why was Elizabeth sentenced for confessed crimes which were quite extraneous to the original charge? Was the Elizabethan public more interested in Mrs. Francis' marital and pre-marital experiences, and in the antics of her white spotted cat, Sathan, which could turn itself into a toad?

Mother Agnes Waterhouse, hanged as a witch at Chelmsford in 1566. A page from the pamphlet describing the first important witch trial in England. From the sole surviving copy, now in Lambeth Palace Library.

First, [Elizabeth Francis] learned this art of witchcraft at the age of twelve years of her grandmother, whose name [was] Mother Eve of Hatfield Peverell, deceased.

Item: when she taught it to her, she counselled her to renounce God and his word, and to give of her blood to Sathan (as she termed it), which she delivered her in the likeness of a white spotted cat, and taught her to feed the said cat with bread and milk. And she did so. Also she [Mother Eve] taught her to call it by the name of Sathan and to keep it in a basket.

When this Mother Eve had given her the cat Sathan, then this Elizabeth desired first of the said cat (calling it Sathan) that she might be rich and to have goods. And he promised her she should, asking her what she would have. And she said sheep (for this cat spake to her, as she confessed, in a strange hollow voice, but such as she understood by use). And this cat forthwith brought sheep into her pasture to the number of eighteen, black and white, which continued with her for a time, but in the end did all wear away, she knew not how.

Item: when she had gotten these sheep, she desired to have one Andrew Byles to her husband, which was a man of some wealth; and the cat did promise she should, but that he said she must first consent that this Andrew should abuse her, and she so did.

And after, when this Andrew had abused her, he would not marry her. Wherefore she willed Sathan to waste his goods, which he forthwith did. And yet not being contented with this, she willed him to touch his body which he forthwith did, whereof he died.

Item: that every time he did anything for her, she said that he required a drop of blood, which she gave him by pricking herself, sometime in one place and then in another; and where she pricked herself remained a red spot, which was still to be seen.

Item: when this Andrew was dead, she, doubting [believing] herself with child, willed Sathan to destroy it. And he bade her take a certain herb and drink it, which she did, and destroyed the child forthwith.

Item: when she desired another husband, he promised her another, naming this Francis whom she now hath, but said he is not so rich as the other, willing her to consent unto that Francis in fornication, which she did. And thereof conceived a daughter that was born within a quarter of a year after they were married.

After they were married, they lived not so quietly as she desired, being stirred (as she said) to much unquietness and moved to swearing and cursing. Wherefore she willed Sathan her cat to kill the child, being about the age of half a year old, and he did so. And when she yet found not the quietness she desired, she willed it to lay a lameness in the leg of this Francis, her husband. And it did in this manner: it came in a morning to this Francis' shoe, lying in it like a toad; and when he perceived it, putting on his shoe, and had touched it with his foot, he being suddenly amazed asked of her what it was. And she bade him kill it, and he was forthwith taken with a lameness whereof he cannot be healed.

After all this, when she had kept this cat by the space of fifteen or sixteen years, and as some say (though untruly) being weary of it, she came to one Mother Waterhouse, her neighbor (a poor woman), when she was going to the oven, and desired her to give her a cake, and she would give her a thing that she should be the better for so long as she lived. And this Mother Waterhouse gave her a cake, whereupon she brought her this cat in her apron, and taught her as she was instructed before by her grandmother Eve, telling her that she must call him Sathan, and give him of her blood and bread and milk as before.

The second of the accused was Mrs. Agnes Waterhouse, a 63-year-old widow, charged with bewitching William Fynee, "who languished until November 1 [1565] when he died." She was linked to Mrs. Francis by having taken her cat, which, because she desperately needed the wool which lined its box, she later changed into a toad. Mother Waterhouse confessed to attempted murder of another neighbor, who, however, "was so strong in faith that she had no power to hurt him." She admitted also numerous petty acts of vindictiveness to livestock. Almost as damaging was her admission to saying her prayers in Latin (not surprising for one born in Catholic England in 1503), a portent of future witch tests.

Apart from the story of a twelve-year-old girl, Agnes Brown, the most damning evidence against Mother Waterhouse came from her own lips. Typical are these confessions:

Also she confessed that falling out with one widow Gooday she willed Sathan to drown her cow, and he did so, and she rewarded him as before.

Also she falling out with another of her neighbors, she killed her three geese in the same manner.

Also being denied butter of another, she caused her to lose the curds two or three days after.

A Detection
of damnable driftes, practi-
zed by three VVitches arraigned at
Chelmifforde in Eſſex, at the
laſte Aſſiſes there holden, whiche
were executed in Apꝛill.
1 5 7 9.

Set forthe to diſcouer the Ambuſhementes of
Sathan, whereby he would ſurpꝛiſe vs
luſſed in ſecuritie, and hardened
with contempte of Gods
vengeance thꝛeatened
foꝛ our offences.

Imprinted at London for Edward White,
at the little North-dore of Paules.

Title page of contemporary tract (1579) on
second major trial of witches at Chelmsford,
Essex. From the copy in the British Museum.

Toward the end of her trial, the Attorney General inquired further about her familiar's sucking blood. Although she made all sorts of other confessions, on this one direct question, Mother Waterhouse denied guilt:

Attorney General: Agnes Waterhouse, when did thy cat suck of thy blood?
Agnes Waterhouse: Never.
Attorney General: No? Let me see. [Then the jailer lifted up her kerchief on her head, and there was divers spots in her face and one on her nose.] Then, in good faith, Agnes, when did he suck of thy blood last?

Agnes Waterhouse: By my good faith, my lord, not this fortnight.

Once again, the pamphlet gives no information about the original indictment; unless it be included in the list of miscellaneous and relatively minor offenses mentioned above: "Item: falling out with another of her neighbors and his wife, she willed Sathan to kill him with a bloody flux, whereof he died." But one would expect the widow, Mrs. Fynee, to give evidence at the trial of a murderer. Mother Waterhouse was examined on two consecutive days, July 26 and 27, found Guilty, and hanged on July 29, 1566, possibly the first woman hanged for witchcraft in modern England. On the scaffold, the old woman "yielded up her soul, trusting to be in joy with Christ her Saviour which dearly had bought her with his most precious blood."

The third defendant was Joan Waterhouse, aged eighteen, who was charged with bewitching the twelve-year-old Agnes Brown, "who on July 21 following became decrepit in her right leg and in her right arm." Joan "put herself on the country" and was found Not Guilty. The chief interest of this part of the trial is the testimony of Agnes Brown about a black dog, claimed to be Sathan, the cat, in disguise!

Agnes Brown testified that

at such a day (naming the day certain) when she was churning of butter; and there came to her a thing like a black dog with a face like an ape, a short tail, a chain and a silver whistle (to her thinking) about his neck, and a pair of horns on his head. And [he] brought in his mouth the key of the milkhouse door.

"And then, my lord," she said, "I was afeared, for he skipped and leaped to and fro, and sat on the top of a nettle. And then I asked him what he would have, and he said he would have butter. And I said I had none for him. And then he said he would have some ere he went, and then he did run to put the key into the lock of the milkhouse door. And I said he should have none. And he said he would have some. And then he opened the door and went upon the shelf, and there upon a new cheese laid down the key. And being a while within, he came out again and locked the door, and said that he had made flap [? churned] butter for me, and so departed."

And then she said she told her aunt of it, and then she sent for the priest, and when he came he bade her to pray to God and call on the name of Jesus. "And so the next day, my lord, he came again to me with the key of our milkhouse door in his mouth, and then I said, In the name of Jesus, what hast thou there? And then he laid down the key and said that I spake evil words in speaking of that name, and then he departed. And so my aunt

took up the key, for he had kept it from us two days and a night, and then we went into the milkhouse; and there we did see the print [pat] of butter upon the cheese, and then within a few days after he came again with a bean pod in his mouth . . ."

And then she said, "My lord, I said, In the name of Jesus what hast thou there? And so then he laid it down and said I spake evil words, and departed and came again by and by with a piece of bread in his mouth. And I asked him what he would have, and he said butter it was that he would have; and so he departed. And, my lord, I did not see him no more till Wednesday last, which was the 24th day of July . . . he came with a knife in his mouth and asked me if I were not dead. And I said, No, I thanked God. And then he said if I would not die, then he would thrust his knife into my heart, but he would make me to die. And then I said, In the name of Jesus lay down thy knife. And he said he would not depart from his sweet dame's knife as yet, and then I asked of him who was his dame, and then he nodded and wagged his head to your house, Mother Waterhouse."

At this point—the only time—Mrs. Waterhouse opposed Agnes' account, claiming she had only a large kitchen knife in her home, and therefore could not be the witch owning the dagger:

Agnes Waterhouse: What manner knife was it?
Agnes Brown: It was a dagger knife.
Agnes Waterhouse: There thou liest!
Queen's Attorney: Why?
Agnes Waterhouse: Marry, my lord, she saith it is a dagger knife, and I have none such in my house but a great knife. And therein she lieth.

This example is one of the earliest in English of spectral evidence, where a specter or devil is connected to the accused by a witness. The big black dog was presumed to be the cat Sathan in disguise, taking his orders from the witch, Mother Waterhouse. One hundred and thirty years later, such evidence was to convict the Salem witches; but Salem also saw such testimony rejected, and the end of the witch mania.

Three feminine dames at-
    tached were,
  Whom Satan did infect
With Belial's spirit, whose
    sorcery did
  The simple so molest.

Title page of contemporary
pamphlet on the third
Chelmsford trial of 1589,
showing Joan Prentice, Joan
Cony, and Joan Upney,
hanged on the gallows.
From the unique copy in
Lambeth Palace Library.

Other celebrated trials held at Chelmsford need only brief mention here. They
show the continuity and tenacity of witch
beliefs and witch hunting, once it had established itself.

The second major trial came in 1579 before John Southcote and Sir Thomas
Gawdy, both Justices of the Queen's Bench,
and involved four women from quite separated localities. Public interest in this
trial was therefore more than local. The
proceedings resembled the first, and produced the customary confessions. Elizabeth
Francis, appearing for the final time, was
convicted and hanged. Ellen Smith, whose
mother had been hanged as a witch in 1574,
was charged with bewitching a four-year-
old child. As the child died, she screamed,
"Away with the witch." Immediately after
her death, the mother, "Goodwife Webbe,
espied a thing like to a black dog go out
at her door, and presently at the sight
thereof she fell distraught to her wits."
Prosecution followed. Notestein suggested
the whole affair may have stemmed from the
whim of a sick four-year-old child. Ellen

Smith put herself on the country and was
convicted and executed. A similar indictment and verdict met Alice Nokes. Margery
Stanton was accused of bewitching to death
"one white gelding valued at three pounds
and one cow valued at forty shillings," the
owner not stated. The court found the indictment insufficient, and since neither man-
slaughter nor murder was alleged, she was
set free.

(Three years after the second trial came
the notorious trial of the witches of St.
Osyth in 1582, conducted at Chelmsford, the
seat of the county assizes. See St. Osyth
Witches.)

The third major trial at Chelmsford in
1589 involved one man and nine women,
most of them charged with bewitching to
death; four were convicted and hanged;
three found Not Guilty on lesser charges
of bewitching persons and goods. The evidence is just as fantastic as in the earlier
Chelmsford trials, and consists largely in
establishing imps or familiars as the cause
of trouble or death. Children gave much of
the evidence, and two boys were praised by

the judges for condemning their unwed mother (Avice Cony or Cunny) and their grandmother (Joan Cony). Three of the witches (Joan Cony, Joan Upney, and Joan Prentice) were executed within two hours of sentencing, confessing their crimes on the scaffold.

The fourth mass trial at Chelmsford came half a century later in 1645, the worst witch trial of the seventeenth century, when, of thirty-two women indicted, nineteen were hanged [see Matthew Hopkins].

Children as Accusers. During the centuries of witch hunting, hundreds of people were sent to their death because of the wanton mischief of undisciplined youngsters. England was especially afflicted with such little monsters, and American children copied their antics. In France, this particular delinquency took the form of girls' accusing priests of immoral conduct [see Catherine Cadière, Louviers Nuns].

Germany was so absorbed with mass executions that children's evidence was incidental. One example, however, surpasses English parallels. In Hagenau (Alsace), the disasters of war and bad harvests were linked to witchcraft, and for witchcraft, on July 16, 1627, three women and a fourteen-year-old girl, Marie Niethin, were executed. Among others, Marie inculpated a thirteen-year-old boy, Peter Roller. Under examination, Roller displayed a fertile imagination, inventing fantastic stories of sabbats, and accusing everyone he knew of being present there. Under torture, those accused could do little except confess and name other accomplices. To protect his own life, the boy claimed he was bewitched, a ruse which sent him to a hospital instead of a death cell. After nine months, on March 23, 1628, Peter Roller was questioned. He was quite able to cope with the situation—in the name of Christ he had just driven away the devil, who came to tempt him outside the hospital window. This brave act was well thought of by the judges, who assigned two Capuchin friars to complete his good beginnings. By May 17, Peter was freed from devils, and in June returned home. This thirteen-year-old was responsible for twenty-

four people being burned, three suicides in prison, and three being dismissed after torture—permanently crippled.

Most examples of young people telling lies under oath occurred in England. They start with the celebrated trial in 1593 of the Warboys Witches, when five hysterical girls sent an old couple and their daughter to the gallows. Four years later, a young impostor, William Somers, the Boy of Nottingham, coached by the false exorcist, John Darrell, accused thirteen women of bewitching him. Exposed before his testimony convicted them, Somers confessed he had studied a chapbook on the Warboys Witches in order to manifest the appropriate symptoms. In 1604, Anne Gunter used this same pamphlet to learn how a bewitched child should act. The circumstances surrounding a hysterical thirteen-year-old boy, John Smith, in 1614, at Leicester, so much resembled the Warboys case that direct stimulation seems likely [see Leicester Boy]. Nine persons had been hanged as witches on Smith's evidence before King James I ordered an investigation, discovered his imposture, and released those still in jail.

Even when young delinquents did not follow the Warboys pattern, they could be influenced by adult conversation about this and similar trials. In 1596, at Burton-on-Trent, thirteen-year-old Thomas Darling had fits, seeing green cats, and accused Alice Gooderidge of witchcraft; Alice was convicted and died in jail [see Burton Boy]. Darling was eventually exposed by Samuel Harsnett, later Archbishop of York. The William Somers who profited by the Warboys pamphlet was sent in 1597 to observe Darling, "that, seeing him in his fits, [he] might the better learn to do them [himself]." In 1597, the children of Nicholas Starkie in Lancashire took on fits and melancholy; a fraudulent exorcist, Hartley, who supposedly imparted a demon to them, was convicted on a separate charge of making magic circles and hanged at Lancaster (George More, *A True Discourse Concerning the Certain Possession*, 1600). In 1620, four years after the exposure of the Leicester Boy, William Perry, the Bilson Boy, also

---

Notable Deceptions: Possessed Adolescents

Discussed by Francis Hutchinson (with some other references)

1533 Elizabeth Barton, the Maid of Kent. A priest encouraged the girl to fake fits and report she was cured by the intercession of the Virgin Mary. In this way, the priest's chapel at Aldington, Kent, would become a shrine, and "pilgrimages being made to it, he might draw those advantages from it." Elizabeth later claimed visions opposing the remarriage of Henry VIII; many priests and gentlemen were implicated and confessed the trick. Before her execution, Elizabeth Barton confessed that "because the thing which I feigned was profitable to them, therefore they much praised me."

1544 Elizabeth Cross, the Girl in the Hole in the Wall, who claimed clairvoyance.

1574 Agnes Bridges, aged eleven, and Rachel Pindar, aged twelve, counterfeited possession and vomited pins. They were exposed and confessed their deception.

1575 Mildred Nerrington of Kent went into hysterics, "so strong that four men could scarce hold her down." She accused an old woman as a witch, but later confessed her deception before the justices of the peace. [Also related by Reginald Scot.]

1579 Elizabeth Orton of Flintshire counterfeited trances. She made a public confession at Chester Cathedral in 1582.

1595 Thomas Darling, the Burton Boy.

1597 William Somers, the Nottingham Boy [see John Darrell].

1604 Thomas Harrison, the Northwich Boy.

1604 Anne Gunter.

1616 John Smith, the Leicester Boy.

1620 William Perry, the Bilson Boy.

1633 Edmund Robinson, the boy in the Pendle Swindle. [Also related by John Webster.]

1697 Richard Dugdale, the Surey (Lancashire) demoniac, possessed by Satan, who struggled with nine ministers of the gospel before being exorcized.

---

simulated possession, but was discovered stuffing his prepuce with inky cotton to make his urine appear blue.

Unfortunately, most such children were never exposed, and throughout the ensuing decades, trials based on children's fantasies continued. In 1634, ten-year-old Edmund Robinson started the notorious Pendle Swindle. Five months later he admitted his hoax; in the meantime, three of the accused had died in prison. In 1644, at Bury St. Edmunds, Rose Cullender and Amy Duny were executed as witches on the allegations of hysterical children, even though fraud was pointed out in court. Over a century after the Warboys case, in 1697, an eleven-year-old girl in Paisley, Scotland, who appeared to vomit trash, accused twenty-one persons of causing her fits; on her say-so, corroborated by three other children, seven of the accused were burned [see Bargarran Impostor].

American children also proved impostors. The four Goodwin Children of Boston recall the Throgmorton children at Warboys. In 1688, they accused an Irish charwoman of bewitching them, going into convulsions at her approach. The Irishwoman was hanged as a witch. In 1720, three young girls at Littleton (Massachusetts) convinced their neighbors they were hexed; eight years later, the eldest daughter confessed it was all a hoax, the girls having picked a woman at random to accuse as a witch. But the classic American example is Salem. Twenty-two people there died from the prank of several "witch bitches." The reason was admitted by one of them: "They must have some sport." Fourteen years later, the ringleader of the girls, Ann Putnam, confessed the fraud: "It was a great delusion of Satan that deceived me in that sad time, whereby I justly fear I have been instrumental . . . to bring upon myself and this land the guilt of innocent blood." Yet the rantings of these young women were considered by Governor Hutchinson "so exact as to leave no room for doubting the stories [of previous possessed children]."

Among the English clergy who fought against accepting childish ravings were Archbishop Samuel Harsnett, author of *Discovery of Fraudulent Practices* (1599), refuting John Darrell, and Bishop Francis Hutchinson, who probably gave the practice its death blow in 1718. A list, partly based on Hutchinson, of notable deceptions is appended here.

In addition to the numerous entries mentioned above, see also Witchcraft in Austria, Dr. Lamb's Darling, Epworth Poltergeist, Edward Fairfax, Glenluce Devil, Sir John Holt, Siri Jørgensdatter, Lille Novices, Mora Witches.

Cideville Case. The disturbances recorded in 1850 at the parsonage of Cideville, in Normandy, eighty miles northwest of Paris, are probably the most varied of any single poltergeist. Moreover, they were confirmed by thirty-four witnesses in a court of law, although the *juge de paix* wisely determined "whatever might be the cause of the extraordinary facts which occurred at the parsonage of Cideville, it is clear, from the sum total of the testimony adduced, that the cause of these facts remains unknown."

A poltergeist became involved in a lawsuit when Felix Thorel, aged forty, charged the village priest with defamation of character for calling him a witch. The unheard-of events at his parsonage, Father Tinel thought, were too complicated to be merely pranks by his two students. Had the bewitching occurred two or three centuries earlier, Thorel, who had boasted that he would bring trouble to the curé, would have been burned as a witch, but in the nineteenth century, Thorel instituted a court action.

The story starts like so many thousands of earlier witch trials as a cut and dried, almost classic, example of threats of evil (*malum minatum*), and evil following (*damnum secutum*). Visiting one of his parishioners who was being treated by an old white witch, Father Tinel advised his going to a physician. A few days later, the witch—referred to only as "G"—was arrested for practicing medicine without a license, largely, as he suspected, because of the priest.

To be revenged, "G" employed Thorel, the village simpleton of Cideville. Thorel had to touch Father Tinel's two pupils. Thereafter the boys became possessed, subjected to invisible beatings, terrified by specters and poltergeist annoyances.

On November 26, 1850, the boys heard rappings, like light blows from a hammer, on the wainscoting of their study. By Sunday, December 1, the blows had become very insistent, and Father Tinel was apprised of them. When he tried saying "*Plus fort,*" the noises grew louder. Monday, Clement Bunel, the older pupil, aged fourteen, thought of telling the rappings to "beat time to the tune of 'Maître Corbeau,'" which they at once did (just like the Drummer of Tedworth who drummed "Roundheads and Cuckolds" for an hour together). They reacted the same way to Father Tinel's command. From then on, for the next two months, until February 15, 1851, when the boys were removed from the parsonage by order of the Archbishop of Paris, the house was infested. Tables moved, tongs and shovel leaped out of the fireplace and jumped back again, a hammer flew across the room and gently came to rest on the floor, a candlestick hurled itself against a *femme de chambre*, doors refused to open, noises in the boys' room became deafening.

Sacheverell Sitwell, in his informative and amusing *Poltergeists*, observes that the Cideville case contains almost every category of poltergeist phenomenon: knockings, answers by knockings, rapping of popular tunes; tables and furniture moved, knives thrown, desks rising and falling; stones thrown; winds rushing; and pillows and bed coverings snatched away. The list reads like a compendium of all the typical poltergeist cases.

Suspicion focused on Thorel as the guilty agent. One day Thorel visited the parsonage (presumably to check on the effectiveness of his sorcery) and Father Tinel forced him to beg pardon of his younger pupil, Gustave Lemmonier. Lemmonier had complained of being hit by a black hand (mysteriously not attached to any body) and to being dragged by his leg. "A kind of human phantasm, clad in a blouse, haunted me for fifteen days wherever I went; none but myself could see it." When confronted with Thorel, the student recognized the phantasm which had haunted him for a fortnight, and said to M. Tinel, "There is the man who follows me." The older student also recognized Thorel as the specter haunting him. Bunel later testified that after this encounter "Lemmonier had a *crise de nerfs* and fainted."

Thorel continued to brag about his uncanny powers, saying if he could just touch one of the boys again, the furniture would dance and the windows break. And so it happened. Even an example of sympathetic magic cropped up: nails were driven into the floor where Lemmonier had seen the specter of Thorel; one nail became red-hot, causing the floor to smoke, and Lemmonier said he saw the nail had hit "the man in the blouse" on the cheek. Soon after, Thorel was observed to have a wound on his face.

The crisis in the relations between Father Tinel and Thorel came when Thorel lost his job as a shepherd in consequence of suspicions of his witchcraft, and when Father Tinel struck him with his walking stick. On this assault, Thorel brought suit for libel. Proceedings opened on January 7, 1851, were adjourned until January 28 for the gathering of evidence, and concluded on February 4, 1851.

Among the witnesses were some well-known and respected men and women: Adolphe Cheval, mayor of Cideville; Father Martin Tranquille Leroux of Saussay; Father Athanase Bouffay of St.-Maclou at Rouen; Father Adalbert Honoré Gobert, also of Rouen; M. Raoul de St.-Victor, lord of the local château; Madame de St.-Victor, Marie Françoise Adolphie Deschamps de Bois-Hébert; and Charles Jules, Marquis de Mirville. Whether for the prosecution or defense, all these witnesses (and a host of local residents) agreed on one thing: the actuality of the happenings.

Father Leroux testified: "I saw things which I have been unable to explain to myself . . . a piece of bread lying on the table darted under the table; and we being placed as we were, it was impossible that any of us could have thrown it in that way." Madame de St.-Victor heard the beating of the tunes and swore she watched the boys very closely. She saw no movement of their feet or hands. "It was impossible that they should have done it." Father Bouffay "took especial notice that the children were motionless when the disturbances occurred, and evidently they could not produce them."

The most detailed evidence came from the Marquis de Mirville, who was known for his research into the occult, and who had come from Paris to investigate. He later published the Cideville story in his *Des Esprits.*

So, after breakfast, the curate having gone to mass and the children being in the room at their studies, he carried out his intention of experimenting alone, thus:

"How many letters are there in my name? Answer by the number of strokes."

Eight strokes were given.

"How many in my given name?"

Five strokes. (*Jules*)

"How many in my *pré-nom?*" (A name, he remarked, by which he was never called, and which was only known from his baptismal record.)

Seven strokes. (*Charles*)

"How many in my younger daughter's name?"

Nine strokes. This time the first error, the name being *Blanche;* but the blows immediately began again and struck seven, thus correcting the original mistake.

"How many letters in the name of my commune? But take care and don't make a common mistake in spelling it."

A pause. Then ten strokes—the correct number of *Gomerville*, often erroneously spelled *Gommerville*.

After hearing the evidence, the court dismissed the case, explaining that although Father Tinel had expressed his suspicions, nevertheless it was "proved by numerous witnesses that the said [plaintiff] had said and done whatever lay in his power to persuade the public" of his being a sorcerer, and consequently the plaintiff could not "maintain a claim for damages for alleged defamation of which he was himself the first author." Thorel was ordered to pay costs, but may have found satisfaction that the curé lost his pupils.

Andrew Lang sums up this whole strange business: "The experienced reader will see that, in the seventeenth century, Thorel

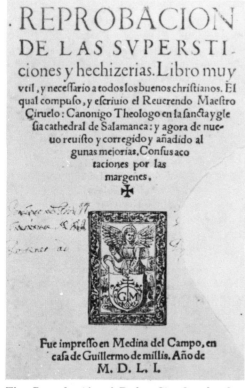

. REPROBACION
DE LAS SVPERSTI-
ciones y hechizerias. Libro muy
vtil, y neceſſario a todos los buenos chriſtianos. El
qual compuſo, y eſcriuio el Reuerendo Maeſtro
Çiruelo: Canonigo Theologo en la ſancta ygle
ſia cathedral de Salamanca: y agora de nue-
uo reuiſto y corregido y añadido al
gunas mejorias. Conſus aco
taciones por las
margenes.

Fue impreſſo en Medina del Campo, en
caſa de Guillermo de millis. Año de
M. D. L. L

The *Reprobación* of Pedro Cirvelo, the first book on witchcraft to be printed in Spanish (1539), and a classic for well over a century. This title page is of the 1551 edition at Medina del Campa, now in Cornell University Library.

would have been burned on the 'spectral evidence' of the appearances to the younger boy. The skeptic will be sure that the boys caused all the trouble because they were tired of staying with M. Tinel."

Cirvelo, Pedro Sanchez. *Opus de Magica Superstitione* [*Book about Belief in Magic*] by Cirvelo (about 1475-1560) remained the classical work on witchcraft in Spain for over a century: his experience for thirty years as Inquisitor at Saragossa and as canon of Salamanca insured its prestige. Its importance also lay in the extensive circulation of the translation, the *Reprobación*, the first book on witchcraft printed in the Spanish language (1539).

Cirvelo wrote that the transvection of witches [*jorguinas*] might actually occur or it might be an illusion of the devil in which the witches imagined themselves flying. However, their trance, because it resulted from a diabolical pact, was just as sinful as the act. Witchcraft, while not a *formal* heresy, should always be treated and punished as such.

Cobham, Eleanor, Duchess of Gloucester. The disgrace of Eleanor Cobham, Duchess of Gloucester, in 1441, satisfied many groups of enemies: those resentful of her previous open concubinage with the Duke, those intriguing against Gloucester himself, and those suspicious of the "new learning" of the Duke's entourage. Although their motives were political, all united in accusations of heresy and witchcraft. Gloucester had charged the Archbishop of York and Cardinal Beaufort, Bishop of Winchester, with malfeasance during the minority of King Henry VI. The bishops immediately hit back by attacking Gloucester's wife, charging "that she by sorcery and witchcraft intended to destroy the King, to the intent to advance her husband unto the crown"—Holinshed, *Chronicle*, 1587. With her were accused Canon Thomas Southwell of Westminster, Father John Hun, Roger Bolingbroke, an Oxford priest, and Margery Jourdain (Jourdemain), "the witch of Eye." The charges rested on the making of a waxen image of the King (Hall, *Chronicle*, 1548). Bolingbroke was one of the world's most famous scholars (according to William of Worcester), an astronomer and alchemist, a favorite of Gloucester, and therefore a likely suspect; he was forced to testify against the Duchess and publicly abjure his instruments of magic in St. Paul's churchyard, "that is to say, a chair painted, wherein he was wont to sit, upon the four corners of which chair stood four swords, and upon every sword an image of copper hanging, with many other instruments." He was hanged, beheaded, and quartered. His accomplice, Southwell, charged with saying mortuary masses against the King, died in prison before sentencing. John Hun was pardoned. Margery Jourdain took the blame for fabricating the image and on October 27, 1441 was burned for high treason, not merely for witchcraft (for which offense she had been lightly punished some years previously).

The accusation against the Duchess of securing her husband's affections by love potions, proposed by a secular tribunal, was dropped before the graver charges "of necromancy, of witchcraft or sorcery, of heresy, of treason," by an ecclesiastical court dominated by her husband's clerical enemies. Neither the Duke nor the Duchess could squash the opposition, and Eleanor Cobham admitted most of the charges. On November 9, 1441, she was sentenced to public penance in London and perpetual imprisonment (Stow, *Annales*, 1631).

Coggeshall Witch. By 1700, indictments for witchcraft in England were rare (although Jane Wenham was convicted, but pardoned, as late as 1712). Popular superstition was probably more deep-rooted than court procedures; a relatively late witch hunt, apparently encouraged by the local minister, resulted in the lynch law murder of a very old woman at Coggeshall, Essex, in 1699.

Old Widow Coman was considered a witch. The vicar of Coggeshall, Rev. J. Boys, decided to save her soul. Over a period of time and in the presence of other villagers, the minister badgered her into confessing most of the paraphernalia of witchcraft: she had made a covenant with the Devil, she had sworn not to go inside a church for five years, she could not accurately recite the Lord's Prayer, she had made a waxen image of a hen and stuck pins in it, and she suckled familiars "at her fundament." Moreover, she would not repeat the simple formula of exorcism suggested by Mr. Boys, "In the name of God I renounce the Devil, his imps or agents."

No doubt encouraged by the attitude of their spiritual leader, a mob took direct action against the old woman. Headed by one James Haines, the crowd tried "fleeting" her in a pond; the vicar reported "she always swam like a cork, as hundreds can testify upon oath." As a result of this ducking she caught cold and died. (Fifty-two years later, in 1751, when the "swimming" of old Ruth Osborne brought on her death, the ringleader of the mob was charged with murder and hanged.)

Mr. Boys raised no protest; still intent on proving Mrs. Coman a witch, he had the corpse examined by a midwife "in presence of some sober women." The minister's persistence was rewarded, for the midwife assured him:

She never saw the like in her life! That her fundament was open like a mouse hole, and that in it were two long biggs [teats], out of which, being pressed, issued blood; that they were neither piles nor emrods [hemorrhoids], for she knew both, but excrescences like to biggs with nipples, which seemed as if they had been frequently sucked.

After this "evidence," Mrs. Coman was buried ignominiously on December 27, 1699.

Cologne Witch Trials. The Free City of Cologne, with the exception of two witch hunt epidemics about 1625-26 and 1630-36, had fewer persecutions than other parts of Germany. This relative freedom was due both to enlightenment and to a milder criminal code, in which the City Council reserved to itself the right of arrest. Hearsay and common talk about sabbat meetings and denunciations by accomplices were generally ignored, and witchcraft punished merely by banishment. To be sure, in 1610 the City Council had taken no action against a mob which stoned a witch to death on this selfsame sabbat rumor.

Of the many trials about 1626, that of Catherine Henot was the most famous. The nuns of St. Clare accused her of bewitching them. In an ecclesiastical court, her counsel (her being allowed counsel was in itself unusual) argued that denunciations by demoniacs were immaterial, and the Adjutant Bishop and the Vicar-General returned a Not Guilty verdict! The Archbishop Ferdinand of Cologne, who resided in Bonn, insisted on a new trial before the secular tribunal and had Catherine Henot condemned and burned.

The second outburst came in 1629 and again met with considerable opposition. One possessed woman, Christine Plum, pointed out many witches. When numerous priests discredited her accusations as those of a demented woman, they found themselves included among the witches. The Archbishop, a weak bigot, encouraged the City Council to increase the tempo of the witch hunt and ordered a commission to examine the scope of the *indicia* or indications of witchcraft. Trials were still relatively humane: no confiscation of property was allowed, although the condemned person's family had to pay all the costs; torture was permitted only by order of the court and not (as elsewhere) at the whim of the hangman. The strategic point of the witch trial remained the initial arrest; but, since the City Council limited arrests, Cologne never had the mass terror of such places as Bamberg or Würzburg.

The Jesuits in Cologne bore an honorable part in opposing the witch delusion. For example, they tried to suppress inflammatory books about magic and witchcraft, and, on the other hand, reprinted moderate books by such writers as the Jesuit Adam Tanner, and Jordonaius, a canon of Bonn, who had written a *Disputatio Brevis et Categorica de Proba Stigmatica*, refuting the value of body marks as evidence of witchcraft, propounded by Ostermann in 1629. Friedrich von Spee was transferred from Paderborn to the Jesuit College in Cologne in November of 1631, and in 1633 the third edition of his humanitarian *Cautio Criminalis* was published in Cologne.

The liberal influence of some of the Jesuits and others was stifled when, after the Battle of Leipzig in 1631, a horde of witch-hunting church dignitaries fled with their treasure to the safety of Cologne, including the Archbishop of Mainz, the four Bishops of Bamberg, Würzburg, Worms, and Speyer, as well as the Abbot of Fulda. Driven from their own dominions by the Swedish army and the Protestants, these prelates set to work hunting witches in Cologne. By 1636, conditions had become so scandalous that the Pope was forced to send Cardinal Giretti and Cardinal Albizzi to Cologne to discourage the trials. On this trip, according to Cardinal Albizzi: "A horrible spectacle met their eyes. Outside of the walls of many towns and villages they saw numerous stakes to which poor, wretched women were bound and burned as witches." This papal mission intensified opposition within the city, and a general change in the religious climate reduced the mania, and for many years after 1636 there were no more witch burnings in Cologne. The last execution took place in 1655.

Confessions. The only sure way to prove crimes of witchcraft was confession. In theory, two methods of proof were acceptable: confession by the accused, and denunciation by one witness, who, under the Continental system of inquisitorial law, did not have to confront the witch. If a confessed witch testified that she had seen the accused at the devil's sabbat, this accusation sufficed. It was argued that if testimony of a sabbat sufficed to condemn the person confessing, similar testimony was sufficient to condemn any others allegedly there. However, not every witch went to a sabbat; some made personal and private pacts with the Devil. "There can be no witness of that crime," wrote Sinistrari as late as 1700, "since the devil, visible to the witch, escapes the sight of all beside." Since Satan himself could not be hailed into court, the only witness available was the accused witch herself. It would be illogical

Stereotyped confession from Alsace about 1620 (1).

These three typical pages from three distinct trials illustrate the stereotyped formulas with which suspected witches were questioned at Steinthal, Alsace. Steinthal was a town in the Vosges Mountains under the sovereignty of the Counts of Lützelstein, a younger branch of the House of Wittelsbach. Sometimes the court records are in French, at other times in German. The scribe knew the order and content of the routine questions so well that he did not bother to write the questions, but merely recorded the answers, which he numbered. In this way, all the confessions followed the same general pattern. This is the confession of Catharine, wife of Philip Marshal de Rote.

The complete collection of these court records, from 1607 to 1675, occupying 550 folios, is in Cornell University Library.

to suppose that a witch would confess voluntarily to a crime involving the death penalty. Therefore the witch had to be tortured into confessing. If the accused, aware of the horrors of torture, confessed immediately on arrest, she still had to undergo torture, for it was held that her first confession might be given falsely, just to avoid the agony of torture. Once accused, the victim had to endure torture and inevitably make a confession of guilt. "Common justice demands that a witch should not be condemned to death unless she is convicted of her own confession," said the *Malleus Maleficarum*.

One quite typical confession, preserved in the court records of Neuerberg, Luxembourg, is that made by one Susanna Stein of Wassweiler over a four-month period from August 6 to November 20, 1627. The manuscript at Cornell includes her confession of a visit from the devil, who did with her as he pleased, and later an account of her aerial trip on a broomstick to the devil's dance.

Every witch trial had its confessions, and many typical specimens are scattered through this *Encyclopedia*. In England, the records of confession are generally not so detailed as those in Europe, but a reasonably full confession is that of Joan Williford, executed in 1645, one of the Faversham Witches. The sensational trial of the Lancashire Witches was reported by the clerk of the court, Thomas Potts, and included the prisoners' confessions. Another good illustration is the confessions of the three women convicted at the third Chelms-

Stereotyped confession from Alsace about 1620 (2).

Confession of Claudette, wife of Vincent de Wilderspach, written in the hand of a second scribe, and parallel to the other confessions, with answers in the same set order. The questions probably started with (1) When did the devil first appear to you? (2) How or where did he appear? (3) What was his name? (4) What did he ask you to do? (5) How much money did he give you? (6) When did he appear the second time? (7) What did he ask you to deny? and so on.

ford trial in 1589; these were read at the scaffold.

A detailed description of how confessions were manufactured in Germany during the first half of the seventeenth century is given by Friedrich von Spee, the humane German Jesuit, who had acted as confessor to hundreds of witches burned at the stake:

> The result is the same whether she confesses or not. If she confesses, her guilt is clear: she is executed. All recantation is in vain. If she does not confess, the torture is repeated—twice, thrice, four times. In "exceptional" crimes, the torture is not limited in duration, severity, or frequency. . . . She can never clear herself. The investigating body would feel disgraced if it acquitted a woman; once arrested and in chains, she has to be guilty, by fair means or foul.

In the sixteenth century, Johan Weyer had described the same kind of procedure.

> Thus these wretched women, whose minds have already been disturbed by the delusions and arts of the devil and are now upset by frequent torture, are kept in prolonged squalor and darkness of their dungeons, exposed to the hideous specters of the devil, and constantly dragged out to undergo atrocious torment until they would gladly exchange at any moment this most bitter existence for death, are willing to confess whatever crimes are suggested to them rather than be thrust back into their hideous dungeon amid ever recurring torture. (*De Praestigiis Daemonum*, 1568)

Behind this irrational legality lay the principle that, apart from any other evidence (such as denunciation by accom-

Stereotyped confession from Alsace about 1620 (3).

Confession of Jean Mougena. Inasmuch as the answers are similar to those of the other two confessions, the questions must be the same; but the scribe, who is not the man who recorded the other trials, has similarly omitted the prescribed questions. In these trials, there are usually thirty questions, which cover the expected activities of a witch—intercourse with the devil, attending sabbats, eating little children, and making ointments from corpses.

plices) which would prove guilt, self-confession was a requisite to execution. Even for accusations of *maleficia* causing personal illness or injury, confessions were necessary. Dr. Franz Joel, professor of medicine at the University of Greifswald in 1580, for example, said that even an experienced physician could not distinguish natural and hexed disease, and that the only sure proof was the confession of the witch herself. Limborch, in his *History of the Inquisition* (1692), pointed out how easy it was

> to extort a confession from such who are most innocent by the cruelty of these tortures, with which the [inquisitors] punish without end of measure those whom these suspect, as the very plagues of human nature, even of crimes they have never thought of and of which they

have never heard so much as the description.

Le Sieur Bouvet, the Provost Marshal of the French armies in Italy in the seventeenth century, added that denial of guilt by a prisoner was an especially good reason why torture should be continued.

No country was free from confessions got by duress, not even Great Britain, which, compared to Europe, was relatively civilized. Torture was forbidden by English common law. Yet in England, for example, in 1645 at Bury St. Edmunds, a seventy-year-old parson, Rev. John Lowes, was forced to keep on running around a room "several days and nights together, till he was weary of his life and was scarce sensible of what he said or did." [See Matthew Hopkins.] In the same year at Bodmin, Cornwall, Anne Jefferies was starved, by order of the court; and in the next year at York, Mary Midgely was beaten until she confessed. In Scotland in 1632, at Commer, the minister and a number of other men took the law into their own hands. They dragged several accused of witchcraft into a private house and

> most cruelly and barbarously tortured the women by waking, hanging them up by the thumbs, burning the soles of their feet at the fire, drawing of others at horse tails, and bringing of them with widdies [halters] about the neck and feet and carrying them so along on horseback to prison, whereby and by other tortures one of them hath become distracted, another by cruelty is departed this life, and all of them have confessed whatever they were pleased to demand of them.

Similarly, the series of trials at North Berwick, Scotland, was set in motion by private torture of his servant by David Seaton in 1590. At the Salem witch trials, John Proctor protested from prison how Martha Carrier's two young sons "would not confess anything till they tied them neck and heels till the blood was ready to come out of their noses. And 'tis credibly believed and reported this was the occasion of making them confess that [which] they never did."

For northern France, the trial of Thomas Looten in 1659 provides a detailed account of the typical means to extort a confession. Another record from northeast France, likewise taken from official court records, is that of Father Dominic Gordel, convicted by his own confession, and burned at St.-Dié in Lorraine in 1631.

Confessions of witchcraft are all false, for they admit to an impossible crime. Just as, after every publicized murder today, several persons surrender to the police and urge their own guilt, so inevitably some of the confessed witches believed their own confessions. So one witch confessed to the theft and murder of a baby—the baby all the time safe with her mother. Nevertheless, the witch was hanged, because she had committed perjury!—Limborch, quoting "Ferrerius." A similar charge involved a Mrs. Kendal at Cambridge, Massachu-

setts, in 1652; only later did the parents reveal the child had died because of neglect by its nurse [see Witchcraft in United States]. Isobel Gowdie's startling confession in 1661 was given quite voluntarily: "I have done so many evil deeds, especially killing of men . . . I deserve to be riven upon iron harrows, and worse if it could be devised." Major John Weir at seventy persisted in a confession which brought about his death. And Agnes Sampson persisted in making a confession to King James, though he thought she was a liar [see North Berwick Witches].

Another illustration of a prisoner's maintaining his confession, even after his conviction and, since this was in England, when no torture would result from recanting, occurred in the report of five men appointed to watch Giles Fenderlyn on the night preceding his execution. The men heard a noise in the prison, and one Robert Todd asked the condemned man what the matter was. He said "he was again tormented" by the devil coming to him as an imp. The men replied they were "all rational men, and [could not] discern anything." Then came this further record:

> The said Giles answered, "But although you see nothing, I am certain I feel it." And did at that instant affirm that he had a familiar come to him. Whereupon the said Robert Todd asked him if he was in his right wits and whether he was sensible what he said or no—"It may be want of rest may beget a distemper in your brain, or the guilt of your own conscience will not suffer you to rest?" Whereupon the said Giles replied: "No, I am in my right wits, and so sensible what I do and what I say, as ever I was in my life!" (*The Trial and Examination of Mrs. Joan Peterson*, 1652)

In France and Germany, confessed witches could not retract their testimony for several practical reasons. If they recanted during the court procedure, they were at once returned to the torture chamber and tortured twice: once, to purge themselves of their retraction, and again to produce a "true" confession, confirming their original admission. If they denied their confession on the way to execution, they were not mercifully strangled before burning, but were burned alive.

In 1460 at Arras, the Inquisition charged several prominent people with witchcraft and finally secured confessions. After sentencing them, the inquisitor read aloud their confessions of attendance at the sabbat, and the prisoners agreed they were true. Then the prisoners were handed over to the secular court for execution. At once they cried they had been promised a light pilgrimage in return for a confession, and death if they denied witchcraft. They firmly maintained they had never been to the sabbat and were no witches. Nevertheless, they were all burned alive, without strangulation, shrieking their innocence to the end [see Arras Witches].

In spite of the dangers of denying the confession, some condemned persons managed to leave word of their innocence. In England, this was somewhat easier. George Sinclair, in *Satan's Invisible World Discovered* (1685), for example, reported how a condemned witch on her way to the scaffold spoke to the crowds who had come to watch her execution:

> Now all you that see me this day, know that I am now to die as a witch by my own confession. And I free all men, especially the ministers and magistrates, of the guilt of my blood; I take it wholly upon myself, my blood be upon my own head. And, as I must make answer to the God of heaven presently, I declare I am as free of witchcraft as any child, but, being delated [accused] by a malicious woman, and put in prison under the name of a witch, disowned by my husband and friends, and seeing no ground of hope of my coming out of prison, or ever coming in credit again, through the temptation of the devil I made up that confession on purpose to destroy my own life, being weary of it, and choosing rather to die than live.

Sinclair gave another example told him by Sir George Mackenzie, Lord Advocate to King Charles II.

He went to examine some women who witches

had confessed, and . . . one of them who was a silly creature [simple person] told him, "under secrecy, that she had not confessed because she was guilty, but, being a poor creature who wrought for her meat, and being defamed for a witch, she knew she would starve, for no person thereafter would either give her meat or lodgings, and that all men would beat her, and hound dogs at her, and that therefore she desired to be out of the world." Whereupon she wept most bitterly, and, upon her knees, called God to witness to what she said.

The Reverend Michael Stapirius in his *Brillentractat,* known only from extracts preserved by Löher, gave examples of forced confessions in Westphalia during the early seventeenth century. After enduring torture twice, a suspect confessed under the third application; just before being thrown into the flames, he cried out, "All that I have confessed is but a network of lies. By subjecting me to this insufferable torture you have forced me to perjure myself." Another woman told the minister she feared her confession would bring her eternal damnation: "I never dreamed that by means of the torture a person could be brought to the point of telling such lies as I have told. I am not a witch, and I have never seen the devil, and still I had to plead guilty myself and denounce others. I beseech you, for God's sake, help me to be saved!"

One further example from Germany is the letter of Burgomaster Johannes Junius, which miraculously has been preserved. Written under great difficulty and intended solely for the eyes of his beloved daughter, the letter from the aged magistrate said: "Now, my dear child, here you have all my acts and confession, for which I must die. And it is all sheer lies and invention, so help me God. For all this I was forced to say through dread of torture beyond what I had already endured." The correspondence between Rebecca Lemp and her husband is equally poignant.

When the Parlement of Normandy in 1670 protested King Louis' reduction of the original death sentence on twelve witches convicted at Rouen, the members argued that the uniformity of the confessions was proof positive of the reality of witchcraft, and consequently of the guilt of the accused:

. . . with so much agreement and conformity between the different cases, that the most ignorant persons convicted of this crime have spoken to the same circumstances, and in nearly the same words, as the most celebrated authors who have written about it. All of which may be easily proved to your majesty's satisfaction by the records of various trials before your parlements.

But the truth is just the opposite. These *ja* confessions agree because they had to conform to the stereotyped idea of witchcraft built up by theologians, inquisitors, lawyers, and judges. A glance at the manner of interrogating witches will clarify this point. The accused were asked questions, answers to which would prove their guilt. In the procès-verbal or court record which reported the questioning, the questions and answers often appear in parallel columns, each list consecutively numbered, as in the illustration of the examination of Catherine Bücher at Gross-Mühlingen (Anhalt-Bernburg) in 1689. Usually the questions did not exceed three dozen; this interrogation, however, shows questions 130 through 133, the questions being in the left-hand column and Catherine Bücher's replies in the right (see p. 177). Interesting too is the confession, made under torture, of Nicholaus Weitlufft in 1650 at Swabian Gmünd, thirty miles east of Stuttgart, a Catholic free city of the Empire. Weitlufft was accused of witchcraft by a beggar boy, Zacherlen. The scribe has not written down the real names of those whom Weitlufft named as his accomplices, but has used Latin pseudonyms. This substitution may have resulted from Weitlufft's implicating court officials, friends of the judges or men present during the torture. The records of this trial do not indicate Weitlufft's fate, but, since he confessed, there can be no doubt of his death.

Sometimes the questions were written by the scribe in advance of the examination, and the accused's replies inserted during the actual torture. A very famous late trial, that of Sister Maria Renata Sänger, subprioress of the Premonstratensian convent of Unter-Zell, Würzburg, 1749, illustrates this aspect. Here eleven questions have been written on the right side of the page, and the left side left blank. The page is headed with the Jesuit initials: O.A.M.D.G. (*Ad majorem Dei gloriam*) and B.V.I.H.

In other European records, only the numbered replies were recorded and the questions omitted, implying that the court had a set prepared list which was so well known to the investigators and scribes that it could be omitted. One such list of obligatory questions was that used by the judges at Colmar in Alsace, year after year throughout the three centuries of the witch mania. It was headed:

QUESTIONS TO BE ASKED OF A WITCH

1. How long have you been a witch?
2. Why did you become a witch?
3. How did you become a witch, and what happened on that occasion?
4. Who is the one you chose to be your incubus [*compagnon*]? What was his name?
5. What was the name of your master among the evil demons?
6. What was the oath you were forced to render him?
7. How did you make this oath, and what were its conditions?
8. What finger were you forced to raise? Where did you consummate your union with your incubus?
9. What demons and what other humans participated [at the sabbat]?
10. What food did you eat there?
11. How was the sabbat banquet arranged?
12. Were you seated at the banquet?
13. What music was played there, and what dances did you dance?
14. What did your incubus give you for your intercourse?
15. What devil's mark did your incubus make on your body?
16. What injury have you done to such and such a person, and how did you do it?
17. Why did you inflict this injury?
18. How can you relieve this injury?

19. What herbs or what other methods can you use to cure these injuries?
20. Who are the children on whom you have cast a spell? And why have you done it?
21. What animals have you bewitched to sickness or death, and why did you commit such acts?
22. Who are your accomplices in evil?
23. Why does the devil give you blows in the night?
24. What is the ointment with which you rub your broomstick made of?
25. How are you able to fly through the air? What magic words do you utter then?
26. What tempests have you raised, and who helped you to produce them?
27. What [plagues of] vermin and caterpillars have you created?
28. What do you make these pernicious creatures out of and how do you do it?
29. Has the devil assigned a limit to the duration of your evil-doing?

When it is remembered that the accused had to answer these questions, that refusal to answer was taciturnity which necessitated still harsher torture, that the judges or other court officials would prompt the accused's memory, there is no mystery about the uniformity of confessions.

The same procedure was followed in England. Matthew Hopkins, for example, in his *Discovery of Witches*, gave leading questions (which he denied using):

Q. You have four imps, have you not?
A. She answers affirmatively, "Yes."
Q. Are not their names so and so?
A. "Yes," saith she.
Q. Did you not send an imp to kill my child?
A. "Yes," saith she.

Still other records show, not the answers of the accused, but merely the word *affirmat* [he admits it]—there is no record of the questions to which the affirmative answers were given. In the illustration of the examination of Agnes Brusse of Brandshagen, widow of Michel Hooge, at Treptow, Pomerania, in 1679, the answers run from 35 through 66. [See illustration on page 502.]

At the conclusion of the trial, after the accused had been found Guilty, the scribe would write the *relatio*, a kind of official memorandum or press release of the entire procès, including the victim's confession, written in the first person as if dictated by the witch herself. This was the standard procedure, even when the witch had responded to the prepared questions only in monosyllables or by nodding the head, probably under torture. Before her death, the accused had to sign the full confession which had been written out for her.

At the burning, under the standard German code of the Emperor Charles (Article 60 of the *Carolina*), the sentences of the judges and the confessions of the condemned were always publicly read. In this way, the theory of witchcraft was taught the mass of the people by those in authority who had themselves propagated it; impressionable children especially would carry these vivid moments with them for the rest of their lives and come to believe in witchcraft without any doubting. For example, at Utrecht, on August 1, 1595, Volkart Dirxen and his daughter, after severe torture, confessed to being werewolves and to killing cattle. The man's three sons, aged eight to fourteen, were sentenced to watch the burning, after which they were to be flogged until the blood flowed.

In fact, uniform confessions, far from proving witchcraft, disprove it.

That there were always some who doubted confessions is clear from the fulminations of the demonologists. Nicholas Jacquier's *Flagellum* (1458) advised judges to examine accusations given under torture, lest they had resulted from terror. In *De Lamiis* (1489), Ulrich Molitor took pains to convince the Archduke Sigismund of Austria that confessions under torture were admissible. Clever lawyers soon found a *rationale* to lull such doubts, and Vignati, for example, in 1468 was already pointing out that confessions under torture must be subsequently confirmed without torture!

As the cruelties increased, apologists felt more and more impelled to silence those who questioned the validity of the confessions. The *Malleus Maleficarum* suggested

A specimen page from the official records showing the final version, neatly and carefully written, of a confession of witchcraft in 1630 at Steinthal, Alsace. "Voluntarily" simply means confession under the first degree of torture (binding and racking). The scribe wrote this confession probably from notes taken during the actual interrogation, and omitted the questions, so that the confession might read continuously.

asking accused persons whether they believe "that there are such things as witches. . . . If they deny it, they must be questioned as follows: 'Then are they innocently condemned when they are burned?' And he or she must answer." Those who did not climb on the bandwagon of hysteria, even though they might be firm believers in witchcraft, were in fact witch lovers, and would soon find themselves accused as accomplices. "He who opposes the extermination of the witches with one single word can not expect to remain unscathed," said Heinrich von Schultheis, a merciless witch hunter. He exposed his

own personal corruption and that of the whole system when he complained: "The devil, the witches and their defenders are the greatest enemies that the commissioners of the Inquisition have. The fact that they say nothing that is good but only things that are bad about me and all inquisitors, we shall not discuss now."

Conjuration: see Divination.

Connecticut Witches. Witchcraft in Connecticut, as in America generally, was scattered and limited both in scope and time, compared to the extent and depth of the delusion in Europe. The Puritans, who had not found the fullest freedom in England to put their religious and political beliefs into practice, suppressed the more rigorously any heresy in New England, as both contrary to God and their own political theocracy. Belief in witches was brought with the early settlers as part of their emotional background, and theory and practice in New England derive from the stricter Protestant writers such as William Perkins and Matthew Hopkins.

From May 26, 1647, when Alse Young was hanged, the first execution for witchcraft in New England, there was a slow trickle of trials. Mary Johnson of Wethersfield was indicted for familiarity with the Devil and condemned "chiefly upon her own confession. . . . She said the devil appeared to her, lay with her, and cleared her hearth of ashes, and hunted hogs out of the corn. 'She could not forbear laughing,' she said, 'to see how he seized them about'"—Hutchinson, *Historical Essay*, 1718. In 1645 and 1650 at Springfield, several people were suspected of witchcraft. One of these, Mary Parsons, confessed after a long examination; she was tried in Boston on May 13, 1651, and sentenced to death, not so much for "divers devilish practices by witchcraft," but for murder of her child. She was reprieved. In the same year Goodwife Bassett was convicted at Stratford. Two alleged witches were executed in New Haven, the last in 1653. In 1658, Elizabeth Garlick of Easthampton, Long Island, was tried in Connecticut, but she was acquitted. In 1669 Katherine Harrison of Wethersfield was imprisoned on suspicion of witchcraft: "Not having the fear of God before thine eyes [thou] hast had familiarity with Sathan, the grand enemy of God and mankind." The jury at Hartford sentenced her to death, but the court overruled it and banished her "for her own safety." [See New York Witches.] And in 1697 Winifred Benham and her daughter, although excommunicated, were acquitted; their accusers were "some children that pretended to the spectral sight." (Calef)

In 1662 at Hartford, young Ann Cole was taken with fits, during which she spoke gibberish and some Dutch, a language not known to her, although some of the neighbors were Dutch-speaking. "Several worthy persons" took down her ravings, which, when interpreted, seemed to implicate a Dutch girl and a "lewd and ignorant woman," Mother Greensmith, already in jail on suspicion of witchcraft. The powerful family influence of Governor Stuyvesant of New Amsterdam [New York] acquitted the Dutch girl; but Mother Greensmith was confronted with the translation and confessed she "had had familiarity with the devil." Increase Mather continued:

> She likewise declared that the devil first appeared to her in the form of a deer or fawn, skipping about her, wherewith she was not much affrighted, and that by degrees he became very familiar, and at last would talk with her. Moreover, she said that the devil had frequently the carnal knowledge of her body. And that the witches had meetings at a place not far from her house; and that some appeared in one shape, and others in another; and one came flying amongst them in the shape of a crow.

On this confession she was executed, along with her husband, although he maintained his innocence. After the hangings, Ann Cole "was restored to health, and has continued well for many years."

Another notable witch trial occurred in Groton in 1671, and again it involved a disturbed adolescent. Sixteen-year-old Elizabeth Knap

was taken after a very strange manner, sometimes weeping, sometimes laughing, sometimes roaring hideously, with violent motions and agitations of her body . . . her tongue for many hours together was drawn like a semi-circle up to the roof of her mouth, not to be removed, though some tried with their fingers to do it. Six men were scarce able to hold her in some of her fits, but she would skip about the house yelling and looking with a most frightful aspect.

Later, without apparently using her lips or tongue, she made strange sounds, reviling the minister. "She cried out in some of her fits, that a woman (one of her neighbors) appeared to her, and was the cause of her affliction." The woman accused, however, was very highly respected and was able to gather public support for her integrity. Elizabeth Knap recovered and admitted that she had been troubled by the Devil himself, who had appeared to her in the shape of a good person. Rev. Samuel Willard, who figured in the Salem trials, was at this time the pastor of Groton and noted the case of possession (which Increase Mather printed in his *Magnalia Christi Americana*). Willard's experience with Elizabeth may have developed his skepticism in 1692, for her behavior was very similar to that of Mercy Short and indeed was a model for the Salem girls.

In Connecticut, all together there were nine certain hangings for witchcraft, from 1647 to 1662, and two probable ones (nine women and two men).

Corpse-Lifting: see Ointment, Killing.

Cory, Giles. Of all the accused at the Salem witch trials, the most courageous was eighty-year-old Giles Cory. He was slowly pressed to death over a period of two days by weights piled on his body. By English law, an accused had to place himself "on God and the country," that is, plead Guilty or Not Guilty. For "standing mute," the penalty was *peine forte et dure*—slow crushing with heavier and heavier iron weights until the naked victim agreed to plead, or died. No food was allowed, "save

Pressing to death, the punishment inflicted on Giles Cory at Salem in 1692 for refusing to plead. From Richard Verstegen, *Theatrum Crudelitatum Haereticorum* (1587).

only on the first day, three morsels of the worst bread, and on the second day, three draughts of standing water that should be nearest to the prison door"—Sir William Blackstone. Robert Calef, a contemporary, relates how as Cory was dying, on Monday, September 19, 1692, in the open field beside the jail in Salem town, "in pressing, his tongue being pressed out of his mouth, the sheriff with his cane forced it in again."

The punishment was actually illegal, for while *peine forte et dure* was not abolished in England until 1827, it was disallowed in Massachusetts by the 1641 Body of Liberties, No. 46: "For bodily punishments we allow amongst us none that are inhumane, barbarous, or cruel."

How much repugnance and opposition to the witchcraft delusion was aroused by this gruesome spectacle cannot be discovered now. But some questioning there must have been, for the next day, in an obvious attempt to show the righteousness of his death by the theory "do unto others as you shall be done by," the Putnam family (the chief *provocateurs* in the witchcraft trials) circulated a fantastic story. As on other occasions in the narrative of Salem, the thought arises of a mastermind (Mrs. Ann Putnam) pulling the strings and devising strategy. The story had a grain of validity in that Cory, sixteen years previously, had been accused of beating a man to death; but few remembered this, for Judge Sewall clearly said, " 'Twas not remembered till Ann Putnam was told of it by said Cory's

specter the Sabbath night [18th], before the execution [19th]."

Of all the nightmare evidence offered at Salem, this story is possibly the most outrageous. It is the great lie of Salem. Thomas Putnam, Ann's father, deposed:

Last night, my daughter Ann was grievously tormented by witches, threatening that she should be pressed to death before Giles Cory; but through the goodness of a gracious God, she had, at last, a little respite. Whereupon there appeared unto her (she said) a man in a winding sheet who told her that Giles Cory had murdered him by pressing him to death with his feet; but that the devil then appeared unto him [Cory] and covenanted with him and promised him that he should not be hanged. The apparition said God hardened his heart that he should not hearken to the advice of the court, and so die an easy death; because, as it said, it must be done to him as he had done to me. The apparition also said that Giles Cory was carried to the court for this and that the jury had found the murder; and that her father knew the man and the thing was done before she was born.

Some critics have ascribed sordid motives to the old man's refusal to plead, contending that a felon's property was confiscated and not inheritable. According to this view (first propounded in 1840), Giles remained mute just to bequeath his property to his heirs. This is contrary to facts: in America property was not confiscated. Condemned and executed witches (John Proctor, for one) made wills and passed on their property. Furthermore, the Statute of 1604 of King James, under which the Court of Oyer and Terminer presumably acted, specifically reserved "to the heir and successor of every such person his or their titles of inheritance, succession, and other rights, as though no such attainder of the ancestor or predecessor had been made."

Giles Cory saw the court was bound by spectral evidence, that it disregarded the laws applicable to all other offenses, and that he could never obtain a fair hearing; so he showed his contempt of it. How can one prove he is not a witch, when confronted by *reported* testimony? By refusing to plead, although he sacrificed himself, he drew increased attention to this evil.

Costs of Witch Trials. All costs of witch trials in France, Germany, and Scotland were paid by the estate of the condemned witch or by his relatives; or, in some few instances where the victim was penniless, by the landlord or citizens of the town. Witch hunting was self-sustaining and became a major trade, employing many people, all battening on the savings of the victims. Witches, especially in Germany, were by no means all poor, and often the wealthiest were the first to be accused. Their property was disbursed to clergymen, judges, physicians, scribes, court attendants, torturers, guards, messengers—even to the laborers who cut the wood for the burning and erected the scaffolds. Less directly, innkeepers and taverners profited by the crowds who came to watch the executions. As well as providing a livelihood for those connected with the courts, the property of the condemned witch provided booty for whatever local authority had jurisdiction. After paying the expenses of the trial, the property of a witch was confiscated by the autonomous town, the local nobleman, the king, the bishop, or the Inquisition, depending on the status of the town or village in which the victim had resided; sometimes several courts, secular and ecclesiastical, shared the loot. In England, under Elizabeth only, a witch's property was confis-

cated by the Crown with a sentence of life imprisonment—not with execution. With such an easy source of funds, it is not strange that the leaders of Germany and France were for a long time content to let witch persecutions continue.

Here are the costs of some typical trials from various regions. In most cases a family of moderate income would be permanently impoverished.

1. Records of witch trials in the seventeenth century at Offenberg, in Baden, a free city of the Roman Empire, furnish interesting sidelights on costs of trials. In 1629, Councilor Philipp Beck, whose wife had been burned as a witch, was fined for contempt of the *Rath* [parliament] when he disputed the costs of her trial as an attack on his property. Everything had to be paid for. Thus, the two attendants guarding an accused each received a weekly wage of ten batzen and seven measures of wine. An executioner was paid ten batzen merely for transporting a prisoner from one jail to another. After every court session the judges enjoyed a banquet, for which they were allowed four batzen a head and the messengers two batzen. In the three days between their sentencing and execution, three woman burned alive at Appenweier on June 22, 1595, had to pay:

	[Florin	Batzen	Pfennig]
For the execu-tioner	14	7	10
For the enter-tainment and banquet of the judges, priests, and advocate	32	6	3
For maintenance of the prison-ers and their guards	33	6	6

Often the costs of the trial were so heavy that virtually all the goods and property of the accused were used up, even before confiscation by the appropriate authorities. For example, on October 8, 1608, the trial of Frau Dietrich had been delayed for lack of evidence; by January 17, 1609, her hus-

REGLEMENT.

Fixed tariff of fees for torture charged by the Prince-Archbishop of Cologne (1757). All the costs of conducting the trial and the torture had to be paid by the prisoner or his relations, after his execution. From Cornell University Library.

band demanded dismissal of the accusation because of the accumulated court costs. Again, the property of the Pabst family was sold by auction in February, 1612, to pay for the costs of the witch trial of Frau Pabst, which had begun on October 15, 1608, and had dragged on for lack of evidence until she died in an insane asylum in April, 1611. Costs had kept mounting each day over the three years she was admittedly wrongfully imprisoned.

2. In the trials in Montebéliard in Franche-Comté, then still part of the Roman Empire, sometimes the property of the condemned was confiscated, at other times only the payment of court costs was demanded. Thus, in 1652, Catherine Jeannot had to pay 480 francs, 3 gros in costs; Pierre Tournier-Faucillier and his wife in 1655 were charged 437 francs, 1 gros, 1 blanc each. Trials in this county rarely amounted to much less than 500 francs, because of the high fees paid to everybody concerned, from the day of arrest to the day of execution. Every act and service performed, for whatever purpose, was charged to the victim. Even after the burning, all the officials had a banquet paid for by the estate of the dead witch. For example, at the execution of Adrienne d'Heur, on September 11, 1646, David Morlot, an innkeeper, was paid 25 francs for furnishing breakfast to the provost, the scribe, the mayor, the four sergeants, and the jailer. François Parau also provided breakfast and dinner, apparently for the burghers and notables who watched the execution, at a charge of 15 francs, 9 gros. Apart from the cost of these meals, the burning, and the executioner's fees, the expenses just for honorariums and wages amounted to 26 francs:

	[Francs	Gros]
To the ministers, two at 1 franc, 8 gros each	3	4
Attorney	1	8
Mayor	1	8
Nine burghers and four notables	13	0
Scribe	1	0
Two assessors and "Jacob" at 9 gros each	2	3
Four sergeants	3	0

3. A complete expense account from Toul, near Nancy, in 1597 itemized the costs for the imprisonment of Cathin Joyeuse, also known as the Mayoress Etienne, which, for less than one month, amounted to 104 francs. Costs for the remainder of her jailing and her execution would appear in a second bill.

	[Francs	Gros]
For her bread from November 14, 1597, to December 11, 1597, when she was handed over to the mayor	2	11
For meat, butter, salt, fish, and other items furnished her during her imprisonment	4	10
For wine [including wine for the guards]	13	0
For straw	0	6
For carrying her belongings when she changed prisons	0	2
For him who conducted the trial	20	0
For the attorney	10	0
For the scribe	10	0
For the sergeants	10	0
Additional for other expenses made by the sergeants who guarded the said Cathin from the announcement of the sentence to torture to the time of that torture	3	6
For inspecting the court record	4	0
For the woman who shaved her	1	0
For the torturer	20	0
For the expenses of the man who had to go to Nancy to fetch the said torturer	4	4

4. The high cost of burning was revealed at the execution of two Aberdeen witches, Janet Wishart and Isabel Crocker, in February, 1596:

Item:	[Shillings	Pence]
For 20 loads of peat to burn them	40	0
For a boll [six bushels] of coal	24	0

Item:	[Shillings	Pence]
For 4 tar barrels	26	8
For fir and iron barrels	16	8
For a stake and dressing of it	16	0
For four fathoms [24 feet] of tows [hangman's rope]	4	0
For carrying the peat, coals, and barrels to the hill	8	4
To one justice for their execution	13	4

5. Another illustration of the cost of burning a witch comes from Kirkcaldy in 1636, when on November 19, William Coke and Alison Dick, his wife, were killed for witchcraft. At Kirkcaldy, witches were placed in tarred barrels to facilitate their burning, and apparently dressed in coats of rough hemp material specially made for their execution. The costs of this execution were shared by the town council and the kirk.

	[Pounds	Shil- lings	Pence]
For ten loads of coal, to burn them, 5 marks or	3	6	8
For a tar barrel		14	0
For tows [hangman's rope]		6	0
For hurden [hemp fabric] to be jumps [short coats] for them	3	10	0
For making of them		8	0
For one to go to Finmouth for the laird to sit upon their assize as judge		6	0
For the executioner for his pains	8	14	0
For his expenses here		16	4

6. The sixth example concerns a condemned witch living as a tenant on a big estate in Scotland in the mid-seventeenth century. The goods of the accused were confiscated and appraised and applied to the total cost of her trial; the balance was paid by the owner of the estate on which she had her cottage. (Notice the reference to John Kincaid who received six pounds Scots for Pricking.) The following sums are for the execution of Margaret Dunhome [also spelled Dinham, Dollmoune] at Burncastle in 1649, from the voucher of the factor or overseer of the estate (inasmuch as the proprietor was a minor). The currency is Scots pounds, valued about one-sixth of the English pound. The bill was padded by £4, the actual total being £88. 14s. 0d. instead of the amount claimed.

More [money due] for Margaret Dunhome, the time she was in prison and was put to death: £65. 14s. 0d.

Count given out by Alexander Louddon in Lylstown, in the year of God 1649 years, for Margaret Dunhome in Burncastell:

	[Pounds	Shil- lings]
Item: in the first [place], to William Currie and Andrew Gray for the watching of her the space of 30 days, each day 30 shillings	45	0
Item: more to John Kincaid for brodding [pricking] of her	6	0
More for meat and drink and wine to him and his man	4	0
More for cloth to her	3	0
More for two tarred trees [gallow stakes]		40
Item: more for two trees and the making of them, to the workmen	3	0
Item: to the hangman in Haddington, and fetching of him, three dollars for his expense, is	4	14
Item: more for meat and drink and wine for his entertainment	3	0
Item: more for a man and two horses, for the fetching of him, and taking of him home again		40

Tariff for Torture, 1757,

Approved by the Archbishopric of Cologne

Even though the Archbishopric of Cologne has previously endowed the high executioner with a permanent yearly income of eighty reichsthaler, twenty albus, twelve malder of grain, and four cords of wood, nevertheless it has turned out that during and after performing executions and other matters connected with them, so many unsubstantiated and exaggerated claims for extra expenses have been made that it has become very costly for the chief court of the Elector Archbishop. Therefore, the archbishopric is compelled, in order to contain these demands, to set up the following rules in which every single operation has been given its due charge, which is forthwith promulgated.

PRICE LIST

	Reichsthaler	Albus
1. For tearing apart and quartering by four horses	5	26
2. For quartering	4	0
3. For the necessary rope for that purpose	1	0
4. For hanging the four quarters in four corners, the necessary rope, nails, chains, and the transport included	5	26
5. For beheading and burning, everything included	5	26
6. For the necessary rope for this procedure, and for preparing and igniting the stake	2	0
7. For strangling and burning	4	0
8. For rope and for preparing and igniting the stake	2	0
9. For burning alive	4	0
10. For rope and for preparing and igniting the stake	2	0
11. For breaking alive on the wheel	4	0
12. For rope and chains for this procedure	2	0
13. For setting up the body which is tied to the wheel	2	52
14. For beheading only	2	52
15. For the necessary rope for this purpose, and for cloth to cover the face	1	0
16. For making a hole and disposing of the corpse	1	26
17. For beheading and tying the body on the wheel	4	0
18. For the necessary rope and chains, together with the cloth	2	0
19. For cutting off a hand or several fingers and for beheading, all together	3	26
20. The same: in addition, for burning with a hot iron	1	26

	Reichsthaler	Albus
21. For the necessary rope and cloth	1	26
22. For beheading and sticking the head on a pole	3	26
23. For the necessary rope and cloth	1	26
24. For beheading and tying the body on the wheel and for sticking the head on a pole, all together	5	0
25. For the necessary rope, chains, and cloth	2	0
26. For hanging	2	52
27. For the necessary rope, nails, and chain needed for that purpose	1	26
28. Before the actual execution starts, for squeezing the delinquent with red-hot tongs, apart from the above-mentioned fee for hanging, for every application	0	26
29. For cutting out the tongue entirely, or part of it, and afterwards for burning the mouth with a red-hot iron	5	0
30. For this procedure, the usual rope, tongs, and knife	2	0
31. For nailing to the gallows a cut-off tongue or a chopped-off hand	1	26
32. For one who has hanged himself, or drowned himself, or otherwise taken his own life: to take down, remove, and dig a hole to dispose of the corpse	2	0
33. For exiling a person from the city or country	0	52
34. For flogging in jail, including the rods	1	0
35. For thrashing	0	52
36. For putting in the pillory	0	52
37. For putting in the pillory, and for whipping, including the rope and the rods	1	26
38. For putting in the pillory, branding, and whipping, including coals, rope, and rods, also the branding ointment	2	0
39. For inspecting a prisoner after he has been branded	0	20
40. For putting the ladder to the gallows, regardless whether one or several are hanged on the same day	2	0

Concerning torture

	Reichsthaler	Albus
41. For terrorizing by showing the instruments of torture	1	0
42. For the first degree of torture	1	26
43. For arranging and crushing the thumb for this degree	0	26

	Reichsthaler	Albus
44. For the second degree of torture, including setting the limbs afterward, and for salve which is used	2	26
45. Should, however, a person be tortured in both degrees of torture, the executioner is to get for both degrees performed at the same time, setting the limbs afterward and for use of the salve, for all this he should be paid	6	0
46. For travel and daily expenses for every day, exclusive, however, of the days of execution or torture, regardless whether on these days one or several criminals are punished	0	48
47. For daily food	1	26
48. For each helper	0	39
49. For hiring a horse, together with fodder and stabling, the daily fee	1	16

50. If a torture or execution takes place in Cologne, the executioner shall receive for this procedure the aforementioned execution fees, without any addition of other extra expenses, such as travel, daily expenses, food, horse hay and fodder; and he has to be satisfied with the above-mentioned execution fee.

51. When he performs executions in Melaten and Deutz, he receives extra expenses for hay for his horse, and nothing else.

52. Since items 16, 32, and 40 of the present rules fall within the province of the weapons master, therefore the weapons master should receive the respective fees.

53. Should the executioner perform functions for those who are vassals or sub-vassals of the archbishopric, he should receive one third more than before specified, the reason being that he enjoys his yearly investiture without any emolument from the aforesaid vassals.

54. Only the executioner and no stranger shall be employed by the vassals or sub-vassals for whatever executions have to be done.

55. Because there have been many complaints that at an execution where an official of the archbishopric presides, the executioner, either in addition to accepting the fees, or instead of accepting them, dared to demand a certain sum of money, and since this demand is regarded as an abuse, it is once and for all forbidden. Therefore, herewith we order that every official of the archbishopric keep strictly to the above-mentioned rules and pay the executioners only the stipulated fees and nothing else, any time there is an execution; and they are asked to submit afterward their accounts with all their vouchers to the treasury of the archbishop.

Given at Bonn, January 15, 1757. L.S.

| | Shil- |
| [Pounds | lings] |

More to her for meat and drink, each day, 4 shillings the space of 30 days, is	6	0
Item: more to the two officers for their fee, each day 6 shillings eight pence, is	10	0

Summa is 4 score 12 pounds, 14 shillings

Ghilbert Lauder
(formerly Lauder Bilzaurs)

Taken of this above written sum, 27 pounds Scots, which the said former Margaret Dunhome had of her own:

£92. 14s. 0d.
£27. 0s. 0d.
£65. 14s. 0d.

7. In comparison, the bills presented at the Salem trials in 1692 seem insignificant, but to farmers with very little ready cash the price was proportionately heavy. Since the prisoners were not officially tortured, this item does not appear, but they had to pay for being chained. Fetters for a man accused of witchcraft cost five shillings; for a woman a set of handcuffs and lighter leg fetters (about eight pounds) cost seven shillings and six pence. A typical charge was that for Sarah Parker of Andover, who was imprisoned for seventeen weeks:

To the prison keeper	£2. 8s. 4d.
Court charges	£1. 10s. 4d.
Expenses attending trials	£1. 4s. 0d.

Even when the accused had been declared innocent, they were done the additional injury of being kept in jail until they paid the expenses of their unlawful incarceration. Margaret Jacobs had to be freed by the generosity of a stranger. Tituba was technically freed in May, 1693, but, having no money to pay for her imprisonment of thirteen months, was sold for expenses as a slave. To recover the body of Ann Foster, who died in jail, her son had to pay £2. 16s. 0d. before he could give his mother a decent burial. And for Sarah Osborne's corpse, another who died under the rigors of the dungeons, £1. 3s. 5d. had to be paid for its delivery.

Coven. Some recent works on witchcraft have described an extensive organization of witches based on covens or underground cells of witches. Margaret Murray and Pennethorne Hughes, for example, believe that to obtain a true estimate of the witch tradition, the evidence of the trials must be related to "the activities of contemporary people in a comparable cultural state." By this means, Hughes finds four groups of adherents of the cult of witchcraft:

1. The remnant of the believers in the Stone Age religion of the "Horned God," the "little people" who often survived in mountainous areas.

2. Women who cherished the survival of an earlier matriarchal society in Europe.

3. Heretical Catharists, influenced by the mystery religions of the East, who parodied Christianity.

4. Later exploiters of the cult.

Margaret Murray, in particular, introduced the idea of the coven of twelve witches headed by a devil or leader masquerading as such. This speculation, as Kittredge said, "will not stand the test of the most elementary historical criticism. There is not the slightest evidence that [witches] were ever organized at all." Offered in support of the Murray thesis are eighteen examples of the twelve-plus-one coven, from 1567 to 1673, one each in France, Germany, Ireland, and North America (!), five in England, and nine in Scotland. The word first appeared in 1662, two centuries after the appearance of witchcraft, when Isobel Gowdie of the Auldearn Witches confessed "there are thirteen persons in each coven."

In 1922, Alex Keiller, "after detailed study of Miss Murray's lists of Scottish and Irish witches designed to evidence the prevalence of covens of thirteen, found in a number of instances the arrangement to be unfounded and the count to be of no value." In 1932, Ewen "checked over the corresponding figures for the alleged covens for

England and found the lady's groups of thirteen had in each case been obtained by an unwarranted omission, addition, or inconcinnous [unsuitable] disposition." Even if the Murray count were accurate, no theory could be based on a mere eighteen instances out of a potential 15,000 covens (estimating, conservatively, about 200,000 witches executed in the entire period of the delusion). It is regrettable that the article on witchcraft in the fourteenth edition of the *Encyclopaedia Britannica* is written by this "authority."

Montague Summers, a true disciple of the classic demonologists, accepted the reality of a coven. In his *Geography of Witchcraft* (1927), for example, Summers referred to Bessie Dunlop, in great distress, meeting a man in Ayrshire, who "was obviously the chief officer of the witches of the district, and was persuading her to join their coven."

The basic cause of these scholars' confusion is the acceptance at face value of the confessions of witches extracted under tor-ture, forced to admit whatever fantasies the minds of the ecclesiastical and lay judges might invent. Inasmuch as witchcraft was viewed as an obscene parody of Christianity, and since a common form of monastic organization was (as Chaucer noted) the "convent" of thirteen (in commemoration of Christ and the apostles), the demonologists finally invented a corresponding "convent" or "coven" of thirteen witches. Such folly is now compounded by writers who claim the existence of present-day covens maintaining an unbroken tradition with Stone Age paganism, and who explain thirteen as the maximum number of people who can dance in a nine-foot circle!

Crouch, Nathaniel. Nathaniel Crouch (?1632-?1728) published the Augustan equivalent of paperbacks, and his series of twelve "penny books" on English history won the praise of Dr. Johnson as "very proper to allure backward readers." Crouch specialized in printing compilations or anthologies, in all, forty-five different works. Said a contemporary publisher, he "prints nothing but what is very useful and very diverting."

Under the pseudonym of "R.B." (Richard Burton), Crouch wrote *The Kingdom of Darkness* (1688), one of the last wild flings of the witchcraft believers, a fantastic mélange of crude stories of witches and devils, to obviate "the common objections and allegations of the Sadducees and atheists of the age, who deny the being of spirits, witches, &c."

Crouch poses as a rational man: It is "beyond the power of all the devils in hell to cause such a transformation . . . since there is a special sort of melancholy which is called lycanthropia, wherein people imagine themselves to be turned into wolves or other beasts." Yet his materials credit every notion made familiar in the witch trials, and then add some, such as the origin of fairy circles [see Demonologists]. The book is illustrated by a number of cuts, and a horrendous frontispiece shows witches in action—making potions from babies, rendering homage to the devil-goat, dancing in a ring, as well as being hanged!

The Four Sorcerers, by Albrecht Dürer.

Frontispiece of Nathaniel Crouch, *The Kingdom of Darkness* (1688), only two copies extant in America. It is the most extreme of all English books accepting the witchcraft mania.

Dalkeith Witch Trial: see Bier Right.

Damnum minatum: see Maleficia.

Darling, Thomas: see Burton Boy.

Darrell, John. In a pamphlet war with Samuel Harsnett, who later became Archbishop of York, John Darrell (about 1562-1602) took the side of exorcism. Darrell is England's one and only exorcist, and his malodorous reputation provoked Canon 72, which in effect prohibited exorcism in the Church of England (1603). Consequently English witchcraft lacks the lurid rites which colored so much of French witchcraft.

Darrell was educated at Cambridge and returned to his home at Mansfield, in Nottinghamshire, to become a free-lance preacher. His first venture at exorcism came in 1586 with hysterical Catherine Wright of Derbyshire; after a day of prayer, at his urging, Catherine accused one Margaret Roper of sending a demon, Middlecub, to possess her. The trick backfired: Catherine admitted she faked her fits and visions, "finding that this made a severe father-in-law more kind." The magistrates threatened Darrell with imprisonment.

Not until ten years had passed did Darrell again venture to dispossess devils, when he achieved notoriety through Thomas Darling, the Burton Boy. The next year, 1597, Darrell was at Clayworth Hall, Leigh, Lancashire, exorcizing seven members of the household of Nicholas Starkie; and, in November, at Nottingham. Here, he attracted attention through his public spectacles exorcizing William Somers. Although invited to preach at St. Mary's Church, Darrell was shortly afterward banned by the Archbishop of York. In 1599, Darrell was questioned at Lambeth Palace, pronounced an impostor, defrocked, and given a year in jail. The rest of his life passed in obscurity.

William Somers, the Boy of Nottingham, disliked being apprenticed to a town musician and ran away. When he found he had to make good the time lost, so that his master would be "glad to get rid of him, he pretended himself sick; and having really got cold in the water, he huffed up his belly." Neighbors immediately suspected possession, and brought copies of the *Witches of Warboys* to compare the symptoms. This pamphlet gave Bill more ideas; now the teen-ager claimed bewitchment "by an old woman that he had met with, because he would not give her a hat band he had found." On November 5, 1597, Darrell, fresh from his exploits at Clayworth Hall, was invited to exorcize the boy. He told Bill how similar he was to the Burton Boy and precisely what form Tommy Darling's hysterics took—gnashing of teeth, writhing so that "their faces stood backward, drawing their mouths away, foaming." Darrell declared the boy suffered for the sins of all Nottingham, and asked for a public fast day. He "desired all the people to refrain from the company of their wives that night, and the next day they would see strange things."

Darrell preached a sermon enumerating fourteen signs of possession, which Bill obligingly demonstrated. "He would speak with his mouth scarce moving; and when they looked, his tongue would seem drawn down his throat." Darrell passed on to the three signs of deliverance, and Bill Somers mimicked them in order—crying, rending, and lying as dead. At the conclusion, the boy appeared recovered, but Darrell hinted at possible recurrences and took up a collection. The next development came when Bill accused thirteen women of bewitching him by demoniacal possession. Some who doubted his story sifted his accusations and caught his deceptions; for example, he did not always have a fit at the approach of every witch. The boy's supporters, however, "had always their excuses ready, that the devil would put in some such appearances of counterfeiting, to save the witches, and make God's work be disbelieved." (Hutchinson)

Darrell's sister-in-law, Mary Cowper, came into the farce and accused as a witch one Alice Freeman, who thought to escape trouble by saying she was pregnant, but Darrell countered that if she was, it was the devil's doing! Her brother, an alderman, had Somers taken to the workhouse, where he told the town council of his deception. Darrell insisted the boy was possessed. In March, 1598, a public inquiry was held, but Bill, scared by a warning that if he was indeed a fraud "he deserved to be hanged," insisted on his possession. Darrell was therefore temporarily vindicated. However, at the trial of the accused witches, Bill Somers confessed his tricks, such as "by working the spittle in his mouth, he foamed till the froth ran down his chin."

Somers and Darrell were examined by the Archbishop of Canterbury and the Bishop of London, two of the Lord Chief Justices, and others. Harsnett, the Bishop's chaplain, described how Bill Somers had "proved" one woman a witch. He knew when she had to appear in court.

> Whereupon, I guessing by the time of Master Darrell's departure, and by the distance of the way, and of the likelihood that she would deny herself to be a witch, said to those that were present by me in one of my fits, about eleven of the clock that Millicent Horsley was in examining and that she denied herself to be a witch.

In spite of the fact that thirty-four of the forty-four witnesses were his friends, Darrell was imprisoned. To Darrell's father-in-law, Robert Cowper, this caused little surprise: "I do verily think and believe in my conscience that William Somers did counterfeit all he did, that he was never possessed, dispossessed, nor repossessed; and that Mr. Darrell dealt very unjustly in all his course."

Yet Darrell had his admirers. Bishop Hall, for example, in his *Invisible World Newly Discovered* (1659), spoke of him as a "goodly and zealous preacher, [who] undertook and, accordingly through the blessing of God upon his faithful devotion, performed these famous ejectments of evil spirits . . . which exercised the press and raised no small envy from the gainsayers." And over a century later, Richard Boulton in his *Complete History* (1715) repeated the story of the Nottingham boy as if it had never been disproved.

Dee, John. John Dee (1527-1608) was such a remarkable man, with so many diverse interests, that any study of the Elizabethan era must contain some reference to "Queen Elizabeth's Merlin." His reputation as a magician has obscured his brilliance. He went to Cambridge University at the age of fifteen, and thereafter, to his death at the age of eighty-one, set as his goal eighteen hours a day study, two hours eating, and four hours sleeping. Most of his seventy-nine works, however, remain in manuscript; one of them, longer than the Bible, was "so dreadful to the printers" they refused to publish it! But he made very sensible proposals. For example, Dee unsuccessfully tried to use his enormous prestige to induce Protestant England to accept the

1582 papal bull on calendar reform (not adopted until 1752). Dee proposed collecting the manuscripts dispersed at the dissolution of the monasteries, anticipating the Historical Manuscripts Commission (1869). He proposed a royal library, anticipating the British Museum (1753). He proposed making copies of important works in the Vatican Library, anticipating the St. Louis University microfilm project (1954). He freely gave his enormous scientific knowledge about navigation (he was a friend of Mercator) to the Arctic explorer, Captain John Davis, anticipating the opening of the Northwest Passage by the *Nautilus* (1958).

John Dee put out many tendrils which justify his inclusion in a study of witchcraft:

1. Although befriended by Queen Elizabeth, he had been imprisoned under Queen Mary as "a companion of the hellhounds, and a caller and a conjurer of wicked and damned spirits." Charges of killing children by sorcery were brought but dismissed.

2. During his ten years of traveling all over Europe in the service of the Count Palatine of Siradz, King Stephen of Poland, the Emperor Rudolph, and Count Rosenberg of Bohemia, he searched for books on magic and witchcraft. His comments on dealers are still amusing: "I long sought before I could meet with [a very rare book]. And such was the ignorance of some booksellers, that I could not persuade them there was any such book extant; but now I have got it." During his travels, his library at Mortlake, outside London, was pillaged; but Dee salvaged some 3,000 volumes, most of them now reposing in the Ashmolean Museum, Oxford, and the British Museum.

3. Dee personally met several of the great demonologists: the skeptic Johan Weyer at Louvain, and Jean Bodin on his visit to the English court in February, 1581. These contacts no doubt encouraged the building of his library.

4. Through Dee and his library, the ideas of the Continental demonologists entered English thought and life. When Dee was Warden of Manchester College in Lancashire, the local justices of the peace bor-

rowed books on witchcraft from him. For example, about 1596, Edmund Hopwood, the Deputy Lieutenant of Lancashire, borrowed Weyer's *De Praestigiis Daemonum*, a *Fustis Daemonum*, Menghi's book on exorcism, *Flagellum Daemonum*, and the celebrated *Malleus Maleficarum*.

5. Dee was asked for advice about the alleged possession of the Starkie family, who were being exorcized by a charlatan, Hartley [see John Darrell]. Dee's curate, Rev. Matthew Palmer, asked Hartley what he was doing to Starkie's children.

Hartley: Praying.
Palmer: Thou pray! Thou canst not pray. What prayer canst thou say?
Hartley: None, but the Lord's prayer.
Palmer: Say it.

Hartley could not say it. Dee "utterly refused to meddle with the affair, and advised the father to consult with goodly preachers and appoint a private fast." He "so sharply rebuked [Hartley] that the children had more ease for three weeks after." Later, John Darrell took over the case.

Dr. John Dee and Edward Kelly practicing necromancy.

6. Less reputable, possibly, was Dee's connection with John Kelly, a mountebank with whom, in 1581, at Wootton-in-the-dale, he tried to evoke spirits to discover hidden treasure.

In spite of his erudition, or because of it, Dr. Dee was easily duped. The most astounding example of his naïveté was swapping wives with his assistant Kelly, twenty-eight years his junior. Kelly, eying Dee's younger and beautiful wife, Jane, reported a spirit communication recommending "the common and impartial using of matrimonial acts amongst any couple of us four." Jane demurred, but Dee told her, "There is no other remedy, but as hath been said of our cross-matching, so it must needs be done. . . . She showed herself prettily resolved to be content for God his sake and his secret purposes to obey the admonishment."

As he maintained in an interesting letter to Archbishop Whitgift in 1594, Dee considered himself a faithful Christian in spite of his Hermetic researches. But his absorption in looking for specters in magic stones and burrowing into the most esoteric aspects of alchemy places Dr. Dee primarily in the history of magic rather than in the history of witchcraft.

De Lancre: see Lancre, Pierre de.

Del Rio, Martin Antoine. Del Rio (1551-1608) was a famous Jesuit scholar and author of the encyclopedic *Disquisitionum Magicarum*, in many ways the most complete of all the works on witchcraft and as renowned as the *Malleus Maleficarum*. He was born at Antwerp, Belgium, of a distinguished Castilian father and wealthy Aragonese mother. His father, a royal official, had his castle pillaged in the native rebellions against Spanish domination, and Martin lost his library. Del Rio was well educated in the classics, Hebrew and Chaldean, five modern languages, and in law; at nineteen he had published an edition of Seneca (citing over 1,300 authorities). At twenty-four he was made Vice-Chancellor and Attorney General for Brabant—later, Voltaire satirized this appointment as Attorney General for Beelzebub. In 1580, however, Del Rio decided to enter the Jesuit order, and studied and taught at various Jesuit centers such as Valladolid, Douay, Liége, Louvain (where he gathered the material for his demonology), Graetz (Styria), Salamanca, and Brussels, dying there in 1608. During these twenty-six years of study and research, he wrote at least fifteen books of sermons and commentaries.

The *Disquisitionum Magicarum Libri Sex* was written about 1596 and first published in Louvain in 1599, dedicated to the Prince-Bishop of Liége; it was constantly reprinted, and was translated into French in 1611. By 1747, when it was last printed, there had been about twenty editions. Its six sections discussed the following topics:

1. Magic in general, and the distinctions between natural and artificial magic; alchemy.

2. Diabolical magic; witches at the sabbat; incubus demons; real and false apparitions.

3. *Maleficia* and how accomplished. How and why God allows men to be tormented by evil spirits.

4. Prophecy, divination (when heresy, when merely superstition), ordeals (Del Rio is somewhat dubious of the value of the *bain des sorciers* or swimming).

5. Instructions to judges: indications and proofs of witchcraft follow practices for heresy, but judges are allowed some latitude.

6. Function of the confessor; natural (coral, onyx) and supernatural (exorcism, amulets) means to oppose *maleficia*.

Under a veil of moderation—he permitted legal counsel for witches and he rejected lycanthropy—Del Rio revived the theories and procedures of the *Malleus Maleficarum* with credulity and blind intolerance. For example, Del Rio told "another quite well-founded story."

In the year 1587, a soldier on guard shot into a dark cloud, and lo, a woman fell to his feet. Now what do those say who deny that witches ride to meetings? They will say that they do not believe it; let them remain incredulous, because

"Who would not hate and destroy witches?"

Title page of the 1604 edition of the famous work by the Jesuit, Martin Del Rio, *Disquisitionum Magicarum*, first published in 1599, urging speedy extirpation of witches. The illustrations in the borders represent the plagues visited on Egypt through the intercession of Moses.

they will not believe eyewitnesses of whom I could adduce many.

By 1600, the venom of witch hunters was directed against the witch lovers who questioned the theory and practice of the witch trials. Said Del Rio:

Judges are bound under pain of mortal sin to condemn witches to death who have confessed their crimes; anyone who pronounces against the death sentence is reasonably suspected of secret complicity; no one is to urge the judges to desist from the prosecution; nay, it is an *indicium* of witchcraft to defend witches, or to affirm that witch stories which are told as certain are mere deceptions or illusions.

Like Bodin, Del Rio was acceptable to Protestant witch hunters because of his friendship with Justus Lipsius of Leyden. Consequently he became well known in England. He was linked with Perkins in the rebuttal by Sir Robert Filmer.

"If, as is not uncommon, God permits children to be killed before they have been baptized, it is to prevent their committing in later life those sins which would make their damnation more severe. In this, God is neither cruel nor unjust, since, by the mere fact of original sin, the children have already merited death."

—Martin Del Rio, S. J. (1599).

Demandolx, Madeleine de: see Aix-en-Provence Nuns.

Demoniacal Possession: see Possession.

Demonologists. After the early writers on witchcraft (before 1550) had established the main features of the heresy of witchcraft and their principles had filtered down to local judges, the theory was refined and deepened from about 1580 to 1620 by various writers of voluminous handbooks. These demonologists might better be called "witch-ologists," for they were more concerned with the crimes of witches than with the wiles of devils. The following are the most famous writers of this group, all discussed in separate entries. Remy, Boguet, Guazzo, and Sinistrari are available in English translations.

> Jean Bodin, *De la Démonomanie des sorciers* (Paris, 1580)
> Peter Binsfeld, *Tractatus de Confessionibus Maleficorum et Sagarum* (? Treves, 1589)
> Nicholas Remy, *Demonolatreiae* (Lyons, 1595)
> Martin Antoine Del Rio, *Disquisitionum Magicarum* (Louvain, 1599)
> Henri Boguet, *Discours des sorciers* (Lyons, 1602)
> Francesco-Maria Guazzo, *Compendium Maleficarum* (Milan, 1608)
> Pierre de Lancre, *Tableau de l'inconstance des mauvais anges* (Paris, 1612)
> Ludovico Maria Sinistrari, *De Demonialitate* (1700)

The arguments, anecdotes, trial reports, personal experiences, and the prestige of the authors assured the popularity of these books. Their influence was heightened by frequent reprintings and by continued borrowings by lesser writers. During the height of the witchcraft delusion, many similar books were published which, however, did not attain the authoritative status of the foregoing. Among the minor demonologists are:

> Lambert Daneau, *Les Sorciers* ([Geneva ?] 1564)
> Ludwig Lavater, *De Spectris, Lemuribus, et Magis* (Geneva, 1570)
> Pierre Nodé, *Déclamation contre l'erreur exécrable des maléficiers, sorciers* (Paris, 1578)
> Johan Georg Godelmann, *Disputatio de Magis* (Frankfort, 1584)
> Giovanni Lorenzo Anania, *De Natura Demonum* (Venice, 1589)
> Henningus Grosius, *Magica* (Eisleben, 1597)
> Petrus Valderama, *Histoire générale du monde* (Paris, 1619)

The Logic of the Demonologists

"[Their] opinions, on the other hand, had been sustained or revived by apostles raised for the purpose, illuminated by special inspiration, and triumphing by the force of theological arguments."—Lecky, *History of Rationalism in Europe*.

The Fact	The Explanation
An aged priest, ninety years old, is imprisoned, waiting to be burned as a witch. In desperation, he commits suicide by slashing his throat.	"Afterwards, as he was sleeping in a tower in a state of despair because he was to be burned for the crime which he had confessed, a demon appeared to him and tempted him so that on Sunday morning, the 25th September of the year 1605 now passed, he cut his own throat with his knife; and although the wound was not serious enough to cause instant death, yet the demon, in that very act of desperation, seized violently on his soul and carried it to hell, to the great astonishment of all. I saw the man dead, and still warm, lying on the straw; and as he had led the life of a beast, so he lay upon the provender of beasts. For so did Divine Justice dispose, which rewards every man according to his works; and God willed that he, who had for ninety years lived a follower of Satan, should also end his life at the hands of Satan." —Guazzo, *Compendium Maleficarum* (1626).
Tracks of cattle are often found in lush meadows.	Witness testifies she saw men and women dancing in a ring, some with "cloven feet like oxen or goats —it should seem they were spirits in the shape of lusty satyrs." A herdsman confesses he had "played upon his crooked staff and struck on it with his fingers as if it had been a pipe . . . Add to all this that there was found in the place where they danced a round circle, with the manifest marks of the treading of cloven feet." —Remy, *Demonolatreiae* (1595); copied by Henry More (1653); Nathaniel Crouch (1688).
A man gets tired of his wife and refuses to sleep with her.	"Ligatures are of two kinds . . . The husband may, as I have seen frequently, be made to conceive such aversion for her as not to endure her presence, so much does the ligature torture him, and he is forced to go away, even with loud cries." —Jacquier, *Flagellum Haereticorum Fascinariorum* (1581).
A man is subject to hallucinations especially when he is starving, very nervous, or deranged.	"For if his health is not robust, if he suffers from a retching of the black bile, if his body is wasted through excessive fasting or want of sleep; if he is injured in the brain, or is excessively timid and subject to violent clouding of the imagination, none such [visions] are to be credited. For such men, even when awake, think they see, hear or taste that which is not there to be seen or heard or tasted; for the devil very easily deludes them, since they eagerly accept and believe the images of false appearances." —Guazzo, *Compendium Maleficarum* (1626).
A person kept in a strong prison is not likely to escape.	Why does not the devil, who enables witches to fly through the air and crawl through a keyhole, help accused witches to escape? "The reason why no witch can escape from prison is that, when the devil has once got control over them, he is eager that they should be put to death, in order that they should not escape him by recanting and penitence." —Grillandus, *Tractatus de Sortilegiis* (1536).
In mountainous areas, heaps of broken glaciers are often found.	"Some of those who were burned confessed that in stormy weather the devil took many of them to the mountains to break ice, and great heaps of ice were often found in the mountains." —*Errores Gazariorum* (about 1450).
Oxen, left in the fields unattended, are found in good condition some time later.	Witches slay and feast on an ox, and then revive it by putting the skin over its bones. —Bartolommeo Spina, *Quaestio de Strigibus* (1523).
A woman cannot endure the agonies of torture and confesses her guilt.	The devil hides in the hair net of a woman undergoing torture, encouraging her to hold out longer. "But when there was no end to her pain and it became more than could be endured by the toughest person, she said: 'Take me away, for he who deceived me has said enough. I am now ready to confess the truth.' And so when she was freed from the devil, whom she was told to renounce very solemnly, she told the whole truth from the first time she had given herself to the devil." —Guazzo, *Compendium Maleficarum* (1626).
Erasmus found his house in Freiburg infested with fleas, so numerous he could not sleep, read, or write (November 19, 1533).	A witch in nearby Kylchove confessed she sent great sacks of fleas to plague Freiburg. She was burned.

Processus Juridicus contra Sagas ([Cologne,] 1629), sometimes erroneously attributed to Paul Laymann.

Heinrich von Schultheis, *Eine aussführliche Instruction* (Cologne, 1634)

Benedict Carpzov, *Practica Nova Rerum Criminalium* (Wittenberg, 1635)

Jacques d'Autun, *L'Incrédulité savante et la crédulité ignorante au sujet des magiciens et des sorciers* (Lyons, 1671)

Bartholomäus Anhorn, *Magiologia* (Basel, 1674)

The demonologists constructed the myth of witchcraft, repeating each other as if repetition could establish veracity. Thus, Del Rio repeated from the *Malleus Maleficarum*, the font of inspiration for all later authorities, the view that the incubus demon asked the witch whether she desired pregnancy or not. Sinistrari (1700), the last of the demonologists, borrowed from Guazzo (1608) the description of a witch's mark as "the imprint of a hare, a toad, a spider, a little dog, or a dormouse." But Guazzo himself had taken this description from Del Rio (1599).

Since many of these writers were, in addition to being lawyers or theologians, judges in witch trials, they had unrivaled opportunity to develop the theory of witchcraft as they themselves wished. Their accounts of the confessions they secured are therefore reflections of their own minds, and not of hallucinations of tortured women—still less of any objective reality.

In England, the witchcraft delusion was mild compared to that in France or Germany, and consequently the English theorists are relatively sober. Furthermore, extremist books appeared very late in England, at a time when belief in witchcraft was almost at an end; King James is the only early parallel to the European authorities. The English demonologists never had the tremendous influence of the French demonologists who wrote at the crest of the witchcraft persecutions. Among the English writers are:

King James I, *Demonology* (Edinburgh, 1597)

The logic of the demonologists: How fairy rings are made.

Henry More (1653) inquired "into the nature of those large dark rings in the grass which they call fairy circles, whether they be the rendezvous of witches, or the dancing places of those little puppet spirits which they call elves or fairies." From Nathaniel Crouch, *Kingdom of Darkness* (1688).

Richard Bovet, *Pandaemonium* (London, 1684)

Nathaniel Crouch, *The Kingdom of Darkness* (London, 1688)

Richard Baxter, *The Certainty of the World of Spirits* (London, 1691)

Richard Boulton, *A Complete History of Magic* (London, 1715)

The promoters of the delusion were opposed by brave writers who risked their fortunes and lives, but their number is few. Without their advocacy of humanitarian decency and of one law for all crimes, and their maintenance of reason against obscurantism, however, the passing of witchcraft would have occurred even later than it did. These opponents include:

Samuel de Cassini, *Question de le Strie* (? Pavia, 1505)

Johan Weyer, *De Praestigiis Daemonum* (Basel, 1563)

Reginald Scot, *The Discovery of Witchcraft* (London, 1584)

Hermann Witekind, *Christlich Bedencken und Erinnerung von Zauberey* (Heidelberg, 1585)

Cornelius Loos, *De Vera et Falsa Magia* (Cologne, 1592)

Alonzo Salazar de Frias, [Regulations for Spanish Inquisition, 1611]

Adam Tanner, *Disputationes* (Ingolstadt, 1617)

Johann Grevius, *Tribunal Reformatum* (Hamburg, 1622)

Gabriel Naudé, *Apologie pour les grands hommes soupçonnez de magie* (Paris, 1625)

Antonius Praetorius, *Gründlicher Bericht von Zauberey und Zauberern* (Frankfort, 1629)

Friedrich von Spee, *Cautio Criminalis* (Rinteln, 1631)

Johann Matthäus Meyfarth, *Christliche Erinnerung* (Schleusingen, 1635)

Hermann Löher, *Hochnötige* (Amsterdam, 1676)

Balthasar Bekker, *De Betoverde Weereld* (Amsterdam, 1691)

Robert Calef, *More Wonders of the Invisible World* (London, 1700)

Christian Thomasius, *De Crimine Magiae* (Halle, 1701)

Laurent Bordelon, *Histoire des imaginations extravagantes de Monsieur Oufle* (Paris, 1710)

Francis Hutchinson, *An Historical Essay Concerning Witchcraft* (London, 1718)

Demonology. Demonology, the "ology" or scientific study of demons, is treated here as the complement of witchcraft, not as the antithesis of theology, the study of God. Theologians could assume some knowledge of the problem of good and evil in their learned readers, but the demonologists bowdlerized this most difficult theory into simple language for priests and magistrates on local levels. The trial of Joan of Arc was an international event, and her replies were examined not only by her judges, all scholars, but by the combined faculties of the Sorbonne. The subtleties of the questions—e.g., did St. Michael seem warm to her—were weighed by Europe's experts to determine her guilt. Similarly, the distinctions in addressing the Devil were clear to the scholastic mind: supplication was to admit his power and was therefore heretical; a command, knowing that God

permitted Satan certain powers (e.g., over weather), was not, at least on this count, heretical. Among many others, the lawyer Paulus Grillandus (1525) probed the niceties of this dilemma of dualism [see Sorcery].

In practice, the priests and judges who examined the witches were not highly educated—Carpzov complained that most judges in Saxony were boorish and semiliterate. The accused themselves, while they might have property and be literate, were generally ordinary town or country folk with little religious training beyond that acquired at the parish church. To judges and victims, the Devil was simply a superhuman figure, the apotheosis of evil, who acted like the ruthless brigand familiar enough in war years, especially in the early seventeenth century. The theologians might debate at length on how the devil could steal semen from a man and keep it warm long enough to impregnate a woman [see Sexual Relations with Devils], but practicing judges found an enforced admission of copulation with the devil—icy cold though it was—sufficient for conviction. "The vulgar opinion," Bishop Hutchinson summarized in 1718, and it was valid for earlier centuries, "is that the devil is something like a man, but with tail, and claws, and horns, and a cloven foot."

Thus such experts as Bodin, Del Rio, or Remy, although themselves highly learned and sophisticated, enlarged on the craft of witches (the pact and the sabbat) rather than the deviltry of demons. The premise of the Devil was not contested, but his agent appeared in court.

The Devil had power, even if its extent was debatable. Johan Weyer, the skeptical physician, wrote (1563):

Satan possesses great courage, incredible cunning, superhuman wisdom, the most acute penetration, consummate prudence, an incomparable skill in veiling the most pernicious artifices under a specious disguise, and a malicious and infinite hatred toward the human race, implacable and incurable.

Jean Bodin, the French witch judge, was willing to extend Satan's attributes to lesser devils (1580):

Vessels of Iniquity: heads of devils from Francis Barrett, *The Magus* (1801).

It is certain that the devils have a profound knowledge of all things. No theologian can interpret the Holy Scriptures better than they can; no lawyer has a more detailed knowledge of testaments, contracts and actions; no physician or philosopher can better understand the composition of the human body, and the virtues of the heavens, the stars, birds and fishes, trees and herbs, metals and stones.

About the time Bodin was writing, many little pamphlets appeared in France testifying to the strange prowess of the Devil. For example, one booklet, published in Paris in 1619, had for its title: *Shocking but True History, Occurring in Soliers in Provence, about a man who had dedicated himself to the Church, but, not having fulfilled his obligations, the devil cut off his privy parts.*

Michaelis Psellus had classified devils by their habitat [see Devil], but at least two

of his species could have no communication with witches. Other demonologists tried to bring such groupings into line with demoniacal power. Alphonsus de Spina found ten varieties of devils:

1. *Fates.* Some say they have seen Fates, but if so they are not women but demons (and Augustine says the only fate is the will of God).

2. *Poltergeists,* commonly called the *duende de casa,* who do little tricks at night, like breaking things, pulling off bedclothes, making footsteps overhead. They move things but do little damage. [Binsfeld held that a poltergeist justified a tenant's breaking his lease.]

3. *Incubi* and *Succubi.* Nuns are especially subject to these devils. When they awake in the morning, they "find themselves polluted as if they had slept with men."

4. *Marching hosts,* which appear like hordes of men making much tumult.

5. *Familiar demons,* who eat and drink with men, in imitation of the angel of Tobit.

6. *Nightmare demons,* who terrify men in their dreams.

7. *Demons* formed from semen and its odor when men and women copulate. These demons also cause men to dream of women so the demons can "receive their emission and make therefrom a new spirit." [Spina did not believe this.]

8. *Deceptive demons,* who sometimes appear as men and sometimes as women.

9. *Clean demons* (but really most foul) who assail only holy men.

10. *Demons* who deceive old women (called *xorguinae* or *bruxae*) into thinking they fly to sabbats [see Transvection].

Other demonologists drew up a hierarchy of devils and ascribed to them power to provoke people to commit the seven deadly sins. Binsfeld (1589), for example, gave one such list:

Lucifer	—	Pride
Mammon	—	Avarice
Asmodeus	—	Lechery
Satan	—	Anger
Beelzebub	—	Gluttony
Leviathan	—	Envy
Belphegor	—	Sloth

In *The Magus or Celestial Intelligencer*, published in London, 1801, Francis Barrett, an occultist born two centuries too late, changed the roster of devils and attributed sins. Mammon became prince of tempters and ensnarers, Asmodeus of revengers of evil, Satan of deluders (serving conjurers and witches), and Beelzebub of false gods. In addition, Pytho was introduced as prince of the spirits of lies, Belial of vessels of iniquity (cards and dice), Merihim of spirits causing pestilence, Abaddan of evil war, and Astaroth as prince of accusers and inquisitors.

Part of the procedure in the service of exorcism, still included in the *Rituale Romanum* printed in 1947, was the interrogation of a possessing devil. The priest demanded his name and rank, and the devil, like a prisoner of war, was in honor bound to respond. In the celebrated exorcism in Auch (1618), the devil gave his name as "Mahonin, of the third hierarchy, and the second order of archangels, and that his living, before he entered the body of the possessed, was in the water." [See Exorcism.] Knowledge of a devil's name was considered to give the exorcist, by a primitive animistic theory, control over him.

Behemoth, demon of the delights of the belly. From Collin de Plancy, *Dictionnaire infernal* (1863).

Under exorcism, people regularly gave the names of the devils possessing them [see Jeanne Fery]. Being acquainted with the current nomenclature, either by reading or sermons, the energumens generally gave names familiar to the exorcists—if the devil was himself reluctant to reveal his identity. Thus, when the Louviers Nuns were bewitched, Sister Mary of the Holy Sacrament said she was possessed by Putifar, and Sister Mary of the Holy Ghost by Dagon, both devils sent by the witches, Father Picard and Sister Madeleine Bavent (*Récit véritable*, 1643). Other nuns added to the roster:

Sister Anne of the Nativity by Leviathan
Sister Barbara of St. Michael by Ancitif
Sister Louise de Pinteville by Arfaxat
Sister Anne by Consague
Sister Marie Cheron by Grongade
Sister Mary of Jesus by Phaëton
Sister Elizabeth by Asmodeus
Sister Françoise by Calconix

One of the most complete lists of devils and their functions was reported by the celebrated exorcist Father Sebastien Michaëlis, in his *Admirable History* (1612). Balberith, a demon possessing Sister Madeleine, at Aix-en-Provence, obligingly told the priest not only the other devils possessing the nun, but added the special saints whose function was to oppose them. Since the devils were angels who had rebelled and fallen, they maintained their rank as ex-angels. The angelic court had been invented in the fourth century, out of the writings of Paul (Col. i. 16; Eph. i. 21), by the Pseudo-Dionysius, and consisted of nine orders of angels (three hierarchies each of three orders):

First Hierarchy:	Seraphim
	Cherubim
	Thrones
Second Hierarchy:	Dominions
	Principalities
	Powers
Third Hierarchy:	Virtues
	Archangels
	Angels

Balberith gave many lesser devils occupying Sister Madeleine, but the most important listed by Michaëlis were as follows:

First Hierarchy

1. *Beelzebub* was Prince of the Seraphim, and next unto Lucifer. For all the princes, that is to say all the chief of the nine choirs of angels, are fallen; and of the choir of Seraphim there fell the three first, to wit, Lucifer, Beelzebub, and Leviathan, who did all revolt. But the fourth, who was Michael, was the first that resisted Lucifer, and all the rest of those good angels followed him, so that now he is the chiefest amongst them all. Lucifer, when Christ descended into hell, was there chained up, where he commands all. . . . Beelzebub tempts men with pride. And as John the Baptist holds Lucifer's place in Paradise . . . by his singular humility, so Beelzebub has Francis for his adversary in heaven.

2. *Leviathan* is the Prince of the same order, and is the ringleader of the heretics, tempting men with sins that are directly repugnant unto faith. [Adversary: Peter the Apostle]

3. *Asmodeus* is of the same order. He continues a Seraphin to this day, that is, he burns with the desire to tempt men with his swine of luxuriousness, and is the prince of wantons. [Adversary: John the Baptist]

4. *Balberith* is Prince of the Cherubim. He tempts men to commit homicides, and to be quarrelsome, contentious, and blasphemous. [Adversary: Barnabas]

5. *Astaroth*, Prince of the Thrones, is always desirous to sit idle and be at ease. He tempts men with idleness and sloth. [Adversary: Bartholomew]

6. *Verrine* is also one of the Thrones, and next in place unto Astaroth, and tempts men with impatience. [Adversary: Dominic]

7. *Gressil* is the third in the order of Thrones, and tempts men with impurity and uncleanness. [Adversary: Bernard]

8. *Sonneillon* is the fourth in the order of Thrones, and tempts men with hatred against their enemies. [Adversary: Stephen]

Second Hierarchy

9. *Carreau*, Prince of Powers, tempts men with hardness of heart. [Adversaries: Vincent and Vincent Ferrer]

10. *Carnivean* is also a Prince of Powers, and does tempt men to obscenity and shamelessness. [Adversary: John the Evangelist]

11. *Oeillet* is a Prince of Dominions. He tempts men to break the vow of poverty. [Adversary: Martin]

12. *Rosier* is the second in the order of Dominions, and by his sweet and sugared words, he tempts men to fall in love. His adversary in Heaven is Basil, who would not listen to amorous and enchanting language.

13. *Verrier* is Prince of Principalities, and tempts men against the vow of obedience, and makes the neck stiff and hard as iron, and incapable to stoop under the yoke of obedience. [Adversary: Bernard]

Third Hierarchy

14. *Belias*, Prince of the order of Virtues, tempts men with arrogance. His adversary is Francis de Paul for his great and dove-like humility. He also tempts gentlewomen to prank up themselves with newfangled attires, to make wantons of their children, and to prattle unto them while mass is saying, and so to divert them from the service of God.

15. *Olivier*, Prince of the Archangels, tempts men with cruelty and mercilessness toward the poor. [Adversary: Lawrence]

16. *Iuvart* is Prince of Angels, but he is in another body [of another nun at Louviers] and hath not his abode here [in Sister Madeleine].

Such lists were common in the works of theologians and demonologists, and the celebrated Ambroise Paré, in the chapter on monsters in his *Opera Omnia* (1572), described devils in a similar fashion. Knowing the saint who opposed the devil had practical use, not only for prayers to help the exorcism, but in less reputable dealings with devils. Devils could be invoked with greater security if prayers were first made to their adversaries; many *grimoires*—do-it-yourself books on conjuration of spirits —include such charms.

The number of devils was legion. St. Macarius of Alexandria prayed to God to let him see the hosts of evil; the saint's eyes were opened, and he saw a multitude of devils "as numerous as bees." Alphonsus de Spina in 1459 thought one-third of the original angels became devils, specifically 133, 306, 668. One sixteenth-century cybernetician (1567) counted 66 princes commanding 6,660,000 devils. Another estimated more precisely 7,409,127 demons commanded by 79 infernal princes. Johan Weyer corrected his figures to 7,405,926 demons and 72 princes of hell. A few years later, another researcher said the devils numbered more than half the population of the world.

Devil. The word "Devil" means the personification of supreme evil, the foe of the Christian God. When used in the plural, however, "devils" are synonymous with demons or fiends, malignant beings of superhuman power, so that *the* Devil, or Beelzebub, becomes "the prince of devils" (Matt. xii. 24).

(In this *Encyclopedia*, when the Devil is considered theologically as the supreme embodiment of evil, the word is capitalized. A person signs a pact with the Devil or sells his soul to the Devil. On the other hand, a witch may work with a demon or minor devil: a person is accused of fornicating with a devil, receiving a devil's mark, or asking help of a devil in working acts of *maleficia;* the possessing agent in demoniacal possession is also presumed to be one of these representatives of Satan. Here, devil has not been capitalized. The distinction, however, remains subtle.)

Devil derives from Greek *diabolos*, which also gives Italian *diavolo*, Spanish *diablo*, and French *diable*, originally meaning an accuser or traducer.

In translating the Old Testament into Greek, the Egyptian Jews of the third century B.C. used the word *diabolos* for the Hebrew *satan*, an angelic entity whose

function was to test men's fidelity to God. He was not evil, but became evil by identification with his functions. Thus *satan* was given power to inflict sufferings on Job (Job i. 6-12; compare I. Chron. xxi. 1). When this Greek "Septuagint" Old Testament was turned into Latin, *diabolos* became either *diabolus* (in the early translations) or *Satan*, in the standard Vulgate text (except in Psalm cix).

In the New Testament, however, the Greek word *satanas* was used to mean something different, not an adversary against man (as in Job), but an adversary against God, as employed by Christ at the temptation on the mountain: "Get thee hence, Satan" (Matt. iv. 10). Throughout the New Testament, *Satanas* meant the Devil, and in Revelation xii. 9 was described as "the great dragon . . . that old serpent, called the Devil, and Satan . . . cast out into the earth, and his angels . . . with him."

In the English translations, the Old Testament Hebrew *satan* as well as the New Testament Greek *satanas* were, following the Latin, both rendered "Satan" (except by Wycliffe in Psalm cix, where he used "devil"). Thus two different conceptions were fused, causing many people errone-

A very early drawing of a devil. From Mandeville's *Travels*, printed at Strasbourg (1484), in Cornell University Library.

ously to believe that the Christian idea of an evil demi-God was known to the Hebrews before the Babylonian captivity, whereas the idea of an arch-fiend developed only later under Persian influence.

A further step equated devil with demon, although originally the words were distinct. The Greek *demon* meant a guardian spirit or source of inspiration, and is sometimes used in this sense in English (spelled *daemon*), as in Shakespeare: "O Anthony! Thy daemon, that thy spirit which keeps thee, is noble, courageous, high unmatchable." But the Greek Septuagint used *demon* for the Hebrew words meaning vengeful idols (*schedim*) and hairy satyrs (*seîrim*) and also for the "destroyer" in the late story of Tobit, which killed the seven husbands of Sara before being overcome by the angel Raphael (Tobit vi. 14; viii. 3). The Vulgate latinized the Greek into *demon* or *demonium*. The English Authorized Version (1613) translated both by "devil," but Wycliffe sometimes also used the old Anglo-Saxon word *fiend*, meaning enemy. The Revised Version (1881) substituted "demon" in Deuteronomy and the Psalms, but retained "devil" in the New Testament.

Thus originally distinct species of spirits were unified by interchangeable translations of devil, demon, fiend. All these terms

Judgment Day. The soul is weighed in the balances before God the Father and the Virgin Mary. From a manuscript in the Bibliothèque nationale, Paris.

devolved on Satan, who absorbed into himself all biblical references to any enemy of God, from the serpent of Genesis (iii), the ruler of a rival kingdom of evil (Enoch), to "the prince of the power of the air" (Eph. ii. 2). In addition, the Devil was given names: Beelzebub, "the chief of devils" (Luke xi. 15); Asmodeus, "the evil spirit" of the Tobit legend (iii. 8); Apollyon, "the angel of the bottomless pit, whose name in the Hebrew tongue is Abaddon [a destroyer]" (Rev. ix. 11); Behemoth and Leviathan (Job xl. 15; xli. 1); Belial (II Cor. vi. 15); or Lucifer, the name patristic writers called Satan before his fall (Isa. xiv. 12). The doctors of demonology invented different personalities for each of

Devils holding a council in hell, at lower left. In the house at the right, the child Merlin is born, the offspring of a woman and the Devil. From a manuscript in the Bibliothèque nationale, Paris.

Angels rescuing a soul pursued by devils. From the legend of Theophilus in a collection of miracles in the Bibliothèque nationale, Paris.

these names, and from these examples created and named legions of new devils.

Man makes his divinities, good or evil, in his own image, the result depending on the stage of his personal development and that of the age he lives in. The concept of the Christian Devil was largely fixed by the so-called desert fathers, the hermits of the Egyptian deserts, in the third and fourth centuries, who pieced together from their hallucinations and recollections of replaced gods (such as the cloven-footed Pan) the visualization of the Devil as the grotesque man illustrated in the plates in this *Encyclopedia*. The Devil was legalized by the Council of Toledo in A.D. 447, and later writers contributed little that was new.

But these early Christians did not always conceive a devil in human form. For example, in the *Life of St. Anthony* (about A.D. 360), attributed to Athanasius, devils appear in many guises in addition to a black boy and a huge man. They come as "a beast like to man having legs and feet like those of an ass," and as leopards, bears, horses, wolves, and scorpions. "The lion was roaring, wishing to attack, the bull seeming to toss with its horns, the serpent writhing." The shapes of the dove and the lamb, holy symbols, were forbidden. Devils frequently changed their shape, "taking the forms of women, wild beasts, creeping things, gigantic bodies, and troops of soldiers . . . at another time they assumed the appearance of monks and feigned the speech of holy men." The most dangerous manifestation of a devil was his appearance as an angel, the dreaded "midday devil" of the Psalms; it was such a suspi-

cion that caused St. Mary her fear at the Annunciation.

Generally devils were heralded by a great commotion, "with sounds and crying such as the disturbances of boorish youths or robbers" (*Life of St. Anthony*) or with "wailing of infants, bleating of flocks, lowing of oxen . . . the roaring of lions, the noise of an army" (Jerome's *Life of St. Hilary*, about A.D. 390). Athanasius testified that devils came and went at will, though the doors were shut. Often they emitted a foul stench, and St. Hilary professed "to tell from the odors of bodies and garments . . . by what demon . . . the individual man was distressed."

At other times, the devil did not create a body for himself out of the air, but took possession of a human or animal, as in the story of the devil named Legion entering the Gaderene swine (Mark v). Michaelis Psellus told of demons living under the earth, unable to endure the extreme cold and equally unable to endure the rays of the sun, who sought "shelter and lodgings in the bodies of beasts." The *Life of St. Hilary* described the exorcism of such a devil lodged in a camel [see Exorcism].

Psellus elaborated on the kinds of devils and distinguished six varieties, according to their habitation, whether in the air or sea, etc. His list was quoted by Guazzo and later by Henry Hallywell in his *Melampronoea* (1681). The following account is from Guazzo's *Compendium Maleficarum* (1608).

The first is the fiery, because these dwell in the upper air and will never descend to the lower regions until the

Day of Judgment, and they have no dealings on earth with men.

The second is the aerial, because these dwell in the air around us. They can descend to hell, and, by forming bodies out of the air, can at times be visible to men. Very frequently, with God's permission, they agitate the air and raise storms and tempests, and all this they conspire to do for the destruction of mankind.

The third is terrestrial, and these were certainly cast from Heaven to earth for their sins. Some of them live in woods and forests, and lay snares for hunters; some dwell in the fields and lead night travelers astray; some dwell in hidden places and caverns; while others delight to live in secret among men.

The fourth is the aqueous, for these dwell under the water in rivers and lakes, and are full of anger, turbulent, unquiet, and deceitful. They raise storms at sea, sink ships in the ocean, and destroy life in the water. When such devils appear, they are more often women than men, for they live in moist places and lead an easier life. But those which live in drier

Minor devils—rural gods, satyrs, and hobgoblins. From Olaus Magnus, *Historia de Gentibus Septentrionalibus* (1555).

and harder places are usually seen as males.

The fifth is the subterranean, for these live in caves and caverns in the mountains. They are of a very mean disposition, and chiefly molest those who work in pits or mines for treasure, and they are always ready to do harm. They cause earthquakes and winds and fires, and shake the foundations of houses.

The sixth is the heliophobic, because they especially hate and detest the light, and never appear during daytime, nor can they assume a bodily form until night. These devils are completely inscrutable and of a character beyond human comprehension, because they are all dark within, shaken with icy passions, malicious, restless, and perturbed; and when they meet men at night they oppress them violently and, with God's permission, often kill them by some breath or touch. . . . This kind of devil has no dealing with witches; neither can they be kept at bay by charms, for they shun the light and the voices of men and every sort of noise.

In practice, this type of classification had little relevance for the actual business of witchcraft and discovering witches. Judges were not erudite theologians and lawyers who could appreciate such niceties, and the devil to them and to their prisoners was very human. How human is seen in the accounts of the two main species of devils who figured in the trials, the male Incubus and the female Succubus devils, occasionally appearing as an animal (a goat), but nearly always in human form. The entries

Eliphas Levi's celebrated drawing of the horned god of the witches (1861).

The Temptation of St. Anthony, by Martin Schongauer.

"On the lives of St. Anthony and his compeers [was] founded . . . the whole science of demonology, with the peculiar literature, its peculiar system of criminal jurisprudence."— Charles Kingsley (1868).

Sexual Relations with Devils, Nightmare, and Sabbat describe further the evil but human-like projection of Satan. Other aspects of the personality of the Christian Devil, when he possessed humans, are seen in the entries for Exorcism and Possession —a rational, determined foe, but sensitive to insults and aware of his own insecurity. A very minor devil was the Poltergeist, but records are not numerous or documented until after the decline of the witchcraft delusion, and the Poltergeist falls more into the field of spiritualism. Further discussion of devils appears under Demonology.

Devil's Mark. Devil's marks [*stigmata diaboli*] or the devil's seal [*sigillum diaboli*] occur in nearly all reports of witches or witch trials and illustrate how perverted intelligence and hysterical stupidity could misinterpret natural phenomena and so bring about the murder of thousands of men and women and children.

The devil's mark was often confused with the witch's mark, and later witch hunters accepted either as sufficient proof to establish witchcraft. The terms came to be used interchangeably throughout the persecutions, even by some demonologists; the distinction was that the devil's mark resembled a scar, birthmark, or tattooing, whereas the witch's mark was a protuberance on the body at which the familiars were supposed to suck—an essentially English conception.

According to the theories current in the sixteenth and seventeenth centuries, the devil sealed the compact with the witches by giving them some mark of identification on the body, just like a rancher branding his cattle. One of the earliest writers to stress these marks was the famous Calvinist theologian, Lambert Daneau, in his *Les Sorciers* (1564), translated into English as *A Dialogue of Witches* (1575). There is not a single witch, said Daneau, "upon whom [the devil] doth not set some note or token of his power and prerogative over them." Judges should always, when suspects are presented to them, "pull [out hair] and shave, where occasion shall serve,

all the body over, lest haply the mark may lurk under the hair in any place." Sinistrari, one of the later demonologists, similarly believed:

The demon imprints on [the witches] some mark, especially on those whose constancy he suspects. That mark, however, is not always of the same shape or figure; sometimes it is the likeness of a hare, sometimes like a toad's foot, sometimes a spider, a puppy, a dormouse. It is imprinted on the most secret parts of the body; with men, under the eyelids or perhaps under the armpits, or on the lips or shoulders, the anus, or elsewhere; with women, it is generally on the breasts or private parts. Now, the stamp which makes these marks is simply the devil's talon. (*De Demonialitate*)

Finding such marks was the best proof of a witch and was in itself sufficient to justify torture (as Nehring wrote in 1666) or sentence of death (Scot, *Discovery of Witchcraft*, 1584). Cotton Mather threw his weight with the witch prickers:

I add, why should not witch marks be searched for? The properties, the qualities of those marks are described by divers weighty writers. I never saw any of those marks, but it is doubtless not impossible for a surgeon, when he sees them, to say what are magical.

Most human beings have some blemish which could be considered a devil's mark. Warts, moles, and various kinds of nevus (forming spots or elevations of red or purplish color) are common, as are other kinds of dry tough excrescences on the skin, and the various species of corns. Old wounds might leave scarred tissue. Any unusual pigmentation would be interpreted as a curious shape; a later age would see strawberries in birthmarks.

Such natural features were considered potential devil's marks, made to signalize the recipient's subjection, his constant fear and obedience, to the Devil. The experts held that if a man or woman, knowing the danger of being found with such a mark, consented to be so branded, he had voluntarily entered into a pact with the Devil and was therefore a witch. The priest Gaufridi in 1611 confessed: "These marks were made as a sign that I shall be a good and faithful servant to the Devil all my life long."

The marks were sought in any part of the body, perhaps on the left shoulder (according to Boguet), or, especially in England, on a finger. A victim of Inquisitor Jacquier (about 1450) had on his hip a mark made by the devil's hoof. But if the mark was not immediately visible, the witch prickers pried into more intimate hiding places, as Del Rio suggested in his *Disquisitionum Magicarum* (1599), searching the sexual and excretory organs. To assist discovery, as well as to expose hidden amulets, the witch was generally shaved round the genitals, often in public. At North Berwick, the witches participated in a sort of ceremony, at which "the devil doth lick them with his tongue in some privy part of their body, before he doth receive them to be his servants, which mark commonly is given them under the hair in some part of their body." When Agnes Sampson, one of the accused, was shaved, "the devil's mark was found upon her privities." In 1658, another Scottish witch, Margaret Taylor, at Alloa, confessed that the devil, "in the likeness of a young man with gray clothes and a blue cap . . . gave her his mark . . . in her secret member."

Jacques Fontaine, doctor to King Henry IV of France, in his *Des Marques des sorciers et de la réele possession que le diable prend sur le corps des hommes* (1611), maintained that "writers . . . who say that it is difficult to distinguish devil's marks from natural blemishes, from a carbuncle, or from impetigo, clearly show that they are not good doctors." Presumably one of the best educated and most scientific men in France at the beginning of the seventeenth century, Dr. Fontaine gave details of how the devil made these marks.

Some say that Satan makes these marks on them with a hot iron and a certain unguent which he applies under the skin of witches. Others say that the devil marks the witches with his finger, when he appears in human form or as a spirit. If it were done with a hot iron, it would

necessarily follow that on the part so marked there would be a scar, but the witches testify that they have never seen a scar over the mark. . . . But it is not necessary to prove this, for the devil, who does not lack knowledge of medications and has the best of them, has only to mortify that place. As for the scar, the devil is such a skillful worker that he can place the hot iron on the body without causing any scar.

Fontaine was one of the four doctors appointed to examine Father Louis Gaufridi, the priest charged with witchcraft, on whose body he found three devil's marks.

As might be expected, a wart or corn would not bleed and would be insensitive to pricking with a needle; such a reaction proved witchery. An old scar might be similarly insensitive. Guazzo, in his *Compendium Maleficarum*, related such an instance at Brindisi in November, 1590:

When Claudia Bogarta was about to be tormented, she was shaved to the skin, as the custom is, so that a scar was revealed on the top of her bare brow. The inquisitor then suspecting the truth, namely, that it was a mark made by the devil's claw, which had before been covered by her hair, ordered a pin to be thrust deep into it. And when this was done, she neither felt any pain, nor was the slightest drop of blood seen at the wound. Yet she persisted to deny the truth, saying that the insensitivity [*torporam*] was caused a long time ago by a blow from a stone.

Later, she was tortured until she confessed.

A refinement of the visible devil's marks was the invisible devil's marks. These could also be discovered by pricking with a needle until some insensitive spot which did not bleed was allegedly found.

The tremendous emotional shock of being publicly stripped and examined amidst the jeering of a crowd of morbid curiosity-seekers could well produce temporary anesthesia. One such example was spotted by a perspicacious judge at the 1649 witch trial at Newcastle-on-Tyne, promoted by a roving professional "finger man" who was ultimately exposed, but not before he had caused the death of 220 persons, for each of whom the authorities paid him at least twenty shillings:

> The said reputed witch finder acquainted Lieutenant Colonel Hobson that he knew women, whether they were witches or no by their looks, and when the said person was searching of a personable and good-like woman, the said Colonel replied and said, Surely this woman is none and need not be tried. But the Scotsman said she was, for the town said she was, and therefore he would try her. And presently in sight of all the people, [he] laid her body naked to the waist, with her clothes over her head, by which fright and shame, all her blood contracted into one part of her body. And then he ran a pin into her thigh, and then suddenly let her coats fall, and then demanded whether she had nothing of his in her body but did not bleed. But she being amazed replied little. Then he put his hand up her coats and pulled out the pin, and set her aside as a guilty person and child of the Devil. And [he] fell to try others, whom he made guilty.
>
> Lieutenant Colonel Hobson, perceiving the alteration of the foresaid woman, by her blood settling in her right parts, caused that woman to be brought again, and her clothes pulled up to her thigh, and required the Scot to run the pin into the same place, and then it gushed out of blood, and the said Scot cleared her, and said she was not a child of the Devil. [See further, Pricking.]

One or two orthodox demonologists discounted the importance of the devil's mark. Del Rio argued that devil's marks were not always insensitive, and sometimes real witches might pretend to feel pain when pricked, a deception against which other authorities warned (e.g., Michaëlis in 1582). Binsfeld, in his *De Confessionibus Maleficorum* (1589), suggested examiners might imagine a mark; and if the Devil knew his followers could be so easily recognized, he would not insist on the stigma (hence the development of the theory of invisible marks). Del Rio agreed on this point with Binsfeld and added that the

mark was often of short duration, and that innocent people with birthmarks or moles were sometimes unjustly punished.

Binsfeld and Del Rio did not understand what dangerous heresy lay in their slight demurrals. One grain of common sense might have destroyed the whole theory of witchcraft. Therefore, against these two demonologists, whose opinions exercised some influence, a professor of law at the University of Cologne, Peter Ostermann, wrote (in 1629) a whole treatise on the necessity and validity of devil's marks, drawing heavily upon and summarizing all the earlier authorities (e.g., Bodin, Remy, De Lancre). Not one person could be produced, he said, who, having the mark, had lived a blameless life; no one convicted of sorcery had ever been found without the mark. It was the proof of proofs and more infallible than either accusations or confessions. His *Commentarius Juridicus* was a summary of both popular and official opinions at the height of the witch belief.

Divination. The history of witchcraft begins and ends in sorcery—the earliest laws punished claims to reveal hidden treasure, and the latest laws punished such fortune-finders as frauds. The crime in divination was the deception of the naïve, not the diabolical means employed. Consequently, when diviners were prosecuted, their punishment was generally light. In England,

A man consulting a witch. The devil is putting a fool's cap on him. From the Douce Collection, Bodleian Library, Oxford.

Magicians disemboweling a goat. From a German edition of Petrarch's *De Remediis Utriusque Fortunae,* in the Douce Collection, Bodleian Library, Oxford.

for example, in 1467 a William Byg was convicted of using a crystal stone to locate stolen property; his punishment was to appear in public with a paper scroll on his head, *"Ecce sortilegus* [Behold the fortune-teller]." In 1546, Henry Neville, the son of the Earl of Westmorland, was investigated for complicity in magical operations and for using a ring to find hidden treasure. In 1560 two priests and several highly-placed men were convicted for conjuring spirits by three magic circles, in order to find a supposed chest of gold; one only was excommunicated. In 1598 Robert Browning, a laborer of Aldam, Sussex, was placed in the pillory for defrauding the king's subjects, "persuading them that by conjuration and invocation of evil spirits they might discover hidden hoards of gold and silver, and regain lost goods."

Such efforts to unearth treasure-trove or to discover the secrets of the future, part of the pagan practices of ancient Greece and Rome, easily became Christian heretical witchcraft. "Divination," wrote William Perkins (1608), "is a part of witchcraft, whereby men reveal strange things, either past, present, or to come, *by the assistance of the devil.*" Divination could be performed with or without "means." True means were the "creatures of God," that is, natural objects or phenomena, such as the flight of

birds, inspection of entrails, astrology, dreams, or the casting of lots (or dice). False or counterfeit means could also be used, as in necromancy or "the black art, because the devil being sought unto by witches, appears unto them in the likeness of a dead body." The classic instance of necromancy was the Endor witch, "which example declareth plainly that there is a kind of divination, whereby witches and sorcerers reveal strange things by means of the devil appearing unto them in the shapes or shadows of the dead." The more wicked kind of divination, according to Perkins, was without means, "by the alone and immediate assistance of a familiar spirit. This kind is mentioned and expressly forbidden (Leviticus xix. 31) . . . [and] is practiced two ways: either inwardly, when the spirit is within the witch; or outwardly, when being forth of the witch, he doth only inspire him or her." Either way, the diviner exposed himself to charges of a pact.

Just as the white witch was held equally guilty as the malicious witch, so the theurgist was condemned with the necromancer. The theurgists' claim "to have to do only with good spirits," said Henry Hallywell (1681), made them "justly exposed to the illusions of the devil or evil spirits." That they did not realize the spirits were evil, and did not make any "solemn compacts"

Divining for metals, from George Agricola, *De Re Metallica* (1556): "Among miners there are many great arguments about the forked twig, for some say it is of the greatest use to them in discovering veins, while others deny this."

was no mitigation. In invoking spirits, both black magic or goety and white magic or theurgy were damnable, as Augustine had pointed out. While "divination without means" was based on a pact, the trials of witches seldom stress this crime, and div-ination remains essentially a facet of ceremonial magic. Henry C. Lea did not recall "in any of the innumerable witch trials any case in which the witch raised the spirits of the dead."

The Kinds of Divination

Aeromancy, or divining by the air.
Alectryomancy, by cocks or poultry.
Alphitomancy, by meal, flour, or bran.
Antinopomancy, by the entrails of women and children.
Arithmancy, by numbers.
Astragalomancy, by dice.
Axinomancy, by saws.
Botanomancy, by herbs.
Capnomancy, by smoke.
Carromancy, by melting of wax.
Catoxtromancy, by looking glasses.
Cattabomancy, by vessels of brass or other metal.
Cephalonomancy, by broiling of an ass's head.
Chartomancy, by writing in papers.
Chiromancy, by the hands.
Chrystallomancy, by glasses.
Cleromancy, by lots.
Coscinomancy, by sieves.
Crithomancy, by grain or corn.
Dactylomancy, by rings.

Demonomancy, by the suggestion of evil demons or devils.
Gastromancy, by the sound of or signs upon the belly.
Geomancy, by earth.
Gyromancy, by rounds or circles.
Hydromancy, by water.
Icthyomancy, by fishes.
Idolomancy, by idols, images, figures.
Lampadomancy, by candles and lamps.
Lecanomancy, by a basin of water.
Lithomancy, by stones.
Livanomancy, by burning of frankin-cense.
Logarithmancy, by logarithms.
Macharomancy, by knives or swords.
Oinomancy, by wine.
Omphilomancy, by the navel.
Oniromancy, by dreams.
Onomatomancy, by names.
Onychomancy, by the nails.
Ornithomancy, by birds.
Podomancy, by the feet.

Psychomancy, by men's souls, affections, wills, religious or moral dispositions.
Pyromancy, by fire.
Roadomancy, by stars.
Sciomancy, by shadows.
Spatalamancy, by skins, bones, excre-ments.
Stareomancy, or divining by the ele-ments.
Sternomancy, from the breast to the belly.
Sycomancy, by figs.
Theomancy, pretending to divine by the revelation of the Spirit and by the Scriptures or Word of God.
Theriomancy, by beasts.
Tuphramancy, by ashes.
Tyromancy, by the coagulation of cheese.
And in one word for all nagomancy or necromancy, by inspecting, consulting and divining by, with, or from the dead.

—John Gaule, *Mysmantia* (1652).

Dr. Lamb's Darling. Dr. Lamb, until his death in 1640, was the Duke of Bucking-ham's personal physician. Like Dr. John Dee, Queen Elizabeth's protégé, he experi-mented in alchemy and esoteric magical practices. Richard Baxter's *World of Spirits* (1691) gave several anecdotes.

Once Dr. Lamb invited his friends, Sir Miles Sands and Mr. Barbor, for a morning *apéritif*, and showed them some "sport." He conjured a tree growing in his room and three little men with axes chopping it down. Although warned not to touch anything, Mr. Barbor pocketed a chip of wood which had fallen on his suit. At night, he was troubled with frightening noises. His wife, according to Baxter, said: "Husband, you told me you were at Dr. Lamb's this day, and I fear you meddled with something."

"I put a chip into my pocket," he replied.

"I pray you," said she, "fling it out, or we shall have no quiet." When her husband did so, the house immediately became quiet, and everybody went back to sleep.

Such was the reputation of Dr. Lamb. Perhaps it should be no surprise that in 1640 a mob pursued him through the streets of London to St. Paul's Cross and stoned him to death as a wizard. Charles I rode out to stop the riot, but he arrived too late. For failing to punish the ringleaders, the King fined the city of London £600.

Dr. Lamb's "darling" was his servant, Mrs. Anne Bodenham, who, though mar-ried, had occasioned some scandal by living in the house of her unmarried master. To Mrs. Bodenham, an uneducated woman, he had taught some tricks. After his death, profiting by his notoriety, by a little book of charms, and by a garden of medicinal herbs, she got a reputation as a wise woman. To give verisimilitude to her claims of oc-cultism, she wore about her neck a toad in a green bag. She moved to the village of Fisherton Anger in Wiltshire. Neighbors consulted her about coming events and oc-casionally about poisons. She became in-volved with the family of Richard Goddard, a connection which brought about her death. Mrs. Goddard, from all acounts a psychopath, feared her two daughters were trying to poison her; in turn, she tried to poison them, at one time procuring from Anne Bodenham three packets of dried vervain, dried dill, and nail parings.

In 1653, a Mr. Mason sought information from Mrs. Bodenham about an impending lawsuit against his father-in-law, Mr. Goddard. Nathaniel Crouch, in his *Kingdom of Darkness* (1688), gave a description of one of the relatively few incidents of divination in English witchcraft. Anne Bodenham

took her staff and therewith drew a circle about the house, and then took of a book, carrying it over the circle with her hands. After that, she laid a green glass on the book, and placed within the circle an earthen pot of coals wherein she threw something which caused a very noisome smell . . . and so calling Beelzebub, Tormentor, Satan, and Lucifer [to] appear, there suddenly arose a very high wind which made the house shake. And presently, the back door flying open, there came five spirits . . . in the likeness of ragged boys, some bigger than others, and ran about the house where she had drawn the staff; and the witch threw upon the ground crumbs of bread which the spirits picked up, and leaped often over the pan of coals in the midst of the circle, and a dog and a cat of the witch's danced with them.

After this performance, she said Mr. Mason should demand £1500 and £150 yearly, or else sue. Mrs. Bodenham was paid three shillings for this advice.

The go-between in these enterprises of Mrs. Bodenham and the Goddards was a servant, Ann Styles. This girl had bought arsenic for Mrs. Goddard's attempts at poisoning; when the intended victims, her two daughters, learned of this, they started inquiries. In fear, Ann Styles fled, having first stolen some silverware. She was soon apprehended, and, to save herself from punishment, accused Mrs. Bodenham of witchcraft. Ann Styles described how Mrs. Bodenham had changed herself into a black cat to tempt her into the Devil's service. Mrs. Bodenham pricked Ann's finger and wet a pen with her blood; she made her sign a red book containing the names of all those who had sold themselves to the Devil. One of the imps, like "great boys with long

Anne Bodenham divines the future.
"And the witch threw upon the ground crumbs of bread which the spirits picked up, and leaped often over the pan of coals in the midst of the circle, and a dog and a cat of the witch's danced with them." From Nathaniel Crouch, *Kingdom of Darkness* (1688).

shagged black hair," guided her hand. After the signing, all said Amen, and the imp gave Ann a silver coin.

At the trial, the mark on Ann's finger where she had been pricked and the piece of silver were conclusive evidence against Mrs. Bodenham. To give added weight to her accusations, Ann went into fits, describing how a black man without a head battled for her soul. She went into trances at the approach of Mrs. Bodenham, waking up quite well when the witch was removed. The accused was searched, and two witch's marks were found, one on her shoulder and the other in her pudenda. Mrs. Bodenham was condemned and hanged at Salisbury (Wiltshire) in 1653. On the way to the scaffold, the eighty-year-old woman pleaded to be given beer so she could become drunk for the hanging; she cursed her accusers and jailers, forgiving none; she refused to let a psalm be sung for her; and she completely denied all accusations of traffic with Satan.

Drummer of Tedworth. Drummings which could be heard a long way from the house, children lifted up into the air, a Bible hidden in ashes, shoes flung at a man's head, chamberpots emptied onto beds, a horse with one of its rear legs forced into its mouth—all this typical poltergeist display in the home of John Mompesson, a magistrate of Tedworth, Wiltshire, from March, 1662, to April, 1663.

Could these things be?

> Mr. Mompesson is . . . a discreet, sagacious and manly person . . . the scene of all being his own house, himself a witness and that not of a circumstance or two, but of an hundred, not for once or twice only, but for the space of some years, during which he was a concerned and inquisitive observer . . . .

> And what interest could any of his family have had (if it had been possible to have managed it without discovery) to continue so long so troublesome and so injurious an imposture?

> Nor can it with any whit of more probability be imagined, that his own melancholy deluded him, since (beside that he is no crazy nor imaginative person) that humor could not have been so lasting and pertinacious . . . .

> Or if it were so in him, can we think he infected his whole family, and those multitudes of neighbors and others, who had so often been witnesses of those passages?

> In these and such like instances, it is not to be conceived how tricks could have been put upon so many, so jealous, and so inquisitive persons as were witnesses of them.

With these arguments, Joseph Glanvill vouched for the veracity of the disturbances at the home of John Mompesson, after he had compiled from divers eyewitnesses and his own inspection the story of the Drummer of Tedworth.

The commotion started in March, 1662, with the arrest of William Drury, a vagrant drummer, who "went up and down the country to show hocus-pocus, feats of activity, dancing through hoops and such like devices." Drury was accused of using counterfeit documents to obtain money while traveling to Portsmouth. The local magistrate, John Mompesson, set him free but confiscated his drum—Drury had been a regimental drummer. From the time of Mompesson's taking away the drum, the strange phenomena at Mompesson's home

at Tedworth commenced, becoming more annoying after the drum had been destroyed. Early in the following year, Drury was apprehended at Gloucester for stealing pigs, but although found Guilty escaped hanging. Sentenced to transportation, he jumped overboard from the convict ship and made his way home to Uffcot, only a few miles from Tedworth. Here he bought a new drum and started beating it. Within twenty-four hours, Magistrate Mompesson had him seized and put in Salisbury jail. Drury was charged with practicing witchcraft, but was acquitted on this charge for lack of evidence, although several local gentry, including the parson, testified against him. On the original charge of pig-stealing, the drummer was found Guilty and condemned once again to transportation to Virginia.

The first to comment on the Tedworth Drummer was Rev. Joseph Glanvill, chaplain to Charles II and a Fellow of the Royal Society, who went to Tedworth to investigate. The following extracts are taken from his *Saducismus Triumphatus*.

> The noise of thumping and drumming was very frequent, usually five nights together, and then it would intermit three. It was on the outsides of the house, which

"From eight till four in the morn,
With a rattling thundering noise."
—*A Wonder of Wonders* (1662).

The Drummer of Tedworth. From Joseph Glanvill, *Saducismus Triumphatus* (1683).

is most of it board. It constantly came as they were going to sleep, whether early or late. After a month's disturbance without, it came into the room where the drum lay, four or five nights in seven, within half an hour after they were in bed, continuing almost two. The sign of it, just before it came, was . . . an hurling in the air above the house, and at its going off, the beating of a drum like that at the breaking up of a guard. . . .

On the fifth of November, 1662, it kept a mighty noise, and a servant observing two boards in the children's room seeming to move, he bid it give him one of them. Upon which the board came (nothing moving it that he saw) within a yard of him. The man added, "Nay, let me have it in my hand." Upon which, it was shoved quite home to him. He thrust it back, and it was driven to him again, and so up and down, to and fro, at least twenty times together, till Mr. Mompesson forbade his servant such familiarities. This was in the daytime, and seen by a whole room full of people. . . .

Mr. Mompesson perceiving that it so much persecuted the little children, he lodged them out at a neighbor's house, taking his eldest daughter, who was about ten years of age, into his own chamber, where it had not been a month before. As soon as she was in bed, the disturbance began there again, continuing three weeks drumming, and making other noises, and it was observed that it would exactly answer in drumming anything that was beaten or called for. After this, the house where the children were lodged out, happening to be full of strangers, they were taken home, and no disturbance having been known in the parlor, they were lodged there, where also their persecutor found them, but then only plucked them by the hair and night clothes without any other disturbance. . . .

After this, it was very troublesome to a servant of Mr. Mompesson's, who was a stout fellow and of sober conversation. This man lay within, during the greatest disturbance, and for several nights something would endeavor to pluck his clothes off the bed, so that he was fain to tug hard to keep them on, and sometimes they would be plucked from him by main force, and his shoes thrown at his head. And now and then he should find himself

forcibly held, as it were bound hand and foot, but he found that whenever he could make use of his sword, and struck with it, the spirit quitted its hold. . . .

The drummer was tried at the Assizes at Salisbury upon this occasion. He was committed first to Gloucester Jail for stealing, and a Wiltshire man coming to see him, he asked what news in Wiltshire. The visitant said he knew of none. "No," saith the drummer. "Do not you hear of the drumming at a gentleman's house at Tedworth?" "That I do enough," said the other. "I," quoth the drummer, "I have plagued him (or to that purpose) and he shall never be at quiet, till he hath made me satisfaction for taking away my drum." Upon information of this, the fellow was tried for a witch at Salisbury, and all the main circumstances I have related were sworn at the Assizes by the minister of the parish, and divers others of the most intelligent and substantial inhabitants, who had been eye and ear witnesses of them, time after time for divers years together.

Two comments in Glanvill's narration of the fantastic aerial drummings may be overlooked, and Glanvill himself tended to disregard their significance. Whenever a weapon was employed as defense against the poltergeist, the "drummer" drew back. A "stout fellow," one of Mompesson's servants, "found that whenever he could make use of his sword, and struck with it, the spirit quitted its hold." The human origin of the drummer is also implied in the account of Mompesson, who, "seeing some wood move that was in the chimney of a room, where he was, as of itself, discharged a pistol into it, after which they found several drops of blood on the hearth, and in divers places of the stairs."

Attention to such details, however, would have robbed the legend of its supernatural authority for Glanvill, who thereafter became, one might say, the father of modern psychical research. John Beaumont, in his *Historical, Physiological and Theological Treatise of Spirits, Apparitions, Witchcrafts, and Other Magical Practices* (1705), says he was told the disturbances were committed by "two young women in the house with a design to scare thence Mr. Mompesson's mother." Maybe Mompesson and Glanvill were being imposed upon. A committee sent by King Charles heard no unusual noises.

Reports of cannon and rifle shots and beating of drums in Yorkshire and Lincolnshire were widespread in 1658, two years before the Tedworth trouble. These alleged noises, however, were not linked to any individual, but their fame may have prepared credence in Drury (*A True Relation of a Very Strange and Wonderful Thing That Was Heard in the Air*, 1658).

Ducking: see Swimming.

Early Writers on Witchcraft (to 1550). The thirty writers noted here illustrate the development of the theory of witchcraft, and show how, with only a few exceptions, the weight of educated opinion had by 1550 evolved the concept of witchcraft as heresy, to be extirpated with all ruthlessness. Nearly all these early works were written in Latin, but translations soon spread the theory to the general public: German in 1517, Italian in 1523, and Spanish in 1539. Manuscripts originally written in the vernacular, though not printed until later, include one in German in 1456 and one in French in 1460. England was relatively free from persecution and therefore from theoretical manuals until the end of the sixteenth century.

The obstacle all these theologians had to overcome was the Canon Episcopi, in which belief in women riding with Diana through the skies was declared a superstition. This had to be discarded before witchcraft persecutions could occur. The Canon was circumvented by three common theses: (1) present-day witches were not the same as those mentioned in the Canon; (2) the Canon Episcopi was not approved by a General Church Council and therefore not binding; and (3) supporting the Canon interfered with getting rid of the witches (as Jacquier honestly put it). Later, Spina, in a massive attack, added a fourth argument: that the Canon was not authentic. The work of these opponents was made easier by a succession of papal bulls con-

demning witchcraft: by Gregory IX (1231), Alexander IV (1258), John XXII (1320), Innocent VIII (1484), Julius II (1504), Leo X (1521), and Adrian VI (1523). The result of all this debate was to make witchcraft a *new* heresy (as many writers so called it—*nova*); this emphasis shows that simple acts of magic—though these led into—were not the *essence* of witchcraft, which was defined as a pact with the Devil to abjure and renounce the Christian God and the Catholic Church.

From the works of these early writers emerges the witches' sabbat. This theory resulted from the questions set by the inquisitors to which the accused were forced to agree. The inquisitors then published the confessions. Other inquisitors elaborated on these and, of their own invention, devised further details. Nider, the earliest writer, in 1435 did not even mention the sabbat, but by 1450 the inquisitor in French Savoy was able to give particulars. Bernard de Como in 1510 elaborated further, and Prierias topped them all in 1521. By the time of Grillandus (1536), some anticipation of the Black Mass could be discerned. The reasons for the alleged growth of the new heresy were uniformly ascribed

One of the earliest illustrations of a book on witchcraft, Ulrich Molitor's *De Lamiis* (1489), showing a witch "inoculating" a man through his foot. From Cornell University Library.

A

DISCOVRSE

OF THE DAM-

NED ART OF WITCH-
CRAFT; SO FARRE FORTH
as it is reuealed in the Scriptures, and
*manifeſt by true expe-
rience.*

FRAMED AND DELIVERED
by M. WILLIAM PERKINS, *in his ordi-
narie courſe of Preaching, and now publiſhed
by* THO. PICKERING *Batchelour of
Diuinitie,* and Miniſter of Fin-
ching field in Eſſex.

WHEREVNTO IS ADIOYNED
a twofold Table; one of the order and Heades
of the Treatiſe; another of the texts of Scripture
explaned, or vindicated from the cor-
rupt interpretation of the
Aduerſarie.

"Now if any man doubt whether there be such witches indeed as have been described, let him remember that, besides experience in all ages and countries, we have also sundry examples of them even in the Scriptures."— William Perkins, *Discourse* (1608).

to increased activity by the Devil. Only Mamor suggested that, in France, the cause was the Hundred Years' War and sorcery brought in by foreigners.

Throughout all this trend toward the glorification of superstition, some stood up to oppose it. Before 1550 it was possible to do so and live; after 1550 and for the next century, opponents were silenced—by fear or by death. So in the roster of the heroes of humanity must be placed the French physician Symphorien Champier (about 1500), the Franciscan Samuel de Cassini (1505), the Milanese lawyer Andreas Alciatus (about 1514), and finally the Florentine lawyer Gianfrancesco Ponzinibio, who utterly rejected both witchcraft and Inquisition [see Demonologists].

Magic or sorcery was not an issue: everybody accepted it, and some thought it might even have its uses. The civil law, for example, did not prosecute a good witch who un-hexed and stopped tempests. In introducing the theory of the heresy of witchcraft, the theologians knew they were breaking new ground. Prominent were the Domini-

can inquisitors, especially Nicholas Eymeric (in the fourteenth century), Nicholas Jacquier, Jean Vineti, and Girolamo Visconti. Playing up the authority of Thomas Aquinas, the Dominicans, it might be said, must bear the responsibility for swinging the Church to a belief in witchcraft.

The inquisitors met considerable opposition, about which they frequently complained. Nider and Vineti said many disbelieved in the incubus demons; Jacquier that "many" opposed the inquisitors; Visconti (as did Pico) that "many" believed confessions were only extorted by torture (and so he wrote a book to refute them). Spina likewise had to write a book against the disbelievers. Thomas Murner (1499) accused some theologians of explaining misfortunes by natural causes rather than by witchcraft; and one Oranus (quoted in Del Rio) lamented that so many learned men in France were skeptics (naming, among others, Montaigne). And Alciatus (about 1514) said the peasants in the subalpine valleys broke into rebellion at the wholesale burnings by the local inquisitor.

This evidence is important, for it disproves a common conception that the less educated people were prone to believe in witchcraft and that the educated opposed it. The reverse is true. Witchcraft was a notion evolved primarily by the Inquisition and opposed by the people (with a handful of lawyers and physicians); it was learned, not popular. Only later, after decades of pounding in the new doctrine, did public support for the delusion grow.

Edward VI: Statute of 1547. In December, 1547, the sixth year of the reign of Edward VI, a general bill was passed to repeal statutes for treason and felony passed under Henry VIII, most of which had been directed against premature Protestants. Among the statutes so revoked was the act of 1542 making witchcraft a felony.

The repeal noted that men in other countries might consider certain laws passed under Henry VIII "very straight, sore, extreme, and terrible." Edward VI, therefore, wished that "the severity of certain laws here following be mitigated and re-

Early Writers on Witchcraft
to the publication of the *Malleus Maleficarum*

DATE OF WRITING	AUTHOR	POSITION	TITLE OF BOOK	DATE, PLACE OF PUBLICATION	REMARKS
c. 1435	Nider, Johannes*†	Dominican professor and prior	*Formicarius*	c. 1475 ? Augsburg	Second book ever printed about witchcraft. No comments on sabbat.
c. 1450	Vineti, Jean	Inquisitor at Carcassonne	*Tractatus contra Demonum Invocatores*	—	First book to identify witchcraft as heresy.
c. 1450	—	Inquisitor in French Savoy	*Errores Gazariorum*	—	Idea of sabbat highly developed.
c. 1456	Hartlieb, Johann	Physician to King of Bavaria	*Buch aller verbotenen Kunst, Unglaubens und der Zauberei*	—	First work written in German.
1458	Jacquier, Nicholas*	Inquisitor in France and Bohemia	*Flagellum Haereticorum Fascinariorum*	1581	First major definition of witchcraft as new heresy.
1458	Alphonsus de Spina*†	Franciscan (converted Jew)	*Fortalicium Fidei*	1467 Strasbourg	First book ever printed about witchcraft.
1460	—–	Inquisitor at Lyons	*La Vauderye de Lyonois*	—	First work written in French.
1460	Visconti, Girolamo*†	Inquisitor, professor, provincial of Lombardy	*Lamiarum sive Striarum Opusculum*	1490 Milan	Even defending witches is heresy.
c. 1460	Martin de Arles	Frenchman, professor and canon in Spain	*Tractatus de Superstitionibus*	1517 Paris	
c. 1462	Mamor, Petrus	Canon, regent of University of Poitiers	*Flagellum Maleficorum*	1490 Lyons	Spread of witchcraft in France due to Hundred Years' War and magic introduced by foreigners. Sabbat described.
c. 1468	Vignati, Ambrogio de	Jurist and professor at Padua, Bologna, Turin	*Tractatus de Haereticis* (lectures)	1581	Urges caution with accusations by accomplices.
c. 1470	Jordanes de Bergamo	Master of theology at Cortona (Italy)	*Quaestio de Strigis*	—	Accepts witchcraft as heresy, but tries to reconcile Canon Episcopi.
c. 1475	Vincent, Jean	Prior at Vendée (France)	*Liber Adversus Magicas Artes*	—	Accepts magic; rejects witchcraft.

[* entry for these writers; † illustration of manuscript or printed book]

Early Writers on Witchcraft
from the *Malleus Maleficarum* to 1550

AUTHOR	POSITION	TITLE OF BOOK	DATE, PLACE OF PUBLICATION	REMARKS
Innocent VIII*†	Pope	*Bull: "Summis desiderantes affectibus"*	1484 Rome Printed in *Malleus*	Appointed Sprenger and Kramer as inquisitors to intensify witchcraft trials, using torture.
Sprenger, Jakob Kramer, Heinrich	Inquisitors	*Malleus Maleficarum**†	c. 1486	The most evil book of the witchcraft delusion. Developed theory of the heresy of witchcraft into rigid code and set pattern for 300 years.
Molitor, Ulrich	Professor of Law University of Constance	*Tractatus de Pythonicis Mulieribus*	1489 ? Constance	If witchcraft is illusion, should be punished as if real.
Champier, Symphorien	Physician	*Dialogus in Magicarum Artium Destructionem*	c. 1500 Lyons	Sabbat a delusion; *maleficia* due to natural causes. Physicians should treat deluded. Remarkable enlightenment.
Prierias, Sylvester	Inquisitor in Lombardy; papal spokesman against Luther	*Sylvestrina Summa*	1504 Bologna	Influenced by *Malleus*. Devoted to explaining away Canon Episcopi.
		De Strigimagarum Daemonumque Mirandis	1521 Rome	Accepts full-blown theory of witchcraft; gives rules for trials, in which condemnation is inevitable.
Cassini, Samuel de*†	Franciscan (opposed Savonarola)	*Question de le Strie*	1505 ?	The first book to attack the identification of witchcraft as heresy, calling inquisitors the heretics.
Geiler von Kaysersberg*†	Priest	*Die Emeis* (1508)	1517 Strasbourg	First book about witchcraft printed in German (collected sermons). Advocates burning white witches as well.
Trithemius	Abbot	*Liber Octo Questionum*	1508 ? 1515, Oppenheim	Follows *Malleus*. All trouble caused by witches, who must be burned.
		Antipalus Maleficiorum	1508 ? 1555, Ingolstadt	
Bernard de Como	Inquisitor at Como	*De Strigiis* [in *Lucerna Inquisitorum*]	(1510) 1566 Milan	Accepts full-blown theory of sabbat as real and corporeal.
Tengler, Ulric*†	Lawyer	*Layenspiegel*	? 1509 ? Augsburg	Follows *Malleus*; secular courts should follow procedure of Inquisition in witchcraft trials.
Alciatus, Andreas	Lawyer at Milan	*Parergon Juris*	(c. 1514) 1558 Basel	Skeptic: witches' delusions about sabbat can be cured by herbs.

Early Writers on Witchcraft
from the *Malleus Maleficarum* to 1550   (continued)

AUTHOR	POSITION	TITLE OF BOOK	DATE, PLACE OF PUBLICATION	REMARKS
Pompanazzi, Pietro	Professor at Padua	*De Naturalium Effectuum Causis*	(1520) 1556 Basel	Inclined to skepticism; escaped punishment by plea that as *philosopher* he might doubt, yet as Catholic he truly believed everything the Church taught.
Ponzinibio, Gianfrancesco *†	Lawyer (? at Florence)	*Tractatus de Lamiis*	(c. 1520) 1563 Venice	Very important work, completely opposing witchcraft delusion and conduct of trials by Inquisition. Accepts simple sorcery.
Pico della Mirandola, Gianfrancesco*†	Lawyer	*Strix*	? 1523	
		Strega (Italian)	1524, Bologna 1555, Pescia	First book about witchcraft printed in Italian. Accepts witchcraft delusion, stressing incubi.
Spina, Bartolommeo*	Theologian, Master of Sacred Palace	*Quaestio de Strigibus*	(1523) 1525 Venice	Disciple of Prierias. Most violent promulgation of extreme witchcraft delusion to date. Opposed Ponzinibio.
Grillandus, Paulus*†	Papal judge in witch trials in Rome area	*Tractatus de Hereticis et Sortilegiis*	(1525) 1536 Lyons	Major work treating in detail all aspects of extreme witchcraft delusion from viewpoint of ecclesiastical law.
Cirvelo, Pedro*†	Inquisitor at Saragossa	*Opus de Magica Superstitione*	1521 Alcala	
		Reprobación (Spanish)	1539	First book about witchcraft printed in Spanish, a classic for a century; relatively moderate.
Vitoria, Francisco de	Professor of theology, University of Salamanca	*Relationes xii Theologicae*	(1540)	Inclined to skepticism.

[* entry for these writers;   † illustration]

mitted . . . repealed and utterly void and of none effect."

From 1547 to 1563, when a second bill against witchcraft was passed, there was no specific law against sorcery, except insofar as sorcery involved murder or treason. The 1547 bill, in fact, specifically mentioned as still felonious "willful killing by poisoning." However, as beforetime, political witchcraft could be taken care of in any highhanded manner, law or no law. *The Autobiography of Edward Underhill* (1859) tells of a sixteenth-century prognosticator's prophesying the life expectancy of Edward VI, and being rushed off to jail:

When we had dined, the mayor sent two of his officers with me to seek Alan, whom we met within [St.] Paul's [Cathedral], and took him within unto his chamber, where we found figures set to calk [calculate] the nativity of the

King, and a judgment given of his death, whereof this foolish wretch thought himself so sure that he and his counselors the papists bruited it all over. The King lay at Hampton Court the same time, and my Lord Protector at the Sion, unto whom I carried this Alan, with his books of conjuration, circles, and many things belonging to that devilish art, which he affirmed before my Lord was a lawful science, for the statute against such was repealed. "Thou foolish knave," said my Lord, "if thou and all that be thy science tell me what I shall do tomorrow, I will give thee all that I have."

Alan was sent to the Tower for a year, but was "by friendship delivered. So escapeth always the wicked."

Eichstätt Witch Trial. The following report of a witch trial in the bishopric of Eichstätt, near Ingolstadt, in 1637 was written down by the official scribe during the actual trial in the courtroom and in the torture chamber. It was first published, with four others, in 1811, but, possibly out of respect to the descendants, the names of all concerned were omitted from the text (being indicated only by N.N.). The original manuscript which would have supplied these names is now, unfortunately, lost. The scribe reported the whole trial in the third person, introducing the evidence of the accused with "*Sagt*" [she says]. The English has been freely translated from the German; two or three passages have been rearranged, where a literal translation would not have made sense.

In this trial, the procedure follows every approved cliché of witchdom: the accused first denies, then is tortured; she invents what she thinks the judges want; then, released from the torture, she recants her confession, and straightway is tortured again. Soon she becomes half demented and ends up by believing herself a witch. None of the crimes of which she was accused—night rides, sabbat banquets, storm-raising, exhumation of corpses, passing through locked doors—was real or possible of proof; nor was any proof offered. Once faced with fifteen denunciations, probably

The concept of the sabbat in the trial at Eichstätt; an engraving from the German translation (1693) of Nicholas Remy's *Demonolatreiae*.

made by other simple persons themselves under torture, or even taken from a stock list of crimes of witchcraft, she was doomed. The judges, as this record shows, were interested only in extorting a confession of guilt and securing the names of alleged accomplices, who sooner or later would be subjected to similar procedures. During this time, the accused was allowed no legal aid; she was not confronted by witnesses, and only after her sentencing was a priest permitted her.

The accused is clearly a poor peasant woman, distracted by terror and perhaps by the unique importance of her role—many highly paid officials devoted three weeks of their time to killing this creature. When she hesitates, she is shown the instruments of torture, and her memory revives. The Spanish boots are put on, and in fright she answers while awaiting the tightening of the screws which will crush her legs. When particularly un-co-operative, she is hoisted on the strappado. She becomes almost incoherent, and semi-meaningless phrases tumble forth, mingled with shrieks of "O Jesus Christ, be with me. . . . Dear God, open your ears again to me." After two weeks' interrogation and torture, she is flogged to the sound of bells ringing the Angelus; she stumbles into a recital of "the long belief," or the creed; and then the phrases the judges want to hear come out.

Verbatim reports of other trials may prove more horrifying, more shocking, more revolting. This trial of the unknown woman at Eichstätt is just pathetic and sickening.

This and other court records included in this *Encyclopedia* are typical of tens of thousands of such trials all over western Europe. For any reader who wants to understand witchcraft, this record gives a very clear introduction.

TRIAL AT EICHSTÄTT

Present: the Herr Chancellor, the Herr Municipal Judge, the Herr Doctor, the Herr Secretary, and the Herr Recorder.

Monday, November 15, 1637

After serious consideration by the civil councillors of the court, the prisoner, N.N., commonly known as N.N., having been taken into custody on suspicion of witchcraft, and on fifteen sworn depositions, meriting death, is thoroughly examined as follows:

Q. What is her name?

A. N.N., aged forty years, does not know the names of either her father or mother, where they were born, where they were brought up, or when they died. She has lived with her husband twenty-three years, and during that time has borne eight children, five of whom are still living. Of the three deceased, one died of smallpox twenty-one years ago at the age of two; another died eight or

nine years ago at the age of six; and the third lad died six years ago also of smallpox. Because of these suspicious circumstances of death, she was told to appear at the Town Hall.

Q. Whether she knows the reason why she was commanded to appear at the Town Hall?

A. She knows of no reason other than the accusation of being a witch.

Q. That is true: otherwise she would not have been brought here. Therefore she should make a start at admitting her guilt, and not look round for any excuses.

A. She will suffer anything, but cannot admit that she is a witch.

Then the judges try to persuade and exhort her as strongly as possible to confess, but all is unavailing; so the prepared list of depositions and completed indictment are read to her and specifically discussed.

While the first deposition is being read to her, she laughs heartily at the charge and declares she prefers death. She replies how could she have done anything when she had not been anywhere. She admits she might possibly have been guilty of the second denunciation. Regarding denunciations 3, 4, 5, and 6, she says that never during her entire life has she been at a sabbat. Says she has no knowledge of denunciations 7, 8, 9, 10, and 11. Again, to denunciations 12, 13, 14, and 15, denies again any participation.

Thus, although she is in no way answerable or responsible for these charges, yet again she states she will gladly accept death.

Q. Whether she wishes to die like a witch?

A. Whatever God wishes, that is her wish too.

Q. Indeed. Therefore she should start making her confession and tell how long she has been engaged in this vice, and how she was first enticed into it.

A. Yes, your worships, I will go willingly wherever you want me, but I am not a witch, as true as Christ was tortured and made to suffer on the cross.

Then she is examined for the devil's mark, which is found on the right side of her back, near the shoulder blade, about the size of a half-kreutzer. Then the mark is pricked and found to be in-sensitive; however, when she is pricked in other places, she immediately behaves like crazy. Many more suspicious marks are observed. She is questioned:

Q. Where had she received these devil's marks?

A. She does not know. She had noth-ing to do with the devil.

Inasmuch as the accused does not re-spond to merciful treatment, she is brought into the torture chamber.

*Evidence taken down
in the torture chamber*

After being put on the ladder, and the ropes tightened a little, she says, Yes, she could be a witch. When released, she announces she is not a witch. Therefore she is put back on the ladder and drawn once, twice, and thrice; finally, she is re-leased on the admission that she is a witch. But immediately she becomes stubborn and denies she is a witch. Then again she is drawn even more tightly on the ladder.

She confesses it is true that fourteen years ago when she was unmarried she had become a witch.

Q. But since she had testified that she had been married for twenty-three years, how could it be only fourteen years ago that she became a witch?

A. At this, she asked to be taken off the ladder, when she would tell the truth.

Q. No, she must first make a start at confessing; she deserves to remain on the ladder.

When she finds out she is not going to be released, she says that about eight-een years ago, once her husband had come home drunk and wished the devil would take her (at that time she had just given birth to another child) and her children, young and old alike. [*Her statements start to become confused.*] And she thought, Oh, when would he come! Oh, soon! And at one time she had an illicit love affair with a hangman, and the devil presented himself the next day during the night in the guise of this same hangman. In fact, he arrived dur-ing the first night, but since a light was burning continuously, therefore he could not get anywhere with her. And since she was under the impression that he was the hangman, the next night about ten

o'clock she had intercourse [*ungebühr*] with him, and his member was very cold. After having had intercourse a second time, the devil revealed who he was, talking lewdly, and demanded she give herself to him, and deny God and our dear Lady and all the holy saints. He threatened her so she had to submit to him, but now she was penitent and wanted to turn to God again.

Q. Whether the devil did not demand anything more of her?

A. To do evil everywhere.

Q. What methods was she supposed to employ to work evil?

A. Eight days after her seduction, the devil gave her a green powder and a black ointment in an earthen dish, which she used on man and beast.

Q. Whether she still has any of this material?

A. No. She threw it into the water four weeks ago.

Q. Whether she had been forewarned of her impending arrest?

A. No, nothing beyond what her sister had warned her.

Q. Whether she had flown also with her sister?

A. No. But they had seen each other at the devil's sabbat.

Q. What did the devil call her, and what name did she call the devil?

A. She called the devil *Gokhelhaan* [rooster] and he called her *Shinterin* [bone-breaker]. Three weeks after her seduction, the devil baptized her and poured something over her head.

Q. Is all what she is saying true?
A. Yes.

She is led out of the torture chamber.

Tuesday, November 16, 1637

Present: The Deputies, the Herr Mu-nicipal Judge, the Herr Doctor, and the Herr Recorder. The accused is brought in, and the usual prayers are said.

Q. Whether she could truly confirm with heart and mouth what she had con-fessed yesterday?

A. Yes, her whole confession is true. By the way, she is afraid that because of her great sins she will not get to heaven. Because of her seduction, she cannot pray to God any more. The devil made her obey him by beating her often and severely. Only last night she twice heard a rustling sound in her cell. Even now during this examination she hears rustling sounds.

The court then gave her good advice how to protect herself from the wicked enemy and insure her salvation.

A. Yes, this is true. If she had remained outside the Church, she would never have found salvation. If it is the will of God that the whole world should be a witness to her evil doings, she is willing to make a public confession; and she desires to pray for their worships the Herr Chancellor and the Herr Doctor because they ordered her to appear in this court. The devil often caused her pain while they were in bed together, so that she screamed out and wakened her husband, who soon after began to sleep in a separate bed. [*She is quoted directly.*]O Jesus Christ, be with me, and because I have grievously sinned against thee, please, dear God, open your ears again to me.

Q. How often did she receive powder and ointment from the devil? Whether she had any more powder and ointment in her possession?

A. Yes. In her store, to the left as one enters from the alley, there is a box which has four drawers on top; in one of these is the ointment.

After searching the store, a court officer found three small boxes of ointment and one box with powder, which he delivered to the Town Hall.

Q. Whom did she injure with this material?

A. First, about eight or nine years ago, she was ordered by the devil to smear the ointment on a cherry and give it to her six-year-old daughter to eat, intending to poison her. Then the child became ill, and within one hour passed from life to death. As a result of this, she was told to appear at the Town Hall. Incidentally, if her husband had not been so religious, the devil would have killed him too.

Second, about thirteen or fourteen years ago, one night while her husband was asleep, the devil sprinkled a powder on him so that he should not wake up, and smeared ointment on his feet and hands, back and neck so that he should die. Within three days her husband got

bladder incontinence [*peissende*]which still troubles him to this day. She says she did not confess this crime, because, if she confessed, the devil would appear and give her no peace. [*Testimony becomes confused.*] A witch only finds salvation when she comes before the court, and she wants to tell them this to their faces.

Third, three years ago she mixed the devil's ointment into a stew and gave it to the four-year-old son of her former mistress. The boy instantly caught the gangrenous plague and died within two days.

Q. Is what she has said true?

A. Yes, she wishes to confess not only this but much more.

[*Then she relates three other instances of maleficia using ointment, and implicates one of her victims, whom she says she introduced to witchcraft. Later denies this. She tells how her little daughter took sick through this ointment. On the next day she thinks a sore on the side of her body is a symptom of the plague, but the hangman Mathess reports this is not any matter for concern. The court then asks what does concern her?*]

A. Last night our dear Lady appeared to her so beautiful and snow white.

Since the prisoner feigns sickness and seems to want to deny her evidence, and since the signs of her piety of yesterday seem to fade, she is ordered to be flogged in the torture chamber to induce fear and a true testimony. After three floggings she says that the devil, dressed in black, came to her prison cell last night and this morning. Last night he arrived precisely between eleven and twelve o'clock and had intercourse with her, but he caused her so much pain, that she could hardly hold him, and she thinks her back and thighs are falling apart. Furthermore, she promised to surrender her body and soul to him again, to reveal nothing of this pact, and to remain true to him only, and to oppose the judges as long as she can. In return, her incubus promised to help her and ordered her to think how she could commit suicide. To this end, she continued scratching open with her fingernails the middle veins on her right arm, a half *bazen* wide, where she had had a blood-letting two weeks ago, because the scars were very recent and the veins could be opened very easily. In this way she could kill herself without attracting attention and go to the devil in both body and soul.

[*Then comes some unimportant testimony about how the devil told her to ascribe the fatal results of the ointment to the plague, and how the devil forced her to surrender herself to him.*]

Now this has been recorded, she is told to answer the following questions:

Q. What do these four boxes delivered to the Town Hall represent—they include two boxes filled with red ointment, one with a whitish ointment, and one with a whitish powder? Inasmuch as at the beginning of her testimony, she mentioned only one, and when confronted with these four she said that the real one is missing, what testimony is true?

A. She received these little boxes from her incubus devil, Gokhelhaan, in order to harm humans and animals. What she said yesterday, namely, that the real box was missing, was done to confuse the judges.

Now she renounces again the Devil and is ready to go a step further toward her salvation by requesting the most severe punishment. She is ready to bear the responsibility before God and the world that her new testimony will be true.

After a discussion of a specific point, she gives the final two examples of her evil-doing using ointment and powder:

Seventh, eight years ago she killed her own black cow using a devilish powder which she mixed in its mash. It was healthy but died within two or three days.

Eighth, six years ago, she sprinkled the powder on her brown horse and it collapsed.

Q. Whether her preceding testimony is true?

A. Yes.

She is led away into custody and put under closer surveillance.

Friday, November 19, 1637

The prisoner is led out again and questioned.

She says and announces publicly that all her life she never saw the devil nor had intercourse with him. All her previous testimony was untrue. Neither her conscience nor her devotion and love to Jesus Christ permit her to continue these lies. She reached this decision just last night. If she could have found a knife to thrust into her breast, she would have killed herself. Indeed, she had asked the guard twice to let her have a knife, giving as an excuse that the collar of her smock was too tight and she wanted to loosen it.

The judges listened to this revocation and recognized her stubborn devilish heart. Her eyes were red as if the devil had tried to pull them out of their sockets. The hangman was ordered to stretch her on the ladder. Soon after, she asked to be released and promised to tell everything she had done during her life.

Q. Is her preceding testimony true?

A. Yes; unfortunately, not only this but everything else she will reveal.

Q. What was the cause of her revocation?

A. The devil visited her last night at twelve o'clock and committed lewdness with her and commanded her to deny everything she had testified previously, saying he would help her.

Thereupon she was released from the rack as one made penitent by torture.

Interrogation continued after the midday meal

Q. Why did she contradict herself this morning? When questioned, she must tell the whole truth. Ordered to swear whether testimony is true or false, and when she started to make a true confession.

A. She indicates willingness by saying Yes. She says the devil was with her all through the night; he not only consoled her and promised to help her again, but also ordered her to think seriously how she might do away with herself. At his prompting, she then decided to ask for a knife so as to make a noose from the collar band of her smock and hang herself. Later, she thought she would pull her tongue out of her mouth, and finally she tried to suffocate herself with her index-finger.

Not satisfied with all her efforts to please him, the devil beat her severely, poked her eyes (which are black and blue and bloodshot) so that they started to bleed and demanded that she sign a pact written in her own blood, brutally guiding her left hand to write a new contract, reading, "I, Shinterin, will be yours in soul, flesh and blood, skin and hair, everything that I am, for ever and ever."

Then the devil took the contract and ordered her to repeat it in her own words. This she did, promising to reveal nothing. The devil said he would not forsake her [*testimony becomes incoherent here*] and again encouraged her to continue with her devilish deeds and then disappeared. She is sorry from the bottom of her heart to have done this and will not do it again. The judges gave her a long sermon, telling her if she was again assailed by the wicked enemy, they could bless and protect her.

[*Two depositions are omitted here, of children injured with magic ointment: her own child still sick in the head, and another boy killed.*]

Saturday, November 20, 1637

She is summoned before the court and to begin with she is asked:

Q. What is her mode of life?

A. Well . . . being alone, she feels afraid and does not know why.

Q. Whether the devil had not attacked her again last night?

A. No.

Q. How often during each month and each year did she fly? Where did she go, and for what purpose?

A. Twice a month, twenty-four times a year. To prevent her husband from waking up and interfering, the devil sprinkled a powder over him, so the devil and she could meet each other wherever they wished, in the kitchen, the bedroom, hall, or loft. The devil presented her with a pitchfork [*Gabl*], to be used exclusively for flying, which he smeared with some magic ointment. The devil always sat in front, and she sat behind. Whenever she wanted to depart for the sabbat, she recited this charm:

Hui! Up the chimney, up the window hole!

In the name of the Devil, out and onward!

While riding the pitchfork, the devil emitted fiery streams so that she could see very little. The assembly places, so far as she knew, were the N. pastures, the gallows, and the N. mountain. At first it seemed they had lots to eat and drink, roasts and stews, served in green dishes. But the food was insipid as well as moldy [*hilz*], completely black, very sweet, indistinguishable, and badly prepared. She never saw bread or salt, and she drank white wine from wooden or clay cups. The wine was brought in pitchers or leather skins. They sat on seats and benches as well as on the gallows. During the meal they blasphemed God and plotted how to commit *maleficia*.

They also talked about the municipal judge and the commissars, and how they should go among the people and have no pity on them. The witches were admonished to continue boldly and not to become confused or give up. The man who gave the sermon was short and fat, with a black beard, and he preached from a wooden pulpit. These sabbats occurred on Thursdays and on Saturday nights at ten or twelve o'clock, according to the season of the year. The place was illuminated by lights held by poor old women; she herself had once held up a light with one hand. After that the dancing began. The chief devil was seated in an easy chair, and special honor was paid him by curtsying with their backsides. After dancing round together in no set pattern, couples paired off to commit lewdness on the side lines. She thought the musicians were pipers and fiddlers, but she did not know any of them. About fifty people, some wearing masks, attended these sabbats. A certain person, N.N. from N., was present. They all sat at a round table.

But when a big sabbat took place, the witches were so numerous they could not be counted. When the time for departure came, the chief devil said, "Hui! Away with you, in the name of the Devil!" They left in the same way they came. Specifically she saw at the sabbat the following:

Accomplices

1. N.N. of N. Little Lane. She saw her two years ago on the N. Mountain during winter, and the last time in the N. pasture eating the sabbat banquet. This woman danced with an incubus devil in the guise of a blacksmith's apprentice and also had intercourse with him. He wore a leather apron and a cap, and she wore a fur [*Belz*] and a black skirt pulled over it.

Tuesday, November 23, 1637

2. She had seen the N.N. woman eight or ten times, the first time six years ago in the N. pastures and the last time a year and a half ago inside the N. Mountain at a sabbat banquet. She ate, drank, danced, and jumped. Specifically, a year ago she flew with her into the cellar of N.N. and drank wine. Her two incubus demons had been present, and the woman, N.N., had appeared in a black dress. Her incubus was disguised as a tanner.

[*During the following days, to November 26, the accused identified 45 accomplices. For every person named, she described characteristic clothing and actions, and the attendant incubus or succubus.*]

Q. Is all this previous testimony true?
A. Yes. She can truly justify this informing before God and the world; she wishes to receive the sacrament of penance and the holy communion, and then give up her body and soul.

Friday, November 26, 1637

Sacrilegious Acts

The accused says that during the time she was under the influence of the devil, she had been to confession and had received holy communion fifteen times. But fourteen years ago, while receiving communion, she put the sacred host into a handkerchief and took it home and threw it away into a nasty place [*Garstiges*]. Twelve years ago, she had dishonored the sacred host in the same way.

Six years ago, when she had received communion, she retained the sacred host in her mouth and took it into her garden and placed it on the cover of the well.

She stabbed it with a knife many times until the holy and pure blood ran out; then she threw it with a little cloth into the well. Instead of saying her prayers she prayed that thunder and hail might bring on destruction.

She called our dear God a murderer, our dear Lady a godless woman, and all the holy saints she called Jews, hangmen, slaves, lackeys, and the most infamous names she could think of.

Q. Whether her testimony so far is true?
A. Yes.

She is suspected of storm-raising and of passing through locked doors into cellars.

Saturday, November 27, 1637

Storm-Raising

The accused said she had thought about storm-raising for a long time, and had helped cause eight tempests. The first storm she had made fifteen years ago, between midday and one o'clock, in her own garden, spurred on by the devil to make the fruit drop so that it would not ripen. This happened.

Q. With what materials did she raise storms, or how else did she do it?
A. She does not want to divulge her secret.

Since she also tries to recant, she is confronted with the hangman, and again asked:

Q. Whether she wants to confess voluntarily or under torture. It was discussed.

A. She will confess voluntarily.

So the hangman leaves, and she is questioned again.

A. She says that the devil supplied her with a powder made from children's corpses and told her to use it for raising storms. She gave the powder to N.N., her loyal accomplice, who buried it in the ground but it popped out. Then she herself buried it, but she pretends to be uncertain what happened. She says her testimony so far is true, but then she sighs heavily.

This seems to be another revocation. So she is again confronted with the hangman and questioned.

Q. How did she influence the weather?
A. She does not know what to say and

can only whisper, "Oh, Heavenly Queen, protect me!"

Q. How did she get the scratch on the right eye?

The Spanish boots were applied to one foot, but the screws were not tightened.

A. The devil in the guise of the hangman came to her last night at twelve o'clock and comforted her, saying that things would improve and that she should not be afraid for nothing would happen to her. Then they had intercourse twice, and she again promised to be his. Then she said that the devil did not order her to do anything, but that he had been with her and had intercourse with her.

Inasmuch as her answers are unsatisfactory [*kalt*], and she still seems to be under the domination of the devil, she is tied with ropes in order to receive a flogging. Several lashes arc administered. Thereupon she confesses that she and N.N., fifteen years ago, buried in her garden the powder she had received from the devil, in the hope that it would cause bad weather and prevent the fruit from ripening that year. And thus it happened.

She does not want to continue.

She says the devil commanded her not to say anything else. Whatever they asked her, she balked at, and recited the creed. And after long and repeated orders to confess, she was lashed three times with the whip while the bells tolled the Ave Maria. But she kept on saying black was white, and finally announced that the devil had forced her to make evasions and deviations in her testimony, but now she does not want to follow his advice any more. Last night the devil had given her a scratch over her left eye with his claw or flat foot. Then she was led back into the courtroom and questioned about storm-raising.

A. The first storm she invoked occurred immediately, and the fruit fell from the trees the same day. She raised another storm fourteen years ago by burying the same powder in the evening in the N. pasture, with the hope that it would drown the hay. It began to thunder and rain, and the hay was completely submerged.

[*A few confessions about storm-raising and plagues of caterpillars are omitted.*]

She is led away. Discord is suspected between her and her husband.

Wednesday, December 1, 1637

Called for examination so that the foregoing point may be discussed. She says she does not feel guilty of causing any discord. She is now furthermore suspected of exhuming children's corpses.

Friday, December 3, 1637

Exhuming corpses of children

She says that once, seven—eight—or nine years ago, she helped N.N. to exhume her own child from the cemetery. The child had lain in the grave for six years, and its body had all rotted away. They took the remains home and put them in a pot and stirred them for two days and nights, then pounded them into a powder with a snath. They gave the powder to the devil. N.N. is not implicated, for even though the devil asked for more powder, she refused to make it and was beaten by the devil.

She is led away and suspected of subornation.

Saturday, December 11, 1637

She says she did not suborn [*verfiehrt*] anybody.

Passage into cellars

She passed through closed doors into the wine cellars of [five names given] about forty times. Also present were two witches, identified by name, who drank wine from the measuring cup or right from the bung.

She also flew into the stable of N.N., and with the help of the devil rode the animals so that they should die. They did not die.

She also went often into the servant's room, and seduced her servant, N.N.; indeed, he had let her show it to him often.

Q. What other crimes can she think of, and are there other things she can remember? This question is discussed.

A. No. But what she has testified is the truth, for which she is responsible before God and the world. Wishes to live and die according to this testimony and be justified by the verdict of the court.

Whereupon she is led back to the torture chamber and the list of her accomplices is read to her, and she confirms it.

Monday, December 13; Tuesday, December 14; Wednesday, December 15: she again confirms all the foregoing testimony as true.

Friday, December 17, 1637

She dies penitent.

Eichstätt suffered also in 1590 and from 1603 to 1630. In twenty-four years to 1627, for example, 113 women and 9 men were burned. In 1629, an Eichstätt judge said he had sentenced 274 witches. These witch hunts were promoted by the Bishop of Eichstätt, Johann Christoph. Evidently he aroused some dissent, for on December 11, 1627, the Bishop stopped confiscating the estates of his victims, many of them upperclass, to show his zeal was solely to honor God. Typical of these earlier trials is that of Anna Käser of Eichstätt, executed September 29, 1629, at Neuburg. The sole charge against her—attendance at the sabbat—had been built up on the forced confessions of other accused, going back almost ten years to the first denunciation in 1620. This, with later accusations in 1624, 1626, and 1627, had been carefully hoarded and finally used to behead and burn her. She told her confessor her testimony had been extorted by torture, and that she and all the others were innocent. The priest reported this to the court, and Anna was tortured a fifth time, more brutally than ever.

Elizabeth: Statute of 1563. Between 1547 and 1563 no laws against witchcraft were on the statute books in England. But there was plenty of discussion about sorcery. In fact, there were more interest and more concern than ever before. Some critics—for example, Notestein, followed by Summers and Davies—ascribe the spurt in activity against witches to the return of the 472 exiled Protestant leaders (many of whom later became bishops in the Episcopal Church or otherwise influential in state affairs) who had witnessed the witch-burnings at such notorious centers as Strasbourg, Frankfort, Zurich, Geneva, and Basel. Bishop John Jewel's sermon before Queen Elizabeth at Oxford about 1560 attacked

that kind of people (I mean witches and sorcerers) [who] within these last few years are marvelously increased within your Grace's realm. These eyes have seen most evident and manifest marks of their wickedness. Your Grace's subjects pine away even unto death, their color fadeth, their flesh rotteth, their speech is benumbed, their senses are bereft. Wherefore, your poor subjects' most humble petition unto your Highness is that the laws touching such malefactors may be put in due execution.

Kittredge, who minimized the influence of such extreme Protestants, pointed out that the wording of the act of 1563 followed the act of Henry VIII. Furthermore, an attempt was made to pass a witchcraft control bill in March, 1559 (when the Marian bishops were still in control), and it was dropped only because of the excitement in passing the Supremacy Act and the Act of Conformity. However, extremists of both left and right, Calvinists and Romanists, were ever indefatigable in combating the devil—and his witches. Most of the indictments for witchcraft during the reign of Elizabeth occurred in Essex, part of the diocese of Bishop Edmund Grindal, a witch-hunting Calvinist, who once complained "our ecclesiastical punishment is too slender" for sorcery.

Clearly, the clergy of all persuasions were not averse to a bill punishing sorcery; they were, indeed, theologically committed to its support. The Convocation of the Church of England, in effect a third "house," met simultaneously with the Lords and Commons at the opening of Parliament in 1563 and advocated "that there be some penal, sharp, yea, capital pains for witches, charmers, sorcerers, enchanters, and such like." The bishops, from about 1550 on, included questions on sorcery in their episcopal visitations. One of the Articles of Enquiry of 1559 asks the churchwardens and parishioners: "Whether you know any that do use charms, sorcery, enchantments, invocations, circles, witchcrafts, soothsaying, or any like crafts or imaginations invented by the Devil, and specially in the time of women's travails?"

It is more probable, however, that the immediate impetus to pass the act was political, and originated in the Privy Council. The danger of sorcery to the English government, as to the Roman Empire, lay not in petty acts of harming cattle or even people, but in the very real menace of political prophecy. Only a year or two prior to the passage of the witchcraft bill, nine men were tried at Westminster before the Queen's Bench for conjuration and sorcery. They confessed their wickedness, but were merely bound over to stand in the pillory and to swear "to abstain from the like acts for the future."

On the other hand, Hutchinson (*Historical Essay,* 1720) noted the condemnation for treason in 1562 of the Countess of Lennox and four others who "had consulted with some pretended cheating wizards to know how long the Queen should live." Such wizardry was the true threat. It is noteworthy that the act preceding the statute against witchcraft was directed against "fond and fantastical prophecies," by writing, printing, singing or any other open speech or deed, using arms, beasts, cognizances, and prophesying bloodshed or war.

Protestant Elizabeth had been on the throne only a month when Sir Anthony Fortescue was arrested for casting a horoscope of the Queen's life. Later, in 1563, he was indicted, along with Arthur and Edmund Pole (nephews of the Cardinal) and five others, for treason; they pleaded "they meant to attempt nothing in the Queen's lifetime, who by conjuration they had found should not live passing the next spring." A prophecy of impending demise could easily provoke a rebellion, and in the still unsettled times Elizabeth could not afford to take risks. Prognostications increased during the reign (especially after 1578), so that a further statute in 1581 decreed that "if any person . . . shall by setting or erecting any figure or by casting of nativities or by calculation or by any

prophesying, witchcraft, conjurations . . . seek to know . . . how long her Majesty shall live . . . that then every such offense shall be felony." Protestant England was generally quite willing to believe that the Roman Catholic supporters of Mary Queen of Scots were resorting to sorcery against Elizabeth. "Witchcraft became at once the most dangerous and detested of crimes," concluded Notestein.

A bill aimed at the political implications of witchcraft could count on popular support for quite different reasons. There were always the common suspicion of and hostility to witches, natural enough at a time when any misfortune not traceable to clearly discernible causes was considered the result of *maleficia;* in fact, there are scattered records of local courts (town courts, archdeacon's courts) acting against witches even before 1563. Physicians, too, were strongly opposed to "wise women" dabbling in medicine. Thomas Gale in 1562 blamed such witches for permanently disabling over 300 people whom he found in two London hospitals. Furthermore, the main area of witch persecutions in this reign was the populous and industrial southeast, especially affected by Calvinist doctrines, and therefore ideologically conditioned to damn witchcraft as the work of the Devil.

In January of 1563, an attempt to revive the statute of Henry VIII against witchcraft failed—Henry's statute had been repealed in 1547 under Edward VI. By March 19, a new bill passed both houses of Parliament. The Scottish Parliament, with the Roman Catholic Mary as Queen, in June, 1563, passed a similar bill (repealed much later under George II). The Elizabethan statute was replaced by a more stringent act under James I; in Ireland (passed in 1586) it continued law until its repeal in 1821. The chief provisions of Elizabeth's act were the death penalty for murder by sorcery, and a year's imprisonment and the pillory for witchcraft not deadly. Property was forfeit only on conviction for a second offense, and only in crimes of divination, attempted murder, and unlawful love. Under the act of 1604, confiscation of property was entirely removed from the penalties. On the surface Elizabeth's statute seemed mild, merely enforcing the death penalty for murder; but this act started the whole witch mania in England. The first major trial resulting from it was that of the Chelmsford Witches. But for this bill, the 535 known indictments for witchcraft in the reign of Elizabeth, and the 82 known executions, might never have taken place.

AN ACT AGAINST CONJURATIONS, ENCHANTMENTS, AND WITCHCRAFTS (5 Eliz. cap. 16).

[Preamble] Where[as] at this present, there is no ordinary or condign punishment provided against the practicers of the wicked offenses of conjurations and invocations of evil spirits, and of sorceries, enchantments, charms, and witchcrafts, the which offenses by force of a statute made in the 33rd year of the reign of the late King Henry VIII were made to be felony, and so continued until the said statute was repealed by the act and statute of repeal made in the first year of the reign of the late King Edward VI; since the repeal whereof many fantastical and devilish persons have devised and practiced invocations and conjurations of evil and wicked spirits, and have used and practiced witchcrafts, enchantments, charms, and sorceries, to the destruction of the persons and goods of their neighbors and other subjects of this realm, and for other lewd intents and purposes contrary to the laws of Almighty God, to the peril of their own souls and to the great infamy and disquietness of this realm:

I. For reformation whereof, be it enacted by the Queen's majesty, with the assent of the Lords spiritual and temporal, and the Commons, in this present Parliament assembled, and by the authority of the same, that [a] if any person or persons after the first day of June next coming, use, practice, or exercise, any invocations or conjurations of evil and wicked spirits, to or for any intent or purpose, or else [b] if any person or persons after the said first day of June shall use, practice, or exercise any witchcraft, enchantment, charm, or sorcery, whereby any person shall happen to be killed or destroyed, that then as well every such offender or offenders in invocations or conjurations as is aforesaid, their counselors and aiders, as also every such offender or offenders in witchcraft, enchantment, charm, or sorcery whereby the death of any person doth ensue, their aiders and counselors, being of either of the said offenses lawfully convicted and attainted, shall suffer pains of death as a felon or felons, and shall lose the privilege and benefit of sanctuary and clergy. Saving to the wife of such person her title of dower, and also to the heir and successor of such person his or their titles of inheritance, succession and other rights, as though no such attainder of the ancestor or predecessor had been had or made.

II. And further be it enacted by the authority aforesaid, that if any person or persons, after the said first day of June next coming, shall use, practice, or exercise any witchcraft, enchantment, charm, or sorcery, [a] whereby any person shall happen to be wasted, consumed, or lamed in his or her body or member, or [b] whereby any goods or chattels of any person shall be destroyed, wasted, or impaired; then every such offender or offenders, their counselors and aiders, being thereof lawfully convicted, shall for his or their first offense or offenses suffer imprisonment by the space of one whole year, without bail or mainprize [surety], and once in every quarter of the said year shall in some market town, upon the market day or at such time as any fair shall be kept there, stand openly upon the pillory by the space of six hours, and there shall openly confess his or her error and offense, and for the second offense, being as is aforesaid lawfully convicted or attainted, shall suffer death as a felon, and shall lose the privilege of clergy and sanctuary. Saving to the wife of such person her title of dower, and also to the heir and successor of such person, his or their titles of inheritance, succession, and other rights, as though no such attainder of the ancestor or predecessor had been had or made.

III. Provided always, that if the offender, in any of the cases aforesaid for which the pains of death shall ensue, shall happen to be a peer of this realm, then his trial therein to be had by his peers, as it is used in cases of felony or treason, and not otherwise.

IV. And further, to the intent that all manner of practice, use, or exercise of witchcraft, enchantment, charm, or sorcery should be from henceforth utterly avoided, abolished, and taken away; be it enacted by the authority of this present Parliament, that if any person or persons shall, from and after the first day of June next coming, take upon him or them by witchcraft, enchantment, charm, or sorcery, to tell or declare in what place any treasure of gold or silver should or might be found or had in the earth, or other secret place; or where goods, or things lost or stolen should be found or be come; or shall use or practice any sorcery, enchantment, charm or witchcraft to the intent to provoke any person to unlawful love; or to hurt or destroy any person in his or her body, member, or goods; that then every such person or persons so offending, and being thereof lawfully convicted, shall for the said offense suffer imprisonment by the space of one whole year without bail or mainprize, and once in every quarter of the said year shall in some market town, upon the market day or at such time as any fair shall be kept there, stand openly upon the pillory by the space of six hours, and there shall openly confess his or her error and offense. And if any person or persons, being once convicted of the same offense, as is aforesaid, do eftsoons perpetrate and commit the like offense, that then every such offender, being thereof the second time convicted as is aforesaid, shall forfeit unto the Queen's majesty, her heirs and successors, all his goods and chattels and suffer imprisonment during life.

Endor Witch. Believers in witchcraft sought justification in the Bible, especially in the Old Testament. One widely discussed illustration was the so-called Witch of Endor described in I Samuel xxviii. King Saul, dismayed about an attacking Philistine army, sought advice from a medium. Although necromancy was a felony, the woman agreed to summon the spirit of his predecessor, Samuel, who might advise him:

And the woman said unto Saul, I saw gods [i.e., demons] ascending out of the earth.

And he said unto her, What form is he of?

And she said, An old man cometh up; and he is covered with a mantle.

And Saul perceived that it was Samuel, and he stooped with his face to the ground, and bowed himself.

Then Saul supposedly heard the voice of Samuel, projected in some ventriloquial manner by the medium, just as if he had been at a modern spiritualist séance. Celebrated theologians debated whether Saul heard the "soul" of Samuel or merely an evil spirit impersonating him (see also I Kings xxii. 22).

The Latin Vulgate calls the woman a *pythonissa* or *mulier pythonem habens*, that is, a woman telling fortunes by the inspiration of a python or conjured spirit. The Greek Septuagint translated the Hebrew *'ôbh* by *heggastramythos* [ventriloquist]. The Acts of the Apostles (xvi. 16) refer to Paul at Philippi meeting "a certain girl having a pythonical spirit, who brought to her masters much gain by divining."

Saul had failed to receive guidance from his professional seers (I Samuel xiv. 37). Striving to retain a monopoly on their divination, they had outlawed clandestine mediums: "Neither let there be found among you anyone . . . that consulteth soothsayers . . . pythonic spirits, or fortunetellers, or that seeketh the truth from the dead. For the Lord abhorreth all these things." (Deuteronomy xviii. 10-12, Douay Version; see also Leviticus xx. 6, 27.) Such was the Witch of Endor.

In the English Authorized Version, the woman medium is referred to as "a woman that had a familiar spirit," not in the sense that she had a "control" through which she could produce materializations of dead people, but in the brand-new seventeenth-century sense of a Christian witch who enjoyed the services of a personal demon disguised as some little animal or familiar. To the story of the Witch of Endor, King James's translators in 1611 added running titles or headings, e.g., "Saul consulteth a witch," thereby sanctifying the recent law of 1604 with the quite bogus authority of the Holy Scriptures. Reginald Scot, one of the first (1584) to show that the diverse meanings of Hebrew and Greek words could not sustain witchcraft, dismissed the theological debates:

> Samuel was not raised from the dead, but . . . it was an illusion or cozenage practiced by the witch. . . . I confess that Augustine and the residue of the doctors that deny the raising of Samuel conclude that the devil was fetched up in

The Witch of Endor. The frontispiece of *The History of Witches, Ghosts, and Highland Seers* (Berwick, about 1803).

his likeness. From whose opinions, with deference I hope I may dissent.

The Witch of Endor. Engraving from the German translation (1693) of Nicholas Remy's *Demonolatreiae* (1595).

England, Witchcraft in. Scattered laws against witchcraft were made in England from very early times, both by church and state. The concept of witchcraft, in Anglo-Saxon and Medieval England, however, differed from the later sophisticated idea of a conspiracy to overthrow the Christian God, involving a compact with the Devil. Consequently, to about 1500, while the punishments might be savage, the crime was not serious (no matter how heinous some might consider it). Witchcraft was sorcery—evildoing. Witchcraft was damage to crops or cattle caused by spells, poisons, or storm-raising. It was damage done to people, ranging from sickness and sterility to death. In the early regulations, witchcraft involved a specific malicious act which could be seen and proved. Black magic was as tangible as white magic, and both were reprehensible. When prayer to the Christian God failed, the wise man or wise woman gave help with some concrete object by which *beneficia* might overcome the physical evidences of *maleficia*. Witchcraft was a crime against man, rather than (as later in the sixteenth and seventeenth centuries) a crime against God. Consequently, the standards of evidence, the rules of trial, and the penalties tended to be like those for any other anti-social act. At the end of the tenth century a law of King Aethelred exiled witches along with whores. Under Edward I, those who burned a neighbor's house or crops were themselves burned; if such people were called "witches," it was not particularly significant. What witches *did* counted, not what they *thought* they did.

Probably the first legislation against witches occurred in the *Liber Poenitentialis* of Theodore, Archbishop of Canterbury (668-90); a typical penance, such as for divination, was a prescribed time of fasting. Similarly, the *Confessional* of Ecgberht, Archbishop of York (735-66), provided that a woman slaying by incantation fast seven years. On the other hand, the secular penalty two centuries later under King Athelstan (925-39) made death the penalty for murder by witchcraft—or murder by any other means. William the Conqueror (1066-87) reduced the sentence to banishment. As in all other crimes, the witch could claim trial by ordeal. Thus Agnes, the wife of Odo, the earliest known person accused of sorcery in England (in 1209), was freed after the ordeal of grasping a red-hot iron.

To about 1200 or 1300, suspected witches were generally tried in an ecclesiastical court and turned over to the secular arm for punishment. In the fourteenth and fifteenth centuries, the accused might be tried in a church court, in a local court, or in the superior court. In practice, conviction carried a relatively light punishment, and few suffered death. In 1371, for example, a man arrested for possessing a skull, the head of a corpse, and a *grimoire*, was released on promise never again to perform magical rites; his props were publicly burned. In 1390, for soothsaying in London, John Berking was sentenced to one hour in the pillory, two weeks' imprisonment, and banishment from the city. As late as 1467, by which time thousands of witches had been burned in France, one William Byg, for gazing in a crystal to lo-

cate thieves, merely had to appear in public with a scroll on his head, *"Ecce sortilegus* [Behold the fortuneteller]."* Under the Statute of Henry VIII he would have been hanged, as under the law of James I (for a second offense). In 1525, twenty men were acquitted for murder by use of a waxen image. In 1560, eight men (including two in orders) confessed to conjuration and sorcery. They were released after swearing to abstain from such acts in the future and a brief appearance in the pillory. The forbidden acts were precisely those which three years later became punishable by imprisonment or death. Their oath read:

> Ye shall swear, that from henceforth ye shall not use, practice, devise, or put in use, or exercise, or cause, procure, counsel, agree, assist, or consent to be used, devised, practiced, put in use or exercised, any invocations, or conjurations of spirits, witchcrafts, enchantments, or sorceries, or any thing whatsoever touching, or in any wise concerning the same, or any of them, to the intent to get, or find any money or treasure, or to waste, consume, or destroy any person in his members, body or goods, or to provoke any to unlawful love, or to know, tell or declare where goods lost or stolen be come, or for any other purpose, end or interest whatsoever, so help you God and the holy contents of this Book.

Before 1563, if the accused was outside the court circles, he met light punishment for all those practices described as "witchcraft." If the accused was a nobleman, however, a charge of sorcery was serious because it implied treason. To burn an effigy or poppet of a monarch was high treason because it revealed *intent*. A man so conspiring would as readily resort to arms. A diviner who made a horoscope of the life of a monarch also committed high treason, for enemies could profit by a pessimistic prognostication. Queen Elizabeth was particularly sensitive to this danger, especially toward the end of her reign, and in 1581 a special statute laid down the same severe penalties for prognostication as for satanic witchcraft.

Thus in England many noblemen suspected of political opposition were accused of witchcraft. In 1324, twenty-seven defendants at Coventry were charged with employing two necromancers to kill King Edward. This was the first trial for witchcraft in a secular court. The dowager Queen Joan and Friar Randolph conspired against Henry V in 1417. Eleanor Cobham (the Duchess of Gloucester), Margery Jourdain (the Witch of Eye), Roger Bolingbroke, and Thomas Southwell sought the death of Henry VI in 1441. In 1478, the Duchess of Bedford was accused of sorcery. In 1483, the former Queen, Elizabeth Woodville, and Jane Shore were accused by Richard III of withering his arm; and the Countess of Richmond and Dr. Morton (later Archbishop of Canterbury) with other Lancastrian leaders were tried in the same year for using sorcery. Some later noble trials involved divination of the life expectancy of the king: the Duke of Buckingham in 1521, Sir William Neville in 1532, Lord Hungerford (who was beheaded) in 1541, Henry Neville in 1546, and the Countess of Lennox in 1562.

Witchcraft emerges in different lands at different times because it reflects the change and turbulence of a society, especially when new ideas and new values are replacing the old. In an age of implicit faith, the Devil can do little harm to believers; a prayer or amulet will protect them. Only when talismans fail are the powers of the Devil recognized. In England, such doubt and questioning became widespread in the reign of Elizabeth.

Witchcraft came to England in 1563, much later than elsewhere, although there had been a statute against witchcraft under Henry VIII; it had been of brief duration and was repealed by Edward VI in 1547. Only one conviction under this act is recorded (and this was remitted). Queen Elizabeth's Statute of 1563 resulted from the pressure of the clergy, and made the Devil an acknowledged factor in the laws of the state. To malicious actions causing injury it attached a smear of "witch"; soon this label or accusation was held sufficient proof of felony even when the malicious actions could not be proved. The act

of Elizabeth, like that of Henry VIII, made death the penalty for invoking or conjuring an evil and wicked spirit "to or for any purpose." Having included this catchall clause, it went on to list specific acts, "whereby any persons shall be killed or destroyed . . . or wasted, consumed or lamed in his or her body or matter." But the invocation of evil spirits *per se* (even without injury resulting) was a felony. This attitude crystallizes the contrast between the primitive and the later conceptions, between *sorcery* (such as existed in all primitive societies) and *witchcraft* (sorcery plus herësy, which can exist only in a Christian society).

The growth of superstition and credulity in the reign of Elizabeth can be followed in the entries on such famous and typical trials as the Chelmsford Witches (1566), the first major trial in England; the St. Osyth Witches (1582), one of the first to disregard conventional rules of evidence; and the horrible trial of the Warboys Witches (1593), when the whims of five sick children sent three harmless people to their death. [See separate entries for these trials.]

Under Elizabethan practice, a woman accused of bewitching children would face their allegations, and some attempt would be made to sift the charges (no matter how ridiculous these were). The witch might be acquitted. In the same year (1582) as the St. Osyth witches were hanged, Allison Laws, notorious as a sorceress, was merely sentenced to do penance in the market place at Durham "with a paper on her head." Just when the new, harsher statute of James I was being enacted, in 1604, fourteen-year-old Anne Gunter of North Moreton (Berkshire) accused an old woman of bewitching her. The trial ended with the acquittal of the accused, the court disallowing the use of the children's test charm, "I, Mary Pepwell, charge thee, white toad, to come out of thee, Anne Gunter." After the trial, Anne was examined by a doctor, who diagnosed hysteria from *natural* causes; Anne confessed she had counterfeited supernatural possession, and was charged with conspiracy. From about 1600 on, many such children were exposed: the Burton Boy (1597), the Northwich Boy (1604), the Leicester Boy (1616), the Bilson Boy (1622), and Edmund Robinson of the Pendle Swindle (1633). [See Children as Accusers.]

Later, the act of James I (1604), while retaining the phraseology, imposed more severe penalties for the same offenses. The act developed the idea of invoking a spirit into the idea of a pact with the Devil; it became a felony to "*covenant* with . . . any evil and wicked spirit." This covenant was the core of the witchcraft delusion, although many indictments still charged simple acts of *maleficia*.

Fantastic as the Elizabethan trials had been, they were based on some groping effort to distinguish right from wrong. "Wrong" was the Devil busily working to destroy men's souls, even if knowledge of the Devil came chiefly through the mouths of children. As legal procedures under the later statute solidified, evidence concentrated on finding the devil's mark, given by the devil only to those who had professed allegiance to him in a covenant. So at Chelmsford in 1645, for example, Matthew Hopkins, who made a career of discovering witches, replaced children's ravings with warts. Perhaps he evolved his techniques to circumvent the by now suspect evidence of children, who admitted accusing old women for gain or (like the Salem girls in America) for "fun."

Authorities differ as to when the witch mania raged most fiercely. Kittredge, for example, believed the republican Calvinists (and hence the New England Puritans) were no more intolerant than anyone else; his evidence is tendentious. On the other hand, Notestein believed the Protestant leaders exiled under Queen Mary introduced the fanatical views on witchcraft they had learned on the Continent. He is supported, more recently, by Trevor Davies, who stresses the downward trend of witch trials under the first two Stuarts (James I and Charles I), and the sudden revival of the delusion under the Calvinists in the Great Rebellion of 1642-60. This much is sure: the more intolerant the belief in God,

the greater hostility to heresy—and witches, as servants of the Devil, were the worst heretics: they were apostates.

Delusions fostered by the Church became the beliefs of the people. If the Devil existed, it was a small step to the supposition that personal acquaintance was possible and that agreements and liaisons could be made. Protestants were as superstitious as Catholics, and the Reformation in no way lessened the persecutions arising from these ridiculous beliefs. (Ewen, *Witch Hunting and Witch Trials*, 1929)

Pioneer research by Ewen into the indictments surviving in the (London) Public Record Office and elsewhere has shown several peaks of persecution, with the *greatest number of accusations* of witchcraft in the reign of Queen Elizabeth. Then the accusations rose again under the Commonwealth. The *proportion of hangings to indictments* for the five counties forming the Home Circuit (Essex, with the most hangings, and Hertford, Kent, Surrey, Sussex) shows the most dangerous time for a witch was the closing years of Queen Elizabeth's reign and the first years of Charles I (41 per cent hanged), as well as the early Commonwealth. The *greatest slaughter of witches* came in the summer of 1645 in the Matthew Hopkins campaign. The following table shows the per cent of those indicted who were hanged in various decades, ending

1567 —	20	1627 —	6
1577 —	32	1637 —	0
1587 —	21	1647 —	42
1597 —	21	1657 —	15
1607 —	41	1667 —	4
1617 —	17		

After 1667 in the Home Circuit there were no executions. Records for other circuits are too scattered to be of much use. The changed attitude in the second half of the seventeenth century is clear, however, from the trials in the Norfolk sessions. For example, in 1668 the jury dismissed charges against Mary Banister of bewitching thirteen-year-old John Stocking, who shrieked whenever she approached him. In the remaining Norfolk sessions from 1661 to

1679, there were fifteen indictments of bewitching; six cases were thrown out, eight
found Not Guilty, and one accused died in
prison. These verdicts would have been
impossible a few years earlier. In the Western Circuit between 1670 and 1712, there
were only fifty-two trials for witchcraft,
and of these only seven resulted in convictions (one of which was reprieved). As
charges of witchcraft decreased, however,
charges of malicious damage increased.

The prevalence of witch trials varied according to the determination of the local
justices and to the fear of the local residents. In London, for example, in 1640 a
mob murdered Dr. Lamb, the alchemist, a
protégé of the Duke of Buckingham, on
rumors of witchcraft [see Dr. Lamb's Dar-
ling]. Major prosecutions against witches
occurred in Essex in 1583, Lancashire in
1633, Scotland in 1643-50, East Anglia in
1645, Newcastle in 1649, Kent in 1652, and
Scotland again in 1661. Ewen summarized:

> There was, in fact, no clearly defined
> periodic wave of witch-mania sweeping
> throughout the country, but rather a
> succession of sporadic outbursts. The un-
> derlying current of superstition always
> present manifested itself unpleasantly
> whenever and wherever fanaticism was
> unusually rampant, the influence of one
> man often being sufficient to raise the
> excess of zeal to the danger point.

Two examples of an individual's influence on the course of witchcraft may be
studied in the decisions of Sir Matthew
Hale (1609-76) and Sir John Holt (1652-
1710), both in turn Chief Justices of England. Hale believed wholeheartedly in the
menace of witches, and accordingly he
manipulated court procedure to secure
convictions. His contempt of orderly proc-
esses was seen at Bury St. Edmunds in
1645, where, by admitting "spectral evidence," Justice Hale made possible the
Salem hangings. On the other hand, Holt
swayed the courts in the opposite direction;
no one accused of witchcraft was ever convicted in his sessions. Because of his prestige, lower judges followed his example,
just as they had imitated Hale. These men
exercised more influence in the long run

than the notorious Matthew Hopkins, the
Witch Finder General, who was directly
responsible for the hanging of at least
sixty-eight persons known by name, and
probably of many others whose records
have not been preserved. The Hopkins delirium lasted less than a year (1645).

Various estimates have been given of the
number of persons hanged for witchcraft
in England, ranging as high as Robert
Steele's ridiculous estimate in *Social England* (1903) of 70,000 under the Statute
of James I alone. During the period of the
laws against witchcraft, i.e., 1542 to 1736,
which in practice is reduced to the hundred-
odd years of hangings between 1566 and
1685, Ewen "guesses" the number at less
than 1,000. No doubt this is the closest
approximation possible from extant records.

The first person definitely known to
have been hanged for witchcraft in England in modern times was Agnes Waterhouse at Chelmsford in 1566. Elizabeth
Howes was convicted of bewitching to
death in 1564 and may have been hanged
at the Essex assizes, although she pleaded
pregnancy. And in 1565 Joan Byden may
have been hanged in Kent for the same
offense. The last to be hanged was Alice
Molland at Exeter in 1684. After the restoration of the Stuart kings in 1660, there
were very few executions, and all indictments for witchcraft charged physical destruction or murder. The last hanging in
the Home Circuit was that of Joan Neville
on September 3, 1660, for murder by
witchcraft. After the executions at Bury St.
Edmunds in 1662, the next execution was
not until 1674, when Ann Foster was
hanged at Northampton for burning barns.
Mary Baguley was hanged at Chester in
1675, and in 1682 three women were
hanged at Exeter (sentenced by Sir Francis
North). However, in 1693 at Beccles, Suffolk, a Widow Chambers, accused of witchcraft, died in jail apparently as a result of
torture by "walking"—Hutchinson. The
last woman to be found Guilty as a witch
was Jane Wenham at Hertford in 1712;
she was reprieved. And in September, 1717,
at Leicester, Jane Clerk of Great Wigton

and her son and daughter became the last persons charged with witchcraft; the jury rejected the indictments. In 1751 a mob beat Ruth Osborne, a suspected witch, to death, but the ringleader was indicted for murder and hanged. After 1700, an accuser might himself be jeopardized. In 1701, Richard Hathaway accused Sarah Moredike of witchcraft; Sarah was acquitted on payment of fees, but Hathaway, "having falsely accused Sarah Moredike of witchcraft without any reason or color for the same," was jailed until he found bail for his appearance at the next assizes (*State Trials*). By the middle of the eighteenth century, witchcraft had been legislated out of existence.

Essentially, the basic philosophy of witchcraft varied little from country to country, or from time to time, no matter how this philosophy was legislated. The *Flagellum Haereticorum Fascinariorum* of Nicholas Jacquier in 1458 covered the same areas as Richard Bovet's *Pandaemonium* in 1684; the works of the classic Continental demonologists, such as Kramer and Sprenger, Bodin, Remy, and De Lancre, circulated widely in England [see John Dee].

Yet the English Channel preserved England from the grosser manifestation of the delusion in the rest of Europe, and English witchcraft took on national characteristics.

In England, there were no barbarous tortures: no strappado, no squassation, no rack, none of the unspeakable devices of the German prisons or of the Inquisition. Brutality was employed, and confessions (especially during the Hopkins terror) extorted. But there is a distinction between squassation and the slowly heated iron chair of Bamberg, on the one side, and enforced wakefulness (watching and waking), trussing of the limbs, and a diet of bread and water—the limit of the English tortures for witches.

Nor in England were *witches* as such ever burned alive at the stake—the universal practice elsewhere, including Scotland. Under English law burning was the penalty for treason, and scattered instances are found until its repeal in 1790. Margery

Jourdemain (Jourdain) was burned in 1444 for high treason against the king; that she employed witchcraft was incidental. Indeed, in 1432 she had been charged as a witch, then released on bail, and the charges dropped; two priests then arrested with her were also freed. Mother Lakeland in 1654 at Ipswich and Mary Oliver in 1659 at Norwich had been burned for petty treason—murdering their *husbands*. Murder of any other man by any means, including witchcraft, under the law would have warranted hanging but not burning. The canard about burning witches may have been spread by the misleading title of the contemporary pamphlet, *The Confession of Mother Lakeland of Ipswich, who was arraigned and condemned for a witch, and suffered death by burning at Ipswich in Suffolk on Tuesday, the 9th September, 1645.*

Nor were there at any time in England the mass executions that disfigured France and Germany, when hundreds were burned within a few weeks, as De Lancre boasted, or as the town records of Bamberg or Würzburg revealed. The largest mass executions in England comprised nineteen witches hanged at Chelmsford in 1645, and the nine Lancashire witches hanged in 1612.

The detailed descriptions of sabbat orgies which became the staple of confessions in all French trials were absent in the English trials. The sabbat feast in England consisted of the mutton consumed by the conspirators at Malking Tower [see Lancashire Witches]. A Continental-type sabbat cropping up in an English trial turned out to be an inspired story taught to a young boy by a Roman Catholic priest. Missing too from English records—and for this the Reformation is responsible—are those sad cases of possessed nuns whose frustrations led them to accuse priests of immorality. Apart from the routine statement (seldom elaborated) that the devil had carnal knowledge of the accused (testified by hags of eighty), sex was discreetly hushed in merry England. "Covens and devil priests and satanic orgies," wrote Kittredge, "are, for England, out of the question."

Penalties for Witchcraft in England, 1543-1736

For	1542-1547 33 Hen. VIII viii (1542)		1563-1604 5 Eliz. xvi (1563)	1604-1736 I Jas. I xii (1604)	
THOSE WHO PRACTICE INVOCATIONS OR CONJURATIONS OF EVIL SPIRITS					
Any purpose	Death Forfeit property		Death	Death	
THOSE WHO PRACTICE WITCHCRAFTS, ENCHANTMENTS, SORCERIES, CHARMS					
Divination of treasure trove	Death Forfeit property	1547-1563 I Ed. VI xii repealed all penalties for witchcraft.	1st: One year 2nd: Life Forfeit property	1st: One year 2nd: Death	1736 Anti-witchcraft bill of James I repealed by 9 Geo. II v.
Recovery of lost or stolen property	Death Forfeit property		1st: One year 2nd: Life	1st: One year 2nd: Death	
Murder	Death Forfeit property		Death	Death	
Bodily injury	Death Forfeit property		1st: One year 2nd: Death	Death	
Intent to cause murder, bodily injury, destruction of goods	Death Forfeit property		1st: One year 2nd: Life	1st: One year 2nd: Death	
Destruction of goods (and livestock)	Death Forfeit property		1st: One year 2nd: Death Forfeit property	1st: One year 2nd: Death	
Unlawful love	Death Forfeit property		1st: One year 2nd: Life Forfeit property	1st: One year 2nd: Death	
Destruction of cross	Death Forfeit property		———	———	
Theft of corpses	———		———	Death	

Benefit of clergy and protection in sanctuary were denied those charged with witchcraft. In the statutes of Elizabeth and James I, the widow of the executed witch retained her dower and the heirs the titles of their inheritance. Under Elizabeth, a witch condemned to life imprisonment forfeited his property. One year's imprisonment always included a public confession and four appearances in the pillory. The statute of James I added five new death penalties for witchcraft, making it much more severe than that of Elizabeth. The repeal bill of 1736 retained the penalty of one year in jail for pretending to locate stolen property or to tell fortunes.

England had some distinctive features. The English witch and wizard, like all the English, loved their animals, and every trial was replete with little domestic animals cherished as pets, referred to in the trials as imps, familiars, or devils. The art of pricking or discovering the devil's mark on the body of a witch, though practiced on the Continent, was especially English; again, hardly a trial lacked this testimony. Those children who at the sight of a witch took on fits, who recovered when allowed to draw blood by scratching the accused, who forced the witch to recite formulas that established her guilt, were also peculiarly English.

The relative simplicity of confessions and the absence of satanic rigmarole in English witch trials were due to the absence of a centralized, highly organized persecuting body, such as the Inquisition, which made all confessions conform to the pattern its demonologists had dreamed up. In addition, too, the continuing stream of Church

Writers Take Sides

Some Notable Books in the Witchcraft Controversy in England

In general, accepting the actuality of witchcraft and the necessity of punishment.	In general, skeptical of witchcraft and of the evidence presented at trials.
	A1. 1584 Reginald Scot, *Discovery of Witchcraft.*
	A2. 1590 Henry Holland, *Treatise Against Witchcraft.*
	A3. 1593 George Gifford, *Dialogue Concerning Witches and Witchcraft.*
1. 1597 King James I, *Demonology* (answers A1).	
	A4. 1599 Samuel Harsnett, *Discovery of the Fraudulent Practices.*
2. 1608 William Perkins, *Discourse of the Damned Art of Witchcraft.*	
3. 1616 Alexander Roberts, *Treatise of Witchcraft.*	A5. 1616 John Cotta, *Trial of Witchcraft.*
4. 1617 Thomas Cooper, *Mystery of Witchcraft* (based on 1, 2, A3; answers 1).	
5. 1619 Michael Dalton, *Country Justice.*	
6. 1627 Richard Bernard, *Guide to Grandjurymen.*	
	A6. 1646 John Gaule, *Select Cases of Conscience Concerning Witches.*
7. 1647 Matthew Hopkins, *Discovery of Witches* (answers A6).	
	A7. 1650 Nathaniel Homes, *Demonology and Theology.*
8. 1653 Henry More, *Antidote Against Atheism.*	A8. 1653 Robert Filmer, *Advertisement to the Jurymen of England* (answers 2).
	A9. 1656 Thomas Ady, *Candle in the Dark* (answers 1, 5).
	A10. 1669 John Wagstaffe, *Question of Witchcraft Debated.*
	A11. 1677 John Webster, *Displaying of Supposed Witchcraft.*
9. 1680 John Brinley, *Discovery of the Imposture of Witches.*	
10. 1681 Joseph Glanvill, *Saducismus Triumphatus.*	
11. 1681 Henry Hallywell, *Melampronoeia, or a Discourse on the Polity and Kingdom of Darkness.*	
12. 1684 Richard Bovet, *Pandaemonium* (answers A10, A11).	
13. 1691 Richard Baxter, *Certainty of the World of Spirits.*	
14. 1705 John Beaumont, *Treatise of Spirits.*	
15. 1715 Richard Boulton, *Complete History of Magic.*	
	A12. 1718 Francis Hutchinson, *Historical Essay Concerning Witchcraft* (answers 15).

Major English Witch Trials as Recorded in Contemporary Pamphlets

Queen Elizabeth I, 1558-1603

(Publication date of pamphlet in parentheses)

*1566 First Chelmsford Trials
The Examination and confession of certain witches at Chelmsford in the county of Essex before the Queen's majesty's judges, the 26th day of July, anno 1566. (1566)

1566 Dorset Trial
The Examination of John Walsh, before Master Thomas Williams, commissary to the Reverend Father in God, William, Bishop of Exeter, upon certain interrogatories touching witchcraft and sorcery, in the presence of divers gentlemen and others, the 20th August, 1566. (1566)

1579 Abingdon or Windsor Witches
A Rehearsal both strange and true of heinous and horrible acts committed by Elizabeth Stile, alias Rockingham, Mother Dutten, Mother Devell, Mother Margaret. Four notorious witches apprehended at Windsor in the county of Berks, and at Abingdon arraigned, condemned, and executed on the 26th day of February last, anno 1579. (1579)

*1579 Second Chelmsford Trials
A Detection of damnable drifts, practiced by three witches arraigned at Chelmsford in Essex at the late assizes there holden, which were executed in April, 1579. (1579)

*1582 St. Osyth (St. Osees) Witches
A True and just record of the information, examination and confessions of all the witches taken at St. Osees in the county of Essex; whereof some were executed, and other some entreated according to the determination of law. Written orderly, as the cases were tried by evidence, as by W. W., 1582. (1582)

*1589 Third Chelmsford Trials
The Apprehension and confession of three notorious witches arraigned and by justice condemned and executed at Chelmsford, in the county of Essex, the 5th day of July last past, 1589, with the manner of their devilish practices and keeping of their spirits, whose forms are herein truly proportioned. (1589)

1592 Mother Atkins of Pinner
A Most wicked work of a wretched witch (the like whereof none can record these many years in England) wrought on the person of one Richard Burt, servant to Master Edling of Woodhall in the parish of Pinner in the county of Middlesex, a mile beyond Harrow. Lately committed in March last, anno 1592, and newly recognized according to the truth by G. B., Master of Arts. (1593)

*1593 The Warboys Witches
The Most strange and admirable discovery of the three witches of Warboys, arraigned, convicted, and executed at the last assizes at Hundington. (1593)

*1597 The Burton Boy (Thomas Darling)
The Most wonderful and true story of a certain witch named Alice Gooderidge of Stapenhill, who was arraigned and convicted at Derby, at the assizes there. As also a true report of the strange torments of Thomas Darling, a boy of thirteen years of age that was possessed by the devil, with his horrible fits and terrible apparitions by him uttered at Burton-upon-Trent, in the county of Stafford, and of his marvellous deliverance. (1597)

[For the pamphlet war between John Darrell and Samuel Harsnett, see separate entries.]

King James I, 1603-1625

1612 The Northampton Witches
The Witches of Northamptonshire: Agnes Browne, Joan Vaughan, Arthur Bill, Helen Jenkinson, Mary Barber, witches, who were all executed at Northampton the 22nd of July last, 1612. (1612)

*1612 The Lancashire Witches (Old Demdike and Old Chattox)
The Wonderful discovery of witches in the county of Lancaster: with the arraignment and trial of nineteen notorious witches, at the assizes and jail delivery, holden at the Castle of Lancaster, upon Monday, the 17th of August last, 1612, before Sir James Altham and Sir Edward Bromley. [By John Potts] (1613)

1613 Three Bedford Witches
A Book of the witches lately condemned and executed at Bedford, 1612-13. (1613)

*1618 Margaret and Philippa Flower (and Rutterkin and the Earl of Rutland)
The Wonderful discovery of the witchcrafts of Margaret and Philip Flower, daughters of Joan Flower near Bever Castle; executed at Lincoln, March 11, 1618, who were specially arraigned and condemned . . . for confessing themselves actors in the destruction of Henry, Lord Rosse, with their damnable practices against others the children of the Right Honorable Francis, Earl of Rutland; together with the several examinations and confessions of Anne Baker, Joan Willimot, and Ellen Greene, witches of Leicestershire. (1619)

*1620 The Bilson Boy (William Perry)
The Boy of Bilson, or a true discovery of the late notorious impostures of certain Romish priests in their pretended exorcism or expulsion of the devil out of a young boy, named William Perry. (1622)

King Charles I, 1625-1642

[The only major scandal of this reign, Edmund Robinson, in the *Pendle Swindle, was not reported in a pamphlet.]

The Civil War and the Commonwealth 1642-1660

*1643 The Newbury Witch
A Most certain, strange and true discovery of a witch, being overtaken by some of the Parliamentary Forces, as she was standing on a small plank-board and sailing on it over the River of Newbury, together with the strange and true manner of her death. (1643)

*1645 The Hopkins Chelmsford Trial (Manningtree Witches) [See Hopkins]
A True and exact relation of the several informations, examinations, and confessions of the late witches arraigned . . . and condemned at the late session, holden at Chelmsford before the Right Honorable Robert, Earl of Warwick, and several of his majesty's Justices of the Peace, the 29th of July, 1645. (1645)

*1645 The Faversham Witches
The Examination, confession, trial, and execution of Joan Williford, Joan Cariden, and Jane Holt, who were executed at Faversham in Kent . . . all attested under the hand of Robert Greenstreet, mayor of Faversham. (1645)

*1645 The Hopkins Bury St. Edmunds Trials [See Hopkins]
A True relation of the arraignment of eighteen witches at St. Edmundsbury, 27th August 1645 . . . as also a list of the names of those that were executed. (1645)

1646 The Hopkins Huntingdon Trials
The Witches of Huntingdon, their examinations and confessions [by William Davenport]. (1646)

*1647 Summary of the Hopkins Witch Hunt [See Hopkins]
The Discovery of witches, in answer to several queries, lately delivered to the Judges of Assize for the County of Norfolk. And now published by Matthew Hopkins, witch finder, for the benefit of the whole kingdom. (1647)

1649 The St. Albans Witches
The Devil's delusions or a faithful relation of John Palmer and Elizabeth Knot, two notorious witches lately condemned at the sessions of Oyer and Terminer in St. Albans. (1649)

*1652 The Wapping Witch
The Witch of Wapping, or an exact and perfect relation of the life and devilish practices of Joan Peterson, who dwelt in Spruce Island, near Wapping; who was condemned for

practicing witchcraft and sentenced to be hanged at Tyborn, on Monday the 11th of April, 1652. (1652)

1652 The Maidstone (Kent) Trials
A Prodigious and tragical history of the arraignment, trial, confession, and condemnation of six witches at Maidstone, ir Kent, at the assizes there held in July, Friday 30th, this present year, 1652 . . . Collected from the observations of E. G., Gent., a learned person, present at their convictions and condemnation. (1652)

*1652 Dr. Lamb's Darling: the trial of Anne Bodenham
Doctor Lamb's Darling, or strange and terrible news from Salisbury, being a true exact and perfect relation of the great and wonderful contract and engagement made between the devil and Mistress Anne Boden-

ham; with the manner how she could transform herself into the shape of a mastiff dog, a black lion, a white bear, a wolf, a bull, and a cat . . . The trial, examinations, and confession . . . before the Lord Chief Baron Wild . . . by [Edmond] Bowen, Cleric. (1653)

King Charles II, 1660-1685

*1662 The Bury St. Edmunds Witches (Rose Cullender and Amy Duny)
A Trial of witches at the assizes held at Bury St. Edmunds for the county of Suffolk, on the 10th day of March, 1664 [=1662]. (1682)

1674 Ann Foster, witch
A Full and true relation of the trial, condemnation, and execution of Ann Foster . . . at the place of execution at Northampton. With the manner how she by her malice and

witchcraft set all the barns and corn on fire . . . and bewitched a whole flock of sheep. (1674)

1682 The Exeter Witches
The Trial, condemnation, and execution of three witches, viz., Temperance Lloyd, Mary Lloyd, and Susanna Edwards, who were arraigned at Exeter on the 18th of August, 1682. (1682)

A Later Pamphlet

*1712 Jane Wenham, the Witch of Walkern
An Account of the trial, examination, and condemnation of Jane Wenham, on an indictment of witchcraft, for bewitching of Matthew Gilston and Anne Thorne of Walcorne, in the county of Hereford. (1712)

Trials marked with an asterisk are treated in appropriate separate entries. In the reigns of Elizabeth and James I, there were about 50 pamphlets of famous witch trials in England. There were only some half-dozen executions for witchcraft during the reign of Charles I; then witch trials increased during the Civil War, reaching the highest peak in England in 1645. About 30 pamphlets record the trials during the Civil War and Commonwealth. After 1660, although the trials tapered off, pamphlets became numerous (perhaps because of the increasing rarity of charges of witchcraft), and literary wars were waged around famous trials, such as those of the Exeter witches in 1682 and Jane Wenham in 1712.

of England skepticism and the relatively brief domination of intransigent Calvinists kept an alternative Protestant pattern from forming in England.

The pros and cons of belief in witchcraft had been openly debated in England for about 150 years (from 1584) by eminent men, not only judges and theologians. Writers took sides. No such prolonged exchange of ideas appeared on the Continent. England could not escape the delusion which spread over western Europe—it is shocking to count the illustrious men who believed in witchcraft—but it was spared the most horrible features of the French and German trials. Even in the worst hysterias, some decent people opposed the irregularity of court procedures, if not the whole theory of witchcraft. To speak against witch hunts even when hunting witches was a patriotic sport, this was England's distinction in the history of witchcraft.

A convenient short history of witchcraft in England is found in the sixty entries contained in this *Encyclopedia.* For discussion and texts of the Statutes against witchcraft see Henry VIII, Edward VI, Elizabeth, James I, George I; for accounts of celebrated trials see Chelmsford Witches (1566), St. Osyth Witches (1582), War-

boys Witches (1593), Lancashire Witches (1612), Faversham Witches (1645), and, for the Bury St. Edmunds and Chelmsford Trials (1645), see Matthew Hopkins; Bury St. Edmunds Trials (1662). See also Margaret Flower (1618), Ruth Osborne (1751), Mary Bateman (1809). See Alice Kyteler (1324), Eleanor Cobham (1441). For notorious youthful impostors see Burton Boy (1597), Anne Gunter (1604), Leicester Boy (1616), Bilson Boy (1620), Pendle Swindle (1633, for Edmund Robinson); also John Darrell, Samuel Harsnett, Children as Accusers. For the work of two prominent jurists see Sir Matthew Hale and Sir John Holt; for the Witch Pricker General see Matthew Hopkins. For significant writers on witchcraft, accepting the delusion, see Richard Baxter, Richard Bovet, Nathaniel Crouch, Edward Fairfax, Joseph Glanvill, James I, Henry More, William Perkins; and, for those questioning belief, Thomas Ady, Sir Robert Filmer, George Gifford, Francis Hutchinson, Reginald Scot, John Wagstaffe, John Webster. See also John Dee, William Hogarth. For court procedures see Evidence in Witch Trials (England), Indictments. Much material on English witchcraft will be found under Familiars, Pricking, Scratching, Swimming,

John Wesley (1703-1791)

"The infidels have hooted witchcraft out of the world."—*Journal* (July 4, 1770).

Waxen Image, Witch's Mark. Poltergeist disturbances were recorded in England; in addition to main entry, see also Drummer of Tedworth (1662) and Epworth Poltergeist (1716).

Energumen: see Possession.

Epworth Poltergeist. The prestige of John Wesley as a founder of a major religious sect has added luster to a poltergeist which under other circumstances might not have become so famous. As it was, the letters written to Wesley's brother Samuel at the time of the haunting (December 2, 1716 to January, 1717), the later depositions from members of the family, collected by John in 1726, and the account by John's father Samuel were not published until seventy-five years later, in 1791, by Joseph Priestley, F.R.S., in his *Original Letters by the Reverend John Wesley and His Friends*. John Wesley had previously published an abbreviated version in the *Arminian Magazine*, the earliest religious periodical in Britain, in 1784. Priestley suspected that Wesley tried to suppress the letters of his sister Hetty (Mehitabel) about this affair—they are still missing. Nineteen years old at the time, Hetty was even then suspected of being the nexus or medium which fomented the phenomena. The disturbances centered around Hetty's bed, and were marked by Hetty's "trembling strongly in her sleep."

Wesley, however, had no doubt about the genuineness of the poltergeist, as of the whole spirit world. "The giving up of witchcraft is, in effect, giving up the Bible," he wrote in his *Journal* for May 25, 1768. Robert Southey, in his *Life* of Wesley, wrote of him:

A belief in witchcraft naturally followed from these premises; but, after satisfying his understanding that supernatural acts and appearances are consistent with the order of the universe, sanctioned by Scripture, and proved by testimony too general and too strong to be resisted, he invalidated his own authority, by listening to the most absurd tales with implicit credulity, and recording them as authenticated facts.

Later critics, on the other hand, have ascribed the alleged facts of the Epworth Poltergeist to a theory of exaggerative memory with "hallucination begotten of excited expectation" or (as Samuel Taylor Coleridge said) "contagious epidemic hallucination of witnesses."

The scene of these manifestations was the parsonage at Epworth, Lincolnshire, where John's father, Rev. Samuel Wesley (1662-1735), was minister.

Here are the Wesley family telling son Samuel, who was away at the time, about "Old Jeffery" (so called by Emily Wesley, after someone who had died in the house). The words are their own, rearranged from original letters and recollections in dialogue form.

Samuel: My mother tells me a very strange story of disturbances in your house. I wish I could have some more particulars from you.

Mr. Wesley: There were some surprising circumstances in that affair. It would make a glorious penny book for Jack Dunton.

Mrs. Wesley: On the first of December—

Molly, a maid: I have always thought it was in November.

Mrs. Wesley: On the first of December, our maid heard at the door of the dining room several dismal groans, like a person in extremes at the point of death.

Susannah: She said it was like the groans

of one expiring. These so frightened her that for a great while she durst not go out of one room into another, after it began to be dark, without company.

Molly: We thought it was Mr. Turpine, who had the stone, and used sometimes to come and see us.

Mrs. Wesley: We gave little heed to her relation, and endeavored to laugh her out of her fears.

The Other Maid: [I] laughed heartily and said, What a couple of fools are you! I defy anything to fright me.

Mrs. Wesley: Some nights (two or three) after, several of the family heard a strange knocking in divers places, usually three or four knocks at a time, and then stayed a little. This continued every time for a fortnight; sometimes it was in the garret, but most commonly in the nursery, or green chamber.

Susannah: I believed nothing of it till about a fortnight after the first noises. The first night I ever heard it, my sister Nancy and I were set in the dining room. We heard something rush on the outside of the doors that opened into the garden, then three loud knocks, immediately after other three, and in half a minute the same number over our heads.

Emily: My sisters in the paper chamber had heard noises, and told me of them, but I did not much believe, till one night, about a week after the first groans were heard, which was the beginning, just after the clock had struck ten, I went down stairs to lock the doors (which I always do). Scarce had I got up the best stairs, when I heard a noise, like a person throwing down a vast coal in the middle of the fore kitchen, and all the splinters seeemd to fly about from it. I was not much frighted but went to my sister Sukey, and we together went all over the low rooms, but there was nothing out of order.

Mrs. Wesley: I was a great while ere I could credit anything of what the children and servants reported concerning the noises they heard in several parts of the house.

Samuel: Could not cats, or rats, or dogs be the sprites?

Mrs. Wesley: Nay, after I had heard them myself, I was willing to persuade myself and them that it was only rats or weasels that disturbed us.

Samuel: I understand my father did not hear it at all but a fortnight after the rest.

Mr. Wesley: Till, I think, the 21st night, I heard nothing of it.

Mrs. Wesley: We all heard it but your father, and I was not willing he should be informed of it lest he should fancy it was against his own death, which, indeed, we all apprehended.

Mr. Wesley: They would not tell me for some time, because, according to the vulgar opinion, if it boded any ill to me, I could not hear it.

Mrs. Wesley: But when it began to be so troublesome, both day and night, that few or none of the family durst be alone, I resolved to tell him of it, being minded he should speak to it.

Emily: [My] father smiled and gave no answer but was more careful than usual from that time to see us in bed, imagining it to be some of us young women that sat up late and made a noise. His incredulity and especially his imputing it to us or our lovers made me, I own, desirous of its continuance till he was convinced.

Mrs. Wesley: I was entirely convinced that it was beyond the power of any human creature to make such strange and various noises.

Mr. Wesley: [I] said, I am ashamed of you! These boys and girls fright one another, but you are a woman of sense and should know better. Let me hear of it no more.

Mrs. Wesley: At first he would not believe but somebody did it to alarm us; but the night after, as soon as he was in bed, it knocked loudly nine times just by his bedside. He rose and went to see if he could find out what it was, but could see nothing.

Mr. Wesley: The next night I heard six knocks but not so loud as the former.

Emily: I heard frequently between ten and eleven something like the quick winding up of a jack at the corner of my room by my bed's head, just the running of the wheels and the creaking of the iron work. This was the common signal of its coming.

John: Whether our clock went right or wrong, it always came, as near as could be guessed, when by the night it wanted a quarter to ten.

Mrs. Wesley: One night it made such a noise in the room over our heads as if several people were walking, then run up and down stairs—

Mr. Wesley: Something like the steps of a man was heard going up and down stairs, at all hours of the night.

Mrs. Wesley: —and was so outrageous that we thought the children would be frighted, so your father and I rose and went down in the dark to light a candle. Just as we came to the bottom of the broad stairs, having hold of each other, on my side there seemed as if somebody had emptied a bag of money at my feet, and on his as if all the bottles under the stairs (which were many) had been dashed to a thousand pieces.

Mr. Wesley: We heard, as Emily had done before, a clashing among the bottles as if they had been broke all to pieces.

Samuel: Was the whole family asleep?

Mrs. Wesley: All the family were asleep when your father and I went down stairs, nor did they wake in the nursery when we held the candle close by them, only we observed that Hetty trembled exceedingly in her sleep, as she always did, before the noise awaked her. It commonly was nearer her than the rest, which she took notice of and was much frightened, because she thought it had a particular spite at her.

Mr. Wesley: Hetty and two of her younger sisters were much affected though asleep, sweating and trembling exceedingly.

Samuel: My sister Hetty, I find, was more particularly troubled?

Emily: My sister Hetty, who sits always to wait on my father going to bed, was still sitting on the lowest step on the garret stairs, the door being shut at her back, when soon after there came down the stairs behind her something like a man, in a loose night gown trailing after him, which made her fly rather than run to me in the nursery.

Mrs. Wesley: The next night your father

would get Mr. Hoole [the Vicar of Haxey] to lie in our house, and we all sat together till one or two o'clock in the morning and heard the knocking as usual. Sometimes it would make a noise like the winding up of a jack, at other time, as that night Mr. Hoole was with us, like a carpenter planing deals. But most commonly it knocked thrice and stopped, and then thrice again, and so many hours together.

Susannah: The latter end of the night that Mr. Hoole sat up on, I lay in the nursery, where it was very violent. I then heard frequent knocks over and under the room where I lay and at the children's bed head, which was made of boards. It seemed to rap against it very hard and loud so that the bed shook under them. I heard something walk by my bedside, like a man in a long night gown. The knocks were so loud that Mr. Hoole came out of their chamber to us.

Mr. Hoole: As soon as we were in the kitchen, the sound was above us in the room we had left. We returned up the narrow stairs and heard at the broad stairs' head some one slaring [dragging] with their feet (all the family now being in bed beside us) and then trailing as it were and rustling with a silk night gown. Quickly it was in the nursery at the bed's head, knocking as it had done at first, three by three.

Mrs. Wesley: We persuaded your father to speak and try if any voice would be heard. One night about six o'clock he went into the nursery in the dark, and at first heard several deep groans, then knocking. He adjured it to speak if it had power and tell him why it troubled his house, but no voice was heard; but it knocked thrice aloud.

Mr. Wesley: Wednesday night, December 26, I went up stairs and found it still knocking, heard, though with some respite, sometimes under the bed, sometimes at the bed's head. I observed my children that they were frighted in their sleep and trembled very much till it waked them. I stayed there alone, bid them go to sleep, and sat at the bed's feet by them, when the noise began again. I asked it what it was and why it disturbed innocent children and did not come to me in my study, if it had anything to say to me. Soon after it gave one knock on the outside of the house. All the rest were within, and knocked off for that night.

Mrs. Wesley: Thus it continued till the 28th December, when it loudly knocked (as your father used to do at the gate) in the nursery and departed.

Samuel: I cannot think any of you very superstitious.

Emily: I am so far from being superstitious that I was too much inclined to infidelity, so that I heartily rejoice at having such an opportunity of convincing myself past doubt or scruple of the existence of some beings beside those that we see.

Samuel: Was there never a new maid or man in the house, that might play tricks? Was there nobody above in the garrets, when the walking was there?

Emily: A whole month was sufficient to convince anybody of the reality of the thing and to try all ways of discovering any trick, had it been possible for any such to have been used.

Samuel: I want to know whether nothing was ever seen by any.

Emily: Something was thrice seen. The first time by my mother, under my sister's bed, like a badger.

Mr. Wesley: I know not whether it was in the morning after Sunday the 23rd. My wife looked under the bed and thought something ran from thence, but could not well tell of what shape but thought it most like a badger.

Mrs. Wesley: Something ran out pretty much like a badger and seemed to run directly under Emily's petticoats.

Emily: The same creature was sat by the dining room fire one evening; when our man went into the room, it ran up by him through the hall under the stairs. He followed with a candle and searched, but it was departed. The last time he saw it in the kitchen, like a white rabbit, which seems likely to be some witch.

Mr. Wesley: After nine, Robert Brown sitting alone by the fire in the back kitchen, something came out of the cooper hole like a rabbit, but less, and

turned round five times very swiftly. Its ears lay flat upon its neck, and its little feet stood straight up. He ran after it with the tongs in his hand, but when he could find nothing he was frightened and went to the maid in the parlor.

Samuel: Has it never at all disturbed you since the 28th of December?

Mr. Wesley: From that time till January the 24th we were quiet. This day at morning prayer, the family heard the usual knocks at the prayer for the king. At night they were more distinct, both in the prayer for the king and for the prince; and one very loud knock at the "Amen" was heard by my wife and most of my children at the inside of my bed. I heard nothing myself.

Emily: Then it intermitted a fortnight or more, and when it began again it knocked only on nights.

Mr. Wesley: Sunday, January 27: two soft strokes at the morning prayers for King George, above stairs.

Emily: [It] grew less and less troublesome, till at last it went quite away.

Mr. Wesley: As for the noises, etc., in our family, I thank God we are now all quiet.

Essex Witches: see Chelmsford Witches; St. Osyth Witches.

Evidence in Witch Trials, England. In England, it was not until after a body of trial records had accumulated that clergymen and judges started compiling handbooks of directions on how to detect or discover a witch. Reginald Scot, writing in 1584, gave a specimen of the type of evidence which would be thrust before the court—a typical witness is giving evidence against one accused of witchery:

She was at my house of late, she would have had a pot of milk. She departed in a [rage] because she had it not. She railed, she cursed, she mumbled and whispered, and finally she said she would be even with me. And soon after, my child, my sow, or my pullet died, or was strangely taken. Nay, if it please your worship, I have further proof: I was with a wise woman and she told me I had an ill neighbor, and that she would come to my house yet it were long, and so she did. And that she had a mark above her waist, and so had she; and, God forgive me, my stomach hath gone against her a great while. Her mother before her was counted a witch. She hath been beaten and scratched by the face till blood was drawn upon her, because she hath been suspected and afterwards some of these persons were said to amend.

Out of such "certainties" came the guides to witchcraft. The chief such books in England were as follows:

William Perkins (Calvinist divine), *Discourse of the Damned Art of Witchcraft* (published posthumously, 1608).

Thomas Potts (clerk to law court), *Wonderful Discovery of Witches* (1613), a court report of the Lancashire witch trials of 1612.

Michael Dalton (justice of the peace), *The Country Justice* (1618; 4th ed. 1630 followed Bernard), a standard manual for lower courts.

Richard Bernard (clergyman), *Guide to Grand Jurymen* (1627).

John Gaule (clergyman), *Select Cases of Conscience Touching Witches and Witchcraft* (1646).

Matthew Hopkins (professional witch hunter), *Discovery of Witches* (1647).

Robert Filmer (knight and judge), *Advertisement to the Jurymen of England* (1653), replaced Perkins with simpler proofs of witchcraft.

Cotton Mather (New England divine), *Memorable Providences* (1689), based on Potts, Bernard, and Gaule.

On these works, and on the stories in Baxter's *Certainty of the World of Spirits* or Crouch's *Kingdom of Darkness*, was formulated public opinion about evidence.

Perkins' book remained very influential throughout the first half of the seventeenth century. It distinguished between (1) "false or uncertain signs" of witchcraft; (2) "presumptions" of guilt; and (3) "just and sufficient proofs."

Under the first head of "uncertain . . . or less sufficient" proofs, Perkins included ordeal by the red-hot iron, scratching a witch to draw blood, and ducking a witch in water to see if she would float [see Swimming]. Also not to be regarded as proof was evidence from a witness claiming injury from a witch who had cursed him, or from a dying man. Yet these accusations might "move the judge to examine the party, but [be] of no moment for conviction."

The "presumptions of guilt" justified a judge's examining a person about witchcraft; these "at least probably and conjecturally note one to be a witch; and these are certain signs whereby the party may be discovered":

1. Notorious defamation is a common report of the greater sort of people with whom the party suspected dwelleth, that he or she is a witch. This yieldeth a strong suspicion.

2. If a fellow-witch or magician give testimony of any person to be a witch, either voluntary, or at his or her examination, or at his or her death.

3. If after cursing there followeth death, or at least some mischief; for witches are wont to practice their mischievous acts by cursing and banning.

4. If after enmity, quarreling, or threatening, a present mischief doth follow.

5. If the party suspected be the son or daughter, the manservant or maidservant, the familiar friend, near neighbor, or old companion of a known and convicted witch. [Guilt by association.]

6. If the party suspected be found to have the devil's mark.

7. If the party examined be inconstant or contrary to himself in his deliberate answers.

Both in England and Europe, the "presumptions" (corresponding to the *indicia* of European theorists) sufficed for a judge to examine a person; but in English law some evidence against the accused was generally presented in court, and since the torture was nothing like as ferocious, many accused were able to resist making confessions of guilt.

For true evidence proving witchcraft, Perkins demanded:

1. Free and voluntary confession of the crime, made by the party suspected and accused after examination. [If the accused refused to confess, then the following evidence sufficed:]
2. The testimony of two witnesses, of good and honest report, avouching before the magistrate upon their own knowledge, these two things:
   a) Either that the party accused hath made a league with the devil;
   b) Or hath done some known practices of witchcraft. [Such as, the accused] hath invocated and called upon the devil; hath entertained a familiar spirit, and had conference with it in form or likeness of a mouse, cat, or some other visible creature.
   c) Or used glasses [crystal balls for divination].

In English trials, at the height of the mania, Perkins' criterion of a familiar spirit became dominant, and as cats and mice were everywhere, it was never difficult to discover and prove a witch. Likewise, in Michael Dalton's and Richard Bernard's handbooks to judges and juries, possession of a familiar determined witchcraft. Dalton based his *Country Justice* on Thomas Potts's court report of the Lancashire trials in 1612, and copied Potts's seven signs of witchcraft. He warned judges "not always [to] expect direct evidence, seeing that all their [witches'] works are the works of darkness, and no witnesses present with them to accuse them." In his fourth edition (1630), Dalton extended these signs to include eight others which he took from Richard Bernard's *Guide to Grand Jurymen* (1627), a relatively cautious work. Familiars and the devil's mark remained primary evidence of witchcraft, and Dalton stressed: "These first two are main points to discover and convict these witches; for they prove fully that those witches have a familiar and make a league with the Devil." Dalton's further indications included possession of waxen images, testimony of children, and spectral evidence.

From his experience as self-appointed Witch Finder General during the Civil War, Matthew Hopkins discussed the value of confessions. With mealy-mouthed hypocrisy he denied the validity of confessions drawn out by torture, promise of immunity, or leading questions—his disclaimer is evidence enough he used these methods (apart from the records of the trials in which he assisted). If a witch were found with any kind of skin blemish—here again the emphasis on devil's marks as evidence—she might be brought to confess her guilt by questions such as Hopkins must have himself used hundreds of times:

What was the occasion of the devil appearing to her—whether ignorance, pride, anger, malice?
What speech they had?
What likeness he was in?
What voice he had?
What familiars he sent her?
What number of spirits?
What names they had?
What shape they were in?
What employment she set them about?

"All these mischiefs being proved to be done is testimony enough against her for all her denial." By such interrogation, after enforcing nights of sleeplessness and trussing the victim like a chicken, Hopkins managed to hang probably 200 persons between 1645 and 1646—sixty-eight are known by name. His list of questions is very similar to the previously prepared lists used in Continental trials [see Confessions].

Finally, Sir Robert Filmer, in his *Advertisement to the Jurymen of England Touching Witches* (1653), ridiculed Perkins' presumptions, but actually repeated Perkins' old touchstones. First, confession, although he admitted "many confess of themselves things false and impossible, that they are carried through the air in a moment, that they pass through keyholes and clefts of doors; that they be sometimes turned into cats, hares, and other creatures and such like—all which are mere fables and things impossible." Second, familiars and spectral evidence: "Two witnesses avouching upon their own knowledge either that the party accused hath made league with the Devil, or hath done some known practices of witchcraft, or hath invoked the Devil or desired his help."

In what is probably one of the last books defending thc witch delusion, swallowing the principles of Continental demonologists, Richard Boulton in 1715 said the surest proof of witchcraft was the "insensible mark" (devil's mark), "the sucking of the witch's body by her demon" (witch's mark), and the water ordeal. The inclusion of the water ordeal is indicative that the popular belief in witchcraft was changing back from religious heresy into folklore fables.

In addition to the proofs discussed in these handbooks, there were a few other methods, such as the evidence provided by a witch's being unable to recite the Lord's prayer without stumbling. A few judges were prepared to forego any evidence at all. Thus Sir Edmund Anderson in 1603 charged a jury:

> The malice [of witches] is great, their practice devilish, and if we do not convict them without their own confession or direct proof, where the presumptions are so great and the circumstances so apparent, they will in a short time overrun the whole land.

While Bernard is among the first English writers to discuss spectral evidence, such evidence had long been admitted in the trials. Spectral evidence was the accusation that the witch had appeared to the bewitched in a vision; or (more common in Europe) that an accused witch had seen some other person at a witches' sabbat or consorting with the devil. In most trials, this evidence was decisive. [For an extended discussion, see Spectral Evidence.]

Possibly the most amazing evidence ever admitted at an English witch trial was that which convicted Mrs. Julian Cox, tried before Justice Robert Archer at Taunton, Somerset, in 1663. It shows how completely credulous judges could be, even when the delusion was declining, and how even the meager safeguards for evidence provided in the handbooks could be swept to one side. One witness was a huntsman who, while following a rabbit behind a bush,

"The blowing witches are the most revolting and most stupid in the Devil's league. If they had any sense they would not blow."—Goya (1799).

found Mrs. Cox there, but no sign of the rabbit. A second witness said that, while smoking his pipe in the house of Mrs. Cox, he saw a toad between his legs. Returning to his own home, and smoking again, he saw what he thought was the same toad between his legs. "He took the toad out to kill it," said Glanvill, who reported the trial in his *Saducismus Triumphatus* (1681), "and to his thinking cut it in several pieces, but returning to his pipe, the toad still appeared. . . . At length, the toad cried and vanished." A third witness had seen Mrs. Cox flying in at her window "in her full proportion." "This tissue of evidence was perhaps the absurdest ever used against even a witch," commented Notestein, "but the jury brought her in guilty."

See further, Evidence in Witch Trials (Europe), Spectral Evidence. Also Confessions, Witnesses.

Evidence in Witch Trials, Europe. In

French and German trials, evidence against a witch was relatively unimportant, and frequently no witnesses were called to testify against the accused. Indeed, the learned lawyer Henri Boguet admitted that "witches work at night and in secret, and a clear proof of such deeds is . . . impossible." What mattered were the *indicia* or indications that a person was a witch. These *indicia* ranged from ugliness and deformity, through common report, to being caught *flagrante delicto* throwing water backward into the air to cause a tempest.

Anybody could have a person arrested on suspicion of witchcraft; furthermore, judges had the duty to look for and arrest such suspects. As early as 1254, Pope Innocent IV decreed that the person making the accusation need not confront the accused, unless the accuser so wished. The suspect was normally not allowed counsel,

although rarely the court appointed a lawyer. No evidence in his favor was admitted, although irrelevant and adverse gossip should be introduced, said the *Malleus Maleficarum*, to engender suspicion. There was no cross-examination of witnesses, if any were called, and consequently no evaluation of the charges.

The suspect, even when he confessed immediately, was always put to torture to make valid his own confession of guilt. Moreover, under torture, he had to provide names of alleged accomplices in his witchcraft, who could, on this evidence, then be charged with suspicion of witchcraft, tortured to confess and give more names. In this way, trials speedily snowballed, and the courts never lacked suspects. The confession was thus in fact the only evidence required, and even the confession was less important than the *indicia*. For when once

The recording of a confession.

Examination of Catherine Bücher, of Gross-Mühlingen (Anhalt-Bernburg) in 1689. The page shows two parallel columns, part of her interrogation, the questions in the left-hand column and her replies in the right. From the notable manuscript collection in Cornell University Library.

accused, "nobody escapes, though he were an earl," as Burgomaster Johannes Junius said; the verbatim report of his trial is exceedingly revealing.

The *Commentarius* (1622) of Bishop Peter Binsfeld, a notorious demonologist, provides a convenient résumé of the typical presumptions justifying arrest on suspicion of witchcraft, some of which go back to Prierias (1521). These *indicia* might be slight (*remota*), serious (*propinqua*), or incriminating (*propinquissima*); but much discretion was given the judge. The most serious indications were:

1. Denunciation by an accomplice.
2. Pact with the Devil.
3. Association with known witches.
4. Common report.
5. Acts of evil following threats (*damnum minatum*).
6. Possession of magical equipment, especially flying ointment.

In addition, flight to avoid arrest, habitual blasphemy, and ignoring common report of witchcraft were all weighty presumptions. Less serious were devil's marks, being the child of a witch, and bewilderment or fear on being questioned.

Boguet summed up the common procedure: "In the crime of witchcraft it is lawful at times to proceed on the strength of those indubitable indications and conjectures, neither more or less, which are applicable to other atrocious crimes committed in secret"—*Discours des sorciers*, 1602. And the same lawless position had been stated by the even more eminent Jean Bodin in 1580: "Inasmuch as the proof of such crimes is so obscure and so difficult, not one witch in a million would be accused or punished if the procedure were governed by the ordinary rules."

Executions. In Continental Europe, both the ecclesiastical and secular courts burned the convicted witch. This practice was based on the theology of Augustine, expanded and developed by later leaders in the theory of persecution, such as Thomas Aquinas, and the Inquisitors Bernardus Guidonis and Nicholas Eymeric. In his *Liber de Fide ad Petrum Diaconum*, Augustine had written that he

> most firmly holds and in no way doubts that not only every pagan, but every Jew, heretic, and schismatic, will go to the eternal fire, which is prepared for the Devil and his angels, unless before the end of his life he be reconciled with and restored to the Catholic Church— *non solum omnes paganos, sed et omnes Judaeos, et omnes hereticos atque schismaticos, qui extra Ecclesiam catholicam praesentem finiunt vitam, in ignem eternum ituros, qui paratus est diabolo et angelis eius.*

This position, incorporated in the *Decretals* of Pope Gregory IX, was reaffirmed toward the height of the persecutions by Cardinal Bellarmine (1542-1631), justifying the death penalty for witchcraft and heresy: "Finally, it benefits obstinate heretics that they be cut off from this life; for the longer they live, thinking their various errors, the more people they pervert, and the greater the damnation they lay up for themselves."

Originally the punishment decreed by the Inquisition (which, of course, had the secular court actually perform the killing), burning was adopted by Catholic lay authorities and by Protestants—Calvin was one of the foremost in burning those he called witches. In the fifteenth century, Girolamo Visconti wrote a book proving witches had to be burned as heretics, also the contention of *De Lamiis* (1571) by Thomas Erastus. The great authority on criminal law in the sixteenth century, Joost Damhouder, in his *Enchiridion* (1554), expressed the accepted opinion:

> Whoever kills by sorcery, or by charms, should be burned in the conflagration of fire, for that is not simple homicide, because sorcery degrades homicide so that it merits death by burning. In the same way, he who hinders by magic the natural power of generation in men or women, or brings it about that a woman is not able to conceive, or to give birth to the child in her womb, or who dries up the milk of a wet nurse, or by whatever means of sorcery or *maleficia* kills anyone either through the body by food or drink, or outside the

body [by other means] is to be considered a murderer.

All countries except England (and New England) executed the witch by burning. In Italy and Spain, the heretic was burned alive. In Scotland, Germany, and France, it was customary first to strangle the witch (by garroting or hanging) and then immediately to light the pyre, always provided that the witch did not recant the confession she had made under torture. The trial of Janet Reid in 1643 is typical of Scottish procedure: she was "to be taken by the lockman [public executioner], her hands bound behind her back, conveyed to the place of execution, worried [strangled] at a stake, and burned to ashes." If the witch revoked her confession or was impenitent, she was left alive on the stake. Another Scottish account, one by the Earl of Mar protesting to the Privy Council on December 1, 1608, described this second method:

> Albeit they persevered constant in their denial [of guilt] to the end, yet they were burned quick [alive] after such a cruel manner that some of them died in despair, renouncing and blaspheming; and others, half burned, broke out of the fire and were cast in alive in it again until they were burned to the death. (*Register of Privy Council of Scotland*, 1624)

If the witch had been un-co-operative in court, the fire was made of green wood to prolong the dying. This method, following cutting and maiming the prisoner, was endorsed by the eminent French lawyer Jean Bodin, whose *Démonomanie* (1580) became a standard authority:

> Whatever punishment one can order against witches by roasting and cooking them over a slow fire [*brusler à petit feu*] is not really very much, and not as bad as the torment which Satan has made for them in this world, to say nothing of the eternal agonies which are prepared for them in hell, for the fire here cannot last more than an hour or so until the witches have died.

On the act of charity of strangling before burning, Henry C. Lea commented: "Hu-

man weakness led to persistence in confession to avoid the awful death by fire. The whole system was one to encourage belief in witchcraft and to multiply the number of victims."

It is impossible to state how many persons were executed as witches in Europe during the period of the witchcraft delusion, from 1450 to 1750, the approximate beginning and ending dates. While many court records have been kept in minute detail from about 1600, or earlier, and are still available, the degree of preservation varies considerably from place to place and from year to year. A visitor to Scotland in 1644 wrote, "I remember that I saw nine witches burned at one time in Leith Links" —Dalyell, *Darker Superstitions of Scotland*, 1834. Yet Trevor Davies found "only one capital conviction for witchcraft" in the records of the Supreme Court of Scotland for that year. On the other hand, unimpeachable records show that in 1583 at Osnabrück in Germany 121 witches were

Various methods of execution, showing beheading, hanging, whipping to death, burning alive. From the book of the celebrated jurist, Joost Damhouder, *Enchiridion* (1554), in the Reserve Book Room, New York Public Library.

burned, and in 1589 some 133; in 1612 at Ellwangen 167 witches burned; and at Würzburg in 1628 and in January and February of 1629 there were 158 burnings. Bartolommeo Spina, a Vatican official, quoted at first hand an inquisitor who said in one year at Como he and his ten assistants had burned 1,000 witches (the actual year is not specified, but it is probably 1523). In the five years from 1631 to 1636, the records of three little villages in the jurisdiction of the Archbishop of Cologne—Rheinbach, Meckenheim, and Flerzheim—show that from 300 households between 125 and 150 persons were executed as witches. In Lorraine, the Attorney General Nicholas Remy, whose office could be presumed to keep accurate accounts, boasted he had burned 900 persons in the ten years from 1581 to 1591. Another example of detailed figures is preserved at Colmar, where, for example, in 1571—

the Thursday following St. Margaret's Day, six women were burned at Hattstatt, among whom were a mother and an eighteen-year-old unmarried daughter. The mother, after having had intercourse with the devil, ended up by marrying her daughter to him. November 3, five witches burned at Herrlisheim. December 4, three witches burned at Ammerschweier. December 12, a witch found dead at Colmar in the Witches Tower.

Many monographs have been written on witchcraft in some particular county or town, or for some particular period, but often these books, many of them paperbound pamphlets, were published by a local printer and had little circulation outside the area they discussed. Again, some famous trials have been described in detail and have had international circulation. Because of the varying condition of historical records, all figures of executions must remain approximations. Ludovicus à Paramo, in his *De Origine et Progressu Officii Sanctae Inquisitionis* (Madrid, 1598), said the Inquisition alone within the space of 150 years had burned 30,000 witches (quoted by Limborch, 1692). If an approximation of those executed as witches be insisted on,

the most reliable suggestion is that of George L. Burr, who estimated a *minimum* of 100,000 men and women and children burned in Germany alone. One might double this figure for the whole of Europe.

Because the number of burnings on the continent was, even at the most conservative estimate, very considerable, there is a danger of assuming an unduly high number for England. Thomas Ady estimated "some thousands" burned in Scotland; Zachary Grey (in 1744) quoted a figure of 3,000 to 4,000 between 1640 and 1660; and Robert Steele (in 1903) gave 70,000 between 1603 and 1628! C. L'Estrange Ewen, one of the few writers on witchcraft to examine original documents, made this pertinent comment:

The very occasional nature of a trial for witchcraft led the curious to take down and preserve the most sensational of the statements of witnesses and accused. A considerable amount of such material is available, mainly in the form of chapbooks, prima facie evidence that witchcraft trials with evidence of a hair-raising nature were sufficiently unusual events to excite the interest of the reading public. (*Witchcraft and Demonianism*)

Ewen "guesses" about 1,000 witches were hanged during the whole period in England.

Evil Eye: see Fascination.

Exorcism. Unlike witchcraft, a Christian aberration restricted to western Europe, possession and exorcism are universal, common to all religions and beliefs at all times and places. Demoniacal possession is a convenient portmanteau term to describe one theory of deranged personality; exorcism, the means which sometimes restored the afflicted person to normal behavior. The function once exercised by priests—curing disturbed persons—is now performed by psychiatrists. The comparison may be taken a stage further: Just as the psychiatrist should himself undergo analysis, so the exorcist had often been possessed. *L'Histoire des diables de Loudun* (1716) noted that "exorcists almost all participate, more or less, in the effects of the demons, by vexations which they suffer from them, and few persons have undertaken to drive them forth who have not been troubled by them."

A pagan witch doctor is to sorcery what a Christian exorcist is to witchcraft. In Catholic demonology, possession by any evil spirit became limited to possession by a Christian devil. As a *Christian* devil, he admitted the superior power of the Christian God and therefore obeyed the commands of a Christian priest acting through exorcism on behalf of God and the Church. Yet the Christian rites of exorcism are not fundamentally different from similar ceremonies in other religions against possession by the demons of those religions. Only the elemental and primitive poltergeist, demonologists observed, was not able to acknowledge Christianity and was little responsive to exorcism; nevertheless, Catholic service books contained exorcisms against noisy demons infesting houses and even bridal suites!

Exorcism grew out of the New Testament accounts—e.g., "In my name shall they cast out devils" (Luke xvi. 17; also Luke ix. 1; x. 17). The practice was introduced into the Christian church at a very early date, and exorcists formed one of the four minor orders of the Church. Their reputation helped spread the new faith. Wrote Justin Martyr in his *Apology* in the second century A.D.:

> For many of our Christian men exorcized numberless demoniacs throughout the whole world and in the city of Rome in the name of Jesus Christ. . . . [They] have healed and do heal them, rendering the possessing devils helpless and driving them out of the men, who could not be cured by all the other exorcists or by those who used incantations and drugs.

Contemporary allusions establish the early ceremonies of exorcism as similar to the later forms which ultimately crystallized in the *Rituale Romanum*, but simpler, with merely a litany, prayers, and the laying on of hands in exorcism. Origen (third century A.D.) stressed the magical efficacy of the letters of the word Jesus, "whose name has already been seen, in an unmistakable manner, to have expelled myriads of evil spirits from the souls and bodies [of men], so great was the power it exerted upon those from whom the spirits were driven out."

The power of the early exorcists extended to beasts. Jerome's *Life of St. Hilary* (about A.D. 390) told how

> brute animals were also daily brought to him in a state of madness, and among them a Bactrian camel of enormous size, amid the shouts of thirty men or more who held him tight with stout ropes. He had already injured many. His eyes were bloodshot, his mouth filled with foam, his rolling tongue swollen, and above every other source of terror was his loud and hideous roar. Well, the old man ordered him to be let go. At once those who had brought him as well as the attendants of the saint fled away without exception. The saint went by himself to meet him, and addressing him in Syriac said, "You do not alarm me, devil, huge though your present body is. Whether in a fox or a camel you are just the same." Meanwhile he stood with outstretched hand. The brute, raging and looking as if he would devour Hilary, came up to him, but immediately fell down, laid its head on the ground, and to the amazement of all present showed suddenly no less tameness than it had exhibited ferocity before. But the old man declared to them how the devil, for men's account, seizes even beasts of burden; that he is inflamed by such intense hatred for men that he desires to destroy not only them but what belongs to them.

When, by various signs or indications, possession had been established, the exorcist had then to decide whether the possessing spirit were good or evil. Vincentius von Berg, who compiled a famous manual of exorcism, the *Enchiridium*, gave a list of tests. The spirit was held to be wicked if it—

An incident in the life of St. Lambert: a possessed man is taken to the altar, while a devil stands on his forehead and torments him. From a book of miracles in the Bibliothèque nationale, Paris.

Fled at the sign of the cross, holy water, the name of Jesus, etc.

Said anything against the Catholic faith.

Excited the mind of the possessed to pride, vainglory, despair, etc.

Refused to discuss the possession with a priest.

Appeared with a loathsome or dejected appearance, or departed leaving a stench, noise, frightfulness, or injury.

Approached mildly, but afterward left behind grief, desolation, disturbance of soul and clouds of the mind.

The next concern of the exorcist was to determine how the evil spirit entered the body. A person could be possessed in one of two ways, summarized Polidori (1587): first, by the devil (with the permission of God) entering the body by his own volition; second, by a witch using incantations to induce the devil to take possession [see entry on Possession]. Berg gave a list of "indications, by which it could be ascertained if anyone were bewitched into possession":

1. The bewitched desire the worst food.
2. They are unable to retain their food, are irked by continual vomiting, and are unable to digest.
3. Others experience a heavy weight in the stomach, as if a sort of ball ascended from the stomach into the gullet, which they seem to vomit forth, yet nevertheless it returns to its original position.
4. Some feel a gnawing in the lower belly; others feel either a rapid pulsation in the neck or pain in the kidneys. Others feel a continuous pain in the head or brain, beyond endurance, on account of which they seem oppressed, shattered, or pierced.
5. The bewitched have trouble with their heart, which feels as if torn by dogs, or eaten by serpents, or pierced by nails and needles, or constricted and stifled.
6. At other times, all parts of their head swell up, so that throughout their body they feel such lassitude that they can scarcely move.
7. Some experience frequent and sudden pains, which they cannot describe, but they shriek aloud.
8. In others, the body is weakened and reduced to a shadow on account of extraordinary emaciation, impotency of vigor, and extreme languor.
9. At other times, their limbs feel whipped, torn, bound, or constricted, especially the heart and bones.
10. Some are accustomed to feel something like the coldest wind or a fiery flame run through their stomach, causing the most violent contractions in their entrails and intense and sudden swelling of the stomach.
11. Many bewitched are oppressed by a melancholy disposition. Some of them are so weakened that they do not wish either to speak or converse with people.
12. Those injured by witchcraft may have their eyes constricted, and the whole body, especially the face, almost completely suffused by a yellow or ashen color.
13. When witchcraft has by chance befallen the sick, he is generally attacked by some serious trouble, seized with fear and terror; if he is a boy, he immediately bewails himself and his eyes change to a dark color, and other perceptible changes are observed. Wherefore the discreet exorcist takes care to disclose the

recognized signs of this sort to the relatives and those present to avoid scandal.

14. It is especially significant if skilled physicians are not sure what the affliction is, and cannot form an opinion about it; or if the medications prescribed do not help but rather increase the sickness.
15. Some times the only indications of bewitching are considered circumstantial and inferential, as employing witchcraft for hatred, love, sterility, storm-raising, ligature, or [harm to] animals.

Even though the exorcist suspected that possession had been brought on by a witch, he was technically forbidden to seek the name of the suspect, for to do so would be to receive help from the devil. Partly as a result of the trial of Father Louis Gaufridi [see Aix-en-Provence Nuns], convicted by demoniacs, the Sorbonne in 1620 proclaimed that the testimony of demons should never be accepted. Completely opposing their parallel justification of Spectral Evidence, the university pointed out that the devil would never tell the truth, even under exorcism. This ruling, however, was not always observed, and the central figure of the Gaufridi case, Sister Madeleine de la Palud, years later in 1653, was herself named by a demoniac as a witch. Evidence of energumens was also admitted in the trial of Father Urbain Grandier in 1634 [see Loudun Nuns].

If, after all the tests, the exorcist thought the evidence insufficient to reach a conclusion, he might pronounce a general exorcism.

Fixing his eyes firmly on the possessed person, and laying his hand on his head, in this position, with a secret command to the devil, because the devil himself is the originator of evil, the exorcist makes a certain sign, urging the possessed man publicly:

"I, N., minister of Christ and the Church, in the name of Jesus Christ, command you, unclean spirit, if you lie hid in the body of this man created by God, or if you vex him in any way, that immediately you give me some manifest sign of the certainty of your presence in possessing this man . . . which heretofore in my absence you have been able to accomplish in your accustomed manner." (*Enchiridium*)

When convinced of the reality of the possessing devil, the exorcist was to follow certain general rules. He was to ask the devil his name; he was to enquire how many devils were possessing the sufferer; he was to seek out the cause of the possession and whether the devil proposed staying a specified time or forever; and finally he was to determine the exact hour the demon entered the body.

Practicing exorcists followed these instructions. For example, a corps of Dominicans, Jesuits, and Capuchins exorcized a noblewoman in the chapel of Notre-Dame-de-Guérison, in the diocese of Auch. On November 16, 1618, they expelled a demon

Blessed Andreas de Conti, died in 1302, beatified in 1724, receiving a stole from two angels, symbolizing his fame in exorcizing demons. The figures on his right illustrate possessed persons, with a devil in the shape of a serpent departing from one of them. From Vincentius von Berg, *Enchiridium* (1743).

Mass public exorcisms by Nicole de Vervins at Laon, in 1569. The possessed people, in various stages of contortion, are displayed on a platform outside the church, while priests pray for them. At the top left, the devils are seen escaping from the bodies they possessed.

called Magot. Four days later, they resumed their exorcism against a second devil:

> The spirit . . . commenced to speak with great difficulty through the mouth of the patient, and we commenced to interrogate it in this manner:
> What was his name; where he came from, and what region. He replied to this command given him through the power of God that his name was Mahonin, of the third hierarchy, and the second order of archangels, and that his living, before he entered the body of the possessed, was in the water.
> Conjured to say what saint in heaven was his adversary, he replied it was St. Mark the Evangelist. . . .
> Interrogated of what place he was native, said Beziers, town in Languedoc, on the Spanish frontier. . . .
> Questioned on what day he had entered the body, said it was the third Tuesday of last Easter in the month of March, when the said possessed lady was in the town of Agen. . . .
> Questioned how long was the bewitchment, said for two years. . . .
> Commanded to give a sign when he would depart, replied he would give one by throwing a stone from the tower into the water of the moat. (*Les Conjurations faites à un démon possédant le corps d'une grande dame*, 1619)

At the height of the witchcraft delusion, numerous anthologies of rites for exorcisms were published, most of them claiming *"cum permissu superiorum."* The best-known was Girolamo Menghi's *Flagellum Demonum: Exorcismos Terribiles, Potentissimos et Efficaces* (1582), with seven different exorcisms. Menghi was probably himself an exorcist, and his *Scourge of the Devils* was widely quoted by subsequent demonologists. Later, it was included with the works of four other authorities, Valderio Polidoro, Zacharias Vicecomes, Pietro Antonio Stampa, and Maximilian van Eynatten, in a 1232-page *Thesaurus Exorcismorum* (1626), and, oddly enough, for a short time (1709) placed on the *Index* of prohibited books.

The *Thesaurus Exorcismorum* included exorcisms for nearly all possible eventualities: an exorcism against a demon vexing a house, introduced by a prayer to bless the place, then the conjuration against the "antique serpent" to leave, concluding with a litany; exorcisms against the drying up of cows, noxious pests (such as caterpillars and locusts), various sicknesses (including "stomach-aches and belly pains"), and ligature. "In no other exorcism is the work of the exorcist more usefully expended than when he tries to remove that *maleficium* [ligature] which destroys matrimony." The exorcist prayed for blessing on "those married people . . . who copulate together," and that "by thy piety thou wouldst deign to free them from all ligature, fascination, and satanic witchcraft, that they may partake of good health, fertility, and the generation of progeny." Vincentius von Berg included a "spiritual remedy against succubus and incubus demons," which could be banished by sorrowful contrition of the afflicted, frequent communion, holy water, acts of charity, placing amulets on the four corners of the bed, blessing of the bed, visiting shrines, exorcism, and two potions of wine with medicinal herbs (recalling Sinistrari's brew for fumigation against an incubus—see Charms).

As presented in the manuals, the rite of exorcism of a person possessed by an evil spirit was lengthy and impressive. It was not to be undertaken lightly, and certain safeguards were recommended, such as the presence of witnesses, especially with women demoniacs. A warning was also given to the priest not to say or do anything that "might provoke obscene thoughts." The ceremony was divided into various sections, alternating prayers and exorcism; some modern critics have seen sound psychological justification in the contrast between encouragement and threatening. The "litanies of billingsgate" reviled the fiend as a lean sow, mangy beast, dingy collier, swollen toad or lousy swineherd, and prayed that God "set a nail in your skull and pound it with a hammer, as Jael did unto Sisera."

The service of exorcism is still practiced today in the Roman Catholic Church. (Most

Protestant churches reject the theory of possession and exorcism.) The 1947 New York edition of the *Rituale Romanum* (with an introduction by Francis, Cardinal Spellman) reproduced verbatim the rite as printed by Maximilian van Eynatten in 1619, and included in the *Thesaurus Exorcismorum*, from which the following abstract is translated.

THE ORDER OF EXORCISM FROM THE RITUALE ROMANUM SET FORTH BY ORDER OF THE SUPREME PONTIFF, PAUL V [1605-21]

The priest, robed in surplice and violet stole, one end of which is placed round the neck of the possessed person, bound if he is violent, sprinkles those present with holy water. Then the service begins.

1. The Litany.
2. Psalm 54 ("Save me, O God, by thy name").
3. Adjuration imploring God's grace for the proposed exorcism against the "wicked dragon" and a caution to the possessing spirit to "tell me thy name, the day, and the hour of thy going out, by some sign."
4. The Gospel (John i; and/or Mark xvi; Luke x; Luke xi).
5. Preparatory prayer.

Then the priest, protecting himself and the possessed by the sign of the cross, placing part of his stole round the neck and placing his right hand on the head of the possessed, resolutely and with great faith shall say what follows.

6. First Exorcism:

"I exorcize thee, most vile spirit, the very embodiment of our enemy, the entire specter, the whole legion, in the name of Jesus Christ, to ✠ get out and flee from this creature of God ✠ ✠.

"He himself commands thee, who has ordered those cast down from the heights of heaven to the depths of the earth. He commands thee, he who commanded the sea, the winds, and the tempests.

"Hear therefore and fear, O Satan, enemy of the faith, foe to the human race, producer of death, thief of life, destroyer of justice, root of evils, kindler of vices, seducer of men, betrayer of nations, inciter of envy, origin of avarice, cause of discord, procurer of sorrows. Why dost thou stand and resist, when thou knowest that Christ the Lord will destroy thy strength? Fear him who was immolated in Isaac, sold in Joseph, slain in the lamb, crucified in man, and then was triumphant over hell.

(*The following signs of the cross should be made on the forehead of the possessed.*) "Depart therefore in the name of the ✠ Father, and of the ✠ Son, and of the Holy ✠ Ghost; give place to the Holy Ghost, by the sign of the ✠ Cross of Jesus Christ our Lord, who with the Father and the same Holy Ghost liveth and reigneth one God, for ever and ever, world without end."

7. Prayer for success, and making the signs of the cross over the demoniac.

8. Second Exorcism:

"I adjure thee, thou old serpent, by the judge of the quick and the dead, by thy maker and the maker of the world, by him who has power to send thee to hell, that thou depart quickly from this servant of God, N., who returns to the bosom of the Church, with fear and the affliction of thy terror. I adjure thee again (✠ *on his forehead*), not in my infirmity, but by the virtue of the Holy Ghost, that thou depart from this servant of God, N., whom Almighty God hath made in his own image.

"Yield therefore; yield not to me, but to the minister of Christ. For his power urges thee, who subjugated thee to his cross. Tremble at his arm, who led the souls to light after the lamentations of hell had been subdued. May the body of man be a terror to thee (✠ *on his chest*), let the image of God be terrible to thee (✠ *on his forehead*). Resist not, neither delay to flee from this man, since it has pleased Christ to dwell in this body. And, although thou knowest me to be none the less a sinner, do not think me contemptible.

"For it is God who commands thee ✠.

"The majesty of Christ commands thee ✠.

"God the Father commands thee ✠.

"God the Son commands thee ✠.

"God the Holy Ghost commands thee ✠.

"The sacred cross commands thee ✠.

"The faith of the holy apostles Peter and Paul and of all other saints commands thee ✠.

"The blood of the martyrs commands thee ✠.

"The constancy of the confessors commands thee ✠.

"The devout intercession of all saints commands thee ✠.

"The virtue of the mysteries of the Christian faith commands thee ✠.

"Go out, therefore, thou transgressor. Go out, thou seducer, full of all deceit and guile, enemy of virtue, persecutor of innocence. O most dire one, give place; give place, thou most impious; give place to Christ, in whom thou hast found nothing of thy works, who hath despoiled thee, who hath destroyed thy kingdom, who hath led thee captive and hath plundered thy goods, who hath cast thee into outer darkness, where for thee and thy ministers is prepared annihilation.

"But why, truculent one, dost thou withstand? Why, rash creature, dost thou refuse?

"Thou art accused by Almighty God, whose statutes thou hast transgressed.

"Thou art accused by his Son, Jesus Christ, our Lord, whom thou didst dare to tempt and presume to crucify.

"Thou art accused by the human race, to whom by thy persuasion thou hast given to drink the poison of death.

"Therefore I adjure thee, most wicked dragon [*draco nequissime*] in the name of the ✠ immaculate lamb, who trod upon the asp and basilisk, who trampled the lion and dragon, to depart from this man (✠ *let the sign be made on his forehead*), to depart from the Church of God (✠ *let the sign be made on those standing by*). Tremble and flee at the invocation of the name of that Lord at whom hell trembles, to whom the virtues of heaven, the powers and dominions are subject, whom cherubim and seraphim with unwearied voices praise, saying, Holy, holy, holy, Lord God of Sabaoth.

"The word made flesh ✠ commands thee.

"He who was born of the Virgin ✠ commands thee.

"Jesus of Nazareth commands thee, who, although thou didst despise his disciples, bade thee go, crushed and prostrate, out of the man, and in his presence, when he had separated thee from the man, thou didst not presume to go into a herd of swine.

"Therefore, adjured now in his ✠ name, depart from this man, whom he has created. It is hard for thee to wish to resist. It is hard for thee to kick against the pricks ✠. Because the more slowly thou go out, the more the punishment against thee increases, since thou despisest not men but him who is Lord of the quick and dead, who shall come to judge the quick and the dead and the world by fire."

9. Prayer.

10. Third and final Exorcism:

"Therefore, I adjure thee, most vile spirit, the entire specter, the very embodiment of Satan, in the name of Jesus Christ ✠ of Nazareth, who, after his baptism in Jordan, was led into the wilderness, and overcame thee in thine own habitations, that thou stop assaulting him whom he hath formed from the dust of the earth to the honor of his glory, and that thou tremble not at the human weakness in miserable man but at the image of Almighty God.

"Therefore, yield to God, who by his servant Moses drowned thee and thy malice in Pharoah and in his army in the abyss.

"Yield to God, who made thee flee when expelled from King Saul with spiritual songs through his most faithful servant, David.

"Yield to God ✠ who condemned thee in Judas Iscariot the traitor. For he beats thee with divine ✠ scourges, in whose sight, trembling and crying out with thy legions, thou hast said: What art thou to us, O Jesus, Son of the most high God? Art thou come hither to torture us before our time? He presses on thee with perpetual flames, who shall say at the end of time to the wicked: Depart from me, ye cursed, into everlasting fire, which is prepared for the devil and his angels.

"For thee, impious one, and for thy angels are prepared worms which never die.

"For thee and thy angels is prepared the unquenchable fire; because thou art the chief of accursed murder, thou art the author of incest, the head of sacrilege, the master of the worst actions, the teacher of heretics, the inventor of all

Title page of the *Alexicacon* (Venice, 1668), by the Franciscan friar, Candidus Brognolus, dealing with the expulsion of evil spirits. From Cornell University Library.

obscenities. Therefore, O impious one, go out. Go out, thou scoundrel, go out with all thy deceits, because God has willed that man be his temple.

"But why dost thou delay longer here?

"Give honor to God, the Father Almighty, to whom every knee is bent.

"Give place to the Lord Jesus Christ ✠ who shed for man his most precious blood.

"Give place to the Holy Ghost, who through his blessed apostle Peter manifestly struck thee in Simon Magus, who condemned thy deceit in Ananias and Sapphira, who smote thee in Herod the King because he did not give God honor, who through his apostle Paul destroyed thee in the magician Elymas by the mist of blindness, and through the same apostle by his word of command bade thee come out of the pythoness.

"Now therefore depart. ✠ Depart, thou seducer. Thy abode is the wilderness, thy habitation is the serpent. Be humbled and prostrate. Now there is no time to delay. For behold the Lord God approaches quickly, and his fire will glow before him and precede him and burn up his enemies on every side. For if thou hast deceived man, thou canst not mock God.

"He expels thee, from whose eye nothing is secret.

"He expels thee to whose power all things are subject.

"He excludes thee, who hast prepared for thee and thy angels everlasting hell; out of whose mouth the sharp sword will go, he who shall come to judge the quick and the dead and the world by fire."

11. Final prayers, including canticles, creed, and various psalms.

In addition, fumigation and flagellation were sometimes employed. Sanchez (1661) distinguished between their superstitious use to expel demons and their religious use to show contempt for devils. Brognolus Bergomensi (1651) quoted many authorities, but still cautioned a "prudent and moderate" application of whipping, more to scorn the devil than afflict the demoniac.

A Mocking View of Exorcism

Holy water come and bring,
Cast in salt for seasoning,
Set the brush for sprinkling;
Sacred spittle bring ye hither,
Meal and it now mix together,
And a little oil to either.
Give the tapers here their light.
Ring the saints' bell to affright
Far from hence the evil sprite.

—Robert Herrick (1591-1674).

Elizabeth Fletcher and her imps, a sketch attributed to Rev. Miles Gale, vicar of Keighley, in an account by Edward Fairfax in 1621 of the bewitching of his children by six women in the Forest of Knaresborough. From a manuscript in the British Museum, London.

Fairfax, Edward. In 1621, the elegant Elizabethan gentleman, Edward Fairfax, of Fewstone, scholar and translator of Tasso, persisted in charging six women living in the Forest of Knaresborough with bewitching his children with fits and visions. Though the women were released at the York assizes, Fairfax brought them to trial; the justices allowed them to escape, since the evidence "reached not to the point of the statute." Fairfax raged at the "best, able, and most understanding" of his neighbors, who suggested to the judges "doubts inferring a supposal of counterfeiting and practice in the children, and that it was not serious but a combination proceeding out of malice."

What is of most interest for this entry is the transcript of the trial, made by Fair-

"Each one of us has a spirit to wait upon us, when we please to call upon him," declared Isobel Gowdie, a Scottish witch. A witch might also inherit a familiar from another witch. The little creature was in constant attendance on its mistress, who was responsible for its care. The faithful "familiar" demon is therefore to be distinguished from the occasional visitations of the Devil disguised as a small animal. Guazzo in 1608 explained: "The Devil manifests himself in many various forms of specters, such as dogs, cats, goats, oxen, men, women, or a horned owl. . . . But because the human form is in all ways the most perfect and beautiful, therefore he usually appears in that form to us." Lady Alice Kyteler's "Robert Artisson," who appeared as a black man, cat, or shaggy dog was not a familiar, but the Devil.

Reginald Scot, in his *Discovery of Witchcraft* (1584), was the first to use the words "familiar" and "imp" in this restricted sense, although "familiar spirit" had appeared in print twenty years earlier. In America, Cotton Mather was the first to mention "imps sucking persons." The two venomous toads which sucked the breasts of the Fair Rosamond, while Queen Eleanor and four witches held her captive, apart from being fable, are not examples of twelfth-century familiars. In Elizabeth's statute of 1563, familiars were not mentioned; but by 1604 it had become a felony "to consult, covenant with, entertain, employ, feed, or reward any evil and wicked spirit." Between these dates, the theory of familiars had developed; the witch trials are all crammed with reports of imps, apparently reckoned as the counterparts of guardian angels. Since the familiar was always some creature found in a house or farm, there was never a witch without her imp. And if she had no cat, the judges usually discovered a bee or fly or mouse to be the Devil's emissary to her. As a result of this assumption, every common animal became suspect as potentially evil. In Gifford's *Dialogue* (1593), the farmer says:

"The witches have their spirits, some hath one, some hath more, as two, three, four, or five, some in one likeness and some in another, as like cats, weasels, toads, or mice, whom they nourish with milk or a chicken, or by letting them suck now and then a drop of blood."—George Gifford, *Dialogue Concerning Witches* (1593).

fax, which was illustrated by Rev. Miles Gale, vicar of Keighley. Two of these sketches, included here, depict the imps or familiars which pestered his children, and one of the supposed witches, Elizabeth Fletcher, herself the daughter of a witch, Mother Foster.

Familiars. The familiar, familiar spirit, or imp is an almost exclusively English (and Scottish) contribution to the theory of witchcraft; the concept is seldom discussed in European trials or handbooks. The Devil, so it was held, having made a compact with the witch, gave her a low-ranking demon in the shape of a small domestic animal to advise her and perform small malicious errands, including murder.

When I go but into my closes [gardens], I am afraid, for I see now and then a hare, which my conscience giveth me is a witch, or some witch's spirit—she stareth so upon me. And sometime I see an ugly weasel run through my yard, and there is a foul great cat sometimes in my barn, which I have no liking unto.

Ursula Kempe's confession in *A True and Just Record* of the St. Osyth Witch Trials in 1582 set the pattern for a familiar.

> She had four spirits, whereof two of them were hes, and the other two were shes: the two he spirits were to punish and kill unto death, and the two shes were to punish with lameness and other diseases of bodily harm. . . . One he, like a gray cat, is called Tittey; the second, like a black cat, is called Jack; one she, like a black toad, is called Pigin; and the other, like a black lamb, is called Tyffin.

These creatures carried out her *maleficia*: the black cat Jack plagued the wife of a neighbor; the toad Pigin caused a young child to become ill; and the black lamb Tyffin spied on people, informing her that one Elizabeth Bennet had "two spirits, one like a black dog, named Suckin, and the other like a red lion, named Lyerd." As a reward, Ursula Kempe allowed these imps to suck her blood from her left thigh, "the which when she rubbeth, it will at all times bleed."

The Chelmsford Trials are very rich in accounts of familiars. At the second trial in 1597, the young son of Ellen Smith said his mother kept three spirits: Great Dick in a wicker bottle; Little Dick in a leather bottle, and Willet in a wool-pack. Unfortunately, when searched for, "the spirits were vanished away." At the same trial, Elizabeth Francis cursed her neighbor's wife for refusing her some yeast, whereupon "a spirit of a white color in seeming like to a little rugged dog" appeared, promising to hurt the miserly neighbor. For its reward, the familiar spirit received a piece of bread.

In the celebrated Warboys trial in 1593, Alice Samuel was accused of bewitching some children. The following account comes from Richard Boulton in 1715:

First, being demanded what the names of those spirits (wherewith she bewitched) were called, she said they were called Pluck, Catch, and White, the which names she often repeated. Being asked whether she had bewitched the Lady Cromwell to death or not, she answered that she had. Being asked with which of her spirits she did bewitch the said Lady to death, she said with Catch. And being demanded for what cause she did it, she answered: For that the said Lady had caused some of her hair and her hair-lace to be burned. And that she said, Catch willed her to be revenged of the said Lady. And that thereupon the said Mother Samuel bid him go and do what he would. And being asked what Catch said to her when he came back again, she confessed that he said that he had been revenged of her. Moreover, she confessed, and upon her death did say for truth, that she was guilty of the death of the said Lady Cromwell.

Another illustration comes from Potts's description of the Lancashire Witches in 1613:

> Jannet Device, daughter of Elizabeth Device, late wife of John Device, of the Forest of Pendle aforesaid, widow, confesseth and saith that her said mother is a witch, and that this she knoweth to be true: for that she hath seen her spirit sundry times come into her said mother in her own house, called Malking Tower, in the likeness of a brown dog, which she called Ball. And at one time amongst others, the said Ball did ask this examinate's mother what she would have him to do; and this examinate's mother answered that she would have the said Ball to help her to kill John Robinson of Barley, alias Swyer. By help of which said Ball, the said Swyer was killed by witchcraft accordingly.

The classic account of familiars, however, occurs in Matthew Hopkins' *Discovery of Witches* (1647). After keeping her awake for four nights, Hopkins saw the familiar spirits come to Elizabeth Clark:

> 1. Holt, who came in like a white kitling [kitten].
> 2. Jamara, who came in like a fat spaniel without any legs at all. She said

Witches and their Familiars

Frontispiece to Matthew Hopkins' *Discovery of Witches* (1647), the work of "an unmitigated scoundrel who preyed upon the fears of the Essex franklins whilst he emptied their pockets."

she kept him fat, for she clapped her hand on her belly, and said he sucked good blood from her body.

3. Vinegar Tom, who was like a long-legged greyhound, with an head like an ox, with a long tail and broad eyes, who when this discoverer spoke to and bade him go to the place provided for him and his angels, immediately transformed himself into the shape of a child of four years old without a head, and gave half a dozen turns about the house, and vanished at the door.

4. Sack and Sugar, like a black rabbit.

5. News, like a polecat. All these vanished away in a little time.

Hopkins swore on oath that he had personally seen these imps while he was watching Elizabeth Clark in her cell; this evidence was accepted, and Mrs. Clark was convicted. At these sessions, seven women were hanged on no other count but that of harboring familiar spirits.

Rev. John Gaule, who opposed Hopkins' methods, ridiculed his ways of securing proof of familiars. He wrote:

A little hole is likewise made in the door [of the prison] for the imp to come in at. And lest it might come in some less discernible shape, they that watch are taught to be ever and anon sweeping the room, and if they see any spiders or flies to kill them. And if they cannot kill them, then they may be seen they are her imps.

Trial records produce other curious names of familiars. Hopkins also reported:

"Elemanzer, Pynewacket, Peckin the Crow, Grizzel, Greedigut . . . which no mortal could invent." An Essex indictment of 1583 named "three imps otherwise called spirits . . . Pygine, resembling a mole, Russoll, resembling a gray cat, and . . . Dunsott, resembling a dun dog." In 1588 another Essex witch had three spirits: Lightfoot, a cat; Lunch, a toad; and Makeshift, a weasel. Isobel Gowdie identified Swein, Rorie, MakHector, Robert the Rule, and others.

The witch had to feed her imps. She could give them choice delicacies, as did Mrs. Heard, who in 1582 at St. Osyth was accused of feeding her blackbirds and rats ("like cows having little short horns") on "wheat, barley, oats, bread and cheese . . . and water and beer to drink." Margaret Cotton, on trial at Cambridge in 1602, allegedly fed "certain things in the likeness of chickens . . . on roasted apples and claret wine." In 1651 Anne Bodenham fed her imps with crumbs of bread; she was hanged [see Dr. Lamb's Darling].

All imps craved human blood, and every witch fed them from her fingers or little protuberances on her body. These were the witch's marks, for which every suspect was meticulously searched. These little teats or wens must be distinguished from devil's marks, with which the devil branded those who had made a pact with him, and which form part of European demonology.

In seventeenth-century England the theory was that such teats formed prima-facie evidence of witchcraft. Mother Agnes Waterhouse, one of the Chelmsford witches, employed her cat "Sathan" in an attempt to kill a tailor named Wardel, but the cat confessed it was unable to break down Wardel's faith and injure him! When asked, "When did thy cat suck of thy blood?" Mrs. Waterhouse replied, "Never." Nevertheless she was searched, and the appropriate marks discovered on her head. Ann Usher at the Suffolk trials in 1645, after Hopkins had kept her two nights without sleep, confessed:

About a year since, she felt a thing like a small cat come over her legs once or twice, and that it scratched her mightily.

After that she felt two things like butterflies in her secret parts, with itchings, dancings, and sucking. And she felt them with her hands, and rubbed them, and killed them.

A scientific explanation for imps' sucking blood was attempted by a Master of Arts of Cambridge University, Henry Hallywell, in his *Melampronoea* (1681). Answering the skeptics, he argued that the confessions of witches have made sucking an "unquestionable matter of fact." The demons

being so mightily debauched . . . wear away by a continual deflux of particles, and therefore require some nutriment to supply the place of the fugacious atoms, which is done by sucking the blood and spirits of these forlorn wretches [witches]. . . . And no doubt but these impure devils may take as much pleasure in sucking the warm blood of men or beasts, as a cheerful and healthy constitution in drawing in the refreshing gales of pure and sincere air!

To all such arguments, Thomas Ady made the rational observation that most poor people needed all the blood they had to keep alive, let alone give it to familiars.

For accounts of familiars in English witch trials, see especially Chelmsford Witches, St. Osyth Witches.

Fascination. Of the various magical folk beliefs which were incorporated into the theological framework of witchcraft, fascination or the "evil eye" was one of the most primitive and extensive. Every civilization has believed that evil can be effected merely through hostile looks; and a word for this conception occurs in nearly all languages, European and non-European— *mauvais oeil* in France, *mal occhio* or, more picturesque, *la iettatura* in Italy, *böser Blick* in Germany, or *glamour* in Scotland (a word introduced into English by Sir Walter Scott). Fascination simply means bewitching or enchanting, from the Latin *fascinum;* this word was also used for the countercharm against the evil eye, generally a phallus.

The Power of the Evil Eye. The frontispiece of *Tractatus de Fascinatione* (1675) by Johannes Christian Fromann, Doctor of Medicine in the Province of Saxe-Coburg.

The superstition was enshrined in the Bible: "From within, out of the heart of men, proceed evil thoughts . . . an evil eye"—Mark vii. Matthew made the link between the evil eye and the evil person or witch: "If thine eye be evil, thy whole body shall be full of darkness." Christ himself gave an example when he cursed the fig tree so that it withered (Matthew xxi). In the thirteenth century, Thomas Aquinas noted that children were especially vulnerable to glares from old women, and he was echoed by a succession of demonologists, Vineti (1450), Nider (1470), and the Inquisitor Bernard de Como (1510). The *Malleus Maleficarum* (1486) warned "that there are witches who can bewitch their judges by a mere look or glance from their eyes, and publicly boast that they cannot be punished." Del Rio in 1599 finally summarized the accepted views: "Fas-cination is a power derived from a pact with the Devil, who, when the so-called fascinator looks at another with an evil intent . . . he infects with evil the person at whom he looks."

This power of fascination entered many witch trials. Janet Wishart, who was burned in 1597, is a classic example in Scotland [see Aberdeen Witches], and Bridget Bishop provides a good illustration of the power of the evil eye in American witchcraft. Mrs. Bishop was charged with casting her eyes at the Salem girls so that "they were presently [immediately] struck down."

Faversham Witches. The confessions of Joan Williford, Joan Cariden, and Jane Holt, executed at Faversham, Kent, on September 29, 1645, illustrate the typical crimes alleged in witch trials. On the Continent, the forced confessions of witches, made publicly before their execution, helped mold popular notions; the pamphlets with similar confessions served the same purpose in seventeenth-century England. The verbatim court records were never extensively available, and so witchcraft was known mainly in chapbook accounts.

The following "confession" of Joan Williford, taken on September 24, 1645, sufficed to send her to her death. Her implication of others should be noted, for only in this way could the vested interests of the witch hunters be maintained.

She confessed that the Devil about seven years ago did appear to her in the shape of a little dog, and bid her to forsake God and lean to him. [She] replied that she was loath to forsake him. She confessed also that she had a desire to be revenged upon Thomas Letherland and Mary Woodruff now his wife. She further said that the Devil promised her that she should not lack, and that she had money sometimes brought her—she knew not whence—sometime òne shilling, sometimes eight pence, never more at once. She called her devil by the name of Bunnie. She further saith that her retainer Bunnie carried Thomas Gardler out of a window, who fell into a backside [cesspool]. She further saith that near twenty years since she promised her soul to the Devil. She further saith that she gave some of her blood to the devil, who wrote the covenant betwixt them. She further saith that the devil promised to be her servant about twenty years, and that the time is now almost expired. She further saith that Jane Holt, Elizabeth Harris, Joan Argoll were her fellows. She further saith that her devil told her that Elizabeth Harris, about six or seven years since, cursed the boat of one John Woofcott, and so it came to pass. She further saith that the devil promised her that she should not sink, being thrown into the water. She further said Goodwife Argoll cursed Mr. Major, and also John Mannington, and said that he should not thrive. And so it came to pass. She likewise saith that the devil sucked her twice since she came

into the prison; he came to her in the form of a mouse.

Fery, Jeanne. The possession of Sister Jeanne Fery at Mons from 1573 to about 1585 by eight devils reads almost like a clinical diagnosis of hysteria. This may be why the published brochure of 1586 (by the Archbishop of Cambrai, François Buisseret) attracted the attention of Dr. Magloire Bourneville, who reprinted it 300 years later; for the symptoms of Sister Jeanne closely paralleled those of the deranged minds he cared for as a doctor, such as Louise Lateau.

Jeanne said she was seduced by the devil at the age of fourteen; thereafter, to the age of twenty-five, when she was helped by exorcism, she suffered hystero-epileptic fits, or, as the contemporary narrative writes, torment by *malings esprits* (which assumed the odd names of Hérésie, Traitre, Art magique, Béléal, Vraye Liberté, Namon, Sanguinaire, and Homicide).

These torments consisted of convulsions and delirious frenzy.

To reduce her convulsions she was given

Successful exorcism, showing devils escaping through the mouth of a possessed nun. This engraving depicts the exorcism of a nun in Hainaut, whose capital was Mons (where Jeanne Fery lived), in the archbishopric of Cambrai. This exorcism followed Jeanne Fery's by about four years (1589).

holy baths, during which she regurgitated through the mouth and nostrils "a great quantity of filth, like hair-balls of goats and other animals in the form of hairy worms," accompanied by a loathsome stench. Frequently she threw herself out of windows or into the river. Her frenzy generally occurred "between sleep and waking." She had visions of hell, recapitulating what she had heard in sermons. She experienced hallucinations of sight, sound, and smell: "There were fire, burning sulphur, darkness and a stinking abominable smell." She had pains in her stomach, as if a serpent were gnawing her so cruelly that "for relief [she] consented to rejoin the devils, just to stop the unendurable agony." She uttered outrageous language (for which the devils were responsible). She alternated between *douleurs continuelles* and *grand joye*. In her ecstasy, she could neither talk, eat, nor feel any sensation or pain from her self-inflicted (or demon-inflicted) lacerations. At one period she regressed to the "true simplicity of infancy, and forgot all her knowledge of God . . . only speaking such simple words as Father, Joan, sweet Mary, and pointing with her finger at the objects about her." She acted like a naughty child. She played with a statue of St. Mary Magdalene like a girl with a doll, "as if she wanted to give it her breast."

The most exact account of her hysteria appears in the account of the exorcism on May 24, 1585. Sister Jeanne had been let out of the infirmary to hear mass. During the post-communion her torments began. She uttered a sad unhappy cry.

A priest found her on her knees, with the rest of her body bolt upright, transfixed into immobility, her complexion pallid and sallow, much altered, her eyes wide open and riveted on the holy statue of St. Mary Magdalene above the altar. . . . Some time later, he saw the nun bend her body and laugh very softly to herself, remaining all the time in ecstasy . . . with trembling shaking her whole body and with excessive pounding of the heart. Not being able to declare by words, because of her extreme weakness,

she made signs with her hand . . . one of the nuns rubbed her hands, which had become stiff and dry, like wood. A little later, still trembling, she was led to her room, and warmed in front of a fire, whereupon her debility passed slowly from her.

Fian, John. Dr. John Fian (also called John Cunningham) was the best known of all the seventy persons implicated in Scotland's most celebrated witch trial, that of the North Berwick Witches in 1590, and probably the bravest of all those Scots who suffered torture. Commenting on his trial, E. Lynn Linton, in *Witch Stories* (1861), wrote: "John Fian, a schoolmaster of Saltpans, with no great idea to support him, and no admiring friends to cheer him on, bore himself as nobly as any hero of them all, and vindicated the honor of manhood and natural strength in a way that exalts our common human nature into something godlike and divine." Dr. Fian's strength of character in refusing to confess to witchcraft contrasts sharply with the conduct of the judicial council and of King James VI of Scotland (James I of England), who personally watched his agonies and himself condemned the schoolteacher to death.

The original informer in this series of trials, a servant girl, Gilly Duncan, was cruelly tortured by her employer, without any pretense of legality and before any interest by the courts. She involved others, and gradually a fantastic story was built up of an extensive plot on the life of the King. In this plot, Dr. Fian was alleged to have acted as secretary or recorder of the "coven" or conspiratorial group planning the murder, and hence the ringleader. On December 26, 1590, he was arraigned for witchcraft and high treason on twenty counts. The "dittay," or indictment, recorded in Pitcairn's *Criminal Trials* (1833), charged, among other things:

1. Conspiracy with Satan to wreck the ship carrying King James to Norway, on a visit to his future queen, by throwing a dead cat into the sea.

2. Making an agreement with Satan,

who appeared to him as he lay "musand and pansand" [musing and thinking] how to be revenged on a workman for not having whitewashed his room on time; and receiving the devil's mark.

3. Rendering homage in North Berwick church to Satan, a "mickle black man, with a black beard sticking out like a goat's beard, and a high ribbed nose, falling down sharp like the bill of a hawk, with a long rumpled tail."

4. Having "ecstasies and trances, lying by the space of two or three hours dead, his spirit taken, and suffered himself to be carried and transported to many mountains."

5. Looting graves for corpses to be used in charms (according to confessions under torture by others accused).

The other counts covered various magical acts committed by Dr. Fian, such as opening locked doors by breathing on them, carrying at night powerful magic candles on his horse, seducing a widow, flying through the air, storm-raising, using love charms (which came to naught), and casting horoscopes.

A contemporary pamphlet, *News from Scotland* (1591), a unique copy extant in the Lambeth Palace Library, London, described how John Fian was tortured. "First, by thrawing of his head with a rope." Thrawing consisted of binding the head with a rope, and then roughly jerking the rope in all directions. After an hour of this, Dr. Fian was admonished to confess "by fair means," but he refused.

Then he was "put to the most severe and cruel pain in the world, called the boots," a sort of vise to crush the legs. After the third pressing, Dr. Fian lost consciousness. The court officials interpreted this as taciturnity, a trick of the devil; accordingly, prompted by some other suspects, they searched his mouth for a charm, and found two pins "thrust up into the head." The pamphlet undoubtedly reverses cause and effect: the torturers themselves stuck the pins into his tongue until he succumbed. After the torture with the pins, in the presence of King James, he confessed whatever was suggested to him as "most true, with-

Two incidents in the charges against John Fian at the trial of the North Berwick Witches in 1590, showing Dr. Fian's lovesick cow (bewitched in mistake for a young lady) and his horse with the brilliant magic candles. From *News from Scotland* (1591), the unique copy in Lambeth Palace Library.

out producing any witness to justify the same," and renounced "conjuring, witchcraft, enchantment, sorcery and such like."

The next night, according to *News from Scotland*, Dr. Fian escaped from prison and made his way home to Saltpans. At this news, the King "commanded diligent inquiry to be made for his apprehension. . . . By means of whose hot and hard pursuit, he was again taken and brought to prison." This escape, in view of the condition of Dr. Fian's legs, is probably an editorial addition to heighten the narrative. Nevertheless, all reports agree that when he was again brought before the King and his council, Dr. Fian recanted his confession. Thereupon he was searched a second time, because in the interval he might have "entered a new conference and league with the Devil." Nothing new was found. Then, to erase his denial and force an acknowledgment of his first admissions, he was "commanded to have a most strange torment."

His nails upon all his fingers were riven and pulled off with an instrument called in Scottish a *turkas*, which in England we call a pair of pincers, and under every nail there was thrust in two needles over even up to the heads. At all which torments notwithstanding, the doctor never shrunk any whit, neither would he then confess it the sooner for all the tortures inflicted upon him.

Torture was heaped on torture, and the "Spanish boots" were again resorted to. Dr. Fian "did abide so many blows in them, that his legs were crushed and beaten together as small as might be, and the bones and flesh so bruised, that the blood and marrow spouted forth in great abundance, whereby they were made unserviceable for ever."

He still denied the accusations and maintained his original confession "was only done and said for fear of pains which he had endured." In spite of his denials and in the absence of a confession, nevertheless the King's council determined to execute him "for example sake, to remain a terror to all others hereafter, that shall attempt to deal in the like wicked and ungodly actions, as witchcraft." The trial ran true to form: the accusation once made, death was inevitable. It came within five weeks. Dr. Fian refused to confess and was burned; his alleged chief collaborator, Agnes Sampson, made a confession and was burned. The only distinction was that Dr. Fian was more horribly tortured before execution.

As was generally the custom, Dr. Fian was first strangled and "immediately put into a great fire, being ready provided for that purpose, and there burned in the Castle Hill of Edinburgh, on a Saturday in the end of January last past [January 23 or 30, 1591]."

Filmer, Sir Robert. Sir Robert Filmer, a country gentleman, educated at Cambridge University (1604), was a prominent political writer in the middle of the seventeenth century. A staunch Royalist, he opposed Hobbes, Milton, and Locke, and held absolutist political views, but on such controversial subjects as usury and witchcraft was very rational. His chief political work, *Patriarcha, or the Natural Power of Kings*, remained in manuscript to 1680. His sole work on witchcraft, a little tract of only

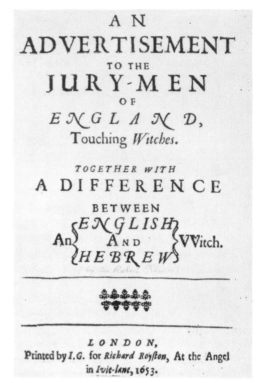

Title page of Sir Robert Filmer's little tract (1653) addressed to jurymen, urging moderation at witch trials.

twenty-four pages, *An Advertisement to the Jurymen of England Touching Witches, together with a difference between an English and Hebrew witch*, was published anonymously in London in 1653.

"Without expressly denying witchcraft, [Filmer] writes satirically against Perkins, its defender," and Del Rio. To this extent, Filmer exercised a progressive and moderating influence. Spurred by the hangings in Maidstone, Kent, he sought to clarify "the great difficulty in discovering what or who a witch is." Del Rio stated, "The main foundation . . . is a contract with the Devil, and renunciation of God and the Blessed Virgin." Therefore, said Filmer, "none can be witches but such as have first been Christians, nay, Roman Catholics, if Del Rio say true, for who else can denounce the patronage of the Virgin Mary." If witchcraft is "an art working wonders," it must be a witch's art; otherwise it is the Devil's craft. "It is a rare art for a witch by her art to be able to do nothing herself, but to command another to practice the art." But how can an accessory (a witch) be convicted without the principal (the Devil) ; and how can the Devil be "lawfully summoned according to the rules of our common law?" Jurymen would certainly have problems to ponder here, and be less ready to convict on accusation.

William Perkins had proposed eighteen signs or proofs of witches, and his tests had been very influential in court trials. Filmer analyzed Perkins' "rules" and demolished them.

> His seven first he himself confesseth to be insufficient for conviction of a witch. His eight next proofs (which he saith men in [high] place have used) he acknowledgeth to be false or insufficient. Thus of his eighteen proofs, which made a great show, [fifteen] of them are cast off by himself. There remains then his sixteenth, which is the confession of a witch, yet presently he is forced to yield that a bare confession is not a sufficient proof. And so he cometh to his seventeenth proof, which is, two credible witnesses. And he here grants that the league between the Devil and the witch is closely made and the practices of witches be very secret, that hardly a man can be brought which (upon his own knowledge) can aver such things. Therefore at last, when all other proofs fail, he is forced to fly to his eighteenth proof, and tells us, that yet there is a way to come to the knowledge of a witch, which is, that Satan useth all means to discover a witch. Which how it can be well done, except the Devil be bound over to give in evidence against the witch, cannot be understood.

Finland, Witchcraft in. Christianity was introduced into Finland from Sweden in 1157. Heathen beliefs in natural and magic powers consequently continued longer there than elsewhere in Europe, and formed a fertile background for new doctrines of Christian demonology. During the early seventeenth century, belief in witches was spread partly by Swedish vagabonds making a living by sorcery, by German craftsmen who brought with them the delusions of their homeland, by Finnish youths returning after study in Germany, by veterans returning from the Thirty Years' War, and by some Finns, trading on the reputation of Laplanders for raising storms, who claimed similar occult powers.

All early references to witchcraft in Finland emphasized sorcery. Bishop Conrad Bitz (1460-89) condemned as deadly sins the casting of lots, prophesying, interpreting dreams, and using charms. About a century later, in 1573, the synod in Turku [Åbo], at that time the capital, excommunicated fortunetellers and witches, turned them over to the secular authorities for punishment, and, failing their reform, banished them. Even during the seventeenth century, witchcraft seldom developed the theories of pact and sabbat. In 1640, Bishop Fsak Rothovius, in a sermon at the new Turku University, lamented the superstition of witches—not their heresy. "When people fall ill, they seek help from the devil by laying wax figures, candles, squirrel skins and other things on the altars, and on certain days sacrifice sheep and coins."

Simultaneously with the Lutheran Church's condemnation, sorcery was opposed by the civil government. King Gustavus Vasa's *Acta Ecclesiastica* (1554) imposed a fine of forty marks on those who housed witches and other tramps without reporting them to the minister or sheriff [Swedish: *lansman*]. In 1575, King Johan III of Sweden gave orders that on their tours of inspection the administrators of his Grand Duchy watch for idolaters and witches. Those detected, for the first and second offenses, were to be whipped at the church door, and, for the third, condemned before the judges. In 1618, King Gustavus Adolphus ordered Bishop Olaus Elimaeus to take similar action in his diocese of Viipuri, where apparently sorcery was prevalent. The Court of Appeals proposed in 1641 that clergy in Vehmaa and Lower Satakunta preach against witchcraft; a suggestion repeated in 1649 by Per Brahe, the Governor-General of Finland, and again in 1669, following the savage outburst against the Mora Witches in Sweden. Special prayers against witchcraft (identified with unexpected calamities) were to be read on all Sundays and holy days. To assist the clergy in their sermons, Bishop Ericus Erici (Sorolainen) in 1621 and Laurentius Petri in 1644 published homilies; both collections, however, were moderate in their outlook. The destruction of servants of the Devil by fire and sword was advocated in Swedish by Andreas Hasselqvist.

In spite of all these attacks, forbidden occult books of magic, such as Paletz' *Kabbala*, the *grimoire—Clavis Salomonis* [*Key of Solomon*], and Cornelius Agrippa's *De Occulta Philosophia*, had wide circulation among professors and clergymen. Scholars, especially experimental scientists, as elsewhere, were often suspected of excessive interest in magic. One of the best-known trials in the late sixteenth century was that of Professor Martin Stodius and two undergraduates, Eolenius Gunnerus and Johannes Arwidi, before the University Council of Turku. Another famous trial was that of the widow of Dean Alanus, accused by Bishop Gezelius the Elder.

In Finland, the laws against witchcraft followed those of Sweden. The provincial laws [*Ostgota*] inflicted the death penalty for *maleficia*, and fines for superstition (e.g., prophesying, sacrificing to trees), and became both the land law [Swedish: *landslag*] and the town law. Persons were indicted under these laws, various royal statutes (especially that of 1575), and "God's law" of the Old Testament. The Articles of War of 1683 stated that a man causing death by witchcraft should be hanged, a woman burned. It was not until 1687 that a statute made death the penalty for both witchcraft and the pact with the Devil, and punished "superstition," according to the crime and offender, by imprisonment on bread and water, running the gauntlet [Swedish: *gatlopp*], or whipping. A decisive factor in sentencing was the general reputation and standing of the accused; thus persons able to procure witnesses for their innocency would be freed, but the poor and lonely, tramps and beggars, were inevitably condemned. Behind these laws lay the principle, not of the deterrent effect of punishment on potential witches, but of the appeasement of God's wrath.

The first trial for witchcraft in Finland was recorded on August 1, 1595, at Pernaja, when a woman was condemned to death, charged that her threats to bring misfortune on people had come true and that she had caused illness which she later claimed to cure. Whether the sentence was carried out is not known. Not until the the late 1620's, however, were witch trials numerous—most frequent in two Swedish-speaking regions, Pohjanmaa [Swedish: Österbotten] and Ahvenanmaa [Swedish: Åland].

In Pohjanmaa the persecutions reached their peak in the 1650's, when fifty cases were tried at the assizes; at this time in other parts of Finland only eleven trials took place. Toward the end of the seventeenth century trials generally decreased in Pohjanmaa, but elsewhere they increased. But in Finland as a whole, only fifty or sixty people received death sentences (but not all were carried out), about thirty of them in Pohjanmaa. Of the total, about ten were men. Most of the men had Finnish names; the women, Swedish names.

Customarily, Finland did not create special tribunals to convict witches, that operated under different procedures from those used for other crimes. Trials were decorously ordered, and torture prohibited, although occasionally mutilation was ordered as a punishment. Finland had no systematically organized persecutions, and charges of witchcraft usually arose out of some presumed individual act of *maleficia*, and not from denunciations.

Only in one area did Finnish trials approximate the lawlessness and torture of inquisitorial procedures. In the late 1660's, stories of the witches' orgies at the Blockberg or Blocula [Swedish: *Blakulla*; Finnish: *Horna*] fanned out from the Swedish province of Dalecarlia. The pattern spread to Stockholm, where a Finnish woman, Magdalena Mattsdotter, was among the witches burned there in 1675, and to Pohjanmaa and Ahvenanmaa.

In Ahvenanmaa persecutions flared from

"The Finlanders were wont formerly among their other errors of [paganism] to sell winds to merchants that were stopped on their coasts by contrary weather. And when they had their price, they knit three magical knots . . . bound up with a thong, and they gave them unto the merchants, observing that rule, that when they unloosed the first, they should have a good gale of wind; when the second, a stronger wind; but when they untied the third, they should have such cruel tempests that they should not be able to look out of the forecastle to avoid the rocks."— Olaus Magnus, *Historia de Gentibus Septentrionalibus* (1555).

1666 to 1678, fostered by overzealous judges and clergy under German influence. Sentences often quoted German demonologists (not otherwise prominent), such as Michael Freudig, Mengering, Kester, and Ludwig Dunte. In 1666, ten women were condemned to be executed and their bodies burned. The first victim was Karin Persdotter, the sick and foolish wife of a beggar, Sigfrid Eriksson; she provided the names of thirteen other women brought to trial as witches. Karin was sentenced at an extraordinary session at Finström in April, 1666; God's law (in Exodus xxii. 18) had become the sole authority to execute witches. The inquisitorial methods used at Ahvenanmaa, however, were isolated and not adopted elsewhere in Finland. Thus, James I erred when he said in his *Demonology* that the power of the Devil was greatest in Lapland, Finland, the Orkney and Shetland Islands, because there the ignorance of the people was the greatest. On the contrary, Finland met the delusion with far greater composure, common sense, and integrity of its legal system than most of Europe. In the eighteenth century, witch-

craft in Finland, as indeed throughout all Europe, was coming to an end. While a law of 1734 still prescribed the death penalty for witchcraft, it seems never to have been invoked, and in 1779 the statute was abolished.

Flade, Dietrich. "Though two centuries of witch-burning followed [1589], Dietrich Flade remains to our day its most eminent victim in the land of its greatest thoroughness." So wrote George L. Burr in 1891 after he had discovered the lengthy documents of the trial, 245 pages in all, lost for the preceding 300 years.

Of prominent family himself and married into a family of wealth and social position, Dr. Dietrich Flade was trained for high office. In 1559 he was chosen by the Prince-Archbishop of Treves to suppress the Protestants there; for twenty years he headed the secular courts; in 1580 he became Vice-Governor of Treves; and in 1586 Rector of the University (the only layman ever to hold that office). "By his civic zeal, and by his proved loyalty to his sovereigns," wrote a contemporary historian, the Jesuit Christoph Brouwer, "he had earned the judge's position in the city; learned both in public and private law, greatly valued for his counsels, he had won favor, and fame as well, among the princes of the Empire, and had gathered to himself riches." Yet in spite of his prestige, Flade was burned in 1589, like thousands of others accused of witchcraft.

The dilemma in which Dr. Flade found himself has been paralleled in later times— an eminent man serving as subordinate to a ruthless fanatic. Not disagreeing in theory, he came only later to disagree in practice and delay the job he was supposed to do. He became an obstacle, had to be removed, and was therefore falsely charged as one of the opposition. A leader in the witch delusion, Suffragan Bishop Peter Binsfeld, hinted at the real reason for the attack on Flade: "I remember myself to have heard from a certain jurist, whether in earnest or in jest I cannot say, that he cared naught for a thousand denunciations." Another contemporary, the famous demonologist Del Rio, also used Flade as an example of a witch-protector being a witch: "In our own times, Dr. Flade, one of the councilors of the Elector at Treves, tried with all his might and main [to obstruct the trials], but being arrested at last confessed his crime and deceit, and was burned at the stake."

The succession of Johann von Schönenburg to the See of Treves in 1581 brought about the suppression of the heretics—the Protestants; then the banishment of the Jews; and finally the extirpation of the witches. At first, with Flade as Vice-Governor, there was little action; the first witch to be accused in the city (1582) was merely banished. But the persecutions were intensified by the Jesuit-trained Suffragan Bishop [*Weihbischof*], Peter Binsfeld, author in 1589 of the authoritative code for witch judges throughout Germany, and by the new Governor (1584), Johann Zandt, an experienced witch-hunter in the country districts of Treves.

Popular support for these leaders was stimulated by calamities (bad weather, plagues of mice, snails, and grasshoppers) which destroyed all but two harvests during the nineteen years from 1580 to 1599. In addition, Protestant and Spanish mercenaries and robbers were ravaging the countryside, and supplies from the Lower Rhine were cut off. Witchcraft was the explanation. Satan's witches had been able "to wreak cruel woes on mortals, to bewitch to death the cattle, to ruin the harvests, and to stir up the horrible thing to the uttermost." Brouwer's chronicle continued, "Both rich and poor, of every rank, age, and sex, sought a share in the accursed crime."

To counteract the restraining influence of Dr. Flade on the severity of the trials, Governor Johann Zandt had to get rid of Flade. He slowly went to work to build up a case:

1. Zandt prejudiced the Archbishop by accusing Flade of plotting against the Archbishop. Zandt produced a boy who swore he had heard Dietrich Flade at a sabbat boasting he had administered "a deadly potion, his Grace being accessible, because contrary to his habit he had on going to bed laid on the table the amulets of sacred wax which he wore about his neck; but that there being not enough of the drug, the Archbishop would this time escape death." The lad, as revealed in the secret correspondence of the Jesuits (who had him under their protection), had "a great imbecility of his own brain," because he had eaten "a cat's brain at the [sabbat] feast."

How confessions were secured in witch trials. One judge questions the prisoner as he endures torture, while another directs the scribe to write the confession. Many confessions thus recorded in the torture chamber are still extant. From *Bambergische Halsgerichtsordnung* (1508).

2. Of the 118 women and two men he had burned in his jurisdiction at Pfalzel in 1587, Zandt found one, "Maria the old Meieress," who on promise of being strangled before burning, on June 5, kept shouting that Dr. Flade was a witch.

3. Zandt procured a host of similar accusations from condemned persons, who repeated the celebrated name revealed by Maria.

4. After Flade had been warned of these charges and the Archbishop had publicly rebuked Flade's reluctance in prosecuting witches, Zandt struck his final blow. Making full use of the plight of the country, on April 15, 1588, he produced one Margarethe of Euren, who swore that at a sabbat Dr. Flade had urged the destruction of crops by hailstorms and snails. Dr. Flade had made the witches present eat a fritter of a child's heart to make them taciturn under torture; Margarethe, however, ate only a little.

Flade had still a year to live, but his fate was inevitable.

July 4, 1588. Commission appointed to examine the accusations, including those of twenty-three persons sentenced by Flade for witchcraft. A notary, Peter Ormsdorf, found in witch trials a good source of income. One of his victims who escaped burning testified that while hanging in torture, she saw the judge bribe the notary, who then questioned her about suspects he named. Angered at her failure to name names, Ormsdorf seized the torturer's pike and poked her breasts until they were bloody. Most of the evidence against Flade was written down, and possibly inspired, by Ormsdorf.

August 21, 1588. Commission reports fourteen witches accused Flade.

September 4, 1588. Archbishop orders commission to continue; it takes six more depositions.

October 3, 1588. Flade attempts flight, is intercepted and brought back to a city now hostile. Most of his relatives and friends are dead. Under house arrest, he is watched by four citizens, whom he must pay. Binsfeld considers his attempt to escape an *indicium* of guilt.

January 5, 1589. Second appeal by Flade to purge himself.

January 14, 1589. Archbishop asks theological faculty of Treves for advice on how to proceed. Faculty resists Archbishop's bias and delays reply.

March 23, 1589. Archbishop by-passes faculty and orders arrest of Flade; but court, reluctant, also delays.

April 22, 1589. Flade finally imprisoned in *Rathaus* by Governor Zandt.

May 10, 1589. Flade confronted by two accused priests who confessed they had seen him at a sabbat. Flade argues, "It can

---

*Form of sentence or "Protocol"
on Dietrich Flade*

In the criminal case between the noble and well-born Johann Zandt von Merll, squire of Hamme, representative of the Archbishop of Treves, councilor and commissioner at Paltzell and Grymburg, by virtue of his office and superior authority as prosecutor, on the one hand, and Dr. Dietrich Flade as the defendant, on the other hand:

In reply to the charge, by his own confession, after all judicial procedures, and by the experience and finding of the Inquisition, therefore, according to the public regulations of King Charles V and the Holy Empire, we, the judges and jury of this supreme high court, have finally recognized it just that Dietrich Flade, the accused, presently standing before this court, because of his evil doings, whereby he defied Almighty God and made himself partisan and servant to the fiend, occupied himself with witchcraft and by vile devices damaged crops and plants, which were destined for the common good, should be punished with fire from life to death, and we herewith anathemize, sentence, and condemn him thereto, recommending his soul to the mercy of Almighty God.

Witnessed: The lords Sultzbach, Enschnegen, Fiedler, Schoder, Fath, Kilburgh, Wolff, and Tholes. Boitzheim gave his vote although absent because of ill health.

Facsimile of a page of the court record passing judgment on Dietrich Flade and ordering his execution and burning. The handwriting is the neat official calligraphy of the scribe at Treves in 1589. From a manuscript in Cornell University Library.

and may be that you saw my figure, but my person surely not."

July 11, 1589. Flade again questioned.

July 29, 1589. Archbishop instructs secular court to charge Flade with witchcraft.

August 5, 1589. Assessors and acting judge rounded up from country districts to try Flade; they argue Flade is still legally their judge, but their protests are overruled.

August 17, 1589. Formal trial opens, Flade tortured. Because of a hernia his sufferings under strappado are very intense. Ultimately Flade confesses his presence at sabbats, intercourse with the devil, acts of *maleficia.* "He, Flade, was also present when it was proposed to make the slugs, so that the seeds would rot. When it had been agreed to do this, he had helped make them, by molding little clods of dirt and throwing them into the air in the name of the Devil, whereupon slugs formed out of them. He thinks he can remember the pact had taken place on Longwicher Hill" (MS. of his confession). Flade names accomplices, qualifying each person named with "whether it was himself in person or only the evil one in his form I cannot say." Accuses prominent people and judges, but only names of those not present at torture recorded. Archbishop dissatisfied with Flade's confession, orders further torture.

September 16, 1589. Court passes judgment, and Flade forced to confess his plot on life of Archbishop.

September 18, 1589. Execution carried out, Flade first "mercifully and Christianly strangled, and the body burned to ashes. May God Almighty have mercy and compassion on his soul."

Concluded Burr:

Dietrich Flade was not a martyr—scarcely even a hero. Little as we know of him, it is clear that he died for something less than a principle, and flinched at last before the end came. Yet it is something to know that, even in that most drearily doctrinaire of ages, there lived plodding men of affairs, who, in spite of dogma and panic, clung to their common sense and their humanity, and with such firmness as was in them breasted the fate that came.

Fleeting: see Swimming.

Flower, Margaret and Philippa. "Specially arraigned and condemned before Sir Henry Hobart, and Sir Edward Bromley, judges of assize, for confessing themselves actors in the destruction of Henry, Lord Rosse, with their damnable practices against others, the children of the Right Honorable Francis, Earl of Rutland." (*Wonderful Discovery*)

This tract, printed in London in 1619, after a stilted rehearsal of views and examples of witchcraft, narrates the trial which resulted in the execution of the Flower sisters at Lincoln in March, 1618. Mother Joan Flower was a "monstrous malicious woman" with the reputation of a witch. Her two daughters, Margaret and Philippa ("Philip" in the pamphlet), apparently followed their mother's shiftlessness. Dismissed from service at the Castle, they turned to magic and hexed the family of the Earl of Rutland, whereby his eldest son died.

Philippa's confession details the steps in working *maleficia*. She

> brought from the Castle the right-hand glove of the Lord Henry Rosse, which she delivered to her mother, who presently rubbed it on the back of her spirit Rutterkin; and then put it into hot boiling water. Afterward she pricked it often and buried it in the yard, wishing the Lord Rosse might never thrive. And so her sister Margaret continued with her mother, where she often saw the cat, Rutterkin, leap on her shoulder and suck her neck.

Three English witches: Anne Baker, Joan Willimot, Ellen Greene.

In the same tract are confessions of three witches apparently linked to the Flower scandal: Anne Baker, Joan Willimot, and Ellen Greene. Their "confessions," however, contain little of note—the usual roster of familiars (white dog, white mouse, owl, and a kitten called "Pusse") and *maleficia* —but the tract is illustrated with a cut of these three women showing the typical conception of the hag and her familiar.

Flying: see Transvection.

Fontaine, Françoise. Françoise Fontaine had just as lurid frenzies as any of the celebrated possessed nuns of the late sixteenth and early seventeenth centuries. Her convulsions resembled those of most other demoniacs: Elizabeth Allier (1639) or Jeanne Fery (1585), for example, or the Burton Boy in England (1596), or Margaret Rule in America (1693). Although a brief account had been given in the *Memoires* of Pierre-Victor Palma Cayet (about 1600), the official transcript of 1591 remained unpublished until 1883. It was dictated during her trial by Louis Morel, the Provost General of Normandy, to the *greffier*, Loys Vauquet; even his asides are recorded, such as the order to bring in candles and torches *"pour nous esclairer"* so the interrogation could continue after dusk.

The editor of the manuscript claimed, with little exaggeration, that it described all the classic symptoms of hysteria and epilepsy: tremblings, faintings, falls, leapings, anesthesia, paralysis, tetanus-like rigidity, exaggerated movements (sometimes culminating in the form of a crucifixion), cataleptic contortions, analgesia, loss of memory, and so forth.

While it is thus valuable in the history of mental disorders, in the history of witchcraft the record is notable for several other reasons. First, Françoise, although admitting a pact and copulation with the devil, was freed by a secular court. Second, no attempt was made to ferret out some woman to accuse of bewitching her. Third, Françoise had convulsions as well as sexual fantasies—most other accounts stress one or the other. Fourth, Françoise, apart from pricking, was not tortured, but even considerately treated by the Provost, the Protestant physician, and the Catholic priests who exorcized her. Fifth, Françoise recovered from her derangement and was able to get married and lead a normal life.

In April, 1591, Louviers was in a state of civil war, about to be taken by the royalist forces. The inhabitants were tense and excited. When Françoise Fontaine created a disturbance by claiming a spirit came down the chimney to molest her and another girl, and when poltergeist-like activities occurred, she was put in prison. The other captives protested that unusual happenings followed her into jail; and it was then decided that Françoise was a witch. During her trial, two priests tried exorcism, and on September 2, 1591, before an audience of 1,200 assembled in the church of Notre-Dame, Françoise was publicly stripped and completely shaved all over her body to remove hiding places for the devils and to facilitate pricking her.

The trial opened on August 17, 1591. While being examined, Françoise "fell on her back, her arms stretched out tense on the ground like a person crucified . . . We noticed that her throat swelled up, her eyes nearly came out of her head, and her face was bathed in huge drops of sweat." The Provost observed she was not breathing, although he found her pulse and temperature normal. However, when he tried to move her arms, still locked in the form of a cross, "it was impossible, without putting our feet on

them, and tugging her hands with all our force."

Showing how impressionable young girls were, Françoise repeated the stock confessions of witches about a demon lover and even embellished them. The Provost was so shocked by her amours, which she said took place even in jail, that he climbed on the roof to examine the chimney for signs of entry; he saw many little marks which might have been newly made.

The devil came as "a *grand homme*, clad in black with a black beard and flashing eyes." She gave herself to him gladly, "*de bon coeur*," as she stated; she even exposed her breasts in the courtroom to show where the devil had given her love-bites. On his first visit, "he ordered her to take off her clothes, and when she had done so, the *grand homme* threw her on the bed and slept with her, lying on the belly of the said witness, and knew her carnally two times —each time for the duration of half an hour."

Françoise then rattled off a string of clichés:

He had a black *membre viril* very stiff, and so thick that the witness experienced considerable pain when he copulated with her, because the said *membre* was hard as flint [*dur comme vn caillou*] and extremely cold. . . . As the said man was leaving her, he kissed her repeatedly and fondled her breasts and private parts.

However, she added a detail not found in other confessions:

She said also that once when the aforesaid *grand homme* enjoyed her favors, he had much trouble pulling out his *membre viril* from the *nature* of the said witness, which she could not relax, as he had already done with his, so that they remained nipped together, like a dog and a bitch when they enjoy the company of each other.

On his second visit, the devil varied his techniques:

He drew her toward him and placed her between his knees, and kissed her many times, and, not even making her take off her clothes, had intercourse with her. He did it only once, but it lasted almost half an hour, and he finished off by emitting something very cold into her stomach. Since then the aforesaid *grand homme* has regularly visited the said witness every night, enjoying her company on each occasion just once.

After such a freely given confession, that Françoise was not burned is incredible. And that she recovered and lived happily ever after is likewise remarkable.

France, Witchcraft in. Each country reacted to witchcraft according to its national conditions—economy, religion, politics, and other complex factors. The over-all development of witchcraft in France may conveniently be telescoped into five major areas, none of which is duplicated precisely in England or Germany:

I. The identification by the Inquisition of witchcraft as heresy, and the extirpation of the Knights Templars in 1307.

II. The political trials of national figures on charges of heresy, involving sorcery, to the mid-fifteenth century (e.g., Joan of Arc and Gilles de Rais).

III. The epidemics of witch hunting whipped up by civil judges in the "great days of witchcraft [1450-1670]," producing the classical descriptions of witchcraft by the French demonologists.

IV. The prevalence of demoniacal possession in the first half of the seventeenth century, especially among nuns subject to lurid sexual fantasies. These scandals resulted in many people's questioning the theory of witchcraft.

V. The wholesale corruption of the French nobility, involving the use of poisons and black masses, revealed in the police investigations in 1682 (fully described in the Chambre Ardente Affair), leading to the end of the witchcraft delusion.

I. The Identification of Witchcraft as a Heresy

Even before witchcraft was equated with heresy, early laws prosecuted sorcerers. The Salic Law (about A.D. 500), however, demanded proof of a definite evil act, such as poisoning; even when the poison resulted in death, the sorcerer was permitted to pay a specified sum of money to compensate the victim's family. Failure to pay this wergild resulted in the murderer's being burned. In unsuccessful attempts at poisoning or ligature, a smaller fine was imposed. While admitting the folklore notion of nocturnal assemblies, the Salic Law, in complete contrast to inquisitorial law, decreed that anyone defaming a person as a *strix* or *lamia* or *stioportius* [male sorcerer] and not being able to prove it would pay damages. Had the Salic Law remained in force, not one of the thousands accused of attending a sabbat would have been burned.

In the eighth century, the Laws of Childeric III aided the Church in suppressing manifestations of paganism, including magic. An edict of the Carolingian period allowed the Church to seize sorcerers, sell them as slaves, and keep the profit. Repression was more or less spasmodic, however, and penalties were imposed, not for witchcraft, but for poisoning or magic.

The witchcraft heresy started in France. The theological basis for witchcraft had been provided by a continuing discussion by theologians, ranging from Archbishop Guillaume d'Auvergne of Paris (1228-49), through Thomas Aquinas (died 1274) and Duns Scotus (died 1308), to Pierre de Palude (died 1342) and Gabriel Biel (died 1484). On their speculation, theologians and lawyers built their laws of procedure, finally creating a detailed concept of the pact with the Devil, the essence of the justification of witchcraft trials [see Early Writers on Witchcraft]. With this formulation, first suggested in France by the University of Paris in 1398, sorcery passed from magic to religion, and witchcraft became an anti-Catholic heresy and therefore subject to the Inquisition.

When the Inquisition had crushed the religious deviations in southern France (Albigensians and Waldensians, for example), it had little justification to continue to exist. Its work was done. The Inquisition, however, set about to introduce and develop the parallel heresy of witchcraft, thereby widening its scope. As a base, it combined the fantastic and impossible allegations scattered throughout earlier trials. During the fourteenth century, before witchcraft had crystallized, individual trials for heresy included charges later to become the standard pattern for the mass witchcraft trials (conducted under the civil code). Trials were held as early as 1245 at Toulouse. In 1275, Angèle de la Barthe, supposed to have eaten babies and have had relations with the devil, was burned by Hugues de Baniols, Inquisitor at Toulouse. She may be considered the first person executed for witchcraft. A series of papal bulls to the inquisitors in southern France codified the heresy of the *sect* of witches: in 1318 against the black art, especially in Lyons; in 1320, 1326, and 1330 against Satanism [see Pope John XXII] in Toulouse and Narbonne. After 1331, Paris was included as a region of sorcery.

The attack on the military and religious order of the Knights Templars, which anticipated so much of the ensuing attack on witches, was authorized by the Pope in 1307. The commission was headed by Guillaume de Nogaret, minister to King Philip IV (le Bel), and Friar Guillaume Imbert, confessor to the King and Grand Inquisitor for France. The charge was heresy, but the counts included acts typical of witches 300 years later, such as worship of the devil in the guise of a cat (the witches' goat god), trampling on the cross, indiscriminate intercourse with succubus demons, and the "kiss of shame" wherein the novice kissed his leader on the mouth, the posteriors, and penis. Admission of these allegations was easily secured by torture, but most of the Templars retracted their confessions. The Grand Master, Jacques de Molay, and the Preceptor of Normandy, Geoffroy de Charnay, revoked their confessions before being burned alive in Paris on March 14, 1314. The reason for the destruction of the order was not only to obtain its great wealth—the King

was bankrupt—but to erase any successful non-sacramental religious system such as the Templars had developed. The attack occurred, incidentally, at the same time as pressure on the Jews was increased.

If trained military men, disciplined in a religious ideal, could capitulate under torture, the confessions of witches, when subjected to similar torments, should occasion no surprise. The success of the extermination of the Templars set the pattern for the subsequent persecution of witches.

After 1390, the Parlement of Paris encouraged the secular courts to try cases of witchcraft, without prejudice, of course, to the courts of the Inquisition. Hitherto, the civil law had concerned itself only with demonstrable acts of injury, in which sorcery was almost incidental—the act, not the intention, was punished. But since the royal courts became so energetic in prosecuting witches for the pact, the ecclesiastical courts (inquisitorial and episcopal) did not forbid this extension of jurisdiction. Several early trials are noted in this *Encyclopedia:* the first secular trial in 1390 at Paris; and the inquisitorial trials in 1459 at Arras, in 1529 at Luxeuil, in 1582 at Avignon [see Sentence], and in 1631 at Toul.

II. The Noble Trials Involving Political Heresy

Just as in England, so in France charges of witchcraft were brought for political purposes, as being certain to succeed. For example, in 1278 Bishop Peter of Bayeux and his nephew were accused of using sorcery against King Philip III; the Bishop was acquitted, but his nephew executed. In 1308 Bishop Guichard of Troyes was similarly charged with using sorcery against the wife of King Philip le Bel and others. In 1314, King Louis X heard charges against Alips de Mons, wife of d'Enguerrand de Marigny, and her sister of plotting his death by waxen images. They implicated a magician, Jacques Dulot, and his wife. Madame Dulot was burned alive, Dulot done to death in prison, and the d'Enguerrands executed. Just a few years later, Count Robert d'Artois made a waxen image, intending to kill King Philip's son, Jean, getting a priest to baptize the figurine to make his sorcery more effective. Robert was banished in 1331. In 1340 came the attempted bewitching of Philip of Valois, involving two monks. In 1398, charges of a pact with the Devil resulted from a prolonged scandal involving the insane French monarch (father-in-law to England's Henry V) and the Duke of Orléans. Witches were called in to cure the King's malady; then two Augustinian monks, professing skill in magic. The King got worse, and the "experts" were beheaded. The list of such trials could be continued. Only the nobility was involved, but the trials hastened the spread of witchcraft throughout all the estates.

The two most famous political trials using witchcraft as the device for prosecution brought Joan of Arc (1431) and Gilles de Rais (1440) to the stake. These trials are noted in separate entries in this *Encyclopedia*.

III. Typical French Witchcraft Trials

Trials for witchcraft continued at intervals throughout the fifteenth and sixteenth centuries. Gradually, the secular courts replaced those of the Inquisition, which nevertheless continued to try some cases (e.g., in 1592, Gilles Garnier) and to take cognizance of religious deviations by priests and nuns (e.g., in 1611 at Aix-en-Provence). The Inquisition also influenced the philosophy of the secular judges, who followed such theorists as Jean Vinetus, Inquisitor at Carcassonne (1450); Nicholas Jacquier, Inquisitor of France (1458); Petrus Mamor (1462), and Jean Vincent of La Vendée (1475).

From 1500 to 1670 hardly a year passed without the execution of some witches. Some of them were no doubt held responsible for the death of men and animals from ergotism, a disease caused by eating infected grain, frequent throughout France in the sixteenth and seventeenth centuries. The following are some typical trials; an asterisk indicates a separate entry. Trials involving possession are listed separately [see Possession].

1275-1500: Witchcraft Delusion Not Generally Accepted

*1390 First trial for witchcraft by a secular court in Paris; some measure of legality observed, in contrast to trials by the Inquisition.

1428 In Briançon, Dauphiné, 110 women and 57 men burned alive as witches in the two decades to the mid-century.

1453 Inquisition at Evreux sentenced Guillaume Edeline, prior of Saint-Germain-en-Laye, to perpetual imprisonment for intercourse with a succubus, flying on a broomstick, and kissing a goat under its tail.

1456 Robert Olive burned at Falaise for flying to sabbats.

*1459 Inquisition investigated outbreak of *vauderie* in Arras, burning four old women and one man. So flagrant were its actions that the Parlement of Paris and three bishops intervened and ultimately forced release of remaining prisoners. In 1491 Parlement rehabilitated those executed.

1479 A Mâcon priest executed for heresy, sorcery, and diabolic art.

1490 King Charles VIII issued edict against fortunetellers, enchanters, and necromancers; their property to be forfeit.

1500-1575: Growth of Trials for Witchcraft

1508 Mass trials in Béarn.

*1521 The werewolves of Poligny, tried by the Inquisition.

*1529 The trial at Luxeuil by the Inquisition.

1556 Witch at Bièvres, near Laon, burned alive in error; Bodin explained this mistake as the secret judgment of God.

1557 Forty witches burned at Toulouse.

1564 Four witches (three men and a woman) burned at Poitiers for kissing the goat and dancing back to back.

An incantation for Queen Catherine de' Medici. From the Douce Collection, Bodleian Library, Oxford. "It is reported that Queen Catherine had much contact with sorcerers and magicians who made her a magic mirror, in which she could see the future monarchs of France. She saw first Henry IV, then Louis XIII, and after him Louis XIV, and finally a horde of Jesuits who sought to overthrow the monarchy and rule themselves. This mirror may still be seen today in the Palace of the King."

1571   Execution at Paris of the magician Trois-Echelles, who said there were a hundred thousand witches in France.

*1574   Gilles Garnier burned alive at Dôle, January 18, 1574, for lycanthropy.

1575-1625: The Peak of the Witchcraft Delusion in France

1579   Church Council at Melun declared: "Every charlatan and diviner, and others who practice necromancy, pyromancy, chiromancy, hydromancy, will be punished by death."

1581   Church Council at Rouen bans *grimoires* under pain of excommunication.

*1582   Eighteen witches burned by the Inquisition at Avignon. [For form committing them to death, see Sentence.]

1583   Trial of lycanthropes at Orléans.

1584   Church Council at Bourges extended decisions of previous councils to makers of ligatures, and added death penalty for those who consulted *les devins*. In general, church councils (as distinct from Inquisition) attacked divination and sorcery, almost ignoring the heresy of witchcraft.

1588   Lycanthropy in the Auvergne mountains—a hunter wounded a wolf which later turned out to be the wife of a nobleman. The woman was burned at Riom.

1589   Fourteen witches at Tours appealed to King Henry III; the King's doctor found no devil's marks, as alleged, and decided the accused were "poor stupid folk." "Our advice was to purge them with hellebore rather than to punish them, and the Parlement [of Paris] discharged them as we recommended" —Bayle. The King was thereupon accused of protecting witches.

1597   At Riom, two men burned for making ligatures against men as well as against cats and dogs.

*1598   Jacques Roulet burned at Paris as a lycanthrope [see Lycanthrope of Angers].

1598   Jacques d'Autun, lycanthrope, burned at Rennes.

*1598   The werewolves of St.-Claude.

*1603   Jean Grenier, lycanthrope of Les Landes (Bordeaux).

1625-1682: Decline of the Witchcraft Delusion

*1631   Father Dominic Gordel tortured (? to death) by the Inquisition in Lorraine.

*1659   Thomas Looten of Bailleul dies under torture by secular court.

*1670 The Rouen witch trials [see Louis
    XIV: Edict of 1682].

But the main interest of the central period
of witch trials, between 1580 and 1620, lies
in the mass persecutions by civil judges, resulting in the classic works of the French
demonologists, e.g., Bodin (1580), Remy
(1595), Boguet (1602), and De Lancre
(1612).

Alsace, at that time mostly part of the
Empire. Many burnings in small villages
occurred after 1575; for example, at Thann,
in the south, 102 witches burned from 1572
to 1620 (some records give 152, if outlying
districts included). At St. Amarin, over
200 witches burned by 1596. Throughout
the region, thousands killed [see also
Witchcraft in Germany].

Lorraine. Nicholas Remy, Attorney General of Lorraine, personally condemned
900 witches between 1581 and 1591.

Normandy. Two severe witch epidemics
in 1589-94 and again in 1600-1645, when
many witches were burned at Rouen.

Burgundy (Franche-Comté), under the
domination of the Inquisition, although the
chief judge was always a layman. Henry
Boguet, chief judge at St.-Claude, waged
an intensive campaign (killing about 600
witches). As a result of his fury, trials continued in Burgundy longer than elsewhere.

Béarn. In 1609, King Henry IV commissioned Judge Pierre de Lancre and
President d'Espagnet to extirpate witchcraft in the Basque-speaking Pays de Labourd [see Basque Witches]. De Lancre
said all 30,000 inhabitants were infected,
and he claimed burning 600 witches in four
months. From Labourd the persecution
spread to Bordeaux.

The central areas of France experienced
no mass terrors. The Parlement of Paris
discouraged witch hunts; as early as 1601
it forbade the use of "swimming" to discover witches and, to prevent abuses by
overzealous judges, claimed jurisdiction
over all cases of sorcery. Where the only
accusation was attendance at a sabbat, with
no charge of *maleficia*, it refused to prosecute. However, sorcery involving sacrilege
was punished by death. A practical result of

these restrictions was the acquittal of fourteen persons condemned to death by a lower
court for sorcery. While the Parlement's
jurisdiction was limited, its influence
and prestige were considerable. Consequently, throughout France in the seventeenth century, there was nothing approaching the wholesale executions of Germany,
nor after the early demonologists was there
much continuing debate on witchcraft.

IV. Witchcraft and Demoniacal Possession

While the punishments for witches who
allegedly brought on possession were very
severe, few persons suffered thus. The most
famous French trials for causing possession
are described separately and in the general
entry.

V. The Chambre Ardente Affair and the End of the Witchcraft Delusion

The amazing practices of the court circle
revealed by the police in the *Chambre ardente* led to the Edict issued by King Louis
XIV in 1682. This act denied the reality of
witchcraft and made fortunetelling and
magic practices involving sacrilege the only
crimes. The dominant view agreed with the
Encyclopedists that "witchcraft [was] a
shameful or ridiculous magical act, stupidly
attributed through superstition to the invocation and power of devils."

In certain areas, however, the delusion
lingered, and scattered trials occurred during the next fifty years: in Normandy, in
1684, 1692, 1699 (at Rouen, when the
Parlement commuted a death sentence to
banishment), and 1730; at Paris in 1701;
at Toulouse in 1702; and at Vesoul in 1707.
In 1691 three shepherds at Brie were condemned to be burned for causing distemper
in cattle; two others were banished, and
one died in jail; all sentences were ratified
by the Parlement of Paris. In 1718 at Bordeaux, a man was executed for inflicting a
ligature; this case is often quoted as the
last execution for witchcraft in France, but
other executions took place later. In 1728
at Lorient, several men, including a priest,
were sent to the galleys or banished for
pretending to reveal hidden treasure by

making a pact with the Devil; the women implicated were merely reprimanded. A similar trial for divination of treasure occurred at Dijon in 1742, when Father Bertrand Guillaudot was burned alive. His confession led to the arrest of twenty-nine accomplices; after a long trial at Lyons ending in 1745, five were sentenced to death, and the others either to the galleys or banishment. Father Louis Debaraz, who had said sacrilegious masses to locate treasure, was burned alive. This was the last execution for witchcraft in France (Beaune, *Les Sorciers de Lyon*).

A convenient short history of witchcraft in France is provided by the forty entries in this *Encyclopedia:* The development of the theory of heretical sorcery and the earliest trials in France are discussed under Inquisition, Trials, Pope John XXII, Paris Witch Trial (1390), Arras Witches (1460), and Luxeuil Witch Trial (1529). Further theories in Early Writers on Witchcraft and Nicholas Jacquier (1458). Some of the foregoing entries contain extracts from court records; in addition, two seventeenth-century trials are given in detail from the procès-verbal, Dominic Gordel (1631) and Thomas Looten (1659). Two of the celebrated political trials are those of Joan of Arc (1431) and Gilles de Rais (1440). The case of the Chambre Ardente (1680) is recorded from the secret police blotter; the exposure led to the Edict of Louis XIV (1682). Some of the famous French writers on witchcraft are Jean Bodin (1580), Nicholas Remy (1595), Henri Boguet (1602), Pierre de Lancre (1612)—continued in the entry on Basque Witches, Le Sieur Bouvet (1659), and the general entry on Demonologists. An opponent of the delusion is Laurent Bordelon (1710).

The famous epidemics of possession in French convents, which generally included accounts of sexual perversions, are discussed in Aix-en-Provence Nuns (1611), Lille Novices (1613), Loudun Nuns (1634), Louviers Nuns (1647), and Auxonne Nuns (1661). Celebrated individual cases of possession include Jeanne Fery (1585), Françoise Fontaine (1591), Elisabeth Allier (1639), Catherine Cadière

(1731), and Louise Lateau (1868) in Belgium. Other material about the French nuns is found in the entries on Exorcism, Possession, and Sexual Relations with Devils.

Examples of werewolves, not infrequent in French demonology, are described in the main entry, Lycanthropy, and under Flying Ointment, and, individually, Werewolves of Poligny (1521), Gilles Garnier (1573), Lycanthrope of Angers (1598), Werewolves of St.-Claude (1598), and Jean Grenier (1603). A typical French poltergeist occurs in the Cideville Case (1849).

Gandillon Family: see Werewolves of Poligny.

Garnier, Gilles. Attacks on young children reached epidemic proportions in 1573 in Dôle, Franche-Comté. So serious were the molestations, that the local parlement issued the following proclamation:

> According to the advertisement made to the sovereign court of Parlement at Dôle, that, in the territories of Espagny, Salvange, Courchapon, and the neighboring villages, has often been seen and met, for some time past, a werewolf, who it is said has already seized and carried off several little children, so that they have not been seen since. And since he has attacked and done injury in the country to some horsemen, who kept him off only with great difficulty and danger to their persons, the said court, desiring to prevent any greater danger, has permitted, and does permit, those who are abiding or dwelling in the said places and others, notwithstanding all edicts concerning the chase, to assemble with pikes, halberds, arquebuses, and sticks, to chase and to pursue the said werewolf in every place where they may find or seize him; to tie and to kill, without incurring any pains or penalties . . . Given at the meeting of the said court, on the thirteenth day of the month of September, 1573. (Bourquelot)

In a remote hovel near Armanges lived Gilles Garnier, originally from Lyons, "the hermit of St. Bonnot," and his wife, Appoline, impoverished and sullen recluses. Two

From the first page of the sermon on witches in Geiler von Kaysersberg's *Die Emeis* (1517), the first work on witchcraft printed in German.

months after the proclamation, on November 9, some peasants rescued a little girl, already badly bitten in five places, from a huge wolf; on their approach, the wolf fled into the dusk, but some thought they recognized the features of Garnier. On November 15, a ten-year-old boy was missing. Rumor and suspicion had quickly spread, and Garnier and his wife were arrested and tried at Dôle for lycanthropy.

Gilles Garnier made the following confessions, confirming two of the accusations:

On or about August 24, 1573, in a pear orchard near the village of Perrouze, Garnier had killed a twelve-year-old boy. "In spite of the fact that it was Friday," he wanted to eat the flesh, but was prevented by the approach of some men. The men testified, and Garnier admitted, that he appeared as a man, and not as a wolf.

On or about October 6, in a vineyard near a wood, La Serre, a mile from Dôle, Garnier in the shape of a wolf had attacked a ten-year-old girl. He killed her with his teeth and claws, stripped her naked, then ate her—an excellent example of parthenophagy, a vice exclusive to lycanthropes. He enjoyed the flesh so much that he took some of it home to his wife.

On or about November 9, Garnier in the shape of a wolf attacked a girl in the meadow of La Poupée, between Authune and Chastenoy. He was interrupted by three passers-by and forced to flee.

On or about November 15, between Gredisans and Menoté, a mile from Dôle, Garnier in the shape of a wolf strangled a ten-year-old boy. He tore off a leg with his

fangs, and ate the flesh of the thighs and most of the belly.

On these confessions, Garnier was executed at Dôle on January 18, 1574, being burned alive without the mercy of strangulation.

Gaufridi, Louis: see Aix-en-Provence Nuns.

Geiler von Kaysersberg, Johann. Johann Geiler (1445-1510), a doctor of theology of both Basel and Freiburg, became the cathedral preacher at Strasbourg (1478). His raciness of style and spiritual fervor made him very popular with the congregation. *Die Emeis* [*The Ants*] is a collection of his Lenten sermons delivered at Strasbourg in 1508, copied by Friar Johann Pauli and published in 1517. One sermon treats of werewolves, which Geiler allows may be devils acting as wolves; he rejects the transformation of men into wolves. In the seventeenth sermon, one of the twenty-six dealing with witchcraft, Geiler stresses the belief that acts of *maleficia* are done only with the permission of God, and that the devil, not the witch, actually does them. For example, it is not the witch's ointment nor her incantation that makes her forked stick fly through the air, but the power of the devil, allowed by God. The *beneficia* of the good witch are likewise due to the devil, and the secular law should not exempt her from being put to death too.

Die Emeis is notable as the first book on witchcraft in German (1517). The sermons are illustrated, and two cuts are reproduced here: preparations for the sabbat, attributed to Baldung, and a werewolf attacking a man, illustrating Lycanthropy. Luther quoted from this book in his sermons at Wittenberg in 1518. An earlier set of German sermons (in 1505) by Martin Plantsch had been printed in Latin translation in 1507. Both collections accept the witchcraft delusion wholeheartedly, and show how the conception was spread downward to the people from the ecclesiastics.

George II: Statute of 1736. The last execution for witchcraft in England was that of Alicia Molland in 1684 at Exeter; the last indictment was in 1717 in Leicestershire of Jane Clerk, but the jury threw it out. By the end of the seventeenth century, belief in witchcraft as a practical affair was generally dead, although it lingered among the ignorant credulous and the educated religious. As late as 1770 John Wesley was lamenting that "the infidels have hooted witchcraft out of the world."

The law finally caught up with practice, and in 1736 the statute of 1604 was repealed. The men of honor who introduced the bill were Alderman Heathcote, Mr. Conduit, and Mr. Crosse.

The new act completely reversed the old; no longer did the law punish witches; it punished, instead, those who thought they were witches. In some respects, this *volte-face* recalls the turning upside down of the doctrine of the Canon Episcopi by the bull of Innocent VIII in 1484, when belief in witches was transformed from heresy into orthodoxy.

Oddly enough, the final clause in this statute is the justification for the occasional prosecution of fortunetellers at the present day—not because they are witches, but because they pretend to be witches! It follows the wording of earlier statutes. The Irish Statute of 1587 against witchcraft was not repealed until 1821.

I. Be it enacted by the King's most excellent Majesty, by and with the advice and consent of the Lords spiritual and temporal, and Commons, in this present parliament assembled, and by the authority of the same, that the statute made in the first year of the reign of King James I, entitled "An act against conjuration, witchcraft, and dealing with evil and wicked spirits," shall, from the 24th day of June next, be repealed and utterly void and of non effect (except so much thereof as repeals the statute made in the fifth year of the reign of Queen Elizabeth, entitled "An act against conjuration, enchantments, and witchcrafts").

II. And be it further enacted by the authority aforesaid, that from and after the said 24th day of June, the act passed in the parliament of Scotland in the ninth parliament of Queen Mary [1562], entitled "Anentis [against] witchcraft," shall be and is hereby repealed.

III. And be it further enacted, that from and after the said 24th day of June, no prosecution, suit, or proceeding, shall be commenced or carried on against any person or persons for witchcraft, sorcery, enchantment, or conjuration, or for charging another with such offense, in any court whatsoever in Great Britain.

IV. And for the more effectual preventing and punishing any pretenses to such arts or powers as are before-mentioned, whereby ignorant persons are frequently deluded and defrauded, be it further enacted by the authority aforesaid, that if any person shall, from and after the said 24th day of June, pretend to exercise or use any kind of witchcraft, sorcery, enchantment, or conjuration, or undertake to tell fortunes, or pretend from his or her skill or knowledge in any occult or crafty science, to discover where or in what manner any goods or chattels, supposed to have been stolen or lost, may be found, every person so offending, being thereof lawfully convicted on indictment or information in that part of Great Britain called England, or on indictment or libel in that part of Great Britain called Scotland, shall for every such offense suffer imprisonment by the space of one whole year without bail or mainprize [surety], and once in every quarter of the said year in some market town of the proper county, upon the market day, there stand openly on the pillory by the space of one hour, and also shall (if the court by which said judgment shall be given shall think fit) be obliged to give sureties for his or her good behavior, in such sum, and for such time, as the said court shall judge proper according to the circumstances of the offense, and in such case shall be further imprisoned until such sureties be given.

Germany, Witchcraft in. Germany was the classic land of witchcraft. In England, not more than 1,000 people were executed as witches; in Germany, at least 100,000 were executed. Torture was forbidden by English law. In Germany, the law ordered torture; one woman (George L. Burr reported) was tortured fifty-six different times. In England, no witch was ever burned, alive or after strangling. In Germany, burning was the prescribed method of death. A contemporary chronicler wrote of Wolfenbüttel (Brunswick) in 1590: "The place of execution looked like a small wood from the number of the stakes." In 1631 on a trip to Cologne, Cardinal Albizzi wrote: "A horrible spectacle met our eyes. Outside of the walls of many towns and villages, we saw numerous stakes to which poor, wretched women were bound and burned as witches." At Neisse (Silesia), the executioner anticipated the Nazis of the twentieth century; he constructed an oven, in which in one year (1651) he roasted to death forty-two women and young girls suspected of witchcraft. Within nine years he had roasted over a thousand persons, including young children two to four years of age. This was the nature of witchcraft in Germany.

Centralized authority was lacking in Germany, and therefore the treatment accorded witches often varied in precept and practice from year to year and from state to state.

Germany consisted of about 300 autonomous territories, large and tiny, constituting the Holy Roman Empire, and all technically recognizing the Empire's Carolina Code (1532), which demanded death and torture for witchcraft. Actually, each state administered whatever laws it chose. Not only the Protestant states such as Saxony (whose law of 1572 far exceeded the Carolina), but even the Catholic states like Bavaria, ignored the imperial code. Sometimes this was good. The Prince-Bishop of Münster, Bernard von Raesfeld, permitted a witch trial in 1563, but was so opposed to further prosecutions that in 1566 he resigned. In 1582, the General Synod of Protestant Hesse-Kassel declared the Devil had power only if people feared witchcraft, and no one could be injured by sorcery (Längin). In 1657 at Amorbach (Mainz), the Bailiff, Daniel von Frankenstein, refused to prosecute alleged raisers of storms (which had destroyed the vines), because the enlightened Prince-Archbishop of Mainz, Johann Philipp von Schönborn (a friend of Spee), had freed witches previously arrested.

Rulers enforced or changed laws according to their individual whim. The Protestant Duke of Juliers-Berg, William III, was much influenced by his personal physician, Johan Weyer, a skeptic, and consequently the duchy stood out by its freedom from persecution; however, in his old age the Duke had an apoplectic fit, dismissed Weyer, and (in 1581) sanctioned the torture of witches. The Prince-Bishop of Würzburg, Philipp Adolf von Ehrenberg, ruthlessly burned hundreds of witches, including (on the advice of the Jesuits) his young heir; but soon after this family loss, about 1630, the bishop apparently changed his views, ordered commemorative services for the executed, and stopped the trials. About 1700, Frederick I of Prussia came under the influence of Christian Thomasius, with the result that the King personally took action against one of his barons who had executed a fifteen-year-old girl for self-confessed intercourse with a devil.

Furthermore, since witchcraft persecutions were at their height following the Counter Reformation (1570) and during the Thirty Years' War (1618-48), and since many areas rapidly changed from Protestant to Catholic, or vice versa, the method of dealing with witchcraft might switch from year to year. At Hagenau (Alsace), a woman accused of witchcraft in 1573, when the judges were Protestant, was not tortured and was freed. In 1577, the same

woman was again accused, but now the judges were Catholic. Her trial lasted a year; she was tortured seven times, finally confessed, and was burned. An accomplice was burned, and six other women were implicated (Tuetey). The Catholic bishopric of Bamberg was a notorious center of witch persecutions under Prince-Bishop Gottfried Johann Georg II (1623), but when the populace rebelled and welcomed the Protestant Swedish Army, witch trials halted from 1632 to 1636.

Often no fixed policy existed even among coreligionists. The Jesuits at first promoted witchcraft, and their leading theologians, such as Del Rio, wrote horrible books advocating extermination of witches. Later, some Jesuits advocated a minority view, and Father Adam Tanner (1617) and Father Friedrich von Spee (1631) led the fight against obscurantism. The Lutheran Carpzov, "the lawgiver of Saxony," who boasted he had read the Bible fifty-three times and was said to have burned 20,000 witches, was followed by the liberal Christian Thomasius. Prince-Abbot Balthasar von Dernbach of Fulda appointed a savage witch judge, Balthasar Ross, to hunt for witches, hoping in this way to terrify the Protestants into submission. Ross rivaled Franz Buirmann in his sadism, thrusting red-hot skewers into women as they hung in strappado. From 1603 to 1606 he executed 300 persons. However, in 1606 a new abbot, Johann Friedrich von Schwalbach, stopped the trials and kept Ross in prison until his execution in 1618—not for burning the innocent, but because "he had deducted exorbitant expenses which he appropriated for his own use."

Further divergence arose from the custom of reporting dubious cases to law or theological faculties for arbitration. But the universities were not always of one mind. For example, when Duke Maximilian I of Bavaria wanted to introduce torture into witch trials, three of his councilors op-

posed him. Thereupon he appealed to the universities; Cologne opposed torture, but Freiburg and Ingolstadt approved. Even within one or two decades the intellectual trends of a university could swerve very sharply. In the Blanckenstein trial, the university recommended acquittal for a woman charged with murder by witchcraft in 1676, but burning alive for her daughter on a similar charge and on similar outlandish evidence in 1689, only thirteen years later and at a time when elsewhere the hysteria was diminishing.

Witchcraft in Germany, therefore, means witchcraft in many independent states. Some of these are represented in this *Encyclopedia:* great and influential duchies like Austria and Bavaria, the electoral archbishopric of Treves, prince-bishoprics like Bamberg and Würzburg, and the imperial free city of Cologne. In addition, certain individual trials are described to show typical practices against witches in these and other states over a period of two centuries:

Dietrich Flade (1588, Treves)

Rebecca Lemp (1590, Nördlingen, Swabia)

Else Gwinner (1601, Offenburg)

Johannes Junius (1628, Bamberg)

Christine Böffgen (1631, Rheinbach, Cologne) [see Franz Buirmann]

Unnamed woman (1637, Eichstätt) [see Eichstätt Witch Trial]

Johann Schüler (1663, Lindheim, Hesse-Darmstadt)

Chatrina Blanckenstein (1676, Naumburg, Saxony)

Althe Ahlers (1694, Saxony) [see Mouse-Maker]

Maria Renata (1749, Würzburg)

Anna Maria Schwägel (1775, Kempten, Bavaria)

All these entries make shocking and terrifying reading.

Map (English, about 1680) of Rhineland area of Germany, the heart of the witch persecutions.

In spite of the many different approaches to witchcraft, however, from the records of these various states a general pattern of German witchcraft emerges that is valid for all areas, and different from the pattern in France or England. In fact, were each state separately described, this pattern would change only little. Horror would follow horror, as it does in the entries given here, and the repetition might even stale.

Witchcraft came late to Germany, and trials are not common until after 1570 or 1580. Elsewhere in Europe, witches had been tried from the fifteenth century, especially in southern France, and in the Italian Alpine regions, overflowing into Switzerland, France, and the Tyrol. A law professor at Constance, Ulrich Molitor, addressed a book on witchcraft (1489) to the Archduke Sigismund of Austria, based on the witch hunts of the Inquisitor Kramer [see *Malleus Maleficarum*] in the Tyrol. From here, witchcraft spread desultorily throughout southern Swabia into Württemberg and Franconia, and on into the Rhineland. Scattered single trials for witchcraft were reported in Heidelberg in 1475, Metz in 1488, Völs in 1506, Waldsee in 1518, Hamburg in 1521, and elsewhere. From southern France, where the original Inquisition against the Albigensians had by the fourteenth century turned against witches, the search moved up the Rhone Valley, through Lyons, and joined the Tyrolean wave in Franche-Comté, Alsace, and Lorraine.

A common fallacy imagines witchcraft to be of popular origin. But ordinary people never took revenge on sorcerers by bringing them to trial. Certainly, some baleful sorcerers were lynched here and there, but there was no *organized* persecution. Nor would there ever have been any, without priests and pastors, who forced on an indifferent or hostile public the hypothesis of sorcerers subversively collaborating with the Devil. The Inquisitor Kramer was chased out of the Tyrol by an angry populace. The concept of the witch trials—faceless informers, a crime so secret and terrible that normal legal procedures were

suspended, torture to secure confession, and burning of the victims—was foreign to Teutonic common-law justice. In England, the comparable Anglo-Saxon system endured; in Germany, Roman imperial and Canon Law replaced it. The new idea was propagandized throughout Germany in thousands of sermons (like those of Plantsch, 1507, or Geiler von Kaysersberg, 1517) and hundreds of laws and vade mecums (to instruct the judges), until witchcraft finally became an accepted fact of life.

Witchcraft did not fully materialize in Germany until after the Council of Trent (1563) had determined to win back Germany from Protestantism; the Society of Jesus (Jesuits) provided the organization for this Counter Reformation. Just as the Dominican inquisitors introduced the theory of witchcraft throughout Europe in the fourteenth and fifteenth centuries, so the Jesuits introduced witchcraft into Germany in the sixteenth and seventeenth. Jesuits first gained strength in Austria, and then in 1590, in spite of the apathy of the secular clergy, inspired the laws which started Bavaria persecuting witches. Jesuits dominated the bishoprics of Bamberg, Würzburg, and Treves. In 1589, the General of the Society, Claudio Aquaviva, ordered its members in the Rhineland to encourage local rulers to bring trials for witchcraft, and citizens to inform on their neighbors; the priests, however, were not to get mixed up in the trials. Similar admonitions were made by two other Jesuits, George Scherer and Jeremiah Drexel. And Jesuit theologians like Petrus Thyraeus (1594) spread propaganda from the universities.

This sudden reversal is clearly shown in the records of witch burnings before and after the third quarter of the sixteenth century; for example:

Waldsee	1518 - 1581	2
(Württemberg)	1581 - 1594	28
Ensisheim	before 1571	2
(Alsace)	1571 - 1620	88
Thann	before 1572	4
(Alsace)	1572 - 1620	150

The burning alive of Frau Peller and Burgomaster Lirtzen in a straw hut in 1631. From Hermann Löher, *Hochnötige Klage*.

Osnabrück	1583	 21
(Hanover)	1589	133

Yet Catholics had no monopoly on witchcraft; Protestants became just as eager to destroy witches—sometimes more eager. At that time, belief in God was commensurate with belief in God's adversary, and fear and hatred of those who had made a pact with the Devil smothered all the states of the Empire, Protestant and Catholic. The Lutherans might even be said to have been "devil oriented"—Luther's *Greater Catechism* named the Devil sixty-seven times, but Christ only sixty-three—and were just as principled as the Catholics in deciding who were God's enemies. For example, in Protestant Saxony, at Quedlinburg, out of a population of 12,000, in one day (in 1589), 133 witches were burned, one of the biggest holocausts recorded. Four beautiful girls were spared by the executioner, who gave out that the devil had spirited them away.

It is dangerous to say that one religion persecuted more than another, for degraded individuals who cared little for any faith often exercised personal authority. For a Bishop Gottfried Johann Georg of Bamberg there was a Professor Benedict Carpzov of Leipzig. Nevertheless, the trials gave the appearance of being worst—in intensity and duration—in the Catholic states, and probably worst of all in those territories ruled by the princes of the Church: the bishops of Mainz, Bamberg, Würzburg, Treves, and Strasbourg, and the abbot of Fulda. For example, in twenty-two villages under the jurisdiction of the Abbey of St. Maximin outside Treves, 368 witches were executed between 1587 and 1594; two villages were absolutely blotted from the map, and in two others, said the *Gesta Trevirorum*, in 1586 only two women were left alive. Between 1615 and 1635, in Strasbourg 5,000 witches were burned (Klélé). According to the Catholic scholar Carl Haas, the Protestant states of Württemburg and Swabia had comparatively the fewest persecutions. The Protestant states, furthermore, generally discarded witchcraft earlier. In Prussia, witch trials were practically ended by King Frederick William in 1714 (the last trial was held in 1728), whereas in Austrian Tyrol the most severe law against witches to that time was adopted in 1707. In the Catholic districts of Lutheran Württemberg, witchcraft flared up in 1746-47, and in Catholic Englingen, Baden (a city belonging to Austria), a woman was burned alive on April 24, 1751, with the blessing of the University of Freiburg. Sister Maria Renata was sentenced by an ecclesiastical court at Würzburg in 1749, and the execution carried out by the bishop's secular court. And the last execution for witchcraft in Germany, of Anna Maria Schwägel, in Kempten, 1775, was confirmed by its Prince-Abbot, Honorius, who endorsed the sentence in his own hand: *"Fiat justicia* [Let justice be carried out]."

During the Thirty Years' War, witchcraft

persecutions reached their zenith. The ruthlessness of the combatants and the intensity of their religious hatreds stimulated their zeal for destroying witches; yet in many states the war brought about at least a temporary cessation of burnings—wherever the Swedish Army took over occupation. After this, the hysteria seldom regained its earlier momentum. Some states, especially those impoverished by the war, seemed to set the clock back, however. Severe outbreaks came in the imperial city of Esslingen (Württemberg) in 1662-65, and in Salzburg (Austria) in 1677-80. But the war years were the worst. For example, in a single year (1629), in Miltenburg, a small town of 3,000 in the archdiocese of Mainz, 56 executions took place in the village and another 178 in the township; in Burgstädt, with less than 3,000 population, 77 were burned in 1629, and in the little village of Eichenbühel, 19 witches burned.

Not only was witchcraft more widely spread in Germany than in other lands, but its persecution was here more ruthless. The most outrageous witch trial described in this *Encyclopedia* took place in Lindheim in 1661; it reads like a nightmare [see Johann Schüler].

Without torture, witch hunters would have found few victims. Margrave Philipp in 1526 forbade torture in Hesse, and witchcraft was unheard of there until 1564, when torture produced a victim who was burned as a witch. Trials for witchcraft multiplied only after the opposition to torture had been squelched. Germany was the land of torture. Bamberg, the shrine of horror, was not exceptional; many towns had their special witch prison or witch tower [*Hexenturm*] and used the same tortures. In Tettwang (Württemberg), near Constance, in 1608, a father died in prison from torture, his wife was hoisted in strappado eleven times before confessing, and their twenty-year-old daughter was hoisted eleven times in one day, with a fifty-pound weight attached to her legs. It was ten weeks before the torturer thought she, had recovered sufficiently to stand more torture without dying under it. In Hagenau (Alsace), a 65-year-old widow, Anna Schödler, was imprisoned

for four months (1627-28), and tortured many times by strappado with heavy weights and by the Spanish boots. These were commonplace practices; more original methods are described elsewhere [see Bibliography].

The records of trials in the city of Offenburg made special mention of an iron torture chair studded with points, under the seat of which a fire was lit. This device almost always produced confessions, generally within fifteen minutes. Records at Offenburg told of only two who did not confess: Jakob Linder, three times on the chair in January, 1629; and, later in 1629, a woman, Gotter Ness, also thrice tortured. When she was put in the chair for the third time, on December 3, she was so weak it was expected she would die at any moment. In contrast, some experts believed the most efficient method of forcing confession and naming of accomplices was sleeplessness (used in England by Matthew Hopkins). A handbook for witches, circulated in Alsace in the early seventeenth century, observed this simple method had the advantage that the accused would never die under the torture.

Another fallacy, that witches were poor riffraff, is also disproved by the documents of German witchcraft. A notable side light on the type of people accused as witches comes in two letters from a priest named Duren in the village of Alfter, near Bonn (the official residence of the Archbishop of Cologne), to Count Werner von Salm. One letter described the situation in the early seventeenth century as follows:

That I haven't written for so long is because nothing unusual has happened, only that they have begun violent burning of witches in Bonn. At the present time there is imprisoned a wealthy woman, whose husband had formerly been a magistrate in Bonn, named Kurzrock, who was the sole owner of the inn *At the Sign of the Flower*. I don't know whether your Grace knew him or not. Be that as it may, she is a witch, and daily the opinion grows that she will be executed, and without doubt some more of these [Lutheran-minded] blockheads must follow her.

In Germany, the instruments of torture were blessed by a priest before being used on the prisoner. From Hermann Löher, *Hochnötige . . . Klage.*

A later letter showed the persecutions in full swing:

> The victims of the funeral pyres are for the most part male witches. Half the city must be implicated; for already professors, law students, pastors, canons, vicars, and monks have been arrested and burned. His Princely Grace has seventy seminarians training to become priests, one of whom, eminent as a musician, was arrested yesterday; two others were sought, but have escaped. The Chancellor and his wife and the Private Secretary's wife have already been apprehended and executed. On the Eve of Our Lady's Day [September 7] there was executed here a girl of nineteen who had the reputation of being the loveliest and most virtuous in all the city, and who from her childhood had been brought up by the Prince-Bishop himself. A canon of the cathedral, named Rotensahe, I saw beheaded and burned. Children of three or four years have devils for their paramours. Students and boys of noble birth, of nine, ten, eleven, twelve, thirteen, and fourteen years of age, have here been burned. To sum up, things are in such a pitiful state, that one does not know with what people one may talk and associate [*mit was Leuten man conversiren und umgehen soll*].

A very similar report was given by the Chancellor of Würzburg, writing a few years later, in 1629 [see Würzburg Witch Trials].

Witches, according to these letters from Bonn and Würzburg, included the richest citizens. This was no oversight. Both secular and ecclesiastical courts adopted the Inquisition's second weapon (torture was its first) of confiscating a heretic's property. When money was involved, Protestants could be as religious as Catholics. Moreover, without the bait of quick profits, few secular courts would have followed so facilely the lead of the clerics. Soldan-Heppe thinks the Protestant rulers of very small territories surpassed all others in the violence of their persecutions.

An illustration of how the witch persecution was linked to monetary gain is seen in the city of Offenburg (Baden), a small town of some 2,000-3,000 inhabitants. In 1627, some women of Offenburg were implicated by condemned witches from neighboring Artenberg as being present at a sabbat on the Blocksberg. The Offenburg *Rath* or town council, acting through a committee, then started looking for witches, especially wealthy ones, and gained much loot from five persons it burned on January 12, 1628. Then followed a lull of six months while the Swedish Army occupied the town; but on June 27, the council took up where it had left off, and stimulated the hysteria by offering a reward of two shillings for each witch apprehended. By July 7, it had found and burned four rich women. At this point, officials of Austria, which owned much property in the town, claimed the witches' properties in the name of the Emperor. The Offenburg town council saw no point in contributing to the Emperor's coffers, so it ceased condemning witches until the confiscation issue was settled. After litigation, Austria withdrew its claims, and the *Rath* recommenced the burnings. It expropriated the properties of four wealthy women burned on October 23, of four more on December 13, and of three rich men on January 22, 1629. Some of the citizens realized that soon everybody would be deemed a witch, and complained about the arbitrary naming of names under torture. This dissent hit at the basis of witchcraft, and the town council quickly silenced the opposition by burning two of its spokesmen. Then it resumed business. May 4, three women burned. May 25, four women and a man. June 8, two women and two men. July 4, five women and a man. August 29, five more witches. Then another obstacle: the clergy complained that their share of the confiscations was too little. Once again witch trials were halted until the *Rath* reached an agreement with the clergy. In October burnings started again: four on October 19, and another four on November 23. But the clergy felt they had been short-changed, and secretly encouraged the condemned witches to revoke their denunciations. Since their pocket was involved, now they decided to protest the morality of torture. A scandal ensued, and the people of Offenburg succeeded in curbing the *Rath*, at least for a few years. In these two years of 1628 and 1629, in this one small town, seventy-nine persons had been burned as witches (Carl Lempens, quoting the *Offenburger Rathsbücher*).

Another such quarrel over the spoils arose in Hagenau (Alsace) in 1629. On January 13, four wealthy persons were executed, producing a dispute between the *Hexenausschuss*, or city witch commission, and the *Reichsschultheiss*, representing the Emperor; the suit was settled by a three-way division, between the Hagenau commissioners, the Emperor, and the Archduke Leopold as *Oberlandvogt* [High Sheriff]. The city observed that if the payments were not made, many witches would escape execution, and God's honor would be besmirched.

Just as the bishopric of Bamberg excelled in torture, so it excelled in making easy money. A list compiled in 1631, after the executions had ceased late in 1630, gave particulars of the property taken from some of the witches burned the preceding year. All were wealthy, including such persons as:

Georg Neudecker, worth 100,000 florins
Barbara Schleuch, worth 2,000 florins
Christina Miltenberger, worth 9,000 or 10,000 florins
Margareta Ofeler, worth 7,000 or 8,000 florins
Margareta Edelwert, worth 10,000 florins
Caspar Cörner, Bailiff of Münchsberg, worth 9,000 or 10,000 florins
Wolfgang Hoffmeister, Treasurer of Bamberg, worth 50,000 florins

The document stated the Prince-Bishop and his men collected 500,000 florins from those they had executed, and 222,000 florins from those still in jail (April, 1631).

When confiscation was disallowed, witch hunts fell off. When the Emperor Ferdinand II (1619-37) forbade all confiscation as *schmutzig* [dirty business], in those areas where he could enforce his mandate, the zeal for witch hunting abated.

Schrecken—horror—is the word for witchcraft in Germany. A few courageous men strove against it—priests, lawyers, businessmen—and found themselves suspect of the only crime worse than being a witch: being a witch lover. They were threatened, tortured, silenced, exiled, or burned. Probably the clearest insight into witchcraft in Germany comes in a few intimate letters which have fortuitously survived, such as those of Rebecca Lemp and her family or the frightening missive of Burgomaster Johannes Junius to his daughter. Even the day-by-day court record of the torture and confession of a nameless woman at Eichstätt is similarly disturbing. Theory seldom strikes the heart; these letters are not only heartrending, but, better than any lists of executions, communicate the evil core of German witchcraft.

Ghirlanda della streghe: see Ligature.

Gifford, George. Three years after the bombshell against the witch hunters by Reginald Scot came George Gifford's *Discourse of the Subtle Practices of Devils by Witches and Sorcerers* (London, 1587). Gifford (died 1620), a noted Nonconformist preacher at Maldon, Essex, in the heart of the witch country, followed with *A Dialogue Concerning Witches and Witchcrafts* (London, 1593, repr. 1603), his major work. Cast in the form of a conversation among a superstitious countryman and his wife, a schoolmaster who accepts witchcraft, and Daniel, a cautious doubter, the *Dialogue* is a somewhat abstruse discussion of delusion. "The Devil hath bewitched your mind with blindness and unbelief, to draw you from God, even to worship himself." Gifford, as Ady noted, is the modern man when he says, "A witch cannot by a familiar, or by any craft, any way hurt or weaken the life, health, or estate of any man by witchery with disease or infirmity." Gifford "yieldeth to those strong delusions which have deceived many" in admitting that witches have familiars, even though only the witch herself is deceived. "Because the hogs and the cow died, are you sure the cat [the witch's familiar] did hurt them? Might they not die of some natural causes, as you see both men and beasts are well, and die suddenly?"

Gifford's position is basically that the Devil is so powerful that he does not need old women to work his evil; the danger is that deluded Christians accept the old women's claims at face value, and ascribe undue power to Satan, and run for help to "white" witches. "I say God alone, and not the witch, giveth power unto the devils to plague and torment." The witch is the accessory; the devil the principal. But the Bible is correct in demanding that witches be put to death, simply because they are "the blasphemous enemies of God." "Although they never mind to kill or to hurt any, but to do them good, as they imagine, yet if they deal with devils they ought to die for it." Gifford concludes with cautioning juries to use "special care and wisdom." A witch's confession is not to be relied on, because her main source of information is

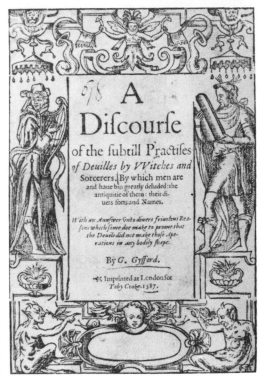

Title page of George Gifford's *Discourse* (1587), the second major book in English on witchcraft. From Cornell University Library.

the devil ("Men must beware that they proceed not upon his testimony"), nor is common report of sorcery reliable. "Many guiltless are upon men's oaths condemned to death, and much innocent blood is shed."

Ady, who really expanded and complemented Gifford (in dealing with the basic issues rather than individual cases), summed up his status by saying Gifford "had more of the spirit of truth in him than many of his profession."

Girard, Jean-Baptiste: see Cadière, Catherine.

Glanvill, Joseph. The "ablest advocate" of superstition and author of the very popular *Saducismus Triumphatus, or full and plain evidence concerning witches and apparitions.* "It was thought to have put the belief in apparitions and witchcraft on an unshakable basis of science and philosophy," wrote Kittredge. "No other English

Joseph Glanvill (1636-1680).
The father of modern psychical research.

work on the subject had a more powerful influence."

Joseph Glanvill (1636-80) took his M.A. at Oxford in 1658—he regretted not having gone to Cambridge—and ultimately became chaplain to King Charles II. His interest in the occult was fostered by his belief that science could explain the supernatural, and was reinforced by his personal experience of the drummer fiend of Tedworth.

The *Saducismus Triumphatus* refuted such disbelievers as John Wagstaffe and John Webster. Said Glanvill: "Atheism is begun in Sadducism. And those that dare not bluntly say there is no God, content themselves (for a fair step and introduction) to deny there are spirits or witches." Glanvill's book achieved its success, not by its reasoning, but by its collection of twenty-six witch "relations." This "small collection of the most credible and best attested stories" was written "to confirm and prove the main subject," that is, the actuality of witchcraft. However, Glanvill received only one story *firsthand*, and that from an epileptic. Some of these stories were discussed at the informal séances which met at Ragley Castle, the home of Lady Anne Conway, and were attended by her physician, Dr. Francis van

Helmont, Dr. Henry More, Lady Roydon, and the scientist Robert Boyle. To this circle came notorious mediums who demonstrated their prowess.

Unfortunately, Glanvill's standards of credibility were hardly scientific, as his acceptance of the evidence at witch trials showed. For example, Florence Newton, accused of witchcraft, felt severe pain when a tile from her prison was heated and the urine of a bewitched woman poured over it. Or again, the owner cut off and burned the ears of some bewitched cattle, forcing Juliana Cox, a seventy-year-old witch, to rush in agony to snatch them from the flames. Other equally unreasonable facts were acceptable to this Fellow of the Royal Society: "The more absurd and unaccountable these actions seem, the greater confirmations are they to me of the truth of those relations and the reality of what the objectors would destroy." Such legends were no way to answer the logical arguments of Webster or Wagstaffe, and it is no wonder that, as Glanvill ruefully admitted—

of all relations of fact there are none like to give a man such trouble and disreputation as those that relate to witchcrafts and apparitions, which so great a party of men (in this age especially) do so rally and laugh at and, without much ado, are resolved to explode and despise as mere winter tales and old wives' fables.

It is easy to laugh at Glanvill's gullibility; yet theoretically he tried to be skeptical and objective, and to sift the evidence for the supernatural in the anecdotes told him. In this respect, he may be regarded as the father of modern psychical research.

Glenluce Devil. The story of the Devil of Glenluce in 1654 is a typical example of poltergeist tricks, but the part played by a young adolescent is very obvious. It was coincidentally framed by *damnum minatum* —the *"evil threat"* of an old beggar, Andrew Agnew, refused an alms—and *malum secutum*, the "following evil." Indeed, the threat may have suggested to Master Tom Campbell the devilish pranks which plagued his father and mother off and on for nearly two years. Ultimately the troubles ceased,

Frontispiece of the second part of Glanvill's *Saducismus Triumphatus* (second edition, 1683), showing six devilish happenings. "Probably the ablest book ever published in defense of the superstition."—W. E. H. Lecky (1865). The boxes represent the Drummer of Tedworth, the Somerset Witch (Julian Cox), levitation of Richard Jones at Shepton Mallet, the rendezvous of witches at Trister Gate (Wincanton), Margaret Jackson, a Scottish witch, devoting herself to the devil, and celestial apparition at Amsterdam.

and, again coincidentally, the beggar was hanged.

The youth in question, Thomas, was the son of Gilbert Campbell, a weaver in Glenluce, near Newton Stewart, in Galloway. Tom had been sent to grammar school (the "College") in Glasgow, but, because of family problems, feared he might be withdrawn and forced to follow his father's trade. So when the boy came home, hearing of the beggar, he started the typical tricks made familiar in other poltergeist manifestations—throwing stones in doors, windows, down chimneys; cutting the thread on the loom and tearing clothes; pulling off bedclothes and ransacking closets; spanking the younger children; and setting little fires. The weaver asked the local minister to pray for relief, and a day of prayer and fasting was held.

When a neighbor suggested sending the children away, the disturbances stopped; but the minister rebuked Campbell for withdrawing the children from God's punishments and forced him to bring them back home. "The children that were nigh, by being brought home," wrote George Sinclair, who first reported the case, "no trouble followed, till one of his sons called Thomas that was farthest off came home. Then did the devil begin afresh, for upon the Lord's Day following, in the afternoon, the house was set on fire." Neighbors put out the fire. The minister then took Thomas to his house—apparently this is what the boy wanted—but in the meantime the other children had picked up the tricks, and so the irritations continued. When other ministers urged that Tom return again, "the boy, returning home, affirmed that he heard a voice speak to him, forbidding him to enter within the house, or in any other place where his father's calling was exercised. Yet he entered, but was sore abused, till he was forced to return to the minister's house again."

All the so-called poltergeist disturbances were keyed to the intellectual and emotional level of a bright young adolescent who wanted to go on with his schooling. The "devil" showed off his learning: when some gentlefolk visited the haunted house, "at their first incoming, the devil says, '*Quum literarum* is good Latin.' These are the first words of the Latin rudiments, which scholars are taught when they go to the grammar school"—Sinclair. The boy named four or five persons "that went under a bad report" as being the "witches of Glenluce." When some visitors suspected the children were responsible for the troubles, saying, "We think this voice speaks out of the children," the devil answered: "You lie. God shall judge you for your lying," and dismissed them, adding he would speak only with the minister (who was doubtless the most professionally credulous). As if to underline Tom's purpose, after the minister had prayed, the devil's voice was heard: "If the goodman's son's prayer at the College of Glasgow did not prevail with God, my father [Satan]

and I had wrought a mischief here ere now." An indication that the children shared Tom's plan comes from the calm with which a young daughter went on dressing her dolls, when the devil swore he would "ding out her harns" [brain her]. A battle of wits ended to Tom's credit, when, having forced the minister to remain in the house under threats of burning it down, the devil scored the minister: "You have now, sir, done my bidding." And, just like an adolescent, the devil became very peeved when the family decided to ignore his altercations. The fracas, which had started about November of 1654, continued, with intervals while Thomas was in Glasgow, until about September of 1656, when it stopped. By this time, Thomas had apparently won his point.

Gloucester, Duchess of: see Cobham, Eleanor.

Godelmann, Johann Georg. One of the Protestant writers on witchcraft, Dr. Godelmann, Professor of Law at Rostock University, in 1591 expanded an earlier dissertation into *De Magis, Veneficis et Lamiis* [*Sorcerers, Poisoners, and Witches*]. He tried, without success, to distinguish various kinds of witches, some guilty and some less guilty, holding that those most often executed were simply foolish and deluded old women. At that period, although completely credulous, his opinions were more enlightened than those generally accepted. Godelmann nullified them, however, by admitting the power of the Devil, the existence of witches, and the reality of the pact. While their stories of sabbat and incubi resulted from delusions sent by the devil and from the hallucinatory effects of their ointments, yet witches could work *maleficia* (including ligature, but not stormraising). In fact, physicians could learn from witches how to counter disease and how to use waxen images in a kind of inverse sorcery to restore health.

Godelmann's sentimental defense of the harmless old crone could not protect her when judges held delusions equally culpable with the acts. His list of suggested questions for an accused witch was not much different from that recommended by the demonologists. For example, he asked, "Whether it is not true that on Walpurgis Night a year ago she threw sand crosswise over N.'s cattle?" or "Whether it is not true that by sorcery she poisoned the pasture of her accuser so that most of the cattle died?" In attacking the flouting of legal procedures and the reliance on torture to secure convictions, however, Godelmann helped diminish the delusion. Opposing Bodin, he argued that the same rules should apply in all trials, and that it were better that many escape than that one innocent be wrongly condemned.

Gooderidge, Alice: see Burton Boy.

Goodwin Children.

I think it will not be improper to tell the world that one thing in the children's deliverance was the strange death of an horrible old woman, who was presumed to have a great hand in their affliction. Before her death and at it, the almshouse where she lived was terrified with fearful noises, and she seemed to have her death hastened by dismal blows received from the invisible world.

A classic American example of possession by the devil in Boston in 1688—what would now be called epileptic fits, perhaps with some admixture of childish deceit—the story of John Goodwin's four children, as told by Cotton Mather in his *Memorable Providences* (Boston, 1689), anticipates by a few years similar happenings at Salem, and, in addition, is another typical illustration of the eagerness of otherwise sober men to accept the most farfetched explanation of a regrettable but natural malady. As with the Warboys Witches, the unpopular scapegoat suffered, and one more old woman was executed.

John Goodwin of Boston had (in addition to a grown-up son and an infant) four children—two boys, five and eleven, and two girls, seven and thirteen—brought up strictly and religiously. In the summer of 1688, the older daughter questioned their Irish washerwoman about some missing

linen; the mother of the laundress, Goody Glover—

a scandalous old woman . . . in her daughter's defense bestowed very bad language upon the girl that put her to the question; immediately upon which, the poor child became variously indisposed in her health, and visited with strange fits, beyond those that attend an epilepsy, or a catalepsy, or those that they call the diseases of astonishment.

Very soon, all the children were similarly affected; the physicians were nonplused, and (just as in the Warboys case) concluded "nothing but an hellish witchcraft could be the origin of these maladies."

The children were sometimes deaf, dumb, and blind.

One while, their tongues would be drawn down their throats; another while, they would be pulled out upon their chins to a prodigious length. They would have their mouths opened unto such a wideness that their jaws went out of joint; and anon they would clap together again with a force like that of a strong spring lock. The same would happen to their shoulder blades, and their elbows, and hand-wrists, and several of their joints. They would at times lie in a benumbed condition, and be drawn together as those that are tied neck and heels; and presently be stretched out, yea, drawn backwards, to such a degree that it was feared the very skin of their bellies would have cracked. They would make most piteous outcries that they were cut with knives and struck with blows that they could not bear. Their necks would be broken, so that their neckbone would seem dissolved unto them that felt after it; and yet on the sudden it would become again so stiff that there was no stirring of their heads. Yea, their heads would be twisted almost round, and if main force at any time obstructed a dangerous motion which they seemed to be upon, they would roar exceedingly.

Throughout all the time of these symptoms, however, the children managed to sleep well; commotions seldom occurred after ten o'clock.

After some time, their father complained

to the magistrates about his neighbor, Goody Glover, whom he suspected of bewitching his children. Cotton Mather, an eyewitness of the whole affair, states very clearly that "Goodwin had no proof that could have done her any hurt."

> The hag had not power to deny her interest in the enchantment of the children. . . . Order was given to search the old woman's house, from whence there were brought into the court several small images, or puppets, or babies, made of rags and stuffed with goat's hair and other such ingredients. When these were produced, the vile woman acknowledged that her way to torment the objects of her malice was by wetting of her finger with her spittle and stroking of those little images.

The magistrates found further that she could not recite the Lord's Prayer in English. Little attention was given the fact that the old woman was Irish and spoke Irish (the trial was conducted through interpreters), said her prayers in Latin, and that, as an Irish immigrant in the middle of the seventeenth century, she must have been steeped in crude folk beliefs (such as hexing). In a talk with Mather, she rambled on but "confessed very little about the circumstances of her confederacies with the devils." Mother Glover was condemned by a court which included Judge Stoughton, the Deputy Governor of Massachusetts, who later sent the Salem witches to the gallows.

Harassed parents of today may find the devil as good an explanation as any for the following little perversities.

> Upon the least reproof of their parents for any unfit things they said or did, most grievous woeful heart-breaking agonies would they fall into. If any useful thing were to be done to them, or by them, they would have all sort of troubles fall upon them. It would sometimes cost one of them an hour or two to be undressed in the evening, or dressed in the morning. For if anyone went to untie a string, or undo a button about them, or the contrary, they would be twisted into such postures as made the thing impossible. And at whiles, they would be so managed in their beds that no bed clothes could

for an hour or two be laid upon them; nor could they go to wash their hands, without having them clasped so oddly together there was no doing of it. But when their friends were near tired with waiting, anon they might do what they would unto them. Whatever work they were bid to do, they would be so snapped in the member which was to do it, that they with grief still desisted from it. If one ordered them to rub a clean table, they were able to do it without any disturbance; if to rub a dirty table, presently they would with many torments be made incapable.

Such was Mather's rigid conviction that the devil was prompting these blocks, that he ignored the significance of the preceding account as well as of the following, instead offering it as evidence that the devil does not know our thoughts:

> We could cheat [the devils] when we spoke one thing and meant another. This was found when the children were being undressed. The devils would still in ways beyond the force of any imposture wonderfully twist the part that was to be undressed, so that there was no coming at it. But if we said, "Untie his neck-cloth," and the parties bidden at the same time understood our intent to be, "Untie his shoe," the neckcloth and not the shoe had been made strangely inaccessible.

Gradually the fits, which had lasted over a year, petered out. Mather equates their cessation with the death of a second old woman suspected of sorcery. "I am resolved after this," he concluded, "never to use but just one grain of patience with any man that shall go to impose upon me a denial of devils or of witches."

Robert Calef, a Boston merchant, in his *More Wonders of the Invisible World* (1700), published in England because of the censorship of Increase Mather, then President of Harvard, wrote:

> Mr. Cotton Mather was the most active and forward of any minister in the country in these matters, taking home one of the children, and managing such intrigues with that child, and after printing such an account of the whole in his *Memorable*

"When I prayed in the room . . . her postures were exactly such as the chained witch had before she died."—Cotton Mather (1688).

Providences, as conduced much to the kindling these flames, that in Sir William's [Phips] time [1692] threatened the devouring this country.

Mather has left two other detailed accounts of "possession," that of Mercy Short and that of Margaret Rule. His father, Increase Mather, in his *Illustrious Providences* related the case of John Stiles in 1679, who plagued his grandfather, William Morse, with poltergeist phenomena as well as fits resembling those of the Goodwin and other possessed children. "He barked like a dog and clucked like a hen . . . his tongue likewise hung out of his mouth." As a result, two suspects, Goody Morse and Caleb Powell, were charged with witchcraft. In 1720 at Littleton (Mass.) three young girls, eleven, nine, and five, displaying similar phenomena to the Goodwin children, convinced their neighbors they were under an evil hand. Eight years later, the eldest daughter, about to join the church at Medford, was moved to confess the hoax; the girls picked on a woman at random to name as the witch. For an English counterpart, well-known in America, which may have proved suggestive to the Goodwin children, see Bury St. Edmunds Witches.

Gordel, Dominic. Father Dominic Gordel, a parish priest charged with witchcraft in 1631 in northeast France, provides an excellent example of an ecclesiastical trial. What is in fact a verbatim report, signed by the Bishop of Sitie acting as Vicar-General in Lorraine, shows step by step the revolting methods of procedure. Unlike Anglo-Saxon jurisprudence, which was accusatory, Continental law (adopted by the Roman Catholic Church) was inquisitorial; that is, the burden of proof lay not with the accusers to prove the defendant guilty (as in English law), but on the accused to prove himself innocent. The Inquisition had long held that in charges as serious as sorcery, the ordinary rules of evidence might be suspended; thus the testimony of infamous criminals and of children of the age of two years was admitted as valid [see Witnesses]. Refusal on the part of the accused to admit his guilt was considered presumptive evidence of the stranglehold the devil possessed over him; and torture was applied until the victim broke down and confessed whatever was demanded of him. Once an accusation had been leveled, very rarely, during the heyday of the witch trials, was the accused vindicated. Either, fearing the torture, he confessed almost immediately and was burned, or he was tortured until he did confess and was burned.

The trial of Father Gordel shows the inquisitorial process at its worst. The accused had to admit the charge of witchcraft; his accusers were four children and persons already convicted as witches; evidence was extracted under duress; the torture became progressively more severe, stopping only at the point of death. This seventeenth-century report is agonizing in its record of the terrified stupefaction of the honest village priest protesting his innocence, calling to God, the Blessed Virgin, and the Saints to aid him. The relentless bludgeoning of the question, over and over, becomes a nightmare of unreason.

The following report is the procès-verbal —the testimony taken down at the depositions, then read to each witness, who attests to its accuracy.

"After this, we had him put to the squassation and pulled up." From Richard Verstegen, *Theatrum Crudelitatum Haereticorum* (1587).

We, the Bishop of Sitie, Vicar-General of Monsignor the Cardinal of Lorraine at his bishopric in Toul, having seen the trial with torture made at the request of the Promoter-General of the said bishopric against Master Dominic Gordel, parish priest at Vomécourt, accused of and indicted for witchcraft and other crimes and the black arts, to wit:

Preliminary testimony charged against the said priest, the oral hearings on the resultant charges, confessions, contradictions, and denials;

Verification and comparison of the evidence of the foregoing preliminary testimony with the accusations especially of Claude Cathelinotte and Hanry, wife of Didier Gaubart of Béthencourt, burned for the crime of witchcraft, who supported the charge of sorcery against the said Gordel and maintained it to the end; other accusations of Bastin Claude and Mengeotte, children of Claudon Pelletier of Hymont, also of Toussaine and Jeane, children of Jean Noël of Mataincourt, both convicted of witchcraft by their own confessions and for this reason held prisoners at Mirecourt, all of whom sustained the charges against the said Gordel, upon confronting him, that several times they had seen him at the satanic gatherings and that he had committed acts of deviltry there;

Interrogations made of the said accused on the impieties and exorcisms committed by him, along with his replies thereto, the documentary evidence alleged by the accused, our inquiry concerning its validity, with other pieces of evidence presented for his vindication; the report of the legal proceedings and torture of the accused made today, in the presence of the doctor and the surgeon who examined his body for any kind of devil's mark, for the judgment of the said Promoter-General on the said trial, and all other relevant matters;

After deliberation, having established full jurisdiction in the aforementioned proceedings, without prejudice to the charges established by them, we have condemned and do condemn the said Gordel, accused, to be subjected to torture, ordinary and extraordinary, by the thumbscrews, strappado, and vise, in order to coerce from him information and answers about all the charges resulting from these preliminary proceedings, and the naming of his accomplices and other secret charges. The whole report to be drawn up and transmitted to the said Promoter-General, as required by him, for whatever judgment he shall determine.

G. de Gournay, Bishop of Sitie,
and Vicar-General.

In the Tower called La Joliette in the episcopal palace of Toul, April 26, 1631, at one o'clock in the afternoon, in the presence of the Reverend Master Jean Midot, Grand Archdeacon and Canon of the said Church of Toul, Master Antoine d'Antan, priest almoner of the Squire of Sitie, and in addition Charles Mathiot, Doctor of Medicine, and Jean Marson, surgeon of Toul, whom we asked to assist in conducting the trial and to see that no unreasonable violence be inflicted on the said Gordel. Declared to the said Gordel, after being seriously admonished about the gravity of the charges laid against him, that he should freely confess his crime without forcing us to resort to the tortures which were being prepared for him, and, after we had made him swear on the Holy Gospels of Our Lord, laying his hands on the book, speak the truth. He replied that he was no sorcerer and that he never had any pact, implicit or professed, with the Devil.

Upon which, we ordered Master Poirson, hangman [*exécuteur des hautes oeuvres*] of the town of Toul, to apply the thumbscrews on the left hand (except the fingers used for benediction). The accused called on "Jesus, Maria" and said that he had never been a sorcerer. Then we had the thumbscrews applied to the same fingers of the right hand, whereupon he said, "St. Nicholas!"

Questioned if he had any kind of pact with the Devil, he said No, and that he wished only to die in the arms of God.

Then we caused the aforesaid screws to be applied to his big toes, at which he said he had never seen nor been at a sabbat, and cried out, "Jesus, Maria! St. Nicholas!" and "St. Mary, Mother of God! Sweet Jesus!"

Questioned if he had not conducted Claude Cathelinotte to a sabbat, he replied he had not and that he had never been to one.

After this, we had him put on the ladder and stretched out, and we ordered him hoisted to the first rung. Questioned if he had ever been to a sabbat and made a pact with the Devil, he said only "Jesus, Maria!" adding "I am dying!" Admonished to tell if he had ever committed any act of sorcery or pretended to act as a priest joining persons in matrimony at a sabbat, he said No. We observed, however, that all this time he had said nothing but "Jesus, Maria!" and that he had never made any compact, implicit or professed, with the Devil and that he had not been to a sabbat.

Then we ordered him to be loosened and then again for the second time drawn on the aforesaid ladder; all the time he kept on saying, "Jesus, Maria! St. Nicholas! Mother of God, help me!" Questioned if he had been present at a sabbat, he said No. Stretched somewhat more severely, he cried aloud, "Jesus! I am dying!" Again reprimanded to tell the truth and we would release him, he replied that he had never been to a sabbat, unable to say anything else except "Mother of God, help me!" Admonished to renounce all the pacts that he must have made with the Devil, he said he renounced them all and that he had never been at a sabbat. Questioned how many times he had been at a sabbat and what people he had seen there, he said he had never seen anybody and did not know what a sabbat was and had never been there, crying out "St. Nicholas! Sweet Jesus! My God have pity on me! They are breaking the body of an innocent man!"

Then we had him released a little and then drawn for the third time on the aforesaid ladder and admonished him to speak the truth. To this he had no other response than to say, "I am dying! St. Nicholas! Jesus! Maria! They are killing me! Mother of mercy, do not desert me!" Interrogated how he had cured a person whose eye was out of its socket, he said he had done it by using olive oil and invoking the name of the Lord. He continued to cry on Jesus, Mary, Mother of God, and St. Nicholas, praying they would not desert him and would bring his soul into the arms of God. "I have never seen a sabbat, nor a waxen image, nor have I distributed magic powder." Then he recited in Latin, "*Libera me a calumniis hominum, Maria mater gratiae, mater misericordiae!*" and afterwards, "St. Dominic, my patron saint, aid me! *Maria, mater gratiae, mater misericordiae, tu nos ob hoste protege et hora mortis suscipe!* Mercy! Mercy! I am dying, I am dying! St. Mary be my help that I speak the truth. I have never seen a sabbat nor know what it is. I have never pricked a waxen image nor seen one nor have ever had a pact with the Devil of any kind whatsoever."

Warned not to be so trusting of the Devil who would surely deceive him, he repeated he never had made a pact with the Devil. Whereupon we had him released somewhat, while he cried, "Oh, oh, I am dying. I cannot take any more!" We repeatedly admonished him to take heed for his spiritual salvation, because it was not possible he could be other than a sorcerer in view of the numerous accusations against him, and to have pity on himself since, because he had made impious use of exorcism, he must be guilty of witchcraft or of heresy. He replied that if he had ever exorcised indiscreetly he begged for pardon, all the time stating he had never been a sorcerer.

After this, we ordered the vise applied to his left arm, thigh, and left leg; to all this he said that he had never been at a sabbat and "I am dying! I am broken! Jesus, Maria! I renounce the Devil!" With this we ordered him to be crushed more severely, whereupon he cried that he told the truth and that he had never been at a sabbat, always saying, "Jesus! Maria! Mother of God have pity on me! Never have I had any compact with the Devil, secret or otherwise. I have never consented to his temptings!" Pressed more tightly, he shrieked, "Jesus! Maria! Father everlasting, help me! I am broken! I never saw a sabbat. I was never at a sabbat. I renounce the Devil and confess the Holy Trinity. I deliver myself into the hands of the good angels. Mercy, I beg God for mercy!"

Finally we ordered that he be taken down from the ladder on which he had been stretched for about a quarter of an hour while the vise had been agonizingly applied, and that he be placed near the fire. We admonished him that he must remember the judgments of God which he could not avoid, although he might escape those of men, and that he must confess to his crime in order to save his soul. But he continued to answer that he had always been a worthy man and a faithful priest and that he had never done any of the crimes of which he had been accused. Thereupon we left him in the said Tower of La Joliette near a fire with a guard we had given him, and made him sign this record of the proceedings with us, the year and day subscribed.

Signed: J. Midot; C. Mathicot;
J. Marson; C. de Gournay,
Bishop of Sitie and Vicar-General.
Dom Husson, Scribe.

We request the Promoter-General of this bishopric to take notice of this present report of all the proceedings to reach a final decision or to summon further evidence as he believes necessary for justice.

At Toul, the year and day stated.
Signed: C. de Gournay, Bishop
of Sitie and Vicar-General.
Dom Husson, Scribe.

Gowdie, Isobel. In four separate confessions, made apparently without torture between April 13 and May 27, 1662, Isobel Gowdie gave what amounted to a résumé of popular beliefs about witchcraft in Scotland. The woman appeared clearly demented, although by her statements it is plain she believed what she confessed, no matter how impossible (such as turning herself into a jackdaw or a cat, and flying through the air to the sabbat). Her imagination was as powerful as Zola's! Unfortunately, on these meanderings of an old woman, two serious scholars, Margaret Murray and Montague Summers, relied to bolster theories of witchcraft no less irrational than Isobel Gowdie's confessions. Thus Summers believed that her account "is substantially true," and regretted he could not identify the coven leader!

Her personal history as a witch went back to 1647, when she met the devil in the church at Auldearne. Here she made a pact, denying Christian baptism, receiving the new name of Janet, the devil's mark on her shoulder, and rebaptism in her own blood which the devil sucked from her. She swore allegiance by placing one hand on her head and the other on the sole of her foot. The ceremony concluded with the devil, just like the minister, reading from the pulpit.

Isobel confessed how a broomstick or stool left in bed would delude her husband whenever she left for the sabbat. She rode on any bit of straw, crying, "Horse and hattock, in the Devil's name." While aloft, she could shoot down any Christian who saw her and did not bless himself. At the sabbat, before the feast, grace was said:

We eat this meat in the Devil's name,
With sorrow and sighs and mickle
[much] shame;

Black John Chastising the Witches,
by Cruikshank.

"The others chiefly took refuge in crying
'Pity! Mercy!' and such like, while Satan kept
beating them with wool cards, and other
sharp scourges, without attending to their en-
treaties and complaints."—Sir Walter Scott
(1830).

We shall destroy both house and hold;
Both sheep and cattle in the fold,
Little good shall come to the fore,
Of all the rest of the little store.

From her ravings comes the most direct
evidence for the idea of a *coven* of thirteen
witches. Each witch had her own special
devil, going by names as curious as those
ascribed to witches' familiars: Swein,
Rorie, Roaring Lion, Robert the Rule, or
Red Riever. The group or coven spent its
time raising storms by hitting a stone with
a wet rag, and reciting a charm, which
Isobel faithfully told to the judges:

I knock this rag upon this stone
To raise the wind in the Devil's name;
It shall not lie, until I please again.

At other times, the witches would change
themselves into animals, by repeating another charm [see Metamorphosis]. Or they
would shoot elf arrows, which Isobel had
seen little elf boys sharpening, to injure or
kill people; occasionally they missed their
target, and the devil would be very angry.
The devil kept strict control over his
witches, said Isobel, and beat them, saying,
"I ken well enough what you were saying
about me." He was especially incensed if
they were absent from a meeting or disobeyed his orders. Alexander Elder was
often beaten, and he was too weak to resist.
But Margaret Wilson fought back, and

Bessie Wilson "would speak crusty with
her tongue and would be belling against
him soundly." Generally the witches fled,
crying, "Pity! Pity! Mercy! Mercy, our
Lord!" The humor of this account attracted
Cruikshank, and his portrayal of Black
John, the devil, chastising the Auldearne
witches is found in some editions of Scott's
Letters on Demonology and Witchcraft.

The court records do not give Isobel
Gowdie's fate, but there seems no reason
that she was not executed. It is noteworthy
that while the Restoration in England
brought a reduction of witch trials, the
first years of Charles II marked a high
point in the number of prosecutions in Scotland.

Grandier, Urbain: see Loudun Nuns.

Grenier, Jean. The story of Jean Grenier
in the département of Les Landes is one of
the classic examples of lycanthropy; it was
reported in detail by Pierre de Lancre, a
wealthy magistrate of Bordeaux.

In 1603, in a village in the southwest of
France, some girls were tending their sheep,
when they were surprised by an odd-looking
fourteen-year-old boy, who told them he was
a werewolf. Jeanne Gaboriant, the eldest
of the girls, questioned the boy. He replied:

[A man] gave me a wolf-skin cape;
he wraps it round me, and every Monday,
Friday, and Sunday, and for about an
hour at dusk every other day, I am a
wolf, a werewolf. I have killed dogs and
drunk their blood; but little girls taste
better, and their flesh is tender and sweet,
their blood rich and warm.

Jean Grenier apparently brought on his
trouble by boasting he was a werewolf;
since several children had been killed in the
St.-Sever district of Gascony, and since
three girls had testified against him (May
29, 1603), he was believed. The district
attorney of Roche Chalès brought Jean before the local judge, who found his admissions, his denunciations of others as
lycanthropes, and the evidence of parents
whose children had disappeared so shocking that he sent the case on to a higher
judge at Coutras (June 2). This superior

court searched the houses of those Jean accused, for magic ointment; although nothing was found, nevertheless Jean's father and a neighbor, M. del Thillaire, were imprisoned. M. Grenier persuaded the court that his son was a well-known idiot, who would say he had slept with every woman in the village. The judge found that M. Grenier's reputation was good, as was that of M. del Thillaire—*gens de bien.*

The court officers spent considerable care in checking Jean's stories. They retraced the steps of all his alleged exploits and interrogated each one concerned—all that this evidence proved, however, was that Jean roamed the neighborhood and knew it and the local inhabitants intimately. Several children who had been present when one of their playmates was seized by a wolf linked these circumstances to Jean's story. So determined was Jean Grenier in his confession, and so incriminating the circumstantial evidence, that the court ordered him hanged and his body burned to ashes. The guilt of M. Grenier and M. del Thillaire was in doubt, so they were tortured; they confessed they had sought out little girls only *pour en jouir et non les manger.*

The Parlement of Bordeaux decided to review the case and all the testimony. "The investigation which followed was as complete as could be desired," wrote Judge De Lancre, and gave the following summary:

Jean deposed: When I was ten or eleven years old, my neighbor, del Thillaire, introduced me, in the depths of the forest, to the Maître de la Forêt, a black man, who signed me with his nail, and then gave me and del Thillaire a salve and a wolf skin. From that time I have run about the country as a wolf.

When questioned touching the children, whom he said he had killed and eaten as a wolf, he allowed that he had once, on the way between St.-Coutras and St.-Anlaye, entered an empty house in a small village, the name of which he did not remember, and had found a child asleep in its cradle; and, as no one was within to hinder him, he dragged the baby out of its cradle, carried it into the garden, leaped the hedge, and devoured

as much of it as satisfied his hunger. What remained he had given to a wolf. In the parish of St.-Antoine-de-Pizon he had attacked a little girl, as she was keeping sheep. She was dressed in a black frock; he did not know her name. He tore her with his nails and teeth, and ate her. Six weeks before his capture he had fallen upon another child, near the stone bridge in the same parish. In Eparon he had assaulted the hound of a certain M. Millon, and would have killed the beast, had not the owner come out with his rapier in his hand.

Jean said that he had the wolf skin in his possession, and that he went out hunting for children, at the command of his lord, the Maître de la Forêt. Before transformation he smeared himself with the salve, which he preserved in a small pot, and hid his clothes in the thicket.

The local Parlement acted in a surprisingly intelligent and sensible manner. It sent two physicians to examine Jean Grenier; they decided the boy was suffering from "a malady called lycanthropy," induced (and here the doctors slipped back into superstition) by an evil spirit, which deceived men's eyes into imagining such things.

On September 6, 1603, the Parlement merely condemned him to life imprisonment in a local monastery.

The court, in conclusion, takes into account the young age and the imbecility of this boy, who is so stupid and idiotic that children of seven and eight years old normally show more intelligence, who has been ill fed in every respect and who is so dwarfed that he is not as tall as a ten-year-old. . . . Here is a young lad abandoned and driven out by his father, who has a cruel stepmother instead of a real mother, who wanders over the fields, without a counselor and without anyone to take an interest in him, begging his bread, who has never had any religious training, whose real nature was corrupted by evil promptings, need, and despair, and whom the devil made his prey. (De Lancre)

Seven years later, in 1610, De Lancre visited the monastery of the Franciscan

Cordeliers at Bordeaux where Grenier had been imprisoned, and found him still diminutive in stature, very shy, and unwilling to look anyone in the face. His eyes were deep-set and restless, his teeth long and protruding, his nails black and in places worn away; his mind was completely blank, and he seemed unable to comprehend even the simplest things. He still maintained that he had been a werewolf, and that he would like to eat children, if he could do so. He also liked to look at wolves. In November, 1610, Jean Grenier died, "as a good Christian."

Grierson, Isobel. The best way to acquire an understanding of witchcraft, what it meant to ordinary people, to judges and ministers, and above all to the people charged with witchcraft, is to read the court record of a trial. Specimens from England, France, and Germany are accordingly included in this *Encyclopedia*. The present entry describes the indictments in a trial at Edinburgh, Scotland, in 1607, made before the Supreme Criminal Tribunal and recorded in the Books of Adjournal. Its first editor called it, of all the trials he printed, "perhaps the most absurd and *outré*"; but actually the accusations are the same as those which sent hundreds of Scottish men and women to their doom during the height of the witch mania.

The accused was Isobel Grierson, wife of John Bull, workman in Prestonpans, indicted on March 10, 1607. The six counts are given below from the court record; editorial comment is not needed.

1. Conceiving cruel hatred and malice against Adam Clark for over a year and a half, Isobel Grierson used all devilish means to be avenged on him. Especially, during November, 1606, between eleven and twelve o'clock, Isobel Grierson, "in likeness of her own cat, accompanied with a great number of other cats, in a devilish manner, entered within their house, where they made a great and tearful noise and trouble; whereby the said Adam, then lying in bed with his wife, and servants that were then in the house, apprehended such a great fear that they were likely to go mad." At this time, the

devil, like a black man, dragged the servant around the house by her hair, so that she was sick for six weeks.

2. For rancor against William Burnet, husband of Margaret Miller, widow, Isobel Grierson sought to kill him "by devilish and ungodly means—as a manifest sorcerer and witch." In January, 1650, she threw a piece [*ane tailzie*] of raw meat at his door, whereafter the devil as a naked infant appeared nightly in his house for half a year. The devil also appeared in the likeness of Isobel Grierson, who "in a most unhonest and filthy manner, pissed upon the said Margaret Miller and in diverse parts of the said house." William Burnet pined away and died in 1605, "in great dolor and pain"; Isobel was accused as "art and part of the said former William's death and sickness."

3. Isobel Grierson was indicted for casting sickness on Robert Peddan in October, 1598, nine years previously. After pining away for some time, he remembered he owed Isobel nine shillings and fourpence; he had refused to pay his debt, whereon Isobel said "he should repent it." Peddan paid Isobel the money and asked her to restore his health. He recovered.

4. Robert Peddan charged that in June, 1606, while passing an open window in his house, Isobel had stretched out her hand to stroke the cat. Peddan was at the time brewing ale, but immediately the brew turned sour, "altogether rotten and black, thick like gutter dirt, with a filthy and pestilent odor, that no man might drink nor feel [endure] the smell therof."

5. Isobel was charged with conceiving a deadly intent against Margaret Donaldson, the wife of Robert Peddan, in 1600. Following a sickness, Margaret thought Isobel might have bewitched her, and asked neighbors to arrange a reconciliation, after which she recovered. But Isobel thought Margaret was defaming her as a witch, and returned, saying, "The faggot of hell light on thee, and Hell's cauldron may thou seethe in." Margaret took sick again, but she recovered in nine weeks. In December, 1606, she encountered Isobel, who again cursed her: "Away, thief, I shall have thy

heart, for spreading rumors about me so falsely." At this, Margaret took sick again.

6. The final indictment was that Isobel Grierson was "a common sorcerer and a witch, and abuser of the people, by laying in and taking off of sickness and diseases, and using all devilish and ungodly means to win her living; and [a] user of charms and other devilish practices."

After the relevant witnesses had been heard (the sixth charge needed none), the jury found her "culpable and convicted of all and sundry the heads and points of the dittay [indictment] above written." Isobel Grierson was strangled and burned to ashes on Castlehill, Edinburgh, and her goods forfeit to the king.

Grillandus, Paulus. The *Tractatus de Hereticis et Sortilegiis* [*Treatise on Heretics and Witches*] is, after the *Malleus Maleficarum*, probably the most influential work on witchcraft published before the middle of the sixteenth century, and because it was so frequently quoted, continued a dominating influence on all later demonologists. Paulus Grillandus was a papal judge in the witch trials in the Rome district, and in this tractate he includes many of his own experiences.

Grillandus covers a very wide area: demonology, pacts with the Devil, possession, the sabbat—nearly all theologians, he says, believe in bodily transvection—metamorphosis, amatory and mortuary masses (a very early reference), and *maleficia*, including ligature, poppets, and potions. All this discussion is bolstered in the scholastic fashion with theological and legal citations. His logic is somewhat undermined, however, by his admission—which most authorities would delete—that he has never seen or heard of any witch caught *"in flagrante crimine."*

In connection with divination, Grillandus cites an amusing punctuation trick. A general consulted a demon as to whether he should go to battle and received this answer· *"Ibis redibis non morieris in bello."* Depending on whether the comma is placed after *redibis* or *non*, the prophecy could mean either: "Go, you will return, you will

not die in battle," or "Go, you will not return, you will die in battle."

Another anecdote, which he gives at first hand, concerns a husband who persuaded his wife to take him with her to a sabbat. He had to promise that under no circumstances would he offend the devil by uttering the name of God or Christ. At the banquet, he found his food insipid and called for salt (which devils fear, for it is used in exorcism). Eventually he got some, and in delight cried out, "God be praised, here comes the salt!" At these words, the assembly vanished and he found himself a hundred miles from home. He denounced his wife to the Inquisition, and she was burned.

Since Grillandus was much respected, anecdotes like these were copied by later writers, and so the fabric of witchcraft was buttressed by the crassest fables of the preceding century. And yet Grillandus was a Doctor of Laws.

Guazzo, Francesco-Maria. Francesco-Maria Guazzo [also Guaccio, Guazzi], an early seventeenth-century friar (exact dates not known), joined the Brethren of St. Ambrose ad Nemus and St. Barnabas in Milan at a time when superstition was allegedly riding rampant. As Lea comments, "the credulity of the period was insatiable." Guazzo himself is an example: he repeats with the utmost seriousness the legend that Luther was the offspring of a nun and the Devil. Discussing "whether witches can by their art create any living thing," he borrows from Del Rio the following *exemplum*:

There was a lewd fellow in Belgium who had to do with a cow, and the cow soon became pregnant and after some months gave birth to a male foetus, which was not a calf but human. There were many present who saw it come from its mother's womb, and they picked it up from the ground and gave it to a nurse. The boy grew up and was baptized and instructed in the Christian life, and applied himself seriously to piety and works of penance for his father; and so came to manhood. But he felt in himself certain bovine

An illustration from Francesco-Maria Guazzo's *Compendium Maleficarum* (Milan, 1626), first printed in 1608. "The greater the wickedness in which demons can involve men, the more God is offended and the greater the power he grants to demons to punish them."

propensities, as that of eating grass and chewing the cud. What must be thought of this? Was he not a man? Certainly I believe he was; but I deny his mother was a cow. What then? The devil was aware of his father's sin, and at his pleasure made the cow appear pregnant: he then secretly brought an infant from elsewhere, and so placed it by the laboring cow (which was big only with wind) that it seemed to be born from the cow.

These anecdotes are typical of the man and his times.

At the request of the Bishop of Milan, Guazzo wrote his encyclopedic *Compendium Maleficarum* [*Handbook of Witches*] to confute and expose, classify and illustrate the practices of witchcraft. Guazzo was well-known as an assessor in trials for witchcraft (though he seldom describes his experiences), and in 1605 went to Cleves to promote charges against one accused of bewitching the Serene Duke John William, long active in persecuting suspected witches. For his handbook, Guazzo borrowed from previous demonologists, especially Del Rio and Remy, and quoted in all from 322 authorities. The *Compendium*, by reason of this load of stock scholarship, became one of the standard demonologies

of the seventeenth century, and was later heavily drawn on by Sinistrari.

Guibourg, Abbé: see Chambre Ardente Affair.

Gunter, Anne. Anne Gunter provides a curious illustration of how a young girl, subject to hysteria, could be so incited that her sickness would seem due to witchcraft. In 1604, at her home in North Moreton, Berkshire, fourteen-year-old Anne Gunter had fits, but the medical diagnosis of "falling sickness" (epilepsy) or "suffocation of the mother" (hysteria) failed to satisfy the credulous. Her father, a prominent local gentleman, brought in eminent Oxford physicians and experts in bewitchment. Anne suffered from swellings of her body, foaming at the mouth, temporary blindness and deafness; she sneezed, voided, and exuded pins from her throat, breasts, and fingers; she fasted as long as ten or twelve days; and she foretold simple domestic events. The cause of her misery Anne ascribed to three witches, Agnes Pepwell, Elizabeth Gregory, and Mary Pepwell, all of whom, with their familiars, spectrally annoyed her.

The fits attracted widespread attention, and the three women were arraigned at Abingdon in 1605; but the court found them Not Guilty. Soon after the trial, Anne was entrusted to the care of Henry Cotton, Bishop of Salisbury and father of nineteen children, who discovered her fraud by marking the pins she claimed to vomit. On August 27, 1605, King James personally examined her, and sent her to be cared for by Rev. Samuel Harsnett (then chaplain to the Archbishop of Canterbury), who had previously exposed the quackery of John Darrell. In the following months, Agnes admitted to Harsnett and to Dr. Edward Jorden that while she suffered from "a natural distemper," her father had encouraged her to counterfeit more extreme manifestations, and that she had been accustomed to hide the pins which later came from her body. Rev. Richard Neile, later (1631) Archbishop of York, was also active in exposing the imposture. After a year's further consultation, Sir Edward Coke, the Attorney General, charged Mr. Brian Gunter and his daughter with conspiracy. A number of witnesses, including the local vicar, testified to Anne's supernormal activities, including the ability of her garters, unassisted, to tie "themselves in knots like chitterlings." The outcome of the conspiracy charges is not known.

Noteworthy, because it provides a clue to other similar adolescents' fits, is the fact that on her "bewitchment," friends brought pamphlets and books about witchcraft to Anne's house. One of these was a work by the self-styled exorcist Darrell, and another was the tract on the Warboys Witches. From such books, Anne got her ideas; in fact, the familiar she assigned to Elizabeth Gregory she called "Catch," the name of the familiar described in the Warboys trial. In addition, the child forced the three women to recite the same charm invented by the Throgmorton girls to gain relief from the Warboys Witches, with the names of the local North Moreton women substituted: "In the name of the Son and Holy Ghost, so be it. Amen. I, Mary Pepwell, charge thee, white toad, to come out of thee, Anne Gunter."

See further, Children as Accusers.

Gwinner, Else. In Germany, procedures against witches varied from state to state. The witch trial in 1601 of Else Laubbach, wife of Martin Gwinner, a baker, shows the common practice in an imperial city or *Reichsstadt* of the Holy Roman Empire. Offenburg, in (modern) Baden, was a town of some 2,000-3,000 inhabitants. It was rigidly Catholic and (through its schools) Jesuit-directed; any person not going to Easter confession was jailed three days, and then allowed two weeks to fulfill his obligation or face further imprisonment. Offenburg was governed by a town council [*Rath*] of twenty-two members, ten nominated indirectly by the trade guilds and ten co-opted by the *Rath* itself, with two priests, ex officio. From these came the mayor and four executives who acted as prosecuting judges in the witch trials.

A councilor of the witch-hunting faction,

Rupprecht Silberrad, determined to crush an opposing councilman, George Laubbach, whose wife had already been burned as a witch in 1597, one of the first in Offenburg. On September 7, 1601, Silberrad accused two of Laubbach's daughters, Adelheid and Helene, of causing the death of his son by witchcraft, and on October 31, added the third daughter, Else Gwinner. The "evidence" came from two vagrants, arrested for stealing grapes. Instead of being punished in the pillory as thieves, they were accused as witches, and tortured into denouncing the Laubbach daughters, especially Else, as accomplices in *maleficia*. The two vagrants denounced other prominent townswomen, including Silberrad's sister-in-law, but little attention was paid to these denunciations.

The day of her arrest, Else Gwinner was tortured, but would confess nothing. Although she screamed fearfully during strappado, all she would say was, "Father, forgive them, for they know not what they do." In spite of popular disapproval, the *Rath*, on the advice of the vicar, decided to arrest Else's young daughter, Agathe, hoping to secure from her some statement which would implicate her mother. But Agathe refused to co-operate. Her mother was therefore more severely tortured a second time, on November 7, 1601, but even when the heaviest weights were attached to her body as she hung pinioned by her wrists, she refused to talk. A week later, the judges returned to Agathe, but the child refused to tell lies against her mother until she was flogged into saying what the judges wanted. On November 22, the two vagabonds were executed, and the same day Else was told about Agathe's accusations and confronted with her daughter. In anguish she reproached her, "Why did I not drown my unfortunate child in her first bath?" "Oh, that you had done so," sobbed Agathe.

Still, Else Gwinner had not confessed. She was tortured with thumbscrews, which drew only an admission of copulation with a devil. Then she was thrown into a freezing dungeon. Torture was resumed for the fourth time on December 11, when Else was so exhausted that she had to be revived even during the agony of torture by cold water on her face. To her story of sexual relations and flight to a sabbat she added denunciations of two women as accomplices. However, two days later she revoked this confession, and maintained her innocence despite the urgings of a priest that she admit her guilt. December 15, the judges told her they would now torture her remorselessly until she broke down. The charge of effecting the death of Silberrad's son, for which she had been first arrested, had been lost sight of, and the aim was to force her to name those she had seen at the sabbat. Else would name nobody, and insisted her previous accusations were false. Seeing their efforts fruitless, the judges summarily sentenced her on December 19, and on December 21, 1601, they burned her.

During this time, her young daughter Agathe had been kept chained in a tiny dungeon, while a priest tried to induce her to admit Else's guilt. Her father and in-laws were so horrified by her denunciation of her mother, even under flogging, that they disowned her. The town council now had on its hands an unwanted child, too young to burn. However, three weeks after the execution of his wife, Martin Gwinner relented and made a formal petition to the *Rath* to pardon Agathe, in consideration of her extreme youth. She was freed, on condition of being exiled to some Catholic town in Germany. The Silberrad faction strongly objected to this show of mercy.

Else's two sisters, Adelheid and Helene, apparently did not come to trial, for the other councilors, on February 4, 1602, turned against Silberrad and four of his supporters and arrested them. On the pleas of the Church, however, the men were merely held under house arrest, and Silberrad was soon released, successfully suing for damages and regaining his former status.

Offenburg continued its witch hunts, for they were profitable to the judges, and the trials became even more lawless and brutal. The judges introduced the iron witch's chair, on which the victim was bound and roasted into confession. This new device quickly proved the wealthiest persons witches [see Witchcraft in Germany]. About 1630 the persecution died down, on account of the war, but was later resumed.

This typical trial in a Catholic city in Germany is balanced by the equally ferocious trials in the Protestant city of Lindheim [see Johann Schüler]. In both towns, prosperous citizens, without the slightest evidence of any misdeed, were named as witches, tortured into confessing the whole rigmarole of pact and sabbat, burned, and their properties confiscated. When money was to be made, Catholics and Protestants vied to keep their religions unsullied by the Devil's associates.

Haizmann, Christoph. Christoph Haizmann was a minor Bavarian artist. In 1677 he wrote an account of his Faust-like pact with the Devil; he illustrated it, moreover, with portraits of the Devil. Such an illustrated autobiography of a demoniac is unique; its interest is increased by Sigmund Freud's citing it to explain his theory of paranoia (or schizophrenia).

With a clinical history of visions, Haizmann was seized by "a certain unnatural convulsion" on August 29, 1677, while engaged as a painter at Pottenbrunn, and taken to the police. He made an amazing confession. Nine years earlier he had twice sold himself to Satan. Fearing the day of reckoning near, he begged the police to send him for protection to the nearby shrine of Mariazell. His story was believed, and on September 5, very contrite, Haizmann arrived in Zell. After continuous exorcism for three days and nights, Haizmann saw the Virgin Mary triumph over the Devil, and snatch the very pact he had written in blood "taken from the palm of his right hand." The pact was endorsed: "Christoph Haizmann. I sell myself to this Satan, to be his own bodily son, and belong to him both body and soul in the ninth year." Seemingly cured, the painter went to live with his married sister in Vienna, but within a month his anxieties returned. By May, 1678, he was back at Zell, where this time the Virgin regained another pact, signed in ink, which Haizmann saw torn in four pieces and thrown on the steps of the altar. After this experience Haizmann entered a monastery, and although tempted by devils, lived a devout life to his death on March 14, 1700, at Neustadt on the Moldau in Bavaria.

His portraits of the Devil are murky with stormy, reddish backgrounds (and therefore unsatisfactory for reproduction here). The Devil is depicted with a human torso, with horns, a woman's breasts, and bird's legs and claws. While they show the stages of his illness, these pictures are not especially different from the conventional conceptions of the Devil—nor would one expect them to be.

> The first time, [the devil] appeared before me in this his guise as a burgher, having with him a black dog, and asked me why I was so dismayed and sad. He would help me out of my distress if I were willing to subscribe myself in ink to him to be his son; he would assist and help me in every possible way.

The eighth time the Devil appeared as a dragon, again with breasts and bird's legs. Haizmann's hallucinations included a vision of hell—

A nineteenth-century conception of the Devil appearing to Collin de Plancy as he was compiling his *Dictionnaire infernal* (1863).

filled with burning flames and terrible stench. In it there was a large cauldron from which came the heart-rending moans and groans of human beings; on its edge sat a hellish devil who did nothing but pour flaming resin, sulphur and pitch over them.

In this autobiography, Freud found evidence of Haizmann's having had an Oedipus complex and castration anxieties, but the two psychiatrists who lavishly edited the manuscript in 1956 questioned this diagnosis.

Hale, Sir Matthew. One of England's most famous judges, "the most profound lawyer of his time," who by his legal decisions helped continue belief in witchcraft. Chief Justice Matthew Hale (1609-76) was given the opportunity to strike obviously perjured testimony; he preferred rather to omit a summation of the evidence and direct the jury according to his own prejudices. In this he fell far below the stature of his successor as Chief Justice of the King's Bench, Sir John Holt, who, over thirty years later, at the same Bury St. Edmunds where Hale in 1662 had encouraged witch hunters, resolutely secured the acquittal of an accused witch. Hale, with all his reputation, could have given a similar lead. That he did not rise above his age is poor testimony to his alleged great legal mind. Even a few years after his death, his judgments in witch trials seemed so dubious that his biographer, Bishop Gilbert Burnet, in 1682 omitted all mention of the notorious trial at Bury St. Edmunds.

Hale had been brought up by his guardian as a Puritan, but, worldly-wise, he straddled the fence in the Civil Wars, accepting appointment from Cromwell as Justice of the Common Pleas in 1654, later becoming a negotiator for the return of Charles II, who rewarded him as First Baron of the Exchequer and subsequently (1671) as Chief Justice. He was a member of Parliament from 1654. In the pamphlet on the trials at Bury St. Edmunds, a note to the reader praised Hale as "a judge, whom for his integrity, learning, and law,

Sir Matthew Hale (1609-76), Lord Chief Justice of England, who encouraged persecution of witches and allowed false testimony to secure convictions. From Harvard University Law Library.

hardly any age, either before or since, could parallel."

At the trial of the witches of Bury St. Edmunds, Hale was the presiding judge, and, as a believer in the crime of witchcraft, accepted hearsay evidence five to seven years old, unsupported testimony of children, evidence as a professional witch pricker from an interested witness (the mother of the children), and spectral evidence from single witnesses. Moreover, when some of the assisting judges (such as Sergeant Keeling) discovered fraud by the accusing children, Hale accepted the lamest excuse from their father. He told the jury there were but two questions for decision: Were the children bewitched? Were the accused guilty of bewitching them? Then he made this statement:

> That there were such creatures as witches he made no doubt at all. For first, the Scriptures had affirmed so much. Secondly, the wisdom of all nations had provided laws against such persons, which is an argument of their confidence of such a crime. And such hath been the judgment of this kingdom, as appears by that act of Parliament which hath provided punishments proportionable to the quality of the offense.

On the Sunday following the executions, Sir Matthew meditated on the trial and later published his "Discourse concerning the great mercy of God, in preserving us from

the power and malice of evil spirits." Cotton Mather followed this trial closely and observed, "It was a trial much considered by the judges of New England." To this extent, the example of Hale fortified the judges at Salem.

His reputation would have been greater, had Hale's conduct not required the whitewash with which Lord Campbell sought to cover up his bias: "I would very readily have pardoned him for an undoubting belief in witchcraft, and I should have considered that this belief detracted little from his character for discernment and humanity."

Hand of Glory. Many *grimoires* and handbooks of magic describe the hand of glory, a gruesome device sometimes featured in trials for witchcraft. The sorcerer wrapped the hand of a hanged man in a piece of shroud, drew it tight to squeeze out any remaining blood, and pickled the hand in an earthenware jar with salt, saltpeter, and long peppers. After two weeks, the hand was removed and exposed to the sun until parched, or dried in an oven with vervain and fern. One recipe suggested using the hand as a candleholder for candles made from the fat of a hanged man, virgin wax, and Lapland sesame.

The Jesuit demonologist Del Rio related how a thief lit the fingers of a hand of glory to put to sleep the inmates of a house. He was observed by a servant girl. While the thief ransacked the house, the girl tried to extinguish the flames, blowing on them and throwing beer or water over them, and finally she dowsed them with milk. Immediately the household awakened and captured the thief. This story was widespread in folklore and was retold in the *Ingoldsby Legends*.

Guazzo, another demonologist, borrowing from Remy, told of a trial (in 1588 at Guermingen) of two witches, Nichel and Bessers, accused of digging up corpses. They prepared a hand of glory; while the fingers were burning, they could successfully poison people; when they had finished their *maleficia*, they extinguished the flames and saved the hand for use a second time.

Jasper's Abomination of Sorcerers, from the Douce Collection, Bodleian Library, Oxford. The Hand of Glory is above the fireplace. "Nothing is more damnable nor more worthy of the fire of hell than this abominable brood of the ministers of Lucifer. From their black mysteries, emerge horror, hatred, strife; and their execrable sabbat reeks with blood. These cursed souls are preparing their own tortures and fanning up the flames which burn eternally."

Harsnett, Samuel. "One of the most rational men of his time," was how George L. Burr characterized Samuel Harsnett (1561-1631), who rose to become Archbishop of York. Educated at Cambridge and ordained priest, Harsnett early (1584) made a name for himself by preaching against the Calvinist doctrine of "absolute predestination," declaring the opinion "monstrous" that "saith that not one or two, but millions of men should fry in hell, and that [God] made them for no other purpose." He returned to Cambridge for advanced theological study and was appointed chaplain to Bishop Bancroft of London. In this capacity he investigated the exorcism practiced by John Darrell and the deceptions of the Burton Boy. As a result, he wrote his slashing attack on fraud and superstition, *Discovery of the Fraudulent Practices of John Darrell* (1599). Later, by order of the Privy Council, he wrote another attack on exorcism, *A Declaration of Egregious Popish Impostures* (the source of the spirits mentioned by Edgar in *King Lear* III.iv). "In this work, Harsnett shows himself a thoroughgoing disciple of Reginald Scot (whom he cites), and scoffs openly at the whole body of witchcraft superstition, declaring it delusion and humbug"—Burr. In 1603 the Church of England prohibited ministers from casting out of devils, except by special license of the bishop, "under pain of the imputation of imposture or cozenage."

In 1605, Harsnett succeeded his friend, Launcelot Andrewes, as Master of Pembroke Hall, Cambridge, a position he held, though absent and often at variance with the professors, until 1616. He was elected Vice-Chancellor of Cambridge in 1606, became Bishop of Chichester in 1609, and Archbishop of York in 1628. His last years were embittered by the growth of Puritanism, which, unlike the Episcopal church, fomented the witch persecutions of the mid-century.

See further, Burton Boy, John Darrell.

Hatfield Peverell Witches: see Chelmsford Witches.

Henry VIII: Statute of 1542. The first bill in modern England against witchcraft; previously, witchcraft was considered either a religious offense, to be tried by minor ecclesiastical courts, or (especially with prominent nobles) a political offense to be punished by the King's Privy Council or the Bishops. Some laws against sorcery had been passed very early in Anglo-Saxon times [see Witchcraft in England].

Although the Statute of 1542 was the most sweeping of any English law against witchcraft, there is record of only one conviction under it (the offender was pardoned). Within six years, in 1547, it was removed under an omnibus repeal of recent statutes for treason and felony [see Edward VI], apparently provoking no dissent. The phraseology of this bill, however, was continued in all succeeding legislation, down to James I.

The stress laid on certain aspects of witchcraft in this bill acts as a significant barometer of the isolation of English witchcraft. For example, there is no mention of any pact with the Devil, so essential in the fully developed Continental and New England conceptions. What occasioned this bill were the acts of witches—divination for precious metals, simple *maleficia*, sympathetic black magic using waxen images, and using rings and bottles or overturning wayside crosses in the hope of finding treasure buried underneath. Witchcraft per se was not an offense; Chief Justice Catlin ruled, in 1561, that making love philters was no grounds for trial. The bill is also curious because, unlike later statutes, it did not differentiate between various crimes, including all, both major and minor, in a blanket condemnation as felonies, and hence punishable by death.

THE BILL AGAINST CONJURATION AND WITCHCRAFTS AND SORCERY AND ENCHANTMENTS

I. Where[as] divers and sundry persons unlawfully [a] have devised and practiced invocations and conjurations of spirits, pretending by such means to understand and get knowledge for their own lucre in what place treasure of gold and silver should or might be found or had in the earth or other secret places;

and [b] also have used and occupied witchcrafts, enchantments, and sorceries to the destruction of their neighbor's persons and goods; and [c] for execution of their said false devices and practices have made or caused to be made divers images and pictures of men, women, children, angels or devils, beasts or fowls; and also, [d] have made crowns, scepters, swords, rings, glasses, and other things, and, giving faith and credit to such fantastical practices, have digged up and pulled down an infinite number of crosses within this realm, and taken upon them to declare and tell where things lost or stolen should be become; which things cannot be used and exercised but to the great offense of God's law, hurt, and damage of the King's subjects, and loss of the souls of such offenders, to the great dishonor of God, infamy and disquietness of the realm.

II. For reformation whereof, be it enacted by the King, our sovereign Lord, with the assent of the Lords spiritual and temporal, and the Commons in this present Parliament assembled, and by authority of the same, that if any person or persons, after the first of May next coming, use, devise, practice, or exercise, or cause to be used, devised, practiced, or exercised, any invocations or conjurations of spirits, witchcrafts, enchantments or sorceries to the intent [a] to get or find money or treasure, or [b] to waste, consume, or destroy any person in his body, members, or goods, or [c] to provoke any person to unlawful love, or for any other unlawful intent or purpose, or by occasion or color of such things or any of them, or [d] for despite of Christ or for lucre or money, dig up or pull down any cross or crosses, or by such invocations or conjurations of spirits, witchcrafts, enchantments or sorcery, or any of them, take upon them to tell or declare where goods stolen or lost shall become, that then all and every such offense and offenses, from the said first day of May next coming, shall be deemed, accepted, and adjudged felony. And that all and every person and persons offending as is aforesaid, their counselors, abettors, and procurers, and every of them from the said first day of May, shall be deemed, accepted, and adjudged a felon

and felons. And the offender and offenders contrary to this act being thereof lawfully convicted before such as shall have power and authority to hear and determine felonies, shall have and suffer such pains of death, loss, and forfeiture of their lands, tenants, goods, and chattels as in cases of felony, by the course of the common laws of this realm, and also shall lose privilege of clergy and sanctuary.

Heresy. Witchcraft was a heresy. Heresy (from a Greek word meaning "free choice") was one of several degrees of divergence from the Catholic Church:

Schism: Departure in matters of government but not in the basic principles of faith, or, as Augustine established, outward separation rather than inner differences.

Heresy: According to Aquinas and Canon Law, "religious error held in willful and persistent opposition to the truth after it had been defined and declared by the Church in an authoritative manner."

Apostasy: Denial of the divine authority of the Bible, or the truth of the Christian religion, especially by one in religious orders.

All these disagreements imply only one permitted philosophy of life, and are possible only in a monolithic Christian society which controls the state and which can therefore enforce penalties for free choice. The terms do not apply to persons who have never professed Christianity: *infidels* (members of religions opposed to Christianity, especially Mohammedans and Jews), *heathens* (neither Christians, Mohammedans, or Jews), or *pagans* (believers in polytheistic gods).

The two heresies most frequently linked to witchcraft were the Albigensian, a form of Catharism, and the Waldensian:

Cathars (Catharists, Catharites). A widespread movement, comprising many groups, prominent from the tenth to the fourteenth century, originating in eastern Europe and gradually spreading over most of the Continent. Common tenets included a belief in the Manichaean or dualist principle of a God of good and a God of evil, both eternal. Satan, the God of evil, controlled the world, which was therefore the same as hell, in opposition to the good God, ruler of the eternal world of Heaven. Cathars generally accepted the universal salvation of all men who had been "reborn" by spiritual baptism in Christ. Standards of life and conduct varied according to class of membership, either Professed (or Perfect) or Believers.

Albigenses (Albigensians). So-called from their predominance in Albi, a town in Provence, (and at Toulouse) in the twelfth and thirteenth centuries. The heresy made its way into southern France about 1020 by the trade routes from eastern Europe— *bougres* [Bulgarians] was a name often applied to Albigensians, and, from the enormities alleged against them, took on the modern connotation of sexual perversion. Protected by Duke William IX of Aquitaine, these heretics became dominant in southern France about 1150. Pope Innocent III tried pacification, and then directed the nobles of northern France in a "crusade" (1209-1229). The southern nobles were largely crushed or bought, but the heresy managed to survive, necessitating the introduction of the Inquisition in 1232 by Pope Gregory IX. The suppression was completed about 1330, about the same time as sorcery began to be identified as a heresy (e.g., the letter of Pope Benedict XII in 1336 to the Bishop of Carcassonne ordering him to step up the hunt for witches).

Waldenses (Waldensians, Vaudois). Named after their founder, Peter Waldo, a rich merchant of Lyons. About 1170 he had a "conversion," and decided to preach the Gospel in the vernacular. At first, his followers were tolerated, but later the parish clergy protested. The Waldenses were condemned for holding the Bible as the final authority for a Christian and for opposing clerical immorality. They differed from the Albigenses in stressing opposition to sacerdotalism. During the Albigensian crusade, the Vaudois in southern France were also persecuted, but some managed to flee to the valleys in the Piedmont, where they gave their popular name (Vaudois) to these areas. Pope Eugenius IV in 1440

and 1445 urged an attack on "these people who are commonly called *stregulae* or *stregones* [witches] or Vaudois." In 1487 Pope Innocent VIII encouraged their extermination, really the first blow in the battle against witchcraft.

The significance of heresy lay in the theory that it was not merely a sin, but a crime punishable by death. This theory was elaborated in the eleventh and twelfth centuries. Innocent III, for example, in 1198 wrote to the King of France that it was "necessary to use the spiritual sword of excommunication against heretics; if this did not suffice, the physical sword was to be employed." The Lateran Council of 1215 embodied this edict into Canon Law and declared all heretics should be excommunicated and turned over to the civil authorities to be punished (by death). Five years later, Frederick II, the Holy Roman Emperor, embodied this church law into civil law; and later ecclesiastical and secular codes reaffirmed these principles. The phrase, "to curse by bell, book, and candle," summarized the Church's resources for excommunicating heretics; it has no specific connection with witchcraft.

The theory of heresy, therefore, was at the bottom of all the anguish and suffering and mental sterility produced by the witchcraft delusion. When men replaced a religious frame of reference with a political or economic Weltanschauung, imagined pacts with devils became unimportant, and witchcraft disappeared.

For the identification of sorcery as the heresy of witchcraft, see especially Executions, Witchcraft in France, Inquisition, Sabbat, Sorcery, Trials, and Witchcraft.

Hex: see Maleficia.

Hogarth, William. Many of the later classic examples of witches and spirits discussed in this book are satirized in "A Medley—Credulity, Superstition, and Fanaticism" by the great English painter and engraver, William Hogarth (1697-1764). Hogarth issued this print in 1762 (when he was sixty-four) as his contribution to the Age of Reason's attack on superstition. The

A Medley—Credulity, Superstition, and Fanaticism, by William Hogarth (1762).

caption quotes the Bible to stress the spirit of skepticism against which so many theologians railed, and to ridicule "the popular credulities of his own day." This was the year of the Cock Lane poltergeist, and Mr. Kent's deceased wife, "Scratching Fanny," is seen knocking on the wall of Elizabeth Parson's bedroom (at the extreme right, over the thermometer). The Drummer of Tedworth forms a headpiece for this thermometer of "a Methodist's brain," which rests on Wesley's sermons [see Epworth Poltergeist] and Joseph Glanvill. In the foreground, Mary Tofts of Godalming, Surrey, another sensation of 1762, gives birth to rabbits. Her claims to unorthodox progeny impressed two doctors, but Sir William Manningham, personal physician to King George I, exposed her! By her side, the Bilson Boy spits forth pins and nails. His basket rests on the *Demonology* of King James and the *Journal* of Whitfield (whose hymn is read by the verger standing above). Two cherubic choirboys, taking very literally the word "cry" from the *Te Deum*, exhibit the contortions of possessed children everywhere [see Children as Accusers]. In his exuberance, the preacher's wig flies off and reveals a Jesuit's shaven crown, and his gown opens, revealing the costume of a clown. His text, "I speak as a fool," adequately describes him. To delude the congregation from reality, he dangles effigies of a typical witch with a cat, her familiar, suckling an exaggerated teat, and a demon complete with pitchfork. At the preacher's left is a scale of vociferation, ranging from a natural tone at the bottom to the bull roar from the distended mouth at the top. The three panels of the pulpit represent, from left to right, Defoe's famous short story of the apparition of Mrs. Veal to Mrs. Bargrave; the ghost of Julius Caesar appearing to Brutus at Philippi; and Sir George Villiers' ghost forewarning the Duke of Buckingham of his impending death. From the chandelier hangs a map of hell (recalling the diagrams of Antonio Rusca's *De Inferno*, 1621). In the congregation men and women are in various stages of fear and frenzy. Through the window, the heathen Turk, smoking his

Sir John Holt (1642-1710), "an ardent supporter of civil and religious liberty." From Harvard University Law Library.

pipe, watches the scene with astonishment. "A Medley" was redrawn on the original copper of an earlier print, somewhat similar, attacking "the superstitious absurdities of popery."

Holt, Sir John. The most influential judge in the history of English witchcraft, by his own strength of will in directing verdicts, contributed very greatly to stopping the delusion. The *Encyclopaedia Britannica* (11th ed.) states: "In judicial fairness, legal knowledge and ability, clearness of statement and unbending integrity, he has had few if any superiors on the English bench. Over the civil rights of his countrymen he exercised a jealous watchfulness."

Himself the son of a lawyer, Sir John Holt (1642-1710) at first passed a dissolute undergraduate life at Oxford, but then studied law at Gray's Inn with much diligence. He soon became known for his impartiality in allowing defendants their due rights; once, when he opposed King James II (who had knighted him), he was kept on as a king's counsel to prevent his defending those the state accused. Active in inviting William of Orange to England, Holt became, with the new régime, Chief Justice.

At a time when other judges were not discouraging convictions of witches (like Widow Chambers in Suffolk in 1693 or Ann Hart in Kent in 1694), Holt directed jury after jury to render acquittals. His opinions as Chief Justice persuaded lower courts, which might otherwise have continued in the footsteps of such witchcraft believers as Chief Justice Matthew Hale. Furthermore, Holt's cases were widely distributed, from Suffolk to Cornwall. In all, Holt dismissed at least eleven witch trials, and in a final case even had the plaintiff (a possessed youth) examined for deceit. A year later the boy and his employers were convicted for fraud. The best account of these trials is that of Bishop Francis Hutchinson, who had access to Holt's own court records:

1691. Three women accused of bewitching a young girl, Mary Hill of Frome, Somersetshire. "One of them died in jail, the other two were tried before the Right Hon. the Lord Chief Justice Holt, and were acquitted. And the maid that was thought to have been bewitched, in a little time did well and was fit for service."

1694. Mother Munnings tried at Bury St. Edmunds for *maleficia*. The chief charge was already seventeen years old! Another was made by a man on his way home from the alehouse.

It was sworn that Thomas Pannel, her landlord, not knowing how to get her out of his house, took away the door, and left her without one. Sometime after, he happening to pass by, she said to him, "Go thy way, thy nose shall lie upward in the churchyard before Saturday next!" On Monday following her landlord sickened, and died on Tuesday, and was buried within the week, according to her word. In her indictment, she was charged to have an imp like a polecat; and one witness swore that, coming from the alehouse about nine at night, he looked in at her window and saw her take out of her basket, two imps, a black and a white.

Sir John Holt so well directed the jury that Mother Munning was acquitted. It was suggested that the white imp was "a lock of wool, taken out of her basket to spin; and its shadow (it is supposed) was the black one."

1694. Margaret Elnore tried at Ipswich. Evidence against her included her acceptance of familiars from her grandmother, who, with her aunt, had been hanged for witchcraft. "A midwife who had searched her grandmother . . . said this woman had plainer marks than she. Others made oath of their being covered with lice after quarrels with her. But notwithstanding these depositions, the jury brought her in Not Guilty."

1695. Mary Guy at Launceston (Cornwall). "It was deposed that the appearance of the said Mary Guy was often seen by that [possessed] girl, and that she vomited pins, straws, and feathers. But notwithstanding such depositions, the prisoner was acquitted."

1696. Elizabeth Horner at Exeter, a case involving three possessed children.

Another had her legs twisted, and yet from her hands and knees she would spring five foot high. The children vomited pins. . . . The mother of the children deposed that one of them walked up a smooth plastered wall till her feet were nine foot high, her head standing off from it. This, she said, she did five or six times. . . . Many other odd things were deposed, but the jury brought her in Not Guilty, and no inconvenience hath followed from her acquittal.

1701. Sarah Morduck at Guildford, for bewitching Richard Hathaway, a blacksmith's apprentice. "Cleared, and Hathaway was indicted for an impostor." Sarah Morduck had been "scratched" several times by Hathaway, who manifested the customary acts of possession (vomiting of pins, contortions of the body, foaming at the mouth, etc.), and public hostility had been so worked up against her that she had to remove to London. Even here, she "was followed in the streets, and often thought herself in danger of being pulled to pieces." When the judges acquitted her, they were

"slandered as if they had not done fairly."
Accordingly Justice Holt committed the
boy for observation, and six months later
brought him to trial. A long list of impostures, all carefully accredited "by many
and substantial witnesses," was produced:
he secreted pins in his trousers, he made
mysterious noises with "his own feet
scratching the bedpost," he pretended to
fast while actually procuring much food.
His employers were prosecuted at the same
time for assaulting Sarah and for riot. Very
seldom are the accusers of a witch brought
into court.

It is, of course, true that the temper of
England had changed since the Commonwealth, when Matthew Hopkins engineered
his mass trials; the last execution had taken
place in 1684, and the shock of Salem was
influencing the English against witchcraft.
But the delusion still flourished—many of
the molders of public opinion were believers. Executions for witchcraft might well
have continued in England another two or
three decades (as they did in Scotland, to
1722), had it not been for the stand taken
by Justice Holt.

Hopkins, Matthew. In one year from
1645 to 1646 Matthew Hopkins acquired
an evil reputation which in later days made
his name synonymous with fingerman or
informer paid by the authorities to commit
perjury. With John Stearne, his fellow
"witch pricker," Hopkins "in fourteen
months' time sent to the gallows more
witches than all the other witch hunters of
England . . . have hung in the hundred
and sixty years during which this persecution flourished in England." (Notestein)
Montague Summers hits Hopkins' insin-
cerity "which made his name stink in men's
nostrils . . . as the foulest of foul para-
sites, an obscene bird of prey of the tribe
of Judas and Cain."

Like other ruthless men, he managed to
turn an early failure into a career of notoriety by irritating a sore spot in the public conscience to his own advantage. Very
little is known of his early years. The son
of a Suffolk minister, he became a lawyer,

Matthew Hopkins (died 1646), the Witch
Finder General. From the Pepysian Library,
Magdalene College, Cambridge.

"but of little note"; not being able to make
a living at Ipswich, he removed to the village of Manningtree in Essex. In Essex and
the other eastern counties of England, ten-
sion and anxiety were particularly high,
for this area formed the backbone of the
Roundheads in the Civil War, "hot" since
1642. The republican side stood for Protestantism without equivocation, against an
established episcopy claiming to be the
Catholic Church in England; but in the
early days of the fighting no one could be
sure about the outcome. As in all times of
change, men were on edge. Given the right

moment, a demagogue could put aside the worries of wartime, put pressure on local authorities to get rid of the subversives (claiming he had the Devil's list of all the witches in England), demonstrate unity behind Puritanism, and provide a horrible circus by attacking the enemies of Parliament and God. It was easier to attack "stupefied, ignorant, unintelligible, poor silly creatures" as witches than to hunt for Roman Catholics—Guy Fawkes was a later diversion of a strong central government. Besides, it was more profitable: anyone could discover a Catholic; it took skill to detect a witch—they were so subtle. And people paid very well for skill: Hopkins received, for example, six pounds for a trip to Aldeburgh and twenty-three pounds for visiting Stowmarket. The average wage at that time was sixpence a day.

So it was that about March, 1645, Matthew Hopkins, with no knowledge of demonology other than the work of James I, Potts's account of the Lancashire Witches, and Bernard's *Guide to Jurymen*, set up as a witch finder. For his first discovery, he picked on a one-legged hag (Elizabeth Clarke), roused his neighbors to denounce others, devised methods of torture to get confessions without leaving incriminating mangled limbs, and wound up with six victims: Mother Clarke herself and five other women she had accused. Hopkins was joined by John Stearne, and the number of suspects grew until it reached thirty-two, who, on examination by the local justices, were remanded to the county sessions at Chelmsford.

Hopkins seized on one passage in King James's *Demonology* as a shibboleth for detecting witches: witchcraft meant keeping imps. Witches suckled imps or familiars, not primarily to feed these agents of the devil, but "more to aggravate the witches' damnation." How this theory worked out in practice is seen in the first deposition Hopkins made (March 25) against Elizabeth Clarke. On this complaint of "entertaining" evil spirits, Elizabeth Clarke was hanged:

The said Elizabeth forthwith told this informant and one Master Stearne, there present, if they would stay and do the said Elizabeth no hurt, she would call one of her white imps and play with it on her lap. But this informant told her they would not allow of it. And that staying there a while longer, the said Elizabeth confessed she had carnal copulation with the devil six or seven years; and he would appear to her three or four times a week at her bedside, and go to bed with her and lie with her half a night together, in the shape of a proper gentleman, with a laced band, having the whole proportion of a man. And [he] would say to her, "Bessie, I must lie with you." And she never did deny him.

Then Hopkins made the amazing sworn statement that "within a quarter of an hour" four imps appeared, seen by him and Stearne, in the forms of a white dog, a greyhound, a polecat, and a black imp which soon vanished. Hopkins' assistant witch finder, Mary Phillipps, and Edward Parsley, and Frances Mills all swore they too had seen these familiars.

All the depositions followed this pattern. A man while crossing a bridge had heard a cry "much like the shriek of a polecat" and been nearly thrown off his horse. A child nursed by a woman who lived near two suspected witches died; the father believed the two witches caused its death. A woman said "something fell down on her right side" while she was in bed. "Being dark she cannot tell in what shape it was, but she believeth Rebecca West and Ann West the cause of her pain." Rebecca testified that her mother (who had previously been imprisoned as a witch) threatened her, whereupon the next night she "felt something come into the bed about her legs . . . but could not find anything." This was the kind of evidence Hopkins produced for the court. And he took trouble to get it; he even visited Colchester and secured Rebecca West's confession that she had married the devil.

Most of the "Chelmsford Witches" made confessions; this is not strange, for Hopkins and his associates developed techniques to secure whatever confessions they needed. "Swimming" was a favorite, but the parliamentary commission of oyer and terminer in August of 1645 frowned on it, and Hopkins was forced to discontinue throwing trussed-up women into a pond to see if they sank! But his other methods were countenanced, and confessions poured forth after starvation, prolonged sitting cross-legged on a stool, solitary confinement, prevention of sleep, and forced continuous walking until the feet blistered. At Hopkins' later investigation at Bury St. Edmunds in Suffolk in August, 1645, of fifteen examinations where the manner of confession is recorded, four were said to have been given freely, two after one day's "watching," four after two days, and five after three days (which seems to be the maximum period of enforced walking a prisoner could stand before breaking down).

The most frequent charge at the county sessions at Chelmsford on July 29, 1645, was bewitching to death; but against eight, additional charges of entertaining evil spirits were added. However, indictments of entertaining spirits, with no accusation of murder or intent to murder or to cause damage or injury to cattle or property, were entered against nine women. [See Section IIa of the Statute of 1604 of James I.] Two were found Guilty but reprieved. The other seven were found Guilty and hanged. The imps or familiars regarded as the evil spirits were simply domestic pets or small animals—a squirrel, a yellow cat, red or gray mice, a mole. Bridget Mayers, for example, the wife of a seaman, who pleaded Not Guilty, was condemned for entertaining on May 6, 1645, an evil spirit in the likeness of a mouse called "Prick-ears."

Bishop Francis Hutchinson told of one woman who was forced into confessing she had an imp called Nan. Some neighbors, incensed at her treatment, rescued her; when the victim had recovered—

she knew not what she had confessed, and had nothing she called Nan but a pullet that she sometimes called by that name . . . My opinion is that when the witch finders had kept the poor people without meat or sleep till they knew not

well what they said, then, to ease themselves of their tortures, they told them tales of their dogs and cats and kittens.

Under the overcredulous judges, Robert Earl of Warwick and Sir Harbottle Grimston, nineteen of the accused witches were sentenced and "hanged by the neck until they be dead." Five found Guilty were reprieved. Eight were remanded to the next sessions; at least four were still in jail three years later in March, 1648. Only one was found Not Guilty. Four of the thirty-two accused had previously died in prison before the sessions opened; their ages were 80, 65, 60, and 40.

Hopkins did not await the conclusion of the Chelmsford trial; he was busy visiting towns and villages, occasionally by request, more often on his own initiative, and growing rich ferreting witches. After Essex, he turned to Norfolk and Suffolk. By the next year, he had extended his operations with a team of six—himself, John Stearne, and four prickers—to the counties of Cambridge, Northampton, Huntingdon, and Bedford. He had become indeed the Witch Finder General.

For the 1645 Suffolk sessions at Bury St. Edmunds, almost 200 persons had been detained as suspected witches, including a seventy-year-old parson, John Lowes. A confession was wrung from Lowes by teams of watchers who "kept him awake several nights together, and ran him backwards and forwards about the room until he was out of breath. Then they rested him a little and then ran him again. And thus they did for several days and nights together, till he was weary of his life and was scarce sensible of what he said or did." (Hutchinson) In this state of mind, he confessed he had covenanted with the Devil, suckled familiars (Tom, Flo, Bess, and Mary) for five years, and had bewitched cattle. Moreover, he had caused a ship to sink off Harwich, on a calm sea, with the loss of fourteen lives. Stearne's pamphlet says Lowes "was joyfull to see what power his imps had." Afterward, the parson retracted this confession, and, since he was not allowed a clergyman to read the burial service over him, recited it himself on his way to the scaffold. This

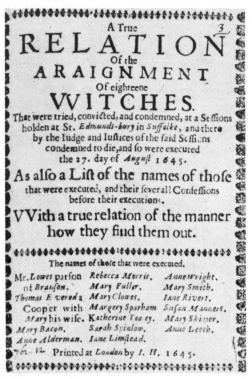

A True
RELATION
Of the
ARAIGNMENT
Of eighteene
WITCHES.

That were tried, convicted, and condemned, at a Seffions holden at St. *Edmunds-bury* in *Suffolke*, and there by the Iudge and Iuſtices of the ſaid Seffions condemned to die, and ſo were executed the 27. day of *Auguſt* 1645.

As alſo a Liſt of the names of thoſe that were executed, and their ſeverall Confeſſions before their executions.

VVith a true relation of the manner how they find them out.

The names of thoſe that were executed.

Mr. *Lowes* parſon   *Rebecca Morris*.   *Anne Wright*.
of *Branſon*.   *Mary Fuller*.   *Mary Smith*.
Thomas E vered a   *Mary Clowes*.   *Iane Rivett*.
Cooper with   *Margery Sparham*   *Suſan Manners*.
Mary his wife.   *Katherine Too ey*. *Mary Skipper*.
Mary Bacon.   *Sarah Spinlow*.   *Anne Leech*.
Anne Alderman.   *Iane Limſtead*.

Printed at *London* by *I. H.* 1645.

Title page of contemporary tract on mass trial at Bury St. Edmunds, Suffolk (1645), instigated by Matthew Hopkins. From the British Museum, London.

infamous trial is perhaps the best illustration of how demented the judges were: no suggestion was ever made to check whether any ship had foundered that day.

During the remainder of 1645, the Hopkins committee was investigating through Suffolk and Norfolk, with Hopkins hurrying from town to town and back again. He visited, for example, Aldeburgh in Suffolk on September 8 (leaving his assistant pricker, Mary Phillipps, to gather evidence) and December 20, and again on January 7, 1646. In Suffolk alone, it is estimated that he was responsible for arresting at least 124 persons for witchcraft, of whom at least 68 were hanged.

Not until April of 1646 did he receive the setback which led to the sudden termination of his career. Some earlier opposition there must have been, for in September, 1645, a Parliamentary news magazine (*The Moderate Intelligencer*) commented on the Suffolk executions: "Divers are con-demned and some executed and more like to be. Life is precious and there is need of great inquisition [inquiry] before it is taken away." However, the first open blast came in April, 1646, from John Gaule, a clergyman who resented Hopkins' incursions into Huntingdon and preached against him. Hopkins blustered and threatened: Hopkins would make a sudden descent on the town; Gaule would be forced to recant. Soon after, Gaule published his *Select Cases of Conscience*, where he exposed, *inter alia*, Hopkins' methods of torture. Hopkins' somewhat lame answers to his critics were published in a little pamphlet, *Discovery of Witches* (1647), in which he wraps up his excesses in a mantle of sanctity and legality.

As quickly as it had flared up, all at once enthusiasm and backing for Hopkins seemed to wane. He had overshot himself and, like the Salem girls when they went to Andover, accused too many. People began to suspect his integrity; judges queried him about his torturing and about his fees (which, with Stearne's, may have totaled a thousand pounds).

> And has not he, within a year,
> Hanged three score of them in one shire?
> Some only for not being drowned;
> And some for sitting above ground
> Whole nights and days upon their
> breeches,
> And feeling pain, were hanged for
> witches;
> And some for putting knavish tricks
> Upon green geese and turkey chicks,
> Or pigs that suddenly deceased
> Of griefs unnatural, as he guessed.
> —Samuel Butler, *Hudibras* (1664).

While witch trials continued, there were very few more mass trials—at least not in the eastern counties. There was an isolated outburst in Kent in 1652, when six were hanged at the Maidstone sessions. Here, however, the jurors exercised a little caution. Elizabeth Hynes of Thorpe was indicted for employing two evil spirits, one in the likeness of a white kitten called Bess and the other in the likeness of a black kitten called Katt. The jurors reported:

Difpellam

The frontispiece of the German translation (1726) of Bishop Francis Hutchinson's *Historical Essay Concerning Witchcraft* (1718), symbolizing the book's role in "dispelling" error. Devils and witches disappear in the shadows on either side.

"We do not find this to be a true bill." On the other hand, those accused of bewitching to death were still found Guilty and hanged.

Hopkins retired in the summer of 1646 to his home in Manningtree, and within a year died of tuberculosis. The legend that he himself was "swum" on suspicion of witchcraft is apocryphal. Stearne was afraid of public animosity at Manningtree and retired to Bury St. Edmunds.

The records of the years of 1645 and 1646 are incomplete, not preserved, or else lost; the pamphlet literature (including Stearne's) is not statistically reliable. It is therefore impossible to estimate how many witches were hanged as a result of Hopkins and Stearne. Thomas Ady, writing in 1656, says about a hundred were hanged at Bury St. Edmunds. One might hazard a guess of several hundreds throughout the eastern counties.

Huntingdon Witches: see Hopkins, Matthew.

Hutchinson, Francis. The man who gave the *coup de grâce* to the witch delusion in England, Francis Hutchinson, was born in Derbyshire in 1660 and educated at Cambridge. In 1692, he became vicar of St. James's at Bury St. Edmunds, the scene of the notorious witch trials in 1662 in the reign of Charles II, and earlier during the Commonwealth, in 1645, of Matthew Hopkins' mass roundups. Many local stories about these events still persisted and quickened Dr. Hutchinson's interest in witchcraft; his epoch-making *Historical Essay Concerning Witchcraft* (1718) is especially valuable for its personal records of survivors. Of this work, the American critic Notestein wrote that it "levelled a final and deadly blow at the dying superstition. Few men of intelligence dared after that avow any belief in the reality of witchcraft; it is probable that very few men even secretly cherished such a belief."

Although "the subject was irksome and unpopular, and very unpleasant," Hutchinson dedicated his *Historical Essay* to the three highest justices in England. He pointed out the large proportion of accusations, in the early witch trials, for political purposes, and later, the many trials arising from children's claiming demoniacal possession. This was one device, of course, for fighting the delusion and the *Historical Essay* was, in fact, a collection of famous trials interpreted from a pronounced skeptical point of view. By this means, it answered Boulton's credulous *Complete History of Magic* (1715). Hutchinson suggested turning the tables on the believers in witchcraft by charging those who "scratched" witches as sorcerers!

An excellent summary of the viciousness of the witchcraft trials may be gathered from Hutchinson's dedication:

If the same notions were to prevail again (and superstition is never far off), no man's life would be safe in his own house, for the fantastic doctrines that support the vulgar opinions of witchcraft rob us of all the defenses that God and Nature have placed for our security against false accusations. For in other cases, when wicked or mistaken people charge us with crimes of which we are not guilty, we clear ourselves by showing that at that time we were at home, or in some other place, about our honest business. But in prosecutions for witchcraft, that most natural and just defense is a mere jest; for if any wicked person affirms, or any crackbrained girl imagines, or any lying spirit makes her believe, that she sees any old woman, or other person pursuing her in her visions, the defenders of the vulgar witchcraft tack an imaginary, unproved compact to the deposition, and hang the accused parties for things that they were doing when they were, perhaps, asleep upon their beds, or saying their prayers, or, perhaps, in the accuser's own possession, with double irons upon them.

Hutchinson was promoted to the bishopric of Down and Connor in 1721, and immediately threw himself into administering his diocese and learning about Irish history and language. In all, he published some nineteen works, not including his sermons. Bishop Hutchinson died in 1739 at Portglenone in Ireland.

Impostors: see Children as Accusers.

Incubus. According to many Church Fathers, an incubus is an angel who fell because of lust for women. Essentially the incubus is a lewd demon or goblin which seeks sexual intercourse with women. It is also termed *follet* (French), *alp* (German), *duende* (Spanish), and *folletto* (Italian). The corresponding devil who appears to men is the succubus. When associated with one particular witch or sorcerer, both incubus and succubus are known as *magistellus*, or familiar. Inasmuch as the nightmare dream is sexual in latent content, incubus is often used interchangeably with the mare demon; in fact, the Latin word for nightmare is *incubo* (< to lie upon; compare Mod. Eng. *incubator*). The "Description of Wales" in Caxton's *Chronicle* gives an early definition in English:

That fiend that goth a-night
    Women full oft to guile,
Incubus is named by right;
    And guileth men other while,
Succubus is that wight.

The learned Guazzo, who in his *Compendium Maleficarum* (1608) discussed at some length the niceties of the theory, wrote: "[The incubus] can assume either a male or a female shape; sometimes he appears as a full-grown man, sometimes as a satyr; and if it is a woman who has been received as a witch, he generally assumes the form of a rank goat."

While the temptation to lechery was itself never doubted, considerable discussion took place in the earlier Middle Ages about the corporeal manifestation of these devils, taken over into Christianity from Hebrew lore and classical mythology. The development of the theory may have been retarded by the hesitancy of Augustine, who admitted only that these demons were "affirmed by such persons [of indubitable honesty and report], and with such confidence that it were impudence to deny it." However, Augustine believed that devils "have often injured women, desiring and acting carnally with them." One of the later demonologists, Sinistrari (died 1701), ex-

Merlin was supposed to have been fathered by the Devil. In this fourteenth-century French manuscript, the Devil is seen copulating with a woman in bed. From the Bibliothèque nationale, Paris.

plained how a spirit could become a body:

> If we seek to learn from the authorities how it is possible that the devil, who has no body, yet can perform actual coitus with man or woman, they unanimously answer that the devil assumes the corpse of another human being, male or female as the case may be, or that, from the mixture of other materials, he shapes for himself a body, endowed with motion, by means of which body he copulates with the human being.

By the thirteenth century, however, the great doctors of the Church conceded that such beings existed. Thomas Aquinas (1225-74) wrote:

> Nevertheless, if sometimes children are born from intercourse with demons, this is not because of the semen emitted by them, or from the bodies they have assumed, but through the semen taken from some man for this purpose, seeing that the same demon who acts as a succubus for a man becomes an incubus for a woman. (*Summa Theologica*)

Elsewhere, in the *De Trinitate*, it was claimed:

> Devils do indeed collect human semen, by means of which they are able to produce bodily effects; but this cannot be done without some local movement, therefore devils can transfer the semen which they have collected and inject it into the bodies of others.

Caesarius of Heisterbach believed that devils collected human semen emitted in nocturnal emissions or masturbation and used it to create new bodies for themselves. Bonaventura similarly wrote:

> Devils in the form of women [succubi] yield to males and receive their semen; by cunning skill, the demons preserve its potency, and afterwards, with the permission of God, they become incubi and pour it out into female repositories.

The incubus demons took pains to get the best quality semen. Sinistrari (without approving) summarized two late sixteenth-century writers, the Dominican Thomas Malvenda and Dr. Franciscus Valesius:

> What incubi introduce into the womb is not any ordinary human semen in normal quantity, but abundant, very thick, very warm, rich in spirits and free from serosity. This, moreover, is an easy thing for them, since they merely have to choose ardent, robust men, whose semen is naturally very copious, and with whom the succubus has relations; and then the incubus copulates with women of a like constitution, taking care that both shall enjoy a more than normal orgasm, for the greater the venereal excitement the more abundant is the semen.

Just as the ingenuity of demonologists was taxed to prove that the acts of witches were more than illusions, as the Canon Episcopi averred, so did the theorists have to labor to make the theory of the incubus as an actual lover displace the earlier idea of erotic dream. But at last they succeeded, and the rational views of Gervais of Tilbury (1214), for example, did not return until the centuries of witch hysteria were over. Only then, by the time of Louis XV, could his personal physician, De Saint André, again suggest that the incubus was partly the result of an overstimulated imagination and partly an excuse for illicit relations:

> The incubus is most frequently a chimera, which has no more basis than a

dream, a perverted imagination, and very often the invention of a woman. . . . Trickery has no less a place in the history of the incubus. To conceal her sin, a woman, a girl, a nun in name only, a debauchee, who affects the appearance of virtue, will palm off her lover for an incubus spirit which haunts her. (*Lettres au sujet de la magie, des maléfices et des sorciers*, 1725)

Such comment was a far cry from the position taken in the *Malleus Maleficarum*, which told how a nun slept with an incubus appearing to her in the shape of one Bishop Sylvanus, and "in lickerish language declared lyingly that he was the bishop." The convent accepted the bishop's explanation that some incubus had assumed his appearance. Reginald Scot, repeating the legend in his *Discovery of Witchcraft* (1584), is of the age to come, in his satirical comment: "Oh, excellent piece of witchcraft or cozening [deception] wrought by Sylvanus!"

Johann Klein (1698) related a historical trial in which the honor, not of a man, but of a woman was in question. A nobleman, Jerôme Auguste de Montléon, was absent from his wife for four years. Soon after his death, about 1636, she bore a child, which she claimed she had conceived by her husband, who impregnated her in a dream. A lower court decided the son was not the lawful heir, but the Parlement of Grenoble reversed that decision on the advice of physicians and midwives of Grenoble, who said such occurrences were possible and not infrequent. But, in a further appeal, the Faculty of the Sorbonne in Paris decided that the Grenoble court merely wished to save the lady's reputation.

The standard demonologists of the time echoed each other as they developed some new facet of the doctrine, and, as Montague Summers wrote, "range themselves in a solid phalanx of assent" about the actuality of incubi.

Martin Del Rio, S.J., in his *Disquisitionum Magicarum* (1599), wrote: "For so many have regarded this belief as axiomatic, that it must be respected, and to disagree with them is only obstinacy and fool-

Heads of Evil Demons, including the Incubus, from Francis Barrett, *The Magus* (1801). From the Library of Mr. Gerritt Lancing, New York.

hardiness; for this is the universal opinion of the fathers, theologians, and writers on philosophy, the truth of which is generally acknowledged by all ages and peoples."

Peter Binsfeld, in his *De Confessione Maleficarum* (1589), wrote: "This is an indisputable truth which not only is proved most certain by experience, but also is confirmed by history, whatever some few doctors and legal writers may suppose."

Nuns were especially subject to lecherous assaults, and as early as 1467, Alphonsus de Spina told how nuns would be visited during the night by incubi and, waking up in the morning, "find themselves polluted just as if they had commingled with a man [*si cum viris miscerentur*]." The confession box, according to Thomas of Cantimpré, was also a favorite place of solicitation by the incubus. Sinistrari told of a nun who was observed to lock herself in her cell after dinner. An inquisitive sister followed her and "presently she heard a sound, as of two voices conversing in subdued tones (which she could easily do, since the two cells were divided but by a slight partition), then a certain noise [*une sonorété vaginal*], the creaking of a bed, groans and sighs, as of two lovers in an orgasm of love." Inspection by the abbess revealed no one in the cell. But the inquisitive nun bored a hole in the partition, "and what should she espy but a comely youth lying with the nun, a sight she took good care to let the others enjoy by the same means." Threats of torture produced a confession that the nun had long been "indecently intimate with an incubus."

Stories of attacks by incubi on women saints in the early Church are not uncommon. St. Margaret of Cortona, for example, was beset just like St. Anthony and St. Hilary [see Succubus]: "Following her about her cell as she wept and prayed, the devil sang the most dirty songs, and indecently encouraged this handmaid of Christ, crying and commending herself to God, to sing along with him . . . but by prayers and tears she repulsed and drove out the tempter."

Two stories about incubi warrant retelling.

One occurs in *Sancti Bernardi Vita Secunda.* When St. Bernard arrived at Nantes in 1135 for a visitation, a distraught woman implored him for help. It appeared that for six years she had enjoyed intercourse with an incubus; in the seventh year her husband discovered her infidelity and left her. The devil persisted in his attentions. Bernard advised her to take his staff to bed with her. That night the devil was unable to get near her, and in rage threatened dire reprisals after Bernard had left. But Bernard called together the congregation and solemnly anathematized the incubus never to solicit this or any other woman again. As the congregation extinguished the lighted candles they held in their hands, the powers of the incubus were likewise snuffed out. The *Vita* does not report whether the husband rejoined his wife. Her liaison might have remained undiscovered, had she been like the women questioned by the Inquisitor Sylvester Prierias, who by sleeping on the left side of the bed never awakened the husband during their extra-marital activities. Intercourse with an incubus justified annulment (i.e., divorce)—it also justified burning. Pott, however, quoted a rare trial from Meiningen in 1613, where the woman was not burned and the husband was told he was free to remarry [see Jewish Witchcraft].

Another story was given by the Cistercian prior Caesarius of Heisterbach (who repeated the St. Bernard legend) in his *Dialogus* (about 1230). Caesarius vouched for this tale, as did his abbot and his fellow monk Gerard. A priest at Bonn had a very lovely daughter whom, to preserve from the excessively ardent desires of the young canons, he kept locked in an upper story of the house whenever he was absent. But a devil in the shape of a man had no trouble gaining access and enjoying her. At last the girl repented and confessed to her father, who sent her to the other side of the Rhine. The incubus then appeared to her father, saying, "Wicked priest, why have you taken my wife from me? You have done this to your own hurt." Thereupon he smote the priest on the chest so that he died the third day afterward.

The attitude of the incubus of Caesarius' story implied some gratification on the devil's part, but from Thomas Aquinas on, it was generally believed that devils had such connections only to degrade the human and show their hatred of God (*Summa Theologica*). The early apocryphal *Acts* of the Apostle Thomas contained a story similar to that told of Bernard: When Thomas bade an incubus depart, the demon complained that he would have to find another woman after the apostle had gone away or else return to his original lady (whom he had possessed every single night for five years!). And there was evidence that the demons must have felt some physical pleasure in that they were strongly attracted to women with beautiful hair (compare I Corinthians xi. 10, where *angelos* was equated with *incubos*). William of Auvergne commented, with a touch of wit, that it was not lust alone that made demons seek women, for if they so desired they could be better served among themselves. Prierias, in *De Strigimagis* (1521), carried William's suggestion much further in ascribing a remarkable vice to the demons: "It is obvious that everywhere the *strigimagae* demons, who practice obscenities of every kind, add another most foul, that is, an incubus demon makes use of a double penis [*membro genitali bifurcato*] so that he abuses himself simultaneously with both organs."

The Church was concerned to know the attitude of the women in order to classify their sin. The *Malleus Maleficarum* (1486) made three divisions: (1) those who submit voluntarily, as witches; (2) those brought against their will by witches to sleep with incubi; and (3) those assaulted against their will. Priests sometimes noted that girls were not quite as eager as they might be to rid themselves of their obsession, even when they asked for spiritual help.

> In 1643 I was ordered by my ecclesiastical superiors to exorcize a young girl of twenty years of age, who was pursued by an incubus. She acknowledged without evasion everything this impure devil had done with her. But after what she told me, I came to the opinion that in spite of her denials she had given the demon some indirect encouragement. Indeed, she was always forewarned of his coming by a violent over-excitation of the sexual organs, and then, instead of having recourse to prayer, she ran straight to her room and threw herself on her bed. I tried to rouse in her some feeling of trust in God, but I did not succeed, and she seemed almost to be afraid of being delivered from the devil. (Delassus, *Les Incubes*, 1897)

A young witch at Rostock, in 1698, had a new demon lover every few years; she summoned her incubus whenever she wished by calling, *"Komm Raster und Knaster mie."*

When the inquisitorial witch trials reached their full stride, copulation with an incubus was an act expected of a witch, and so women were tortured until they made such a confession. At this stage the most fantastic and wild accounts were related, and incubi litter the reports of the demonologists [see further, Sexual Relations with Devils].

Because the incubus was a different species, intercourse with him was condemned as buggery or bestiality, a far worse sin than fornication or adultery (contrast Sinistrari). As Alphonsus Liguori, followed by numerous jurists of the seventeenth century, in his *Theologia Mo-*

ralis explained, "Sin with a succubus or incubus is called bestiality; to which sin is added also malice against religion, sodomy, adultery, and incest." To bolster this theory, many accounts of the monsters, half human, half animal, born of such unions, were freely circulated.

Some of the above accounts show that the incubus demons were repulsed by the powers of the Church, for example, through anathema or by prayer. But Sinistrari believed incubi and succubi "do not obey the exorcists, have no dread of exorcisms, show no reverence for holy things, at the approach of which they are not in the least overawed. . . . Sometimes they even laugh at exorcisms, strike at the exorcists themselves, and rend the sacred vestments." Sinistrari drew from his personal experience to tell how a persistent incubus wooed a beautiful and virtuous matron of Pavia, tempting her with amorous words and loving kisses so light and soft "that she might have fancied being stroked by the finest feather-down." Even after exorcism and benediction of the house, the demon lover continued his attentions, and, now irked, resorted to poltergeist actions. He collected roofing stones and built a wall round the bed so high that "the couple were unable to leave their bed without using a ladder." Some of the later demonologists held that only the lowest order of devils functioned as incubi. This belief may have been related to the idea that the less intelligent and less sensitive devils could not be exorcized. A partial parallel is seen in the poltergeists, which hold little respect for Christian rites. Indeed, the twentieth-century demonologist Montague Summers suggested that the Drummer of Tedworth, the Epworth Poltergeist, and other similar agents might be the incubus, "a very pestering and pothersome bogle."

The superstitions of incubus, mare, werewolf, and vampire are all related, since in each the desire for sexual satisfaction is in varying degrees repressed [see further, Nightmare]. Repression ranges from the slight substitution in the incubus dream to the most complete transmutation in the nightmare and the morbid reactions of sad-

ism in the werewolf obsession. But, because
the conception of a demon lover is of such
universal appeal, the incubus, in the literature of the demonologists, takes first place.

Indictment. The indictments printed below are typical of the formal charges made
against persons accused of witchcraft in
England (and America). The indictment
differed from a presentment, which, according to William Lambard's *Eirenarcha*
(1614), was a "mere denunciation [by] the
jurors themselves . . . without any other
information." The indictment, however, was
"the verdict of the jurors grounded upon the
accusation of a third person . . . their
finding of a bill of accusation to be true."
William West in his *Simboleography*
(1594) added that the indictment "is made
to the end to compel the party accused to answer thereunto." In Scotland, the indictment
was called a *dittay*. In England, present-
ments were generally written in English,
and indictments (except from 1651 to
1659) in Latin; after 1731 English was
used for both.

Since many local courts seldom encountered certain crimes, and since court officials
might be uncertain of the correct Latin
forms and references, William West's volume reproduced several hundred typical indictments. All that was necessary was to fill
in the names and dates, copy the Latin, and
the court would have an adequate legal
document. Witchcraft is only one of many
crimes West recognized, such as "taking
of pheasants and partridges with nets and
other engines in another man's freehold
without license," "absence from church for
six months," "forcible entry," and "man-
slaughter." One wonders what kind of society Elizabethan England comprised if
West included specimen indictments which
he expected to be much used:

An inquisition of murder found before a coroner upon the view of the body
slain, against one for killing of his mistress with a hatchet on the head, she
being then great with child.

Against one for publishing that the
Queen hath two or three children by the
Lord R.D.

Buggery committed by a minister,
being an Italian, born in the city of
Rome, with a boy of fifteen years.

Against one for breaking of a house,
and murdering of one with a cudgel in
his bed, by privity and consent of the
wife of the murdered.

West's sample Latin indictments for
witchcraft correspond to those used, for
example, in the trial of the Lancashire
Witches in 1612, and, curiously enough,
in the indictments of Ralph Hall and his
wife in New York in 1665 and of Martha
Cory in Salem in 1692, which translated
almost word for word one of West's examples.

SPECIMEN INDICTMENT I, TRANSLATED
FROM THE LATIN

For bewitching a horse, whereby he
wasted and became worse.

It is enquired, for our sovereign lady
the Queen, whether N.N. of N. town,
in the country of N., widow, on the x
day of the x month in the x year of the
said reign of our sovereign lady Elizabeth, &c., some most malicious arts,
called in English enchantments and
charms, within the said town of the abovesaid county of N., maliciously and
diabolically, in, upon, and against a
certain horse, of white color, valued at
four pounds of the goods and chattels
of one M.M. of the said town of N., in
the said county of N., exercised, practiced, and used. Through which the same
horse of the said M.M. on the said x
day, within the said town of N., became
much worse and wasted, against the
peace of our said sovereign lady the
Queen and against the laws of the statute
in such cases made and provided.

SPECIMEN INDICTMENT II, TRANSLATED
FROM THE LATIN

For killing a man by witchcraft upon
the statute of Anno 5 of the Queen.

The jurors for our sovereign lady the
Queen present that N.N., of N. town,
in the county of N., widow, the x day
of the x month, in the x year of the
reign of our sovereign lady, Elizabeth,

by the grace of God, Queen of England, &c., and divers other days since the said day, certain detestable arts, called in English witchcraft and sorcery, did maliciously and feloniously practice and exercise, at and within the town of N., in the county of N. aforesaid, in, upon, and against one M.M., of N. town, in the said county of N., laborer, through which same arts the said M.M. from the x day of the x month, the x year abovesaid, most dangerously and mortally sickened and languished; and on the x day of the x month of the year abovesaid, the same M.M. through the aforesaid arts died in the said county of N. And so the said jurors do present that the same N.N., of the aforesaid town, by ways and means above stated, by her malice, as is suspected, voluntarily, maliciously, and feloniously through the said arts killed and murdered the same M.M. within the town of N., against the peace of our said sovereign lady the Queen and against the laws of the statute in the said Parliament of our lady the Queen, held at Westminster in the county of Middlesex in the fifth year of her reign aforesaid, in such cases made and provided.

After trial, the indictment was endorsed with the verdict, either *billa vera,* a true bill, or *ignoramus,* ignored or thrown out, or "no true bill." The prisoner usually pleaded Not Guilty—*Po[nit] se [super patriam de bono et malo]*. The verdict was given as (*non*) *cul[pabilis]*, with the standard notation: *ca[talla nulla]*, has no goods for forfeiture. Execution was indicated by *Jud[iciu]m [secundum formam statuti]*.

The following document against Martha Cory in 1692 is typical of the later American indictments and shows the English pattern still in use nearly a hundred years after the statute of 1604 (Woodward, *Records,* 1864).

INDICTMENT AGAINST MARTHA CORY OF SALEM, 1692.

Province of the Massachusetts Bay in New England, Anno Regis et Reginae Willm. et Maria, nunc Anglice &c., Anno quarto.

Essex SS.

The jurors for our sovereign lord and lady, the King and Queen, present that Martha Cory, wife of Giles Cory of Salem, husbandman, the 21st day of March, in the fourth year of the reign of our sovereign lord and lady, William and Mary, by the grace of God, of England, Scotland, France, and Ireland, King and Queen, Defenders of the Faith, &c., and divers other days and times as well before as after, certain detestable arts, called witchcrafts and sorceries, wickedly and feloniously hath used, practiced, and exercised, at and within the township of Salem, in the county of Essex, aforesaid, in, upon, and against one Elizabeth Hubbard of Salem, single woman, by which said wicked arts the said Elizabeth Hubbard, the 21st day of March, in the year abovesaid, and divers other days and times as well before as after, was and is tortured, afflicted, pined, consumed and tormented; and also for sundry other acts of witchcraft by the said Martha Cory, committed and done before and since that time, against the peace of our sovereign lord and lady, the King and Queen, their crown and dignity, and against the form of the statute in that case made and provided. Witnesses:

Elizabeth Hubbard and Jury of Women's Return.

Mercy Lewis; Ann Putnam; Edward Putnam; Ezechiel Cheever.

Informers. At St. Albans in 1649, John Palmer, before he was hanged as a witch, named fourteen men and women as accomplices:

In Hitchin, he reckons two, Mary Bychance and Widow Palmer. In Norton, John Salmon, senior, Joseph Salmon, and Judith his wife; John Lamen, senior, and Mary his wife; John Lamen, junior; Mary the daughter of John Lamen, senior; Joan Lamen, the daughter of the aforesaid John Lamen; and the wife of one Mayer in Weston. And at the place of execution he confessed two more, Sarah Smith and Anne Smith, servants, the one to Mr. Beaumont, the other to Mr. Reynolds. (*The Devil's Delusions,* 1649)

What is unusual in this account is that all fourteen were not hanged as witches, for being accused by a convicted witch was strong presumption of guilt. Yet, for example, John Lamen died in 1688, Mary Lamen in 1706, Joseph Salmon in 1684, and Judith Salmon in 1692. Such laxity or neglect in pursuing leads would not have happened on the Continent. Again, at the trial of the St. Osyth witches in 1582, Ursula Kempe was accused of laming a servant girl. On interrogation by a determined judge, Mrs. Kempe named as witches some of her acquaintances, who in turn implicated others, until fourteen women were imprisoned. But out of this alleged coven, only two were hanged, on indictments of multiple murders.

Informers had more success in Scotland. Writing of the witches indicted in 1678 for bewitching Sir George Maxwell, Bishop Francis Hutchinson (1720) noted that "one who was the first that confessed, was pardoned, and used for a witness against the others." All six named by the pardoned witch were executed. A century earlier, at the North Berwick trials in 1590, Gilly Duncan, after severe torture by her employer, confessed to being a witch and named many people as notorious witches. The charges mushroomed until seventy people were accused. At the Aberdeen Trials in 1597, many of the twenty-four men and women burned were originally accused by a convicted witch, who tried to extend her life span by co-operating with the judges.

Scotland encouraged faceless informers by a practice praised by the French demonologist Bodin, who wished it copied throughout Europe, and not merely in Milan. It was described by Reginald Scot in his *Demonology* (1584):

A hollow piece of wood or a chest is placed in the church into which anybody may freely cast a little scroll of paper, wherein may be contained the name of the witch, the time, place, and fact, etc. And the same chest, being locked with three several locks, is opened every fifteenth day by three inquisitors or officers appointed for that purpose, which keep three several keys. And thus the accuser need not be known, nor shamed with the reproach of slander or malice to his poor neighbor.

Informers were most widespread in Germany. In the early seventeenth century, Friedrich von Spee, the Jesuit confessor to so many burned as witches in the Rhineland, wrote how the prisoner was "compelled to accuse others whom she does not know, whose names are frequently put into her mouth by the investigators or suggested by the executioner, or of whom she heard as suspected or accused. These in turn are forced to accuse others, and these still others." A notary kept a record of all names mentioned during the trial. The special witch judge, Balthasar Ross, appointed in 1603 by the Prince-Abbot of Fulda, secured new victims by this kind of questioning:

Refresh your memory! Have you not seen at the sabbat so-and-so from such-and-such a street? Don't be afraid to name them. You have not been spared, not you! And the rich will get what's coming to them just like the poor."

In 1628, the burgomaster of Bamberg, Johannes Junius, pleaded he did not know the names of those with him at the witches' sabbat. The judges thereupon ordered him taken through the streets to recognize witches. On one street alone he was forced to pick out eight persons.

From his vast knowledge of the manuscripts of court trials in Germany, George L. Burr summed up the prevailing practices:

No confession was complete and no witch released from her agony until accomplices had been named. Nor were they satisfied with one or two only. I have read a list of no less than 150 accomplices taken down from the lips of a single witch; and I know of several others who accused upward of 100 each. A record of confessions kept by one local court during the space of seven years . . . contains some 6,000 accusations from about 300 witches, that is to say, an average of twenty apiece. Under such circumstances you can see how the witch trials must go on multiplying, when once the ball was set rolling.

In spite of the prohibition by the imperial law, the Carolina Code (1532) of Charles V, in the German cities people were tortured to secure names. This inquisitorial practice was justified by most of the demonologists. Thus, Bodin believed that "no rules should be observed in so heinous a crime," and that informers should be encouraged, even with promises of immunity or diminished punishment (if the informer was likewise a witch). The pattern had been set in the mid-fifteenth century when a professor of law, Vignati (1468), told how one man confessed to witchcraft and implicated many others, on the strength of which accusations the inquisitors tortured those named into confessions of guilt. This incident Vignati related from firsthand knowledge.

If a man or woman knew he was reputed to be a witch, he had to appeal to the local civil or ecclesiastical court for a hearing; otherwise his silence would be taken as admission of guilt. When the alleged witch appealed to the courts, he would be tortured into confessing he was so indeed. Le Sieur Bouvet observed that denial of guilt was a valid reason for increasing and continuing the torture. Once accused, there was very little hope of escape.

In England it was legally possible for a wealthy person accused as a witch to fight back at the perjurer, but most people lacked the money to seek redress and had to suffer the consequences of ill repute. C. L'Estrange Ewen, who has done so much original research on seventeenth-century English witch trials, commented:

There is ample evidence that a great number of the informations laid originated in nothing more than spite, it becoming recognized that a person once apprehended on a charge of witchcraft might remain in jail until death from cold, hunger, or disease terminated his or her suffering, even if the hangman did not have occasion to exercise his office. (*Witchcraft in the Star Chamber*, 1938)

"But one needed only to be envied in those days. It was malice and jealousy which oftenest dictated the names denounced in that torture chamber. Wealth, learning, beauty, goodness, these were often the very conditions of accusation."
—George Lincoln Burr (1886)

There was a trickle of lawsuits where an alleged witch won damages. For example, in the King's Bench in 1614, Richard Ellson took action against Richard Moore for saying, "Richard Ellson is a witch and he hath bewitched my son," and was awarded damages and £6 1s. 2d. costs. John Lowes, the parson who was finally hanged in the Hopkins hysteria in 1645, had some years earlier won the considerable sum of £45 18s. 10d. for damages and costs for defamation as a witch. In 1658, Rosamond Swayne sued Richard Atkinson for calling her a witch and claimed £100 damages for clearing her name; the verdict is not known.

A few similar cases occurred in the United States.

In 1656 in Virginia, a clergyman from Scotland brought action for slander against William Harding, who had called him a witch. Harding was sentenced to ten lashes and banishment from the colony.

At Cambridge in 1660, Mrs. Winifred Holman, an aged widow, sued her neighbors, the Gibson family, who said she was a witch. The result of her suit is not known.

Ralph and Mary Hall [see New York Witches] were accused of witchcraft in 1664, but the Brookhaven magistrates not only dismissed the charges, but decided that the plaintiff "hath not sufficiently made good what he hath said of her, and therefore [he] is ordered to pay the woman five marks."

At the Andover trials, contemporaneous with Salem, "a worthy gentleman" of Boston was accused. He brought action for defamation of character and claimed £1,000 damages. When his friends at Andover started collecting evidence for his suit, the accusations ceased, and in fact similar accusations of witchcraft against others decreased.

The final discrediting of false witnesses or informers came on October 17, 1711, when the General Court reversed "several convictions, judgments, and attainders" against some of those executed at Salem, and in December appropriated £578 12s. 0d. to pay reparations.

See also Confessions, Evidence, Torture, Witnesses.

Innocent VIII, Pope. Pope Innocent VIII (1484-92) issued one of the key documents in the history of witchcraft, the papal bull of December 5, 1484, "*Summis desiderantes affectibus* [Desiring with the most profound anxiety]." "It fastened on European jurisprudence for nearly three centuries the duty of combating the Devil and saving mankind from his clutches . . . it served as justification for pitiless persecution." (Hansen)

Not until several centuries after the Canon Episcopi of A.D. 906, did the Popes begin to promulgate belief in witchcraft, expressly forbidden by this earlier canon. One of the first papal bulls was that of 1233 by Pope Gregory IX to the Dominican Conrad of Marburg, who, in effect (according to Montague Summers), introduced the Inquisition into Germany. Two bulls by Pope Alexander IV in 1258 and 1260 cautioned both Franciscan and Dominican inquisitors to distinguish witchcraft from heresy. During the fourteenth and fifteenth centuries, almost every pope issued bulls against sorcery, most of them against specified individuals or groups, for example: John XXII (1316-34); Benedict XII (1334-42); Gregory XI (1370-78); Alexander V (1409-10); Martin V (1417-31); Eugenius IV (1431-47) with four bulls; Nicholas V (1447-55); Calixtus III (1455-58); and Pius II (1458-64). Only one of these bulls need be noted here, that of Eugenius IV in 1437 addressed to all inquisitors, which shows the growing belief in the varied aspects of *maleficia*, but which makes no mention of transvection, incubi, or the sabbat (perhaps first remarked in a papal bull in 1500 by Alexander VI).

Sixtus IV, refuting certain Carmelites,

was the first to equate sorcery and black magic positively with heresy, thereby facilitating the task of the witch hunters, in three bulls in 1473, 1478, and 1483.

Thus the bull of Innocent VIII follows a long line of apostolic letters condemning witches, but assumes far greater importance than these earlier pronouncements because of the rapid spread of printing. As Sir Walter Scott said, "It rang the tocsin against this formidable crime." This bull was prefixed to the textbook of the two inquisitors Innocent VIII had appointed to Germany, *Malleus Maleficarum* [*The Hammer of Witches*]. Since this book went into new editions every few years, the letter of Innocent VIII had a circulation never before possible with earlier bulls. Furthermore, the previous bulls had been restricted to specific localities; the new one covered whole provinces.

In this respect, "*Summis desiderantes affectibus*" is a milestone that finally marked the reversal of the Canon Episcopi. This Canon was retained in Canon Law, however, and hence was a potential block to the inquisitors.

In this bull, the Pope complains that the work of his two Dominican inquisitors, Heinrich Kramer and Jakob Sprenger, lacked support because—a surprising admission—neither clergy nor laity were convinced of the extent and crime of witchcraft in Germany; hence, now, everyone will support their investigations, or else "upon him will fall the wrath of God Almighty."

Innocent VIII, Giovanni Battista Cibo (1432-92), a Genoese, took service under a cardinal, became a bishop by thirty-five, and by forty-one a cardinal himself. In August, 1484, he was elected Pope, and reigned until his death. In his last months he kept alive by sucking milk from a woman's breasts. An attempt to rejuvenate him by blood transfusions resulted in the deaths of three boys. Contemporary Catholic chroniclers (like Burchard) hold no brief for his character, noting that he kept a mistress by whom he had two children; he married the boy into the Medici family and the girl to his Papal treasurer. Such was the man who within a few months of

Tenoz bulle apoſtolice aduerſus hereſim
maleficarum cum approbatione t ſubſcriptione doctozũ alme vniuerſitatis Colonien. in ſequentem tractatum Incipit feliciter.

Innocentius epus ſeruus ſeruozũ dei. Ad futuram rei memozia3. Summis deſiderantes affectib3, put paſtozalis ſollicitudinis cura requirit. vt fides catholica noſtris potiſſime tpibꝰ. vbiꝗ augeaf t flozeat. ac omnis heretica prauitas. de finibꝰ fideliũ pcul pellatur. ea libenter peclaramus. ac etiũ de nouo concedimus. ꝓ que bmõi pui ꝺeſideriũ noſtrũ votiuũ ſoztiatur effectũ. cũctiſꝗ ꝗ erea ꝓ noſtre opationis miniſteriũ. quaſi per puidi opatiois ſarculũ. errozibꝰ ertirpatis. ciuſdẽ fidei zelus. t obſeruantia in ipoz cozda fideliũ foztius imprimatur. Sane nup ad noſtrũ nõ fine graui moleſtia puenit auditu. ꝗ in nõnullis ptibꝰ Alamanie ſupiozis. necnõ in Woguntin. Colonien. Treuerẽ. Salzburgẽ. t Bremeñ. puinciꝗs. ciuitatibꝰ. terris locis t ꝺiocceſibꝰ. qã plurescv triuſꝗs ſexus perſone. ꝓpe ſalutis immemozes ta fide catholica deui antes. cum demonibꝰ incubis t ſuccubis abutẽ. ac ſuis incantationibꝰ. carminibꝰ. t cõiurationibꝰ alyſꝗs nephandis ſupſticys t ſoztilegys. ececeſſibꝰ.criminibꝰ t ꝺelictis. mulierũ ꝓtus. animaliũ fetus. terre fruges. vinearũ vuas. t arbozũ fructus. nec nõ homines mulieres. iumenta. pecoza.pecudes. talia ꝺiuerſozũ generũ animalia. vineas quoꝗs pomeria. prata. paſcua. blada. frumẽta talia terre legumina pire ſuffozari. tettingui facere t pcurare. ipaſꝗs hoies mulieres. iumenta. pecoza. pecudes. t an̄malia. ꝺiris tam intrinſecis ꝗ ettrinſecis doloribꝰ t tozmentis afficere t ecruciare. ac eoſd bores ne gignere. t mulieres ne concipe. viroſꝗs ne vrozibꝰ. t mulieres ne viris. actus cõiugales reddere valeant impedire. Fidem pterea ipam quã in ſacri ſuſceptione baptiſmi ſuſceperũt oze ſacrilego abnegare. Aliaꝗs quãplurima nefandẜ. ececeſſus. zer umina uitꝗsgaate hamini generis inimico cõmittere t ꝓpetrare nõ vereatur. in animarũ ſuaꝗ piculum. ꝺiuine maieſtatis offenſam. ac pniicioſum ececemplũ t ſcandalũ plurimozꝗ. Qⁿ ꝗ3 licꝗs dilectⁱ fily Henrici inſtitozis in ꝓdictis ptibꝰ Alamanie ſupiozis. i quibꝰ etiã puincie. ciuitates. terre. ꝺyoc. t alia loca bmõi cõꝓhenſa foze cenſentur. necnõ Jacobus ſprenger ꝓ certas partes lineã rheni oʒdinis fratrũ pꝺicatoz t theologie pſeſſoʒes. heretice prauitatis inꝗſitozes. ꝓ lꝉas apoſtolicas ꝺeputati fuerint. put adhuc etiãt. tñ nõnulli clerici t layci. illarũ pⁱũ qrentes plura ſapere ꝗ ꝯopozteat. ꝓ co ꝗ̃ in litteris ꝺeputationis bmõi. puincie. ciuitates. ꝺyoc. terre talia loca pꝺicta. illarũꝗ3 pſone. ac ececeſſus bmõi. noiatim t ſpecifice ececꝓeſſa nõ fuerunt. illa ſub eiſdem ptibꝰ minime cõtineri. t ꝓpterea pſatis inꝗſitozibꝰ.in puinciys ciuitatibus.ꝺyoce. terris t locis pꝺictis. bmõi inꝗſitionis officiũ. erequi nõ licere. t ad pſonarũ carũdem.super ececeſſibus t criminibus antedictis. punitionẽ.incarceratione. t correctione admitti nõ ꝺebere ꝓtinaciter aſſerere nõ erubeſcũt. Proter ꝗd in puinciys.ciuitatibus. ꝺyoc.terris t locis pꝺictis ececeſſus t crimina bmõi.nõ ſine animarũ carũdem euidẽti iactura. teterne ſalutis diſpendio remanẽt impunita. Flos igitur impedimẽta ꝗlibet ꝗ̃ per ipozũ inquiſitoz officiũ erecutio.quomõlibet retardari poſſet ꝺe medio ſubmouere. t ne labes heretice prauitatis alioꝗsꝗs ececeſſuũ bmõi in pniciem alioꝗ. innocentiũ ſua venena diffundat.opoztunis remedys put noſtro incũbit officio.puidere volentes.fidei zelo ad hoc maime nos impellente. ne ꝓterea ꝓtingat. Prouincias.ciuitates. ꝺyoc.terras. tloca pꝺicta ſub eiſdẽ ptibꝰ Alamanie ſupiozis ꝺeb.to inquiſitõnis officio carere eiſdẽ inquiſitozibus.in illis officiũ inquiſitionis.bmõi erequi licere. t ad pſonarũ carũdem ſup ececeſſibus t criminibus pꝺictis. correctione incarceratione. t punitione admitti ꝺebere. ꝓinde in omnibus t p omnia. ac ſi in litteris pꝺictis. puincie. ciuitates. ꝺyoc. terre t loca ac pſone t ececeſſus bmõi. noiatim t ſpecifice ececꝓeſſa fozent. auctoritate aplica tenoze pſentiũ ſtatuimus. ꝓcꝗs potioⁱ cautela. litteras t ꝺeputationis pꝺictas.ad puincias ciuitates ꝺyoc.terras t loca.necnõ pſonas. t crimina bmõi ececendẽte. Prefatis inꝗſitozibus.ꝗ̃ ipi t alter coꝗ.accerſito ſecũ dilecto filio Johanne gremper clerico Conſtañ. ꝺyoc.magiſtro in artibus coꝗ moderno. ſeu quouis alio notario publico.ꝓ ipos t quemlibet coꝗ.ꝓ tpe ꝺeputando in puinciys ciuitatibus ꝺyoc.terris.tlocis pꝺictis.ꝗstra quaſcũꝗs pſonas. cuiuſcũꝗs cõditionis ꝗ pemineⁿte fuerint. bmõi inꝗſitionis officiũ erequi. ipaſꝗs pſonas quas in pmiſſis culpabiles repererint. iuꝗta earũ ꝺemerita.cozrigere incarcerare.punire.t mulctare. Flecnõ in ſingulis puinciaꝗ bmõi par

The Bull of Pope Innocent VIII, printed in the second edition of the *Malleus Maleficarum*, about 1490 somewhere in southern Germany, which gave great prestige to the inquisitors, Kramer and Sprenger. From Cornell University Library.

his election started the inquisition against witches.

THE BULL OF INNOCENT VIII

Innocent, bishop, servant of the servants of God, for a perpetual remembrance.

Desiring with the most profound anxiety, even as pastoral solicitude requires, that the Catholic Faith should especially in our time everywhere increase and flourish, and that all heretical depravity should be driven away from the territories of the faithful, we very gladly proclaim and even restate those particular means and methods whereby our Christian endeavor may be fulfilled; since, when all errors have been rooted out by our toil as with the hoe of a provident husbandman, a zeal for and devotion to our Faith may take hold all the more strongly on the hearts of the faithful.

It has recently come to our attention, not without bitter sorrow, that in some parts of northern Germany, as well as in the provinces, townships, territories, districts, and dioceses of Mainz, Cologne, Treves, Salzburg, and Bremen, many persons of both sexes, unmindful of their own salvation and deviating from the Catholic Faith, have abused themselves with devils, incubi and succubi, and by their incantations, spells, conjurations, and other accursed superstitions and horrid charms, enormities and offenses, destroy the offspring of women and the young of cattle, blast and eradicate the fruits of the earth, the grapes of the vine and the fruits of trees; nay, men and women, beasts of burden, herd beasts, as well as animals of other kinds; also vineyards, orchards, meadows, pastures, corn, wheat, and other cereals of the earth. Furthermore, these wretches afflict and torment men and women, beasts of burden, herd beasts, as well as cattle of all other kinds, with pain and disease, both internal and external; they hinder men from generating and women from conceiving; whence neither husbands with their wives nor wives with their husbands can perform the sexual act. Above and beyond this, they blasphemously renounce that Faith which they received by the Sacrament of Baptism, and at the instigation of the Enemy of the human race they do not shrink from committing and perpetrating the foulest abominations and excesses to the peril of their souls, whereby they offend the Divine Majesty and are a cause of scandal and dangerous example to very many.

And although our beloved sons Heinrich Kramer [Institor] and Jakob Sprenger, Professors of Theology, of the Order of Friars Preachers, have been by Letters Apostolic delegated as inquisitors of these heretical depravities, and still are inquisitors, the former in the aforesaid parts of northern Germany, wherein are included those aforesaid provinces, townships, districts, dioceses, and other specified localities, and the latter in certain territories which border the Rhine, nevertheless not a few clerics and lay folk of those countries, seeking to know more than concerns them, since in the aforesaid delegatory letters there is no express and individual mention by name of these provinces, townships, districts, dioceses, and other specified localities; and further since the two delegates themselves and the abominations they are to encounter are not designated specifically and expressly, these persons are not ashamed to pertinaciously assert that these enormities are not practiced in these provinces, and consequently the aforesaid inquisitors have no legal right to exercise their power of inquisition in the provinces, townships, districts, dioceses, and territories, which have been rehearsed, and

that the inquisitors may not proceed to punish, imprison, and correct those convicted of the offenses and wickednesses set forth. Accordingly, in the aforesaid provinces, townships, districts and dioceses, the abominations and enormities in question remain unpunished not without evident danger to their souls and loss of eternal salvation.

Wherefore we, as is our duty, desirous to remove all hindrances and obstacles whatsoever by which the work of the inquisitors may be impeded, as also to apply potent remedies to prevent the disease of heresy and other turpitudes diffusing their poison to the destruction of other innocent souls, as our position demands and marked by the greatest zeal for the Faith, lest the provinces, townships, dioceses, districts and territories of those parts of northern Germany, which we have specified, be deprived of the benefits of the Holy Office of the Inquisition thereto assigned, by the tenor of these presents by our apostolic authority, we decree and enjoin that the aforesaid inquisitors be empowered to proceed to the correction, imprisonment, and punishment of any persons for the said abominations and enormities, without let or hindrance, in every way as if the provinces, townships, dioceses, districts, territories, yea, even the persons and their crimes in this kind were named and specifically designated in our letters.

Moreover, for greater surety we extend these letters deputing this authority to cover all the aforesaid provinces, townships, dioceses, districts, and territories, and also persons, and crimes newly rehearsed, and we grant permission to the aforesaid inquisitors, to each separately or to both, as also to our dear son John Gremper, priest of the diocese of Constance, Master of Arts, their notary [*modernus*], or to any other public notary, who shall be by them, or by one of them, temporarily delegated to these provinces, townships, dioceses, districts, and aforesaid territories, to proceed, according to the regulations of the Inquisition, against such persons of whatsoever rank and high estate they may be, and to correct, punish, imprison, and mulct, as their crimes merit, those whom they have found guilty.

Moreover, they shall enjoy a full and

perfect faculty of expounding and preaching the word of God to the faithful, so often as opportunity may offer and it may seem good to them, in cach and every parish church of the said provinces, and they shall freely and legally perform any rites or execute any business which may appear advisable in the aforesaid cases. By our supreme authority we grant them once again full and complete faculties.

And by Letters Apostolic we require our venerable brother, the Bishop of Strasbourg, [Albrecht von Bayern], that he himself shall announce, or by some other or others cause to be announced, the substance of our bull, which he shall solemnly publish when and as often as he considers necessary or when he shall be requested to do so by the inquisitors or by one of them. Nor shall he permit them to be molested or hindered by any authority whatsoever, in disobedience to the tenor of these letters presented, but he shall threaten all who hinder or harass or oppose the inquisitors, all rebels, of whatsoever rank, estate, station, preeminence, dignity, excellence, or condition they may be, or whatsoever privilege or exemption they may claim, with excommunication, suspension, interdict, and yet more terrible penalties, censures, and punishments, as may seem good to him, without any right of appeal, and also by our authority proceed to and heed these decisions as frequently as he pleases, calling in, if it is necessary, the help of the secular arm.

Let no obstacle whatever be set against these apostolic letters and ordinances. Let no man therefore in any way rashly oppose this page contrary to this declaration extending our authority and injunction. But if any man dare do so, let him know that on him will fall the wrath of God Almighty and the blessed Apostles Peter and Paul.

Given at Rome, at St. Peter's, on December 5 of the Year of the Incarnation of Our Lord one thousand four hundred and eighty-four, in the first year of our pontificate.

Inquisition. Were it not for the Inquisition, the Catholic tribunal charged with exposing and punishing religious unorthodoxy, not one person would have died for witchcraft. All later trials, secular and ecclesiastical, Protestant and Catholic, stem from early inquisitorial patterns, culminating in the Bull of 1484 of Pope Innocent VIII.

When Christianity became the state church of the Roman Empire, the new religion extended the intolerance to which hitherto it had been subject. By A.D. 430 the civil code was ordering death for heresy, although such laws were not rigorously enforced until many centuries later. In 1144, Pope Lucius II was uncertain and unconcerned about the proper penalty for heresy. Yet only forty years later, in 1184, Pope Lucius III created the earliest *episcopal* inquisition and ordered bishops to make systematic inquiry or *inquisitio* into deviation from the official teaching of the Church. Any persons "found marked by suspicion alone" had to prove their innocence or else be punished by the secular authorities; all law officers had to co-operate or suffer excommunication.

These local inquisitions proving inadequate, however, Innocent III appointed *inquisitores* directly from the Vatican, with absolute authority to override local administrators. The decree, later part of Canon Law, came as a bull (March 25, 1199) to the town of Viterbo.

Inasmuch as the laws, when men are condemned to death for high treason, confiscate their goods and reserve a livelihood for their children only as an act of mercy, how much more should those, who by straying from the faith offend against Jesus Christ, God and Son of God, be cut off by ecclesiastical rigor from our head, who is Christ, and be despoiled of their earthly goods, since it is far more grievous to sin against the king of heaven than against an earthly ruler.

In a decree of 1215, *"Excommunicamus* [We excommunicate]," Innocent III reinforced his earlier orders, stressing that the secular authorities take a public oath to "strive in good faith, to the utmost of their power, to exterminate from the lands subject to their obedience all heretics who have been marked by the Church."

Horrors of the Inquisition,
according to Samuel Clarke,
Martyrology (1651).

The work of strengthening the new tribunal was continued by Pope Gregory IX, who in 1233 proclaimed that the *"inquisitores hereticae pravitatis"* were henceforth to be Dominicans, appointed by and subject only to the pope. The inquisitors remained in an area until they had stamped out the heresy; their headquarters were the local Dominican (sometimes Franciscan) monastery.

The Inquisition emerged about 1200 because of the mounting insecurity, weakness, and immorality of the Roman Church, manifested by the apostasy of the most civilized parts of Europe, especially southern France and the rich cities of central France and the Rhineland. At the end of the twelfth century, Peter des Vaux of Cernay wrote that "almost all the barons [of Provence] had become harborers and defenders of heretics," and the Inquisition first (1204) attacked the Albigensians of that region, the majority of the population [see Heresy].

The procedure of the Inquisition's investigation of heresy was repeated in its

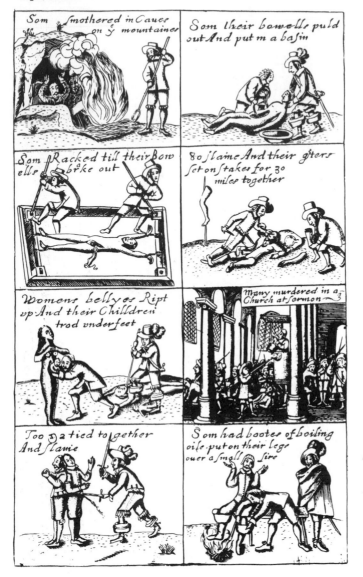

Tortures of the Inquisition, according to Samuel Clarke, *Martyrology* (1651).

later trials for witchcraft, which, when the Inquisition took upon itself to decide that sorcery was a form of heresy, came under its jurisdiction. The inquisitorial method, which developed slowly, may be summarized as follows:

1. The accused was presumed guilty until he had proved his innocence. The Inquisition adopted this pivot of Roman Imperial law; but in matters of belief, vindication was almost impossible [see Evidence in Witch Trials, Europe].

2. Suspicion, gossip, or denunciation was sufficient indication of guilt to hail a person before the Inquisition [see Luxeuil Witch Trial of 1529].

3. To justify the activity of the Inquisition, the offense, whatever it might have been, was correlated with heresy. Thus, the men who killed the bigoted Inquisitor Peter Martyr in 1252 were tried, not for murder but for heresy (as opponents of the Inquisition).

4. Witnesses were not identified; often their accusations were not made known to the defendant. In 1254 Pope Innocent IV

granted accusers anonymity [see Evidence in Witch Trials, Europe].

5. Witnesses disallowed in other offenses were encouraged to inform against heretics: convicted perjurers, persons without civil rights, children of tender years, and excommunicates (including condemned heretics). If a hostile witness retracted his evidence, he was prosecuted for perjury, but his testimony was allowed to stand. However, according to the Inquisitor Nicholas Eymeric (1360), if the retraction was less favorable to the accused, the judge could accept this second testimony.

6. No witnesses were allowed to testify on behalf of the accused; nor was his previous good reputation as citizen or Christian taken into account.

7. The accused was permitted no counsel, since the lawyer would thereby be guilty of defending heresy. (For a short time lawyers had been allowed, especially when inquisitors were sitting on episcopal courts, and this privilege was resumed in the seventeenth century.)

8. The judges were inquisitors. Occasionally bishops or even laymen were allowed to sit on the *inquisitio*.

9. The judges were encouraged to trip the accused into confessing. The Inquisitor Sylvester Prierias in 1521 told how this could be done [see Witnesses].

10. Although technically allowed only as a last resort, in practice torture was regularly used, and could be inflicted on any witness. Civil authorities employed torture, but the Inquisition extended and systematized its use. Torture had been sanctioned as a means to discover heresy by Pope Innocent IV in 1257, in a bull, *"Ad extirpanda,"* and was confirmed by later popes; it was not abolished until 1816 by Pope Pius VII.

11. Legally, torture could not be repeated, but it could be, and was, legally "continued" until the accused confessed whatever was demanded of him. Three sessions of torture were usual. Somewhat milder regulations for conducting witchcraft trials were circulated by the Inquisition about 1623. This *Instructio pro Formandis Processibus in Causis Strigum* was printed several times, but the original document is now extremely rare. A copy printed in 1657 in Rome, probably the only one surviving, is preserved at Cornell University Library. It reveals that the Inquisition, under pressure from the milder views of some Jesuits as well as from its opponents, admitted that over the preceding two centuries its judges had resorted to torture, even prescribing death, without careful scrutiny of the evidence. The Preface stated:

> The gravest errors in trials for witchcraft are daily committed by inquisitors, so that the Inquisition has scarcely found one trial conducted legally, with women convicted on the most slender evidence, with confessions extorted by illegal means, and has had to punish its judges for inflicting excessive tortures. In future, all inquisitors must keep strictly to the rules.

Apologists for the Inquisition sometimes quote only the newer regulations—e.g., the accused should receive a daily copy of the proceedings and be assigned a lawyer (with his expenses paid if the accused were indigent). However, even the "milder" regulations permitted torture.

12. Having confessed under torture, the accused, in sight of the torture chamber, had to repeat his confession "freely and spontaneously, without the pressure of force or fear." Thus he was considered, and the court records so stated, to have admitted his guilt *without torture* [see Friedrich von Spee].

13. Every accused had to give or invent names of accomplices or those whom he suspected of heresy.

14. Generally no appeal was countenanced.

15. The property of the accused was confiscated by the Inquisition. All popes praised this practice as one of the strongest weapons in the fight against heresy. Innocent IV said it hung like a sword suspended over the heads of heretics and princes. Because confiscation was routine, it was seldom expressly mentioned, save in sentences of excommunication against the dead (Tanon).

Som had their harts pulled out which the Papists gnawed with their teeth

A Smith had his braines beaten out on his Anvill with a hamer.

Som had their throtes cut with Butchers knives, others knocked on the head with Axes.

Som had their right hands and feet crushed betweene red hot Irons

Som their Noses and brestes pulld of with red hot pincers.

Som were hanged up by one Foote their heads and brests in the water

Som were torne in peeces by Horses

More tortures of the Inquisition, according to Samuel Clarke, *Martyrology* (1651).

As a result, as all records show, and as even inquisitors admitted, once accused, the chances of escaping death were almost nil. "There was never any case of an acquittal pure and simple," observed Henry C. Lea, still the major historian of the Inquisition. Not Proven was the alternative verdict to Guilty. At first, instead of having the convicted heretic burned, the Inquisition sometimes punished by public ignomity, anticipating the ostracizing of Jews by the Nazis; the *Inquisitor's Manual* of the celebrated Bernardus Guidonis (1261-1331), who himself convicted 930 heretics, described the method.

We enjoin you for your penance the wearing of two crosses of yellow felt, one in front and one behind, on each garment except your shirt. You shall never go about, whether indoors or without, without these crosses being visible; one arm of each shall be twenty inches in length and the other sixteen inches; and each arm of the cross shall be twelve inches in breadth. If they become torn or worn out, you shall repair them.

But when torture could be continued until the victim confessed, lesser punishments gave way before the ultimate penalty of burning at the stake. Even though the Inquisition, after it had blazed a trail for civil and episcopal courts, actually prosecuted few witches in the sixteenth century, Ludovicus à Paramo in 1598 said the Inquisition had burned 30,000 witches within 150 years [see Executions].

Although it maintained and staffed its own dungeons and torture chambers (sometimes leased), and sentenced to life imprisonment, the Inquisition seldom itself pronounced or performed the actual execution of those it condemned. By a legal fiction, begun in 1231, it surrendered or "relaxed" the heretic to the appropriate civil authority, making a great show of requesting mercy. "We ask, and that with urgency, the secular court to moderate its sentence so that effusion of blood and peril of death may be avoided." Should the secular judges show mercy, however, they were charged with favoring heretics. When the Senate of Venice in 1521 refused to sanction executions ordered by the Inquisition in Brescia, Pope Leo X promulgated a bull blasting them with "the Church's censure and other appropriate legal measures."

Whether or not the accused was executed, his property was confiscated by the Inquisition. Seeing the potentiality in this rule, secular authorities raised no objections. Fingering by alleged accomplices made certain a continuous supply of further victims, whose property would in due course be expropriated. In this way a vested interest was built up, comprising men whose sole function and training was to extirpate persons who, rightly or wrongly, were reputed to disagree in some way with what the Church at that particular moment advocated. Sometimes the booty was shared with the episcopal court and/or the civil government; at other times, the local inquisitor seized everything for himself, not even sending a share to the officials of the Inquisition at Rome. So extensive was this confiscation that in a little over a century, the Inquisition had exhausted the major sources of wealth, and Inquisitor Eymeric complained in 1360: "In our days there are no more rich heretics; so that princes, not seeing much money in prospect, will not put themselves to any expense; it is a

pity that so salutary an institution as ours should be so uncertain of its future."

The eagerness of the Inquisition and the co-operation of the state in seeking heretics were proportionate to the opportunities for confiscation. "In the north of France," said the *Encyclopaedia Britannica* (11th ed.), "the workings of the Inquisition were very intermittent; for there were fewer heretics there than in the south, and as they were poorer there was less zeal on the part of the secular arm to persecute them."

Graft became common, and money might sometimes buy off torture and death. Cornelius Agrippa, the celebrated physician, in his *De Incertitudine et Vanitate Scientiarum* (1531), told of the contemporary corruption of the Inquisition at Milan.

> For it is not unusual that the inquisitor commutes physical into monetary penalties, which act has created very considerable revenue for him. Some unfortunates have to surrender a yearly fine; if they cease to pay they are once again hauled before the Inquisition. Moreover, the property of heretics being confiscated to the profit of the public treasury, the inquisitor gets a very good percentage of all this. Finally, a sole accusation, only a suspicion of heresy or of sorcery, or a citation by the Inquisition leads to infamy, from which one is only free by giving much silver to the inquisitor. While I was in Italy [about 1511-18], the majority of the inquisitors of the Duchy of Milan were in this way mulcting the most noble ladies as well as poor but honest women, terrorized with fear, from whom they received huge sums of money.

Agrippa, not surprisingly, was continually in trouble with the Inquisition, who regarded him as a magician.

The Roman Catholic De Cauzons' *Histoire de l'Inquisition* (1909) stated the Inquisition "had invented the crime of witchcraft and . . . relied on torture as the means of proving it." This process took time. First came the request in 1257 to extend the field of heresy to include sorcery. This was refused by Pope Alexander IV, unless sorcery savored manifestly of heresy —a nice point, since sorcery almost inevitably involved the Devil. The secular

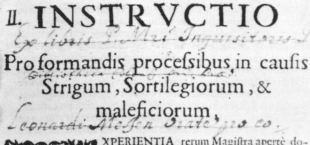

II. INSTRVCTIO

Ex libris P. Mei Inquisitionis S.

Pro formandis procefsibus, in caufis
Strigum, Sortilegiorum, &
maleficiorum,

Leonardi Mefsen Inate pro eo.

XPERIENTIA rerum Magiftra apertè do-
cet, grauiffimos quotidie committi errores
in formandis Proceffibus contrà Striges, fiuè
Lamias, & Maleficas in notabile præiudicium
tàm 'iuftitiæ, quàm huiufmodi mulierum in-
quifitarum, ità vt in Sanctæ Romanæ, & Vni-
uerfalis Inquifitionis aduersùs hæreticâ pra-
uitatem Generali Cógregatione longo tem-
pore obferuatum fuerit, vix vnquam repertum fuiffe aliquem
proceffum fimilem rectè, & iuridicè formatum, imò ple-
rumquè neceffe fuiffe quamplures Iudices reprehendere,
ob indebitas vexationes, inquifitiones, carcerationes, nèc
non diuerfos malos, & impertinentes modos habitos in formandis proceffibus, reis interrogandis, exceffiuis torturis infe-
rendis, ità vt quandoquè contigerit iniuftas, & iniquas proferri
fententias, etiam vltimi fupplicij, fiuè traditionis Brachio Sæcu-
lari, & re ipfa compertum eft, multos Iudices ità faciles, &
procliues fuiffe ob leue, aùt minimum inditium credere aliquam
mulierem effe Strigem, & ideò nihil omninò prætermififfe, vt ab
huiufmodi muliere, etiàm modis illicitis talem confeffionem,
extorquerent, cùm tot tamèn, tantifque inuerifimilitudinibus,
varietatibus, & contrarietatibus, vt fuper tali confeffione nulla,
aùt modica vis fieri poffet; Quapropter vt Iudices de cætero magis cauti effe poffint in conficiendis huiufmodi proceffibus, in-
fraferipta diligentèr, & accuratè præ oculis habeant, & confi-
derent.
Error principalis, & peculiaris omnium ferè Iudicum in hac mate-
ria eft deuenire nedum ad inquifitionem, & carcerationem, fed
fæpe etiàm ad torturâ contrà aliquàm mulierè de maleficio im-
puta-

A

Probably the only copy in existence of the official *Instructions* of the Holy Roman Inquisition in 1657. The opening paragraph warns inquisitors to interrogate witches with caution. Very significantly, these *Instructions* admit that for the past two hundred years the Inquisition had used excessive torture and given unjust sentences, including burning at the stake, because the judges had too lightly assumed the guilt of any woman brought before them as a reputed witch. This proclamation further admits that the Inquisition extorted confessions illegally, using many pernicious and unrighteous methods, instead of exercising only a moderate application of torture. This precious document is now in Cornell University Library.

courts, he held, were competent to deal with simple sorcery, and the Inquisition should let them do it. For a decade, from 1320, on the authority of Pope John XXII, the Inquisition at Carcassonne was empowered to investigate magic and sorcery, especially worship of demons; but in 1333 the former restriction demanding suspicion of heresy was reimposed. However, throughout southern France, and especially at Carcassonne and Toulouse, the Inquisition was active in hunting witches as heretics, not merely in 1326 and 1330 at Toulouse and Narbonne, but regularly thereafter. In 1451 Pope Nicholas V allowed the Inquisition control over sorcery even when heresy was not involved. This latitude was reaffirmed in 1505 by Sixtus V in his bull, *"Coeli et terrae creator,"* which denounced astrology, divination, incantation, keeping of demons, and all forms of magic, even those which had not formerly been prohibited. All through the fifteenth and early sixteenth centuries, the popes repeated the authority of the Inquisition over witchcraft. Alexander VI in 1501 encouraged the persecution in Lombardy, Julius II (1503) in Cremona, and Adrian VI (1523) in Como, permitting inquisitors to act without cooperating with local bishops.

The crucial question of when sorcery became heretical was later discussed by a leading inquisitor, Caesar Carena, in his *Tractatus de Officio Sanctissimae Inquisi-*

tionis (1636). Sorcery, he argued, was heretical when—

It made use of any holy object such as holy water, blessed oil, or used Christian prayers.

It asked the Devil to do something beyond the powers allowed him by God (e.g., to resuscitate a corpse).

It paid the Devil the adoration due only to God.

It was performed by a sorcerer who had made a pact with the Devil.

However, the Inquisition could also punish non-heretical sorcery, Carena continued, such as simple cures used for a good purpose, or the use of Christian prayers for superstitious ends (e.g., to escape disease). In all charges, the inquisitor was the sole judge whether an act was heretical. Some inquisitors, like Lupo da Bergamo, recommended that cases of non-heretical sorcery be tried in episcopal courts.

Until the first groping attempts in Paris in 1390, no secular court had prosecuted witchcraft [see Paris Witch Trial]. In that year, the University of Paris had sanctioned such trials by civil authorities, and in 1398 had declared that all magical practices effecting more than could reasonably be expected in nature implied a pact. The history of witchcraft is the gradual assumption by episcopal and secular courts of the work started by the Inquisition. Apart from trials involving priests and other religious, the Inquisition (except in Spain) conducted relatively few trials for witchcraft after 1500. The growth and development of the delusion was sporadic, so that while the Inquisition in southern France had been trying witches for over a century without official protests, the inquisitorial trial in 1459 at Arras, in the north of France, aroused considerable opposition and was condemned by several bishops and by the Parlement of Paris.

Although the institution and administration of witchcraft trials passed largely into secular hands, the dual techniques—torture to secure admission of guilt, and confiscation of property of the guilty—had been so perfected by the Inquisition that they were taken over without major change.

Town courts and bishops' courts could not improve on them. More remarkable, in the various component states of the Roman (i.e., German) Empire, was their use by Protestant tribunals; Saxony in 1572 and the Palatinate in 1582, for example, promulgated basically inquisitorial methods of conducting witch trials.

The prosecution, by secular courts, of offenses originally religious was facilitated by the prospect of additional sources of revenue to the principality controlling the courts, for the civil administration naturally adopted the Inquisition's policy of sequestrating the property of those it convicted. In France, for example, a special royal official [*procureur des encours*] was designated to make sure the estates of heretics were incorporated with the crown lands, and that their movable property and moneys went to the king's coffers. It is significant that where confiscation of property was not allowed, as in the German state of Juliers-Berg, witch trials were unknown.

Even after the spate of handbooks for conducting witch trials, the seventeenth century still saw many works by inquisitors, most of them paying stricter attention to the legal safeguards but just as obscurantist as the earlier. Among these writings, of interest only to special readers, are:

Ignatius Lupo da Bergamo, *Nova Lux in Edictum Sanctissimae Inquisitionis ad Praxim Sacramenti Penitentiae* (1633).

Caesar Carena, *Tractatus de Officio Sanctissimae Inquisitionis et Modo Procedendi in Causis Fidei* (1636).

Giovanni Alberghini, *Manuale Qualificatorum Sanctae Inquisitionis* (1642).

Franciscus Bordonus, *Sacrum Tribunal Judicum in Causis Sanctae Fidei* (1648) and *Manuale Consultorum in Causis Sanctae Officii* (pub. posth. 1693).

Sebastian Salelles, S.J., *De Materiis Tribunalium Sanctae Inquisitionis* (1651).

Thomas Delbene, *De Officio Sanctae Inquisitionis Circa Haeresim* (1666).

Bordonus listed indications of witchcraft,

most of them sufficing for torture: books containing charms, brands burned by the Inquisition on the suspect's body for a previous offense, a pot of human remains or sacred objects, reported conversation with an invisible devil, offers to teach sorcery, sudden death of a person after meeting a suspected witch, invocation of the Devil, stripping corpses on the gallows, ugly or deformed appearance, being the child of a witch, threats followed by evil, and gathering poisonous herbs (*Sacrum Tribunal*). These writings continued to be printed throughout the seventeenth century, and the Inquisition must therefore take the responsibility, not only of initially formulating the concept of witchcraft, but of maintaining it.

> "Faith must be persuaded to men, and not imposed upon them. Yet it would be better that they were coerced by the sword of that [magistrate] who beareth not the sword in vain, than that they should be allowed to bring many others into their own error."
> —Bernard of Clairvaux (1091-1153).

The position of the Inquisition in the history of Europe was summarized by the nineteenth-century Roman Catholic historian, Lord Acton:

> The principle of the Inquisition is murderous. . . . [Liberalism] swept away that ·appalling edifice of intolerance, tyranny, cruelty, which believers in Christ built up to perpetuate their belief. There is much to deduct from the praise of the Church in protecting marriage, abolishing slavery and human sacrifice, preventing war, and helping the poor. No deduction can be made from her evildoing toward unbelievers, heretics, savages, and witches. Here her responsibility is more undivided; her initiative and achievement more complete. (*Letters to Mary Gladstone*)

For major entries on the Inquisition's development of sorcery as heresy, see Evidence in Witch Trials, Heresy, Trials, Torture, and Witchcraft. For the papal bulls confirming and authorizing the Inquisition's position, see John XXII (1320), Innocent VIII (1484), Alexander VI (1501), and Leo X (1521). For early inquisitors who developed the theory of witchcraft, see Early Writers on Witchcraft, and Nicholas Jacquier (1458), Girolamo Visconti (1460), the *Malleus Maleficarum* (1486), Pedro Cirvelo (1521), and Bartolommeo Spina (1523). For the form of sentencing a witch, see Sentence. For typical inquisitorial trials, see Arras Witch Trial (1459) and Luxeuil Witch Trial (1529); for joint trials, see Joan of Arc (1431) and Gilles de Rais (1440). For the Spanish Inquisition, an organization acting independently of the Papal Inquisition and exercising a moderating influence on the mania, see Witchcraft in Spain and Alonzo Salazar de Frias.

Institor, Heinrich: see *Malleus Maleficarum*.

Ipswich Witchcraft Case. On May 14, 1878, 186 years after America's only important witch trial, a suit alleging *maleficia* was instituted at Salem, Massachusetts. "Between this and the power of witches to stick pins into people and otherwise to afflict them, there is nothing to choose," one religious journal commented some years later (*Advance*, October 4, 1917). The contemporary papers dubbed the suit the "Ipswich Witchcraft Case."

In the infancy of Christian Science, some disagreement among the followers of Mary Baker Eddy had led Lucretia Brown of Ipswich to believe herself physically harmed by the "malicious animal magnetism" of a dissenting student, Daniel Spofford. Miss Brown's "healer," a Miss Dorcas Rawson, urged the afflicted girl to bring suit against Spofford as a mesmerist who "by means of his said power and art" caused her bodily suffering. The indictment reads like a seventeenth-century document, charging that Spofford "wrongfully and maliciously and with intent to injure" brought on Lucretia Brown "great suffering of body and mind and severe spinal pains and neuralgia and a temporary suspension of mind." The plaintiff feared Spofford's continued mesmerism because she was "wholly unable to escape from the control and influence he so exercises upon her." According to the official *Life* (1907), by Sibyl Wilbur, Mrs. Eddy opposed filing the action; however, she joined the plaintiff in the courthouse at Salem, ostensibly supporting her. The case was thrown out on the grounds that the court had no power to control Spofford's mind.

One of the followers, Edward Arens, had argued the case for Lucretia, and he became the protégé of Mrs. Eddy's husband, Asa Gilbert Eddy. In October of that year (1878), Mr. Eddy was arrested for attempted murder of Arens, but in a mass of conflicting and unreliable evidence, the indictment was not sustained. Two years later, Mrs. Eddy tried to dissociate herself from the Ipswich Witchcraft Case, claiming utter ignorance of the legal proceedings, and showing an affidavit that Arens started the affair.

Ireland, Witchcraft in. Witchcraft almost, but not entirely, bypassed Ireland. The relative isolation of the country, the separation between the ruling Protestant minority and the indigenous Roman Catholic majority, and the total absence of writings or controversy about witchcraft are some circumstances that might account for Ireland's immunity. Between the first and last trials in 1324 and 1711, not more than half a dozen others are recorded. Curiously, with the exception of the first, they were all of Protestants by Protestants.

In 1317, Bishop Richard de Ledrede of Ossory, described by the Seneschal of Kilkenny as a "vile, rustic, interloping monk [*trutannus*]," had found in his diocese "a certain new and pestilential sect . . . who attempt to hinder the salvation of souls." By 1324, he charged Dame Alice Kyteler for heretical sorcery. After prolonged legal and physical battling, in which the nobles opposed the clerics, Dame Alice fled to England, her maid and several other "accomplices" were burned, and others whipped, banished, or excommunicated. The trial was widely discussed, and was followed by other occasional burnings for heresy (e.g., 1327 and 1353). The Bishop

too fell a victim to closed thought, but ultimately cleared himself of heresy and resumed administration of his diocese. The Kyteler case preceded by two years the bull against sorcery of Pope John XXII, who was always fearing plots on his life by waxen images or rings enclosing a devil.

The next reference to Irish witchcraft came in 1447, when Parliament remonstrated to the King that "ruining or destroying any man by sorcery or necromancy . . . they [Lords and Commons] think and believe impossible to be performed in art"; furthermore, "no such art was attempted at any time in this land."

Even during the sixteenth century, when the witchcraft mania was elsewhere raging, Ireland was spared. An odd trial occurred (again at Kilkenny) in November, 1578, when two witches and a "blackamoor" were executed "by natural law, for that we found no law to try them by in this realm." A Negro witch in the British Isles is unique. His execution may have resulted from false etymology, necromancy (divination by the dead) being confused with divination through Negroes! Natural law was soon replaced by statute, and in 1586 the Irish Parliament passed Queen Elizabeth's bill of 1563, not repealed until 1821.

Similarly, during the early seventeenth century, incidents are few and relate to sorcery. In 1606 a minister invoked "wicked and lying spirits" to divine the whereabouts of "the most wicked traitor, Hugh of Tyrone." In 1609 a possessed girl was cured by a holy girdle from Holy Cross Abbey, near Thurles. At some unspecified date, a servant girl divined stolen silverware by magic circles and reading backward passages from scripture. A poltergeist near Limerick in 1644 anticipated the Drummer of Tedworth by eighteen years; another followed sixteen years later (1678) in Dublin. Bare are the records indeed. Nothing of importance in Irish witchcraft occurred from 1324 to 1661, in which year Florence Newton, the witch of Youghal, was charged with hexing a young servant girl.

Prior to the last trial for witchcraft in Ireland in 1711, there is but one other note-

A young witch roused and taken off to the sabbat. Ascribed to Hans Baldung Grün.

worthy incident, another case of possession, described in a contemporary pamphlet, *The Bewitching of a Child in Ireland* (1699), later retold by Glanvill. Having given alms to a beggar woman, a nineteen-year-old girl received in return some sorrel leaves. Scarce had she swallowed a leaf, "but she began to be tortured in her bowels, to rumble all over, and even was convulsive, and in fine to swoon away as dead." The physician in despair sent for the minister, whose presence only increased the hysteria.

> She began first to roll herself about, then to vomit needles, pins, hairs, feathers, bottoms of thread, pieces of glass, window nails, nails drawn out of a cart or coach wheel, an iron knife about a span long, eggs, and fish shells.

The old beggar woman was assumed to have bewitched the girl, was apprehended, condemned, and, says Glanvill (reproducing the pamphlet), burned.

See further, Magee Island Witch Trial, Alice Kyteler, Florence Newton.

Jacquier, Nicholas. Nicholas Jacquier was a famous Dominican inquisitor, at Tournay (1465), against the Hussites in Bohemia (1466), and at Lille (1468-72). In 1452, at the age of fifty, while Inquisitor in northern France, Jacquier wrote a *Tractatus de Calcatione Demonum* against numerous heretics whom he later equated with the Vaudois at Arras as *haeretici fascinarii*. Jacquier is the first demonologist

in the classical pattern of such men as Bodin, Remy, or Del Rio. Perhaps "witchologists" would be a fitter description, for, while they were all concerned with the basis of witchcraft—i.e., the pact with the Devil—in practice they were more interested in the results of the pact, the witch. The Devil could not be brought into court, but his sworn friend could be sentenced.

The *Flagellum Haereticorum Fascinariorum* [*A Flail Against the Heresy of Witchcraft*], written in 1458 to destroy the Canon Episcopi, is known from its inclusion in an anthology of 1581. Jacquier's contribution to witch theory was establishing witchcraft as a new heresy; witches fulfilled the prophecy of John xii. 31 and with their sabbats were building a new empire for the Devil. Of all heresies, witchcraft was the worst, for the witches renounced God and the Catholic Church *knowingly*. Better become a Jew or Mohammedan or sun-worshiper than a witch! Stop the persecutions? Not only are witches idolaters, but they commit the foulest of other crimes. What justice were this, to discharge a witch for heresy so she could go free for sodomy and murder?

One example of Jacquier's reasoning should be quoted—how to make evidence lead to a foregone conclusion [for other examples, see Demonologists]:

A confessed witch accuses a woman of being at the sabbat.

The woman replies that the devil impersonated her.

The judge should accept the accusation unless the accused woman can prove her rebuttal. And the devil, if subpoenaed, would rightly say he acted with God's permission. The woman now has to prove God gave the devil permission to impersonate her. Otherwise, she is "adjudged a falsifier and inventor."

The value of this spectral evidence by an accuser was the problem of the Salem trials; and so, for three hundred years, unreason pursued its course.

The Inquisition, it might be observed, did not deny the possibility of the Devil's impersonating the innocent (so Inquisitor Bernard de Como, about 1510), but argued further that, if the evidence of a witch was good enough to send her to the stake, it was sufficient to burn those she accused (Inquisitor Spina, about 1523).

James I. At the beginning of his reign in Scotland, King James was a firm believer in witchcraft; at the end of his reign in England in 1628, James had become just as firm a skeptic. The King's credulity was confirmed by the trial of the North Berwick Witches, who were made to confess they had gone to sea in sieves and had tried to raise a storm to wreck the King's ship en route to Norway for his bride. James—he was then only twenty-four—accepted this fantastic account because Agnes Sampson, one of the accused:

> declared unto him the very words which had passed between the King's majesty and his Queen at Oslo in Norway the first night of their marriage, with their answer each to other. Whereat the King's majesty wondered greatly, and swore by the living God that he believed that all the devils in hell could not have discovered the same, acknowledging her words to be most true, and therefore gave the more credit to the rest which is before declared. (*News from Scotland*, 1591)

When the jury acquitted one of the accused, a woman of noble birth, James was so incensed that he charged the jury with "an assize of error." Thereupon, on June 7, 1591, they agreed to "yield themselves to the King's will." James, who had personally supervised the torture of some of the accused, explained he intervened only "for an example in time coming, to make men to be more wary how they give false verdicts," and because "witchcraft, which is a thing grown very common among us . . . [is] a most abominable sin." The original document, published the day following, June 8, is reproduced here (the Tolbooth Speech).

His interest in the North Berwick Witches no doubt led James to start on his *Demonology* (published in Edinburgh, 1597), a dialogue in three parts, written in the classical tradition of European demonologists; the King's Tolbooth Speech is, in fact, like a précis of the book. The *Demonology* was, of course, written to refute the *Discovery of Witchcraft* (1584) of Reginald Scot, and *De Praestigiis Daemonum* (1563) of Johan Weyer, and to prove that "such assaults of Satan are most certainly practiced and that the instruments thereof merit most severely to be punished." In 1603, the King tried to have extant copies of Scot's *Discovery* destroyed. James's disbelief in lycanthropy gave his work an air of disinterested judgment which it did not deserve; he stressed both swimming and devil's marks as evidence for rooting out "so odious a treason against God." A similar point of view pervades the *Basilikon Doron*, written for his son Prince Henry (who died in 1612); the young prince was advised that witchcraft was among the "horrible crimes that [he was] bound in conscience never to forgive." At the same time, James also cautioned "how wary judges should be in trusting accusations without an exact trial."

When James VI of Scotland became James I of the united kingdoms of Scotland and England in 1603, he brought out a new edition of his *Demonology* (at London); a Dutch translation appeared in 1604, and two Latin editions in 1604 and 1607 (printed at Hanover). Within one year of his accession, he had coerced Parliament to pass a new witch act. The 1604 statute changed the emphasis from *maleficia* to the pact with the Devil, in line with Continental thinking, and certainly heightened the attack against witches.

King James's Tolbooth Speech

[King James charged the Edinburgh jury with "an assize of error" for dismissing the indictment of witchcraft against Barbara Napier, one of the North Berwick witches, on June 7, 1591.]

For witchcraft, which is a thing grown very common amongst us, I know it to be a most abominable sin, and I have been occupied these three quarters of this year for the sifting out of them that are guilty herein. We are taught by the laws both of God and men that this sin is most odious. And by God's law punishable by death. By man's law it is called *maleficium* or *veneficium*, an ill deed or a poisonable deed, and punishable likewise by death.

The thing that moved [the men of the assize] to find as they did, was because they had no testimony but of witches; which they thought not sufficient. By the civil law I know that such infamous persons are not received for witnesses, but in matters of heresy and *lesae majestatis*. For in other matters it is not thought meet, yet in these matters of witchcraft good reason that such be admitted. First none honest can know these matters. Second, because they will not accuse themselves. Thirdly, because no act which is done by them can be seen.

Further, I call them witches which do renounce God and yield themselves wholly to the Devil; but when they have recanted and repented, as these have done, then I account them not as witches, and so their testimony sufficient.

Demonology no doubt received special attention because of its royal author; it was quoted in contemporary trials. A court in Dorset in 1602 found an accused woman had done "things worthy to be . . . punished for that the King's most excellent Majesty in his book against witches intituled the *Demonology* hath set forth that the things practiced by Joan [the accused] are the very qualities and marks whereby to know a witch or a sorcerer." Again in 1613, Potts's *Lancashire Witches* found justification for the conclusions of the court in the pages of the *Demonology*. "What hath the King's Majesty written and published in his *Demonology* by way of premonition and prevention, what hath not here by the first or last been executed, put in practice, or discovered."

The King's bias influenced the translation of the Bible; whenever the Septuagint had "one that consulteth pythonic spirits," the Authorized Version (1603) used James's definition of a witch in his *Demonology*, "a consulter with familiar spirits." The Bible was thus angled to justify conceptions completely unknown to it.

Possibly the first break in James's credulity came in 1605 with the trial of the Abingdon women accused by a fourteen-year-old girl, Anne Gunter. The King learned of the case, and had Rev. Samuel Harsnett talk to the girl, providing £300 toward the costs of the proceedings. Anne confessed she had feigned hysteria and had falsely accused three witches. The next case of imposture was John Smith, the Leicester Boy, interrogated by the King himself after the lad's accusations had resulted in the hanging of nine witches in 1618; the King took the trial away from Chief Justice Sir Edward Coke and stopped the execution of the remaining women accused by Smith. In 1620 the Stafford judges dismissed similar accusations by the Bilson Boy.

In 1621, another young impostor examined by King James, Katherine Malpas of Westham, Essex, counterfeited diabolical possession, so visitors would come to see her and donate money. She accused two women of bewitching her. Ultimately, a woman confessed she had taught Kate various tricks, such as heaving up her stomach, wringing her hands, leaping, and skipping. Especially "she would have a rising-up in her stomach to the bigness of a halfpenny loaf, and would beat her head against the wainscot and would shrug up her shoulders and would make her bones to crackle within her skin, and sometimes her mouth would be drawn to one side." (Ewen, *Witchcraft in the Star Chamber*, 1938)

These instances of adolescents' falsely charging people as witches were largely responsible for the change in the King's views. Dr. Thomas Fuller, in his *Church History of Britain*, noted: "The frequency of forged possessions wrought such an alteration upon the judgment of King James that . . . he grew first diffident of, and then flatly to deny, the workings of witches and devils as but falsehoods and delusions." Among other influences on the King were his own wider reading to include the moderates (such as Cornelius Agrippa), and the skeptical outlook of such courtiers as Francis Bacon, Florio (the translator of Montaigne), and of his personal physician, Dr. Harvey. In addition, the religious climate was changing and a reaction against Calvinism setting in.

The most graphic indication of the alteration in the political situation, however, is the fact that in the last nine years of the King's reign, only five persons were executed for witchcraft. Yet despite the King's change of heart, the witchcraft law of 1604 remained on the statute books. After passing almost into desuetude under Charles I, it became the basis for the Cromwellian persecutions.

James I: Statute of 1604. Most important English witch trials were conducted under this decree—the Lancashire mass trials of 1612 and 1633 (where most of the accused were acquitted) and the Leicester trials of 1616 (where nine were hanged). The act continued in force during the Civil War and the Commonwealth (1642 to 1660) and was the basis of the indictments at the notorious trials in 1645 throughout the eastern counties (Chelmsford, Norfolk, Bury St. Edmunds, Great Yarmouth) and in 1649 at Huntingdon, Berwick, and Newcastle.

This bill of James I repealed the similar act of 1563 under Queen Elizabeth (although retaining most of the phraseology) and substituted even harsher laws. It made

". . . or take up any dead man, woman, or child out of his, her, or their grave, or any other place where the dead body resteth . . ." —Statute of 1604. From Joost Damhouder, *Enchiridion* (1554).

hanging mandatory for the first offense for *maleficia* even where the bewitched person did not die; under the Elizabethan law the penalty was a year's imprisonment. However, for divination of stolen property, making love philters, or damaging property, the penalty remained, for a first offense, one year's imprisonment and appearance in the pillory. The new statute tried to spell out the pact with Devil, making it a felony (entailing the death penalty) to "exercise any invocation or conjuration of any evil and wicked spirit, or [to] consult, covenant with, entertain, employ, feed, or reward any evil and wicked spirit to or for any intent or purpose."

Witchcraft was not merely the vulgar prejudice of uneducated people; this bill was framed by some of the ablest and most learned men in England, including the Earl of Northumberland, the Bishop of Lincoln, the Chief Justice of the Court of Common Pleas, the Attorney General, the Chief

Baron of the Exchequer, and the Chief Justice of the King's Bench.

Sir Robert Filmer, the great lawyer, writing fifty years later in his *Advertisement to the Jurymen of England Touching Witches* (London, 1653), ridicules the difficulty of defining witchcraft, or distinguishing (as the act tried to) witchcraft, conjuring, and sorcery. "This statute presupposeth that every one knows what a conjurer, a witch, an enchanter, a charmer, and sorcerer is, as being to be learned best of divines, [although] they have not described or distin-guished between them." Then Filmer adds, to show the impossibility of securing convictions under this statute, "And yet the law is very just in requiring a due and lawful conviction." Filmer comments that intent to kill was generally necessary to secure conviction:

Although the statute runs in the disjunctive *or*, and so makes every single crime capital, yet the judges usually by a favorable interpretation take the disjunctive *or* for the copulative *and*, and therefore ordinarily they condemn none for witches unless they be charged with the murdering of some person.

However, the jail deliveries show that at Chelmsford in 1645 seven women were hanged for the sole charge of entertaining evil spirits. Kittredge, *Witchcraft in Old and New England* (Cambridge, Mass., 1929), adds: "No case has ever been cited in which a man or woman was put to death for this offense alone [digging up the dead, a new clause], and we may therefore disregard that clause as of no practical effect."

Most of the Salem witch trials were prosecuted under this statute, the later indictments mentioning it by name. On December 14, 1692, the Massachusetts General Council enacted substantially the 1604 bill to give "more particular direction in the execution of the law against witchcraft." It remained law until 1695.

The act of 1604 was repealed in England in 1736 under George II.

AN ACT AGAINST CONJURATION, WITCH-CRAFT, AND DEALING WITH EVIL AND WICKED SPIRITS.

I. Be it enacted by the King, our sovereign lord, the Lords spiritual and temporal, and the Commons in this present Parliament assembled, and by the authority of the same, that the statute made in the fifth year of the reign of our late sovereign Lady of most famous and happy memory, Queen Elizabeth, intituled "An Act against conjurations, enchantments, and witchcrafts," be from the Feast of St. Michael the Archangel next coming, for and concerning all offenses to be committed after the same feast, utterly repealed.

II. And for the better restraining the said offenses, and more severe punishing the same, be it further enacted by the authority aforesaid, that if any person or persons, after the said Feast of Saint Michael the Archangel next coming, [a] shall use, practice, or exercise any invocation, or conjuration, of any evil and wicked spirit, or shall consult, covenant with, entertain, employ, feed, or reward any evil and wicked spirit to or for any intent or purpose; or [b] take up any dead man, woman, or child out of his, her, or their grave, or any other place where the dead body resteth, or the skin, bone, or any other part of any dead person, to be employed or used in any manner of witchcraft, sorcery, charm, or enchantment; or [c] shall use, practice, or exercise any witchcraft, enchantment, charm, or sorcery, whereby any person shall be killed, destroyed, wasted, consumed, pined, or lamed in his or her body, or any part thereof; that then every such offender or offenders, their aiders, abettors, and counselors, being of any the said offenses duly and lawfully convicted and attainted, shall suffer pains of death as a felon or felons, and shall lose the privilege and benefit of clergy and sanctuary.

III. And further, to the intent that all manner of practice, use, or exercise of witchcraft, enchantment, charm, or sorcery should be from henceforth utterly avoided, abolished, and taken away, be it enacted by the authority of this present Parliament, that if any person or persons shall, from and after the said Feast of St. Michael the Archangel next coming, take upon him or them by witchcraft, enchantment, charm, or sorcery, [a] to tell or declare in what place any treasure of gold or silver should or might be found or had in the earth or other secret places, or where goods or things lost or stolen should be found or become; or [b] to the intent to provoke any person to unlawful love; or [c] whereby any chattel or goods of any person shall be destroyed, wasted, or impaired; or [d] to hurt or destroy any person in his or her body, although the same be not effected and done; that then all and every such person and persons so offending, and being thereof lawfully convicted, shall for the said offense suffer imprisonment by the space of one whole year, without bail or mainprize [surety], and once in every quarter of the said year shall in some market town, upon the market day or at such time as any fair shall be kept there, stand openly upon the pillory by the space of six hours, and there shall openly confess his or her error and offense.

IV. And if any person or persons being once convicted of the same offenses as is aforesaid eftsoons perpetrate and commit the like offense, that then every such offender, being of any the said offenses the second time lawfully and duly convicted and attainted as is aforesaid, shall suffer pains of death as a felon or felons, and shall lose the benefit and privilege of clergy and sanctuary. Saving to the wife of such person as shall offend in anything contrary to this act her title of dower; and also to the heir and successor of every such person his or their titles of inheritance, succession, and other rights, as though no such attainder of the ancestor or predecessor had been made.

V. Provided always that if the offender in any of the cases aforesaid shall happen to be a peer of this realm, then his trial therein to be had by his peers, as is used in cases of felony or treason, and not otherwise.

Jewish Witchcraft. There was no such thing as Jewish witchcraft. Witchcraft was a blasphemous parody of Christianity with relevance only to a Christian. Because a witch was considered a heretic—that is, a baptized Christian who persisted in disagreeing with official Catholic dogma—no Jew could, by definition, be a witch. Nor, in fact, were Jews often persecuted for witchcraft. They were, of course, attacked as adherents of Satan and, with pagans (i.e., Mohammedans) and witches, bracketed as the main targets of the Faith. Allegations against Jews paralleled the typical accusations against witches (and other heretics), especially the use of poisonous herbs and of human bodies ritually murdered for magical potions and ointments. Conversely, witches were accused of attending a *sabbat*, often (especially in the earliest accounts) called a *synagogue*. These words representative of the Jewish religion were considered opprobrious enough to use against witches.

If Christianity precluded Jews from witchcraft, Jews, for their part, had no concern with witchcraft. First, although they had a developed demonology, with hosts of evil spirits (whose existence was never questioned), neither in their religion nor folklore had they any personification of evil like the Christian Devil, the opponent of God. Satan was an abstraction. Thus the basis of witchcraft, the pact with the Devil, was inconceivable to Jews. Second, whereas Jews had an international reputation for magic, this tradition was kept in a religious framework; angels, not devils, were responsible for effects beyond nature and were, with the names of God, invoked to this end. Magic never rivaled orthodoxy. The talmudic tradition classified various kinds of sorcery, admitting the power of demons as well as angels; but it condemned only sympathetic or "homeopathic" magic. Third, Jewish magic was not malevolent. Devils were not employed to work harm, but to help discover hidden treasure or lost property. Jewish thought could not conceive of black magic, for all magic was white and, since magicians were drawn from the ranks of scholars, not disreputable. Fourth, Jewish religion condemned informers, who, so far as the practice of witchcraft went, were indispensable for the continuation of the trials.

While completely rejecting any Jewish approximation of witchcraft, Jews continued their own traditions of sorcery or magic, the non-essential trappings of Christian witchcraft. There was, for example, a Jewish incubus. In Christian doctrine, intercourse (whether voluntary or enforced) with a devil merited death for bestiality, because the devil was not human. Jewish thought viewed it less seriously (e.g., it could not justify divorce) simply because the relationship was with a devil. Jews made waxen images—not, like Christians, to injure or kill one's enemy, but to recover stolen goods. The Jewish theory differed from the Christian: Pricking of figurines was not sympathetic or diabolical magic, but rested on an involved theory of "angel deputies" (assigned to every person or animal). The angel of the aggrieved would transfer the intended pain (from pricking the image with pins) to the angel of the thief, who in turn would cause pain to the thief himself, who would thereupon return what he had stolen. Among other superstitions, Jews believed in the evil eye, necromancy and other divination, divining rods (taken over from Germany), bier right, treasure-trove, ligature (also from Germany), the magic of herbs, and possession (the "dibbuk" devil did not appear until the sixteenth century). So renowned were their amulets, that at the end of the fourteenth century the Bishop of Salzburg asked a Jew for a mezuzah to place on the gate of his castle!

Very occasionally, the reputation of the Jews to work magic brought them trouble. For example, in 1573, the master minter of Berlin was tortured into confessing he had murdered the Elector by magic drinks. The Jew was fiendishly killed by being torn asunder. The pieces of his corpse were burned with a book on magic allegedly in his possession. In 1579, twenty-four Jews were likewise accused of sorcery and burned at Frankfort-on-Oder.

What aspects of demonic witchcraft existed in Jewry came from a dominating Christian culture; for example, the names of witches, *estrie, broza, mare* (German or French), were transliterated into Hebrew and served for devils. To this extent only, a statement in the thirteenth-century manual on ethics, *Sefer Hasidim*, held true for Jewish "witchcraft": "As the Gentiles do, so do the Jews."

Joan of Arc. Just as in 1590 King James of Scotland believed in Agnes Sampson when she told him what he said to his bride on their wedding night, so in 1429 Charles VII of France believed in Joan of Arc when she repeated his personal daily prayer to God. But a superstitious king is a feeble reed, and when Joan was captured, Charles did nothing to rescue or ransom her. Instead, he transferred his trust in some mystic savior to a young shepherd boy, who was speedily captured by the English and drowned in the Seine. Joan of Arc's trial by the English and Burgundian allies was clearly political, designed to discredit the successes she had brought the French King: she was a witch and he owed his crown to witchcraft. The priests who conducted her trial were for this reason more than usually scrupulous in restricting the process to matters of faith, i.e., heresy.

The literature on Joan of Arc now amounts to over 4,000 items. The New York Public Library catalogues nearly 700 entries, but only one (a minor magazine article) mentions witchcraft. It is often supposed that Joan of Arc was condemned as a witch. This is inaccurate. She was popularly bruited a sorceress and originally alleged a witch; but she was officially condemned as a heretic and legally burned as a relapsed heretic. This fact indicates the embryonic concept of witchcraft in 1431, when it was simpler to secure conviction for heresy than for sorcery. Within the century the reverse would be true.

Joan of Arc [Jehanette or Jehanne Darc] was captured trying to raise the siege of Compiègne on May 23, 1430, by the Bastard of Wandomme, a knight in the service of Jean de Ligny (of the house of Luxembourg). Three days after her capture, the Inquisitor General of France, Friar Martin Billorin, claimed inquisitorial jurisdiction over Joan "as one violently suspect of several errors savoring heresy." On July 14

Procès de condamnation, from a late fifteenth-century manuscript in the Bibliothèque nationale, Paris.

"In the name of the Lord, Amen. Here beginneth the trial regarding her beliefs against a certain woman Joan, commonly called La Pucelle. To all those who may see this present document, Pierre, by divine grace Bishop of Beauvais, and Brother Jean Lemaître, Dominican inquisitor, a man of great piety and prudence, eminent teacher of sacred writings. . . ."

Pierre Cauchon, Bishop of Beauvais, a renegade Frenchman acting for the English, claimed episcopal jurisdiction over Joan as suspect of sorcery and invocation of devils. For her person, he offered Ligny 10,000 francs in cash and to Wandomme an annuity of £300, money raised by taxes in Normandy. Her captors, waiting for a counter offer as ransom from the French King, hesitated. The English-oriented University of Paris assuaged their conscience by pointing out they should act "for the preservation of Holy Church and safeguarding divine honor, and for the utmost benefit to this most Christian kingdom." In mid-November, Joan was surrendered to Bishop Cauchon. The Inquisitor, who had not been willing to compete in the bidding, had to be content with joining the Bishop in trying her.

Joan was imprisoned in the castle of Rouen, the English occupation forces claiming the ecclesiastical prison insecure. En route, she was exhibited in a specially constructed iron cage, barely big enough for her to stand upright, chained by the neck, hands, and feet.

On January 9, 1431, Joan was given an informal hearing before a small, handpicked court. The nine ecclesiastics were well known and erudite, and pro-English, accepting the somewhat irregular jurisdiction of Bishop Cauchon, from a different diocese. During the four sessions, Joan's high-minded answers created a favorable impression, enhanced by the testimony of women appointed by the Duchess of Bedford that Joan was a virgin (and therefore by implication not a witch), and by the favorable reports brought back by royal notaries from her neighbors at Domremy, her birthplace. "They found nothing, they said, which they would not have wished to find in their own sister." But Bishop Cauchon repressed this evidence and drew up several "articles."

After this informal hearing, the regular preparatory interrogations [*procès d'office*] began in Rouen Castle on February 21, 1431, before forty-two priests (seldom all present at the same time). The Bishop of Beauvais presided but turned over the duty of "promoting" or prosecuting to his canon, Jean d'Estivet. At the second session, February 22, the court was joined by the deputy of the Inquisitor General, the Inquisitor Jean le Maistre. After the sixth session, Bishop Cauchon decided to conduct further hearings *in camera* before a few reliable examiners, "in order not to fatigue the rest." From March 10, Joan was examined in her prison cell. Her examination revolved round her claim that her voices or revelations from St. Michael, St. Catherine, and St. Margaret were divine, and on her refusal to accept the authority of the Church in such matters. The implication was that these voices came from the Devil, an interpretation heightened by questions about fairies, a holy tree, mandrakes, and catching butterflies.

As usual in such trials, the judges thought in scholastic terms and, to test Joan's orthodoxy, tried to confuse her by tricky questions. Here are some random examples from the sixteen sessions (the last on March 17, 1431), later offered as proof of her heresy:

Q. Does she see St. Michael and the angels corporeally?

A. I see them with my own corporeal eyes, as well as I see you. And when they leave, I weep, and I wish they would take me with them.

Q. What proof does she have the revelations come from God, and that St. Catherine and St. Margaret are really involved?

A. I have told you often enough that they are St. Catherine and St. Margaret. Believe me if you want to.

Q. Does St. Margaret speak English?

A. Why should she speak English since she does not belong to the English party?

Q. How does she know that St. Catherine and St. Margaret hate the English?

A. They love what God loves and hate what God hates.

Q. Does God hate the English?

A. I know nothing about God's love or hatred for the English or what he will do about their souls. But I do know they will be expelled from France, save those who die here.

Q. Does St. Michael have hair?

A. Why? Do they want to cut it?

Q. Has she kissed St. Michael and St. Catherine?

A. Yes.

Q. Do they smell pleasant?

A. It's good to know they smell pleasant.

Q. In embracing them, does she ever feel any warmth or anything else?

A. It is not possible for me to embrace them without feeling or touching them.

Q. What part has she embraced, the upper or lower?

A. It is more decorous to embrace them above rather than below.

Q. Was St. Michael nude?

A. Do you think then that God has nothing to clothe him with?

Some especially difficult questions were posed, but Joan evaded the traps with a casuistry worthy of her inquisitors. To the demand, "Who is the true pope?" (referring to the three rival popes), she replied she "believed in the true pope at Rome." One priest protested at her being forced into a dilemma: "Are you in a state of grace?" Foreseeing her quandary—"No" would be a confession of guilt; "Yes" proof of her diabolical arrogance—she countered: "If I am not, may God be pleased to lead me to a state of grace; and if I am, may God be pleased to keep me in it."

As a result of this preliminary process, on March 27 Joan of Arc was brought to formal "trial in ordinary" [*procès ordinaire* or *procès de droit inquisitorial*] in Rouen Castle before thirty-seven clerical judges (including two English priests, William Bralbester and John de Hampton), headed again by the Bishop of Beauvais and the Inquisitor. Seventy counts were made against her:

Vehemently suspected, rumored, and notoriously delated by virtuous and sober persons . . . denounced and declared sorceress, witch, diviner, pseudo-prophetess, invoker of evil spirits, conjurer, superstitious, implicated in and given to the arts of magic, doubting the Catholic faith, schismastic . . . blasphemer against God and the saints, scandalous and seditious, perturber of the peace, inciter to war . . . indecent and shameless, seducer of princes and people . . . heretic or at least vehemently suspect of heresy.

After considerable testimony about her earlier life and the magic-ridden customs of Domremy, the main attack turned to her revelations. Joan was trapped when she admitted disobeying her "voices" when she sought to escape from prison, jumping from a high tower at Beaurevoir Castle, and when she had urged an attack on Paris. Logically she was caught in a dilemma: either she had no revelations from God, or she had disobeyed revelations from God. Furthermore, she admitted feeling *impelled* to jump from the tower; in this she had denied free will and had obeyed the Devil.

After thorough inspection of the evidence on these original seventy counts, on April 2 the court struck out all allegations of sorcery or witchcraft (which could hardly be sustained) and reduced the charges to twelve. One covered her belief in apparitions, noting, "On all sides, men and women are rising up, feigning to have revelations of God and his angels, sowing lies and errors." The two principal charges were her wearing of men's costume and her refusal to accept the Church militant. "In case the Church wished her to do something contrary to the commandments she said came from God, she could not do it." In this respect, Joan of Arc was simply a premature Protestant.

Reports on these twelve items were submitted to sixteen doctors of theology and six licentiates of law. After three days, they declared the charges proved. "She sets herself up as an authority, a doctor, a master," they complained. With this backing, the chapter of Rouen Cathedral found Joan a heretic.

On April 18, 1431, the Bishop and the Inquisitor appealed to Joan to reconsider. She refused. Joan fell sick, but physicians cured her, for, as the Duke of Warwick was reported to have said, "the King of England had paid too much for her to be deprived of the pleasure of seeing her burn." Another opportunity for Joan to recant came on May 2 at a solemn session in Rouen Castle before sixty theologians. Joan was still obdurate. On May 9 the instruments of torture were prepared, but on May 12 the judges decided against torture, on the curious grounds that since the whole procedure had been so meticulously conducted, no opportunity should be given for calumny that her confession was forced.

In an effort to hasten her execution, the Cardinal Bishop of Winchester had referred her case to the University of Paris. From April 29 to May 14, the combined four faculties of the Sorbonne deliberated on the records of her trial. The rector, Pierre de Gonda, returned their unanimous verdict: if she would not admit her errors, she should be "relaxed" to the secular authority. This decision was pronounced at Rouen on May 23, 1431. A canon of Rouen, Pierre Maurice, pleaded with Joan:

> Suppose the King of France, by his authority, had entrusted to you the defense of some place, warning you to prevent any chance comer from entering. Some one says he comes by authority of the King, without presenting to you any letter or certain token. Well, should you believe him and admit him? In the same way, God has delivered the rule of his Church to St. Peter and his successors. . . . Thus you should not have given credit to those who you say appeared to you. Obey the Church and submit yourself to her judgment.

To all his persuasion, Joan replied:

> Whatever I have said about my deeds and words in this trial, I let it stand and wish to reaffirm it. Even if I should see the fire lit, the faggots blazing, and the hangman ready to begin the burning, and even if I were in the pyre, I could not say anything different.

On May 24, 1431, in the cemetery of St. Ouen in Rouen, before the English Cardinal Bishop of Winchester and the Bishop of Norwich and a host of distinguished clerics and laymen, the Rector of the University of Paris, Guillaume Erard, delivered a sermon, taking as his text, John xv. 6: "If a man abide not in me, he is cast forth as a branch and is withered; and men gather them, and cast them into the fire, and they are burned." The executioner was standing by to translate this metaphor into reality. Unexpectedly, Joan tried to make a last-minute appeal to the Pope, and then suddenly capitulated, promising to abjure her visions and obey the Church. The English soldiery was furious at losing its victim and stoned the French ecclesiastics.

Joan of Arc's retraction of her confession, which brought about her condemnation as a relapsed heretic and consequent death by burning alive. In the right-hand margin, the scribe has noted her "fatal words"—*Responsio mortifera.* From the Bibliothèque nationale, Paris.

"Questioned what her voices had said to her, Joan replied: That through St. Catherine and St. Margaret, God had shown her the most wretched mistake she had made by this great treason, by agreeing to abjure and revoke her former confession in order to save her life, and that in so trying to save her life she had damned herself. Similarly she said her voices had told her, before last Tuesday, what she would do and what would be done to her at this time. She said furthermore her voices told her, when she would be on the scaffold before the people, to reply courageously to whatever the chaplain said. And Joan said also that he was a false preacher, and that he would reproach her for doing many things she had not done. Finally, she declared that if she said that God had not sent her, she would damn herself, for it was the truth that God himself instructed her.—I notarize the above-written. Boisguillaume."

Joan signed her mark against a hastily written confession:

I, Joan, called La Pucelle, a miserable sinner, after I realized the snare of the error in which I was held, and by the grace of God have returned to our mother Holy Church, in order that all may see that I have re-entered the fold, not feigning but with good heart, I confess that I have previously sinned, in falsely pretending to have had revelations from God and his angels, St. Catherine and St. Margaret. And I revoke all my words and deeds which are contrary to the Church, and I wish to live in union with the Church, without ever straying from it. In witness whereof my mark.

At the start of her life imprisonment "on the bread of grief and the water of affliction"—not in the church prison she had expected—her English guards took away the female attire she had resumed, and substituted men's clothes. The *Procès de réhabilitation*, as biased as the process condemning her, said that eventually she was forced to put them on in order to go to relieve herself. The ecclesiastical court, instantly informed of her change of dress, condemned her on May 28 as a relapsed heretic. Joan retracted her confession and insisted her revelations were divine. On May 29, two friars labored to induce her to repent. The next day, May 30, 1431, the Bishop of Beauvais and the Inquisitor read the sentence of excommunication, "casting her forth and rejecting her from the communion of the Church as an infected limb, and handing her over to the secular justice." There was no secular court, however, and as soon as the priests had left the Old Market Place, the Bailiff of Rouen ordered the execution. The twenty-year-old girl, her head crowned with a miter reading "Relapsed, heretic, apostate, idolater," was placed high on the pyre so the flames would reach her slowly. When her dress had been burned, the hangman slaked the fire so the mob could gaze on "all the secrets which can or should be in a woman. . . . And when the people had satisfied themselves and watched her die, tied to the stake, the hangman built up a huge fire on the poor corpse, which was soon completely burned, and bones and flesh turned to ashes."

Just as this trial had been essentially political, to satisfy the dominant English, so the later process annulling it, on June 16, 1456, was similarly political, to justify the victorious French. In the nineteenth century, interest in Joan of Arc was revived by the clerical party in France, as the *Encyclopaedia Britannica* (11th ed.) noted, "to advertise . . . the intimate union between patriotism and the Catholic faith." On June 6, 1904, Joan was decreed "venerable" by Pope Pius X, and beatified on December 13, 1908. On May 9, 1920, she was canonized by Pope Benedict XV, and on July 10, 1920, the French government declared her festival (May 30) a national holiday.

John XXII, Pope. One of the most superstitious of all popes, always imagining his enemies were plotting to take his life by sorcery, Pope John XXII in 1317 tortured those he suspected into confessing such an attempt. Three years later, on August 22, 1320, John XXII at Avignon had Cardinal William Goudin, in his name, order the Inquisition at Carcassonne to take action against magicians, sorcerers, and those who invoked demons or made waxen images or abused the sacraments, as heretics, and to confiscate their property. In this way, although earlier bulls had been promulgated against practitioners of magic (e.g., by Alexander IV in 1258), John XXII was the first to promote the theory of witchcraft and spread obscurantism.

[Pope John,] desiring fervently that all evildoers, infecting the flock of Christ, be put to flight from the house of God, wishes, orders, and commissions you, by his authority, to seek out and otherwise proceed against those who sacrifice to devils or worship them, or render homage to them, by giving them a charter or something else signed with their name; those who make an open avowed pact with the devils; those who fashion or cause to be fashioned any waxen image, or anything else to bind the devil, or by invocation of devils to commit any kind of *maleficium;* those who, by misusing the sacrament of baptism, baptize a figurine of wax or one made of something else, or cause it to be baptized, or by invocation of devils make or cause anything similar to be done . . . and also those sorcerers and witches who use the sacrament of the mass or the consecrated host as well as other sacraments of the church, or any one of them, in form or matter, for sorcery or witchcraft.

Many times John XXII spurred on the witch hunts, as he did in 1323, 1326, 1327, and 1331. His bull of 1318 allowed trials against dead heretics—"the memory even of a man who is dead must be assailed." In 1330, in a letter to the inquisitors of Toulouse and Narbonne, he lumped together magic and heresy as crimes against God. His bull of 1326 (or 1327) further detailed the crimes of witches and asserted that these crimes were real. By this credulity, doctrine was degraded to superstition:

Some people, Christian in name only, have forsaken the first light of truth to ally themselves with death and traffic with hell. They sacrifice to and adore devils; they make or obtain figurines, rings, vials, mirrors, and other objects by which they command demons through their magic art, getting replies to their questions from them, asking their aid in carrying out their wicked ends, giving themselves up to the most shameful subjection for the most shameful of ends.

Jørgensdatter, Siri. Siri Jørgensdatter provides a documented illustration of how accounts of celebrated witch trials many years later influenced young children, and put ideas into their minds to accuse people as witches. Siri Jørgensdatter was a thirteen-year-old Norwegian girl who in 1730 parroted the myth of the Blakulla [Blocula] invented by the Swedish children at Mora sixty-one years earlier, in 1669. Whether Siri got this story direct from her grandmother, whom she described as a witch, and who would certainly have heard about the Swedish mania which influenced all Scandinavia, or whether she learned it through some history or sermon, cannot

"The Devil told her grandmother that he wanted to take her away." From Olaus Magnus, *Historia de Gentibus Septentrionalibus* (1555).

be decided. The magistrate, however, observed that Siri's description tallied exactly with those given by Cappelio in his *Relationes Curiosae* of the Mora and Elfdale witches.

The magistrate sent the girl to the dean and parson for examination. Their credulous acceptance of the narrative was dismissed by the Bishop and Governor, so that she never came into court. In 1669, however, the same story had brought on the execution of nearly a hundred persons condemned as witches on this kind of evidence.

REPORT OF THE DEAN AND PARSON

Siri told them that when she was seven years old, her grandmother took her to a pigsty, where she smeared a sow with some ointment she took from a horn, whereupon they both mounted and after a short ride through the air arrived at a place that her grandmother called Blaakullen. On the way they met three men dressed in black whom the grandmother referred to as "grandfather's boys." At Blaakullen they left the sow outside the building and went in and sat down at table next to the devil, whom her grandmother called "grandfather." They were served cream pudding, butter, cheese, bread, and both fresh and dried fish, as well as beer to drink. There were seven tables and all the seats were filled.

After eating, the guests began to fight with pieces of bread. Then a trap door in the floor was opened and a blue flame flared up, within which were small people who moved around and made piping noises. The devil, dressed in black and wearing a hat, sat at the head table. Around his waist he wore iron chains which he kept filing, but as soon as a link was filed through, it became whole again. The devil talked with the guests continuously, and, after he had spoken to her grandmother, they went home. . . .

Last New Year's Eve, Siri again went with her grandmother to Blaakullen. They feasted as before, and this time the devil marked her on the little finger. The procedure was as follows: the devil cut the end of her finger with a knife, sucked out some blood and with it wrote the girl's name in a big book, and then bit her on the right ear. There is a visible scar on her finger, and it has been noticed that she has no feeling where the devil cut her and bit her.

Then the grandmother died after a short illness. While she was sick she gave the girl a wooden cup with ointment in it, which she said had been given to her by the devil, and was to be used for riding to Blaakullen with Anne Holsten-stad and Goro Braenden next Whitsun Eve. After the grandmother's death, the girl moved in with her uncle.

Shortly after this, her aunt found the ointment and burned it along with the broom she had ridden on. Siri had confessed to two girls, who told her aunt. Her uncle now took her to the Dean. Three times the devil's boys came to talk to her, one at a time. The first asked her not to reveal anything, the other two threatened to tear off her head because she had revealed what she knew. . . .

She also said she saw her grandmother stick a knife in the wall, tie to it three straps which the devil had given her, and milk any cow in the district that she wanted to.

Finally, she said that Anne Holstenstad came to her in the summer and forbade her to tell anything on pain of losing her health.

Junius, Johannes. The trial in 1628 of Johannes Junius, Burgomaster of Bamberg, is described in contemporary court records. Even more harrowing is the letter he smuggled out of prison to his daughter, which has miraculously been preserved. In all the horrors of the witch delusion, no more soul-shattering document exists than this. It crystallizes the insanity and evil of the whole conception of witchcraft, while at the same time it shows a man's capacity for nobility of spirit. Of this letter, Henry C. Lea wrote: "The very incoherencies of some passages assure the authenticity of what is written under so awful a strain of mind and body."

Bamberg was a notorious center of persecution, especially under Prince-Bishop Johann George II (1623-33), who was responsible for at least six hundred being burned alive, including many of the town's foremost citizens: the Chancellor of the principality and five of its burgomasters. Johannes Junius had served in that capacity from 1608 until the day of his arrest. He was then fifty-five. Shortly before his arrest, his wife had been executed as a witch; hence he wrote to his daughter rather than to his spouse.

The account of his trial, typical of thousands of others throughout Germany, is translated here from the official transcript:

MINUTES OF THE TRIAL OF BURGOMASTER
JOHANNES JUNIUS

On Wednesday, June 28, 1628, was examined without torture, Johannes Junius, Burgomaster at Bamberg, on the charge of witchcraft: how and in what fashion he had fallen into that vice. Is fifty-five years old, and was born at Niederwayisch in the Wetterau. Says he is wholly innocent, knows nothing of the crime, had never in his life renounced God; says that he is wronged before God and the world, would like to hear of a single human being who has seen him at such gatherings [as the witch sabbats].

Confrontation of Dr. George Adam Haan. Tells him to his face he will stake his life on it [*er wolle darauf leben und sterben*] that he saw him, Junius, a year and a half ago at a witch gathering in the electoral council-room, where they ate and drank. Accused denies the same wholly.

Confronted with a servant Ellse. Tells him likewise that he was on Hauptsmorwald at a sabbat, but first the holy wafer was desecrated. Junius denies. Hereupon he was told that his accomplices had confessed against him and was given time for thought.

On Friday, June 30, 1628, the aforesaid Junius was again without torture exhorted to confess, but again confessed nothing; whereupon . . . since he would confess nothing, he was put to the torture, and first

Thumb screws were applied. Says he has never denied God his Saviour nor suffered himself to be otherwise baptized; will again stake his life on it; feels no pain in the thumb screws.

Leg vises [Beinschrauben]. Will confess absolutely nothing; knows nothing about it. He has never renounced God; will never do such a thing; has never been guilty of this vice. Feels likewise no pain.

Is stripped and examined; on his right side is found a bluish mark, shaped like a trefoil, is thrice pricked without sensation or drawing blood.

Strappado. He has never renounced God. God will not forsake him. If he were such a wretch he would not let himself be so tortured. God must show some token of his innocence. He knows nothing about witchcraft. . . .

On July 5, the above-named Junius is without torture, but with urgent persuasions, exhorted to confess, and at last begins and confesses:

Confession of Burgomaster Johannes Junius

When in the year 1624 his lawsuit at Rothweil cost him some six hundred florins, he had gone out, in the month of August, into his orchard [*Baumfeld*] at Friedrichsbronnen; and, as he sat there in thought, there had come to him a woman like a grass-maid, who had asked him why he sat there so sorrowful. He had answered that he was not despondent, but she had led him by seductive speeches to yield to her will. . . . And thereafter this wench had changed into the form of a goat, which bleated and said, "Now you see with whom you have had to do. You must be mine or I will forthwith break your neck." Thereupon he had been frightened, and trembled all over for fear. Then the transformed spirit had seized him by the

throat, and demanded that he should renounce God Almighty, whereupon Junius said, "God help me," and thereupon the spirit vanished through the power of these words. Yet it came straightway back, brought more people with it, and persistently demanded of him that he renounce God in Heaven and all the heavenly host, by which terrible threatening he was obliged to speak this formula: "I renounce God in Heaven and his host, and will henceforth recognize the Devil as my God."

After the renunciation he was so far persuaded by those present and by the evil spirit that he suffered himself to be baptized by the devil in the evil spirit's name. The *Morhauptin* had given him a ducat as dower-gold, which afterward became only a potsherd.

He was then named Krix. His succubus was called Vixen [*Füchsin*]. Those present had congratulated him in Beelzebub's name and said that they were now all alike. At his baptism, among others, were the aforesaid *Morhauptin* Christiana, the young Geiserlin, Paul Glaser, Caspar Wittich, and Claus Gebhard, who were both gardeners. After this they had dispersed.

At this time, his paramour had promised to provide him with money, and from time to time to take him to the sabbats.

Whenever he wished to ride to the sabbat, a black dog would come to his bed, and tell him to come; whereupon he would mount it, and the dog would raise himself in the devil's name and so fly off.

About two years ago, he was taken to the electoral council-room, at the left hand as one goes in. Above, at a table, were seated the Chancellor, the Burgomaster Neudecker, Dr. George Haan, [and twenty-four others]. Since his eyes were not good, he could not recognize more persons.

More time for consideration was now given him.

On July 7, 1628, the aforesaid Junius was again examined, to know what further had occurred to him to confess. He confessed that about two months ago, on the day after an execution was held, he was at a witch dance at the Black Cross,

The most moving document recorded in the history of witchcraft. The first page of the letter of Burgomaster Johannes Junius to his daughter, written on July 24, 1628, and smuggled out of prison just before he was burned as a witch.

where Beelzebub had shown himself to them all and said expressly to their faces that they must all be burned together on this spot, and had ridiculed and taunted those present. Names four more witches.

Crimes of Burgomaster Johannes Junius

Immediately after his seduction, his succubus had demanded that he should make away with his youngest boy Hans Georg, and had given him a gray powder for this purpose; this, however, being too hard for him, he had made away with his brown horse, instead.

His succubus had also repeatedly urged him to kill his two daughters . . . and because he refused he had been beaten therefor.

Once, at the suggestion of his succubus, he had taken the holy wafer out of his mouth and had given it to her. Was obliged occasionally to have intercourse with his succubus.

A week before his arrest, as he was going to St. Martin's church, the devil met him on the way, in the form of a goat, and told him that he would soon be imprisoned, but that he should not trouble himself—he would soon set him free. Besides this, by his soul's salvation, he knew nothing further; but what he had spoken was the pure truth, on that he would stake his life.

On August 6, 1628, there was read to the aforesaid Junius this his confession, which he then wholly ratified and confirmed, and was willing to stake his life upon it. And afterward he voluntarily confirmed the same before the court.

This was the end of the trial, and Junius was burned at the stake.

Before he was burned, Junius, his hands scarce able to hold a pen because of the torture, on July 24, 1628, sent his last letter to his daughter, Veronica. He was kept incommunicado, but his guard smuggled out the note—he was to receive a thaler for his risk. At the end of the letter, Junius advised Veronica to collect whatever money she could and get out of town until the terror diminished, giving out she was going on a pilgrimage.

Junius added a postscript:

Dear child, six have confessed against me at once: the Chancellor, his son, Neudecker, Zaner, Hoffmeister Ursel, and Höppfen Ellse—all false, through compulsion, as they have all told me, and begged my forgiveness in God's name before they were executed. . . . They know nothing but good of me. They were forced to say it, just as I myself was.

LETTER OF BURGOMASTER JOHANNES JUNIUS
TO HIS DAUGHTER VERONICA

July 24, 1628.

Many hundred thousand good-nights, dearly beloved daughter Veronica. Innocent have I come into prison, innocent have I been tortured, innocent must I die. For whoever comes into the witch prison must become a witch or be tortured until he invents something out of his head and—God pity him—bethinks him of something.

I will tell you how it has gone with me.

When I was the first time put to the torture, my brother-in-law, Dr. Braun, Dr. Kötzendörffer, and two strange doctors were there. Then Dr. Braun asks me, "Kinsman, how come you are here?" I answered, "Through falsehood and misfortune." "Hear, you," he retorts, "you are a witch. Will you confess it voluntarily? If not, we'll bring in witnesses and the executioner for you." I said, "I am no witch; I have a pure conscience in the matter. If there are a thousand witnesses, I am not anxious, but I'll gladly hear them."

Then the Chancellor's son was set before me, who said he had seen me. I asked that he be sworn and legally examined, but Dr. Braun refused it. Then the Chancellor, Dr. George Haan, was brought, who said the same as his son. Afterward Höppfen Ellse. She had seen me dance on Hauptsmorwald, but they refused to swear her in. I said: "I have never renounced God, and will never do it—God graciously keep me from it. I'll rather bear whatever I must."

And then came also—God in highest heaven have mercy—the executioner, and put the thumbscrews on me, both hands bound together, so that the blood spurted from the nails and everywhere, so that for four weeks I could not use my hands, as you can see from my writing.

Thereafter they stripped me, bound my hands behind me, and drew me up on the ladder. Then I thought heaven and earth were at an end. Eight times did they draw me up and let me fall again, so that I suffered terrible agony. I said to Dr. Braun, "God forgive you for thus misusing an innocent and honorable man." He replied, "You are a knave."

And this happened on Friday, June 30, and with God's help I had to bear the torture. When at last the executioner led me back into the cell, he said to me, "Sir, I beg you, for God's sake, confess something, whether it be true or not. Invent something, for you cannot endure the torture which you will be put to; and, even if you bear it all, yet you will not escape, not even if you were an earl, but one torture will follow another until you say you are a witch. Not before that," he said, "will they let you go, as you may see by all their trials, for one is just like another."

Then came George Haan, who said the commissioners had said the Prince-Bishop wished to make such an example of me that everybody would be astonished.

And so I begged, since I was in wretched plight, to be given one day for thought and a priest. The priest was refused me, but the time for thought was given. Now, my dearest child, see in what hazard I stood and still stand. I must say that I am a witch, though I am not—must now renounce God, though I have never done it before. Day and night I was deeply troubled, but at last there came to me a new idea. I would not be anxious, but, since I had been given no priest with whom I could take counsel, I would myself think of something and say it. It were surely better that I just say it with mouth and words, even though I had not really done it; and afterwards I could confess it to the priest, and let those answer for it who compel me to do it . . . And so I made my confession, as follows, but it was all a lie.

Now follows, dear child, what I confessed in order to escape the great anguish and bitter torture, which it was impossible for me longer to bear.

[*Here follows his confession, very much as it appears in the minutes of his trial.*]

Then I had to tell what people I had seen [at the witch sabbat]. I said that I had not recognized them. "You old knave, I must put the torturer at your throat. Say—was not the Chancellor there?" So I said yes. "Who besides?" I had not recognized anybody. So he said: "Take one street after another. Begin at the market, go out on one street and back on the next." I had to name several persons there. Then came the long street [*die lange Gasse*]. I knew nobody. Had to name eight persons there. Then the Zinkenwert—one person more. Then over the upper bridge to the Georgthor, on both sides. Knew nobody again. Did I know nobody in the castle—whoever it might be, I should speak without fear.

And thus continuously they asked me on all the streets, though I could not and would not say more. So they gave me to the torturer, told him to strip me, shave me all over, and put me to the torture. "The rascal knows one on the market-place, is with him daily, and yet won't name him." By this they meant Burgomaster Dietmeyer; so I had to name him too.

Then I had to tell what crimes I had committed. I said nothing. . . . "Hoist the knave up!" So I said that I was to kill my children, but I had killed a horse instead. It did not help. I had also taken a sacred wafer, and had buried it. When I said this, they left me in peace.

Now, my dearest child, here you have all my acts and confession, for which I must die. And it is all sheer lies and inventions, so help me God. For all this I was forced to say through dread of torture beyond what I had already endured. For they never cease the torture till one confesses something; be he ever so pious, he must be a witch. Nobody escapes, though he were an earl. If God send no means of bringing the truth to light, our whole kindred will be burned. God in heaven knows that I know not the slightest thing. I die innocent and as a martyr.

Dear child, keep this letter secret, so that people do not find it, else I shall be tortured most piteously and the jailers will be beheaded. So strictly is it forbidden. . . . Dear child, pay this man a thaler. . . . I have taken several days to write this—my hands are both crippled. I am in a sad plight. . . .

Good night, for your father Johannes Junius will never see you more.

Klein, Johann. A professor of law at the University of Rostock, Klein was consequently on the board which, at the end of the seventeenth century, reviewed difficult witch cases submitted by courts in the state of Mecklenburg. A major problem concerned sexual relations between the witch and the devil, and to clarify this difficulty Klein wrote a dissertation. He believed in actual intercourse, although not in offspring (except by delusion by the devil). Some of his arguments and examples are noted in other entries, especially in Sexual Relations with Devils, where there is a reproduction of the title page of the 1731 edition of his *Examen*.

Kramer, Heinrich: see *Malleus Maleficarum*.

Kyteler, Alice. The first witch of Ireland, Lady Alice Kyteler, was in 1324 charged with heretical sorcery, some counts being very similar to the charges common two centuries later. The instigator was Bishop Richard de Ledrede of Ossory, a Franciscan who had been trained in France; the probability is strong that he learned about witch trials there and prematurely tried to introduce them into Ireland. The Bishop chose as his target the wealthiest lady of Kilkenny; the possible confiscation of a heretic's property no doubt spurred his zeal. Lady Alice had acquired her wealth by the death of her various husbands: William Outlaw, Adam le Blound, and Richard de Valle. Her fourth husband, John le Poer, was at the time of her arrest in poor health.

Bishop de Ledrede made seven indictments against Lady Alice, her son by her first marriage (William Outlaw), and several accomplices:

1. To make their sorcery effectual, they denied God and the Catholic Church for various periods of time and abstained from all Christian duties.

2. They sacrificed living creatures, especially cocks, to Robert Artisson (*filius Artis*), a demon, "one of the poorer classes of hell."

3. They sought knowledge of the future from the devils.

4. They parodied religious ceremonies in nocturnal meetings, which they concluded by extinguishing candles and saying "Fi! Fi! Fi! Amen."

5. To incite love and hatred or to kill or injure men and beasts, they made powders and ointments from intestines of sacrificial cocks, "certain horrible worms," herbs, nails of dead men, hair, brains of unbaptized children, all boiled in the skull of a beheaded robber over a fire of oak wood.

6. Lady Alice possessed magic powders. These were found by her fourth husband,

John le Poer, and forwarded to the Bishop. All her other children joined in a complaint that she had killed her husbands and by magic robbed them of their inheritance.

7. Lady Alice had sexual relations with Robert Artisson, who sometimes appeared as a cat, a black shaggy dog, or a black man carrying a rod of iron.

Later chroniclers elaborated on these original charges.

Lady Alice was strong enough to defy the Bishop, who retaliated by excommunicating her. Then Lady Alice imprisoned the Bishop, who countered by placing the whole diocese under interdict and summoning her son, William Outlaw, to his court. To this move, the Lord Justice (a supporter of Alice Kyteler) charged an illegal ban, and the Bishop was forced to lift his censure. In a few days Bishop de Ledrede appeared in full regalia with a train of friars at the secular court, but he was physically ejected. A determined man, the Bishop returned and demanded the civil arrest of those he had accused of sorcery. He was thrown out a second time. Nevertheless, De Ledrede persevered, so that Lady Alice withdrew to England. John le Poer helped the Bishop imprison his stepson, William Outlaw, for nine weeks. The real victim of all this confusion, however, was the lady's maid, Petronilla de Meath, who served as a scapegoat. She was flogged six times and confessed whatever the Bishop wanted. She had sacrificed to Artisson and had been to nocturnal orgies, and Lady Alice was the most wicked and skillful sorcerer alive. Petronilla was excommunicated and burned alive November 3, 1324, at Kilkenny, the first victim of the delusion in Ireland.

Lea made the following important observation on this trial:

The case is interesting as developing a transition state of belief between the earlier magic and the later witchcraft; and it illustrates one of the most important points in the criminal jurisprudence of the succeeding centuries, which explains the unquestioning belief universally entertained as to the marvels of sorcery. Torture administered with unlimited repetition not only brought the patient into a condition in which he would confess whatever was required of him, but the impression produced was such that he would not risk its renewal by retraction even at the last.

The conduct of this ecclesiastical trial in Ireland is in contrast to the common law trial, in the same year (1324), of twenty-seven men and two necromancers at Coventry, England. Although these men conspired to destroy King Edward III by making waxen images, they were acquitted by the jury.

Labourd Witches: see Basque Witches.

Ladder. A method of torture employed throughout France and Germany generally in the preliminary stages of "questioning." It was followed by strappado and squassation.

The accused, garbed only in a shirt or underpants, was placed horizontally on his back, resting on the ladder [*échelle*] or rack [sometimes called *le grand tresteau*], or on the ground between two fixed posts. His legs were fastened with ropes to one end, and his arms, bound together and extended over his head, were attached to the other end by a kind of tourniquet. When the tourniquet was tightened, the ropes contracted so that his body was suspended taut in the air.

A more severe use of the ladder involved twistings [*tortillons*] of the rope to increase the pain. The prisoner, man or woman, was bound to the two uprights of the ladder by relatively thin ropes from his shoulders, arms, and fingers down to his toes. The ropes were wound round and round the limbs and the uprights. By this means, little sticks could be inserted into the ropes and rotated as in a tourniquet. The cords were twisted and tightened so that the limbs and joints were squeezed in many places, and the knots in the ropes forced into the flesh.

Lamia. A common Latin word describing a witch. In classical legend, Lamia was a queen of Libya whose beauty charmed

Stretching the prisoner on a rack, ladder, or (as here) with ropes attached to two fixed hooks, was the first stage of torture. In this illustration, the hangman is causing additional pain by applying the tourniquet to the thighs. From Joost Damhouder, *Enchiridion* (1554).

Zeus, by whom she bore several children. Hera, angry at her husband's infidelity, transformed Lamia's beauty into ugliness and killed her children. In despair, Lamia turned to killing the children of others. Lamia also had the power to resume her original loveliness to seduce men and suck their blood. The word *lamia* was used in the Vulgate Latin to translate the Hebrew Lilith, originally a Babylonian night spirit, in Hebrew lore the first wife of Adam, and in the Book of *Emek hammelech* a spectral whore. In Isaiah xxxiv, the Authorized Version translates *ibi cobavit lamia* as "the screech owl also shall rest there," while the Revised Version has "night monster."

Thus the word has numerous associations in folklore and legend. In the writings of the demonologists, *lamia* often implies a vampire or (night-)mare. Gervais of Tilbury (about 1218) saw in *lamia*, vulgarly called *masca*, a simple nocturnal hallucination like the mare, "which disturbs the minds of sleepers and oppresses with weight." The meaning of *lamia* is further complicated by being linked to *striga* or *strix* (screech owl), a vampire which attacks children, all being used for evil creatures which disturb sleep. The word seems to have served a dual use, one stressing a diabolic aspect (as a succubus demon), and the other (as early as the ninth century) a witch. Nicholaus of Jauer, professor of theology at Prague and Heidelberg (1402-35), said *lamiae* were really demons in the shape of old women who stole children and roasted them over a fire. Johannes Pott, in his study of intercourse between humans and demons (1689), distinguished several kinds of *lamiae:* unstable women deceived by the devil into *thinking* they can do various tricks of magic, and women who consciously enter a pact with the Devil to gratify their exorbitant sexual desires.

Lancashire Witches. Of all the many pamphlets and chapbooks describing witch trials in England, *The Wonderful Discovery of Witches in the County of Lancaster* (London, 1613) is outstanding. This mass trial of twenty alleged witches was the largest to that date (1612) in England, and created considerable stir throughout the northern counties. The chapbook was unusually long (188 pages in the original) and detailed; it was a semiofficial record written by the clerk of the court (Thomas Potts) and was approved by the judge (Sir Edward Bromley) as being "carefully set forth and truly reported." The document thus became a kind of textbook on the conduct of witch trials.

Old Demdike, as eighty-year-old, blind Mrs. Elizabeth Sowthern was known, confessed she became a witch about 1560, when a "spirit or devil in the shape of a boy" received her soul. Five years later, this "wicked firebrand of mischief" persuaded a friend and neighbor, Mrs. Ann Whittle ("Old Chattox") to join her in "most barbarous and damnable practices, murders, wicked and devilish conspiracies." These two were aided by their daughters—Old

Demdike by Elizabeth Device, and Old Chattox by Anne Redfearne—with other relatives and neighbors.

Potts made each of the four principals a caricature of a chapbook witch. Old Chattox, also about eighty, was a "withered, spent, and decrepit creature, her sight almost gone." Old Demdike was the "rankest hag that ever troubled daylight." Elizabeth Device "was branded with a preposterous mark in nature, even from her birth, which was her left eye standing lower than the other, the one looking down, the other looking up, so strangely deformed, as the best that were present in that honorable assembly and great audience did affirm, they had not often seen the like."

In March, 1612, Old Demdike was brought before a local justice, Roger Nowell, for examination on suspicion of witchcraft by common report. This examination was a "fishing expedition." Old Demdike implicated her granddaughter, Alison Device, and her rival, Old Chattox. All three were committed to Lancaster Castle for the assizes. Alison Device was indicted for laming an itinerant peddler. To her evil intention was ascribed what seems to have been a stroke:

> But by this devilish art of witchcraft his head is drawn awry, his eyes and face deformed, his speech not well to be understood, his thighs and legs stark lame; his arms lame, especially the left side, his hands lamed and turned out of their course; his body able to endure no travail.

Alison confessed, and the link between cause and effect was welded. Old Chattox was indicted

> For that she feloniously had practiced, used, and exercised divers wicked and devilish arts called witchcraft, enchantments, charms, and sorceries, in and upon one Robert Nutter of Greenhead, in the Forest of Pendle in the county of Lancaster, and by force of the same witchcraft feloniously had killed the said Robert Nutter.

In addition, Old Demdike's daughter, Elizabeth Device, and Old Chattox's daughter,

Anne Redfearne, were involved in charges of bewitching Robert Nutter to death.

The account of the trial (on August 17) is exceptional only in the fullness of its presentation, and in its cops-and-robbers story of a plot to blow up the jail to free the prisoners—the novelty of this charge lent verisimilitude to the other more hackneyed items.

Early in April, on Good Friday, it was charged that Elizabeth Device called an emergency meeting of the two families at her mother's home, Malking Tower in the Forest of Pendle, for "some speedy course for the deliverance of her mother (Old Demdike), her daughter [Alison], and other witches at Lancaster." About eighteen women and two or three men attended; sixteen were identified by name (but only about half of these were indicted). There was "great cheer, merry company, and much conference." This first English sabbat seems not much more than a solid English repast. "The persons aforesaid had to their dinner, beef, bacon, and roasted mutton." The mutton was a wether admittedly stolen by James (an act sufficient to hang him, apart from witchcraft). The group planned to kill the jailer at Lancaster, blow up the Castle (an idea clearly borrowed from Guy Fawkes' Gunpowder Plot seven years before to blow up the Houses of Parliament), and free the accused. Potts's record says all "went out of the said house in their own shape and likeness," rode off on horseback, and "presently vanished out of . . . sight." This sounds like an attempt to add metamorphosis (and perhaps transvection) to the witches' crimes. The next meeting was arranged for the following year. Rumor of such an assembly got to the ears of Justice Nowell, who, on April 27, arrested and sent to Lancaster nine witches (some others who were accused fled).

The Court prided itself on its objectivity and fairness, but to secure conviction of all the accused it actually relied almost exclusively on the evidence of Elizabeth Device and her children, James (in his early twenties) and Jannet (aged nine). Elizabeth Device refused to confess "until it pleased God to raise up a young maid,

Jannet Device, her own daughter, about the age of nine years, a witness unexpected, to discover all their practices, meetings, consultations, murders, charms, and villainies." When her other two children joined Jannet, Elizabeth made "a very liberal and voluntary confession." Although she retracted this, her confession still stood and became the chief evidence against her. She died maintaining her innocence.

Jannet told how a "spirit in likeness of a brown dog," called Ball, helped her mother kill people. James Device testified he too had seen the brown dog as well as the making of magic clay images, and had heard his grandmother say Elizabeth had bewitched a man to death for refusing alms. James told a weird story of stealing the communion bread on Maundy Thursday. When he returned home, a hare asked him for the bread; James crossed himself, and the hare vanished.

James and Jannet identified most of the witches at the alleged dinner at Malking Tower. In spite of his co-operation with the Court in accusing his mother and naming names, James faced two indictments. On nine-year-old Jannet's word, further indictments were added: James, she said, had employed another dog named Dandy to bewitch to death. While held a prisoner in the Castle, James confessed in front of three witnesses. He was, says Potts, "as dangerous and malicious a witch as ever lived in these parts of Lancaster."

On charges of bewitching to death Robert Nutter, "the evidence being not very pregnant against her," Anne Redfearne was found Not Guilty. This verdict displeased both the court and the mob, and she was tried again for bewitching to death Robert's father, Christopher Nutter. She was convicted. The evidence appears the same in both cases, much of it hearsay gossip going back "eighteen or nineteen years."

Alice Nutter, the mother of the dead Robert, was "a rich woman and had a great estate." She appeared "of good temper, free from envy and malice." She was fingered as present at Malking Tower. Mrs. Nutter was proved a witch because James Device said his grandmother said she was a witch, because Jannet Device said her mother had told her Alice was a witch, and because Elizabeth Device said she and Alice bewitched a man to death. To be very certain that Jannet identified Alice Nutter correctly, Judge Bromley, "being very suspicious of the accusations of this young wench," presented a number of prisoners "and some other strange women" to Jannet. Jannet (who had seen Mrs. Nutter, a prominent figure in the county, many times, and who only a few minutes before had been giving testimony against her in court) passed this test successfully. "This could be no forged or false accusation," reported Potts, "but the very act of God to discover her." Mrs. Nutter died protesting her innocence, convicted, as Notestein said, on "the flimsiest [evidence] ever offered to a court."

Similar evidence was presented against the others accused. The evidence of confessing witches was readily accepted, because "who but witches can be proofs and so witnesses of the doings of witches?" It is not known how these confessions were secured; Old Demdike died in jail. Old Chattox, "being openly charged with all this in open court, with weeping tears she humbly acknowledged them to be true." Nearly all the other accused, however, insisted on their innocence, "crying out in very violent and outrageous manner, even to the gallows, where they died impenitent (for anything we know)."

In all, ten of the accused were hanged, including Old Chattox and her daughter Anne Redfearne; Elizabeth Device (daughter of Old Demdike, who died in jail) and her son James, and her eleven-year-old daughter Alison; and Mrs. Alice Nutter. Two others were sentenced to one year in jail with four appearances in the pillory; the rest of the twenty were acquitted.

On the third day, the trial of the Lancashire witches was interrupted by the trial of the three Salmesbury witches, accused of afflicting a young woman. Taking advantage of a flicker of doubt evidenced by the judge, the three women urged him to interrogate the girl. She admitted her accusations were false, and had been prepared by a Roman Catholic priest incensed at the three women's apostasy to Protestantism. This interruption made no impression on the major trial.

The Lancashire witches of 1612 are to be distinguished from the infamous swindle in 1634 at Pendle, in which the words of a young boy convicted seventeen persons, eventually reprieved by Charles I. Among those accused was Jannet Device.

Lancre, Pierre de. "Our fathers lived in this error, based on erroneous conceptions, that witches should not be condemned to death, but simply sent back to their pastors and curés as if it were simply illusion and false imagination." Pierre de Lancre (1553-1631) as a trial judge tried to remedy such error, and boasted of burning 600 victims. Today he becomes especially valuable for his detailed eyewitness account of a witch hunt in his *Tableau de l'inconstance des mauvais anges* [*Description of the Inconstancy of Evil Angels*] (1612). His other works on witchcraft are *L'Incredulité et mescréance du sortilège* [*Incredulity and Misbelief of Enchantment*] (1622) and *Du Sortilège* [*Witchcraft*] (1627).

Pierre de Rosteguy, Sieur de Lancre, was born in Bordeaux in 1553, the son of a rich winegrower who became a royal official and adopted the name of De Lancre. Pierre studied law at Turin and in Bohemia, becoming in 1579 a doctor of laws, and in 1582 a lawyer for the Parlement of Bordeaux. In 1588, he married Jehanne de Mons, the grandniece of Montaigne. Montaigne had also been a lawyer for the Parlement, and, possibly with De Lancre's legal activities in mind, wrote in his *Essays:* "The witches of my part of the country go in danger of their lives, as every new author transforms fantasies into realities. . . . Our life is too real and essential to warrant these supernatural and fantastical accidents." De Lancre started on a pilgrimage to the Holy Land in 1599, but got only as far as Naples. While passing through Rome, he saw a girl changed by the devil into a boy; undoubtedly this metamorphosis deepened his belief in witchcraft.

At the end of 1608 (December 10), King

Henry IV commissioned Pierre de Lancre, now a wealthy magistrate, to investigate the Pays de Labourd, a Basque-speaking territory in the southwest part of Guienne [see Basque Witches]. On February 4, 1609, the Parlement of Bordeaux restricted his investigations to witchcraft, and added its president, D'Espagnet, to his committee. Their tenure was to run to November 10, 1609. However, D'Espagnet resigned by June 5, and his partner continued alone, searching out witches by the devil's mark. De Lancre discovered that the whole population of 30,000, including all the priests, were infected by witchcraft. Apparently this heresy had been introduced into Labourd from Béarn at the end of the fifteenth century (since the Basque words for witchcraft were borrowed from Romance languages); once implanted, because of the isolation of the area, it had supposedly developed freely.

The *Tableau* consists of nearly 600 pages relating the highlights of De Lancre's experiences at the trials in Labourd, interspersed with some discussion on demonology. In addition to the sabbat, De Lancre devoted some 150 pages to lycanthropy based on the case of Jean Grenier. Almost a century later, the Abbé Laurent Bordelon singled out De Lancre for especial ridicule in his *Histoire . . . de Monsieur Oufle* (1610). Bordelon mocked the *Tableau*, parodying its double-page engraving of the sabbat with an even more sensational illustration, and paying tongue-in-cheek tribute: "There is such an ample and very particular description of all that passes at the sabbat, that I don't believe I should be better informed concerning it if I had been there myself."

At the age of sixty-three, De Lancre retired to Loubeur-sur-Garonne, near Cadillac, and there wrote his other works on witchcraft. He died in 1631, his tomb being inscribed in Basque. He had no legitimate son, so his estate went to his grandnephews; he bequeathed his library, however, to his bastard son, a Jesuit.

Lateau, Louise. Louise Lateau, the "Belgian stigmatic," manifested many of the classic symptoms of bewitched children, in addition to her celebrated hemorrhages or stigmata. Because she lived in the second half of the nineteenth century, however, her condition was recorded by medical men rather than by demonologists or exorcists. Consequently her "ecstasies" became a standard of comparison for the many young women in the history of witchcraft who had fits and visions, from the girls in the Warboys trial to the Goodwin children. Perhaps the closest parallel was Jeanne Fery (about 1580), possessed by eight devils.

Louise was born in Hainault in 1850, and, although both parents were healthy, was a sickly child. Just after she had entered service with her 78-year-old grandaunt, at the age of eleven, she was gored by a bull; at sixteen, she nursed a dying household in a cholera epidemic, removing the corpses herself. At seventeen an attack of angina nearly killed her. She made her first communion at eleven, and communicated nearly every week thereafter; five years later she joined the Third Order of St. Francis. Apparently, Louise was a simple girl and very charitable: religion was the main force in her life.

The *grande maladie* which made her celebrated began when she was eighteen, a few weeks before the onset of her first menstruation. She had an urge to suffer the agonies of Christ's crucifixion. She lost her appetite, spouted blood through the mouth, and existed for a month on water. On April 15, 1868, she had a vision of the Christ Child and went into an ecstasy; on April 19 her menses began. In May she had the first of the hemorrhages from her side and feet, which recurred at more or less regular intervals for the next seven years.

Dr. Bourneville, the alienist, analyzed these symptoms into two groups: the stigmata, of minor concern for witchcraft; the ecstasies, typical marks of possession—

1. Hemorrhages or stigmata.
Pustules formed under the skin, like blisters, containing blood with a very high proportion of white corpuscles. These pustules broke and continued bleeding up to twenty-four hours, with an

The very rare illustration in the second edition of Pierre de Lancre's *Tableau de l'inconstance des mauvais anges* (Paris, 1613), showing a very elaborate conception of the sabbat. De Lancre gave the following explanation of the details:

A. Satan preaching in the likeness of a goat, seated in a golden chair. One of his five horns is lighted to kindle all the candles and fires of the sabbat.

B. The Queen of the sabbat, crowned, at his right; one less favored at his left.

C. In front of the throne, a witch presents a child she has abducted.

D. Here are the guests at the sabbat feast, each having a demon next to her. The only meat is that of corpses, hanged men, hearts of unbaptized children, and unclean animals never eaten by Christians. Everything is insipid and without salt.

E. At the extreme right, poor witches, who dare not approach the high ceremonies, are admitted only as spectators and shoved away into corners.

F. After the feasting follows the dancing; for having been filled up with food, whether unsatisfying or illusory, and most pernicious and abominable in any case, each devil leads the one who was seated next him at the banquet table under a cursed tree. There, the first devil turns his face inward toward the dancers, and the second faces outward, while the rest alternate in the same way. Then they all dance, stamping their feet, and moving with the most salacious indecencies they can imagine.

G. These are the musicians performing their concert, to whose music and song the witches leap and dance.

H. Below is a troop of women and girls who dance in a circle, back to back.

average loss of about 250 grams of blood. Other bleeding came from cracks or little swellings, hard to the touch, and looking like toughened pimples. The surrounding skin was not turgid or inflamed. Louise also had a "crown of thorns," twelve to fifteen points in her forehead from which she could make a little blood flow.

2. Ecstasies or frenzies, some like diabolical possession of earlier times, characterized by three stages:

a) Contortion: Louise threw herself to the ground, as if distracted, dislocated and choking. This stage was followed by periods of insensibility.

b) Genuflexion: Louise fell on her knees, one hand on her stomach, her head high as if watching an invisible spectacle. This lasted about fifteen minutes, and was followed by pallor and flushes, weeping, lowered pulse and body temperature.

c) Prostration: Louise appeared in deep sleep with all her limbs extended. She developed convulsive movements causing complete rigidity of the body in the position of crucifixion. After several hours, Louise began to relax her body; her eyes were closed, her face very pallid, covered with cold sweat, and her hands icy.

In addition to these two main symptoms, Louise frequently went without food or water, sleep, or urination and defecation (allegedly as long as twenty or thirty days). After she reached twenty-five, her hysteria apparently ceased.

From his long experience at the Salpêtrière, the mental hospital in Paris, Dr. Bourneville cited patient after patient whose

The first stage of demoniacal possession: contortion followed by insensibility.

condition paralleled that of Louise. He diagnosed "hemorrhage of the stomach and skin combined with convulsions." This he defined as "hysteria."

Leicester Boy. A rare instance of fraud exposed (1616).

In the decades around 1600, the testimony of young adolescents sent many old women to the gallows. The Leicester Boy is as incredible as the Burton Boy, the Boy of Northwich, the Bilson Boy, or Edmund Robinson [see Pendle Swindle]. The trials which grew out of the accusations of these young people all followed the precedent established in 1593 at the conviction of the witches at Warboys, save that the evidence of the Leicester Boy (like that of the Bilson Boy) was shattered, and those so blatantly stigmatized were rehabilitated.

The Boy of Leicester was John Smith, of Husbands Bosworth, Leicestershire, young son of Sir Roger Smith (an ancestor of the Earls of Derby). In 1607, when only four

---

I. Here is a pan over a fire to make all sorts of poisons, to bring death and disease to men, or to waste the flocks. One witch holds serpents and toads in her hand, and the other cuts off their heads and skins them and then throws them in the pot.

K. During the sabbat, several witches arrive on pitchforks and broomsticks, others on goats with their children, whom they have instructed in and incited to witchcraft, to present before Satan. Others are leaving and, carried aloft, are going over the sea to raise storms and tempests.

L. At the left are the noble lords and ladies, and other rich and powerful witches who conduct the important business of the sabbat, where they often appear disguised or masked, so that they will not be recognized.

M. Young children assist the witches who brought them to the sabbat ceremonies by using sticks and white switches to prevent the toads from getting out of a little stream.

or five, he had accused several women of bewitching him, but no convictions resulted. As his hystero-epilepsy progressed —in which lying and imposture are familiar symptoms—he was able to develop his imagination and document his visions so that, at the age of thirteen, his word alone could procure the conviction and execution of nine witches. Just like the Salem girls, John Smith claimed the witches tormented him; like Margaret Rule, his fits were of such force that men could not restrain him. Like Madeleine de Demandolx [see Aix-en-Provence Nuns], whose possession had become widely known in England by 1613, he made cries like a horse whenever a demon or witch in such shape affected him. Like the Throckmorton children [see Warboys Witches], he had a similar formula ready for recitation by the accused, probably picked up from the conversation of his elders about the most famous cause célèbre in England for many years.

A contemporary letter describes his seizures:

> A young gentleman of the age of twelve or thirteen years old . . . hath had divers wonderful strange fits. . . . Sir Henry Hastings hath done what he could to hold him in his fit, but he and another as strong as he could not hold him. If he might have his arm at liberty, he would strike himself such blows on his breast, being in his shirt, that you might hear the sound of it the length of a long chamber, sometimes fifty blows, sometimes one hundred, yea, sometimes two or three hundred blows, that the least of them was able to strike down a strong man. And yet he did to himself no hurt.

He had accused nine women of bewitching him.

> Six of the witches had six several spirits, one in the likeness of a horse, another like a dog, another a cat, another a foumart [polecat], another a fish, another a toad, with whom every one of them tormented him. He would make some sign according to the spirit, as, when the horse tormented him he would whinny; when the cat tormented him, he would cry like a cat &c. When he was in his fit, [the witches] were sometimes brought to him, and then were charged to speak certain words, and to name their spirits, and one of them to speak it after another, as thus: "I such a one charge thee, horse, if I be a witch, that thou come forth of the child." And then another by her spirit to do the like, and so till all had done. If any of them would speak a word contrary to that "charm," [the boy] should be mightily tormented; but if [they] would speak as he had first directed them, at the end of the last he would fall out of his fit as quietly as if one lay him down to sleep.

Like most of the other Children Accusers, his deception might have passed unnoticed, had not chance brought King James I to Leicester on one of his "progresses" (August 15, 1616), a few weeks after the hanging of the nine witches named by Smith (July 18, 1616). Ever interested in the occult, James I examined the boy, "whereupon John Smith began to falter, so as the King discovered a fallacy; where the servants of [Archbishop Abbot of Canterbury] did in a few weeks discover the whole deceit"— Osborne. The King was informed of the imposture, for "upon a small entreaty, [the boy] would repeat all his tricks oftentimes in a day."

Six other witches still remained in prison as a result of John Smith's allegations; October brought a new trial (with a representative of the Archbishop present) and their release—too late for one, unhappily, for she had died in prison.

This was not the first time the superstitious King had exposed fraud. Early in his reign he had detected the imposture "of a woman [who] pretended to be bewitched, that cast up at her mouth pins, and pins were taken by divers in her fits out of her breast." In April, 1605, James revealed the sham of Richard Haydock, the so-called Sleeping Preacher at Oxford.

The gullible magistrate, Sir Humphrey Winch, and his Sergeant Crew, who had countenanced John Smith's ravings, were discredited by the King's overriding them, but were not punished. James, however, allowed Ben Jonson the liberty of satirizing them in his *The Devil Is an Ass*. This play poked fun at credulous acceptance of the witch belief, where "a boy of thirteen year old made [the devil] an ass but t'other day."

Lemp, Rebecca. Rivaling in poignancy the intimate farewell letter of Johannes Junius to his daughter is the letter by Rebecca Lemp, jailed in 1590 for witchcraft, to her husband, Peter Lemp, a well-educated accountant of Nördlingen, Swabia. The persecutions were promoted here, not by pastors or priests, but by local lawyers, Sebastien Roettinger and Conrad Graf, led by Burgomaster Georg Pheringer. In spite of the favorable testimony of neighbors who took the risk of appearing in their defense, in 1590 thirty-two prominent and well-placed women were burned. Among them were Frau Lemp and the wives of a former burgomaster, a senator, the town clerk, and an important administrator.

The four documents translated here were read in court and incorporated in the trial record.

I

The first, a moving letter to Rebecca Lemp from her six young children, was written very soon after her arrest in April, 1590, while her husband was away. The children could not comprehend what was happening and, after a few days, their father still absent on business, wrote to their mother. John, the little scholar of the family, showed off his schooling by signing his name in Latin.

Our dutiful greeting, dearly beloved Mother! We let thee know that we are well. Thou hast informed us that thou art well too. We expect that father will come home today, God willing. So we will let thee know as soon as he gets home. Almighty God grant thee his grace and Holy Spirit that, if it please God, thou mayest come back to us hearty and well. God grant it! Amen.

Dearly beloved Mother, let beer be bought for thee, bread for soup, and little fried fish got, and send to us for a little chicken. I have just killed two. The Rev. Rummel [a friend of the family] has dined with us. If thou needest money, send for it; thou hast some in thy purse. Fare thee well, my beloved Mother; do not be worried about the housekeeping till thou comest back to us.

Rebecca Lempin, thy loving daughter
Anna Maria Lempin, thy loving daughter
Maria Salome Lempin, thy loving daughter
Joannes Conradus Lempius, *tuus amantissimus filius*
Samuel Lemp, thy loving son
X [mark of Peter Lemp]
For the thousandth time, God grant thee a good night.

II

The second is Rebecca's letter to her husband, in which she fears he may believe the accusations against her. Naïvely, she tells him not to worry; since she has done nothing wrong, she will not be tortured!

My dearly beloved Husband, be not troubled. Were I to be charged by thousands of accusations, I am innocent, else may all the demons in hell come and tear me to pieces. Were they to pulverize me, cut me in a thousand pieces, I could not confess anything. Therefore do not be alarmed; before my conscience and before my soul I am innocent. Will I be tortured? I don't believe it, since I am not guilty of anything. Husband mine, if I am guilty of anything, may God reject me forever far from his sight. If they do not believe me, Almighty God, who knows everything, will work a miracle so they will believe me. Otherwise, if I have to stay in this anxiety, there is no God in heaven. Don't hide thy face from me, thou knowest my innocence. In God's name, do not leave me in this anguish which is choking me.

III

Third is Rebecca's note to her husband, some months later, after she had been tortured five times and had confessed. How she wrote this letter and smuggled it out of jail is not known, but it was intercepted and read in court as evidence of an additional crime, suicide, because she asked her husband to bring her poison.

O thou, the chosen of my heart, must I be parted from thee, though entirely innocent? If so, may God be followed throughout eternity by my reproaches. They force one and make one confess; they have so tortured me, but I am as innocent as God in heaven. If I know the least thing about such matters, may God shut the door of heaven against me! O thou, dearly beloved Husband, my heart is nearly broken! Alas, alas! My poor dear children orphans! Husband, send me something that I may die, or I must expire under the torture; if thou canst not today, do it tomorrow. Write to me directly.—R. L.

[*On the reverse.*] Oh, Husband of thine innocent Rebecca, they take me from thee by force! How can God suffer it? If I am a witch, may God show no pity to me. Oh, what wrong is done me! Why will God not hear me? Send me something, else may I peril even my soul.

IV

The court then dictated a letter which Rebecca had to write to her husband, swearing she had lied and that she was indeed a witch, unworthy of him and her children. Peter Lemp, however, knew his wife too well to be deceived by this ruse, and resolutely replied to the court in the following letter:

Honorable and esteemed lords, most wise and magnanimous!

Recently, on June 1, I addressed to the court a humble petition relating to my dear wife, in which I requested that she be set free; but my request was turned down. May my petition this time have a different result. Since then, I have received from my wife a true report, in which she tells me she is closely confined in prison for something of which she is not guilty, and asks me to come to her help—me, her closest, dearest, and best friend, her husband, spouse—and to succor her in her tribulation and suffering. In truth, I would not be a Christian, if I did not seek how to comfort and assist her. [*Peter Lemp then asked for confrontation by witnesses, because he believed the accusations were secured by torture.*] I hope, I believe, I know that during all our life, my wife has never even thought about what she is accused of, let alone having done it. I swear this by my soul. Very many well-respected people, who know me and my wife, testify, as I do, that she has always been a pious, chaste, honest housewife, foe to any evil; that she has always cherished me faithfully as her dear spouse. She has, moreover, as a good mother to her family carefully raised our dear little ones, taught them—together with me—not only their catechism, but furthermore the Holy Bible, especially the beautiful psalms of David. Indeed, thanks to God—and I say this without boasting—all the children with which God has blessed us, without exception, know and can recite several psalms.

No one in the world—this I say to the best of my belief—can maintain that my wife ever worked the least ill, no matter what, or that anyone had the slightest suspicion about her. . . .

This is why, in my name and in the name of my dear little children, who now number six—God be forever praised—I humbly pray you, for the love of God and the prospect of the last judgment at which Jesus Christ will himself appear as judge, and I beg you, who manifest in yourselves wisdom and duly constituted authority, to show a favorable regard for my dear wife and to set her free.

After it had received this petition of Peter Lemp, the court further tortured Rebecca and condemned her to be burned on September 9, 1590.

Then the witch hunt intensified, and the prisons overflowed. The persecutions ceased only in 1594 when Maria Hollin, who owned the Crown tavern in Nördlingen, maintained her innocence during eleven months in a stinking dungeon, being subjected *fifty-six times* to the most cruel tortures the court could imagine—among the highest number recorded where the victim survived. Its use of torture, the court argued, was actually in the interests of the accused, because it quickly terminated the suspense of uncertainty and indefinite anxiety. Maria Hollin was ultimately rescued by the intervention of Ulm, the city of her birth, which claimed jurisdiction over her. But her resistance at Nördlingen gave courage to Pastor Wilhelm Lutz to speak out in the name of the Protestant churches and, supported by public opinion, force the infuriated lawyers to stop their illegal trials. "The proceedings will never end," preached Lutz, "for there are people who have informed on their mothers-in-law, their wives or husbands, denouncing them as witches. What can come of all this?"

Leo X, Pope. In trials for witchcraft, the Inquisition, having found the accused guilty of heresy, released him to the secular authority with a formal recommendation for mercy. Should the civil court show mercy, its officials were then guilty of favoring heretics and equally culpable. The fiction that the Inquisition did not in effect sentence to death is exposed by a bull of Pope Leo X on February 15, 1521. In that year, the Senate of Venice refused to sanction some very numerous executions ordered by the Inquisition in Brescia, and summoned the acting papal legate, the Bishop of Capo d'Istria, to explain the severity of the burnings. The dispute between church and state flared into the open. Thereupon, Leo X, "the Maecenas of Renaissance Humanism" (as Montague Summers called him), wrote to his inquisitor as follows:

And therefore, on account of the said letters [of the Senate of Venice], in which the said legate was restricted, some have hesitated whether you can proceed with your power thus diminished, as you were able before the transmission of the [Venetian] letters. And as it is indecent and contrary to the disposition of law and the sacred canons, prejudicial to the liberty of the church, that laymen interfere in ecclesiastical proceedings and refuse to carry out an execution ordered by us, unless they have seen and examined the court records and sentences, as if they had authority and jurisdiction over priests and in religious matters, whereas, however, their competency has never been recognized in any similar case, the only thing they have to do being to do as they are told and to perform the execution, without any right of questioning. Wherefore among the faithful of Christ no little scandal has arisen.

We, therefore, in order that what has been introduced for the salvation of souls and for the simplest expediting of the said trials may not degenerate into injury and destruction, and moreover, on account of the delays, that these unhappy souls be not more heavily charged with such sins, and that all doubt about such procedures may be removed,

We decree and declare, by virtue of our apostolic authority, that you should continue, as is your bounden duty, to take action, just as before the said letters [of the Venetian Senate] were issued, according to law, custom, and privilege, against all witches and sorcerers, apostates from the faith, depending on the extent of their crime.

And we declare and order you to exhort and command the aforesaid Senate of Venice, their Doge and his officials, to intervene no more in this kind of trial, but promptly, without changing or inspecting the sentences made by the ecclesiastical judges, to execute the sentences which they are enjoined to carry out. And if they neglect or refuse, you are to compel them with the Church's censure and other appropriate legal measures. From this order there is no appeal.

Levitation: see Transvection.

Ligature. Ligature is a state of impotency produced by sorcery, generally accomplished by tying knots in threads or hanks [Latin: *licia*], and also by administering potions. The fear of impotence was traditional; Vergil in his eighth *Eclogue* referred to the nine knots which affected copulation, and Petronius (first century A.D.) wrote of the restoration of virility. That ligature was merely an addition to witchcraft is clear from its previous existence and from its survival after the trials came to an end.

Guazzo, whose *Compendium Maleficarum* (1608) usefully summarized previous authorities, classified ligature under seven general heads:

1. When one of a married couple is made hateful to the other, or both hateful to each other.

2. When some bodily hindrance keeps a husband and wife apart in different

places, or when some thing or phantasm is interposed.

3. When the vital spirit is hindered from flowing to the penis and the emission of semen is prevented.

4. When the semen is not fertile.

5. When a man's penis becomes flabby whenever he wishes to perform the sex act.

6. When certain natural drugs are given a woman to prevent her from conceiving.

7. When the female genitals become narrow or close up, or when the male organ retracts.

Domenic de Soto noted that, because the Devil did not wish to discourage fornication, ligature was not as common as other sorts of witches' *maleficia*.

The typical method of ligature—*vaecordia* [Latin], *aiguillette* [French], or *ghirlanda delle streghe* [Italian]—was to tie knots in a cord or a strip of leather and hide it. This "detestable impiety which merited the witch's death" (in Bodin's words) would continue until the cord was discovered and untied; the ligature would remain permanent if the cord were not found or if the knots could not be loosened.

Another method involved potions. At the Château de Bassompierre an old man married a beautiful young wife, but kept his mistress. The wife became jealous and sought advice from a neighbor, who gave her a herb to put in her husband's soup. When the husband woke up the following morning, he found himself impotent. "Since he could not hope to conceal it from her for long," he told his wife. Realizing her own forfeit of connubial pleasures, the wife confessed what she had done, "saying that it was all due to the great love which she had for him." The lord of the manor was informed; he discovered the witch and forced her to administer another herb to restore virility. The witch, "guilty by her own showing," was soon afterwards burned to death.

Most demonologists, especially De Soto, Bodin, Remy, and Guazzo, discussed impo-

tence caused by magic. In 1567 a woman told Bodin there were more than fifty ways of knotting the *aiguillette*—varying in application (to affect urination, copulation, or procreation; one, both, or all partners) and duration (for a day, month, forever). In a person under ligature, swellings would appear on the body, indicating the children who would otherwise have been born. Bodin, however, disbelieved the *Malleus Maleficarum* that witches could hide a man's penis in his belly. This was apparently a specialty of the German witches. In Scotland, in 1590, Janet Grant and Janet Clark were convicted of taking away the privy members from some men and bestowing them on others [see also Reginald Scot].

Since the intended injury was diabolical, cures were difficult. The *Malleus Maleficarum* recommended coming to friendly terms with the witch. Grillandus told of a respected citizen, unable to consummate his marriage, who sought help from a white witch or *magus*. The magician gave him a potion which produced a frightening nightmare but enabled him eventually to raise a large family. Other authorities forbade any attempt to cure ligature by any kind of sorcery.

Ivo of Chartres (died 1115) was the first Catholic theologian to discuss the impediment at any length. Thomas Aquinas (1227-74) also accepted the idea of ligature. In his discussion of impediments to matrimony, he wrote:

> Of witchcraft, however, be it known that certain have said there is no such thing [as ligature] and that this proceeded from infidelity, because they would have it that there are no demons, save by the imagination of men—inasmuch, that is, as men imagined them and, terrified by that imagining, were distressed. But the Catholic faith teaches both that there are demons and that by their doings they can inflict injury on men and prevent carnal copulation. (*Quodlibeta*)

The theologians found a supernatural reason to explain natural events. Ulrich

Molitor (1489) related how wives brought deficient spouses into court; the husbands were examined by physicians and their impotence deemed the result of witchcraft. Earlier, Petrus Mamor (1462) complained that many people in Aquitaine abused the plea of *impotentia ex maleficio* to secure annulments. This followed the distinction (established by Aquinas) between natural *frigiditas*, where a man (*frigidus*) could not sleep with any woman at all, and ligature, where a man (*maleficiatus*) could not perform copulation with just one woman. The Canon of the Church (Gratian's *Corpus Juris Canonici*, about 1140) established four points:

1. Copulation can be prevented by malice.
2. Ligature is allowed only by permission of God.
3. The Devil effects the ligature. (Curiously enough, God allowed the Devil power only over the genitals.)
4. Relief can come with God's help, by abstinence and prayers. White witches are to be avoided.

The celebrated Franciscan, Father Candidus Brognolus Bergomensi, in his *Manuale Exorcistarum* (1651), gave a French prayer against impotence caused by the Devil in a partner who entered matrimony only to satisfy the lusts of the flesh: "Please, God, deliver me from this *maleficium* with which I am ligatured. . . . I do not want to make use of marriage only as a remedy for avoiding the sins of lechery."

Ligature was, of course, recognized (outside of Rome) as a just cause for dissolution of marriage: "If by chance they are not able to be healed, the spouses are allowed to separate"—*Decretum*. "Ligature, if it is perpetual and precedes matrimony, renders void a union about to be made and annuls one already contracted." (*Hostiensis*, and Alphonsus de Vera Cruz)

Lille Novices. Witchcraft is closely linked to young women afflicted with genuine or fraudulent physical or mental abnormalities. Of the many deceptions, possibly the most obvious concerns the deluding of An-

toinette Bourignon by the thirty-two girls she had befriended in her convent home at Lille (Département du Nord, northern France).

Antoinette Bourignon (1616-80) started a foundling home about 1653 and soon had fifty orphan girls under her care. Being very devout, she decided to start a convent, and in 1658 the majority of her charges joined her cloister "where she kept her girls under strict discipline and to very good orders." Madame Bourignon later became famous as a mystic; she was exiled from Flanders and died in Friesland, much revered. She wrote voluminously, her two best-known books being *La Parole de Dieu* [*The Word of God*] and *La Vie extérieure* [*Mysticism for the Layman*]. Perhaps her preoccupation with the mystical life kept her mind from administering the convent, for very soon her wards turned out to be witches! When a pastor examined the girls, aged from eight to twenty-two, all thirty-two of them "declared that they had daily carnal cohabitation with the devil, that they went to the sabbats or meetings, where they ate, drank, danced, and committed other whoredom and sensualities."

The novices of Lille had discovered how to exploit the credulity of Madame Bourignon. A thirteen-year-old girl explained: "She was to have been whipped [for stealing]; but saith she, 'Do not do it, and I'll tell you who it is that makes me do this mischief.'" She escaped punishment, and Antoinette Bourignon heard about the girl's temptation by the devil, who appeared as "a handsome young youth a little bigger than herself." A twelve-year-old also found the devil a good excuse to avoid punishment for misdemeanors. Her account of the sabbat is actually a touching fairy story of a sad little orphan's daydreams of the gay life of the rich folk:

Being very young and playing with the girls in the village, they asked her if she would go with them to the dedication [sabbat]; that she should have good cheer and a sweetheart into the bargain. And as soon as she consented, her said lover came upon a little horse, and took her by the hand, asking her if she would be his mistress. And she saying "Ay," she was catched up into the air with him and the other girls; and they flew all together to a great castle, where they played upon instruments, danced, feasted, and drank wine.

Madame Bourignon, incredibly credulous, had a kind heart. She summarized her predicament:

I was mightily perplexed to find myself confined to a house with two and thirty creatures who declared that they had all given their souls to the devil . . . I proposed to dismiss them by degrees, but then I feared I should be guilty of the mischief that they would do among mankind when they were abroad. . . . Upon this, I was greatly dispirited, and could not see what was the will of God in this point.

After her death, the cult of Bourignianism grew, and infiltrated Scotland. It is surprising that Madame Bourignon was never threatened as a witch, for among the reasons Jack Cockburn, who wrote about Bourignianism, gave for her fame were secret knowledge of men's thoughts, foretelling, and supernatural acquiring of knowledge without books or teachers. Cockburn, however, dismissed her acts and sayings as "the effects of a melancholy head or crazy brain."

Löher, Hermann. To fall into the hands of a witch judge, wrote Hermann Löher about 1650, "is just as if a condemned person were forced to fight with lions, bears, and wolves for his life, and were prevented from protecting himself, since he is deprived of weapons of every description." This quotation comes from a book existing in only one copy, *Hochnötige unterthänige wemütige Klage der frommen Unschültigen* [*Most Pressing Humble Complaint of the Pious Innocents*]. Löher was not letting his imagination run wild; he had been an official of the law court at Rheinbach, near Bonn, during the two fantastic waves of persecution in 1631 and 1636, which killed one person out of every two families. In the preceding hundred years, the village had not known one case of imprisonment,

let alone an execution. But things changed with the visitations of a special itinerant judge, Franz Buirman. Löher, as one of the court's seven local assessors, saw terror grip the village, and contributed to a common bribe to get the judge to go elsewhere. Buirmann went, but returned in 1636. Löher then joined the mayor and one other official in opposing Buirmann, but they received little support; and Löher, having quietly liquidated as much of his property as he could, barely escaped with his family to Amsterdam. Buirmann brazenly confiscated the remainder of Löher's property on August 3, 1636. Löher became a Dutch citizen, set up business again, and lived to be over eighty.

Löher felt impelled to record his own experiences "to enlighten the authorities for justice in a uniform criminal procedure among humble folk in small towns and villages." He stressed three points: (1) innocent people who are tried in the witch courts are tortured and die innocent; (2) victims lie when tortured; (3) all victims can be forced to confess anything, especially when the torture is repeated. Löher urged the local princes in Germany to scrutinize the court records, to reduce the high fees the officials received for trying each witch, and above all to stop the torture.

> "The early Christian martyrs were falsely accused of grievous crimes; but in our day Christian witches are far more unjustly accused of mortal sins that they have not committed—and that they could not possibly commit."
> —Hermann Löher, *Hochnötige* (1676).

In a memorable passage, Löher describes how a witch judge conducted a trial, raging at the accused:

You apostate, you witch, you dumb dog [*du stummer Hund*]! Confess your sin of witchery [*Zauberlaster*]; reveal the names of your accomplices! You filthy whore, you devil's wanton, you sackcloth-maker, you dumb toad [*du alte garstige Hur, du Teuffelsbuhlin, du Rupffenmachersche, du stumme Krotte*]! Speak and confess in God's name! Swal-

An illustration of the horrors of the witch trials included by Hermann Löher in his exposé, only one copy of which is extant today.

low the holy salt! Drink the holy water! Tell who it was that taught you witchcraft [*Zauberen*], and whom you saw and recognized at the witches' sabbat [*Zaubertanz*]. Then you will not be tortured any more, but have eternal life.

Although he started collecting his materials when he came to Amsterdam, Löher did not publish his book until 1676, when he was eighty-one. He delayed for fear of reprisals from the authorities.

Who would assume such a dangerous task? Should anyone undertake it out of Christian charity, then people would somehow manage to prevent him from being heard; and if he were heard, then those who began the unjust witch burnings would cry out that they mistrust him as a witch lover.

At long last he realized he must speak out, and so that the book could have wide circulation, he himself subsidized the publication. The *Hochnötige* was illustrated with plates of witch tortures, seven of which are reproduced here.

Loos, Cornelius. Father Cornelius Loos, the first man in Germany who raised his voice against the witch hunts, was a celebrated theologian; he was tortured and banished.

What he had to say was so damning that the Inquisition raided the Protestant printshop at Cologne where Loos in 1592 had secretly sent his manuscript. For almost 300 years his work was thought destroyed, known only by what its opponents said of it, until in 1886, by a stroke of good luck, two of its four sections were found by the great American scholar of witchcraft, George L. Burr.

Cornelius [Callidus] Loos was Dutch, born in Gouda in 1546. He quickly distinguished himself at the universities of both Louvain and Liége. Because of the religious struggles in Holland, Loos accepted a professorship at the Catholic College of Mainz; here he wrote many denunciations of the Protestants, and, his prestige spreading, was rewarded with a professorship at Treves.

At that time Treves was a center of the witch persecution. Loos's firsthand experience of the trials horrified him, and he determined to try to halt them. He may have been influenced by the Dutch skeptic, Johan Weyer (1563), whose works were available. Loos spoke to important people; he wrote letters to the civil and ecclesiastical authorities.

When these steps proved fruitless, he took to writing a tract. In *De Vera et Falsa Magia* [*True and False Sorcery*], he attacked the notion of a physical devil—"Devils do not assume bodies"—and the use of torture to produce confessions. "Wretched creatures are compelled by the severity of the torture to confess things they have never done, and so by cruel butchery innocent lives are taken and by a new alchemy gold and silver coined from human blood." Loos was especially vehement against the *Mal-*

leus Maleficarum, blaming it for introducing persecution into Germany, and attacked the influential Suffragan Bishop of Treves, Peter Binsfeld, for bolstering a sagging system. Only occasionally did his indignation flare up, as when he wrote about the alleged pact with Satan: "One can but exclaim, O Christian Religion, how long shalt thou be vexed with this direst of superstitions? and cry aloud, O Christian Commonwealth, how long in thee shall the life of the innocent be imperiled?"

Word of Loos's unorthodoxy got about, and by order of the Papal Nuncio, Bishop Ottavio, the polemic was suppressed, and Loos jailed in the dungeons of the local Benedictine Abbey of St. Maximin. After a long imprisonment, during which his health was broken, on Monday, March 15, 1593, publicly kneeling before a swarm of dignitaries, Loos made his recantation (written for him by his opponent, Binsfeld). Del Rio, a Jesuit demonologist, printed the text to discredit his ideas; it was heresy *not* to believe in witchcraft—pact and copulation, flight through the air, and all.

The nature of this still unpublished work can be gathered from its "Propositions" or chapters. Book I: the nature of magic, essence of demons, diversity of witchcraft, divine permission, consent of witches, imaginary compact. Book II: power of devils, impotence of devils, poisoning and magic, disparity of devils, incorporeal substances, assumption of bodies.

Father Loos was banished, and he found a curacy at Notre-Dame-de-la-Chapelle in Brussels. Although aware of the dangers, he would not be silent, and he was soon seized as a relapsed heretic. Surprisingly, he was not executed, but after many months was set free. His death, on February 3, 1595, forestalled a third incarceration and probable burning. He was, by his wish, buried in an obscure chapel in the parish, before a figure of Christ bearing the Cross.

Looten, Thomas. Thomas Looten (1599-1659) was convicted of sorcery at a civil trial in 1659 at Bailleul, a small town lying between Dunkirk and Lille (Département du Nord).

Contemporary court records of witch trials are not too common, and those from Bailleul are especially welcome. The documents provide a useful chronology of the several steps of a trial, from the first preliminary investigation to the final burning of a corpse forty-seven days later. They comprise the official account of Bailiff Jacques Vandewalle the Younger of Meteren, official prosecutor in the "sovereign court of the town and lordship of Bailleul," on the conduct of the trial, the torture of garrote, and the confession inevitably extracted after forty-eight hours of torment. In addition, there is the day-by-day listing (with further brief comments on the trial) of the expenses incurred by the court, which had to be paid by the estate of the prisoner. Together these court records and notes (written in Flemish) form an invaluable original source for our knowledge of a civil process. This trial is doubtless typical of thousands of similar cases.

The procedure may be reconstructed as follows:

September 21. Thomas Looten, an old man living in Meteren, is suspected by his neighbors of causing the death of a child by offering it bewitched plums. Hounded by the villagers, he surrenders to the bailiff and asks for a trial in order to clear himself. Local citizens (*les hommes de fief*) sitting as judges order him guarded by two constables and held in prison.

September 23. The bailiff reports he has found twelve witnesses against Looten, and is told by the judges to search Looten's house for magic ointment and powder.

September 25. Three witnesses are examined.

September 27. First public examination of the prisoner, before eleven judges (the number varied from four to twenty-one).

Q. When were you born, who are your parents, and where have you lived since marriage?

A. I was born at Zudberquin and am about sixty years old; my father was called Maillard and my mother Nannette Heyeman, and I have lived in the parish of Meteren since my marriage.

Q. What caused you to give yourself up as a prisoner?

A. Because a child of Adam Wycaert, a neighbor in the parish, died about a month ago, and folk suspected me of having killed it by sorcery, and therefore I wish to clear myself.

September 30. Bailiff requests a trial to show proof or disproof of witchcraft.

October 11. Another witness is examined.

October 16. Recall of a previous witness.

October 28. Bailiff announces he has the necessary evidence to prove sorcery; judges to ask prisoner if he wishes to introduce counterevidence.

October 29. Judges to interview prisoner about engaging services of a lawyer.

October 31. M. Pierre Boddaert and M. François Hysenbrant, two of the judges acting for the whole bench, visit the prisoner in jail, and tell him that the Bailiff, prosecutor by reason of his office, has gathered sufficient evidence to prove sorcery, and that the defendant has the right to prove the contrary, if he thinks fit. To these same men sent to ask him if he desires to offer opposing evidence for his vindication, he replies in the negative. He also declines the services of a lawyer, saying only that

> he is not guilty either in word or deed of any of the enormities attributed to him and that he will accept whatever verdict the judges choose to render in this action, but they should strive to reach a judgment so scrupulously that afterwards they will not themselves be condemned in the life to come.

November 1. The judges (eight members present) avail themselves of the Dunkirk torturer [*bourreau*], who happens to be passing through town, "to see whether he had been marked with the *stigma diaboli.*" The torturer finds a mark

> in which the aforementioned torturer has several times thrust a pin as far as its head without the same prisoner feeling it or shedding a single drop of blood, although the aforesaid torturer squeezed the spot from underneath to make it bleed. And the aforesaid torturer declared under oath that the prisoner had the aforesaid devil's mark, and that he

himself had examined and executed between 500-600 witches, so that he was very certain that this was a real devil's mark.

He signed his affidavit with a cross. In view of this discovery, the judges order the prisoner "put to torture to obtain by this means his sworn oath on the deeds charged against him."

November 2. Looten is put to torture by the garrote, "seated on a wooden chair with his arms stretched out, his feet twisted under another chair and tightly bound," and his neck enclosed in an iron collar which could be tightened by screws. He affirms that in Jean Boone's tavern one Robert Beicqué said that Jean Merlinck had said Looten was a witch; that he had given plums to many children, including Adam Wycaert's child; and that he had heard that this child had become sick and died a few days later. Asked why he had not complained to the judges about such accusations, he replies that he had and that was the reason he was in prison. The torture to continue until further notice.

November 4. The torture is continued, the torturer testifying that the constitution of the prisoner is such that he can stand much more rigorous torture. The prisoner is placed

> on another chair previously blessed, his shirt is removed and burnt in his presence, and another blessed one put on, while his whole body is sprinkled with holy water by Father Martin, a Capuchin friar, who had exorcized him; finally the judges stay close by the side of the prisoner, so that, when it appears necessary, they can call the doctor to survey the case and determine the capacity of the victim.

At eight o'clock in the evening, Looten breaks down and confesses. His confession is a stereotype: all the well-known crimes are listed and a few local names are inserted for verisimilitude. Looten says he has been a sorcerer for eight years, that he had signed a pact with the devil in blood "drawn from his right thumb," and had been marked on the shoulder, and that the devil, called Harlakyn, appeared to him dressed in green and with a deformed foot. Then Looten gives a list of places where he had attended the sabbat, always in the company of three or four beautiful women, with one of whom he always had intercourse, and says he had feasted on beer and hard cider and veal (but without salt). He had received green ointments from the devil so that he could fly wherever he wished. The devil had endured in his stead the pains of the torture, and given him large sums of money to buy cows and horses for resale. He had given Wycaert's child "three plums on which he had previously spat, for which he received five coins from the devil."

November 5. About eight o'clock in the evening, the body of Looten is found with the neck broken, "suffocated by the Devil himself," some twenty hours after he had been released from the garrote. The bailiff and judges order the dead body to be dragged to the scaffold to be burnt, and then taken on a cart to the 's Gravensberg Gibbet for public spectacle on the wheel [*roue*].

November 6. The sentence is carried out as ordered.

For each time the judges sat they received an honorarium of 2 livres 10 pattars, probably the cost of a banquet; on one day (November 1) they assembled four times. For each meeting there was a levy of 10 pattars, no doubt for court expenses. The two doctors received 12 livres; the bailiff received 22 pattars for examining each of sixteen witnesses; the three guards, at 8 pattars a day, were paid the sum of 68 livres and 8 pattars—a padded expense account: they worked 47 days and were paid for 57. In addition the prisoner was charged the cost of searching his house for witch powders; the expense of his transportation from Bailleul to Meteren; the cost of the paper for recording his trial (on September 27, eleven leaves at 8 pattars each); the travel expenses for two judges to escort the burnt body to 's Gravensberg; and even the wood consumed during the torturing. Looten would also have to pay for the food he ate while imprisoned, but a space is left

blank in the manuscript for this amount. The fees of the torturer and the scaffold-maker were paid separately by the bailiff. In all, the cost to Looten of his own execution was far more than the 197 livres and 10 pattars (3,950 pattars) itemized. This value may be approximated from the cost of a cow, which in this same document ranges from 10 to 16 or 20 pattars (one livre), or of a heifer, which was priced at 5 pattars. The judges ordered confiscation of Looten's goods to pay for these expenses and any other debts.

One final comment on the Looten case is called for. The court of the nearby lordship at Cassel, hearing of the work of the torturer while at Bailleul, wrote for the names of its residents whom Looten named. The court of Bailleul quickly sent the names of six persons said by Looten to have been with him at the sabbat. This document does not indicate the disposition.

Loudun Nuns. In seventeenth-century France, many priests lived little differently from laymen; some few rivaled the urbanity and license of men of the world. One such was the handsome Father Urbain Grandier, appointed in 1617 parish priest of St.-Pierre-du-Marché in Loudun. Compounding the difficulties which he might have anticipated as a result of his notorious amours, Father Grandier gibed at the powerful Cardinal Richelieu, then temporarily in disfavor with King Louis XIII. The priest was suspected of being the father of the child of Philippa Trincant, daughter of the public prosecutor of Loudun, and he openly made a mistress of one of his young penitents, Madeleine de Brou. It caused little surprise that, after thirteen years as a parish priest leading this gay and scandalous life of "marriages of conscience," Father Grandier on June 2, 1630, was charged with immorality before his enemy, the Bishop of Poitiers, and found Guilty. But Father Grandier had political connections and was able to have his suspension from clerical duties lifted within the year by order of Archbishop Sourdis of Bordeaux.

His opponents, to forestall his revenge,

Father Urbain Grandier, accused by the Nuns of Loudun in 1633 of witchcraft.

then had recourse to Father Mignon, another enemy, confessor to the nuns of a small Ursuline convent at Loudun. The plan was to persuade a few sisters they were possessed and, under exorcism, get them to swear that Father Grandier had bewitched them. The Mother Superior, Sister Jeanne des Anges (Madame de Béclier), and a nun co-operated; they went into fantastic convulsions, holding their breath to swell to a huge size and altering their looks and voices. Sister Jeanne said they were possessed by two devils, Asmodeus and Zabulon, sent by Father Grandier. The plot misfired, however, and the outcome was merely a prohibition by the Archbishop on March 21, 1633, against any further exorcism by Father Mignon and Father Pierre Barré, his confederate.

Although the nuns were allowed to resume their regular quiet lives, the conspiracy against Father Grandier continued. Monsieur Jean de Laubardemont, a relative of the Mother Superior's and an important crony of the now omnipotent Cardinal Richelieu, came to Loudun on government business to supervise the pulling down of the fortified keep. Laubardemont was told that Father Grandier had published a virulent satire which enraged Richelieu; Laubardemont was also aware that one of the nuns, Sister Claire de Sazilly, was related to the Cardinal. The chance of humiliating the parish priest was not to be foregone, and Richelieu was eager to

show his power. Accordingly, Laubardemont was ordered to form a kangaroo commission with two complaisant magistrates, the seneschal and the civil lieutenant, to arrest and convict Father Grandier as a witch.

The original plot was revived. Under exorcism by the Franciscan Father Lactance, the Capuchin Father Tranquille, and the Jesuit Father Surin, the nuns took up their accusations against Father Grandier. Some of his rejected mistresses helped prejudice his case. "Sixty witnesses deposed to adulteries, incests, sacrileges, and other crimes, committed by the accused, even in the most secret places of his church, as in the vestry, where the holy host was kept, on all days and at all hours." (Des Niau) The priests took care to exorcize the nuns in public, and great crowds came to watch and hear the denunciations of Father Grandier.

Finally, Father Grandier was himself forced to exorcize the nuns, because they claimed he had caused their possession. Since one of the sure signs of demoniacal possession was the ability of the energumens to speak foreign languages, Father Grandier spoke to one of the nuns in Greek. But the nun had been coached. "Ah, you are subtle. You know full well that one of the first conditions of the pact between us was never to speak Greek." Des Niau reported that the priest "did not dare to question her or the others in Greek, though they dared him to it; whereon he remained very embarrassed." At the end of the scene, the nuns moved on the priest, accusing him of witchcraft. The Mother Superior swore that Father Grandier had bewitched them by throwing a bouquet of roses over the convent walls.

During the building up of charges against him, Father Grandier took no counter steps, thinking he could not be convicted of an imaginary crime. On November 30, 1633, however, he was thrown into the jail of the castle of Angers. According to the later account compiled by Nicholas Aubin, devil's marks were quickly discovered by the expedient of cutting the priest with a

RECIT

VERITABLE

DE CE QVI S'EST

PASSE' A LOVDVN.

Contre Maiſtre Vrbain Grandier
'Preſtre Curé de l'Egliſe de S. Pierr
de Loudun, attaint eſ conuaincu di
crime de Magie, maleſice eſ poſſeſio:
arriuée par ſon fauct és perſonne
d'aucunes des Religieuſes Vrſeline
de la ville de Loudun.

A   PARIS,
De l'Imprimerie de PIERRE TARGA, ru
Sainct Victor au Soleil d'or.

M. DC   XXXIV.

Title page of one of the many contemporary
tracts written for and against Father Urbain
Grandier on charges of bewitching the nuns
at Loudun.

sharp lancet in one part of his body, causing him to cry out in considerable pain, and
then immediately lightly touching his body
elsewhere with the blunt end, causing no
pain. The procés-verbal recorded four such
areas on the buttocks and testicles. An
apothecary from Poitiers witnessed the
hoax and, snatching the lancet, quickly
proved the sensitivity of the priest's flesh;
the surgeon who prepared him for torture,
Dr. Fourneau, likewise testified he found
no such devil's marks.

The trial at Loudun was irregular and a
mockery of justice. In the first place, Urbain Grandier should legally have been
tried by the secular court and permitted an
appeal to the Parlement of Paris (traditionally lukewarm to accusations of witchcraft). Hence the Cardinal used the shoddy
device of an investigating committee. In the

second place, customary legal procedures
were cast aside. The prosecution produced
Father Grandier's pact with the Devil, allegedly written in his own hand, which the
demon Asmodeus had rifled from Lucifer's
cabinet and given to the court. (The manuscript was preserved for many years as a
curio; it is reproduced and translated here
under the entry for Pact.) The court refused to allow several nuns to retract their
previous statement against the priest, explaining their volte-face as an attempt by
the Devil to save his servant. The nuns insisted their testimony had been dictated by
the friars who hated the parish priest. The
Mother Superior was ignored when she appeared in court with a noose round her
neck, threatening to hang herself to ex-
piate her previous false witness. Such
friends of Father Grandier's as wished to
appear in his defense were pressured by
Laubardemont into keeping silence, on pain
of their own inculpation as witches. A local
physician, Dr. Claude Quillet of Chinon,
had detected impostures at the public exorcisms wherein Father Grandier was accused and wanted to give his testimony
before the commission; Monsieur Laubardemont immediately ordered his arrest, and
Dr. Quillet saved himself by flight to Italy.
Laubardemont issued warrants for Father
Grandier's three brothers, two of whom
were parish priests; all three were similarly
forced to flee. A public meeting in support
of the priest, organized by the Bailli of
Loudun, complained of the arbitrary procedure of the committee; Laubardemont
squelched it as an attack on the King, implying treason.

On August 18, 1634, sentence was pronounced, both degrees of torture followed
by burning alive, as follows:

We have ordered and do order the said
Urbain Grandier duly tried and convicted of the crime of magic, maleficia, and of causing demoniacal possession of several Ursuline nuns of this
town of Loudun, as well as of other
secular women, together with other
charges and crimes resulting therefrom.
For atonement of which, we have condemned and do condemn the said Gran-

dier to make *amende honorable*, his head bare, a rope round his neck, holding in his hand a burning taper weighing two pounds, before the principal door of the church of St.-Pierre-du-Marché, and before that of St. Ursula of this town. There on his knees, to ask pardon of God, the King, and the law; this done, he is to be taken to the public square of St. Croix, and fastened to a stake on a scaffold, which shall be erected on the said place for this purpose, and there to be burned alive, together with all the compacts and magical apparatus used by him, as well as the manuscript book composed by him against the celibacy of priests, and his ashes scattered to the wind. We have ordered and do order that each and every article of his movable property be acquired and confiscated by the King; the sum of 500 livres first being taken for buying a bronze plaque, on which will be engraved the abstract of this present trial, to be set up in a prominent spot in the said church of the Ursulines, to remain there for all eternity. And before proceeding to the execution of the present sentence, we order the said Grandier to be submitted to the first and last degrees of torture [*la question ordinaire et extraordinaire*], concerning his accomplices. Given at Loudun against the said Grandier, and executed August 18, 1634.

Even under torture so severe that the marrow of his bones oozed out of his broken limbs, Father Grandier maintained his innocence and refused to bear false witness by naming imaginary accomplices. A contemporary manuscript at Poitiers said Father Tranquille and other Capuchins assisted in the torture and smashed his legs. So furious were they at his fortitude, they proved him a witch by arguing that every time he prayed to God he was in reality invoking the Devil—his God! Father Grandier had been promised permission to make a dying statement and to receive the mercy of strangulation before burning. The friars who accompanied him to his death, however, prevented him from speaking by deluging him with holy water. One account, which has indeed been disputed, said the friars made sure he kept quiet by smashing his face with a heavy crucifix, under

A contemporary sketch of Father Urbain Grandier being burned alive at Loudun in 1634.

pretext of making him kiss it. At any rate, they arranged that the halter for his garroting was so knotted that it could not be drawn tight. The Franciscan Father Lactance himself lit the pyre and, with Madame de Laubardemont, gloated over Grandier's struggles as he burned alive.

Some slight retribution came in the fate of his tormentors: Father Lactance died insane within the month, his last words being, "Grandier, I was not responsible for your death." Father Tranquille died insane within five years; Dr. Mannouri, the witch pricker, was so haunted by his false findings that he died in horrible delirium; and Father Barré was banished from France in 1640 for collusion with pretended demoniacs at Chinon [see Possession].

Even after the murder of Father Grandier, at whose death the demoniacal possession of the nuns should have ceased, the sisters continued their displays, and the town and the convent profited by becoming a tourist attraction.

Typical of the nuns' conduct under

The receipt for the wood used to burn Father Urbain Grandier. "I, the undersigned, state I have had and received the sum of nineteen livres and sixteen sous for wood that was used to make the pyre for Monsieur Urbain Grandier, for the stake to which he was bound, and for other wood which I left there. Done at Loudun, this twenty-fourth day of August, 1634. Deliard."

exorcism was the behavior of one young nun, Sister Claire.

She fell on the ground, blaspheming, in convulsions, lifting up her petticoats and chemise, displaying her privy parts without any shame, and uttering filthy words. Her gestures became so indecent that the audience averted its eyes. She cried out again and again, abusing herself with her hands, "Come on, then, *foutez-moi!*"

She called the prior by name, though it was said she had never seen him before, asking him to be her lover. This demonstration lasted an hour.

[At other times, the nuns] struck their chests and backs with their heads, as if they had their necks broken, and with inconceivable rapidity. They twisted their arms at the joints of the shoulder, the elbow, or the wrist, two or three times round. Lying on their stomachs, they joined the palms of their hands to the soles of their feet; their faces became so frightful one could not bear to look at them; their eyes remained open without winking. Their tongues issued suddenly from their mouths, horribly swollen, black, hard, and covered with pimples, and yet while in this state they spoke distinctly. They threw themselves back till their heads touched their feet, and walked in this position with wonderful rapidity, and for a long time. They uttered cries so horrible and so loud that nothing like it was ever heard before. They made use of expressions so indecent as to shame the most debauched of men,

while their acts, both in exposing themselves and inviting lewd behavior from
those present, would have astonished the
inmates of the lowest brothel in the
country. (Des Niau)

The English nobleman Lord Montagu
was so impressed by the exorcisms conducted by the Jesuit Jean Joseph Surin that
he was converted to Roman Catholicism.
However, when Cardinal Richelieu's niece,
the Duchess d'Aiguillon, visited Loudun,
she realized the imposture and told her
uncle. Richelieu had now lost interest in
the affair, and he discontinued the "pension" he had granted the demoniacs for de-
claiming against Grandier. With no regular
subsidy for their performances, the nuns
themselves lost interest; and money—or
lack of it—succeeded in curing their possession where exorcism had failed.

Louis XIV: Edict of 1682. A turning
point in the history of the witch mania in
France was the Edict of Louis XIV in 1682,
which practically put an end to all trials for
witchcraft. It followed closely the terrific
outburst of satanic degeneracy in the King's
own court, exposed by the trials in the
Chambre ardente and, after an interval of
twelve years, the rebuke the King had given
to the Parlement of Normandy in 1670.
The Edict served several purposes: it classified witchcraft on a very low level as
*pratiques superstitieuses, superstition, pré-
tendues magies, prétextes,* and thereby dismissed the lurid apparatus of the sabbat
which the demonologists had made the
basis of all trials. To a certain extent it
aimed at protecting those duped by fortunetellers or magicians. It hit hard at blasphemy and sacrilege, which demonstrably
mocked religion or violated church procedure. The crime itself became the offense
to be prosecuted, not suspicion of witchcraft. Finally, it provided a code to be
followed by all the regional courts or parlements. Previously, the laws against witchcraft depended on local customs and precedents, and punishment varied according to
the attitude of the judges and the extent of
local fears. On such an accumulation of

individual decisions, in fact, the Parlement of Normandy had justified its stand
against the accused witches. Yet even this
Edict, by the vagueness of its second article,
allowed much leeway to local courts.

When Louis XIV in 1670 reprieved the
twelve persons condemned as witches, the
Parlement at Rouen sought reconsideration
of his clemency. Yet the original charges
had been more than usually ridiculous. An
epidemic of nervous maladies occurred in
the districts of Coutances, Caretan, and La
Haye de Puits in Basse-Normandie. Local
physicians, unable to cure, took refuge in
the traditional diagnosis of sorcery. Origi-
nators of the sorcery had therefore to be
sought out; many recollected seeing their
neighbors at the sabbat. Among the depositions taken in May, 1669, and in the following months, were those of James le
Boulenger, who had seen a flight of naked
people through the air lasting half an hour;
of Michael Marais, who had seen over 200
persons dancing naked near La Haye de
Puits; of Isaac Marais, who, asleep in a
cabin in the woods, was awakened by a
troop of naked people surrounding a goat
and holding black candles. Certain peasants claimed to have seen priests with the
naked hordes, some celebrating black
masses while standing on their heads. A
local curé wrote a letter in which he summarized the accusations:

This sabbat was just the same as those
described in all the books, at all times
and in all places. The witches anointed
themselves, and a tall man with horns
carried them up the chimney. Their activities followed the established pattern:
dancing, what they call their "pleasure,"
cutting infants into little bits, boiling
them with snakes over the fire, taking
devil's powder to work *maleficia,* signing
the pact with [the Devil] their master in
their own blood, the huge goat, right
down to the black candles. The only
thing peculiar to this sabbat at La Haye
de Puits was that the devil, for greater
protection, frequently put his mark on
his vassals. It was also most unusual
that more than a hundred priests were
identified. For my part, I am convinced
of the truth of everything that was said

The original proclamation of King Louis XIV in 1682, which virtually put an end to witch persecutions in France. This illustration shows the preamble to the three articles. From Cornell University Library.

ÉDIT DU ROI,

POUR la punition de différens crimes, notamment des Empoifonneurs, ceux qui fe difent Devins, Magiciens & Enchanteurs; & portant reglement pour les Épiciers & Apothicaires.

Donné à Verfailles, au mois de Juillet 1682.

Regiftré en Parlement le 31 Août audit an.

LOUIS, par la grace de Dieu, Roi de France & de Navarre : A tous préfens & à venir, SALUT. L'exécution des Ordonnances des Rois nos prédéceffeurs, contre ceux qui fe difent Devins, Magiciens & Enchanteurs, ayant été négligée depuis long-temps, & ce relâchement ayant attiré des Pays étrangers dans notre Royaume, plufieurs de ces Impofteurs, il feroit arrivé que fous prétexte d'horofcope & de divination, & par le moyen des preftiges des opérations des prétendues magies & autres illufions femblables dont cette forte de gens ont accoutumé de fe fervir, ils auroient furpris diverfes perfonnes ignorantes ou crédules, qui s'étoient infenfiblement engagées avec eux, en paffant des vaines curiofités aux

at the trial, and I believe that [the devil in the shape of] a rat had really spoken to one of the accused, a boy of ten years.

Finally, 525 persons were indicted for witchcraft. Some of these were named twice and were therefore counted twice. Nine informers had provided the names:

Jean le Coustelier	154
Marguérite Marguérie	90
Jacques le Gastolois	85
Siméon Marguérie	78
Jean le Marchand	43
Charles Champel	35
Anne Noël	20
René le Marchand	15
Catherine Roberde	5

The court saw to it that most of the arrested confessed. The Parlement had confirmed the death sentence of the first twelve convicted (thirty-four more awaited such confirmation), when their families appealed to the King for clemency. On the advice of his minister, Colbert, Louis remitted their sentences to banishment from the province and restored their property.

The Parlement of Normandy, which had been burning witches at Rouen since Joan of Arc, was scandalized, and, suggesting "State's rights," sent its request to Louis XIV to rescind his pardon. The King ignored the request and forced Normandy to obey his orders. Some twelve years later, partly on Colbert's advice to strengthen the authority of the central government, partly on La Reynie's determination to control fortunetelling and sacrilege, Louis published his famous Edict:

EDICT OF JULY, 1682,
REGISTERED BY PARLEMENT
ON AUGUST 31, 1682

Article 1.
All persons practicing divination, or calling themselves fortunetellers, will, after publication of this edict, immediately vacate their houses, on pain of corporal punishment.

Article 2.
All practices and acts of magic or superstition, in word or speech, either profaning the text of Holy Writ or the Liturgy [by charms], or saying or doing things which cannot be explained naturally [in prophecies], are forbidden. Those who have taught as well as those who have practiced or made use of such acts for whatever purpose are to be summarily punished according to the gravity of their offense.

Article 3.
If, after publication of this edict, evil-minded persons augment and compound superstition with impiety and sacrilege, under pretext of working fancied acts of magic or other deceptions of similar nature [such as necromancy], they are to be punished, and subject to the penalty of death.

The provincial parlements in general obeyed. Paris burned three shepherds charged with spreading epidemics among sheep in 1691, but they apparently mixed their spells with arsenic. Bordeaux took until 1718 before it burned its last witch (a man charged with making a ligature). While Louis XIV could not have issued his Edict had there been no support for its skeptical attitude, nevertheless the prestige of the King was a major factor in securing obedience to the order and so stopping the witch hunts throughout France.

Louviers Nuns. "It may be open to question whether the poor nuns are possessed— I have not examined them; but there can be no question that this state of affairs is a terrible scandal." The Bishop of Evreux's initial reaction seems reasonable.

In seventeenth-century France, witchcraft manifested itself chiefly in the hysterics of young nuns, bewitched into immorality and even blasphemy by their spiritual directors. To such reports, three approaches are possible: they are completely false, the fantasies of young women living a conventual life that forbade ordinary sexual activities; they are completely true, and the priests who advised the nuns were monsters of degradation; or the reports are misconstructions of odd happenings or exaggerations of isolated abuses. Each major flare-up of Satanism in the convents therefore saw the adherents of the accusing nuns and the accused priests fiercely battling for public approval. The case of the Nuns of Louviers in Normandy in 1647 was the third of the series of great scandals, all of which followed one pattern. The two protagonists, Sister Madeleine Bavent and Father Thomas Boullé, had their exemplars at Loudon in 1634 (Sister Jeanne des Anges and Father Urbain Grandier), and at Aix-en-Provence in 1611 (Sister Madeleine de la Palud de Demandolx and Father Louis Gaufridi). All three trials were complicated by bitter rivalry between the secular clergy (the parish priests) and the religious (the monks and friars). Almost a parody of these involved proceedings came nearly a hundred years later, in 1731, when the accusations of Sister Catherine Cadière were rejected, and the accused Father Girard was not (as was Father Boullé) burned alive.

At least thirty-four contemporary books and pamphlets were circulated about Madeleine Bavent and the three successive directors of the convent at Louviers, Father David, Father Picard, and Father Boullé. The chief sources of information are the court records and Madeleine Bavent's own written autobiography or confession—"There is no more important or more terrible book," wrote Michelet. Both authorities, however, are suspect, for Madeleine asserted that her testimony before the court had been "based upon nothing else than the vivid suggestion she retained from the questioning" of the

Exterior of old chapel of convent at Louviers, prior to the alterations in 1867.

investigators. At her interrogation, she had been forced "to say both what she knew and what she did not know, and to notarize her statements." And, in her autobiography, Madeleine asked her readers "to distinguish what they thought real from what seemed to be hallucinations."

From various contemporary sources, often contradictory, the following narrative can be assembled:

Madeleine Bavent, early an orphan, was brought up by her aunt and uncle in Rouen, and in 1620, at the age of thirteen, was apprenticed to a dressmaker. Here, while Dame Anne catered to the customers downstairs, Madeleine and some half-dozen other young girls in the upstairs atelier sewed church vestments, and were often visited by priests inspecting their work. When she was about eighteen, Madeleine was seduced by one such, a Father Bontemps, a Franciscan, who had previously become intimate with three other girls. To evade the suspicions of her aunt, Madeleine decided to enter the little convent of the Franciscan Tertiaries at Louviers, founded in 1616 as a charitable home for the poor. Since she was deeply religious, her act caused little surprise.

The first chaplain of this convent dedicated to St. Louis and St. Elizabeth of Hungary was Father Pierre David. A contemporary account (*Récit véritable*, 1643) said: "Under the appearance of a saintly life, he sowed the seeds of the pernicious doctrine professed by the Illuminati." This heretical mystical sect, along with the Adamites and Quietists, believed that a person filled or illuminated by the Holy Ghost could do no sin, that he should worship God naked after the example of Adam, and that when practicing inward quietness or devotion any act was irreproachable. Apparently, Father David was at least interested in these heresies, for after his death, the Bishop burned his books. The nuns at Louviers were, in token of poverty and humility, accustomed to receive holy communion naked and then fast for eight or ten days. Practices such as these, originally perhaps pure in intent, easily lent themselves to misinterpretation and perversion.

Madeleine passed three years as a novice under the guidance of Father David and from him learned about these heresies. He ordered her, for example, "to strip [herself] to the waist and communicate with breasts exposed." The other nuns prevented her from covering herself with the communion cloth and forced her to stretch up her arms. Of Father David, she wrote:

> The most holy, virtuous, and faithful nuns were held to be those who stripped themselves completely naked and danced before him in that state, appeared naked in choir, and sauntered naked through the gardens. Nor was that all. He habituated us to fondle one another with lustful embraces, and, what I dare not whisper, to give ourselves up to the most foul and sinful [Lesbian] infamies . . . I have witnessed a mock act of circumcision performed upon a huge phallus, which seemed made of a paste, which afterwards some nuns seized upon to gratify their fancies.

Yet Father David never had intercourse with her and took only immodest liberties, contenting himself with "certain indecent caresses and mutual masturbation."

Her instruction was continued by another parish priest, Father Mathurin Picard, who had succeeded Father David as chaplain in 1628, and his assistant, Father Thomas Boullé. "The obscene practices [of Father David] were continued and were held in great repute." According to her confession, Madeleine resisted these customs, and the nuns considered her intractable. At her Easter confession, Father Picard revealed to her his passion and toyed with her. "After that, I never had any other kind of confession from him . . . Generally, all the time he handled the most private parts of my body, although I was always respectably covered, never, as the nuns maliciously report, undressed." Madeleine always tried to refuse him the ultimate favor; but sometimes Father Picard forced her, and at last she became pregnant.

Other nuns were involved in the chaplains' amours. Father Picard was accustomed to make love philters of sacramental wafers sopped up with "several clots of menstrual blood," and bury these in the ground. Fascinated by such charms, at these locations the nuns supposedly "committed the most filthy acts" with him. For other philters, Father Picard added entrails of slain babies, broken limbs of dead bodies, and "blood which trickled from the holy wafer."

Once or twice a week, Madeleine confessed, she went to the sabbat. About eleven o'clock at night, she said, she would lose consciousness, and fall "into a kind of trance or ecstacy." Present at the sabbat were the two chaplains, Father Picard and Father Boullé, and three or four nuns from her convent, with a few lay people, and some half-human and half-bestial demons. The priests recited a Black Mass from a "paper of blasphemy," in effect parodying the regular liturgy. After a feast, which twice included roast human flesh, the nuns copulated with the specter of Father David or with some living priest. Once Madeleine lay with Father Boullé, while Father Picard watched and "held my hands tightly while Father Boullé lay on top of me."

At these midnight sabbats, the priests brought large communion wafers. What happened next must be given in Madeleine's own words. Having said a Black Mass, from these consecrated hosts the priests

> cut out a round piece of about the size of a half-sou from the center, and attached it to a piece of vellum or parchment cut and trimmed in the same way, securing it in position with some kind of greasy adhesive, similar to shoemaker's wax. Then they put this gadget over their genitals, reaching to the stomach, and thus

arrayed gave themselves to the women present . . . At the sabbat, [Father Picard] had intercourse with me five or six times . . . but only once or twice in the manner I have just described.

For several years Madeleine was visited by the devil in the form of a huge black cat.

> On no fewer than two occasions, having entered my cell, I found that damned incubus of a cat on my bed in the most indecent postures it is possible to imagine, exhibiting a huge penis just like a man's. I was terrified and tried to fly, but in an instant it leaped toward me, dragged me forcibly on the bed, and then violently ravished me, causing me to experience the most peculiar sensation.

All these fantastic orgies allegedly continued from 1628 to 1642, when Father Picard died. No complaint or rumor had ever percolated to the outside world, although for several years Madeleine herself (while a novice) was gatekeeper for the convent and went into town several times every week, and although visiting priests regularly heard confession. Only after Father Picard's death did the nuns evidence diabolical possession which forced ecclesiastical attention. The credulous provincial of the Capuchin Fathers, Père Esprit de Bosroger (who in 1652 wrote an account of the fits), said the young women, while apparently healthy, had

> suffered the most frightful convulsions night and day during four years, and for three or more hours daily been subjected to exorcisms during a term of two years, although they have been subsisting in these paroxysms of constantly recurring frenzy, contortions, animal howlings, clamors, and outcries. And besides all these excessive torments, they have experienced the peculiar motions of their own demon, their special tormentor, three or four times a day.

Out of fifty-two nuns, at least fourteen said they were possessed (giving the name of their own particular demon—Putiphar, Dagon, Grongade, and so forth), and another four tormented [see Demonology]. In the hopes of avoiding severe punish-

The exorcism of Sister Madeleine Bavent by Monseigneur de Péricaud, Bishop of Evreux, from a contemporary print.

ment, the nuns confessed to everything asked them and put the blame on Madeleine Bavent. Crowds thronged the churches where public exorcisms were conducted by the various orders of monks; and the nuns, flattered or terrified by the publicity, exhibited the most strange behavior. Preaching a sermon, Father Esprit de Bosroger said the devil's malice was like the buzzing of a fly. Immediately a voice (no doubt one of the demented nuns) rang through the church: "Say you so? Flies! Flies! You shall soon see what power this fly the devil has!" The assembled nuns went into an uproar, shouting and contorting their bodies. Not everybody accepted these hystero-epileptic fits as demoniacal possession. Dr. Yvelin, a royal physician, reported that in no instance did the nuns truly manifest the various approved signs; he detected imposture and deceit and thought the nuns were rehearsed for their exorcisms.

The Bishop of Evreux, Monseigneur de Péricaud, examined the convent for witchcraft, and in March, 1643, charged Sister Madeleine Bavent with sorcery, attendance at the sabbat, signing a pact with the Devil, stealing the host, and copulating with devils. Under duress, Madeleine confessed to being a witch and was expelled from the order; she was confined in perpetual imprisonment in an underground dungeon, with bread and water her only sustenance for three days every week. The corpse of Father Picard, as instigator of this witchcraft and immorality, was secretly exhumed and excommunicated. When Picard's brother and nephew came across the priest's corpse in a refuse heap, they demanded redress. Because of the scandal of the disinterment, and because of suspicion of witchcraft, on the advice of a royal investigating commission, the local Parlement at Rouen took the case in hand. The resulting investigations, both civil and ecclesiastical, dragged on for four years to 1647.

Madeleine Bavent was held in the Ursuline convent at Rouen, where she was cruelly mistreated. The Grand Penitentiary of Evreux (a sort of inquisitor) personally searched her, "roughly and indecently," for devil's marks on two separate occasions and witnessed other searchings. She tried to commit suicide, stopping up her menstrual discharge with bandages, swallowing spiders, and bribing a boy to bring her arsenic. In August, 1647, the court postponed formal sentence, but continued her solitary incarceration. She endured such treatment for only a short time, and died in prison at the age of forty, the same year.

One witness, before being burned as a heretic, confessed he had prompted Madeleine Bavent about the sabbat orgies, but everything he told her was "merely gossips' twaddle." The story of the "paper of blasphemy," supposedly recited at the Black Mass, "had been suggested to him by his interrogator, the Grand Penitentiary of Evreux, who bribed him with six sous to give evidence against Madeleine and besmirch her name. Being utterly destitute, he agreed to bear false witness for the sake of money."

Father Thomas Boullé, chaplain after the death of Father Picard, had been arrested on suspicion of witchcraft on July 2, 1644. After three years' imprisonment, he was sentenced, on this sort of evidence, for bewitching the nuns. On the other hand, it must be noted that two other priests, also accused with Boullé, were exculpated because the only evidence against them came from convicted criminals. Father Boullé was condemned to be tortured "in order that he might reveal his accomplices," and to make *amende honorable*, "his head and feet being bare, clad only in his shirt, having a cord about his neck, and holding in his hand a lighted taper of two pounds weight," to be drawn on a hurdle to the Old Market Square. There, on August 21, 1647, he was burned alive, and his ashes scattered to the four winds.

At the same time, the Parlement at Rouen declared the exhumation of Father Picard illegal, but found him guilty of witchcraft; his corpse was to be shamefully and publicly burned (with Father Boullé). Burned at the same time was another priest, Duval, similarly accused by Madeleine Bavent. The nuns of Louviers whom the two chaplains had bewitched for immoral practices were to be dispersed to other convents to remove the "dryness" of their souls.

Lowestoft Witches: see Bury St. Edmunds Witches.

Luxeuil Witch Trial. In the history of witchcraft, the trial of Madame Desle la Mansenée, the 27-year-old wife of Jean de la Tour, in the bailiwick of Luxeuil, Franche-Comté, is important for documenting the continuing work of the Inquisition in initiating witch hunts.

The Inquisitor-General of Besançon in 1529, in circumstances of great secrecy, visited the village of Anjeux and took down hearsay gossip from the villagers. Their charges were unsifted; when a sufficient number had been collected, not one of which could by itself be proved, the person involved was considered a witch by common report and therefore subject to torture. The Inquisition, of course, insisted on secrecy to protect its sources of information; to disclose its witnesses would wreck its operations.

Complaints and accusations focused on one woman, Desle la Mansenée; they comprised unexplained misfortunes and the customary *maleficia* preceded by the deadly threat. A child sickened; the witch was blamed. Her young son was pressed to give incriminating evidence against his mother. Typical of the depositions was that of Antoine Godin:

Antoine Godin, of the said Anjeux, aged about forty years, remembering back some thirty years, as he says from a clear distant recollection, sworn and questioned like the preceding on what was formerly said, says and deposes on his oath to have knowledge that Desle la Mansenée is held and reputed in the said neighborhood a witch [*genosche*], a wicked common woman, and a sorcerer. . . . Says furthermore to have heard that Mazelin, son of the said Desle, had said in the fields that his mother went backwards on a twisted osier stick to the meeting. Also testified he had heard people say that the said Desle had caused three threads to be drawn from the distaff of a woman called Prince, while she was in childbed, and the said Desle took them and said they were for doing some sorcery and witchcraft in the said Anjeux. . . . In May his testimony was read back to the aforesaid Antoine, and he has persisted and does persist in his said deposition.

Armed with such rumors from some two-dozen neighbors, in March, 1529, the Inquisitor began interrogating the suspected woman before a six-man commission, including the parish priest, the Lieutenant, and the Governor of Luxeuil. In several prolonged sessions, Desle maintained her innocence, and nothing pointed to her guilt. The Inquisitor, however, suspected something and confined her *en prison ferme*. Finally, he turned her over to the civil authorities to be tortured by squassation. Very soon Desle la Mansenée confessed and told her judges what they had been wanting to hear: the devil's broken promises of wealth, her denial of the Catholic faith, making hailstorms, flying through the air on an anointed stick, dancing at the sabbat, copulation with Monsieur Rondot, the devil, cold as ice [*froid comme glace*], and using black powder to poison cattle. By April 8, the witch was naming her accomplices at the *sabbats et sinagogues des diables*. The report of her trial was submitted to theologians for confirmation, and on December 18, 1529, Desle la Mansenée was hanged and her body burned on conviction of homicide, renouncing the Catholic faith, and committing the crime of heresy. Witchcraft was not even mentioned in the sentence.

Lycanthrope of Angers. In France, in the year 1598, occurred several celebrated trials for lycanthropy. One of these accused werewolves was Jacques Roulet, a beggar of Caude, near Angers. His behavior in jail showed he was feeble-minded and epileptic. His testimony in court was as contradictory as it was fantastic; he involved his brother John and his cousin Julien in his alleged crimes, though they were proved many miles distant at the time—just as fantastic was the fact that this evidence was admitted. Roulet was accused as a werewolf after being found (by a soldier and some peasants) in some bushes, half-naked, his hair unkempt, his hands smeared with blood, and his nails clotted with shreds of human flesh. Nearby was the mutilated corpse of a fifteen-year-old boy named Cornier. Roulet confessed to murdering the youth, and described the victim and the place of the killing in circumstantial details. On August 8, 1598, Judge Pierre Hérault questioned the prisoner:

Q. What is your name and what your estate?

A. My name is Jacques Roulet, my age thirty-five; I am poor and a beggar.

Q. What are you accused of having done?

A. Of being a thief; of having offended God. My parents gave me an ointment; I do not know its composition.

Q. When rubbed with this ointment, do you become a wolf?

A. No. But for all that, I killed and ate the child Cornier. I was a wolf.

Q. Were you dressed as a wolf?

A. I am dressed as I am now. I had my hands and face bloody, because I had been eating the flesh of the said child.

Q. Do your hands and feet become paws of a wolf?

A. Yes, they do.

Q. Does your head become like that of a wolf—your mouth become larger?

A. I do not know how my head was at the time; I used my teeth. My head was as it is today. I have wounded and eaten many other little children. I have also been to the sabbat.

The secular court sentenced Roulet to death, but, oddly enough, he appealed to the Parlement of Paris, which commuted the sentence to two years in the insane asylum of St.-Germain-des-Près, with instruction in religion, "which he had forgotten in his utter poverty." This approach to lycanthropy as a mental disease looks forward to the trial of Jean Grenier five years later.

In the same year, on December 14, the Parlement of Paris sentenced a tailor of Châlons to death as a lycanthrope. He decoyed children into his shop, it was charged, attacked them there or else murdered them when they strayed into the woods, and ate their flesh. In his shop a cask of bones was allegedly found. The trial was so full of horrors that the judges ordered the court records to be burned.

Lycanthropy. The salient features of lycanthropy, arising out of hallucinations and a sadistic craving for blood, were (1) transformation into animal, (2) nocturnal excursions through the countryside, (3) attacks on animals and humans to devour their flesh, and (4) retransformation into human form.

The increase in trials for witchcraft at the end of the sixteenth century led also to more trials for lycanthropy. Most people believed a man actually became a lycanthrope or werewolf [German: *Währ-Wölffe*; French: *gerulf* or *loup-garou*; Italian: *lupo manaro*]. Some few held with Reginald Scot (1584) that "lycanthropia is a disease and not a transformation." In such mental derangement a man imagined himself to be and indeed acted like a wild beast. Epidemics of such madness have been recorded. Thus, in Luc in the parish of

Béarn, in the seventeenth century, an outbreak of men barking like dogs was cured, not by doctors, but by the afflicted wearing round their necks the agnus castus plant.

The concept of metamorphosis was old. A Greek myth told of Lycaon, who, having sacrificed a child at the altar of Zeus Lycaeus, was changed into a wolf. Plato expanded the legend: eating the flesh of a man sacrificed at that altar effected transformation. Vergil, too, described how a sorcerer turned himself into a wolf.

The most famous classical story of lycanthropy was told by Petronius in his novel *Cena Trimalchionis* [*Feast of Trimalchio*]. One of the characters, Trimalchio, goes out at night to visit his mistress Melissa, and asks an acquaintance to accompany him part of the way. As they pass a cemetery, Trimalchio is amazed to see the man stop, strip, put his clothes on the ground and urinate in a circle around them, and then change into a wolf. "Do not think I jest; I would not lie for all the money in the world," affirms Trimalchio. The werewolf begins howling and races into the woods. Trimalchio goes to take up the clothes, but they are turned to stone. Sweating with fear, he rushes to Melissa, who tells him: "Had you only come sooner you might have helped us, for a wolf broke in and worried our cattle. But he got the worst of it, although he escaped; for our hired man ran a spear through his neck." Trimalchio's suspicions anticipate the conclusion, and when morning comes he returns home, noting en route that the clothes have gone but that the ground is covered with blood. At home he finds his acquaintance bleeding profusely from the neck and a doctor dressing his wounds. "Then I knew he was a werewolf [*versipella*], and after that I could never eat with him again, no, not if you had killed me."

This story of the first century A.D. was repeatedly told by the demonologists, and its four essential features appear in most later stories of lycanthropes: transformation in moonlight, removal of all clothes, urination or some other charm to permit regaining human shape, and sympathetic wounding.

Werewolf attacks a man. Engraving from the first work on witchcraft printed in German, Geiler von Kaysersberg's *Die Emeis* (Strasbourg, 1517). From Cornell University Library.

The old Norse sagas show how fact mingled with fable. For warmth and appearance of ferocity, a warrior or outlaw would dress himself in the skins of the bears he had slain [*berserker*, man in a bear shirt]. From this natural act it was a short step to ascribing to the man the savage qualities of the beast and even supernatural powers. Ultimately, the meaning of this word was extended to anyone *berserk* or afflicted with the madness of imagining himself a wild beast. This explanation sheds light on many of the stories of metamorphosis to a wolf that are preserved in western Europe. Significantly, the earliest meaning of werewolf in English, about 1000, is "outlaw."

Another relic of folklore incorporated into lycanthropy was the idea of the reversal of the pelt. In 1541, in Pavia, a maniac who imagined himself a wolf was apprehended; he told his captors that he differed from a real wolf in that his fur grew not outside but on the inside. To test the truth of his contention, the authorities promptly cut off his arms and legs. Although proved innocent, he died not many days after, said Job Fincelius (1556).

The full-blown conception of witches' going to a sabbat led to the assumption of parallel gatherings of wolves (as told by Boguet in 1603). Casper Peucer, a Protestant physician, in his *Commentarius de Praecipibus Divinationum Generibus* (1560), told a typical Baltic story from Livonia (Latvia), a favorite haunt, of the night march of thousands of werewolves led by the devil:

At Christmas a boy lame of a leg goes round the country summoning the Devil's followers, who are countless, to a general conclave. Whoever remains behind, or goes reluctantly, is scourged by another with an iron whip till the blood flows, and his traces are left in blood. The human form vanishes, and the whole multitude become wolves. Many thousands assemble. Foremost goes the leader armed with an iron whip, and the troop follow, firmly convinced in their imagination that they are transformed into wolves. They fall upon herds of cattle and flocks of sheep, but they have no power to slay men. When they come to a river, the leader smites the water with his scourge, and it divides, leaving a dry path through the midst, by which the pack go. The transformation lasts twelve days, at the expiration of which period the wolf skin vanishes, and the human form reappears.

Just as they had to explain a witch's being at home while simultaneously attending a sabbat, so investigators had to account for the visible presence of the accused during the time he was presumed to be a lycanthrope. This illusion or impossibility was explained in a similar manner: the spirit left the body (so Bodin, opposed by De Nynauld); or a dummy body was substituted; or a demon assumed the shape of the wolf. Rhanaeus, for example, like Olaus Magnus earlier (1555), discussing the Latvian lycanthropes, explained there were three classes of werewolves:

1. Men who act like wolves and do damage to cattle. They are not changed into wolves, but believe themselves transformed into wolves, and are so regarded by some others suffering similar hallucinations. [This is also the opinion of Petrus Thyraeus, S.J., 1594.]

2. Men who, dreaming in their sleep, imagine they injure the cattle, while the devil incites wolves actually to commit the mischief these men dream they do.

3. Men who imagine they are wolves and commit damage which is really done by the devil, who has changed himself into a wolf. [This is basically the position of Augustine, in his *De Civitate Dei*.]

The stories about the lycanthropes of Kurland (Latvia), Rhanaeus added, were so powerful that only a Scythian adventurer would not be horrified by them.

To exemplify the hallucination of his first category, Rhanaeus told a story of the year 1584. A farmer shot at a wolf stealing his sheep, and later discovered one of his tenants wounded.

On inquiry, the tenant's wife, called Lebba, related the following circumstances, which were fully corroborated by numerous witnesses. When the husband had sown his rye, he had consulted with his wife how he was to get some meat, so as to have a good feast. The woman urged him on no account to steal from his landlord's flock, because it was guarded by fierce dogs. However, he rejected her advice and fell upon his landlord's sheep, but he had suffered and had come limping home, and in his rage at the ill success of his attempt, had fallen upon his horse and had bitten its throat completely through.

The sympathetic wounding of a wolf and the subsequent discovery of a similar wound in a human (as in Petronius) is a recurring motif in tales of lycanthropy. Thus Bodin related how the royal prosecutor, Bourdin, had assured him that he had shot a wolf, and that the arrow had stuck in the beast's thigh. A few hours later, the arrow was found in the thigh of a man in bed. Jean de Nynauld, a skeptical physician, in *De la Lycanthropie* (1615), told of a woodsman's cutting off the leg of a wolf which had attacked him; immediately the "wolf" turned into a woman lacking her arm. She was burned alive.

Guazzo, the learned Italian monk who wrote the *Compendium Maleficarum* (1626), tried to reconcile a belief that lycanthropy was an illusion with the belief that humans received sympathetic wounds parallel to those inflicted on werewolves. He cited the following example:

In Flanders at a town not far from Dixmuide, a certain peasant was drinking at a tavern with his young son, and watched the hostess scoring up the beer which she brought him. He noticed that she marked up twice as much as he drank, but he kept quiet until he had finished drinking. At the end of the round, he called the hostess and asked what he owed; and she demanded the amount that she had scored. He refused to pay it and, thrusting many persons aside, threw on the table what he knew to be a sufficient sum of money, and started to leave. The enraged hostess cried out, "You will not go home today, or my name is not so-and-so." But he went away despising the woman's threats. He came to a stream where he had left his boat, but, even with the help of his son (who was a strong lad), he could not budge it from the bank, however much they tried, so that you would have said it was nailed to the ground. Two or three soldiers happened to pass that way, and the father called to them, saying, "Good friends, come and help me launch this boat from the bank, and I promise you a good drink as your reward." They came and exerted themselves as much as they could for a long time in vain, until one of them, panting and sweating, said, "Let us take out these heavy packages. Perhaps when the boat is empty we shall manage better." And behold, when the goods were exposed to view, they saw an immense lurid toad in the hold looking at them with gleaming eyes. One of the soldiers at once slit its throat with the point of his sword and threw it into the water, where it floated belly upwards on its back as if dead. The others gave it more wounds as it floated, and suddenly the boat was launched. The overjoyed peasant led his helpers back to the same inn and ordered beer. A serving maid brought it. The man asked where the hostess was, and learned she was confined to her bed very ill. "What!" said he. "Do you think I am drunk, you fool? It is scarcely half an hour since I left her as well as you are. I am going to see what the trouble is." He went into the bedroom and found that the woman had died from wounds and slashes in her neck and stomach. "How did she get these wounds?" he asked. The serving maid said she did not know and that, to her knowledge, the woman had not set foot outside the house. They went to the magistrate, and the cuts and stabs were found in the very same places as those where the soldiers had killed the toad, which was never found.

"Now, how should this story be explained?" inquired Guazzo. "No one must fall into the delusion a man can really be changed into a beast, or a beast into a real man," he said, "for these are magic portents and illusions which have the form but not the reality of those things they appear to be." How, then, could this illusion take place? Guazzo exerted his faculties to prove the impossible.

Sometimes the devil substitutes another body, while they are absent or hidden somewhere in a secret place, and himself assumes the body of a sleeping wolf formed from the air and enveloping him, and does those actions which men think are perpetrated by the wretched absent witch who is asleep.

The devil had an alternative trick, even more farfetched. "Sometimes he surrounds a witch with an aerial effigy of a beast, each part of which fits onto the corresponding part of the witch's body." If this aerial effigy is attacked, "the enveloping air easily yields, and the true body receives the wound." But if the witch is asleep (as Guazzo had first suggested), "then the devil wounds her in that part of her absent body corresponding to the wound which he knows to have been received by the beast's body." This explanation covered all eventualities.

Not everybody was satisfied with this tricky reasoning. Robert Burton, in his *Anatomy of Melancholy* (1621), developed Reginald Scot's view that lycanthropy was a mental disease: some "call it a kind of melancholy; but I should rather refer it to madness, as most do." This rationalism came easier to Englishmen, for in England wolves had become extinct very early, the cat or hare replacing the wolf for purposes of transmogrification. The twelfth-century English writer, Gervais of Tilbury, was able to recall: "In England we often see men changed into wolves at the changes of the moon." In his *Topographica Hibernica* (about 1188), he told an anecdote which he evidently accepted as factual. A priest journeying in Ireland was lost in a wood and accosted by a wolf claiming to be human. The animal explained that in the sixth century the Abbot of St. Natalis had cursed the village of Ossory, so that every seven years two of its residents had to live as werewolves. If they survived, they were permitted to resume human form and return, whereupon another couple had to take their place. The werewolf wished the priest to give the sacrament to his dying wolf-wife. The terrified priest went with the werewolf. "Moreover, to remove all doubt, using his claw as a hand, [the werewolf] drew off the pelt from the head of the wolfess and folded it back even as far down as the navel, whereupon there was plainly to be seen the body of an old woman." The wolf thanked the priest and guided him safely out of the forest.

In England the belief survived in literature, and the romance *William of Palerne* (translated from the late thirteenth-century French) related one of the few examples of the admirable werewolf:

In order to retain the succession to the throne for her own son, a jealous stepmother by magic salve and charms transformed Alphonsus, son of the King of Spain, into a werewolf. As a werewolf, Alphonsus rescued a baby, William, the heir to the throne of Sicily, from a wicked uncle, and gave it to the care of a cowherd. Some years later, the werewolf enticed the Emperor of Rome, while hunting, to approach the place where William was tending kine. The Emperor brought up William with his own daughter. When he reached manhood, William eloped with the Emperor's daughter, both disguised as white bears. The werewolf, unknown to the couple, led them back to Sicily, where William regained his throne. Then the werewolf went back to Spain, and forced his wicked stepmother to restore him to his original form by means of a ring tied with red thread placed about his neck. Now acknowledged as the rightful heir, Alphonsus married William's sister.

In both these stories, and in the *Lai de Bisclavaret*, the reader's sympathies lie with the lycanthrope, because he has been involuntarily transformed. In Marie de

Pray thee, what's his disease?
A very pestilent disease, my lord;
They call it lycanthropia.

What's that?
I need a dictionary to it.

I'll tell you:
In those that are possessed with it, there o'erflows
Such melancholy humor, they imagine
Themselves to be transformed into wolves,
Steal forth to church yards in the dead of night,
And dig dead bodies up. As two nights since
One met the duke, 'bout midnight, in a lane
Behind St. Mark's church, with the leg of a man
Upon his shoulder; and he howled fearfully;
Said he was a wolf; only the difference
Was, a wolf's skin was hairy on the outside,
His on the inside. Bade them take their swords,
Rip up his flesh, and try.

—John Webster, *The Duchess of Malfi* (1614).

France's *Bisclavaret* (the Breton word for *garou*), the animal is savage only against his enemies, a faithless wife and her perfidious lover. A knight of Brittany is married to a fair lady, but he leaves her three nights every week. The wife insists on learning why he goes away and finds her husband is a werewolf. The knight admits he takes his clothes off but will not tell where he hides them. "I can recover human form only at the moment I put them on." The wife persists and learns that the clothes are left under a bush near an old stone cross in a corner of a chapel. The wife has her lover steal the clothes; when her husband fails to return, the wife marries her lover. A year later, the king hunts a wolf and wounds it, but the wolf licks the king's foot. At this gesture, the king takes the wolf (the husband in disguise) as a domestic pet. It has the run of the court and hurts nobody, save once it attacks the wife and lover when they visit the king. On a return visit to the couple, the wolf manages to bite off the woman's nose. These acts rouse suspicions, and under arrest the wife confesses her crime. The clothes are restored to the wolf, and the knight materializes. The king restores him to his honors and lands, and banishes the faithless wife. As a punishment for her infidelity, thenceforth all her daughters are born without noses.

Transformation into a wolf was effected by putting on a wolf's skin, or a magic belt of wolf's skin, or by rubbing the body with special ointments (as De Lancre explained). Or spells might serve: in the trials of the Scottish witches, Isobel Gowdie recited incantations for turning into animals and for returning to human form. Pierre Gandillon [see Werewolves of Poligny] came back by rubbing himself in the dewy grass or by washing with water.

Lycanthropy was not simply folklore or legend. It was, just as much as witchcraft, a sin against God, and was even more ruthlessly punished by the law. Several of the most celebrated trials for lycanthropy are included in this *Encyclopedia*. The following are outstanding for their careful recording by standard demonologists from personal knowledge or contemporary accounts, described in separate entries:

Werewolves of Poligny (1522)
Gilles Garnier (1573)
Peter Stubb (1589)
Lycanthrope of Angers (1598)
Werewolves of St.-Claude (1598)
Jean Grenier (1603)

Magee Island Witch Trial. In 1710-11 the final witch trial took place in Ireland. The Magee Island case (near Carrickfergus, Antrim) was unusual in linking witches to poltergeists. The "noisy ghost" formed a preamble for alleged demoniacal possession, which in turn laid the basis for the trial. In this prologue, the actors included the widow of a Presbyterian minister, staying with her son James Haltridge and his wife, a young servant, a child (who entered

very briefly), and either an actual or imagined young urchin. One of these last three was responsible for the tricks—throwing stones and turf at windows, stealing books, and pulling off bedclothes (and sometimes even making them up like corpses). Yet it was noted at the time that no strange event ever occurred when anybody was in the bedroom. The alleged disturbances came in two waves: the first was stopped by the return of Mr. Haltridge and his dog, which for a time frightened away the poltergeist. Then in February, 1711, the troubles recommenced with increased vigor. One night, Widow Haltridge, who bore the brunt of these irritations, felt a stabbing pain in her back. Within a few days she died.

The introduction of witchcraft followed her demise. An eighteen-year-old girl, Mary Dunbar, "a very intelligent young person," was hired to look after the young Mrs. Haltridge in her mourning. A rumor that the widow had been killed by witchcraft apparently gave the young helper ideas: she had fits and saw specters of various women tormenting her. By the end of March, she had described seven local women as witches, all of whom were arrested. Mary identified an eighth suspect: "As soon as she came into the room the said Mary fell into such a violent fit of pains that three men were scarce able to hold her, and cried out, 'For Christ's sake, take the devil out of the room.' And being asked, said . . . she was 'the woman that did torment her.'" But apparently the judges had sufficient prisoners, and this woman was not arrested.

The trial took place at Carrickfergus on March 31, 1711, from six in the morning to two in the afternoon. The chief evidence against the accused witches comprised various accounts of Mary's fits. A Dr. Tinsdall, vicar of Belfast, left an eyewitness account:

There was a great quantity of things produced in court, and sworn to be what she vomited out of her throat. I had them all in my hand, and found there was a great quantity of feathers, cotton, yarn, pins, and two large waistcoat buttons, at least as much as would fill my hand. They

The Rage of Witches: an old print in the Douce Collection, Bodleian Library, Oxford.

gave evidence to the court they had seen those very things coming out of her mouth, and had received them into their hands as she threw them up.

The prisoners had no lawyer; but many of them were found "laborious, industrious people, and had frequently been known to pray with their families, both publicly and privately; most of them could say the Lord's Prayer, which it is generally said they learned in prison, they being every one Presbyterians."

The two judges were divided. Judge Anthony Upton

seemed entirely of the opinion that the jury could not bring them in Guilty upon the sole testimony of the afflicted person's visionary images. . . . Had the accused been really witches and in compact with the Devil, it could hardly be presumed that they should be such constant attenders upon divine service.

Judge James MacCartney thought the accused Guilty; the jury agreed with him, and the women were sentenced to one year's imprisonment with four appearances in the pillory.

Magic: see Sorcery.

Maleficia. Misfortunes, injuries, and calamities suffered by persons, animals, or property, for which no immediate explanation could be found, were called *maleficia*. These mishaps were attributed to the vindictive malice of witches. Witches, angered by their neighbors or simply delighted at doing wrong, made a threat of evil [*damnum minatum*]; any ensuing misfortune [*malum secutum*] was regarded as their fault. This attempted explanation of the numerous natural troubles, from petty inconveniences such as a headache to national disasters such as loss of crops, gained popular approval for the burning of friends and neighbors whose executions as heretics would otherwise have been furiously opposed. Charges of concrete acts of malefice could be understood by all; and, in prosecuting the alleged perpetrators, otherwise hated witch hunters could pose as protectors of public welfare. Thus, allegations of wrong doing were made to bolster what were essentially trials for alleged wrong thinking.

Hermann Löher noted how rapidly the witchcraft delusion changed public opinion. In 1610, in the Bonn region, the late May frost which killed the crops was ascribed to an act of God or nature; by 1631, after the witch judge Buirmann had been active, similar disasters were universally ascribed to the malice of witches. Only by associating physical damage experienced by ordinary, simple people with the complicated theory of heresy, could the civil and ecclesiastical inquisitors maintain their control over Europe for so long. "These things are done by virtue of a covenant or compact between the witch and an evil spirit," said the Protestant Glanvill. Jannet Reid, at the Orkney Islands trial in 1643, was condemned to be strangled and burned to ashes for *maleficia* committed with the aid of Satan, making retribution to man and God: "By your cursings and imprecation ye wrong both man and beast, which evils are brought to pass by the power and working of the devil, your master." Thomas Murner, in *De Pythonico Contractu* (1499), is one of the few demonologists to allow that injuries, as well as being caused by witches, might sometimes be due to the Devil working independently of witches, the character of the individual sufferer, or God himself.

Witches were classified *malefici* and, according to Nider in 1435, could work malefice and injure men and property in seven ways:

1. Inspiring love
2. Inspiring hatred
3. Causing impotence
4. Causing disease
5. Taking life
6. Depriving of reason
7. Injuring property or animals

Consequently, all the above acts were, in the broadest sense, acts of evil, since they were perpetrated by *malefici*. (Ligature to cause impotence is discussed more fully in a separate entry.) The word *maleficia* was generally limited, however, to causing disease and injuring property or animals (items 4 and 7). The Inquisitor Bernard de Como (1510) decreed all diseases which a physician could neither explain nor cure were attributable to sorcery; and Martin de Arles (1460) defined as *maleficia* all occurrences where the effect was more than could reasonably be expected in nature. On this basis, he concluded that all *maleficia* involved an implicit pact to serve Satan. Hence those trials, especially in England, which depended on evidence of harm or injury to people were brought into line with the basic principle that witches were condemned for worshiping the Devil, whether or not evil-doing was alleged.

In his *Discourse of Damned Art of Witchcraft* (1608), William Perkins spelled out specific acts, including mental as well as physical harm:

1. The raising of storms and tempests, winds and weather, by sea and land [see Storm-Raising]
2. The poisoning of air
3. Blasting of corn

4. Killing of cattle, and annoying of men, women, and children
5. The procuring of strange passions and torments in men's bodies and in other creatures, with the curing of the same [see Possession]
6. Casting out of devils [see Scratching]

These crimes against men were the counterpart, on a popular folklore basis, of the crimes against God, on a learned ecclesiastical basis, detailed in the Pact with the Devil.

Horrible examples of these more-than-natural injuries were the stock in trade of demonologists. Alexia Belheure quarreled with her husband because he did not make enough money; so she asked the devil to punish him. One Christmas Eve he went to town to buy some staples, and on his way

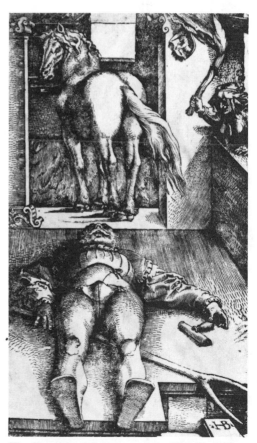

The Bewitched Groom and the Witch's Curse, by Hans Baldung Grün.

home was beaten up, in accordance with the devil's promise. Alexia, forewarned of the event, found her husband and gave out that he had been attacked by robbers. "And they all easily believed her," added Guazzo in his *Compendium Maleficarum* (1626), "because she was not young or beautiful enough to be suspected of having entertained adulterers."

Guazzo described another common anecdote of *maleficia*, involving the *damnum minatum*, the threat to work ill, and the ensuing evil, the *malum secutum*. A certain woman, Apra Hoselotte—

> had a son in the service of Jean Halecourt, whom his master had cruelly punished for a theft of which he, more than the rest of the servants, was suspected. This grieved the mother and made her wish for revenge, the chance for which she eagerly grasped. When the master was bringing his horses home from pasture and was carelessly riding upon one of them, she and her familiar came invisibly and so bore upon the horse's neck that the rider fell to the ground and broke his leg; and he was still lame and crippled by that fall when he appeared as a witness against the witch.

In New England, Cotton Mather in his *Remarkable Providences* found evidence of *maleficia* in the following example, which he reported in good faith at first hand. A very good man offended two women who threatened him with harm. Soon after, some of his cattle died in a strange manner and he himself "was haunted with sights of the women." He tried to explain his troubles at a church meeting, but was prevented by an epileptic fit.

> One or two more such fits he had after that, but afterwards a more private sort of torture was employed upon him. He was advised by a worthy man to apply himself unto a magistrate; and warned that he would shortly be murdered if he did not. He took not the counsel; but languished for some weeks; yet able to walk and work. But then, he had his breath and life suddenly taken away from him, in a manner of which no full account could be given.

An example of *maleficia* in England was given by W. Drage in his *Daimonomageia* (1665). In Bedford, in 1637, Goodwife Rose was ducked in a river because she had bewitched some peas into being worm-eaten, in revenge for being refused a portion of them, and had also infested a man with lice.

Witches were often accused of setting fire to buildings and towns by means of their magical arts.

Throughout these illustrations, no mention is made of how the witch accomplished her designs. Presumably she was aided by the Devil—specifically, in England at least, by her imp or familiar, the little animal assigned by Satan to do the witch's wicked commands. Alternatively the explanation might be found in the old notion of fascination or the evil eye. William Perkins, in his *Discourse*, elucidated:

> It is an old received opinion, that in malicious and ill-disposed persons, there proceed out of the eye with the beams noisome and malignant spirits, which infect the air, and do poison or kill not only them with whom they are daily conversant, but others also whose company they frequent, of what age, strength, or complexion so ever they be.

Though Perkins found it possible to accept the pact with the Devil, he dismissed this theory "as fond [foolish] as it is old."

In addition to this indefinable and unprovable ability to cause harm, witches were presumed to use other and more tangible physical means from time immemorial associated with magic and sorcery, such as ointments, dust, herbs, or potions, knotted cords or ligature, waxen images, or the frightening hand of glory. Or they might try to obtain something personal belonging to their victim—a tooth, nail clippings, hair, or bits of clothing—for use in working evil. Inasmuch as these techniques are described elsewhere in separate entries, only a few generalized examples are included here.

About the middle of the eighteenth century (August 13, 1746), John Wesley recorded in his *Journal* an instance of bewitching he had encountered in Cornwall. After his sermon, a woman told Wesley how his preaching that day had given her "respite or ease" from what sounds like arthritis or rheumatism. It appeared that seven years previously, a wizard, at the request of a woman whom she had affronted, had cast a spell on her. During a "sudden storm of thunder, lightning, and rain . . . she [had] felt all her flesh shudder, and knew the devil was close to her . . . from thenceforth she had no rest, day or night, being not only in fear and horror of mind, but in the utmost torment of body, feeling as if her flesh was tearing off with burning pincers."

At the Salem trials, Roger Toothaker was accused by Thomas Gage of having procured some of his daughter's urine, which he put in an earthen pot into a hot oven. "And the next morning said child was dead."

Joan Peterson was charged at London on April 7, 1652, of being "a practitioner in physic [medicine] but suspected to be a witch," and with having administered a potion or posset to an old lady "who soon after the drinking thereof died." The chapbook account, published the day after the indictment and before the verdict, noted, "Many conjecture she died a natural death, being aged eighty years." [See Wapping Witch.]

Another story came from Metz, where a woman, having been refused credit by the baker, asked help from the devil. Guazzo wrote that the devil—

eager for any chance of doing ill, gave her some herbs wrapped in a paper, telling her to scatter them in the place most often used by the baker and his family.

She at once took them and spread them in the doorway by which they had to go to the village; and the baker, and after him his wife and children, walked over them and were all afflicted with the same sickness. And they did not recover until the witch, moved by pity, obtained from the demon another herb to restore them. This she hid secretly in their beds, as she had been told to do, and they were soon all restored from sickness to their former health.

At a visitation or inspection of his diocese in 1543, Archbishop Cranmer of Canterbury was presented with Joanna Meriweather on a curious charge of evil-doing. "She had made a fire upon the dung of Elizabeth Colsey, and dropped a holy candle upon it, and told her neighbors it would make the cule [buttocks] of the maid divide in two parts." (*Memoirs of Archbishop Cranmer*)

Colorful allegations were more general in European witchcraft. Johann Müller of Welferdingen at the end of the sixteenth century deposed about his year-old child.

" 'Be revenged or die!' The devil gives the witches a powder and ointment, and makes them promise to destroy fruit and crops—or at least makes them think they can do so."—Guazzo (1626).

Agatina of Pittelingen and Miatte of Hohenech stole this child from its cradle and placed it on a burning pyre which they had prepared for that purpose on a steep hill called La Grise and carefully collected its calcined ashes. These they mixed with dew, shaken from the ears of corn and the heads of grasses, into a mass that could be easily crumbled, and with this they dusted the vines and crops and trees, causing their flowers to fade and preventing them from bearing fruit. (*Compendium Maleficarum*)

Sometimes personal grievances were added to sorcery, as in 1533 when a servant dismissed from his job allegedly burned the town of Schiltach, in Württemberg, in revenge.

Poisonous ointment or drugs and waxen poppets were the most frequently charged methods of working *maleficia*. A classic instance of the sympathetic magic of effigies was given at the trial of the Abington witches, executed in 1579. One Mother Dutton was accused of murdering four persons by "pictures" or figurines, "about a span long and three or four fingers broad." Mother Dutton stuck the prick or thorn of a hawthorn bush into the left sides of these images, "where they thought the hearts of the persons to be set, whom the same pictures did represent." Allegedly, the four victims suddenly died.

John Palmer and Elizabeth Knott, executed at St. Albans in 1649, were charged with murder by witchcraft; they had agreed "to frame the picture"—that is, to fashion a figurine—of a woman in clay, "which was forthwith laid upon the fire and duly raked up in the embers; while it was consuming and moldering away, the woman lay in miserable torments. When it was quite consumed, the woman immediately died." (*The Devil's Delusions*, 1649)

Fortunately for law enforcement officials, the demonologists invented the theory that as soon as an officer touched her, the witch lost her powers to inflict *maleficia*. However, Prierias (1521) warned that the witch might possibly bewitch them, and suggested officers carry exorcized salt and consecrated wax. Other theorists even suggested carrying the witches to the prison in a large basket so their feet could not touch the ground [see Ulric Tengler].

One of the worst features of blaming everything on witches was that witchcraft became a kind of "finagle factor" introduced to explain what could not be ex-

Ronwe, the demon who gives knowledge of languages. From Collin de Plancy, *Dictionnaire infernal* (1863).

plained. The imputation could be made retroactive; thus, at the trial of the North Berwick witches in 1590, the death of Archibald, Earl of Angus, was introduced as evidence of witchcraft, yet at the time of his death "the same was not suspected." Thomas Ady complained that

> seldom hath a man the hand of God against him in his estate, or health of body, or any way, but presently he crieth out of some poor innocent neighbor, that he, or she, hath bewitched him; for, saith he, such an old man or woman was lately to my door, and desired some relief, and I denied it, and God forgive me, my heart did rise against her at that time, my mind gave me she looked like a witch. And presently my child, my wife, myself, my horse, my cow, my sheep, my sow, my hog, my dog, my cat, or somewhat was thus and thus handled, in such a strange manner, as I dare swear she is a witch, or else how should these things be, or come to pass. (*A Candle in the Dark*, 1656)

Similarly, Reginald Scot, the first Englishman to oppose the delusion, in 1584, bluntly stated: "Evil humors, etc., and not strange words, witches, or spirits are the cause of such diseases. Also, some of their cattle perish either by disease or mischance."

The denial of logic in associating witchcraft and *maleficia* is illustrated by Matthew Hopkins, as well as by his European counterparts. How should the death of a man from an incurable illness be explained? That the doctors could not cure his sickness? Yes, but . . . In his *Discovery of Witches,* Hopkins reasoned thus:

1. Witches fear they are about to be apprehended.
2. Witches ask devil's help.
3. Devil tells them to bewitch a certain man who is their deadly enemy. (The devil knows this man is "liable to some sudden disease.") "What will you have me do for you, my dear and nearest children, covenanted and compacted with me in my hellish league, and sealed with your blood, my delicate firebrand-darlings?"
4. The man dies by natural means.
5. The devil tells the witches they have killed their deadly enemy by the power he has given them.
6. The witches praise the devil for helping them.

> Next, news is heard that the party is dead, [the devil] comes to the witch, and gets a world of reverence, credence, and respect for his power and activeness, when and indeed the disease kills the party, not the witch nor the devil (only the devil knew that such a disease was predominant), and the witch aggravates her damnation by her familiarity and consent to the devil, and so comes likewise in compass of the laws.

A witch's malefice often produced symptoms very similar to those of possession, where a devil entered or possessed a person's body. It was considered very important to be able to distinguish the two maladies, for each needed a different cure. In possession, exorcism might bring relief. In bewitching, prayer might help, or, some few demonologists suggested, the witch or a "white witch" might be consulted to lift the *maleficia.* The great authority on witchcraft, Francesco-Maria Guazzo, in his *Compendium Maleficarum* (1626), gave the following twenty indications of bewitchment by simple *maleficium,* in contrast to demoniacal possession:

SIGNS OF MALEFICIA

1. First, when the bewitched patient's illness is very difficult to diagnose, so that the physicians hesitate and are in doubt, and keep changing their minds, and fear to make any positive statement.
2. If, although remedies have been applied from the beginning, the sickness does not diminish, but rather increases and grows worse.
3. If it does not, like natural sicknesses, worsen little by little; but the sick man frequently suffers the severest pains immediately at the outset, although there is no apparent pathological reason for it.
4. If the sickness is extremely erratic; although it may occur periodically, it is seldom regular; and although it may resemble a natural disease, nevertheless it differs in many respects.
5. Although the sick man often suffers the greatest pain, yet he cannot say in which part he feels the pain.
6. From time to time, the sick utter the most mournful sighs [*quae luctuosa vocant*] without any manifest cause.
7. Some lose their appetite, and some vomit their food and are so upset in the stomach that they often are constricted with pain; and a sort of lump may be observed rising and falling from the stomach to the throat; and if they try to expel it when it is rising in the throat all their efforts are futile, although it may very soon come out by itself.
8. They feel sticking pains in the region of the heart, so that they assert it is being torn in two.
9. In some the pulse may be seen beating and, as it were, trembling in their necks.
10. Others have excruciating spasms in their necks or kidneys or the bottom of their stomachs, and often an ice-cold wind goes through their stomach and quickly comes back; or they feel a vapor like the hottest flame of fire infesting them in the same manner.
11. Some become sexually impotent.
12. Some are seized with a light sweat,

especially at night, even though the weather and the season are cold.

13. Others seem to have certain parts of their bodies twisted as if in knots.

14. The sicknesses with which those who are bewitched suffer are most often a wasting or emaciation of the whole body and a loss of strength, with a deep languor, dullness of mind, various melancholy ravings, different kinds of fever, causing much work for the physicians; certain convulsive movements like an epileptic; a sort of rigidity of the limbs presenting the appearance of convulsions; sometimes the whole head swells; or such a lassitude pervades the whole body that they can hardly move at all.

15. Sometimes the whole skin, but generally only the face, turns yellow or ashen-colored.

16. Some have their eyelids so gummed up that they can scarcely open them; they can be recognized by certain tests.

17. Those bewitched can hardly bear to look at the face of a priest, at least not directly; for they shift the whites of the eyes in different ways.

18. When the charms are burned, the sick usually change for the worse, or take some greater or less harm as their bewitchment was slight or severe; so that often they are forced to utter terrible cries and roars. But if no change or any new lesion can be observed, there is a good chance that the sick man will with a little attention be restored to good health.

19. If by chance the witch should approach the sick man, the patient is immediately affected with great uneasiness and seized with terror and trembling. If it is a child, it immediately cries. The eyes turn black in color, and other remarkable changes are to be seen in the sick man.

20. Finally, when the priest, to heal the disease, applies certain holy liniments to the eyes, ears, brow, and the other parts, if a sweat or some other change appears in those parts, it is a sign that the patient is bewitched.

This entry may be concluded with a few examples of more recent evil-doing; such reports are still occasionally seen in the newspapers. A few other illustrations are entered under Sorcery.

In 1879 in Wratschewe, a village in the jurisdiction of Novgorod, Agrafena Ignatjewa, a woman over fifty, was suspected of bewitching cattle. The villagers locked her in her cottage and set fire to it. When the ringleaders came to trial, the jury sentenced them merely to slight ecclesiastical penance; the other villagers were dismissed scot free.

> "*Maleficium* is a vicious act directed against the body, through the power of the Devil in a tacit or public pact entered into with the witch, through the control of nature, and through the assistance of some person satisfying his own malice, done always, rightly even if obscurely, with the judgment of God permitting."
> —Candidus Brognolus Bergomensi, *Manuale Exorcistarum*, 1651.

In the very same year, at East Dereham in Norfolk, England, a man was sued for assault and battery on an eighteen-year-old girl. In his defense, he claimed the girl and her mother were witches. In spite of her youth, he said the girl "would bewitch any one; she charmed me and I got no rest day and night for her, till I found this walking-toad under the turf." Then he described how the girl had allegedly worked the spell:

She dug the hole and put it there to charm me, gentlemen, that is the truth. I got the toad out and put it in a cloth and took it upstairs, and showed it to my mother, and throwed it into the pot in the garden. She went round this here walking-toad after she had buried it, and I could not rest by day or sleep by night till I found it. (Quoted in Christina Hole, *Mirror of Witchcraft*)

An example from the mid-twentieth century was reported in the [London] *News Chronicle* for January 6, 1947. An old man was charged with assault on an old woman. She claimed she was gathering parsley on his property, but he said she was hexing him: "You know that this is going back to the witchcraft of the Dark Ages. I dare

Urobach, one of the lower orders of demons. From Collin de Plancy, *Dictionnaire infernal* (1863).

not tell you half the terrible things she has done to me. I have been tortured for five years."

This aspect of witchcraft thus lingers to the present day, but it must be clearly realized as being magic or sorcery, and be separated from the concept of witchcraft known and described over the three centuries of the witchcraft delusion. Both in America and Europe accounts of *maleficia* are still being reported, and because of the confused use of the word, many believe that witchcraft has been continuous from classical Greek and Roman times to now. But these incidents and reports, familiar to all, properly belong to folklore rather than to witchcraft, which is fundamentally a religious heresy.

Malleus Maleficarum. *Malleus Maleficarum*, the *Hammer of Witches* or *Hexenhammer* (first printed in 1486), without question the most important and most sinister work on demonology ever written. It crystallized into a fiercely stringent code previous folklore about black magic with church dogma on heresy, and, if any one work could, opened the floodgates of the inquisitorial hysteria. It sought to make effective the biblical command of Exodus

xxii. 18, "Thou shalt not suffer a witch to live." This handbook for witch hunters was republished and republished, in at least thirteen editions up to 1520, and revived in another sixteen between 1574 and 1669—many early editions lack place and date of publication. There were at least sixteen German editions, eleven French, two Italian, and several English (mainly late, e.g.: 1584, 1595, 1604, 1615, 1620, 1669). The *Malleus Maleficarum* was the source, inspiration, and quarry for all subsequent treatises on witchcraft, and still held its pre-eminent position even after Remy (1595) and Del Rio (1599) had become the recognized authorities.

It owed its authority and pride of place over other contemporary works to several features: first, the scholastic reputation of its two authors, both Dominicans, Jakob Sprenger (1436-95), Dean of Cologne University, and Prior Heinrich Kramer [Latinized as Institor] (about 1430-1505); second, the papal bull of 1484 which Kramer obtained from Innocent VIII to silence opposition to the witch hunt; and third, the detailed procedure for witchcraft trials, "in order, then, that the judges, both ecclesiastical and civil, may have a ready knowledge of the methods of trying, judging, and sentencing." Much of its argument was taken from the *Formicarius* (1435) and the *Praeceptorium* of the Dominican prior, Johannes Nider.

The *Malleus Maleficarum* is divided into three parts. Part I discusses the need for administrators thoroughly comprehending the enormity of witchcraft, which generally comprised the renunciation of the Catholic faith, devotion and homage to the Devil, the offering of unbaptized children, and carnal intercourse with incubi or succubi [see Pact with Devil]. Disbelief in witchcraft is (*pace* the Canon Episcopi) heresy. The Bible says there are witches; therefore, "any man who gravely errs in an exposition of Holy Scripture is rightly considered a heretic." The form of abjuration (given later in Part III) for those who are strongly suspected of heresy (but against whom there is no legal evidence) includes: "I abjure, renounce, and revoke that heresy, or rather infidelity, which falsely and mendaciously maintains that there are no witches in the world." The law allows that any witness whatsoever is to be admitted to give evidence, inasmuch as witchcraft is high treason against God's majesty. Consequently, witnesses not ordinarily admitted are allowed to give evidence on suspicion of witchcraft: excommunicates, criminals, and even convicted perjurers; and furthermore, their names may be kept secret.

Part II treats the three types of *maleficia* of witches and how these evils may be counteracted. Here Sprenger and Kramer sanction all the fables about the doings of witches: the compact with the Devil, sexual relations with devils, transvection, metamorphosis, ligature, injury to cattle and crops—in fact, the whole wide range of sorcery.

Part III (probably the work of Kramer, who had much practical experience) gives formal rules for initiating legal action against witches and securing a conviction and passing sentence. The *Malleus* distinguishes the jurisdiction of inquisitorial, episcopal, and civil courts, and incites the two latter to be active in prosecuting witches. There was a point to this generosity: witches who could not, on some technicality, be prosecuted by the Inquisition as heretics, could be taken care of by the other two courts. Part III concludes with discussing witnesses, their examination, the arrest, imprisonment, questioning, and torture of a witch; and such practical issues as how to break down the taciturnity of a witch—technically a witch could not be condemned without her own confession. It also establishes that the identity of an accuser could be withheld from the prisoner (and defending counsel, if any).

Throughout the whole quarter of a million words, the argument depends on the fantastic sacrifice of logic and common sense to a preconceived theological line. For example, *femina* [woman] is derived, quite erroneously, from *fe* [faith] and *minus* [less]; and *diabolus* [devil] from *dia* [two] and *bolus* [death], which kills body and soul. Even in the first chapter, rational arguments are ignored. Those are heretics who say "the imagination of some men is so vivid that they think they see actual figures and appearances which are but the reflection of their thoughts, and then these are believed to be the apparitions of evil spirits or even the specters of witches." The *Malleus*, however, rejoins: "But this is contrary to the true faith, which teaches us that certain angels fell from heaven and are now devils, and we are bound to acknowledge that by their very nature they can do many wonderful things which we cannot do." Although Charles Williams calls it "almost of the first order," Lea summarizes the intellectual caliber of the book: "The wretched style is fairly uniform throughout and the divagations endless and perplexing, representing a wandering mind, unused to concentration of thought and diverted to following every intrusive idea."

Apologists for the demonologists, as well as independent thinkers, point out that it is illogical and unfair for the twentieth century to judge the sixteenth by modern standards of right and wrong. In this, they are correct; but since a rational, humanist, and scientific approach was being offered as an alternative *at that time* and was rejected, then a thinking man has the right and duty to condemn the demonologists as obscurantists who set back the orderly development of civilization several hundred years.

Kramer was first active in the Tyrol, where he aroused great hostility from the local populace. To justify his witch hunt, Kramer had encouraged a dissolute woman to hide in an oven, making believe the devil lodged there. Her voice denounced many people, whom Kramer cruelly tortured. The Bishop of Brixen finally managed to expel Kramer, not before he had been rewarded by the Archduke Sigismund (for whom Ulrich Molitor wrote his book in 1489).

Another side light is thrown on the in-

Title page of a late edition (Lyons, 1669) of the *Malleus Maleficarum*, "a perfect armory of judicial murder." This edition included numerous works of early demonologists.

MALLEVS

MALEFICARVM,

MALEFICAS ET EARVM

haeresim frameâ conterens,

EX VARIIS AVCTORIBVS COMPILATVS,
& in quatuor Tomos iustè diſtributus,

QVORVM DVO PRIORES VANAS DÆMONVM verſutias, præſtigioſas eorum deluſiones, ſuperſtitioſas Strigimagarum cæremonias, horrendos etiam cum illis congreſſus; exactam denique tam peſtiferæ ſectæ diſquiſitionem, & punitionem complectuntur. Tertius praxim Exorciſtarum ad Dæmonum, & Strigimagarum maleficia de Chriſti fidelibus pellenda; Quartus verò Artem Doctrinalem, Benedictionalem, & Exorciſmalem continent.

TOMVS PRIMVS.
Indices Auctorum, capitum, rerúmque non deſunt.

Editio nouiſsima, infinitis penè mendis expurgata ; cuique acceſsit Fuga Dæmonum & Complementum artis exorciſticæ.

Vir ſiue mulier, in quibus Pythonicus, vel diuinationis fuerit ſpiritus, morte moriatur Leuitici cap. 10.

I.P.Auer in.   I.I.Thourneyſer ſc.

LVGDVNI,
Sumptibus Claudii Bourgeat, ſub ſigno Mercurij Galli.

M. DC. LXIX.
CVM PRIVILEGIO REGIS.

An illustration from the 1497 Paris edition of the *Malleus Maleficarum*.

tegrity of the two inquisitors by what purports to be an official letter of approbation from the Theological Faculty of the University of Cologne in 1487, appended to the *Malleus*. This letter is purposely misleading, however, for, as Hansen shows, only four teachers in the whole university signed it, and their approval was limited to saying that nothing in Parts I and II was repugnant to Catholic teaching, and that Part III was held true because of the character of the eminent witnesses quoted there. Another four teachers, according to the university beadle, approved a further statement against incautious preachers who denied witchcraft. This statement, however, does not appear in the Cologne editions until 1494, the year of the beadle's death, whereas it was inserted (in an unusual position) in early editions for sale outside Cologne. The inference is that the letter is a forgery to add prestige to the book. Sprenger, at his death on December 6, 1495, was not given a requiem mass by his colleagues on the university faculty; this omission may have been due to his de-

mise away from Cologne, but on the other hand may have been occasioned by his academic dishonesty. The authors of the *Malleus Maleficarum* would go to any lengths to make sure the witches burned.

What is especially significant is that the Protestants, who otherwise so strongly opposed the Inquisition, accepted the *Malleus* as their authority and code against witches.

Malum secutum: see Maleficia.

Mare. The supposed mare (demon) which during the night sits on the chest and causes feelings of suffocation. Very occasionally mare refers to the nightmare dream itself. *Mare* is an Old Teutonic stem (Old English *mare*, demon, quite distinct from Old English *mere*, a female horse); it is found also in the French word for nightmare, *cauchemar* (*caucher*, to trample). Very often it is used interchangeably with *incubus*, as in the early *Anglo-Saxon Glosses* (about 700) and in Bacon (1626): "The incubus, which we call the mare." The mare (as well as the incubus) was also known by the scientific name, *ephialtes* (Greek = to leap upon); and in German by *alp* or *mara*.

The picture of the mare remains very constant in all accounts; the early nineteenth-century work, *The Philosophy of Sleep*, by Robert Macnish (1830) gives the common picture:

A monstrous hag squatting upon his breast—mute, motionless and malignant; an incarnation of the evil spirit—whose intolerable weight crushes the breath out of his body, and whose fixed, deadly, incessant stare petrifies him with horror and makes his very existence insufferable.

While the reality of the mare was accepted by the standard demonologists, King James I in his *Demonology* (1597) denied it, answering his own question: Is the "mare, which takes folks sleeping in their beds, a kind of these spirits?" No, it is

but a natural sickness, which the mediciners have given that name of *incubus* unto, *ab incubando*, because it is a thick phlegm, falling into our breast upon the heart, while we are sleeping, intercludes so our vital spirits, and takes all power from us, as makes us think that there were some unnatural burden or spirit, lying upon us, and holding us down.

The mare also attacked horses, and Sir Thomas Browne (1646) tells how a stone hung up in stables prevents the disease. [See further, Nightmare, Night Spell.]

Mary, Queen of Scots: Statute of 1563. In the same year that Queen Elizabeth's act against witchcraft was passed in England, a parallel statute was enacted in Scotland under Mary, Queen of Scots. The wording is very vague and witchcraft seems to imply sorcery (*beneficia* or *maleficia*) or fortunetelling; the one who seeks such help is culpable along with the witch.

Item: forasmuch as the Queen's majesty and the three Estates in this present Parliament being informed'that the heavy and abominable superstition used by divers of the lieges of this realm by using of witchcrafts, sorcery, and necromancy;

And credence given thereto in times bygone against the law of God, and for avoiding and away-putting of all such vain superstition in times to come;

It is statute and ordained by the Queen's majesty and three Estates foresaid:

That no manner of person or persons of whatsoever estate, degree, or condition they be of, take upon hand in any times hereafter to use any manner of witchcrafts, sorcery, or necromancy;

Nor give themselves forth to have any such craft or knowledge thereof, therethrough abusing the people;

Nor that no person seek any help, response, or consultation at any such users or abusers aforesaid of witchcrafts, sorceries or necromancy.

Under the pain of death as well to be execute against the user, abuser, as the seeker of the response or consultation.

And this to be put to execution by the justice, sheriffs, stewards, bailiffs, lords of regalities and royalties, their deputies and others, ordinary judges competent within this realm, with all rigor having power to execute the same.

This act was ratified and confirmed in 1649, and repealed in 1736.

Mass of St. Sécaire: see Black Mass.

Mather, Cotton. "So horrid and hellish is the crime of witchcraft, that were God's thoughts as our thoughts, or God's way as our ways, it could be no other but unpardonable." So wrote Cotton Mather (1662-1728), a lasting example of the wickedness and harm that sincere, God-fearing men can cause when they become fanatics in what they regard as the battle between eternal right and wrong, between God and Satan.

The brilliant son of an illustrious father, Increase Mather, likewise a minister, Cotton Mather entered Harvard at twelve, and at twenty-five was left in charge of the North Church in Boston, the largest in New England, during his father's mission to England to represent the colony. When the Governor and Council asked the advice of the Boston clergy in regard to the Salem witchcraft trials, Cotton Mather formulated the reply or "Return," by which the prosecutions were encouraged. This leadership was not surprising, for he had already made his mark with *Memorable Providences Relating to Witchcrafts and Possessions* (1689), showing that "there is both a God and a Devil and witchcraft." The reader of this book, Mather hoped, would thereby learn "to work out his own salvation with fear and trembling."

Mather investigated many cases of sorcery, and used his influence to ferret out and bring to punishment any suspected of traffic with the devil. When the spectators at the execution of Rev. George Burroughs seemed moved to free him, Judge Sewall implies that Mather persuaded the crowd of his guilt. Called upon by the Governor to justify the trials, his *Wonders of the Invisible World* (1693), an "account of the sufferings brought upon the country by witchcraft" [i.e., at Salem], actually fostered the popular delusion and fanned the hysteria.

It must be observed, however, in mitiga-

Cotton Mather (1662-1728)

"Witchcraft is the most nefarious high treason against the Majesty on high. A witch is not to be endured in heaven or on earth."—Cotton Mather.

tion of Mather's concept of witches, that he hesitated over "spectral evidence," and demanded additional proofs. He recorded in his *Diary* about Salem:

The devils, after a most preternatural manner, by the dreadful judgment of heaven, took a bodily possession of many people in Salem, and the adjacent places; and the houses of the poor people began to be filled with the horrid cries of persons tormented by evil spirits. There seemed an execrable witchcraft in the foundation of this wonderful affliction, and many persons, of divers characters, were accused, apprehended, prosecuted, upon the visions of the afflicted. For my own part, I was always afraid of proceeding to commit and condemn any person, as a confederate with affecting demons, upon so feeble an evidence as a spectral representative. Accordingly, I ever testified against it, both publicly and privately.

Yet, having studied the trial of Rev. George Burroughs, he found a fair trial: "Had I been one of his judges, I could not have acquitted him."

In 1696, only four years after the Salem witch trials, the presiding judge, Samuel Sewall, realized his own participation a mistake and set his influence against Cotton Mather because he had originally encouraged the allegations. Mather's reputation was further damaged by Robert Calef's *More Wonders of the Invisible*

Excerpts from "The Return of Several Ministers consulted by the Excellency, and the Honorable Council upon the present witchcrafts in Salem Village" (1692)

V. When the first inquiry is made into the circumstances of such as may be under any just suspicion of witchcrafts, we could wish that there may be admitted as little as is possible, of such noise, company, and openness, as may too hastily expose them that are examined; and that there may nothing be used as a test for the trial of the suspected, the lawfulness whereof may be doubted among the people of God.

VI. Presumptions whereupon persons may be condemned as guilty of witchcrafts, ought certainly to be more con-

siderable than barely the accused person being represented by a specter unto the afflicted; inasmuch as 'tis an undoubted and notorious thing that a demon may, by God's permission, appear even to ill purposes in the shape of an innocent, yea, and a virtuous person. Nor can we esteem alterations made in the sufferers by a look or touch of the accused to be an infallible evidence of guilt; but frequently liable to be abused by the devil's legerdemains.

VIII. Nevertheless, we cannot but humbly recommend unto the Government, the speedy and vigorous prosecution of such as have rendered themselves obnoxious, according to the directions given in the laws of God and the wholesome statutes of the English nation for the detection of witchcrafts.

World (completed in 1696, printed in London, 1700), even though his father, Increase Mather, as President of Harvard, had Calef's "wicked book" publicly burned [see Goodwin Children]. The slow growth of religious toleration and skepticism regarding witchcraft all told against Cotton Mather; several times he was passed over for the presidency of Harvard. Finally, in 1721, embittered by Harvard's liberal trends, he persuaded a London merchant, Elihu Yale, to found a Calvinist college along his own lines at New Haven. Mather's later years, although he still poured forth new writings, were filled with personal misfortune. He was still maintaining his stand against witchcraft, although repudiated and finally ignored, as late as 1723. His diary for 1724 complains that "some, on purpose to affront me, call their Negroes by the name of 'Cotton Mather,' so that they may, with some shadow of truth, assert crimes as committed by one of that name, which the hearers take to be me."

That Mather merely reflected the prejudices and limitations of his age is an explanation but not an excuse, and as a leader of men he must be placed far below those others who (like Robert Calef), using better judgment, spoke out against the delusion.

Mather, Increase. The youngest son of a family distinguished in Puritan circles, Increase Mather (1639-1723) was graduated from Harvard (1656) and Trinity College, Dublin (1658); he ministered in England until 1661, when he refused to conform to the recently restored Church of England. He became pastor of the North Church in Boston until his death, and President of Harvard from 1685 to 1701. Mather labored hard, in a mission to England, for the interests of the colonists against the British. The *Encyclopaedia Britannica* (11th ed.) ranks him with Jonathan Edwards and Benjamin Franklin as "the greatest Americans of the period before the War of Independence."

Alarmed at the decline of religion in New England and the apparent growth of rationalism, Mather started to collect contemporary moralizing examples of God's works or "illustrious providences" to demonstrate "the real existence of apparitions, spirits and witches" and thus convert skeptics to belief in the supernatural. The resulting collection was entitled *An Essay for the Recording of Illustrious Providences.* "Modern relations," wrote Mather, "being fresh, and near, and attended with all the circumstances of credibility, it may be expected they should have more success upon the obstinacy of unbelievers." Among his stories are the Drummer of Tedworth, George Walton's Stone-Throwing Devil, and a student's pact with the Devil. For each story, Mather was "well assured it is according to truth." Mather's book was an American parallel to *A Blow at Modern Sadducism* by Joseph Glanvill, with whom he corresponded. His famous son, Cotton Mather, extended his father's fight for narrow Congregational orthodoxy, and has the dubious distinction of being the most active witch hunter in America.

Metamorphosis. The belief that humans could be changed into animals is as widespread as it is primitive. It is basic to the totemist conception of the American Indians, for example, each tribe claiming descent from some animal or bird. In the Old Testament, Nebuchadnezzar grew animal's hair. The followers of Odysseus were transformed into swine on Circe's island. Erysichthon sold his daughter over and over as a cow or as a horse. Apuleius' *Golden Ass* (90 B.C.) is another great classical example. Metamorphosis appears early in the work when Lucius, a visitor to Thessaly, watches his hostess Pamphile strip herself naked, smear ointment on her body, and fly through the air. Lucius tries to follow suit, but uses the wrong ointment and is changed into an ass. From this point, the *Golden Ass* is a recital of both fantastic and realistic adventures of Lucius in his new shape as an ass. Apuleius described the scenes of magic so closely that he was charged with sorcery; his successful defense has been preserved. Vergil, in his eighth *Eclogue*, speaks of herbs and baneful plants growing in Pontus. "By these have I seen Moeris transform himself into a wolf, and skulk into the woods."

The commonest metamorphosis in witchcraft is man into wolf; lycanthropy is discussed in a separate entry. A few other transformations are also known by their technical designations, such as aeluranthropy (cat), boanthropy (cow), kuanthropy (dog), lepanthropy (hare), but these terms are rarely used.

The typical transformations in England were human into cat, dog, or hare. Isobel Grierson was burned at Edinburgh in 1607 for entering a house in the form of a cat, a common allegation in Scottish trials (as late as 1752). In various accounts of trials, witches were alleged to appear in the guise of almost all small animals and birds. John Palmer, executed on July 16, 1649, for example, confessed that "falling out with a young man, he transformed himself into a toad, and lying in the way where the young man came, he kicked it; immediately Palmer complained of a sore shin, whereupon he bewitched the young man for many years to his great woe and torment"—*The Devil's Delusion*, 1649. *A True and Exact Relation*, in 1645, described witches taking the shape of dogs, polecats, kites, rats, snakes, gray birds, mice, and black rabbits. Amazing evidence of change into a rabbit convicted Mrs. Julian Cox in 1663 [see Evidence in Witch Trials, England].

So extensive was the common belief in shape-shifting that one of the characters in Gifford's *Dialogue Concerning Witches* (1593) saw witches thus disguised wherever he went in his garden: "I am afraid, for I see now and then a hare, which my conscience giveth me is a witch, or some witch's spirit, she stareth so upon me. And sometimes I see an ugly weasel run through my yard, and there is a foul cat sometimes in my barn, which I have no liking unto." In Europe, Guazzo stated, "Witches can turn themselves into mice or cats or locusts or other small animals and creep through little holes and afterwards resume

"Wait until you have been properly anointed." —Goya (1799).

their shape." This ability was supposed to be reserved for especially devoted witches as a reward by the devil. One sorcerer, Scavius, about 1375, always escaped his enemies by turning himself into a mouse, until one day he was slain with a sword while absentmindedly sitting at a window, before he could effect his transformation (Nider, *Formicarius*, about 1435).

Any injury to the supposed animal would cause a parallel injury to the human when he resumed his own body; this legend of sympathetic magic occurs again and again. Very early, Gervais of Tilbury wrote: "Women have been seen and wounded in the shape of cats by persons who were secretly on the watch, and the next day the women have shown wounds and loss of limbs." Over 400 years later, Stearne, the henchman of.Matthew Hopkins, told just the same fable of an old crone who displayed the wound she had received when in the likeness of a dog (*Confirmation and Discovery of Witchcraft*, 1648).

Rare throughout the worst of the witch mania was the man who questioned metamorphosis. The Anglican bishop Samuel Harsnett was one such, writing in his *Declaration of Egregious Popish Impostures* (1603):

> What man judging according to wit, understanding, or sense, can imagine a witch can transform herself into the likeness of a cat, a mouse, or an hare; and that she being hunted with hounds, in the form of an hare, and pinched in the breech [buttocks], or whipped with scourges in the similitude of a cat, the same pinch or mark should be found in the breech of the witch, that was before made by the hounds in the breech of an hare.

Fifty years later such opinions were more common, and Sir Robert Filmer said: "Many confess of themselves things false and impossible . . . that they be sometimes turned into cats, hares, and other creatures and such like; all which are mere fables and things impossible."

But because such things were impossible, the upholders of witch hunts held all the more firmly to their beliefs, on the analogy of *credo quia impossibile*. Joseph Glanvill, for example, even at the end of the seventeenth century, in his *Saducismus Triumphatus*, discussing witches' being "sucked in a certain private place in their bodies by a familiar," wrote: "The more absurd and unaccountable these actions seem, the greater confirmations are they to me of the truth of those relations and the reality of what the objectors would destroy."

The position of Glanvill regarding transformation was that of most of the sixteenth- and seventeenth-century demonologists. Proponents had the same difficulty, however, regarding the opposition of the early and authoritative Canon Episcopi as they had with transvection. Some like Bodin and Boguet accepted metamorphosis without any reservations about its actuality, but others (e.g., Bernard de Como and Binsfeld) equivocated by arguing with Augustine and Thomas Aquinas that transformation was not actual, but an illusion of the Devil in which men *appear* to have the shape of animals. The early Ulrich Molitor (1489) explained it in this way:

> Devils, thus deceiving men's eyes, make appear before them chimerical forms which men believe to be real, in such a way, for example, that he who looks at a man sees in place of him an ass or a wolf, yet nevertheless the man is not cloaked in either of these shapes. . . . The eyes alone are dupes of phantasmagoria to the extent of taking their error for reality.

All this was done only with the permission of God. Guazzo, in his *Compendium Maleficarum* (1626), summed up: "No one must fall into the delusion that a man can really be changed into a beast, or a beast into a real man; for these are magic portents and illusions [*praestigias*], which have the form but not the reality of those things which they appear to be."

This distinction is subtle, and how far it would be understood by unlearned men and women accused in courts, or even accepted in practice by their judges, cannot be ascertained. But to William Perkins, for a long time an authority on witchcraft in England, the argument was incomprehensible. He wrote in his *Discourse of Witchcraft* (1608):

Sometimes a horse I'll be, sometimes a hound,
A hog, a headless bear, sometimes a fire,
And neigh, and bark, and grunt, and roar and
    burn
Like horse, hound, dog, bear, fire, at every
    turn.
    —Shakespeare, *A Midsummer Night's Dream* (1594).

The inquisitions of Spain and other countries wherein these and such like things are recorded, touching witches really metamorphosed into such creatures, cannot be true; considering that it is not in the power of the Devil thus to change substances into other substances.

Metamorphosis was supposed to be effected by means of a magic ointment similar to that used for transvection. In addition, in the trials of the Scottish witches in 1662, Isobel Gowdie revealed a number of charms for transformation into various animals and, providently, also for resuming human form. She confessed:

When we go in the shape of a hare, we say thrice over:

I shall go into a hare,
With sorrow and sigh and mickle
    [much] care;
And I shall go in the Devil's name
Ay while I come home again.

And instantly we start in a hare. And when we would be out of this shape, we will say:

Hare, hare, God send thee care.
I am in a hare's likeness just now,
But I shall be in a woman's
    likeness even now.

When we would go in the likeness of a cat, we say thrice over:

I shall go into a cat,
With sorrow and sigh and a
    black shot.
And I shall go in the Devil's name
Ay while I come home again.

She gave similar formulas for changing into a crow or any other likeness. Other witches could be transformed into the same shapes simply by saying. "I conjure thee, go with me . . . and presently they become as we are, either cats, hares, crows."

Meyfarth, Johann Matthäus.

Listen, you money-hungering judges and bloodthirsty prosecutors, the apparitions of the Devil are all lies. It is high time the rulers appointed better judges and put faith in more moderate preachers, and then the Devil with his deceiving illusions would be put to shame.

Johann Meyfarth, who wrote the above, was the early seventeenth-century Protestant counterpart to the Roman Catholic Friederich von Spee (from whom Meyfarth drew some of his arguments). Both had witnessed hundreds of witch trials and burnings and had come to despise and oppose the whole procedure. Dr. Meyfarth would have given a thousand thalers, he said, to forget the tortures: he had seen feet wrenched off legs, and eyes torn from their sockets, and the prisoner burned with brimstone and basted with oil. He had seen torturers apply flaming balls of brimstone to the genitals of a woman while she was hanging in strappado. He had watched them revel in horror until their victims confessed—or died (strangled by the Devil, the judges explained). Because they are vivid firsthand accounts, Meyfarth's *Christliche Erinnerung* (1635) and Spee's *Cautio Criminalis* (1631) make illuminating introductions to the theory and practice of witchcraft.

Addressing preachers, administrators, and judges of Thuringia and Franconia, Meyfarth, a Lutheran professor of theology at Erfurt, drew a picture of the hatred and suspicion and terror wrought in Germany by the witchcraft delusion. Once introduced, the persecution spread from house to house, village to village, and city to city. Not only were the poor disgraced, but many landed and merchant families were ruined, because once an accusation had been made, the judges strove only to establish guilt and seize property. Like Spee, Meyfarth exposed the dilemmas used by the judges to prove the guilt of any accused. If their reputation were bad, they were clearly witches; if good, equally so, for witches always tried to appear virtuous. If, on arrest, the suspects were frightened —surely witches, fearing merited punishment; if resolute—no less witches, because witches always pretend innocence.

The accused had to name other witches. One victim, after three days of torture, confronted a burgher's wife of irreproachable character. She pleaded:

I have never seen you at the sabbat, but to end the torture I had to accuse someone. You came into my mind because, as

I was being led to prison, you met
me and said you would never have believed it of me. I beg forgiveness, but
were I tortured again, I would accuse you
again.

Thereupon the judges returned her to the
torture to make her repeat her charges, and
the burgher's wife was prosecuted. Many
would have withdrawn their accusations,
had they not feared a repetition of torture.
"Oh, God," they cried, "it would be unendurable."

In a biting description Meyfarth scored
the professional witch finder confiding to
his wife:

Liza, you should thank God you belong to
me, for I could not be higher than I am.
I hold full power over rich and poor,
over young and old, man and woman,
boy and girl, servant and maid, citizen
and peasant, knight and noble, doctors,
licentiates, masters, and bachelors. I
know all the tricks, and you should
thank God for that.

By 1635, protests like Meyfarth's were
possible; they anticipated the end of the
witchcraft mania; had they not been made,
however, the vested interests of those who
made a business of finding witches might
have prolonged the persecutions. Even so,
in Germany, witch trials continued into the
eighteenth century.

Molitor, Ulrich. Ulrich Molitor was one
of the earliest writers on witchcraft. Though
he adopted a moderate position, Molitor in
practice was equally hostile to sorcerers
"suspected of heresy." He found nothing
wrong with burning at the stake a man
charged with bewitching a neighbor and
sometimes riding a wolf.

Molitor was Doctor of Laws of Padua
and professor at the University of Constance, where his book was first published
(1489). *De Lamiis et Phitonicis Mulieribus*
[*Concerning Female Sorcerers and Soothsayers*], a dialogue, was written to allay the
doubts of those like the Archduke Sigismund of Austria and "the most illustrious
doctors." Sigismund had learned about
witchcraft from the Dominican inquisitors,

Witch going to the sabbat, one of the six
illustrations in Ulrich Molitor's book on
witches, *De Lamiis* (1489).

Sprenger and Kramer, who had come to the
Tyrol to root out witchcraft. The heresy
of witchcraft was by no means universally
accepted. Thus Sigismund (in the dialogue)
dismisses evidence extracted by torture:
"For the fear of punishments incites men
to say what is quite contrary to the nature
of the facts." If sorcerers could produce
tempests, princes like himself could disband
their armies and maintain a few witches.
All those confessions of intercourse with
the devil arise because "the loquacity of
women is flattered by many foolish things,
which they ultimately believe true."

To these objections Molitor puts up very
weak rejoinders, generally quoting the
Bible, a few Church Fathers, and even the
History of King Arthur and Vergil (for
poets tell the truth!). Overriding is Molitor's belief in the power of the Devil, always
acting by permission of God, to deceive
men, who are thereby culpable. He explains
Merlin, not as the offspring of a woman

and a demon (as most authorities held), but as a real human. The woman indeed gave herself to the devil and thought she was pregnant; God allowed the devil to blow up her stomach with wind and cause her birth pangs. At the critical moment, the devil substituted a real infant he had just stolen. The mother thought the child her own and the devil its father. Molitor observes that the devil cannot procreate, even if he serves first as a succubus and then uses the semen so received as an incubus, because he could not keep the semen fresh!

On the question of attendance at the sabbat, Molitor concludes:

> It is untrue that witches go thousands of furlongs in the silence of the night to gather for the sabbat. They are the playthings of dreams or some powerful illusion . . . which the devil has impressed on their minds. Thus deceived by vain appearances, they believe, on waking, that such things really happened to them.

Illusion was just as sinful as real flight to a sabbat, for they had abandoned God and were therefore heretics.

Montespan, Madame de: see Chambre Ardente Affair.

Mora Witches. The sudden flare-up of witch persecution at Mora, in Dalecarlia or Dalarna (Sweden), in 1669, one of the most amazing incidents in the history of witchcraft, resulted in the burning of eighty-five persons, who had seduced three hundred children into flying to the Blocula. "Is it not plain," asked the skeptical Bishop Hutchinson, "that the people had frightened their children with so many tales, that they could not sleep without dreaming of the devil, and then made the poor women of the town confess what the children said of them?"

The original documents of the trial were printed by Balthasar Bekker in his *World Bewitched,* and translated from High Dutch into English by Dr. Anthony Horneck (1641-97), as an appendix to Glanvill's *Saducismus Triumphatus.*

Reports that the Devil had made some

hundreds of children "subject to his power" and had "been seen to go in a visible shape through the country" brought on an investigation in August, 1669. The trouble had started on July 5, 1668, when the pastor of Elfdale, in Dalecarlia, reported that an eighteen-year-old girl, Gertrude Svensen, had been accused by Eric Ericsen, fifteen, of stealing several children for the Devil. Others, similarly charged, pleaded innocent, except one seventy-year-old woman.

Interest grew, and by May, 1669, King Charles XI appointed a commission to redeem the accused witches by prayers, avoiding imprisonment or torture. The prayers, however, merely spread mass hysteria, and when the Royal Commission first met on August 13, 1669, three thousand people assembled to hear the sermons and assist the investigators. The next day, having heard the stories of the children, the commissioners discovered seventy witches. Twenty-three freely confessed and were condemned and burned within a fortnight; the forty-seven others were sent to Falun, where they were burned a little later. In addition, fifteen children were burned; thirty-six children between nine and fifteen were judged less guilty and had to run the gauntlet; and twenty others "who had no great inclination" to witchcraft, because they were very young (under nine), were condemned "to be lashed with rods upon their hands, for three Sundays together at the church door; and the aforesaid six and thirty were also doomed to be lashed this way, once a week for a whole year together."

On August 25, "the day being bright and glorious, and the sun shining," twelve days after the commission had begun, the condemned were executed *en masse.* Before being burned, the witches as a group were forced to confess the truth of the children's accusations. "At first, most of them did very stiffly, and, without shedding the least tear, deny it, though much against their will and inclination." When questioned individually, most continued "steadfast in their denials."

The evidence for what can only be called legalized mass murder fell into three areas:

A contemporary illustrated jacket of a book describing the witchcraft at Mora, Sweden,
*Der Königs Herren Commissarien gehaltenes Protocol über die entdeckte Zauberey in dem
Dorff Mohra* (The Hague, 1670).

(1) transvection to the sabbat, (2) the
sabbat, and (3) the *maleficia* proposed.

The witches carried the children, dressed
in red or blue, on goats or sticks or sleeping
men! They flew through windows, the devil
previously having removed the glass "so
they had room to go." If the children later

repented and revealed the names of the
witches, they were beaten, but "the marks
of the lashes, the judges could not perceive
in them . . . but the witches said they
would quickly vanish."

The assembly point was the Blocula, "a
delicate large meadow, whereof you can see

no end. The place or house they met at had before it a gate painted with divers colors; through this gate they went into a little meadow distinct from the other, where the beasts went that they used to ride on."

This fairy-story land, however, was given over to the devil's rites, consisting of seven acts:

1. Denial of God, by cutting the finger and writing the name with blood in the devil's book.

2. Baptism by the devil.

3. Oath of fidelity. The witches threw filings of clocks into water, and recited: "As these filings of the clock do never return to the clock from which they are taken, so may my soul never return to heaven."

4. Banquet. The menu included "broth with coleworts and bacon in it, oatmeal, bread spread with butter, milk, and cheese."

5. Dancing, ending with "fighting one with another."

6. Music and copulation.

7. Building a stone house to preserve the witches at the Day of Judgment, but the walls were perpetually falling down.

The witches promised the devil to work evil, but their proposals were merely simple acts of *maleficia*. In this grim narration one amusing note told how a witness got a headache.

> The minister of Elfdale declared that one night these witches were, to his thinking, upon the crown of his head; and that from thence he had a long continued pain of the head. One of the witches confessed, too, that the devil had sent her to torment that minister; and that she was ordered to use a nail, and strike it into his head, but it would not enter very deep, and hence came that headache.

As might be expected, the witches could perform none of the magic tricks ascribed to them, but the witch believers had a ready answer: "The Lords Commissioners were indeed very earnest and took great pains to persuade them to show some of their tricks,

but to no purpose; for they did all unanimously confess that since they had confessed all, they found that all their witchcraft was gone."

From Mora, the hysteria spread through Norrland to the two Swedish-speaking provinces of Finland, and by 1675 to Stockholm. Here it was finally stopped when the young doctor Urban Hjärne succeeded in demonstrating that the whole craze depended on morbid imagination, confused and half-mad thoughts, or pure malice and a desire to attract attention. Even educated people became involved, either by hallucinations or external pressures: a schoolteacher, later Dean of Mora, insisted that the devil had carried him to the Island of Blakulla [Blocula], and a professor at Uppsala named Lundius and an assessor named Anders Stjernhök believed that the devil had appeared to them three times in one night.

A curious epilogue to the Mora witch trials came sixty years later, when a thirteen-year-old Norwegian girl, Siri Jørgensdatter, repeated the details about Mora (which she had heard or read about) and accused several old women of witchcraft.

More, Henry. Henry More (1614-87) spent his life within the confines of Christ's College, Cambridge, emerging only for Lady Ragley's séances [see Glanvill] and local witch trials. A retiring scholar, More refused two bishoprics. He was the leader of the Cambridge Platonists, philosophers opposed to medieval scholasticism, unbending Calvinism, as well as ritualistic Episcopalianism. Like Plato and Plotinus, he turned to mysticism, stressing the "world" soul, the "actual knowledge of eternal truths" always in the mind, and the substantiality and immortality of the soul.

Influenced by the new scientific thinking of the seventeenth century (which tended to materialism), More tried to prove the existence of God by visible indications, the clearest of which were witches and demons. "No spirit, no God," he declared. In *An Antidote Against Atheism* (1653), More accepted the reality of witches because of testimony for their existence by disinterested witnesses, agreement of eyewitnesses, and the sensory effects which witchcraft produced. Even this position was in advance of that of his contemporary, Meric Casaubon, D.D., who believed in witches because everybody believed in witches. (*Of Credulity and Incredulity*, 1668)

Such opinions were harmless in the study. Yet More provided the philosophic justification for the excesses of the most extreme witch hunters. No English writer accepted so completely and unreservedly the whole paraphernalia of witchcraft constructed by such men as Remy and Bodin. Even Meric Casaubon admitted these authorities were more credulous than he. More believed literally in transvection, metamorphosis, sabbats, familiars, and sexual intercourse with devils.

More's advocacy of witchcraft in the seventeenth century was as fantastic as belief in "bug-eyed monsters" by any twentieth-century atomic scientist. As one of England's most learned and most respected professors, More countenanced ignorance and superstition, instead of using his intellectual leadership to turn the less gifted and fortunate away from witchcraft. He personally interrogated a girl accused of witchcraft at Cambridge. She made a fantastic confession of a devil's assembly. Wrote More:

> As for my own part, I should have looked upon this whole narration as a mere idle fancy or sick man's dream, had it not been that my belief was so much enlarged by that palpable satisfaction I received from what we heard from four or five witches which we lately examined before. And yet what I heard was but such matters as are ordinarily acknowledged by such witches as will confess.

Instead of applying scientific methods to break down superstition, More used these methods to reinforce witch beliefs. He explained the devil's coldness as due to coagulated air. He rationalized lycanthropy as follows:

> For I conceive the devil gets into their body, and by his subtle substance, more operative and searching than any fire or putrefying liquor, melts the yielding compages [structures] of the body to such a consistency, and so much of it as is fit for his purpose, and makes it pliable to his imagination; and then it is easy for him to work it into what shape he pleaseth, as it is to work the air into such forms and figures as he ordinarily doth.

Most writers on More praise him as "one of the finer spirits of English philosophy," but pass very lightly over his views on witchcraft. Yet his whole philosophy rested fundamentally on a belief in demons, witches, and wonders.

Morton, Patrick : see Pittenweem Witches.

Mouse-Maker. Toward the end of the seventeenth century, a rational approach was often taken to a completely irrational problem. This mixture of common sense and fantasy in a witch trial in Saxony in 1694 (the records do not specify the town), happily ending without executions, illustrates the intellectual confusion caused by growing skepticism about witchcraft.

Ten-year-old Althe Ahlers had learned a conjuring trick, and mystified the other children at school by producing a live mouse from a handkerchief, using some small yellow contraption as a prop. News of the trick spreading, the little girl was arrested, but made no secret of her skill, saying she learned it from Elsche Nebelings, aged sixty-three. On August 25, 1694, the trial opened, with Elsche testifying that, although reputed a witch, she was only a poor widow and knew nothing about mouse-making. Both Althe and Elsche were held in jail. On August 30, three children described the trick for the benefit of the court. On September 11, the prosecutor questioned Althe, and a week later formally accused her of sorcery and, in accordance with Exodus xxii. 15, demanded the death penalty [see Bible Witchcraft]. Since Althe was only a child, the court appointed a defense counsel. The two lawyers debated her case. The prosecution showed the enormity of mouse-making and, referring to Remy and

Carpzov, the need for torturing the accused girl with whips and thumbscrews to elicit the truth. The defense countered that mouse-making was sleight of hand and, even if sorcery, was done in innocence, without any concealment.

On October 1, 1694, the judge forwarded the court reports to the law faculty of an impartial university for instructions. He asked three questions:

1. Since both the woman and the child deny sorcery, should they be tortured (either by showing them the horrible instruments or applying screws and strappado) and should they be searched for the devil's mark?

2. If devil's marks were found, how should Althe be punished?

3. If Althe were not tortured, what should be done to her?

The answer came: to release the prisoners. Althe had been in prison for six weeks, and that was sufficient punishment. The university's sobriety is still commendable, for witch trials and executions on similar evidence continued into the eighteenth century.

Necromancy: see Divination.

Newbury Witch. An incident in the Civil War in England in 1643 provides an example of lynch law and a very unusual execution of a witch by shooting. Some of the Cromwellian army, under command of the Earl of Essex, while loitering in Newbury, saw a woman apparently walking on the waters of a river, no doubt on stilts. "They could perceive there was a plank or deal overshadowed with a little shallow water that she stood upon . . . turning and winding it which way she pleased." Seizing the woman, the soldiers decided she was a witch, "so they resolved themselves to make a shot at her." At this point, legend takes over completely, and the printed account tells how "with a deriding and loud laughter at them, she caught their bullets in her hands and chewed them." Finally, one soldier slashed her forehead, as a sure method that "would prevail against the strongest sorcery," and "discharged a pistol under-

Title page of contemporary tract on the Witch of Newbury (1643). From the British Museum, London. "Her soul we ought not to judge of, though the evils of her wicked life and death can escape no censure."

neath her ear, at which she straight sunk down and died."

Newton, Florence. The trial of Florence Newton, the "witch of Youghal," at the Cork assizes in Ireland in September, 1661, was first related by Joseph Glanvill from the notes of the presiding judge, Sir William Ashton. It is therefore a unique eyewitness account of an actual witch trial in Ireland in the mid-seventeenth century. No matter how ridiculous the evidence and how illogical the reasoning, it forms the antithesis of German trials: here, the trial was public, witnesses (including the mayor and minister) were presented and sworn, torture was not used to force a confession or denunciations, and an attempt was made to approximate the legal procedure of any other trial.

The counts against Florence Newton

were two: bewitching a young servant girl, Mary Longdon, into fits, and causing the death of David Jones by bewitchment. Mary's refusal to give her a piece of pickled beef for Christmas, 1660, sent Florence Newton away mumbling a threatened evil [*damnum minatum*]. A week later, as Mary was carrying some laundry, the "witch of Youghal" accosted her, knocked down her basket, and "violently kissed her." Soon after the kissing, Mary was troubled with visions: By her bedside stood a veiled woman, whom a "little old man in silk clothes" revealed as Goody Newton. Mary refused to obey the male specter, whereupon she manifested the usual symptoms of demoniacal possession or hysteria: abnormal strength, loss of memory, and vomiting "needles, pins, horsenails, stubs, wool, and straw." An additional—and uncommon—feature was the poltergeist-like showers of stones which "would follow her from place to place." Skeptics might regret that no one "could ever take them, save only some few which she and her master caught in their hands. Amongst which, one that had a hole in it she tied (as she was advised) with a leather thong to her purse, but it vanished immediately, though the latter continued tied in a fast knot." Throughout all these disturbances, Mary Longdon said she saw Florence Newton tormenting and sticking pins into her. When the witch was manacled, Mary stopped her fits.

After a preliminary hearing by the mayor, on March 24, 1661, Goody Newton was imprisoned. Some amateur witch finders tried their skill at proving guilt. One of them stabbed Mother Newton's hand, "but could not enter it, though the awl was so bent that none of them could put it straight again. Then Mr. Blackwall took a lance, and lanced one of her hands an inch and a half long, and a quarter of an inch deep, but it bled not at all. Then he lanced the other hand, and then they bled."

Glanvill did not give the conclusion of the trial, but, undoubtedly, Florence Newton was executed.

New York Witches. Except for the two trials noted here, New York remained free from the witchcraft delusion throughout the seventeenth century. During the Salem trials, New York became the haven for those able to make their escape from the Massachusetts Bay Colony. Hospitably received were such refugees as Nathaniel Cary and his wife, and Philip and Mary English, who had introductions to Benjamin Fletcher, the Governor. The presence of a little colony of exiles may have encouraged Joseph Dudley, the former Deputy Governor of Massachusetts under Andros, living in New York after his expulsion in 1689, to canvass the New York Dutch pastors to send a rational report on evidence used against witches to the new governor at Boston, Sir William Phips.

The main factor in New York's freedom from witch trials was the Dutch influence, suggests Burr, pointing to the long line of Dutch intellectual leaders who had opposed witch hunting—Weyer, Grevius, Bekker—and the consequent absence of witch trials in Holland after 1610.

Even when accusations of witchcraft were made in New York, the charges were greeted by both juries and magistrates with sobriety. In 1670, for example, a complaint was laid by the residents of Westchester against Katherine Harrison, a rich widow recently moved from Wethersfield, Connecticut, that she return to her former abode. "That contrary to the consent and good liking of the town, she would settle amongst them; and she being reputed to be a person lying under the suspicion of witchcraft hath given some cause of apprehension to the inhabitants there." A month later, in August, she was summoned to appear in New York, with a Captain Richard Panton, "at whose house she resideth." However, the magistrate decided:

The reasons [for this suspicion] do not so clearly appear unto me; yet, notwithstanding, to give as much satisfaction as may be to the complainants who pretend their fears to be of a public concern, I have not thought absolutely to determine the matter at present, but do suspend it until the next General Court of Assizes.

By October, 1670, Katherine Harrison was vindicated.

In the case of Katherine Harrison, widow, who was bound to the good behavior upon complaint of some of the inhabitants of Westchester until the holding of this court: It is ordered that, in regard there is nothing [that] appears against her deserving the continuance of that obligation, she is to be released from it, and hath liberty to remain in the town of Westchester where she now resides, or anywhere else in the government [of New York] during her pleasure.

One other record (1665) comes from Long Island, settled (in Suffolk County) by New Englanders but since 1664 wholly administered by New York. It is valuable, first, as a specimen of a typical seventeenth-century American indictment for witchcraft (following the specimen printed in West's *Simboleography* in 1594: see Indictment). Second, because it concerns itself solely with sorcery or *maleficia*—there is no mention of any pact with the Devil or any convention of witches. Indeed, the law of New York did not recognize witchcraft per se as an offense; when witchcraft was alleged to result in murder, then it was accounted murder and so prosecuted. Third, because the jury found the evidence unsatisfactory, and the Court merely bound the defendants to be of good conduct. The same charges in England—or New England—would no doubt have secured conviction and execution.

At the Court of Assizes held in New York, the second day of October, 1665.
The trial of Ralph Hall, and Mary his wife, upon suspicion of witchcraft.
The names of the persons who served on the Grand Jury: Thomas Baker, Foreman of the Jury, of Easthampton; Captain John Symonds of Hempstead; Mr. Hallet; Anthony Waters [of] Jamaica; Thomas Wandall of Marshpath Kills [Maspeth]; Mr. Nicolls of Stamford; Balthazar de Haart, John Garland, Jacob Leisler, Antonio de Mill, Alexander Munro, Thomas Searle, of New York.
The prisoners being brought to the bar by Allard Anthony, Sheriff of New York, this following indictment was read, first against Ralph Hall, and then against Mary his wife, viz.:
"The Constable and Overseers of the town of Seatallcott [Setauket, now Brookhaven] in the East Riding of Yorkshire [Suffolk County] upon Long Island, do present for our sovereign Lord the King, that Ralph Hall of Seatallcott aforesaid, upon the 25th day of December, being Christmas day last was twelve months [1663] in the fifteenth year of the reign of our sovereign Lord, Charles II, by the grace of God, King of England, Scotland, France, and Ireland, Defender of the Faith, &c., and several other days and times since that day, by some detestable and wicked arts, commonly called witchcraft and sorcery, did (as is suspected) maliciously and feloniously practice and exercise at the said town of Seatallcott in the East Riding of Yorkshire on Long Island aforesaid, on the person of George Wood, late of the same place, by which wicked and detestable arts the said George Wood (as is suspected) most dangerously and mortally sickened and languished. And not long after by the aforesaid wicked and detestable arts, the said George Wood (as is likewise suspected) died."

A second indictment charged that Ralph Hall did

"maliciously and feloniously practice and exercise . . . on the person of an infant child of Ann Rogers, widow of the aforesaid George Wood deceased, by which wicked and detestable arts, the said infant child (as is likewise suspected) most dangerously and mortally sickened and languished, and not long after by the said wicked and detestable arts (as is likewise suspected) died; and so the said Governor and Overseers do present that the said George Wood and the said infant child, by the ways and means aforesaid, most wickedly and feloniously were (as is suspected) murdered by the said Ralph Hall at the times and places aforesaid, against the peace of our sovereign Lord the King and against the laws of this government in such cases provided."
The like indictment was read against Mary, the wife of Ralph Hall.
Thereupon, several depositions accusing the prisoners of the fact for which they were indicted were read, but no witness appeared to give testimony in court viva voce.
Then the Clerk, calling upon Ralph Hall, bade him hold up his hand, and read as follows:

"Ralph Hall, thou standest here indicted for that, having not the fear of God before thine eyes, thou didst upon the 25th day of December, being Christmas day last was twelve months [1663], and at several other times since (as is suspected), by some wicked and detestable arts commonly called witchcraft and sorcery, maliciously and feloniously practice and exercise upon the bodies of George Wood and an infant child of Ann Rogers; by which said arts the said George Wood and the infant child (as is suspected) most dangerously and mortally fell sick and languished unto death. Ralph Hall, what does thou say for theyself: Art thou Guilty or Not Guilty?"

Mary, the wife of Ralph Hall, was called upon in like manner.

They both pleaded Not Guilty and threw themselves to be tried by God and the country.

Whereupon, their case was referred to the jury, who brought into the court this following verdict, viz.:

"We, having seriously considered the case committed to our charge, against the prisoners at the bar, and having well weighed the evidence, we find that there are some suspicions by the evidence, of what the woman is charged with, but nothing considerable of value to take away her life. But in reference to the man we find nothing considerable to charge him with."

The Court thereupon gave this sentence: That the man should be bound body and goods for his wife's appearance at the next sessions, and so on from sessions to sessions, as long as they stay within this government. In the meanwhile to be of their good behavior. So they were returned unto the Sheriff's custody, and upon entering into a recognizance, according to the sentence of the court, they were released.

On August 21, 1668, a release was signed at Fort James freeing the Halls, who resided on Great Miniford's Island [City Island, New York], from all "bonds of appearance or other obligations . . . there having been no direct proofs nor further prosecution of them or either of them since."

Nider, Johannes. *Formicarius* [*The Ant-hill*], by Johannes Nider (about 1380-

The second book ever printed discussing witchcraft (1475): Johannes Nider's *Formicarius*, written about 1435. This is the first page of the second edition (Augsburg, about 1484), now in Cornell University Library.

1438), Dominican professor of theology at the University of Vienna (1425) and Prior at Nuremberg and at Basel (1431), is (following Alphonsus de Spina) the second printed book in the world to deal explicitly with witchcraft. It is written as a dialogue between a theologian and a skeptic discussing the problems faced by the Church Council of Basel. Many of Nider's anecdotes are contemporary and show that trials for sorcery were already in progress.

Nider finished the book about 1435, and it was printed six times up to 1692. The fifth book or part, which described "witches and their deceptions," was sometimes appended to the *Malleus Maleficarum*. While Nider discussed the evil powers of witches, he did not stress those features found in the later demonologists—the sabbat, pact, night flight, and copulation with the devil. Nider was almost a skeptic; indeed. in his earlier *Praeceptorium Divinae Legis*, he had said transvection was the delusion of a dream, real metamorphosis was impossible, and visions of heaven and hell merely superstitions created by devils.

Night Flight: see Sabbat; Transvection.

Nightmare. A word popularly used for (1) the demon or mare alleged to cause the dream; and (2) the dream itself. The attacking demon was often regarded as an incubus or succubus; thus Bayley's *English Dictionary* (1785) defined incubus as "the nightmare, a disease when a man in his sleep supposes he has a great weight lying upon him; a devil who has carnal knowledge of a woman under the shape of a man." This conception is of great antiquity, for in the Hebrew *Zohar* it was said that a man's erotic dreams are caused by a succubus lying with him to bear evil spirits.

Although both the mare and incubus demons are projections of repressed sexual desires, for convenience of treatment the two complementary conceptions are distinguished: with the mare-demon, terror predominates; but with the incubus-demon, the main element (although mingled with dread) is pleasure. Both experiences seem real—in fact, "a daylight vividness of vision that was all but being awake," as Charles Lamb said in his essay on witchcraft.

The nightmare—demon and dream—had provoked at least sixteen treatises from 1627 to 1740, but it was not until 1763 that the first classic description of the dream appeared in English:

> The nightmare generally seizes people sleeping on their backs, and often begins with frightful dreams, which are soon succeeded by a difficult respiration, a violent oppression on the breast, and a total privation of voluntary motion. In this agony they sigh, groan, utter indistinct sounds, and remain in the jaws of death, till, by the utmost efforts of this nature, or some external assistance, they escape out of that dreadful torpid state. As soon as they shake off that vast oppression, and are able to move the body, they are affected by strong palpitation, great anxiety, languor, and uneasiness; which symptoms gradually abate, and are succeeded by the pleasing reflection of having escaped such imminent danger. (J. Bond, *An Essay on the Incubus or Nightmare*)

All writers on the subject agree on three characteristics of the nightmare dream:

1. A very terrible and indescribable fear, called in medical writings *Angst* (used by Freud in 1895 to include a neurosis linked to the unconscious repression of sexual desires and activities), often accompanied by voluptuous feelings.

2. A feeling of a heavy weight on the chest which interferes with breathing.

3. A feeling of complete helplessness in the face of these terrors.

This dream is generally accompanied by such physical manifestations as described above by Bond, as well as a rise in blood pressure. On the other hand, the more common ordinary terror dream lacks features 2 and 3, and is characterized by an emotion so intense that waking results; the completion of the dream is blocked by waking, and recall of the dream is difficult. The nightmare dream of today invariably follows the typical pattern which old scholars attributed to the demon mare.

Since the dread, fundamental to the nightmare, is based on repression of sexual desires, the nightmare will become the more terrifying according to the degree of repression. Ernest Jones, *On the Nightmare*, explained the underpinning of the dream from a Freudian standpoint:

> The latent content of a nightmare consists of a representation of a normal act of sexual intercourse, particularly in the form characteristic for women; the pressure on the breast, the self-surrender portrayed by the feeling of paralysis, and the genital secretion directly indicate its sexual nature, and the other symptoms, the palpitation, sweating, sense of suffocation, etc., are merely exaggerations of manifestations commonly experienced in some degree during coitus when fear is present.

Jones's comments are not too different from those of Gervais of Tilbury (about 1218), who identified nocturnal fancies arising from timidity and melancholy as *lamiae*, "which disturb the minds of sleepers and oppress with weight." Gervais continued: "Others assert that they have seen such imaginations in dream so vividly that they seemed to be awake. But I am moved against this because I know women, my neighbors, who have told me they had seen with shame at night the naked organs of males and females."

The same kind of sexual experience was described by a nun of Louviers, Sister Marie-du-St.-Sacrament, after she had been molested by Father Picard:

Once Father Picard passed by me and put his hand on my stomach, and immediately I was beset with the most disturbing fantasies. After I had gone to bed, about nine o'clock in the evening, three times I saw huge fairy sparkles fall from the ceiling on the bedcover. I was very frightened. Another day, a tremendous weight rested on my shoulders so that I thought I was going to choke. I dragged myself as best I could to the cell of the Mother Superior, and I felt this weight fall to the ground with a loud noise. In the same instant I myself was thrown down and injured, with blood gushing from my nose and mouth.

Desire for intercourse by most men and women does not normally result in nightmares, although it would probably encourage erotic dreams. However, in persons with a predisposition to emotional instability, severe repression of such erotic desires leads to dreams where humans are replaced by superhuman figures or even by unpleasant animals typifying strength and energy.

A "stupendious account" of this kind of nightmare was described by Richard Bovet, in his *Pandaemonium* (1684):

We saw the poor young man lying speechless on the bed, his eyes were staring very wide, and fixed on one side of the room, his hands were clutched, his hair erected, and his whole body in so violent a sweat, as if he had been in the *bagnio*. . . . At length . . . he gave us this surprising account. He told us that he lay about half an hour, endeavoring to compose himself to sleep, but could not, because of the pain in his head, that about that time there came into the room to him two in the appearance of very beautiful young women, whose presence enlightened the place . . . they endeavored to come into the bed to him, being one on the one side, the other on the other side thereof, which he resisted with all the power he could, striking at them several times with his fists, but could feel nothing but empty shadows; yet were they so strong, that they drew all the bedclothes off him, though he endeavored with all his force to hold them, that after that they had stripped him of his shirt; and he had contested so long with them,

The Nightmare: an old print by Simonet from the Douce Collection, Bodleian Library, Oxford.

that he concluded within himself he should die under their violencies, during all that time he had no power to speak, or call for aid.

A woman vowed to chastity might experience a nightmare by repressing a natural urge, and in fact the most vivid accounts of nightmares and incubi come from convents. Paracelsus in the early sixteenth century said that demons were produced from menstrual flux, and therefore convents were seminaries of nightmares. Perverse sexual wishes produce other kinds of repressions and consequently different hallucinations and projections [see Lycanthropy and Vampire].

The relation between longing and fear, and the resulting conflict in a person's mind are illustrated by Bond's anecdote of the nightmare of a young woman:

A young lady, of a tender, lax habit, about fifteen, before the menses appeared, was seized with a fit of this disease, and groaned so miserably that she awoke her father, who was sleeping in the next room. He arose, ran into her chamber, and found her lying on her back, and the blood gushing plentifully out of her mouth and nose. When he shook her, she recovered and told him that she thought some great heavy man came to her bedside, and, without further ceremony, stretched himself upon her. She had been heard moaning in sleep several nights before; but, the next day after she imagined herself oppressed by that man, she had a copious eruption of the menses, which, for that time, removed all her complaints.

In his *Anatomy of Melancholy* (1621), Burton suggested the symptoms of nightmare were often removed by marriage.

> So on his nightmare, through the evening fog,
> Flits the squat fiend o'er fen, lake, and bog;
> Seeks some love-wildered maid with sleep oppressed,
> Alights, and grinning sits upon her breast . . .
> Back o'er her pillow sinks her blushing head,
> Her snow-white limbs hang helpless from the bed;
> While with quick sighs and suffocative breath
> Her interrupted heart pulse swims in death.
> —Erasmus Darwin (1731-1802).

Modern analysts and historians alike agree with the testimony of earlier accounts on the acute impression of reality during the nightmare. In his *Treatise on the Incubus or Nightmare* (1816), J. Waller wrote: "Indeed, I know no way which a man has of convincing himself that the vision which has occurred during a paroxysm of nightmare is not real, unless he could have the evidence of other persons to the contrary who were present and awake at the same time." A psychiatrist, discussing the nightmare of suffocation, confirmed this testimony: "I find that the victims of claustrophobia have a very vivid dream life and may pack almost incredible horrors into their dreams"—Fodor, *Journal of Nervous and Mental Disease*, Vol. CI. These comments illuminate also the "confessions" of some witches about the sabbat, after the general pattern had been established by the inquisitors.

As suggested above, the mare becomes fused with the incubus. The analogy between experiences in the temptations of St. Bernard or St. Margaret of Cortona and the delirium of the insane in the Salpêtrière was observed as early as 1834:

> These hallucinations manifest such a correspondence, that the beings evoked by them differ only in incidentals. The descriptions given by the insane in our hospitals resemble those given earlier by saints and mystics . . . only the names are different. Thus, to understand the incubus, it is only necessary to listen to one of these sick people who complain they are visited during the night. The incubus still is just what it was in times past, and acts in just the same way. (Leuret, *Fragments psychologiques sur la folie*, 1834)

The nightmare was indirectly related to witchcraft by two assumptions. It could be brought on by demoniacal possession, perhaps at the request of some witch. The Franciscan Father Candidus Brognolus in his *Manuale Exorcistarum* (1651) gave a prayer that the devil "would not be able to molest me in phantasies, either in the imagination or in the flesh, especially in those members designed for procreation." This petition resembles the hymn, *"Procul recedant omnia"* (mentioned in the entry for Succubus). Alternatively a link was taken for granted, as by Bodin, in his *Démonomanie* (1580), who was told by Nicholas Nobet, a rich farmer of Valois, that he often experienced visits from the nightmare succubi or *coche-mares*, and always the next morning an old witch would come to him asking for alms.

Night Spell. A charm against harm by night, especially against the nightmare or mare. In Chaucer's *Miller's Tale*, the carpenter recites a white paternoster as a charm against the night *verye* [monster]:

> Jesu Christ and Saint Benedict,
> Bless this house from every wicked wight.

Another invocation was mentioned by Fletcher in one of his plays (1619):

St. George, St. George. . . .
He walks by day, he walks by night.

In his *Compendium Maleficarum* (1626),
Guazzo gave directions for securing protection during sleep

> by reciting holy psalms and prayer, such
> as *Qui habitat in adiutorio altissimi* or
> *In te Domine speravi,* or some such orison. Let them make the sign of the cross,
> reciting the *Salve regina mater misericordiae,* the paternoster, and the *Ave
> Maria,* &c., if they would be safe from
> such snares. Let them have by them a
> waxen Agnus Dei blessed by the pope, or
> some holy relics. For such devotions are
> the safest protection and rampart against
> all the wiles of the prince of darkness.
> [See further, Charms.]

North Berwick Witches. The trials of
the North Berwick witches in 1590-92
mushroomed out of some unexpected, seemingly miraculous, cures wrought by a servant woman, through confessions torn out
of one person after another, into accusations which eventually implicated some
seventy persons, including the Earl of
Bothwell, on charges of high treason. To
rely on reports of this Scottish trial for
proof of organized covens of witches and
sabbat orgies, as do several well-known
writers on witchcraft, is preposterous. The
interrogations of the accused were conducted in the presence of a superstitious
king, who aspired to be a counterpart of
the French demonologists; and, furthermore, the confessions were extracted by
violent tortures.

The genesis of the trials was the curiosity
of David Seaton, the deputy-bailiff of Tranent, a small town ten miles from Edinburgh, about suspicious nocturnal movements of his young servant, Gilly [Geillis]
Duncan. Gilly had rapidly acquired a reputation for curing "all such as were troubled
or grieved with any kind of sickness or infirmity." Her skill, it seemed to Seaton, was
unnatural and devilish; so, to find out her
connection with Satan, he tortured her by
jerking her head with a rope tied round it,
crushing her fingers in a vise, and examining her for the devil's mark, which he de-

The deeds of the North Berwick Witches from
the contemporary tract, *News from Scotland*
(1591), the unique copy in Lambeth Palace
Library. Dr. John Fian, as recorder of the
coven, sits at a desk in the center; at the
bottom right the witches make merry with
wine.

cided was on her throat. After this, she confessed to him "the wicked allurements and
enticements of the devil."

Only then did her employer turn her over
to the authorities, and soon after, she was
forced to name her accomplices, forthwith
"apprehended one after another." Among
the "innumerable" persons she fingered,
living near Edinburgh and Leith, prominent were the elderly and well-educated
Agnes Sampson and Dr. John Fian, the
schoolteacher at Saltpans, and two women,
Euphemia Maclean and Barbara Napier,
"reputed for as civil honest women as any
that dwelled within the city of Edinburgh."

Agnes Sampson, "of a rank and comprehension above the vulgar, grave and settled
in her answers," was examined at Holyrood
Castle by King James himself. "She stood
stiffly in the denial of all that was laid to
her charge." So Agnes had "all her hair
shaven off, in each part of her body," was
roughly searched, and a devil's mark discovered in the pudenda. She was fastened to
the wall of her cell by a witch's bridle, an
iron instrument with four sharp prongs
forced into the mouth, so that two prongs
pressed against the tongue, and the two
others against the cheeks. She was kept without sleep. She too was "thrawed" with a

rope about her head, "a pain most grievous." Only after these ordeals did Agnes
Sampson confess to the fifty-three indictments against her, mostly relating to curing
disease by charms. She started with admitting simple charms, a white paternoster
("Open, heaven's gates"), and the black
paternoster:

> Four nooks in this house, for holy angels,
> A post in the midst, that's Christ Jesus,
> Lucas, Marcus, Matthew, Joannes,
> God be into this house and all that be-
> longs us.

And in this trial, her simple, devout bedtime
prayer was dubbed a devilish incantation:

> Matthew, Mark, Luke, and John,
> The bed be blessed that I lie on.

Then came the anticipated stories of magic
powders, a familiar in the form of a dog
called Elva, who lived in a well. Finally,
worn out by torture and questioning, Agnes
Sampson related a gathering of some ninety
women (*News from Scotland* says 200) and
six men on Allhallows Eve. Making merry
with flagons of wine, they sailed in "riddles
or sieves" to North Berwick. Here they
landed and danced a reel, with Gilly Duncan playing a Jew's harp, the men turning
"nine times widdershins [counter-clock-
wise] about, and the women six times." The
church was illuminated with black candles,
and the devil, in the habit of a man, ordered
"that they should kiss his buttocks, in sign
of duty to him, which being put over the
pulpit bare, every one did as he enjoined
them." Then they discussed ways of harming the King, and raising the storm that
should destroy his ship sailing to Denmark.

The credulous monarch was so fascinated
by this story that he had Gilly Duncan play
"Gyllatripes" on her Jew's harp before him,
"to his great pleasure and amazement."
King James, continuing the interrogation
of Agnes, decided the witches "were all extreme liars." When Agnes whispered to him
the words he had spoken to his fifteen-year-
old queen, Anne of Denmark, on their
bridal night at Oslo, Norway, James acknowledged "her words to be most true,
and therefore gave the more credit to the

King James I interrogates the accused women
at the North Berwick trial in 1590, an illustration from *News from Scotland* (1591).

rest which is before declared." It should be
remembered that the only witness of this
extrasensory perception was James himself;
and a fanatic could be easily persuaded,
particularly when a possible plot against
his life was introduced.

Her confessions became more incredible:
Agnes Sampson hung up a black toad for
three days and collected its venom in an
oyster shell; she tried to procure some intimate garment of the King's in order to bewitch it with the venom and make the King
"as if he had been lying upon sharp thorns
and ends of needles." She and other witches
made a waxen image of the King and
melted it. She received a shroud and two
joints from a corpse to make a magic powder. She assisted in raising the most celebrated storm in witchcraft by baptizing a
cat, attaching dead men's limbs to each of
its paws, and throwing it in the sea. The
web of fabrications poor Agnes Sampson
wove for her tormentors stopped the torture, but she was strangled and burned as a
witch.

Barbara Napier, a sister-in-law to the
Laird of Carschoggill, was accused of associating with Agnes Sampson and Richard Graham, allegedly a notorious sorcerer.
Specifically, she was indicted "for many
treasonable conspiracies undertaken by
witchcraft to have destroyed the King's person by a picture of wax . . . and for

drowning a boat between Leith and King-horne, wherein were sixty persons lost." After hearing these accusations, the jury of the assizes dismissed the case. This action so enraged King James that he reassembled the court, and ordered Barbara Napier to be strangled and burned at the stake, her property to be forfeit to him. Those jury-men who had voted for acquittal were then tried for "willful error on assize, acquitting a witch," provoking the Tolbooth Speech of King James. Mrs. Napier pleaded preg-nancy, and, after a lapse of time, "nobody insisting in the pursuit of her, she was set at liberty."

Dame Euphemia Maclean was another prominent woman accused, the daughter of Lord Cliftonhall and wife of Patrick Mos-crop, a man of wealth and influence. Six lawyers took the risk of defending her. She refused to confess anything (bewitchings and cures were mainly alleged). The jury deliberated all night, and the foreman had to be dismissed before a Guilty verdict was returned. Probably because she was a friend of the Earl of Bothwell and a Roman Catholic, King James saw that she was burned without the mercy of being first strangled—"burned in ashes alive to the death"—on July 25, 1591. The Earl of Bothwell, although kept in Edinburgh Castle, apparently escaped without harm. Later, Richard Graham, accused with Bar-bara Napier, was alleged to have helped Bothwell bewitch the King. After interroga-tion by James himself, Graham was burned in February, 1592, with many of the others accused, "for witchcraft and sorcery."

It seems likely that his experience with these North Berwick witch trials encour-aged King James to write his *Demonology*, first published in Edinburgh, 1597—"to resolve the doubting hearts of many" on the reality of witchcraft.

Norway, Witchcraft in. As in other Scandinavian countries, in Norway witch-craft was never the major social problem it was in lands beset by the Inquisition. Belief in sorcery and demons, however, was well established and drew on the seafaring tradi-tions of the country. Thus, witches were credited with ability to raise storms, upset boats, or drive away shoals of fish. These feats they accomplished by flying about as swans or geese, by throwing a knotted towel into the sea, by opening a bag of winds, or by whistling. The great sabbats at Christ-mas and midsummer, when sixty witches might assemble, took place in the northern countries: the Lyderhorn, a mountain near Bergen; Balvolden and Domen Mountain in East-Finnmark; Dovrefjeld; and Hekla in Iceland. Some of these places were far distant, but the Norwegian witches, trans-formed into cats, dogs, wolves, or ravens, traveled to them with ease, riding a broom, poker, black sheep, or dog. At the sabbat they drank beer and mead, danced, and played cards. Sometimes the devil played a tune for them on the *langspil* (a native stringed instrument played with a bow), or fife and drum, or horn [*lur*]. Witchcraft in Norway took on the air of myth or legend rather than religious heresy, and sorcery and *maleficia* rather than pact and sabbat became the bases of the few scattered witch trials.

Probably less than two-dozen witch trials took place in Norway. The earliest recorded was in 1592, when Oluf Gurdal was sen-tenced to death in Bergen. Two years later, also in Bergen, three other witches were condemned: Ditis Røncke was outlawed, and Johanne Jensdatter Flamske [the Flem-ish] and Anne Knutsdatter, wife of Kirsten Jyde [the Jute], were both burned. Nearly thirty years passed before another trial; in 1622 Synneve [no last name] strangled herself in prison while awaiting trial; her body was burned.

In 1650 Karen Thorsdatter confessed that at the age of twenty-six she had entered the service of a man who called himself Lucifer. He taught her how to steal milk by magic (e.g., by sticking a knife into the wall) and prevent harm to her own cows. She named several persons who had flown in the air with her: Christen Klod, their leader, rode a calf; Sidsel Mortensen (widow of the burgomaster), a poker; and she, a cat. Once they tried to kill two magis-trates, but failed because the men feared God very fervently and because one of them

Peoples of the North had the reputation of raising storms to destroy ships. From Olaus Magnus, *Historia de Gentibus Septentrionalibus* (1555).

wore a cross on a gold chain. A woman accused by Karen, Bodil Kvams, admitted riding a poker and trying to kill the magistrates. Another woman, denounced by Karen as a storm-raiser, was arrested at her wedding to a country judge; when she came before the court, her husband vigorously defended her, and successfully insisted that in so grave a charge the testimony of felons (as he called Karen and Bodil) should not be believed. Karen and Bodil were sentenced to be burned in Kristiansand.

In 1670, the year of the Nypen trial, another case occurred in Kristiansand. Councilman Niels Pedersen, in Copenhagen on official business, racked with pain and losing his speech, thought himself bewitched. After prolonged examination, Karen Snedkers confessed she had tried to injure him by making herself invisible and sprinkling fine salt on his clothes. With her companion, Dorthe Fudevik, she flew to Copenhagen and emptied a vial into his mouth as he lay sleeping. As a raven, she had buried hair, nails, bones, and feathers in the garden of the city clerk, Johan Worm, so that his chickens and animals might sicken. "The hairs she had plucked from her boy, Whitegoose, who is shaped like a horse's colt and on whom she rides when she wants to 'get somewhere in a hurry.'" Many witnesses testified against her. At a later hearing, Karen Snedkers confessed to flying as a raven with two other witches to raise a wind to destroy Councilman Pedersen's ship. One witch alighted on the rudder, and the others on

each railing, but they could not harm him, for he held a prayer book in his hand. Karen was burned, along with six other women whom she had accused as witches.

Probably the last witch trial in Norway resulting in execution occurred in 1680 in the Sondmore district—another trial took place in 1684 at Jaederen, but the fate of the accused is not known. A man named Ingebrigt confessed that, by walking three times backward round a graveyard, he had forsworn Christianity before the devil. Using the tails of two calves, he had played a drum at several sabbats at Dovrefjeld. Moreover, he had stolen the communion wafer so he could poison cattle. Ingebrigt accused others, but withdrew his accusations. He was sentenced to be burned.

One further related case might be included here: In 1687, a girl was accused by the ghost of her child of murder done fourteen years previously. Apparently she confessed when the ghost led her and the court to the scene of the crime. The girl was executed. In 1701 came a parallel, described in detail by the principal of the Bergen high school. He realized the ghost was a hoax, but many people believed in it and, furthermore, the accused confessed! The ghost of 1687 stayed on even after the execution of its mother, and talked with the Governor, who asked it to show how terrible it could sound. The ghost let out a tremendous roar, but the Governor was not impressed; the ghost replied that was the best it could do. It demanded aquavit and food, threatened the household, and then acted like a poltergeist by throwing clay and rocks down the chimney.

Several other instances of Norwegian poltergeists occurred in the eighteenth century. From August 1722 to May 1723 the home of Stefan Olsen in Andenaes was beset with strange noises and kitchen upsets, including throwing of plates and blowing out the fire. The contemporary account (by the parish parson, Rev. Jens Weding) failed to notice that the spirit replied, when questioned if it were of God or the Devil, "in the same words in a childish voice." The household included two young boys, who were frequently the major witnesses of the alleged troubles. At its last demonstration, the poltergeist beat loudly on all the walls, and lifted up the roof for a while; something like a skin bag flew out of the house into the fields, and ravens and crows gathered round for some hours following. After this, everything was quiet.

A similar "demon" plagued the household of a parson in Vaagen in Nordland in 1726, from February to Easter. Here again a fourteen-year-old boy was the center of the disturbances. He said that he heard Danish and Latin whispered in his ear, that water was poured on him during the night, and that sometimes he was dragged across the yard. The boy showed abnormal strength, and often people had to lie on top of him to hold him down. After eight weeks, the parson's threats brought the troubles to a stop.

One final poltergeist might be mentioned, from Hellesø, in Senjen, about 1730. While the fishermen were away on a protracted voyage, loud knockings were heard in a house, but nothing was to be found except the marks of clubs on the walls. While the inhabitants were in bed, the fire would be scattered on the floor, doors opened, and rocks thrown into the rooms. When they read the Bible and sang hymns, the knockings became louder. When and if the noises ceased, the parson of the parish, who vouched for the story, did not record.

Nottingham Boy: see Darrell, John.

Nypen, Ole and Lisbet. In places not reached by the Inquisition, witchcraft remained basically sorcery with a veneer of Christianity. All over western Europe witchcraft had been designated a subversive movement to overthrow the Christian God (Catholic and Protestant), but in the few outlying areas of Europe, pact and sabbat, torture and denunciation, were rarely encountered. The case of Ole and Lisbet Nypen in 1670 at Leinstrand, Trondheim, one of the dozen in Norway, shows the form a witch trial took in a country free from the pall of the witchcraft delusion. Here, acts of white magic, imagined *maleficia*, and the spites and jealousies of village life

brought about the Nypens' punishment. The couple were condemned to death on hearsay, prejudice, and guesses. Yet there was no organized heresy hunt, no rigged court, and no monetary profit from the execution. The Nypen trial grew out of folklore and magic; it was not a concomitant of religion, although the indictment charged *signeri* [witchcraft; literally, "making the sign of the cross"] and "contemptuous abuse of God's word." The trial was recorded in detail, but only a summary is given here.

In 1667, at a christening party, Erik Kveneld slandered Ole Nypen by calling him a witch. Erik blamed Ole for the rheumatism in his hands, and threatened to let "the red cock crow over him" if Ole did not cure him. In the brawl which followed, harsh words passed, and Ole Nypen felt Kveneld was setting the minister and the neighbors against him. Three years later, on April 30, 1670, Ole Nypen hailed Kveneld into court for slander. This first hearing brought a rebuttal by Kveneld, testimony of witnesses about Ole and Lisbet Nypen's alleged sorcery, and an admission from Lisbet of her use of charms and salt to cure sickness.

As an example of Ole's hexing, Kveneld complained he had been unable to raise his arms, and his breasts had grown big like a woman's; his wife's eyebrows hung over her eyes so that she could not see, and her ears hung down to her shoulders like a dog's ears. Three neighbors testified Ole or Lisbet had recited charms over afflicted limbs, while rubbing them with salt; more or less cured, they had paid Lisbet a small fee. Lisbet argued that since her charms used God's words they could not do much harm; the power was not in the salt, but in the "prayers" she read over it. One charm or prayer was to cure grippe:

Christ walked to the church with a book in his hand. Came the Virgin Mary herself walking. "Why are you so pale, my blessed son?" "I have caught a powerful grippe [? *greb*]." "I cure you of powerful grippe—cough grippe, intestinal grippe, back grippe, chest grippe— from flesh and bone, to beach and stone, in the name of the Father, Son, and Holy Ghost."

Four months passed, and in August Lisbet was charged with reputation for witchcraft and use of sacrilegious prayers. Four witnesses appeared against her, but merely added further examples of Lisbet's use of charmed salt, and of her relieving aches and pains by transferring them to animals or other humans. The parson of the parish swore he had heard the Nypens trafficked in witchcraft; and the court itself said all the common people "could not deny there had been rumors for many years about the Nypens, and that many had fed animals for them out of fear."

Lisbet was interrogated:

1. Had she willingly served Satan with her forbidden prayers? No, nor had she thought they could possibly be so misconstrued; she blamed her ignorance and lack of understanding of these matters. Directed by the court to curse Satan, she did.
2. By whose power had she helped or harmed men or beasts? If she had helped anyone, that was by God's power; but she had harmed no one.
3. Did she know others, in or out of the district, who knew these prayers, besides Ane Fergstad? She knew only one other; she had heard Ane read one for frostbite.
4. Had she intended the evil that hit a girl really for the girl or for the girl's mistress, Kari Oxstad? She insisted she was innocent of the whole matter.

A third hearing was held on August 27, 1670, during which the girl swore she had been crippled in mistake for Kari Oxstad (who Lisbet thought had slandered her daughters).

In his report to the district judge, the prefect, Hans Edvardsen, indicted both Ole and Lisbet on four counts:

1. Taking the Lord's name in vain.
2. Harming their neighbors, driving some mad, crippling others, disfiguring still others (e.g., the hanging ears and eyebrows), or blinding them, and then helping their victims when it happened to suit the Nypens.

3. Curing people by transferring the devil from them to their enemies or, having failed in this, to animals.
4. Their general evil reputation, testified to by the minister and the population of the district.

The prefect suggested to the judge that the couple had forfeited their lives and should be burned, after having been tortured into fuller confession. The couple were convicted on more or less the four counts, with special emphasis on their taking the name of God in vain and on their bad reputation. Their failure to confess was stressed (whether torture was used is not stated). After God's law and the King's statutes based on it had been consulted, Ole and Lisbet Nypen were sentenced to be burned; but Ole was first to be beheaded.

Obsession: see Possession.

Ointment, Flying. To achieve transvection or metamorphosis, witches rubbed their bodies with ointment. An early story by Nider, before 1435, told how a woman rubbed herself with ointment while seated in a large kneading trough; she immediately went to sleep and dreamed of flying, shaking the trough so much that she fell out and injured her head. On the other hand, nearly all the later demonologists believed in the physical actuality of transvection.

Probably basing their accounts partly on popular folklore of medicinal herbs, partly on the repelling ingredients of classical magic, and partly on their own imagination, the Continental demonologists described some of the ways to prepare these salves.

For example, Prierias, the papal champion against Luther, in 1521 said that the ointment used for flying through the air was made chiefly from the thick stew of boiled children, preferably unbaptized. Guazzo, in 1608, repeated this fantasy. Francis Bacon enlarged on this hint, and in *Sylva Sylvarum* satirically noted that "the fat of children digged out of their graves" could be mixed with fine meal and "the juices of smallage, wolfbane, and cinque-

DE
LA LYCANTHROPIE,
TRANSFORMATION, ET
EXTASE DES SORCIERS.

Où les aſtuces du Diable ſont miſes tellement en
euidence, qu'il eſt preſque impoſſible, voire
aux plus ignorants, de ſe laiſſer
doreſenauant ſeduire.

Auec la refutation des argumens contraires,
que Bodin allegue au 6. chap. du ſecond
liure de ſa Demonomanie, pour ſou-
ſtenir la realité de ceſte pretenduë
transformation d'hommes
en beſtes.

Le tout compoſé par I. DE NYNAVLD,
Docteur en Medecine.

A PARIS,
Chez IEAN MILLOT, Imprimeur & Libraire,
demeurant en l'Iſle du Palais, au coing de la
ruë de Harlay, vis à vis les Auguſtins.

M. DC. XV.
Auec Priuilege & Approbation.

Title page of Jean de Nynauld's celebrated book on metamorphosis, which includes recipes of magic ointments for flying through the air and for turning into animals. From Cornell University Library.

foil." He added, scientifically, that "the soporiferous medicines are likest" to drug the witches into delusions of flight. This hallucination was induced, "not by incantations . . . but by ointments and anointing themselves all over." Later Fellows of the Royal Society were not all so scientific as Bacon. Glanvill, for example, believed in transvection. Another scientist, Henry More, in 1653 explained how the magic ointment, in "filling the pores, keeps out the cold and keeps in the heat and spirits, that the frame and temper of the soul may continue in fit case to entertain the soul again at her return"—*Antidote Against Atheism*. On the other hand, Jean de Nynauld in 1615 said the ointment must be rubbed until the body was red [*à rougir*], so that the medication could penetrate the pores more deeply.

While the English theorists discussed ointments, the English witches tried in the courts apparently knew very little about these unguents. One of the very few trials at which ointments were introduced was that of the Salmesbury witches (Lancashire) in 1612. Jannet Bierley and Ellen Bierley were charged with bewitching a child to death. Fourteen-year-old Grace Sowerbutts testified that these women dug up a little corpse, and

> having it there did boil some thereof in a pot, and some did boil on the coals, of both which the said Jannet and Ellen did eat. . . . And afterwards the said Jannet and Ellen did seethe the bones of the said child in a pot, and with the fat that came out of the said bones, they said they would anoint themselves, that thereby they might sometimes change themselves into other shapes.

The only flaw in this sworn deposition was that the witness had been rehearsed by a Jesuit priest who sought revenge on the accused women as renegades from Roman Catholicism.

A French trial was reported from Cressy, near the Cité de Lausanne, in 1604. A child was seized by werewolves and brought to the devil, who sucked its blood from the big toes. Then witches cut up the body and boiled it; some they ate and some "they made into their unguents, with other ingredients." All this the witches confessed, so they were rightfully burned. Actually, this myth was one of the earliest in witchcraft, and almost two centuries previously, Nider, in similar phrases, had told how babies were stewed by *malefici*. The horror story was repeated time and time again in the works of the demonologists and in the confessions at witch trials. At Bamberg, for example, the witches exhumed the infant's body on Walpurgis night. Del Rio (*Disquisitionum Magicarum*) explained that by so using the fat of slain children, the witches in addition mocked the chrism (the mixture of oil and balm) used in baptism.

No doubt the most complete account of ointments was that by Jean de Nynauld in *De la Lycanthropie &c.* [*Lycanthropy*,

Witches anointing themselves with flying ointment, according to Hans Baldung Grün. The witch on the right is passing into a hypnotic state; behind her, a voluptuous young hussy is whisked off to her paramour by an older witch.

Metamorphosis, and Ecstasy of Witches] in 1615. De Nynauld, unlike More, denied "that the devil can separate the soul from the body of the sorceress" and keep the body alive for its return. He classified ointments under three heads:

1. For going to the sabbat in imagination. This ointment produced a fantastic dream world, remembered when the witch awakened. Like Weyer and Guazzo, De Nynauld gave the fat of a child as the main ingredient, to which were added juice of water parsnip [*ache*], aconite, cinquefoil, deadly nightshade, and soot. De Nynauld cited typical examples where women anointed with this ointment had been watched all night, yet on waking related minute details of a sabbat many miles away (just like Nider's woman in the kneading trough). A similar recipe was given by Weyer, the skeptical physician, in 1563, who pointed out the natural soporific properties of medicinal herbs, which often brought on "a great disorder in the mind." (*De Lamiis*)

2. For riding on a broomstick and flying through the air. This ointment produced

physical sensations of riding and consisted of simple narcotics such as belladonna. There were other ways: one could eat the brain of a cat or get drunk. De Nynauld shrewdly avoided exact details, "for fear of giving wicked persons an opportunity to do ill." The efficacy of such an ointment was reported to De Nynauld in 1603 by a Frankfort physician, who, on realizing his aunt was a witch, watched her preparations for night flight. He had similarly rubbed himself with his aunt's salve and had attended a sabbat; on his return, as punishment for his intrusion, the calf on which he was flying dropped him in the Rhine, from which he was rescued by a friendly miller. He informed against his aunt, but nobody would believe him because, said the physician, many influential people were themselves witches.

3. For metamorphosis into a beast (the witch firmly retained belief in her shapeshifting when awake). This salve comprised a whole roster of Macbeth-type objects: parts of toads, serpents, hedgehogs, wolves, and foxes, and human blood, all mixed up with herbs, roots, and other similar ingredients "which have the property of disturbing and deceiving the imagination." Such an ointment was spread all over the body "about two inches thick," according to the Sieur de Beauvoys de Chauvincourt, describing the capture of a werewolf— *"couvert de graisse de deux doigts d'espais par tout le corps."*

Some physicians believe that the drugs used in the witches' preparations are those recognized as producing delirium. Aconite and deadly nightshade (belladonna), however, are highly poisonous, and De Nynauld's water parsnip [*ache*] may refer to the water hemlock, similarly toxic. Guazzo included as "natural soporific drugs" belladonna, darnel, mandragora, castor, and poppy. In an Appendix to Margaret Murray's *Witch Cult in Western Europe* (1921), Professor H. S. Clark stated that aconite in small doses upsets the heartbeat, belladonna produces delirium, and hemlock paralysis and excitement; further, that rubbing such ointments into the skin would intensify any physiological properties. Recently, interest in drug-producing plants has been stimulated by the publication of R. Gordon Wasson's book on the magic mushrooms of Mexico. On the other hand, Otto Snell in 1891 reported his personal experiments with these drugs and observed no symptoms from *small* doses except headaches.

Ointment, Killing. As part of the *maleficia* of witches, it was commonly believed that witches poisoned people. In addition to deadly potions, they employed special killing ointments. The composition of such poisonous concoctions was given by Guazzo in his *Compendium Maleficarum:* leaves, stalks and roots of plants, animals and fishes, venomous reptiles, metals and stones. The ointment could be administered as a poison orally or by inhalation, or else rubbed into the body while the victim slept.

The fat of roasted dead babies also made a good *Pinguedo Pagini*, according to Grillandus in his *Tractatus de Sortilegiis* (1536), and diseases so produced were incurable and could cause death. Witches were assumed to rifle graves for bodies, especially those of children and executed criminals, to use as ingredients in magic potions, powders, and killing ointments.

Crazy Sister Marie de Sains, having heard about Father Gaufridi when visiting Aix-en-Provence, returned to her convent at Lille, her head filled with witchcraft. She told how Gaufridi had made a concoction to cause demoniacal possession, from "sacred hosts and consecrated wine, with powdered goat, human bones, skulls of children, hair, nails, flesh, and wizard's semen, with bits of goose, female rat, and brains." (Jean Lenormant de Chiremont, *Exorcismes de trois filles possedées*, 1623)

In England, at Chelmsford in 1616, one of the indictments against Susan Barker was that she

> feloniously did take up a skull out of a certain grave in the burying ground of the parish church of Upminster aforesaid, being part of the body of a certain deceased man lately buried there, with intent to use the said skull in certain evil and devilish arts, namely, witchcrafts,

"In order to cause men to perish with an evil death, witches are accustomed to exhume corpses, especially those which have been executed and hanged on the gallows. From these dead bodies, along with all the instruments of torture the hangman uses, they obtain materials for their magic, endowing them with a curious power by their incantations."—Guazzo (1626).

charms, and sorceries, with intent to bewitch and enchant a certain Mary Stevens.

Other formulas for deadly ointments were recorded by Weyer, the skeptic physician of the Duke of Cleves:

Hemlock, juice of aconite, poplar leaves, soot.

Water hemlock, sweet flag, cinquefoil, bat's blood, belladonna, oil.

Baby's fat, juice of water hemlock, aconite, cinquefoil, belladonna, soot.

The trials before the *Chambre ardente* revealed widespread use of poisons, coupled with black magic. The salves had an arsenic base, which in acid form was tasteless and indetectable in the corpse. In addi-

Witches attempting to kill a sleeping woman. From Guazzo, *Compendium Maleficarum* (1626).

A plague in Milan in 1630 was ascribed to sorcerers' smearing the city walls with poison. Those suspected were cruelly tortured and killed.

tion, the professional poisoners used red and yellow sulphur, vitriol, all mixed with horrific ingredients such as the blood of bats and toads, various toxic or aphrodisiac plants, semen, and menstrual blood.

Witches' killing ointments served to explain outbreaks of the plague. The Calvinists at Geneva in the middle of the sixteenth century could explain the spread of infection only by witchcraft; thus in 1545 a man confessed to smearing the foot of a hanged man with a magic ointment and rubbing the bolts of doors with it. In this way the disease spread. A conspiracy was detected. More severe punishments were ordered: condemned men were to have the flesh torn from their bodies by pincers, and condemned women their right hands cut off before burning. Especially were poor people with unsavory reputations to be tortured to find out if they spread the pestilence; those who would not confess were to be walled up and left to die. Although thirty-one persons were executed as witches within three months (1545), Calvin complained: "Notwithstanding, the conspirators do not cease to smear the locks of doors with their ointments. Behold the perils that beset us." (Trevor Davies, *Four Centuries of Witch Beliefs*, 1947)

Opponents of Witchcraft: see Demonologists.

Osborne, Ruth. In England, although the last execution of a witch occurred in 1682 and the last official conviction for witchcraft in 1712 [see Jane Wenham], yet as late as 1751, at Tring, Hertfordshire, an old couple were lynched by a mob which claimed they were witches.

Ruth Osborne and her husband were both very old and very poor, supporters of the unpopular Stuart rebellion of 1745, and moreover regarded as witches. When any trouble happened, the Osbornes were blamed. Especially were they blamed by a farmer named Butterfield, who, having refused to give Mother Osborne some buttermilk, found his cows dying. Butterfield then sold his farm and opened a tavern at Gubblecot, in the hope of diverting the spell he assumed Ruth Osborne had cast on him. But things got worse, and Butterfield himself was taken with fits. A white witch from Northampton told him he was indeed bewitched.

Without any apparent motive, word went round three market towns that suspected witches were to be put to the ordeal of fleeting or ducking in a stream at Longmarston. On April 22, 1751, a mob started looking for victims. Local officials had taken the Osbornes into the workhouse for their safety, but the mob found their location, "broke the workhouse windows, pulled down the pales, and demolished part of the house." The mob even searched the salt box, "supposing she might have concealed herself within less space than would contain a cat." When the crowd threatened to burn the building, the superintendent was forced to reveal their hiding place. The two Osbornes were stripped naked, bound crosswise hand to foot, and dragged two miles to the stream and thrown in. Mrs. Osborne, tied up in a sheet, did not sink; so the ringleader, a chimney sweep called Thomas Colley, poked and prodded her. At length, this old woman of over seventy years was "thrown quite naked on the bank, almost choked with mud, and expired in a few minutes, being kicked and beat with sticks after she was dead." Her husband was similarly abused and died some time later. Colley, a great hero to the mob, took up a collection for himself.

At the Hertford assizes, on July 30, a verdict of willful murder was returned against Colley; he was found Guilty and hanged in chains on Saturday, August 24, 1751.

Pact with the Devil. The pact with the Devil was the essence of witchcraft. The pact pinpointed sorcery as heresy, and thereby brought witchcraft under the jurisdiction of the Inquisition. But to every demonologist, Protestant as well as Catholic, the agreement to work with the Devil to deny and oppose the Christian God was the core of the crime. Thus Gifford gave the common opinion among Protestant Englishmen: "A witch by the word of God ought to die the death not because she killeth men—for that she cannot, unless it be those witches which kill by poison, which

"Do you swear to obey your masters or those in authority . . . to honor them, to sweep, to spin, to beat drums, to howl, to yell, to fly, to cook, to suck, to bake, to roast, and everything else whenever you are ordered? . . . I swear . . . Very well, you are a witch, my dear. Congratulations!" —Goya (1799).

either they receive from the devil, or he teacheth them to make—but because she dealeth with devils." The pact, not any acts of evil-doing, constituted the offense. And so-called white witches were just as damnable as doers of evil. William Perkins in 1608 amplified this connection:

> In like manner, though the witch were in many respects profitable, and did no hurt but procured much good, yet, because he hath renounced God his king and governor and hath bound himself by other laws to the service of the enemies of God and his church, death is his portion justly assigned him by God: he may not live.

Take out the pact, and the witchcraft heresy disappears. The American skeptic Robert Calef underlined this connection: "However irrational or unscriptural such assertions are, yet they seem a necessary part of the faith [of] such as maintain the belief of such a sort of witches."

The early Catholic demonologists and all Protestant authorities modeled the diabolic pact on the church ceremonies they knew; these accounts are relatively sober. To Henry More in 1653 it was "not at all unreasonable that such ceremonies should pass betwixt a spirit and a man, when the like palpable rites are used for the more firmly tying of man to God"—*Antidote Against Atheism*. But the later Catholic writers added whatever fantasies their own imaginations could invent.

The first extended description by a demonologist occurred in Johannes Nider's *Formicarius* (about 1435), the second book on witchcraft to be printed, which told about a young man burned as a witch:

> First, on a Sunday, before the holy water is consecrated, the future disciple, with his masters, must go into the church, and there in their presence must renounce Christ and his faith, baptism, and the Catholic Church. Then he must do homage to the *magisterulus*, that is, to the "little master" (for so, and not otherwise, they term the devil). Afterwards he drinks from the flask [of liquid from murdered infants]; this done, he forthwith takes himself to conceive and hold

within himself an image of our art and the chief rules of this sect.

Almost 200 years later comes an English Protestant description, parallel except for regional variations. Thomas Cooper, in *The Mystery of Witchcraft* (1617), copied an evangelical ritual. The witch

> must be covenanted solemnly in the house of God, there to make open testimony of her subjection unto him [the Devil], by renouncing all former covenants with the Lord. And here, usually these things are performed in their order. Satan blasphemously occupying the place whence the holy oracles are delivered, doth thence:
>
> First: require of his proselyte an acknowledgment of her covenant, causing her usually in her own person to repeat the form thereof, as "I, N., do here acknowledge that upon such conditions I have given myself unto Satan to be disposed of him at his pleasure."
>
> Secondly: when this acknowledgment is made, in testimonial of all this subjection, Satan offers his back-parts to be kissed of his vassal. . . .
>
> Fifthly: for their confirmation, he yet enjoins them another ceremony, namely, to compass about the font divers times, there solemnly to renounce the Trinity, especially their salvation by Jesus Christ,

Solemn Public Pact

"The witches abjure their baptism, the Christian faith, withdraw their obedience to God, and repudiate the protection of the Blessed Virgin, whom in derision they call 'La Rousse.' Finally, they deny the sacraments of Holy Church and trample under foot the Cross of Christ and the statues of the Virgin and other saints."—Guazzo (1626).

and in token thereof to disclaim their baptism.

The German Peter Binsfeld, a witch-hunting bishop, whose influential *Tractatus* went through eight editions from 1589 to 1623, likewise made witchcraft revolve round the pact: witches renounce God and their baptism, make a covenant with the Devil to worship and perpetually serve him. His views were one with those of the violently anti-papist Englishman William Perkins, who, about the same period (1608), wrote: "The ground of all the practices of witchcraft is a league or covenant made between the witch and the Devil, wherein they do mutually bind themselves to each other."

This uniform conception of the pact had been slowly developed by the Church Fathers out of the symbolic language of Isaiah xxviii. 15: "We have entered into a league with death; we have made a covenant with hell." Both Origen (A.D. 185-254) and Augustine (A.D. 354-430) link augury, ligature, and charms to a *pacta cum daemonibus*. Augustine's formulation passed into Canon Law, and thus, as Henry C. Lea noted, "remained a permanent part of the Church's jurisprudence." "Therefore, all superstitions of this kind, either trivial or noxious," Augustine declared, "arising out of the damnable consorting of men and demons, as if formed by a faithless pact of treacherous friendship, are to be intrinsically repudiated"—*De Doctrina Christiana*. Also concentrating on divination, Thomas Aquinas stressed the pact: "Any divinations and semi-magic measurements count as superstitions in so far as they arise from any operations of demons, and therefore come under some pact or other entered into with them." (*Summa Theologica*)

Most of the early legends of pacts with the Devil for help in this world at the expense of the next, which became the stock examples of the later demonologists, passed into the Western tradition about the ninth century from Byzantine sources. In this diffusion, the Crusades helped; legends of transvection also appeared. Hincmar of Rheims (died 882) was the first to tell a

Solemn Public Pact

"The witch is rebaptized in the name of the Devil, and, having renounced his Christian name, takes another."—Guazzo (1626).

story, in the *Life of St. Basil*, of a senator's valet who fell in love with his master's daughter. By signing away his soul, the valet won her. He was saved only by the assistance of the saint, who forced the Devil to give up the contract. The legend frequently appeared in later centuries. By the thirteenth century, an earlier story of an agreement between Theophilus of Adana and the Devil had developed into the writing of the document in human blood. Other early writers whose stories of pacts were borrowed by the witchcraft writers were the Benedictine Thomas of Cantimpré, Walter Mapes, Caesarius of Heisterbach, and Vincent of Beauvais.

By the end of the fourteenth century (1398), the University of Paris had ap-

Solemn Public Pact

"The Devil confirms the witch's decision by scratching the witch on the forehead to erase the baptismal chrism."—Guazzo (1626).

proved the theory that witchcraft involved the pact with the Devil. Everything was in readiness for the Inquisition to spread the heresy of sorcery and start the delusion which crippled Europe for over two centuries.

Theologians distinguished two kinds of pact: the implicit, tacit, or Private Pact (*Professio Tacita*), and the professed or Solemn Public Pact (*Professio Expressa*). The influential witch judge Paulus Grillandus was one of the first (1525) to develop this classification, using as evidence his own prepared statements, which he tortured his victims into confirming. In a tacit pact the witch gave allegiance to the Devil indirectly through some other witch; ultimately, it was expected that the witch would make a public acknowledgment. The Public Pact (*Professio Expressa*) could be administered with all due rites at a sabbat (*solemnis sive publica*) or made without an audience by signing a written agreement (*privata*). "That which is called solemn or public," wrote the skeptic Reginald Scot, "is where witches come together at certain assemblies, at the times prefixed, and do not only see the devil in visible form, but confer and talk familiarly with him." By the time of Binsfeld (1585), the pact had become so formalized by lawyers that it resembled "a contract between two merchants or landowners."

Protestant demonologists, as indicated

Solemn Public Pact

"The witches give the Devil some part of their clothing, in token that the Devil separates them from spiritual, corporal, natural, and terrestrial things."—Guazzo (1626).

previously, had no compunction about taking over Roman Catholic witch theories, but, not willing to rely on the tradition of the Church, skirted the omission from the Bible of any mention of this all-essential pact. William Perkins brushed this difficulty aside thus:

> The express and manifest compact is so termed, because it is made by solemn words on both parties. . . . And it is not so expressly set down in Scriptures, as in the writings of learned men, which have recorded the confessions of witches. . . . For the ratifying hereof, he gives to the devil for the present, either his own handwriting, or some part of his blood, as a pledge and earnest penny to bind the bargain.

The pact with the Devil, written in the blood of the witch, is the most spectacular aspect of the theory, and the Faust legend, in all its variations, has perpetuated it. It certainly encouraged lurid authentication: one young man who sold his body and soul for twelve years of pleasure came to sign the contract. "The devil squeezed his left hand as he put it out, with such force that he filled his hand with blood pressed from the ends of three fingers." (Guazzo, 1608) Again, as in nearly all theories of the witchcraft delusion, there is little to distinguish Catholic and Protestant. The very early tract *Errores Gazariorum*, written by an inquisitor in French Savoy about 1450, told of the confession of one Jean de Stipulis, burned at the stake, that he gave blood from his left hand to the devil to write the pact. Nearly two and a half centuries later, Cotton Mather was still accepting the fable, although toning it down to accord with Protestant sobriety. In his account of the possession of Margaret Rule, Mather related how a Christian Indian was tempted by the devil to sign the Book of Death— "with pen and ink."

Cotton's father, Increase Mather, President of Harvard University, firmly believed in a tangible document. In his *Illustrious Providences* (1684), the following story was included to strengthen the readers' belief in God. In 1658, at Caen (France), a young student who had squan-

Solemn Public Pact

"The witches swear allegiance to the Devil within a circle marked out on the ground, possibly to indicate that the Devil wants them to believe he is lord of heaven and earth, or possibly because the circle is the symbol of divinity and the earth the footstool of the Lord."
—Guazzo (1626).

dered away his allowance was "in his discontent walking solitary." A stranger, on learning the cause of his distress, gave him money. "That being quickly consumed upon his lusts, as soon as his money was gone, his discontent returned." The devil—for such was the stranger—returned and gave him further money on condition the student "sign the contract with his blood." Later, the student repented of his action and begged some Protestant ministers to recover the contract. The ending may be given in Increase Mather's own words.

> Hereupon, the ministers resolved to keep a day of fasting and prayer in that very place of the field where the distressed creature had made the woeful bargain, setting him in the midst of them. Thus they did, and being with special actions of faith much enlarged to pray earnestly to the Lord to make known his power over Satan, in constraining him to give up that contract, after some hours' continuance in prayer, a cloud was seen to spread itself over them, and out of it the very contract signed with the poor creature's blood was dropped down amongst them; which being taken up and viewed, the party concerned took it and tore it in pieces.

The actual signing of a document, however, was but one part of the pact (not even

always included in the public profession). In what was probably the most elaborate description, Guazzo, in his *Compendium Maleficarum* (1608), classified the parts of the ceremony, modeled of course on the Catholic liturgy. The 1626 edition added illustrations of seven of these steps [reproduced here].

1. Denial of the Christian Faith. Guazzo gave a typical oath: "I deny the creator of heaven and earth; I deny my baptism; I deny the worship I formerly paid to God. I adhere to the Devil and believe only in thee." Trampling the cross, which accompanied this oath, had been from very early times an important part of the ritual (e.g., Jacquier).

2. Rebaptism by the Devil with a new name.

3. Symbolic removal of the baptismal chrism (the consecrated oil mingled with balm).

4. Denial of godparents and assigning of new sponsors.

5. Token surrender to the Devil of a piece of clothing.

6. Swearing allegiance to the Devil while standing within a magic circle on the ground. Limborch, in his *History of the Inquisition* (1692), gave a slightly different procedure: "As a token of all this [allegiance], they put their left hand behind their back and touch the Devil's hand, and offer him somewhat as a mark of their subjection."

Solemn Public Pact

"The witches request the Devil that their names be struck out of the book of life and inscribed in the book of death."—Guazzo (1626).

Solemn Public Pact

"The witches promise sacrifices of little children, killing one by sorcery every month or sucking its blood every fortnight."—Guazzo (1626).

7. Request to the Devil for their name to be written in the Book of Death.

8. Promise to sacrifice children to the Devil, a step which led to the stories of witches murdering children. The early *Errores Gazariorum* specified children under three years of age.

9. Promise to pay annual tribute to the assigned demon. Only black-colored gifts were valid.

10. Marking with the Devil's mark in various parts of the body, including the anus in men, and the breasts and genitals in women, so that the area marked became insensitive. The mark might vary in shape—a rabbit's foot, a toad, or a spider. Only those—and in this Guazzo disagreed with most other authorities—were thus marked whom the Devil suspected as unreliable.

11. Vows of service to the Devil: never to adore the sacrament; to smash holy relics; never to use holy water or candles; and to keep silence on their traffic with Satan.

Sinistrari, the last of the classic demonologists, followed Guazzo's list. However, he omitted steps 3, 4, 8, and 9, and substituted three others: throwing away sacred medals, swearing allegiance on "a foul black book," and promising to proselytize others.

As an illustration of the pact, Guazzo told of a twelve-year-old girl, Dominique Falvet, who, while picking rushes with her mother, was accosted by a strange man. "The girl

was made to swear an oath to this man, and he marked her on the brow with his nail as a sign of her new allegiance, and then he lay with her in the sight of her mother. The mother in her turn offered herself to be defiled by him in the daughter's presence."

Another example Guazzo took from Raymond's *Antichrist* (1597). A young girl confessed before the inquisitors of Aquitaine in 1594 that her Italian lover took her to a sabbat on the eve of St. John the Baptist's Day (June 24). Having made a magic circle, the Italian invoked a large black goat, two women, and a man vested like a priest. When the Italian told the devil-goat the girl desired to become his subject—

the goat ordered her to make the sign of the cross with her left hand, and all present to venerate him. At which all kissed him under the tail. Those present lit the candles they were holding from a black candle burning between the goat's horns and dropped money in an offertory bowl.

At a second visit, the girl offered the goat a lock of her hair.

By the terms of the pact, "the witch as a slave," wrote Sir Robert Filmer in 1653, "binds herself by vow to believe in the Devil, and to give him either body or soul, or both." In return, "the Devil promiseth

Solemn Public Pact

"The witches promise never to adore the Blessed Sacrament, always to abuse the Virgin and the saints, spit on and destroy holy relics as much as possible, not to use holy water or holy candles, never to make full confession of all their sins, and finally to maintain the strictest silence about their traffic with the Devil."—Guazzo (1626).

to be ready at his vassal's command, to appear in the likeness of any creature, to consult and to aid him for the procuring of pleasure, honor, wealth, or preferment; to go for him, to carry him any whither, and to do any command." An example of the Devil's help was given by Jane Weir, sister of Major Weir, at her trial in 1670; she had a familiar spirit which did her spinning "in a shorter time than three or four women could have done the same."

Filmer toyed with the question of who got the best of the bargain: the Devil was not bound to keep his promise, and the witch could make a deathbed repentance. The Devil was handicapped, however, because he could work his evil tricks only with God's permission; if the witch requested the Devil to do something which God forbade, the "Devil may lose his credit and give occasion of repentance"!

In view of the importance of the pact, it is remarkable that there have survived so few documents claiming to be the actual contract written by the Devil. Any demonologist, of course, would explain that the Devil, to protect his disciples, always destroyed such incriminating evidence. However, at the celebrated trial of Father Urbain Grandier [see Loudun Nuns] such a document was introduced as evidence! It is in two parts: one, the oath of allegiance subscribed by Father Grandier, and the second, the acceptance of the priest's allegiance by a panel of devils. This latter is written backward in abbreviated Latin. A facsimile, a word for word Latin transcription, and the English translations are given here.

A Pact with the Devil

A Pact between the Devil and a nobleman in Pignerole in 1676. This highflown, Faust-like document was apparently written by a lawyer and introduced into the trial "as a description of this loathsome sin." Thanks to this evidence, the knight was convicted and imprisoned.

1. Lucifer, you are bound to deliver to me immediately 100,000 pounds of money in gold!
2. You will deliver to me the first Tuesday of every month 1,000 pounds.
3. You will bring me this gold in current money, of such kind that not only I, but also all those to whom I may wish to give some, may use it.
4. The foresaid gold must not be false, must not disappear in one's hand, or turn to stone or coals. It should be metal stamped by the hands of men, legal and valid in all lands.
5. If I need a considerable sum of money, no matter when or for what purpose, you are duty bound to deliver to me secret or buried treasure. Nor need I fetch it myself from wherever it may be hidden or buried, but you must deliver it into my hands, without any trouble to me, to wherever I happen to be at the time, to

dispose of according to my own wishes and pleasure.
6. You are bound to cause no injury to my body and limbs, and do nothing to weaken my health, but preserve me from human illnesses and injury for fifty years.
7. If, contrary to our expectations, I should happen to become ill, you are bound to procure for me proved remedies to help me regain my previous good health as soon as possible.
8. Our agreement is to begin on this date . . . in the year 1676, and to end on the same day in 1727. You are not to tamper with this period or encroach on my rights, or make a false reckoning (as you have often formerly been accustomed to do).
9. When my time has finally run out, you are to let me die like all other men, without any shame or disgrace, and be honorably buried.
10. You are bound to make me loved and accepted by the King and all the aristocrats, by high and low, men and women, so that I may always be assured of good will and affection, and that everybody

A Pact with the Devil

(Continued from previous page)

will grant without question what I may desire of them.

11. You are bound to transport me (and any other) without injury to the ends of the world, wherever I desire, no matter how far distant. You are to make me immediately so expert in the language of that place that I shall be able to speak it fluently. When I have satisfied my curiosity sufficiently, you will bring me back again, uninjured, to my home.

12. You are bound to protect me from all harm from bombs, firearms, and other weapons, so that nothing may strike me and injure my body or limbs.

13. You are bound to assist me in my dealings with the King and help me prevail over my special enemies.

14. You are bound to provide me with a magic ring so that whenever I put it on my finger I shall become invisible and invulnerable.

15. You are bound to give me true and thorough information, without distortion or ambiguity, about any question I ask of you.

16. You are bound to give me advance warning of any secret plot against me, and to give me ways and means to thwart those plots and to bring them to naught.

17. You are bound to teach me whatever languages I may desire to learn so that I can read, converse, and express opinions as perfectly as if I had known them thoroughly from childhood.

18. You are bound to endow me with good sense, understanding, and intelligence, so that I can discuss all problems logically and can give an informed opinion about them.

19. You are bound to protect and look after me in all courts of justice and council chambers of King, Bishop or Pope, before whom I might be summoned.

20. You are bound to protect me and my household from injury, whether domestic or foreign, from theft, and from harm.

21. I am to be permitted to lead my life in outward appearance like a good Christian, and to attend divine service without your interfering.

22. You are bound to teach me how to prepare medical prescriptions and the correct use and administering of them in dosage and weight.

23. If on any occasion, skirmish or fight, I should be attacked and set upon, you are to take up the challenge for me and produce help and assistance against all enemies.

24. You are bound to prevent anyone, no matter whom, from knowing about our accord and compact.

25. As often as I desire your presence, you are to appear to me in a loving and agreeable form, never in a frightening or horrible shape.

26. You are to see that each and every person shall do my bidding.

27. You are to promise me and bind yourself to keep unbroken these clauses, individually and collectively, and to comply assiduously with all of them. If you fail me in the slightest degree or display any negligence, then this pact and accord is null and void and of no force whatever.

28. In return for the foregoing promises, I swear and vow to deliver into your power several men and women. Furthermore, I renounce God, the most Holy Trinity; I wholly renounce the vows made for me at baptism. I step forward with you in a new alliance and submit myself to you both in body and soul, forever into eternity.

The pact between the devils and Urbain Grandier, introduced as evidence at his trial at Loudun in 1634. This pact is written in Latin, using looking-glass letters, from right to left (since the devils did most things in reverse, to show their opposition to Christianity). The signatures of Satanas, Beelzebub, Lucifer, Elimi, Leviathan, and Astaroth are subscribed.

Pact between the devils and Father Urbain Grandier

[Written from right to left, with words spelled backward, and using conventional Latin contractions.]

mlE ntvL bbzlB ntS etnvuj rfcL snetpp soN tcap tpecca smebah eidh qsila toratsA qta ciuh te .e sibon iuq rdnarG brU siredeof munigriv merolf lum meroma mecillop oudirt bacinrof .po te pulov noh mon suced ona ni lemes terffo sboN .re arac illi teirbe sbon te ealccE as baclucoc sdep bus gis gas xilef giv na teviv tcap q ;ture suispi tagor

Pact between the devils and Father Urbain Grandier

[The same text, written from left to right, retaining the conventional contractions.]

Nos pptens Lcfr juvnte Stn Blzbb Lvtn Elm atq Astarot alisq hdie habems accept pact foederis Urb Grandr qui nobis e. et huic pollicem amorem mul florem virginum decus mon hon volup et op. fornicab triduo ebriet illi cara er. Nobs offret semel in ano sag sig sub peds coculcab sa Ecclae et nobs rogat ipsius erut; q pact vivet an vig felix

.D delam son tni aetsop nev te moh art ni
mead ssoc tni fni ni tcaF
[Signatures of the demons:]
rfcL bubezleB sanataS
nahtaiveL imilE
htoratsA
mod pcnirp mead te baid gam sop giS
tprcs htrblB

in tra hom et ven postea int nos maled D.
Fact in inf int coss daem
[Signatures of the demons:]
Satanas Belzebub Lcfr
Elimi Leviathan
Astaroth
Sig pos mag diab et daem princp dom
Blbrth scrpt

[Translation into English:]
We, the all-powerful Lucifer, seconded by Satan, Beelzebub, Leviathan, Elimi, Astaroth, and others, have today accepted the pact of alliance with Urban Grandier, who is on our side. And we promise him the love of women, the flower of virgins, the chastity of nuns, worldly honors, pleasures, and riches. He will fornicate every three days; intoxication will be dear to him. He will offer to us once a year a tribute marked with his blood; he will trample under foot the sacraments of the church, and he will say his prayers to us. By virtue of this pact, he will live happily for twenty years on earth among men, and finally will come among us to curse God. Done in hell, in the council of the devils.

[Signatures of the demons:] Satan, Beelzebub, Lucifer, Elimi, Leviathan, Astaroth.

Notarized the signature and mark of the chief devil, and my lords the princes of hell. Countersigned, Baalberith, recorder.

[Expansion of contracted Latin into conventional writing:]
Nos praepotens Lucifer, juvante Satan, Belzebub, Leviathan, Elimi, atque Astaroth, aliisque, hodie habemus acceptum pactum foederis Urbani Granderi qui nobis est. Et huic pollicemur amorem mulierum, florem virginum, decus monacharum, honores, voluptates et opes. Fornicabitur triduo; ebrietas illi cara erit. Nobis offeret semel in anno sanguinis sigillum, sub pedibus conculcabit sacra ecclesiae et nobis rogationes ipsius erunt; quo pacto vivet annos viginti felix in terra hominum, et veniet postea inter nos maleficere Deo.

Factum in infernis, inter consilia daemonum.

[Signatures of the demons]

Sigilla posuere magister diabolus et daemones principes domini.
Baalberith scriptor.

Urbain Grandier's pact of allegiance, allegedly in his own hand, introduced as evidence against him at his trial at Loudun in 1634. It is written in Latin, regularly from left to right. Father Grandier was convicted and burned to death.

Urbain Grandier's pact with the devils

Domine magisterque Lucifer te deum et principem agnosco, et polliceor tibi servire et obedire quandiu potero vivere. Et renuncio alterum Deum et Jesum Christum et alios sanctos atque sanctas et Ecclesiam Apostolicam et Romanam et omnia ipsius scramenta et omnes orationes et rogationes quibus fideles possint intercedere pro me; et tibi polliceor quid faciam quotquot malum potero, et attrahere ad mala per omnes; et abrenuncio chrismam et baptismum, et omnia merita Jesu Christi et ipsius sanctorum; et si deero tuae servitui et adorationi; et si non oblationem mei ipsius fecero, ter quoque die, tibi do vitam meam sicut tuam.
Feci hoc anno et die.

Urb. Grandier. Extractum ex infernis.

My lord and master Lucifer, I acknowledge thee as my God and prince, and promise to serve and obey thee as long as I shall live. And I renounce the other God, as well as Jesus Christ, all the saints, the apostolic and Roman church, all the sacraments, and all the prayers and petitions by which the faithful might intercede for me. And I promise thee that I will do as much evil as I can, and that I will draw everyone else to evil. I renounce chrism, baptism, all the merits of Jesus Christ and his saints. And if I fail to serve and adore thee, and if I do not pay thee homage thrice every day, I give you my life as thine own. Made this year and day.

Urbain Grandier. Extracted from hell.

Orgies: see Sabbat.

Oufle, Monsieur: see Bordelon, Laurent.

Paisley Witches: see Bargarran Impostor.

Pamphlet Literature: see England, Witchcraft in.

Paris Witch Trial. Over 500 years later, it is possible to read the verbatim record, preserved in the manuscripts from the Grand Châtelet, the criminal court of Paris, of the first secular trial in Europe for witchcraft. It took place in Paris in 1390, after the Parlement of Paris had decided that witchcraft was a civil as well as an ecclesiastical offense. The early secular trials form a striking contrast to the early ecclesiastical trials (such as the inquisitorial trial in 1460 at Arras) and to the later trials in both types of court (e.g., Father Dominic Gordel; and the civil trial at Eichstätt). In the early secular trials at Paris, specific acts of *maleficia* were charged, great care was taken to ascertain the degree of guilt of the defendants, the proceedings were public, and nearly two-dozen judges and lawyers were engaged. The Parlement of Paris heard an appeal

and reopened the case. Nevertheless, torture was employed to force confessions. The Châtelet heard two cases of witchcraft in 1390; the one described here is the second, lasting almost a year.

October 29, 1390. The court produced a deposition by Jehan de Ruilly that Jehenne de Brigue, called La Cordière, having used sorcery to heal him, was a witch [*devine*]. Given only a week to live, Ruilly had learned from Jehenne he was bewitched by one Gilette, by whom he had two children. Jehenne tried to help him by making a waxen figure [*voult*] of Gilette, and by suckling two toads. Ruilly recovered and agreed he had been "unhexed" by the accused. In rebuttal, 34-year-old Jehenne denied any knowledge of witchcraft and admitted only to acquaintance with one Marion, of Rozay-en-Brie, who had taught her to cast charms, using "In the name of the Father, the Son, and Holy Ghost," and to avoid washing or saying her paternoster on Sundays. She had once intervened with Marion for a man who had lost his purse.

February 9, 1391. The trial was put off for over three months. On this date, Jehenne admitted she had learned the elements of witchcraft from her aunt. To summon the devil, named Haussibut, she had merely to say, "Come to me and tell me and instruct me about what I shall demand of you." Taking pity on Ruilly's sickness, she had learned from this devil about his bewitchment by Gilette. As payment for the devil's services, Jehenne gave Haussibut, not his customary promised tribute of an arm or a finger at death, but a handful of hemp seed and a handful of cinders from her hearth. She admitted being jailed at Meaux two years later for sorcery, but was freed on her promise to abstain in the future. On this evidence, the provost consulted the assessors and sentenced Jehenne to burning. Since she appeared to be pregnant, and midwives found her five months advanced, sentence was postponed.

Jehenne was not executed until eight months later; the calendar of events read as follows:

April 5, 1391. Other midwives decide Jehenne not pregnant, and that "bad humors had accumulated in her body, whereby she had become swollen."

June 13, 1391. Jehenne admits she had slept with a man eight days before her imprisonment, but she knew she was not pregnant.

June 16, 1391. Provost confirms his original sentence. Jehenne immediately appeals to the Parlement of Paris.

August 1, 1391. Parlement orders the provost to re-examine the trial reports with the help of two court lawyers.

August 2, 1391. The trial is reopened before three members of Parlement and nine other high officials. Jehenne gives further particulars about her relationship with Haussibut. Two years before, she had invoked him at a tavern at Villeneuve-Saint-Denis to discover hidden silver.

The court decides that Jehenne seems to be holding something back, and that therefore she should be "put to the question," that is, tortured into confession. Jehenne pleads she has nothing more to reveal. She is stripped stark naked, bound to the trestle (or ladder). At once she wishes to confess, so she is released and, as was customary, warmed before a fire. Her statement puts an entirely different complexion on the case. Jehenne had been approached by Macette,

the wife of Ruilly, to bewitch the husband so Macette could be free to pursue an affair with the curate at Guerart. Macette had ceased to love her husband because he beat her. Together the two women had prepared a philter from a recipe of Macette's to kill Ruilly, and also made a waxen image to the accompaniment of Christian prayers.

August 3, 1391. Seeing Jehenne persist in her accusations, the court arrests Macette, the wife of Ruilly.

August 4, 1391. Macette de Ruilly, confronted with Jehenne, at first denies all allegations. When placed on the rack, however, she agrees the charges are true. Thereupon, her case is joined with that of Jehenne.

August 5, 1391. The two accused reiterate their confessions, presumably without torture. However, two legal problems have to be resolved before sentence can be passed: (1) Was their offense subject to the civil code or should it be judged by the church courts? (2) If the civil jurisdiction were granted, what should be the punishment? All the lawyers consulted, save one, agreed in recognizing the jurisdiction of the civil court; the dissenting lawyer argued that no injury or death had resulted from the attempted bewitchment (thereby implying the offense one of wrong intention and therefore heretical). Only one lawyer held out for the punishment of pillory and six months' imprisonment on bread and water instead of burning. In consequence of these recommendations, the provost accepted the responsibility of the civil court and pronounced sentence of burning.

August 6, 1391. Walter the Seneschal, representing the Parlement of Paris, demands a review of the trial to re-examine the question of jurisdiction.

August 8, 1391. Parlement determines the case comes within the purview of a secular court.

August 11, 1391. Final appearance of the two prisoners in court; they repeat their confessions. The provost draws up the manner of their execution; they are to be led to the Châtelet aux Halles, mitered as sorcers, put in the pillory; then led to the Pig Market to be burned alive.

August 12, 1391. Before passing sentence, the provost consults three lawyers of the Parlement of Paris. Two favor the death sentence; one, in view that no murder was involved, a lengthy imprisonment. The lawyers decide to give further consideration to the question, "which is serious and weighty."

August 16, 1391. The provost consults five other superior lawyers, including the President of Appeals, and finds all favoring the execution of the witches.

August 17, 1391. A supplementary hearing is accorded an official advocate to question the husband, Ruilly, who states that he never saw his wife trying to poison him. Then Ruilly adds that his page recently found two toads in his courtyard and killed them. The advocate presents as evidence upholding the conviction several articles, such as a piece of a host, three leaves of periwinkle, a piece of charcoal, two shoots of a mustard plant, a splinter of wood, wax, and hair.

August 19, 1391. These articles are shown to the prisoners. Macette explains their magical use, but denies using them in any witchcraft. The death sentence is finally pronounced and carried out the same day.

Pendle Forest Witches: see Lancashire Witches.

Pendle Swindle. The first great witch hunt in the north of England ended with the mass execution of the nine Lancashire Witches in 1612. The second great scare in 1633 at Hoarstones (likewise in the Pendle Forest district of Lancashire) saw over thirty arrested and seventeen (on whom devil's marks were found) convicted of witchcraft. One girl, twenty-year-old Mary Spencer, was convicted because, on her way to the well for water, she often rolled her pail down the hill, running before it and in fun calling it to follow her.

The chief witness was a young lad named Edmund Robinson, who testified that when he had beaten two greyhounds for not coursing a hare, they turned into a woman and a boy. On his refusing a bribe to keep quiet, the woman had taken Edmund on the boy, now transformed into a white horse, to a sabbat gathering. Here he saw about sixty persons. They all went into a barn. What he saw there reads like the erotic night symbolism of a boy on the threshold of manhood. Edmund swore

> he saw six of [the witches] kneeling and pulling, all six of them, six several ropes, which were fastened or tied to the top of the barn. Presently after which pulling, there came into this informer's sight, flesh smoking, butter in lumps, and milk as it were flying from the said ropes. All which fell into basins' that were placed under the said ropes . . . And during all the time of their several pulling they made such ugly faces as scared this informer, so that he was glad to run out and steal homewards.

Edmund's deposition was endorsed by his father. Not knowing the names of all the people he saw at the sabbat, Edmund was authorized to go about the countryside, visit market places and churches, and pick out the witches by their appearance. For each witch he recognized, he received a fee. The vicar of Kildwick, Rev. John Webster, described how young Robinson came into his church during the sermon. Robinson

> was set upon a stall (he being but about ten or eleven years old) to look about him, which moved some little disturbance in the congregation for a while. And after prayers, I enquiring what the matter was, the people told me that it was the boy that discovered witches. Upon which, I went to the house where he was to stay all night, where I found him, and two very unlikely persons that did conduct him and manage the business. I desired to have some discourse with the boy in private, but that they utterly refused. Then in the presence of a great many people, I took the boy near me and said, "Good boy, tell me truly, and in earnest, did thou see and hear such strange things of the meeting of witches as is reported by many that thou dost relate? Or did not some person teach thee to say such things of thyself?" But the two men, not giving the boy leave to answer, did pluck him from me, and said he had been examined by two able justices of the peace, and they did never ask him such a question.

To whom I replied, "The persons accused had therefore the more wrong."

Ironically enough, one of those fingered by Robinson was Jannet Device, who, twenty-two years earlier, had been the key child witness in the first Lancashire witch trials.

Dubious about the propriety of the Guilty verdict, the local justices sent the cases forward to the King's Council for further consideration. First, the accused and accusers were interrogated by the Right Rev. John Bridgeman, the Bishop of Chester (whose diocese included Lancashire); the Bishop concluded that blackmail and vindictiveness lay behind most of the accusations. Four of the accused (including Mary Spencer) and Mr. Robinson and Edmund were then sent to London, where the King's physician, the skeptical Dr. Harvey, and King Charles I himself looked in vain for the critical devil's marks. When Edmund was questioned, he confessed, like his exemplars at Leicester, Burton, Nottingham [see John Darrell], and Bilson, that his stories about the witches were prompted by his father and were wholly fabricated "for envy, revenge, and hope of gain." At the time of the alleged sabbat, he had, in fact, been picking plums. The accusations exposed as frauds, all the convicted were happily acquitted. What became of Edmund Robinson is not known.

Perkins, William. William Perkins (1555-1602) was a prominent English demonologist and Puritan preacher, whose *Discourse of the Damned Art of Witchcraft* was published posthumously in 1608. His other numerous and uncompromising writings combatted Roman Catholicism and maintained the extreme evangelical position. Like several witch believers, such as Henry More and Henry Hallywell, he was a Fellow of Christ's College, Cambridge.

By English and Continental Protestants, according to the *Dictionary of National Biography*, "he continued to be studied throughout the seventeenth century as an authority but little inferior to Hooker or Calvin." By 1610, his *Discourse* had been translated into German. Consequently, Per-

kins surpassed King James as an authority against those who "receive it for a truth that witchcraft is nothing else but a mere illusion, and witches nothing but persons deluded by the Devil." This popularity may have been caused by the King's later defection as a witch hunter, as well as by Perkins' neglect of the European demonologists (except Remy) and almost exclusive appeal to the Bible. Thomas Fuller, in his *Holy State* (1642), selected him as best combining the qualities of "the faithful minister." Robert Filmer, in his *Advertisement to the Jurymen of England* (1653), still thought it necessary to refute Perkins' arguments of half a century earlier; and in 1693 Cotton Mather approvingly summarized the *Discourse* (in his *Wonders of the Invisible World*).

The seven chapters of the *Discourse* cover true and false miracles, the league between Satan and the witch, divination, the good witch ("the worser of the two"), and the discovery and punishment of witches. Perkins' editor, Thomas Pickering, asked "special notice of these particulars," which in fact summarize Perkins' views on witchcraft:

1. That they do grossly err who either in express terms deny that there be witches . . . avouching that there is no league between them and the Devil, or affirming they can do no such miraculous works as are ascribed to them.
2. That the witch truly convicted is to be punished with death, the highest degree of punishment, and that by the law of Moses, the equity whereof is perpetual.
3. That the miracles of the popish church at this day are indeed either no miracles, or false and deceitful works.

For other opinions of Perkins, see entry on Evidence in Witch Trials, England.

Perry, William: see Bilson Boy.

Perth Witch Trial. Verbatim reports from official court records are relatively inaccessible; the following report of a trial at Perth in 1623 is valuable for indicating some of the allegations which in Scotland would bring about arrest for witchcraft:

here, simple folk charms, generally of a beneficent nature, and washing and bathing were charged. The basic pact with the Devil was assumed. In other Scottish witch trials, however, the pact was spelled out, as in the indictment against the six women burned at Borrowstones, December 23, 1679, which referred to Leviticus xx and Deuteronomy xviii. These women were charged with entering "in paction with the Devil, the enemy of your salvation, and have renounced our blessed Lord and Saviour, and your baptism, and have given your selves, both souls and bodies, to the Devil."

The following is the verbatim report of the trial of Isobel Haldane, at the sessions of Perth, 1623.

May 15, 1623

Isobel Haldane, suspect of witchcraft, being convened before the Session of Perth, after prayers made to God to open her heart and loose her tongue to confess the truth:

Q. If she had any skill of curing men, women, or bairns that were diseased?
A. None.
Q. If she cured Andrew Duncan's bairn?
A. According to the direction of Janet Kaw, she went with Alexander Lokart down to the Turret-port, took water from thence, being down [there]; brought it to Andrew Duncan's house, and there, upon her knees, in the name of the Father, Son, and Holy Ghost, washed the bairn. After that, took the water, with the bairn's sark [dress], accompanied by Alexander Lokart, and threw both in the burn [river]; but in the going, she spilled some, which she regrets bitterly, because had any one stepped over the place, the disease would have been transferred from the sick child to him.
Q. If she had any conversation with the fairy folk?
A. Ten years since, lying in her bed, she was taken forth, whether by God or the Devil she knows not, [and] was carried to a hillside. The hill opened and she entered in there. She stayed three days, viz., from Thursday to Sunday at twelve o'-clock. She met a man with a gray beard, who brought her forth again.

Witness John Roch swears: About the same time, he being in James Christie the wright's shop, having the wright make a cradle for him, because his wife was near down lying [childbirth], the said Isobel Haldane came by, desired him not to be so hasty, for he needed it not; his wife should not be delivered of her child till that time five weeks. And then the bairn should never lie in the cradle, but be born, baptized, and never suck, but die and be taken away. And as the said Isobel spoke, so it came to pass in every point.
Q. How she knew it?
A. The man with the gray beard told her.

Witness John Roch swears: The said Isobel Haldane came to Margaret Buchanan, spouse to David Rind, being in health, at her ordinary work, and desired her to prepare for death, for before Fastings Eve, which was within few days, she should be taken away. And as she said, so it was: before that term, the woman died.
Q. How she knew the term of her life?
A. She had enquired at that same man with the gray beard, and he had told her.

May 16, 1623

Witness Patrick Ruthven, skinner in Perth, swears: He being bewitched by Margaret Hornscleugh, Isobel Haldane came to see him. She came in to the bed and stretched herself above him, her head to his head, her hands over him, and so forth, mumbling some words, he knew not what they were.

Confessed. Before the said Patrick was bewitched, she met him and forbade him to go until she had gone with him.

May 19, 1623

Witness Stephen Ray of Muirton, swears: Three years since, that Isobel Haldane having stolen some beer forth of the Hall of Balhoussie, he followed her and brought her back again. She clapped him on the shoulder, saying, "Go thy way! Thou shalt not win thyself a bannock [morsel] of bread for a year and a day." And as she threatened, so it came to pass. He pined away, heavily diseased.

Confesses taking away the beer and the disease of the man. She only said, "He that delivered me from the fairy folk shall take amends on thee." . . .

Confesses she went silent to the Holy Well of Ruthven, and returned silent, bringing water from thence, to wash John Gow's bairn. When she took the water from the well, she left a part of the child's dress at it, which she took with her for that effect; and when she came home, she washed the bairn therewith, in like manner she had done the like to John Powryis' bairn.

May 21, 1623

Confessed. She had given drinks to cure children, among the rest, that David Morris' wife came to her, and she sent forth her son to gather fochsterrie [star grass] leaves, whereof she directed the child's mother to make a drink.

Witness Mrs. David Morris swears: The said Isobel Haldane, unrequested, came to her house and saw the child. Said "it was a changeling taken away." Took in hand to cure it; and to that effect gave the child a drink, after the receipt whereof the bairn died.

> William Young, scribe to the Presbytery of Perth, at command of the same, with my hand.
> Jonathan Davidson, notary public and clerk to the Session of Perth, at their command and direction, with my hand.

Her trial was continued on two later dates, May 22 and May 26, and included similar confessions, for example:

Q. Where had she learned her skill?
A. When I was lying in child bed lair, I was drawn forth from my bed to a dub [stagnant pool] near my house door in Dunning, and was there puddled [confused] and troubled.
Q. By whom was this done?
A. By the fairy folks, who appeared some of them red, some of them gray, and riding upon horses. The principal of them that spake to me was a bonny white man, riding upon a gray horse. He desired me to speak of God, and do good to poor folks; and he showed me the means how I might do this, which was by washing,

bathing, speaking words, putting sick persons through hasps [skeins] of yarn, and the like.

The records are incomplete, but it would be safe to assume that Isobel Haldane was found guilty, strangled, and burned.

Pico della Mirandola, Gianfrancesco. *Strix* [*The Witch*] shows very clearly that by the beginning of the sixteenth century the theory of witchcraft was already fully developed; later demonologists merely embellished it. Although Pico della Mirandola (1469-1533) had studied at the University of Ferrara, Lea could write of him: "The credulity of so learned a man is scarce conceivable." He was the nephew and namesake of the famous humanist, the count of the tiny principality of Mirandola, near Modena. Pico hurdles the Canon Episcopi by saying modern witches are somewhat different from the followers of Diana men-

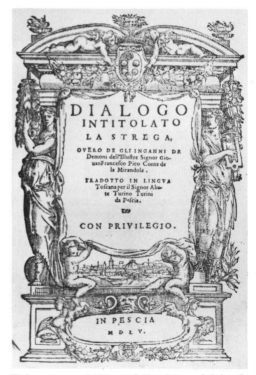

Title page of Pico della Mirandola's *La Strega*, the first work on witchcraft to be printed in Italian (Pescia, 1555). From Cornell University Library.

tioned there. He accepts a fantastic witches' sabbat: "This rite is not an empty tale, but in essence very old, and only changed, in respect to new elements, according to the wishes of the Devil."

Pico della Mirandola stressed intercourse between witches and devils; copulation with incubi is much more enjoyable than with humans. The explanation is given through the character of the inquisitor, Dicaste:

> The witches claim to derive so much pleasure that they assert there is no other like it on earth. And I think this may be for several reasons. First, because of the very great beauty and grace of countenance which those evil spirits assume; second, for the extraordinary largeness of their members [*la grandezza straordinaria de' membri*]. For with the former they attract the eye, and with the latter they cause delight in the most secret parts. Beyond that, the demons pretend to be greatly enamored of the witches, which to these wretched silly women is dearest above all things. The devils can even agitate the thing when it is inside, wherefore the women derive more pleasure than they do with men. I believe the same sort of explanation applies to those men who use demons as their lovers, inasmuch as that most villainous priest (of whom I spoke a while ago) said that he derived much greater pleasure from sleeping with a succubus demon who called herself Armellina than with any other woman he might ever have had. And lest you think he had to do with only few women, he had to do even with his own sister, and they say that he had a son by her. That poor man was so blinded by the love of Armellina that very often, walking in the piazza, she kept him company.

The *Strix* is especially important in the history of witchcraft because it was the first book on this subject to be printed in Italian. Originally published in Latin, it was translated in 1524 and again *in lingua toscana* in 1555. A German version appeared in 1612. The introduction to the 1524 edition by the Dominican Alberti bewailed the widespread opposition by ordinary folk to the persecutions in 1523 at Bologna; many had protested the burnings because they believed that the accused admitted only under torture going to the sabbat, and that later they revoked their confessions. Witchcraft was the Church's idea, not the people's.

Pittenweem Witches. None of those accused as witches at the small seaport town of Pittenweem, in the east of Scotland, was judicially murdered, but two died in horrible circumstances as a result of the accusations, and a third died after severe torture in virtual banishment. The cause of these troubles was a sixteen-year-old youth, Patrick Morton. His case paralleled that of Christine Shaw in 1697, the story of whose fits had been recounted and widely circulated. Since the minister had read these pamphlets at least twice to Patrick, the supposition is strong that the lad consciously imitated the young Bargarran impostor. Indeed, the minutes of the kirk session state, "His condition is much about the same with that of Bargarran's daughter in the west."

In 1704, while working for his father, a smith, young Morton was asked to forge some nails for Beatrix Laing, the wife of a former treasurer of Pittenweem. Patrick was too busy with another job to oblige her, so she left him, "threatening to be revenged, which did somewhat frighten him." The next day, he observed Beatrix throwing hot coals into water and knew his fate was being determined by witchcraft. He was soon seized with weakness in his limbs; he lost his appetite and became emaciated. By May, 1704, he manifested symptoms of epileptic fits: troubled breathing, swelling of the stomach, rigid spasms, swallowing of the tongue. He made wild accusations of haunting him against Beatrix Laing, Mrs. Nicholas Lawson, and others. Like the Salem children, he showed the marks on his arm where the witches had pinched him. On May 19, 1704, he informed the minister he would have no relief until Mrs. Laing was punished.

Patrick's hysteria was described in detail in a contemporary manuscript, *Narrative of the Trouble of Patrick Morton*. This manuscript records how Patrick wrote with his own hand an account of one of his halluci-nations:

He said he saw Satan standing in the bed, and said unto him, "My child, I will give you a silver suit and silver tressing about your hat, if you will confess that there is no Saviour; though two of my dear children [Beatrix Laing and Mrs. Nicho-las Lawson] suffer punishment, yet it shall be well with you hereafter."

After a petition to the Privy Council on June 13, 1704, the accused were imprisoned. In spite of her social position, Beatrix Laing was very grievously tortured. She was searched for the devil's mark, then kept without sleep for five days and nights. Her confession followed, implicating Janet Cornfoot (Corfeitt, Corphat, or Carset), Mrs. Nicholas Lawson, Isobel Adam, and others; but she immediately retracted it. In revenge, the magistrates put her in the stocks, transferred her to the "Thieves' Hole," and then kept her in "a dark dun-geon where she was allowed no manner of light or human converse" for five months. At length, the influence of two members of the Privy Council curbed the zeal of the local judges, and Beatrix Laing, with some other accused, was freed on the fine of £8 Scots. (About 1700 a pair of blankets cost £3 Scots or five shillings sterling.) But the anger of the local population was so great that she could not go home but had to wan-der abroad, dying "undesired" at St. An-drews.

The kind of confession which the judges finally forced is exemplified by Isobel Adam, who, after imprisonment, was also permitted to buy her freedom by the com-pletely illegal fine:

Confesses that about a fortnight after Martinmas [November 11], she came to Beatrix Laing's, and that she saw a little black man with a hat and black clothes, sitting at the board end, and Beatrix said: "Here is a gentleman that will fee [hire] you." . . . Upon which she engaged, and the devil kissed her, and told her that he knew she was discontent with her lot, and that in his service she should get riches as much as she could wish. And that upon New Year's Day there-

after, the devil appeared to her in Thomas Adam's house, and there she renounced her baptism vows; and like-wise acknowledges that she was in Mac-gregor's house with Beatrix Laing, [Mrs.] Nicholas Lawson, Janet Cornfoot, and Thomas Brown, upon a design to strangle the said Macgregor.

The second to lose his life was Thomas Brown. He was starved to death in the dungeon.

> "In places where the minister was in-flamed with a holy zeal against the Devil and his emissaries (such as Pittenweem), the parish became a perfect hotbed for the rearing of witches; and so plentiful a crop did it produce, that it appeared nothing else could thrive. But in places where the minister had some portion of humanity, and a little common sense, the Devil very rarely set foot on his terri-tories, and witchcraft was not to be found."
> —Thomas George Stevenson (1871).

The third person to die as a result of Patrick Morton's hallucination was Janet Cornfoot. She was tortured, on new accu-sations of bewitchings by Alexander Mac-gregor. Janet Cornfoot confessed under torture, which included a flogging by the minister of the parish, Patrick Cowper, but she recanted. Lest her defection encourage other accused persons to revoke their con-fessions, she was removed from the tol-booth [jail] and placed in the steeple. She escaped, but was returned to the minister (a notorious witch hunter), who refused to give her shelter. Thereupon, Janet sought refuge at the home of one of the accused witches.

On the night of January 30, 1705, a mob, enraged by her escape, seized her, tied her up, beat her, and dragged her to the shore. Here she was strung on a line from the shore to a ship, swung to and fro, and pelted with stones. Janet Cornfoot was re-leased, beaten again, and finally covered with a door piled with stones and crushed to death. "And to be sure it was so, they called a man with a horse and a sledge, and made him drive over her corpse backward and forward several times." Neither the magistrate nor the minister made any attempt to prevent the lynching, although earlier in the evening a bailiff had dispersed the rabble. The minister refused her a Christian burial, and the leaders of the mob were not prosecuted.

Patrick Morton was eventually exposed as an impostor, and shortly after, a Scottish gentleman said, "All men of sense are ashamed for giving any credit to such a person."

Poltergeist. *Poltergeist* is a German word signifying literally a spirit [*geist*] that makes a noise or uproar [*polter*]. Used in German by Luther, it was first adopted into English in 1848 (by Catherine Crowe), but became popular only after 1926, when a medium, Eleonore Zugun, received extensive press notice as the "Poltergeist Girl." Of the legion of demons once generally credited, whose tricks were ascribed to witchcraft, the poltergeist is the only demon left commanding even limited acceptance among the credulous.

The poltergeist lies outside the mainstream tradition of Christian witchcraft, but its manifestations have been known from the earliest centuries and have been absorbed into the *maleficia* of witches. Thus the Drummer of Tedworth was blamed for the aerial noises at the house of Mr. Mompesson and "tried for a witch." The accepted view was given by the gullible Nathaniel Crouch, in his compendium of superstition, *The Kingdom of Darkness* (1688): "And as there are witches so they are many times the causes of those strange disturbances which are in houses haunted by evil spirits." Only in the eighteenth and nineteenth centuries, when belief in witchcraft had become discredited, do independent accounts of poltergeists become numerous and separated from witches.

The classic demonologists of the sixteenth and seventeenth centuries recorded some poltergeist phenomena and attributed them to demons. As early as Alphonsus de Spina (1460) and Nider (1470), the mischievous pranks of the *duende de casa* were arranged in the demonic hierarchy. Girolamo Menghi

The mischievous pranks of the poltergeist, an engraving from the German translation (1693) of Nicholas Remy's *Demonolatreiae* (1595). Illustrations of poltergeist phenomena are rare.

recorded at Bologna in 1579 a naughty poltergeist who made noises and upsets and played tricks on a young servant girl. Peter Binsfeld (1589) justified a tenant's breaking a lease if his house was troubled with noisy demons. Guazzo, in his *Compendium Maleficarum* (1608), described strange happenings following the death of a young girl at Callas:

A servant girl was struck on the shoulder by a stone . . . a vessel, which stood on the table, was hurled at her. And over the greater part of the town, tiles and slates were seen to be hurled about with a great uproar to a distance of two miles (not that there are many tiles or slates in the suburbs of Callas, as nearly all the houses of that city are roofed with palm leaves) . . . in the garden, a brick was hurled and overturned a whole dinner table.

The Spanish writer, Turrecremata, whose romance was discovered in Don Quixote's library and burned by the curate, in his *Jardin de las Flores Curiosas* (1570), translated into French as the *Hexameron*, described a typical poltergeist haunting at Salamanca in a house occupied by "two young girls of no mean beauty." Aroused by the disturbances, the mayor and twenty men searched the house.

> And lo! Hardly had they reached the place before there was a great noise, and stones began to be hurled at them and swept them off their legs, but without harming them. So they were sent again to see where this shower of stones came from; and although they found no one in the place, the shower of stones kept falling. . . . One of [the men], feeling bolder, threw one particular stone into the house, saying, "If this came from you, O devil, throw the same stone back at me." And when this was at once done, there was no more room for doubt that the house was haunted by demons as the matron had said.

Some inevitable doubters thought the incidents had been fabricated by the girls to facilitate their assignations with their lovers.

Father Herbert Thurston, S.J., commented in 1954 that the Catholic Church "has never taken very much account of these spectral appearances—ghosts in fact —which are said at times to disturb the peace of some ordinary dwelling house." The poltergeist, furthermore, was found unresponsive to the Christian faith and resisted exorcism; indeed, there are very few authorized rituals for the casting out of demons from houses [see Exorcism]. Robert Boyle, a founder of the Royal Society and discoverer of "Boyle's Law" in physics, witnessed the experiences of François Perrault, the Huguenot minister of Mâcon, in 1612; he had Dr. Peter du Moulin publish the story in 1658 at Oxford. On one occasion, this French poltergeist mocked the Protestant minister and satirically suggested that the minister send for the Roman Catholic curé, "to whom he would confess himself, and that he should not fail to bring holy water along with him for that, said he, could send me packing presently."

From the various accounts of what are termed poltergeist phenomena emerge the following typical manifestations—not every

A late seventeenth-century German conception of a poltergeist demon.

one, of course, being found in each example:

1. Noises or knockings without apparent natural origin, on walls or ceilings, or footsteps on floors and staircases.

A typical description was given by Rev. Joseph Glanvill about the Drummer of Tedworth in 1662:

> Having one night played some little tricks at [the owner's] bed's feet, it went into another bed, where one of his daughters lay. There it passed from side to side, lifting her up as it passed. At that time there were three kinds of noises in the bed. They endeavored to thrust at it with a sword, but it still shifted and carefully avoided the thrust, still getting under the child when they offered at it. The night after, it came panting like a dog out of breath. Upon which, one took a bedstaff to knock, which was caught out of her hand, and thrown away; and company coming up, the room was presently filled with a bloomy noisome smell, and was very hot, though without fire, in a very sharp and severe winter. It continued in the bed panting and scratching an hour and a half, and then went into the next chamber, where it knocked a little, and seemed to rattle a chain.

2. Uncontrolled movement [telekinesis] of small objects (such as dishes or bric-a-

brac), which are sometimes broken and at other times come to rest slowly, in apparent defiance of gravity; also spontaneous movement of other small articles (such as bells); and hurling of small stones [lithobolia], both inside and outside a house. Under the heading of telekinesis should also be included the supposedly uncontrolled movement of heavier objects, such as tables, beds, heavy kitchenware; or the pulling off of bedclothes (an old prank, known in the thirteenth century to Guilielmus Alvernus, the Bishop of Paris). The seventeenth-century Demon of Spreyton (Devon) played with shoestrings:

> At another time one of his shoestrings was observed, without the assistance of any hand, to come of its own accord out of his shoe and fling itself to the other side of the room. The other was crawling after it, but a maid espying that, with her hand drew it out, and it was strangely clasped and curled about her hand like a living eel or serpent. (Bovet, *Pandaemonium,* 1684)

Throwing stones is another common manifestation of the poltergeist, and certainly the earliest recorded, for Livy reported "showers of stones" in the sixth century B.C., and in A.D. 530 St. Cyprian told how the physician to King Theodoric endured "diabolic infestation," particularly flight of stones within his house. Increase Mather attested to the Stone-Throwing Devil in New Hampshire.

3. Disappearance of small objects, and their subsequent recovery in unexpected hiding places.

Increase Mather told how at Newbury, Massachusetts, in 1679 William Morse with his young grandson, John Stiles, after innumerable curious happenings, was eating cheese, but "the pieces which he cut were wrested from them, but they were afterward found upon the table under an apron and a pair of breeches"—*Illustrious Providences,* 1684. On another day, an "inkhorn was taken away from him while he was writing, and when by all his seeking he could not find it, at last he saw it drop out of the air down by the fire." Like other possessed children, John Stiles had fits, in which "he barked like a dog and clucked like a hen . . . his tongue likewise hung out of his mouth." In this instance, as a result of poltergeist and possession, Goodwife Morse and a Caleb Powell were charged with witchcraft (both managed to escape hanging).

Sinistrari, one of the last of the demonologists, gave a classic story of these tricks. An incubus demon, furious that his advances had been repulsed, caused a table prepared for a dinner party to vanish, along with all the food in the kitchen. As the guests were going sadly away, the incubus restored a better table and even provided new and superior foods and wines. "All the guests were fully satisfied, so that no one could think of supper after such a magnificent dinner."

4. Occasional major disasters, such as arson.

In his *Demonolatreiae* (1595), Nicholas Remy told the following story:

> Not twenty years ago a certain wanton demon began to throw stones incessantly by day and night at the servants of an inhabitant of [Dolmar, Lorraine]; but after he had done this for a long time

The Persecuted Butler, by Cruikshank.

"But in spite of the exertions of my Lord Orrery, in spite of two bishops who were his guests at the time, in spite of the celebrated Mr. Geatrix, it was all they could do to prevent the butler from being carried off bodily from amongst them by the fairies, who considered him as their lawful prey. They raised him in the air above the heads of the mortals, who could only run beneath, to break his fall when they pleased to let him go."—Sir Walter Scott (1830).

without effect, they began to treat it as a joke and did not hesitate to hurl back taunts and insults at him. Therefore at the dead of night he set fire to the whole house in a moment, so that no amount of water was enough to prevent it from being immediately burned to the ground.

The early tendency would be to ascribe such troubles to witchcraft; then, when credulity had taken a different form, to the equally mystic poltergeist. In those disasters where a definite cause has been discovered, either spontaneous combustion is clearly responsible, or a very human, even if unconscious, pyromaniac is discovered— modern believers in the spirit world identify him, not as the originator, but as the accompaniment of such outbreaks by the poltergeist demon.

These foregoing four types of disturbances will be found in most examples of the poltergeist.

In most recorded cases, poltergeist phenomena are found associated with some one person, often with younger children, especially girls, such as Hetty Wesley in the Epworth Poltergeist. Accounts of many children during the manifestations describe symptoms of hysteria similar to those encountered in demoniacal possession. Where fraud has been positively proved, the agency responsible for what seemed supernatural or extra-normal acts turned out to be either a naughty and cunning child or a mentally sick adult. Sometimes reading the story of an earlier disturbance has provoked new phenomena. The Derrygonnelly poltergeist, notable because it was investigated by Professor Sir William Barrett in 1877, had its analogue in Epworth, for the five young children, Methodists, may have heard John Wesley's account of Jef. In the same way, public familiarity with the pamphlet about the Warboys Witches (1593) inspired many other young impostors to fake fits and accuse old women as witches.

People are not often physically injured by poltergeists, although some serious injuries have resulted from fires. Young people, the mediums through which the poltergeist disturbances are supposed to crystallize, are sometimes ill-treated. Petrus Thyraeus, S.J., in his *Loca Infesta* [*Haunted Places*] (1598), told of some nuns being molested by a fun-loving poltergeist which tickled them "nearly to death." The poltergeist's acts are not usually malicious or dangerous but mischievous, and are the sort of tricks with which a young child would try to annoy adults. In fact, the poltergeist responds to treatment fitting a lively pre-adolescent or even teen-ager. John Wesley said his mother warned their Epworth Poltergeist not to disturb her between five and six, when she was at evening prayers; and thereafter "it was never heard in her chamber from five till she came down stairs, nor at any other time when she was employed in devotion." The Bargarran Impostor was a schoolboy who convinced several clergymen of a poltergeist demon—his own mental age and with his own limitations.

That many investigators ascribe all acts of poltergeists either to fraud or self-deception by the witnesses should not prove surprising. In this, they have taken to heart the mechanistic explanation of one of the earliest books printed in English to include poltergeist phenomena. Ludwig Lavater, *Of Ghosts and Spirits Walking by Night, and of strange noises, cracks, and sundry forewarnings* (1572, translated from the Latin of 1570), warned strongly against an uncritical credulity:

Melancholic persons and mad men imagine many things which in very deed are not. . . . Many natural things are taken to be ghosts, as for example, when they hear the crying of rats, cats, weasels, martens, or any other beast, or when they hear a horse beat his feet on the planks in the stable at midnight, by and by they sweat for fear, supposing some bugs [specters] to walk in the dead of the night. . . . If a worm which fretteth wood, or that breedeth in trees, chance to gnaw a wall or wainscot, or other timber, they will judge they hear one softly knocking upon an anvil with a sledge [hammer].

Eight of the classic historical accounts of poltergeists linked to witchcraft have been selected for presentation as separate

TRACTATVS SVBTILIS ET
ELEGANS DE LAMIIS ET EXCEL-
LENTIA VTRIVSQVE IVRIS, CVM
*nonnullis conclusionibus ad materiam hæresis in practica vtili-
bus, spectabilis & egregii Iuris vtriusque doctoris •
domini Ioan.Francisci Ponzinibii Placentini.*

Title page of Gianfrancesco Ponzinibio's *Tractatus de Lamiis* (1520), from the 1563 edition at Venice. Ponzinibio was an outstanding opponent of the witch delusion and exerted much influence. Over a century and a half after his book was written, it was still being debated in 1672 by Sir George Mackenzie, the Lord Advocate of King Charles II. From Cornell University Library.

entries; not only do they make amusing reading, but they illustrate the common elements in poltergeist visitations:

The Glenluce Devil (1654)
The Drummer of Tedworth (1662)
The Stone-Throwing Devil (1682)
The Salmon Falls Assaults (1683)
The Bargarran Impostor (1697)
Magee Island Trial (1711)
The Epworth Poltergeist (1716)
The Cideville Case (1849)

Ponzinibio, Gianfrancesco. Fifteen years after Cassini's attack on the Inquisition for promoting the witchcraft delusion, came a still stronger condemnation in 1520. Ponzinibio, a prominent lawyer in northern Italy, is known only by his *Tractatus de Lamiis* [*Treatise on Witches*]. Although accepting sorcery, he opposed the witch trials because non-legal procedure was used to secure convictions. Only in witch trials was evidence accepted from excommunicates and accomplices, the last confession paramount, and prisoners not allowed to know the charges or evidence against them. Not only condemning the methods of the trials, Ponzinibio also condemned their basis: witchcraft was simply a delusion and witches did not fly to the sabbat or murder children.

Ponzinibio's major offense was as a lawyer to reprove the theologians for improper conduct. Soon he was answered by Bartolommeo Spina, the "Master of the Sacred Palace" of the pope: by his skepticism and his attack on the Inquisition, Ponzinibio was in fact aiding the witches, and ought himself to be prosecuted.

Ponzinibio's beliefs crop up again in Judge Dietrich Flade, who doubted the validity of evidence given by accomplices; he was himself accused as a witch and burned (1589). Binsfeld recognized this revival of Ponzinibio's theories by Flade, and (like Spina) wrote his book to refute them. After 150 years, Ponzinibio was still regarded as a valid authority in 1672 by Sir George Mackenzie, the Scottish lawyer and King's Advocate.

Poppet: see Waxen Image.

Possession. Numerous entries in this *Encyclopedia* describe the demoniacal possession of nuns in France or of individual children in England or America, and the concomitant persecution of priests or old women as witches.

Possession was technically distinguished from obsession. Both were considered states of mind in which the victim could not be held responsible for what he said or did. In obsession, the devil was presumed to "besiege" or "sit without" the body of the afflicted [Latin: *ob-sedere*]. In possession, the devil beset the person inside the body. Bishop Montague, after Shakespeare one of the first to use the words, in 1642 contrasted the power of Satan "to move [and] actuate" [obsession] and "to possess and really inhabit" his victim [possession].

Because a virtuous person was supposed immune to possession, the early saints suffered only obsession. The theorists observed that attacks were strongest when the victims were destitute, alone, or depressed; and in fact Christian demonology was largely developed in the Egyptian deserts by hermits with these characteristics. The *Life of St. Hilary* (about A.D. 390) told how "his temptations were numerous; day and night the demons varied their snares. . . . How often when he lay down did naked women appear to him." And St. Athanasius described how the devil attacked St. Anthony, "at night assuming the form of a woman and imitating a woman's gestures [*feminaeque gestus*] to beguile him."

In the Western Christian tradition, the theory of possession stemmed from the New Testament, where, for example, Christ cured a man suffering, as Mark v (and Mat-

thew viii and Luke viii) said, "with an unclean spirit." "He had been often bound with fetters and chains, and the chains had been plucked asunder by him, and the fetters broken in pieces; neither could any man tame him. And always, night and day, he was in the mountains and in the tombs, crying, and cutting himself with stones." Descriptions of demoniacs or energumens [people "worked on" by the devil] multiplied in the writings of the early Church Fathers. Cyril of Jerusalem in the fourth century A.D. described how the devil

> tyrannically uses another's body, another's instruments, as his own property; he throws down him who stands upright; he perverts the tongue and distorts the lips. Foam comes instead of words; the man is filled with darkness; his eye is open, yet his soul sees not through it; and the miserable man quivers convulsively before his death. (*Catechisms*)

In the seventh century, the *Life of St. Gall* related how a young girl rolled on the ground, "and rending herself in a lamentable fashion, began to utter loud and terrible cries accompanied by the most filthy words."

Involuntary possession (as contrasted with the induced trances of shamans and modern spiritualist mediums) resembled epilepsy or hysteria, at least in external manifestations, typically:

1. Writhings and contortions of the face and body which could not be produced except under abnormal conditions;
2. Vomiting of strange objects (*allotriophagy*, common in the mentally deranged and hysterical, often to induce suicide); and
3. Change of voice (to deep and gruff). In England, such "belly speaking" was common, and Thomas Ady (1656) observed that "by this imposture, [young people] do make the people believe that they are possessed by the devil speaking within them."

Henry More, in his *Antidote Against Atheism* (1653), noted that all these symptoms and signs were proof that "the devil got into the body of a man . . . making use of the organs of the body at his own pleasure, for the performing of such pranks and feats as are far above the capacity, strength, or agility of the party thus bewitched or possessed." There was some discussion, for example, as in Robert Burton's *Anatomy of Melancholy* (1621), as to whether the devil acted directly on the mind, or indirectly by means of the body which affected the mind. Some demonologists, noting the clinical fact that hysterical epileptics stank, inclined to the latter view. Bodin thought the stench came from the devil's assumption of a corpse; but Sir Matthew Hale, from "the sympathy betwixt the body and the soul."

While the devil could (with God's permission) initiate possession of his own will, the demonologists generally credited a witch with causing possession. Any kind of strange fit in a child immediately started a hue and cry for some helpless neighbor, presumed to have sent her familiar demons to plague him from within [see Scratching]. The witch tempted her victim with food; Henri Boguet found that apples, in which the devil could hide and be unsuspectedly consumed into the body, were best. "In this, Satan continually rehearses the means by which he tempted Adam and Eve in the earthly paradise." In 1585, continued Boguet, frightened passers-by pushed into the river at Annecy, Savoy, an apple that gave out a "great and confused noise. . . . It cannot be doubted that this apple was full of devils, and that a witch had been foiled in an attempt to give it to someone."

In Europe, possession was especially prevalent in convents. One hysterical nun rapidly infected the whole flock, and by direct stimulation or autosuggestion the entire nunnery would be plagued with devils, and only later quieted by exorcism. Guazzo noted that among women "those especially afflicted were bound by a vow of virginity; it was wonderful with what wiles the devil surrounded them . . . to deter them from chastity." Writing in 1580, Bodin thought demoniacal possession most common in Spain and Italy; however, in the early seventeenth century, possession was more frequent in France.

MAJOR GROUP EPIDEMICS
(asterisks indicate separate entries)

1491 Cambrai. A rare occurrence at so early a date. The nuns showed superhuman strength, barked like dogs, and foretold the future. The originator of the outbreak, Jeanne Potier, a hysterical nymphomaniac, was eventually revealed as a witch; after her removal, the convent resumed normalcy (De Lancre, Del Rio).

1526 Lyons. Typical demoniac possession; nuns exorcized.

1550 Wertet, in the county of Hoorn, Brabant. Nuns lent a poor woman three pounds of salt, and received six pounds in return. Immediately, the nuns climbed trees like cats, were invisibly pinched and beaten, and levitated several feet in the air without harm. A reputable woman of the town was tortured into confessing she had bewitched the convent (Weyer).

1552 Kentorp, near Strasbourg. Highborn nuns freed from possession when the cook, Elisabeth Kama, was revealed as a witch and the daughter of a witch. Weyer examined the accused at Cleves (Weyer, Bodin).

1554 Rome. Eighty-two possessed women, converted Jews, accused their relatives of sending devils into them in revenge for their apostasy. Pope Paul IV wanted to banish all Jews but was dissuaded (Bodin).

1555 Rome. Eighty children in orphanage afflicted (Weyer).

1560 Xante, Spain. Nuns bleated like sheep, tore off veils, had convulsions in church; behavior resembled that of nuns at Wertet (Weyer).

1565 Cologne. Nuns at Nazareth convent had lovers, but averred that devils, masquerading as dogs, shamefully abused them [see Sexual Relations with Devils]. Dr. Henry Weyer, the son of the famous skeptic, attended the sisters (Weyer, Boguet, Michaëlis).

1566 Amsterdam. Thirty boys in foundling hospital possessed. Under exorcism, they vomited "needles . . . shreds of cloth, pieces of pots, hair, glass." (Weyer, Michaëlis, More)

1577 Oderheim on Rhine. Nuns plagued by lascivious devils, who as dogs fawned on sisters to the accompaniment of soft night music (Weyer).

*1585 Mons. Sister Jeanne Fery exorcized by the Archbishop of Cambrai.

1590 Milan. Thirty nuns possessed. Here, as in most of these reports, rapidly spreading mass hysteria was indicated.

*1611 Aix-en-Provence. Sister Madeleine Demandolx de la Palud and Sister Louise Capel accused Father Louis Gaufridi of bewitching nuns. Gaufridi tortured and burned; the two nuns expelled (Michaëlis).

*1613 Lille. Epidemic spread from related Brigittine house at Aix. Three nuns accused another, Marie de Sains, of bewitching them; spoke foreign tongues, had paroxysms, attended shocking orgies. Celebrated exorcist, Father Francis Domptius, in attendance. Sister Marie de Sains imitated the confession of Sister Madeleine of Aix, and itemized the intimacies of the sabbat. On Mondays and Tuesdays, the witches copulated *"par voie ordinaire."* On Thursdays, they practiced sodomy. "On this day, everybody, men and women, commits the sin of the flesh in other than the vessel provided by nature. They pollute themselves in many strange and abominable ways, women with women, and men with men." Saturday was reserved for bestiality. "On this day, they have to do with all kinds of animals, like dogs, cats, pigs, goats, and winged serpents." Wednesdays and Fridays the witches sang litanies to the Devil (Michaëlis).

1628 Madrid. Here, the Spanish Inquisition dispersed the affected nuns to other convents (Juan Antonio Llorente).

*1634 Loudun. The most famous of all cases of possession. Mother Superior displayed the classical symptoms of possession. Father Urbain Grandier, foe of Cardinal Richelieu, accused of bewitching nuns and burned. Hysteria continued after his execution and spread to other convents.

1640 Chinon. Father Bauré, notorious at Loudun, continued his exorcism at Chinon, but was suspected by Archbishop of Lyons —the girls "believe themselves to be really possessed on your word alone, so that the reason for their affliction is the confidence they place in your opinion." Father Bauré finally banished for conniving with Mademoiselle Beloquin in accusing a priest of rape on the altar, whereas stains on altar cloth turned out to be merely blood of a chicken.

*1642 Louviers. Eighteen nuns possessed on promptings of Sister Madeleine Bavent. Father Boullé accused and later (1647) burned alive.

1656 Paderborn. Mass hysteria affecting whole diocese. Demoniacs, speaking many languages, accused especially Capuchin friars, who became suspect. Burgomaster's maid arrested and found to possess articles allegedly used in sorcery (toad, hair, needles).

*1662 Auxonne. Three bishops and five physicians decided the convent was possessed. Sister Denise felt no pain from needles thrust under her fingernails (probably an example of analgesia common to hysterics). Angry mob lynched women accused of bewitching nuns.

*1669 Mora, Sweden. Epidemic involving many children, with hallucinations about the sabbat.

1670 Hoorn, Holland. Children under twelve years old, in orphanage, possessed.

1681 Toulouse. Marie Clauzette and four other novices possessed and exorcized. Parlement investigated and found the girls impostors, but the nuns accused the government lawyers of having strayed from the Catholic religion and become libertines and atheists.

*1682 Salem. America's only mass epidemic of possession.

1687 Lyons. Mass hysteria of about fifty nuns.

1744 Les Landes. Father Heurtin, desirous of working miracles, exorcized young girls who thought themselves possessed.

*1749 Unterzell, Lower Franconia. Possession of nuns for several years, with convulsions, swellings, and delirium. Sub-prioress Maria Renata burned as a witch.

Typical instances of individual possession

1566. On August 27, King Charles IX of France witnessed the exorcism by the monks of Vervins of Madame Nicole Autry at Laon, where she was publicly whipped "to obtain through God the expulsion of the devils from her body."

1583. In Vienna, sixteen-year-old girl suffered from cramps; considered demoniac. After eight weeks of exorcism, Jesuits expelled 12,652 living demons, which her grandmother kept in the form of flies in glass jars! The seventy-year-old grandmother was tortured into confessing intercourse with the devil in the shape of a ball of thread. She was dragged at the horse's tail to the place of execution and burned alive. The Jesuits lauded the sentence and urged judges to intensify the witch hunts.

1586. A later King of France, Henry III, the son of Catherine de' Medici, raised in a household of superstition, sent three physicians to examine a girl allegedly possessed by a devil. According to her mother, the girl had *des fleurs blanches* during menstruation. The doctors, however, examined the discharges and found a virulent gonorrhea [*chaudepisse*]; midwives found the girl no virgin. Two years previously, she had been discovered faking possession, when a priest, to trick her, read a passage in Latin from Cicero. She, thinking it from the Bible, put on a fit. The girl was condemned to be publicly whipped at Amiens.

1598. At Paris, Marthe Brossier claimed to be possessed. The Capuchin monks decided her possession was genuine, but the doctors disagreed, and Bishop Miron of Angers, using Vergil as a standard, also decided she was fraudulent. The monks forwarded the case to the papal court, but when the Jesuits sided with the physicians, they dropped it, leaving the girl and her father stranded in Rome.

1691. Marie Volet of Bourg acted as if possessed. Dr. Rhodes and Canon d'Estaing of Lyons found no demoniacal cause and recommended convalescence.

1816. A late example of deception near Amiens, when a girl tried to divert attention from her pregnancy by claiming to be possessed. She named the three devils infesting her: Mimi, Zozo, and Crapoulet. A Jesuit priest tried exorcism. Mimi left quietly. Zozo broke windows in the church before flying away. Crapoulet, however, remained and took up a position in the girl's pudenda. At this point, the Jesuit was forbidden to continue exorcism, under pain of arrest.

Such mentally disturbed people naturally attracted theologians who tried to classify their symptoms. One treatise (Rouen, 1644), provoked by the disorders at Louviers, suggested eleven *indications* of true possession:

1. To think oneself possessed.
2. To lead a wicked life.
3. To live outside the rules of society.
4. To be persistently ill, falling into heavy sleep and vomiting unusual objects (either natural objects: toads, serpents, worms, iron, stones, etc.; or artificial objects: nails, pins, etc., which may also be illusions caused by witches and not inevitably signs of possession by the devil).
5. To blaspheme.
6. To make a pact with the Devil.
7. To be troubled with spirits ("an absolute and inner possession and residence in the body of the person").
8. To show a frightening and horrible countenance.
9. To be tired of living [*s'ennuyer de vivre et se désespérer*].
10. To be uncontrollable and violent.
11. To make sounds and movements like an animal.

These indications should alert the priest for the *sure signs* of demoniacal possession: revealing secret and hidden information; speaking or comprehending strange languages; displaying phenomenal strength and extraordinary bodily movements; and reacting to sacred objects.

Another treatise on the same troubles at

Louviers, by Père Esprit de Bosroger, gave a variant list of sure signs (perhaps more generally representative of possession):

1. Denial of knowledge of fits after the paroxysm has ended.
2. Incessant obscenities and blasphemies.
3. Circumstantial descriptions of the sabbat.
4. Fear of sacred relics and sacraments.
5. Violent cursing at any prayer.
6. Lewd exposure and acts of abnormal strength.
7. Similar manifestations in other demoniacs.

The most convenient summary of the signs of possession, however, was that given by Guazzo in his *Compendium Maleficarum* (1608, 1626):

A demoniacal attack, or hystero-epileptic fit, showing the classic symptoms of contortion, tearing of garments, lacerating the body, and extending the tongue.

The following is the customary practice to determine whether a sick man is possessed [*energumenus*] by a demon. [Priests] secretly apply to the sick man a writing with the sacred words of God, or relics of the saints, or a blessed waxen Agnus Dei, or some other holy thing. A priest places his hand and his stole upon the head of the possessed and pronounces sacred words. Thereupon the sick man begins to shake and shudder with fright, and on account of his pain makes many confused movements, and says and does many strange things. If the demon lodges in his head, he feels the most piercing pains in his head, or else his head and his face are suffused with a hot red flush like fire. If the demon is in his eyes, he makes them roll wildly. If in the back, he brings on convulsions in his limbs, in front and behind, and sometimes makes the whole body so rigid and inflexible that no amount of force can bend it.

Sometimes the [possessed persons] fall down as if dead, as if they were suffering from tertiary epilepsy and a vapor rushing into their head; but at the priest's command they arise, and the vapor goes back where it came from. If the demon is in their throats, they are so constricted that they appear to be strangled. If the devil is in the nobler parts of the body, as about the heart or lungs, he causes panting, palpitations

and syncope. If he tends more to the stomach, he provokes hiccoughs and vomiting, so that sometimes they cannot take food, or else cannot retain it. And he causes them to pass something like a little ball by the anus, with roarings and other discordant cries; and afflicts them with wind and gripings in the abdomen. They are also sometimes known by certain fumes of sulphur or some other strong-smelling stuff.

If, after consideration of all the signs and symptoms, it was decided that the afflicted was truly possessed by a devil, then exorcism was called for. Guazzo's parallel list of symptoms of bewitchment is given here under the entry Maleficia.

Paralleling the possessed young nuns on the Continent were the possessed girls and boys in English and American homes. The most famous examples are listed elsewhere [see Children as Accusers]. But these English youngsters reacted much like the Continental. Richard Baxter's description (from Cornelius Gemma) of fifteen-year-old Catherine Gualter, possessed at Louvain in January, 1571, would be apt for any of the boys exposed in England.

She voided a living eel by stool. It lay as dead in the excrements at first, but put into water revived. When it was dead, and laid up to keep, it vanished away. . . . Then she vomited great flocks of hair, with filthy water, such as in ulcers, and sometimes like the dung of doves and geese, and in them pieces of wood, and those like new chips lately cut off an old tree, and abundance of skins like parchment shavings. . . . After this she vomited innumerable stones, some like walnuts, like pieces broken out of old walls and with some of the lime on them.

Baxter, a Protestant, added: "That she was cured by the priest's means does not render the story incredible, though there be many deceits."

In Protestant countries, exorcism was not used, and in England the attempts at exorcism by an unattached preacher, John Darrell (about 1600), led to Canon 72 of the Episcopal Church, in practice forbidding exorcism. Apart from an occasional individual, such as the priest at the 1958 Lambeth Conference who maintained possession as an explanation of certain mental disorders, the Anglican communion has rejected the theory of the Devil's power to enter into human bodies. The evangelical Protestants in general adopted Luther's recommendation to cure demoniacal possession by prayer alone, for Almighty God knows when the devil ought to depart. Luther, it is reported (Snell), showed his contempt for a possessing devil by vigorously kicking a demoniac presented to him, a shock treatment which was apparently successful. Cotton Mather relied on prayer for the Goodwin Children, Mercy Short, and Margaret Rule, the most famous of the American possessed children. In his *Memorable Providences*, Mather undertook to show "the near affinity between witchcraft and possession." He gave an example of a young boy about sixteen, born in Holland, and resident at Branford, near New Haven, who had fits and communications with a devil, who wanted him to sign a pact. When the boy refused—

the devil took a corporal possession of him, and hath not ceased to torment him extremely ever since. If anything be spoken to him, the devil answereth (and

many times he barks like a fox, and hisseth like a serpent) sometimes with horrible blasphemies against the name of Christ; and at some other times the boy is sensible.

George L. Burr observed that Mather's account resembled a description of epilepsy.

Just as the Catholics gave directions for ascertaining possession, so the Protestants had their handbooks. The very popular Michael Dalton's *Guide to Jurymen* (1627) gave seven signs of bewitchment (Dalton's conception of possession):

1. When a healthful body shall be suddenly taken, and without probable reason, or natural cause appearing.
2. When two or more are taken in the like strange fits, in many things.
3. When the afflicted party in his fits doth tell truly many things, what the witch or other persons absent are doing or saying, and the like.
4. When the parties shall do many things strangely, or speak many things to purpose, and yet out of their fits know not anything thereof.
5. When there is a strength supernatural, as that a strong man or two shall not be able to keep down a child, or weak person, upon a bed.
6. When the party doth vomit up crooked pins, needles, nails, coals, lead, straw, hair, or the like.
7. When the party shall see visibly some apparition, and shortly after some mischief shall befall him.

George L. Burr made an important distinction between witchcraft and possession.

Insanity, or even suspicion of it, was the best possible *defense* against the charge of witchcraft; and Johan Weyer, who first attacked the persecution, not daring (as now seems proven) to speak the full truth about the torture, sought to *save* the witches by making them out demented. . . . The distinction between the demoniac and the witch was fundamental: the former was the devil's unwilling *victim*, the latter his conscious and sane ally. In the former the *possessing devil* was sometimes harshly treated; but only to *drive him out* and relieve the sufferer—*never* with mutilation or death. The latter was punished for crimes committed by his (or her) *own volition*; and for none more often than for having *brought* possession upon others. . . . Nay, the plea of insanity was the one thing that *could*—aye, and in one or two cases actually *did*—exculpate them; if they were the victims of Satan, they could not be his willing accomplices.

When credence in witchcraft ceased, belief in possession, since it was similarly predicated on a personal devil, also stopped. When the two daughters, sixteen and eighteen years old, respectively, of James Williams, of Fitts Hill, Illinois, in 1871 acted as if crazy, "seeing" witches riding on horses and asking the girls to give their souls to the Devil, they attracted considerable publicity. The girls, normal during the day, possessed throughout the night, actually swallowed pins, caught and ate flies, and had convulsions. But no credence was given to any diabolical agency. Oesterreich wrote (1930):

Possession begins to disappear amongst civilized races as soon as belief in spirits loses its power. In modern Europe this point of time was marked by the advent of the Age of Enlightenment. Not all its rationalistic exaggerations can prevent the unprejudiced from seeing in that drastic intellectual criticism . . . a great turning-point in the conception of the world, inasmuch as at this stage European thought achieved complete liberation from the older theological system or at least made definite and final preparations to do so.

For further discussion of the theory of demoniacal possession, see Exorcism; also James I, John Darrell, Samuel Harsnett, Francis Hutchinson. For examples of demoniacal possession, epilepsy or hysteria, real or feigned, see:

Belgium: Louise Lateau (1868).
England: Warboys Witches (1595), Burton Boy (1597), Anne Gunter (1604), Leicester Boy (1616), Bilson Boy (1620), Pendle Swindle (for Edmund Robinson,

1633), Bury St. Edmunds Witches (1662).
France: Jeanne Fery (1585), Françoise Fontaine (1591), Aix-en-Provence Nuns (1611), Lille Novices (1613), Loudun Nuns (1634), Elisabeth Allier (1639), Louviers Nuns (1647), Auxonne Nuns (1662), Catherine Cadière (1731).
Germany: Christoph Haizmann (1677), Sister Maria Renata (1749).
Ireland: Witchcraft in Ireland; Florence Newton (1661), Magee Island Witch Trial (1711).
Norway: Siri Jørgensdatter (1730).
Scotland: Glenluce Devil (1654), Bargarran Impostor (1697), Pittenweem Witches (1704).
Sweden: Mora Witches (1669).
United States: Connecticut Witches (1662), Goodwin Children (1688), Ann Putnam (1692), Salem Witch Trials (1692), Mercy Short (1693), Margaret Rule (1693).

Potions. Witches supposedly accomplished their *maleficia* by a pact with the Devil or by magic powders, potions, and ointments. From classical times, herbs and exotic ingredients have been employed as poisons or aphrodisiacs, and in themselves are not peculiar to witches. As the famous lawyer Sir George Mackenzie observed in 1678: "Not only witches but even naturalists may give potions that incline men and women to lust." The magic power of a witches' brew is more a part of the literature and folklore of sorcery than of historical witchcraft. The people of Leicester who accused an old woman of stealing a pot of "rosemary balm and marigold flowers . . . in a quart of ale" were not, in 1717, too concerned with any pact with the Devil. Indictments sometimes mentioned hellish liquids, as when Agnes Sampson of the North Berwick Witches confessed "she took a black toad, and did hang the same up by the heels, three days, and collected and gathered the venom as it dropped and fell from it in an oyster shell." More often charges covered the possession or making of flying ointment, which led directly into the main charge of sabbat-going. The ingredients for potions are discussed further in the en-

"Double, double, toil and trouble,
Fire burn, and cauldron bubble."

Witches at work, by Hans Baldung Grün.

tries for Ointment (Flying and Killing), and Charms.

Pott, Johannes Henricus. *Specimen Juridicum de Nefando Lamiarum cum Diabolo Coitu* (Jena, 1689) of Johannes Henricus Pott, professor of law at the University of Jena, is a fantastic storehouse of the extravagant legends of intercourse between devils and witches. Very learnedly, Pott related stories of witches giving birth to worms which they later used as legs or arms for men, of monstrous unions (such as Guazzo's account of the offspring of a man and a cow who grew up a pious man with a tendency to enjoy browsing among herds), and of prodigies (women bearing lions, dogs, and serpents). Pott also included an account of Faust, as a wicked magician who, among other tricks, showed a man how to get a smooth skin without shaving. Unfortunately, the arsenic depilatory took off, not only the beard, but the skin and flesh! For any man or woman lusting

with the devil, with or without a pact, death by burning was the penalty.

In addition to his seventy pages discussing sex, Pott printed the text of a pact with the Devil made in 1676, translated here under Pact.

Pricking. In the wave of witch persecutions in England during the Civil War, Matthew Hopkins had a brief inglorious career as a professional witch finder, swimming and pricking suspects. This latter method was linked to the theory of devil's marks, those areas on the skin disfigured by some mole or birthmark or scar, supposedly indicating the possessor's branding by Satan. If a suspected witch had no such obvious marks, she might still have invisible marks, discovered only by pricking. All such devil's marks were reputedly morbid; thus, if a long pin were stuck into them, no pain would be felt and no blood would run out. Generally, as a preliminary to being searched for the devil's mark, the suspect was completely shaved [see Shaving], to reveal anything hidden by hair. Hopkins profited considerably from the fees towns and villages paid him for discovering witches; so great was his business in 1645-46 that he and his partner, John Stearn, hired four assistants to prick likely suspects. Probably Hopkins used a trick of European prickers. Spee had warned that the torturer should be watched very closely, lest he only pretend to prick and then cry out he had distinguished a devil's mark, and lest he employ "cheating pricks, whether magic or charmed, or *so made* that at pleasure they enter and wound or only seem to do so *by sliding back into themselves.*" (*Cautio Criminalis*)

Scotland spawned many prickers about the second quarter of the seventeenth century, such as John Kincaid of Tranent, and John Balfour of Corhouse, and John Dick. The career of one of these men, who may be taken as typical, is told in detail in Ralph Gardiner's *England's Grievance Discovered in Relation to the Coal Trade* (1655), from which the following account is taken. It is the sworn petition by three witnesses at

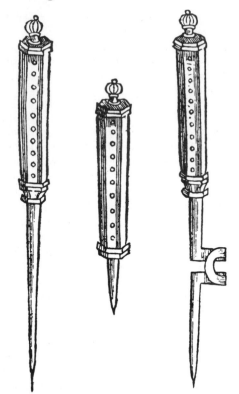

The Tricks of Witch Prickers. Examples of two false bodkins, left, and genuine bodkin, "for show," right. The center specimen has a retractable blade and hollow shaft, so that the accused witch would feel no pain when it was put against her flesh.

Newcastle, questioning the legality of the procedure (the verdicts were not attacked). Confirmation of the incident is given in the parish register of St. Andrew's, Newcastle, which names fifteen women who "were executed in the town moor for witches" at that time. In March, 1650, the magistrates at Newcastle decided to invite "the man that trieth the witches in Scotland"—his name is not recorded—to give his tests in Newcastle, to be paid "twenty shillings a piece for all he could condemn as witches, and free passage thither and back again."

Gardiner's testimony continued:

When the sergeants had brought the said witch finder on horseback to town, the magistrates sent their bellman through the town, ringing his bell and crying: All people that would bring in any complaint against any woman for a witch, they should be sent for and tried by the person appointed. Thirty women were brought into the townhall and stripped, and then openly had pins thrust into their bodies. And most of them were found guilty, near twenty-seven of them, by him and set aside.

As a result of this very literal witch hunt, one man and fourteen women were executed.

These poor souls never confessed anything, but pleaded innocence. And one of them, by name Margaret Brown, beseeched God that some remarkable sign might be seen at the time of their execution, to evidence their innocency; and as soon as ever she was turned off the ladder, her blood gushed out upon the people to the admiration [astonishment] of the beholders.

During the pricking, one magistrate, Lieutenant Colonel Hobson, intervened, and managed to save the life of one "personable and goodlike" woman [see Devil's Mark].

Following this triumph, the witch pricker went into Northumberland, here increasing his tariff to £3 for each witch convicted. But finally he was stopped. "Henry Ogle, Esquire, a late member of Parliament, laid hold on him, and required bond of him to answer the sessions, but he got away for Scotland. And it was conceived if he had stayed he would have made most of the women in the North witches, for money." Justice pursued him to Scotland, however, and he was indicted. "And upon the gallows he confessed he had been the death of above 220 women in England and Scotland, for the gain of twenty shillings a piece."

John Balfour was another taken to task by the Lords of the Scottish Privy Council, in 1632, who decided Balfour was "abusing simple and ignorant people for his private gain and commodity." Furthermore, "his art was only conjectural, and [he was] forbidden to practice his trade."

Pricking for devil's marks, it might be added, was common all over Europe; but since the accused was there always tortured into confession, evidence got from pricking

Four executed witches, with the witch finder receiving his wages for discovering them. From Columbia University Library. "This mark is discovered among us by a pricker, whose trade it is and who learns it as other trades; but this is a horrid cheat, for they allege that if the place bleed not, or if the person be not sensible, he or she is infallibly a witch . . . and a villain who used this trade with us, being in the year 1666 apprehended for other villainies, did confess all this trade to be a mere cheat."—Sir George Mackenzie, *Laws and Customs of Scotland* (1678).

was not essential even for the appearances of legality. In the reports of the tortures, pricking is therefore simply noted, passed over lightly, or assumed. To this extent, the following account of pricking in Switzerland in 1652 is atypical. A country woman, Michelle Chaudron of Geneva, was accused of bewitching two young girls, who said they felt a continual itching in parts of their bodies. Michelle was searched by physicians for devil's marks, and long needles were stuck into her flesh, but blood flowed from each puncture and Michelle cried out in pain. Not finding a devil's mark, the judges ordered the woman to be tortured; overcome with agony she confessed everything demanded. After her confession, the physicians returned to hunt the devil's mark, and this time found a tiny black spot on her thigh. Michelle Chaudron, at this point in a state of exhaustion following the torture, did not shriek. This evidence confirmed her confession, and she was immediately condemned to be strangled and burned.

Putnam, Ann. Of all the young women who were the accusers in the Salem witch trials of 1692, Ann Putnam was the youngest and the most precocious. She testified

at every trial except one. For a girl of twelve, she revealed a surprisingly vivid literary imagination. Her evidence is as convincing in its use of circumstantial details as Defoe's account of Mrs. Veal. At the examination of Rev. George Burroughs on May 3, 1692, for example, she swore on oath she had seen two ghosts with their bloody wounds stopped with sealing wax.

And one [apparition] told me that she was [Mr. George Burroughs'] first wife, and [Mr. Burroughs] stabbed her under the left arm and put a piece of sealing wax on the wound. And she pulled aside the winding sheet and showed me the place; and also told me that she was in the house Mr. Parris now lived where it was done. And the other [apparition] told me that Mr. Burroughs and that wife, which he hath now, killed [her] in the vessel as she was coming to see her friends, because they would have one another. And they both charged me that I should tell these things to the magistrates before Mr. Burroughs' face.

Throughout the trials, hovering behind Ann Putnam is her mother Ann, aged thirty. She was the wife of Thomas Putnam, constable of Salem Village, a former judge and an important person. It cannot be decided at this late date whether or not she coached her child—the phraseology of little Ann's description of Mr. Burroughs' two wives and Mrs. Putnam's own testimony of "murders" committed by John Willard might suggest this.

There was collusion somewhere, when Edward Putnam, Ann's uncle, swore on oath that he "saw the mark, both of bite and chains," with which Ann was allegedly afflicted by Mrs. Nurse. Rebecca Nurse, while in jail several miles distant, bit Ann and struck her with a spectral chain, leaving a mark "being in a kind of a round ring, and three streaks across the ring; she had six blows with a chain in the space of half an hour; and she had one remarkable one, with six streaks across her arm." Is this one of Mrs. Putnam's inventions?

Some fine hand is behind the sequence of events in the visit to sixty-year-old Martha Cory by two detectives, one of them Ann's uncle. Who suggested to this Edward Putnam that he first find out from little Ann how Martha Cory's apparition was dressed, so that he could make positive identification by their dress between the living Martha and the specter Martha? Who thought up Ann's story that the specter "told her that her name was Cory and that she [Ann] should see her no more before it was night, because she should not see what clothes she had on"?

Suspicion of Mrs. Putnam is not just interpreting history in the light of the present. She was suspected as the *agent provocateur* at the time of the trials. John Tarbell, for example, testified that one day at the Putnams' house, he

asked this question, whether the girl that was afflicted [Ann] did first speak of Goody Nurse before others mentioned her to her [Ann]. They said she told them she saw the apparition of a pale-faced woman that sat in her grandmother's seat, but did not know her name. Then I replied and said, "But who was it that told her that it was Goody Nurse?" Mercy Lewis said it was Goody [Mrs. Thomas] Putnam that said it was Goody Nurse; Goody Putnam said it

was Mercy Lewis that told her. Thus they turned it upon one another, saying, "It was you" and "It was *you* that told her." This was before any was afflicted at Thomas Putnam's beside his daughter, that they told his daughter it was Goody Nurse.

Another deposition in the case of Elizabeth Proctor was made by two men, Samuel Barton, twenty-eight, and John Houghton, twenty-three—that Mr. and Mrs. Putnam inspired Mercy Lewis to name Elizabeth Proctor as a witch.

Charles Sutherland Tapley in his biography of *Rebecca Nurse* (Boston, 1930): "I have never known a Putnam to name his daughter, Ann."

Fourteen years after the trials came Ann Putnam's confession of the part she had played. But for this, direct evidence of wholesale fraud and deception by the girls would be lacking. The confession was read in Salem Village church by the new pastor, Rev. Joseph Green; it is worth noting that Ann Putnam still did not deny witchcraft—she merely acknowledged her delusion by Satan.

I desire to be humbled before God for that sad and humbling providence that befell my father's family in the year about 1692; that I, then being in my childhood, should by such a providence of God be made an instrument for the accusing of several persons of a grievous crime, whereby their lives were taken away from them, whom now I have just grounds and good reason to believe they were innocent persons. And that it was a great delusion of Satan that deceived me in that sad time, whereby I justly fear I have been instrumental, with others, though ignorantly and unwittingly, to bring upon myself and this land the guilt of innocent blood; though what was said or done by me against any person I can truly and uprightly say before God and man, I did it not out of any anger, malice, or ill-will to any person, for I had no such thing against one of them, but what I did was ignorantly, being deluded of Satan.

And particularly as I was a chief instrument of accusing of Goodwife Nurse and her two sisters, I desire to lie in the dust, and to be humbled for it, in that I was a cause, with others, of so sad a calamity to them and their families; for which cause I desire to lie in the dust and earnestly beg forgiveness of God, and from all those unto whom I have given just cause of sorrow and offense, whose relations were taken away or accused.

See also George Burroughs, Giles Cory, and Salem Witch Trials.

Quaker Witchcraft. The Quakers hold an honorable record in the history of witchcraft. No Quaker wrote in favor of the delusion; several wrote against. Although George Fox, the founder of the Society of Friends, never questioned "the spirit of witchcraft," he ridiculed such superstitions as witches' raising storms. In 1676 he told "seafaring men" not to be deluded.

> Let New England professors [of religion] see whether or no they have not sometimes cast some poor simple people into the sea on pretense of being witches. . . . For you may see that it was the Lord who sent out the wind and raised the mighty storm in the sea, and not your witches, or ill-tongued people, as you vainly imagine.

During the seventeenth century, the sect suffered much abuse, and to physical violence were added satires linking them to witchcraft. "For the Quaker revelation doth arise in them only when the witchcraft fit is upon them." The Quakers were accused, in German and English works, of using a nostrum called Quaker powder to gain converts.

By the time the Quakers were established in America, belief in witchcraft was fading everywhere. Their rationalism was therefore not exceptional. In 1718 Pennsylvania revived the English statute of James I, but it was never invoked. Pennsylvania had only one trial, on December 27, 1683, involving two old Swedish women charged with bewitching animals. The case, hardly one of witchcraft, was dismissed on a technicality. The apocryphal legend of William Penn's

handling of the trial should be recorded. Penn asked one of the accused: "Art thou a witch? Hast thou ridden through the air on a broomstick?" The confused old woman said she had. Penn then told her she had a perfect right to ride on a broomstick, there was no law against it, and he ordered her dismissal.

Benjamin Franklin satirized witchcraft in the *Pennsylvania Gazette* (October 22, 1730) with a description of a purported witch trial near Mount Holly, New Jersey. Many regarded the hoax as historical, and it was reprinted in the British *Gentleman's Magazine* of 1731.

Question: see Torture.

Rais, Gilles de. Gilles de Laval, Baron de Rais [Rays, Rayx, or Retz] (1404-40), belongs more to the history of alchemy and magic than witchcraft, for he invoked devils to learn how to make gold. It was charged "he adored and sacrificed to spirits, conjured them and made others conjure them, and wished to make a pact with the said evil spirits, and by their means to have and receive, if he could, knowledge, power, and riches." For this, he was executed. His notoriety, however, rests largely on his alleged sexual perversions.

At the height of his power, Gilles de Rais was the richest noble in Europe, and in 1420 his fortune was increased by his marriage to a fabulously wealthy heiress, Catherine de Thouars. As a marshal of France, he played an honorable part in fighting against the English, but after the coronation of Charles VII, he retired to his estates, at Machecoul, Malemort, La Suze, Champtocé, and Tiffauges. Here he lived like an emperor, with a bodyguard of two hundred knights and a private chapel of thirty canons, and an extensive library of rare manuscripts. But profligate expenditure on his lavish establishments forced him to start selling his lands. In 1436, his heirs obtained an order from King Charles VII of France forbidding further sales, but the decree was ignored in Brittany, where both Duke John V and his Chancellor, Bishop Malestroit, were eager to acquire the

The trial of Gilles de Rais (at right) before the Bishop of Nantes and the Inquisitor General of France, from a manuscript in the Bibliothèque national, Paris.

properties. Thus, to counteract the financial drain of his luxury, Gilles de Rais turned to alchemy, seeking the philosophers' stone which would transmute base metals into gold.

When Gilles de Sillé, a priest, failed in such an attempt, his employer turned to other mountebanks who employed less science and more magic. For example, Jean de la Rivière and Du Mesnil preyed on him and further wasted his fortunes. In 1439, another necromancer, Father Francesco Prelati of Florence, joined three other Italians at Tiffauges and organized terrifying séances, invoking a demon named Baron. As failure followed failure, Prelati (it was later charged) turned to rarer materials to cajole the spirits, especially young children, whose blood propitiated the devils and whose bones became magic powders.

Although his evil fame was becoming notorious, the downfall of Gilles de Rais started from a relatively minor misdemeanor. The Treasurer of Brittany, Geoffroi le Ferron, was another with eyes on the castles; in September, 1440, he bought St. Etienne de Malemort. Foolishly, De Rais refused admission to Geoffroi's

brother, Jean le Ferron, who had come to take title, and beat and imprisoned him. This treatment would have gone unnoticed, had not Jean le Ferron been a priest. Bishop Malestroit seized on this pretext to bring Gilles before his court, on charges which he had been secretly preparing since July 29. The Bishop was joined by the Inquisition, which pressed heresy, and a simultaneous civil trial was promoted in the ducal court. Bishop, inquisitor, and duke stood to gain a tremendous fortune by declaring Gilles de Rais a heretic, for they thereby confiscated his property. Taking was simpler than buying. At first, Gilles dismissed their accusations as "frivolous and lacking credit," but so certain were the principals of finding him guilty that on September 3, fifteen days before the trial began, the Duke disposed of his anticipated share of the Rais lands. Under these circumstances, it is difficult to place any credence in the evidence against him, among the most fantastic and obscene presented in this *Encyclopedia*.

The forty-seven initial charges made by the Bishop of Nantes, Jean de Malestroit, and the Inquisitor, Jean Blouyn, acting for the Inquisitor General of France, Guillaume Merici, resolved into three major areas: abuse of clerical privilege (by his violence against Jean le Ferron), conjuration of demons, and sexual perversions against children. Charge No. 16, for example, alleged that

in a certain low room of the castle or fortress of Tiffauges, in the diocese of Nantes, belonging to the wife of the aforesaid Gilles, about five years ago, Monsieur Francesco Prelati, self-styled expert in the prohibited art of geomancy, and Jean de la Rivière, made many magic signs, circles, and characters. Also, in a certain wood near the said fortress of Tiffauges, Antoine de Palerme, of Lombardy, and one named Louis, with other magicians and conjurers of demons, practiced divinations and summons to evil spirits, named Orion, Beelzebub, Satan, and Belial, with fire, incense, myrrh, aloes, and other fragrant substances.

The invocation of spirits was embellished

with accusations of human sacrifices. Charge No. 15 read:

> According to initial reports of public gossip, resulting in a secret inquiry by the Right Rev. Bishop of Nantes, in his town and diocese, by the agents of the Deputy Inquisitor, and by the Prosecutor of the ecclesiastical court, into the following charges, all crimes and offenses governed by ecclesiastical law, and according to the lamentable outcries, tears and wailings, denunciations coming from many persons of both sexes, crying out and complaining of the loss and death of children, the aforesaid Gilles de Rais, accused, [and his accomplices] have taken innocent boys and girls, and inhumanly butchered, killed, dismembered, burned and otherwise tortured them, and the said Gilles, accused, has immolated the bodies of the said innocents to devils, invoked and sacrificed to evil spirits, and has foully committed the sin of sodomy with young boys and in other ways lusted against nature after young girls, spurning the natural way of copulation, while both the innocent boys and girls were alive or sometimes dead or even sometimes during their death throes.

Other charges elaborated these crimes. One said he had ordered "the bodies of the said innocents burned, and had them thrown in the trenches and ditches about the said castles, and in the cesspool of the said castle of La Suze." Another alleged that Gilles offered "the hand, the eyes, and the heart of one of these said children, with his blood in a glass vase, to the demon Baron, in sign of his homage and tribute." A third prosecuted him for obtaining and reading prohibited books of magic.

In sum, Gilles was accused of being a "heretic, apostate, conjurer of demons . . . accused of the crime and vices against nature, sodomy, sacrilege, and violation of the immunities of Holy Church."

On September 13, 1440, the Bishop summoned Gilles (who offered no resistance) before his court. Preliminary hearings took place on September 28, October 8, 11, and 13, and the formal trial opened on October 15. The Duke of Brittany, John V, sanc-

tioned a concurrent trial which started on September 17; after six sessions, on October 19 Gilles de Rais was put to torture, and to procure the necessary damning evidence, his servants and four alleged accomplices were also tortured. In all, 110 witnesses (including informers) were heard.

The depositions in the civil court concerned the disappearance of children. The testimony of Thomas Aysée was typical:

> Thomas Aysée and his wife, living at St. Peter's Gate, go on record under oath, that they have lived at Machecoul for a year and that they were living there last Easter. And about that time, since they are poor folk, they had sent their son, aged about ten years, to seek alms at the castle of Machecoul, where the Sire de Rais was then, and that since that time they have not seen the said child nor had news of him. Except that the wife of the aforesaid Aysée said that a little girl, whose name nor parentage she does not know, had told her she had seen her son at the almsgiving at the said castle, and that alms had first been given to the girls and then after to the boys. This little girl said she had heard that one of the people belonging to the castle said to the son of the aforementioned Aysées that he had no meat, but that if he went in the said castle, he would have some, and that after this conversation he had entered the said castle.

The two personal attendants of Gilles de Rais, Henry Griart, aged twenty-six, and Etienne Corillaut, called Poitou, aged twenty-two, gave evidence before both tribunals on the fate of the missing children. Poitou said he had counted about thirty-six to forty-six heads of dead children, and that he had seen his master

> in order to practice his debauches with said children, boys and girls, against the use of nature, first with licentious passion take his rod in his left or right hand, rub it so it became erect and sticking out, then place it between the thighs or legs of the said boys or girls, not bothering with the natural female receptacle, and rub his said rod or virile member on the belly of the said boys and girls with

much gratification, heat and libidinous excitement, until he emitted his sperm on their stomachs.

At the civil trial, Poitou added some extra details, which it was claimed he gave "without either the first or second degree of torture." He testified he had heard that Gilles de Rais said

> after having had an orgasm on the stomach of the said children holding their legs between his, he had considerable pleasure in watching the heads of the children separated from the body. Sometimes he made an incision behind the neck to make them die slowly, at which he became greatly excited, and while they were bleeding to death he would sometimes masturbate on them until they were dead, and sometimes he did this after they had died while their bodies were still warm. . . . In order to stifle the cries of the children when he wished to have relations with them, he would first put a rope round their neck, and hang them up three feet off the floor in a corner of the room, and just before they were dead he would cause them to be taken down, telling them they would not utter a word, and then he would excite his member, holding it in his hand, and afterwards have an emission on their stomach. When he had done this, he had their throats cut and their heads separated from their bodies. Sometimes he would ask, when they were dead, which of these children had the most beautiful head.

After the fifth session of the secular trial, starting at 2:00 P.M. on Friday, October 21, 1440, Gilles de Rais was tortured until he promised to confess "voluntarily and freely" (as the court records stated). Everything charged against him he now admitted, confessing how he had enjoyed his vice, sometimes personally cutting off the head of a child with a dagger or knife, at other times beating the youngsters to death with a stick, then kissing voluptuously the dead bodies, gloating over those who had the loveliest heads and the most attractive limbs. His greatest pleasure was to sit across their stomachs and watch them slowly pass away. Gilles concluded his re-

Execution of Gilles de Rais in 1440. From a manuscript in the Bibliothèque nationale, Paris.

cital with an appeal to "the fathers and mothers of those so piteously slain [to] pray for me," and a request that his sins be publicly proclaimed in the vernacular—a sure way of securing popular support for his execution.

Closely co-operating with each other, the joint episcopal-inquisitorial court, with four local bishops among the judges, and the civil court apportioned the crimes and convictions between them. The Inquisitor found Gilles de Rais guilty of apostasy, heresy, and invocation of demons; the bishop convicted him of sodomy, sacrilege, and violation of ecclesiastical privileges. The ecclesiastical trials lasted nearly forty days and resulted in Gilles being handed over to the secular arm for punishment. Meanwhile, the civil court, under Pierre de l'Hospital, the Chancellor of the Breton Parlement, reintroduced the charge of murder (with which the church courts could not deal), and quickly sentenced him on that count.

On October 26, 1440, at Nantes, after prayer and penitence (he had been excommunicated the day before), Gilles de Rais was strangled and his body placed on the pyre with two of his associates (Henri Griart and Poitou). His relatives, however, were permitted to remove the body before the flames touched it and to inter it in the nearby Carmelite church.

The proceedings were highly irregular, even for trials of heresy. Not one of the 500 servants of Gilles was summoned to give evidence; very little evidence was not hearsay; and his own attendants were tortured and, having testified against their associate, freed. Prelati, who was equally guilty as Gilles, after a few months in a church prison, was set free by the Duke of Anjou. In return for not revoking his confession, Gilles was granted the mercy of strangulation before burning. The fifteenth-century chronicler Monstrelet indicated his suspicion of the motives of the trial, noting, "The greater part of the nobles of Brittany, more especially those of his own kindred, were in the utmost grief and confusion at his disgraceful death. Before this event, he was much renowned as a most valiant knight at arms."

Remy, Nicholas. Nicholas Remy was one of the standard French demonologists, and his *Demonolatreiae*, first published in 1595 at Lyons, was frequently reprinted. Remy's claims as an expert were emphasized by the title page, wherein he boasted he had condemned 900 witches in fifteen years—actually, since he made no allusions to any trials before 1581 or after 1591, in a period of ten years. Remy mentioned by name 128 condemned witches, but his figures and names cannot be documented, for the records for these years have been lost. Remy might well have borrowed the documents for his book and failed to return them.

Remy was born about 1530 at Charmes in the Département des Vosges in Lorraine. He came from a family of lawyers: his father, Gérard Remy, was Provost of Charmes; and his uncle, Lieutenant General of Vosges. It was only natural that the young Remy follow this tradition, so he studied law at the University of Toulouse, where Jean Bodin taught. From 1563 Remy worked in Paris, leaving in 1570 to become Lieutenant General of Vosges on the retire-

ment of his uncle. In 1575 he was made, in addition, Privy Councilor to Duke Charles III of Lorraine, and in 1584 Seigneur de Rosières-en-Blois et du Breuil. In 1591 he was elevated to Attorney General of Lorraine, in which position he was able to influence and override local magistrates too lenient with witches, keeping up his hatred of witches to the last. He died in the service of the Duke in April, 1612. Remy married Anne Marchand and fathered at least seven children.

The *Demonolatreiae* was one in the chain

Title page of the added second part to the German translation (1693) of Nicholas Remy's *Demonolatreiae* (1595).

"Among them that have lately written on demons and spirits, and their instruments, men and women, witches and sorcerers, Bodin and Remy are most known, I think, and read. Learned men both . . . yet for all this, I do not think myself bound to believe everything that they believed and thought truth . . . in some things, perchance, more credulous than I should be."—Meric Causabon, *Credulity* (London, 1668).

Nicholas Remy, Attorney General of Lorraine, who boasted he had burned 900 persons as witches between 1581 and 1591.

of celebrated French studies on witchcraft by such authorities as Bodin (1580), Le Loyer (1586), Crespet (1590), Del Rio (1599), Boguet (1602), and De Lancre (1612). Remy had much personal contact with witches. For example, as a child he had watched the trials of old women so accused. Again, in 1582, he personally prosecuted a beggar woman as a witch, because his eldest son had died some days after Remy refused her alms. When the plague hit Nancy in 1592, Remy left for the country, where he wrote his book. So eager was he to publish his warning about the evils of witchcraft that he neglected the formal organization of his work. As a result, the *Demonolatreiae* remained a hodgepodge of impressions, lecture notes, anecdotes, court records, and quotations, although Remy tried to categorize his material in three sections or books: (1) a study of Satanism, (2) an account of the activities of witches, stressing their sex life, and (3) examples and practical conclusions.

Typical of all demonologists is Remy's attempted use of rationality to prove and justify obscurantism. "Everything which is unknown," he wrote, "lies, as far as I am concerned, in the cursed domain of demonology; for there are no unexplained facts. Whatever is not normal is due to the Devil."

Thus Remy answered the question, Why should witches be punished? by arguing that laws existed ordering punishment, and that many authorities—Remy quoted altogether some 800—corroborated these laws. Along with his contemporary, Jean Bodin, Remy to some extent replaced the *Malleus Maleficarum* as the final authority on witch hunting.

Renata, Sister Maria. One of the later victims of the witch delusion, caught in the final swirl of ebb tide which sometimes sweeps with greater force just because it is on the way out, was the sub-prioress of the Premonstratensian convent of Unterzell, near Würzburg. Sister Maria Renata Sänger von Mossau, having successfully, strictly, and creditably devoted herself to the convent for fifty years, was accused of bewitching some hysterical nuns, tortured into fantastic confessions, beheaded, and burned as a witch on June 21, 1749.

For several years certain nuns had showed signs of demoniacal possession. Cecilia Pistorini, of an Italian family resident at Hamburg, was especially troubled with cramps and contortions and hallucinations. As one of the senior members of the convent, Sister Maria Renata had doubts of Cecilia's fitness to be professed, and she recommended further probation. In fact, she considered Cecilia gave way to hysteria and that her possession was pretended. Nevertheless, Cecilia became a nun in 1745. When other nuns copied her disturbed actions, shrieking during the service, writhing, and foaming at the mouth, and when one of the older nuns, on her deathbed, publicly accused the sub-prioress, Sister Maria Renata, of bewitching her, the prioress and the confessor had reluctantly to take notice and action, and withstand the inevitable scandal.

The abbot of the neighboring Premonstratensian monastery at Oberzell, Father Oswald Loschert, an assessor at the trial, wrote an eyewitness account of the whole affair, which he forwarded to the Empress Maria Theresa. Father Loschert was completely credulous as well as antagonistic to Sister Maria Renata. The nuns, he wrote—

preferred to suffer in patience rather than allow themselves to be persuaded that a religious, at any rate a person wearing the religious habit, could be guilty of such abominations. However, the demon declared by the mouth of a possessed nun that he seized Renata even in her mother's womb, that she was his slave and a cursed thing.

Priests attached to the convent increased their ceremonies and intensified the devotions to control the possession; finally, they tried exorcism. After three days, however, the nuns were worse than ever, and their contortions and shrieking became extreme. They displayed all the classical signs of demoniacal possession, about which they had read and been told all their lives. Through

their mouths the demons cried out, "Our time is come! Our time is come! We cannot lie longer hid." They even revealed their strange-sounding names—Datas Calvo, Dusacrus, Nataschurus, Nabascurus, Aatalphus, Elephatan. Wrote Abbot Loschert:

From this moment, no one could doubt that the six nuns were possessed by the devil. One could only in all humility wonder that heaven had permitted so terrible a curse to fall upon a convent where day and night the occupation of all was the praise of God and prayer. This hour, however, had been ordained by providence to expose that foul witch who hid her sorceries beneath the holy habit, to expel her from that fair community to

A death warrant signed by Nicholas Remy, Attorney General of Lorraine, on May 4, 1596, for a witch to be burned at Nancy, Lorraine.

"The undersigned Attorney General of Lorraine, who has witnessed the present examination and torture made by Messieurs the Provost and officers of justice of St.-Dié upon George de Haut, of Claingotte, held prisoner at the aforementioned St.-Dié on charges of witchcraft, of which he was apprized, to discover information about the fact, hearing, etc., and who has witnessed the statements, reading of depositions, confrontations, and procès-verbal of the torture given him, holds this person to have been duly arraigned and convicted of the aforesaid charges of witchcraft, for satisfaction of which crime it is deemed and judged that he be condemned to be burned alive, that he be bound to a stake expressly erected for the purpose at the appointed place for such executions, so that at least he will feel the flames keenly before being suffocated, his goods to be declared forfeit and confiscate to whom they belong, reasonable expenses for the trial first being deducted. Given at Nancy, May 4, 1596.   Remy."

which in spirit and in truth she had never belonged.

As visitor to the convent, Abbot Loschert made formal inquiries and, though Sister Maria denied all these charges, put her in confinement. Her room in the convent was searched, and ointments alleged to be witch salves, herbs supposed to be noxious, and a yellow robe said to be her sabbat-going dress were found and used as evidence against her. Over several months, 69-year-old Sister Maria Renata was interrogated and, finally, on the advice of the Jesuit theologians at the University of Würzburg, tortured until she made a confession. First, she received "twenty lashes with a consecrated rawhide [*Karbatsche*]," a new technique recently introduced into German torture from the Orient.

In her confession, Sister Maria gave the conventional summary of the crimes expected of a witch. She had given herself to Satan at the age of eight, been seduced at eleven, intrigued with two officers (demons in disguise) at thirteen, and as a teen-ager had learned the craft of Satanism. At nineteen, on Satan's orders, she entered the convent to bring about its destruction. She went out almost every night to a sabbat in Würzburg, rubbing her body with magic ointment, riding on a broomstick, and wearing the yellow robe found in her room. She publicly renounced God and the Church; she had been rebaptized with the name of Ema, had received the devil's marks, and copulated indiscriminately with devils. She had recruited three others to the Devil's service. In addition, she had bewitched several persons with sickness and caused six nuns to be possessed with demons, and had desecrated the host.

PART OF THE VERBATIM REPORTS OF HER TRIALS

Q. Why is she in prison?

A. Because of the godless life which she led.

Q. How could she have led or been led into a godless life, since she had been a nun in a convent for so long?

A. It had never been any different;

Prepared questions used at the trial of Sister Maria Renata in 1749. Her answers to these questions could be filled in at the left in the blank column or written on a separate sheet. The page is headed with the Jesuit initials, A.M.D.G. and B.V.I.H. From a manuscript in Cornell University Library.

because her vows were not taken through inner conviction, and she had always lived a godless life. While she had taken vows, yet her thoughts remained in the world, and her profession did not come from the heart. . . .

Q. Why did she enter the convent, if she had no desire for the religious life?

A. She was born to poor but noble parents. Consequently, her parents had easily seen that she would be cared for if she went into the convent.

Q. How then did she lead her godless life?

A. In witchcraft [*Zauberei*] and other devilish arts.

Q. Was she a witch?

A. Yes.

Q. Where did she learn this and from whom?

A. A grenadier had taught her in Vienna, where she and the whole household had gone with her father during the Hungarian War.

Q. How did she meet this grenadier?

A. As happens in wartime. The grenadier had often given her bread when she was hungry, and finally he promised to teach her something.

Q. What then did this grenadier finally teach her?

A. He gave her a paper, on which all sorts of letters were written. On this paper she had to draw a circle and stand inside it. In addition, she had received a charm [*Zetel*] with various words on it; and if she read these words, then she could make the passers-by in the street lame and crippled.

Q. Did she ever do such things and did any man become crippled?

A. Yes, she had done it several times; but whether the people had become lame she did not know.

Q. Where then are this circle and paper?

A. She had torn up and thrown away this circle and paper, when once she had acknowledged the devil and knew more [about witchcraft].

Q. Did she then sign the devil's book? Where and when?

A. Yes, when she had been conveyed from Vienna to Prague, where indeed this grenadier had taken her. This man had transported her to Prague to a room in a palace, where quite a gathering was assembled. The grenadier had brought her to the highest lord who sat in the midst, requesting him to accept her as one of his fellowship.

Q. Who then was this great lord?

A. Without doubt he was the devil.

Q. Did the devil then admit her into his fellowship?

A. No. He answered that she was still somewhat too young, and gave her a picture on which two witches were painted. On these two witches she had to write her name in ink.

Q. What did she use to make her signature?

A. Nothing. She had used her own blood to sign her pledge to him, namely, the devil.

Q. Whether she had there and then with her own blood signed herself to the devil?

A. Yes. In her fourteenth year, the forementioned grenadier had brought her to Prague in the above-mentioned salon, where she had been accepted by him and had inscribed herself with her own blood.

At the behest of the devil, she had registered herself in a big book, with blood from her hand between the little finger and the ring finger. Instead of Maria, she had written Ema Renata. By this act, in the presence of "many countesses and nobility from Vienna," she had to forswear the Holy Trinity and all the heavenly host. For this she received a new robe, in which she went to the witches' sabbat, and an ointment, powder, and charm with divers letters, with which she could bewitch people within the sound of her voice. In spite of her godlessness, she had entered the convent because of pressure from her parents. There she had so performed her religious functions that no one could notice her vicious life, to which the devil introduced her. So she had amazingly desecrated seven consecrated hosts; four of these she had concealed in her arms and in her feet, one she had thrown into the cesspool, and another into the sea, and the last one she had taken with her to the witches' sabbat.

Q. How or in what way did she hide these hosts?

A. She had made a cut in her arms and legs with a penknife, and had placed the holy hosts under the skin, lifting it up, and thus she had concealed them. She had endured terrible pains until the wounds were healed. [*She displayed the scars.*] At the sabbat, the hosts were stuck through with nails, from which spots clear water flowed.

Under questioning, she told of her journey to the witches' sabbat, which corresponded to customary accounts.

Q. Does she believe that this was not a delusion, but actually so?

A. Often it was a delusion, but more often it was truth.

In an agreeable forest, or else in a large, lovely meadow, high honor was lavished on the devil, who was present in the form of a great lord and potentate. Among those present were Count von X. from Prague and other notables from Vienna. They ate biscuits, anise bread, and such like, drank sour wine, and entertained themselves with dancing, leaping, and other revels to the music of the devils. Some of the dancers were dressed, but the majority stark naked. Once she got a gold thaler from the devil. She named two additional participants, one a nun and the other a mass priest. The Lord Chancellor Reibelt had let loose a severe inquisition against this priest. Every Monday the devil visited her in the convent.

Q. What did he do with her?

A. Every Monday he lay with her for fornication.

Q. How was such a thing possible, since the devil was a spirit and unserviceable for such depraved acts?

A. He always had a body and was only too real, and he copulated with her; but she experienced horrible and most intense pain. He had often stayed with her two or three hours without anyone knowing it.

Now came leading questions concerning her bewitching the nuns. She confessed everything. Her spells consisted of "disturbance of the mind, and paroxysms of the body, pain from this, and torments of all five senses." Out of envy she had also bewitched three court ladies and a knight. Her enmity against the nuns began when they confessed to the abbot of the Premonstratensian monastery, whom she did not like. God did not allow her to make him lame and blind through sorcery.

A. She could not cure those whom she had bewitched, for, as soon as her witchcraft had been revealed, she had immediately burned her robe, ointment, charm, etc. Now she could no longer harm any other person.

Q. How then are such persons to be freed from these evils?

A. Through the ceremonies of holy church, exorcism, and religious means.

Q. How then was her depraved life found out?

A. Through cats, which she was forced to give up.

Q. What sort of cats were these?

A. The convent and all the rooms were infested with so many vermin, mice, and rats, that they did not know what to do. They had complained so much to the abbot that he had then allowed each nun to keep a cat in her room to exterminate the vermin.

Q. How then was her wickedness discovered through such cats?

A. Instead of one, she had kept three cats. However, these three cats were three devils, who spoke to her in her room as well as in the cloisters. The nuns had heard these cats talking in the evening and at night and were concerned about them. One nun told another and complained about this talking, and the convent was in great terror, so they notified the abbot that her three cats talked.

As a result, the abbot had all the cats removed and gave her a "most stinging" reprimand. Since her arrest, the devil had not visited her.

After hearing this confession, six priests, including Abbot Loschert, the almoner of the convent (also hostile to Sister Maria), and two Jesuits, condemned her on thirteen counts of sorcery, heresy, and apostasy. The Bishop of Würzburg confirmed the sentence and defrocked her on May 28, 1749. His secular court ordered her burned as a witch, but the Bishop, "in consideration of the extreme youth of the accused when she was first seduced to the heinous sin of witchcraft," let her be first executed.

Sentence of the Inquisition pronounced against Sister Maria Renata Sänger von Mossau for witchcraft on May 28, 1749. She was defrocked and turned over for trial to a secular court, thus assuring her condemnation to death. From a manuscript in Cornell University Library.

On June 17, 1749, Maria Renata, now no longer a nun, clad in a long black robe, white apron and a white neckerchief, and a white and black hood, was conducted by Father Maurus and Father Gaar to Marienberg. Here she was beheaded, and her body thrown on a bonfire of tar barrels and wood. The executioner, according to an eyewitness report, cut off her head so dexterously that the onlookers roared their bravos in admiration. During the burning, the Jesuit, Father George Gaar, preached a sermon justifying the execution, relating details of her wickedness and her sin of witchcraft. So proud was he of his speech that he published it in German and (in translation) in Italian. However, this dissemination provoked some controversy, in which the Italian jurist Tartarotti joined, and Father Gaar became the recipient of unfavorable comment. Shocking as the trial is, it is a sign of the change in public opinion that opponents were able to ward off an epidemic of similar trials.

Renfrew Witches: see Bargarran Impostor.

Reynie, Monsieur Nicholas de la: see Chambre Ardente Affair.

Rio, Del: see Del Rio, Martin.

Rule, Margaret. Cotton Mather called his adversary Robert Calef's work on witchcraft an "abominable bundle of lies, written on purpose, with a quill under a special energy and management of Satan, to damnify my precious opportunities of glorifying my Lord." What provoked this outburst was Calef's skepticism about Mather's account of the alleged diabolical possession of Margaret Rule, who, after a period of depression, had been carried shrieking from Mather's church in North Boston on September 10, 1693. Mather had circulated a report in manuscript, apparently to whip up a witch panic in Boston. Margaret provided him with names of witches, including one woman recently freed from such charges, but Mather was reluctant to initiate charges on spectral evidence alone. He recognized the accused, however, as the "sort of wretches who for these many years have gone under as violent presumptions of witchcraft as perhaps any creatures yet living upon earth." Calef, to be sure, did not believe in the power of witches to command devils to possess people.

The diagnosis of Margaret Rule paralleled that of Mercy Short. The outward symptoms were analogous in the young women, "resembling [each other] in almost all the circumstances . . . that the relation I [Mather] have given of the one, would almost serve as the full history of the other." She had spastic fits, clenching her teeth to refuse food for several days, at other times gulping as if swallowing quantities of liquid, and manifesting black and blue marks from some invisible pinching. This seventeen-year-old also produced poltergeist-like phenomena, including stealing Mather's sermons and subsequently finding them in the street, the presence of a small moving object [an imp!] on her bed, her production (apparently from nowhere) of pins, and her levitation from bed to ceiling. Like Mercy Short, one of the bewitched Salem girls, Margaret had hallucinations, not only of the inevitable black man or devil, but of a White Spirit (discussed by Increase Mather, *Illustrious Providences*).

> She says that she could never see his face, but that she had a frequent view of his bright, shining and glorious garments; he stood by her bedside continually heartening and comforting of her and counselling her to maintain her faith and hope in God.

Mather thought Calef's commentary on his description of Margaret so full of mistakes and falsehoods that "were they willful and designed, [they] might justly be termed gross lies." He was particularly incensed when Calef reported that Mather quietened the girl by rubbing "her stomach, her breast not covered with the bedclothes, and bid others do so too." When a girl offered to help thus, Margaret cried: " 'Don't you meddle with me!' and hastily pushed away her hand." Nor did Calef indicate sympathy toward Margaret by his observation that thirty or forty spectators came daily to watch Mather's exorcism.

> Soon after [the ministers] were gone, the afflicted desired the women to be gone, saying that the company of the men was not offensive to her; and having hold of the hand of a young man, said to have been her sweetheart formerly, who was withdrawing, she pulled him again into his seat, saying he should not go tonight.

A few nights later, again after Mather had left, Calef found her engaging another young man, "saying that she liked his company, and . . . she would not have him go till she was well, adding, 'For I shall die when you are gone!' " Mather issued a warrant for libel against Calef but failed to press it.

Perhaps because of his medical training, Mather was aware that even then some witnesses doubted witchcraft as the cause of Margaret's fits, so he stressed that it was "unchristian and uncivil, yea, a most unreasonable thing to imagine that the fits of the young woman were but mere impostures." In one of her "laughing times," Margaret "said she wondered any people should be so wicked as to think she was not afflicted, but to think she dissembled." After two or three months, Margaret's fits passed, Mather believed, as the consequence of his prayers and fastings. He was indeed vitally concerned with her recovery, for, very ironically, "the young woman . . . began in her fits to complain that [he] threatened her and molested her."

One of the more interesting features of the Margaret Rule case is Mather's report of the New England Puritan version of the classic pact with the Devil.

> These cursed specters [demons] now brought unto her a book about a cubit long, a book red and thick, but not very broad, and they demanded of her that she would set her hand to that book, or touch it at least with her hand, as a sign of her becoming a servant of the Devil.

This book is frequently met in confessions and charges in American witch trials.

Sabbat. Of all the aspects of witchcraft, the sabbat has attracted the most attention, from both the curious layman as well as the professional demonologist. The sabbat combined into one system old legends of sorcery and new ideas of heresy: blasphemous parodies of Christian rites, allegedly licentious orgies otherwise considered taboo subjects, an underground conspiracy against law and order, aided by all the powers of evil, and the theological twist that these assemblies of witches and demons were the nadir of Satanism.

The conception of the sabbat seems to

have been fabricated during the fourteenth and fifteenth centuries, largely by the investigators and judges connected with the Inquisition. A rudimentary form was introduced at a trial at Toulouse in 1335. Martin le Franc (about 1440) included in his *Champion des dames* a confession of a developed sabbat from an old woman who said she had attended such meetings since she was sixteen, which places the sabbat as early as 1400. To the early demonologist Johannes Nider (1435), the sabbat was unknown, but the anonymous French tract *Errores Gazariorum* (1450) has a detailed account of the "synagogue." Nicholas Jacquier about 1458 used the actual word "sabbat," although his account was sketchy; "sabbat" also appeared in a report of the witch persecutions at Lyons in 1460 (*La Vauderye de Lyonois*). In northern Italy about 1460, two inquisitors managed to gain admittance to a sabbat; however, the enraged crowd of witches discovered and attacked them so that they died before they could report their experiences. Pope Innocent's Bull of 1484, however, made no allusion to the sabbat, and the *Malleus Maleficarum* was also reticent. Yet by the sixteenth century the sabbat was an established part of witchcraft. Bernard de Como (1510) and Bartolommeo Spina (1523) both held advanced ideas of the sabbat. Complicated and detailed analyses were found in the works of the classic demonologists, for example, in the French writers, Bodin (1580), Remy (1595), and De Lancre (1612), and in the Italian, Guazzo (1608).

Various derivations have been given for the word. It may best be regarded as simply the Hebrew word for the seventh day, transferred by hostile association to witches—Jews, witches, and Mohammedans were three traditional targets for Catholic opposition. In early works, even the word *synagoga* was often used for sabbat.

More important than its derivation or definition, however, were all the connotations that came to surround the word—not simply an assembly of witches to honor the devil, but also the celebration of diabolical rites and the indulgence of licentious orgies. Three trends were fused.

1. First, when the idea of witches as an organized group or sect was formulated about 1400, largely by the Inquisition, it was easy to transfer to them rites and ceremonies which, because the witches were traitors to God, could be pictured as inverse parodies of the Christian liturgy. (Centuries later, the black mass became a sophisticated mocking of the Catholic mass.) Many accounts were quite humdrum, and the sabbat was an anti-Christian ritual clandestinely conducted in a church [see Pact]. Inquisitor Sebastian Michaëlis, for example, had the witches singing hymns: "The magicians and those that can read [music] sing certain psalms as they do in church, especially *'Laudate Dominum de coelis'* . . . transferring all to the praise of Lucifer" —*Admirable History*, 1613. In Protestant Scotland in 1678, the devil administered to the Loudian witches "the communion or holy sacrament, the bread was like wafers, the drink was sometimes blood, sometimes black moss water."

2. Second, to excite popular curiosity and, it was hoped, hostility to this new sect of witches, theologians attributed to them abominations previously attached to other heresies, such as the Albigensians, Cathars, or Bulgarians (from whom the modern word *buggery* is derived). Thus, about 1336 and again in 1387, are seen premonitions of the witches' sabbat in the secret assemblies of the Austrian Waldenses, which ended in indiscriminate intercourse; or in the similar confessions extracted from the heretical Cathari in the mid-fifteenth century, or from the Italian Fraticelli (the strict Franciscans who could not tolerate the laxity of the regular friars). The Fraticelli were likewise accused of squeezing babies to death in their hands, and then burning the bodies to make a sacramental powder. At the close of the fifteenth century, Pope Innocent VIII organized a crusade against the Waldenses of Dauphiné and Savoy, and unearthed, he said, the synagogue of Satan.

3. Third, and less important, old classical and pagan associations gathered round the theological conception of a sabbat. Pe-

"When worshiping the Devil, the witches assume different postures. Sometimes they beg on bended knees; sometimes they fall down on their back; sometimes they kick their legs in the air and bend their head to the belly, always moving so that the chin points to the sky."—Guazzo (1626).

tronius, Apuleius, and Horace had all described a kind of sabbat, perhaps recollected from old feasts of Bacchus and Priapus. Throughout the early Middle Ages, from about 1100, scattered comments appeared on nocturnal assemblies, all of which probably contributed to the development of the idea of a sabbat. Such, for example, was Odericus Vitalis' curious story of a throng of men and women, on foot and riding, of all ranks and conditions, traveling through the night. They said they were spirits, suffering pain for the sins they did on earth. Walter Mapes, a little later, alluded to the legend of the Host of Herla (an Anglo-Saxon king), which traversed the skies at night—a host which after 200 years' feasting with the gnomes was forced to remain on horseback. These riders were last reported seen on December 19, 1154. Similar apparitions were seen in Brittany. Other groups of nocturnal voyagers included the harmless good women who followed Dame Habounde, Domina Abundia or Lady Abundance, an extension of the Roman goddess Hera, conceived as a kind of feminine Santa Claus. Many women, said Giacopo Passavanta (mid-fourteenth century), imagined they joined this company and did wonderful things. That little trouble resulted for such deluded women is evi-

dence that the heretical witches' sabbat was not yet developed (1353).

Some writers linked to witchcraft the two traditional druid festivals, October 31, Allhallows Eve, and April 30, the eve of May Day, or the Walpurgis Night, the vigil of St. Walburga, a Devonshire saint who reputedly died in Germany in A.D. 777. In addition, *grand sabbats* were supposed to take place on the four pagan seasonal festivals (which had been incorporated into the Christian calendar), loosely associated with witchcraft: the winter festival of February 2 (Candlemas), the spring festival of June 23 (Eve of St. John the Baptist), the summer festival of August 1 (Lammas Day), and the fall festival of December 21 (St. Thomas). The Scottish Forfar witches in 1661 allegedly met at great sabbats on Candlemas, Holy Cross (May 3), Lammas, and All Saints (November 1). Occasional mention is made of national or regional gatherings of witches on these or similar festivals at such fearful locations as the Brocken or Blocksburg in the Harz Mountains in Germany, the Venusberg mountain in central Germany (Geiler von Kaysersberg and Albertini), the Heuberg in the southern Black Forest, the river Jordan or the oak at Beneventura (Spina), the Swedish Blocula —a house with a wide meadow, and the Puy-de-Dôme in the Auvergne (France), mentioned by Raymond and Guazzo. Such associations, however, were largely folk beliefs, were seldom introduced in trials or treatises, and were not essential to the theory of witchcraft.

For convenience of treatment, the sabbat may be considered under five heads:

1. The assembly for the sabbat. [See further, detailed entries for (Flying) Ointment and Transvection.]
2. The homage to the Devil. Religious worship of the Devil reputedly came first at the sabbat; at this time the public profession of the pact would be administered, and the new witches signed with the devil's mark.
3. The banquet.
4. The festivities, especially dancing.
5. Indiscriminate intercourse, the con-

The witches' sabbat on the Brocken. From the Douce Collection, Bodleian Library, Oxford.

clusion of every sabbat. [For further detailed discussion, see Incubus, Succubus, Sexual Relations with Devils.]

1. *The assembly*. The witch made her own arrangements to attend the sabbat; she smeared herself with flying ointment to facilitate transvection, and rode on a forked stick or broom through the air. Alternatively, she might receive from the devil a goat, ram, or dog for this purpose. Sabbats were held in various places—crossroads, woods, wild fields, or even churches.

The demonologists were not agreed that any special day of the week was favored for the assemblies, save that Saturday was less often mentioned because it was sacred to the Virgin Mary. Nicholas Jacquier (about 1458) gave Thursday; Bernard de Como (1510) also suggested "the night preceding Friday." Spina (1523) said Wednesday and Sunday were the days for sabbats; Louis Gaufridi at his trial testified to Wednesday and Friday; the Essex witches, according to Hopkins, met on Friday; De Lancre said witches met on Mondays, Wednesdays, and Fridays. These were the three days most often mentioned in the confessions of witches tried at Bamberg. Guazzo believed the sabbat was celebrated variously according to the region: in Italy on Thursdays, in Lorraine on Wednesdays. Boguet, devoting a whole chapter to *"Du jour du sabbat,"* specified Thursday, but he also found that witches assembled on Monday, Friday, and

Sunday nights—in fact, they gathered whenever they pleased.

Remy was one of the minority who believed that most sabbats were held on Saturdays. A curious rationalization for this day was given by a nineteenth-century historian of the Béarn (the De Lancre country), the Abbé Cartier, who suggested that the *bal masqué* of the peasants formed the basis for accounts of the sabbat. Their dances were always held on Saturday nights, so the participants could rest on the official Sunday holiday, and at night, because that was their only free time.

The revels of gypsies, or beggars, George B. Harrison suggested, gave rise to tales of sabbats in England. He quoted the diary of John Manningham for 1603:

> About three years since there were certain rogues in Berkshire, which usually frequented certain sheepcotes every night. A justice having intelligence of their rabblement, purposing to apprehend them, went strong, and about midnight found them in the sheepcote, some six couple men and women dancing naked, the rest lying by them.

Sabbats were always held at night. Traditionally women first went to bed and then left for the sabbat. Guazzo and Remy set the time at two hours before midnight; most of the Bamberg witches at eleven at night. The sabbat lasted till dawn or cockcrow. One witch named Latoma told Remy

The sabbat, a Brueghelesque fantasy of witchcraft. From the Douce Collection, Bodleian Library, Oxford.

that the crowing of the cock was the signal to terminate the gathering.

There was never any prescribed number of witches attending a sabbat; it depended on the imagination of the witch and the prosecutor. Nowhere is there any serious evidence for a coven of thirteen. At St.-Dié, according to court depositions, 50 to 100 witches assembled together. Some few judges reported huge mass meetings. A famous physician of Ferrara told Spina of 6,000 people dancing and feasting near bonfires at night. One unusual confession in 1440 mentioned 10,000 women riding on sticks to an assembly at Valpute (Burgundy). De Lancre, using the confessions he extorted from his victims, let his fancy run wild: "The sabbat resembles a fair of merchants, mingling together, angry and half crazed, arriving from all quarters, a surging crowd of some one hundred thousand devotees of Satan."

As the demonologists gained experience, the sabbat became excessively formalized. Sister Madeleine de Demandolx [see Aix-en-Provence Nuns], possessed by devils, told the Inquisitor Sebastian Michaëlis of the three social classes at the sabbats, ranging from "people of sordid and base condition" to "gentlemen." Sister Madeleine confessed:

Since my conversion [to witchcraft] there is a sabbat held every day, but before, it was kept but three times in the week, beginning at eleven of the clock at night, and continuing until three of the clock after midnight. . . . The sorcerers by the power of a certain ointment which they use are carried in the air by devils in the midway, and passing by him they bow unto him, and make him reverence, and so are hurried to the synagogue at the place designed.

Where, being assembled, the hags and witches, who are people of a sordid and base condition, and whose trade and custom is to murder infants, and to bring them to the sabbat, after they have been buried in their grave, are the first that come to adore the Prince of the Synagogue . . . next they go and worship the devil who is seated in a throne like a prince. In the second place come the sor-

cerers and sorceresses, who are people of a middle condition, whose office is to bewitch and spread abroad charms. . . . In the third place come the magicians who are gentlemen and people of a higher rank; their office is to blaspheme God as much as they can.

2. *The homage to the Devil.* Whether or not special observances, such as rebaptisms by the devil or witches' marriages, were to be celebrated, all sabbats included a ritual of allegiance to Satan. In England, where the sabbat played a minor part in witch trials, the reverence was somber and confined in a Protestant tradition. For example, King James I in his *Demonology* (1597) has Epistemon, the expert in these matters, describe a sabbat thus:

As to their consultations thereupon, they use them oftest in the churches, where they convene for adoring; at what time their master enquiring of them what they would be at, every one of them proposes unto him what wicked turn they would have done, either for obtaining of riches, or for revenging them upon any whom they have malice at, who granting their demand (as no doubt willingly he will, since it is to do evil), he teacheth them the means, whereby they may do the same.

Some witches, such as those tried at Bamberg, confessed that the devil called the roster of those present, reading off the names from a red book. This role was allegedly taken by the recorder of the North Berwick Witches, John Fian. At this time, any weddings between witches would be celebrated. "In place of the customary wedding gifts, the couple were only required to stoop down and blow on each other's posteriors."

Guazzo described the Continental sabbat, centering round the obeisance paid the devil in his classic manifestation as a goat. In his *Compendium Maleficarum* (1626), this adoration is depicted by a cut:

When these members of the devil have met together, they generally light a foul and horrid fire. The devil is president of the assembly and sits on a throne, in some terrible shape, as of a goat or a

Obeisance to the Devil, from a fifteenth-century French manuscript on witchcraft in the Bodleian Library, Oxford.

dog; and they approach him to adore him, but not always in the same manner. For sometimes they bend their knees as suppliants, and sometimes they stand with their backs turned, and sometimes they kick their legs high up so that their heads are bent back and their chins point to the sky. They turn their backs and, going backwards like crabs, put out their hands behind them to touch him in supplication. When they speak they turn their faces to the ground; and they do all things in a manner altogether foreign to the use of other men.

Then came the *osculum infame* or *osculum obscoenum*, the celebrated kiss of shame:

> Then they offer him pitch-black candles, or infants' navel cords; and kiss him upon the buttocks in sign of homage [*ad signum homagii eum in podicem osculantur*]. Having committed these and similar execrable abominations, they proceed to other infamies.

The kiss was featured prominently by most authorities; the circumspection of the eminent lawyer, Jean Bodin, was unusual: "There is no greater disgrace, dishonor, or villainy than that which these witches endure when they have to adore Satan in the guise of a stinking goat, and to kiss him in

that place which modesty forbids writing or mentioning." The kissing even appeared in Scottish trials, when, for example, Agnes Sampson swore "the devil caused all the company to come and kiss his arse, which they said was cold like ice."

The synthetic character of the sabbat is indicated by the fact that the same accusations of the kiss of shame were made against the Waldenses, and the Knights Templars in 1307. Their leaders were tortured by the Inquisition to force confessions very similar to those drawn from witches. Among the charges were trampling the cross, the obscene kiss, veneration of an idol (sometimes a cat), sodomy, and possession of devils as familiars. Just like many witches, Templars recanted their confessions at the stake. Sorcerers are lumped together with the heretical Cathari and Waldenses in the *Errores Gazariorum* (1450); and in the district of Lyons, throughout the fifteenth century, witches were called Vaudois.

3. *The banquet.* The demonologists inflated the sabbat into an orgy of gluttony and lust, but unwilling, even in their own filthy imaginations, to allow their victims the slightest enjoyment, promptly proceeded to force confessions that the banquets were insipid and copulation painful. Yet Alphonso de Castro (1547) maintained that voluptuous pleasures were the main incentives for women to become witches. Guazzo, again, has given a classic account of the feasting:

> There are tables placed and drawn up, and they sit and start to eat of the food which the demon has provided, or which they have themselves brought. But all who have sat down to such tables confess that the feasts are all foul either in appearance or in smell, so that they would easily nauseate the most hungry stomach. . . . They say that there is plenty of everything except bread and salt.

Guazzo was paralleled by Remy: "They say the taste is disagreeable, harsh, and bitter, so that they are immediately forced to spit it out in disgust."

Sister Madeleine de Demandolx about 1611 furnished fuller details:

The drink which they have is malmsey, to provoke and prepare the flesh to luxurious wantonness. . . . The meat they ordinarily eat is the flesh of young children, which they cook and make ready in the synagogue, sometimes bringing them thither alive by stealing them from the houses where they have opportunity to come. They have no use of knives at table for fear lest they should be laid across . . . they have also no salt, which figureth out wisdom and understanding; neither know they the use of olives or oil which represent mercy.

After the banquet, the witches might partake of the magic cake, made of black millet mixed with flesh of unbaptized infants, supposed to induce taciturnity under torture.

The first confession of a sabbat banquet in England, coming after fifty years of witch hunting, occurred in the extended trial of the Lancashire Witches in 1612. One of the chief defendants, Old Chattox, told of her family's meeting with that of another witch, Old Demdike, at the Malking Tower.

> There was victuals, viz., flesh, butter, cheese, bread and drink . . . and after their eating, the devil called Fancy, and the other spirit calling himself Tibbe, carried the remnant away. And she said, although they did eat, they were never the fuller nor better for the same; and that at their banquet, the said spirits gave them light to see what they did, although they neither had fire nor candle light; and that they were both she spirits and devils.

The charges brought by fourteen-year-old Grace Sowerbutts against the Salmesbury witches (involved with the Lancashire group), of dancing and copulation in a Continental-style sabbat were later found to be prompted by a Jesuit. Anti-Roman sentiment saved the accused. At the second Lancashire trials in 1638, the fabricated Pendle Swindle, a young impostor concocted a version of a sabbat attended by sixty persons, decorated with adolescent sexual fantasies of flying butter and milk. The comparative absence of sabbats in English witchcraft is remarkable, for the Latin authorities (such as the *Malleus Maleficarum* and Bodin) had wide circulation in England, and are quoted by most of the English writers. In Scotland, however, a sabbat was described at the trial of the North Berwick Witches in 1590; and in 1661 the Forfar witches first drank ale and followed up with whiskey [*aqua vitae*], "and thus made themselves merry."

4. *The festivities.* Following the banquet came "dances, which are performed in a circle but always to the left. . . . Sometimes they dance before eating and sometimes after the repast. . . . All the rites are performed with the utmost absurdity in a frenzied ring with hands joined and back to back"—*Compendium Maleficarum*, 1626. Back-to-back dancing was one form of medieval folk dancing, often practiced by the rougher elements in towns; it was apparently considered indecent. It was first mentioned in connection with sabbats by Paulus Grillandus (1525), perhaps to indicate the reversal of the customary Christian procedures, similar to making the sign of

A young seated witch goes through the ritual of lighting a candle, while grasping a mock rosary of bones and dice, held by a buxom lascivious witch rising from the ground on the right. At the left, a third witch holds up a bowl of exhumed bones to complete the spell. By Hans Baldung Grün.

Tenier's Departure for the Sabbat.

the cross from right to left, or jumbling the words of consecration at the mass (*"hoc est corpus"*) into hocus-pocus.

Music was provided by some of the witches: "viols and other instruments, which are brought thither by those that were skilled to play upon them." (Michaëlis) In Scotland a jew's harp was played. Guazzo included an illustration of a musician seated in a tree. Henry More, in his *Antidote Against Atheism* (1653), told a fable of Remy's with evident approval:

As a boy, John of Heinbach, also seated in a tree, had piped for a sabbat. To the lad, the dancing seemed so ridiculous that he said to himself, "Good God, what a mad company have we here." The holy name made the whole company vanish, and John fell out of the tree. Henry More found tangible proof of the dances of witches and devils with cloven hooves, evidence which, as a master of arts of Cambridge University, More considered irrefutable.

Add unto all this, that there was found in the place where they danced a round circle wherein there was the manifest marks of the treading of cloven feet, which were seen from the day after Nicolea had discovered the business till the next winter that the plough cut them out; these things happened in the year 1590. [See illustration in Demonologists.]

5. *Indiscriminate intercourse.* The preoccupation of celibate priests with the niceties of intercourse was insatiable; since this subject is discussed in other entries, only specimen examples are given here. "The dancing over, the witches gave themselves over to copulation: the son did not spare the mother, neither the brother the sister, nor the father the daughter; incest went on everywhere." Most witches, according to the demonologists, found intercourse painful. De Lancre, for example, gave the sworn testimony of sixteen-year-old Jeanette d'Abadie:

At the coupling, she deposed she had seen every one mix incestuously and in violation of the laws of nature . . . she blamed herself for having been deflowered by Satan and carnally known an infinity of times [*une infinité de fois*] by one of her relations and others who condescended to go in to her. She said she feared intercourse with the devil, because his member was scaly and caused extreme pain; furthermore, his semen was extremely cold, so cold that she had never become pregnant by him; in fact, she was never made fat by the other ordinary men at the sabbat.

Inquisitor Michaëlis introduced a new aspect into the accounts. Sister Madeleine de Demandolx confessed to him she went every night to a sabbat, and every night there was a different form of sexual activity:

Upon Sundays they pollute themselves by their filthy copulation with devils that are succubi and incubi; upon Thursdays they contaminate themselves with sodomy; upon Saturdays they do prostitute themselves to abominable bestiality; upon other days they use the ordinary course which nature prompteth unto them.

This account of the sabbat may be concluded with a confession reproduced by De Lancre which covered the whole range of activities, starting with the preparations for transvection and finishing with copulation. It could be duplicated many times:

Marguerite Brement, wife of Noel Laveret, deposed that last Monday, after dusk, she had been with her mother Marion at a gathering, near the mill of Franquis de Longny in a meadow. Her mother had taken a broom between her thighs, and, saying words she did not understand, they were both suddenly carried through the air to a place where they found Jeanne Robert, Jeanne Guillemin, Marie the wife of Simon d'Agneau, and Guillemette wife of a man named Le Gras, and each one had her own broomstick. In this place there were also six devils, in the form of men, but very ugly to look on. . . . When the dancing was done, the devils slept with them and enjoyed their company. One of them, who was her partner in the dancing, took her and kissed her twice, and cohabited with her for the period of over half an hour; but his emission was extremely icy. Jeanne Guillemin likewise deposed about this matter, and said the two of them were joined in the sex act for a good half hour, and that her devil discharged very cold semen.

Illustrations of sabbats in the standard works on witchcraft depicted the typical alleged crimes and so helped foster the witch mania. A very curious plate was that included in the 1613 edition of the *Tableau des mauvais anges* by De Lancre, now very rare. Another engraving [see Treves Witch Trials] gave a German engraver's idea of the sabbat about 1594. These two illustrations show the resemblance in the two countries. A hundred years later, public opinion had changed, and attacks on the theory were illustrated by witty satires. The German translation of the *Displaying of Supposed Witchcraft* (1677) by John Webster was provided with a frontispiece (1719). On the wall (in the engraving) hangs a portrait of Mr. Oufle, alluding to the Abbé Laurent Bordelon's satire of 1710. Bordelon's *L'Histoire des imaginations extrava-*

"The black goat carried a lighted candle in his fundament, and all the witches had candles which they lighted at his, and danced in a circle back to back."—Francis Hutchinson (1720).

gantes de Monsieur Oufle was itself adorned with a mocking fantasy of the doings of witches.

The power of pictures is shown by what George L. Burr called "one of the most remarkable books in the history of witchcraft." *Christlich Bedencken und Erinnerung von Zauberey*, printed in 1585, with a second edition in 1586 at Strasbourg, was written by "Lercheimer," a pseudonym to protect the identity of the author, Hermann Witekind, a professor at Heidelberg University and a friend of Melanchthon. Since his book was really a "bold and startlingly eloquent protest against the worst features of the persecution," he concealed its true nature by an engraving on the title page of witches and devils in a ring dance. Witekind hoped that readers would be deceived by this trick and start reading; only later in the book would they be confronted by its arguments.

Salmesbury Witches: see Lancashire Witches.

St. Osyth Witches.

The use of evidence in this trial would lead one to suppose that in England [in 1582] no rules of evidence were yet in existence. The testimony of children ranging in age from six to nine was eagerly received. No objection indeed was made to the testimony of a neighbor who professed to have overheard what he deemed an incriminating statement . . . Expert evidence was introduced in a roundabout way by the statement offered in court that a physician had suspected that a certain case was witchcraft. Nothing was excluded.

Such is Wallace Notestein's description of the trial of the witches of St. Osyth at the county sessions at Chelmsford in 1582. According to the pamphlet written by the presiding judge, Bryan Darcy, thirteen women were accused, ten with bewitching to death. Reginald Scot, moved by such conduct to write his famous attack on belief in witches two years later, says seventeen or eighteen were executed. However, recent research by Ewen into the Essex records has shown only two women hanged, and the rest reprieved (if found Guilty) or acquitted.

Nevertheless, in spite of the few executions, it still remains, as Kittredge described it, "one of the most notorious of Elizabethan cases." With its psychologically interesting women informers, the St. Osyth case is a barometer of English witchcraft, falling between the famous Chelmsford trial of 1566 and the equally famous trial of the Warboys Witches in 1593. It illustrates the spread of credulity and the formation of a specifically indigenous tradition of sorcery, without transvection, metamorphosis, or sabbats—not noted in trials until May 19, 1612 (and a tame affair these Lancashire witches had, dining on English mutton)— a tradition parochial in outlook, and limited to petty acts of spite and strange domestic animals who served as familiars to do the witches' malicious biddings. The abnegation of the rules of evidence shows where the lead given at Chelmsford by the Attorney General was to wind up. In 1566 twelve-year-old Agnes Brown had been allowed to introduce spectral evidence; in 1579 a four-year-old had cried, "Away with the witch"; by 1593 the Throckmorton children had established the formula used by Abigail Williams and Ann Putnam a century later. By 1582 the search for witch's marks was routine, and often conducted by accusing witches (as with Ursula Kempe and Cicely Celles). These trends were accentuated by the St. Osyth affair; yet, although presented with evidence of this nature, the jury found four Not Guilty.

The origin of this hunt which swept through the remote marshland villages of the Essex coast—the region so lovingly described in Paul Gallico's *The Snow Goose* (1941)—was an everyday occurrence. Ursula Kempe (no better than she should have been) eked out a living by nursing and "unwitching." A child being sick, Ursula had cured the lad by incantations. "I warrant thee, I, thy child shall do well enough." she had told Davy's mother, Grace Thorlowe. When refused the nursing of Grace's newborn daughter, she was indignant; and when the baby fell out of its crib and broke its neck, "Ursley" was suspected of witchcraft. However, soon afterward, Grace accepted Ursula's help in alleviating her arthritis, but, refusing to pay the witch her fee of twelve pence, she found the "lameness in her bones" returning. Grace then complained to her master, Bryan Darcy, a county sessions judge. After a preliminary examination by the local justices of the peace, Ursula Kempe was committed to the county sessions. At this point, the witch trial commences.

Having induced Ursula's bastard eight-year-old son to tell some fantastic stories about his mother, Judge Darcy broke down Ursula's denials with false promises of clemency: "They which do confess the truth of their doings, they shall have much favor; but the other they shall be burned and hanged." Mother Kempe, "bursting out with weeping," elaborated her son's description of familiars and then named some of her acquaintances as witches. So Elizabeth Bennet, Alice Hunt and her sister Margery Sammon, and Alice Newman, all of St. Osyth, came before the court. In turn, these women implicated themselves and others. Alice Hunt dragged in not only her sister (who was thus twice accused) but Joan Pechey. Margery Sammon hit back at her sister, and confirmed Joan Pechey. Alice Newman named Elizabeth Bennet as a witch. And so it went on.

In a short time, Judge Darcy had uncovered a nest of witches. Indictments are extant for fourteen women, most of them pretty disreputable and impoverished characters. Their names are not especially important; what happened to the women is important:

Two were not indicted, for No True Bill was found, although one of the accused, Margery Sammon, herself the daughter of a reputed witch, made a confession.

Two were discharged, for no indictment had been made. They were held in prison on suspicion of divers felonies, which both denied. Judge Darcy heard charges of bewitching to death two people and bewitching cattle, against one of these women, but the jail delivery roll notes that nothing evil warranting further imprisonment was found against either of them.

Four were acquitted—these had entered initial pleas of Not Guilty. Three were indicted on charges of bewitching to death, and evidence against two was taken from a seven-year-old daughter and an eight-year-old granddaughter. Two of the women confessed during the trial to damaging property. In one case, the accusation concerned a death five years earlier.

Four were convicted after pleading Not Guilty, but were reprieved. It is curious that Alice Newman, charged for a joint crime with Ursula Kempe and likewise found Guilty, was reprieved, whereas Mother Kempe was hanged. According to Judge Darcy, Alice Newman was further charged (although the indictments have not been found) with bewitching to death four other persons and her own husband, "as it is thought." Agnes Glascock was formally indicted on three counts, all of bewitching to death. The indictment against Cicely Celles was likewise bewitching to death. The fourth reprieve is not clear: Joan Turner was apparently charged with bewitching (*per fascinacione*), sentenced, and returned to prison for a year.

Two were hanged: Elizabeth Bennet indicted for killing a man and his wife, who died a few weeks before the trial, and (according to Darcy) two others. She confessed. Ursula Kempe was indicted for three deaths occurring between October 1580 and February 1582. She eventually confessed, was found Guilty on all counts, and hanged.

This breakdown of the disposition of the accused illustrates Ewen's contention that the proportion of executions to charges was relatively small: in the counties bordering London, when tried by regular justices, only 19 per cent (from 1558 to 1736). Between 1598 and 1607, however, Ewen finds 41 per cent of those indicted were hanged. Again in 1645 the percentage was very high, thanks to the work of Matthew Hopkins.

In most of the English trials, the reason for a woman's being accused of witchcraft was some simple accident or annoyance, and these relatively minor irritations took up more attention than the really serious charges of bewitching to death. So in St. Osyth there were village vendettas. Falling out with Elizabeth Ewstace, a neighbor had trouble with a cow and with his geese. Elizabeth Bennet was supposed to have killed a man who refused to sell her milk and called her an "old trot, old whore." Alice Manfield bewitched a cart in front of her house, so that it could not be moved for an hour. After displeasing Margaret Grevell, one neighbor had trouble with brewing, another with churning.

The rational explanation of these troubles was given by Margaret Grevell herself, as she fought back. She said that "she herself [had] lost several brewings and bakings of bread, and also swine, but she never did complain thereof." Agnes Heard responded similarly.

Such real or fancied acts of *maleficia* might be linked to murder. Like other witnesses, John Wade testified that "after speaking to Agnes Heard, he had many losses among his cattle and sheep." "After words, [Thomas Cartwright] had trouble with his cattle, caused, he thought, by the witchery of Agnes Heard." Others complained that after some trivial encounter with Agnes, their butter would not churn or else their beer would not brew. All such accusations culminated in the charge of bewitching to death the wife of a minister:

Richard Harrison, cleric, parson of Beaumont, saith that he and his late wife did dwell in Little Oakley in a house of his said wife, and that he, the said Richard Harrison, had also the parsonage of Oakley in farm. And about summer twelve-month, he being at London, his wife had a duck sitting on certain eggs under a cherry tree in a hedge. And when the said duck had hatched, his said wife did suspect one Agnes Heard, a light woman and a common harlot, to have stolen her ducklings; and that his said wife went unto the said Agnes Heard and rated her and all-to [soundly] chid her. But she could get no knowledge of her ducklings, and so came home, and was very angry against the said Agnes.

And within a short time after, the said Richard Harrison went into a chamber and there did read on his books for the space of two or three hours, bidding his wife go to bed with the children, and that he would come to her. And she so did. And being awhile laid down in her bed, his wife did cry out, "Oh, Lord, Lord, help me and keep me!" And he running to her asked her what she ailed. And she said, "Oh, Lord! I am sore afraid, and have been divers times, but that I would not tell you." And said, "I am in doubt, husband, that yonder wicked harlot, Agnes Heard, doth bewitch me." And the said Richard Harrison said to his wife, "I pray you be content and think not so, but trust in God, and put your trust in him only, and he will defend you from her, and from the Devil himself also." And [he] said moreover, "What will the people say, that I, being a preacher, should have my wife so weak in faith?"

This examinate saith that within two months after, his said wife said unto him, "I pray you, as ever there was love between us (as I hope there hath been, for I have five pretty children by you, I thank God), seek some remedy for me against yonder wicked beast (meaning the said Agnes Heard). And if you will not, I will complain to my father, and I think he will see some remedy for me. For," said she, "if I have no remedy, she will utterly consume me." Whereupon this examinate did exhort his wife as he had before, and desired her to pray to God, and that he would hang her, the said Agnes Heard, if he could prove any such matter.

And after, he went to the parsonage, and there he saith he gathered plums. And the said Agnes Heard then came to the hedge side, and Anwick's wife with her, and said unto him, "I pray you give me some plums, sir." And this examinate saith unto her, "I am glad you are here, you vile strumpet!" Saying, "I do think you have bewitched my wife, and, as truly as God doth live, if I can perceive that she be troubled any more as she hath been, I will not leave a whole bone about thee. And besides, I will seek to have thee hanged!" And [he] saith he said unto her that his wife would make her father privy unto it, and that "Then, I warrant thee, he will have you hanged, for he will make good friends, and is a stout man of himself." And [he] saith that then he did rehearse divers things to her that were thought she had bewitched, as geese and hogs. And as he was coming down of the tree, she, the said Agnes, did depart suddenly from him without having any plums.

This examinate saith (after which speeches so by him used unto her, and before Christmas) his said wife was taken sore sick, and was at many times afraid both sleeping and waking. And [she] did call this examinate, her husband, unto her not above two days before her death and said unto him: "Husband, God bless you and your children, for I am now utterly consumed with yonder wicked creature" (naming the said Agnes Heard). Which words, he saith, were spoken by her in the presence of John Pollin and Mother Poppe. And within two days after, his said wife departed out of this world in a perfect faith, repeating these words, "Oh, Agnes Heard, Agnes Heard! She hath consumed me!"

Agnes Heard was found Not Guilty by the jury, and acquitted.

Apart from the acceptance of very questionable testimony, the striking feature of the trial of the St. Osyth Witches is the prevalence of familiars or imps in nearly all the accusations and confessions. Alice Hunt had "two spirits, like unto little colts, the one black, and the other white, called by the names of Jack and Robin." Her granddaughter said "she kept [them] in a little low earthen pot with wool, color[ed] white and black . . . and that she hath seen her mother to feed them with milk." Elizabeth Bennet confessed to having two "spirits, one called Suckin, being black like a dog, the other called Liard, being red like a lion." Agnes Heard's illegitimate daughter, aged seven, testified Agnes had six blackbirds. Alice Manfield and Margaret Grevell were alleged to keep four imps, named Robin, Jack, Will, and Puppet, "like unto black cats."

One other striking story of familiars was invented by the perverse imagination of nine-year-old Henry Celles, in a fantasy studded with homely, concrete details. A spirit came to his brother John, and

took him by the left leg, and also by the little toe, which was like his sister but that it was all black. At which time his brother cried out and said, "Father, father, come help me! There is a black thing hath me by the leg, as big as my sister!" Whereat his father said to his mother, "Why, thou whore, cannot you keep your imps from my children?" Whereat she presently called it away from her son, saying "Come away, come away." At which speech it did depart.

The boy was so frightened "that he sweat for fear, and that he could scarce get his shirt from his back." His mother merely said, "Thou liest, thou liest, whoreson!"

To men of Elizabeth's reign, such testimony might not seem strange—sober if limited citizens thought it convincing enough to bring indictments against the women they hated and suspected. The jurymen cannot have been too different from such plaintiffs as Rev. Richard Harrison or John Wade or Thomas Cartwright. Therefore the remarkable aspect of this trial is that the jury found Not Guilty many of the accused (like Agnes Heard), and that, after a verdict of Guilty had been brought in, four of the six condemned were reprieved (like Cicely Celles).

Salazar de Frias, Alonzo. On May 22, 1611, Alonzo Salazar de Frias, a ranking inquisitor of Spain, started what H. C. Lea called "the turning point in the history of Spanish witchcraft." The previous year the secular judges at Logrono, Navarre, embarked on a witch hunt, rare in Spanish history, quickly gathering victims, forcing confessions, and burning the accused. The all-powerful Spanish Inquisition, jealous of its authority, immediately sent three inquisitors and other theologians to the area of Cigarramundi to make a report. The inquisitors were infected by the credulity of the judges, and found over 280 adults and many children (too young to be burned) worshiping the Devil. Forty of these witches were taken before the local tribunal of the Spanish Inquisition. Many others, however, were suspected to be in neighboring areas, and twenty large sabbat assemblies or *aquelarres* were named.

The Spanish Inquisition determined to join with the King, the Archbishop of Burgos, local bishops, and the leaders of the monastic orders in a wholesale campaign to inform the populace of the dangers of witchcraft and to get rid of witches, just as De Lancre was doing in Bordeaux. To stimulate public co-operation, an elaborate two-day auto-da-fé was arranged for November 7, 1610, when the witches would be publicly burned. The festival was not so impressive as planned: King Philip III did not attend; many witches recanted and were "reconciled," so that only six obdurates were executed; and their forced confessions were so farfetched—they had eaten the decaying bodies of their relatives—that the more influential clergy and laity recovered their traditional skepticism. Royal officials arrested the local judges for exceeding their powers; and the Suprema, the central committee of the Inquisition, failed to support its own tribunal when it protested against the arrest of the civil judges. Furthermore, on March 26, 1611, the Suprema decreed an Edict of Grace, during which time witches could confess their crimes without penalties. Salazar was one of the inquisitors sent into the suspected areas on May 22 to administer the Edict.

Salazar was familiar with the situation, for he had been a member of the original commission which led to the Logrono auto-da-fé. At that time he had been dissatisfied with the evidence, and now he was able to examine the charges in detail. He spent nearly eight months talking to 1,802 penitent witches, 1,384 of whom were children from twelve to fourteen! Salazar promised secrecy and immunity to those who took advantage of the grace period, so that eighty-one revoked their original confessions of guilt. Others would also have retracted, had they not feared execution for perjury.

Salazar's report covered 5,000 large sheets and was grouped into four heads: transvection, the sabbat, proofs of witchcraft, and evidence for punishment. He found the proofs illusory. One eighty-year-old woman, who slept in the same bed with her daughter, maintained that no one saw the daughter on her nightly trips to the sabbat. Another woman said that while waiting to see Salazar she was carried to the *aquelarre*, although many companions kept on talking to her all the time she said she was absent. A mother told how she touched her daughter throughout her supposed presence at the sabbat. Many girls who confessed to intercourse with devils were found to be virgins. Boys described an *aquellare* at a certain place, when at that very time two secretaries of Salazar happened to be there and saw nothing. Thirty-six people who gave the location of the *aquellare* all disagreed on the place. Unguents, alleged to be given by the devil for transvection, were examined by apothecaries and found useless and harmless. There was no external evidence. Furthermore, the confessions were gathered by torture; one witch said he was burned with live coals. Others were bribed to denounce someone's enemies; in one place a young beggar had accused 147 persons. In all, 1,672 persons were known to have been accused on perjured testimony.

After such interviews, Salazar came to one conclusion: the delusion had been provoked by the presence of an inquisitor looking for witches. He summed up his findings:

I have not found even indications from which to infer that a single act of witchcraft has really occurred, whether as to going to *aquelarres*, being present at them, inflicting injuries, or other of the asserted facts. This enlightenment has greatly strengthened my former suspicions that the evidence of accomplices, without external proof from other parties, is insufficient to justify even arrest. Moreover, my experience leads to the conviction that, of those availing themselves of the Edict of Grace, three-quarters and more have accused themselves and their accomplices falsely. I further believe that they would freely come to the Inquisition to revoke their confessions, if they thought that they would be received kindly without punishment, for I fear that my efforts to induce this have not been properly made known.

The other inquisitors who worked with Salazar in promulgating the Edict of Grace disagreed with his conclusions, but the Suprema accepted his statement and suppressed further investigations. On August 31, 1614, it issued a set of thirty-two instructions, drawn up by Salazar, for the guidance of inquisitors in dealing with witchcraft. It insisted on external evidence to confirm the accusations made by accused witches; witnesses could retract their confessions without fear of torture; confessions were to be thoroughly investigated, but there was to be no confiscation of property in a matter of such doubt. No action was to be taken in any tribunal of the Spanish Inquisition without a unanimous vote, and all such actions involving witchcraft were to be forwarded to the Suprema for review. In addition, all pending cases of witchcraft were to be dropped. Some amends were to be made to the victims of the 1610 Logrono auto-da-fé: their properties were not to be expropriated, nor their descendants penalized.

As a result of this striking statement by Salazar, witchcraft in Spain virtually came to an end, and only a handful of scattered and isolated trials were recorded later.

See further, Inquisition, Witchcraft in Spain.

Salem Witch Trials. The year 1692 seems to have been a particularly troubled one in New England. It was a time of political uncertainty, with Increase Mather at the English court, seeking clarification of the colony's government. The French were waging war, and the Indians were on the warpath. Taxes were intolerable (in 1691 the colonial government had demanded £1,346), the winter was cruel, pirates were attacking commerce, and smallpox was raging. In addition, the ingrown irritations of a small village, where ownership of land and boundaries were in dispute, increased the tensions.

To men and women brought up in a restricting evangelical world, the troubles of 1692 were caused by the Devil. The Puritan New England mind was alerted to devils and to their agents on earth, witches. Belief in the supernatural was unquestioned. The Bible told about witches and demoniacal possession; the Mosaic codes of Massachusetts turned legend into law. Witchcraft was part of the *Weltanschauung* of the colonists, especially strong since Massachusetts was not a monarchy or a republic, but a theocracy. The party line of the church ministers became both the law of God and the law of the land. Any traffic with Satan was treason to God—and the colony. This religious control of the state accounts in part for the panic in Massachusetts at a time when elsewhere the witchcraft delusion was waning (the last witch had been executed in England in 1685). When one of those accused as witches, William Barker, added political to religious heresy, the Puritans believed him: "The design was to destroy Salem Village, and to begin at the minister's house, and to destroy the Church of God, and to set up Satan's kingdom" —Hale, *Modest Inquiry into Witchcraft*, Boston, 1702. The same realization occurred to an Englishman, John Evelyn, who recorded in his diary (February 4, 1693): "Unheard of stories of the universal increase of witches in New England; men, women, and children devoting themselves to the Devil, *so as to threaten the subversion of the government.*"

The immediate cause of this "subversion" was a group of unmarried young women, who visited the house of Rev. Samuel Parris to listen to his slave Tituba's tales of West Indian lore. His daughter Elizabeth, aged nine, and her cousin Abigail Williams, aged eleven, the two youngest girls, were so emotionally excited by these get-togethers, coming at the onset of puberty, that they went into fits of uncontrollable sobbing and convulsions. Even after Elizabeth had been sent to live with Stephen Sewall (brother of Judge Samuel Sewall, who later abjured his part in the trials), her fits continued. In the first published account of the Salem troubles, *A Brief and True Narrative* (Boston, 1692), Deodat Lawson, Rev. Samuel Parris' predecessor, told how he saw Abigail "run to the fire, and begin to throw fire brands about the house; and run against the back as if she would run up the chimney."

Elizabeth Parris and Abigail Williams were the bellwethers in this defiance of the whole adult world, showing lawlessness, disobedience, flouting of authority, delinquency, to an extent no one in the twentieth century can envision. Little Elizabeth, brought up by the strictest of fathers, flung the holy Bible across the room—and got away with it. Abigail, who lived at the Parris home, took the limelight at a solemn day of fasting on March 11 for relief from the bewitchment—shrieking, romping, and disrupting the prayers. On Sunday, March 20, at a guest sermon by Rev. Deodat Lawson, Abigail gave a performance of audacious impudence—and everybody marveled. Lawson himself described it:

> After psalm was sung, Abigail Williams said to me, "Now stand up, and name your text." And after it was read, she said, "It is a long text." . . . And in the afternoon, Abigail Williams, upon my referring to my doctrines, said to me, "I know of no doctrine you had. If you did name one, I have forgot it."

Later, at the examination of John Proctor, Parris (who was then acting as recording secretary) wrote:

> So great were the interruptions of John [Indian] and Abigail by fits, while we were observing these things to notify [record] them, that we were fain to send them both away that I might have liberty to write this without disturbance.

This was the start, but out of this hysteria of high-strung personalities developed the contrived artfulness of the later fits of the older girls. Robert Calef, a Boston merchant who observed the proceedings, noted how from the first the girls acted in their homes, using "sundry odd postures and antic gestures, uttering foolish ridiculous speeches, which neither they themselves nor any others could make sense of."

Of these older girls, Ann Putnam was the youngest—twelve. Elizabeth Hubbard, who worked for her aunt and uncle (Dr. William Griggs), was seventeen; Mary Walcott, sixteen; Mary Warren, who worked for John and Elizabeth Proctor, twenty; Mercy Lewis, another servant girl (of the Putnams'), nineteen; and Susan Sheldon and Elizabeth Booth were both eighteen. These eight "witch bitches" (as one of the accused, old George Jacobs, called them) were the ringleaders. In addition, other young people also acted strangely and joined in accusing their neighbors—Sarah Churchill, a twenty-year-old servant of George Jacobs'; Sarah Trask, nineteen; Margaret Reddington, twenty; Phoebe Chandler, only twelve; and Martha Sprague, sixteen.

These girls were not children, but late teen-agers, and by the time the trials ended were almost a year older. They were, as the court called them, "grown persons." Even Ann Putnam, twelve, was precocious, designated by the court, not as a child, but as a "single woman."

As recently as 1668, public opinion had been concerned with possession, and had ascribed the affliction of John Goodwin's children in Boston to the Devil. The Goodwin children stem from the long line of Children Accusers. Governor Hutchinson of Massachusetts observed: "The behavior of the [Salem] children is so exact as to leave no room for doubt [that] the stories [of previous possessed children] had been read by the New England persons, or had been told to them."

In view of this tradition which consid-

> To the Honourable Committee
>
> of the humble representation of William Good of the Damage
> sustained by him in the year 1692. by reason of the suffering
> of his family upon the account of supposed Witchcraft.
> 1 My wife Sarah Good was in prison about four months & then Executed
> 2 a sucking child dyed in prison before the mothers Execution.
> 3 a child of 4 or 5 years old was in prison 7 or 8 months and
>   being chain'd in the dungeon was so hardly used and terrifyed
>   that she hath ever since been very chargeable having little or
>   no reason to govern herself. — And I leave it unto the Honourable
>   Court to Judge what damage I have sustained by such a
>   Destruction of my poor family — And so rest
>
>   your Honours humble servant
>
> Salem. Sept. 13. 1710.   William Good
>
>   30. proposed for to be
>   allowed

Petition of William Good, September 13, 1710, for damages by reason of the trial and execution for witchcraft in 1692 of his wife, Sarah Good, and the imprisonment for witchcraft of his daughter, Dorothy, "a child of four or five years old," who, "being chained in the dungeon was so hardly used and terrified that she hath ever since been very chargeable, having little or no reason to govern herself." William Good's petition is endorsed with a note allowing him thirty pounds.

ered rebellious adolescents as bewitched, the opinion in Salem about the girls was not surprising. The local physician, Dr. Griggs, who himself harbored a possessed girl in his home, and the local ministers diagnosed witchcraft. The local judges found suspects responsible for the girls' antics, and thereby proved witchcraft.

If the doctor and ministers could offer no explanation save witchcraft, at least one citizen had a practical suggestion to stop the *manifestations* of witchcraft. "If [the girls] were let alone, we should all be devils and witches quickly; they should rather be had to the whipping post." His procedure had proved effective, for John Proctor added that when his Mary Warren "was first taken with fits, he kept her close to the [spinning] wheel and threatened to thrash her; and then she had no more fits—till the next day he had gone forth, and then she must have her fits again, forsooth."

Proctor's suggestion was disregarded, and folk preferred the explanation of witch-

craft. Mary Sibley, the aunt of Mary Walcott, inadvertently forced attention on the matter. She had Tituba's husband, John Indian, make a "witch cake." A contemporary New England almanac gives a recipe: "To cure ague. Take a cake of barley meal and mix it with children's water, bake it, and feed it to the dog. If the dog shakes, you will be cured." Mrs. Sibley may also have hoped that, alternatively, if the dog got sick, the girls would tell who or what afflicted them. When Rev. Samuel Parris finally realized what was going on under his nose, the affair became dynamite.

What may have begun as a teen-age prank had developed into a *cause célèbre.* It may be—motives are very elusive—they initially hit upon the idea of specters haunting them in order to escape punishment for their fantastic behavior. This device was developed little by little. Tituba was actually the first to tell in court about specters or shapes of neighbors trying to win them to the Devil. When the question "Who torments you?" failed to produce names, suggestive questions followed, and answers had to be given. So the girls named first the obvious scapegoats of the community, the vulnerable and weak—Tituba, the Negro slave; Sarah Good, the pipe-smoking beggar; and Sarah Osborne, a thrice-wedded cripple. Martha Cory, the fourth to be accused, had an illegitimate half-caste son. Having taken the first steps in accusing people and seen their horrifying effects, the girls still more feared to reveal the truth.

Sarah Good was charged on February 29, 1692, with feloniously using and practicing "certain detestable arts called witchcrafts and sorceries," whereby Sarah Bibber, Elizabeth Hubbard, and Ann Putnam were "tortured, afflicted, pined, consumed, wasted, and tormented." Her preliminary examination of March 1, 1692, was a trial balloon of public sentiment and the testing ground for future accusations; the girls' techniques improved with experience. Judge Hathorne (an ancestor of Nathaniel Hawthorne) and Judge Corwin, both of Salem, firmly believed in deviltry and sorcery:

"What familiar hath Sarah Osborne?"
"She had a thing with a head like a woman with two legs and wings."

Q. Sarah Good, what evil spirit have you familiarity with?

A. None.

Q. Have you made no contract with the Devil?

A. No.

Q. Why do you hurt these children?

A. I do not hurt them. I scorn it!

Q. Whom do you employ then to do it?

A. I employ nobody.

Q. What creature do you employ then?

A. No creature—but I am falsely accused.

This formula became the standard gambit for interrogation. When Judge Hathorne saw that his questions to Sarah Good were not creating evidence for a conviction, he sought help from the girls. "Judge Hathorne desired the children, all of them, to look upon her and see if this were the person that had hurt them. And so they all did look upon her and said this was one of the persons that did torment them." To demon-

strate the torment, the girls cried out as if in pain, claiming pinchings, bitings, and paralysis. Apparently at this first trial not all the girls were sure about their spectral evidence, for the record adds: "Presently they were *all* tormented."

Having produced visible evidence of Sarah's powers to bewitch, Judge Hathorne then demanded names of her accomplices:

Q. Why, who was it?

A. I do not know, but it was some you brought into the meetinghouse with you.

Q. We brought you into the meetinghouse.

A. But you brought in two more.

Q. Who was it, then, that tormented the children?

A. It was Osborne.

In addition to going into fits whenever an accused was presented in court, the girls corroborated each other by prognosticating some other's contortions. At the examination of William Hobbs, "Abigail Williams said he was going to Mercy Lewis, and quickly after the said Lewis was seized with a fit. Then said Abigail cried, 'He is coming to Mary Walcott.' And said Mary presently fell into a fit also." Without realizing the implications, Judge Hathorne characterized the girls in his interrogation of Rebecca Nurse: "They accuse you of hurting them, and if you think it is not unavailingly but by design, you must look upon them as murderers."

The sworn depositions of all the young women are much of a piece. Erase the name of the accused, and the evidence would apply to any other. Thus Elizabeth Booth accused John Proctor:

> The deposition of Elizabeth Booth, aged eighteen years, who testifieth and saith that since I have been afflicted, I have been most grievously tormented by my neighbor, John Proctor, senior, or his appearance. Also I have seen John Proctor, senior, or his appearance most grievously torment and afflict Mary Walcott, Mercy Lewis, and Ann Putnam, junior, by pinching, twisting, and almost choking them. *Jurat in curia* [She swears to it in court].

Over three months later, Mary Walcott was repeating this formula against Abigail Faulkner:

> The deposition of Mary Walcott, who testifieth and saith that about the 9th August, 1692, I was most dreadfully afflicted by a woman that told me her name was Abigail Faulkner. But on the 11th of August, being the day of the examination of Abigail Faulkner, she did most dreadfully afflict me during the time of her examination. I saw Abigail Faulkner, or her appearance, most grievously afflict and torment Sarah Phelps and Ann Putnam. And I verily believe in my heart that Abigail Faulkner is a witch, and that she has often afflicted me and the aforesaid persons by acts of witchcraft.

Whenever the young women became un-

certain of a course of action, a lead was given them by another witness, Ann's mother, Mrs. Thomas Putnam. A close reading of the court records points strongly to her masterminding the accusations [see Ann Putnam].

A second older witness who frequently testified was 36-year-old Sarah Bibber, mentioned as a complainant in the first indictment of February 29. Ten of her depositions against highly respected persons are extant. Generally she contented herself with backing the girls. At the trial of Rebecca Nurse, for example, she was the second witness of a specter: "I saw the apparition of Rebecca Nurse . . . most grievously torture and afflict the bodies of Mary Walcott, Mercy Lewis, and Abigail Williams by pinching them and almost choking them to death." This she swore on oath before the court.

But friends and relatives of Mrs. Nurse were scrutinizing her. Sarah Nurse, Rebecca's daughter, detected chicanery and came forward to swear: "I saw Goody Bibber pull pins out of her clothes and hold them between her fingers, and clasp her hands round her knees. And then she cried out and said Goody Nurse pinched her. This I can testify."

Some time later, certain neighbors made statements about this Sarah Bibber. John and Lydia Porter said she was "a woman of an unruly turbulent spirit, and she would often fall into strange fits when she was crossed of her humor." Richard Walker confirmed this. Some people with whom the Bibbers had lodged made highly damning comments on her credibility as a witness. For example, she "would be very often speaking against one and another very obscenely and those things that were false, and wishing bad wishes and very often." Other neighbors said she "could fall into fits as often as she pleased."

Those who beat the gun by confessing were the only accused against whom the girls did not testify at length. The Salem victims were hanged not because they admitted to being witches, *but because they denied it.* No one who confessed to being a witch was ever hanged, yet, if witchcraft were a punishable offense, a confessed criminal should have been punished.

A confession meant a reprieve, for then the accusers did not make a scene. At the examination of Mary Warren, "not one of the sufferers was afflicted during her examination after once she began to confess, though they were tormented before." After Tituba confessed, Ann Putnam, as well as Elizabeth Hubbard, said: "She left off hurting me and has hurt me but little since." And Rev. Francis Dane noted "the common speech that was frequently spread among us, of their liberty, if they [the accused] would confess." On the other hand, Samuel Wardwell, who first made a confession but later denied it, was hanged. In all, 55, of the 150 accused, confessed in order to get reprieves (Thomas Brattle's *Letter*).

The course of the trial shocked only two of the "witch bitches" into confessing their deception; and the public performance of the other girls, terrified that they would be exposed, was so outrageously hostile that both penitents recanted, and were taken back into the ranks of the accusers.

Sarah Churchill, twenty, servant to George Jacobs, was one of the less vocal accusers. When Jacobs was apprehended and examined, she refused to continue the imposture. The other girls immediately accused her as a witch. Frightened by this twist of events, she quickly reversed herself and rejoined the afflicted.

Her conscience bothered her, however, and she poured out her doubts to Sarah Ingersoll, the spinster daughter of Deacon Ingersoll, a pillar of the church and proprietor of the Salem Village "ordinary" or inn. Sarah filed a deposition, but the court ignored it, just as it had ignored the exposure of Sarah Bibber:

> The deposition of Sarah Ingersoll, aged about thirty years, saith that seeing Sarah Churchill, after her examination, she came to me crying and wringing her hands, seeming to be much troubled in spirit. I asked her what she ailed. She answered she had undone herself. I asked her in what. She said in belying herself and others in saying she had set her hand to the devil's book; whereas, she said, she

never did. I told her I believed she had set her hand to the book. She answered, crying, and said, "No, no, no. I never, I never did!" I asked her then what made her say she did. She answered because they threatened her, and told her they would put her into the dungeon, and put her along with Mr. Burroughs. And thus several times, she followed [me] up and down, telling me that she had undone herself in belying herself and others. . . . She said also that if she told Mr. Noyes but once she had set her hand to the book, he would believe her. But if she told the truth and said she had *not* set her hand to the book, a hundred times, he would not believe her.

The other defector—temporarily—was Mary Warren, the maid at the Proctors'. The fate of the Proctor family was enough to bring sanity to a half-wit. John and his wife Elizabeth were in jail. Mary Warren was left with their five children (the youngest aged three). An overzealous sheriff, taking the law into his own hands, had appropriated the family property. Long before the trial, he came

> to the house and seized all the goods, provisions, and cattle that he could come at, and sold some of the cattle at half price and killed others and put them up for the West Indies; threw out the beer out of the barrel and carried away the barrel, emptied a pot of broth and took away the pot, and left nothing for the support of the children.

Like Sarah, she could not bring herself to testify against her employer. Instead of supporting the fifty-two neighbors who boldly upheld his innocence in a public petition, however, she uttered her thoughts to her girl friends. Detecting a dangerous weak reed, Ann Putnam, Mercy Lewis, Mary Walcott, and Abigail Williams accused Mary Warren as a witch.

From April 21 to May 12, Mary Warren was hounded by the magistrates and "witch bitches" until she confessed that John Proctor's apparition afflicted her. Most of the questioning turned round her signing the devil's book, which she eventually admitted, her finger making a black mark. But whether her finger was wet with spittle, with sweat, or "with cider that she had been drinking of," she could not say. While in jail, and momentarily free from the judges' pressures, she admitted:

When I was afflicted I thought I saw the apparitions of a hundred persons; for she said her head was distempered that she could not tell what she said. And the said Mary told us that when she was well again, she could not say that she saw any of the apparitions at the time aforesaid.

Mitigation of their sins could be found for other young witch finders who actually suffered epileptic or spastic fits, or who were mentally deranged. But there can be no mitigation of the crimes of the Salem girls. Never at any time, even during the hangings, was the slightest compunction or contrition shown (with the possible exception of Sarah Churchill and Mary Warren). They knew exactly what they were doing. Their acts during 1692 imply a state of utter delinquency, causing death without rhyme or reason, for sport. On March 28, at Ingersoll's inn, one girl said she saw Mrs. Proctor afflicting her. Mrs. Ingersoll "told the girl she told a lie, for there was nothing. Then the girl said she did it for sport—'They must have some sport.'"

Some of these young accusers continued their evil-doing after the trials, so that, as the Reversal of Attainder in 1711 stated, "some of the principal accusers and witnesses . . . have since discovered [shown] themselves to be persons of profligate and vicious conversation." The only document which proves the irrational viciousness of the accusations is Ann Putnam's confession made fourteen years later, when she was twenty-six. [See Ann Putnam.]

In addition to the accusations of injuring the young women by appearing as evil specters, most "witches" were accused also by adults with acts of *maleficia*. Such alleged misdeeds were never directly included in the indictment, and seem to have been allowed as evidence on the theory that any stick was good enough to beat the dog. The deposition of Sarah Holton against Rebecca

Nurse is typical of the rest, and no whit more stupid. In all the accusations of harming persons or cattle, the plaintiff was completely unable to link cause and effect, and united two incidents related only in time, to try to prove a causal relationship.

The deposition of Sarah Holton, relict [widow] of Benjamin Holton, deceased, who testifieth and saith that about this time three years, my dear and loving husband, Benjamin Holton, deceased, was as well as ever I knew him in my life, till on Saturday morning that Rebecca Nurse, who now stands charged for witchcraft, came to our house and fell a-railing at him, because our pigs got into her field (though our pigs were sufficiently yoked, and their fence was down in several places). Yet all we could say to her could no ways pacify her, but she continued railing and scolding a great while together; calling to her son, Benjamin Nurse, to go and get a gun and kill our pigs, and let none of them go out of the field, though my poor husband gave her never a mis-beholding word. And within a short time after this, my poor husband going out very early in the morning, as he was a-coming in again, he was taken with a strange fit in the entry, being struck blind and stricken down two or three times. So that when he came to himself, he told me he thought he should never have come into the house any more. And all summer after, he continued in a languishing condition, being much pained at his stomach and often struck blind. But about a fortnight before he died, he was taken with strange and violent fits, acting much like to our poor bewitched persons, when we thought they would have died. And the doctor that was with him could not find what his distemper was. And the day before he died, he was very cheerly, but about the midnight he was again most violently seized upon with violent fits, till the next night about midnight he departed this life by a cruel death.

But crimes were petty compared to *sin;* the pact with the Devil, rather than the evil accruing from the pact, was what mattered. Cotton Mather defined witchcraft as "a renouncing of God and advancing of a filthy

Examination of Rebecca Nurse

Devil into the throne of the Most High; 'tis the most nefandous high treason against the majesty on high."

A large part of the hysteria which blanketed Salem and its environs was due to the indiscriminate accusations of the girls, whereby anyone might find himself labeled a witch. Some who possibly approved the arrest of such "inferiors" as Tituba or Sarah Good were only weeks later themselves accused, like Martha Cory, who had said: "I could not blame the Devil for making witches of *them;* for they are idle, slothful persons and minded nothing that was good."

The accused were, in fact, a cross section of society in the Salem area, from farm laborers to landowners.

John Willard, farmer and deputy constable of Salem Village, had arrested the first suspects, but he came to see that the real culprits were the girls in the informers' box. "Hang *them*," he had cried. This was talk unendurable in a police officer, and Willard realized it. He fled from Salem, but was picked up ten days later, accused by six girls and Mrs. Putnam on seven indictments (the most against any defendant), tried at the third session of the court on August 2, and hanged on August 19.

John Proctor had a house and cattle and a hired girl (Mary Warren it was) to help with his five children. He had no patience with believers in witchcraft, and this was his undoing. Sam Sibley, the uncle of Mary Walcott, informed how Proctor had dealt with Mary Warren. It was dangerous to speak one's mind, even to friends. "If he

[Proctor] had John Indian in his custody, he would soon beat the devil out of him." This comment too was offered (by Deacon Nathaniel Ingersoll) as evidence in court. A man's skepticism and dissent from a majority prejudice made him a witch.

The most distinguished victim was the former minister of Salem Village, Rev. George Burroughs, who had left the village about 1682. The man and his trial are noted in a separate entry.

Rebecca Nurse was another classic figure. Her husband, Francis, had been a plain yeoman who did not mind hard work, and with his four sons and four sons-in-law had almost paid off a 300-acre estate. Rebecca was the eldest of three sisters; the other two, again both substantial citizens, Sarah Cloyce and Mary Esty, were also accused and convicted. Sarah made a confession and was reprieved. When charged (by the Putnam clan) with bewitching the girls, Rebecca Nurse was seventy-one years old and bedridden. Through the verbatim reports of her trial a picture emerges of this old matriarch—maintaining her integrity to the last, puzzled over the search for "preternatural marks":

Q. How came you sick? For there is an odd discourse of that in the mouths of many.
A. I am sick at my stomach.
Q. Have you no wounds?
A. I have not but old age.

At the first, many of those accused were residents of Salem Village or Salem Farms —the equivalent of a township of about thirty square miles, with a population of less than a hundred households. Many others came from neighboring Topsfield, significant because there was considerable bitter talk between the men of the two districts. As the girls' notoriety in spotting witches grew, witches were later discovered in more distant places.

Andover became the chief scene of these extended exploits. One John Ballard, whose wife's sickness defied diagnosis or cure, suggested the Salem girls investigate this and other mysterious maladies. Ann Putnam and Mary Walcott were handicapped by not knowing the names of the local residents, but they found an even more effective substitute in the "touch" test. Ann and Mary went into fits, and the suspects lined up to touch the girls. If the girls became quiet, the toucher was a witch. "Ann Putnam said she had never seen her, but since she [the accused] came to Salem Town last, said Putnam fell into a fit, and said [Ann] Pudeator was commanded to take her by the wrist, and did. And said Putnam was well presently." Ann Pudeator was hanged on September 22. When Mary Parker of Andover "came before the justices, she recovered all the afflicted out of their fits by the touch of her hand." She was hanged on September 22.

The cause of Mrs. Ballard's sickness, said Ann and Mary, was clearly bewitching by Ann Foster, her daughter Mary Lacy, and her granddaughter Mary. Mrs. Foster died in jail from ill treatment and exposure, but Mary Lacy saved her life by confessing. The examinations of these three women are valuable evidence to show how the mind and will can be broken by the pressures of imprisonment and tricky questioning. Mrs. Foster confessed the "devil appeared to her in the shape of a bird at several times, such a bird as she never saw the like before." She had "tied a knot in a rag and threw it into the fire to hurt Timothy Swan, and that she did hurt the rest that complained of her by squeezing poppets like them, and so almost choked them." She confirmed the broomstick legend:

She and Martha Carrier did both ride on a stick or pole when they went to the witch meeting at Salem Village, and that the stick broke as they were carried in the air above the tops of the trees, and they fell. But she did hang fast about the neck of Goody Carrier and were presently at the village, that she was then much hurt of her leg.

A few days later, unaware that her daughter, Mrs. Lacy, had made just as lurid a confession, Mrs. Foster refused to implicate her. Then Goodwife Lacy was called in, and began thus:

"Oh, mother, how do you do? We have left Christ, and the Devil hath got hold of us. How shall I get rid of this evil one? I desire God to break my rocky heart that I may get the victory this time."

After Mrs. Foster and Mrs. Lacy had been questioned and removed, young Mary Lacy was brought in, and immediately Mary Warren had a violent fit which lasted until Mary Lacy touched her. Then she berated her parent: "Where is my mother that made me a witch, and I knew it not." To accuse another was the best way of showing co-operation with the court and earning consideration.

Judge Hathorne still hankered after names:

Q. Your mother and your grandmother say there was a minister there. How many men did you see there?

A. I saw no one but Richard Carrier.

Q. Did you see none else?

A. There was a minister there, and I think he is now in prison.

Q. Were there not two ministers there?

A. Cannot tell.

Q. Was there not one Mr. Burroughs there?

A. Yes.

In Andover, after Justice Dudley Bradstreet had issued forty warrants, he refused to sign any more. Because of his lack of co-operation in hunting down enemies of chapel and state, which suggested sympathy for the witches and therefore made him a witch, he was indicted for committing nine murders. He fled with his wife. His brother John, though likewise the son of a former governor, was also indicted; his offense— inciting a dog to afflict. "The said dog was tried and hung for a witch."

After Andover, the girls moved into the Boston area.

Mrs. Nathaniel Carey of Charlestown visited Salem Village to clear herself of incriminating rumors. Mr. Carey reported:

Being brought before the justices, her chief accusers were two girls. My wife declared to the justices that she never had any knowledge of them before that day. She was forced to stand with her arms stretched out. I requested that I might hold one of her hands, but it was denied me. Then she desired me to wipe the tears from her eyes and the sweat from her face, which I did. Then she desired she might lean herself on me, saying she should faint. Justice Hathorne replied she had strength enough to torment these persons, and she should have strength enough to stand. I speaking something against their cruel proceedings, they commanded me to be silent or else I should be turned out of the room. (Calef, *More Wonders of the Invisible World*)

Captain John Alden of Boston was named. Then, of course, he did not have the romantic glamour which Longfellow's poem gave him. But he was known and respected as a sea captain and a fighter in the Indian wars, so much in esteem that Lieutenant Governor Stoughton himself signed the warrant. The girls went through their routines, and one of them pointed out a Captain Hill, but she was prompted by a bystander and then correctly identified Alden. "There stands Alden! A bold fellow with his hat on before the judges. He sells powder and shot to the Indians and French, and lies with Indian squaws and has Indian papooses."

Brought back into the courtroom, he was ordered to stand on a chair and face the girls: they all fell flat on their faces. Alden's hand was placed on them: at once they recovered. At this juncture, he asked the judges a question which, if answered, would have ended all the trials: "What's the reason *you* don't fall when I look at you? Can you give me one?" Alden's sword was taken away, and he was imprisoned in Boston jail. After fifteen weeks, he escaped.

In spite of the growing distrust of the girls everywhere else, in October Gloucester sent for them; but there they discovered only four witches. The panic caused by the French and Indian attacks in July was subsiding. Summoned again in November, the girls met a rather chilly reception, and no one was arrested. En route, at Ipswich, they went into their usual fits at an old woman, but the people of Ipswich ignored them.

During the hysteria, almost 150 people were arrested; a search of all the court records would no doubt add to this number. Because of the time taken to convict each prisoner, only thirty-one were tried in 1692 (not including Sarah Churchill and Mary Warren, two accusers who briefly recanted). The court of Oyer and Terminer [hear and determine] sentenced to death all thirty-one (of whom six were men). Nineteen were hanged. Of the remaining twelve, two (Sarah Osborne and Ann Foster) died in jail; one (Giles Cory) was pressed to death; one (Tituba) was held indefinitely in jail without trial; two (Abigail Faulkner and Elizabeth Proctor) postponed execution by pleading pregnancy and lived long enough to be reprieved; one (Mary Bradbury) escaped from jail after sentencing; and five made confessions which secured reprieves for them.

An especially shocking detail about these trials is that the accused had to pay for their maintenance in jail, even when acquitted! A reprieve cost a fee; a discharge another. The relatives paid the hangman's fee for the execution. Many remained in prison after the general jail delivery because their possessions had been sold to maintain their families in the meantime. Sarah Dustin was acquitted in January, 1693, but, having no one to come to her aid, died in prison. Margaret Jacobs was acquitted, but the property of her parents had been seized, and she was kept in jail until at length a generous stranger (a Mr. Gammon) heard of her plight and bought her freedom. William Buckley spent his last shilling paying £10 to release his wife and daughter. He survived another ten years. His pastor, Rev. Joseph Green, made the following entry in his diary: "January 2, 1702. Old William Buckley died this evening. He was at meeting the last Sabbath, and died with the cold, I fear, for want of comforts and good tending. Lord forgive! He was about eighty years old. He was very poor." Tituba remained in jail until May, 1693, when an *ignoramus* [we cannot decide] technically freed her; after thirteen months' imprisonment, she was finally sold for prison expenses as a slave. Ann Foster died in jail; her son had to pay £2 16s. 0d. costs before he could get the body for

Samuel Wardwell, hanged September 22, 1692, according to a nineteenth-century conception. "At execution, while he was speaking to the people, protesting his innocency, the executioner being at the same time smoking tobacco, the smoke coming in his face interrupted his discourse; those accusers said the Devil hindered him with smoke."—Robert Calef (1700).

burial. For Sarah Osborne's body, costs of £1 3s. 5d. were demanded. When finally Elizabeth Proctor and Abigail Faulkner, reprieved for pregnancy, were released, they found themselves legally dead and unable to claim their own property and inheritance.

The sins of the court of Oyer and Terminer are legion: confessions forced by binding neck and heels until blood oozed from the nose; admittance of testimony of a seven-year-old daughter by which her mother (Martha Carrier) was hanged, and evidence of another seven-year-old, Lydia Nichols, which confirmed the conviction of Abigail Hobbs; denial of advice and lawyers to the accused; loaded questioning and browbeating—in short, a determination to stretch every device to find the accused guilty. Yet Cotton Mather believed the Salem trials were conducted more impartially than the famous Lancashire trials.

The fundamental evil of the trials, however, was not so much the miscarriage of justice in particular instances, shocking as these were, but the underlying philosophy on which the trials were based and against which Mary Esty and Sarah Cloyce had vainly protested: the theory that the Devil used the shapes or bodies only of the wicked (those who had made a pact with him) as specters to torment and even kill the innocent. Tied in with spectral evidence were two other anti-legal premises: guilt by association, and guilt by accusation.

The first major published discussion of spectral evidence was by Rev. Samuel Willard, minister of the Old South Church in Boston, who late in 1692 published *Some Miscellany Observations.* Willard had three of the judges in his congregation, and his tolerance and perspicacity may have helped them free themselves of bigotry.

"The New England panic at Salem was but a last bright flicker of the ghastly glare which had so long made hideous the European night."
—George Lincoln Burr, *The Literature of Witchcraft* (1890).

The immediate problem was how to detect witches and avoid false accusation of the innocent. On the one hand were those diehards and officials who held that the Devil worked only through those who had made a pact with him; therefore spectral evidence was proof of witchcraft. The clergy generally maintained that the Devil would confuse people by appearing in the shape or specter of a good person. Spectral evidence was therefore unreliable. Witches, Willard said, must be expressly charged for specific acts, and there must be "a full and clear legal discovery that the party accused hath done the fact by which the crime is evidenced . . . The thing testified [must] be that which [the witness] came to the knowledge of, after the manner of men"— not by God's revelation or the Devil's insinuation.

Increase Mather was another to oppose the sort of evidence on which the court of Oyer and Terminer had convicted. On October 3, 1692, he addressed a group of Boston ministers (who supported his position) and strongly opposed evidence based on specters, "touching" to cure fits, or confessions of possessed persons. He admitted only two classes of proof: voluntary confession, and two witnesses to the accused's saying or doing something that only "such as have familiarity with the devil ever did or can do." Perhaps aware he was holding open the door for dubious testimony by this second proof, he added a highly important caveat:

It were better that ten suspected witches should escape than that one honest person should be condemned. . . . It is better a guilty person should be absolved than that he should without ground of conviction be condemned. I had rather judge a witch to be an honest woman, than judge an honest woman as a witch.

An even stronger attack on spectral evidence and the conduct of the court came from a wealthy and educated Bostonian, Thomas Brattle, who also in October, 1692, circulated a very lengthy letter among his friends. He applied common sense rules to the court procedure, and asked some embarrassing questions. Since the judges have made touching the test of witchcraft, why do they bother with so much other evidence? Why do the witches afflict only some girls and not others? Why are confessions full of lies and flat contradictions accepted by the court? Why is the evidence of confessed witches, admitted agents of the Devil, accepted against Christian persons? "That such as confess themselves to be witches, to have renounced God and Christ and all that is sacred, should yet be allowed and ordered to swear by the name of the great God! This indeed seemeth to me to be a gross taking of God's name in vain." Why is the distinction between a specter and a real person ignored? Why are all sorts of extraneous evidence allowed at trials for witchcraft? Why are highly placed persons who are accused of witchcraft (such as Margaret Thatcher, the mother-in-law of Judge Corwin) not prosecuted? Why are fugitives not extradited from New York? Why are children so encouraged by zealous adults? "Now no man will be so much out of his wits as to make

The Wonders of the Invisible World.

OBSERVATIONS

As well *Historical* as *Theological*, upon the NATURE, the
NUMBER, and the OPERATIONS of the

DEVILS.

Accompany'd with,

I. Some Accounts of the Grievous Molestations, by DÆ-
MONS and WITCHCRAFTS, which have lately
annoy'd the Countrey; and the Trials of some eminent
Malefactors Executed upon occasion thereof: with several
Remarkable *Curiosities* therein occurring.

II. Some Councils, Directing a due Improvement of the terrible things, lately done, by the Unusual & Amazing
Range of EVIL SPIRITS, in Our Neighbourhood: &
the methods to prevent the *Wrongs* which those *Evil
Angels* may intend against all sorts of people among us;
especially in Accusations of the Innocent.

III. Some Conjectures upon the great EVENTS, likely
to befall, the WORLD in General, and NEW-EN-
GLAND in Particular; as also upon the Advances of
the TIME, when we shall see BETTER DAYES.

IV A short Narrative of a late Outrage committed by a
knot of WITCHES in *Swedeland*, very much Resembling, and so far Explaining, *That* under which our parts
of *America* have e laboured !

V. THE DEVIL DISCOVERED: In a Brief Discourse upon
those TEMPTATIONS, which are the more Ordinary *Devices*
of the Wicked One.

By **Cotton Mather.**

Boston Printed by *Benj. Harris* for *Sam. Phillips.* 1693.

Title page of first Boston edition (1693) of
Cotton Mather's *Wonders of the Invisible
World*. From New York Public Library.

this a legal evidence; and yet this seems to
be our case." The whole thing was nonsense: "The witches' meetings, the devil's
baptisms and mock sacraments, which the
accusing and confessing witches oft speak
of, are nothing else but the effect of their
fancy, depraved and deluded by the devil,
and not a reality to be regarded or minded
by any wise man."

The influence of Brattle's letter was so
extensive that those upholding the court,
William Stoughton, John Hathorne, Stephen Sewall, Cotton Mather, and Captain
John Higginson, decided to publish an
apologia. Mather, indeed, stated that Governor Phips had asked him for such a
volume. Thus *The Wonders of the Invisible
World* came to be written as a semiofficial
history of the Salem trials. Its publication
date was held up by the Governor (because "people were dissatisfied . . . some
[hanged] were thought by many persons to

be innocent") until the new "reformed"
court had softened the memory of the old.
Yet early in January, 1693, over a hundred
were still in jail. Mather's work is invaluable for its almost stenographic reports of
five typical trials—George Burroughs,
Bridget Bishop, Susanna Martin, Elizabeth
How, and Martha Carrier.

The only trouble with the book was that
it was completely tendentious and seemed
to whitewash the court. Furthermore,
Mather still wrote with complete credulity
in witches. Indeed, in his accounts of Mercy
Short and Margaret Rule, written after the
exposure of the Salem girls, Mather never
once questioned the demoniac origin of
their fits. On the other hand, Robert Calef,
a Boston businessman, saw in them only
exhibitionism. Later, he expanded his views
with suppressed information about the
Salem trials as *More Wonders of the Invisible World* (London, 1700), a clear at-

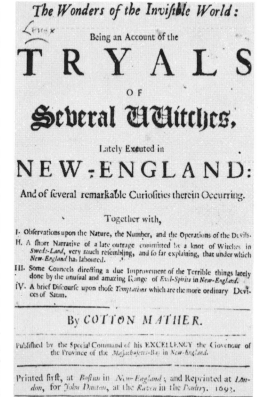

The Wonders of the Invisible World:

Being an Account of the

TRYALS

OF

Several Witches,

Lately Executed in

NEW-ENGLAND:

And of several remarkable Curiosities therein Occurring.

Together with,

I. Observations upon the Nature, the Number, and the Operations of the Devils.

II. A short Narrative of a late outrage committed by a knot of Witches in
Sweds-Land, very much resembling, and so far explaining, that under which
New-England has laboured.

III. Some Councels directing a due Improvement of the Terrible things lately
done by the unusual and amazing Range of *Evil-Spirits* in *New-England*.

IV. A brief Discourse upon those *Temptations* which are the more ordinary Devices of Satan.

By *COTTON MATHER.*

Published by the Special Command of his EXCELLENCY the Governour of
the Province of the *Massachusetts-Bay* in *New-England.*

Printed first, at *Boston* in *New-England*; and Reprinted at *London*, for *John Dunton*, at the *Raven* in the *Poultry*. 1693.

Title page of first London edition (1693) of
Cotton Mather's *Wonders of the Invisible
World*. From New York Public Library.

tack on Mather. In turn, Calef was excoriated by a group of pro-Mather clergymen in Obadiah Gill's *Some Few Remarks upon a Scandalous Book* (Boston, 1701), and was forced to move from Boston to Roxbury.

When spectral evidence had been discredited, conviction for witchcraft was impossible. By January, 1693, the judges who had accepted spectral evidence in the summer and fall of 1692 now rejected it. When a juror asked how much weight should be given it, he was told "as much as chips in wort [beer]." Out of fifty-two accused, the judges condemned only three persons, of feeble mind, who had confessed to being witches. Chief Justice Stoughton ordered these three to be hanged, along with five others held over from 1692 (including Elizabeth Proctor, now no longer pregnant), but Governor Phips overrode him and reprieved all eight. Later, in April, 1693, Mary Watkins, a servant girl, confessed at Boston to witchcraft, but the jury returned an *ignoramus*. Sent out to recon-

---

Rebecca Nurse
Yarmouth, England, 1621
Salem, Massachusetts, 1692

O Christian martyr, who for Truth
    could die
When all about thee owned the
    hideous lie,
The world redeemed from Superstition's sway
Is breathing freer for thy sake today.
        —John Greenleaf Whittier.

---

sider their verdict, since the accused had voluntarily confessed, the jurymen again returned the same dismissal. On January 15, 1697, the jurors who had brought in the verdicts of Guilty made their amends. That day was a day of fasting in the colony to show repentance for all the wrongdoings of the trials. Ten years after the executions, Judge Samuel Sewall confessed the guilt of the court, desiring "to take the blame and shame of it, asking pardon of men." In July, 1702, twelve ministers from Essex county

---

Condemned at the Salem witch trials, 1692

Bishop, Bridget *Hanged June 10*

Bradbury, Mary *Convicted September 6; Escaped*

Burroughs, Rev. George *Hanged August 19*

Carrier, Martha *Hanged August 19*

Cloyce, Sarah *Convicted September 6; Reprieved*

Cory, Giles *Pressed to death September 19*

Cory, Martha *Hanged September 22*

Eames, Rebecca *Convicted September 17; Reprieved*

Esty, Mary *Hanged September 22*

Faulkner, Abigail *Convicted; Pleaded pregnancy*

Foster, Ann *Died in jail*

Good, Sarah *Hanged July 19*

Hoar, Dorcas *Convicted September 6; Reprieved*

Hobbs, Abigail *Convicted September 6; Reprieved*

How, Elizabeth *Hanged July 19*

Jacobs, George *Hanged August 19*

Lacy, Mary *Convicted September 6; Reprieved*

Martin, Susanna *Hanged July 19*

Nurse, Rebecca *Hanged July 19*

Osborne, Sarah *Died in jail*

Parker, Alice *Hanged September 22*

Parker, Mary *Hanged September 22*

Proctor, Elizabeth *Convicted; Pleaded pregnancy*

Proctor, John *Hanged August 19*

Pudeator, Ann *Hanged September 22*

Reed, Wilmot *Hanged September 22*

Scott, Margaret *Hanged September 22*

Tituba *Held in jail*

Wardwell, Samuel *Hanged September 22*

Wilds, Sarah *Hanged July 19*

Willard, John *Hanged August 19*

supported the petition of the surviving witches in Andover and Topsfield for vindication, since "their names were exposed to infamy and reproach while their trial and condemnation stand on the public record." The General Court at last declared that the use of spectral evidence was unlawful, and on October 17, 1711, reversed the attainders of twenty-two of the thirty-one convicted in 1692, whose relatives (or themselves, if surviving) so petitioned. The act was not perfect, for it was never signed by the Governor; there is some suspicion, too, that the act was intended to protect the Salem lobby against civil suits. The reinstatement of those without survivors or without friends (such as Bridget Bishop and Sarah Osborne) to plead their memories had to wait 150 years; in 1957 the Commonwealth of Massachusetts finally reversed the attainders of all those not covered by the earlier act. In 1709, nearly two dozen accused or their descendants,

joined later by others, sought financial compensation for their losses sustained during the trials. These claims were admitted in 1711, although the infinitesimal sum of less than £600 was all that was allocated to reimburse the survivors and their families.

Charles W. Upham, who in 1867 wrote his two-volume *Salem Witchcraft*, still the definitive work on this subject, summed up the historic importance of Salem:

Error is seldom overthrown by mere reasoning. It yields only to the logic of events. No power of learning or wit could have rooted the witchcraft superstition out of the minds of men. Nothing short of a demonstration of their deformities, follies, and horrors, such as here was held up to the view of the world, could have given their death blow. This was the final cause of Salem witchcraft, and makes it one of the great landmarks in the world's history.

A Partial List of the Accused at the Salem witch trials

Abbott, Goodman (Billerica)
Abbott, Nehemiah (Andover)
Abbott, Nehemiah, Jr. (Topsfield)
Alden, Capt. John (Boston)
Andrews, Daniel (Salem Village)
Andrews, M. (Billerica)
Baker, Mrs. Ebenezer (Andover)
Barker, Abigail (Andover)
Barker, Mary (Andover)
Barker, William (Andover)
Barker, William, Jr. (Andover)
Barry, William (Andover)
Bassett, Sarah (Lynn)
Bishop, Bridget (Salem Village)
Bishop, Edward (Salem Village)
Bishop, Sarah (Salem Village)
Black, Mary [slave] (Salem Village)
Bradbury, Mary (Salisbury)
Bradstreet, Justice Dudley (Andover)
Bradstreet, John (Andover)
Bridges, Sarah (Andover)
Bromidge, Goodwife (no address)
Buckley, Sarah (Salem Village)
Buckley, Sarah, Jr. (Salem Village)
Burroughs, Rev. George (Wells, Maine)
Buxton, John (Salem Village)

Candy [slave] (Salem)
Carey, Elizabeth (Charlestown)
Carey, Nathaniel (Charlestown)
Carrier, Martha (Andover)
Carrier, Richard (Andover)
Carrier, Sarah (Andover)
Carter, Bethiah (Woburn)
Carter, Bethiah, Jr. (Woburn)
Cave, Sarah (Andover)
Clark, Mary (Haverhill)
Clinton, Rachel (no address)
Cloyce, Sarah (Salem Village)
Coffin, Mary (Gloucester)
Cole, Sarah (Lynn)
Colson, Elizabeth (Reading)
Cory, Giles (Salem Village)
Cory, Martha (Salem Village)
Dane, Deliverance (Andover)
Dane, Mrs. Nathan (Andover)
Derick, Mary (Lynn)
Derrill, Mary (Lynn)
Doliver, Ann (Gloucester)
Dustin, Lydia (Reading)
Dustin, Sarah (Reading)
Eames, Rebecca (Bixford)
Eames, Robert (Bixford)

(Continued)

(Continued from previous page)

English, Mary (Salem)
English, Phillip (Salem)
Esty, Mary (Topsfield)
Farrar, Thomas (Lynn)
Faulkner, Abigail (Andover)
Faulkner, Abigail, Jr. (Andover)
Faulkner, Dorothy (Andover)
Flood, Capt. John (Romney Marsh)
Fosdick, Elizabeth (Malden)
Foster, Ann (Andover)
Frye, Eunice (Andover)
Good, Dorothy (Salem Village)
Good, Sarah (Salem Village)
Greene, Mary (Haverhill)
Hardy, Thomas (Great Island)
Harrington (Andover)
Hart, Elizabeth (Lynn)
Hawkes, Sarah (Salem)
Hoar, Dorcas (Beverly)
Hobbs, Abigail (Topsfield)
Hobbs, Deliverance (Topsfield)
Hobbs, William (Topsfield)
How, Elizabeth (Topsfield)
How, James (Topsfield)
Hubbard, Elizabeth (Salem Village)
Hutchinson, Mrs. Francis (Haverhill)
Ireson, Mary (Lynn)
Jackson, John (no address)
Jackson, John, Jr. (no address)
Jacobs, George (Salem Village)
Jacobs, George, Jr. (Salem Village)
Jacobs, Margaret (Salem Village)
Jacobs, Martha (Salem Village)
Jacobs, Rebecca (Salem Village)
Johnson, Abigail (Andover)
Johnson, Elizabeth (Andover)
Johnson, Elizabeth, Jr. (Andover)
Johnson, Stephen (Andover)
Lacy, Mary (Andover)
Laundry, John (Andover)
Marston, Mary (Andover)
Martin, Susanna (Amesbury)
Merrill, Sarah (Beverly)
Morey, Sarah (Beverly)

Osborne, Sarah (Salem Village)
Osgood, Mary (Andover)
Parker, Alice (Salem)
Parker, Mary (Andover)
Payne, Elizabeth (Charlestown)
Pease, Sarah (Salem)
Post, Mary (Rowley)
Post, Sarah (Andover)
Prince, Martha (Salem)
Proctor, Benjamin (Salem Village)
Proctor, Elizabeth (Salem Village)
Proctor, John (Salem Village)
Proctor, Sarah (Salem Village)
Proctor, William (Salem Village)
Pudeator, Ann (Salem)
Reed, Wilmot (Marblehead)
Rice, Sarah (Reading)
Rich, Mary de (Salem Village)
Riels, Mary de (Salem)
Riste, Sarah (Beverly)
Roote, Susanna (Beverly)
Scott, Margaret (Rowley)
Sears, Ann (Woburn)
Somes, Abigail (Gloucester)
Sparks, Martha (Chelmsford)
Tituba [slave] (Salem Village)
Toothaker, Jason (Billerica)
Toothaker, Mary (Billerica)
Toothaker, Roger (Billerica)
Toothaker, Miss (Billerica)
Tukey, Job (Beverly)
Tyler, Hannah (Andover)
Tyler, Joanna (Andover)
Tyler, Martha (Andover)
Usher, Hezekiah (no address)
Wardwell, Mary (Andover)
Wardwell, Samuel (Andover)
Warren, Mary (Salem Village)
White, Mrs. (Salem)
Whittredge, Mary (Salem Village)
Wilds, Sarah (Topsfield)
Willard, John (Salem Village)
Wilson, Sarah (Andover)
Wilson, Sarah, Jr. (Andover)

Death Warrant for Bridget Bishop
The first of the Salem accused to be hanged as a witch

To George Corwin, Gentleman, High Sheriff of the County of Essex. Greeting. Whereas Bridget Bishop (alias Oliver), the wife of Edward Bishop of Salem in the county of Essex, sawyer, at a special court of Oyer and Terminer held at Salem the second day of this instant month of June for the counties of Essex, Middlesex, and Suffolk, before William Stoughton, Esquire, and his Associate Justices of the said court, was indicted and arraigned upon five several indictments for using, practicing, and exercising on the 19th day of April last past and divers other days and times before and after, certain acts of witchcraft in and upon the bodies of Abigail Williams, Ann Putnam, junior, Mercy Lewis, Mary Walcott, and Elizabeth Hubbard, of Salem Village, single women, whereby their bodies were hurt, afflicted, pined, consumed, wasted, and tormented, contrary to the form of the statute in that case made and provided.

To which indictments the said Bridget Bishop pleaded Not Guilty, and for trial thereof put herself upon God and her country; whereupon she was found Guilty of the felonies and witchcrafts, whereof she stood indicted, and sentence of death accordingly passed against her as the law directs. Execution whereof yet remains to be done.

These are therefore in the name of their Majesties William and Mary, now King and Queen over England, &c., to will and command you that upon Friday next, being the tenth day of this instant month of June, between the hours of eight and twelve in the afternoon of the same day, you safely conduct the said Bridget Bishop (alias Oliver) from their Majesties' jail in Salem aforesaid to the place of execution, and there cause her to be hanged by the neck until she be dead, and of your doings herein make return to the clerk of the said court and precept. And hereof you are not to fail at your peril.

And this shall be your sufficient warrant. Given under my hand and seal at Boston the eighth day of June in the fourth year of the reign of our soverign lord and lady, William and Mary, now King and Queen over England &c. Annoque Domini 1692.

William Stoughton.

An Accused Witch Explains Her Confession

Goodwife Tyler did say that when she was first apprehended she had no fears upon her, and did think that nothing could have made her confess against herself. But since, she has found to her great grief that she had wronged the truth and falsely accused herself.

She said that when she was brought to Salem, her brother Bridges rode with her; and that all along the way from Andover to Salem, her brother kept telling her that she must needs be a witch, since the afflicted accused her and at her touch were raised out of their fits, and urging her to confess herself a witch.

She as constantly told him that she was no witch, that she knew nothing of witchcraft, and begged of him not to urge her to confess.

However, when she came to Salem, she was carried to a room, where her brother on one side and Mr. John Emerson on the other side did tell her that she was certainly a witch, and that she saw the devil before her eyes at that time (and accordingly the said Emerson would attempt with his hand to beat him away from her eyes). And they so urged her to confess that she wished herself in any dungeon, rather than be so treated.

(Continued on next page)

(Continued from previous page)

Mr. Emerson told her once and again, "Well! I see you will not confess! Well! I will now leave you, and then you are undone, body and soul forever."

Her brother urged her to confess, and told her that in so doing she could not lie. To which she answered, "Good brother, do not say so, for I shall lie if I confess, and then who shall answer unto God for my lie?" He still asserted it, and said that God would not suffer so many good men to be in such an error about it, and that she would be hanged if she did not confess. And [he] continued so long and so violently to urge and press her to confess, that she thought verily her life would have gone from her, and became so terrified in her mind that she owned at length almost anything that they propounded to her.

But she had wronged her conscience in so doing. She was guilty of a great sin in belying of herself, and desired to mourn for it as long as she lived.

This she said and a great deal more of the like nature, and all of it with such affection, sorrow, relenting, grief, and mourning as that it exceeds any pen for to describe and express the same.
—Account, perhaps by Thomas Brattle, dated October 19, 1692.

Methods of Securing Evidence for the Salem Witch Trials

Salem Prison
July 23, 1692

Mr. Mather, Mr. Allen,
Mr. Moody, Mr. Willard, and
Mr. Bailey.

Reverend Gentlemen:

The innocency of our case with the enmity of our accusers, and our judges, and jury, whom nothing but our innocent blood will serve their turn, having condemned us already before our trials, being so much incensed and engaged against us by the devil, makes us bold to beg and implore your favorable assistance of this our humble petition to his Excellency, that if it be possible our innocent blood may be spared, which undoubtedly otherwise will be shed, if the Lord doth not mercifully step in.

The magistrates, ministers, juries, and all the people in general, being so much enraged and incensed against us by the delusion of the devil, which we can term no other, by reason we know in our own consciences we are all innocent persons.

Here are five persons who have lately confessed themselves to be witches and do accuse some of us of being along with them at a "sacrament," since we were committed into close prison!—which we know to be lies.

Two of the five are [Martha] Carrier's sons, young men who would not confess anything till they tied them neck and heels till the blood was ready to come out of their noses. And 'tis credibly believed and reported this was the occasion of making them confess that [which] they never did, by reason they said one had been a witch a month and another five weeks, and that their mother had made them so—who has been confined here this nine weeks!

My son William Proctor, when he was examined, because he would not confess that he was guilty, when he was innocent, they tied him neck and heels till the blood gushed out at his nose, and would have kept him so twenty-four hours, if one more merciful than the rest had not taken pity on him and caused him to be unbound.

These actions are very like the popish cruelties. They have already undone us in our estates, and that will not serve their turns without our innocent bloods.

(Continued from opposite page)

(Continued from previous page)

If it cannot be granted that we can have our trials at Boston, we humbly beg that you would endeavor to have these magistrates changed, and others in their rooms, begging also and beseeching you would be pleased to be here, if not all, some of you at our trials, hoping thereby you may be the means of saving the shedding our innocent bloods, desiring your prayers to the Lord in our behalf, we rest your poor afflicted servants,

John Proctor.

—Robert Calef, *More Wonders of the Invisible World* (1700).

False Witness Acceptable in Witch Trials

On the self-confessed false testimony of Margaret Jacobs, her grandfather George Jacobs, John Willard, and Rev. George Burroughs were executed for witchcraft.

The humble declaration of Margaret Jacobs unto the honored court now sitting at Salem, sheweth that

Whereas your poor and humble declarant being closely confined here in Salem jail for the crime of witchcraft, which crime, thanks be to the Lord, I am altogether ignorant of, as will appear at the great Day of Judgment,

May it please the honored court, I was cried out upon [accused] by some of the possessed persons as afflicting of them. Whereupon I was brought to my examination, which persons at the sight of me fell down, which did very much startle and affright me.

The Lord above knows I knew nothing, in the least measure, how or who afflicted them. They told me, without doubt I did, or else they would not fall down at me. They told me if I would not confess, I should be put down into the dungeon and would be hanged, but if I would confess I should have my life. The which did so affright me, with my own vile wicked heart, to save my life made me make the confession I did; which confession, may it please the honored court, is altogether false and untrue.

The very first night after I had made my confession, I was in such horror of conscience that I could not sleep, for fear the devil should carry me away for telling such horrid lies. I was, may it please the honored court, sworn to my confession, as I understand since; but then, at that time, was ignorant of it, not knowing what an oath did mean. The Lord, I hope, in whom I trust, out of the abundance of his mercy, will forgive my false forswearing myself.

What I said was altogether false, against my grandfather, and Mr. Burroughs, which I did to save my life and to have my liberty. But the Lord, charging it to my conscience, made me in so much horror, that I could not contain myself before I had denied my confession, which I did, though I saw nothing but death before me—choosing rather death with a quiet conscience than to live in such horror, which I could not suffer.

Whereupon my denying my confession, I was committed to close prison, where I have enjoyed more felicity in spirit a thousand times than I did before in my enlargement.

And now, may it please your honors, your poor and humble declarant having in part given your honors a description of my condition, do leave it to your honors' pious and judicious discretions to take pity and compassion on my young and tender years; to act and do with me as the Lord above and your honors shall see good, having no friend

(Continued on next page)

(Continued from previous page)

but the Lord to plead my cause for me; not being guilty in the least measure of the crime of witchcraft, nor any other sin that deserves death from man; and your poor and humble declarant shall forever pray, as she is bound in duty, for your honors' happiness in this life and eternal felicity in the world to come. So prays your honors' declarant.

Margaret Jacobs.

—Governor Thomas Hutchinson, *History of the Colony of Massachusetts Bay* (1764).

Confession of Error by the Jurors at the Salem Witch Trials, Four Years Later (January 14, 1696)

We whose names are under written, being in the year 1692 called to serve as jurors, in Court at Salem, on trial of many who were by some suspected guilty of doing acts of witchcraft upon the bodies of sundry persons:

We confess that we ourselves were not capable to understand, nor able to withstand, the mysterious delusions of the Powers of Darkness and Prince of the Air; but were, for want of knowledge in ourselves and better information from others, prevailed with to take up such evidence against the accused, as on further consideration and better information we justly fear was insufficient for the touching the lives of any (Deut. xvii.6).

Whereby we fear we have been instrumental with others, though ignorantly and unwittingly, to bring upon ourselves and this people of the Lord the guilt of innocent blood—which sin the Lord saith in Scripture he would not pardon (II Kings xxiv.4), that is, we suppose in regard of his temporal judgments.

We do therefore hereby signify to all in general, and to the surviving sufferers in especial, our deep sense of, and sorrow for our errors, in acting on such evidence to the condemnation of any person. And we do hereby declare that we justly fear that we were sadly deluded and mistaken, for which we are much disquieted and distressed in our minds; and do humbly beg forgiveness, first of God for Christ's sake for this error, and pray that God would not impute the guilt of it to ourselves nor others. And we also pray that we may be considered candidly and aright by the living sufferers as being then under the power of a strong and general delusion, utterly unacquainted with, and not experienced in matters of that nature.

We do heartily ask forgiveness of you all whom we have justly offended, and do declare according to our present minds we would none of us do such things again on such grounds for the whole world; praying you to accept of this in way of satisfaction for our offense; and that you would bless the inheritance of the Lord, that he may be entreated for the land.

[Signed]

Thomas Fisk, *Foreman*
William Fisk
John Batcheler
Thomas Fisk, Junior
John Dane
Joseph Evelith
Thomas Perly, Senior
John Pebody
Thomas Perkins
Samuel Sayer
Andrew Elliott
Henry Herrick, Senior

—Quoted in Robert Calef, *More Wonders of the Invisible World* (1700).

Salmon Falls Assaults. A strange anecdote at Salmon Falls in Berwick, Maine, included in Increase Mather's *Illustrious Providences* (1684), provides a curious story of an American poltergeist in 1683. It was reported to Mather by Rev. Joshua Moody, who transcribed it from Thomas Broughton, a well-known Boston merchant, who took it "from the mouth of the woman and her husband."

A brief narrative of sundry apparitions of Satan unto and assaults at sundry times and places upon the person of Mary, the wife of Antonio Hortado, dwelling near the Salmon Falls. Taken from her own mouth, August 13, 1683.

In June, 1682 (the day forgotten), at evening, the said Mary heard a voice at the door of her dwelling, saying, "What do you here?" About an hour after, standing at the door of her house, she had a blow on her eye that settled her head near to the doorpost. And two or three days after, a stone (as she judged) about half a pound or a pound weight, was thrown along the house within into the chimney, and [she] going to take it up, it was gone. All the family was in the house, and no hand appearing which might be instrumental in throwing the stone. About two hours after, a frying pan, then hanging in the chimney, was heard to ring so loud, that not only those in the house heard it, but others also that lived on the other side of the river near an hundred rods distant or more.

Whereupon the said Mary and her husband going in a canoe over the river, they saw like the head of a man newshorn and the tail of a white cat, about two or three foot distant from each other, swimming before the canoe, but no body to join head and tail together. And they returning over the river in less than an hour's time, the said apparition followed their canoe back again, but disappeared at landing.

A day or two after, the said Mary was stricken on her head (as she judged) with a stone, which caused a swelling and much soreness on her head, being then in the yard by her house. And she presently entering into her house was bitten on both arms, black and blue, and one of her breasts scratched, the impressions of the teeth (being like man's teeth) were plainly seen by many.

Whereupon, deserting their house to sojourn at a neighbor's on the other side of the river, there appeared to said Mary in the house of her sojourning, a woman clothed with a green safeguard [outer coat], a short blue cloak, and a white cap, making a proffer to strike her with a firebrand, but struck her not. The day following, the same shape appeared again to her, but now arrayed with a gray gown, a white apron, and white head-clothes, in appearance laughing several times, but no voice heard. Since when, said Mary has been freed from these satanical molestations.

But the said Antonio being returned in March last with his family to dwell again in his own house, and on his entrance there, hearing the noise of a man walking in his chamber, and seeing the boards buckle under his feet as he walked, though no man to be seen in the chamber—for they went on purpose to look—he returned with his family to dwell on the other side of the river. Yet planting his ground, though he forsook his house, he hath had five rods of good log-fence thrown down at once, the feeting of neat cattle plainly to be seen almost between every row of corn in the field, yet no cattle seen there, nor any damage done to his corn, not so much as any of the leaves of the corn cropped.

Schüler, Johann. From his extensive knowledge of witchcraft, Henry C. Lea selected the Blanckenstein Tragedy as the embodiment of "the blind and stupid cruelty of this superstition." That trial of 1676 in Naumburg, however, was gentle and civilized compared with the trial of Johann Schüler and his wife in 1663-64 in Lindheim, an imperial town in the Wetterau district of Protestant Hesse-Darmstadt, subject to the authority of the *Herrenschaft:* Hermann von Oynhausen, High Bailiff of Brunswick-Lüneburg, Hartmann von Rosenbach, Dean of Würzburg Cathedral, and several other noblemen. The Schüler case is probably the most atrocious in this *Encyclopedia.*

The administration of Lindheim was left by the absentee lords to a chief magistrate,

Geiss, a vulgar and rapacious veteran of the Thirty Years' War. In 1661, Geiss persuaded Baron Oynhausen that Lindheim was swarming with witches. "The majority of the citizens are very much upset and offer, if his Lordship just expressed a desire to burn them, gladly to provide the wood and pay all the costs." In this projected witch hunt, Geiss saw great profit: "His Lordship might also acquire much money thereby, so that the bridge as well as the church could be brought into good repair. Furthermore, his Lordship might also have so much wealth that in future his officials might be so much better paid."

So prompted, Baron Oynhausen and the other *Herrenschaft* assented to resuming the witch trials (in abeyance for eight years), and in July, 1661, Geiss appointed as his assistant judges [*Blutschöffen*] four of the lowest and most vicious scum of the town. These judges arrested whom they would: wealthy men and women as well as children from eight to twelve. One timid woman, who always fled when she saw one of the new judges, was arrested, tortured into insensibility, and burned within a few weeks. Generally the victims were manacled by short chains to a wall, about fifteen feet from the ground, while a fire slowly charred them. It is a curious coincidence that the scene of these atrocities, the Witches' Tower, was later owned by the novelist Sacher-Masoch.

The Schüler troubles started in 1663. Geiss wanted the property of this wealthy and respected miller, whose wife the preceding year had had a stillborn child. From the midwife, Geiss extracted a confession that she had killed the infant by witchcraft and been aided by six other persons. These six were arrested and, under torture, all swore they had exhumed the little corpse, cut it up, and rendered the pieces in a pot for witch ointment. The Schülers insisted no one was to blame for the death of their child, and demanded the grave be opened for proof. In the presence of the father, the judges found the corpse unviolated. Geiss forced the miller to keep quiet under threats of direst torture, and then, because confessions made under torture must be

true, burned the midwife and the six she had implicated.

Toward the end of the year, Geiss arrested an old woman known as Becker-Margareth. One of his henchmen promised that free confession would exempt her from torture and allow her body, after execution, burial in the churchyard. The unfortunate woman knew she was lost and submitted to her fate; she accused fourteen more persons, including Schüler's wife, of complicity in the death of the child, desperately remarking that these too would get to know what burning bodies smelled like. Frau Schüler was immediately put in prison on suspicion of witchcraft, and an old scar from a fall, which had been treated by the barber-surgeon of Hanau, was identified as a devil's mark. Johann Schüler, however, managed to get out of town and hasten to Würzburg, to persuade the Dean of the Cathedral, as co-administrator of the town, to rescue his beloved wife. But in his absence, Geiss tortured her into confessing complicity in the murder and accusing her husband as a witch. Geiss was waiting for Schüler, and, on his return, threw him into the freezing Witches' Tower, without straw, covering, or stockings. After five days, Schüler was tortured with barbarities specially prepared for him, and admitted his guilt. Freed from his agony, he immediately revoked, whereupon he was tortured a second time. Schüler again retracted his confession, but just as Geiss was ready to stretch him a third time on the rack, angry townspeople started to riot. In the ensuing disorder, during the night Schüler managed to get free, and, with several others liberated by their friends, on February 18, 1644, struggled to Speyer, the seat of the Imperial Supreme Court [*Reichskammergericht*]. The sight of the tortured bodies of the women who escaped raised popular indignation, and a noted lawyer petitioned the Court on their behalf. Meanwhile, in the face of rising hostility in Lindheim, Geiss continued his fury, and on February 23, 1664, with her husband still in Speyer, burned Frau Schüler alive. In early March, a popular rising forced Geiss and his men to flee. The Dean of Würzburg advised Oynhausen to caution Geiss. Seeing the hatred against his appointee, however, and bowing to the decision of the Supreme Court that the Lindheim witch hunt stop, Oynhausen dismissed his judge, whom he could no longer protect. However, although Geiss had executed thirty innocent persons, he was not punished.

The records at Lindheim revealed that Geiss had received in ready cash alone the huge sum of 188 thalers and 18 albus from those he had burned. Of the livestock he had acquired, he did not bother to keep a reckoning. Whatever he did in connection with his duties was exorbitant; for a visit to a village two hours distant (to look for witches), he charged five thalers. Geiss took care of his strong-arm men too: "For the Inn at Hainchen [half an hour from Lindheim]: what the guards sitting next to the Queen of the Witches [*Hexenkönigin*] drank—two thalers and seven albus." "July 29. To the cellarer in connection with the witch hunt [*Hexenverfolgung*], in the presence of the steward—twelve thalers, fifteen albus."

In his defense, Geiss made the typical pleas of a gauleiter. He had received only his regular pay (usually a third of the confiscations). He had not embezzled. He had sent the due shares (about two-thirds) of everything he had confiscated to the *Herrenschaft*. No matter how much Geiss had defrauded the co-administrators, they got something. This fact may explain why both Baron Oynhausen and the Dean of Würzburg Cathedral were slow to stop Geiss's witch hunt.

Schultheis, Heinrich von. Schultheis' *Detailed Instructions how to proceed in the inquisition against the horrible vice of witchcraft* (1634), according to George L. Burr, is "the most gruesome in all the gruesome literature of witch persecution." Written by the secretary to several witch-hunting bishops in the Rhineland, a doctor of both civil and ecclesiastical law, it is "the most pious and the most cruel of all such handbooks" for the pursuit and the conviction of witches. The instructions appear as answers by a doctor [Schultheis]

"With the same, in fact with even greater indifference do I regard torturing you than I do bending this reed out of my path with my stick; for by so doing I earn nothing. But when I have you tortured, and by the severe means afforded by the law I bring you to confession, then I perform a work pleasing in God's sight; and it profiteth me."—Heinrich von Schultheis, a notorious witch hunter in the Rhineland, in the first half of the seventeenth century. There is only one known copy of his book (1634) in the world, now in the Cornell University Library.

to questions by a mythical baron [*Freyherr*] named Philadelphus, on the procedure against witches.

One curious passage shows how, under witch law, convictions were obtained by evidence which in any other trial would never have been admitted. The impact is greater than that of parallel distortions elsewhere, because the dialogue includes the rational comments of the *Freyherr*. Four witnesses testify they have seen a Mr. "Alpha" at a sabbat: Gretta says he rode a black horse, Thomas a red piebald horse; Kurt swears Alpha was on a gray horse, and young Fundemann says a brown horse. "Since there are four conflicting testimonies, how can the charge stand," inquires the Baron, "for a man cannot sit on four different horses at one time?" Dr. Schultheis explains that people who see a white stallion belonging to a neighbor would all agree it was white, but a *witch* has a horse of a different color. "That is very odd," ponders the Baron. "Surely it is impossible that a horse should be seen as white by one, black by another, sorrel by another, and yellow by someone else." Schultheis then says Alpha's horse was really Satan, with whom, as with a conjurer, many such strange things are possible. He tells the Baron to look at a gray horse through some green-tinted spectacles. "The horse is green!" exclaims the Baron. "But what have these spectacles to do with the horse we are talking about? Those witnesses weren't looking through tinted glasses." Schultheis answers that if manmade spectacles can cause a change in color, how much more powerfully can the devil work to confuse the senses. The accusation is therefore valid evidence.

Schultheis met with opposition, and then he became especially enraged. At Paderborn in 1631, he convicted a number of wealthy citizens; he was much infuriated at one "Pisano," who confessed he asked the devil to permit the appearance of many innocent persons at the witch sabbat, so that they might be denounced. By this very multiplicity of names, the procedure of the court might be brought into question, the validity of the denunciations doubted, and the prosecution discontinued. Schultheis was naturally incensed at a gibe which might prevent his confiscating the property of those he burned.

This "false witch judge" (so called by Löher) was a bitter opponent of the Jesuits, Adam Tanner (1572-1632) in his *Theologia Scholastica* (1617) and Friedrich von Spee. His virulence in advocating the extermination of accused witches indicates the opposing influence of the skeptics, as well as the entrenched position of the Inquisition and the Prince-Archbishop of Mainz (Peter Ostermann), whose approbations are featured in the book.

Schwägel, Anna Maria. The grandfather of a man living today could have seen a woman beheaded as a witch! Just three generations separate the world of the mid-twentieth century from the obscurantism of witchcraft. The death of Anna Maria Schwägel at Kempten (Bavaria), a prince-abbacy, on April 11, 1775, was the last official execution for witchcraft in Germany; the evidence for her beheading—her demented confession that she had copulated with the devil.

Getting on in her thirties, well past the age a girl expected marriage, Anna Maria fell easy prey to a fellow servant, a coachman. He promised marriage if she would turn Lutheran, and accordingly Anna Maria journeyed to Memmingen formally to renounce her Catholicism. The coachman seduced and then abandoned her. In despair at the twin loss of her faith and virginity, she sought absolution from an Augustinian friar. When some time later she learned the friar had himself been converted to Protestantism, her doubts and fears increased. Only the devil could have doublecrossed her so. She wandered about the countryside, dazed and crazed. Finally, she was picked up and put in a bedlam at Laneggen, near Kempten. Here, the matron, Anna Maria Kuhstaller, herself unbalanced, beat her and forced her to admit intercourse with the devil (whom Anna Schwägel identified as the coachman). On this confession, Matron Kuhstaller denounced her to the magistrates, and on February 20, 1775, Anna Maria, now crippled in body as well as in mind, was thrust into jail.

Two weeks later, her trial for witchcraft began. Apparently torture was not used. Anna, completely befuddled and under insistent questioning, admitted to a pact and sexual relations with the devil, in dreams and in reality. No charge of *maleficia* was made. On March 30, three judges sentenced her to execution, after a discussion whether she should be burned, hanged, or beheaded. The Prince-Abbot of Kempten examined the procès-verbal and confirmed the verdict. On April 11, 1775, Anna Maria Schwägel was judicially murdered.

Schweidler, Maria: see Amber Witch.

The diſcouerie of
Witchcraft.

¶ *The firſt Booke.*

An impeachment of Witches power in me-
teors and elementarie bodies, tending to the rebuke of ſuch as attribute too much vnto them.

The firſt Chapter.

Ꜧ Ꜫ fables of Ꮃitchcraſt haue taken ſo faſt hold and dæpe rœt in the heart
of man, that ſewe oꝛ none can(nowadaies)
with patience indure the hand and coꝛecti-
on of God. Foꝛ if any aduerſitie, græfe, ſick-
neſſe, loſſe of childꝛen, coꝛne, cattell, oꝛ liber-
tie happen vnto them; by & by they exclaime
vppon witches. As though there were no God in Iſrael that oꝛdereth all things ac- Iob.5.
coꝛding to his will ; puniſhing both iuſt and vnuiſt with græfs,
plagues, and afflictions in maner and foꝛme as he thinketh gœd:
but that certeine old women hære on earth, called witches,
muſt næds be the contriuers of all mens calamities, and as
though they themſelues were innocents, and had deſerued no
ſuch puniſhments. Inſomuch as they ſticke not to ride and go
to ſuch, as either are iniuriouſlie tearmed witches, oꝛ elſe are
willing ſo to be accounted, ſæking at their hands comfoꝛt and
remedie in time of their tribulation, contrarie to Gods will and
commandement in that behalfe, who bids vs reſoꝛt to him in all Matth.11.
                                    C.i.   our

The first page of the first edition (1584) of Reginald Scot's *Discovery of Witchcraft*, the most important book in English to attack the witchcraft delusion. It is now comparatively rare, for on his accession to the throne of England in 1603, King James I ordered all copies to be destroyed. The second edition did not appear until 1651. From Cornell University Library.

Scot, Reginald. King James called Scot's opinions "damnable" and very likely had all copies of his book burned (there are no first editions in either Lambeth Palace or St. Paul's Cathedral libraries). "Scot's *Discovery of Witchcraft* [1584] dismasketh sundry egregious impostures," wrote Gabriel Harvey in 1593, "and in certain principal chapters and special passages hitteth the nail on the head." In 1688, the credulous Meric Casaubon found Scot, whose "book, I must confess, I never had, nor ever read," an "illiterate wretch . . . a very inconsiderable man." In spite of the fact that Scot cited twenty-three English writers, such as Chaucer, Bale, Fox, and Thomas More, none of these was primarily concerned with witchcraft. Apart from the translations of Lavater's *De Spectris* (in 1572), Daneau's *Les Sorciers* (in 1575), and *The World Possessed with Devils* (1583) of Pierre Viret, Scot's is the first book in English devoted to witchcraft. From it, Shakespeare got hints for his witches in *Macbeth,* and Middleton for his play, *The Witch.*

Born of a Kentish country family in 1538, Scot attended Oxford University, but left without a degree to live the life of a country gentleman. He held briefly a government post as collector of subsidies, was a member of Parliament for a year, and managed the estate of his cousin, Sir Thomas Scot. He was twice married, to women of good families. His death came in 1599. His cultured and practical interests led to his writing *The Hop Garden* (1574); this manual stimulated the development of Kent as the hop-producing county of England.

Probably the shock of the mass executions in 1582 of the witches at St. Osyth in Kent, or else the trial of Margaret Symons, a Kentish witch, prompted Scot to write his *Discovery of Witches,* in the same way that the trial of Jane Wenham stimulated the work of Bishop Hutchinson. Since Scot attacked a conception which had been defined as a felony, he published the book on his own responsibility; it was not entered in the Stationers' Register, nor did a publisher's name appear (only the printer's name at the end of the book). Scot thought the whole delusion the invention of the Inquisition:

> And because it may appear unto the world what treacherous and faithless dealing, what extreme and intolerable tyranny, what gross and fond [foolish] absurdities, what unnatural and uncivil discourtesy, what cankered and spiteful malice, what outrageous and barbarous cruelty . . . what abominable and devilish inventions, and what flat and plain knavery is practiced against these old women, I will set down the whole order of the Inquisition, to the everlasting, inexcusable, and apparent shame of all witch mongers. (Book I)

Scot's position was that "spiritualistic manifestations were artful impostures or illusions due to mental disturbance in the observers." His whole attitude was skeptical and sarcastically mocking, save where he credited precious stones and fabulous objects (like a unicorn's horn) with power to cure sickness. Not all the sixteen divisions or books discuss witchcraft; the last four take up charms, and explanations of impostures and jugglers' tricks.

Since Scot was not writing to advise judges or theologians but to ridicule witchcraft in the eyes of the general public, his *Discovery* is lightly handled and easier reading than the works of the standard demonologists. Among his biting anecdotes (illustrating Ligature) is that of a young man who, after fornicating, later found himself emasculated. He

> went to a witch for the restitution thereof. She brought him to a tree, where she showed him a nest, and bade him climb up and take it. And being in the top of the tree, he took out a mighty great one, and showed the same to her, asking her if he might not have the same. Nay, quoth she, that is our parish priest's tool, but take any other which thou wilt. And it is there affirmed, that some have found twenty, and some thirty of them in one nest, being there preserved with provender, as it were at a manger. . . . These are no jests, for they be written by them that were and are judges upon the lives and deaths of those persons.

Henry C. Lea summarized the work thus: "It has the honor of being the first of the controversial works which resolutely denied the reality of witchcraft and the power of the devil."

Scotland, Witchcraft in. Scotland is second only to Germany in the barbarity of its witch trials. The Presbyterian clergy acted like inquisitors, and the church sessions often shared the prosecution with the secular law courts. The Scottish laws were, if anything, more heavily loaded against the accused. Finally, the devilishness of the torture was limited only by Scotland's backward technology in the construction of mechanical devices. Suppression of any opposition to belief in witchcraft was complete.

To the end of the sixteenth century, while there is evidence of considerable magic and sorcery of a simple folklore nature (which has survived in various customs and superstitions to the present), trials for witchcraft were few. Up to the Reformation, there was not one case of burning for witchcraft. As in England, the early trials charged witchcraft for political ends, and Scotland had its own series of "Noble trials." So, in 1479, the Earl of Mar was accused of trying to kill his brother, King James III, by witchcraft. Lady Glamis was burned in 1537 for using charms against King James V. In 1590 Lady Foullis was charged with employing charms, waxen images, and poisons against Lady Balnagowan so that Lady Foullis could marry Lord Balnagowan; a jury of her tenants acquitted her.

Witchcraft was introduced into Scotland by Mary, Queen of Scots, in 1563, but in accordance with the country's own traditions, the new statute concentrated its opposition against beneficent sorcery and fortunetelling; he who sought help from a witch was as culpable as the witch herself. After this statute, there was a steady trickle of trials. Bessie Dunlop of Lyne, Ayrshire, was burned in 1576 for being a member of a conclave of witches, "eight women and four men," and for receiving herbal cures from the Queen of the Fairies. In 1588, Allison Peirson of Byre Hills, Fifeshire, was burned for converse with the Queen of Elfame and prescribing magic potions—she had recommended the Bishop of St. Andrews cure his hypochondria with spiced claret and boiled capon. In these and later trials, there is a marked absence of spectral evidence and of charges of sexual relations with the devil.

Scottish witchcraft did not take hold until the reign of King James VI of Scotland (James I of England) who himself supervised the notorious trial and torture of the North Berwick Witches in 1590, and by his *Demonology* (1597) set the pattern for Scottish witch trials in the line of European demonologists. While the King toward the end of his life veered to almost skeptical views, nevertheless the records of witchcraft in Scotland affirm the truth of Lynn Linton's summation:

Whatever of blood-stained folly belonged specially to the Scottish trials of this time—and hereafter—owed its original impulse to him; and every groan of the tortured wretches driven to their fearful doom, and every tear of the survivors left blighted and desolate to drag out their weary days in mingled grief and terror, lie on his memory with shame and condemnation ineffaceable for all time. (*Witch Stories*, 1861)

The usual method of procedure in Scotland was for the Privy Council to appoint a commission of eight local gentlemen, any three (or five) of whom could act, to investigate alleged witchcraft. This commission might have only investigative powers or it might (more commonly) have power to sentence to death. These commissions were the bane of Scottish law; for example, on November 7, 1661, fourteen such commissions were authorized, and another fourteen on January 23, 1662. If the evidence seemed to warrant, the commission authorized the sheriffs to summon an assize of no more than forty-five local men, from whom fifteen were selected as a jury. The commissioners acted as the judges. Often the minister and the elders of the church met in session as a "presbytery" to initiate charges of witchcraft, and then apply to the Privy Council for civil judges to pass sentence. The General Assembly of the Kirk of Scotland in 1640 and 1642 encouraged vigilance and ordered all ministers to search out suspected witches and punish them. Indeed, the worst periods of persecution— 1590-97, 1640-44, and 1660-63—coincide with the dominance of Presbyterianism.

The costs of the trial and execution had to be borne by the condemned person, paid out of his own property before it was confiscated by the king. If the victim was a tenant on an estate, the owner of the house was responsible for the costs. If the victim was living in a town or village and was a pauper, the costs of imprisonment and burning were divided equally between the town council and the church sessions. For a poor community these costs could be very heavy [see further, Costs].

In Scotland the law against witchcraft included some distinctive features. In no other country was a prisoner permitted a lawyer (but most witches were too poor to retain counsel). On the other hand, again differing from German custom, a confession was not necessary before conviction and execution. General reputation as a witch was considered evidence without further proof and, if entered on an indictment (as it generally was), made conviction certain. Sometimes this practice was opposed, as in the East Lothian trial of Isobel Young of Eastbarns in 1629, where—of all authorities!—Jean Bodin was appealed to for "a clear probation" involving notoriety of the fact, voluntary confession, and deposition of witnesses. But a general charge of "habit and repute" remained in force into the early eighteenth century.

Once a dittay [indictment] had been drawn, the accused could not dispute its accuracy, even when clearly untrue. Thus, for example, Isobel Young was accused of stopping a water mill twenty-nine years previously and of maligning a man who thereby lost the use of his legs (1629). In her rebuttal, she urged that a mill could break down through natural causes, and that the man had been lame before she cursed him. Sir Thomas Hope, the prosecutor, argued that this defense was "contrary to the libel," that is, she contradicted what was charged by the prosecutor in his indictment. He was upheld, and Isobel Young was convicted, strangled, and burned.

Examples of torture, some of it extralegal, used in Scottish witch trials have been given in other entries [see Torture, Margaret Barclay, John Fian, North Berwick Witches, Pittenweem Witches]. Keeping the prisoner without sleep for several days and nights, keeping her naked on a cold stone for as long as twenty-eight days, immuring in solitary confinement in an underground dungeon, were passive torments compared with flogging, crushing the legs in stocks, jerking the head with ropes, crushing the fingers in a vise, squeezing the legs in iron boots, or pulling out the fingernails with pincers. One specifically Scottish torture was to put a hair shirt steeped in vinegar on the accused, so that the skin would be pulled off the body. For each act of torture the victim had to pay a fee; thus the 1597 Aberdeen trials record a charge of six shillings and eight pence for branding on the cheek.

And the Scottish judges combined mental with physical cruelty. On June 4, 1596, Ali-

son (or Margaret) Balfour, "a known notorious witch," was kept forty-eight hours in the "caspie claws," an iron vise crushing the arms. While under this torture at Edinburgh Castle, she had to watch her 81-year-old husband pressed under 700 pounds of iron bars, her son placed in the "Spanish boots" and given fifty-seven blows, each blow directed at a wedge which tightened the boots to render his bones into pulp, and her seven-year-old daughter tortured with pilliwinks [thumbscrews]. Her servant, Thomas Palpa, who was also implicated, was kept 264 hours in the caspie claws, and scourged with "ropes on such sort that they left neither flesh nor hide upon him." Both Alison Balfour and Thomas Palpa recanted their confessions when released from torture, but both were burned, Alison on December 16, 1596.

Another disgraceful episode was recorded in 1652 by the "English Commission for administration of justice," which heard two fugitive witches from the Highlands relate how they had been hung up by their thumbs, whipped, and burned between the toes, in the mouth, and on the head. Four of the six accused had died under this torture.

In Scotland belief in witchcraft continued beyond the end of the seventeenth into the eighteenth century. Sir George Mackenzie, King's Advocate, wrote as late as 1678: "That there are witches, divines cannot doubt, since the word of God hath ordained that no witch shall live; nor lawyers in Scotland, seeing our law ordains it to be punished with death." Rev. Robert Kirk, minister at Aberfoyle, in 1691 accepted without hesitation the devil's mark (*Secret Commonwealth*), as did Rev. John Bell, minister of Gladsmuir, as late as 1705 (*Trial of Witchcraft*). But, at the same time, opposition to the delusion was mounting. In 1678, Sir John Clerk refused to sit on a commission to investigate witchcraft. In 1718, Robert Dundas, the King's Advocate, rebuked the deputy sheriff of Caithness for proceeding against witches without first notifying him, because of the difficulty of the charges (William Montgomery was plagued by cats; he slashed at

The Most Significant Scottish Trials

1590   North Berwick Witches: a fantastic story of many witches sailing over the sea in sieves, and invoking tempests to shipwreck the King.

1590   Fian, John: the alleged ringleader of the North Berwick group, subjected to horrible torture.

1597   Aberdeen Witches: witch mania resulting from King James's *Demonology*.

1607   Grierson, Isobel: a typical witch trial, at the height of the mania, of a woman reputed "a common sorcerer and witch."

1618   Barclay, Margaret: a gruesome trial, based on *damnum minatum* or witch's threat, resulting in the torture and death of four persons accused.

1623   Perth Witch Trial: a verbatim report of a trial involving simple acts of beneficent sorcery.

1654   Glenluce Devil: typical poltergeist tricks by a young adolescent.

1662   Gowdie, Isobel: imaginative and freely given confession embracing entire range of witchcraft; two accused presumably condemned.

1670   Weir, Thomas: a seventy-year-old man becomes demented and confesses to monstrous perversions.

1697   Bargarran Impostor: twenty-four persons indicted and seven witches of Renfrew burned following charges of witchcraft by eleven-year-old Christine Shaw.

1704   Pittenweem Witches: illustration of mob violence, condoned by clergy and judges, resulting in death of two accused witches.

two cats, and as a result two witches were said to have died). And in 1720 he refused to act against women imprisoned on accusations of the son of Lord Torphichen, a possessed child who accused some women of Calder as witches; although the charges were eventually dismissed, two of the accused died in jail.

Certain dates fix the end of Scottish witchcraft. On May 3, 1709, Elspeth Ross was the last person tried before the Court of Justiciary on a general charge of being a notorious witch and of making threats. She was branded and banished. In June, 1727, Janet Horne was burned at Dornoch, Ross-shire, for having used her daughter as a flying horse, the devil shoeing her so that she was permanently lamed. The judge, Captain David Ross, dismissed charges against the daughter, however. In June, 1736, the "Acts anentis witchcraft" was formally repealed. Almost forty years later (1773), the divines of the Associated Presbytery passed a resolution declaring their belief in witchcraft—just one more indication of the part of the ministers in encouraging superstition.

Various estimates have been made of the number of witches executed in Scotland. Thomas Ady said the Presbytery of Scotland admitted burning some 4,000 witches. In the *Scottish Review* (1891), F. Legge gave 3,400 from 1590 to 1680. George F. Black in 1938 gave the names of 1,800 witches, but not all of these were executed; his estimate of 4,400 witches burned is probably the closest that can be made.

Scratching. Scratching was a minor form of torture practiced on a witch with the object of curing the person she had allegedly bewitched. It was confined almost exclusively to England. "To scratch and fetch blood of such as do harm in that quality is a means to cure them that be hurt." The recovery of the afflicted person after the blood of the witch had been let was generally taken to imply the guilt of the suspect. Behind this popular belief was the theory that a witch's imp or demon, whom she had sent into the body of the afflicted to possess and torment it, would come out of the body to suck the blood of its mistress. A ballad based on this belief, "The Scratching of Witches," was composed in 1579. A similar belief fostered the search for witch's marks, from which the familiars or imps suckled blood.

While primarily undertaken by relations or friends as a practical measure to relieve the sufferer, scratching was apparently permitted as evidence in court. In 1615 the accusers of Alice Smewen scratched her face with their nails "in such furious manner that the blood ran down in abundance." At this they scoffed, saying forebodingly, "This blood shall not serve our turn, we will have thy heart's blood." In 1717 at Leicester a suspect resisted scratching, and consequently was held down by force. The report of the trial noted: "The old woman's skin was so tough that they could get no blood of her by scratching, so they used great pins and such instruments for that purpose."

The Throckmorton children, who had picked on Mrs. Alice Samuel with her daughter Agnes, were allowed to sit on her lap and scratch and tear her face "for the breadth of a shilling." The son of the jailer in this case took sick during the trial and was also allowed to scratch Mrs Samuel. After he had done so, he recovered his health. Another example told of Mother Atkins in the preceding year (1592): Richard Burt, a farmhand in Pinner (Middlesex), was eating apple pie in a barn, when he saw a monstrous black cat. He was suddenly jerked into the air, carried a long way off to Harrow, dropped in a fire and scorched; after four days he found his way home, speechless and able only to point at Mother Atkins' house. After he had drawn blood from the witch, he "mended reasonably." (*A Most Wicked Work of a Wretched Witch*, 1593)

Most women would resist or at least resent being scratched, but some had quiet reactions. When the young upstart Thomas Darling clawed at Alice Gooderidge until "blood came out apace," she gently said, "Take blood enough, child. God help thee." To which the brash youth retorted: "Pray for thyself, thy prayer can do me no good." [See Burton Boy.] George Gifford told

how the father of a boy bewitched with sores forced the return of the witch by burning the boy's hair in a cloth in an open space. "The woman came home with all speed, came to his house, came to the boy, and said, 'John, scratch me.' He scratched her until the blood flowed, and whereas before nothing would draw his sores, they healed of themselves." (*Dialogue*, 1593)

Sir Robert Filmer in 1653 quoted the authority of William Perkins' *Discourse of Witchcraft* (1608) that "scratching of the suspected party and the present recovery therefrom" constituted one of the "less sufficient proofs" of witchcraft. Perkins, while not entirely ruling out scratching as a presumption of guilt, found it godless: "For it is a means which hath no warrant or power thereunto, either by the word of God, or from nature, but only from the Devil; who, if he yieldeth either at crossing or scratching, he doth it willingly and not by compulsion."

Sentence. The sentence relaxing or remitting a condemned heretic to the secular authority was a terrifying formula. Albeit the Inquisition employed the most barbarous tortures in its own dungeons, it never executed those it found guilty; these it handed over to the secular courts with a technical recommendation for clemency and the practical advice that clemency by the secular judges would be indicative of their own heresy.

A typical specimen of such a sentence was given by the Dominican Inquisitor, Sebastian Michaëlis, against eighteen men and women at Avignon in 1582, which he later "set down in Latin just as it was then read and pronounced."

We, N.N., having considered the counts wherewith you stand charged and accused before us, and having examined both the statements of yourselves and your accomplices, and your own confessions made before us and often sworn according to law, as well as the depositions and accusations of the witnesses and other legitimate proofs, basing our judgment on what has been said and done during this trial.

We lawfully agree that you and your accomplices have denied the one and triune God, the creator and maker of all things, and that you have worshiped the devil, the ancient and implacable enemy of mankind.

You have vowed yourselves to him forever, and have renounced your most holy baptism and those who were your sponsors therein, together with your part of paradise and the eternal heritage which our Lord Jesus Christ bought for you and the whole human race by his death.

All these you renounced before the said devil existing in the species of a man, and that raging devil baptized you anew with water, which you accepted, and you did change the name given you in baptism at the holy font, and so took and received another false name in the guise of baptism.

And as a pledge of your fealty to the devil you gave him a fragment and particle of your clothing; and that the father of lies should take care to delete and obliterate you from the book of life, at his order and behest you with your own hands wrote your names in the black book there prepared, the roll of those damned to eternal death.

And that he might bind you with stouter bonds to so great perfidy and impiety, he branded each of you with his mark or stigmata as belonging to him, and you did swear homage and obedience to his orders within a circle (which is the symbol of divinity) traced upon the earth (which is God's footstool); and you and your accomplices bound yourselves to tread under foot the image of the Lord and the cross.

And in obedience to Satan, with the help of a staff, smeared with some nefarious ointment given you by the devil himself, and placed between your legs, you were enabled to fly through the air at dead of night to the place ordained, at an hour fit for vilest criminals, and on stated days you were so carried and transported by the devil himself;

And there in the common synagogue [synagoga] of all the witches, sorcerers, heretics, conjurers, and devil worshipers, you did kindle a foul fire, and after many rejoicings, lively dancings, eating and drinking, and games in honor of your president Beelzebub, the prince of devils, in the shape and appearance of a deformed and hideous black goat, you adored him in deed and word as God and did approach him on bended knees as suppliants and offered him lighted candles of pitch; and (fie, for shame!) with the greatest reverence you did kiss with sacrilegious mouth his most foul and beastly backside; and did call upon him by the name of the true God, and invoke his aid to avenge you on all who had offended you or denied your requests.

And, taught by him, you did wreak your spite in *maleficia* and charms against both men and beasts, and did murder many newborn children, and with the help of the said serpent Satan you did afflict mankind with curses, loss of milk, the wasting sickness, and other most grave diseases.

And your own children, many of them with your own knowledge and consent, you did by the said *maleficia* suffocate, pierce, and kill, and finally you dug them up secretly by night in the cemetery, and so carried them to the aforesaid synagogue and college of witches.

Then you did offer them to the prince of devils sitting on his throne, and did draw off their fat to be kept for your use, and cut off their heads, hands, and feet, and did cook and stew the trunk, and sometimes roast them [*assari curastis*], and at the bidding and hest of your aforesaid evil father did eat and damnably devour them.

Then, adding sin to sin, you the men did copulate with succubi, and you the women did fornicate with incubi; by most icy coitus with demons you did commit the unspeakable crime of sodomy.

And, most hateful of all, at the bidding of the aforesaid serpent thrust forth from paradise, you did keep in your mouths the most holy sacrament of the eucharist received by you in the sacred church of God, and did nefariously spit it out on the ground with the greatest contumely, impiety, and contempt; you did dishonor our true and holy God, and promote the glory, honor, triumph, and kingdom of the devil himself, and worship, honor, and glorify him with all honor, praise, majesty, dignity, authority, and adoration.

All which most grave, abhorred and unspeakable crimes are directly contumacious and contemptuous of Almighty God, the creator of all.

Wherefore we, Brother Florus, Provincial of the order of Friars Preachers, Doctor of Sacred Theology, and Inquisitor General for the holy faith within the jurisdiction of Avignon, having the fear of God before our eyes, sitting in tribunal, have caused to be written this our definitive sentence according to the lawful precept of revered theologians and jurists, piously having invoked the names of our Lord Jesus Christ and the Blessed Virgin Mary, we say, declare, pronounce, and formally sentence all you above named and your accomplices who have been or are truly apostates, idolaters, rebels from the most holy faith, deniers and mockers of Almighty God, sodomites, and perpetrators of the foulest crimes, adulterers, fornicators, sorcerers, witches, profaners, heretics, workers of the evil eye, murderers, infanticides, worshipers of devils, satanists, adherents of diabolical and infernal law and damnable and reprobate faith, blasphemers, perjurers, infamous livers, and those convicted of all the evil crimes and offenses.

Wherefore by this sentence we relax you and your accomplices as limbs of Satan to the secular court, actually and effectually, for most worthy and legitimate punishment according to its own secular provisions.

The sentencing and execution by the secular authority were also made an occasion for terror. At Neuchâtel, for example, the accused was led in formal procession to receive judgment on the terrace of the castle. The Châtelain opened the ceremony:

Q. Do you know, Monsieur le Lieutenant, that the time and hour are now at hand to administer justice for the crime committed?

A. I indeed know, Monsieur le Châtelain, that now is the time and hour to administer criminal justice.

Q. This is likewise your view, Gentlemen of the Court?

A. Yes.

The church bells tolled, sometimes wrapped in wet cloth to make the peals more lugubrious. The witch was brought forward. Kneeling before the spectators, she was forced to recite a résumé of her trial. In response to admonishment from the mayor, the prisoner assented to its accuracy—if she refused, she was taken back to jail for further torture. Then one of the attendant priests delivered a sermon, after which the scribe read the sentence, and the prisoner was formally delivered to the executioner. The execution was a public spectacle, with the school children getting a holiday so they too could witness the fate of witches. The proceedings concluded with a banquet (paid for by the victim) for the Châtelain, the mayor, four court officials, twelve court assessors, two guards [*sautiers*], and the two schoolteachers.

In the Protestant states of Germany, the execution was likewise transformed into a never-to-be-forgotten drama. Benedict Carpzov (1635), for example, held the proceedings were invalid if all the formalities were not strictly observed, and he described the common form throughout Saxony. The public was summoned by the blare of trumpets and the ringing of bells. The judge, holding his staff of office, demanded of the court officials or councilors whether the trial had been according to law. One by one, the accused were brought forth, and an official asked for their condemnation. The prisoners publicly confirmed their guilt. Then the judge pronounced sentence: "Since you, N.N., confess that you, N.N., have [committed the crime specified], so I, N.N., judge at N.N., under the jurisdiction of the Saxony electoral judges at Leipzig, decree that you, on account of the [crimes] committed, should be sentenced by [method of execution] from life to death." The judge then broke his staff of office, and ordered the executioner to carry out his orders. At the conclusion of the public sentencing, the bailiff asked those who wished to denounce anyone to come forward and inform the judge.

In Protestant Prussia the execution was also formal. A contemporary document described a ceremony in 1687 at Arendsee (Altmark). The magistrate [*Amtmann*] asked the prisoners if they were guilty. They admitted their guilt. The notary then read the sentence. The executioner asked for police protection should he bungle the beheading (if he missed at the first stroke, the crowd might stone him). Then the magistrate broke his wand, and the tables and chairs in the courtroom were ceremonially upturned. A procession formed, headed by a company of men, with the executioner leading the prisoners by ropes, surrounded by armed guards, then the preachers, followed by men of the town bearing arms. En route, the whole procession prayed and sang psalms. A choir of school children led the singing of hymns—*"Gott der Vater wohn uns bei"* ["God the Father abide with us"], while the victim was led to the block, and *"Nun bitten wir den heiligen Geist"* ["Now pray we to the Holy Ghost"] after the execution. The bodies were pulled by chains onto the pyre and burned to ashes, while the spectators continued to sing hymns.

Sexual Relations with Devils. According to the confessions extracted from witches by the courts, women attending sabbats always had sexual intercourse with the devil. Theologians accepted the reality of intercourse between humans and the devil, either as a male incubus or as a female succubus, and debated on the nature of the devils (whether corporeal or spirit), the extent of the sin, and the techniques of the act. "The curiosity of the judges [at witch trials]," wrote Henry C. Lea, "was insatiable to learn all the possible details as to sexual intercourse, and their industry in pushing the examinations was rewarded by an abundance of foul imaginations." Thus a combination of prurient inquisitors and hysterical young women about to be burned produced most of the accounts, which are completely the product of erotic and neurotic imaginations.

Theologians and demonologists were puzzled as to how demons, who were spirits, could have relations with humans. The fact itself was accepted, for it had the authority of the Bible and Church behind it. Augustine, in his *De Civitate Dei,* expounded

Genesis vi. 4: "The *sons of God* came unto the daughters of men, and they bare children to them." He was the first to consider fully "whether the angels, since they are spirits, are able bodily to have intercourse with women." Augustine inclined to the affirmative, although he denied that the angels of God so sinned. Later, Pope Benedict XIV, in *De Servorum Dei Beatificatione,* commented:

> This passage has reference to devils known as incubi and succubi . . . for while nearly all authorities admit copulation, some writers deny that there can be offspring. . . . Others, however, asserting that coitus is possible, maintain that children may result, and say that this has actually occurred, although in some new and unusual way not ordinarily known to men.

Pope Innocent VIII and Bonaventura also agreed that intercourse between devils and humans was possible. Augustine, and in particular Thomas Aquinas, affirmed that demons as evil spirits either entered into corpses or else made new bodies out of the elements. Sometimes, as Boguet noted, the devil used the body of a man recently hanged. This traditional view appeared throughout all the literature on demonology, and as late as 1665 the Carmelite manual, *Theologia Moralis,* complained that "some deny this opinion, holding it impossible that devils could practice effectual intercourse with humans. But the opposite opinion is very certain and must be accepted."

To reconcile the difficulties inherent in physical relations between spirit and human being, a later writer, Sinistrari (died 1701), in his *De Daemonialitate et Incubis et Succubis,* developed Augustine's account of "rural spirits and sylvan deities, commonly known as incubi," and conceived of them, not as evil angels, but as beings of a different (and lower) nature, motivated solely by lasciviousness. Here he departed from the orthodox position that since the demons are spirits, "they can feel no joy or pleasure" (De Lancre) and act thus solely to degrade man. In Sinistrari's view, acquiescence by a human won favors from the

Incidents in the begetting of Merlin. The center and bottom panels of the first column shown a devil seducing a woman, and are followed by panels of the woman confessing to her priest and being chased out of the house by her husband. From an old French manuscript in the Bibliothèque nationale, Paris.

demon, while rejection caused hostility. According to Sinistrari, the incubus demons simply wanted to satisfy their desires; however, frequently they urged the human partners to abjure the Faith, to indulge in sorcery, and to perpetuate crimes "as preliminary conditions to the infamous intercourse." When there was no offense against religion, however, "it is hard to discover a reason why it should be more grievous than bestiality and sodomy." Yet, concluded Sinistrari, when men and women believed the incubi to be devils, then their guilt was what the Church said it was.

From about 1430, the Inquisition, while not yet making it a major feature of the witchcraft trials, prosecuted women for relations with the devil. Even young girls could have such intercourse. Johannes Henricus Pott, at the end of the seventeenth century, told how a girl of nine or ten, under the influence of her stepmother, was seduced by a devil, but on account of her youth was merely scourged while forced to witness her stepmother's being burned as a witch. Bodin, in his *Démonomanie* (1580),

said girls of six, "which is the age of consent for women," had intercourse. And at Würzburg, in January, 1628, three children —Anna Rausch, twelve, Sybille Lutz, eleven, and Mürchin, eight and a half—all confessed to sexual relations with incubi. Anna declared she had intercourse six times with Master Hämerlein ("Jack Catch, the devil") ; the court records noted "this copulation the child has *formalissime* described." Sybille copulated with Master "Federlein." Little Mürchin testified *formaliter* she had *coitus cum demone*. Sybille and Anna were put to death; Mürchin and seven others, between eight and thirteen, after interrogation were remanded to their fathers for reformation—Diefenbach, *Der Hexenwahn*, 1886. The *ne plus ultra* of this fantasy was surely reached in a letter written by the Chancellor of Würzburg in August, 1629: "The witch affair has sprung up again in a manner beyond description. . . . There are some 300 children of three or four years who have had intercourse with devils."

The devil could appear in whatever form

he pleased. He might imitate a man's mistress or unattainable ideal, as when Mephistopheles conjured for Faust the image of Helen of Troy. Brognolus, in his *Alexicacon*, had a classical story of a succubus. In 1650 he heard the confession of a young man to whom his beloved had appeared, claiming she had been driven away from home. After a night's pleasures, the youth realized his Teresa was actually a succubus, but his enjoyment was such that he continued this "monstrous commerce" night after night for several months.

This young fellow was luckier than the hermit whose succubus was so demanding that he lasted only one month [see Succubus], or the two men reported by Remy in his *Demonolatreiae* (1595):

But on this point those who have told us about copulation with demons, whether in male or female form, all with one voice say that nothing could be imagined or described as being more cold and unpleasant. Petronius Armentarius said that as soon as he embraced his "Abrahel" all his limbs became rigid; and Hennezel proclaimed it was like putting his instrument into an ice-cold cavity [*speculum*] and that he had to leave his "Schwartzburg" without having an orgasm—these odd names were what the succubi were really called.

But men's experiences were not often discussed, and interest centered in women.

Some authorities (for example, Weyer, 1563; Carpzov, 1635; and Pott, 1689) stated that even when the devil appeared as an animal or bird, especially serpent, goat, or raven, intercourse was possible. Boguet reported how Françoise Secretain admitted copulation with the devil, sometimes as a black man, but also as a dog, cat, or fowl. Before they were burned, the Scottish witches at Borrowstones in 1679 testified to the commissioners how the devil "would have carnal dealing with [them] in the shape of a deer, or in any other shape, now and then. Sometimes he would be like a stork, a bull, a deer, a roe, or a dog, and have dealing with [them]." One of these witches, Margaret Hamilton, was accused of having had "carnal copulation with the

devil in the likeness of a man, but he removed from [her] in the likeness of a black dog"—Pitcairn, *Criminal Trials*. Pott quoted an earlier anecdote (1605) of the wife of a Wittenberg merchant whose lover one night exclaimed, "Behold your lover, transformed into a woodpecker," flew off, and was seen no more. When the demon appeared in animal form, the Church held it was technically no longer an incubus; but the ordinary man or woman did not understand this distinction.

Nuns were supposedly specially subject to this kind of bestial temptation, imagined or real. Boguet, in his *Discours des sorciers*, believed the devil frequently assumed the shape of a dog to abuse women, and gave a "remarkable example" from a convent in the diocese of Cologne, in 1566, where a dog, said to be a devil, lifted up the robes of the nuns in order to abuse them. Bodin, however, who told the same story, was somewhat less credulous: "In my opinion, it was certainly not a demon but an ordinary dog." In his *Démonomanie*, he gave further examples.

He came to the convent of Mont de Hesse in Germany, where the nuns were supposed to be possessed by demons, and saw lying on their cots dogs shamelessly awaiting those suspected of having been assaulted and having committed that sin called the secret sin [*le péché muet*, i.e., sodomy, because the word is too shocking for honest ears]. At Toulouse, he found a woman who abused herself in this manner; and in front of everybody the dog wanted to mount her. She confessed to the truth and was burned.

Bodin gave another case in Paris in 1540.

One of the few descriptions of how such an act of bestiality could be performed was given by De Lancre in his *Tableau* (1612) from what was claimed to be an eyewitness account. Johannes d'Aguerre swore:

The devil in the form of a goat, having his member in the rear, had intercourse with women by joggling and shoving that thing against their belly. Marie de Marigrane, aged fifteen years, a resident of Biarritz, affirmed that she had often seen the devil couple with a multitude of women, whom she knew by name and surname, and that it was the devil's custom to have intercourse with the beautiful women from the front, and with the ugly from the rear.

Another witness examined by De Lancre, seventeen-year-old Marguerite de Sare, testified that whether the devil appeared as man or goat—

he always had a member like a mule's, having chosen to imitate that animal as being best endowed by nature; that it was as long and as thick as an arm . . . and that he always exposed his instrument, of such beautiful shape and measurements.

De Lancre added:

Quite the opposite is told by Boguet, who says the witches in Franche-Comté have never seen one longer than a finger and correspondingly thin. All that can be said is that Satan serves the witches of Labourd better than he does those of Franche-Comté!

Since demons had no sex, the traditional position, propounded by Thomas Aquinas, held that they could appear either as men or as women. The Dominican Charles René Billuart (1685-1757), in his *Tractatus de Angelis*, wrote: "The same evil spirit may serve as a succubus to a man; and as an incubus serve a woman." By this duality they were able to re-use semen received while acting as succubus for later emission as incubus. In his *Compendium Maleficarum*, Guazzo summarized the theory thus:

For devils can assume the bodies of dead men, or re-create for themselves out of air and other elements a palpable body like that of flesh, and to these they can impart motion and heat at their will. They can therefore create the appearance of sex which they do not naturally have, and abuse men in a feminine form and women in a masculine form, and lie on top of women or lie under men; and they can also produce semen which they have brought from elsewhere, and imitate the natural ejaculation of it.

Martin of Arles suggested that the incubi squeezed out semen from corpses; other

Title page of academic dissertation by Johann Klein in 1731 discussing the possibility of offspring resulting from coitus between a witch and a demon.

demonologists, such as Guazzo, that they stole it from men's nocturnal emissions, and "by speed and experience of physical laws preserved that semen in its fertilizing warmth." However, the influential Nicholas Remy (1595) believed that all incubi were sterile, and so also did other authorities, such as Ulrich Molitor (1489).

If a woman desired impregnation, the preserved semen was used; otherwise the demon "emits something like semen, yet warm so that the deception will not be discovered"—Guazzo. Jeanne d'Abadie confessed before De Lancre that "the devil's semen was extremely cold, therefore she never became pregnant by him." Sinistrari maintained, "as a mere expression of private opinion," that the incubus was itself able to procreate; in this he followed the standard *Malleus Maleficarum* and Del Rio. Other writers, such as Pott (1689), believed that the devil was sterile, but that he supplied a stolen child at parturition.

The relatively late dissertation of Johann

Klein (submitted to the University of Rostock in 1698) gave some of the most detailed accounts of the monstrous offspring of these unions. A magisterial report told of the confession of a woman who claimed to have given birth first to a tapeworm and later to a girl the size of a jug [*Pottkrug*], which sucked her breast. Her incubus, David, removed both. By another incubus, Hansen, she had a boy and girl, both of which Hansen took away from her. She confessed that her incubi continued to consort with her in prison, and that she bore there a further child, which was also removed. "Although there was copious flooding which stained the clothes and the floor, all traces of it disappeared." Bodin gave further stories of monsters resulting from such generation. And at Toulouse in 1275, it was alleged that Angela de Labarthe gave birth to a monster with a wolf's head and a snake's tail; she was presumably the first woman burned for intercourse with the devil. Carpzov and Pott also told many stories of this nature, including one of a woman at Augsburg, who in 1531 gave birth to a two-footed serpent.

Legends, perhaps arising from rumors circulated by their enemies, credited many well-known historical figures with devilish origin: Robert (the father of William the Conqueror), Luther, Alexander the Great, Plato, Caesar Augustus, Scipio Africanus; also Romulus and Remus, Merlin, and the whole race of Huns, and the inhabitants of the Island of Cyprus (Sinistrari). One early writer believed that Merlin was not fathered by the devil, but was a human child substituted by the devil (Molitor).

Other witches confessed their children were fathered by the devil. Holinshed's *Chronicle* told of a young Scots woman discovered copulating with a monster; she later gave birth to "such a misshapen thing as the like before had not been seen." To avoid dishonor, the family burned the foetus. *A Prodigious and Tragical History of the arraignment, trial, confession, and condemnation of six witches at Maidstone in Kent . . . 1652* noted that "Anne Ashly, Anne Martin, and one other of their associates, pleaded that they were with child

pregnant, but confessed it was not by any man, but by the devil." The generally credulous Boguet, however, used common sense in regard to such confessions and asked: "Why should we not rather believe that these women [Rhea and Leda] used the gods as a screen to cover their incests and adulteries? And therefore I maintain that the widow of whom Bodin speaks was made pregnant by a natural man, and not by a devil."

Some of the early accounts had emphasized the intense pleasure of diabolic intercourse. The Inquisitor Nicholas Jacquier, writing in 1458, said it was *inordinate carnaliter*, and that many witches "for several days afterward remain worn out [*afflicti et debilitati*]." Italian accounts generally concurred; Grillandus, the famous papal lawyer, reported confessions made to him personally by women who enjoyed the devil "*maxima cum voluptate.*" William of Paris, in his *De Universo*, said the devil could delude women into thinking that relations

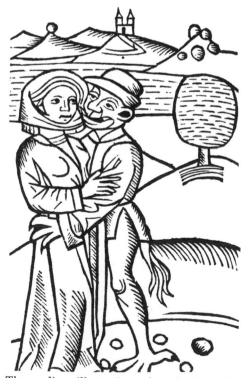

The earliest illustration of a devil making love to a woman in a book on witchcraft, Ulrich Molitor's *De Lamiis* (1489).

performed only once or twice were repeated fifty or sixty times a night. On the other hand, *La Vauderye de Lyonois* (1460) gave the later and more general view, that witches had intercourse with "great fear [*timore et pavore*]." This assertion of fear and pain first appeared in print about 1470, when the techniques of demonology were still a novelty, in Jordanes de Bergamo, who wrote: "These self-same witches confess and assert that the tool of the devil as well as his semen is always frigid."

In nearly all the later accounts, however, those accused of witchcraft said intercourse was painful and lacking in pleasure. So Boguet reported:

> Thievenne Paget said, moreover, that when Satan copulated with her she had as much pain as a woman in labor. Françoise Secretain said that, while she was in the act, she felt something burning in her stomach; and nearly all the witches say this intercourse is by no means pleasurable to them, both because of the devil's ugliness and deformity, and because of the physical pain which it causes them, as we have just said.

Remy likewise quoted a witch as saying that copulation was devoid of satisfaction and painful. In his *Tableau*, De Lancre gave some of the reasons:

> Marie de Marigrane, a girl of Biarritz aged fifteen years, affirmed that it seemed that the member of this devil for its full length was of two parts, half of iron, half of flesh, and similarly his testicles; and she testified to have seen it many times at the sabbat as she described it. Furthermore, she had heard many women, who had slept with the devil, say that he made them cry out like women in travail with child, and that he always held his tool exposed. Petry de Linarre testified that the devil had his instrument made out of horn, or at least it looked like that, and that is why he made the women cry out so much.

Another of De Lancre's witnesses added further details of the devil's penis:

> This was generally sinuous, pointed, and snake-like, made sometimes of half-iron and half-flesh, at other times wholly of

horn, and commonly forked like a serpent's tongue; he customarily performed both coitus and pederasty at once, while sometimes a third prong reached to his lover's mouth.

A devil *"cum membro bifurcato"* was mentioned as early as 1520.

Similar confessions from Lorraine were recorded by Remy in his *Demonolatreiae:*

> The female witches also all maintain that when they are laid by their demons, they can admit, only with the greatest pain, what are reputed their tools, because they are so huge and rigid. Alexia Drigie examined her devil's penis when it was sticking up, and said it was always as long as some kitchen utensils which then happened to be in view and which she pointed out with her finger; but that there was nothing where the testicles and scrotum should be hanging. Claudia Fellet said she herself had often experienced something forced into her, swollen to such a size, that no matter how capacious a vagina a woman might have, she would not be able to hold it without extreme pain. And nearly all the other witches complain they are very unwilling to be embraced by their demons, but that it is useless to struggle against them.

One witch, Antide Colas, reported by Boguet, reputedly had a hole below her navel, through which she had intercourse with the devil; she had relations with her husband by the vagina. However, when examined by the court, only a scar on her stomach was visible.

Testimony is almost unanimous as to the coldness of the devil. Boguet quoted Jacquema Paget, a witch of Franche-Comté, who

> had several times taken in her hand the member of the devil which slept with her, and that it was as cold as ice and a finger's length, but not as thick as that of a man. Thievenne Paget and Antoine Tornier also added that the members of their devils were as long and big as one of their fingers.

Another girl quoted by Boguet said that the semen "kept its original warmth," but this comment is not typical. For example, Sylvine de la Plaine, aged twenty-three, con-

A young witch shamelessly acquiescing to relations with the Devil's emissary.

demned to be burned by the Parlement of Paris in 1616, described her experiences: "The devil had known her once before, and his member was like that of a horse, and on insertion it was as cold as ice and ejected ice-cold semen, and on his withdrawing it burned her as if it had been on fire."

Guazzo related how a "wench of intelligent appearance" was tried before the Parlement of Aquitaine in 1594. After describing the preparations for the witches' sabbat, she continued her testimony:

> Afterwards, the Italian [boy friend] again took the girl to the same place; and then the goat asked her for a tress or lock of her hair, which the Italian cut and gave to him. By this token the goat led her apart as his bride into a neighboring wood, and, pressing her against the ground, penetrated her. But the girl said that she found this operation quite lacking in any sensation of pleasure, for she rather experienced a very keen pain and sense of horror of the goat's semen, which was as cold as ice.

A few similar reports came from England. Mother Bush of Barton in 1649 said that the devil who visited her in the form of a young man "was colder than man, and heavier, and could not perform nature as man"—Stearne, *Confirmation and Discovery of Witchcraft*. In 1662 Isobel Gowdie (Janet Breidheid, too) of Auldearne, Scotland, described the devil as "a mickle, black, rough man, very cold, and found his 'nature' as cold within [her] as spring well water." (Pitcairn, *Criminal Trials*, 1833)

In Treves, in 1572, Eva of Kenn admitted intercourse with a devil, but "it was like an icicle." And Johann Klein (1698), while admitting that women may imagine intercourse in erotic dreams, nevertheless believed in the reality of the reports of actual intercourse *"cum semine frigidissimo."* Guazzo explained, "As for the cold semen, that is only found in the case of witches who are fully aware that he is a devil."

The coldness of the devil rapidly became part of folk literature, so that in the *Strange and Wonderful History of Mother Shipton* (London, 1686), a kind of "merry tale," Agatha Soothtell, when sixteen, was seduced by the devil

> in the shape of a very handsome young man . . . [who] prevailed so far as to gain her, but his touches (as she afterwards confessed to the midwife) were as cold as ice or snow. From this time forward, she was commonly once a day visited by her hellish gallant, and never wanted money.

The famous English philosopher Henry More, in his *Antidote Against Atheism* (1653), gave what he imagined a scientific reason for this characteristic.

> It stands to good reason that the bodies of devils, being nothing but coagulated air, should be cold, as well as coagulated water (which is snow or ice): and that it should have a more keen and piercing cold, it consisting of more subtle particles than those of water, and therefore more fit to insinuate, and more accurately and stingingly to affect and touch the nerves.

Whatever Sinistrari might have thought about the classification of the incubus—spirit, human, or animal—intercourse with a devil was held the equivalent of buggery, for which the penalty was burning. In a few of the confessions, a distinction of the type of intercourse was made. In 1624, Marie-de-Sains, self-styled princess of magic, said she had committed sin "in the usual way," and also "the crime of sodomy and bestiality," that is, with the devil in the form of an animal—*Histoire véritable*, Paris, 1624. The Provost Marshal of the French armies, Le Sieur Bouvet, lumped together intercourse with the devil and sexual relations between Christians and "Jews, Turks, pagans, and other infidels, because of the strange hatred these have for the Catholic Church, for which reason they are treated as animals lacking the way to salvation." The sinning couple should be burned together—the devil, of course, would leave the witch to go to the stake alone.

An early Latin tract (1460) on the Arras witches summarizes the curious beliefs about sexual relations with devils:

At the sabbats of the Vaudois, the presiding devil took aside the neophyte and carried her off to one side of the grove, so that in his own fashion he might make love to her and have carnal knowledge of her; to whom he said maliciously that he would lay her down on the ground supporting herself on her two hands and feet, and that he could not have intercourse with her in any other position; and that was the way the presiding devil enjoyed her, because at the first sensation by the neophyte of the member of the presiding devil, very often it appeared cold and soft, as very frequently the whole body. At first he put it in the natural orifice and ejaculated the spoiled yellowing sperm, collected from nocturnal emissions or elsewhere, then in the anus, and in this manner inordinately abused her. . . . Upon her return to the sabbat, the neophyte, before the banquet, entered into sexual relations with any other man. . . . Then, the torches (if there are any) being extinguished, each one at the order of the presiding devil takes his partner and has intercourse. Sometimes indeed indescribable outrages are perpetrated in exchanging women, by order of the presiding devil, by passing on a woman to other women and a man to other men, an abuse against the nature of women by both parties and simi-

larly against the nature of men, or by a woman with a man outside the regular orifice and in another orifice. . . . Indeed a man experiences no pleasure with a she-devil, neither a woman with a he-devil; but they only consent to copulate out of fear and obedience. . . . In the second intercourse, however, the woman neophyte herself is known carnally by some demon, intimately and thoroughly, in the same way it was first done by the presiding demon; but in other succeeding copulations no more by a demon; except when on account of the paucity of men to complete the pairings (which happens whenever the greater part of the group there consist of women rather than men) the demons take over the part of the men in copulation, as it happens sometimes, though only occasionally. When the women are fewer, the complement is filled by she-devils, and this happens very frequently in other unions, in addition to the first two couplings, in the first of which, after admission to the group, in returning to the presiding devil, a man has intercourse with a female devil. . . . Indeed, as sometimes happens, yet only occasionally, a certain man always has copulation with a she-devil, and it is an indication of extreme vileness in him; and likewise in any woman who has all her unions with a devil rather than with a man. (Hansen, *Quellen*)

Shaving. Whenever a person was imprisoned on suspicion or charges of witchcraft, his head and body would be completely shaved. This was standard procedure throughout Europe and Britain, from the beginning of the witch delusion. One early reference occurs in Jordanes de Bergamo, about 1470.

Three reasons were adduced for this simple form of torture:

1. The suspect might conceal tiny charms or amulets in the hair, as well as under the nails, in the mouth or ears or any other body orifices, to confer taciturnity or insensibility to the pain of torture. Such was the reason commonly advanced on the Continent. The whole body, "even the secret parts, not to be named," had to be thoroughly examined. The *Malleus Maleficarum*

said some inquisitors merely cut off the hair and, to induce confessions, forced the accused to drink holy water on an empty stomach. Some authorities (e.g., Prierias) said women should be employed to search women, but this advice was not always followed. Guazzo referred to the trial of a man called Benignus who was implicated in the murder of a councilor of the Queen of Denmark. Although abroad at the time of his indictment, he returned to stand trial, trusting in the efficacy of a magic charm he had hidden on his body. "He came through all sorts of torture unhurt and without confessing, and was acquitted." However, just as he was being released from prison, his conscience smote him, and he confessed his guilt and was executed. (*Compendium Maleficarum*, 1626)

2. The devil might be hiding in the hair of the witch, and thus unobserved advise her what to do and say and thwart the judges. In victims of possession, who would not be punished by shaving, another technique was used to get rid of the devil. A wig would be placed on the head of the possessed, and when the hysteria came on, it would quickly be snatched off and put into a bottle, along with—one hoped—the devil.

3. Hair had to be removed so the body could be more closely inspected for devil's marks. This justification for shaving applied especially, but not exclusively, in England. In France, for example, Father Gaufridi was very meticulously shaved and three devil's marks, previously unobserved, were discovered [see Aix-en-Provence Nuns].

Sherwood, Grace. Witchcraft beliefs survived past the beginning of the eighteenth century in isolated Princess Anne County, Virginia. Grace Sherwood had acquired a reputation as a witch and resented the slur. In 1698, she and her husband sued John and Jane Gisburne for £100 damages for slandering her: "She is a witch and bewitched their pigs to death." The jury found for the defendants. The Sherwoods also sued Anthony and Elizabeth Barnes, asking the same damages, for say-

ing that Grace "went out of the keyhole or crack of the door like a black cat." Again the jury found for the defendants. In 1705, Grace herself sued Luke Hill and his wife for assault, and this time she was awarded twenty shillings damages; however, she had to pay the expenses of several witnesses for four days each.

In 1706 Luke Hill hit back and charged Mrs. Sherwood on "suspicion of witchcraft." Hill was ordered to pay the costs of the trial, but Grace Sherwood was held to be searched for witch's marks. On March 7, 1706, a jury of women found "two things like teats with several other spots." On May 2, the justices asked for a new indictment to avoid the vagueness of the original, and had Mrs. Sherwood's home searched for waxen images. At the new trial on June 6, a jury of women now refused to search her for witch's marks; these women were charged with contempt and another jury impaneled.

By her own consent, on July 5, Grace Sherwood asked "to be tried in the water by ducking. But the weather being very rainy and bad, so that possibly it might endanger her health, it [was] therefore ordered that the sheriff request the judges personally to appear on Wednesday next by ten of the morning at the court house." On July 10 they took Mrs. Sherwood to Jonathan Harper's plantation for the water ordeal, "always having care of her life to preserve her from drowning," and for "ancient and knowing women" to look for witch's marks. Grace swam and the women found "two things like teats on her private parts of a black color, being blacker than the rest of her body." She was kept in irons in the common jail to await trial, but the case apparently petered out.

Short, Mercy. Mercy Short, the subject of a monograph by Cotton Mather, was a prime example of diabolical possession. That she had such extraordinary hallucinations is not surprising, for her father and mother, brother and sister, and other relatives had been killed by Indians at Salmon Falls, New Hampshire, on March 18, 1690, and Mercy taken captive to

Canada. At the end of the year, she was rescued and brought to Boston, where she entered domestic service.

From the end of November, 1692, until her "deliverance" on March 16, 1693, she was subject to savage fits, so violent that "many strong men with an united force could not well carry her," and so vocal that her "direful shrieks" made "many people quit the room." At other times, she was gay and "extravagant as a wild-cat . . . always excessively witty [and] took an extraordinary liberty . . . to animadvert upon all people that had anything in their apparel that savored of curiosity or ornament." Contrariwise, she suffered periods of depression, when she "imagined herself in a desolate cellar, where day or night could not be distinguished." She would not eat for days together, once fasting for fifteen days. If food were offered, "her teeth would be set, and she thrown into hideous torments." In addition, Mercy swallowed pins, and by breathing heavily could make her abdomen swell, "just like one poisoned by ratsbane."

Among her hallucinations was the devil, who appeared to her in the classic form of a black man with a cloven foot, although Mather says "she had no sort of acquaintance with histories of what has happened elsewhere." However, Mather's own sermons contain similar pictures. Nor is it surprising that, to a girl whose family had been massacred by Indians, the symbol of evil should be "of a tawny or an Indian color . . . with straight hair." Mather ascribes her possession to the Salem witch, Sarah Good, who, when Mercy taunted her in Boston jail, "bestowed some ill words upon her."

Mercy Short provides one of Cotton Mather's three detailed accounts of possession, all written from personal observation over a period of months. All furnished the names of their bewitchers, but apparently Mather could not find additional evidence to press charges of witchcraft. The symptoms in all three cases might well be noted among the manic depressives in any mental institution [see also Goodwin Children, Ann Putnam, Margaret Rule].

Sinclair, George. Sinclair's *Satan's Invisible World Discovered* (1685), a fabulous collection of witch stories, went through many editions, and, said Lea, "formed during the eighteenth century a part of every cottage library in Scotland." It thus helped perpetuate a belief in witchcraft, long after it had been discarded in England. George Sinclair was a professor of philosophy and mathematics at the University of Glasgow, from which he was dismissed from 1666 to 1688 for nonconformity to the Episcopal Church. During this period he worked as a mining engineer, but even in his technical work, *Hydrostatics* (1672), he introduced the story of the Devil of Glenluce. If disbelief in witchcraft spread, wrote Sinclair, "farewell all religion, all faith, all hope of a life to come." *Satan's Invisible World Discovered* sought to confute the "Sadducees," and hoped to convert them by the fable of the Pied Piper of Hamelin.

Sinistrari, Ludovico Maria. The last of the demonologists in the inquisitorial tradition of Remy, Boguet, and the others, Sinistrari (1622-1701) was known in his own day as a scholar and gentleman, a good linguist and an urbane conversationalist. At the age of twenty-five, he became a Franciscan friar, and then, successively, professor of theology at Pavia University, consultant to the Supreme Tribunal of the Inquisition at Rome, and Vicar-General to the Archbishop of Avignon. In 1688 he compiled the statutes of the Franciscan order. His greatest work, *De Delictis et Poenis* [*On Crimes and Punishments*], was published at Venice in 1700, but it went on the Index of prohibited books until it was posthumously corrected in 1753 (Rome). The work by which Sinistrari is known today, *De Daemonialitate* [*Demoniality*], an expansion of a section in his *De Delictis*, was not available to his contemporaries. The manuscript was discovered only about 1875 in a London bookshop by a French publisher, Isidore Liseux, who paid sixpence for it.

Demoniality is devoted to the problems

Andras, grand marquis of hell, who provokes discords and quarrels. From Collin de Plancy. *Dictionnaire infernal* (1863).

arising from relations between humans and devils. To Sinistrari, incubi and succubi are not evil angels or devils, but *folleti* or *duendes*, similar to humans, having emotions and being capable of redemption by Christ; they differ because they can make themselves invisible and can pass through walls (just like Blessed Clara d'Agolanto). Intercourse with incubi or succubi is therefore neither pollution, sodomy, or bestiality. While young women sometimes have erotic dreams, their stories of incubi are generally to be taken literally.

Somers, William: see Darrell, John.

Sorcery. Sorcery must be differentiated from witchcraft. As indicated in the entry for Witchcraft, sorcery is timeless and world-wide, whereas witchcraft is specifically limited to approximately three centuries from 1450 to 1750 and to Christian western Europe (with an excursion to Salem). Sorcery is an attempt to control nature, to produce good or evil results, generally by the aid of evil spirits. On the other hand, witchcraft embraces sorcery, but goes far beyond it, for the witch contracts with the Devil to work magic for the purpose of denying, repudiating, and scorn-

ing the Christian God. The crimes both sorcerer and witch are supposed to commit —that is, the whole range of *maleficia*— appear to be alike, but the motives are distinct. This is the basis on which the Inquisition built up the theory of witchcraft as a heresy—a conscious rejection of God and the Church; witchcraft became not a question of deeds (did the witch hex the cows so their milk dried up?) but a question of ideas. Witchcraft took its place among crimes of conscience. Witchcraft "was but a shadow, a nightmare; the nightmare of a religion, the shadow of a dogma." (George L. Burr)

In the early years, while the theory was being formulated, some inquisitors and judges were unsure of this distinction. Their confusion was not surprising, for the Catholic Church had its own traditions of sorcery and tended to view man against a backdrop of magic. For example, the Old Testament is replete with sacred magic. In spite of the legend that all sorcery stopped with the birth of Christ, in the first few centuries after Christ an extensive literature developed about Simon Magus, a magician whose attempts to fly were foiled by his contemporary and rival, the Apostle Peter. The inquisitors investigated sorcery very searchingly to discover the intention or motives of the accused. By the mid-thirteenth century, a Summa de Officio Inquisitionis minutely probed all facets of sorcery and fortunetelling, with a view, presumably, to extending its jurisdiction. Inasmuch as the Inquisition made use of torture, it could extort from the accused whatever it needed.

From about 1321, there is a succession of ecclesiastical trials, mainly in southern France, at Toulouse and Carcassonne, seeking heresy in acts of sorcery. By 1330, women were confessing to sabbats, transvection, and intercourse with the devil, to eating babies and adoring the goat. Between 1320 and 1350, 200 people accused of heretical sorcery, that is, witchcraft, were burned at Carcassonne and 400 at Toulouse. Yet more than half a century later, about 1395, the civil judge, Peter of Bern (Peter von Greyerz), was burning what he

Vandervelt's Sorceress, from an old print (1626) in the Douce Collection, Bodleian Library, Oxford.

thought *malefici* or witches, when they were really sorcerers—for there is no mention of any pact or sabbat. (Nider, *Formicarius*, 1435)

Certainly the bull of Pope Innocent VIII in 1484 should have removed uncertainty. The influential lawyer, Paulus Grillandus (1525), also devoted many pages of his *Treatise on Witches* to determining when sorcery became heresy. Much of his argument was based on Joannes Andreae, the most prominent canon lawyer of the first half of the fourteenth century. God allowed the Devil certain powers, such as to tempt people to sin, to know the nature of things, and to cure disease. Asking help of the Devil to do these "permitted" acts was sorcery; asking the Devil to do other acts which God reserved for himself was heresy. For example, asking the Devil to help in seducing a woman was not heretical, since this aid came within the Devil's province. Yet the manner of asking was very important: if a person *ordered* the Devil to do the evil permitted by God, he was not a heretic; but if he *implored* the Devil, the same request made him a heretic. Moreover, if a person who was thought to have contracted with the Devil asked in any way even for the permitted acts, he was a witch and a heretic. The Franciscan Father Candidus Brognolus Bergomensi gave a very full discussion of what may lawfully be required of the Devil in his *Manuale Exorcistarum* (1651). Lea wryly com-

mented: "These subtleties [of intention] were not attended to in practice." *All* wonders were eventually held due, as Thomas Blount defined in his *Glossographia* (1674), to "the assistance of the Devil." Toward the end of the sixteenth century, Peña included as heretical all charms or incantations using sacred things, not only holy water but even recitation of the paternoster or Ave Maria. So the Scottish court which damned Agnes Sampson in 1590 for reciting a bedtime prayer was acting in a universal church tradition [see North Berwick Witches].

From about 1700 the secular state took over where the church (both Catholic and Protestant) left off in its endeavor to control thoughts. However, inasmuch as the modern world does not function in terms of religion, but of economics and politics, witchcraft involving a pact with a personal devil is not the medium in which modern heresy hunters operate. The word *witchcraft* has continued in use after the *thing* has ceased to exist and has become again equated with *sorcery*. Thus one can speak loosely of African or Haitian "witchcraft." To avoid confusion, throughout this book *witch* and *witchcraft* are used exclusively for the heresy dominant in the sixteenth and seventeenth centuries, and *sorcery* or *magic* for the acts of *maleficia* found throughout the whole world.

Comparative folklore may heap parallel on parallel to the *magical* practices of European witches, and find, for example, a Mexican demon, Tlazolteote, who wears a peaked hat and flies through the air on a broomstick. The Mexican legend illustrates sorcery, not witchcraft, because it has nothing to do with denying the Christian God. But to call it *witchcraft*, as the word was used throughout Europe from 1500 to 1700, is simply to cause confusion.

Every month or so, newspapers and magazines report outbreaks of "witchcraft." Such reports would be out of place in this book, but a few scattered specimens may be given by way of illustrations of sorcery.

About 1816 at Nyack, New York, a stranger to the community, who gathered herbs and practiced a homeopathic kind of medicine, was held responsible for the drying up of cows and the souring of milk. The farmers therefore tried Goody Caniff at the Old Mill and started to weigh her on the miller's scales against the heavy brassbound Bible from the church. If she failed the test she was to be drowned in the millpond. Apparently, more rational advice prevailed, and Goody Caniff was not drowned.

At Wratschewe, in the government of Novgorod, in 1879, a woman of fifty, Agrafena Ignatjewa, was suspected of bewitching cattle. The villagers took matters into their own hands, and locked her in her cottage, and set fire to it. The ringleaders were tried for murder, but the jury so sympathized with them that they were set free with a slight ecclesiastical penance. (Philadelphia *Evening Telegraph*, December 20, 1879)

In 1885, an elderly widow, Madame Lebon of Sologne, France, who had saved a few thousand francs, went to live with her daughter, who coveted the money. Shortly after her arrival, the cow calved prematurely and the eggs addled. The obvious conclusion was that old Madame Lebon was a witch. The daughter had the parish priest hear the mother's confession, then bound her tightly, put faggots, dry furze, and wood in the open fireplace, poured on kerosene, and there burned her mother alive. "It is greatly borne upon me," she rationalized, "that now is the time to kill the hag. If we delay, she may commit a sin in thought or deed and the confession will go for nothing." While watching the old lady burn, the daughter told her children to recite the litany for the dying and ask God to forgive their grandma for being a witch. The fire, she added, "shows you what hell is like." Madame Lebon screamed and writhed in the flames, but the son-in-law pounded her down with his sabot. The couple then confessed to the priest, who was bound by vows of silence, and then reported to the mayor that, while they were working in the fields, their old mother had fallen into the fire and had been burned.

In Massachusetts, in April, 1892, Edwin A. Brown of Exeter was ill with tuberculosis. He believed evil spirits lodging in the heart and liver of his dead sister were sapping his life. Accordingly he had his sister's body exhumed from Shrub Hill Cemetery, and the heart and liver burned. Brown rallied, but soon failed and died on May 5 of the same year.

In Havana, on March 10, 1905, fourteen persons were accused of witchcraft. A sick woman, because of some evil inflicted on her when she had been a slave, had to obtain the blood of a white person to effect her cure. A two-year-old baby was stolen and dismembered; the blood from its heart was applied as a poultice to the woman's stomach, and the heart itself was eaten. Several of the accused were convicted and two executed. (Nevins, *Witchcraft in Salem*)

At Horseheath, in Sussex (England), a tale was current in the nineteen-twenties about an old woman.

> One day a black man called, produced a book, and asked her to sign her name in it. The woman signed the book, and the mysterious stranger then told her she would be the mistress of five imps who would carry out her orders. Shortly afterwards the woman was seen out accompanied by a rat, a cat, a toad, a ferret, and a mouse. Everybody believed she was a witch, and many people visited her to obtain cures. (London *Sunday Chronicle*, September 9, 1928)

Again, this incident represents sorcery with

A witch pouring water over two drowning monsters; an engraving by Ertinger, in the Douce Collection, Bodleian Library, Oxford.

a veneer of the stereotyped witch. Ewen, who reproduced the clipping in his *Witch Hunting and Witch Trials*, commented: "Such an account might well have been taken from a seventeenth century deposition."

In July, 1950, Martha Minnen of Witgoor, Flanders, sued her neighbors for slandering her as a witch. The church warden refused her offering at the services; neighbors refused to let their children play with hers. No particular act of *maleficia* was alleged—at most, eccentricities. Mrs. Minnen kept cats. "It's just beyond belief, the number of black cats you see around Martha's house at night," testified one witness against her. Mrs. Minnen gave a neighbor's child the somewhat unusual present of a nest of baby sparrows. Maria Deckx, one of the defendants, testified: "I have always been nice to Mrs. Minnen, but I don't want a lot of birds around my house." She apparently expressed the local feeling when she said, "I believed in witches and I still believe in witches. If the shoe fits, too bad [for Martha Minnen]." The court awarded Mrs. Minnen half the damages she asked for.

This contrast between sorcery and witchcraft might be summed up in the words of the widely-read English Puritan, William Perkins, typical of all inquisitors, judges, lawyers, scientists, and men of letters who accepted the witch delusion. "The very thing that maketh a witch to be a witch," Perkins wrote in 1608, is "the yielding of consent upon covenant." He excluded from this definition of witch those "tainted with frenzy or madness," those with weak brains, and

> all such superstitious persons, men or women, as use charms and enchantment for the effecting of anything upon a superstitious and erroneous persuasion, that the charms have virtue in them to do such things, not knowing that it is the action of the Devil by those means, but thinking God hath put virtue into them, as he hath done into herbs for physic.

Spain, Witchcraft in. Sorcery and witchcraft were sharply distinguished in Spain, and whereas sorcery was prosecuted rigorously for centuries, the attack on witchcraft was restricted. The moderation resulted from the Spanish Inquisition's complete control over the country. This Inquisition was nationalistic and independent of the Inquisition of Rome. By a curious quirk, this country, in which a heresy-hunting organization wielded greater authority than the parallel organization in France and Germany and actually burned the greatest number of heretics in Europe, suffered the least, so far as witchcraft persecutions went.

Sorcery was everywhere. Because of the mingling of cultures—from the Christianized paganism of the Roman domination, the superstitions of the Visigoth conquerors in the fifth to the seventh centuries, the intrusion of the Moors with their heritage of astrology and divination, to the occult traditions of the Jews—superstition had become deeply engrained in Spain. Astrology and necromancy were formal courses in the universities. The acceptance of superstition's external manifestations, magic and sorcery, continued to a late date.

In Castile, for example, diviners and those who consulted them were declared heretics in 1370; if laymen, they were to be punished by royal officials, and if clergy, by bishops (law of 1387). The prohibition was intensified in 1414. But apparently it was little heeded, and as late as 1539, Cirvelo, who wrote the first book in Spanish on witchcraft, regarded sorcery as coming under secular control (thereby dismissing its essential heresy). The problem of heresy and sorcery was earnestly debated, but the area of legitimate doubt remained extensive, as was granted by the *Repertorium Inquisitorum* in 1494, and Francis Pegna, who in 1585 edited the Inquisitor Eymeric.

In this period of uncertainty over definitions, inquisitors exercised considerable personal latitude, and the same offense might be punished quite differently by different tribunals. Individual inquisitors worked under the strict observance of the Suprema, the supreme policy-making body of the Spanish Inquisition, which as late as 1568 reproved an inquisitor for imposing a fine for the recital of charms to cure sickness (apparently to be regarded as non-heretical sorcery). On the other hand, in 1585, the Saragossa inquisitors were not reprimanded when they concluded that keeping a dead man's finger as a good luck charm was heretical.

The layman's course of action was resolved by an edict of the Grand Inquisitor, Alfonzo Manriquez, early in the sixteenth century. A Catholic's duty was to denounce to the Inquisition any person who entertained familiars or spirits, who used any kind of divination or made circles to conjure demons, who employed astrology for fortunetelling, who kept mirrors or rings to bind some spirit, or who had *grimoires* or any other books of magic.

Those who equated sorcery with heresy, however, were heartened by the bull of Pope Sixtus V in 1585, condemning all divination (including astrology), incantations, alleged control of demons, and all sorceries, magic, and superstitions, as heresy. The Suprema held up circulation of this bull until the beginning of the next century. Three years previously, in 1582, the Spanish Inquisition had attacked the University of Salamanca for teaching astrology (which, because of its use in divi-

nation, was regarded as heretical), and placed works on this subject on the Index of forbidden books. During the seventeenth century, the measures against astrology increased, and as late as 1796 the Spanish Inquisition charged a lay brother with computing the position of the planets. From 1600 on, the Spanish Inquisition assumed jurisdiction over all types of sorcery, even when suspicion of heresy was only·light, and often forced episcopal or civil courts to deliver their prisoners. Consequently, an accused was seldom tried by two or three courts (as was Gilles de Rais), and in general the penalties of the Spanish Inquisition were lighter than those of the secular courts.

Since the implied pact with the Devil justified the concern of the Spanish Inquisition with sorcery, various sets of instructions were promulgated for questioning suspects. In one of these, *Praxis Procedendo* (1655), the Suprema gave a sample of how a *zahori*, one who can see through matter (such as earth) to find hidden objects, should be questioned. Since it was commonly believed that demons guarded treasure-trove, the *zahori* would soon find himself guilty of a pact.

When the time came that the rest of Europe was ridiculing sorcery and punishing sorcerers as impostors, the Spanish Inquisition still retained its conviction in the reality of magic into the nineteenth century. On October 15, 1818, for example, the Seville tribunal sentenced Ana Barbero, for superstition, blasphemy, and a pact with the Devil, to two hundred lashes and six years' exile (later remitted to eight years in a penitentiary for prostitutes). A similar sentence was meted out to Francisca Romero on June 18, 1819. Perhaps because in the nineteenth century there were fewer trials of Moriscos and Jews, the Spanish Inquisition found more time to prosecute sorcery (just as the papal Inquisition in southern France, having successfully removed the Albigenses, found it necessary to make witchcraft into a heresy). Henry C. Lea noted that in Toledo from 1575 to 1610, only one and a half per cent of the cases related to sorcery, but in the years from 1648 to 1749 the proportion

An auto-da-fé in Spain. From Philip van Limborch, *Historia Inquisitionis* (1692).

rose to over eight per cent. In the forty years preceding the temporary suspension of the Spanish Inquisition, 1780-1820, nearly seventy per cent of the trials were for superstition (not involving *maleficia*).

That Spain was spared the horrors of the witchcraft persecution that plagued France and Germany was due partly to geography (since Spain lay outside the mainstream of European thought) and partly to the Spanish Inquisition. Other fringe countries (e.g., the Scandinavian lands) were spared for the opposite reason, that the papal Inquisition never reached them. When France and Italy were already burning women for attending a sabbat, the Bishop of Avila, the learned Alfonso Tostado, in 1436 was saying the sabbat was a delusion brought on by drugs. Even the credulous Alphonsus de Spina in 1467 thought the sabbat no more than a delusion evoked by the malice of the Devil. In 1494, however, the *Repertorium Inquisitorum* argued that if the sabbat [Spanish, *aquelarre* = field of the goat] were true, the witches

or *jorguinas* were apostates; if a delusion, heretics; in any case subject to the Spanish Inquisition. The first execution of a witch by the Spanish Inquisition occurred in 1498, when Gracia la Valle was burned in Saragossa; other executions took place in 1499, 1500 (three women), 1512 (two), and 1522. Llorente, the early nineteenth-century historian, said thirty witches were burned in Biscay in 1507.

In 1526 secular courts held mass trials for witchcraft in Navarre, whereupon the Suprema investigated the indictments. The rational approach, even in broaching these topics for discussion, and the skeptical attitude of the ten members of the Suprema explain the absence of any obscurantist witchcraft panic in Spain until the beginning of the seventeenth century. The questions discussed in 1526 included:

1. Do witches really commit the crimes they confess or are they deluded? The vote was six to four on the reality of the crimes.

2. If their crimes are real, should the witches be treated like penitents in all

other crimes and be "reconciled" to the Church, or should they be delivered to the secular courts for execution? The majority favored reconciliation; if murder was alleged, the secular courts could try them for homicide.

3. If their crimes are illusions, how should witches be punished? No decision was reached.

4. Do their crimes come within the purview of the Inquisition? The majority said yes.

5. Are witches' confessions, without further evidence, sufficient for conviction? A split vote ensued. Valdes, the future Inquisitor General, said self-incrimination sufficed only for minor punishments.

6. How can witchcraft best be removed? Only three of the Suprema advocated increased prosecution; most favored more preaching. In addition, Valdes stated that witches' accusations against others should not be accepted.

These restraining conclusions were not promulgated until 1530, after two mass outbreaks, in 1527 at Navarre and in 1528 in Biscay, initiated by individual inquisitors. In 1530 the Suprema quietened a threatened witch hunt in Navarre, and in spite of opposition squelched its own zealous inquisitors in Barcelona in 1537, in Navarre in 1538, and in Galicia in 1551. During the rest of the century, episcopal and civil courts and certain tribunals of the Inquisition sometimes tried to adopt the usual European methods of persecuting witches, but the Suprema held the irregularities down, plainly implying witchcraft was an illusion.

In 1610, however, a witch panic broke out in Navarre. The secular judges, to forestall the Spanish Inquisition, speedily burned their victims. Pierre de Lancre, judge in the mass persecutions of the Basque Witches in 1609, thought the outbreak in Navarre had spread from the Pays de Labourd, and favored his harsh treatment of witches in France over the lenient treatment (as he considered it) of the Spanish witches. The Spanish Inquisition reversed its skepticism of the preceding seventy-five years, and determined on a crusade jointly with the Crown and the bishops against these collaborators of Satan. But informed opinion hesitated, and on March 26, 1611, the Suprema reversed itself and ordered an Edict of Grace, or period of repentance without penalty. To receive evidence and confessions, it delegated Alonzo Salazar de Frias. Salazar's report, while not denying the crime of witchcraft, made conviction almost impossible, and led to the cessation of witchcraft trials in Spain. A few isolated trials occurred in 1622, 1637, 1640 and 1641, but there were no convictions. The Suprema consistently advocated leniency or withdrawal of charges, sometimes openly countering the delusion, as in 1641 when it ordered an inquisitor to prosecute those who beat alleged witches. In the following decades perhaps some half-dozen trials for witchcraft occurred, but no person was executed for witchcraft after 1611; trials and convictions for sorcery, however, continued.

See further, Alonzo Salazar de Frias, Pedro Cirvelo, Alphonsus de Spina.

Spectral Evidence. Because the essence of witchcraft was the pact with the Devil, to secure proof of guilt, ideally the Devil should have been subpoenaed to give evidence against the accused. Since not even the most rabid witch hunter expected to be able to do this, evidence of association with the devil had to be supplied by the suspect himself (through torture), by other confessed witches who would testify (under torture) the suspect was with them in the presence of the devil at a sabbat, or by innocent victims who claimed to see the spirit or specter or shape of the suspect tormenting them. John Cotta justified this ability to identify the spirits of witches by an analogy: "Experience doth show us that the same eye which saw the shape, proportion and figure together with the true substance, doth as perfectly both see and know it, when it is separated from the substance by the art of the painter." (*The Trial of Witchcraft*, 1616)

On such evidence, tens of thousands of people were executed.

From the beginning of the witch trials, however, some people held that such evidence was untrustworthy. The demonologists were constantly battling to prove that although a husband testified his wife did not move from her bed all night, or although reputable citizens vouched that they had guarded a woman who had never stirred from the room, nevertheless such a woman did go to a sabbat, and witnesses testifying to that effect must be believed. They explained the apparent contradiction by the devil's impersonating the body of the woman lying in bed, while the real woman attended the sabbat. Those authorities who retreated to the position that the woman just imagined she went to a sabbat, nevertheless, found her Guilty because she maintained such claims when fully awake in the questioning and because she believed the sabbat to be true.

As early as 1523, Bartolommeo Spina was arguing against the skeptical views by pointing out that, with very few exceptions, persons accused by a witch of being at a sabbat ultimately confessed. Furthermore, he added, God's mercy would not permit the devil to assume the form of an innocent person. Bishop Francis Hutchinson in 1718 could have answered this: "Hath God anywhere promised that he will save credulous men from being deceived because otherwise the blood of the innocent man will be in danger?"

And as late as 1692, the Protestant historian, Limborch, in his *History of the Inquisition,* did not oppose such evidence on the basis of the unreality of the sabbat, but on the grounds that the devil can impersonate the guiltless; hence judges, who are aware of this dilemma, are forced to convict on even more unreliable "conjectures and presumptions" such as bewitchings and threats. Bishop Hutchinson again had the only possible answer; he wrote in 1718: "Many a man hath verily believed he hath seen a spirit externally before him when it hath been only an internal image dancing in his own brain."

But the reality of attendance at a sabbat was not the major issue of spectral evidence. This crux was whether the devil could impersonate an innocent person in working evil. A brief illustration may be quoted from Increase Mather's *Illustrious Providences* (1684). Elizabeth Knap of Groton, Connecticut, had violent fits and uttered strange blasphemies. "She cried out in some of her fits that a woman (one of her neighbors) appeared to her and was the cause of her affliction." Elizabeth could identify the woman with her eyes closed. (For various reasons, the girl's accusations were not decisive, and the accused woman luckily escaped.) This is the pattern of many—perhaps a majority—of the English witch trials, and certainly of most of the American trials.

The most famous controversy about spectral evidence was that provoked by Salem in 1692, where young girls just like Elizabeth Knap said they were tormented by specters of the people they accused. It was assumed that the devil was given no power to impersonate a virtuous person, and that consequently all those named by the girls had given permission for the devil to use their bodies. On this theory, they were found Guilty and hanged. A typical contribution to the debate was Rev. Samuel Willard's *Some Miscellany Observations* (1692), which maintained that the evidence must be human. In order to prove guilt, two things were needed: First, "a free and full confession made by the accused person of the fact, being in his right mind, not frighted or forced into it." Second, "the testimony of two sufficient human witnesses to one and the same individual fact, as done by the party accused." His hypothetical believer in spectral evidence entered the dialogue now with "if this rule be always followed, it will be hard to punish wickedness."

In time, the majority of educated people came to doubt spectral evidence. The Dutch clergymen in New York advised Governor Phips of Massachusetts that "the devil can assume the shape of a good man." In April of 1693, after the trials, the men of Salem forced Rev. Samuel Parris to acknowledge his error in encouraging the accusations. He now believed, he said, "God sometimes suffers the devil, as of late, to afflict in shape of not only innocent but pious persons." He still quibbled, however, adding ". . . or so to delude the sense of the afflicted, that they strongly conceit [imagine] their hurt is from such persons, when it is not." Even Cotton Mather retracted some-

what, and he declared spectral evidence must be used with caution.

See Confessions. Evidence in Witch Trials (England), Evidence in Witch Trials (Europe), Witnesses.

For the fantastic doctrines that support the vulgar opinions of witchcraft rob us of all the defenses that God and nature have placed for our security against false accusation.

For in other cases, when wicked or mistaken people charge us with crimes of which we are not guilty, we clear ourselves by showing that at that time we were at home, or in some other place, about our honest business. But in prosecutions for witchcraft, that most natural and just defense is a mere jest. For if any wicked person affirms, or any crackbrained girl imagines, or any lying spirit makes her believe, that she sees an old woman, or other person, pursuing her in her visions, the defenders of the vulgar witchcraft tack an imaginary unproved compact to the deposition, and hang the accused parties for things that were doing, when they were perhaps asleep upon their beds, or saying their prayers, or perhaps in the accuser's own possession with double irons upon them.

But such fantastic notions are so far from raising their sickly visions into legal evidence, that they are grounded upon the very dregs of pagan and popish superstitions, and leave the lives of innocent men naked without defense against them.
—Bishop Francis Hutchinson, *Historical Essay Concerning Witchcraft* (1718).

Spee, Friedrich von. Spee's *Cautio Criminalis [Precautions for Prosecutors]* is a major attempt by a German in the first half of the seventeenth century to stem the tidal wave of terror against witches. His summary of the nightmarish legal proceedings deserves careful attention, coming from a trained theologian who had lived through the horrors of those accused, for it exposes the whole sleazy fabric of the witchcraft delusion.

The *Cautio*, according to Cardauns, the biographer of Spee, "formed in some sort a line of demarcation separating the minds of men from each other, a victorious memorial of reason and humanity triumphing over hallucination and bestiality." Lea, however, cautioned against exaggerating the importance of the work; since all Catholics were bound to believe in the existence of devils, effective opposition to the witchcraft persecutions could come only from a Protestant. Later opponents of witch trials tended to read into the *Cautio* their own advanced views.

Asked by young Johann Philipp von Schönborn, later Archbishop of Mainz, why his hair had turned prematurely gray,

Friedrich von Spee (1591-1635) replied: "Grief has turned my hair white—grief on account of the witches whom I have accompanied to the stake." Not only grief at such inhuman punishments, but grief at the malice and stupidity of the whole procedure of witch hunts, then raging throughout Franconia and Westphalia. Many prosecutions, continued Spee (according to the philosopher Leibnitz, who years later reported the conversation), he had personally and diligently investigated, and, after considering the charges and confessions, never once had he found anything about the accused that would make them guilty of witchcraft.

Father Spee spent his whole life in the center of the German witch trials. He attended the Jesuit College at Cologne (near his birthplace at Kaiserswerth), entered the novitiate in 1611, then studied philosophy at Würzburg, (a center of the persecutions), and theology at Mainz (another hotbed), in 1624 became a missionary preacher at the cathedral of Paderborn, and in 1627 was made a professor at Würzburg. Here he acted as confessor to those charged with witchery. Following two bad harvests

The judge was technically responsible for the death of a prisoner under torture, although the manuals warned him not to risk losing the chance of obtaining a confession. Said Spee: "If the prisoner dies under so much torture, they say the Devil broke his neck." From Hermann Löher, *Hochnötige . . . Klage.*

in 1626 and 1628, popular frustration sought an outlet in witch charges; in the succeeding years, at nearby Bamberg 600, and at Würzburg 900 (during the rule of Bishop Philipp Adolf) had been burned alive as witches. Father Spee died August 7, 1635, at the age of forty-four, having caught the plague in Treves while serving as a parish priest to the afflicted.

Although his lyric poetry, *Trutznachtigall* [*In Disregard of the Nightingale*] and *Güldenes Tugendbuch* [*Golden Book of Virtues*], both published posthumously, give Spee a minor place in German literature, his claim on posterity rests on his *Cautio Criminalis* (1631), a stringent indictment of the German princes and judges who encouraged the atrocities. Spee could not, of course, deny the existence of witches, but in the fifty-one "Doubts" or "Questions" into which he divides his book, he exposes the methods by which convictions were obtained; once a whisper of witchcraft was heard against any man or woman, the foregone result was death by burning.

His attack was as head-on as was possible at the time. He concentrated on the general disregard of even those thin legal safeguards allowed the accused and on the universal use of torture to extract confessions. "The innocent zealots who encourage witch hunts should realize that, since the tortured have to denounce some persons, trials will become more and more numerous, until at length accusations will encompass them, and in the end everybody will be burned." Spee portrays a vividly grue-

some picture of the common practices in witch trials. Inquisitors and judges assumed guilt in anyone calumniated by "common fame." They made it their business to prove guilt, holding it a disgrace if any were acquitted. For this work they were well paid, four or five thalers a head. The accused was generally held *incommunicado*, allowed no counsel, frequently not even informed of the specific charges or witnesses, and tortured until confessing guilt —in words suggested by the investigators. Moreover, says Spee, "a single innocent person, compelled by torture to confess guilt, is forced to denounce others of whom she knows nothing; so it fares with these, and thus there is scarcely an end to accusers and accused, and, as none dares retract, all are marked for death." Yet on such forced confessions the opinions of all the authorities are based (Spee especially refutes the *Malleus Maleficarum*, Binsfeld, Remy, and Del Rio, a Jesuit). Spee concludes: "Previously I never thought of doubting that there were many witches in the world; now, however, when I examine the public record, I find myself believing that there are hardly any."

Since many of the princes and judges attacked by Spee were benefactors of the Jesuits, the *Cautio Criminalis* was published anonymously, but within the Society of Jesus his authorship was hardly any secret. He was fought by many of his order —one Father Roestius tried to have him placed on the Index of prohibited books; and the General (Father Mutius Vitelleschi) and the Provincial told him he had sinned in publishing a book without permission and must "earnestly guard his manuscripts better in future." A note by the anti-Jesuit "false witch judge," Heinrich von Schultheis, in an attack on the *Cautio*, indicates that Spee was imprisoned for his opposition. Dr. Schultheis complains of "the horrible abuse he poured out regarding the Inquisition and authorities who were taking action against the witches." Not too long after, Spee was transferred to the Jesuit College at Cologne.

That the *Cautio Criminalis* had some practical effect is seen in the preface to the second edition by Johannes Gronäus, who noted that after its publication Prince-Bishop Philipp von Schönborn and the Bishop of Brunswick abandoned persecutions. Yet the mania in effect continued almost another thirty years after Spee's death. The popularity of the *Cautio* among Protestants as well as Catholics, however, surely helped diminish the delusion: a German translation appeared in 1632, and others in 1647 at Bremen and Posen, and in 1649 at Frankfort; a Dutch in 1657, a French in 1660, and a Polish version in 1680; in all, sixteen editions (including translations in German, Dutch, French, and Polish) within a hundred years (the last in 1731).

"How, now, in summary, are the trials against witches conducted today?—This is a question worthy Germany's consideration." (Question 51) Father Spee's answer constitutes a major document in the history of witchcraft; the following condensation is freely translated from the original Latin (1631).

QUESTION 51 OF THE CAUTIO CRIMINALIS

1. Incredible among us Germans, and especially (I am ashamed to say) among Catholics, are popular superstitions, envy, calumnies, backbitings, insinuations, and the like, which, being neither punished nor refuted, stir up suspicion of witchcraft. No longer God or nature, but witches are responsible for everything.

2. Hence everybody sets up a clamor that the magistrates investigate the witches—whom only popular gossip has made so numerous.

3. Princes, therefore, bid their judges and counselors bring proceedings against the witches.

4. The judges hardly know where to start, since they have no evidence [*indicia*] or proof.

5. Meanwhile, the people call this delay suspicious; and the princes are persuaded by some informer or another to this effect.

6. In Germany, to offend these princes is a serious offense; even clergymen approve whatever pleases them, not caring by whom these princes (however well-intentioned) have been instigated.

7. At last, therefore, the judges yield to their wishes and contrive to begin the trials.

8. Other judges who still delay, afraid to get involved in this ticklish matter, are sent a special investigator. In this field of investigation, whatever inexperience or arrogance he brings to the job is held zeal for justice. His zeal for justice is also whetted by hopes of profit, especially with a poor and greedy agent with a large family, when he receives as stipend so many dollars per head for each witch burned, besides the incidental fees and perquisites which investigating agents are allowed to extort at will from those they summon.

9. If a madman's ravings or some malicious and idle rumor (for no proof of the scandal is ever needed) points to some helpless old woman, she is the first to suffer.

10. Yet to avoid the appearance that she is indicted solely on the basis of rumor, without other proofs, a certain presumption of guilt is obtained by posing the following dilemma: Either she has led an evil and improper life, or she has led a good and proper one. If an evil one, then she should be guilty. On the other hand, if she has led a good life, this is just as damning; for witches dissemble and try to appear especially virtuous.

11. Therefore the old woman is put in prison. A new proof is found through a second dilemma: she is afraid or not afraid. If she is (hearing of the horrible tortures used against witches), this is

sure proof; for her conscience accuses her. If she does not show fear (trusting in her innocence), this too is a proof; for witches characteristically pretend innocence and wear a bold front.

12. Lest these should be the only proofs, the investigator has his snoopers, often depraved and infamous, ferret out all her past life. This, of course, cannot be done without turning up some saying or doing of hers which men so disposed can easily twist or distort into evidence of witchcraft.

13. Any who have borne her ill now have ample opportunity to bring against her whatever accusations they please; and everyone says that the evidence is strong against her.

14. And so she is hurried to the torture, unless, as often happens, she was tortured on the very day of her arrest.

15. In these trials nobody is allowed a lawyer or any means of fair defense, for witchcraft is reckoned an exceptional crime [of such enormity that all rules of legal procedure may be suspended], and whoever ventures to defend the prisoner falls himself under suspicion of witchcraft—as well as those who dare to utter a protest in these cases and to urge the judges to exercise prudence, for they are forthwith labeled supporters of witchcraft. Thus everybody keeps quiet for fear.

16. So that it may seem that the woman has an opportunity to defend herself, she is brought into court and the indications of her guilt are read and examined—if it can be called an examination.

17. Even though she denies these charges and satisfactorily answers every accusation, no attention is paid and her replies are not even recorded; all the indictments retain their force and validity, however perfect her answers to them. She is ordered back into prison, there to consider more carefully whether she will persist in obstinacy—for, since she has already denied her guilt, she is obstinate.

18. Next day she is brought out again, and hears a decree of torture—just as if she had never refuted the charges.

19. Before torture, however, she is searched for amulets: her entire body is shaved, and even those privy parts in-

dicating the female sex are wantonly examined.

20. What is so shocking about this? Priests are treated the same way.

21. When the woman has been shaved and searched, she is tortured to make her confess the truth—that is, to declare what they want, for naturally anything else will not and cannot be the truth.

22. They start with the first degree, i.e., the less severe torture. Although exceedingly severe, it is light compared to those tortures which follow. Wherefore if she confesses, they say the woman has confessed without torture!

23. Now, what prince can doubt her guilt when he is told she has confessed voluntarily, without torture?

24. She is therefore put to death without scruple. But she would have been executed even if she had not confessed; for when once the torture has begun, the die is already cast: she cannot escape, she has perforce to die.

25. The result is the same whether she confesses or not. If she confesses, her guilt is clear: she is executed. All recantation is in vain. If she does not confess, the torture is repeated—twice, thrice, four times. In exceptional crimes, the torture is not limited in duration, severity, or frequency.

26. If, during the torture, the old woman contorts her features with pain, they say she is laughing; if she loses consciousness, she is sleeping or has bewitched herself into taciturnity. And if she is taciturn, she deserves to be burned alive, as lately has been done to some who, though several times tortured, would not say what the investigators wanted.

27. And even confessors and clergymen agree that she died obstinate and impenitent; that she would not be converted or desert her incubus, but kept faith with him.

28. If, however, she dies under so much torture, they say the devil broke her neck.

29. Wherefore the corpse is buried underneath the gallows.

30. On the other hand, if she does not die under torture, and if some exceptionally scrupulous judge hesitates to torture her further without fresh proofs or to burn her without her confession, she is

kept in prison and more harshly chained, there to rot until she yields, even if it take a whole year.

31. She can never clear herself. The investigating committee would feel disgraced if it acquitted a woman; once arrested and in chains, she has to be guilty, by fair means or foul.

32. Meanwhile, ignorant and headstrong priests harass the wretched creature so that, whether truly or not, she will confess herself guilty; unless she does so, they say, she cannot be saved or partake of the sacraments.

> "The most robust who have thus suffered have affirmed to me that no crime can be imagined which they would not at once confess to, if it would bring ever so little relief, and they would welcome ten deaths to escape a repetition."
> —Spee, *Cautio Criminalis* (1631)

33. More understanding or learned priests cannot visit her in prison lest they counsel her or inform the princes what goes on. Nothing is more dreaded than that something be brought to light to prove the innocence of the accused. Persons who try to do so are labeled troublemakers [*justitiae turbatores*].

34. While she is kept in prison and tormented, the judges invent clever devices to build up new proofs of guilt to convict her to her face, so that, when reviewing the trial, some university faculty can confirm her burning alive.

35. Some judges, to appear ultra scrupulous, have the woman exorcized, transferred elsewhere, and tortured all over again, to break her taciturnity; if she maintains silence, then at last they can burn her. Now, in Heaven's name, I would like to know, since she who confesses and she who does not both perish alike, how can anybody, no matter how innocent, escape? O unhappy woman, why have you rashly hoped? Why did you not, on first entering prison, admit whatever they wanted? Why, foolish and crazy woman, did you wish to die so many times when you might have died but once? Follow my counsel, and, before undergoing all these pains, say you are guilty and die. You will not escape, for this were a catastrophic disgrace to the zeal of Germany.

36. When, under stress of pain, the witch has confessed, her plight is indescribable. Not only cannot she escape herself, but she is also compelled to accuse others whom she does not know, whose names are frequently put into her mouth by the investigators or suggested by the executioner, or of whom she has heard as suspected or accused. These in turn are forced to accuse others, and these still others, and so it goes on: who can help seeing that it must go on and on?

37. The judges must either suspend these trials (and so impute their validity) or else burn their own folk, themselves, and everybody else; for all sooner or later are falsely accused, and, if tortured, all are proved guilty.

38. Thus eventually those who at first clamored most loudly to feed the flames are themselves involved, for they rashly failed to see that their turn too would come. Thus Heaven justly punishes those who with their pestilent tongues created so many witches and sent so many innocent to the stake.

39. Now many of the wiser and more learned judges are opening their eyes to this enormity, and proceed more slowly and cautiously.

40. Judges need not deny that they torture on mere denunciations.

41. When denunciations become common knowledge, those denounced can seek flight or remain. If they fly, it is a strong presumption of guilt; if they stay, it is all the same, for the devil detains them so that they cannot get away.

> "Experienced confessors know that there are those who have made false denunciations under torture and, when told that they must withdraw the accusations of the innocent, will say that they would willingly do so, if there were any way without incurring a second torture, but they cannot risk it even to avoid damnation."
> —Spee, *Cautio Criminalis* (1631)

42. Moreover, if one defamed goes to the investigators and asks whether what is rumored is true, so that he may prepare his defense, this is proof that his conscience is bothering him.

43. Whatever he does he incurs common

fame, which after a year, coupled with denunciations, suffices for torture.

44. It is the same with those who are calumniated maliciously; if they do not seek redress, their silence is proof of guilt; if they do seek it, the calumny is spread, suspicions are aroused, and it becomes common fame.

45. Thus those forced under torture to denounce are likely to name names.

46. From all which follows this corollary, worthy to be noted in red ink: that, if only the trials be steadily continued, nobody is safe, no matter of what sex, fortune, condition, or dignity, if any enemy or detractor wishes to bring a person under suspicion of witchcraft.

> "There is a frequent phrase used by judges, that the accused has confessed without torture and thus is undeniably guilty. I wondered at this and made inquiry and learned that in reality they were tortured, but only in an iron vise with sharp-edged bars over the shins, in which they are pressed like a cake, bringing blood and causing intolerable pain, and this is technically called without torture, deceiving those who do not understand the phrases of the inquisitors."
>
> —Spee, *Cautio Criminalis* (1631)

Spina, Bartolommeo. Spina (about 1475-1546), a student of Sylvester Prierias, was among the leading theologians of the mid-sixteenth century appointed by the Pope to evaluate the Council of Trent. That a Dominican of such prestige answered the skeptic Ponzinibio indicates the widespread apathy and even resistance to the witch delusion in Italy and elsewhere.

His major work, *Quaestio de Strigibus* [*On Witches*] (1523), against a background of specifically Italian magic, upheld belief in witches, especially their flight by night, sexual intercourse with demons, and transformation into animals. Like all other apologists, he had to whittle away the Canon Episcopi, in which *disbelief* in witches had been the law of the Church. To this end he advocated spectral evidence, observing that if the confessions of witches

sufficed to burn them, their confessions must be accepted as valid evidence against those they named (under torture) as accomplices. Such accomplices all confessed; furthermore, God would not allow truly innocent people to be so defamed.

Spina cited two examples to prove the reality of witchcraft; a modern reader might place another interpretation on them:

One morning a young girl of Bergamo was found naked in the bed of a man in Venice. She explained she had watched her mother apply flying ointment; following suit, she had arrived just in time to stop her mother from murdering the man's child. Her mother scolded her and flew off. The mother was seized by the Inquisition and burned. This story passed into common lore and was retold, for example, by Binsfeld in 1589.

One morning a man was found drunk in a nobleman's wine cellar. He explained he had imitated his wife's preparations for a sabbat flight and found himself among witches. When they saw him they disappeared, leaving him alone among the casks. The wife was seized by the Inquisition and burned. This story passed into common lore and was retold, for example, by Remy in 1595.

Sprenger, Jakob: see *Malleus Maleficarum*.

Squassation. In the *question extraordinaire*, the final torture designed to make prisoners inform on their alleged accomplices, the accused was hoisted as in strappado, his hands bound behind his back to a cord secured to a pulley in the ceiling of the torture chamber. The victim was raised off the ground, and then suddenly released a few feet so that he almost, but never quite, touched the ground. This jerking caused intense pain and complete dislocation of the limbs. The higher the drop, the greater the pain. More than three applications ("severe torture") usually caused death. "Very severe" torture consisted of adding weights to the feet of the prisoner as he hung, and twisting the ropes binding his hands. In France, stones or lead weighing from 40 to 220 pounds were employed; at Mâcon, 660-pound weights were attached to the hanging body.

Philip Limborch, in his *History of the Inquisition* (1692), has left a detailed description:

> The prisoner hath his hands bound behind his back, and weights tied to his feet, and then he is drawn up on high, till his head reaches the very pulley. He is kept hanging in this manner for some time, that by the greatness of the weight hanging at his feet, all his joints and limbs may be dreadfully stretched, and on a sudden he is let down with a jerk, by the slacking the rope, but kept from coming quite to the ground, by which terrible shake his arms and legs are all disjointed, whereby he is put to the most exquisite pain —the shock which he receives by the sudden stop of his fall and the weight at his feet stretching his whole body more intensely and cruelly.

Stapirius, Michael. Michael Stapirius was no great hero, but a simple minister of Hirschberg (Paderborn) who came to hate the persecution for witchcraft after he had acted as chaplain to many of those condemned in Westphalian trials. In his indignation, probably about 1628, he wrote a little *Brillentractat*, known today only through the description of it by Hermann Löher in a book which itself exists in a single copy. Pastor Stapirius had similar experiences to those of Father Friedrich von Spee, Father Kircher of Bamberg, and Pastor Winand Hartmann of Reinbach. Stapirius reports many dying confessions of those burned as witches, all telling how their testimony had been wrested from them by torture. When he pleaded with them to recant and save their souls from perjury, he met with such answers as this of one Wolrath:

> I was tortured, and I was asked, "What do you know about so-and-so and so-and-so who live by the cemetery?" I was asked so often that I could not help seeing what people he [the inquisitor] wanted me to denounce. So I mentioned the names of the persons about whom people had been whispering. But I

Instruments of torture used in the trials witnessed by Michael Stapirius: (above) the heating chair and (below) the choking-pear.

> really don't know anything bad about them. . . . I begged the commissioner to strike out their names, but he answered that if I should declare them innocent I should be tortured again.

Little is known about Rev. Michael Stapirius beyond what his writings reveal, but Lois Gibbons has summarized this brave man, who surely helped destroy the witch delusion, in this way:

> Stapirius' intensity, his profound reli-

gious feeling, clear mind, and singularly keen sense of justice are reminiscent of Cornelius Loos and Friedrich von Spee. In vivid colors he has portrayed these lurid, heart-rending scenes. Few arguments against the cruelty and stupidity of this procedure could be more cogent than are these cases as he describes them.

For further quotations from Stapirius, see Introduction, Confessions, and Torture.

Stigmata Diaboli: see Devil's Mark.

Stone-Throwing Devil. The Stone-Throwing Devil (1682) provides a classical illustration of typical poltergeist phenomena. The rumpus was affirmed by two contemporary writers, Increase Mather in his *Essay for the Recording of Illustrious Providences* (1684), and R[ichard] C[hamberlain], Secretary of the Province of New Hampshire, in a tract published in London in 1698, with a very long and descriptive title:
  Lithobolia, or the Stone-Throwing Devil: Being an exact and true account, by way of journal, of the various actions of infernal spirits, or—devils incarnate—witches, or both; and the great disturbance and amazement they gave to George Walton's family, at a place called Great Island [Newcastle] in the province of New Hampshire in New England, chiefly in throwing about, by an invisible hand, stones, bricks and brickbats of all sizes, with several other things, as hammers, mauls, iron crows, spits, and other domestic utensils, as came into their hellish minds, and this for the space of a quarter of a year.
  Several prominent people, including Samuel Jennings, Governor of West Jersey, Walter Clerk, Deputy-Governor of Rhode Island, and some six others, signed their names to Chamberlain's narrative to "attest the truth of their being eyewitnesses of at least half a score stones that evening thrown invisibly into the field, and in the entry of the house, hall and one of the chambers of George Walton's."
  Mather described the stone-hurling as continuing throughout the summer of 1682, with some recurrence in the spring of 1683:

On June 11, 1682, being the Lord's Day, at night, showers of stones were thrown both against the sides and roof of the house of George Walton. Some of the people went abroad, found the gate at some distance from the house wrung off the hinges, and stones came thick about them, sometimes falling down by them, sometimes touching them without any hurt done to them; though they seemed to come with great force, yet did no more but softly touch them; stones flying about the room, the doors being shut; the glass windows shattered to pieces by stones that seemed to come not from without but within, the lead of the glass casements, window bars, etc., being driven forcibly outwards and so standing bent.

Chamberlain's report, seemingly made from rough eyewitness notes, ran parallel to Mather's. In the evening of June 24, 1682, while he was a guest at Walton's house:

About midnight . . . two very great stones weighing about 30 pounds a piece (that used to lie in the kitchen, in or near the chimney) were, in the former wonted rebounding manner, let fly against my door and wall in the antechamber, but with some little distance of time. This thundering noise must needs bring up the men from below, as before (I need not say to wake me) to tell me the effect, which was the beating down several pictures, and displacing abundance of things about my chamber. But the repetition of this cannon-play by these great rumbling engines, now ready at hand for the purpose, and the like additional disturbance by four bricks that lay in the outer room chimney (one of which having been so employed the first Sunday night, as has been said) made me despair of taking rest and so forced me to rise from my bed.

This experience so moved Chamberlain that it

confirmed [him] and others in the opinion that there are such things as witches and the effects of witchcraft, or at least the mischievous actions of evil spirits, which some do as little give credit to as in the case of witches, utterly rejecting both their operations and their beings. . . . Who that peruses these preternatural occurrences can possibly be so much an enemy to his own soul, and irrefutable reason, as obstinately to oppose himself to, or confusedly fluctuate in, the opinion and doctrine of demons, or spirits, and witches. Certainly, he that does so . . . must temerariously unhinge or undermine the fundamentals of the best religion in the world.

There is a simpler explanation of the New Hampshire poltergeist. Chamberlain was a very unpopular character. New Hampshire had for fifty years been in a state of administrative chaos; Chamberlain had been "secretary" or acting governor for two years and had done nothing to clear up the confusion. The shower of stones was not directed against Walton, who was merely the host to Chamberlain. Stone-throwing, indeed, is often used to express popular disapproval.

Storm-Raising. That witches could raise storms is another traditional folklore belief tagged on to witchcraft and, in the thirteenth century, accepted as true by such Church authorities as Thomas Aquinas and Bonaventura. With such approval, popular acceptance of the heresy of witchcraft spread rapidly. "It were but fruitless labor, and ill spent, to bestow long time in confirming this so manifest a truth," wrote Alexander Roberts in his *Treatise of Witchcraft* (1616). As early as about 700, in the *Liber Poenitentialis* of Archbishop Theodore of Canterbury, Article 21 ordered five years penance, one of them on bread and water, for causing storms. By this penance, the Church admitted the power of sorcerers to control weather, a high compliment. Ulrich Molitor in 1489 said it was common belief that witches provoked lightning and hail. Popular superstition associated the Laplanders with storm-raising, and Richard Eden, in his *History of Travel in the West and East Indies* (1577), copying Olaus Magnus, described how Finnish witches achieved their effects:

They tie three knots on a string hanging at a whip. When they loose one of these,

"Witches have confessed that they made hailstorms at the sabbat, or whenever they wished, to blast the fruits of the earth. To this end, according to their confessions, they beat water with a wand, and then they threw into the air or into the water a certain powder which Satan had given them. By this means, a cloud was raised which afterwards turned to hailstones and fell wherever the witches wished. When water was lacking, they used their urine."—Guazzo, *Compendium Maleficarum* (1626).

they raise tolerable winds. When they loose another, the wind is more vehement. But by loosing the third, they raise plain tempests, as in old time they were accustomed to raise thunder and lightning.

In 1563, the King of Sweden included four witches in his army against the Danes, presumably for their prowess in this direction.

The ability to accomplish such a miracle, and to succeed perhaps when the Church's prayers for rain had failed, was a power not lightly to be disavowed. Consequently many witches confessed to this distinction. They told the demonologist Remy, for example, that they would beat water in a pond with a rod, whereupon the water would rise to form clouds which could be directed to make lightning, hail, or rain, wherever the witches desired. Remy, following Caesalpinus, described another way of producing rain. A little girl helping her father in the field was upset by his complaints about the drought. She quickly resolved to help him by doing what she had seen her mother do: she urinated into a little hole, stirred up the resultant mud, and produced the needed rain. The father in-

Witches raising a storm, from Ulrich Molitor, *De Lamiis* (1489). "But now for the truth of this, that certain words or ceremonies do seem at least to cause an alteration in the air or to raise tempests."—Henry More (1653).

formed on the mother, who was burned alive as a witch. Nider described a third method: a man under torture confessed how he threw a sacrificial pullet into the air, at which the devil produced a storm.

Reginald Scot, who ridiculed the witchcraft delusion, made a long roster of other means by which every "doting old woman" thought she affected the weather. Scot listed casting a flint stone over the left shoulder toward the west, throwing a little sea sand into the air, wetting a broom and shaking it, digging a hole in the ground and pouring water in it, boiling hog bristles, laying sticks on a dry river bank, or burying sage till it be rotten. "All which things are confessed by witches, and affirmed by writers, to be the means that witches use to move extraordinary tempests and rain." Scot omitted other techniques mentioned in various records, such as boiling eggs in a pail of water, reciting a charm, whistling on a ship, boiling a baby in a cauldron, or beating a wet rag against a stone.

Another Englishman, but a firm advocate of the powers of witchcraft, Henry More, told a well-known story current among the demonologists about the malicious witch of Constance. Like the wicked fairy, she was angry at not being invited to a wedding. Left out of the drinking and merrymaking, solitary and neglected, she asked the devil "to transport her through the air" to a hill overlooking the village. Here, "digging a hole and putting urine into it, [she] caused a great tempest of hail, and directed it so that it fell only upon the village, and pelted them that were dancing with [such] violence that they were forced to leave off their sport." Constance also featured in Bodin's reference to a storm which destroyed the corn crop; Anne Mindelen and one Agnes were accused: they confessed and were burned.

More, after telling a number of similar anecdotes (including some from Weyer) about raising tempests, admitted, "But whether there be any causal connection betwixt these ceremonies and the ensuing tempests I will not curiously decide. But that the connection of them is supernatural is plain at first sight." This acceptance in 1653 is quite a contrast to a much earlier view, one of several contending opinions, introduced by Molitor in his dialogue, *De Lamiis*, in 1489, that "tempests, hails, or poisoned air are not the work of some malicious women, but purely the movements of nature or the toleration of divine will which allows the Devil to afflict us, possibly to punish us or perhaps to enable us to acquire merit in the favor of ineffable grace."

A unique pamphlet in the Bodleian Library, Oxford, dated 1716, *The Whole Trial and Examination of Mrs. Mary Hicks and her daughter Elizabeth but of nine years of age, who were condemned at the last assizes held at Huntingdon for witchcraft and there executed on Saturday the 28th of July, 1716,* referred to raising a storm in which ships were almost lost. To accomplish this feat, Mrs. Hicks pulled off her stockings and made a lather with soap. However, this incident is fictitious, for no independent record of the facts is preserved, and there are several internal contradictions.

In the history of witchcraft, there are two well-known instances of storm-raising in Britain. One classic example is part of the involved trial of the North Berwick Witches in 1590. Apparently a group of dissident Scots attempted by magical means to bring on a storm to wreck the ship in which King James was coming back from Denmark. The contemporary pamphlet *News from Scotland* tells how Agnes Sampson "took a cat and christened it, and after bound to each part of that cat the chiefest part of a dead man and several joints of his body." The cat was then thrown into the sea. The witches felt sure that they were responsible for the contrary wind which slowed down the King's ship. "For when the rest of the ships had a fair and good wind, then was the wind contrary and altogether against his Majesty."

The other is uncomplicated: the forced confession in 1645 of Reverend John Lowes, aged seventy, pastor of Brandeston, Suffolk, who was tortured by Matthew Hopkins to say he had caused a tempest to sink a sailing ship off Norwich, in which fourteen persons were drowned. The broken, half-crazed old man, when asked if he were sorry, answered: "No, he was joyful to see what power his imps had!"—Stearne, *Confirmation and Discovery of Witches*. Richard Baxter in 1691 repeated the story to prove the existence of devils. Bishop Francis Hutchinson, however, in the early years of the eighteenth century, commented: "A monstrous tale, without any tolerable proof to support it."

Strappado. Strappado [*Zug*] was a common form of torture to force confessions and naming of accomplices. The prisoner's arms were tied behind his back with a rope attached to a pulley, and he was then hoisted in the air. Frequently, weights were attached to his feet to pull his shoulders from their sockets without leaving visible marks of rough treatment. Sometimes toe-

screws and thumbscrews were applied while the victim was suspended. Strappado (from Latin, *strappare* = to pull) was customarily one of the "lighter" measures used by the Inquisition and civil authorities, but could easily develop into squassation, a more severe variant. Squassation differed from strappado in that the victim was suddenly dropped from a height to within a few inches of the floor; the consequent jerking of his trussed-up limbs caused even more intolerable pain. Limborch, quoting Julius Clarus (*Practica Crimina*), lists strappado as the second degree of torture used by the Inquisition—the first being stripping and severe binding, and the third squassation. Strappado, said Limborch, "is done by hoisting a person up, and keeping him hanging for a considerable time," and is for the purposes of interrogation rather than torture (*History of the Inquisition*, 1692). Lea suggests that the *tratti di corde* (Ital. for strappado) was first used in witch trials in 1474 in Piedmont. Strappado was not used in England, but was used (e.g., in 1652) in Scotland.

Stubb, Peter. The trial of Peter Stubb or Stump (his name is also spelled Stumpf and Stube) in 1589, near Cologne, as a lycanthrope attracted much attention throughout Europe—Del Rio, Rowlands, and Fairfax all commenting on it. Generally it conformed to the traditional ideas about werewolves, but two aspects are worthy of note: the ease with which otherwise intelligent persons rationalized the impossible and made negative evidence positive proof, and the accumulation of death torments meted out to Stubb. The English account quoted here is "truly translated out of the High Dutch"—werewolves are rarely found in English witch trials.

Peter confessed how he changed his shape by means of a magic belt which transformed him into "a greedy devouring wolf, strong and mighty, with eyes great and large, which in the night sparkled like unto brands of fire, a mouth great and wide, with most sharp and cruel teeth, a huge body, and mighty paws." While a wolf, he committed many murders. Removal of the belt restored him "to the proportion of a man."

At his trial, Stubb said he left this belt in a certain valley. The magistrates searched in the spot indicated and found nothing. However, Stubb's story was not disbelieved, "for it may be supposed that [the belt] was gone to the devil from whence it came, so that it was not to be found."

> A German, called Peter Stump, by charm
> Of an enchanted girdle, did much harm,
> Transformed himself into a wolfish shape,
> And in a wood did many years escape
> The hand of justice, till the hangman met him,
> And from a wolf, did with an halter set him.
> —Samuel Rowlands, *Knave of Hearts* (London, 1612).

On October 28, 1589, sentence was pronounced, and on October 31, in the town of Bedburg, carried out "in the presence of many peers and princes of Germany." The judgment is probably the most severe to be encountered. Stubb was condemned

> first to have his body laid on a wheel, and with red-hot burning pincers in ten several places to have the flesh pulled off from the bones; after that, his legs and arms to be broken with a wooden axe or hatchet; afterward to have his head struck off from his body; then to have his carcass burned to ashes.

Guazzo told a very similar story but moved it forward to 1615 at Treves.

Succubus. A devil in female form, the succubus specializes in seducing men. Although feminine in meaning, in form this medieval Latin word, *succubus*, is masculine (because demons were supposedly sexless); the feminine form *succuba* [strumpet] is occasionally found. Since women were allegedly more licentious than men, the male incubi appear more frequently in works on demonology; it was supposed that incubi outnumbered succubi by nine to one.

A personal and imaginative explanation of the succubus appeared in 1801, in *The Magus,* a curious book by a believer in magic and demons, Francis Barrett. He thought a succubus was really a wood nymph, although he gravely agreed that Satan could himself appear as a young lady:

> And seeing the fauni and nymphs of the woods were preferred before the other [spirits] in beauty, they afterwards generated their offspring among themselves, and at length began wedlocks with men, feigning that, by these copulations, they should obtain an immortal soul for them and their offspring; but this happened through the persuasions and delusions of Satan to admit these monsters to carnal copulation, which the ignorant were easily persuaded to; and therefore these nymphs are called succubi; although Satan afterwards committed worse, frequently transchanging himself, by assuming the persons of both incubi and succubi in both sexes; for they conceived not a true young by the males, except the nymphs alone.

The first accounts of the succubus made her much more desirable than a mortal. Pico della Mirandola told of a man who had slept with a succubus for forty years, and would rather die in prison than give her up. The *Malleus Maleficarum* related an incident at Coblenz. In front of his wife and friends, a man was forced to have intercourse with a succubus. He kept at it three times; but when the succubus wanted to recommence, the man fell to the floor worn out. Later writers, probably desiring to parallel the allegations that witches found intercourse with the devil cold and painful, made relations with a succubus similarly frigid. Guazzo told how a couple procured a succubus for their son. Although she had hooves for feet, the boy was eager for initiation, "but it was as if he had entered an icy cavern."

Most of the primitive saints were tempted by such devils, especially, as Girolamo Cardano (1550) observed, when both mind and body were enfeebled by prolonged asceticism in the desert. St. Anthony of Egypt (A.D. 251-356) was plagued at night by a devil "throwing filthy thoughts in his way" and "imitating all the gestures of a woman." Again, according to his biography by Athanasius, "the devil, unhappy wight, one night even took upon him the shape of a woman and imitated all her acts simply to beguile Anthony." His disciple, St. Hilary, was, on lying down to sleep, "encircled by naked women." (*Life*, by St. Jerome)

The saints struggled, of course; but it is recorded that one, St. Victorinus, succumbed. The Bishop Ermolaus of Verona (1453-71) is the authority for the story of a hermit who yielded to the blandishments of the devil disguised as a woman; the hermit so gave himself to lechery that he died within a month. St. Hippolytus (died A.D. 236) was once visited by a nude woman, but when he threw his chasuble over her to conceal her nakedness, the woman became a corpse (which the devil had animated to tempt the saint to sin). In consequence of such visions, the fear of the succubus became enshrined in a famous Ambrosian hymn (*"Procul recedant somnia"*)—"Let all dreams and phantasms of the night . . . fade away, lest our bodies be polluted."

Stories of succubi recur throughout medieval times; in the sixteenth and seventeenth centuries they are found chiefly in reports of trials. Although the charge appears in prosecutions from about 1430, it is not until the later centuries that intercourse with demons features prominently.

Perhaps the most notorious fable was that spread by Walter Mapes, in his *De Nugis Curialium* [*Courtiers' Trifles*] (about 1185), concerning Gerbert of Aurillac, who became Pope Sylvester II (999-1003). As a young man, Gerbert fell in love with the daughter of the Provost of Rheims. The girl rejected him, and Gerbert despaired so long that he became impoverished and at his wit's end. One day he came across a beautiful maiden seated on silks and surrounded by hoards of money. She told him her name was Meridiana, and that if he would only be faithful to her, he could possess her, her magical knowledge, and her money. Gerbert gladly accepted and

The succubus demon, from Father Mathias de Giraldo, Order of Preachers, *Histoire curieuse et pittoresque des sorciers, augmentée par M. Fornari* (Paris, 1854).

prospered rapidly, becoming Archbishop of Rheims, Cardinal, Archbishop of Ravenna, and ultimately Pope. All this time he secretly enjoyed the company of Meridiana every night, and was even forgiven by his succubus when the Provost's daughter, finding him inebriated, seduced him. At last Meridiana prophesied Gerbert's approaching death at such time as he celebrated mass in Jerusalem (to which holy place he had vowed to make a pilgrimage). However, it was a Jerusalem nearer home, a church known by this name from its possession of an alleged piece of the Cross. Realizing his end was near, Gerbert made a public confession of his sins and died repentant. Mapes said his tomb in the Lateran sweats copiously before the death of a pope.

Another farfetched anecdote was given by the Dominican Johannes Nider (1435). Many harlots, he said, offered their services to those attending the Council of Constance (1414-18), but the most sought-after call girl was a succubus, who even boasted of the money she had earned. Such fantasies as these, however, in 1468 condemned to death a man at Bologna for running a brothel staffed by succubi. Two centuries later, George Sinclair, in *Satan's Invisible World Discovered* (1685), related the execution in 1655 in Scotland of William Barton and his wife. "He confessed that he lay with the devil in the shape of a gentlewoman, and [she] had fifteen pounds of him in good money; but he denied it again before his execution."

See further, Incubus, Sexual Relations with Devils.

Sweden, Witchcraft in. The outstanding occurrence of witchcraft in Sweden took place at Mora in 1669. In spite of, or perhaps because of, the severity of the repression, the hysteria spread in the following years to other parts of the kingdom. Special commissions were appointed in 1670 for Uppsala and Helsinki, in the Swedish province of Finland, and apparently continued the witch hunting. A little later, between 1674 and 1675, seventy-one persons were beheaded or burned in three parishes; and in 1676 Stockholm was hit with the mania. Accusations were rife; many were jailed; the churches by public fasts and prayers reinforced the panic. Finally, when it was found some young informers had acted out of envy and greed, King Charles XI forthwith banned all further prosecutions. Miraculously, witchcraft disappeared.

These prosecutions had been made under laws of Charles IX in 1608 and of Gustavus Adolphus in 1618, covering attempted poisoning or sorcery and working *maleficia*. Accusations of sorcery had to be substantiated by six witnesses, and an accused could purge himself if supported by twelve compurgators or character witnesses. The death penalty was abolished in 1779.

Notwithstanding his mildness and skepticism, King Charles XI has to take responsibility for this major outbreak in Swedish history. His initial order for the Mora commission discountenanced torture; his reply to the Duke of Holstein hinted that the acts of the accused witches were imaginary. Positive leadership at this late date was not difficult; yet Charles XI made a poor showing in comparison to his predecessor, Queen Christina. During the Thirty Years' War, after ascending the throne, she banned witch trials. To one of her ministers she wrote that experience demonstrated persecutions merely increased the number of accused witches; he was consequently to free all such prisoners, except those clearly guilty of murder. She was convinced, she said, that women who confessed to the pact suffered either from diabolical illusions or from female internal disorders. Her letter is notable as the first legislation curbing witch hunts (February 16, 1649).

See also Mora Witches, Witchcraft in Finland, Witchcraft in Norway.

Swimming. Ordeal by immersion in water is a very ancient means of determining innocence or guilt. In his edition of Matthew Hopkins' *Discovery of Witches* (1647), Montague Summers collected a sampling of the early laws, beginning with the Code of Hammurabi, King of Babylon, in the third millennium B.C.

> If a man charges another with black magic and has not made his case good, the one who is thus taxed shall go to the river and plunge into the water. If the river overcometh him, then shall his accuser possess his property. If, however, the river prove him innocent and he be not drowned, his accuser shall surely be put to death, and the dead man's property shall become the portion of him who underwent the ordeal.

The ordeal moves closer to witchcraft in the Anglo-Saxon laws of King Athelstan (925-39) and of King Edward the Confessor (1042-66), where the trial by water (*iudicium aquae*) became a general test for all crimes, sinking now establishing innocence. However, in 1219 under Henry III, ordeal by water was abolished, although it continued in nonofficial use.

Swimming, like so many traditional beliefs incorporated in the heresy of witchcraft, both antedated and postdated the height of the mania. It reached its peak about the first half of the seventeenth century, especially (in England) from the approval of this test by King James:

> So it appears that God hath appointed, for a supernatural sign of the monstrous impiety of the witches, that the water shall refuse to receive them in her bosom, that have shaken off them the sacred water of baptism and willfully refused the benefit thereof.

Matthew Hopkins, the self-styled Witch Finder General, encouraged swimming, but wrote that he never presented evidence based on it. Hopkins evaded the charge that swimming was "an abominable, inhumane, and unmerciful trial of these poor creatures . . . a trial not allowable by law or conscience." About the same time in France (1601 and again in 1641), the Parlement of Paris forbade swimming as evidence; and on August 10, 1642, it condemned to death the judges of Braguelon for having submitted a witch to the water ordeal, during which she died.

As described by Sir Robert Filmer in 1653, the method consisted of tying the right thumb to the left big toe, so that the witch was "cross bound," and immersing her three times in water. In earlier times, the right thumb had been bound to the right toe. If she fleeted [floated] and did not sink, she was guilty. If she sank, she was innocent; but, of course, she might drown if not rescued by her tormentors. Some men knew of a special technique which would tend to make a person float and therefore be found guilty. Thomas Ady said the Bible never ordered a witch tried by sinking or swimming, and he pointed out that laying the victim "flat on the back and [holding] up their feet with a string" would ensure that "their forepart will not sink." (*A Candle in the Dark*, 1656)

The chief European exponent of the water ordeal was William Adolf Scribonius, a Hessian schoolmaster, who wrote *De Sagarum Natura et Potestate, deque his recte cognoscendis et puniendis physiologia* [*The Nature and Power of Witches, and the theory both of correctly discovering and punishing them*] (1588). This work passed into English much later through Richard Baxter's *Certainty of the World of Spirits* (1691). However, a majority of Continental jurists and theorists did not stress swimming as evidence against witches, and Binsfeld, in fact, says it was prohibited, along with the other traditional ordeal by the red-hot iron. Thus, tests by swimming appear late, are generally at the insistence of the accused, and are thrown out by the civil judges.

The first admission of swimming as evidence in an English trial came in 1612 at

The swimming of Mary Sutton (1612), part of the title page of a Bodleian pamphlet, *Witches Apprehended, Examined, and Executed* (London, 1613).

Northampton against Arthur Bill and his parents, and the final official use in 1717 at Leicester—both the accused, a mother and daughter, "swam like a cork, a piece of paper, or an empty barrel, though they strove all they could to sink." This last incident apparently just avoided the prohibition of the Chief Justice, Lord Parker, who in 1712 gave "all men warning, that if any dare for the future to make use of that experiment, and the party lose her life by it, all they that are the cause of it are guilty of willful murder . . . neither King James's book nor all other past precedents will save them from an halter." Action had been taken, in fact, in 1694 against three men for swimming Ann Waddan.

In America, a couple implicated with Goodwife Greensmith, hanged for witchcraft at Hartford in 1633, "swam after the manner of a buoy, part under, part above the water . . . [believing] that an halter would choke them, though the water would not, they very fairly took their flight." [See Connecticut Witches.] Grace Sherwood, the Virginia witch, in 1706 sought to prove her innocence by being "tried in the water by ducking." The court agreed, "always having care of her life to preserve her from drowning."

After Lord Parker's ban, swimming lingered in mob action. In 1751 a mob killed a couple of old beggars at Tring, Northamptonshire [see Ruth Osborne]. Action against mob leaders for swimming was taken in 1760 at Leicester. In 1785 at Northampton, Sarah Bradshaw, popularly regarded as a witch, pleaded to be ducked; luckily for her, she quickly sank. In 1829 at Monmouth, several persons were tried for swimming a supposed witch. E. Lynn Linton in *Witch Stories* (1861) told about "an old gentleman who died . . . not so long ago, [who] when a boy had seen a witch swum in Polstead Ponds, 'and she went over the water like a cork.' " In 1865 at Castle Headingham, Emma Smith and Samuel Stammers were charged with having led a crowd of sixty or seventy in the swimming of an old deaf-and-dumb Frenchman. The Frenchman died the following day of exposure, and the couple was committed to Chelmsford Assizes [London *Times*, September 24, 1865]. Throughout the nineteenth century, there crop up other scattered incidents, showing the survival of sorcery after the demise of witchcraft as heresy.

Tedworth Drummer: see Drummer of Tedworth.

Tengler, Ulric. Governor of Höchstädt on the Danube, Ulric Tengler in 1509 wrote a handbook of law that was reprinted many times during the sixteenth century. The second edition (1511) was augmented by his son, Christoph, a professor of Canon Law at Ingolstadt, and by other theologians. In the chapters on witchcraft, derived from the *Malleus Maleficarum*, secular judges were urged to encourage informers, who were not punished even if their accusations were false. A number of illustrations in the book depict contemporary tortures.

Tengler's *Layenspiegel* [*Mirror for Laymen*] paralleled the Bamberg laws on which the Carolina Code was based. He was the first to issue a vernacular handbook including procedure against witches, the forerunner of similar guides for the next 200 years. Two sections are translated here, a proclamation urging people to inform against suspected witches, and a set of suggested questions to be asked an accused witch.

FORM OF CITATION AGAINST WITCHES

I, *N.*, the judge, make known to all, to each and every person subject to the authority of the court of *N.*, as subjects, relatives, and inhabitants, that rumor and gossip have reached my ears that there are certain witches and other such within this jurisdiction who, with the help of the evil spirit, secretly wreak injury on and bring damage to young and old people, to beasts and to crops, and who also traffic in other types of sorcery and heretical practices.

Whereas, by virtue of my obligations and by the special command of the Almighty God, for whose praise and honor as well as in duty to my holy Christian faith, I am obliged to root out and crush under foot such heretical evil, as far as I am able, I herewith give notice [as follows]:

Therefore, on pain of serious punishment, I admonish you one and all, and especially those in the district of *N.*, that everyone within twelve days, which I have set up so that the first four are assigned to subjects, four to relatives, and four to inhabitants, to reveal and to give notice to me, whether to anyone's knowledge, any one has seen or heard of such a person who has been denounced or suspected or rumored as a witch or as any other heretic or as one who traffics in such things as working evil to men, animals, or crops, or causing damage against the common good.

No one needs to be worried about proving his accusation or fearing, should his denunciation not be proved, that he will be punished or called to account. But if it turns out that someone has been guilty of these things, now and henceforth, he shall fall victim to all the prescribed pains and punishments. This should be known for the guidance and judgment of everyone.

Dated under my signature.

A specific citation against a particular person may be formulated in the following manner, with any necessary changes.

If any person who wishes to make an accusation comes forward, the judge, who shall be assisted by a notary and two honorable anonymous persons, shall assume his duties, and shall make the accuser swear an oath [to make him aware of the gravity of his charges], and ask him furthermore the basis of his knowledge and accusations, and especially where and in what places he heard these things, and in what way, how often, and at what time, and (where the accused had been found under suspicious circumstances or in bad company) what else he might have seen. But should someone say that he had only heard something, then he ought to be further questioned concerning from whom, where, when, how often, and also who else had been present, etc. And in conclusion [the judge] should admonish each one under oath to keep everything secret.

Thereupon, in such a case, if such evidence appears, the secular judge must decide whether it would be proper to refer the matter to secular or clerical authority.

And where [the judge] fears that one or more of the accused persons may flee, he may take them into custody or otherwise secure them. And when they take them into custody, they should look into the place of abode of such accused witches or otherwise suspected persons; and they should be careful to look into all corners and crevices and hiding places, above and below, on the chance that perhaps certain instruments or signs [of witchcraft], if they have not been [carefully] hidden, might doubtless be found.

And if the [suspects] have daughters, servant girls, or domestics, to be careful also to take these people into custody, and to question them. And wherever such people are apprehended in their place of abode, to be careful that they are not permitted to remain alone in any chamber or other room where they might dispose of any evidence they might have, and also to prevent them casting any spell that might enable them to remain silent. It is sometimes the custom to carry these people off in a sheet [so that if their feet do not touch the ground they will have no magic powers].

When such suspected persons have been apprehended in this manner, they should initially be gently questioned in prison in a general manner, so that they are not told by whom and how they have been accused. In particular, [they should be questioned] where they were born, raised, lived, and where they are now residing, and in what places and with whom they have been, if they have friends, if they are still alive, and if they have died a natural death or otherwise.

Item: specifically, if they have left their homeland.

Item: particularly, why their cows give more milk than those of their neighbors whom they dislike or who have more cattle than they have, and why people have become their enemy.

Item: whether they have not heard or suspected that the place where they have their dwelling is unholy; and why they have been wandering in the midst of the fields even in bad weather.

Item: why the animals, children, or men have at once become infirm, which has distressed the people.

Item: whether they knew that these persons who had to do with such things were evil.

Item: whether they knew that such persons had been apprehended and burned in certain areas.

Item: why the people in these areas were their enemies.

Item: why [their enemies] had drowned several of these accused persons.

Item: why they had stolen [something] from [someone], which they could very well have got otherwise. And for what purpose they had used these things.

Item: why they have thus remained in adultery and unhallowed love.

Item: why they had done this or that at the childbirth of Frau N.

The skilled judge on the basis of his experience will be able to formulate similar lines of inquiry about the charges which have been made against the suspect. Should the suspected persons make improper responses to the questions by denial or silence, then the judge may presume they have been bewitched and are not telling the truth, and then he may take further counsel against them. When it is a question of proceeding against such sorcery, no fixed rule can be given here, otherwise the evil spirit would be able to anticipate what was coming and would be able to escape the snare set for him.

In cases where these people being questioned indicate a desire to confront the persons who have accused them, for many reasons this is not to be permitted. . . .

This and other problems can be found [discussed] in the previously mentioned *Malleus Maleficarum.*

Any judge and his assistant may through diligent labor prepare themselves and take precautions that they do not touch the evil person on the naked flesh, but equip themselves with dissolved soft soap, wax, and other things, that the Christian Church has prescribed against such and other devilish tricks and spells. And as they go to question this unhallowed backslider, let them cross themselves and diligently see to it that the evil and poison of the old serpent may, through God's help, be kept apart from them.

Thomasius, Christian. Christian Thomasius (1655-1728) first attracted notoriety by his advocacy of mixed marriages. The son of a professor at Leipzig, he studied law; he delivered his first lectures at Leipzig in German rather than in Latin, early indicating his nonconformity. When the Lutheran Duke of Saxony wished to marry the daughter of the Calvinist Frederick III, Elector of Brandenburg, and later first King of Prussia, the Saxon universities of Leipzig and Wittenberg opposed the union. For his support of the Lutheran Duke, Thomasius lost his position and had to flee to Calvinist Brandenburg, where he found a post at the insignificant *Ritterschule* of Halle. But his best students from Leipzig followed him, and others joined them. Soon Frederick III made Halle a university and placed Thomasius at its head. The new institution was scorned by the older academies and was nicknamed the University of Hell [Hölle]. Here Thomasius fostered the liberal traditions of the Protestant lawyer Pufendorf and the Catholic lawyer Grotius (both on the Index of prohibited books), based on the Law of Nature, the moral law of God as discerned by right reason, and the Law of Nations, the contractual agreements between countries. Thomasius stressed the historical method of study, that things were only intelligible in their historical growth.

An early eighteenth-century conception of the flight of witches to the sabbat: the satirical frontispiece of *Kurze Lehr-Sätze* (1712) by Christian Thomasius.

In his teaching and study, Thomasius dealt with major issues of the day. One of these was belief in witchcraft. In September, 1694, he took part in a review by the law faculty of Halle of the 150 procedures followed in the witch trial of Barbara Labarenzin. Thomasius voted to use light torture to induce confession, but the majority decided that she should be discharged with a warning. Thomasius studied the grounds of his opponents and became convinced he had been wrong; further study brought him to disbelief in the whole superstition of a personal Devil. Under theological pressure, he modified his stand to admit the existence of witches, but he denied the possibility of a pact. This compromise satisfied no one. Thomasius, however, continued to spread his original skepticism through dissertations by his students, such as Johann Reiche (1701) and Johann Paul Ipsen (1712). Thomasius also opposed torture (although he favored its application in certain trials) and intolerance. "The duty of princes is not to save souls," he wrote, "but to preserve peace." In spite of such hesitations, Thomasius was, according to Andrew D. White, "the greatest and bravest German between Luther and Lessing." Lea commented that, considering "the absolute nature of the Scriptural assertions, and the character of the Imperial laws on the subject, the wonder is, not that men trained in reverence to such authorities should believe in witchcraft, but that any intellects should be found sufficiently bold to shake off the traditional superstitions."

The *De Crimine Magiae* was printed in Latin in 1701, and in a German translation in 1703, with frequent reprintings. Thomasius especially opposed the theologian Theophilus Spitzel (1687), and the celebrated Protestant lawyer Benedict Carpzov (influential since 1635). In numerous asides, Thomasius showed his unusual perspicacity. For example, he noted that when a pious man resisted oppression and could not be burned for heresy, the theory of the pact served to condemn him; false witnesses would swear to his being a witch and so send him to the stake. Since there never was any pact, all witches had been burned for a nonexistent crime, their confessions being the result of torture. Anybody would confess under torture to whatever the judges demanded.

Thumbscrews. Also known as thumbikins, the screws, pilliwinks, and (in France) *grésillons*. A common and effective method of forcing confessions. In the simplest form, pressure was applied on the thumb, or toe, by a piece of string. A metal thumbscrew, however, exerted such pressure as to crush the thumb to pulp. During the sixteenth century the device was used in France, where it was recommended that only the tip of the finger, to the end of the nail, be placed in the vise. It was apparently introduced into England at the end of the seventeenth century, for in 1684 it was

called a "new invention and engine" that "had never been used before." Bishop Gilbert Burnet, in *History of His Own Times* (1724), writes of two men, Spence and Carstairs (not accused of witchcraft), among the first to be thus tortured:

> When the torture had its effect on Spence, they offered the same oath to Carstairs. And upon his refusing to take it, they put his thumbs in the screws, and drew them so hard, that as they put him to extreme torture, so they could not unscrew them, till the smith that made them was brought with his tools to take them off.

"And then came also—God in highest Heaven have mercy!—the executioner and put the thumbscrews on me, both hands bound together, so that the blood spurted from the nails and everywhere, so that for four weeks I could not use my hands, as you can see from my writing."—Johannes Junius, writing to his daughter (1628). Examples of thumbscrews and bone vises used at this period.

Thyraeus, Petrus. Distinguished Jesuit preacher and Professor of Theology at the University of Mainz, Thyraeus published his *De Spectris Apparitionibus* [*On Spectral Apparitions*] in 1594 at Cologne. It is chiefly concerned with Spectral Evidence. The Devil has power to represent the likeness (or simulacrum) of an innocent person at a sabbat; but since the Devil is circumscribed by God, in practice he represents only the wicked. God protects the innocent; if the Devil were allowed to represent these at the sabbat, he would also represent them outside the sabbat doing other crimes, such as adultery and robbery. But, says Thyraeus, this does not happen. And if the Devil did this, honest men would live in constant fear of wrongful arrest and torture —and men do not live like this. Spectral evidence is therefore valid proof of witchcraft.

Torture. Torture was intellectually justified for use in witch trials by the following theory:

First, certain premises had to be granted. Truth and goodness, the attributes of God, were eternal verities, revealed to and by the Christian Church, and not subject to the fluctuations of men's opinions about right and wrong. This Church, while it might modify and deepen these concepts of the way and the life to be followed by all men, had the exclusive key to man's basic purpose in living. All other ideas were false and not to be tolerated. Not only was there one God, but only one just God. A real Devil was continually striving to gain converts among humans and set up a rival system. Anyone who supported the Devil was obviously fighting the Christian God and must consequently be stopped by the Christian Church before he spread these wrong ideas further. As early as A.D. 382, the Christian Church decreed that anyone convicted of opposition, i.e., heresy, was to be executed.

Then followed certain conclusions, all quite logical if the major assumptions were accepted. Since the crime of aiding the Devil—witchcraft—was not physical but spiritual, it could not be proved by the ordinary rules of evidence followed in other crimes. Under Continental and Roman law, witchcraft was regarded as a *crimen excepta*, an exceptional crime, so grave and difficult of proof that all normal legal procedures were superseded. The best way to prove connections between a human and the Devil, since the Devil would not appear to give evidence against one of his own supporters, was to get a confession from the human. Inasmuch as working against the Christian Church, the representative of God, was considered treason, meriting death, no human would voluntarily admit an act which would automatically result in such severe punishment. Therefore the human suspected of trafficking with the Devil, because of certain signs and presumptions [*indicia*], had to be tortured until he confessed his guilt. For the general good of the world, he had to be killed to stop the Devil's subversion of God's kingdom. For his own good, he had to be killed, so that, dying penitent before a relapse into greater error, he might be saved from more severe torments after his death and ultimately be accepted into God's plan for the world.

In his *Démonomanie* (1580), Jean Bodin summarized the orthodox views:

> Now, if there is any means to appease the wrath of God, to gain his blessing, to strike awe into some by the punishment of others, to preserve some from being infected by others, to diminish the number of evil-doers, to make secure the life of the well-disposed, and to punish the most detestable crimes of which the human mind can conceive, it is to punish with the utmost rigor the witches.

If witchcraft were considered simply as primitive magic or sorcery (as it always had been to the year 1200), in which a devil might be asked to assist in performing acts beyond what could reasonably be expected in nature, but without any thought of denying the supremacy of the Christian God, then the offense of witchcraft would not be heresy, and would be punished by the civil courts as a minor crime. However, since all such requests implicitly acknowledged the power of the Devil against a Christian world-order, all witchcraft was potentially opposition to the Christian God and therefore heresy. "In her desperation, the Church hit upon that last expedient for the detection of wrong thinking; she devised the Holy Inquisition and put in its hand the torture." Having rooted out the heresy, "the hungry organization cast its eyes about for other victims." (Gibbons, *Some Rhenish Foes of Credulity*, 1920)

"Heresy," said Bernardus Guidonis (1261-1331) in his *Manual of the Inquisitor*, "is a crime of divine lese majesty which consists in the knowing rejection of a dogma or the rigid adherence to a sect whose doctrines have been condemned by the Church as contrary to faith." As heresy, the sect of witches came within the province of the papal Inquisition, whose business it was to extirpate any opposition to or deviation from the revelations of God through the Church. The Inquisition, first established in Toulouse in 1233 and in Aragon in 1238, over the thirteenth and fourteenth centuries had built up an efficient and successful institution for this purpose; when it had suppressed most of the major here-sies, the Inquisition realized that witchcraft might be a heresy too. In 1257 it had requested permission to proceed against divination and sorcery, but it was not until 1320 that Pope John XXII asked the Inquisition to destroy the devil-worshipers. Guidonis collected all the previous justifications for burning heretics into one big manual, *Practica Inquisitionis Heretice Pravitatis*. When Pope Clement V sought to moderate the severity of torture employed by the Inquisition, Guidonis protested that the papal constitution was obstructing the work of the Inquisition and should therefore be amended!

During the fifteenth century, the Inquisition set about to prove witchcraft a heresy and superimpose this view on all western Europe. The same methods that had been employed to get rid of earlier heresies (without magic) were in existence and waiting to be used against the new heresy (with magic) of witchcraft. Torture was a well-proved method, and therefore torture was naturally used against the adherents of the new sect, the witches. This position

Writ of the Chancellor and Council of the Prince-Bishop of Bamberg, Johann Gottfried von Aschhausin, on September 10, 1621, ordering the examination under torture of Cunz Prütinger of Dachstadt on charges of witchcraft. From a manuscript in Cornell University Library.

had been given support in 1350 by the most eminent jurist of the day, the Italian Professor Bartolo, who applied to witches the words of Christ: "If a man abide not in me [i.e., the Catholic Church], he is cast forth as a branch . . . and men gather them and cast them into the fire and they are burned."

The Inquisition always made a big show of mercy and interceded with secular authorities for the prisoner it had condemned. Nicholas Eymeric (died 1399), in his *Directorum Inquisitorum*, quoted the form of the sentencing:

As in truth one who has relapsed into heretical pravity . . . we expel you from our ecclesiastical court and relinquish or turn you over to the secular arm. Nevertheless, we ask, and that with urgency, the secular court to moderate its sentence so that effusion of blood and peril of death may be avoided.

Yet any secular judge exercising clemency would be accused of sympathy toward heretics and would himself be charged by the Inquisition [see Leo X].

After the religious divisions in Europe, the Protestants broke with the Roman Church on many dogmas and doctrines, but preserved the conception of witchcraft. Protestants and Catholics set the same premises and used the same logic. The only brake on the Protestant persecution of witches, which in many areas was just as savage as that of the Catholics, came, not from the "reformed" religion, but from the pagan common-law traditions of the Teutonic countries. This common law, unlike the Continental Roman law, opposed the use of torture and, incidentally, held it the duty of the prosecution to prove guilt rather than the accused to prove his innocence. Survivals of this tradition were early crushed in Germany, and England and Holland, with the Scandinavian countries, became the only lands to escape the holocaust of the witch mania—and even England was adversely affected by the intellectual climate on the Continent, to tolerate brutality.

As opposition grew and its methods became discredited, however, the Inquisition

had to retract, and a bull of Pope Gregory XV (1623), which gave the official instructions of the Roman Church for procedures in witch trials, necessarily reflected the influence of more humane and enlightened views. In 1657, the Holy Inquisition issued an official set of instructions on how to interrogate witches, even admitting that in the past 200 years judges had too easily and hastily applied torture, even death, without careful scrutiny of the evidence.

To be suspected of witchcraft, no evidence was needed; common report or anonymous accusation was "semi-sufficient proof" and warranted the application of torture. Ponzinibio's protest in 1520 against the use of torture on suspicion arising out of conjectures went unheeded. "Mere suspicion was thus erected into actual crime, for when the torture was once applied the possibility of proof of innocence was removed. No power under heaven could save the prisoner: he was doomed." (Gibbon)

To some extent, merely being in prison was torture. The prison of the sixteenth and seventeenth centuries was not the hygienic, concrete and steel cage of the modern jail; it was a stinking dungeon in which many died of disease. Even in England, which practiced a very lofty legal code, twelve per cent of the prisoners (as at Guildford Castle in 1598) died in jail. For the six years from 1573 to 1579, Stow said in his *Survey of London,* nearly a hundred prisoners in the King's Bench prison in London died through contagion. In 1630 at Colchester Castle: "The miseries of the poor prisoners are so great and lamentable, partly by reason of the cruelty of the jailer, and partly by reason of the extreme wants they suffer that many of them are famished [almost dead]."

It was generally accepted throughout the Continent of Europe that a witch should not be executed without her own confession of guilt, irrespective of the amount of demonstrable adverse evidence against her (laid down by Prierias in 1504). Nor did a voluntary confession suffice; it had to be made under torture, for only then could it be presumed to come from the heart and be genuine. Furthermore, as the *Errores Gazariorum* (1450) had observed, many convicted witches had been regular communicants whom no one would have suspected, had they not been tortured; then they admitted all kinds of crimes. Torture invariably produced confessions; and the verbatim court records of such trials as those of Father Dominic Gordel, Thomas Looten, Burgomaster Johannes Junius, Rebecca Lemp, or the unnamed victim at Eichstätt, all translated here, show how amply pain will force a person to confess *anything*. In Paderborn, in the early 1630's, one tortured woman told her minister, Michael Stapirius, that her confession and denunciations were false. When he pleaded with her to recant and rehabilitate the innocent people she had been forced to name as accomplices, she replied:

> But look, Father, look at my legs! They are like fire—ready to burn up—so excruciating is the pain. I could not stand it to have so much as a fly touch them, to say nothing of submitting again to the torture. I would a hundred times rather die than endure such frightful agony again. I cannot describe to any human being how terrific the pain actually is.

It must be remembered that methods of torture varied from place to place, from century to century, and from hangman to hangman. Generally, the foulest tortures were committed in Germany in the early seventeenth century, when Bamberg became synonymous with horror and shame. Nevertheless, the basic principles and procedures remained fairly constant through Europe over the three centuries.

The first stage of torture was designed to force the victim to confess. This was the so-called Preparatory Torture, the *question préparatoire*. It was generally simple, though horrible and effective. It would start with threatening, and continue with taking the victim to the torture chamber to view the horrors (*"in conspectu tormentorum"*). At this *territio*, or session to induce terror, the torturer would explain the uses of each instrument and the kind of pains each would cause. Often the viewing might finish with binding ropes around the

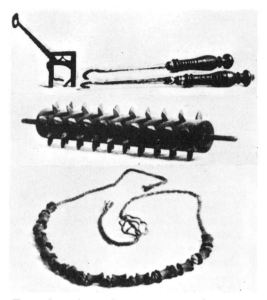

Examples of simple instruments of torture, from Germany, early seventeenth century: eye-gouger and branding iron, a spine roller, and forehead tourniquet.

prisoner, possibly on the ladder or rack. The witch was stripped and bound with ropes that were gradually tightened around the limbs; alternatively, the arms and feet might be tied to the ends of the ladder, and, as the ropes were tightened, the body slowly stretched out.

The bible of the witch hunters, the *Malleus Maleficarum* (1486), gave detailed instructions for this Preparatory Torture:

> The method of beginning an examination by torture is as follows. First, the jailers prepare the implements of torture, then they strip the prisoner (if it be a woman, she has already been stripped by other women, upright and of good report). This stripping is lest some means of witchcraft may have been sewed into the clothing—such as often, taught by the devil, they prepare from the bodies of unbaptized infants, that they may forfeit salvation. And when the implements of torture have been prepared, the judge, both in person and through other good men, zealous in the faith, tries to persuade the prisoner to confess the truth freely; but, if he will not confess, he bids the attendants prepare the prisoner for the strappado or some other torture. The

attendants obey forthwith, yet with feigned agitation. Then, at the prayer of some of those present, the prisoner is loosed again and is taken aside and once more persuaded to confess, being led to believe that he will in that case not be put to death. . . .

But if, neither by threats nor by promises such as these, the witch cannot be induced to speak the truth, then the jailers must carry out the sentence, and torture the prisoner according to the accepted methods, with more or less severity as the delinquent's crime may demand. And, while he is being tortured, he must be questioned on the articles of accusation, and this frequently and persistently, beginning with the lighter charges—for he will more readily confess the lighter than the heavier.

The *Malleus Maleficarum* gave what might be termed idealized conditions of torture; in practice, as records clearly show, trials were simply outlets for the sadism of the prosecutors. Philip Limborch's estimate in his *History of the Inquisition* (1692) is in greater accord with the facts revealed in manuscripts of trials:

The stripping is performed without regard to humanity or honor, not only to men, but to women and virgins, the most virtuous and chaste of whom they have sometimes in the prisons. For they cause them to be stripped, even to their very shifts, which they afterwards take off, forgive the expression, even to their pudenda, and then put on their straight linen drawers.

More likely, the woman, during her stripping, would be raped by the torturer's assistants, as happened to Frau Peller, the wife of a court officer, in her trial at Rheinbach in 1631. She had, incidentally, been accused of witchcraft because her sister had refused to sleep with the witch judge, Franz Buirmann, the appointee of the Prince-Archbishop of Cologne. Or it might be a nun who was molested, as, for example, Sister Madeleine Bavent, who in 1643 was "roughly and indecently" searched for devil's marks by the Grand Penitentiary of Evreux, a sort of inquisitor [see Louviers Nuns].

"Ja" confessions. Part of the examination of Agnes Brusse of Brandshagen, widow of Michel Hooge, at Treptow, Pomerania, in 1679. This page shows a list of numbers (35 through 66), followed generally by *affirmat* [she says yes]. Frequently, the inquisitors or judges interrogated the prisoner from a prepared list of questions used for all suspects. The accused, probably under torture, had merely to murmur "Yes" or nod the head. At the end of the trial, the scribe would write out affirmatively the list of questions so that they would seem a full confession, as if the accused had made it in detail. The prisoner would then sign this *relatio* or fabricated confession.

So little regard was given this preliminary torture that many court records ignored it and simply stated, "The prisoner confessed without torture." The Protestant professor, Johann Meyfarth, from personal knowledge of witch trials, in 1635 told how—

The prisoners are fed only on salted food, and how all their drink is mixed with herring pickle, and no drop of pure, unadulterated wine, beer, or water is allowed them, but raging thirst is purposely kept up in them. . . . But this cruel, raging, devouring thirst the inquisitors do not consider torture.

Even when the prisoners were crushed like grapes in the vise or stretched like leather hides in the rack, "this also must not be reckoned torture."

Dr. Meyfarth explained just what the public, voluntary confessions of witches really meant:

> And what do these words mean? Margaret [the accused witch] of her own free will has ratified before the assembled court the confession she made under torture. This is what the words really mean: When Margaret, after fiendish torture which she could no longer endure, at last confessed, the executioner spoke to her as follows: "You have now made your confession. Will you again deny it? Tell me now while I am still at hand, and if so I'll give you another going over. If you recant tomorrow, or the day after tomorrow, or before the court, you will come back again into my hands, and then you'll learn that up to now I have only been playing with you. I'll plague and torture you in such a way that even a stone would cry out in pity." On the appointed day in court, Margaret is taken in a cart to the judges, with chains on her body, and with her hands bound so tightly that the blood oozes out. Round her are the jailers and torturers, behind her follow armed guards. After her statement has been read aloud, the executioner himself asks Margaret whether she abides by it or not, so that he may know how to proceed. Thereupon Margaret confirms her confession. Is this a voluntary confession? Forced by such inhuman and such brutal torture, watched and guarded by such degenerate men, bound with hard ropes, is her testimony freely made?

To secure a confession of guilt, however, was not the only nor even the primary purpose of torture. The real torture was reserved for the *question définitive*, the Final Torture, which sought to make the witch reveal the names of the accomplices. The torture in 1597 of Clara Geissler of Gelnhausen, a 69-year-old widow, illustrates this aim. She resisted the thumbscrews, but when

. . . her feet were crushed and her body stretched out to greater length, she screamed piteously and said all was true that they had demanded of her: she drank the blood of children whom she stole on her night flights, and she had murdered about sixty infants. She named twenty other women who had been with her at the sabbats, and said the wife of a late burgomaster presided over the flights and banquets.

When released from the rack, Clara retracted her accusations and pleaded: "As to what she had said about others, she had no personal knowledge of them, but had reported rumors spread by other people." The judges, however, arrested those she had accused and tortured them. One of the women admitted more sensational crimes than those Clara had accused her of, so Clara was again tortured to admit the truth of her first denunciations. On release she recanted a second time; tortured a third time with "the utmost severity" for several hours, she admitted what the judges wanted. During the agony she collapsed and died under the torture. The judicial report concluded: "The devil would not let her reveal anything more and so wrung her neck." On August 23, 1597, her corpse was burned.

Final Torture consisted of two phases—first, the Ordinary Torture, followed by the second, the Extraordinary Torture, or *question extraordinaire*. The methods generally employed were the strappado for the ordinary, and squassation for the extraordinary, torture (described in detail in separate entries). Squassation was really a more cruel form of strappado, wherein heavy weights were attached to the feet of the prisoner as he hung, his hands bound behind his back, and was jerked at the end of a rope. Squassation completely dislocated hands, feet, elbows, limbs, and shoulders.

During the torture it was the practice, following the *Malleus Maleficarum*, for the notary to "write down everything in his record of the trial, how the prisoner is tortured, on what points he is questioned, and how he answers." From the old court records, the modern reader can hear the

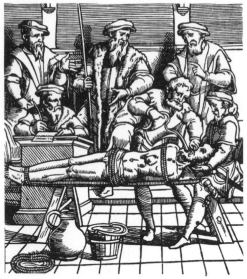

The water ordeal: "Down the throats of some they violently thrust knotted clouts, and then with a string pulled them up again, whereby they displaced their bowels."—Clarke (1651). The judges supervise the torture and the scribe takes down the prisoner's confession.

whimperings and shrieks of the condemned. The trials of Father Dominic Gordel and Father Louis Gaufridi are terrible examples.

After severe torture, the victim would be warmed and clothed, so that he might recover sufficiently to endure the next torture without losing consciousness too soon. Frequently, physicians were in attendance to stop the torture if the victim seemed near death.

These tortures were the logical outgrowth of a theory that there was only one right way of living and that all other ways were wrong; if this theory was firmly believed, torture was justified to remove any divergence of opinion. But beyond this technical approach, in practice, the venom of the judges, both civil and ecclesiastical, made use of torture as a cloak to make death more horrible and violent. An early opponent of torture, Sebastian Costello, said the inquisitors "covered all these things with the robe of Christ and protested that they do these things by his will." (*Traité des hérétiques*)

In Europe there were many supplemen-

tary punishments for alleged acts at which the court took offense. No limits hindered the ingenuity of the witch judges; one of these creatures, Judge Schultheis, at Erwitte cut open a woman's feet and poured hot oil into the wounds. The secular courts at Valenciennes record payment of ten sous to the hangman "for having pierced the tongue of Matthew Godefroy, July 4, 1573." One might glance at some of the special tortures at Bamberg, for example, such as the forcible feeding of the accused on herrings cooked in salt, followed by denial of water —a sophisticated method which went side by side with immersion of the accused in baths of scalding water to which lime had been added. Other ways with witches included the wooden horse, various kinds of racks, the heated iron chair, leg vises [Spanish boots], and large boots of leather or metal into which (with the feet in them, of course) was poured boiling water or molten lead. In the water torture, the *question de l'eau*, water was poured down the throat of the accused, along with a soft cloth to cause choking. The cloth was pulled out quickly so that the entrails would be torn. The thumbscrews [*grésillons*] were a vise designed to compress the thumbs or the big toes to the root of the nails, so that the crushing of the digit would cause excruciating pain.

Witches were often accused of desecrating the sacrament, a charge carried over from earlier heresy trials. The usual punishment for this was tearing with red-hot pincers or chopping off a hand before being burned alive. Thus in 1642, for example, at Chamonix, Jean Gehauds had his foot cut off because he had allegedly trampled the host. In 1629 at Zell, a woman was sentenced to be torn four times with red-hot pincers for four times desecrating the host.

Before burning, witches were by convention first strangled (by garroting or hanging), provided they did not recant their confessions. Knowledge of this custom kept the majority of men and women silent, in order to benefit by even this small mercy. Henry C. Lea commented on this practice: "Human weakness led to persistence in

---

Torture

Steps of torture in witchcraft trials

I. *Preparatory Torture.* To force a confession of guilt. Methods: stripping, threatening, binding, whipping, thumbscrews, stretching on rack or ladder. (In court records, this torture was often not reported, and the accused was said to confess voluntarily.)

II. *Final Torture.* To force confession in cases of taciturnity, and to force naming of accomplices, who, having been defamed, could then be tortured.
   A. *Ordinary Torture.*
      Method: strappado.
   B. *Extraordinary Torture.*
      Method: squassation.
   (Torture could be applied up to three times without new evidence introduced. Refinements could be added to these basic methods, such as flogging, application of fire, thumbscrews, etc.)

III. *Additional Tortures for special offenses.* To cause agony in retribution. Methods: cutting off hands or legs; tearing of flesh with red-hot pincers.

IV. *Occasional Tortures used at individual prisons.* To satisfy sadism of judges or hangmen. Methods: no limit fixed to barbarity, e.g., pressed to spiked chair with fire underneath; scalding water baths, etc.

V. *Execution.* Methods: Burning by fire. Possibility of strangulation before burning if accused did not recant; otherwise burning alive. According to region, accused tied to stake, placed in straw hut, or set on barrel of pitch. Green wood used for slow burning for impenitent witches. Occasionally, desecration of body before burning by smashing on wheel or hacking of limbs.

---

confession to avoid the awful death by fire. The whole system was one to encourage belief in witchcraft and to multiply the number of victims." Binsfeld explained this unexpected charity was allowed lest the agonies of slow death drive the victims to despair and impenitent death. However, if the accused were pertinacious and clearly unrepentant, then they should be burned fully alive (as was always done with every condemned witch in Italy and Spain, Binsfeld observed), because desperation was nothing to worry about with the impenitent. Attempts were made to prolong the agony of death. The celebrated French lawyer and professor, Jean Bodin, recommended burning witches "over a slow fire, since that pain is nothing compared to what Satan is going to make them suffer . . . for the fire here cannot last above half an hour before they are dead." Green bushes in place of dry faggots would slow down combustion and make death come more slowly and painfully. Father Louis Gaufridi's ex-

ecution was specifically ordered in this manner.

Scotland generally followed European rather than English traditions, and witches were severely tortured and burned, following a law attributed to King Kenneth I (died 860), which prescribed burning for those who invoked spirits. In Scotland, too, trials continued to a later date than in England, where the last witch was executed in 1682, whereas the last known execution in Scotland took place in 1727. Probably the Scottish trial which exceeded all others in the severity of the torture was that of the North Berwick Witches.

The demonologists anticipated certain problems arising from torture and tried to help the witch judges on a course of action. These problems can be grouped under seven heads:

1. What should a judge do if the prisoner refuses to talk?

Taciturnity was relatively simple to deal with. The *Malleus Maleficarum* advised:

"If the prisoner will not confess the truth satisfactorily, other sorts of tortures must be placed before him, with the statement that unless he will confess the truth, he must endure these also." Here the lawyers invented a subtle trick to avoid the prohibition against repeating torture. Legally, torture could be repeated only if new indications of guilt were produced. But the lawyers maintained that torture given more than once, without new evidence, was not *repetition*, but a *continuation;* and the judge was to advise the prisoner that "such and such a day for the continuation of the tortures" had been assigned. Nearly two centuries later, in 1659, Le Sieur Bouvet, the Provost Marshal of the French armies in Italy, similarly recommended that the judge increase the torture and continue the interrogation, "all through the cries which the prisoner would undoubtedly make—and the judge could demand the names of his friends to ascertain if they were accomplices [*en le peut encore interroger de ses compagnons et complices pour scavoir s'ils ont participé au délit*]." Torture could be "continued" up to three times; however, in practice, only death determined the upward limit. In 1630, one woman (Barbara Schwartz) was tortured eight times without her confessing, and kept three years in the Bamberg jail.

Taciturnity was itself a crime and was punishable by burning. A man accused as a witch who refused to plead was guilty of contempt—and would therefore be executed, not on the original charge of being a witch, but on an added and incidental charge of taciturnity. This device also evaded the law that an accused witch who maintained her innocence through three torturings must be assumed proved Not Guilty. Friedrich von Spee asked in anger: "Now, in Heaven's name, I would like to know, since she who confesses and she who does not both perish alike, how can anybody, no matter how innocent, escape?" In England the punishment for taciturnity in any criminal case was *peine fort et dure,* pressing to death. Thus in 1654, at Maidstone, a man remained silent on a charge of murder and robbery; he was stripped

and "upon his body must be laid so much iron and stone as he can bear no more." Giles Cory at the Salem witch trials was killed in this manner. *Peine fort et dure* survived in England to 1722.

The demonologists explained taciturnity, not by strength of character, but by charms given by the devil. A well-known story repeated by Guazzo, told how

> a woman of fifty endured boiling fat poured over her whole body and severe racking of all her limbs without feeling anything. For she was taken from the rack free from any sense of pain, whole and uninjured, except that her great toe, which had been torn off during the torture, was not restored, but this did not hinder or hurt her in any way. (*Compendium Maleficarum*, 1626)

The influential jurist Damhouder told how he himself had witnessed a witch who withstood three severe tortures, laughing and mocking the hangman. On a further search of her body, a piece of parchment was discovered; when this was removed, the woman quickly succumbed and confessed her pact with Satan. The equally celebrated Paulus Grillandus gave an example of a Latin charm for taciturnity:

> In the same way that the milk of the Blessed and glorious Virgin Mary was sweet and pleasing to our Lord Jesus Christ, so may this torture be sweet and pleasing to my arms and limbs.

2. How far should the judge promise favor or immunity to a prisoner in order to induce a confession, and to what extent should he abide by his promise?

The *Malleus Maleficarum* took up this problem. Opinion was divided into three schools of thought. With a notorious ringleader, a promise to spare his life, with the implication of exile, might be made—the intended punishment of perpetual confinement on bread and water should not be mentioned at this point. This promise might be honored if the accused co-operated with the court in accusing more witches. A second view maintained "that for a time the promise made to the witch sentenced to imprisonment is to be kept, but that after

Methods of torture in Germany in 1527, including burning, hanging, beheading, disemboweling, breaking with the wheel, trussing, gouging out the eyes, cutting off the ear or hand, and flogging. From Cornell University Library.

a time she should be burned." A third view had the original judge excuse himself from the bench, and let another judge sentence the witch to burning.

3. Should a sick man be put to torture?

Le Sieur Bouvet had experience with such people who said they were too ill to be tortured. The simplest way was to throw boiling water under the armpits; this would restore health so quickly "that it will seem like a miracle." If a prisoner had syphilis, the judge could combine torture with healing. The soles of the feet of the accused should be placed on top of a fire so that the accused would break out in a terrific sweat. The sweat running out of the pores of the skin would cure the disease at the same time it would provoke the prisoner to speak the truth.

4. Should the judge relax torture lest the prisoner die in the torture chamber?

Awareness of his responsibility for a possible death should not sway the judge to mitigate torture. If the prisoner fainted, throw water in his face or force vinegar up his nostrils. The judge should not be moved to pity a disabled prisoner; he must not let his heart rule his conduct. Often witches feigned signs of death, such as foaming at the mouth or collapsing; but the judge should not be gullible.

5. How should a tortured prisoner be prevented from committing suicide?

The *Malleus Maleficarum* warned against possible suicide of a prisoner through desperation, and recommended that throughout the intervals between the torture "guards constantly be with the prisoner, so that she would not be left alone." Suicide was always attributed to the wiles of the devil, who encouraged self-destruction so his promise that a witch should not die at the stake might be technically fulfilled.

6. Should clemency be shown to very young witches?

The mere fact of youth did not in itself call for mitigation. Children under fourteen might receive lighter sentencing. In the trial of the Scottish witches accused of making a waxen image to kill Sir George Maxwell, a girl of thirteen was let off with imprisonment in place of burning. Sir George

Mackenzie, King's Advocate, added: "All this is arbitrary with us"—*Laws and Customs of Scotland*, 1678. Dr. Johannes Pott (1689) mentioned a nine-year-old girl at Rinteln who was convicted of copulation with the devil; she merely had to be flogged while watching her grandmother burn at the stake. But at Würzburg in 1628 two girls of eleven and twelve were burned. And Remy (1595) regretted that instead of burning children along with their elders, he had merely sentenced them to be flogged while watching their parents burn.

"Do but imagine a poor old creature, under all the weakness and infirmities of old age, set like a fool in the middle of a room, with a rabble of ten towns round about her house; then her legs tied cross, that all the weight of her body might rest upon her seat. By that means, after some hours, that the circulation of the blood would be much stopped, her sitting would be as painful as the wooden horse. Then she must continue in her pain four and twenty hours, without either sleep or meat, and since this was their ungodly way of trial, what wonder was it, if when they were weary of their lives, they confessed any tales that would please them, and many times they knew not what."
—Bishop Francis Hutchinson, *Historical Essay Concerning Witchcraft* (1720).

7. Should any consideration be given a pregnant woman?

It was generally agreed in theory to postpone execution of a pregnant woman until one month after the birth of her baby (so Francis Pegna, 1584). In England, women were generally kept until the next assizes, about a year; thus at the third Chelmsford trial in 1589, Joan Cony was executed within two hours of sentencing, but her daughter Avice pleaded pregnancy and was not hanged until 1590. In Germany, however, this custom was not always followed; at Bamberg, in 1630, the wife of Councilor Dümler, though pregnant, was horribly tortured and burned.

A note might be added on torture in England. Although its value was not disputed, it did not follow the pattern of the Continent. William Perkins was of the opinion that it might "no doubt lawfully and with good conscience be used, howbeit not in every case, but only upon strong and great presumptions going before, and when the party is obstinate"—*Discourse of Witchcraft*, 1608. In the first place, torture was not allowed under common law. In the second place, the accused could be executed for witchcraft without a confession—discovery of the witch's mark or familiars was sufficient proof. In the third place, since there was no elaborate organization like the Inquisition which depended for its own survival on a continuous supply of suspects, there was not the same maniacal insistence on identifying accomplices. Torture never developed into a science of applied cruelty, as it did in Germany. In England torture was less crude and violent, and free from the blasphemy of blessing the instruments of torture.

The commonest tortures in England—perhaps indignities is a better word—were pricking and walking and, to a lesser extent, sitting. Pricking was intended to reveal evidence of guilt; the ignominy of being publicly exposed and the pain of being pierced with long pins were incidental. On the other hand, walking was intended to force a confession by preventing the accused from getting any sleep; it was therefore real torture. Matthew Hopkins "walked" the old parson, Rev. John Lowes, for several days and nights until he collapsed and confessed. Binsfeld, however, who was certainly no novice about the efficacy of various kinds of tortures, saw in sleeplessness an almost infallible method, one most efficacious because it could be prolonged without serious bodily injury. Denying sleep was used in some parts of Germany to procure confessions from common criminals (not witches). Walking was still practiced in 1693 at Beccles, Suffolk, but the accused, one Widow Chambers, "a diligent, industrious, poor woman," died in jail (Hutchinson, 1718).

The third method common in England was explained by Rev. John Gaule, who opposed the Witch Finder General, Matthew Hopkins, in 1646; it was a variant of walking designed to produce exhaustion by lack of sleep. "[The suspected witch] is placed in the middle of a room upon a stool, or table, cross-legged, or in some other uneasy posture, which if she submit not, she is then bound with cords; there is she watched and kept without meat or sleep for the space of twenty-four hours." (*Select Cases of Conscience Touching Witches and Witchcraft*)

Records of English witch trials note occasional forms of torture, such as the heated boots used on Alice Goodridge [see Burton Boy]. A man offered to prove Alice a witch: "He put on a pair of new shoes on her feet, setting her close to the fire till the shoes being extreme hot might constrain her through the increase of pain to confess." The woman, "being thoroughly heated, desired a release," offering to confess; but as soon as her feet cooled, she refused. In 1614, Lyon Gleane was put in the stocks and, because he was suspected as a conjurer, was "stripped naked from the middle upward and . . . whipped at the cart's tail until his body be bloody." In 1645, Anne Jeffries was kept in Bodmin jail "without victuals."

Popular animosity against witches sometimes rose to great heights. In 1603 at Catton in Suffolk, Sir Thomas Grosse egged on a mob which molested eighty-year-old Agnes Fenn, accused of bewitching a sick man. The men punched her with the handles of their daggers, tossed her in the air, flashed gunpowder in her face, and "having prepared a stool in the which they had stuck daggers and knives with sharp points upwards, they often times struck her down upon the same stool whereby she was sore pricked and grievously hurt." (Ewen, *Witchcraft in the Star Chamber*)

Burning, it should be observed, was never the punishment in England for witchcraft. Burning was reserved for treason, either petty treason, of a woman killing her husband or a servant his master, or grand treason, of a subject killing or attempting to kill his sovereign, or for counterfeiting. This law was repealed only in 1790. While witchcraft was considered divine treason, it

---

A Typical Day's Torture

Verbatim report of the first day's torture of a woman accused of witchcraft at Prossneck, Germany, in 1629.

1. The hangman bound her hands, cut her hair, and placed her on the ladder. He threw alcohol over her head and set fire to it so as to burn her hair to the roots.
2. He placed strips of sulphur under her arms and around her back and set fire to them.
3. He tied her hands behind her back and pulled her up to the ceiling.
4. He left her hanging there from three to four hours, while the torturer went to breakfast.
5. On his return, he threw alcohol over her back and set fire to it.
6. He attached very heavy weights on her body and drew her up again to the ceiling. After that he put her back on the ladder and placed a very rough plank full of sharp points against her body. Having thus arranged her, he jerked her up again to the ceiling.
7. Then he squeezed her thumbs and big toes in the vise, and he trussed her arms with a stick, and in this position kept her hanging about a quarter of an hour, until she fainted away several times.
8. Then he squeezed the calves and the legs in the vise, always alternating the torture with questioning.
9. Then he whipped her with a rawhide whip to cause the blood to flow out over her shift.
10. Once again he placed her thumbs and big toes in the vise, and left her in this agony on the torture stool from 10:00 A.M. to 1:00 P.M., while the hangman and the court officials went out to get a bite to eat.

In the afternoon a functionary came who disapproved this pitiless procedure. But then they whipped her again in a frightful manner. This concluded the first day of torture.

The next day they started all over again, but without pushing things quite as far as the day before.

—Wilhelm Pressel, *Hexen und Hexenmeister* (1860).

---

did not follow the civil code of execution. When women were burned in England, it was for one of these other offenses (although witchcraft might have been involved). So Mother Lakeland was burned at Ipswich on September 9, 1645, for murdering her husband by sorcery; and May Oliver was similarly punished in 1659 at Norwich. An eyewitness account of the burning, apparently alive, of Prudence Lee on April 10, 1652, is given in the entry for the Wapping Witch.

Likewise, in New England, which followed English usage, no witch was ever burned. Slaves were burned alive for murdering their masters (treason), as was a Negro slave, Phillis, who poisoned John Codman of Charleston and was burned in Cambridge; and in 1691 a slave, Marja, burned for killing his owner.

One final revolting detail should be mentioned in this account of torture in witchcraft. The estate of the accused (before its confiscation by whatever authority held the jurisdiction) or his relations had to pay the costs of the entire trial, including the fees for torture. This practice is more fully described in a separate entry [see Costs of Trials].

See further, Bamberg Witch Trials, Boots, Franz Buirmann, Confessions, Eichstätt Witch Trial, Evidence in Witch Trials (Europe), Executions, Witchcraft in Germany, Dominic Gordel, Inquisition, Johannes Junius, Ladder, Rebecca Lemp, Thomas Looten, Pricking, Sister Maria Renata, Johann Schüler, Heinrich von Schultheis, Shaving, Friedrich von Spee, Squassation, Strappado, Witnesses.

Transformation: see Metamorphosis.

Transvection. The celebrated Canon Episcopi of the tenth century defined as heretical superstition the belief in the claims of "wicked women . . . who profess that in the dead of night they ride upon certain beasts with the pagan goddess Diana, and fly over vast tracts of country." Demonologists had always to explain away this flat statement denying transvection, for a salient feature of witchcraft was the nocturnal flight through the air. They arrived at several solutions (for which see Early Writers on Witchcraft), but generally found the simplest way to prove guilt was to equate the delusion with the act. Consequently, a woman who in her own mind (even if dreaming) considered she had flown to the sabbat was just as guilty as if she had physically mounted a real broom and physically been carried aloft. Sir Charles Mackenzie, the King's Advocate, in 1678 framed it thus: "Because those witches desire to have these dreams, and glory in them when they are awake; nor have any these dreams but such as have entered into a preceding paction"—*Laws and Customs of Scotland*. Prierias (1504) argued that the Canon condemned belief in Diana, not belief in flying. In practice, however, the subtleties of theory were confined to the study, and judges in court got a confession involving transvection, which they assumed to be actual.

Ulrich Molitor (1489) told a story of the relation of body and spirit, which was copied by many later demonologists and applied to various aspects of transvection, metamorphosis, and attendance at the sabbat: "During sleep as well as during a waking state, devils can produce impressions so vivid that men believe they see or act in actuality." Molitor told how St. Germain, while staying at a humble cottage, observed that his host, before retiring, prepared a second sumptuous supper. Later, St. Germain found the meal consumed by evil spirits in the appearance of the cottager's neighbors.

You see by this story that at the precise

The earliest printed picture of witches in flight, from Ulrich Molitor's *De Lamiis* (1489). From Cornell University Library.

moment that a man is in one place, nevertheless he is able to appear in spirit in another, since those neighbors who, during that night slept in their own beds at home, yet by the power of the demon, appeared as images in the house where St. Germain received hospitality."

Popular illustrations of witches have spread the notion of the broomstick as the regular vehicle for flight. However, at the beginning of the delusion the broomstick was but one of several implements, such as a cleft stick (very common), a distaff, or even a shovel. The very early *Errores Gazariorum* (1450) said a stick [*baculum*] with flying ointment was presented to every new witch after she had rendered her kiss of shame. Boguet (1602) found the witch traveled "on a white staff which she placed between her legs." Lambert Daneau in *Les Sorciers* (1564) believed the devil aided only those witches "that are so weak that they cannot travel of themselves"; to these he gave a staff or rod and "a certain oint-

Three witches dancing in the air, by Bonaventura von Genelli (1847).

ment." Bodin, in his *Démonomanie* (1580), said witches rode a broom or a black ram; Guazzo (1608) added goats, oxen, and dogs. Animals were suggested before brooms, and Molitor (1489) told of wolves as transport. The early woodcuts in Molitor's *De Lamiis* show a witch riding a wolf, as well as witches sitting astride a forked stick. Stephen of Bourbon (died 1261) wrote that the "good women," the attendants of a mythical Dame Abundance, rode on sticks, but the evil *strigae*, the prototype of the later witches, on wolves. The broomstick probably won out because of its tradition as the symbol of women (corresponding to the pitchfork for the male), and because it is easily identified as a phallic symbol.

Before travel, the witches rubbed themselves and their stick with a special Flying Ointment. Once out of the chimney—a means of egress first mentioned about 1460 by Petrus Mamor—flight offered few dangers, but occasionally casualties occurred. One difficulty was the sound of church bells, which had power to ground the broom. The speed of flight, according to Grillandus (1525), was generally sufficient to obviate this peril. Grillandus, however, quoted the confession of one Lucrezia, who, returning from a sabbat at Benevento, was unceremoniously jettisoned by her demon at the ringing of the Angelus. Lucrezia was duly burned. Johann Zandt

told Binsfeld that at Treves, in the early seventeenth century, during May the churches were ordered to ring their bells continuously throughout the night to protect the city from flying witches. A blessing for church bells included in his *Pontifical* by Ecgbert, Archbishop of York (732-766), explained why demons feared them so much: "Wherever this bell sounds, let the power of enemies retire, so also the shadow of phantoms, the assault of whirlwinds, the stroke of lightnings, the harm of thunders, the injuries of tempests, and every spirit of the storm winds."

Although agreed on the guilt of witches, the authorities were never unanimous about the reality of transvection (and of the sabbat, too); but the vast majority followed the *Malleus Maleficarum* and believed its actuality. Said Guazzo:

> I hold it to be very true that sometimes witches are really transported from place to place by the devil, who in the shape of a goat or some other fantastic animal carries them bodily to the. sabbat. . . . This is the general opinion of the theologians and jurists of Italy, Spain, and Catholic Germany, while a great many others are of a like opinion.

Prierias explained transvection was possible because corporeal matter obeyed the command of angelic spirits, whether good or bad, on the analogy of the movement of the spheres controlled by the angels. Analogues of transvection were drawn from the Bible, including Satan's carrying Christ to a high mountain. And the classical legend from Apuleius about Pamphile's flight as an owl, after anointing herself with magic grease was not lost on the demonologists. Furthermore, believers could point to the number of condemned witches who confessed to transvection, "which would never have been done, or suffered by the popes, unless these things really did happen." (Limborch, drawing on such writers as Prierias and Spina)

Transvection by witches resembled levitation by saints of the Church. Thus the *Acta Sanctorum* records seventy flights made by St. Joseph of Cupertino (1603-63), who could scarcely read and who from the age of eight had cataleptic fits and convulsions. It was related that he flew eighty yards to a crucifix, and even performed this miracle in the presence of the Spanish

"Sometimes witches are really conveyed from one place to another by the Devil, in the bodily likeness of a goat or some other fantastic animal, and are indeed physically present at their nefarious sabbats. This opinion is commonly held by theologians and lawyers among the Catholics of Italy, Spain, and Germany."—Guazzo (1626).

ambassador. Henry More, in his *Antidote Against Atheism* (1653), told of the reputedly very holy Magdalena Crucia, Abbess at Cordova, Spain, that "she would sometimes be lifted up above the ground three or four cubits high." At other times, "bearing the image of Christ in her arms, weeping savorly [passionately], she would make her hair to increase to that length and largeness that it would come to her heels . . . [and then] would shrink up again to its usual size." Later, she confessed to being a witch, and married to the devil for thirty years.

The celebrated Florentine lawyer, Gianfrancesco Ponzinibio, classified very minutely the arguments pro and con over transvection. He presented them so scholastically, however, that it is doubtful if many would be convinced today by either set. In favor of transvection he listed ten reasons, including witches' confessions and observers' reports, the technical possibility that the devil could accomplish this act, and the assumption of flight as fact rather than fable. Ponzinibio himself favored the opposite view, but his five reasons are more like opinions than arguments—one of his reasons was that witches are corrupt in faith. Ponzinibio was later refuted by Grillandus, who drew up similar lists.

Of the early demonologists, in addition

"Gradually he makes progress. Now he can jump a little. In time he will do even as much as his teacher."—Goya (1799).

"There they go! The witch is riding on a crippled devil. The poor devil whom everyone scorns is sometimes very useful."—Goya (1799).

to Ponzinibio, Jean Vincent, Cassini, and Geiler von Kaysersberg opposed the idea of real movement. Alphonsus de Spina suggested the devil mocked witches by parodying the angels, as when Habakkuk was carried from Judea to Babylon. Bodin held the bodies of witches remained at home, with only the spirit of the witch going to the sabbat; and so did the Protestants Luther and Melanchthon.

In 1560 Giambattista Porta related how a supposed witch promised to bring him information from a distant town. She shut herself in a room, and Porta, peeping through a chink, saw her disrobe, rub herself with ointment, and pass into a trance. He entered the room, tried to rouse her, and finally beat her black and blue, all the time without waking her. Later, the witch told of traveling over seas and mountains and of other impossibilities. Even when shown

her bruises, the woman still maintained she had actually flown.

A parallel tale was told by Dr. Gassendi, a friend of Molière's. He met a shepherd, a self-styled wizard who, after swallowing a magic pill, was then transported through the air on a black cat. The doctor watched the man lying in bed in a state of delirium, and to convince the other villagers of the falsity of the stories which the shepherd was wont to tell, gave them all a comparable drug which produced the same hallucinations as the pill.

All such doubters as these, pontificated Guazzo, "who assert that [transvection] is not true, but only a dream or an illusion, certainly sin in lack of true reverence to our mother the church."

If the woman really flew to the sabbat, she had to deceive her husband. Remy told of one witch who put her husband into a deep sleep by smearing his ear with flying ointment; other witches left in the bed a pillow, broom, or bundle of straw which their husbands took as their wives; and one witch persuaded her demon to stay and impersonate her. An early questioning lawyer, Andreas Alciatus of Milan, about 1515, asked the obvious question: "Why not rather presume the demon to be with his demons [*cur non potius cacadaemonem cum suis daemonibus*] and the woman with her husband? Why invent a real body in a fictitious sabbat and a fantastic one in a real bed?"

That the folk belief in transvection still survives is indicated by the current vogue of such modernistic coinages of the space age as "teleportation" and "astral projection."

Treves Witch Trials. The archbishopric of Treves or Trier (with its seat at Coblenz), an electoral state of the Holy Roman Empire, also included the spiritual jurisdiction of neighboring Lorraine and Luxembourg; the witch delusion spread from these two states into Treves in the latter years of the sixteenth century. Remy, the notorious witch judge, boasted he had burned 900 persons from 1581 to 1595 in

Lorraine; Luxembourg, under Spanish domination, started persecution about 1580. Organized witch hunts started in Alsace in 1570. In Treves, the trials came a little later, although five women had been burned by the Abbey of St. Maximin in 1572; they did not get under way until 1582 in the principality, and 1586 in the city—a date still several decades in advance of the fierce terror in the other church states, such as Würzburg and Bamberg. The theologians linked the witches to heretics, and blamed the Protestant, Albert of Brandenberg, for bringing in witchcraft by his raids in 1552.

Witchcraft in Treves is associated with three names: Flade, Binsfeld, and Loos. The assault on witches was initiated under Prince-Archbishop Johann von Schönenburg (1581-99), abetted by Governor Johann Zandt, notary Peter Ormsdorf, and Suffragan Bishop Peter Binsfeld. The civil court at Treves lacked the enthusiasm of the ecclesiastical court for persecutions, and under the guidance of Dietrich Flade damned fewer witches. Finally, Zandt, frustrated by Flade's hesitancy about the evidence of accomplices, charged Flade with witchcraft, and, after a process lasting two years, had him convicted. Flade's doubts must have been widely shared, for Binsfeld said he wrote his *Tractatus* in 1589 to correct the waverers. Just three years after Flade's execution, the celebrated Catholic theologian, Cornelius Loos, tried to publish his exposé of the procedure followed in the witch trials, but the Papal Nuncio had the book destroyed and Father Loos banished to Brussels. Binsfeld was largely responsible for the troubles of Loos and revised his *Tractatus* to include this new opponent.

According to George L. Burr, "one of the most remarkable relics of the witch persecution" is the witch register of the Benedictine Abbey of St. Maximin, just outside the city walls, which had jurisdiction over twenty villages. It contains detailed court records from 1587 to 1594 of the 306 persons accused as witches, whose denunciations involved about 1,500 different people (6,000 names are recorded).

The rapid spread of the witchcraft epidemic was attributed by Binsfeld to an igno-

A witches' sabbat at Treves, about 1600. This large engraving was supposedly attached to the end of a book on witchcraft by Thomas Sigfried of Erfurt, published at Treves in 1594. The verses attached mention Treves, but the picture is simply an omnibus representation of all acts ever attributed to witches.

rant priesthood and skeptical judges. However, the succession of bad harvests with
the attendant misery was the major cause
[see Flade]. A canon of Treves Cathedral,
Johan Linden, in his *History of Treves*, has
left a graphic description of the spread of
the trials. His comments on the "big business" and "vested interest" aspects of witch
hunting are especially revealing:

> Inasmuch as it was popularly believed
> that the continued sterility of many years
> was caused by witches [*strigibus et male-
> ficis*] through the malice of the Devil, the
> whole country rose to exterminate the
> witches. This movement was promoted by
> many in office, who looked for wealth in
> the ashes of the victims. And so, from
> court to court throughout the towns and
> villages of all the diocese, scurried special
> accusers, inquisitors, notaries, jurors,
> judges, constables, dragging to trial and
> torture human beings of both sexes and
> burning them in great numbers. Scarcely
> any of those who were accused escaped
> punishment. Nor were even the leading
> men spared in the city of Treves. For the
> judge [Flade], two burgomasters, sev-
> eral councilors and associate judges were
> burned. Canons of sundry collegiate
> churches, parish priests, rural deans,
> were swept away in this ruin. So far, at
> length, did the madness [*insania*] of the
> furious populace and of the courts go in
> this thirst for blood and booty that there
> was scarcely anybody who was not
> smirched by some suspicion of this
> crime.
> Meanwhile notaries, copyists, and
> innkeepers grew rich. The executioner
> rode a blooded horse, like a noble of the
> court, and went clad in gold and silver;
> his wife vied with noble dames in the
> richness of her array. The children of
> those convicted and punished were sent
> into exile; their goods were confiscated;
> plowman and vintner failed—hence came
> sterility. A direr pestilence or a more
> ruthless invader could hardly have rav-
> aged the territory of Treves than this
> inquisition and persecution without
> bounds: many were the reasons for
> doubting that all were really guilty. This
> persecution lasted for several years; and
> some of those who presided over the ad-
> ministration of justice gloried in the

multitude of the stakes, at each of which
a human being had been given to the
flames.

> At last, though the flames were still un-
> sated, the people grew impoverished,
> rules were made and enforced restricting
> the costs of examinations and the profits
> of the inquisitors, and suddenly, as when
> in war funds fail, the zeal of the perse-
> cutors died out.

Trials. This entry discusses only the earliest trials for sorcery or witchcraft to illustrate the beginning of the theory of witchcraft as a heresy. The conduct of the later
trials is described in other entries [listed
below].

As early as 1258, the Inquisition had
asked the Pope "whether it ought not to
take cognizance of divination and sorcery."
Pope Alexander IV had said no, *nisi man-
ifeste haeresim saperent*—unless they
smacked of manifest heresy.

The first trials for heretical sorcery were
conducted by the Inquisition under a papal
bull of August 22, 1320, when Pope John
XXII empowered the Inquisitor at Carcassonne to prosecute those who worshiped
demons, entered a pact with them, made
images, or used sacred objects to work
magic. Even earlier, in the thirteenth
century, women had been executed for
sorcery. Angela, Lady of Labarthe, was
probably the first woman to be burned for
"witchcraft," at Toulouse in 1275. At
Carcassonne, a woman confessed she had
a child by the devil, born with a wolf's
head and a snake's tail, to feed which she
stole babies; the *Histoire de Languedoc*
says the woman was burned in 1274.

During the fourteenth century, witchcraft was elaborated into the latest heresy.
Southern France, which had recently been
so severely purged by the Inquisition
against the Albigensians that no more
heretics remained there, stood the first
wave of the hungry Inquisition's attack.
Sorcery trials occurred at Carcassonne in
1330 and 1335 (when seventy-four persons
were accused), and at least once in approximately every succeeding decade to 1400.
Toulouse (the home of the Inquisition)

was the other center where the Inquisition functioned against witches. In 1335 the Inquisitor Bernardus Guidonis tried sixty-three persons, and burned eight of them. This mass trial produced the earliest confessions of the sabbat. (The trials of the six witches executed at Arras in 1460 is often given as the first reference.) After torture, one Anne-Marie de Georgel confessed that a tall dark man had seduced her while she was washing, that he transported her to a sabbat, and that a goat taught her the secrets of evil. By 1350 the Inquisition had prosecuted 1,000 persons in these two towns for sorcery, and had burned 600 of them. Burnings continued in this region throughout the fourteenth century, and spread west to Béarn by 1393.

By the early fifteenth century, the Inquisition (here staffed by Franciscans in place of the customary Dominicans) was investigating in the Dauphiné, covering Lyons to Grenoble. On March 15,1438, an old man, Pierre Vallin of La Tour du Pin, confessed

The Chamber of Justice about 1619 at Valenciennes, a district civil court which tried accused witches. [A. Reserved for the king. B. The Count of Valenciennes, owing allegiance to the Duke of Hainaut, representing the king, and in whose name the accusations would be brought. C. The Regional Provost. D. The Mayor. 1-10. The *échevins*, magistrates nominated by the Count, who, with the Provost, formed the jury. E. Last *échevin*. F. Court officers.]

that sixty-three years before he had given himself to the devil, paying him an annual monetary tribute, that he offered his six-month old daughter to the devil (who killed her), raised tempests, rode on a stick to the sabbat (called here a synagogue), ate children, and had intercourse with a succubus demon in the form of a 22-year-old girl. The examination continued the following day to discover accomplices, and Vallin named three men and one woman, all dead. On March 23, Vallin was questioned further about accomplices and told it was ridiculous that during his sixty-three years of witchcraft he could remember only four dead witches. Under the first degree of torture, he gave another five names. Then under strappado, in the kitchen of the castle of Quinezonasium, he named five more. The record of the trial was sent forward to the civil court.

The trial of Pierre Vallin is significant for its developed concept of witchcraft at so early a date, just like the proceedings of the late sixteenth century. It is also significant that all the accused were wealthy; the Inquisition shared with the civil courts the confiscated properties of the condemned.

Trials for witchcraft spread from southern France, through south and west Switzerland, including French Savoy, to northern Italy, where the diocese of Como had been one of the first centers of inquisitorial activity. Spina in his *Quaestio de Strigibus* (1523) said at least a hundred witches a year were burned at Como, and sometimes more than a thousand. At one of the earliest trials, reported in *La Vauderye de Lyonois* (1460), one of the tests for witches was the later very popular ordeal of saying the paternoster or Lord's Prayer without faltering or making a mistake [see Arras Witches]. In 1462, at Chamonix in Savoy, the inquisitor turned over to the secular courts for burning four men and four women who had confessed under torture to witchcraft. One of the women, Peronette, who had admitted she ate children at the sabbat (or synagogue), was forced to sit naked for three minutes on a red-hot iron before being burned alive. The records of other trials in Savoy are extant. In 1477, for example, a woman of Annecy, named by a convicted witch, was questioned by the inquisitor. Under torture, Madame Antoine gave a detailed account of a sabbat, no doubt prompted by the inquisitor. She rendered homage to a dog by kissing it under its tail; she received the devil's mark; she flew on a stick eighteen inches long, which she rubbed with ointment and placed between her thighs; she had intercourse with men after the manner of animals; she used killing ointments; she ate children; she trampled a sacred host and attempted to fry it. Under the strappado, she named first three, then thirteen, and finally four more, accomplices.

On the basis of such confessions, made under the most agonizing torture, the inquisitors evolved the heresy of witchcraft, and, supported by papal bulls, moved into other lands to extirpate alleged witches. That witchcraft was originally known only to the inquisitors, that it was a belief invented by them, is indicated by the popular opposition to witch trials. Sprenger and Kramer, who firmly established the delusion by their *Malleus Maleficarum*, complained of the apathy and even hostility of rulers and people when they invaded Germany. Further, no secular court before 1390 [see Paris Witch Trial] conducted a trial for witchcraft; the secular trials were concerned merely with poisons or love potions—acts, not ideas. The first treatises on witchcraft, including the first vernacular works in French and Spanish, were written by Dominican inquisitors such as Nicholas Eymeric, Nicholas Jacquier, Jean Vineti, and Girolamo Visconti [see Early Writers on Witchcraft]. Incidentally, the Franciscans frequently opposed the idea of witchcraft—for example, their great theologians Astesanus de Ast (1317) in the fourteenth century, Alphonsus de Spina (1458) in the fifteenth, and Samuel de Cassini (1505) in the sixteenth century.

The theories of the Inquisition about witchcraft were soon adopted by other church courts as well as by the secular courts, which all shared in the profits of the confiscation of the victims' property.

During the fifteenth century, secular courts were also prosecuting witches, parallel to the courts of the Inquisition, starting in Savoy and the Valais, the adjoining region of Switzerland. The Lucerne Chronicle of Johann Fründ recorded the burning of 200 witches in 1428 in Valais. Secular trials continued in Lucerne throughout the fifteenth century. By 1450 witch trials were taking place in scattered parts of Lorraine, especially in Metz and Cologne, and by the end of the century witchcraft had come to Treves. In 1493 at Huy in Belgium, Ysabel Packet, after confessing to sabbat orgies, was burned as *sorceresse* and—very significantly, linking witchcraft to the old heresy —*vaudoise*. The witchcraft delusion spread throughout western Europe like black ink on a tablecloth.

Between 1500 and 1700 all trials followed a set pattern, based on a unified theory originated by the inquisitors, whether the trials were held by a secular or ecclesiastical court, inquisitorial or episcopal, Protestant or Catholic, and irrespective of time or place. The aim was twofold: to secure a confession of guilt (to make the execution legally proper), and to secure names of accomplices (to provide a continuous supply

Accusations of witchcraft were an easy way of proving heresy. In 1509 the Dominicans of Heidelberg opposed the new theory of the Immaculate Conception. The strict Franciscans, who favored the doctrine, charged the Dominicans with signing a pact with the Devil, tortured them into confessing their guilt, and then burned them. An illustration of the execution from a French tract published in Geneva in 1549, *Histoire véritable . . . de quatre Iacopins*.

of suspects so that the courts could continue functioning and making money). The final tortures of strappado and squassation were reserved for naming names. Apart from England, which preserved some safeguards from Anglo-Saxon common law (including an occasional royal pardon for a condemned witch), Holland (which had no trials for witchcraft after 1610), the Scandinavian countries (hardly affected by the witchcraft delusion), and a few other exceptions, all witch trials assumed the guilt of the accused even before any proceedings took place. The prisoner was allowed no lawyer (except very occasionally one appointed by the judges), no right to cross-examine, and generally no right to present favorable evidence. Witnesses unacceptable in other crimes were encouraged; their identity could be concealed; judges were instructed to trick and deceive the prisoner; stool-pigeons were brought in to pump incriminating gossip from the prisoner or to encourage his confession. After all this, even if the prisoner were acquitted, the court did not proclaim his innocence, but said the charges had not been proved and that the case could be reopened at any time.

The law faculties of the universities were involved in many of these trials by acting as referees in cases of doubt, short-circuiting the higher courts. For this reason, the dissertations of scholars were related to the actual phenomenon of witchcraft at first hand, and, by serving as textbooks for the judges, exercised more than academic influence.

The conduct of later trials is discussed in separate entries: Confessions, Costs, Evidence, Executions, Indictment, Informers, Pricking, Sentence, Torture, Witnesses. Actual records of witch trials are reproduced for the various countries as follows:

England: Bury St. Edmunds Witches, Chelmsford Witches, Lancashire Witches, St. Osyth Witches.
France: Arras Witches, Dominic Gordel, Joan of Arc, Thomas Looten, Luxeuil Witch Trial, Paris Witch Trial.
Germany: Eichstätt Witch Trial, Johannes Junius, Rebecca Lemp, Maria Renata.
Scotland: Margaret Barclay, Isobel Grierson, Perth Witch Trial.
United States: New York Witches, Salem Witch Trials.

For other information on witch trials, see also Bamberg Witch Trials, Franz Buirmann, John Fian, Sir John Holt, Friedrich von Spee, Ulric Tengler, Treves Witch Trials.

United States, Witchcraft in. Salem is probably the best-known name in the entire history of witchcraft, yet in America the witchcraft delusion was sporadic and mild and, compared with the holocausts in sixteenth- and seventeenth-century Europe, insignificant. In all, only thirty-six people were executed. Witch trials were practically confined to the northern English settlements in New England. The southern colonies were almost unaffected, perhaps because settled by the more tolerant Episcopalians. There were only a few minor incidents. In Virginia, for example, in 1706, in Princess Anne County, Grace Sherwood was tried but apparently released; and in 1709, in South Carolina, a few persons were punished for witchcraft. Rebecca Fowler was the only one of the five accused of witchcraft in Maryland who was hanged (in 1685). A few accused as witches sued their detractors for slander—sometimes successfully.

The acceptance of witchcraft in South Carolina is suggested by the action of Judge Nicholas Trott of Charleston, who in 1703 gave the following instruction to his jurymen:

But this I think I may very well assert, that they that have given us good proof of apparitions and witches have done service to the common cause of religion, for if there be such creatures as witches, then there are certainly spirits by whose aid and assistance they act, and by consequence there is another invisible world of spirits. . . . Yet that there are creatures as witches I make no doubt, neither do I think that they can be denied, without denying the truth of the Holy Scriptures, or most grossly perverting the sense of them.

The northern Puritans were committed to a theocratic form of government, where the elders of the chapels (the ministers and lay deacons) made and administered the laws according to their interpretation of the Bible. In any society which, for whatever reason, maintains its beliefs with fierce rigidity, non-conformity is always severely punished. Yet even so, there were fewer than fifty trials in New England.

Apart from Salem, from 1648 to 1691, slightly more than a dozen witches were executed in New England, and some few others condemned to whipping or banishment. This relative freedom from witchcraft for the forty preceding years makes the Salem trials overshadow everything else, so that it may be said the history of American witchcraft is Salem. New York was in effect free of the witchcraft delusion; Rhode Island had a law against witchcraft, but no trials; Connecticut executed four alleged witches, including the first witch to be hanged in America, Alse Young, on May 26, 1647. In New Hampshire, Jane Welford was charged at Dover in 1656, and freed on her good behavior; thirteen years later she sued her detractors for damages and was awarded five pounds and costs. Pennsylvania, without any statutes against witchcraft until 1717, had only two trials (charging property damage) in 1684, when Governor William Penn himself directed the jury to return Not Guilty because of a technical defect in the indictment. His act may have arrested an outbreak like that at Salem, for the Swedish and German population inherited strong witch beliefs (see Quaker Witchcraft). Apart from these states, the rest of the few American trials took place in Massachusetts.

Margaret Jones, who used simple medicines to cure the sick, was hanged on June 15, 1648 at Boston. "She was suspected partly because . . . after some angry words passing between her and her neighbors, some mischief befell such neighbors in the creatures or the like." She was accused of bewitching children, and was found to have a witch's mark, "a teat, as fresh as if [it] had been newly sucked." Soon after, a Mrs. Lake was executed in Dorchester. A solemn day of prayer was held in 1651 to consider how far "Satan prevails amongst us in respect of witchcraft." The next year John Bradstreet was indicted at Ipswich for "having familiarity with the devil." He was fined twenty shillings or a whipping. The same year (1652), Hugh Parsons of Springfield was found "not legally guilty of witchcraft" at Boston, but his wife was convicted. At Cambridge a Mrs. Kendal was tried for bewitching a young child to death. The nurse testified that Mrs. Kendal "did make much of the child," but that soon after the child changed color and died. The court did not summon the child's parents, who only later revealed that the child died because of exposure caused by neglect of the nurse. By this time the nurse was in prison for adultery; there she died, and the case fizzled out.

In 1656 Mrs. William Hibbins, a much respected widow, sister of Governor Richard Bellingham, was charged at Salem with witchcraft and hanged on June 19. One Joshua Scottow came to her defense and testified in her favor; his act displeased the judges and he was forced to make a humble apology to the court for giving offense.

During the next two decades (1660-80), most of those cases involving witchcraft were dismissed; the embers of the delusion had almost been extinguished when the girls and the judges at Salem fanned them into a blaze. For example, Eunice Cole at Boston in 1673 was found "legally not guilty" of copulation with the devil, and merely ordered to depart from the jurisdiction of the court. In 1674 at Salem, the judges dismissed Christopher Brown with a caution for discoursing with the devil. In 1680 at Ipswich, Margaret Read did not appear to answer the charges, and apparently no action was taken to apprehend her. Goody Clover, an Irish immigrant, was the last woman hanged for witchcraft in the city of Boston, on November 15, 1688.

One of the later trials (1679) involved

Two statements by her neighbors testifying to their belief that Winifred Holman, of Cambridge, Massachusetts, was not a witch. She had been accused in 1660 of bewitching Rebecca Gibson, the wife of Charles Stearns. The first affidavit is signed by seven persons. The second is very similar and bears eighteen signatures.

poltergeist manifestations at the house of William Morse at Newberry: a sailor, Caleb Powell, suspected of witchcraft causing the disturbances, was dismissed on payment of costs, but Mrs. Elizabeth Morse was found Guilty; she was, however, reprieved and released after a year in jail at Boston.

After the Salem trials, people became ashamed of their credulous stupidity, and accusations ceased. The last trial in Massachusetts was actually an aftermath of Salem: Sarah Post of Andover, in 1693, at Ipswich was found Not Guilty of having "made covenant with the devil and signed the devil's book."

Voisin, La: see Chambre Ardente Affair.

Vampire

It leaned to one side, the skin was fresh and ruddy, the nails grown long and evilly crooked, the mouth slobbered with blood from its last night's repast. Accordingly a stake was driven through the chest of the vampire who uttered a terrible screech whilst blood poured in quantities from the wound. Then it was burned to ashes.

Such was the appearance of a vampire in 1732 in Belgrade. To many modern readers, however, the vampire will recall *Dracula,* the best-selling novel by Bram Stoker, first published in 1897, and turned into a very successful play in 1927. Indeed, since the concept of the vampire is sufficiently diffuse—the product of legends found in folklore throughout all countries and in most centuries, anecdotes of maniacs with unnatural craving for blood, of premature burial, and religious motifs of restless souls—it is not surprising that literary works should have formulated the common conception of a bat-demon which sucks the blood of sleeping women. Such is the monster depicted in Prest's *Varney the Vampire* (1847), a forerunner of *Dracula.* Indeed, from the early nineteenth century, the vampire has been a legitimate subject of serious writers, probably influenced by the university dissertations on the out-breaks of vampirism throughout eastern Europe during the eighteenth century.

Notable treatments of the vampire include Goethe's *"Die Braut von Korinth* [The Bride of Corinth]" (1797), Burgher's ballad *Leonore* (1773), translated by Sir Walter Scott (1794), Southey's *Thalaba the Destroyer* (1801), Lord Byron's *The Vampyre* (1819), and Mary Shelley's *Frankenstein* (1818). Other accounts of vampires are Gautier's poem, *"La Morte amoreuse"* (1836), and Baudelaire's *"Le Vampire"* (1855); *Juliette* by the Marquis de Sade (1796); *Carmilla,* by Sheriden le Fanu (1872); two short stories, one by M. R. James, "Count Magnus" (1905), and the other by E. F. Benson, "The Room in the Tower" (1912); and *For the Blood is the Life* (1911), a best-seller by the prolific American novelist, F. Marion Crawford.

What is behind this fabricated idea of vampire which has so attracted literary men?

The word itself is of Magyar origin, and appears in cognate forms in Slavonic languages; its origin may possibly be from the Turkish *uber* [witch]. Vampire is sometimes rendered in Latin by *strix* [screech owl]; in Portuguese it appears as *bruxsa,* a bird-woman who sucks the blood of children. Vampire was first used in English about 1734, when it was described as follows: "The bodies of deceased persons, animated by evil spirits, which come out of the graves in the night-time, suck the blood of many of the living, and thereby destroy them." It was only later (1762) applied to bats supposed to attack animals.

In western Europe there were only incidental references to vampires prior to the late seventeenth century, and theoretical discussions did not see print until the middle of the eighteenth century. Dom Augustin Calmet in his *Traité sur les apparitions* (1751) said vampires had become known only in the past sixty years and were chiefly reported from Hungary, Moravia, Silesia, and Poland. Greece and Albania were also rich in vampire tales.

The vampire is clearly akin to the were-wolf [see Lycanthropy], but is distinguished by two characteristics: its origin in a dead person reanimated to life, and its sucking blood from a living person to regain vitality.

There are two views of the nature of the vampire: one, that it is a demon which enters a dead body; and the second, perhaps more common, that it is the spirit of the dead person who himself inhabits his own body. Montague Summers wrote: "It partakes the dark natures and possesses the mysterious and terrible qualities of both. . . . [yet] the vampire is not strictly a demon"—*Vampire: Kith and Kin.* Walter Mapes, in his *De Nugis Curialium [Courtiers' Trifles]* at the end of the twelfth century, held the first belief; he tells of a demon impersonating a respected noblewoman and slitting the throats of young children.

The conception of the vampire is extremely ancient, and as it has developed, is an amalgam of various superstitions; as in most folklore there is a slight substratum of fact.

1. The widespread superstition of the revenant, or dead person, returning to his old haunts, crystallized in the legends of Halloween. All Saints' or Allhallows Day, commemorated on November 1, has assimilated many pagan associations, including the Celtic festival honoring Samhain, Lord of the Dead. The following day, November 2, is the feast of All Souls, the traditional date for the return of spirits. Returning dead were to be feared, and hence propitiated. Most burial rites primarily try to make sure the dead will not return; the moral of many stories about people unable to stay buried because the services were irregular or omitted warns the living to perform those essential obsequies. Odysseus had to return many miles to lay the ghost of Elpenor; and Patroclus was very demanding of Achilles. Naturally, the most frequent recipient of vampiric visits are the relatives, especially the wife (whose memory of her husband would be the most vivid). In one of the earliest stories (in 1196) of a vampire (although not the blood-sucking variety) in William of New-

burgh's *Historia Rerum Anglicarum,* a dead man molested his wife; when his tomb was opened in order to allay this living corpse, the body was found quite uncorrupt, just as it had been laid out on the day of his burial.

2. The existence of maniacs who crave for blood. This condition, of course, is very rare and abnormal, and is distinct from the cannibalism occasionally resorted to in extremity, as in the famine in Samaria described in the Bible (II Kings vi. 24-30).

3. Premature burial, or the occasional interment of a person in a state of catalepsy or suspended animation. Summers (giving no reference) says that at the beginning of the twentieth century, in the United States an average of one premature burial a week was reported—*Vampire: Kith and Kin.* Dr. Franz Hartmann's *Buried Alive* (1895) related 700 instances in the doctor's own neighborhood at the end of the nineteenth century; the doctor, it might be mentioned, was an occultist. In early times, when medical knowledge was less advanced, the error must have been more common, as Rohr, *De Masticatione Mortuorum* (1679), admits; and vandals robbing the coffin a short while after burial might easily have been confronted with horror. The struggles of the body to escape from the casket would account for the distorted features and position, and for the blood. Discussing the Belgrade vampires of 1732, Dr. Herbert Mayo, in his *On the Truths Contained in Popular Superstitions* (1851), suggests the bodies "were simply alive in the common way or had been so for some time subsequently to their interment; that, in short, they were the bodies of persons who had been buried alive, and whose life, where it yet lingered, was finally extinguished through the ignorance and barbarity of those who disinterred them." This probability is illustrated by the story quoted by Summers (*Vampire in Europe*). A certain villager, Zaretto, having drunk too well and got rain-soaked, lay down to rest with his wet clothes on. "He was seized with horrible convulsions; toward eleven o'clock, he went into a state of coma: he became cold and his breathing stopped. At last he was dead. . . . At eight

o'clock next morning, he was taken away to be buried." The route lay over rocky ground, and the bouncing of the hearse suddenly brought Zaretto out of his drunken stupor.

4. Popular vindictiveness which seeks to perpetuate punishment for a wrongdoer, a wish often reinforced by religious lore. Thus certain people, outcasts of society while alive, remain outcasts after death. Likely to become vampires were those who have led a "wicked and debauched life, very often one excommunicated by his bishop" (Allatius, *De Graecorum Hodie Quorundam Opinationibus,* 1645); those who have died under any kind of curse or malediction, perjurers, those buried without proper rites (e.g., omission of sacraments), apostates, all suicides, lycanthropists, and (in Hungary) the stillborn illegitimate children of parents also illegitimate. In Slavonic countries, those corpses over which a cat jumped or birds flew, were likely to end up vampires; this belief survives in English folklore in the exclusion of animals from the place where the corpse is waiting burial. Many are the legends that tell how the body of an excommunicate does not decompose; a Scottish folk belief holds that the body of a suicide remains whole until the normal life span has been reached. The incorruption of the bodies of saints is, on the other hand, a miracle. The hostility of tightly knit groups toward the unusual is evidenced by the belief that the old, poor, and deformed were witches, or even vampires; so harelips, hair on the palms of the hands, blue eyes, red hair, have all been, at various times, signs of the vampire.

5. The coincidence of reports of vampirism with plagues and epidemics, both occasioning horrible stench. Dr. Henry More, the celebrated Cambridge Platonist, in his *An Antidote Against Atheism* (1653), tells how a vampire tormented a parson in Pentsch, Silesia. One evening

when this theologer was sitting with his wife and children about him, exercising himself in music, according to his usual manner, a most grievous stink arose suddenly, which by degrees spread itself to every corner of the room. Hereupon he commends himself and his family to God by prayer. The smell nevertheless increased, and became above all measure pestilently noisome, insomuch that he was forced to go up to his chamber. He and his wife had not been in bed a quarter of an hour, but they find the same stink in the bedchamber; of which, while they are complaining one to another, out steps the specter from the wall, and creeping to his bedside, breathes upon him an exceedingly cold breath, of so intolerable stinking and malignant a scent, as is beyond all imagination and expression.

From an early date, the vampire stench was held to herald and accompany plague. William of Newburgh tells the story of a revenant, a lecherous husband, terrifying his home town.

For the air became foul and tainted as this fetid and corrupting body wandered abroad, so that a terrible plague broke out and there was hardly a house which did not mourn its dead, and presently the town, which but a little before had been thickly populated, seemed to be well-nigh deserted, for those who had survived the pestilence and these hideous attacks hastily removed themselves to other districts lest they also should perish.

Two young men located the corpse of the husband, ˙cut it with a spade, whereupon red blood gushed out, and burned it. William continues:

Now, no sooner had that infernal monster been thus destroyed, than the plague, which had so sorely ravaged the people, entirely ceased, just as if the polluted air was cleansed by the fire which burned up the hellish brute who had infected the whole atmosphere. (*Historia Rerum Anglicarum.*)

Vampirism and epidemic alike ravaged southeastern Europe in the late seventeenth and early eighteenth centuries, and continued to the nineteenth century. Epidemics raged in Chios in 1708, Meduegya and Belgrade in 1725 and 1732, Serbia in 1825, Hungary in 1832, and in Danzig as late as 1855. Vampirism was also virulent at other times and provoked academic tracts in German universities, especially at Leipzig. One

such theological discussion, *Dissertatio de Vampiris Serviensibus* (1733) by John Heinrich Zopft [Zopfius], gave a classic description:

Vampires issue forth from their graves in the night, attack people sleeping quietly in their beds, suck out all their blood from their bodies and destroy them. They beset men, women, and children alike, sparing neither age nor sex. Those who are under the fatal malignity of their influence complain of suffocation and a total deficiency of spirits, after which they soon expire.

Calmet complemented this: "Men who have been dead for some considerable time . . . issue forth from the graves and come to disturb the living, whose blood they suck and drain." Any plague where "within a few hours five or six persons fell ill in the village" would be linked to vampirism. *The Jewish Spy of d'Argens* (1729) continued: "Their symptoms were complete exhaustion and a faintness as though from excessive loss of blood. . . . In spite of all that the local apothecary could do, the sick men expired within a few days." In later times, the unknown factor causing death would be called a germ or virus.

6. The existence of certain perversions which parallel the acts of the vampire: necrophagism (eating dead bodies), necrosadism (mutilation of corpses to induce sexual excitement), and necrophilia (sexual intercourse with a corpse, either normal, sodomy, or masturbation). A famous case in France at the end of the nineteenth century was that of Henri Blot, tried in 1886 for vandalism and necrophilia. Blot was

a not unattractive young man of twenty-six years, somewhat sallow in complexion. His hair was pulled over his forehead, like a shaggy dog's. On his upper lip he had a fine mustache, carefully waxed. His deep-set black eyes were always shifting. He had something of the feline in his make-up, something also of a night-bird in his physiognomy. On the night of March 25, 1886, between eleven and midnight, Blot scaled a little door leading to the graveyard of St.-Ouen, approached one of the trenches where persons not entitled to individual graves were buried, and lifted up the boards which held up the earth on the last coffin in the row. An inscribed cross above the grave informed him that the coffin contained the body of a young woman of eighteen years, Fernande Méry, professionally Carmanio, a ballet dancer, buried the preceding evening. Blot moved the coffin, opened it, and took out the body of the young girl, which he carried to the bank at the end of the trench. There, as a precaution, he rested his knees on some sheets of white paper taken from the floral offerings, and had coitus with the corpse. After this, he fell asleep, and awakened in time to get out of the cemetery without being observed, but too late to replace the body.

On June 12, Blot again violated a cadaver, but did not wake up in time; he was discovered and arrested. On August 27, he appeared in court and nonchalantly replied, to the judge's horror: "What would you have? Everyone to his taste. Mine is for corpses." He was sentenced to two years' imprisonment. (Albert Bataille, *Les Causes criminelles et mondaines*, 1886)

> But first, on earth as vampire sent,
> Thy corpse shall from its tomb be rent:
> Then ghastly haunt thy native place,
> And suck the blood of all thy race;
> There from thy daughter, sister, wife,
> At midnight drain the stream of life. . . .
> Wet with thine own best blood shall drip
> Thy gnashing tooth and haggard lip;
> Then stalking to thy sullen grave
> Go—and with the ghouls and afreets rave,
> Till these in horror shrink away
> From specter more accursed than they!
> —Byron, *The Giaour* (1813)

7. Ernest Jones explains the vampire "as a nocturnal spirit who embraces a sleeper to suck his blood from him; he is evidently a product of the nightmare." Just as sexual conflict produces the erotic dream, so when normal aspects of sexuality are repressed, the conflict takes on extreme forms, as in the werewolf and the vampire, where "hate and guilt play a far larger part" and oral sadism is manifested.

The vampire, so goes the superstition,

can be removed by discovering its grave, then exhuming the corpse, which will be found in excellent preservation, and destroying it by running a spear or a spade through its heart with one blow. Calmet, the Benedictine monk, wrote: "Nor can men deliver themselves from these horrid attacks, unless they dig the corpses up from the graves, drive a sharp stake through these bodies, cut off the heads, tear out the hearts; or else they burn the bodies to ashes."

Visconti, Girolamo. Girolamo Visconti (Hieronymus Vicecomes), in his *Little Book on Witches* (manuscript about 1460), was one of the earliest writers to spread the witchcraft delusion. Probably a member of the famous Milanese family, he was Professor of Logic at the University of Milan (1448) and Dominican provincial of Lombardy from 1465 to his death about 1477; he is no doubt the inquisitor at Como whose wholesale burnings of witches were admired in the *Malleus Maleficarum*. Visconti wrote to prove, first, the reality of witchcraft (including transvection and sabbat orgies) and, second, the heresy of witchcraft. That witches may be deranged is no excuse; that they believe their delusions is sufficient to burn them. Those who defend witches are to be excommunicated.

Visconti prepared the ground for the acceptance of the *Malleus Maleficarum*, just as did Nider (1435), Vineti (1450), Jacquier (1458), Alphonso de Spina (1459), Mamorus (1462), Vignati (1468), Bergamo (1470), and Vincent (1475).

Wagstaffe, John. Neglected today, John Wagstaffe in the later seventeenth century saw his attack on the witchcraft delusion go through two editions in two years; thirty-four years after his death in 1677, his reputation was still fresh when *The Question of Witchcraft Debated* was translated into German. Wagstaffe, educated at Oxford, was fortunate in receiving an inheritance from an uncle who left him an estate in Derbyshire; here "he applied himself to the study of politics and learning." Unfortunately, Wagstaffe wrote little and

A page from the manuscript of Girolamo Visconti, written about 1460, and published in Milan in 1490 as *Opusculum in Quo Probantur Lamias Esse Hereticas*. Visconti was a professor and inquisitor who ordered mass burnings of accused witches at Como. To Visconti, even defending witches was heresy. From the manuscript in Cornell University Library.

died young, having ruined his health, by the "continued bibbing of strong and high-tasted liquors."

His book was generous and noble, and many pages rise to impassioned heights. It has been eclipsed, however, by the occult sensationalism of a Glanvill or a Baxter or a Mather, or even by Meric Casaubon who refuted Wagstaffe. Yet his sincerity helped diminish credulity—by such passages, for example, as this:

Surely the blood of men ought not to be so cheap, nor so easily to be shed by those who, under the name of God, do gratify exorbitant passions and selfish ends; for without question, under this side of heaven, there is nothing so sacred as the life of man, for the preservation whereof all policies and forms of government, all laws and magistrates are most especially ordained.

Again, the following remarks emphasize the horror of the persecutions, so frequently veiled by writers on the other side:

I cannot think without trembling and horror on the vast numbers of people that in several ages and several countries have been sacrificed unto this cold opinion. Thousands, ten thousands, are upon record to have been slain, and many of them not with simple deaths, but horrid, exquisite tortures. And yet, how many are there more who have undergone the same fate, of whom we have no memorial extant.

Wapping Witch. Joan Peterson's trial in London was marked by defense witnesses who acknowledged her abilities as a good witch in relieving headaches and unwitching cows. Many defense witnesses, however, were intimidated into staying away, and other witnesses were bribed to testify against her. The prosecution alleged evil threats and familiars, including, in addition to a black cat, the less common squirrel. A servant testified that "her mistress and it talked together a great part of the night; but being demanded what they discoursed on, she replied that she heard her conference very perfectly, but she was so bewitched by it that she could not remember one word." A member of Cromwell's council, Sir John Danvers, unexpectedly sat on the bench to coerce the other magistrates to a guilty verdict. The trial was rigged, and Joan Peterson was hanged at Tyborn on Monday, the twelfth of April, 1652.

The booklet describing her trial also tells of Prudence Lee, who was burned at Smithfield two days earlier for murdering her husband. This crime was held treason and was the only offense to merit this punishment: women in England were never burned for witchcraft *per se*.

Then the executioner setting her in a pitch barrel, bound her to the stake, and placed the straw and faggots about her

Title page of contemporary pamphlet on Joan Peterson, the Witch of Wapping, hanged on April 12, 1652, in London.

. . . and the executioner putting fire to the straw, she cried out, "Lord Jesus, have mercy on my soul." And after the fire was kindled she was heard to shriek out terribly some five or six several times.

Warboys Witches. A notorious plot against three innocent people, and the most widely discussed trial for witchcraft in England before 1600, anticipating in many ways the famous Broadway successes, *The Children's Hour, The Bad Seed*, and Henry James's *The Turn of the Screw*. In essence, the trial of the Warboys family was the story of some little monsters of girls sending the old and poor to death. What made these events so distressing was the credence responsible men gave to the play-acting of children. But the children who made the accusations belonged to a wealthy and influential family, and some cause had to be found to explain their juvenile ravings. "From beginning to end," wrote Notestein, "it had been the strong against the weak . . . all were banded together against this poor but respectable family."

Robert Throckmorton was a prominent squire residing at Warboys in the county of Huntingdon. His daughter suffered violent hysteria, no doubt epileptic fits:

About the tenth of November which was in the year 1589, Mistress Jane, one of the daughters of the said Master Throckmorton, being near the age of ten years, fell upon the sudden into a strange kind of sickness and distemperature of body, the manner whereof was as followeth. Sometimes she would neese [sneeze] very loud and thick for the space of half an hour together, and presently as one in a great trance and swoon lay quietly as long. Soon after she would begin to swell and heave up her belly so as none was able to bend her, or keep her down. Sometime she would shake one leg and no other part of her, as if the palsy had been in it; sometimes the other. Presently she would shake one of her arms, and then the other, and soon after her head, as if she had been infected with the running palsy.

During one of these bouts, an aged

Mrs. Samuel conjuring the Devil, as portrayed in one of the last English books to advocate a belief in witchcraft, the credulous Richard Boulton's *Complete History of Magic* (1715).

neighbor of seventy-six years, Mrs. Alice Samuel, came to pay her respects to the family, and Jane manifested the not uncommon hostility of the rich sub-teen-ager of all centuries against the old and impoverished: "Look where the old witch sitteth . . . Did you ever see (said the child) one more like a witch than she is? Take off her black thrumbed [fringed] cap, for I cannot abide to look on her." At the time, her parents wisely ignored this outburst, and continued the attendance of two celebrated physicians, Dr. Philip Barrow and Master Butler, both of Cambridge University, twenty miles distant. Within two months, Jane's four sisters, ranging from nine to fifteen, started to show similar symptoms; seven servants followed suit. Here is a clear example of imitation, conscious or unconscious (they too said Mrs. Samuel was a witch), in order to get some of the special attentions lavished on Jane, no doubt really mentally and physically sick.

Dr. Barrow, a friend of the family's, realizing his own limitations in effecting any cure of Jane, told the Throckmortons that he himself "had some experience of the malice of some witches, and he verily thought that there was some kind of sorcery and witchcraft wrought toward [their] child." The parents resisted this diagnosis for a long time, but eventually agreed, since their other daughters were behaving in the same way, and forcibly confronted Mother Samuel with the children. The girls

at once acted wild, falling to the ground "strangely tormented," and scratching Mrs. Samuel's hand [see Scratching]. Naturally, Mrs. Samuel denied these allegations and laid them to the children's "wantonness." But the Throckmortons kept on urging her to confess (seeing the plight of their children), and the girls kept on accusing her. At first, the children put on fits only in her presence, but later they reversed themselves, feigning affliction if she were absent. Mrs. Samuel was thereupon forced to live at the Throckmortons', and even denied food there.

The children delighted in badgering Mrs. Samuel:

Many times also as she sat talking with these children, being in their fits by the fire side, they would say unto her: Look you here, Mother Samuel, do you not see this thing that sitteth here by us? She would answer no, not she. Why, they would say again, I marvell that you do not see it. Look how it leapeth, skippeth, and playeth up and down, pointing at it with their fingers here and there as it leaped.

In September, 1590, the most important woman of the region, Lady Cromwell, wife of Sir Henry, paid a courtesy call on the Throckmortons, and seeing the old woman, who was one of her tenants, berated her as a witch, striking off her bonnet and slashing her hair, which she ordered burned. Mrs. Samuel saw the implication of this gesture and said: "Madam, why do you use me thus? I never did you any harm, as yet." After this emotionally-charged encounter, Lady Cromwell suffered bad dreams, and, whether as a consequence or not, her health declined so much that she died some fifteen months later (July, 1592).

The derangement of the children went on until the Christmas of 1592, when, to placate the family, Mother Samuel exhorted the children to stop their fits. They obeyed. Not only was this proof to the family that Mrs. Samuel was a witch, but the effect of her words also shook her own faith in her innocence; having been told so often she was a witch, she almost could believe it herself: "O Sir, I have been the cause of all this trouble to your children . . . Good master, forgive me." On the promptings of the local parson, Dr. Dorrington, she publicly confessed. On the next day, however, after some rest and recovery, she retracted her statement.

Mrs. Samuel was then handed over to the police to be taken before William Wickham, the Bishop of Lincoln, where, thoroughly frightened, she expanded her first confession and gave the names of her familiars: three dun chickens, Pluck, Catch, and White. Brought back to Huntingdon, she was jailed for the assizes along with her daughter Agnes and her husband John Samuel, whom by now the Throckmorton children had implicated with her.

But the five children not only continued their fits, but made up a new insinuation, namely, that Alice Samuel had caused the death of Lady Cromwell (over a year before). The three Samuels were tried at Huntingdon on April 5, 1593, for the witch murder of Lady Cromwell. The story of the children was presented as evidence, and on their own suggestion (as proof of the Samuel family's guilt) the girls demonstrated how they could recover if Alice or Agnes said to them: "Even as I am a witch and consented to the death of Lady Cromwell, so I charge thee, spirit, to depart and to let her be well." If the wording were changed to "As I am no witch," these impudent adolescents continued their masquerade, just as they did if anyone but the three

Samuels spoke the exorcism. In addition, as further evidence, two or three country people reported sickness and death of their livestock. The fact that in all the previous years, when Mother Samuel was presumably practicing witchcraft, no one had ever accused her, was forgotten.

With such conclusive proof, the jury took only five hours to find all three Guilty on the count of "bewitching unto death the Lady Cromwell." Mother Samuel "confessed," and added that the devil "had carnal knowledge of her body." Agnes Samuel was urged to plead pregnancy to stay execution, but her scorn at such deceit commands our respect and admiration to this day: "Nay, that I will not do: it shall never be said that I was both a witch and a whore."

The conviction and hanging can be explained only by the complete stranglehold

Title page of contemporary tract (1593) about Witches of Warboys in the British Museum.

the idea of witchcraft had gained on the English mind by the end of the sixteenth century. The belief in witches was, of course, not new, but by 1600 it had become separated from sorcery—the *maleficia* or harm which could be done to any innocent person—and it was for the first time being extensively discussed in books and pamphlets. If prejudice against an idea or person is strong enough, then any favorable evidence will be so twisted that it serves the ends of the accuser. Thus Sir Thomas Browne, an eminent physician and author of the famous *Religio Medici*, testifying as an expert witness in a similar trial at Bury St. Edmunds in 1662, claimed the Devil could work "upon a natural foundation." Furthermore, Browne "conceived these swooning fits were natural, and nothing else but what they call the mother [hysteria] but"—and here comes the reversal of reason—"only heightened to a great excess by the subtlety of the Devil, co-operating with the malice of these which we term witches, at whose instance he doth these villainies." (*A Trial of Witches at the Assizes Held at Bury St. Edmunds,* 1682)

Some few saw through the deception. "It had been reported by some in the county, those that thought themselves wise, that this Mother Samuel . . . was an old simple woman, and that one might make her by fair words confess what they would." Six years afterward, Samuel Harsnett, later Archbishop of York, in his *Discovery of the Fraudulent Practices of John Darrell* (1599), excoriating a self-styled exorcist of this name who was ultimately imprisoned, hinted at the truth, calling the 1593 tract on the Warboys case, "a very ridiculous book."

The significance of the Warboys witch trial is considerable. The incidents recurred over nearly four years, and involved Cambridge graduates and many highly placed families—the Throckmortons and the Cromwells were very well-connected. Sir Henry Cromwell, grandfather of Oliver Cromwell, was the richest commoner in England. It spread and confirmed the popular superstition of the evil eye, and "produced a deep and lasting impression on the

class that made laws." Kittredge hazards the suggestion that the personal involvement of some of the legislators with the trial may have added impetus to the passage of the 1604 Bill against witchcraft, which provided the death penalty for all so accused and convicted.

The trial was kept fresh by the appropriation of the meager goods of the Samuels by Sir Henry Cromwell (as lord of the manor) to subsidize an annual sermon "against the detestable practice, sin, and offense of witchcraft" at Huntingdon—a practice continued until 1812, although by this time the sermons were warning *against* belief in witches. It was also memorialized in considerable detail in a pamphlet promoted by the hanging judge, *The Most Strange and Admirable Discovery of the Three Witches of Warboys* (London, 1593 —surviving in only one copy, in the British Museum), and in a broadside ballad. The pamphlet was written with so much skill and care, using the notes the Throckmortons kept during the fits, that it was regularly referred to in subsequent disputes on the existence of witches.

Water Ordeal: see Swimming.

Waxen Image. Damage to waxen images, dolls, figurines, or clay poppets, by sympathetic magic produced similar damage on the body of the enemy they represented. The damage might merely be "constant sickness" (as James I allowed) or it might be death. This belief is both primitive and universal and crops up today in more primitive cultures and in pockets of superstition in so-called civilized nations; for example, in 1946 a Mexican sorceress in Colorado substituted a photograph for the figurine. From Egypt the superstition passed to Greece and Rome; from classical Rome, the waxen image came into European sorcery. Horace, for example, in his *Satires* referred to a waxen image made by a witch Canidia for amatory purposes. English and Scottish trials are especially rich in accusations of making figurines, dating from very early times. George Sinclair referred to a group of devil worshipers burning a wax effigy to cause the death of the Scottish King Duffus (A.D. 968), and, perhaps more historically, to twelve witches burning the image of King James III in 1479 at Edinburgh.

Probably the clearest account of waxen images was given by old Mother Demdike at the trial of the Lancashire Witches in 1612. She confessed:

> The speediest way to take a man's life away by witchcraft is to make a picture [figurine] of clay, like unto the shape of the person whom they mean to kill, and dry it thoroughly. And when you would have them to be ill in any one place more than another, then take a thorn or pin and prick it in that part of the picture you would so have to be ill. And when you would have any part of the body to consume away, then take that part of the picture and burn it. And so thereupon by that means the body shall die. (*Wonderful Discovery of Witches in the County of Lancaster*, 1613)

In Scotland, in 1597, Janet Leisk of Fortiefairde put a waxen image on a spit for six hours, "and as the wax melted, at that same time and hour, so his body melted by sweating." In the absence of a poppet [*volt*], the early treatise on witchcraft, *La Vauderye* (1460), suggested that sticking pins into a tree was just as effective.

In indictments charging *maleficia* by use of poppets, tangible evidence could be introduced. At a witch trial in London in 1537, a witness testified he saw a crowd of people in a churchyard gazing at what at first glance looked like an unburied child. "The clerk of the church took out a piece of cloth knit like a winding sheet and ripped it, and found therein an image of wax made in the form of a young child, with two pins in it." The witness then asked a bystander if he knew what it was, and was told it was a device to cause a person to consume away; but to have been really effective, the figurine should have been placed either in horse manure or in a dunghill.

The little images could be made either of wax or clay (called *corp chre* in Scotland). On February 26, 1579, at Abingdon, Mother Stile and three other women were condemned for murder by making "pictures of red wax about a span long and three or four fingers broad," and piercing them with a briar thorn. Other witches, as revealed at Lady Foullis' trial in 1590 in Scotland, shot arrowheads at the effigies. If the wax figurine remained hidden, the victim would suffer sickness during the life of the figurine, estimated generally at about two years. The clay image was made from loathsome ingredients: earth from a new-made grave, bones of a man or woman burned to ashes, black spiders, "with an inner pith of elder, tempered all in water in which toads have been washed"—*Examination of John Walsh*, 1566. A clay image could be placed in a running stream to be worn away by the water. However, if such an image was pierced where the heart should be, the victim would die within nine days.

Waxen images were frequently introduced in the "Noble trials." Eleanor Cobham, the wife of the Duke of Gloucester, in 1442 was accused of "sorcery and necromancy" and being an accessory to treason against King Henry VI. The principals in the trial, Rev. Roger Bolingbroke and Canon Thomas Southwell, were convicted: the former was hanged, beheaded, and quartered; the latter died in prison. The Duchess of Gloucester was implicated because she had allegedly encouraged the two clerics' divination of the life of the King and had ordered one Margery Jourdemain, "The Witch of Ey," to devise "an image of wax, representing the King, which by their sorcery, a little and little consumed, intending thereby in conclusion to waste and destroy the King's person and so to bring him death"—Hall's *Chronicle*, 1548. Margery Jourdemain was burned for treason, and the Duchess sentenced to public penance and perpetual imprisonment.

On April 16, 1594, Ferdinand Stanley, Earl of Derby, died after twelve days of a strange sickness, in which he vomited fifty-two times and had twenty-nine severe bowel evacuations. Five days before his death, in his bedroom was discovered "an image of wax with hair, like unto the hair of his

Thomas Hardy in *The Return of the Native* (1878) has given a classic description of sympathetic magic surviving in England to the middle of the nineteenth century. Susan Nunsuch fears an evil spell has been cast on her son by Eustacia Yeobright. She therefore takes measures to counteract it:

She passed with her candle into an inner room, where, among other utensils, were two large brown pans, containing together perhaps a hundredweight of liquid honey, the produce of the bees during the foregoing summer. On a shelf over the pans was a smooth and solid yellow mass of a hemispherical form, consisting of beeswax from the same take of honey. Susan took down the lump, and, cutting off several thin slices, heaped them in an iron ladle, with which she returned to the living room, and placed the vessel in the hot ashes of the fireplace. As soon as the wax had softened to the plasticity of dough she kneaded the pieces together. And now her face became more intent. She began molding the wax; and it was evident from her manner of manipulation that she was endeavoring to give it some preconceived form. The form was human.

By warming and kneading, cutting and twisting, dismembering and rejoining the incipient image she had in about a quarter of an hour produced a shape which tolerably well resembled a woman, and was about six inches high. She laid it on the table to get cold and hard. . . .

Susan held the object at arm's length and contemplated it with a satisfaction in which there was no smile. To anybody acquainted with the inhabitants of Egdon Heath the image would have suggested Eustacia Yeobright.

From her workbasket in the window seat the woman took a paper of pins, of the old long and yellow sort, whose heads were disposed to come off at their first usage. These she began to thrust into the image in all directions, with apparently excruciating energy. Probably as many as fifty were thus inserted, some into the head of the wax model, some into the shoulders, some into the trunk, some upward through the soles of the feet, till the figure was completely permeated with pins.

She turned to the fire. It had been of turf; and though the high heap of ashes which turf fires produce was somewhat dark and dead on the outside, upon raking it abroad with the shovel the inside of the mass showed a glow of red heat. She took a few pieces of fresh turf from the chimney corner and built them together over the glow, upon which the fire brightened. Seizing with the tongs the image that she had made of Eustacia, she held it in the heat, and watched it as it began to waste slowly away. And while she stood thus engaged there came from between her lips a murmur of words.

It was a strange jargon—the Lord's Prayer repeated backwards—the incantation usual in proceedings for obtaining unhallowed assistance against an enemy. Susan uttered the lugubrious discourse three times slowly, and when it was completed the image had considerably diminished. As the wax dropped into the fire a long flame arose from the spot, and curling its tongue round the figure ate still further into its substance. A pin occasionally dropped with the wax, and the embers heated it red as it lay.

honor's head, twisted through the belly thereof, from the navel to the secrets"—John Stow, *Annales*, 1631. A servant threw the image into the fire, thinking this act would consume the witch; "but it fell out contrary to his love and affection, for after the melting thereof, he more and more declined." The Earl believed he had been bewitched. The figurine, however, was apparently intended as a decoy, for the Earl showed symptoms of poisoning and "his vomit stained the silver and irons." Furthermore, suspicion pointed to his Master of Horse, who precipitately fled. (Hutchinson, *Historical Essay on Witchcraft*, 1718)

One further celebrated case involving the nobility occurred in 1609. Frances, Lady Essex, had employed a Dr. Forman to make her husband impotent and so secure an annulment, and to make unusually virile Sir Robert Carr, whom she wished to marry. In this plot, little dolls were used, one of "a naked woman spreading and laying forth her hair in a looking glass," and another of a woman "sumptuously appareled in silks and satins." In 1613, Lady Essex married Robert, now Earl of Somerset, but both were charged with murdering a gentleman who had discovered their intrigue. Their trial was promoted by a witch believer, Sir Edmund Coke, Chief Justice of England, but it was interrupted and continued by King James I in person with Sir Francis Bacon. The Countess and the Earl of Somerset were found Guilty, imprisoned, but later pardoned.

Sympathetic magic was also practiced on the Continent. For example, King Philip le Bel charged Archbishop Guichard with attempting his life by images, and Philip VI similarly accused Count Robert of Artois. In 1347, Father Etienne Pépin, in the diocese Clermont, was sentenced to fifteen years solitary confinement for making a waxen image. Bishop Francis Hutchinson alluded to an attack on the life of Pope Urban VIII in 1633 by Centini, the nephew of a cardinal, who, with a friar as his associate, stuck pins and needles into a waxen image. Centini was executed. Jean Bodin, the celebrated French demonologist, discounted the value of figurines: in hardly more than two cases out of a hundred were they successful (*Démonomanie*, 1580).

The demonologists, of course, denied the witch had any power to inflict injury. The *maleficium* was done by an invisible demon, said Nider in his *Praeceptorum* (about 1470), with the permission of God. This theory created some dilemmas for the witch. To stick pins into a figurine was not necessarily heresy; it was fundamentally sorcery. The act would turn into heresy if the Devil were *supplicated*, because by this the witch acknowledged the power of the Devil. On the other hand, if the witch *or-*

dered the Devil to work harm by the poppet, it was sorcery, because she did not grant that the Devil shared any authority with God. However, Paulus Grillandus, the famous jurist, believed all sorceries "savoring manifestly of heresy" were punishable as heresy, and any sorceries performed by a witch who made an express profession of her pact with the Devil savored of heresy, if not regarding the act itself, at least regarding the actor. So there was no escape: in practice sorcery was heresy, and heresy, on the advice of the ecclesiastical courts, was punished with death. If, by some chance, sticking pins into an image was considered merely sorcery without heresy, then the witch could be punished by the civil courts; however, the civil courts were more severe than the ecclesiastical courts in their punishment for simple sorcery, and decreed death.

One curious development of the figurine might be noted, showing the influence of magic on Christianity. In exorcism, the priest was to make a waxen image of the possessing devil, adding the devil's name, if known, or any suitable epithet, and throw it on a fire. This act of paganism was rendered Christian by the recital of appropriate texts from Revelations or Jeremiah (Stampa, *Fuga Satanae*, 1597).

Webster, John. John Webster (1610-82) was an evangelical Yorkshireman who passed from teaching and preaching to medicine. He wrote numerous unpublished books on subjects ranging from pedagogy to metallurgy; toward the end of his life came his polemic, *The Displaying of Supposed Witchcraft* (1677). The extended title gives a résumé of its contents and of Webster's position:

> . . . wherein is affirmed that there are many sorts of deceivers and impostors, and divers persons under a passive delusion of melancholy and fancy. But that there is a corporal league made betwixt the devil and the witch, or that he sucks on the witch's body, has carnal copulation, or that witches are turned into cats or dogs, raise tempests or the like, is utterly denied and disproved. Wherein also

"It is clear that one addle-pate dreams up in his own mind the deeds of a thousand witches in the real world."
Frontispiece of the German translation (1719) of John Webster's *Displaying of Supposed Witchcraft* (1677), satirizing the believers in witchcraft. At the top right of the engraving, above the door, is a portrait of Monsieur Oufle, the character created in 1710 by the Abbé Laurent Bordelon to ridicule witchcraft.

is handled the existence of angels and spirits, the truth of apparitions, the nature of astral and sidereal spirits, the force of charms and philters, with other abstruse matters. By John Webster, practitioner in physic.

Weir, Thomas. Long after his execution in 1670, Major Thomas Weir was remembered in popular estimation as one of Scotland's most famous wizards. Public interest was intensified by Weir's previous outstanding reputation as a parliamentary officer, at one time in charge of the guards of Edinburgh, and as an extreme evangelical leader. At the age of seventy, he suddenly confessed, of his own volition and in the face of initial disbelief, to a roster of abominable crimes ranging from fornica-

tion, incest, and sodomy to the worst crime of all, witchcraft. He involved his sixty-year-old sister, Jane Weir, who was burned as a witch on her own confession, there being no independent evidence.

By the nineteenth century, Robert Chambers, in his *Traditions of Edinburgh* (1825), could write: "The conclusion to which the humanity of the present age would come regarding Weir—that he was mad—is favored by some circumstances. What chiefly countenances the idea is the unequivocal lunacy of his sister." This verdict is doubtless correct, but the psychology of the couple has not been satisfactorily explained: an intolerant and opinionated man, living like a bachelor most of his life, immersed in a religion of hell-fire and damnation, suddenly admits to all those sins he had been ostensibly combating. Perhaps a clue to his state of mind is to be found in his statement "that if it were not for the terrors which he found tormenting him within, he should scarce believe there was a God."

His life can be briefly told. He was born of good family in Lanark, about 1600. In 1641 he served as lieutenant in the Scottish Puritan army, and continued during the Civil War as an extreme Covenanter opposing the Royalists. In 1649 and 1650 he was a major commanding the guards defending Edinburgh. (Hickes, *Ravillac Redivivus*) He earned his living in a supervisory civil service post. Besides his military activities, he was very assiduous in prayer meetings of the evangelical Protestants, taking care, however, never to usurp the minister's functions of preaching. Said a contemporary account:

He became so notoriously regarded among the Presbyterian strict sect, that if four met together, be sure Major Weir was one. . . . At private meetings he prayed to admiration, which made many of that stamp count his converse [value his company]. Many resorted to his house to hear him pray.

In his old age, in 1670—some records give his age then as seventy-six—Thomas Weir started to reveal his hideous secret life, which he had concealed so hypocritically and so successfully all those years. At first no one believed him, but, as he persisted, the Provost sent physicians to examine him. The doctors, however, found him sane, and "his distemper only an exulcerated conscience"; the Provost was therefore compelled to arrest him on his own testimony. Major Weir was brought to trial on April 9, 1670, indicted on four counts:

1. Attempted rape of his sister, Jane Weir, when she was ten; and continued incest with her from the time she was sixteen years old to fifty, when he "loathed her for her age."

2. Incest with his stepdaughter, Margaret Bourdon, daughter of his deceased wife.

3. Adultery with "several and diverse persons"; and fornication with Bessie Weems, "his servant maid, whom he kept in his house . . . for the space of twenty years, during which time he lay with her as familiarly as if she had been his wife."

4. Bestiality with mares and cows, "particularly in polluting himself with a mare, upon which he rode into the West Country, near New Mills."

Apparently witchcraft was taken for granted, for although it was not formally charged, it figured in the evidence. Major Weir's sister, Jane, was charged with him, for incest and sorcery, "but most especially consulting witches, necromancers, and devils."

The chief evidence against the Weirs was their own confessions, and evidence of witnesses that the Weirs had made such confessions in their presence. However, the Major's sister-in-law, Margaret, testified that when she was about twenty-seven, "she found the Major, her brother[-in-law], and her sister Jane, lying together in the barn at Wicket-Shaw, and that they were both naked in the bed together, and that she was above him, and that the bed did shake, and that she heard some scandalous language between them." Major Weir confessed to bestiality with a mare in 1651 or 1652, and said a woman saw him in the act and complained; but no one believed her and she

was "whipped through the town [of Lanark] by the hands of the common hangman, as a slanderer of such an eminent holy man."

Jane Weir elaborated with tales of a familiar spirit which helped by spinning "extraordinary quantities of yarn for her, in a shorter time than three or four women could have done the same." Many years previously, when a schoolteacher at Dalkeith, she had given her soul to the Devil, saying in the presence of a little woman, "All my cross and troubles go to the door

The Bow, Edinburgh, the home of Major Thomas Weir. "His house, though known to be deserted by everything human, was sometimes observed at midnight to be full of lights, and heard to emit strange sounds as of dancing, howling, and, what is strangest of all, spinning. Some people occasionally saw the Major issue from the low close at midnight, mounted on a black horse without a head, and gallop off in a whirlwind of flame." —Robert Chambers, *Traditions of Edinburgh* (1825).

with me." As long ago as 1648, she and her brother had been "transported from Edinburgh to Musselburgh, and back again, in a coach and six horses, which seemed all of fire." Jane Weir introduced the subject of the Major's staff, made of thornwood and decorated with carved heads, as his magic wand. After this prompting, people remembered Thomas Weir always leaned on his staff while praying, as if to get inspiration from the Devil.

A majority of the jurors found Major Weir Guilty; Jane Weir was found Guilty unanimously.

Major Weir was strangled and burned at the execution ground between Edinburgh and Leith on April 11, 1670, and his sister Jane the following day at the Grass Market in Edinburgh. On the ladder she addressed the crowds, showing a combination of urbane acumen and pitiable religiosity: "I see a great crowd of people come hither today to behold a poor old miserable creature's death, but I trow there be few among you, who are weeping and mourning for the broken Covenant."

Many pamphlets and personal journals recorded this event, and it continued to be discussed for at least the following century. The Weir house in Edinburgh remained tenantless and became a focal point for the accretion of ghost stories and mysterious happenings. Ghostly coaches were seen driving to the door to take the Major and his sister to hell. After the house had been vacant for over a century, one impoverished couple accepted the low rent and moved in, to the astonishment of the whole city; but the next morning they fled, swearing a calf had gazed at them while they were lying in bed. The Weir house remained empty for another fifty years. Just prior to its demolition, Sir Walter Scott testified to the hold the old house retained on popular imagination as late as 1830: "Bold was the urchin from the high school who dared approach the gloomy ruin at the risk of seeing the Major's enchanted staff parading through the old apartments, or hearing the hum of the necromantic wheel, which procured for his sister such a character as a spinner."

Wenham, Jane. The trial of Jane Wenham in 1712 is important because it was the last trial for witchcraft in England. Although the jury at the Hertford Assizes returned a verdict of Guilty, the judge obtained a pardon. All England was stirred by the trial and eagerly read the numerous pamphlets, pro and con, which argued her case. Fifty—even twenty—years sooner, Jane Wenham would certainly have been convicted and hanged, for the evidence against her was on a par with that presented at all previous trials.

In the first place, Jane Wenham had a bad reputation as "the wise woman of Walkerne." She had already been accused of threatening and bewitching a farmhand, Matthew Gilson. She had asked him for a pennyworth of straw, which he refused. Then Gilson felt impelled to run out of the barn along the highway, asking everyone he met for straw. Getting none, he picked up handfuls of fresh manure and stuffed the dirty stuff into his shirt. Gilson's employer seized this opportunity to call Jane Wenham "a witch and bitch." Jane retaliated with a warrant for defamation of her character, but Sir Henry Chauncey, the magistrate, urged both parties to settle their feud privately before the local minister, Mr. Gardiner. A believer in witches, Mr. Gardiner berated Jane about living peaceably with her neighbors, but, indicative of the changed temper of the times, the farmer had to pay a fine of one shilling.

Some time later when Anne Thorne, a young servant of Mr. Gardiner, fell into fits because she had seen "a little old woman muffled in a riding hood," it could be none other than Jane Wenham. It appeared that Anne, too, was hexed with a "running spell." Although she had a dislocated knee, Anne ran distractedly "with a prodigious swiftness," a long way until she encountered Jane Wenham.

Asked where she was running, Anne replied: "To Cromer for sticks to make me a fire."

"There be no sticks at Cromer," said the old woman in the riding hood. "Here be sticks enough; go to that oak tree and pluck them there."

When Anne had gathered a bundle, the witch, she alleged, told her to take off her gown and apron and carry the sticks in her clothes, giving her a big pin to fasten them. Anne ran home half naked, explaining her condition, "I am ruined and undone."

After several days in jail, Jane Wenham was searched for witch's marks, and, under pressure from the local parson, made a confession implicating three other women (who were only later released). She was then held for the assizes. Sixteen witnesses, including three clergymen, gave evidence against her. A magic ointment made from rendered corpses was discovered under her pillow, and curious cakes made of feathers found in her house. In spite of furious opposition from the clergymen, the lawyers refused to draw up any other indictment save that of "conversing familiarly with the devil in the form of a cat." Of this charge the jury proceeded to find her Guilty. The assize judge, Justice Powell, probably mindful of the lead of Chief Justice Holt a few years earlier, opposed the jury, although he had to pass sentence. He managed to obtain a reprieve, and Jane Wenham was soon pardoned. She was befriended by a local gentleman, who gave her a little cottage where she lived without further molestation until her death in 1730.

An interesting appendix to this trial—which throws some light on all possessed girls—concerns the chief witness against Jane Wenham, the servant girl, Anne Thorne. She had fits; she was troubled with visions of devils in the shape of cats; she vomited pins. A doctor ordered her to wash her hands and face twice a day, and to be watched by a "lusty young fellow" during her convalescence. The young man proved an effective cure for Anne's hysterics, and the two were happily married.

Werewolves of Poligny. One of the most popular stories of werewolves was that first told by Johan Weyer, who dismissed it as a delusion concocted under torture. Boguet and Vairo, however, repeated it to prove the existence of lycanthropes. The story concerned Pierre Bourgot (Big Peter), Michel Verdung (or Udon), and Philibert Mentot, tried in December, 1521, by the Inquisitor General of Besançon, the Dominican friar, Jean Boin (or Bomm). Suspicion fell on these men when a traveler, passing through the Poligny district, was attacked by a wolf; he wounded the animal and followed its trail to a hut, where he found the wife bathing Verdung's wounds. In his confession, Michel Verdung told how he had kept Pierre faithful to the Devil.

Then Pierre Bourgot confessed. In 1502, a terrible storm scattered his flocks. While searching for them, he met three black horsemen to whom he told his sorrows. One of the horsemen (whose name was later revealed as Moyset) promised Pierre relief and help if he would serve him as lord and master, and Pierre agreed to bind the bargain within the week. Very soon, he found his sheep. At the second meeting, Pierre, learning that the kind stranger was a servant of the Devil, denied Christianity and swore fealty by kissing the horseman's left hand, which was black and cold as ice. After two years, Pierre began to drift back to Christianity. At this point, Michel Verdung, another servant of the Devil, was instructed to make Pierre toe the Devil's line. Encouraged by promises of satanic gold, Pierre attended a sabbat, where everyone carried a green taper burning with a blue flame. Then Verdung told him to strip and apply a magic salve; Pierre found himself a wolf. After two hours, Verdung applied another ointment, and Pierre regained his human form. As a werewolf, Pierre confessed (under torture) to various assaults. He attacked a seven-year-old boy, but the lad screamed so that Pierre had to put on his clothes and become a man again to avoid detection. He confessed he ate a four-year-old girl and found her flesh delicious; he broke the neck of a nine-year-old girl and ate her. As a wolf, he mated with real wolves, and, reported Boguet, all three men said "they had as much pleasure in the act as if they had copulated with their wives."

The three men were, of course, burned.

Werewolves of St.-Claude. In the Jura region of France, werewolves were traditional: Pierre Bourgot of Poligny in 1521, Gilles Garnier of Dôle in 1573, and in 1598 the four members of the Gandillon family of St.-Claude—two sisters, a brother, and his son. Their story is very valuable, for it was recorded by an eyewitness, Judge Henri Boguet.

Perrenette was a poor demented creature who no doubt believed she was a wolf. She met her death in this way: Sixteen-year-old Benoît Bidel of Naizan climbed a tree to pick fruit, leaving his younger sister sitting by the trunk. A tailless wolf attacked her; Benoît climbed down to help her. In the struggle, the wolf snatched Benoît's knife and stabbed his neck. The youth noticed that instead of front paws this wolf had human hands, and he was able to pass on this information before he died of his wounds. Perrenette was found in the vicinity of the murder and, guilty or not, was torn to pieces by the enraged peasants.

The second Gandillon, Antoinette, in addition to being a lycanthrope, was alleged to produce hail, attend the sabbat, and sleep with the devil, who came to her as a goat.

Brother Pierre was accused of witchcraft, making hail, enticing children to the sabbat, turning himself into a wolf, and killing and eating animals and men. He confessed—torture may be assumed—how

> Satan clothed them in a wolf's skin which completely covered them, and that they went on all fours, and ran about the country, chasing now a person and now an animal, according to the guidance of their appetite. They confessed also that they tired themselves with running.

One Maundy Thursday, Pierre was seen in a cataleptic state lying in his bed, but on awakening told of going to a wolfish sabbat. His son Georges confessed to covering himself with salve and turning himself into a wolf; in the company of his aunts, he had killed two goats.

Boguet, the presiding judge of St.-Claude, visited the three lycanthropes in jail:

> In company with the Lord Claude Meynier, our recorder, I have seen those I have named go on all fours in a room just as they did when they were in the

fields; but they said that it was impossible for them to turn themselves into wolves, since they had no more ointment, and they had lost the power of doing so by being imprisoned. I have further noted that they were all scratched on the face and hands and legs; and that Pierre Gandillon was so much disfigured in this way that he bore hardly any resemblance to a man, and struck with horror those who looked at him.

This testimony, to be sure, merely established the insanity of the prisoners. All three, Antoinette, Pierre, and Georges, were convicted and burned.

Wesley, John: see Epworth Poltergeist.

Weyer, Johan. Johan Weyer (1515-88) was among the earliest to question the witch hunts, by distinguishing between simple women who worked no evil, even though accused of a pact with the Devil (a possibility Weyer did not deny), and subtle magicians who really conspired with Satan. Whatever evil such women thought they worked was merely a hallucination brought on by the Devil; the actual evil was done by the Devil himself without human assistance. Fundamentally, Weyer

Johan Weyer (1515-88), physician to Duke William of Cleves, and an active opponent of the witchcraft delusion.

was activated by pity rather than by reason. Consequently, his attempted distinction between harmless witches and wicked wizards was easily demolished by his more logical opponents, like Bodin; and in many other ways Weyer accepted as true the most incredible legends. For example, he accepted literally the story of the Pied Piper of Hamelin (as did Glanvill a hundred years later) and dated the incident June 16, 1284. Weyer personally had prevented the Devil from flying off with a young virgin to the castle of Caldenbroch in Gueldres.

Yet in spite of his acceptance of the power of a personal Devil, Weyer opposed so many of the excesses of the witch hunters that, in practice, his was a moderating influence. The Duchy of Cleves and Juliers-Berg, where he was personal physician to the Duke William, consequently became a relative haven of sanity, along with the Palatinate of the Rhine and Nassau, in a Germany increasingly ravaged by executions of the innocent. His views created so much opposition that, without the protection of the Duke, he would have been burned as a witch lover.

Weyer was born in Brabant of a noble family, studied under Cornelius Agrippa, an early scientist reputed a magician, and then at Paris to become a physician. He became tutor to the two sons and a nephew of King Francis I of France, traveling with the boys throughout France and to Africa and Crete. This assignment over, he took a post at Cleves, became renowned as a diagnostician, and wrote his books on witchcraft. As a physician, Dr. Weyer realized that the accounts of sabbats and possession were the products of deranged minds. For this reason, and because nearly all diseases were attributed to sorcery, he felt it especially the duty of doctors to combat such superstition.

As a Protestant, Weyer was especially hostile to ignorant priests and monks, who, at the first sign of illness, pronounced bewitchment and earned money by exorcism. These priests oppressed the guiltless with false accusations and filled the prisons with victims.

Daily experience shows what execrable

DE
PRAESTIGIIS
DAEMONVM, ET IN-
cantationibus, ac uene-
ficijs, Libri v.

Authore IOANNE VVIE-
RO Medico.

Totius Operis Argumentum in Præ-
fatione comperies.

Nolite uos confortes effe dæmoniorum.
1. Corinth. 10.
Refiftite diabolo, & fugiet à uobis.
Iacobi 4.

Cum Cæfareæ Maieft. gratia
& priuilegio.

BASILEÆ, PER IOAN-
nem Oporinum. 1563. *6.*

The title page of Dr. Johan Weyer's *De Praestigiis*, the first edition of 1563 at Basel, the most celebrated of all books exposing the witchcraft delusion. From Cornell University Library.

alienation from God, what fellowship with the Devil, what hatred between relatives, what strife between neighbors, what enmities among the peasants, what feuds between cities, what frequent slaughter of the innocent, are caused by that most fruitful mother of calamities, the belief in the sorcery of witches.

In Book VI of his *De Praestigiis* [*On Magic*], 1563, Weyer inveighed against cruel imprisonment where the prisoners were "constantly dragged out to suffer awful torture until they would gladly exchange this most bitter existence for death," and thus willingly confessed "whatever crimes were suggested to them rather than be thrust back into their hideous dungeon amid ever recurring torture." His denunciation of the typical methods of witch hunters is one of the high points of this work, putting it on a par with Father Spee's.

But very different is the common procedure when simply through malicious accusation or the mistaken suspicion of illiterate and ignorant peasants, old women deceived or possessed by the Devil are put by judges into the horrible dens of thieves and caves of wicked demons, and then turned over to be slaughtered with the most refined tortures that tyrants could invent, beyond human endurance. And this cruelty is continued until the most innocent are forced to confess themselves guilty. So it happens that the time comes when these bloodthirsty men forced them to give their guiltless souls to God in the flames of the pyre rather than to suffer any longer the tortures inflicted on them by these tyrants. If indeed, overcome by the severity of the torture, they die in the hands of their executioners, or if their endurance, exhausted by suffering and incarceration, gives way and they die when brought out, lo, the joyful cry goes up that they have committed suicide (as indeed they might, what with the severity of their agonies and the squalors of the jail), or that the Devil has killed them.

But when the great searcher of hearts, from whom nothing is hidden, shall appear, your wicked deeds shall be revealed, you tyrants, sanguinary judges, butchers, torturers and ferocious robbers, who have thrown out humanity and do not know mercy. So I summon you before the tribunal of the Great Judge, who shall decide between us, where the truth you have trampled under foot and buried shall arise and condemn you, demanding vengeance for your inhumanities.

Fourteen years after his *De Praestigiis*, in 1577, Weyer, seeing a revival of persecution, wrote an abridged and revised version of his earlier work, the *De Lamiis* [*On Witches*], covering more or less the same materials. His emphasis on the uselessness of confessions extracted by torture prepared public acceptance for the later attacks by the Jesuit humanitarians, Fathers Tanner, Laymann, and Spee, and by Father Cornelius Loos. Witches, Weyer summed up in a letter to a doctor in Württemberg in 1565, following heavy losses to crops––

confess many things, especially when subjected to very severe torture, which are just fables, trifles, lies, which are not and never were, nor could be according to the nature of things. Nor should more credence be placed in that part of their confession where they say they are bound to the Devil in one way or another and therefore have agreed to work his evil will, than where they voluntarily confess they have disturbed the air, caused hailstorms, destroyed harvests and vines or have done any other *maleficia*. . . . When there is no proof but the confession of an old woman demented by prison and torture, whom we refuse to believe in other matters, why not in everything else, when nothing positive is to be gained from the deluded confession of a demoniacally possessed old hag?

White Witch. Civil law, observed the famous jurist Paulus Grillandus (about 1525), did not punish sorcery when it was beneficial, such as curing disease or driving away storms. A few demonologists justified this position. Guazzo (1608), for example, distinguished natural magic, a gift from God, from artificial magic, done with the help of the Devil. Natural magic was "no more than a more exact knowledge of the secrets of nature"; and Guazzo pointed to Tobias in the Bible curing his father's blindness with the gall bladder of a fish. Nevertheless, Guazzo admitted that white magic could become evil and unlawful when practiced for an evil purpose, when performed with the help of demons, and when it endangered the body and the soul.

On the other hand, ecclesiastical law, after the year 900, punished curative sorcery or "white magic" with excommunication, resulting in execution by the civil authorities. The church view gradually prevailed. Jean Vincent (about 1475) wrote that those who used herbs for cures did so only through a pact with the Devil, either express or implicit. Gilly Duncan at North Berwick in 1590 was suspected of witchcraft because she was curing "all such as were troubled or grieved with any kind of sickness or infirmity." In fact, the good witch came to be regarded by the theologians as a "more horrible and detestable monster" than the wicked witch. William Perkins wrote (1608):

A shepherd consults a white witch. From the Douce Collection, Bodleian Library, Oxford.

For let a man's child, friend, or cattle be taken with some sickness or strangely tormented with some rare and unknown disease, the first thing he doth is to bethink himself and enquire after some wise man or wise woman, and thither he sends and goes for help. . . . And the party thus cured cannot say with David, "The Lord is my helper," but "The Devil is my helper!" for by him he is cured. Of both these kinds of witches the present law of Moses must be understood.

Perkins continued:

Though the witch were in many respects profitable, and did not hurt, but procured much good, yet because he hath renounced God, his king and governor, and hath bound himself by other laws to the service of the enemies of God and his Church, death is his portion justly assigned him by God: he may not live.

All the English authorities, while admitting that "unbinding" witches existed and were generally consulted if a physician could not heal an illness, were unanimous in their condemnation. Fuller, in his *Holy and Profane State*, wrote, "The white and the black [witch] are both guilty alike in compounding with the Devil"; and Gifford, in his *Dialogue* (1593), felt that white witches "ought to be rooted out, that others might see and fear." Cotton Mather, according to a sermon at Boston in 1689, believed good witches did not exist, that there was "none that doeth good, no, not one."

Wishart, Janet: see Aberdeen Witches.

Witch. The idea of a witch as a heretic (discussed in the entries for Trials and Witchcraft), which was responsible for the judicial murder of thousands in western Europe in the years between 1500 and 1700, did not lend itself to pictorial representation. More easily, the mind's eye conceived, as an embodiment of evil, a woman "old, lame, blear-eyed, pale, foul, and full of wrinkles"—Reginald Scot. Since the majority of accused witches were women, this concept predominated and took hold in words and illustrations, coming down to modern times in the creations of Walt Disney. Nider (about 1435) declared that there were more women than men witches because women have a slippery tongue and tell other women what they have learned; Geiler von Kaysersberg (1510) agreed, adding that women were more credulous and more impressionable than men, and more subject to hallucinations. King James repeated these explanations in Scotland (1597).

Samuel Harsnett, who became Archbishop of York, in his *Declaration of Popish Impostures* (1599), following Scot, described the popular idea of a witch as a crone:

Out of these [impostures] is shaped [for] us the idea of a witch—an old, weather-beaten crone, having the chin and her knees meeting for age, walking like a bow, leaning on a staff; hollow-eyed, untoothed, furrowed on her face, having her limbs trembling with the palsy, going mumbling in the streets; one that hath forgotten her paternoster, and yet hath a shrewd tongue to call a drab a drab.

Noting how any unexplained calamity was attributed to the witch, a charge especially common in English witch trials, Harsnett continued:

If she hath learned of an old wife, in a chimney end, "Pax, Max, Fax," for a spell, or can say Sir John Grantham's curse for the miller's eels—

All ye that have stolen the miller's eels,

Laudate dominum de coelis;
And all they that have consented thereto,
Benedicamus domino.

—why then, beware! Look about ye, my
neighbors. If any of you have a sheep
sick of the giddies, or a hog of the
mumps, or a horse of the staggers, or a
knavish boy of the school, or an idle girl
of the wheel, or a young drab of the
sullens, and hath not fat enough for her
porridge or butter enough for her bread,
and she hath a little help of the epilepsy
or cramp to teach her to roll her eyes,
wry her mouth, gnash her teeth, startle
with her body, hold her arms and hands
stiff, and then, when an old Mother Nobs
hath by chance called her an idle young
housewife, or bid the devil scratch her,
then no doubt but Mother Nobs is the
witch, and the young girl is owl-blasted.

A similar portrait was drawn by Joseph
Addison of "a wrinkled hag," Moll White.

During the seventeenth century, the
storybook caricature was created from the
pictorializations of the idea in contemporary French and German treatises and in
the English pamphlets. So ingrained did
this notion become that Madame Bourignon
(about 1666) said of one of her novices,
declared by three clergymen to be a witch,
that "not knowing what sort of creature a
witch must be, having often thought witches
were ugly, deformed creatures . . . [she]
could not believe that this girl was a witch."
(Matthew Hale, *Modern Relations*)

In turn, the theologians profited from
the popular views, and, as Binsfeld observed, ugliness came to be a sign or indication [*indicium*] of witchcraft. Bodin, in
his *Démonomanie* (1580), quoted the prov-
erb, "as ugly as a witch," and the remark
of Girolamo Cardano (1550), who said he
had never seen a witch not deformed.

A late seventeenth-century comic book,
*The Strange and Wonderful History of
Mother Shipton* (1686), described the birth
of Ursula Soothtell (later to be known as
the witch, Mother Shipton): "The body
was long, but very big-boned, great gog-
gling eyes, very sharp and fiery, a nose of
unproportional length, having in it many
crooks and turnings adorned with great
pimples." Ursula was the offspring of a

Three excited witches, attributed to Hans
Baldung Grün. The young witch at the right
plays leapfrog, skillfully holding aloft a
flaming chamber-pot. This picture was designed as a New Year's greeting card.

witch and a devil; it was generally believed
that, as Boguet noted, children "usually
followed their mother's manner of life." To
be the child of a witch was considered evidence of being a witch. In his *Compendium
Maleficarum* (2d ed., 1626), Guazzo explained:

The infection of witchcraft is often
spread through a sort of contagion to
children by their sinful parents, when
these try to find favor with their devils.
For the greed of Satan was ever limitless
and insatiable; thus, when once he has
entered a family, he will never give up
his foothold except with the greatest difficulty. And it is one among many sure
and certain indications against those accused of witchcraft, if one of their parents were found guilty of this crime.
There are daily examples of this inherited

taint in children, for the Devil is always busy to increase the number of his adherents. And there can be no better way of attaining this end than by urging and compelling those who are already in his power to corrupt their own children.

A few writers and early artists held a minority conception of a witch as young and attractive, obviously more alluring than an old hag to a devil perpetually aiming at seduction. The engravings of Hans Baldung Grün (about 1514) illustrate this limited view. It has been recently revived in the proposed panels for a Witchcraft Museum at Biarritz, and an illustration of the Basque Witches represents a young nude witch in the act of anointing herself for flight. The elimination of the fleshly and comely witch was probably due to the puritanism, both Catholic and Protestant, which feared that associating beauty with witchcraft might encourage converts to the heresy.

> There, in a gloomy hollow glen, she found
> A little cottage built of sticks and weeds,
> In homely wise, and walled with sods around,
> In which a witch did dwell in loathly weeds
> And willfull want, all careless of her needs;
> So choosing solitary to abide,
> Far from all neighbors, that her devilish deeds
> And hellish arts from people she might hide,
> And hurt far off, unknown, whomever she envied.
> -Edmund Spenser, *Faerie Queene* (1590)

The witch in the black pointed hat and cape, riding on a broomstick or talking to her cat, is part of the folklore of witchcraft. Unfortunately, this notion obscures the fact that the majority of persons accused as witches were not old women casting spells; even in England, where the trials no doubt involved many hags, younger women were just as frequently accused. In Scotland, at the North Berwick trials in 1590, women were charged, "reputed for as civil honest women as any that dwelled within the city of Edinburgh." In Germany, the educated,

wealthy, young, and respected were the most numerous of those burned, as is revealed in a letter written by the Chancellor of the Prince-Bishop of Würzburg in August, 1629 [for full text see Würzburg Witch Trials]. One nineteen-year-old girl burned at Würzburg was Barbara Göbel, who was thus described in the hangman's list: "She was the fairest maid in Würzburg." In Cologne, about the same time, another young woman was burned who "had the name that she was the fairest and the purest maiden in all Cologne."

The over-all situation in Germany was summed up by George L. Burr: "But one needed only to be envied in those days. It was malice and jealousy which oftenest dictated the names denounced in that torture chamber. Wealth, learning, beauty, goodness—these were often the very conditions of accusation."

To anyone who had doubts about the crime of these people, the demonologists retorted that a seemingly pious demeanor was a subtle trick of the Devil; the witches did everything a good Catholic should to achieve greater protection to carry on their devilish work.

Accusations of witchcraft might be aimed at any scholar or intellectual, either by the church authorities or else by a mob. Dr. John Dee, Queen Elizabeth's astrologer, had been charged in 1555 by the Privy Council with practicing magic to kill Queen Mary; he was not convicted. However, his reputation as a magician grew, and with it came unpopularity; in 1583 he was attacked by a crowd which later sacked his house and destroyed his library. The Queen continued to support him, and in 1590 gave him £100 for alchemical experiments. Dr. John Lamb, another alchemist, was less fortunate; he was lynched as a wizard in 1640 [see Dr. Lamb's Darling]. Naudé came to the defense of men of superior learning accused of witchcraft, such as Savonarola, Nostradamus, Thomas Aquinas, Roger Bacon, and Albertus Magnus. The English translation by J. Davies, printed in London in 1657, was entitled, *The History of Magic by Way of Apology for all the wise men who have unjustly been reputed*

An Elizabethan conception of a wizard, from a rare tract, *A Most Wicked Work of a Wretched Witch* (1592), in Lambeth Palace Library.

magicians. Catherine Kepler, the mother of the famous astronomer, was prosecuted for witchcraft in 1620 at Guglingen, Swabia (Gunther, *Ein Hexenprozess*, 1906). The complete records of her trial have been preserved, and her forty-nine answers show (by the absence of the questions in the court reports) an established routine for witch suspects [see Confessions].

Throughout the writings of the demonologists, many synonyms are found for witch. Jordanes de Bergamo (1470) noted:

> *bacularia* (from riding on a stick)
> *fascinatrix* (from the evil eye)
> *herberia* (from her baneful herbs)
> *maliarda* (from the evil or *mala* she works)
> *pixidaria* (from her box of magic ointment)

Binsfeld, in 1589, listed other names:

> *femina saga* (wise woman)
> *lamia* (bloodsucking night monster)
> *incantator* (worker of charms)
> *magus* (wise man)
> *maleficius* (worker of evil against men, beasts, or property)
> *sortiariae mulier* (woman who prophesies by lots)
> *strix* (nocturnal bird)
> *venefica* (poisoner)
> *vir sortilegi* (magician)

But, as the Jesuit Gaspar Schott observed, "*lamia* and *strix* mean the same thing, namely, *saga*." (*Physica Curiosa*, 1657) Other Latin terms for "witch" encountered in the classic treatises on witchcraft include *anispix, auguris, divinator, januatica, ligator, mascara, phitonissa, sortilega, stregonis,* and *stregula.*

Johannes Pott included the more familiar German synonyms for "witches": *Hexen, Töchter des Donners, Unholdinnen, Gabelreiterinnen* [riders on pitchforks], *Wettermacherinnen, Zauberinnen,* and sometimes *Truten* and *Wickhersen* [*wicken* = to foretell]. *Hexerei* first appeared in court trials in 1419 in Lucerne, where a man named Gögler was tortured for witchcraft.

A German conception of a witch (about 1709). "A witch must be a hagged old woman, living in a little rotten cottage, under a hill, by a woodside, and must be frequently spinning at the door; she must have a black cat, two or three broomsticks, an imp or two, and two or three diabolical teats to suckle her imps."—*Round About Our Coal Fire* (an English Christmas book, about 1700).

The Kinds of Witches

From William West, *Simboleography*
(London, 1594)

Magicians:

Magicians be those which by uttering of certain superstitious words conceived, adventure to attempt things above the course of nature, by bringing forth dead men's ghosts, as they falsely pretend, in showing things either secret or in places far off, and in showing them in any shape or likeness.

Soothsaying wizards:

Soothsayers or wizards . . . divine and foretell things to come, and raise up evil spirits by certain superstitious and conceived forms of words. And unto such words as be demanded of them, do answer by voice, or else set before their eyes in glasses, crystal stones or rings, the pictures or images of things sought for.

Divinators:

The professors of the art of divination which be puffed up with prophesying spirits. And can manifest who hath stolen things and tell where things lost or stolen be.

Jugglers:

Jugglers and flighty curers of diseases, which for the curing of all sicknesses and sores of man and beast, use either certain superstitious words or writings called charms or spells hanged about the neck or some other part of the body.

Enchanters and charmers:

Enchanters or charmers, through certain words pronounced and characters or images, herbs or other things applied, think they can do what they list, the devil so deceiveth them, or in very deed dispatcheth those things which the enchanters would have done. From these somewhat differ witches or hags, and augurers or soothsayers by birds, diviners by seeing the entrails of beasts sacrificed.

Witches:

A witch or hag is she which being [d]eluded by a league made with the devil through his persuasion, inspiration and juggling, thinketh she can design what manner of evil things soever, either by thought or imprecation, as to shake the air with lightnings and thunder, to cause hail and tempests, to remove green corn or trees to another place, to be carried of her familiar (which hath taken upon him the deceitful shape of a goat, swine, or calf, etc.) into some mountain far distant, in a wonderful short space of time, and sometimes to fly upon a staff or fork, or some other instrument, and to spend all the night after with her sweetheart, in playing, sporting, banqueting, dancing, dalliance, and divers other devilish lusts and lewd disports, and to show a thousand such monstrous mockeries.

A wide range of distinctions occurs in English writings. Wycliffe, in his *Apology for Lollard Doctrines*, for example, listed *arioler* [soothsayer], *augurer* [diviner], *enchantress, haruspex* [prognosticator by entrails], *phytoness* [diviner], *sortileger* [fortuneteller], and a host of *-mancers*— people who profess to forecast coming events by air [*aeromancer*], figures and lines [*geomancer*], water [*hydromancer*], or fire [*pyromancer*]. As the idea of witchcraft developed, it became necessary to clarify the various kinds of witches. Thomas Ady, basing his classification on Deuteronomy xviii, established nine varieties.

John Gaule in 1646 told the jurymen of England there were eight classes of witches:

1. The diviner, gypsy, or fortunetelling witch.
2. The astrologian, star-gazing, planetary, prognosticating witch.
3. The chanting, canting, or calculating witch, who works by signs and numbers.
4. The veneficial or poisoning witch.
5. The exorcist or conjuring witch.
6. The gastronomic witch.
7. The magical, speculative, sciential, or arted witch.

8. The necromancer.

This classification was largely theoretical, for all these wickednesses were regarded as dependent on the Devil, and therefore all were considered heresy. Thus Damhouder, in his *Practica Rerum Criminalium* (1554), concluded: "And thus *sortilegi, divinatores,* and *malefici,* who have professed this dia-bolical superstition, are said to be enemies of man's salvation and believed to be hostile to the human race." And the Englishman Gifford noted: "The conjurer, the enchanter, the sorcerer, the diviner, and whatsoever other sort there is, are indeed compassed within this circle." (*Discourse of the Subtle Practices of Devils by Witches and Sorcerers*)

Charles Lamb on "Witches and other night fears."

We are too hasty when we set down our ancestors in the gross for fools, for the monstrous inconsistencies (as they seem to us) involved in their creed of witchcraft. In the relations of this visible world we find them to have been as rational, and shrewd to detect an historic anomaly, as ourselves. But when once the invisible world was supposed to be opened, and the lawless agency of bad spirits assumed, what measures of probability, of decency, of fitness, or proportion—of that which distinguishes the likely from the palpable absurd—could they have to guide them in the rejection or admission of any particular testimony?—that maidens pined away, wasting inwardly as their waxen images consumed before a fire—that corn was lodged, and cattle lamed—that whirlwinds uptore in diabolic revelry the oaks of the forest—or that spits and kettles only danced a fearful-innocent vagary about some rustic's kitchen when no wind was stirring—were all equally probable where no law of agency was understood. . . . That the intercourse was opened at all between both worlds was perhaps the mistake, but, that once assumed, I see no reason for disbelieving one attested story of this nature more than another on the score of absurdity. There is no law to judge of the lawless, or canon by which dreams may be criticized.
—Charles Lamb, *First Essays of Elia* (1822).

Witchcraft. Witchcraft means different things to different people. Linguistic variations as well as a long-continued looseness in usage have obscured its real significance. For the two centuries of the imposition of the witchcraft delusion on the religious and intellectual life of Europe, the word had a precise meaning, one generally recognized and frequently spelled out:

1587: George Gifford: [The witch is] "one that worketh by the Devil, or by some devilish curious art, either hurting or healing, revealing things secret or foretelling things to come, which the Devil hath devised to entangle and snare men's souls withal unto damnation."

1599: Martin Del Rio: [Witchcraft is] "an art which, by the power of a contract entered into with the Devil, some wonders are wrought which pass the common understanding of man."

1608: William Perkins: "A witch is a magician, who either by open or secret league, wittingly and willingly consenteth to use the aid and assistance of the Devil, in the working of wonders."

1608: Francesco-Maria Guazzo: "Witchcraft is a form of magic whereby with the help of a Devil one man does harm [*damnum*] to another."

1653: Sir Robert Filmer: "Witchcraft is an art serving for the working of wonders, by the assistance of the Devil, so far as God shall permit."

1671: Edward Phillips (the nephew of John Milton): [Witchcraft is] "a certain evil art, whereby with the assistance of the Devil, or evil spirits, some wonders may be wrought which exceed the common apprehension [understanding] of men."

1689: Cotton Mather: "Witchcraft is the doing of strange, and for the most part ill, things by the help of evil spirits, covenanting with . . . the woeful children of men."

1730: William Forbes (Professor of Law at Glasgow University) : "Witchcraft is the black art whereby strange and wonderful things are wrought by a power derived from the Devil."

To these men, who, as theologians, judges, or lawyers, were most concerned either in attacking or defending the belief, witchcraft meant one thing: a league with the Devil to do evil [see Pact]. Whether Catholic or Protestant, to them witchcraft was heresy. "This fact, that witchcraft was heresy, and that persecution for witchcraft was persecution for heresy," wrote George L. Burr, "we cannot bear too carefully in mind, for it is the essence of the matter."

Nothing in these foregoing definitions stressed magic or sorcery, yet magic represented the other aspect of this "cozening art." A belief in magic was the substructure of witchcraft long before the element of heresy was added; it existed as the essence of witchcraft in the popular mind long before and after the centuries of the witch delusion.

The scattered accounts of what passed for witchcraft during the first thirteen centuries after Christ emphasized sorcery. Since nearly all early histories were written by Christians, Christian concepts of a Devil were superimposed on folk beliefs; and later scholars, familiar with the background of a developed demonology, have read into these histories conceptions originally alien to them. One authority for seeing the Devil in everything was Augustine, who accepted every fable about demons and laid a basis for Canon Law as well as a storehouse from which demonologists drew very heavily. He shares with Thomas Aquinas the dubious distinction of being an inventor of demonology and witchcraft.

> Witches are those who, because of the magnitude of their crimes, are commonly called *malefici* or evil-doers. These witches, by the permission of God, agitate the elements, and disturb the minds of men less trusting in God. Without administering any poison, they kill by the great potency of their charms . . . For they summon devils and dare to rouse them so that everyone kills his enemies by evil stratagems. For these witches make use of the blood of victims and often defile the corpses of the dead . . . For the devils are said to love blood, and therefore as often as the witches practice the black arts, they mingle blood with water, so that by the color of blood they can more easily conjure the devils. (Gratian, *Decretum*)

Before 1350, witchcraft primarily meant sorcery, a survival of common superstitions —pagan only insofar as the beliefs antedated Christianity, never pagan in the sense of an organized survival of opposition to Christianity or of some pre-Christian religion. Sorcery or magic is world-wide and world-old; it is simply the attempt to control nature in man's own interests; it is the forerunner of religion before priests appropriated tribal lore for themselves. The same stages of development of any early society, in whatever part of the world, at whatever date, and without transmission or direct influence, will produce similar basic ideas, although, of course, the rationalization of these ideas may vary. Thus, many of the practices of sorcery—invocation of spirits, belief in demons, charms and rituals for fertility of men and crops, charms and rituals for blight and death—found in Europe are duplicated in Africa, Asia, South and Central America. The curious resemblance of these practices and cults suggested the false derivation of the word *voodoo* from the thirteenth-century witch heretics of the Vaudois in southern France; actually, there is no connection, and *voodoo* comes from Ewe, an African language of Dahomey and Togoland.

In the first thirteen centuries, witchcraft was punished by death only if some concrete injury resulted; divination or healing was considered about as bad as prostitution and was punished accordingly. In the fourteenth century, ecclesiastical law started to become more organized against sorcery. In 1310 the Church Council at Treves forbade divination, love potions, conjurations, and the like. In 1432 the Bishop of Béziers excommunicated sorcerers and their ilk. Legislation increased in the fifteenth century. These laws were not directed against

The Black Arts of Witchcraft, a print by C. de Pas. From the Douce Collection, Bodleian Library, Oxford. "You know the future, life and death, the order of the stars, their fatal powers—more than the Devil. You do not know that your knowledge leads you only to the flames of hell."

the later witchcraft of pact and sabbat, although in the inquisitorial trials these crimes were being introduced, even as early as 1330 (at Toulouse).

Christianity was not opposed to a belief in interruptions of the normal course of nature; every saint worked miracles and every desert father had overcome the tricks of devils. The Church was opposed to "miracles" when they were worked by demons. The writings of early and medieval theologians are packed with incidents of sorcery and magic, all treated with serious credulity. In such a climate, sorcery was treated as commonplace, not exceptional.

Some time about the middle of the fourteenth century, witchcraft began to acquire a different form; gradually, out of the old concept of magic grew the new concept of heresy. Heresy was treason against God,

and may be defined in the words of Bernardus Guidonis (1261-1331) as "the knowing rejection of a dogma or the rigid adherence to a sect whose doctrines have been condemned by the Church as contrary to the faith." The first reference to the new witchcraft seems to be in the trials at Toulouse and Carcassonne, before 1350, by which time 600 persons had been burned as heretics. [For earlier trials, see Trials.] The Inquisitor Bernard de Como alluded to an anti-Catholic sect of witches prosecuted in 1360 at Como. Witchcraft, with pact and sabbat, was prosecuted about 1400 in Italian Savoy and the neighboring areas of Switzerland. Apparently the contagion spread from southern France through the Alpine valleys to northern Italy.

Witchcraft was introduced and spread by the Inquisition, which had responsibility in matters of orthodoxy. The secular courts made no contribution at this time to the idea of witchcraft. Little by little, the inquisitors gained for themselves the control over and the determination of witchcraft. At first, however, it was merely sorcery they attacked. In a bull of 1258, Pope Alexander IV allowed inquisitors to prosecute sorcerers when their acts conflicted with articles of faith, a subtle point left to the inquisitors themselves to settle. With the exception of the thirteen years after 1320, when Pope John XXII allowed the Inquisition full control over all kinds of sorcery, this state of affairs, reformulated in various bulls, continued to 1451. Then Pope Nicholas V, in a letter to Hugues Lenoir, Inquisitor of France, gave the inquisitors authority to deal with all sorcery, even when it did not "manifestly savor of heresy." The *Malleus Maleficarum*, in 1486, the work of two such inquisitors, was the first manual to codify the heresy of witchcraft and include pact, sabbat, and nightflight: "A belief that there are such things as witches is so essential a part of the Catholic faith that obstinately to maintain the opposite opinion savors of heresy." Tribute to the effectiveness of the Inquisition was paid by Ludovicus, who said the world would have been destroyed by witches had it not been for the inquisitors, who burned, he estimated, at least 30,000 men and women between 1450 and 1598.

About 1550 witchcraft finally appeared as "an elaborate theological notion," and was enshrined even in civil Protestant regulations. Witchcraft without alleged malefice, if it involved a pact with the Devil, became a capital crime in Lutheran Saxony by the law of 1572, and in the Calvinist Palatinate by a law of 1582. By about 1600 the new witchcraft had reached its full development in the massive treatises of the celebrated theologians and lawyers (by now no longer mainly inquisitors), only possible after many years of torture, confessions, and executions. The impetus of these demonologists continued another hundred years, until about 1700.

Why did the Inquisition need a new heresy of witchcraft? Probably the chief reason why sorcery was turned into heresy was the success of the inquisitors in obliterating previous heresies. All through the thirteenth century, the Inquisition had concentrated its forces on the inhabitants of southern France, and with the work of the notorious inquisitor, Bernardus Guidonis, from 1308 to 1323, the Albigensians and other heretics had been exterminated. About 1320, says the *Encyclopaedia Britannica* (11th ed.), "the persecution stopped for lack of an object." Witchcraft was in fact *invented* to fill the gap; the first trials for sorcery were held in Provence. Between 1350 and 1400 various trials allowed the Dominican inquisitors to think out a theory of sorcery as treason against God; and treason against God, according to Joost Damhouder (1554), the influential criminal lawyer (whose handbook was at one time the prescribed authority for the state of Delaware), was "the gravest and greatest of all crimes." This theory immeasurably increased the number of possible heretics, for sorcery was universal. Everyone throughout Europe was a potential witch, a potential heretic, and therefore a potential source of income to the inquisitors, who shared with the civil authorities the confiscated properties of all those they condemned as heretics.

Once having begun the heresy of

Heads of two devils, from Francis Barrett, *The Magus* (1801).

witchcraft, the Inquisition lost direct control. By the early sixteenth century, in Germany and France, the extirpation of witchcraft was handled by the civil power. A decree of the Parlement of Paris as early as 1390 gave the secular courts the right to try witches, and trials were conducted by inquisitorial, episcopal, and local civil courts. Many of the electoral states of the Holy Roman Empire were governed by Roman Catholic bishops as territorial princes. In such principalities witches were tried in episcopal rather than in inquisitorial courts. Only in Italy, where there was considerable factional opposition, did the Inquisition continue, maintained by the papacy. In Spain, the Inquisition was a separate organization and suppressed divergences of opinion by other means than charges of witchcraft.

In all courts, however, the inquisitorial conception of witchcraft was upheld; nor was there any essential difference between Catholic and Protestant. The Bamberg *Halsgerichtsordnung* of 1507 and Ulric

Tengler's *Layenspiegel* of 1508, and the Carolina Code of the Emperor Charles in 1532, were secular codifications of inquisitorial practice and a standard for the upper Rhineland. Joost Damhouder's *Praxis Rerum Criminalium* of 1544 was but a secularization of the *Malleus Maleficarum* into criminal law, and was adopted in the lower Rhineland. Even Thomas Hobbes was influenced by the traditional thought, writing in his *Leviathan:*

> As for witches, I think not that their witchcraft is any real power, but yet that they are justly punished, for the false belief they have that they can do such mischief, joined with their purpose to do it if they can, their trade being nearer to a new religion than to a craft or science.

As thought of at the time of the witch persecutions in the sixteenth and seventeenth centuries, witchcraft had outgrown its connection with sorcery. Witches were punished primarily for entering into an agreement with the Devil to deny the Christian God, not for raising a storm to damage the crops or for bewitching a neighbor's baby to death. But by allowing such evidence in the trials (where it was taken as proof of the pact), the inquisitors gained some public tolerance of their work in condemning those they called witches. The belief in sorcery accompanied the belief in heresy; but throughout the period of its onset, power, and decline, witchcraft was an intellectual, not a popular, movement. The late George L. Burr, who probably knew more about the history of witchcraft than any other scholar (including the great Henry C. Lea), wrote: "Whatever (in universal human experience) anthropology or folklore may find akin to it, the witchcraft our fathers feared and fought was never universal, in place or time. It belonged alone to Christian thought and modern centuries." Only a *Christian* could be a witch.

The chain of quotations heading this entry is therefore correctly couched in terms of theology; the Roman Catholic Del Rio gives a description identical with those of the Anglican Robert Filmer and the Protestant Cotton Mather. Each saw witchcraft as a diabolical conspiracy against God and interpreted it by his own individual and national religious experience [see Pact]. Sylvester Prierias, the papal champion against Luther, allowed inquisitors to prosecute witches, not so much for night flying to sabbats, but because they denied the Catholic faith and did "much that manifestly savors of heresy." The main crime was knowingly invoking the Devil and opposing the Church; quite secondary was causing disease or death. How far apart was Prierias from his adversary? Luther, who believed he talked personally to the Devil, maintained: "Our ordinary sins offend and anger God . . . What then must be his wrath against witchcraft, which we may justly designate high treason against divine majesty, and revolt against the infinite power of God?"

Witchcraft was an impossible crime because it granted the impossible. To the courts, both spiritual and secular, for over two centuries, the concurrence of a disliked neighbor and a dead cow or sick child were simply cause and effect: a witch working witchcraft. And power to cause such harm could only be acquired through a pact with the Devil. The alleged pact constituted a crime of conscience, of thinking certain ideas. That the ideas were invented by the judges and that the confessions were extorted under torture is something else. It is no wonder, therefore, that the great early jurist, Grillandus (who believed in the reality of witchcraft), said he had never seen or heard of any witch being taken *in flagrante crimine.*

Because the crime was so grave and so difficult to prove, in 1468 witchcraft was declared a *crimen excepta,* an exceptional crime, in which the ordinary legal rules and safeguards were suspended. Evidence never allowed in other cases was admitted in witch trials: testimony of meetings with the devil from young children, accomplices, perjurers, and excommunicates. Torture was permitted to force a confession of guilt; in fact, torture was required, for a confession without torture was considered unreliable. And, to insure employment and money for the whole apparatus of the witch hunters, the accused had to give or invent the names of his accomplices, who in turn would be tortured into confessing and naming still others. In the occasional territory where the idea of *crimen excepta* was rejected, there was no witchcraft. Thus, in the Duchy of Juliers-Berg, for example, not one witch was burned from 1609 to 1682.

The medieval period, the so-called Dark Ages, was relatively free from witch persecution. The delusion was a product of the Renaissance. In the Middle Ages, conditions were more or less stable; in the sixteenth and seventeenth centuries ideas were fermenting, and hence the established social order felt a greater need to maintain itself against possible overthrow. Executions inspired terror, and terror, it was hoped, would guarantee conformity. About 1600, Boguet wrote from his own experience, "Germany is almost entirely occupied with building fires for [the witches]. Switzerland has been compelled to wipe out many of her villages on their account. Travelers in Lorraine may see thousands and thousands of the stakes to which witches are bound."

As feudalism passed into capitalism, the witchcraft mania reached its height. In England, for example, after the severe persecution under Elizabeth, the second peak of persecution occurred under the Commonwealth, which in so many other ways represented the most advanced political, economic, and philosophical thought of the seventeenth century. With the demise of feudalism in 1686, however, and the complete domination of capitalism, symbolized by the new monarch, William of Orange, a German-speaking princeling from Europe's largest banking community, witchcraft ceased. Commerce could not live in a world of uncertainty, where inquisitorial proceedings could be taken against a man long dead, and his property confiscated from his heirs many years later. Businessmen could not put up with a world in which commercial agreements could be capriciously nullified at a whisper of heresy.

The end of witchcraft came at various times in various countries; generally, the date of the last execution may be considered indicative: in Holland, 1610; in England, 1684; in America, 1692; in Scotland, 1727; in France, 1745; in Germany, 1775; in Switzerland, 1782; in Poland, 1793. In Italy, the Inquisition condemned the mountebank Cagliostro to death in 1791, but commuted the sentence to life imprisonment.

> "When we affirm the universality of witchcraft or of the belief in it, it is in a sense which neither the etymology nor the history of that word suffices to explain. . . . It is only in a sense that would make it inclusive of both religion and magic that witchcraft can be demonstrated universal."
> —George L. Burr (1911).

Many factors contributed to the withering away of witchcraft as a heresy. In Germany, the almost total implication of the whole population in many states finally led to calling a halt, if only for self-preservation of the living. In England, the opposition of both clerics and skeptics to the distortion of biblical texts against witchcraft was another help, since the witch believers stressed the Bible rather than church tradition. In Holland, one of the first countries to outgrow feudalism, witchcraft disappeared very early; after 1610 no one was killed as a witch. This rational atmosphere encouraged victims of witch hunts, Catholic as well as Calvinist, to come to Holland, and for writers to oppose the delusion. In France, the edict of King Louis XIV in 1682 was probably more responsible than any other single act for the cessation of witchcraft trials. But in all countries, the delusion would have continued much longer had it not been for the active opposition of the witches who denied their crime and, on their way to the stake, cursed their judges; and of those men who, in advance of their times, by their writings, often at the risk of career, fortune, and sometimes of their lives, gave the lead to their countrymen and became unsung heroes of humanity.

Witch's Mark. Witch's marks are techr

cally the extra breasts (*polymastia*) or extra nipples (*polythelia*), the latter more common in men than in women, considered as proof of witchcraft. Most descriptions, in fact, represent witch's marks as some natural physical malformation. Margaret Murray quotes an experiment where, out of 315 people selected at random, 7 per cent were found to have supernumerary nipples. One of the seventeenth-century skeptics, Thomas Ady, dismissed all piles, long fleshy warts, bleeding tumors, tonsils under the tongue:

> Very few people in the world are without privy marks upon their bodies, as moles or stains, even such as witchmongers call the devil's privy marks . . . and many an honest man or woman have such excrescences growing upon their bodies, as these witch mongers do call the devil's biggs [teats].

The theory in seventeenth-century England presumed that such teats were used by imps or familiars, agents of the devil, and therefore prima-facie evidence of witchcraft. Michael Dalton's *Country Justice* (1618) gave as a second test for discovering witches: "Their said familiar hath some bigg, or little teat, upon their body, and in some secret place, where he sucketh them." Most of the women taken in the Hopkins hysteria, after being kept from sleep for two, three, or four nights, and forced to keep moving continually during this time until they were in a state of exhaustion, confirmed Dalton's law. Thus, at the Suffolk trials of 1645—

> Margaret, wife of Bayts, of Framlingham, after two or three days watching, confessed when she was at work she felt a thing come upon her legs and go into her secret parts, and nipped her in her secret parts, where her marks were found. And at another time when she was in the churchyard, she felt a thing nip her again in those parts; and further that she had but two teats and they might be made at once sucking.

The records of witch trials in England, Scotland, and New England are all especially rich in accounts of witch's marks.

Shadwell, a Restoration playwright, alluded to the common belief: "Their having of biggs and teats all modern witchmongers in England affirm"—*The Lancashire Witches*, 1681. So Elizabeth Sawyer, the witch of Edmonton (1621), was found to possess "a thing like a teat the bigness of the little finger, and the length of half a finger, which was branched at the top like a teat, and seemed as though one had sucked it." Mary Read of Kent (1652) "had a visible teat under her tongue and did show it to many." Temperance Lloyd, one of the last women hanged for witchcraft in England, in 1682 at Exeter, was searched by Ann Wakely: "Upon search of her said body, she, this informant, did find in her secret parts two teats hanging nigh together like unto a piece of flesh that a child had sucked. And that each of the said teats was about an inch in length"—Howell, *State Trials*, 1816. In examining Bridget Bishop, one of the Salem witches (1692), "a jury of of women found a preternatural teat upon her body; but upon a second search, within three or four hours, there was no such thing to be seen." (Cotton Mather, *Wonders of the Invisible World*, 1693)

Pleading that such protuberances were natural availed little. For example, it did not help Elizabeth Wright and her daughter Alice Gooderidge, examined in 1596.

> The old woman they stripped, and found behind her right shoulder a thing much like the udder of an ewe that giveth suck with two teats, like unto two great warts, the one behind under her armhole, the other a handful off toward the top of her shoulder. Being demanded how long she had those teats, she answered she was born so. Then they did search Alice Gooderidge, and found upon her belly a hole of the bigness of two pence, fresh and bloody, as though some great wart had been cut off the place. (*The Most Wonderful Story of a Witch Named Alice Gooderidge*, 1597)

Alice said the wound was caused by a knife when she slipped from a ladder two days previously, but a physician said it "seemed to be sucked." [See Burton Boy.]

The searching generally took place in

public, and as late as 1717 at Leicester an old woman was inspected "publicly before a great number of good women in that town. They deposed there were found on her secret parts two white pieces of flesh like paps; and some swore they were like the teats of an ewe, and some like the paps of a cat." On some occasions, the examination was conducted by prosecution witnesses, as in the trial of Cicely Celles at St. Osyth in 1582. Even the dead were not exempt from public display. Eighty-year-old Alice Samuel was hanged as a witch on the evidence of five hysterical children [see Warboys Witches]. After the execution, the contemporary account of 1593 related:

> The jailer, whose office it is to see them buried, stripped off their clothes, and being naked, he found upon the body of the old woman, Alice Samuel, a little lump of flesh, in manner sticking out as if it had been a teat, to the length of half an inch, which both he and his wife perceiving, at the first sight thereof meant not to disclose, because it was adjoining to so secret a place which was not decent to be seen. Yet in the end, not willing to conceal so strange a matter, and decently covering that privy place a little above where it grew, they made open show thereof unto divers that stood by. After this, the jailer's wife took the same teat in her hand, and seeming to strain it, there issued out at the first as if had been *beesenings* (to use the jailer's word), which is a mixture of yellow milk and water. At the second time, there came out in similitude as clear milk, and in the end very blood itself. (*The Most Strange and Admirable Discovery*, 1593)

Witch's marks were frequently confused with devil's marks, natural blemishes on the skin reputedly insensitive to pain, regarded as brandings identifying the possessor as the child of Satan. Thus John Bell, minister of Gladsmuir, in the early eighteenth century included both marks in one category—"sometimes like a blue spot, or a little teat, or red spots like flea biting, sometimes also the flesh is sunk in and hollow." (Bell, quoting a pamphlet of 1645, *The Laws Against Witches and Conjuration*.) Nor did Michael Dalton distinguish be-

tween teats and other marks which "being pricked will not bleed, and be often in their secretest parts, and therefore require diligent and careful search." And the great expert, Matthew Hopkins, blandly defined teats as devil's marks. (*Discovery of Witches*, 1647)

Witnesses. In France and Germany, an accusation of witchcraft was generally sufficient for condemnation; witch trials were designed not to establish guilt or innocence, but to provide victims for execution. Consequently, the trial, in the sense of an impartial attempt to ascertain the truth of charges, was sham, and often resembled the third-degree police interrogation of a thug. Since derogatory common report or gossip was considered sufficient proof for conviction, the evidence of witnesses was not really needed. Nevertheless, rules were established for witnesses. For example, all witnesses, including accused witches, were sworn. The oath used at Neuchâtel in 1659 is typical; the witness swore "by the belief he has in God, and the expectation he has of paradise, and to the peril and damnation of his soul, that the testimony is true; and may he exchange the abodes of heaven for hell, if he tells a lie"—Lardy. These rules, as well as those for the whole conduct of the trial, were first drawn up by the Inquisition, and were indeed "inquisitorial"—that is, the accused had to prove his innocence. This legal procedure was easily assimilated by the secular courts, for both derived from the same classical Roman codes.

The Inquisitor Sylvester Prierias gave the accepted position on witnesses in his *De Strigimagarum Daemonumque Mirandis* (1521). Ideally, said Prierias, there should be two witnesses. Their identity should not be made known, although the prisoner would be asked if he knew of any mortal enemies; if the prospective witnesses fell into this category, they should not be admitted. Prierias suggested, however, that the judge try to trap the prisoner by a series of moves designed as in a chess game:

> *Judge:* Have you any enemies who would charge you falsely?

Prisoner: [Either] (1) (if taken by surprise): No.
[Or] (2): Yes.
Judge: Why are these witnesses your enemies?
Prisoner: (Gives his reasons.)

The judge then assembled a panel of experts, who might know the relationship between the prisoner and the witnesses, to decide on the validity of the prisoner's bases of mortal enmity. Or the judge might try another gambit:

Judge: Do you know the principal witnesses against you?
Prisoner: [Either] (1): No. (Therefore he cannot later allege mortal enmity.)
[Or] (2) (guessing at possible witnesses): Yes.
Judge: Has this witness ever done any sorcery?
Prisoner: Yes (and describes it).
Judge: Is this witness a friend?
Prisoner: (In order that his previous reply may be believed): Yes. (Therefore he cannot charge a friend as a mortal enemy.)

If the prisoner demanded to be confronted with the witnesses, the judge was not bound to comply; but if the witnesses stated their readiness to repeat their evidence before the prisoner, the judge might permit their appearance. In rare cases, the judge might appoint a defense lawyer; but, if this lawyer defended the prisoner too earnestly, he rendered himself liable to charges of heresy. The names of the witnesses might be kept secret from the defense lawyer, or revealed in a different order from their evidence so the lawyer could not clearly identify them.

As in all trials for heresy, the prisoner was not allowed to call defense witnesses. The rare exceptions establish the rule. The prosecution witnesses could be persons disbarred in all other trials; such "infamous witnesses" were close relatives, such as a wife testifying against her husband, and vice versa, or a child against parents, and vice versa, or a servant testifying against his employer. In addition, evidence was accepted from accomplices (given under torture), perjurers, and—most infamous witnesses of all—excommunicated persons.

Later, but only under pressure, the Inquisition was forced to modify its stand, and in 1683 Cardinal Albizzi's *De Inconstantia in Jure Admittenda vel non* was printed in Rome, giving the official view of the Roman Inquisition on evidence and witnesses.

The English tradition of accusatorial law (that is, the prosecution must prove the guilt of the accused) prevented witch trials in England from becoming the complete mockery they were in Europe. However, England followed Continental custom in permitting infamous witnesses. A great many English men and women were hanged on the unsupported evidence of little children. The legal age of discretion was fourteen, but at the St. Osyth Trial in 1582:

A seven-year-old illegitimate daughter accused her mother, Agnes Heard.

An eight-year-old son accused his mother, Ursula Kemp.

A seven-year-old son and a nine-year-old son accused their mother, Cicely Celles.

At the third Chelmsford Trial in 1589, two young boys testified against their grandmother and their unwed mother (who was hanged on their evidence), and received the praises of the judge. In France, Boguet encouraged very young children to act as witnesses, for, said he, "Numberless witches have been discovered and brought to their just punishment by means of a child." Bodin, too, valued child witnesses because at their tender age they could easily be persuaded or forced to inform.

In Europe, most of those accused as witches were named as such by other accused persons under torture, which had for its chief purpose the identification of accomplices. Thus at Colombier (Neuchâtel), on January 5, 1630, Pierre Perret, about to be burned alive, identified thirty persons by name as present at a sabbat. Instead of witnesses, such persons might more properly be termed informers; and as such are treated in a separate entry [see Informers].

Würzburg Witch Trials

As to this matter of witches, which Your Grace thought over some time ago, it has started up again, and no words can adequately describe it. The woe and misery of it all! There are still 400 of both sexes in the city, of high and low estate, even clergy, so strongly accused that they may be arrested at any minute. It is certain that many of the people of my gracious Prince-Bishop here, of all offices and faculties, must be executed: clerics, electoral councilors and doctors, city officials, court assessors, several of whom Your Grace knows. Law students have been arrested. My lord the Prince-Bishop has more than forty students who should soon become priests, of whom thirteen or fourteen are said to be witches. A few days ago, a dean was arrested; two others who were summoned have fled. A notary of our cathedral consistory, a very learned man, was arrested yesterday and put to the torture. In one word, a third of the city is surely implicated. The richest, most attractive, most prominent of the clergy are already executed. A week ago, a girl of nineteen was burned, of whom it is said everywhere that she was the fairest in the whole city, and universally regarded as a girl of exceptional modesty and purity. In seven or eight days, she will be followed by others of the best and most attractive persons. Such people go in fresh mourning clothes undauntedly to their deaths, without a trace of fear of the flames. And thus many are burned for renouncing God and attending the sabbat, against whom nobody has ever else said a word.

To conclude this horrible matter, there are 300 children of three and four years, who are said to have had intercourse with the devil. I have seen children of seven put to death, and brave little scholars of ten, twelve, fourteen and fifteen years of age. Of the nobles—but I cannot and must not write any more about this misery. There will yet be persons of higher rank, whom you know and admire, and would scarcely believe it true of them. Let justice be done.

Then comes a postscript:

P.S. Many astounding and terrible things are happening. It is beyond doubt that, at a place called the Fraw Rengberg, the Devil in person with 8,000 of his followers, held an assembly and celebrated mass before them all, administering to his congregation (that is, the witches) rinds and parings of turnips in place of the Holy Sacrament of the Altar. I shudder to write about these foul, most horrible and hideous blasphemies. It is also true that they pledged themselves not to be enrolled in the Book of Life, and all have agreed that their decision should be recorded by a notary, who is well known to me and my colleagues. We hope, too, that the book in which they are enrolled will yet be found, and everybody is diligently searching for it.

This remarkable letter describing Würzburg in August, 1629, was written in German by the Chancellor of the Prince-Bishop of Würzburg to some (unidentified) distinguished friend. In its human tones, the stark reality of witchcraft, a facet often ignored by those who picture witches as unwanted ugly old women [see Witch], is graphically portrayed.

At this time, the bishopric of Würzburg paralleled the bishopric of Bamberg in the savagery of its witch hunts, conducted by two cousins, Prince-Bishop Philipp Adolf von Ehrenberg of Würzburg (1623-31), who burned 900 witches, and Prince-Bishop Gottfried Johann Georg II Fuchs von Dornheim of Bamberg (1623-33), who burned 600 witches. As in Austria and Bavaria, the Jesuits (invited into Bamberg in 1612) were mainly responsible for starting the hysteria in the two bishoprics, surrounding Bishop Philipp as policy advisers.

Following the death of Bishop Julius Echter von Mespelbrunn in 1617, a new bishop came from Bamberg, Johann Gottfried von Auschhausen (1617-23), but, although there had been random executions since 1600, the real terror did not break until Bishop Philipp Adolf succeeded to the throne in 1623. Records for 1627 to 1631 are incomplete; for example, one account lists only twenty-nine executions in 1627, but another gives forty-two. A few typical trials may be mentioned:

In 1626 a peasant was accused on com

mon gossip of *maleficia;* under torture he involved seven others, who were burned, one of them being first torn with red-hot pincers. In January, 1628, three children, the oldest thirteen, the youngest eight, confessed to intercourse with the devil; two were burned, and the youngest remanded for correction [see Sexual Relations with Devils]. In October of the same year, a schoolboy named Johann Philipp Schuck was interrogated; after forty-six lashes, he still denied, but after seventy-seven more he made a full confession of attending the sabbat and named his accomplices. He was killed November 9. Another schoolboy, Jacob Russ, aged twelve, after repeated floggings made a similar confession and accused priests of being at the sabbat. He was killed November 10.

Hauber, in his *Bibliotheca Magica* (Lemgo, 1738), printed a list dated February 16, 1629, of twenty-nine separate mass executions at Würzburg, totaling 157 persons. The list included nearly as many men as women, many highly placed and wealthy people, as well as children, thirteen of them aged twelve or younger. Although well known, the partial list from a contemporary document may emphasize the extent of the delusion in one year:

A LIST OF WITCHES WHO SUFFERED DEATH BY THE EXECUTIONER'S SWORD AND WHOSE BODIES WERE THEN BURNED AT WÜRZBURG

Fifth execution, eight persons:
Lutz, a distinguished merchant. A merchant named Rutscher. The wife of the chief provost of the cathedral. Old mother Hof Seiler. The wife of Johann Steinbach. The wife of a senator named Baunach. A woman named Babel Znickel. An old woman.

Seventh execution, seven persons:
A little girl, a stranger, aged twelve. A stranger. A stranger, a woman. A village mayor, a stranger. Three women, strangers. At the same time was executed in the market place a guard who had let some prisoners escape.

Eighth execution, seven persons:
The Senator Baunach, the fattest burgher in Würzburg. The chief provost of the cathedral. A stranger. A man named Schleipner. A woman who sold vizors. Two women, strangers.

Tenth execution, three persons:
Steinacher, one of the wealthiest citizens. Two strangers, a man and a woman.

Eleventh execution, four persons:
A vicar of the cathedral named Schwerdt. The wife of the Provost of Rensacker. A woman named Stiecher. A man named Silberhans, a fiddler.

Thirteenth execution, four persons:
Old Hof-Schmidt. An old woman. A little girl nine or ten years old. Her younger sister.

Nineteenth execution, six persons:
A son of a nobleman from Rotenham was executed at six o'clock in the courtyard of the Town Hall, and his body burned on the following day. The wife of Secretary Schellhar. Another woman. A boy, ten years old. Another boy, twelve years old. A baker's wife named Brügler was burned alive.

Twenty-first execution, six persons:
The Master of the Dieterich hospital, a very learned man. A man named Stoffel Holtzmann. A boy fourteen years old. The young son of Senator Stolzberger. Two seminarians.

Twenty-third execution, nine persons:
The son of David Crot, a boy aged twelve in the upper school. The two young sons of the Prince-Bishop's cook, schoolboys, the elder fourteen and the younger twelve years old. Melchior Hammelmann, parish priest of Hach. Nicodemus Hirsch, a canon of the new cathedral. Christopher Berger, a vicar of the new cathedral. A seminarian. N.B. An officer of the Court of Brembach and a seminarian were burned alive.

Twenty-fifth execution, six persons:
Frederick Basser, a vicar of the cathedral chapter. Stab, parish priest of Hach. Lambrecht, a canon of the new cathedral. The wife of Gallus Haus. A boy, a stranger. A woman named Schelmerey, a shopkeeper.

Twenty-sixth execution, seven persons:
David Hans, a canon of the new cathedral. The Senator Weydenbusch. The

wife of the innkeeper at Baumgarten. An old woman. The young daughter of Valkenberger was executed privately and the body burned in a coffin. The young son of an officer of the Council. Wagner, a vicar of the cathedral chapter, was burned alive.

Twenty-ninth execution, nine persons:
Viertel Beck. Klingen, an innkeeper. The steward of Mergelsheim. The wife of the baker at the Oxen Gate. A fat noblewoman. N.B. A doctor of theology, named Meyer, of Hach, and a canon of Hach were executed secretly at five o'clock in the morning; their bodies were burned. A gentleman of rank, named Squire Fischbaum. Paul Vaecker of Breit-Hüt. Since then there have been two other executions, February 16, 1629.

About this time a young relative of the Prince-Bishop's was beheaded as a witch. The boy was the Prince-Bishop's sole heir, and had he lived would have inherited considerable wealth. The incident is described by a Jesuit, one of the advisers who seemed responsible for it. Ernest von Ehrenberg was a model student with a brilliant future, but, it was said, he suddenly left his studies to run after an older woman. He turned to drink and dissipation. The Jesuits subtly questioned him and decided he was engaged in all kinds of vice, including frequenting the sabbat. Ernest was denounced and, without his knowledge, secretly tried and sentenced. One morning at seven, the boy was awakened and told he was going to lead a better life. Unsuspecting, he was led to the castle and into the black-draped torture chamber. At the sight of the horrors, Ernest fainted. Some of the judges were so moved that they asked the Prince-Bishop for mercy, but Philipp Adolf renewed the order for execution. Ernest resisted the hangman and, in a melee, was hit over the head. The Jesuit who recorded the scene, continued: "He fell to the ground without any sign of grief or any manifestation of piety. *Utinam non etiam in eternum rogum cecidisset*—May God grant he does not fall like this into eternal fires of Hell!"

After the execution, the Prince-Bishop perhaps had a change of heart, for he instituted commemorative services for victims of the witch trials, and the hysteria started to diminish. The march of the Swedish Protestant army also helped to halt, at least temporarily, the executions. Nevertheless, whatever his repentance, and whether he acted with or without the promptings of his Jesuit advisers, the record of Prince-Bishop Philipp Adolf is black. Some writers (like Diefenbach) have tried to whitewash him, calling him "not a man of cruel nature," and blaming "his worldly counselors [who] urged him to decisions which disgraced his name and position." Leitschuh also regarded him as "otherwise noble and pious." With Jules Baissac, however, one falters to accept such standards for judging a man who permitted children of nine and ten to be burned.

Youghal Witch: see Newton, Florence.

Young, Alice: see Connecticut Witches.

BOOKS FOR FURTHER READING

(Numbers refer to titles in SELECT BIBLIOGRAPHY)

Most readers will obtain all the general information they need in this *Encyclopedia*. Those wishing to explore witchcraft further will soon find they need the resources of a major library and the ability to read German, French, and Latin. The following items are recommended for a basic library for a small college or town or for the individual booklover.

General work on witchcraft: 979, though based on original sources, impaired by literal belief in witchcraft delusion. Not recommended: 742, 743, 744, speculative and unscholarly; 531, 709 (tr. 710, 711), accept actuality of witchcraft.

Works on witchcraft in England: 264, best-informed general survey; 343, outstanding work based on original documents;

340, another first-class, reliable study; 512, useful anthology of extracts from original sources.

Works on witchcraft in America: 963, authoritative, well-written, a standard; 150, selections from documents and contemporary books on Salem, essential.

Works on witchcraft in Europe: 978, useful, if allowance made for absurd obscurantism; 945 (German), illustrated, outstanding work emphasizing German witchcraft, essential, scarce; 44 (French), outstanding and authoritative work emphasizing French witchcraft, unfortunately rare.

Work on demoniacal possession: 538, describes typical and most famous of disturbances in French convents.

Translations of standard demonologists: 986, 988, 990, 992, 993, available only in limited editions.

Source books on witchcraft: 607, collections of notes and quotations, many in original languages; little material on England; Burr's introduction an outstanding essay on witchcraft; essential for any public library. 471 (German), comparable and supplementary, source book of original extracts from standard authorities; advanced study only; scarce.

Survey of literature of witchcraft: 149 and 153, repr. 151; both excellent, but specialized.

CLASSIFIED SUBJECT BIBLIOGRAPHIES

(Numbers refer to titles in SELECT BIBLIOGRAPHY)

Aberdeen Witches: 846; partly repr. 5, 644.
Ady, Thomas: 6 (rare). Not listed *DNB*.
Aix-en-Provence Nuns: Detailed account from original documents 649. See also 418. Bibliography 1131 (Items 1260-70). 704 (tr. 705) slanted and tedious. 201 discusses Madeleine de Demandolx and Marie de Sains. Accounts in most standard authorities: 44, 161 (Vol. I), 192 (Vol. III), 400.
Alexander VI, Pope: Text 270. Bull of Adrian VI tr. 978.
Allier, Elisabeth: 859.
Alphonsus de Spina: 15, abstracted 607 (Vol. I).
Amber Witch: 691 (tr. 692); discussed 888.
Aquinas, Thomas: 24, 25. General summary 472, 945; also 670 (by Dominican apologist); all three works reviewed 521. See also 379, 824.
Arras Witches: 640, 844, 856. Latin tract 471.
Austria, Witchcraft in: Code 222; discussed 656, 933 (pro). Trials in Tyrol 1137; see also 841, 870 (Styria). Handbooks of Mozel and Frölich described 607 (Vol. III).
Auxonne Nuns: 403.
Bamberg Witch Trials: 584, 621, noted 607 (Vol. III). Sources for trials 482 (Vol. III), 1123. Exhaustive study for all Rhineland 791. Many MSS. of trials in Cornell Univ. Lib., some used in 411. See Johannes Junius for trial of Bamberg burgomaster.
Barclay, Margaret: 917, 1034.
Bargarran Impostor: 858; 437, repr. 745, included in 508 (by ? Rev. James Dodds, or ? J. Miller), abstracted 30, 120, 607 (Vol. III), 935.
Basque Witches: See Lancre; also 56, 81, 107 (with selections), 176, 589 (briefly noted, 607, Vol. III), 628 (résumé of trials 1393-1672); see also 947, 1067.
Bateman, Mary: 349.
Bavaria, Witchcraft in: 460, 944; 871, noted 607 (Vol. III), opposed 311.
Baxter, Richard: 62; life 822; see also 408.
Bekker, Balthasar: 68 (tr. 70, 71), 69 (English tr.) answered by 65 (German tr. 66). General controversy summarized 607 (Vol. III).
Bier Right: 806 (Vol. III); discussed 609; fictionalized account 916.
Bilson Boy: 128; discussed 533 (1720 ed. only).
Binsfeld, Peter: 86, 87 (tr. 88); both abstracted 607 (Vol. II).
Black Mass: 136, 159, 188, 866, 910 (with invocation). See also 536 (tr. 537).
Blanckenstein Tragedy: 854, abstracted 607 (Vol. III).

Bodin, Jean: 99 (tr. 100, 101), abstracted 607 (Vol. II); 102 (pub. posthumously). Biography 58. Discussion of views on witchcraft 84, 372, 575, 671, 672.
Boguet, Henri: 103 (tr. 104).
Bordelon, Laurent: 113 (English tr. 114); German tr. (Danzig, 1712). Discussed 474. 1064 in same tradition.
Bouvet, Le Sieur: 124.
Bovet, Richard: 125 (rare).
Buirmann, Franz: Gibbons in 410; detailed 303.
Burton Boy: 732; discussed 819 (Harrison's ed.); also 340. See John Darrell, Samuel Harsnett.
Bury St. Edmunds Witches: 1036, repr. 529 (Vol. VI). The dates of certain days of the week (mentioned in the text) correspond, not with 1664, but with 1662, the actual year of the trial. Case devastatingly analyzed 533. Most general works comment on trial, e.g., 763; 568 is more favorable to Hale.
Cadière, Catherine: Almost 100 contemporary accounts, all now rare, listed in 1131 (Items 1407-81); English quotations from original sources. 847 (8 vols., sometimes bound in 6 or 7 vols.) includes *Justification de Demoiselle Catherine Cadière, Memoire instructif de . . . Cadière, Mémoire du Père Girard,* etc., collection of Girard's letters, court reports, etc., 36 items in all. Similar 848, seven texts, including *Justification,* mostly pr. 1731 at various places. Many texts tr. into English, e.g., 183, 218, 274. Trial described in most standard authorities, e.g., 44, 192 (Vol. III), 400. 709 (tr. 710, 711) is unreliable. The nature of the trial, coupled with hostility to Jesuits, produced several obscene illustrated pamphlets; for refs. see 978; see also earlier anti-Jesuit satire 17.
Canon Episcopi: Original text 270, 850; discussed 471, 607 (Vol. I). The Canon remained a point of controversy: see Early Writers on Witchcraft.
Carolina Code: 576; abstracted 471; discussed 295.
Carpzov, Benedict: 175; abstracted 607 (Vol. III). See 294, 792, 976; also 775.
Cassini, Samuel de: 184; abstracted 471, 607 (Vol. I); answered by a Dominican 299, abstracted 471.
Chambre Ardente Affair: Court records 843 (Vols. V, VI, VII). See 328, 391, 722 (good bibliography), 747, 1039. See also 926 (Vol. V). Summarized in English 1111 (without refs.); highly colored account 978.

Channel Islands, Witchcraft in: 807; see also 48, 238.
Charms: 1054 (tr. 1055). Examples of charms 914; early English 212; Scottish 166; others 512, 658.
Chelmsford Witches: 345, unique copy in Lambeth Palace Lib., repr. 343; partly repr. 512, 763, 1111. Second trial 288; partly repr. 216 (rare); outlined 340, 763. Third trial 23, unique copy also in Lambeth; 340 (résumé).
Cideville Case: English tr. of court records by Lang in 832 (Vol. XVIII) and 591. French eyewitness 714; expanded 713; summarized 733, 783. Recent retelling 940.
Cirvelo, Pedro Sanchez: 207 (tr. 208, 209), discussed 607 (Vol. I).
Coggeshall Witch: Detailed account by vicar 129. Later parallel, Ann Izzard manhandled by crowd at St. Neots but saved by a vicar, 758.
Cologne Witch Trials: Exhaustive study based on Cologne archives 791. See also 330, 411.
Confessions: Reproductions of confessions from MSS. in Cornell Univ. Lib. Questions at Colmar 946; other lists of questions 76, 293; confessions and torture 757.
Connecticut Witches: Best contemporary source 687; modern account 1006; Mary Parsons 306. Various local and historical publications deal with individual witches, e.g., Ann Cole 509; Elizabeth Knap 440, 630, 1106.
Cory, Giles: 1051; preliminary examination 307. Longfellow immortalized Giles and Martha Cory in "Giles Corey of the Salem Farms."
Costs of Witch Trials: Seven examples: 1074 (abstracted 607, Vol. III), 1046, 286, 846, 215, 30, 1051. Other costs 75.
Coven: 744; supported 399, 531; refuted 338, 560. See also 523. 789 is a sensible paperback relating European witchcraft and African sorcery.
Crouch, Nathaniel: 234 (very rare). *DNB* errs in dating 1706.
Darrell, John: Three tracts on Somers 253, 255, 254; answered by Harsnett 477, evoking Darrell's 256. Lancashire exorcisms 259; opposed 267, 268; Darrell's equally dull replies 257, 258. Supported by 53 (perhaps by James Barnford, minister of Southwark). Most tracts without place, but probably London. See also 601, Burton Boy, Samuel Harsnett.
Dee, John: For mass of MSS. materials, see *DNB*. Autobiographical materials 271, 272, 273; biographies 430, 943. Modern discussion 360 (stand-

study 344). Political background 35 (English tr. 36); attempted refutation 696; other contemporary accounts 755 (English tr. 756), 996. Modern accounts 83 (full, good bibliography), 96, 365, 627 (attempt to show possessions genuine), 810, 895. Religious background 134 (monumental; English tr. 135). Fictionalized accounts 315, 316 (play), 1038, 1063 (play).

Louis XIV: Edict of 1682: 44, 542; English tr. of Request of Normandy Parlement 978. Trial exposed 889, answered 108, noted 44, 161, 192, 400.

Louviers Nuns: 505 (English tr. 506, with intro. and extensive bibliography), 1132 (with 14 other rare contemporary accounts). Discussed in most standard accounts on French witchcraft, e.g., 44, 161, 192, 400. Detailed 51. 431 (French tr. 432) is not reliable; nor is 709 (English tr. 710, 711; 708 is better). English summary (based on 161) 666.

Luxeuil Witch Trial: Verbatim transcripts of the secret evidence and ensuing trial 59.

Lycanthrope of Angers: 586.

Lycanthropy: See Vampire, which differs from the werewolf by its origin in a revenant or zombi. French demonologists distinguished a special variety of werewolf called loublins, which frequented burial grounds to eat corpses. Early standard works on lycanthropy 200, 325, 367, Rhanaeus in 559, 772 (English tr. 773), 765, 800, 830, 1023. Standard demonologists, especially 99, 103, 589. Typical of German dissertations on werewolves 1018. Modern discussions 44 (3 good chapters, but scarce), 52 (very reliable), 119 (for case in 1595), 123, 468 (good), 768 (credulous and undocumented), 821 (chatty and routine), 983 (pedantic and credulous, but interesting). Stories of early werewolves 409, 420, 675, 1109. See further 80, 321, 323 (psychological approach), 556 (good), 971. Bibliography of fiction 942; fictionalized accounts include 82, 313 (tr. 314), 402, 494, 527, and Guy de Maupassant's well-known short story, Le loup.

Magee Island Witch Trial: 746, quoted 1129. Also 927 (with bibliography).

Malleus Maleficarum: 958 (English tr. 959; German tr. 960), abstracted 607 (Vol. I) from 1580 Frankfort ed. 470, 471, 472, summarized 607 (Vol. I). See also 736, 879. Useful general comments 1111.

Mather, Cotton: 682, 683, 684, 685; with the exception of the curiosities discussed here, few of Mather's 437 published works are now read; original copies scarce. Bibliography 515; same author whitewashes Mather's part in witch hunts 516. "The Return of Several Ministers upon the Present Witchcrafts in Salem Village" appended to Increase Mather 686, and later in Cotton Mather 683. 150 prints from MS., "A Brand Plucked out of the Burning" (1693), narrative of Mercy Short, and selections from other works. Other selections 738. 307 prints 685 and 160 (Calef), superior ed. to 377. Biography using Mather's own words 1090; another biography 98.

Mather, Increase: Among his 150 works, most important here is 687, better known by its changed running title, Remarkable Providences, abstracted 150. 686 in part discusses spectral evidence.

Meyfarth, Johann Matthäus: 703, abstracted 607 (Vol. II).

Molitor, Ulrich: 718 (two German tr. 720, 721). 607 (Vol. I) summarizes from 1580 ed., Tractatus de Phtonicis Mulieribus; many eds. have slightly variant titles, e.g., Tractatus de Lamiis et Pythonicis (Paris, 1561). Molitor wrote lania for the more common lamia. The ed. used here is the first, 1489 (? Cologne), illustrated with six quaint woodcuts; also repr. facs. with French tr. 719.

Mora Witches: 424, 578; and frequently retold, e.g., 533, 684.

More, Henry: 726, most conveniently read (with other selections) 662. Standard biography 1084; see also 19, 408.

—use-Maker: 854, abstracted 607 (Vol. III).

—bury Witch: 729.

—on, Florence: 424 (ed. of 1726); also 132; —lern retelling 927. See also 390.

—York Witches: The Hall documents (de—ed by fire in 1911) first pr. in 1821, then Harrison) in 767; both originals best ac—e 150. Harrison case 786.

Nider, Johannes: 759, abstracted 607 (Vol. I); 760, noted 607 (Vol. I); biography 901.

Nightmare: Freudian account 556.

North Berwick Witches: 754, repr. 215, 806; see further 638, 644, 935.

Norway, Witchcraft in: 42.

Nypen, Ole and Lisbet: 42.

Ointment, Flying: 200, 765 (noted 983), 815. For plants see 415, 519, 1008. See also 944, 1086.

Ointment, Killing: 681.

Osborne, Ruth: Gentleman's Magazine (1751), repr. 512. See also 1129.

Pact with the Devil: The 1676 pact is added at the end of 818.

Paris Witch Trial: 319 (Vol. II), abstracted 373. The first trial described in Cornhill Magazine, Vol. XXX (1874).

Pendle Swindle: 1087 (Appendix); also described 264. Thomas Heywood based his topical play, The Late Lancashire Witches (1634), on this scandal.

Perkins, William: 795.

Perth Witch Trial: May 15 trial 806; later trials 825; Borrowstones trial 846.

Pico della Mirandola, Gianfrancesco: 803 (2 Italian tr. 804, 805), abstracted 471, 607 (Vol. I).

Pittenweem Witches: 935 (1871 ed. with addit. documents); also 215 (quoting from contemporary minutes and proceedings of kirk sessions and "Letter from a Gentleman in Fife"). Confessions 318. See also 882.

Poltergeist: Modern examples are not included here. Succinct and scholarly account by Andrew Lang in 11th ed. Encyclopaedia Britannica, Vol. XXII; also articles, "Haunting" (Vol. XIII), and "Poltergeist" in 832; also 590 (with Celtic examples) and 591 (general). Standard work, with good bibliography, 827 (but occultist in approach); also comprehensive 177, 940 (ten examples using original documents), and 978 (summary of typical cases). Podmore in 832 (Vol. XII) shows trickery as well as rational explanations of poltergeists. See also 235 (English and German examples), 511, 687 (early American stories), 783 (somewhat unreliable). Stone-Throwing Devil 194, repr. 150. Checklist of 375 examples, with articles on "poltergeist psychosis," 178; list to be supplemented by examples from 65, 125, 453 (tr. 454), and 568. Still older authorities discussing poltergeists include 598 (tr. 599), 623 (tr. 624), 1023, 1037. Most general works on demonology include a chapter on poltergeists, but material is largely repetitive. Detailed accounts of specific poltergeists, mostly recent, in 832 (esp. Vols. IV, VII, XII, XVII, XVIII, XXV). Fictionalized account in Sir Walter Scott, Woodstock (1826).

Ponzinibio, Gianfrancesco: 814.

Possession: A standard source book for epidemics, though now outdated, 161; also 487. Modern general survey 770 (with list of sources). See also 14, 199, 203, 365 (esp. for possession in nunneries), 404 (also for nunneries), 753, 799, 944, 979, 1025. For early scientific approach see 260, 276, 289, 335, 490 (with approval of Abp. of Rouen), 502, 868, 873, 895. The story of Martha Brossier tr. into English 480; Marie de Sains 724; 1681 Toulouse case 64. The first Louviers treatise 1029; the other 116.

Pott, Johannes Henricus: 818, abstracted 607 (Vol. II).

Quaker Witchcraft: 358 (Quaker opposition to delusion), 378 (Fox), 380 (Franklin's satire), 457 (general history), 688 (Quaker account of Salem).

Rais, Gilles de: Original Latin documents 118, the basis of later books; French tr. 493. The attribution of Bluebeard rests on an unrelated Breton legend. See also 112, 117, 394 (English tr. 395), 635, 701, 1065, 1072; and 310 (novel).

Remy, Nicholas: 860 (tr. 861, 862, 863). Discussed 41 (trial in 1583), 281 (notes that in court records details of copulation relatively rare), 296, 374, 613, 801.

Renata, Sister Maria: Many original MSS., including Sister Maria's confession, in Cornell Univ. Lib. See 110 (debate between Gaar and Tartarotti, noted 607, Vol. III), 311 (Vol. IV), 392, 431 (tr. 432), 525 (Vol. III for Loschert, repr. 674), 695, 900 (minutes of trial); 945 (Vol. II). Two other executions for witchcraft occurred in Germany in 1749: Anna Maria Baverin at Salzburg and a seamstress at Neumarkt.

Rule, Margaret: Cotton Mather's account and correspondence with Calef 160, summarized 682.

Sabbat: Notable accounts of the sabbat in most demonologists, especially 38, 99, 103, 283, 453, 589. French writers generally detailed; English slight and vague. Confessions of nuns about sabbat 704 (tr. 705), 724. Confessions from trials 198, 653 (six plates and two transcripts). Notes on early nocturnal gatherings 607 (Vol. I). Modern composite accounts 122, 136 (second-hand and over-popular), 157, 709 (unreliable, should be considered fiction). A curious Italian attack on the delusion of the sabbat 1004. Two 19th-century dramas on the sabbat: Jules Bois, Les noces de Satan, and Roland Brévannes, Les messes noires.

St. Osyth Witches: 1043, summarized 644, discussed 340, 343, 512, 568, 763.

Salazar de Frias, Alonzo: 605 (Vol. IV), also discussed 1111.

Salem Witch Trials: Best book for modern reader 963 (documented, readable, authentic, and excellent bibliography). Copies of MSS. of trials collected by Federal Writers Project in typescript at Salem Court House. Best printed collection of court records 1126 (rare). Five trials repr. 633; others 197. Contemporary accounts include Thomas Brattle's letter, 160, 603, 685, 1105, all five repr. with other materials 150 (indispensable). 633 prints extracts. Calef and Mather elaborately ed. 307. Richard Pike's letter 1051 (Vol. II). 603 also in 978. Contemporary Quaker account 688. Standard authority on Salem 1051 (brilliant study, now rare), superseding 1050; deriving therefrom is another classic 752. 1003 is a short biography of Rebecca Nurse. Recommended for young people 544 (derived from 1051, deletes death of Cory). Most other books about Salem are derivative and careless, and need not be perpetuated here. Much detailed information in journals of local historical societies (see 963). Many fictionalized versions, including 47, 186, 371, 401, 469, 485, 855; bibliography 777. Outstanding drama 712; equally outstanding, though neglected, 364.

Salmon Falls Assaults: 687, repr. 978.

Schüler, Johann: 524 (Vol. II), 579, abstracted 607 (Vol. III), 945, 978.

Schultheis, Heinrich von: 909, unique copy in Cornell Univ. Lib., noted 607 (Vol. II).

Schwägel, Anna Maria: 460, abstracted 607 (Vol. III), retold 978.

Scot, Reginald: 914; only English work on witchcraft to be tr. into Dutch 915.

Scotland, Witchcraft in: Excellent detailed bibliographies 92, 362. Contemporary tracts infrequent in Scottish trials, but the best repr. 215 (with other documents). Primary sources are published court records, e.g., 30, 95, 806; also scattered records 1, 140, 195, 715, 825, 831, 846. Best summary of legal system 661. Two essential books, with some primary materials, 917, 935. Special areas in 1, 202, 508, 1125. Selected trials retold in 5, 883; trial of Janet Horne basis of Dmitri Merejkowski's Romance of Leonardo da Vinci. General accounts 166, 244, 644. Good basic history 930. Four tales by Burns, Scott, Stevenson 97; other stories and anecdotes 263.

Sentence: 706 (English tr. with sentence in Latin 707), repr. in Latin 453. Ceremony at Neuchâtel 596, Saxony 175, Prussia 579.

Sexual Relations with Devils: Standard demonologists with especially full accounts 87, 99, 103, 283, 453, 625, 860. Special studies 569, 818, 937 (tr. 938, 939). See also 381, 384. The Vaudois tract is repr. 471.

Sherwood, Grace: 239, 1108.

Short, Mercy: 150.

Sinclair, George: 934, 935.

Sinistrari, Ludovico Maria: 937 (tr. 938, 939), noted 607 (Vol. II).

Spain, Witchcraft in: 206, 606 (Vol. IV), 978.

Spee, Friedrich von: 952, French tr. 953, German tr. 954, another German tr. included in 1017. Biographies 169, 887; connection with witchcraft 225, 320, 1140 (detailed). See also 312, two informative articles 554, 973, and note 857. Mentioned in 1111. Question 51 tr. with some omissions 152; extracts tr. 913, abstracted 607 (Vol. II). Story of Leibnitz quoted in 621. Schultheis' attack on Spee later refuted by Löher.

Spina, Bartolommeo: 956.

Stapirius, Michael: 411.

SELECT BIBLIOGRAPHY

1. *Abbotsford Club Miscellany*, Vol. I (Edinburgh, 1837).
2. *Abdruck aktenmässiger Hexenprozesse: Das Büchlein enthält Berichte von Prozessen aus den Jahren 1590-1637* (Eichstätt, 1811).
3. *Account of the trial . . . of Jane Wenham* (London, 1712).
4. *Account of the Trial . . . of Six Witches at Maidstone* (London, 1645, 1837, ltd. ed.).
5. Adams, William Henry Davenport, *Witch, Warlock, and Magician* (London, 1889).
6. Ady, Thomas, *A Candle in the Dark* (London, 1656; 2d ed., *A Perfect Discovery of Witches*, London, 1661).
7. Ainsworth, William Harrison, *The Lancashire Witches* (London, 1848).
8. Albe, Edmond, *Hughes Géraud, évêque de Cahors: l'affaire des poisons et des envoûtements en 1317* (Cahors, 1904, ltd. ed.).
9. Alberghini, Giovanni, *Manuale Qualificatorum Sanctae Inquisitionis* (Palermo, 1642; Cologne, 1740).
10. Alberti, Valentin, *De Sagis* (Leipzig, [1690]).
11. Albertini, Arnaldo, *De Agnoscendis Assertionibus Catholicis et Hereticis Tractatus* (Rome, 1572).
12. Albizzi, Cardinal, *De Inconstantia in Jure Admittenda vel Non* (Amsterdam [i.e., Rome], 1683).
13. Alciatus, Andreas, *Parergon Juris* (Basel, 1558, 1582).
14. Alexander, William Menzies, *Demonic Possession in the New Testament* (Edinburgh, 1902).
15. Alphonsus de Spina, *Fortalicium Fidei* (Strasbourg, 1467; Nuremberg, 1485, 1494; Venice, 1487; Lyons, 1525).
16. Alphonsus de Vera Cruz, *Speculum Conjugiorum* (Milan, 1599).
17. *Les Amours de Sainfroid, Jésuite, et d'Eulalie, fille dévote* (La Haye, 1729).
18. Anania, Giovanni Lorenzo, *De Natura Demonum* (Venice, 1581; Rome, 1654; Lyons, 1669).
19. Anderson, Paul Russell, *Science in Defense of Liberal Religion* (New York, 1933).
20. Angles, Jos., *Flores Theologicarum Quaestionum* (Venice, 1584).
21. Anhorn, Bartholomäus, *Magiologia: Christliche Warnung für dem Aberglauben und Zauberey* (Basel, 1674).

22. *An Apology for Antonia Bourignon* (London, 1699).
23. *The Apprehension and Confession of Three Notorious Witches Arraigned and by Justice Condemned in the County of Essex* (London, 1589).
24. Aquinas, Thomas, *Opuscula* [including *De Operationibus Occultis Naturae; De Sortibus*] (Paris, 1927).
25. ———— *Quaestiones Quodlibetales* (Paris, 1926).
26. Arbaumont, Joseph d', "Autour d'un procès de sorcellerie au commencement du xvii⁰ siècle," *Académie des sciences . . . de Besançon* (1907).
27. Argentinus, Richardus, *De Praestigiis et Incantationibus Daemonum* (Basel, 1568).
28. Aries, Martinus, *De Superstitionibus Maleficorum et Sortilegiorum* (Rome, 1559).
29. Arles y Andosilla, Martin de, *Tractatus de Superstitionibus* (Paris, 1517; Venice, 1584).
30. Arnot, Hugo, *A Collection and Abridgment of Celebrated Criminal Trials in Scotland, 1563-1784* (Glasgow, 1785, 1812).
31. *Arrest memorable de la cour de parlement de Dôle . . . contre Gilles Garnier* (Sens, 1574).
32. Ashton, John, *The Devil in Britain and America* (London, 1896).
33. [Assier, Alexandre,] *Le diable en Champagne* (Paris, 1869, ltd. ed.).
34. Aubenas, Roger, *La sorcière et l'inquisiteur: épisode de l'Inquisition en Provence, 1439* (Aix-en-Provence, 1956).
35. [Aubin, Nicholas,] *Cruels effets de la vengeance du Cardinal de Richelieu ou histoire des diables de Loudun* (Amsterdam, 1693, 1716, 1737, 1752).
36. ———— (English tr. perhaps by Daniel Defoe) *The Cheats and Illusions of Romish Priests and Exorcists Discovered in the History of the Devils of Loudun* (London, 1703).
37. Automne, Bernard, *La conférence du droit français avec le droit romain* (Paris, 1629).
38. Autun, Jacques d', *L'incrédulité savante et la crédulité ignorante au sujet des magiciens et des sorciers* (Lyons, 1671, 1674).
39. Axenfeld, Alexandre, *Jean Wier et la sorcellerie* (Paris, 1866).

40. Bach, Adolf, *Hexenprozesse in der Vogtei Ems* (Bad Ems, 1923).
41. Badel, Emile, *D'une sorcière qu'aultrefois on brusla dans Sainct-Nicholas* (Nancy, 1891, ltd. ed.).
42. [Baetzmann, Frederick,] *Hexevaesen og Troldskab i Norge* (Oslo, 1865).
43. Baissac, Jules, *Le Diable* (Paris, 1882).
44. ———— *Les grands jours de la sorcellerie* (Paris, 1890).
45. ———— *Histoire de la diablerie chrétienne* (Paris, [1882]).
46. ———— *Satan ou le diable* (Paris, 1876).
47. Baker, Shirley, *Peace, My Daughter* (New York, 1949).
48. Balleine, G. R., "Witch Trials in Jersey," *Société Jersiaise, Bulletin*, Vol. XIII (1939).
49. *Bambergische Halsgerichtsordnung* [compiled by Johann Freiherr von Schwarzenberg und Hohlandsberg] (Mainz, 1508).
50. Bang, Vilhelm, *Hexevaesen og Hexeforfølgelser isaer i Danmark* (Copenhagen, 1896).
51. Barbe, Lucien, "Histoire du couvent de Saint-Louis de Louviers," *Bulletin de la Société d'études diverses de Louviers*, Vol. V (1898).
52. Baring-Gould, *The Book of Werewolves* (London, 1865).
53. [? Barnford, James,] *The Trial of Master Darrell or a Collection of Defenses Against Allegations Not Yet Suffered to Receive Convenient Answer* ([London,] 1593).
54. Barrett, Francis, *The Magus or Celestial Intelligencer, Being a Complete System of Occult Philosophy* (London, 1801).
55. Barrett, Wilfred Phelps, *The Trial of Jeanne d'Arc* (London, 1931; New York, 1932).
56. Barthéty, Hilarion, *La sorcellerie en Béarn et dans le pays Basque* (Pau, 1879).
57. Bataille, Albert, *Les causes criminelles et mondaines* (Paris, 1880).
58. Baudrillart, Henri, *Jean Bodin* (Paris, 1853).
59. Bavoux, Francis, *Hantises et diableries dans la terre abbatiale de Luxeuil d'un procès d'Inquisition, 1529, à l'épidémie démoniaque de 1628-30* (Monaco, 1956).
60. ———— *La sorcellerie en Franche-Comté* (Monaco, [1954]).
61. ———— *La sorcellerie au pays de Quingey* (Besançon, 1947).

62. Baxter, Richard, *The Certainty of the World* of Spirits (London, 1691, 1834).

63. —— (German tr.) *Die Gewissheit der Geister* (Nuremberg, 1691, 1731, 1755).

64. Bayle, François and Henri Grangeron, *Relation de l'état de quelques personnes prétendues possédées faite d'autorité du Parlement de Toulouse* (Toulouse, 1682).

65. Beaumont, John, *An Historical, Physiological and Theological Treatise of Spirits, Apparitions, Witchcrafts, and Other Magical Practices* (London, 1705).

66. —— (German tr.) *Tractat von Geistern* (Halle, 1721).

67. Beaune, Henri, "Les sorciers de Lyon," *Académie des sciences . . . de Dijon, Mém.*, II Série, Vol. XIV (1868).

68. Bekker, Balthasar, *De Betoverde Weereld* (Leeuwarden and Amsterdam, 1691-93; Deventer, 1739).

69. —— (English tr. by B. B. A.) *The World Bewitched* (London, 1695; reissued as *The World Turned Upside Down, or a Plain Detection of Errors*, London, 1700).

70. —— (French tr.) *Le monde enchanté* (Amsterdam, 1694).

71. —— (German tr.) *Die bezauberte Welt* (Amsterdam, 1693; Leipzig, 1781).

72. Bell, John, *The Trial of Witchcraft or Witchcraft Arraigned and Condemned* (Glasgow, 1697, [1705 ?]).

73. Belon, Marie Joseph, *Jean Bréhal, grand inquisiteur de France et la réhabilitation de Jeanne d'Arc* (Paris, 1893).

74. Bénet, Armand, *Procès verbal fait pour délivrer une fille possédée par le malin esprit à Louviers* (Paris, 1883).

75. Benton, Rita, *Franklin and Other Plays* [*Margaret of Salem*] (New York, 1924).

76. Bercet, Gaston, "Sorciers du pays d'Avesnes," *Annales de cercle archéologique de Mons*, Vol. XXIX (1899).

77. Bergstrand, Carl Martin, *Trolldom och klokskap i Västergötland under 1800-talet* (Borås, 1932).

78. Bernard, Richard, *A Guide to Grand Jurymen* (London, 1627, 1629).

79. Bernardus Comensis [de Como], *Lucerna Inquisitorum Haereticae Pravitatis . . . et Eiusdem Tractatus de Strigiis* (Milan, 1566; Rome, 1584).

80. Bernheimer, Richard, *Wild Men in the Middle Ages: A Study in Art, Sentiment, and Demonology* (Cambridge, Mass., 1952).

81. Bernou, Jean, *La chasse aux sorcières dans le Labourd, 1609* (Agen, 1897).

82. Berthet, Elie, *Le loup-garou* (Brussels, 1843).

83. Bertrand, I., *Les possédées de Loudun et Urbain Grandier* (Paris, [c. 1908]).

84. Bezold, Friedrich von, "Jean Bodin als Okkultist und seine Démonomanie," *Historische Zeitschrift* (Munich), Vol. CV (1910).

85. Bienert, Walther, *Die Philosophie des Christian Thomasius* (Halle, 1934).

86. Binsfeld, Peter, *Commentarius de Maleficis* (Cologne, 1622).

87. —— *Tractatus de Confessionibus Maleficorum et Sagarum* (1589; Treves, 1591, 1596, 1605; Cologne, 1623).

88. —— (German tr.) *Tractat von Bekanntnüss der Zauberer und Hexen* (Treves, 1590; Munich, 1592).

89. Binz, Carl, *Augustin Lercheimer (Witekind) und seine Schrift wider den Hexenwahn* (Strasbourg, 1888).

90. —— *Doctor Johann Weyer* (Bonn, 1885; rev. Berlin, 1896).

91. Bizouard, Joseph, *Les rapports de l'homme avec le démon* (Paris, 1863).

92. Black, George F., *A Calendar of Cases of Witchcraft in Scotland 1510-1727* (New York, 1938).

93. —— *List of Works in the New York Public Library Relating to Witchcraft in Europe* (New York, 1911).

94. —— *List of Works in the New York Public Library Relating to Witchcraft in the United States* (New York, 1908).

95. —— *Some Unpublished Scottish Witchcraft Trials* (New York, 1941).

96. Bleau, Alphonse, *Précis d'histoire sur la ville et les possédées de Loudun* (Poitiers, 1877).

97. Bliss, Douglas Percy (ed.), *The Devil in Scotland* (London, 1934).

98. Boas, Ralph Philip and Louise Schultz Boas, *Cotton Mather* (New York, 1928).

99. Bodin, Jean, *De la démonomanie des sorciers* (Paris, 1580, 1582, 1587, 1598; Strasbourg, 1581; Antwerp, Lyons, 1593; Rouen, 1604).

100. —— (German tr. by Johann Fischart) *Daemonomania: vom aussgelassnen wütigen Teufelsheer der Besessenen* (Strasbourg, 1581, 1586; Hamburg, 1698).

101. —— (Latin tr.) *De Magorum Daemonomania* (Basel, 1581; Frankfort, 1603).

102. —— *Le fléau des démons et sorciers* (Niort, 1616).

103. Boguet, Henri, *Discours des sorciers* (Lyons, 1602, 1605, 1610; Paris, 1603; Rouen, 1606).

104. —— (English tr. ed. Montague Summers) *An Examen of Witches* (London, 1929, ltd. ed.).

105. Bois, Jules, *Le Satanisme et la magie* (Paris, 1895).

106. Boissardus, Jan. Jac., *De Divinatione et Magicis Praestigis* (Oppenheim, 1616).

107. Boissell, W., "Le conseiller Pierre de Lancre," *Bullétin du Musée Basque*, Bayonne, No. 15 (1938).

108. Boissier, Le Sieur A., *Recueil de lettres au sujet des malefices et du sortilège, servant de réponse aux lettres du Sieur de Saint-André, médecin à Coutances, sur le même sujet* (Paris, 1731).

109. Bond, John, *An Essay on the Incubus or Nightmare* (London, 1753).

110. [? Bonelli, Benedetto,] *Animavversioni critiche* (Venice, 1751).

111. *A Book of the Witches Lately Condemned and Executed at Bedford* (London, 1613).

112. Bordeaut, A., *Champtocé, Gilles de Raiz* (Rennes, 1924).

113. Bordelon, Laurent, *Histoire des imaginations extravagantes de Monsieur Oufle* (Paris, 1710).

114. —— (English tr.) *The History of the Ridiculous Extravagances of Monsieur Oufle* (London, 1711).

115. Bordonus, Franciscus, *Sacrum Tribunal Judicum in Causis Sanctae Fidei* (Rome, 1648).

116. Bosroger, Père Esprit de, *La Piété affligée . . . Saincte Elizabeth de Louviers* (Rouen, 1652; Amsterdam, 1700).

117. Bossard, Abbé Eugène, *Les derniers jours de Barbe-Bleue* (Nantes, 1899).

118. —— *Gilles De Raiz maréchal de France, dit Barbe-Bleue* (Paris, 1886).

119. Bot, H. de, *Van Heksen en Weerwolven in 1595* (Rotterdam, 1951).

120. Boulton, Richard, *A Complete History of Magic* (London, 1715).

121. Bourneville, Dr. Magloire Désiré, *Louise Lateau ou la stigmatisée belge* (Paris, 1875).

122. —— and E. Tenturier, *Le sabbat des sorciers* (Paris, 1882, ltd. ed.).

123. Bourquelot, Félix, *Recherches sur la lycanthropie* (Paris, 1848).

124. Bouvet, Le Sieur, *Les manières admirables pour découvrir toutes sortes de crimes et sortilèges avec l'instruction solide pour bien juger un procès criminel* (Paris, 1659).

125. Bovet, Richard, *Pandaemonium, or the Devil's Cloister, Being a Further Blow to Modern Sadducism, Proving the Existence of Witches and Spirits* (London, 1684; ed. Montague Summers, Aldington, Kent, 1951, ltd. ed.).

126. Bowen, James [? Edmond], *Doctor Lamb Revived, or Witchcraft Condemned in Anne Bodenham* (London, 1653).

127. —— *Doctor Lamb's Darling, or Strange and Terrible News from Salisbury* (London, 1653).

128. *The Boy of Bilson, or a True Discovery of the Late Impostures* (London, 1622).

129. Boys, Rev. J., *The Case of Witchcraft at Coggeshall, Essex, 1699* (London, 1901, ltd. ed.).

130. Bragge, Francis, *A Defense of the Proceedings Against Jane Wenham* (London, 1712).

131. —— *A Full and Impartial Account of* the Discovery of Sorcery and Witchcraft Practiced by Jane Wenham (London, 1712).

132. —— *Witchcraft Further Displayed* (London, 1712).

133. Brand, John, *Observations on Popular Antiquities* (London, 1813).

134. Brémond, Henri, *Histoire littéraire du sentiment religieux en France* (Paris, 1916-33).

135. —— (English tr.) (London, 1928-36).

136. Brévannes, Roland, *L'orgie satanique à travers les siècles* (Paris, 1904).

137. Brewster, Sir David, *Letters on Natural Magic* (London, 1842).

138. Bricaud, Joanny, *J.-K. Huysmans et le satanisme* (Paris, 1913, ltd. ed.).

139. Brinley, John, *A Discovery of the Impostures of Witches and Astrologers* (London, 1680).

140. Brodie-Innes, John William, *Scottish Witchcraft Trials* (London, 1891, ltd. ed.).

141. Brognolus Bergomensi, Candidus, *Alexicacon, Hoc Est de Maleficiis* (Venice, 1668, 1714).

142. —— *Manuale Exorcistarum* (Bergamo, 1651; Lyons, 1658).

143. —— (Portuguese tr.) *Methodo . . . de Exorcizar* (Lisbon, 1725).

144. Brown, Robert, *Demonology and Witchcraft* (London, 1889).

145. Brugière, Prosper C. F., Baron de Barante, *Jeanne d'Arc* (Paris, 1935).

146. [Buisseret, François,] *La possession de Jeanne Fery, religieuse professe du couvent des soeurs noires de la ville de Mons, 1584* (Paris, 1586, ed. Magloire D. Bourneville, 1886).

147. *Bullarium Diplomatum et Privilegiorum Sanctorum Romanorum Pontificium* (1858).

148. Burnet, Gilbert, *Incidents in the Life of Matthew Hale* (Boston, 1832).

149. Burr, George Lincoln, "The Literature of Witchcraft," *Papers of the American Historical Association*, Vol. IV (1890).

150. —— *Narratives of the Witchcraft Cases, 1648-1706* (New York, 1914, 1959).

151. —— *Selections from his Writings* (ed. Lois Oliphant Gibbons, Ithaca, 1942).

152. —— *Translations and Reprints, University of Pennsylvania*, Vol. III, No. 4 (Philadelphia, 1897).

153. —— "A Witch Hunter in the Book Shops," *Bibliographer*, Vol. I (1902).

154. Burton, Robert, *Anatomy of Melancholy* (London, 1621).

155. Butler, Eliza Marian, *Ritual Magic* (Cambridge, 1949).

156. Byloff, Fritz, *Hexenglaube und Hexenverfolgung in den österreichischen Alpenländern* (Berlin, 1934).

157. Cabanès, Augustin, *Moeurs intimes du passé: le sabbat a-t-il existé?* (Paris, 1935).

158. Caillet, Albert L., *Manuel bibliographique des sciences psychiques* (Paris, 1912).

159. Caleb, S., *Les véritables et les fausses messes noires* (n.p., n.d.).

160. Calef, Robert, *More Wonders of the Invisible World* (London, 1700; Salem, 1796, 1823; Boston, 1828).

161. Calmeil, Louis François, *De la folie* (Paris, 1845).

162. Calmet, Augustin, *Dissertations sur les apparitions . . . et vampires* (Paris, 1746; *Traité*, 1751).

163. —— (English tr. by Henry Christmas), *The Phantom World* (London, 1850).

164. Camfield, Benjamin, *A Theological Discourse of Angels and Their Ministries* (London, 1678).

165. Campbell, John Gregorson, *Superstitions of the Highlands* (Glasgow, 1900).

166. —— *Witchcraft and Second Sight in the Highlands and Islands of Scotland* (Glasgow, 1902).

167. Cannaert, Joseph Bernard, *Olim: Procès des sorcières en Belgique sous Philippe II* (Ghent, 1847).

168. Cardano, Girolamo, *De Subtilitate Rerum* (Paris, 1550; Basel, 1557).

169. Cardauns, Hermann, *Frankfurter zeitgemässe Broschüren*, Vol. V (1884).

170. Cardi, Paulus Maria, *Ritualis Romani Documenta de Exorcizandis Obsessis a Daemonio* (Venice, 1733).

171. Carena, Caesar, *Tractatus de Officio Sanctissimae Inquisitionis et Modo Procedendi in Causis Fidei* (Cremona, 1636; Lyons, 1669).

172. Carerio, Luigi, *Practica Causarum Criminalium . . . Tractatus de Haereticis* (Lyons, 1550).

173. Caristinus, *Diatriba Theologico-Critica* (ed. Bernardus Maria Marsicani, Naples, 1788).

174. Carpenter, William H., "Dietrich Flade," *Library of Cornell University*, Vol. I (1883).

175. Carpzov, Benedict, *Practica Nova Rerum Criminalum Imperialis Saxonica in Tres Partes Divisa* (Wittenberg, 1635, 1657, 1670; Frankfort, 1657).

176. Carré, Henri, "Quelques mots sur la sorcellerie dans les provinces de l'Ouest au xvi⁰ et xvii⁰ siècles," *Société des Antiquaires de l'Ouest, Bullétin* (Poitiers), III Série, Vol. VII (1927).

177. Carrington, Hereward, *Poltergeist Down the Centuries* (London, 1953).

178. ——— and Nandor Fodor, *Haunted People* (New York, 1951).

179. Cart, Jacques, *Le Château de l'Isle et les procès de sorcellerie* (Lausanne, 1908).

180. Casaubon, Meric, *Of Credulity and Incredulity* (London, 1668, 1670).

181. ——— *A Treatise Concerning Enthusiasm As It Is an Effect of Nature, but Is Mistaken by Many for Either Divine Inspiration or Diabolical Possession* (London, 1656).

182. *The Case of the Hertfordshire Witchcraft Considered* (London, 1712).

183. *The Case of Mistress Mary Catherine Cadiere Against the Jesuit Father John Baptist Girard* (10th ed., London, 1732).

184. Cassini, Samuel de, *Question de le Strie* ([? Pavia,] 1505).

185. Castelli, Enrico, *Il Demoniaco nell' arte* (Milan, 1952).

186. Castleton, D. R. [Caroline Rosina Darby], *Salem* (New York, 1874).

187. Caudembergs, Girard de, *Le monde spirituel* (Paris, 1577).

188. Caufeynon and Jaf, Docteurs [pseudonyms], *Les messes noires* (Paris, 1905).

189. Cauz, Constantin Franz de, *De Cultibus Magicis* (Vienna, 1767, 1771).

190. Cauzons, Thomas de [pseudonym], *Les Albigeois et l'Inquisition* (Paris, 1908).

191. ——— *Histoire de l'Inquisition en France* (Paris, 1909).

192. ——— *La magie et la sorcellerie en France* (Paris, [? 1910-12]).

193. Chabloz, Fritz, *Les sorcières neuchâteloises* (Neuchâtel, 1868).

194. [Chamberlain, Richard,] *Lithobolia, or the Stone-Throwing Devil* (London, 1698; Tarrytown, New York, 1923).

195. Chambers, Robert, *Domestic Annals of Scotland* (Edinburgh, 1858).

196. Champier, Symphorien, *Dialogus in Magicarum Artium Destructionem* (Lyons, [c.1500]).

197. Chandler, Peleg Whitman, *American Criminal Trials* (Boston, 1841-44).

198. Chanteau, Francis de, *Notes pour servir à l'histoire du chapitre de Saint-Dié: les sorciers à Saint-Dié et dans le val de Galilée* (Nancy, 1877).

199. Charcot, J. M. and Paul Richer, *Les démoniaques dans l'art* (Paris, 1887).

200. Chauvincourt, Sieur de Beauvoys de [of Angers], *Discours de la lycanthropie* (Paris, 1599).

201. Chiremont, Jean Lenormant de, *De la vocation des magiciens et magiciennes par le ministre des démons* (Paris, 1623).

202. Christie, John (ed.), *Witchcraft in Kenmore [Perthshire,] 1730-57: Extracts from Kirk Session Records* (Aberfeldy, 1893).

203. [Church, Thomas,] *An Essay Toward Vindicating the Literal Sense of the Demoniacs in the New Testament* (London, 1737).

204. Cigogna, Strozzi, *Magia Omnifariae* (Cologne, 1606).

205. Cimber, Louis and François Danjou, *Archives curieuses de l'histoire de France*, I Série, Vol. VIII (Paris, 1836).

206. Cirac Estopañán, Sebastian, *Los Procesos de hechicerías en la Inquisición de Castilla la Nueva* (Madrid, 1942).

207. Cirvelo, Pedro, *Opus de Magica Superstitione* (Alcalà, 1521).

208. ——— (Spanish tr.) *Reprobación de las supersticiones y hechizerías* (Salamanca, 1539, 1556; Medina de Campa, 1551; Madrid, 1952, ltd. ed.).

209. ——— (Spanish tr. by Pedro Jofreu) *Tratado en el qual se repruevan todas las supersticiones y hechizerías* (Barcelona, 1628).

210. Clarke, Samuel, *A General Martyrology* (London, 1651).

211. Closmadeuc, Gustave de, "Les sorciers de Lorient: procès criminel devant la sénéchaussée d'Hennebont en 1736," *Bullétin de la société polymathique du Morbihan* (Vannes), Vol. I (1885).

212. Cockayne, Oswald, *Leechdoms. Wortcunning and Starcraft of Early England* (London, 1864-66).

213. Cockburn, Jack, *An Apology for Antonia Bourignon* (London, 1699).

214. ——— *Bourignianism Detected, or the Delusions and Errors of Antonia Bourignon and Her Growing Sect . . . Narrative I* (London, 1698).

215. *Collection of Rare and Curious Tracts on Witchcraft and Second Sight* (ed. David Webster, Edinburgh, 1820).

216. *Collection of Rare and Curious Tracts Relating to Witchcraft* (ed. J. R. Smith, London, 1838).

217. Collins, D. C., *A Handlist of News Pamphlets* (London, 1943).

218. *A Complete Translation of the Memorial of the Jesuit Father John Baptist Girard . . . Against Mary Catherine Cadiere* (London, 1732).

219. *The Complete Wizard* (London, 1770).

220. *The Confession of Mother Lakeland of Ipswich* (London, 1645; repr. Morley Adams, *In the Footsteps of Borrow and Fitzgerald*, London, [? 1915]).

221. *Les conjurations faites à un démon possédant le corps d'une grande dame* (Paris, 1619).

222. *Constitutio Criminalis Theresiana . . . peinliche Gerichtsordnung* (Vienna, 1769).

223. Conway, Moncure Daniel, *Demonology and Devil Lore* (London and New York, 1879).

224. Cooper, Thomas, *The Mystery of Witchcraft* (London, 1617, 1622).

225. Cornelis van Stockum, Theodorus, *Friedrich von Spee in de heksen processen* (Amsterdam, 1949).

226. Cotta, John, *The Trial of Witchcraft, Showing the True and Right Method of the Discovery* (London, 1616, 1625).

227. Coulange, Father Louis [Joseph Turmel], (English tr. by Stephen Haden Guest) *The Life of the Devil* (New York, 1930).

228. Coulton, George G., *Christ, St. Francis, and Today* (Cambridge, 1919).

229. ——— *The Death Penalty for Heresy* (London, 1924).

230. ——— *The Inquisition and Liberty* (London, 1937).

231. Coynart, Charles de, *Une sorcière au xviii⁰ siècle: Marie-Anne de la Ville, 1680-1725* (Paris, 1902).

232. Crespet, P. Pierre, *De la hayne de Sathan et malins esprits contre l'homme* (Paris, 1590).

233. Cross, Tom Peete, "Witchcraft in North Carolina," *Studies in Philology*, Vol. XVI (1919).

234. Crouch, Nathanial [pseudonym, Richard Burton], *The Kingdom of Darkness* (London, 1688).

235. Crowe, Catherine, *The Night Side of Nature* (London, 1848).

236. Cumont, Franz, *Les religions orientales dans le paganisme romain* (4th ed., Paris, 1929).

237. ——— (English tr.) *The Oriental Religions in Roman Paganism* (New York, [1956]).

238. Curtis, S. Carey, "Trials for Witchcraft in Guernsey," *La société guernesiaise, Reports*, Vol. XIII (1937).

239. Cushing, "Grace Sherwood's Trial for Witchcraft," *Virginia Historical Society Collections* (Richmond), Vol. I (1833).

240. Dacheux, J., *Jean Geiler* (Paris, 1876).

241. Dahlerup, Verner, *Hexe og hexeprocesler i Danmark* (Copenhagen, 1888).

242. Dalnas, Jean-Baptiste, *Les sorcières du Vivarais devant les inquisiteurs de la foi* (n.p., 1865, ltd. ed.).

243. Dalton, Michael, *Country Justice* (London, 1618, 1630, 1647).

244. Dalyell, Sir John Graham, *The Darker Superstitions of Scotland* (Edinburgh, 1834; Glasgow, 1835).

245. Dambielle, Abbé, "La sorcellerie en Gascogne," *Bullétin de la société archéologique de Gers* (Auch), Vols. VII, VIII (1901).

246. Damhouder, Joost, *Enchiridion, Praxis Rerum Criminalium* (Louvain, 1554, 1601).

247. ——— (French tr.) *La practique et enchiridion des causes criminelles* (Louvain, 1554; Antwerp, 1564).

248. Dandolo, Tullio, *La Signora di Monza e le Streghe del Tirolo, processi famosi del secolo decimosettimo* (Milan, 1855).

249. Daneau, Lambert, *Les sorciers* ([? Geneva,] 1564; *Deux traités*, Paris, 1579).

250. ——— (English tr. by R. W. [? Thomas Twyne]) *A Dialogue of Witches* ([London,] 1575).

251. ——— (German tr.) *Von den Zauberern, Hexen und Unholden* (Cologne, 1576).

252. ——— (Latin tr.) *De Veneficis* (Cologne, 1575).

253. Darrell, John, *An Apology or Defense of the Possession of William Somers* [London, ? 1599].

254. ——— *A Brief Apology* ([London,] 1599).

255. ——— *A Brief Narration* ([London,] 1599).

256. ——— *A Detection of That Sinful, Shameful, Lying, and Ridiculous Discourse of Samuel Harsnett* ([London,] 1600).

257. ——— *The Reply of John Darrell to the Answer of John Deacon* ([London,] 1602).

258. ——— *A Survey of Certain Dialogical Discourses* ([London,] 1602).

259. ——— *A True Narration of the Strange and Grievous Vexation by the Devil of Seven Persons in Lancashire and William Somers of Nottingham* ([London,] 1600).

260. Daugis, Antoine Louis, *Traité sur la magie, le sortilège, les possessions* (Paris, 1732).

261. Davanzati, Archbishop Giosseppe, *Dissertazione sopra Vampiri* (Naples, 1774).

262. Davenport, John, *The Witches of Huntingdon* (London, 1646).

263. Davidson, Thomas Douglas, *Rowan Tree and Red Thread* (Edinburgh, 1949).

264. Davies, Reginald Trevor, *Four Centuries of Witch Beliefs* (London, 1947).

265. Davies, T. Witton, *Magic, Divination, and Demonology Among the Hebrews and Their Neighbors* (Leipzig diss., London, n.d.).

266. Davis, George W., *Inquisition at Albi* (New York, 1948).

267. Deacon, John and John Walker, *Dialogical Discourses of Spirits and Devils* (London, 1601).

268. ——— *A Summary Answer* (London, 1601).

269. *A Declaration in Answer to Several Lying Pamphlets Concerning the Witch of Wapping* (London, 1652).

270. *Decretalium Corpus Canonicum Glossatum* (Lyons, 1606).

271. Dee, John, *Autobiographical Tracts of Dr. John Dee* (ed. James Crossley, Manchester, 1851).

272. ——— *The Private Diary* (ed. James Orchard Halliwell, London, 1842).

273. ——— *A True and Faithful Relation What Passed for Many Years Between . . . John Dee . . . and Some Spirits* (pref. by Meric Casaubon, London, 1659).

274. *The Defense of Father John Baptist Girard, Part I* (3d ed., London, 1732); *II* (London, 1731).

275. [Defoe, Daniel,] *History of the Devil* (London, 1727).

276. Delacroix, Frédéric, *Etudes d'histoire, psychologie du mysticisme* (Paris,).

277. ——— *Les procès de sorcellerie au xvi⁰ siècle* (Paris, 1894).

278. ——— *Les procès de sorcellerie ancienne France devant les juridictions séculières* (Paris, 1907).

279. Delassus, Jules, *Les incubes* (Paris, [1897]).

280. Delbene, Thomas, *De Officio Sanctae Inquisitionis Circa Haeresim* (Lyons, 1666).
281. Delcambre, Etienne, *Le concept de la sorcellerie dans le Duché de Lorraine au xviᵉ et xviiᵉ siècle* (Nancy, 1948, ltd. ed.).
282. Delogne, Th., *L'Ardenne méridionale belge, suivi du procès des sorcières de Sugny en 1637* (Brussels, 1914).
283. Del Rio, Martin Antoine, *Disquisitionum Magicarum* (Louvain, 1599, 1600, 1601, 1603, 1606; Lyons, 1604, 1608, 1612; Venice, 1606, 1640, 1747; Mainz, 1612, 1624; Liége, 1612, 1624; Cologne, 1633, 1659, 1679).
284. ———— (French tr. by André Duchesne) *Les controverses et recherches magiques de Martin Delrio* (Paris, 1611).
285. Denis, Albert, *La sorcellerie à Toul* (Toul, 1888).
286. Dennler, J., *Ein Hexenprozess im Elsass vom Jahre 1616* (Zabern, 1896).
287. Dermenghem, Emile, *La vie admirable et les révélations de Marie des Vallées* (Paris, 1926).
288. *A Detection of Damnable Drifts Practiced by Three Witches Arraigned at Chelmsford* (London, 1579).
289. Dethardingius, Georgius, and Christianus Fridericus Stever, *Dissertatio . . . de Obsessione* (Rostock, 1724).
290. Dettling, A., *Die Hexenprozesse im Kanton Schwyz* (Schwyz, 1907).
291. *The Devil's Delusions* (London, 1649; ed. W. B. Gerish, Bishop's Stortford, 1914; ed. J. A. Foster, East Lancing, 1940, ltd. ed.).
292. Déy, Aristide, *Histoire de la sorcellerie au compté de Bourgogne* (Vesoul, 1861).
293. Diefenbach, Johann, *Der Hexenwahn vor und nach der Glaubensspaltung in Deutschland* (Mainz, 1886).
294. ———— *Wetzer und Welte*, Vol. V (1898).
295. ———— *Der Zauberglaube des 16. Jahrhunderts nach den Katechismen Dr. Martin Luthers und des P. Canisius* (Mainz, 1900).
296. Dintzer, Lucien, *Nicholas Remy et son oeuvre démonologique* (Lyons, 1936).
297. Diricq, Edouard, *Maléfices et sortilèges, procès criminels de l'ancien évêché de Bâle pour faits de sorcellerie 1549-1670* (Lausanne, 1910).
298. *Doctrine of Devils* (London, 1676).
299. Dodo, Vincente, *Apologia pro Inquisitoribus* (Pavia, 1506).
300. Donais, C., *Documents pour servir à l'histoire de l'Inquisition dans le Languedoc* (Paris, 1900).
301. Doncoeur, Paul, *La minute française* (Melun, 1952).
302. ———— (English tr. by Walter Sidney Scott) *The Trial of Joan of Arc* (London, 1956).
303. Dornbusch, J. B., *Annalen des historischen Vereins für den Niederrhein*, Vol. XXX (1876).
304. Drage, William W., *Daimonomageia* ([London,] 1665).
305. ———— *A Relation of Mary Hall . . . Possessed of Two Devils* (London, 1664; ed. W. B. Gerish, Bishop's Stortford, 1912).
306. Drake, Samuel G., *Annals of Witchcraft in New England* (Boston, 1869).
307. ———— *The Witchcraft Delusion in New England* (Roxbury, Mass., 1866).
308. Duboin, Eloy, *La justice et les sorciers au xviᵉ siècle* (Nimes, 1880).
309. ———— *Procès de sorciers à Viry, Bailliage de Ternier, 1534-48* [Geneva, 1882].
310. Dubu, Marc, *Gilles de Rays, magicien et sodomiste* (Paris, 1945).
311. Duhr, Bernard, *Geschichte der Jesuiten in den Ländern deutscher Zunge* (Freiburg and Munich, 1907-28), Vol. IV.
312. ———— *Die Stellung der Jesuiten in den deutschen Hexenprozessen* (Cologne, 1900).
313. ———— , Alexandre (père), *Le meneur des ...s* (Paris, 1857).
314. ———— (English tr. by Alfred Allinson) *Wolf Leader* (London, 1904).
315. ———— Alexandre, *Les crimes célèbres: les ...s du Midi—Urbain Grandier ...891).
316. ———— *Urbain Grandier* (Paris, 1856).

317. Dumcke, Julius, *Zauberei und Hexenprozessen* (Berlin, n.d.).
318. Dunbar, Edmund, *Social Life in Former Days, Chiefly in the Provinces of Moray* (Edinburgh, 1865).
319. Duplès-Agier, H., *Registre criminel du Châtelet de Paris* (Paris, 1861-64, ltd. ed.).
320. Ebner, Theodor, *Friedrich von Spee und die Hexenprozesse seiner Zeit* (Hamburg, 1898).
321. Eckels, P. R., *Greek Wolf Lore* (Philadelphia, 1937).
322. Eckertz, G., *Annalen des historischen Vereins für den Niederrhein*, Vols. IX, X (1861).
323. Eisler, Robert, *Man into Wolf* (London, 1951; New York, 1952).
324. Elbarchs, Regius, *Medicatio Viri Incubo Divexati* (Utrecht, 1645).
325. Elich, Philipp Ludwig, *Daemonomagia* (Frankfort, 1607).
326. Elliott, Charles Wyllys, *Mysteries, or Glimpses of the Supernatural* (New York, 1852).
327. Elworthy, Frederick Thomas, *The Evil Eye* (London, 1895; New York, 1958).
328. Emard, Paul and Suzanne Fournier, *Les années criminelles de Madame de Montespan* (Paris, 1938).
329. Emery, Richard W., *Heresy and the Inquisition in Narbonne* (New York, 1941).
330. Ennen, L., *Geschichte der Stadt Köln*, Vol. V (1863).
331. Erastus, Thomas, *Disputatio de Lamiis seu Strigibus* (Basel, 1572, 1577).
332. ———— (French tr.) *Deux dialogues touchant le pouvoir des sorcières* ([Geneva,] 1579).
333. Ernotte, J., "Un procès de sorcellerie à Strée . . . en 1705," *Wallonia* (Liége), Vol. X (1902).
334. Eschbach, Dr. H., "Dr. med. Johannes Wier . . . Ein Beitrag zur Geschichte der Hexenprozesse," *Beiträge zur Geschichte des Niederrheins* (Düsseldorf, 1886).
335. Esquirol, E., *Des maladies mentales* (Paris, 1838).
336. Evans, Edward Payson, *The Criminal Prosecution and Capital Punishment of Animals* (London, 1906).
337. Ewen, Cecil L'Estrange, "A Noted Case of Witchcraft at North Moreton," *Berkshire Archaeological Journal*, Vol. XL (1936).
338. ———— *Some Witchcraft Criticism* ([London,] 1938).
339. ———— *The Trials of John Lowes, Clerk* ([Paignton,] 1937).
340. ———— *Witchcraft and Demonianism* (London, 1933).
341. ———— *Witchcraft in the Norfolk Circuit* ([Paignton,] 1939).
342. ———— *Witchcraft in the Star Chamber* ([Paignton,] 1938).
343. ———— *Witch Hunting and Witch Trials* (London and New York, 1929).
344. Ewers, Hanns Heinz (ed.), *Memoiren einer Besessener von Soeur Jeanne [des Anges]* (Stuttgart, 1911).
345. *The Examination and Confession of Certain Witches at Chelmsford* (London, 1566; ed. Hermann Beigel, 1863).
346. *The Examination, Confession, Trial, and Execution of Joan Williford* (London, 1645, 1837, ltd. ed.; Ingram, Pa., 1939, ltd. ed.).
347. *The Examination of John Walsh* (London, 1566).
348. *Exorcismo* (Brandenburg, 1590).
349. *The Extraordinary Life and Character of Mary Bateman, the Yorkshire Witch* (6th ed., Leeds, 1809).
350. Eymeric, Nicholas, *Directorium Inquisitorum* (ed. Francis Pegna, Rome, 1585; Venice, 1607).
351. Fabre, Joseph, *Procès de condamnation de Jeanne d'Arc* (Paris, 1884).
352. ———— *Procès de réhabilitation de Jeanne d'Arc* (Paris, 1888).
353. Fabre, Lucien, *Jeanne d'Arc* (Paris, 1948).
354. ———— (English tr. by Gerard Hopkins) (New York, 1954).
355. Fairfax, Edward, *A Discourse on Witchcraft* (London, 1858; ed. William Grange, Harrogate, 1882).
356. Falgairolle, Edmond, *Un envoûtement en Gévaudan en l'année 1347* (Nimes, 1892).

357. Farconnet, François, *Relation véritable contenant ce qui s'est passé aux exorcismes d'une fille appellée Elisabeth Allier* (Paris, 1649; Lyons, 1875).
358. Farnsworth, Richard, *Witchcraft Cast Out from the Religious Seed and Israel of God* (London, 1655).
359. Félice, Paul de, *Lambert Daneau* (Paris, 1881).
360. Fell-Smith, Charlotte, *John Dee* (London, 1909).
361. Ferguson, Ian, *The Philosophy of Witchcraft* (London, [1924]; New York, 1925).
362. Ferguson, John, "Witchcraft Literature of Scotland," *Edinburgh Bibliographical Society Papers*, Vol. III (1899).
363. Ferraironi, Francesco, *Le Streghe e l'Inquisizione: superstizioni e realtà* (Rome, 1955).
364. Feuchtwanger, Lion, *Wahn oder der Teufel in Boston* (Los Angeles, 1948).
365. Figuier, Guillaume Louis, *Histoire du merveilleux dans les temps modernes* (Paris, 1860).
366. [Filmer, Sir Robert,] *An Advertisement to the Jurymen of England Touching Witches* (London, 1653, 1679, 1684).
367. Fincelius, Job, *Wunderzeichen, warhafftige Beschreibung und gründlich Verzeichnung schrecklicher Wunderzeichen und Geschichten* (Jena, 1556).
368. Fischer, Wilhelm, *Aberglaube aller Zeiten* (Stuttgart, 1906).
369. Fleischmann, Max, *Christian Thomasius Leben und Lebenswerk* (Halle, 1931).
370. Fontaine, Jacques, *Discours des marques des sorciers et de la réelle possession que le diable prend sur le corps des hommes* (Lyons, 1611; Arras, [c. 1850]).
371. Forbes, Esther, *A Mirror for Witches* (Boston, 1928).
372. Fosses, Castonnet des, "Jean Bodin, sa vie et ses oeuvres," *Revue de l'Anjou* (Angers), n.s. Vol. XX (1890).
373. Foucault, Maurice, *Les procès de sorcellerie dans l'ancienne France devant les juridictions séculières* (Paris, 1907).
374. Fournier, Dr. Alban, "Epidémie de sorcellerie en Lorraine," *Annales de l'Est* (Nancy, 1891).
375. ———— "Note sur la sorcellerie dans les Vosges," *Bullétin, Société philomatique vosgienne* (Saint-Dié), Vol. X (1885).
376. Fournier, Paul, *Les officialités au moyen âge* (Paris, 1880).
377. Fowler, Samuel Page, *Salem Witchcraft* (Salem, 1861; Boston, 1865).
378. Fox, George, *A Declaration of the Ground of Error* (London, 1657).
379. Français, J., *L'église et la sorcellerie* (Paris, 1910).
380. Franklin, Benjamin, *Writings* (ed. Albert H. Smyth, New York, 1905).
381. Freimark, Hans, *Okkultismus und Sexualität* (Leipzig, [post 1900]).
382. Freud, Sigmund, "A Neurosis of Demoniacal Possession in the Seventeenth Century," *Collected Papers* (London, 1949), Vol. IV.
383. Freuler, Kaspar, *Anna Göldi: die Geschichte der letzten Hexe in der Schweiz* (Bern, [1956]).
384. Friedrich, J., *La Vauderye* (Munich, 1898).
385. Frischbier, Hermann, *Hexenspruch und Zauberbann . . . in der Provinz Preussen* (Berlin, 1870).
386. Fromann, Johann Christian, *Tractatus de Fascinatione Novus et Singularis* (Nuremberg, 1675).
387. Fuhrmann, Philip David, *De Conventu Sagarum ad Sua Sabbata* (Wittenberg, 1678).
388. *A Full and True Relation of the Trial . . . of Ann Foster* (London, 1674, 1881; Northampton, 1878).
389. *A Full Confutation of Witchcraft* (London, 1712).
390. Fuller, James F., "Trial of Florence Newton," *Journal of Cork Historical and Archaeological Society*, Series II, Vol. X (1904).
391. Funck-Brentano, Frantz, *Le drame des poisons* (Paris, 1900).
392. Gaar, Georgius, *Christliche Anred nächst dem Scheiterhauffen worauff der Leichnam Mariae Renatae* (Würzburg, [1749]).
393. ———— (Italian tr.) *Maria Renata* (Verona, 1749).

394. Gabory, Emile, *La vie et la mort de Gilles de Rais* (Paris, 1926, ltd. ed.).

395. ———— (English tr. by Alvah C. Bessie) *Alias Bluebeard: The Life and Death of Gilles de Raiz* (New York, 1930).

396. Garçon, Maurice and Jean Vinchon, *Le diable* (Paris, 1926).

397. ———— (English tr. by Stephen Haden Guest) *The Devil* (London, 1929; New York, 1930).

398. Gardiner, Ralph, *England's Grievance Discovered in Relation to the Coal Trade* (London, 1655, 1749).

399. Gardner, Gerald Brosseau, *Witchcraft Today* (London and New York, [1955]).

400. Garinet, Jules, *Histoire de la magie en France* (Paris, 1818).

401. Garis, Howard R., *With Force and Arms* (New York, 1902).

402. Garnett, David, *Lady into Fox* (London, 1922).

403. Garnier, Dr. Samuel, *Barbe Buvée, en religion Soeur Saint-Colombe, et la prétendue possession des Ursulines d'Auxonne 1658-63, étude historique et médicale* (Paris, 1895, ltd. ed.).

404. Gassners, Johann Josef, *Pfarrers zu Klösterle* (Augsburg, 1774).

405. Gaule, John, *Mysmantia, the Mag-astro-mancer* (London, 1652).

406. ———— *Select Cases of Conscience Touching Witches and Witchcraft* (London, 1646).

407. Geiler von Kaysersberg, Johann, *Die Emeis* (Strasbourg, 1517).

408. George, Edward Augustus, *Seventeenth Century Men of Latitude* (New York, 1908).

409. Gervais of Tilbury, *Otia Imperialia* (ed. F. Riebrecht, Hanover, 1856).

410. Gibbons, Lois Oliphant (ed.), *Liberty and Persecution, Essays in Honor of George Lincoln Burr* (New York, 1931, ltd. ed.).

411. ———— *Some Rhenish Foes of Credulity and Cruelty 1620-40* (diss., Ithaca, 1920).

412. Gifford, Edward S., Jr., *The Evil Eye* (New York, 1958).

413. Gifford, George, *A Dialogue Concerning Witches and Witchcrafts* (London, 1593, 1603, 1842; ed. Beatrice White, Oxford, 1931).

414. ———— *A Discourse of the Subtle Practices of Devils by Witches and Sorcerers* (London, 1587).

415. Gilbert, Emile, *Les plantes magiques et la sorcellerie* (Moulins, 1899).

416. ———— *Sorciers et magiciens* (Moulins, 1895).

417. Gill, Obadiah, *Some Few Remarks Upon a Scandalous Book* (Boston, 1701).

418. Gineste, Raoul, *Les grandes victimes de l'hystérie: Louis Gaufridi curé des Accoules et Magdeleine de la Palud* (Paris, 1907).

419. Giraldo, le Père Mathias de (augmented by M. Fornari) [? pseudonyms], *Histoire curieuse et pittoresque des sorciers* (Paris, 1846, [1854]).

420. Giraldus Cambrensis, *Topographica Hibernia* (London, 1867).

421. Giraud, Docteur, *Etudes sur les procès de sorcellerie en Normandie* (Rouen, 1897).

422. Giraud, Victor, *Vie de Jeanne d'Arc* [Avignon, rev. ed., 1948].

423. Glanvill, Joseph, *A Blow at Modern Sadducism* (London, 1668).

424. ———— *Saducismus Triumphatus* (ed. Henry More, London, 1681, 1683, 1689, 1700, 1726).

425. ———— (German tr.) *Vollkommener und clarer Beweiss von Hexen und Gespentern* (Hamburg, 1701).

426. ———— *Some Philosophical Considerations Touching the Being of Witches and Witchcraft* (London, 1661, 1667).

427. Godelmann, Johann Georg, *Disputatio de Magis* (Frankfort, 1584).

428. ———— *Tractatus de Magis, Veneficis et Lamiis* (Frankfort, 1591, 1601; Nuremberg, 1676).

429. ———— (German tr. by Georgius Nigrinus) *Von Zauberern, Hexen und Unholden wahrhaftiger und wohlgegründeter Bericht* (Frankfort, 1592).

430. Godwin, William, *Lives of the Necromancers* (London, 1834; New York, 1835).

431. Görres, Johann Joseph von, *Die christliche Mystik* (Regensburg, 1836-42).

432. ———— (French tr. by Charles Sainte-Foi) *La mystique divine, naturelle, et diabolique* (Paris, 1854, 1861, 1882).

433. Gower, Lord Ronald [Charles Sutherland], *Joan of Arc* (London, 1893).

434. Graf, Arturo, *Il Diavolo* (Milan, 1889).

435. ———— (English tr. by Edward Noble Stone) *The Story of the Devil* (New York, 1931).

436. ———— (German tr. by R. Teuscher) *Geschichte des Teufelsglaubens* (Jena, 1893).

437. Grant, Sir Francis, Lord Cullen, *Sadducismus Debellatus* (London, 1698; pr. as *A True Narrative*, Edinburgh, 1698; Paisley, 1775).

438. Grässe, Johann Georg Theodor, *Bibliotheca Magica et Pneumatica* (Leipzig, 1843).

439. ———— *Trésor de livres rare* (Dresden, 1859).

440. Green, Samuel Abbot, *Groton in the Witch-craft Times* (Groton, Mass., 1883).

441. Greenslet, Ferris, *Joseph Glanvill* (New York, 1900).

442. Grevius, Johann, *Tribunal Reformatum* (Hamburg, 1622; Wolfenbüttel, 1727).

443. Grillandus, Paulus, *Tractatus de Hereticis et Sortilegiis* (Lyons, 1536, 1545; Frankfort, 1592).

444. Grillot de Givry, *La musée des sorciers, mages et alchimistes* (Paris, 1929).

445. ———— (English tr. by J. Courtenay Locke) *Witchcraft, Magic, and Alchemy* (London and Boston, 1931; New York, [1954]).

446. Groff, William, *Etudes sur la sorcellerie ou le rôle que la Bible a joué chez les sorciers* (Cairo, 1897).

447. Grönwald, F. W., *En Skansk Hexenprocess* (Lund, 1899).

448. Gropp, Ignatz, *Collectio Scriptorum et Rerum Wirceburgensium* (Frankfort, 1741).

449. Grosius, Henningus, *Magica, seu Mirabilium Historiarum de Spectris et Apparitionibus Spiritum* (Eisleben, 1597).

450. Grote, Otto Freiherr, *Ortia Lundemann oder der Zaubereiprocess zu Egeln, 1612* (Osterwieck, 1877).

451. Guaita, Stanislas de, *Essais des sciences maudites* (Paris, 1886, 1890).

452. ———— *Le temple de Satan* (Paris, 1891).

453. Guazzo, Francesco-Maria, *Compendium Maleficarum* (Milan, 1608, 1626).

454. ———— (English tr. ed. Montague Summers) (London, 1929).

455. Guidonis, Bernardus, *Practica Inquisitionis Heretice Pravitatis* (ed. C. Douais, Paris, 1886).

456. ———— (French tr.) *Manuel de l'inquisiteur* (Paris, 1926-27).

457. Gummere, Amelia Moth, *Witchcraft and Quakerism* (Philadelphia, 1908).

458. Günther, Ludwig, "Ein Hexenprozess: ein Kapitel aus der Geschichte des dunkelsten Aberglaubens," *Archiv für Kriminal-Anthropologie und Kriminalistik* (Leipzig), Vol. XIX (1905; repr. Giessen, 1906).

459. Guth, Johan Balthasar, *Das Ries wie es war und wie ist, eine historische-städtische Zeitschrift* (Nördlingen), Vol. VI.

460. Haas, Carl, *Die Hexenprozesse: ein cultur-historischer Versuch, nebst Dokumenten* (Tübingen, 1865).

461. Habricht, Hartwig, *Joseph Glanvill* (Zurich, 1936).

462. Haen, Anton von, *De Magia* (Leipzig, 1744).

463. Hainari, O. A. and Kustavi Grotenfelt, *Suoemen historia Ruotsin Mahtavuuden aikakaudella 1617-1721* (Jyväskylä, 1922).

464. Hale, John, *A Modest Inquiry into the Nature of Witchcraft and How Persons Guilty of that Crime may be Convicted* (Boston, 1702, 1771).

465. Hale, Sir Matthew, *Pleas of the Crown* (London, 1716).

466. Hallenberg, George P., *Dissertatio de Inquisitione Sagarum in Svecia 1668-77* (Uppsala, 1787).

467. Hallywell, Henry, *Melampronoea .·. .. With*

a *Solution of the Chiefest Objections Brought Against the Being of Witches* (London, 1681).

468. Hamel, Frank, *Human Animals* (London, 1915; New York, 1916).

469. Hammond, Esther Barstow, *Road to Endor* (New York, 1940).

470. Hansen, Joseph, "Heinrich Institoris, der Verfasser des Hexenhammers, und seine Tätigkeit an der Mosel im Jahre 1488," *Westdeutsche Zeitschrift für Geschichte und Kunst* (Treves), Vol. XVII (1898).

471. ———— *Quellen und Untersuchungen zur Geschichte des Hexenwahns und der Hexenverfolgung im Mittelalter* (Bonn, 1901).

472. ———— *Zauberwahn, Inquisition und Hexenprozess im Mittelalter* (Munich, 1900).

473. Harenberg, Johann Christoph, *Vampirs* (Wolffenbüttel, 1733).

474. Harpe, Jacqueline de la, *L'abbé Laurent Bordelon* (Berkeley, 1942).

475. Harrison, George Bagshawe, *Elizabethan Journal 1591-94* (New York, 1929).

476. Harsnett, Samuel, *A Declaration of Egregious Popish Impostures . . . under the Pretense of Casting out Devils* (London, 1603, 1605).

477. ———— *Discovery of the Fraudulent Practices of John Darrell* (London) 1599).

478. Hartmann, Franz, *Buried Alive* (Boston, 1895).

479. Hartmann, Wilhelm, *Die Hexenprozesse in der Stadt Hildesheim* (Hildesheim, 1927).

480. Hartwell, Abraham, *A True Discourse upon the Matter of Martha Brossier of Romorantin, Pretended to be Possessed by a Devil* (London, 1599).

481. *Harvard University Catalogue of English and American Chapbooks* (Cambridge, Mass., 1905).

482. Hauber, Eberhard David, *Bibliotheca, Acta et Scripta Magica* (Lemgo, 1738-45).

483. Hautefeuille and Santeur, *Les Sieurs de, Plaidoyez sur les magiciens et sur les sorciers, tenus en la Cour de Liége le 16 Decembre 1675, où on montre clairement qu'il n'y peut avoir de ces sortes de gens* (Liége, 1675).

484. Havekost, Ernest, *Die Vampirsage* (Halle, 1914).

485. Hawthorne, Nathaniel, *The House of the Seven Gables* (Boston, 1851).

486. Hearnshaw, F. J. C. (ed.), *The Social and Political Ideas of Some English Thinkers* (London, 1928).

487. Hecker, Justus Friedrich Karl, (English tr. by B. G. Babington) *The Epidemics of the Middle Ages* (London, 1844).

488. Heilig, Otto, "Zur Kenntnis des Hexenwesens am Kaiserstuhl," *Zeitschrift des Vereins für Volkskunde* (Berlin), Vol. XIV (1904).

489. Held, Gerrit Jean, *Magie, Hekserij, Entoverij* (Groningen, 1950).

490. Hélot, Docteur Charles, *Névroses et possessions diaboliques* (12th ed., Paris, 1898).

491. Hennen, Dr. Gerhard, *Ein Hexenprozess aus der Umgegend von Trier aus dem Jahre 1572* (St. Wendel, 1887).

492. Hermann, Ernst, *Die Hexen von Baden-Baden* (Karlsruhe, [1890]).

493. Hernandez, Ludovico (ed.), *Le procès inquisitorial de Gilles de Rais* (Paris, 1921).

494. Hertz, Wilhelm, *Der Werwolf* (Stuttgart, 1862).

495. Hertzberg, Rafaël, *Kulturbilder ur Finlands historia II: Hexprocesser på 1600 talet* (Helsinki, 1888).

496. ———— *Vidskepelsen i Finland på 1600 talet: Bidrag till Finlands kulturhistoria* (Helsinki, 1889).

497. Heywood, Thomas, *The Hierarchy of the Blessed Angels* (London, 1635).

498. [Hickes, Thomas,] *Ravillac Redivivus* (London, 1685).

499. Hildebrand, Wolfgang, *Goetia vel Theurg* (Leipzig, 1631).

500. Hillyer, Anthony [Thomas Perry Stricke] *Elizabeth's Merlin* (Los Angeles, 1947, ed.).

501. Hinschius, Paul, *System des katholi Kirchenrechts* (Berlin, 1893), Vol. V

502. *Histoire admirable de la maladie prodigieuse de Pierre Creusé arrivée en la ville de Niort en 1628* (Niort, 1631, ed. L. Faure, 1881).

503. *L'histoire des diables de Loudun* (Paris, 1716).

504. *Histoire espouventable et véritable arrivée en la ville de Soliers en Provence d'un homme qui s'estoit voué pour estre d'Esglise et qui n'ayant accomply son voeu le diable lui a couppé les parties honteuses* (Paris, 1619; Lyons, 1875).

505. *Histoire de Magdelaine Bavent, religieuse du monastère de Saint-Louis de Louviers, avec sa confession générale et testamentaire* (Paris, 1652; ed. Père Desmarets, Rouen, 1878, ltd. ed.).

506. ——— (English tr. by Montague Summers) *Confessions of Madeleine Bavent* (London, 1933).

507. *The History of Witches, Ghosts, and Highland Seers* (Berwick, [? 1803]).

508. *A History of the Witches of Renfrewshire* (Paisley, 1809, 1877).

509. Hoadly, C. J., "A Case of Witchcraft in Hartford," *Connecticut Magazine*, Vol. V (1899).

510. Hodder, Mabel Elisabeth, *Peter Binsfeld and Cornelius Loos* (diss., Ithaca, 1911).

511. Hole, Christina, *Haunted England* (London, 1940, 1950).

512. ——— *A Mirror of Witchcraft* (London, 1957).

513. ——— *Witchcraft in England* (London, 1945; New York, 1947).

514. [Holland, Henry,] *A Treatise Against Witchcraft* (Cambridge, 1590).

515. Holmes, Thomas James, *Cotton Mather* (Cambridge, Mass., 1940).

516. ——— *Cotton Mather and His Writings on Witchcraft* (Chicago, 1926).

517. Holt, Sir John, *Modern Cases [1702-3] Argued and Adjudged* (London, 1716).

518. ——— *A Report of All the Cases Determined by Sir John Holt 1681-1710* (London, 1738).

519. Holzinger, J. B., *Zur Naturgeschichte der Hexen* (Graz, 1883).

520. Homes, Nathaniel, *Demonology and Theology* (London, 1650).

521. Hopkin, Charles Edward, *The Share of Thomas Aquinas in the Growth of the Witchcraft Delusion* (Philadelphia, 1940).

522. Hopkins, Matthew, *The Discovery of Witches* (London, 1647; Great Totham, Essex, 1837; ed. Montague Summers, London, 1928).

523. Hopper, Vincent Foster, *Medieval Number Symbolism* (New York, 1938).

524. Horst, Georg Conrad, *Daemonomagie, oder Geschichte des Glaubens an Zauberei und daemonische Wunder* (Frankfort, 1818).

525. ——— *Zauberbibliothek* (Mainz, 1821-26).

526. Hort, Gertrude M., *Dr. John Dee* (London, 1922).

527. Housman, Clemence, *The Werewolf* (London, 1896).

528. Howard, Henry, Earl of Northampton, *Defensative Against Poison* ([London,] 1583, 1620).

529. Howell, Thomas Bayle, *State Trials* (London, 1816-28).

530. Howitt, William, *Visits to Remarkable Places* (London, 1840).

531. Hughes, Pennethorne, *Witchcraft* (London, [1952]).

532. Humborg, Ludwig, "Die Hexenprozesse in der Stadt Münster," *Münstersche Beiträge zur Geschichtsforschung*, n.s., Vol. XXXI (1914).

533. Hutchinson, Francis, *An Historical Essay Concerning Witchcraft* (London, 1718, 1720).

534. ——— (German tr.) *Historischer Versuch von der Hexerey* (Leipzig, 1726).

535. Hutchinson, Thomas, *History of the Colony of Massachusetts Bay* (Boston, 1764, 1828; London, 1765; Cambridge, Mass., 1936).

6. Huysmans, Joris-Karl, *Là bas* (Paris, 1891).

7. ——— (English tr. by Keene Wallis) *Down There* (New York, 1958).

Huxley, Aldous, *The Devils of Loudun* (London, 1952).

The Impossibility of Witchcraft Plainly Proving . . . That There Never Was a Witch (London, 1712).

540. Inderwick, F. A., *Side-Lights on the Stuarts* (London, 1888).

541. Ireland, William Henry, *Memoirs of Jeanne d'Arc* (London, 1824).

542. Isambert, François André, *Recueil général des anciennes lois françaises* (Paris, 1821-33).

543. Isolani, Isidoro, *Libellus Adversus Magos, Divinatores, Maleficos* (Milan, 1506).

544. Jackson, Shirley, *The Witchcraft of Salem Village* (New York, 1956).

545. Jacomet, Daniel, *Jehanne d'Arc . . . documents originaux* (Paris, 1933, ltd. ed.).

546. Jacquier, Nicholas, *Flagellum Haereticorum Fascinariorum* (Frankfort, 1581).

547. Jäger, Dr., "Geschichte des Hexenbrennens in Franken," *Archiv des historischen Vereins für den Untermainkreis* (Würzburg), Vol. II (1834).

548. Jäger, Karl, *Die Hexenverfolgung im Amt Homburg* (Bad Homburg, 1931).

549. Jahn, Ulrich, "Hexenwesen und Zauberei in Pommern," *Gesellschaft für Pommersche Geschichte* (Stettin), Vol. XXXVI (1886).

550. James I, *Demonology* (Edinburgh, 1597; London, 1603, ed. G. B. Harrison, 1924).

551. James, Montague Rode, *Lists of Manuscripts Formerly Owned by Dr. John Dee* (Oxford, 1921).

552. Janssen, Johannes, *Geschichte des deutschen Volkes seit dem Ausgang des Mittelalters* (ed. Ludwig von Pastor, Freiburg, 1883-1894), Vol. VIII.

553. ——— (English tr. by Mary A. Mitchell and A. M. Christie) *History of the German People After the Close of the Middle Ages* (London, 1896-1910), Vol. XVI.

554. "A Jesuit Philanthropist," *Church Quarterly Review*, Vol. LVII (1904).

555. Joel, Frank, *De Morbis Hyperphysicis* (Rostock, 1580).

556. Jones, Ernest, *Nightmare, Witches, and Devils* (New York, 1931; 2d ed., *On the Nightmare*, London, 1949).

557. Jordonaius, Joannes, *Disputatio Brevis et Categorica de Proba Stigmatica* (Cologne, 1630).

558. *Judicum Matris Kepleri* ([? Frankfort,] 1860).

559. Kanold, Johann, [*Breslauer-Sammlung:*] *Supplementum III. Curieuser und nutzbarer Anmerkungen von Natur- und Kunst-Geschichten* (Bautzen, 1728).

560. Keiller, Alex, *The Personnel of the Aberdeenshire Witchcraft Covens* (1922).

561. Kerdaniel, Edouard L. de, *Sorciers de Savoie* (Annecy, 1900).

562. Kernot, Henry, *Bibliotheca Diabolica* [Scribner, Sales Cat.] (New York, 1874).

563. Kheuller, Sebastian, *Murke Bund warhafftige Historia* (Munich, [1579]; Vienna, 1885).

564. Kiesewetter, Carl, *John Dee: ein Spiritist des 16. Jahrhunderts* (Leipzig, 1897).

565. Kirk, Robert, *Secret Commonwealth* (Edinburgh, 1815, ltd. ed.; ed. Andrew Lang, 1893, ltd. ed.; ed. R. B. Cunninghame Graham, Stirling, 1933).

566. Kittredge, George Lyman, "English Witchcraft and James I," *Studies in History of Religions Presented to Crawford Howell Toy* (New York, 1912).

567. ——— "King James I and The Devil is an Ass," *Modern Philology*, Vol. IX (1911).

568. ——— *Witchcraft in Old and New England* (Cambridge, Mass., 1929; New York, 1958).

569. Klein, Johann, *Meditatio Academica Exhibens Examen Juridicum Judicialis Lamiarum Confessionis Se ex Nefando cum Satana Coitu Prolem Suscepisse Humanum* (Güstrow, 1698, 1731, 1741).

570. *Kleiner Beitrag zur Geschichte des Hexenwesens im 16. Jahrhundert* (Treves, 1830).

571. Klélé, J., *Hexenwahn und Hexenprozesse in der ehemaligen Reichsstadt und Landvogtei Hagenau* (Hagenau, 1893).

572. Knortz, Karl, *Hexen, Teufel und Blocksbergspuk in Geschichte, Sage und Literatur* (Annaberg, [1913]).

573. Knuttel, W. P. C., *Balthasar Bekker die Bestrijder van het Bijgeloof* (The Hague, 1906).

574. Koch, Hugo, *Hexenprozesse und Reste des Hexenglaubens in der Wetterau* (Giessen, 1935).

575. Kohler, Joseph, "Bodinus und die Hexenverfolgung," *Archiv für Strafrecht und Strafprozess* (Berlin), Vol. LXVI (1918).

576. ——— and Willy Scheel (eds.) *Die peinliche Gerichtsordnung Kaiser Karls V: Constitutio Criminalis Carolina, 1532* (Halle, 1900).

577. König, Bruno Emil, *Ausgeburten des Menschenwahns im Spiegel der Hexenprozesse und der Auto da fé's* (Rudolstadt, 1893; Berlin, 1926, [194-?]).

578. *Der Königs-Herren Commissarien gehaltenes Protocol über die entdeckte Zauberey in dem Dorff Mohra* (The Hague, 1670).

579. Köppen, K. F., *Hexen und Hexenprozesse* (Leipzig, 1844).

580. Kuebert, Hans, *Zauberwahn, die Greuel der Inquisition und Hexenprozesse* (Munich, 1913).

581. Ladame, Paul, *Procès criminel de la dernière sorcière brulée à Genève le 6 avril 1652* (Paris, 1888).

582. Lamb, Charles, *Witches* (London, [1929]).

583. Lambard, William, *Eirenarcha* (London, 1614).

584. Lamberg, M. J. Graf von, *Criminalverfahren vorzüglich bei Hexenprozessen im ehemaligen Bistum Bamberg während der Jahre 1624-30* (Nuremberg, 1835).

585. Lamothe-Langon, Etienne Léon de, *Histoire de l'Inquisition en France* (Paris, 1829).

586. Lancre, Pierre de, *L'incrédulité et mécréance du sortilège* (Paris, 1622).

587. ——— (German tr.) *Wunderbarliche Geheimnüsse der Zauberey* (n.p., 1630).

588. ——— *Du sortilège* (Paris, 1627).

589. ——— *Tableau de l'inconstance des mauvais anges et démons* (Paris, 1612, 1613).

590. Lang, Andrew, *Book of Dreams and Ghosts* (London, 1897).

591. ——— *Cock Lane and Common Sense* (London, 1894).

592. ——— *The Maid of France* (London, 1908).

593. ——— *The Making of Religion* (London, 1898).

594. Längin, Georg, *Religion und Hexenprozess* (Leipzig, 1888).

595. Langton, Edward, *Satan, a Portrait* (London, [1949]).

596. Lardy, Charles, *Les procédures de sorcellerie à Neuchâtel* (Neuchâtel, 1866).

597. Laurent, Charles, *Sainte Jeanne d'Arc* (Paris, 1935).

598. Lavater, Ludwig, *Von Gespänsten vaghüren, fälen und anderen wunderbaren Dingen* (Zurich, 1569).

599. ——— (English tr. by Robert Harrison) *Of Ghosts and Spirits Walking by Night* (London, 1572, 1596; ed. J. Dover Wilson, Oxford, 1929).

600. ——— (Latin tr.) *De Spectris, Lemuribus et Magis* (Geneva, 1570; Leyden, 1659).

601. Law, T. G., "Devil Hunting in Elizabethan England," *Nineteenth Century* (1894).

602. *Laws Against Witches and Conjuration . . . also the Confession of Mother Lakeland* (London, 1645).

603. Lawson, Deodat, *A Brief and True Narrative* (Boston, 1692; London, 1693, 1694).

604. Laymann, Paul, *Theologia Moralis* (Antwerp, 1634; Padua, 1733).

605. Lea, Henry Charles, *History of the Inquisition of the Middle Ages* (New York, 1887, 1955; London, 1888).

606. ——— *History of the Inquisition in Spain* (New York and London, 1906).

607. ——— *Materials Toward a History of Witchcraft* (Philadelphia, 1939, ltd. ed.; New York, 1957).

608. ——— *Studies in Church History* (Philadelphia, 1883).

609. ——— *Superstition and Force* (Philadelphia, 1866; 4th rev. ed., 1892).

610. ——— "The Witch Persecutions in Transalpine Europe" in *Minor Historical Writings* (Philadelphia, 1942).

611. Lecanu, Abbé [pseudonym], *Histoire du Satan* (Paris, 1861).

612. Lecky, William E. Hartpole, *History of the Rise and Influence of the Spirit of Rationalism in Europe* (New York, 1866).

613. Leclerc, L., *Notice sur Nicholas Remy, procureur général de Lorraine* (Nancy, 1869).

614. Lecocq, Ad., *Les sorciers de la Beauce* (Chartres, 1861, ltd. ed.).

615. Legge, F., "The Origin of the Medieval Belief in Witchcraft," *Scottish Review* (1893).

616. Legué, Gabriel, *Médecins et empoisonneurs au xvii⁰ siècle* (Paris, 1896).

617. ———— *Urbain Grandier et les possédées de Loudun* (Paris, 1880, ltd. ed.).

618. ———— and Gilles de la Tourette, *Soeur Jeanne des Anges, autobiographie d'une hystérique possédée* [Paris, 1886].

619. Lehmann, Alfred G. L., *Aberglaube und Zauberei* (Stuttgart, 1898, 1908).

620. Leib, Johann, *Consilia* (Frankfort, 1666).

621. Leitschuh, Friedrich, *Beiträge zur Geschichte des Hexenwesens in Franken* (Bamberg, 1883).

622. Leland, Charles Godfrey, *Arcadia or the Gospel of the Witches* (London, 1899).

623. Le Loyer, Pierre, *Discours et histoires des spectres* (Paris, 1605).

624. ———— (English tr. by Zachary Jones) *A Treatise of Specters* (London, 1605).

625. ———— *Quatre livres des spectres ou apparitions et visions d'esprits* (Angers, 1586).

626. Lempens, Carl, *Geschichte der Hexen und Hexenprozesse* (St. Gall, 1880).

627. Leriche, Abbé, *Etudes sur les possessions . . . et sur celle de Loudun en particulier* (Paris, 1859).

628. Lespy, V., "Les sorcières dans le Béarn 1393-1672," *Bullétin de la société des sciences, lettres et arts de Pau*, II Série, Vol. IV (1875).

629. Leuret, François, *Fragments psychologiques sur la folie* (Paris, 1834).

630. Levermore, C. H., *New Englander*, Vol. XLIV (1885).

631. Lévi, Eliphas Alphonse Louis Constant, *Dogme et rituel de la haute magie* (Paris, 1861).

632. ———— (English tr. by A. E. Waite) *The History of Magic* (London, 1922).

633. Levin, David, *What Happened in Salem?* (New York, 1952).

634. Lévy-Bruhl, Henri, *Revue de folklore français et de folklore colonial*, Vol. I (1930).

635. Lewis, Dominic Bevan Wyndham, *The Soul of Marshal Gilles de Raiz* (London, 1952).

636. Liel, Anselm Franz Joseph, "Die Verfolgung der Zauberer und Hexen in dem Kurfürstenthume Trier," *Archiv für rheinische Geschichte*, Vol. I (1834).

637. *Life of Sir John Holt* (London, 1764).

638. Liisberg, Bering, *Vesten for sø og Østen for Hav 'Trolddom i København og I Edinburg 1590: Ev Bidrag til Hekseprocessernes Historie* (Copenhagen, 1909).

639. Lilienthal, J. A., *Die Hexenprocesse der beiden Städte Braunsberg* (Kaliningrad, 1861).

640. Limborch, Philip van, *Historia Inquisitionis* (Amsterdam, 1692).

641. ———— (English tr. by Samuel Chandler) *History of the Inquisition* (London, 1731).

642. Lindeqvist, K. O., *Taikausto ja noitavainot* (Porvoo, 1924).

643. Linderholm, Emanuel, *De Stora Häxprocesserna i Sverige* (Uppsala, 1918).

644. Linton, Elizabeth Lynn, *Witch Stories* (London, 1861).

645. Llorente, Juan Antonio, *Histoire critique de l'Inquisition d'Espagne* (Paris, 1818).

646. Lodtmann, Justus Friedrich August, "Die letzten Hexen Osnabrücks und ihr Richter," *Mittheilungen des historischen Vereins zu Osnabrück*, Vol. X (1875).

647. Löher, Hermann, *Hochnötige unterthänige wemütige Klage der frommen Unschultigen* (Amsterdam, 1676).

648. Loos, Cornelius, *De Vera et Falsa Magia* (Cologne, 1592).

649. Lorédan, Jean, *Un grand procès de sorcellerie au xvii⁰ siècle: l'abbé Gaufridy et Madeleine de Demandolx* (Paris, 1912).

650. Lorgion, Everard Jan Dienst, *Balthazar Bekker in Amsterdam* (Groningen, 1851).

651. ———— *Balthazar Bekker in Francken* (Groningen, 1848).

652. Loseby, Charles Edgar, *Witches, Mediums, Vagrants and Law* (Manchester, 1946).

653. Louïse, Théophile, *De la sorcellerie et de la justice criminelle à Valenciennes, xvi⁰-xvii⁰ siècles* (Valenciennes, 1861).

654. Ludovicus à Paramo, *De Origine et Progressu Officii Sanctae Inquisitionis* (Madrid, 1598).

655. Lupo da Bergamo, Ignatius, *Nova Lux in Edictum Sanctissimae Inquisitionis* (Bergamo, 1648).

656. Maasburg, Friedrich von, *Theresianische Halsgerichtsordnung* (Vienna, 1880).

657. MacAlpine, Ida and Richard A. Hunter, *Schizophrenia 1677: a Psychiatric Study of an Illustrated Autobiographical Record of Demoniacal Possession* [London, 1956, ltd. ed.].

658. McBryde, John M., "Some Medieval Charms," *Sewanee Review* (1917).

659. McCasland, Selby Vernon, *By the Finger of God* (New York, 1951).

660. Mackay, Charles, *Memoirs of Extraordinary Popular Delusions* (London, 1841; Philadelphia, 1850; Boston, 1932).

661. Mackenzie, Sir George, *Laws and Customs of Scotland in Matters Criminal* (Edinburgh, 1678, 1699).

662. Mackinnon, Flora Isabel, *Philosophical Writings of Henry More* (New York, 1925).

663. Macleod, Malcolm, *History of Witches* (London, 1793; New York, 1804, 1892; Albany, 1814).

664. Macnish, Robert, *The Philosophy of Sleep* (Glasgow, 1830).

665. McWilliams, Carey, *Witch Hunt, the Revival of Heresy* (Boston, 1950).

666. Madden, Richard Robert, *Phantasmata or Illusions and Fanaticism* (London, 1857).

667. *Magnum Bullarium Romanum* (Lyons, 1592; Luxembourg, 1739).

668. Malmquist, H., *Om Hexprocessen i Dalarne 1757-63* (Lund, 1877).

669. Mamor, Petrus, *Flagellum Maleficorum* (Lyons, 1490, 1621).

670. Manser, Gallus M., "Thomas von Aquin und der Hexenwahn," *Jahrbuch für Philosophie und spekulative Theologie*, Vol. IX (1922).

671. Mantz, Harold Elmer, "Jean Bodin and the Sorcerers," *Romanic Review*, Vol. XV (1924).

672. Marchand, George, "Bodin et les sorciers," *Province d'Anjou*, No. 20 (1929).

673. Marchand, Jean, *Le procès d̄e condamnation de Jeanne d'Arc* (Paris, 1955, ltd. ed.).

674. *Maria Renata Singer von Mossau: Die letzte deutsche Hexe* (Leipzig, 1849).

675. Marie de France, *Lai de Bisclaveret* (Paris, 1819).

676. [Marshall, F.,] *A Brief History of Witchcraft with Especial Reference to the Witches of Northamptonshire* (Northampton, 1866).

677. Marx, Jean, *L'Inquisition en Dauphiné* (Paris, 1914).

678. Mary, André, *Paroles authentiques de Jeanne d'Arc tirées du procès du 1431* (Paris, 1931).

679. Mason, James, *The Anatomy of Sorcery* (London, 1612).

680. Massé, Pierre, *De l'imposture et tromperie des diables* (Paris, 1579).

681. Masson, Dr. A., *La sorcellerie et la science des poisons au xvii⁰ siècle* (Paris, 1904).

682. Mather, Cotton, *Diary* (ed. Worthington C. Ford, Boston, 1911).

683. ———— *Magnalia Christi Americana* (London, 1702).

684. ———— *Memorable Providences Relating to Witchcrafts and Possessions* (Boston, 1689; London, 1691; Edinburgh, 1697).

685. ———— *Wonders of the Invisible World* (Boston and London, 1693; extracted Cotton Mather on Witchcraft, Mount Vernon, New York, 1950).

686. Mather, Increase, *Cases of Conscience Concerning Evil Spirits* (Boston, 1693).

687. ———— *An Essay for the Recording of Illustrious Providences* (Boston, 1684, 1856; London, 1890).

688. Maule, Thomas, *The Truth Held Forth and Maintained* (New York, 1695, 1927).

689. Mayo, Dr. Herbert, *On the Truths Contained in Popular Superstitions* (Edinburgh, 1851).

690. Meincke, Daniel, *De Incubo, Dissertationem Medicam Inauguralem* (Jena, 1624).

691. Meinhold, Wilhelm, *Maria Schweidler die Bernsteinhexe: der interessanteste aller bisher bekannten Hexenprozesse* (Berlin, 1843, [192- ?]; Leipzig, [1908]; Schwerin, [1954]).

692. ———— (English tr. by Lady Duff Gordon) *Mary Schweidler, the Amber Witch* (London, 1844; New York, 1845).

693. Mejer, Ludwig, *Ueber den Ursprung des Hexenthums* [extract: n.p., 1867].

694. Mellor, Alex, *La torture* (Paris, 1949).

695. Memminger, A., *Das verhexte Kloster* (Würzburg, 1904, 1908).

696. Ménardaye, Jean Baptiste de la, *Examen et discussion critique* (Paris, 1747).

697. Menghi, Girolamo, *Compendio dell'arte essorcistica* (Bologna, 1580).

698. ———— *Flagellum Daemonum: Exorcismus Terribiles, Potentissimos, et Efficaces* (Bologna, 1582; Bonn, 1588; Venice, 1606, 1644).

699. ———— *Fustum Daemonis* (Frankfort, 1582).

700. Merzbacher, Friedrich, *Die Hexenprozesse in Franken* (Munich, 1957).

701. Meunier, Georges, *Gilles de Rais et son temps* (Paris, 1949).

702. Meyer, Carl, *Der Aberglaube des Mittelalters und der nächstfolgenden Jahrhunderte* (Basel, 1884).

703. Meyfarth, Johann Matthäus, *Christliche Erinnerung* (Schleusingen, 1635).

704. Michaëlis, Sebastian, *Histoire admirable de la possession et conversion d'une pénitente* (Paris, 1613).

705. ———— (English tr. by W. B.) *The Admirable History of the Possession and Conversion of a Penitent Woman* (London, 1613).

706. ———— *Pneumalogie, ou discours des esprits* (Paris, 1587; Lyons, 1614).

707. ———— (English tr.) *A Discourse of Spirits* (London, 1613).

708. Michelet, Jules, *Louis XIV et la Révolution* (Paris, 1860).

709. ———— *La sorcière* (Paris, 1862, 1863, 1865, 1952).

710. ———— (English tr. by L. J. Trotter) *The Witch of the Middle Ages* (London, 1863).

711. ———— (English tr. by A. R. Allinson) *Satanism and Witchcraft* (New York, 1939).

712. Miller, Arthur, *The Crucible* (New York, 1953).

713. Mirville, Jules Eudes, Marquis de, *Des Esprits* (Paris, 1854, 1863).

714. ———— *Fragment d'un ouvrage inédit* (Paris, 1852).

715. *Miscellany of the Spottiswoode Society*, Vol. II (Edinburgh, 1845).

716. Mitchell, J. and J. Dickie, *The Philosophy of Witchcraft* (Paisley, 1839).

717. Molinier, Charles, *L'Inquisition dans le midi de la France au xiii⁰ et au xiv⁰ siècle* (Paris, 1880).

718. Molitor, Ulrich, *De Lamiis et Phitonicis Mulieribus* (n.p., 1489; Paris, 1561).

719. ———— (French tr.) *Des sorcières* (Paris, 1926, ltd. ed.).

720. ———— (German tr.) *Hexen meystere* ([Cologne,] 1544).

721. ———— (German tr.) *Von Hexen und Unholden* ([Strasbourg,] 1575).

722. Mongredien, Georges, *Madame de Montespan et l'affaire des poisons* (Paris, [ ).

723. Monoyer, Jules, *La sorcellerie en Hainaut spécialement aux environs de Mons* (Mons, 1886).

724. [Montmorency, Nicholas de, Comterre,] *Histoire véritable et mémorable de ce qui c'est passé sous l'exorcisme de trois filles possédées és pais de Flandres, en la descouverte et confession de Marie de Sains* (Paris, 1624).

725. More, George, *A True Discourse of the Certain Possession* (Lo[

726. More, Henry, *An Antidote Against Atheism* (London, 1653, rev. ed., 1655).
727. Morelle, Paul, *Histoire de la sorcellerie* (Paris, 1946).
728. Morin, A. S., *Le prêtre et le sorcier* (Paris, 1872).
729. *A Most Certain, Strange and True Discovery of a Witch* (London, 1643; Ingram, Pa., 1939, ltd. ed.).
730. *The Most Strange and Admirable Discovery of the Three Witches of Warboys* (London, 1593).
731. *A Most Wicked Work of a Wretched Witch* (London, 1593).
732. *The Most Wonderful and True Story of a Certain Witch Named Alice Gooderidge of Stapenhill . . . As Also a True Report of the Strange Torments of Thomas Darling* (London, 1597).
733. Mousseaux, Gougenot des, *Moeurs et pratiques des démons ou des esprits visiteurs* (Paris, 1854).
734. Mudge, Zachariah Atwell, *Witch Hill: A History of Salem Witchcraft* (New York, [c. 1871]).
735. Muller, Friedrich, *Beiträge zur Geschichte des Hexenglaubens und des Hexenprocesses in Siebenbürgen* (Brunswick, 1854).
736. Müller, Karl Otto, "Heinrich Institoris, der Verfasser des Hexenhammers, und seine Tätigkeit als Hexeninquisitor in Ravensburg im Herbst 1484," *Württemberg. Vierteljahrshefte für Landesgeschichte* (Stuttgart), Vol. XIX (1910).
737. Mundy, John H., *Liberty and Political Power in Toulouse* (New York, 1954).
738. Murdock, Kenneth B., *Selections from Cotton Mather* (New York, 1926).
739. Murisier, Ernest, *Les maladies du sentiment religieux* (Paris, 1901).
740. Murner, Thomas, *Tractatus Perutilis de Pythonico Contractu* ([? Kirchheim,] 1499).
741. Murray, Douglas, *Jeanne d'Arc* (New York, 1902).
742. Murray, Margaret Alice, *The Divine King in England* (London, 1954).
743. ———— *The God of the Witches* (London, 1933).
744. ———— *The Witch Cult in Western Europe* (Oxford, 1921).
745. *A Narrative of the Sufferings and Relief of a Young Girl Strangely Molested by Evil Spirits* (Paisley, 1775).
746. *A Narrative of the Sufferings of a Young Girl called Mary Dunbar, 1712* (ed. MacSkimin, Belfast, 1822).
747. Nass, Lucien, *Les empoisonnements sous Louis XIV* (Paris, 1898).
748. Naudé, Gabriel, *Apologie pour les grands hommes soupçonnez de magie* (Paris, 1625; Amsterdam, 1712).
749. ———— (English tr. by J. Davies) *The History of Magic by Way of Apology for All the Wise Men Who Have Unjustly Been Reputed Magicians* (London, 1657).
750. Naylor, M. J., *Four Sermons Preached at All Saints Church, Huntingdon, on the 25th Day of March, 1792-3-4-5: The Inanity and Mischief of Vulgar Superstitions* (Cambridge, 1795).
751. Nehring, Johann Christian, *De Indiciis* (Jena, 1666, 1714).
752. Nevins, Winfield Scott, *Witchcraft in Salem Village in 1692* (Salem and Boston, 1892).
753. Nevius, John Livingston, *Demon Possession and Allied Themes* (Chicago, 1894, 1896).
754. *News from Scotland, Declaring the Damnable Life of Dr. Fian, a Notable Sorcerer* (London, 1591; *Gentleman's Magazine*, 1779; Roxburghe Club, 1816; Bodley Head Quartos, 1924).
755. Niau, Monsieur des, *La véritable histoire [de Loudun] . . . par un témoin* (Poitiers, 1634).
756. ———— (English tr. by Edmund Goldsmid) *The History of the Devils of Loudun* (Edinburgh, 1887-88, ltd. ed.).
757. ————s, Augustin, *Si la torture est un moyen à vérifier les crimes secrets* (Amsterdam, 1682).
758. ———— Isaac, *A Sermon Against Witchcraft preached in Great Paxton, Hunting-*...*17, 1808* (London, 1808).
759. ————nnes, *Formicarius* (Augsburg,

1475, [1484]; Strasbourg, 1517; Paris, 1519; Douai, 1602; Helmstädt, 1692).
760. ———— *Praeceptorium* (Basel, [1470]).
761. Niehues, Bernard, *Zur Geschichte des Hexenglaubens und der Hexenprozesse, vornämlich im ehemaligen Fürst-Bistum Münster* (Münster, 1875).
762. Nodé, Pierre, *Déclamation contre l'erreur exécrable des maléficiers* (Paris, 1578).
763. Notestein, Wallace, *History of Witchcraft in England from 1558 to 1718* (Washington, 1911).
764. Nyerup, Rasmus, *Udsigt over Hexeprocesserne her i Norden* (Copenhagen, 1823).
765. Nynauld, Jean de, *De la lycanthropie, transformation, et extase des sorciers* (Paris, 1615).
766. ———— (Dutch tr.) (Haarlem, 1645).
767. O'Callaghan, Edmund Bailey, *Documentary History of the State of New York* (Albany, 1850).
768. O'Donnell, Elliott, *Werewolves* (London, 1912).
769. Odorico, Federico, *Le Streghe di Valtellina e la Santa Inquisizione, con documenti inediti del secolo xvi* (n.p., 1861).
770. Oesterreich, Traugott Konstantin, *Possession, Demoniacal and Other* (London and New York, 1930).
771. Ohle, Rudolf, *Die Hexen in und um Prenzlau* (Prenzlau, 1908).
772. Olaus Magnus, *Historia de Gentibus Septentrionalibus* (Rome, 1555).
773. ———— (English tr.) *A Compendious History of the Goths, Swedes, and Vandals* (London, 1658).
774. Oldekop, Justus, *Observationes Criminales Practicae* (Bremen, 1654; Frankfort-on-Oder, 1698).
775. Oldenburger, Philipp Andreas, *Thesaurus Rerum Publicarum* (Geneva, 1675).
776. Oliverio Vicentino, Carolo, *Baculus Daemonum Conjurationis Malignorum Spirituum* (Perugia, 1618).
777. Orians, G. H., "New England Witchcraft in Fiction," *American Literature*, Vol. II (1930).
778. Osborne, Francis, *Miscellaneous Works* (London, 1722), Vol. I.
779. ———— *Miscellany of Sundry Essays* (London, 1659).
780. Ostermann, Peter, *Commentarius Juridicus* (Cologne, 1629).
781. Oursel, Raymond, *Jeanne d'Arc* (Tours, 1952).
782. ———— *Le procès de condamnation de Jeanne d'Arc* [Paris, 1953].
783. Owen, Robert Dale, *Footfalls on the Boundary of Another World* (Philadelphia, 1860, 1875; London, 1861).
784. Palingh, Abraham, *Het afgerukt mom-aangezicht der Tooverij* (Amsterdam, 1659).
785. Palou, Jean, *La sorcellerie* (Paris, 1957).
786. Paltsits, Victor Hugo, *Minutes of the Executive Council of the Province of New York* (Albany, 1910).
787. Parfouru, Paul, "Un procès de sorcellerie au Parlement de Bretagne: la condamnation de l'abbé Poussinière, 1642-43," *Revue l'Hermine* (Rennes, 1893).
788. Parke, Francis Neal, "Witchcraft in Maryland," *Maryland Historical Magazine*, Vol. XXXI (1936).
789. Parrinder, Geoffrey, *Witchcraft* (London, 1958).
790. Paul, Henry N., *The Royal Play of Macbeth* (New York, 1951).
791. Pauls, Emil, "Zauberwesen und Hexenwahn am Niederrhein," *Beiträge zur Geschichte des Niederrheins*, Vol. XIII (1898).
792. Paulus, Nicolaus, *Hexenwahn und Hexenprozess, vornehmlich im 16. Jahrhundert* (Freiburg, 1910).
793. Payer-Thurn, R., "Faust in Mariazell," *Chronik des wiener Goethe-Vereins*, Vol. XXXIX (1924).
794. Pensa, Henri, *Sorcellerie et religion* (Paris, 1933).
795. Perkins, William, *A Discourse of the Damned Art of Witchcraft* (Cambridge, 1608, 1610).
796. ———— (German tr.) [Hanover,] 1610).
797. Pernoud, Régine, *Vie et mort de Jeanne d'Arc* [Paris, 1953].

798. Perreaud, François, *Démonologie ou traicté des démons et sorciers* (Geneva, 1653).
799. Petersdorff, Egon von, *Daemonologie* (Munich, 1956).
800. Peucer, Casper, *Commentarius de Praecipuis Divinationum Generibus* (Wittenberg, 1560, 1572, 1576).
801. Pfister, Charles, "Nicolas Remy et la sorcellerie de Lorraine à la fin du xvie siècle," *Revue historique* (Paris), Vol. XCIII (1907).
802. Pfister, Oscar, *Calvins Eingreifen in die Hexenprozesse 1545* (Zurich, 1947).
803. Pico della Mirandola, Gianfrancesco, *Strix, sive de Ludificatione Daemonum* (Bologna, 1523).
804. ———— (Italian tr. by Leandro delli Alberto) *Libro detto Strega o delle Illusioni del Demonio* (Bologna, 1524; Venice, 1556).
805. ———— (Italian tr.) *Dialogo intitolato la Strega, overo de gli inganni de' Demoni* (Pescia, 1555; Milan, 1864).
806. Pitcairn, Robert, *Criminal Trials in Scotland from A.D. 1488 to 1624*, Maitland Club (Edinburgh, 1833).
807. Pitts, John Linwood, *Witchcraft and Devil Lore in the Channel Islands* (Guernsey, 1886; partly repr. [by E. Goldsmid] *Confessions of Witches under Torture*, Edinburgh, 1886, ltd. ed.).
808. Plancy, Jacques Albin Simon Collin de, *Dictionnaire infernal* (Paris, 1818, 1825, 6th rev. ed., 1863).
809. Plantsch, Martin, *Opusculum de Sagis Maleficis* (Pforzheim, 1507).
810. Poitiers, Jean de, *Les diables de Loudun* (Paris, 1876).
811. Pollack, Heinrich, *Mittheilungen über den Hexenprozess in Deutschland insbesondere über verschiedene Westphälische Hexenprozessakten* (Berlin, 1886).
812. Pollock, Sir Frederick, "The Theory of Persecution," *Essays in Jurisprudence and Ethics* (London, 1882).
813. Pomponazzi, Pietro, *De Naturalium Effectuum Causis* (Basel, 1556).
814. Ponzinibio, Gianfrancesco, *Tractatus de Lamiis* (ed. Zilotti, Venice, 1563, 1584; Frankfort, 1587, 1592).
815. Porta, Johannes Baptista, *Magiae Naturalis sive de Miraculis Rerum Naturalium* (Antwerp, 1560; Frankfort, 1597).
816. ———— (English tr.) *Natural Magic* (London, 1658).
817. ———— (French tr. by Meyssonnier) *Magia Naturalis* (Lyons, 1688).
818. Pott, Johannes Henricus, *Specimen Juridicum de Nefando Lamiarum cum Diabolo Coitu* (Jena, 1689).
819. Potts, Thomas, *The Wonderful Discovery of the Witches in the County of Lancaster* (London, 1613; ed. G. B. Harrison, *Trial of the Lancaster Witches*, 1929; ed. J. Crossley, Manchester, 1845).
820. *Le pour et le contre de la possession des filles de la parroisse de Landes . . . diocèse de Bayeux* (Antioche, 1738).
821. Pourrat, Henri, *L'homme à la peau de loup* (Paris, 1950).
822. Powicke, Frederick J., *A Life of the Reverend Richard Baxter* (London, 1924).
823. Praetorius, Antonius, *Gründlicher Bericht von Zauberey und Zauberern* (Frankfort, 1629).
824. Pratt, Sister Antoinette Marie, *Attitude of the Catholic Church to Witchcraft* (Washington, D. C., 1915).
825. *Presbytery Book of Strathbogie*, Spalding Club (Aberdeen, 1843).
826. Pressel, Wilhelm, *Hexen und Hexenmeister* (Stuttgart, 1860).
827. Price, Harry, *Poltergeist over England* (London, 1945).
828. Prierias, Sylvester, *De Strigimagarum Daemonumque Mirandis* (Rome, 1521, 1575).
829. ———— *Sylvestrina Summa* (Bologna, 1504; Lyons, 1572; Rome, 1576).
830. Prieur de Laval, Claude, *Dialogue de la lycanthropie ou transformation d'hommes en loups* (Louvain, 1596).
831. *Proceedings of Justiciary Court 1661-69*, Scottish History Society, Vol. XLVIII (Edinburgh, 1908).

832. *Proceedings of the Society for Psychical Research.*

833. *Procès verbal du crime détestable de trois sorcières . . . en Sainct-Germain des Prez* (Paris, 1619, 1876).

834. *Processo originale degli Untori nella peste del 1630* (Milan, 1839).

835. *Processus Juridicus Contra Sagas* ([Cologne,] 1629).

836. *A Prodigious and Tragical History . . . of Six Witches at Maidstone* (London, 1652, 1837).

837. Psellus, Michaelis, (tr. Petrus Morellus) *De Operatione Daemonum Dialogus* (Paris, 1615).

838. Putnam, Allen, *Witchcraft of New England Explained by Modern Spiritualism* (Boston, 1888).

839. Quicherat, Jean (ed.), *Le procès de Jeanne Darc*, Société de l'histoire de France, Vols. XXIX, XXXVII, XLII, XLVI, LX (Paris, 1841-49).

840. —————— (French tr. by Pierre Champion) *Procès de condamnation* (Paris, 1920-21).

841. Rapp, Ludwig, *Die Hexenprozesse und ihre Gegner in Tirol* (Innsbruck, 1874; Brixen, 1891).

842. Rautert, Fr., *Etwas Näheres über die Hexenprozesse der Vorzeit* (Essen, 1827).

843. Ravaisson, François Nicholas Napoléon, *Archives de la Bastille* (Paris, 1866-1904).

844. Raviart, Georges, *Sorcières et possédées: la démonomanie dans le Nord de la France* (Lille, 1936, ltd. ed.).

845. *Récit véritable de ce qui s'est fait et passé à Louviers touchant les religieuses possedées* (Paris, 1643).

846. *Records of the Burgh of Aberdeen*, Spalding Club (Aberdeen, 1841).

847. *Recueil des pièces concernant le procès entre la demoiselle Cadière, de la ville de Toulon, et le père Girard, Jésuite* (La Haye, 1731).

848. *Recueil général des pièces contenues au procez du père Jean-Baptiste Girard, Jésuite* (Aix-en-Provence, 1731).

849. Redgrove, Stanley and I. M. L. Redgrove, *Joseph Glanvill and Psychical Research in the Seventeenth Century* (London, 1921).

850. Regino, *De Ecclesiasticis Disciplinis* (Migne, *Patrologia Latina*, Vol. CXXXII).

851. *Register of the Privy Council of Scotland* (ed. David Masson, Edinburgh, 1877).

852. Régné, Jean, "La sorcellerie en Vivarais et la répression inquisitoriale ou séculière du xvᵉ au xviiᵉ siècle," *Mélanges d'histoire offerts à M. Charles Bémont* (Paris, 1913).

853. *A Rehearsal Both Strange and True of Heinous and Horrible Acts Committed by Elizabeth Stile . . . at Abingdon . . . Executed* (London, 1579; East Lancing, 1940, ltd. ed.).

854. Reiche, Johann, *Unterschiedliche Schriften vom Unfug des Hexen-Processes* (Halle, 1703).

855. Reid, Mildred I., *The Devil's Handmaidens* (Boston, 1951).

856. Reiffenberg, Baron de, *Mémoires de Jacques du Clercq* (Brussels, 1823).

857. Reilly, Pamela, "Friedrich von Spee's Belief in Witchcraft," *Modern Language Review*, Vol. LIV (1959).

858. *A Relation of the Diabolical Practices of above Twenty Wizards and Witches of the Sheriffdom of Renfrew* (London, [1697]).

859. *Relation véritable contenant ce qui s'est passé aux exorcismes d'une fille appellée Elisabeth Allier* (Grenoble, 1649; Lyons, 1875).

860. Remy, Nicholas, *Demonolatreiae Libri Tres* (Lyons, 1595; Cologne, 1596; Frankfort, 1597).

861. —————— (English tr. ed. Montague Summers) *Demonolatry* (London, 1930, ltd. ed.).

862. —————— (German tr.) *Von Unholden und Zaubergeistern* (Frankfort, 1598).

863. —————— (German tr.) *Historien von des Teuffels Hinterlist* (Hamburg, 1693).

864. Reuss, Rudolphe Ernest, *La sorcellerie au xviⁱ et au xviiⁱ siècle . . . en Alsace* (Paris, 1871).

865. Rhamm, Albert, *Hexenglaube und Hexen-*

processe vornämlich in den braunschweigischen Landen (Wolfenbüttel, 1882).

866. Rhodes, Henry Taylor Fowkes, *The Satanic Mass* (London, 1954; New York, 1955).

867. Ricchierus [Ludovicus Caelius Rhodiginus], *Lectionum Antiquarum* (Basel, 1517).

868. Richer, Paul, *Etudes cliniques sur la grande hystérie ou hystéro-épilepsie* (Paris, 1881, 1885).

869. Riegger, Paul Josef, *Dissertatio de Magia* (Vienna, 1773).

870. Riegler, Ferdinand, *Hexenprozesse mit besonder Berücksichtigung des Landes Steiermark* (Graz, 1926).

871. Riezler, Sigmund, *Geschichte der Hexenprozesse in Bayern* (Stuttgart, 1896).

872. Rigault, Abel, *Le procès de Guichard, évêque de Troyes 1308-13* (Paris, 1896).

873. Ringger, Peter, *Das Problem der Besessenheit* (Zurich, 1953).

874. Rios, Señor de los, "De las Artes magicas y de Adivinacia en el suelo Iberico," *Revista de España* (1870).

875. Risco, Vincente, *Satanás, historia del Diablo* (Barcelona, 1956).

876. Roberts, Alexander, *A Treatise of Witchcraft* (London, 1616).

877. Roger, Abbé J., *Histoire de Nicole de Vervins* (Paris, 1863).

878. Rohr, Philippus, *De Masticatione Mortuorum* (Leipzig, 1679).

879. Römer, Wilhelm, *Die Hexenbusse nebst Auszügen aus dem Hexenhammer* (Schaffhausen, 1889).

880. Roosa, William V., *The Significance of Exorcism in the Gospel of Mark* (diss., Chicago, 1937).

881. Roskoff, Gustav, *Geschichte des Teufels* (Leipzig, 1869).

882. Roughead, William, "The Devil in Pittenweem," *Juridicial Review* (Edinburgh), Vol. XXVIII (1916).

883. —————— *The Riddle of the Ruthvens* (Edinburgh, 1919, 1936).

884. Rückert, Georg, "Der Hexenwahn [zu Lavingen]," *Alt-Lavingen, Organ des Altertumsvereins* (Lavingen), Vol. II (1907).

885. Ruland, Wilhelm, "Zwei Hexenprozesse zu Trier," *Quellen und Studien zur Geschichte der Hexenprozesse* (Weimar, 1898).

886. Rusca, Antonio, *De Inferno et Statu Daemonum ante Mundi Exitum* (Milan, 1621).

887. Rüttenauer, Isabelle, *Friedrich von Spee: ein lebender Märtyrer* (Freiburg, 1951).

888. Rysan, Joseph, *Wilhelm Meinhold's Bernsteinhexe: A Study in Witchcraft and Cultural History* (Chicago, 1948).

889. Saint André, François de, *Lettres . . . au sujet de la magie, des maléfices et des sorciers* (Paris, 1725).

890. Salelles, Sebastian, *De Materiis Tribunalium Sanctae Inquisitionis* (Rome, 1651-56).

891. Salillas, Rafael, *La Fascinación en España* (Madrid, 1905).

892. Salomies, Ilmari, *Noitausko ja noitavainot: Suomen kulttuuri-historia*, Vol. III (Jyväskylä and Helsinki, 1935).

893. Sargent, Epes, *Planchette* (Boston, 1869).

894. Sauter, Johann Georg, *Zur Hexenbulle, 1484* (Ulm, 1884).

895. Sauzé, Jean Charles, *Essai médico-historique sur les possédées de Loudun* (Paris, 1839).

896. Schacher von Inwil, Joseph, *Das Hexenwesen im Kanton Luzern* (Lucerne, 1947).

897. Schack, John, *Disputatio Juridica Ordinaria de Probatione Criminis Magiae* (Greifswald, 1706; Jena, 1750).

898. Scharf, Riwkah, *The Figure of Satan in the Old Testament* [London, 1946].

899. Scheltema, Jacobus, *Geschiedenis der Heksenprocessen* (Haarlem, 1828).

900. Scherr, Johannes, *Hammerschläge und Historien* (Zurich, 1878).

901. Schieler, Caspar, *Magister Johannes Nider* (Mainz, [1885]).

902. Schiess, Emil, *Die Hexenprozesse und das Gerichtswesen im Lande Appenzell* (Trogen, [? 1919]).

903. Schilliger, Josef, "Die Hexenprozesse im ehemaligen Fürstbisthum Basel," *Vom Jura zum Schwarzwald* (Aarau), Vol. VIII [1891].

904. Schmidt, Johann Georg, *Die gestriegelte*

Rocken-Philosophia (Chemnitz, 1709).

905. Schneider, Heinrich, "Die Hexenliteratur-Sammlung der Cornell-Universität in Ithaca, New York," *Hessische Blätter für Volkskunde* (Giessen), Vol. XLI (1950).

906. Schnell, Eugen, *Zur Geschichte der Criminal-Justiz und besonders der Hexenprozesse in Hohenzollern* (n.p., 1873).

907. Schott, Caspar, *Physica Curiosa* (Würzburg, 1697).

908. Schreiber, Heinrich, *Die Hexenprozesse zu Freiburg im Breisgau, Offenburg in der Ortenau* (Freiburg, 1837).

909. Schultheis, Heinrich von, *Eine aussführliche Instruction wie in Inquisitions-Sachen des grewlichen Lästers der Zauberei . . . zu procediren* (Cologne, 1634).

910. Schwaeblé, René, *Le problème du mal: la sorcellerie pratique* (Paris, 1911).

911. —————— *Le sataniste flagellé* (Paris, [1912]).

912. Schwager, Johann Moris, *Versuch einer Geschichte der Hexenprocesse* (Berlin, 1784).

913. Schwickerath, Robert, "The Attitude of the Jesuits in Trials for Witchcraft," *American Catholic Quarterly Review*, Vol. XXVII (1902).

914. Scot, Reginald, *Discovery of Witchcraft* (London, 1584, 1651, 1654, 1665; ed. Brinsley Nicholson, 1886; ed. Montague Summers, 1930; New York, 1954).

915. —————— (Dutch tr. by Thomas Basson) *Ontdecking van Tovery* (Leyden, 1609; Beverwyck, 1638).

916. Scott, Sir Walter, *Fair Maid of Perth* (London, 1828).

917. —————— *Letters on Demonology and Witchcraft* (London, 1830; New York, 1831, 1855).

918. —————— (French tr. by A. Defauconpret) *Histoire de la démonologie et de la sorcellerie* (Paris, 1832).

919. —————— (German tr. by Georg Nicolaus Bärmann) *Briefe über Dämonologie und Hexerei* (Zwickau, 1833).

920. Scribonius, Gulielmus Adolphus, *De Examine et Purgatione Sagarum per Aquam Frigidam Epistola* ([? Herborn,] 1589).

921. —————— *De Sagarum Natura et Potestate deque His Recte Cognoscendis et Puniendis Physiologia* (Marburg, 1583, 1588).

922. Secombe, Thomas (ed.), *Twelve Bad Men* (London, 1894).

923. *The Second Part of the Boy of Bilson or a True and Particular Relation of the Impostor Susannah Fowler* (London, 1698).

924. Seligmann, Siegfried, *Der böse Blick und Verwandtes* (Berlin, 1910).

925. Sergeant, Philip Walsingham, *Witches and Warlocks* (London, 1936).

926. Sévigné, Madame de, *Lettres* (Paris, 1863).

927. Seymour, St. John Drelincourt, *Irish Witchcraft and Demonology* (Baltimore and Dublin, 1913).

928. Shadwell, Thomas, *The Lancashire Witches* (London, 1681).

929. Shannon, Albert C., "The Secrecy of Witnesses in Inquisitorial Tribunals and in Contemporary Secular Trials," *Essays in Medieval Life and Thought Presented in Honor of Austin Patterson Evans* (New York, 1955).

930. Sharpe, Charles Kirkpatrick, *Historical Account of the Belief in Witchcraft in Scotland* (London, 1819, 1884).

931. Sharpe, Granville, *The Case of Saul Showing that His Disorder Was a Real Spiritual Possession* (London, 1777, 1807).

932. *A Short History of the Salem Village Witc Trials* (Salem, 1911).

933. Simon, Jordan, *Die Nichtigkeit der Hexe und Zauberkunst* (Frankfort, 1766).

934. Sinclair, George, *Hydrostaticks* (Edinbu 1672).

935. —————— *Satan's Invisible World Disc* (Edinburgh, 1685, 1871).

936. Singer, Charles Joseph (ed.), *Studies History and Method of Science* 1917).

937. Sinistrari, Ludovico Maria, *De D itate et Incubis et Succubis* (F French tr., Paris, 1875, ltd. ed

938. —————— (Latin with English tr

Liseux) *Demoniality or Incubi and Succubi* (Paris, 1879, ltd. ed.).

939. —— (English tr. by Montague Summers) *Demoniality* (London, 1927).

940. Sitwell, Sacheverell, *Poltergeists* (London, 1940; New York, 1959).

941. Smit, Johannes, *De Daemoniacis in Historia Evangelica* (Rome, 1913).

942. Smith, Kirby Flower, "Werewolf in Literature," *PMLA*, Vol. IX (1894).

943. Smith, Thomas, *Vitae Eruditissimorum ac Illustrium Virorum* (London, 1707).

944. Snell, Otto, *Hexenprozesse und Geistesstörung* (Munich, 1891).

945. Soldan, Wilhelm Gottlieb, *Geschichte der Hexenprozesse aus der Quellen dargestellt* (Stuttgart, 1843); 2d ed. rev. Heinrich Ludwig Julius Heppe [Soldan-Heppe], *Geschichte der Hexenprozesse* (Stuttgart, 1880); 3d ed. rev. Max Bauer (Munich, 1912).

946. *La sorcellerie à Colmar* (Colmar, 1869).

947. *Sorciers et loups-garous dans les Landes* (Auch, 1904).

948. Soto, Domenic de, *In Quattuor Sententibus* (Venice, 1598).

949. *Southern Magazine* (Baltimore), Vol. XII (1873).

950. Southey, Robert, *The Life of John Wesley* (London, 1901).

951. Spalding, Thomas Alfred, *Elizabethan Demonology* (London, 1880).

952. Spee, Friedrich von, *Cautio Criminalis* (Rinteln, 1631; Cologne, 1632; ed. Joachim Friedrich Ritter, Weimar, 1939).

953. —— (French tr. by F. B. de Velledor) *Advis aux criminalistes sur les abus qui se glissent aux procès de sorcellerie* (Lyons, 1660).

954. —— (German tr.) (Frankfort, 1632; Bremen, 1647).

955. Spielmann, Karl Heinz, *Die Hexenprozesse in Kurhessen* (Marburg, 1932).

956. Spina, Bartolommeo, *Quaestio de Strigibus* (Venice, 1525; Rome, 1576).

957. Spinetti, Vittorio, *Le Streghe in Valtellina* (Sondrio, 1903).

958. Sprenger, Jakob and Heinrich Kramer [Institor], *Malleus Maleficarum* (Cologne, ? 1486; Nuremberg, 1494,] 1496; Venice, 1576; pub. Claudius Bourgeat, Lyons, 1669).

959. —— (English tr. ed. Montague Summers) (London, 1928, ltd. ed.; 1948).

960. —— (German tr. by J. W. R. Schmidt) *Der Hexenhammer* (Berlin, 1906, 1922; Vienna, 1938).

961. Stade, Reinhold, *Barbara Elizabeth Schulzin: ein Arnstädter Hexenprozess vom Jahre 1669* (Arnstadt, 1904).

962. Stampa, Pietro Antonio, *Fuga Satanae* (n.p., 1597; Lyons, 1619).

963. Starkey, Marion Lena, *The Devil in Massachusetts* (New York, 1949).

964. *Statutes at Large* (London, 1763), Vol. VI.

965. *Statutes of the Realm* (London, 1817; repr. *The Statutes*, 3d ed., London, 1950).

966. Stearne, John, *A Confirmation and Discovery of Witchcraft* (London, 1648).

967. Steck, Rudolf, *Die Akten des Jetzerprozesses* (Basel, 1904).

968. —— *Der Berner Jetzerprozess 1507-9* (Bern, 1902).

969. Stengel, George, *De Judiciis* (Ingolstadt, 1651).

970. Stephen, Edward, *A Collection of Modern Relations of Matter of Fact Concerning Witches and Witchcraft* (London, 1693).

971. Stewart, C. T., *Origin of Werewolf Superstitions*, University of Missouri Social Studies, Series II (1906).

972. Stöber, August, *Zur Geschichte des Volks-Aberglaubens im Anfange des 16. Jahrhunderts* (Basel, 1856).

—. Stone, J. M., "The German Witches and Their Apostle," *Month*, Vol. C (1902).

Strange Witch at Greenwich (London, 1650).

Strange and Wonderful History of Mother Shipton (London, 1686, 1870).

—inzing, R. von, *Geschichte des deutschen Rechtswissenschaft* (Munich, 1884).

—mpff, Johann,] (French tr. by François Bonivard) *Histoire véritable et digne*

978. Summers, Montague, *Geography of Witchcraft* (London, 1927; New York, 1958).

979. —— *The History of Witchcraft and Demonology* (London, 1926; New York, 1926, 1956).

980. —— *Popular History of Witchcraft* (London and New York, 1937).

981. —— *The Vampire in Europe* (New York, 1929).

982. —— *The Vampire: His Kith and Kin* (London, 1928; New York, 1929).

983. —— *The Werewolf* (London, 1933; New York, 1934).

984. —— *Witchcraft and Black Magic* (London and New York, 1946).

985. —— (tr.) *Confessions of Madeleine Bavent* (London, [1933]).

986. —— (ed. English tr.) Henri Boguet, *An Examen of Witches* (London, 1929).

987. —— (ed.) Richard Bovet, *Pandaemonium* (Aldington, Kent, 1951).

988. —— (ed. English tr.) Francesco Guazzo, *Compendium Maleficarum* (London, 1929).

989. —— (ed.) Matthew Hopkins, *Discovery of Witches* (London, 1928).

990. —— (ed. English tr.) Nicholas Remy, *Demonolatreiae* (London, 1930).

991. —— (ed.) Reginald Scot, *Discovery of Witchcraft* (London, 1930).

992. —— (tr.) Ludovico Sinistrari, *Demoniality* (London, 1927).

993. —— (ed. English tr.) Jakob Sprenger and Heinrich Kramer, *Malleus Maleficarum* (London, 1928, 1948).

994. —— (tr.) Noel Taillepied, *Treatise of Ghosts* (London, [1933]).

995. *The Surey Demoniac, or an Account of Satan's Strange and Dreadful Actings in and About the Body of Richard Dugdale of Surey near Whalley in Lancashire* (London, 1697).

996. Surin, Jean Joseph, *Histoire abregée de la possession des Ursulines de Loudun et des peines du père Surin* (Paris, 1828).

997. Taillepied, Noel, *Histoire de l'estat et république des druides* (Paris, 1585).

998. —— (English tr. by Montague Summers) *Treatise of Ghosts* (London, [1933]).

999. Tandlero, Tobia, *Dissertatio de Fascino et Incantatione* (Wittenberg, 1606).

1000. Tanner, Adam, *Disputationes Theologicae* (Ingolstadt, 1617).

1001. —— *Tractatus Theologicus de Processu Adversus Crimina Excepta ac Speciatim Adversus Crimen Veneficii* (Cologne, 1629).

1002. Tanon, Celestin Louis, *Histoire des tribunaux de l'Inquisition en France* (Paris, 1893).

1003. Tapley, Charles Sutherland, *Rebecca Nurse* (Boston, 1930).

1004. Tartarotti, Girolamo, *Apologia del Congresso notturno delle Lammie* (Rovereto, 1749; Venice, 1751).

1005. Tavenner, Eugene, *Studies in Magic from Latin Literature* (New York, 1916).

1006. Taylor, John Metcalfe, *The Witchcraft Delusion in Colonial Connecticut 1647-97* (New York, 1908).

1007. Taylor, Zachariah, *The Surey Impostor: Being an Answer to a Late Fanatical Pamphlet Entituled the Surey Demoniac* (London, 1697).

1008. Teirlinck, Isidoor, *Flora Magica: de Plant in de Tooverwereld* (Antwerp, 1930).

1009. Telfair, Alexander, *A New Confirmation of Sadducism* (London, 1696).

1010. —— *A True Relation of an Apparition* (Edinburgh, 1696).

1011. Tengler, Ulric, *Layenspiegel* ([Augsburg,] 1509; Strasbourg, 1510, 1511, 1530).

1012. —— *Der neu Layenspiegel* (Augsburg, 1512; [Strasbourg,] 1514, 1518, 1527).

1013. Thamm, Melchior, *Fehmgericht und Hexenprozesse* (Leipzig, [1903]).

1014. *Thesaurus Exorcismorum* (Cologne, 1626).

1015. Thiaucourt, Paul, *La sorcellerie au Ban de Ramonchamp au xvii° siècle* (Remiremont, 1908).

1016. Thomasius, Christian, *De Crimine Magiae* (Halle, 1701).

1017. —— (German tr.) *Kurze Lehr-Sätze von dem Laster der Zauberei* (Halle, 1704, 1712; Frankfort, 1717).

1018. Thomasius, Jacob, *De Transformatione Hominum in Bruta* (Leipzig, 1667, 1673).

1019. Thompson, R. Lowe, *The History of the Devil, the Horned God of the West* (London and New York, 1929).

1020. Thorndike, Lynn, *History of Magic and Experimental Science* (New York, 1923).

1021. —— *Place of Magic in Intellectual History of Europe* (New York, 1905).

1022. Thummius, Theodoricus, *Tractatus Theologicus de Sagarum Impietate, Nocendi Imbellicitate et Poenae Gravitate* (Tübingen, 1667).

1023. Thyraeus, Petrus, *Daemoniaci cum Locis Infestis* (Cologne, 1598, 1604; Lyons, 1599).

1024. Tihon, Ferdinand, "Un procès de sorcellerie à Huy en 1495," *Wallonia* (1904).

1025. Tonquédoc, J. de, *Les maladies nerveuses ou mentales et les manifestations diaboliques* (Paris, 1937).

1026. Torreblanca Villalpando, Francisco [Cordubensis], *De Magia* (Lyons, 1678).

1027. —— *Daemonologia* (Mainz, 1623).

1028. Trachtenberg, Joshua, *Jewish Magic and Superstition* (New York, 1939).

1029. *Traicté des marques des possedez et la preuve de la véritable possession des religieuses de Louviers* (Rouen, 1649).

1030. *Transactions of the Ossory Archaeology Society*, Vol. I (1889).

1031. Trask, Willard, *Joan of Arc, Self Portrait* (New York, 1936).

1032. *A Treatise of Witchcraft with True Narration . . . of Mary Smith* (London, 1616).

1033. *The Trial, Condemnation, and Execution of Three Witches . . . at Exeter* (London, 1682).

1034. *Trial, Confession, and Execution of Isobel Insh, John Stewart, Margaret Barclay, and Isobel Crawford for Witchcraft at Irvine, Anno 1618* (Ardrossan, [? 1855]).

1035. *The Trial and Examinations of Mrs. Joan Peterson* (London, 1652; Ingram, Pa., 1939, ltd. ed.).

1036. *A Trial of Witches at the Assizes Held at Bury St. Edmunds . . . 1664* (London, 1682, 1716, 1838).

1037. Triez, Robert du, *Les ruses, finesses et impostures des esprits malins* (Cambrai, 1563).

1038. Trollope, Anthony, *Sketches from French History* (London, 1878).

1039. Truc, Gonzague, *Madame de Montespan* (Paris, 1936).

1040. *A True Discourse, Declaring the Damnable Life and Death of One Stubbe Peter* (London, 1590; East Lancing, 1940).

1041. *A True and Exact Relation of the Several Informations, Examinations, and Confessions of the Late Witches, Arraigned and Executed in the County of Essex* (London, 1645).

1042. *A True and Impartial Relation of the Informations Against Three Witches, Viz., Temperance Lloyd, Mary Trembles, and Susanna Edwards . . . Executed at Exeter, August 14, 1682* (London, 1682).

1043. *A True and Just Record of the Information, Examination, and Confession of All the Witches Taken at St. Oses* (London, 1582).

1044. *A True Relation of the Arraignment of Eighteen Witches at St. Edmundsbury* (London, 1645).

1045. *A True Relation of a Very Strange and Wonderful Thing That Was Heard in the Air* (London, 1658).

1046. Tuetey, Alexandre, *La sorcellerie dans le pays de Montbéliard au xvii° siècle* (Dôle, 1886).

1047. Turberville, Arthur Stanley, *Medieval Heresy and the Inquisition* (London, 1920).

1048. Turmel, Joseph, *Histoire du diable* (Paris, 1931).

1049. Turner, William, *Complete History of the Most Remarkable Providences* (London, 1697).

1050. Upham, Charles Wentworth, *Lectures on Witchcraft* (Boston, 1831).

1051. —— *Salem Witchcraft* (Boston, 1867).

1052. Vacandard, Abbé Elphège, *L'Inquisition, étude historique* (Paris, 1907).

1053. ——— (English tr.) (London, 1908).

1054. Vairo, Leonardo, *De Fascino* (Paris, 1583; Venice, 1589).

1055. ——— (French tr. by Julian Baudon) *Trois livres des charmes, sorcelages ou enchantements* (Paris, 1583).

1056. Valderama, Petrus, *Histoire générale du monde* (Paris, 1619).

1057. Valletta, Niccola, *Cicalata sul Fascino volgamente detto Jettatura* (Naples, 1814).

1058. Verdun, Paul, *Le diable dans la vie des saints, xᵉ au xivᵉ siècles* (Paris, n.d.).

1059. Verner, Gerald (ed.), *Prince of Darkness* (London, 1946).

1060. [Verstegen, Richard,] *Theatrum Crudelitatum Haereticorum* (Antwerp, 1587, 1592).

1061. Vidal, J. M., *Bullaire de l'Inquisition française* (Paris, 1913).

1062. Viglione, J. B., *Enchiridion . . . Tractatus III, De Cacodaemonibus* (Naples, 1734).

1063. Vigny, Alfred de, *Cinq mars* (Paris, 1827).

1064. Villars, Abbé Montfaucon de, *Comte de Gabalis* (Paris, 1670).

1065. Vincent, Albert Leopold and Clare Binns, *Gilles de Rais: the Original Bluebeard* (London, 1926).

1066. Vincentius von Berg, *Enchiridium* (Cologne, 1743).

1067. Vinson, Jules, "La sorcellerie dans le Labourd," *Revue de linguistique et de philologie comparée*, Vol. XLVII (1913).

1068. [Viret, Pierre,] (English tr. by T. Stocker) *The World Possessed with Devils* (London, 1583).

1069. Viriville, Vallet de, *Procès de condamnation de Jeanne Darc* (Paris, 1867).

1070. Visconti, Girolamo, *Lamiarum sive Striarum Opusculum* (Milan, 1490).

1071. Visser, Cassimir K. [Kurt Baschwitz], *Van de Heksenwaag te Oudewater* (Lochem [1941]).

1072. Vizetelly, Ernest Alfred, *Bluebeard* (London, 1902).

1073. Vogt, Gottlob Heinrich, *Kurtzes Bedencken von denen Acten-mässigen Relationen wegen derer Vampiren* (Leipzig, 1732).

1074. Volk, Franz, *Hexen in der Landvogtei Ortenau und Reichsstadt Offenburg* (Lahr, 1882).

1075. Wächter, Carl Georg von, *Beiträge zur deutschen Geschichte* (Tübingen, 1845).

1076. Wächter, Oskar Eberhard Siegfried von, *Vehmgerichte und Hexenprozesse in Deutschland* (Stuttgart, 1882).

1077. Wagner, Robert Léon, *Sorcier et magicien: contribution à l'histoire du vocabulaire de la magie* (Paris, 1939).

1078. Wagstaffe, John, *The Question of Witchcraft Debated* (London, 1669, 1671).

1079. ——— (German tr.) *Gründliche Ausgeführte Materie von der Hexerei* (Halle, 1711).

1080. Waite, Arthur Edward, *Devil Worship in France* (London, 1896).

1081. Waldbrühl, Wilhelm von, *Naturforschung und Hexenglaube* (Berlin, 1867).

1082. Wall, S. Charles, *Devils* (London, 1904).

1083. Waller, John, *A Treatise on the Incubus or Nightmare* (London, 1816).

1084. Ward, Richard, *Henry More* (London, 1710).

1085. *Warhaft und gründtlicher Bericht sehr wunderlich vnnd gleichsam vnerhörter Geschichten . . . auss französischer Sprach in Hochteutsch gebracht* (Munich, 1589).

1086. Wasson, R. Gordon, *Mushrooms, Russia and History* (New York, 1957).

1087. Webster, John, *The Displaying of Supposed Witchcraft* (London, 1677).

1088. ——— (German tr. ed. Christian Thomasius) *Untersuchung der vermeinten und sogenannten Hexereyen* (Halle, 1719).

1089. Weigel, Oswald, *Geschichte der Hexenprozesse* (Leipzig, 1912).

1090. Wendell, Barrett, *Cotton Mather* (New York, 1891).

1091. Weng, Johann F., *Die Hexenprocesse der ehemaligen Reichsstadt Nördlingen in den Jahren 1590-94* (Nördlingen, n.d.).

1092. West, William, *Simboleography* (London, 1594, 1615).

1093. Weyer, Johan, *De Lamiis* (Basel, 1577, 1582; Amsterdam, 1660).

1094. ——— *De Praestigiis Daemonum et Incantationibus ac Veneficiis* (Basel, 1563, 1564, 1566, 1568, 1577, 1583).

1095. ——— (French tr. by Jacques Grévin de Clermont) *De l'imposture et tromperie des diables* (Paris, 1567).

1096. ——— (French tr. by Simon Goulart) *Histoires, disputes et discours des illusions et impostures de diables* (Geneva, 1579; Paris, 1885).

1097. ——— (German tr. by Fuglin) *Von Teufelsgespenst, Zauberern und Giftbereytern* (Frankfort, 1586).

1098. White, Andrew Dickson, *History of the Warfare of Science with Theology* (New York, 1896, 1955).

1099. ——— *Seven Great Statesmen* (New York, 1919).

1100. *The Whole Trial and Examination of Mrs. Mary Hicks* (London, 1716).

1101. Wickwar, John William, *Witchcraft and the Black Art* (London, [1925]; New York, 1926).

1102. Wilbur, Sibyl, *The Life of Mary Baker Eddy* (Boston, 1907).

1103. Wiley, Margaret L., *The Subtle Knot* (Cambridge, 1952).

1104. *Wilhelm Perry, oder der besessene Knabe* (n.p., 1799) [Extract from German tr. of Hutchinson].

1105. [Willard, Samuel,] *Some Miscellany Observations on Our Present Debates Respecting Witchcraft* ([? Philadelphia,] 1692; Boston, 1869).

1106. ——— *Massachusetts Historical Society Collections*, 4th Series, Vol. VIII.

1107. Willey, Basil, *Seventeenth Century Background* (London, 1946).

1108. *William and Mary College Quarterly, Historical Papers*, Vol. III (1894-95).

1109. *William of Palerne* (ed. W. W. Skeat, London, 1867).

1110. Williams, Charles, *Descent into Hell* (London, 1937).

1111. ——— *Witchcraft* (London, 1941; New York, 1958).

1112. Williams, Howard, *Superstitions of Witchcraft* (London, 1865).

1113. Wilson, M. H., "Witch Beliefs and Social Structure," *American Journal of Sociology*, Vol. LVI (1951).

1114. Wilson, Thomas, *Bluebeard* (New York and London, 1899).

1115. Winkler, C., *Die Hexenprozesse in Türkheim in den Jahren 1628-30* (Colmar, [post 1890]).

1116. Winkler, R., "Über Hexenprozesse in Estland," *Baltische Monatschrift* (Riga), Vol. V (1909).

1117. Winwar, Frances, *Gallows Hill* (New York, [1937]).

1118. *The Witch of Wapping* (London, 1652; Ingram, Pa., 1939, ltd. ed.).

1119. *Witches Apprehended, Examined, and Executed* (London, 1613).

1120. *The Witches of Huntingdon* (London, 1646).

1121. *The Witches of Northamptonshire* (London, 1612; ed. Thomas Wright, Northampton, 1867).

1122. [Witekind, Hermann,] *Christlich Bedencken und Erinnerung von Zauberey* (Heidelberg, 1585; Strasbourg, 1586; Speyer, 1597).

1123. Wittman, Pins, "Die Bamberger Hexen-Justiz, 1595-1631," *Archiv für katholisches Kirchenrecht*, Vol. L (1883).

1124. *The Wonderful Discovery of the Witchcrafts of Margaret and Philip Flower* (London, 1619).

1125. Wood, John Maxwell, *Witchcraft and Superstitious Record in the Southwestern District of Scotland* (Dumfries, 1911).

1126. Woodward, W. Elliot, *Records of the Salem Witchcraft* (Roxbury, Mass., 1864, ltd. ed.).

1127. Woolley, Reginald Maxwell, *Exorcism and the Healing of the Sick* (London, 1932).

1128. Wright, Dudley, *Vampires and Vampirism* (London, 1914, 1920).

1129. Wright, Thomas, *Narratives of Sorcery and Magic* (London, 1851; New York, 1852).

1130. ——— *Proceedings Against Dame Alice Kyteler*, Camden Society (London, 1843).

1131. Yve-Plessis, Robert, *Essai d'une bibliographie française . . . de la sorcellerie et de la possession démoniaque* (Paris, 1900).

1132. Yvelin, Docteur, *Examen de la possession des religieuses de Louviers* (Paris, 1643; ed. J. Lemmonnyer, Rouen, 1879, ltd. ed.).

1133. Zakrzeuska, Miroslawa, *Procesy o czary* (Lublin, 1947).

1134. Zehner, Ioachim, *Fünf Predigten von den Hexen* (Leipzig, 1613).

1135. Zilboorg, Gregory, *The Medical Man and the Witch during the Renaissance* (Baltimore, 1935).

1136. Zilotti, Giovanni Battista, *Volumen Praeclarissimum . . . Tractatium Criminalium* (Venice, 1563).

1137. Zingerle, Ignaz, *Barbara Pachlerin die Sarnthaler Hexe und Mathias Perger der Lauterfresser* (Innsbruck, 1858).

1138. Zopft [Zopfius], John Heinrich, *Dissertatio de Vampiris Serviensibus* (Halle, 1733).

1139. *Zwei Hexenprocesse aus dem Jahre 1688 geführt bei dem hochfürstlichen Amte in Ballenstedt* (Quedlinburg, 1863).

1140. Zwetsloot, Hugo, *Friedrich Spee und die Hexenprozesse* (Treves, 1954).